1 MONTH OF
FREE
READING

at

www.ForgottenBooks.com

By purchasing this book you are eligible for one month membership to ForgottenBooks.com, giving you unlimited access to our entire collection of over 700,000 titles via our web site and mobile apps.

To claim your free month visit:

www.forgottenbooks.com/free631373

ISBN 978-0-483-00232-6
PIBN 10631373

THE

HISTORY

OF THE

REIGN OF GEORGE III.

TO WHICH IS PREFIXED,

A VIEW OF THE PROGRESSIVE IMPROVEMENT OF ENGLAND,
IN PROSPERITY AND STRENGTH, TO THE
ACCESSION OF HIS MAJESTY.

IN THREE VOLUMES.

BY ROBERT BISSETT, LL. D.

AUTHOR OF THE " LIFE OF BURKE," &c. &c.

A NEW EDITION,

BROUGHT DOWN TO THE DEATH OF THE KING.

VOLUME II.

PHILADELPHIA:
PUBLISHED BY EDWARD PARKER,
No. 178, MARKET-STREET.

1822.

HISTORY

OF THE

REIGN OF GEORGE III.

CHAP. XXXII.

General .election.—Meeting of parliament—and commencement of Mr.
Pitt's administration.—The king's speech—State of the empire when
Mr. Pitt's ministry commenced.—Objects which he proposes to pursue.
—First efforts directed to finance—Bill for the pr   n   n of smuggling—Commutation act.—Arguments against and fine itie—Regulation
on duties for British spirits.—Preliminary motions for the relief of the
East India Company.—Bill for the regulation of India.—Arguments
against it—Arguments for it—Comparison of the two bills as resulting
from the characters of their authors—Debate on the Westminster election.—Mr. Dundas proposes the restoration of the forfeited estates.—A
law passed for that purpose.—Labours of Mr Pitt in investigating the
public accounts.—Supplies.—Loan and taxes.—Session closes.

BY dissolving the parliament, his majesty virtually asked
the question, Did your late representatives speak your sense, or
not? If they did, you will re-elect them; if not, you will choose
others. Thus interrogated, the greater part of the people answered, No; and a very considerable majority of members
friendly to Mr. Pitt was returned. As far as popular opinion
can be a test of either merit or demerit, it was decidedly favourable to the minister, and inimical to his opponents. The
general conduct of Mr. Fox often has been erroneously estimated by those who considered defects, without comprehending the excellencies of his plans, acts, and character; but
never was he less popular than after his India bill and contest
with the sovereign. Still, however, he retained great favour
in some parts of the kingdom, especially in Westminster, and
his election was the most noted of any that occurred for the new
parliament. The candidates were, lord Hood, who had so eminently distinguished himself with Rodney, Mr. Fox, and sir Cecil
Wray; of whom the two last were the late members. Wray
had been originally chosen through the interest of Mr. Fox,
but now abandoned that gentleman and joined lord Hood.
For several days, Mr. Fox was superior to either of his compe-
titors; but his majority afterwards rapidly decreased, and he
became inferior to sir Cecil Wray, who was far surpassed by

CHAP.
XXXII.

1784.
General
election.

contest for
Westmin-
ster, and
influence
of a beau-
tiful lady.

the naval candidate. On the 11th day of the poll he was three hundred and eighteen behind Wray: but an interference now took place that changed the face of affairs. A lady of very high rank, still more eminent for beauty than for condition, one of our lovely countrywomen, who demonstrate that, in celebrating a Venus or a Helen, poets do not exceed nature and experience, warmly interested herself in the election of Mr. Fox, with a success far beyond the hopes of the favoured candidate. Animated by personal friendship, and inspired with an ardent zeal for what she conceived to be a public benefit, this 'exalted woman undertook a personal canvass in favour of the losing candidate, and was not to be deterred by any inconveniences of the pursuit, or by the strictures of the opposite party, upon active efforts which were so efficacious towards the attainment of the object. Many voters indeed, though far from approving Mr. Fox's political principles and conduct, could notwithstand the fascinating eloquence of so impressive an advocate ; they might have resisted the utmost efforts of the brilliant genius of an Erskine or a Sheridan, but could not withstand the brilliant eyes of the Duchess : these two great masters of the pathetic might have in vain attempted to canvass for their brother orator ; persuasion sat on the lips and dimpled in the smiles of the beautiful Devonshire, pleading for her brother whig. Persons too callous to yield to the application of beauty, were not without other avenues to their hearts, to which the fair friend of Mr. Fox did not fail to apply with effect. The candidate himself extremely well qualified for co-operating with the efforts of his friends, was better known to the lower and more numerous classes of Westminster electors, than any other eminent person existing. He was naturally open, frank, unassuming, and popular in his manners, politically attended all the public meetings, and associated under 'the appearance of most intimate familiarity with tavern keepers, mechanics, and tradesmen, and was, by a great number belonging to these classes, regarded with the warmest affection. He was, besides, connected with many of the principal inhabitants, whose personal exertions and influence were strenuously employed in his favour. After a contest of forty days, Mr. Fox was two hundred and thirty-five superior ; but a scrutiny being demanded by sir Cecil Wray, and granted by the high bailiff, a return was not made. The orator, however, having been chosen by Scottish boroughs, had a voice in parliament.[a]

a The writer was one day present at this celebrated election, and being recently come to London, was forcibly struck with the free and easy terms in which some of the lower adherents of Mr. Fox. especially a party of butchers, accosted a personage of his transcendent superiority. It was not with the veneration due to so extraordinary talents from any rank, that those persons of the very humblest addressed Charles James Fox: it was in the endearing terms of fond comrades, on a footing of perfect

The 16th of May was the day fixed for the meeting of the new CHAP. parliament, in which Mr. Pitt, not twenty-five years of age, may XXXII. be properly said to have commenced the chief executorial direc- tion of British affairs. The probable conduct of a man in an office 1784. depends upon his talents, dispositions, and habits, combined with Meeting of the state of affairs relative to his employment, and his own clear parlia- and full comprehension of its nature, objects, means, and duties: ment, and If a minister takes an exact and complete survey of the actual ment of condition of a nation, and rises to general views of the chief con- Mr. Pitt's stituents of national prosperity, bestowing application and per- efficient ad- severance either in the removal of evil or promotion of good, he ministra- must produce much greater benefit to the state, than he who re- tion. gards and pursues only a part.

The chief constituents of national prosperity are, first, the means of subsistence, through agriculture, mines, fisheries, manufactures, and commerce: secondly, defence in military and naval strength, for securing those advantages; compre- hending also, connexions with foreign countries, when conducive either to benefit or security; thirdly, the preservation and improve- ment of that physical and moral character, which is best fitted for retaining and promoting the advantages; this head requires the encouragement of useful and liberal arts, and in every civi- lized and enlightened country the promotion of science and lite- rature; fourthly, the gratification of prevalent habits of comfort and enjoyments, as far as depends upon government, unless re- striction be necessary for the public good, and the liberty of the subject, without which, to generous and independent spirits, no other blessing of life can afford perfect enjoyment; fifthly, subsidiary to the rest, is provision for the continuance of these, as far as human foresight can extend.[b] A statesman of con- summate wisdom may bestow a greater or less proportion of attention on one or another of these constituents, according to circumstances; but such a minister will have them all in his view. The peculiar situation of Britain, exhausted by the enor-

equality. "Charles, my sweet boy; God bless your black face! do not "be afraid, my lad, wɛ *are your friends!*" The writer recollects, the same day, to have heard a very open avowal of corruption. Being in a bookseller's shop in Covent Garden, a woman, who it seems was a neigh- bour, coming in, was asked by the master of the house, if her husband had polled No, she answered; we are told, votes will bear a higher price next week! The circumstances of this election, in a city wherein votes are so general, and of another in the same place four years after, are by no means favourable to the doctrine of certain political reformists, that universal suf- frage would promote respectability and independence of elections.

b This analysis the reader will perceive to be abridged from Gillies's Frederick, which appears to the author to exhibit a much juster and more comprehensive estimate of national advantage, than those, either of writers or counsellors, who should consider mere opulence, either private or public, or the aggregate of both, as the tests of national prosperity.

CHAP. mous expenses of her late ruinous war, and loaded with an
XXXII. immense public debt, rendered the promotion of trade and im-
〜〜 provement of finance the most immediately urgent objects of
1784. legislative and ministerial consideration. Besides, at this time,
the study of political enconomy occupied the greater number of
scholars, moral and political philosophers, and almost every
able and informed senator and statesman. Such disquisitions,
originating in French ingenuity, had been corrected, enlarged,
and digested into a grand system, by British experience, knowledge, and deduction. Adam Smith was the framer of commercial science and the consequent inculcations; and his estimable work, indeed, was become the text book of political economists in the closet, the cabinet, and senate. A very eminent
writer often gives a tone and fashion to the subjects which he
treats, that procures them an attention, perhaps greater than
may be justified by their comparative value among the various
pursuits of life and constituents of happiness. Dwelling on the
nature and causes of the wealth of nations, both theorists and
politicians, by too exclusive attention to that one subject, have
frequently been led into an imagination that the supreme constituent of national good was opulence; an idea totally inconsistent with a knowledge of human powers and enjoyments, the
experience of happiness, and the history of nations.[c] This
very high estimation of wealth, as the supreme excellence of a
country, co-operated with the mercantile character, so prevalent
in Britain, and many in the various departments of active (especially trading) life considered commerce and finance as the
principal objects of executorial conduct. Mr. Pitt, though too
enlarged in his views to admit that opinion in the common extent, yet regarding trade, and especially revenue, as most immediately urgent in forming his plans for the first session of the
new parliament, directed his mind chiefly to commerce and
finance, and these constitute the principal subjects of his majesty's introductory speech to parliament.

The king's   The new parliament being met, Mr. Cornwall was chosen
speech.   speaker, and on the 19th, his majesty opened the session by a
speech from the throne; he declared the high satisfaction with
which he met his parliament, after having recurred in so important a moment to the sense of his people. He entertained
a just and confident reliance, that the assembly was animated
with the sentiments of loyalty and attachment to the constitution, which had been so fully manifested in every part of the
kingdom. The objects particulary recommended to their at-

c Compare, for instance, the Greeks and Persians, the Romans and Carthagenians, the Europeans and Hindoos. The heroes sent by poverty from the
north, to the dastardly and enervated defenders of the riches of the south.
These, in the monuments of Gillies, of Fergusson, and Gibbon, show how
falsely a political reasoner would conclude, who should measure national
glory and happiness by national receipts.

tention, were the alarming progress of frauds in the revenue,
the framing of such commercial regulations as were immediately necessary, and the providing for the good government of
our possessions in the East Indies. Upon this subject parliament would not lose sight of the effect which the measures they
adopted might have on our own constitution, and our dearest
interests at home. He had no wish but to consult the prosperity of his people, by a constant attention to every object of national concern, by an uniforn adherance to the true principles
of our free constitution, and by supporting and maintaining in
their just balance the rights and privileges of every branch of
the legislature. An address conformable to the speech having
been moved, a debate arose on the expressions of gratitude to
the king, for having dissolved the late parliament: and an
amendment was proposed, to leave out such parts of the address
as referred to that subject, which was negatived by a great
majority. As his majesty's speech implied a censure of the
former parliament, and particularly of Mr. Fox's East India
bill, Mr. Burke undertook the justification of opposition and the
censure of their adversaries, and on the 14th of June, made a
motion for an address to the king, representing and vindicating
the proceedings of the last parliament, and criminating the
present ministers. The remonstrance[d] dwelt particularly on
the rectitude and expedience of the late East India bill, and on
the dreadful consequences likely to ensue from the dissolution.
Though both the speech and proposed statement were replete
with ingenuity, yet the main arguments being necessarily a repetition of what had been frequently urged before, the motion
was negatived without a division. Firmly established as the
minister, supported by the people through their recently appointed representatives, as well as chosen by the king, Mr. Pitt
was called to exercise his talents for performing the duties of
so arduous a situation. Although a year and a half had now
elapsed since the conclusion of peace, the contentions of party
had hitherto prevented the adoption of any effectual measures
to recover the country from the miserable state to which it had
been reduced by an expensive and ruinous war. Commerce
was still stagnant, the national credit depressed, and the funds,
after an interval of peace, at the lowest price of war; the
public income, unequal to the expenditure even in its full amount,
was at present greatly diminished by fraud; and our important
concerns in India without any effectual plan of beneficial ar-

d He said, he intended his motion as an epitaph on his departed friend,
the last parliament; that he had, on some occasions, written long epitaphs
to the memory of those that he honoured and respected; and, on the present occasion he chose to follow the corpse to the sepulchre, and go
through the ceremony of saying, " ashes to ashes, and dust to dust," in sure
and certain hope, through the merit of the good works of the last parliament, that it would have a glorious and joyful resurrection, and become
immortal.

CHAP. rangement; the country, so situated, required the efforts of the
XXXII. minister to raise drooping credit; to revive the funds; to promote the just and beneficial government of India; to improve
1784. the income, by suppressing fraudulent deduction, and by posi-
State of the tive additions; to stimulate the national industry, enterprise,
empire and skill, to the highest improvement of our mercantile capa-
when Mr.
Pitt's mini- bility ; and to promote manufactures and commerce, the sources
stry began of public and private wealth. Such were the objects to which,
Objects partly the circumstances of the country, and partly the preva-
which he lent opinion of the times, called the attention of Mr. Pitt, who
proposes to was just commencing an administration long and important ; in
pursue. which the counsels and conduct of the minister, whether wise
or unwise, right or wrong, stamp the history of these realms,
their dependencies and connexions, for the last sixteen years
of the eighteenth century; an æra more awfully momentous,
involving greater and more extensive interests of enlightened,
energetic, and efficacious MAN, than any century in the annals
of human nature.

His first   The first ministerial efforts of Mr. Pitt, were directed to
efforts are finance. Before he proceeded to new imposts, or new regula-
directed to tion for the advancement of revenue, he attempted to render
finance. the present taxes as productive as possible, by preventing the
defalcations of fraud. · He had bestowed very great pains in
collecting information respecting the various subjects, modes,
and details of smuggling. The former ministers having also in
view the suppression of this unlawful traffic, had in the last
session proposed a committee for inquiring into those illicit
practices ; three reports were delivered, containing very ample
materials ; and Mr. Eden, chairman of the committee, having
employed his usual industry and acuteness in investigating these
minute and complicated topics, had moved the following resolution, declaratory of the result, That the illicit practice had
greatly increased; the public revenue was annually defrauded
to the extent of not less than two millions; and these enormities and national losses merited the early and serious attention
Bill for the of the legislature. Soon after the meeting of the new parlia-
prevention ment, the subjects of these reports, and of the laws in being
of smug- for the prevention of smuggling, were referred to a committee
gling. of the whole house. On the second of June, the chancellor of
the exchequer moved for leave to bring in a bill for the more
effectual prevention of smuggling. The objects of the proposition were, to extend the bounds of the hovering laws, which
had limited the distance from shore within which seizures could
be made; to prevent ships from carrying arms, without a license
from the admiralty; smuggling ships once captured were never
to be returned ; ships of a certain description adapted to smuggling, were never to be built ; and clearances were to be regulated, so as to prevent ships clearing out in ballast, and afterwards
going on the smuggling trade. In the progress of the bill, a

variety of improvements were suggested; and after considerable discussion, it passed into a law.

Among various articles of illicit trade, the principal commodity was tea. It had appeared before the committee on smuggling, that only five millions, five hundred thousand pounds of
tea were sold annually by the East India company, whereas
the annual consumption of the kingdom was believed to exceed
twelve millions; so that the contraband traffic in this article
was more than double the legal. The remedy which the minister devised for this evil, was to lower the duty on tea to so
small an amount, as to make the profit inadequate to the risk.
In this trade the rate of freight and insurances to the shore was
about 25 per cent. and the insurance on the inland carriage
about 10 per cent. more; in all 35 per cent. The duty on tea,
as it then stood, was about 50 per cent. so that the smuggler
had an advantage over the fair dealer of 15 per cent. As this
regulation would cause a deficiency in the revenue of about
600,000l. *per annum*, he proposed to make good the same by
an additional window tax. This tax (he said) would not be
felt as an additional burthen, but ought to be considered as a
commutation, and would prove favourable to the subject.e But
the principal benefit which he expected from this measure, was
the absolute ruin of the smuggling trade, which subsisted almost entirely on the profit of their teas. Another benefit
would be, the timely and necessary relief it would afford to the
East India company. By this regulation they would find a vent
for thirteen, instead of five, millions of pounds of tea, and would
be enabled to employ twenty more large ships in their service.
This was the bill since so well known under the title of the
COMMUTATION ACT.

Opposition in both houses denied this tax to be commutative:
tea, though a commodity of general use, still was an article of
luxury; whereas the admission of light into houses was indispensably necessary; and thus all persons, whether they drank tea
or not, were compelled to pay a tax. The gain to the company
might be considerable, but must be derived from the people,
without any return; the present was a new and positive tax,
and not a substitution of one for another. This bill was farther censured, as a measure of finance; tea, it was said, was a
most eligible object for taxation, which produced to the revenue
near a million sterling annually. If once given up, it could
never be recovered, and five times the quantity of tea consumed yearly that had formerly been used, by the new duty would
not produce an equal revenue. It was farther contended, that

---

* A house (he said,) for instance, of nine windows, which would be rated at 10s. 6d., might be supposed to consume seven pounds of tea; the
difference between the old duties on which, and the new duty proposed,
might at an average amount to 1l. 5s. 10d.; so that such a family would
gain by the commutation 15s. 4d.

CHAP. XXXII.

1784.

it would not affect the suppression of illicit traffic ; the price of tea on the continent was 7½ per cent. cheaper than at the company's sales, and 5 per cent. was allowed to the company ; these added to the 12½ per cent. duty, it was asserted, would be a sufficient compensation for all the risks incurred by the smuggler. Mr. Pitt combated these objections : he denied that tea was a certain and permanent object of revenue ; the present state of finance and public credit did not permit him to barter a certainty for an uncertainty : he was obliged to select an object on which he could build the most entire and confident expectation; and with the invaluable benefits that would result from this measure to the public, notwithstanding the industry with which popular odium was attempted to be stirred up against it, he was ready to risk any unpopularity which it might occasion. The bill was passed by a majority of one hundred and forty-eight to forty.

Regulation of duties on British spirits.

A third bill was also passed into a law for the regulation of duties upon British spirits, and to discontinue during a limited time certain imposts upon rum and spirits imported from the West Indies. These three bills comprehended the whole plan of Mr. Pitt upon the subject of smuggling, as far as it was now submitted to parliament. The effect of the scheme for preventing contraband trade, including several improvements which subsequent experience devised, has been almost the annihilation of that species of fraud, to the great benefit of the revenue[f] and of morals. The commutation act being misinterpreted and misrepresented both by ignorance and sophistical ingenuity, caused at first some dissatisfaction; that, however, was not of long continuance, and the additional duty on windows came to be paid without reluctance.

Preliminary motions for the relief of the East India company.

Meanwhile East India affairs occupied the attention of the minister and parliament; a committee was appointed to collect information ; and its report being presented, was taken into consideration by a committee of the whole house. A bill was proposed, for enabling the company to make a half yearly dividend at the rate of eight per cent. for the year, and passed both houses, with considerable opposition in the house of lords, in which it was said that the company's affairs could not afford such a dividend.[g] On the second of July, Mr. Pitt introduced a bill for the relief of the company : this proposition was to allow the company a further respite of duties due to the exchequer, to enable them to accept bills beyond the amount prescribed by former acts of parliament, and to establish their future dividends.

---

f Visitors of the watering places, or other parts of the coast, who have conversed with elderly or middle aged watermen, or any kind of seafaring men, in those places, must have perceived that they considered smuggling, heretofore their most lucrative occupation, as having received its death blow from the hands of Mr. Pitt.

g Parliamentary Journals.

The proposed indulgence was, that the duties now due should
be paid by instalments, at Midsummer and Christmas 1785.
The principle of the projected accommodation, was the solvency of the company at the specified terms. Mr. Pitt, in supporting the measure, informed the house, that from the late inquiries which he had made into the state of the company's
finances, and from the very ample and satisfactory accounts he
had obtained, he had no room to admit the remotest idea, that
they would not, at the period he had mentioned, be able to fulfil
every engagement. India would now enjoy peace, and parliament would enforce the active economy which the present state
of affairs so strongly recommended; a few years of tranquillity,
and a system of exertion and frugality, would render our Indian
possessions affluent and prosperous. Opposition doubted the
favourable prospect of the company's affairs, and objected to
the relief proposed. A question was started, whether or not
parliament, by authorizing acceptances of bills, guaranteed their
validity? Mr. Pitt contended that they did not; Mr. Fox that
they did, at least so far as to pledge the national honour to their
responsibility, by allowing the acceptance which they had a right
to restrain. The sanction of parliament impressed the public
with an opinion of their goodness, and established their credit.
Mr. Dundas illustrated the subject, by reminding the house of
the circumstances in which the restriction had originated. By
the regulating bill of 1773, the public were to come in for a share
in the profits of the company: in order, therefore, to prevent the
appropriation of any part of their profits to the payment of bills
that might be fraudulently sent over from India, it had been
thought necessary to restrain the amount of those bills; consequently, when a parliament should consent to the acceptance of
bills to a greater amount, it resigned, in behalf of the public, so
much of the national claim to the dividends, as was secured to
them by the bill of 1773. The bill passed without a division.

These measures were preparatory and subordinate to the bill
of the minister for the government of India, which he now introduced, similar in object and principle to the scheme that he
had proposed in January, but more detailed in its provisions,
and more extensive in its applications. On the 6th of July, Bill for the
Mr. Pitt proposed his bill for the better regulation of India : in regulation
his prefatory oration he stated the magnitude of the subject; of India.
and described the vast accession of power which the wealth
of India had for a series of years added to the empire of Great
Britain: our former opulence was owing to the prudent management of our commercial·concerns; and our future hopes
depended on the judicious regulations that were now to be introduced for the government of that country. 'The leading ob-'
ject was to correct and restrain abuses, remedy evils, improve
the condition of British India, and thereby augment the opulence and prosperity of this country, by powers adequate to
those important purposes, without being so great as to endanger

CHAP. the balance of the constitution. The bill undertook to insti-
XXXII. tute a new system of government at home, and to regulate the
different presidencies abroad; to provide for the happiness of
1784. the natives, and to put an end to their misunderstandings and
controversies; to establish a new judicature for trying offences
committed in India, and by strictness of government to prevent
delinquency. The proposed change at home was nearly the
same that has appeared in the narrative.[h] It proposed to leave
the management of commercial affairs to the company, and to
vest the territorial possessions in a board of control. Abroad,
the supreme council and governor-general were to have an absolute power of originating orders to the inferior presidencies,
in cases that did not interfere with the directions already received from Britain, and of suspending members of the other councils in case of disobedience. The supreme government was
restrained from offensive war or alliances, without orders from
home; the subordinate settlements were prohibited from forming even defensive treaties, but with a conditional clause, which
would render their permanency dependent on the ratification of
the governor-general; the servants of the company were required to transmit accounts of all considerable transactions to the
council of Bengal, and the supreme council to convey speedy
intelligence to Britain of every important occurrence. In considering the comfort and security of the natives, inquiry was
ordered to be instituted by the different presidencies into the
expulsions of hereditary farmers, and the oppressive rents and
contributions that might have been extorted; and measures
were directed to be employed for their relief and future tranquillity. Various regulations were added, respecting the debts
of the nabob of Arcot, and the rajah of Tanjore, to private individuals and to the company. The bill further required an examination into the different establishments of the presidencies,
for the purposes of retrenchment, and an annual report of the
same to be transmitted to Britain. The proposition also contained both the description of delinquency and the judicial establishments for its cognizance and punishments. Crimes committed by English subjects in any part of India, were made
amenable to every British court of justice, in the same manner
as if they had been committed in our immediate dominions.
Presents, except such as were merely ceremonial, were forbidden to be received, unless by a counsellor at law, a physician, a
surgeon, or a chaplain, under the penalty of confiscation of the
present, and an additional fine, at the discretion of the court.
Disobedience of orders, unless absolutely necessary, and pecuniary transactions contrary to the interests of the company, were
declared to be high crimes and misdemeanors. The company
were forbidden to interfere in favour of any person legally condemned of the above crimes, or to employ him in their service

[h] See vol. i. chap. xxxi.

for ever. The governors of the several presidencies were empowered to imprison any person suspected of illicit correspondence, and to send him to England if they judged it necessary.
Every person serving in India was required, within two months
after his return to England, to deliver in upon oath to the court
of exchequer, an inventory of his real and personal estates, and
a copy thereof to the court of directors, for the inspection of
the proprietors; and should the validity of the account be doubted, or any complaint to that effect made by the board of control, the court of directors, or three proprietors possessing India stock· to the amount of 10,000l. conjunctively, the court
of exchequer were required to examine upon oath the person accused, and to imprison him until he should have satisfactorily answered interrogatories. Neglect or concealment
were to be punished by the imprisonment of the defendant,
the forfeiture of all his estates, both real and personal, and an
incapacity of ever serving the company. For the more speedy
and effectual prosecution of persons in Great Britain, charged with crimes committed in India, a court was established, to
consist of three judges, nominated respectively by the chancery, king's bench, and common pleas, four peers taken from a list
of twenty-six, and six commoners from a list of· forty (the lists
to be chosen by ballot from their respective houses), a certain
number of whom should be subject to peremptory challenge
both by the prosecutor and the defendant. The judgment of
the court was to extend to imprisonment, fine, and incapacity
of serving the company. Such are the outlines of Mr. Pitt's
legislative, executorial, and judicial arrangement for the government of India.

Opposition reprobated the bill, on the grounds of insufficiency
for the regulation of India, and dangerously extending the
patronage of the crown. Many objections were also made to
particular clauses; the new tribunal was said to be in truth
a screen for delinquents, since no man was to be tried but on
the accusation of the company or the attorney-general; he had
only to conciliate government, in order to attain perfect security.
The obligation to swear to the amount of property, and the
powers granted to the courts of enforcing interrogatories,
tended to compel persons to criminate themselves, and were
modes of inquisitorial proceedings unknown to the subjects of
this island. It was confidently denied that there was any necessity for so alarming a departure from the established principles and practice of the constitution; and it was therefore
presumed that it could have been done with no other than a
corrupt view, to draw the rich and powerful servants of the
East India company into a dependence upon the crown for its
protection. Mr. Fox directed the force of his eloquence
against this measure of his rival. "It prepares (said the ora-
"tor) feebleness at home by a division of power; if there be
"a receipt, a nostrum, for making a weak government, it is

CHAP.
XXXII.

1784.

"by giving the power of contriving measures to one, and the
"nomination of the persons who are to execute them to another.
"Theories that do not connect men with measures, are not
"theories for this world; they are chimeras with which a re-
"cluse may divert his fancy, but not principles on which a
"statesmen would found his system. But, say the ministers,
"the negative provides against the appointment of improper
"officers; the commissioners have a negative, therefore they
"have full power. Here then is the complete annihilation of
"the company, and of the so much vaunted chartered rights.
"The bill is a scheme of dark and delusive art, and takes
"away the claims of the company by slow and gradual sap.
"The first assumption made by the minister, is the power of
"superintendance and control; and what is the meaning of
"this power? Does it mean such a superintendance and con-
"trol as this house possesses over ministers? No; for this
"house has not the power of giving official instructions. It is
"to be an active control, it is to originate measures; and this
"is the next step. At last, to complete the invasion, orders
"may be secretly conveyed to India by the commissioners,
"at the very moment they were giving their open countenance
"to instructions to be sent from the directors of an opposite
"tendency. To suffer such a scheme of dark intrigue will be
"a farce, a child's play, and does not deserve the name of a
"government. To this progressive and underhand scheme,
"I peremptorily object. If it were right to vest the powers
"of the court of directors in a board of privy-counsellors,
"at any rate it should be done openly. A great nation ought
"never to descend to gradual and insidious encroachment.
"Let them do what they wished for explicitly, and show
"the company, that what they dare to do, they dare to
"justify."

Argu-
ments
for it.

The minister declared his conviction, that the ordinary courts
of justice were inadequate to the cognizance of Indian delinquency; and that there were many crimes committed there,
for which the common law had provided no redress: at the
same time he did not conceive, that the principle on which he
proceeded was so totally unknown in the jurisprudence of this
kingdom: it was recognised in the whole code of martial law.
As to the influence of the crown, he trusted he had sufficiently
guarded against any such apprehensions, by the mode directed
for the constitution of the new court of judicature. The whole
plan was efficient to every good purpose, and guarded against

Compari-
son of the
two bills as
resulting
from the
characters
of their au-
thors.

the evil which must have resulted from the scheme of Mr. Fox.
The bill passed both houses by very great majorities.
In the characters of Messrs. Pitt and Fox a diversity has
been remarked, which may perhaps account for a striking
difference in their respective systems. Energetic as Mr. Fox
is in power, he is not always proportionably guarded and considerate in the exertions of his faculties; hence, though his

judgment be exquisite, his actually exerted discrimination does not uniformly keep pace with the strength of his invention: Mr. Pitt, on the other hand, powerful as he is in force, is extremely circumspect and discriminate, as to the extent and bounds of operation most conducive to the purpose. Mr. Fox, adopting a principle in itself right, often adopts it too implicitly, and carries its application to a greater extent than the exact case justifies. Mr. Pitt much more accurately fixes the line of demarcation, which the principle with the existing case requires. The India bill of 1783, considered in relation to certain ends, was ably, skilfully, and effectually devised; but attending to efficacy, its author neglected control. The wheels strongly constructed, but wanting the drag, by the force and rapidity of their motion, might have overturned and crushed the constitution. The plan of 1784, in forming a power for specific use, guarded more cautiously against eventual abuse.

During this session, the Westminster election occupied considerable attention; a scrutiny having been granted by the high bailiff, at the instance of sir Cecil Wray, the unsuccessful candidate, its legality was questioned by Mr. Fox: according to that gentleman, the election ought to have been referred to a committee, under Mr. George Grenville's bill. The discussion produced an astonishing display of legal ability and knowledge, both from Mr. Pitt and Mr. Fox; when the question was put, the arguments of the former were found to have prevailed, and the scrutiny was ordered to be continued.
Debate on the Westminster election.

A very humane and equitable measure was this session proposed by Mr. Dundas, indeed equally meritorious as a scheme of individual justice and national policy; this was the restoration of the estates forfeited in the Scottish rebellions to the representatives of the sufferers. He enlarged on the wisdom and justice of the principle, and adducing the opinion of a Chatham as an authority in favour of his arguments, he quoted the celebrated passage in one of that illustrious orator's speeches, which describes the merits of the Scotch Highlanders. He drew an auspicious omen from reflecting, that the first blow had been given the proscription by the earl of Chatham; and trusted, that the remains of a system, which, whether dictated at first by narrow views or by sound policy, ought certainly to be temporary, would be completely annihilated under the administration of his son.
Mr Dundas proposes the restoration of the forfeited estates.

He made the panegyric of persons under this predicament, who had distinguished themselves in the last war. He said there was not one of those families, in which some person had not atoned for the errors of his ancestors, and spilt his blood in his country's cause; and he would boldly assert, that the spirit which had rendered the inhabitants of the highlands disaffected to the present government, had long since disappeared, and that the king had not at this moment a set of more loyal subjects
A law is passed for that purpose.

1784.

in his dominions. It would be magnanimity to treat them like true and faithful subjects, and cancel for ever the offences of their ancestors; nor would the liberality of the proceeding be greater than its policy. The spirit of emigration in the High-landers was such, that nothing could extinguish it but the return of their long lost patrons, and the affection and reverence which the inhabitants of that part of the island felt for their natural lords. It was obvious, that a property held for the be-nefit of the public, was not so well managed as if possessed by private proprietors: the restoration of the estates would tend very much to the improvement and prosperity of the country. The bill experienced some opposition in the house of lords; the objections proceeded not from the substance, but the lateness of the season, and the form in which it was introduced; all these, however, were overruled, and it was passed into a law.

Labours of Mr. Pitt in investiga-ting the public ac-counts.

Mr. Pitt found himself necessarily engaged in the laborious business of winding up the accounts of the war, and was compelled, by the burthen of floating debt, and the general state of the national finances, to negotiate a loan, though in time of peace; but as this measure was obviously unavoidable, in order to make the terms as favourable as possible, instead of granting enormous profit to private or political favourites, he disposed of it to the best bidders. The sum borrowed was six millions: the taxes were chiefly upon articles of accommoda-tion and ornament in dress, furniture, and equipage, or postage, by the restrictions of franking, with some additional duties on liquors. The principle of impost with which he set out, was to bear as lightly as possible on the poorer classes: besides this loan, there was a large debt unfunded, chiefly in navy and ex-chequer hills, and ordnance debentures. Of these six million, six hundred thousand pounds were funded, and the rest neces-sarily deferred to the following year. On the 2d day of Au-gust, the session was ended, by a speech from the throne; in which his majesty expressed his warmest thanks for the emi-nent proofs exhibited by parliament of zealous and diligent at-tention to the public service. The happiest effects were de-clared to be expected from the provision made for the better government of India, and from the institution of a tribunal so peculiarly adapted to the trial of offences committed in that distant country. The sovereign observed with great satisfac-tion, the laws which were passed for the preservation and im-provement of the revenue. He applauded the zeal and libera-lity with which the house of commons had provided for the exigencies of the state, though he felt and regretted the neces-sity in which their exertions originated. A definitive treaty, the king informed the house, was concluded between Britain and the states-general; and the aspect of affairs, as well as the positive assurances from foreign powers, promised a continu-ance of general tranquillity.

Supplies,

Loan and taxes.

CHAP. XXXIII.

FOR the last twenty years, England had been so much engaged in her own intestine and colonial dissensions, and afterwards with the American war and its consequences, that she bestowed much less attention on the general concerns of Europe, than at any former period of her history since the revolution. From the commencement of Mr. Pitt's administration, while recovering her internal prosperity, she resumed her importance among foreign nations. During the remaining portion of our narrative, her interests became so interwoven with those of continental powers, that the general state of Europe must occupy a larger share of the history than has been hitherto necessary.

The empress of Russia had not been engaged in any great war since the peace concluded in 1774 with Turkey; she nevertheless was actively employed in schemes of external aggrandizement, as well as of internal improvement. Catharine's objects were to extend over Germany, and her more northern vicinity, her influence and power, so much increased by her acquisitions in Poland; on the other side to make herself mistress of the Turkish empire, through the extent of coast which she should then possess on the Euxine and the Mediterranean: in addition to her maritime territories in the north, she proposed to attain a commercial and naval eminence, proportioned to her territorial power, rapidly increase the value of her immense

CHAP. XXXIII.
1784.
Britain resumes her attention to the affairs of the continent.

State of foreign powers.

Situation and views of Catharine.

dominions, and become decidedly superior to every other sovereign. The end was grand, nor were the means ill adapted.
At peace herself, she had carefully surveyed the circumstances,
situation, and character of other states and princes. As the
supreme obstacle to maritime exaltation would be Britain, the
confederacy formed against the mistress of the ocean was consonant to her wishes, and, without open and direct hostilities,
she endeavoured to promote its success. This naturally produced a connexion between her and France, the ancient ally of
Turkey, the chief object of Catharine's ambition. The sagacious empress, penetrating into the characters of other princes,
availed herself of either their strength or weakness, and applied
to their ruling passions to gratify her own. The king of Prussia, she well knew, she never could render an instrument for
effecting her purposes, though she might procure him as a coadjutor when co-operation with Russia suited his own. She was
aware that he would instantly dive into her designs, and effectually obstruct them if they were likely ever remotely to interfere with his interests. Besides, in her principal scheme, his
co-operation could not directly advance her designs, even if he
were so disposed. From the situation and power of his dominions, the emperor would be the most effectual auxiliary;
and to his personal character, she did not doubt she could apply

Character
and pro-
jects of the
emperor
Joseph.

with success. Joseph was fond of distinction, without the means
of acquiring it by great and meritorious qualities. Ardently
desirous of increasing his power, without solid and vigorous
capacity to gratify his favourite passion, he was one of those
secondary characters, bustling, busy, and active, which in all
ages and ranks have been efficacious tools, moved and guided
by superior ability. Joseph, she well knew, from his power
and vicinity, would be a most useful instrument in her designs
upon Turkey, either of encroachment, which she at the time
meditated, or of subjugation, which though at a more distant
period she no less firmly intended. That she might the more
readily win over Joseph to second her views, in the year 1780,
she requested a personal conference; they met at Mohilof, and
there Catharine thoroughly confirmed the opinion which she
had conceived of his abilities and character, and after having
impressed him with the highest opinion of her own genius and
accomplishments, she appeared to make him the repository of

Catharine
courts his
alliance.

her most secret designs. She represented to him the advantages that would accrue to both empires from a close political
union; and the practicability that, by such a connexion, they
might share the spoils of Turkey, and each acquiring both an
extensive and productive accession of dominions contiguous to
their respective territories, their concert, when so increased in
power, would enable them to direct the affairs of the German

and a trea-
ty is con-
cluded.

empire. Joseph very readily acceded, both to the expediency
of the object, and feasibility of the plan. It was agreed that
Catharine should return to her capital, and that Joseph, after

making a circuitous tour through the Russian provinces, should **CHAP.**
repair to Petersburgh. There they more completely digested **XXXIII.**
their schemes, and a firm alliance was established between the
two imperial sovereigns.

1784.

Catharine found that from the late cessions in Turkey she **Catharine's**
derived great and rapid advantages; her commerce on the **invasion of**
Black Sea daily extended its progress; the Russian vessels pas- **the Crimea.**
sed the Dardanelles, and went to traffic at Aleppo, at Smyrna,
and in the Italian ports. By so great and increasing benefits,
the desire of Catharine was inflamed to extend the kind of possessions from which they arose. The Crimea, so well known
in ancient history and poetry as thé Taurica Chersonesus, the
scene of exquisite tragedy, is a peninsula which projects into
the Euxine from the Palus Mœotis, or the sea of Azoff. This
country, celebrated for its fertility and commerce, and filled
with populous towns and cities, was formerly a dependency
upon Turkey, and had been, at the last peace, declared to be a
neutral principality, under one of the Tartarian khans, or chieftains. The empress studiously fomented dissensions between
the ruling prince and his brother, a pretender to the sovereignty, expecting that the former, whom she professed to favour
and protect, would implore her assistance, and thus afford a
pretext for sending Russian troops into the Crimea. The
Tartar solicited the assistance of Catharine, as that ambitious
princess desired. The empress, secure of meeting no interruption from Joseph, and well knowing the feebleness of the Turks,
invaded the peninsula with a powerful army, still professing
that her intention was to relieve the khan. She left him the
shadow of power; but taking all the substance to herself, she
became absolute mistress of the Crimea. Having ascertained **Seizure of**
the success of the iniquitous invasion, she published one of those **that coun-**
manifestoes, in which modern aggressors and conquerors render **try.**
due homage *in words* to that justice and rectitude which THEIR
ACTIONS are grossly violating. In this curious monument of
imperial reasoning she affirmed, that her successes in the late
war had given her a right to the Crimea, which from her sincere desire of peace she had sacrificed to the wishes of the
Ottoman Porte; that she had proposed the happiness of the
Crimeans by procuring to them liberty and independence, under
the authority of a chief elected by themselves. But those
benevolent wishes had been grievously disappointed: revolt
and rebellion had arisen; to suppress which, and restore tranquillity and happiness, from the same philanthropic motives she
had been induced, at a very great expense of money and loss
of troops, to interfere, for the beneficent purpose of preventing
the recurrence of such evils; and had undertaken, once for all,
the firm resolution of terminating the troubles of the Crimea.
The measures which she had employed, the manifesto farther
affirmed, were also intended to perpetuate the peace between
Russia and the Porte. In this bountiful display of virtue, seeking

CHAP.
XXXIII.

1784.

Measures
of internal
improve-
ment.

It is the
interest of
Russia to
cultivate
amity with
Britain.

the temporal comforts of its objects, Catharine did not forget their eternal happiness, and promised her new subjects a full and free toleration of their religion. The Turks were extremely enraged at this usurpation of Catharine, but did not at that time conceive themselves strong enough to commence hostilities.

Meanwhile the empress was engaged in improving her own country, and in connecting herself more closely with Joseph. In pursuing the former of these objects, she promoted manufactures, trade, voyages, and expeditions of discovery; particularly for exploring the resources of those dominions which were remote from the metropolis, and not under her own immediate inspection. She endeavoured as much as possible to facilitate communication between distant parts of Russia, and especially by water conveyance. She had projected to open a navigation between the White Sea and the Baltic, by a line of canals which should join the gulf of Finland, the lakes of Ladoga and Onega, and the river Dwina, and thus save traders with Archangel the dangerous voyage round Cape North, but on a survey of the interjacent country, abounding with rocks and mountains, the scheme was judged to be impracticable. She attempted to establish an intercourse between her eastern and western dominions, by opening a canal between the Pruth, which falls into the Wolga, and the Mista, that communicates by lakes with a river which falls into the Baltic, that so there might be a commercial traffic carried on between the maritime regions of Europe, and the inland recesses of northern Asia; and this great design was fully accomplished.

The policy of Russia respecting foreign alliances, was of much more questionable wisdom, than her schemes of internal improvement. The former princes of Muscovy had uniformly cultivated a close intercourse with England; desirous of naval and commercial aggrandizement, Catharine conceived that the trade and maritime power of Britain were the chief obstructions to her own, and from this opinion rather discouraged than promoted amity with these realms. Were a person in private life to observe, that it is the interest of venders of commodities to cultivate a close connexion with their best customers, he would be charged with advancing a self-evident proposition, which no man in his senses could deny, either as an abstract truth, or as a prudent rule of conduct. Undeniable as it is, yet Catharine was not guided by this principle. The commerce with England is essential to Russia. No merchants, with smaller capitals, or less commercial spirit than the English, will or can advance such sums of money long before the period of return, to invigorate the manufactures, employ the people in a wide and poor country, aud enable the small traders to bring their goods to market from remote districts. Without this application of British capital, industry ceasing to be productive, trade and manufactures would languish, and all the efforts of

Catharine for stimulating the industry of her subjects, must CHAP.
become less valuable, in the proportion that her policy de- XXXIII.
creased the English market. Most of the articles that her dominions could supply, might be procured from America ; and 1784.
should repulsive conduct drive Britain from Russia into other
channels of import, it would be a loss to her commerce, which
from no other source she could compensate. Never could, or
can, Russia profit by disagreement with England. Influenced, Her con-
however, in this important instance by narrow, and unavailing duct to
jealousy, instead of her usual enlarged policy, she conducted Britain not
herself inimically to the nation with which it was her chief in- with her
terest to maintain the strictest friendship. She continued to usual wis-
cultivate an amicable correspondence with France, and the dom.
closest union with Joseph, whom she ardently seconded in
schemes which now occupied the chief attention of Europe.

Since the year 1781, Joseph II. by the death of his mother
the empress-queen, had been the sole sovereign of the Austrian
dominions ; and being now free from restraint, fully exhibited
that character which was before discovered by the discerning,
but had not yet been displayed to the world. Possessing
lively but superficial talents, the emperor was extremely desirous of fame and distinction. Without original genius to Presuming
concert great schemes, Joseph was the creature of imitation, projects of
and had formed himself on the model of the king of Prussia, the empe-
as far as his conception of that extraordinary character reach- ror.
ed. Among many objects which called forth the exertion of
Frederick's astonishing powers, two principally occupied his
attention ; the acquirement of productive territories, and the
improvement of all his possessions, according to their physical,
political, and commercial resources, including the advancement
of the general character of his subjects. His efforts ably,
skilfully, and constantly directed to one or both of these objects, had been so successful as to raise Prussia from being a
small and secondary principality, to the first rank among the
powers of Europe. Joseph attempted both to improve and
extend the Austrian possessions ; his means did not, however,
bear much resemblance to the designs of his archetype. Frederick directed his efforts to increase national prosperity in its
various constituents : whatever opinions he himself might have
formed on the subject of religion, he was far from judging it
expedient to interfere with the established notions of his subjects, or to subvert any of those establishments, which, either in
themselves or by habitual associations, cherish sentiments of
piety, the surest sources of both the private and public virtues
which exalt a people. If he was a deist, he did not apprehend
that his subjects would be the fitter without religion for either
defending or improving his dominions. Like many others of
no great talents, Joseph considered indifference to religion as a
source of distinction ; he was ostentatious in infidelity, and
wished it, under the name of liberality, to spread through his

CHAP.
XXXIII.

1784.

Suppres-
sion of re-
ligious or-
ders.

territories. One measure which he adopted, was certainly in itself equitable; he disclaimed all dependence in secular affairs on the pope of Rome: he justly deemed it totally inconsistent with the rights and dignity of an independent sovereign, to acknowledge subordination to a foreign priest. The emperor greatly increased toleration in the various parts of his dominions, and in general extended religious liberty to Jews and all other sects and denominations. So far his policy appeared wise and liberal; but counsels and acts right in themselves, may be wrong as part of a general system. The emperor was a *reforming projector*, and in the ardour of his zeal for change very far exceeded expediency: the suppression of the religious orders, and confiscation of their property, were the principal objects of his innovating plans. In 1782, he issued imperial decrees for suppressing monasteries, convents, and every species of religious fraternities or sisterhoods, and took possession of all their lands and moveables. A commission was established for the administration of the sequestered estates and effects, which were so considerable, that the most moderate calculators supposed that the emperor could gain four or five millions sterling by the reform.[i] Annual stipends were allotted for the maintenance of the reformed abbots, abbesses, canons, canonesses, monks, and nuns, which were in some degree proportioned to their respective rank and condition; but it was heavily complained, that the portions were so scantily measured, as to be shamefully inadequate to the purpose. A reform, involving in it such an extensive robbery, was by no means applauded by distinguishing and wise men, as consistent with either justice or sound policy. The spoliation rendered the whole measure more particularly odious than it otherwise might have been; and whatever means were at home employed to stifle complaint, they could not restrain the censure of foreigners upon the conduct of this prince. Many conceived that his object was to plunder the church; that the pillage (instead of being applied to any useful or benevolent purpose) was intended merely for the support of his ambitious projects; and that he had concerted with Russia, plans of mutual co-operation, in order to aggrandize both powers. The situation of

i The celebrated Mirabeau makes the following observations upon these changes: The internal revolutions which the emperor has effected in his dominions have been greatly applauded; but what a number of objections might be brought against these eulogiums; at least, the panegyrists of Joseph the Second ought to tell us what justice they find in driving a citizen from the profession which he has embraced, under the sanction of the laws. I will tell them plainly, that there is as much injustice in expelling a friar, or a nun, from their retreat, as in turning a private individual out of his house. Despise the friars as much as you will, but do not persecute them; above all, do not rob them; for we ought not either to persecute or rob any man, from the avowed atheist down to the most credulous capuchin.

maritime Europe had afforded to the Austrian Netherlands CHAP.
mercantile benefit, which inspired Joseph with the hopes of ac- XXXIII.
quiring naval and commercial importance. The war that pervaded western Europe had transferred from Holland to Aus- 1784.
trian Flanders and Brabant that immense trade, which, through His
the canals and great German rivers, England carried on with schemes of
the eastern and northern countries of the continent. The be- naval and
nefits which the Netherlands derived from this transit of so great cial ag-
a commerce, were still farther increased, by the peculiar circum- grandize-
stances of the naval war in which Britain was involved: at- ment.
tacked at once in every part of the world, England was frequently under the necessity of abandoning the protection of
her European commerce, that her foreign fleets might be sufficiently powerful to cover her very numerous distant possessions; and British merchants were obliged to use foreign vessels for the conveyance of their goods. From the operation of
these causes, Ostend became a general mart of all the neutral
as well as belligerent states; and such an influx of trade was
carried into that city and port, that even early in the war it
reached a degree of opulence and commercial importance,
which it never before enjoyed, or was expected to attain. The
spirit of mercantile adventure was rapidly diffused through the
Austrian Low Countries; the desire and hope of acquiring immense riches universally operated: Brussels itself, notwithstanding the habitual ease and love of pleasure incident to its situation, and the long residence of a court, could not escape the in-
fection; and many of its inhabitants, who had never before
engaged in commerce of any kind, now laid out all their ready
money in building ships. The citizens of Antwerp regretted
the loss of their former trade, riches, and splendour; and conceived hopes of the possible recovery of those valuable advantages. Indeed, the spirit now excited was so prevalent, that the
states of the Netherlands presented a memorial to the emperor,
requesting that he would take measures for the re-tablishment
of that port. Meanwhile the growing opulence of Ostend was
immense; the limits of the city became too narrow for its inhabitants, and the buildings were not sufficient to cover the immense quantities of merchandise of which it was become the
temporary depository: traders and speculators continually arrived to participate such benefits, and rapidly rising population
was in proportion to the sudden flow of riches. Elated with
unexpected prosperity, the inhabitants little regarded the circumstance in which it originated, and forgot that, as the cause
was transitory, the effect was not likely to be permanent. Such
was the state of affairs and sentiments in the Netherlands when
the emperor arrived in June 1781 at Ostend: struck with the
flourishing condition in which he found this port, impressed
with the exulting hopes of the inhabitants, and devoid of that
comprehensive sagacity which could distinguish between special and general causes, with the precipitancy of superficial

reasoners, he concluded that the prosperity which was then prevalent must always last. In his tour through the Netherlands
he bestowed the greatest attention upon merchants, and every

object connected with merchandise. Arrived at Antwerp, he in
his conduct exhibited views of interfering in the navigation of the
Scheldt. He went down that river in a boat, as far as to the
first of those Dutch forts, which had been erected to guard the
passage, and to secure to the states the exclusive command of
the river; he had the depth of the channel ascertained in several
places, and he strictly examined all the obstructions of art and
nature which tended to impede its navigation. Joseph had also
farther objects in view, which he thought the situation of Holland, weakened by her impolitic war with her natural ally, would
enable him to accomplish.

At the conclusion of the succession war, as many readers
must know, the principal fortresses of the Austrian Netherlands
were deposited in the hands of the Dutch, for the mutual benefit and security of the court of Vienna and themselves; and
while they formed a powerful barrier to cover the territories of
the states, they were to be garrisoned and defended by them,
and thus serve to obviate the danger apprehended from the
power and ambition of France. During the weakness of Austria in the beginning of Maria Teresa's reign, she derived considerable advantages from this treaty; but now that he was
become so powerful, the emperor thought himself fully competent to protect and defend his own dominions, and, being master
of great armies, he conceived that he did not want fortresses
to impede the progress of an enemy. Thinking it derogatory
to his own honour, as well as to the dignity and power of the
empire, that a great number of his principal cities and fortresses
should be garrisoned, and at his own expense, he proposed to
resume the barrier. To justify the intended measure, he stated
that, in the last war between Austria and France, the Dutch
had shown themselves incapable of maintaining the fortresses;
that, besides, the state of affairs was now so entirely altered,
that none of the causes or motives which originally operated
to the establishment of the barrier, any longer existed. France,
instead of being the common enemy, as then, was now the
common friend of both parties; her ambition was no longer
dangerous, and if it were, was directed to other objects; the
emperor and she were mutually bound in the strictest and dearest ties of friendship and blood. On the side of Holland, it was
alleged that Austria was indebted to Britain and the states-general for the possession of the Low Countries; and that, as
these were the great leaders in the succession war, they compelled France and Spain to cede the Netherlands to Austria.
The settlement of the barrier was the only compensation to
Holland for all these services, and her immense expenses of
blood and treasure to place the grandfather of the present emperor on the throne of Spain. Besides, being a direct breach

of treaty and violation of faith, the proposed measure would be CHAP.
a shameful dereliction of every sense of past service and obli- XXXIII.
gation; and the season chosen for its accomplishment, under
the present embarrassed and depressed state of the republic, 1784.
would render it still more disgraceful. These arguments, how-Disman-
ever strong, were of little avail against the power of Joseph; tles the
and the Dutch were compelled to yield. The emperor dismantled fortresses
the fortresses; and thus Holland, through her folly in going to therlands.
war with England, was stripped of her barrier, for which she
had often and vigorously fought. Her most valuable resources
being exhausted by war, that unhappy country had the additional calamity of being torn asunder by factions; peace had
neither restored vigour and unanimity at home, nor reputation
and importance abroad: on the contrary, their civil dissensions
were every day increasing in magnitude and virulence. The
faction hostile to the stadtholder, and connected with France, was
now become so strong, that no sufficient counterpoise remained
in the state, to restrain the excess and violence incident to the
predominance of political parties. The emperor made various claims upon the Dutch frontiers, and did not want pretexts
that gave a plausible colouring to meditated injustice. But of He propo-
all his claims, the most distressing to Holland were the claims ses to open
upon the city and country of Maestricht, the entire and free the
navigation of the Scheldt from Antwerp to the sea, and a free Scheldt.
and uninterrupted commerce to the factories of Holland in both
the East and West Indies. The Dutch alleged, that the emperor claimed all the benefits which were derived from their colonies in the New World, and their conquests and settlements in
the East, being the fruits of much hard adventure, great risk,
and advance of treasure, of numberless treaties and negotiations, and of many severe wars through the course of near two
centuries. The rights of the republic, and particularly her exclusive sovereignty of the Scheldt, had been confirmed and
guaranteed to her by all the treaties which secure the political
existence of Europe. The claim upon Maestricht was founded
upon obsolete pretences; important as the place was, however, Argu-
it was only a matter of secondary consideration, and altogether ments on
subordinate to the Scheldt. The assertion of the emperor was both sides.
founded on what he called the natural rights of countries to the
navigation and benefit of a river which ran through his territories; whereas the possession of Holland rested on positive and
specific compact. A recurrence to the original rights of man,
the Dutch justly contended, would destroy those social agreements between individuals and political conventions, which constitute and secure all private and public property. Such a principle, practically admitted, would unloose every bond that unites
mankind, throw them into a state of nature, and render the
world a chaos of confusion and disorder. However just these
arguments were, the emperor paid no regard to reasoning so
opposite to his ambitious views. He saw in several concessions

CHAP. the fears of the Dutch, and trusted that their dread of his
XXXIII. power would make them desist from the maintenance of their
own rights. The moral principle, indeed, of his conduct was
1784. very simple: the Dutch are weak, I am strong; I intend to rob
Joseph's them of their property, and they will be afraid to resist. In
allegations this belief, he tried the experiment, by equipping two vessels, of
entirely which one was to proceed down the Scheldt from Antwerp to
contrary to the sea, and the other up the river from the sea, on its course
justice. from Ostend to that city. The captain of the former of these
was furnished with written orders from the emperor, commanding him to proceed in the brig Louis, from Antwerp along the
Scheldt into the sea, and expressly forbidding him and his crew
to submit to any detention, or to any examination whatever
from ships belonging to the republic, which he might meet in
the river, or in any manner acknowledge their authority. The
imperial ship passed the Lilu and some other forts without examination, but falling in with a Dutch cutter that sent a boat
with an officer to the vessel from Antwerp, the imperial captain
told the Dutchman, THAT HE WAS ON HIS PASSAGE TO THE SEA;
and that his instructions forbid his holding any parley whatever
with the officers or ships of the United Provinces. The cutter now
coming up to the brig, the imperialist quoted the instructions of
his master, and refused to give any further satisfaction, persevering to sail towards the sea. The commander of the cutter
entreated, threatened, and employed every means to induce the
other to desist from conduct which would necessarily bring the
affair to a crisis; but finding his efforts unavailing, he determined to prevent such an unjust and insolent usurpation. He
fired first powder without ball, but at length poured a broad-
side, and threatened with the next discharge to sink his opponent, if he continued refractory: the imperialist seeing it was
in vain to contend, relinquished his object. The ship from Ostend was no less disappointed in the expectations of getting
undisputed up the river. The emperor pretended to consider
this spirited defence of their own right, as an aggression on the
part of the Dutch. The imperial ambassador was recalled from
the Hague, and an army of sixty thousand men was under orders and in preparation for marching from the Austrian hereditary dominions to the Netherlands. The troops which were
already there, amounted to about sixteen thousand men; great
trains of artillery, and all the other apparatus of war were in
The Dutch motion. Exhausted as they were by the war with England,
prepare to the Dutch made very vigorous preparations; they employed
defend agents to hire troops from Germany; and at home they exerted
their themselves in recruiting the troops, strengthening the frontiers,
rights. and putting the posts and garrisons in the best posture of defence. They prepared for the last refuge which the nature of
their country peculiarly afforded, and resolved to open the dykes
and la the Flat Countries under water. While they were thus
making provisions for hostility, they endeavoured to appease

Joseph by reasonable and equitable expostulation; though they were very far from being disposed, they said, to go to war with the emperor, they were bound by all the laws of nature, of nations, of justice, and of reason, not to permit a violation of their dearest and most incontrovertible rights.

Russia was at this time closely connected with the emperor, and though she had lately sought the alliance of Holland, and made the republic the tool of her ambition in the armed neutrality, she now warmly and openly seconded the pretensions of Joseph. Catharine, in a letter to the king of Prussia roundly asserted that the Dutch were in the wrong, and the emperor equally just, moderate, and disinterested. The amount of her reasoning was, that the law of nature gave the Austrian Netherlands the exclusive right of the navigation of the Scheldt, and that the Dutch, in quoting specific treaties to support their claims, manifested an avidity which was notorious and blamable in every respect. Nothing well founded (she said, in the conclusion of her letter) can be alleged in favour of Holland; therefore she merits no assistance from any foreign power. The consequences which these republicans are drawing upon themselves by their obstinacy, must be submitted to the moderation of the emperor alone: I am firmly resolved to assist his pretensions with all my land and sea forces, and with as much efficacy as if the welfare of my own empire was in agitation. I hope that this declaration of my sentiments will meet with the success which our reciprocal friendship deserves, and which has never been interrupted.[k] These maxims of imperial ethics were not more contrary to the moral judgment of impartial individuals clearly apprehending and fairly estimating right and wrong, than the imperial politics of both the sovereigns were to the obvious interests of neighbouring potentates. The king of Prussia, it was foreseen, would not be an idle spectator of such an accession accruing to his rival. France, for her own security, would protect Holland against so formidable a neighbour, and was not without farther inducements to oppose the emperor, even should actual hostilities be the consequence. To the arms of France the rich provinces of the Low Countries were most likely to have recourse, especially now that the fortresses on the barrier were demolished. Notwithstanding the affinity between the royal families of Vienna and Versailles, his most christian majesty made very pressing remonstrances to the emperor; he justified the conduct of the Dutch, and urged his imperial majesty not to persevere in violating these important rights, which were so solemnly secured; he hoped the emperor would desist from efforts, which would cause so general an alarm among his neighbours; and other powers would think themselves obliged to take such precautions and measures as circumstances and

k See translation of this letter in the State Papers, 1784, page 352.

CHAP. events might require. The king himself, must, in that case,
XXXIII. be under the necessity of assembling troops on his frontiers,
〜〜〜 and could not, by any means, be indifferent to the fate of the
1784. United Provinces, nor see them attacked by open force in their
rights and possessions. The remonstrances of France made
no impression upon the emperor ; he considered the free navigation of the Scheldt as an incontrovertible right, which was
subject to no discussion or question. The Netherlands was
fast filling with his troops, and winter only retarded hostile
operations.

Britain is   Great Britain observed all those proceedings with a watchful
disposed eye, but did not commit herself by any hasty declaration. The
to protect views of the British cabinet were great and extensive; it was
the rights planned to secure Holland from the aggressions of her neigh-
of Holland. bours, and to detach her from a connexion with France. This
project, however, was then only in contemplation, being by no
means fit for execution.

Britain re-   Britain was now recovering fast from the distresses of the
covers war ; trade was reviving; by the prevention of fraud the reve-
from the nue was becoming much more productive; and industry and
distresses enterprise were again roused by the rekindled hopes of suc-
of the war. cess. So lately drooping, this country now raised her head;
a benignant season added to the improvements of her condition, and in present comfort the people soon forgot recent distress: prospects of returning prosperity opened, and the people were satisfied with government, whose measures they expected would greatly increase and accelerate private and public prosperity. The great demands of our distant possessions,
precluded during the war from regular and sufficient supply,
afforded a very large vent for the productions and acquisitions
of British industry and skill. The Americans too, communication being again opened, eagerly flocked in quest of British
wares, the superior, excellence of which, compulsory disuse had
only imprinted the more deeply on their minds. The restored
islands of the West Indies furnished a considerable market for
our commodities; the want of which, while under the dominion of our enemies, they had so sensibly felt. The settlements also which remained in our possession, had been but sparingly provided while hostile fleets hovered on their coasts, and
not yet having fully recovered from the scourge of the hurri-
canes, called for a great portion of our merchandise. Of our
foreign settlements, the chief vent after the peace was the East,
in which the supply had not been by any means so liberal as
the wants of British India required; but during this, and some
years after the war, the outward trade of the company very far
exceeded the usual periods of peace.[1] Our commerce with

1 This great and general benefit to skilful and judicious adventurers, as well
as to the public, was attended with partial evil in the ruin of those traders,
who did not distinguish the real nature of the case, and who confounded tem-

our late maritime enemies of Europe revived, although it was
easily seen that systems might be formed, respecting every
branch of trade, which would render them much more productive.

    This year England lost one of the brightest ornaments that
had graced her literary annals during a century, with which he
was almost coeval. In December 1784, died Dr. Samuel Johnson, in the 76th year of his age, after a long and tormenting
illness, which he bore with fortitude and resignation, worthy of
his other virtues. Literary history affords few instances of such
a combination of intellectual and moral qualities as constituted
the character, and prompted and guided the efforts of Samuel
Johnson. An understanding perspicacious, powerful, and comprehensive; an imagination vigorous, fertile, and brilliant; and
a memory retentive, accurate, and stored with valuable knowledge, were uniformly directed to render mankind wise, virtuous and religious. The most successful and beneficial exertions
of this illustrious sage were exhibited in philology, criticism,
biography, and ethics. On subjects of language, Johnson
displayed science as well as knowledge; he not only collected
usages, but investigated principles; applying and modifying
general analogies, according to the circumstances of the particular cases, he extremely enriched the English tongue, and improved it in precision and force. The style which his precept
and example formed, bore the stamp of his mind and habits,
being less distinguished for elegance and delicacy, than for perspicuity and strength: his expression, however, was perhaps
not the most useful as a general model, because its excellence
depended on its conformity to his vigorous sentiments and
thought. Since the time of Aristotle few have equalled Johnson as a critic, either in principles of estimation, or in actually
appreciating defect and excellence. Surveying models rather
than considering ends, many critics of distinguished acuteness
and knowledge of literature conceived that meritorious execution consists in resemblance to certain celebrated performances:
but these, justly and highly applauded, do not include every
possible means of deserving applause. Disregarding mere
usage and authority, Johnson followed nature and reason: in
rating the value of a Shakespeare, he did not esteem the mode
of Grecian arrangement the criterion of judgment, but the exhibited operation of passion, sentiment, and character, and its
conformity to real life. He estimated works of imitation by

porary with general causes. Finding that very large profits had been made
by a variety of articles during the first voyages after the war, not a few of
the company's officers in the shipping service, and their connexion at home,
carried out investments of the same kind, until they glutted the market
and lost their former profits, and from their misjudging eagerness of avarice
completely defeated their own purposes and became bankrupts; but skilful
and able traders continued to realize fortunes.

their likeness to originals, combined with the importance of object and difficulty of delineation. As a biographer, Dr. Johnson is unequalled; he indeed possessed the highest requisites for that important species of writing: he thoroughly knew the constitution and movements of the human understanding and will; was intimately conversant with the kind of circumstances in which his subjects acted; and the usual and probable operation of such causes: he completely knew their individual history, comprehended their character, and had the power of clearly conveying to others, and forcibly impressing his thoughts, opinions, and conceptions. Though the most valuable ethics are diffused through all his works, yet two of his productions are more peculiarly appropriated to those subjects. His Rambler showed more of man in his general nature, as he himself says of Dryden; his Idler, as he says of Pope, more of man in his local manners. His Rambler was the work of a profound, comprehensive philosopher; his Idler of genius and learning experienced in life: the former describes men as they always are, the latter as they then were in England. It may be easily and obviously objected to the political writings of Johnson, that they were by no means equal in either knowledge or wisdom to his other productions. A whig zealot might exclaim against the high church bigotry, theological intolerance, and arbitrary politics of this great man, as a tory zealot might depreciate Milton, because a puritan and republican; but this impartial observer, making allowance for human infirmities, will see prejudices and unfounded opinions totally outweighed by transcendent excellencies. The historian of the present reign, if he narrate the truth after balancing the good and the bad, must admit that few either lived or died in it of such great and beneficially directed wisdom as Samuel Johnson. Besides the vast accession of knowledge and instruction accruing to mankind from the individual efforts of this extraordinary man, his conversation and writings stimulated and formed many others to meritorious compositions. The disciples of the Johnsonian school, whatever, might be their several diversities of ability and character, have written to promote religion, order, and virtue. Having made such important additions to the general mass of information and instruction, he taught by precept and example the most efficacious processes of reasoning, and the surest test of truth; he exhibited the close connexion between clearness of conception and precision of expression, and afforded materials and principles of thought and judgment, with directions and examples for estimating fairly, and conveying ideas and sentiments with clearness, force, and effect. Scholars of moderate talents, who neither evince depth of reflection, vigour of invention, or brilliancy of fancy, are now accurate composers, and competent estimators of literary merit. Through Johnson, respectable mediocrity of ability and learning has been prompted and enabled to direct its patient and industrious ef-

forts to the useful purposes, not only of just criticism, but loyal
and patriotic, virtuous and religious, inculcation. Perhaps, however, the literary efforts of Dr. Johnson may have been more
beneficial to other writers, than to his own particular associates;
from the latter, they come to the world tinctured with his particular prejudices; among the former, they have often diffused
unalloyed portions of his general wisdom and virtue.

As the death of Dr. Johnson is an epoch in the literary
history of the times, it may not here be unseasonable to give
a short sketch of literary efforts at this period. The American
war had produced a vast multiplicity of political pamphlets,
of which, though the greater number were of only a temporary
interest, yet some, from the ability of the writers, the importance of the principles, and the receptions of the doctrines,
were of much more permanent consequence. Two men of
considerable talents and high reputation engaging in this controversy, broached opinions of a very unconstitutional tendency: these were, doctors Richard Price and Joseph Priestley,
gentlemen who from nature and study possessed the means of
promoting, to a great extent, the benefit of society, were disposed to use their talents for those meritorious purposes, and
had actually employed them with very great success, in certain paths, to the good of mankind; yet were now active in
exerting them in pursuit of objects, or at least in inculcating
doctrines of a very injurious tendency to the existing establishments. With genius competent to any subject of literary or
scientific investigation, and deeply skilled in calculation, Price
had peculiarly distinguished himself by inquiries into population, and by financial research. Priestley, by his discoveries in
chemistry, electricity, pneumatics, and subjects relative to
these, had made valuable additions to physical knowledge and
science, both for theoretical contemplation and practical use.
These two philosophers were dissenters, and dissenters of a
class which has generally carried dissent beyond theological
opinions, and has incorporated politics.   Men, at once able
and ambitious, if they happen to find themselves in a minority,
very naturally seek to render that minority a majority. In
situations of peace by making converts, as in situations of war
by making conquests, aspiring leaders seek power.   From
calculations and from chemical researches, doctors Price and
Priestley betook themselves to politics, and to theological controversy, which was intended to minister to politics; adopted
the visionary theories which the profound wisdom of Locke
had not prevented from pervading his opinions in politics, with
many of the hypothetical comments which had joined them in
the course of the century: these they inculcated as the just
conclusions of political wisdom, and the proper rules for political conduct. Besides the treatises already mentioned, they
published various works, which refined on Locke's fiction of a
social compact, and represented every system of government

CHAP. as necessarily bad, that had not originated in a convention of
XXXIII. men assembled for the purpose of forming a constitution;
consequently, as no existing government had been so con-
1784. stituted, concluding that every established polity was necessarily unjust. So far as these speculations were merely ex-
ercises of metaphysical ingenuity, they might be accounted
innocent pastimes: but whether intended or not to be harmless, they certainly were not designed to be inefficient: they
were most industriously circulated by the secondary instruments, which, in the literary as well as the political world,
are in such numbers ready to repeat even the errors of conceived genius; and by the authors themselves, among those
who were most disposed to take their assertions as arguments. Price, though constant in his principle, was more desultory and occasional in his operations: eminent in certain
departments of learning, Priestley had attempted to grasp at
every subject of human knowledge, and, in the midst of his
endeavours at universality, directed his principal efforts towards
one great object, the subversion of the ecclesiastical establishment. It is now obvious, by considering the whole series of
his conduct, that he had early formed the design of overturning our hierarchy, which he himself afterwards acknowledged with triumphant exultation for the imagined success.
Priestley appeared to have proceeded on the following principle: "I, and a minority of this nation, do not approve of
" any establishment, especially of the church of England, her
" constitution and doctrines, supported by the majority of the
" nation; as we, a *smaller number* with *not more* than our own
" proportion of ability and property, cannot agree with the
" GREATER NUMBER, we must make THEM agree with our
" creed."[m] Seeking the downfall of the church, Dr. Priestley
formed a plan, consisting of two parts; the first to attack the
articles of her faith, the next the muniments of her establishment. The former part of his scheme, which was indeed
preparatory to the latter, at present chiefly engaged his attention. For several years he had been strenuously labouring
to overturn the Christian doctrine of the Trinity; this being an
article of faith, which the greater number of Christians, and
especially those of the church of England, deem essential to
the gospel, and consequently to every establishment by which
the gospel is cherished. An attack upon so fundamental a
part of our religion, was by no means an impolitical movement; nor was it carried on without great dexterity. In

m It must be admitted by any liberal friend of the church, on the one
hand, that if Dr. Priestley conscientiously intended the temporal and eternal happiness of his countrymen, and not his own aggrandizement, he was
morally justifiable; but a liberal dissenter, on the other hand, must admit,
that all those whose opinion was different, whether moralists or statesmen,
were equally justifiable in impugning his arguments and repelling his
attacks.

adducing the common arguments of often exploded sophistry, his genius gave to triteness a colour of originality,
and to superficial declamation an appearance of profound
reasoning, which, on many even of those not borne down by
the authority of his name, made a very strong impression.
While the generalissimo of heresy was himself thus employed,
he had distributed his officers and troops with great skill in different posts and positions, according to his knowledge of their
ability, skill, and zeal for the cause. Our ecclesiastical establishment, however, did not want a defender, who was at once
ardent, able, and well provided with the means of guarding the
church against the assailant. Dr. Samuel Horsely brought an
acute and powerful mind, disciplined and formed by science,
and stored with general and theological learning, to support
the faith which he had embraced, and the venerable body of
which he was a member. The Unitarian controversy, which
for several years maintained by misconstruing ingenuity, and
re-assertion of often confuted argument; by obstinate itera-
tion of sophistry on the one hand, and on the other, by plain
interpretation, deductive reasoning, fair inference, and firm
adherence to positions so founded; now occupied a great
share of lettered efforts and attention.[n] Controversies arising
from some parts of Gibbon's history were also very prevalent:
the author, however, engaged little in the disputes; he was
persevering in his able, learned, and approved work, in which,
though the pious must disrelish the anti-christian tendency of
several parts, and the acute may discover assertion without
proof adduced to support favourite notions, yet every reader of
judgment, comprehension, and philosophical and political knowledge, must allow that it is an illustrious monument of industry
and genius, which lightens readers through the darkness of the
middle ages, and exhibits man in various stages of declining
society, until he terminated in barbarism, and, regenerating, began to return towards civilization. Another history had at this
time just appeared, that embraced periods much better known
to every classical reader; but though it recited transactions
with which every literary man was well acquainted, it presented
new and profound views, unfolded causes, and marked operations and effects, that even intelligent and profound readers had
not before discovered. The philosophical pen of Fergusson
rendered the affairs of the greatest people of antiquity the
ground-work of the deepest and most expanded moral and political science, to teach mankind that wisdom, courage, enterprise, and skill, uniformly and constantly exerted in the various
departments of a political system, elevate a nation as they exalt an individual, and that folly and vice overturn the fabric
which virtue and wisdom had raised. Works of an inferior

n The Reviews of these years had more than one half of their writings
occupied either with this controversy, or the politics of the day.

CHAP. species to history, though pursuing the same object, travels, and
XXXIII. voyages, much increased our knowledge of the interior and civil
           condition of various countries, with which our acquaintance be-
1784.   fore had been chiefly confined to geographical outlines and political relations. The travels of Messrs. Moore, Wraxal, Coxe,
and others, into various parts of Europe, not only afforded amusement and entertainment, but knowledge of mankind. The
voyages of the renowned circumnavigator, captain Cook, which
displayed human nature in a light showing at once its varieties
and uniformity, were a pleasing and interesting accession of
literary novelty.

Improve.   Physical knowledge and science were making rapid advances,
ment of the while, from former discoveries of philosophy, invention and ex-
presentage perience were fast educing arts which administered to the pur-
in natural poses of life. Doctors Black and Watson were persevering in
philosophy
and chem- their chemical pursuits, and powerfully contributing to the eluci-
istry.   dation of subjects, curious to speculative, and useful to practical
men ; with which, through the abilities and labours of such men,
followed by many others of patient research and useful industry,
who were employed in experimental detail, the public is now
become so conversant.

Invention   The immense improvements of the present age, in the general
of air bal- analysis of material substances, and particularly in the applica-
loons.   tion of chemistry to the qualities of air, produced about this time
an invention that astonished mankind, by an artificial phenomenon, which appeared to realize the fable of Dædalus, and to
find a passage for man through the air. Eminent philosophers
of the sixteenth and seventeenth centuries from the qualities of
air had inferred the practicability of such an undertaking, but
did not explore the means. The discovery was reserved for
the ingenuity of two French manufacturers of paper at An-
nouay in Dauphiny, Messrs. Montgolfier. These gentlemen,
observing the ascent of vapour or smoke in the atmosphere,
concluded that the general principle was the ascent of air rarefied by absorption, and that it must ascend until it arrive at air
of such a tenuity as to prove an exact equilibrium. On this
reasoning they constructed a globular machine of paper and
fine silk, covered with elastic gum ; in short, of the very light-
est terrene materials. This ball, being about thirty feet in circumference, was raised to a considerable height, merely by applying some lighted combustibles to an aperture at its lower
extremity. If so small a power of rarefied air could raise such
a weight, a proportionate increase must raise a proportionably
greater weight; hence it was found, by extending the experiment, that a ball of linen of 23,000 cubic feet° in dimension, being moved by combustibles, would lift about five hundred
weight. Montgolfier soon after presented the experiment at
Paris; a sheep, a cock, and a duck, were placed in a gallery

° About twenty-eight and a half, to a figure exactly cubical.

next the balloon, and returned without hurt. On the 23d of
November 1783, two human beings adventured to essay an element hitherto unexplored by man. The marquis de Landes
and Monsieur Drosier undertook this extraordinary navigation:
at 54 minutes past one o'clock, the machine ascended into the
air before an immense number of astonished spectators. When
it had reached 250 feet, the intrepid travellers waving their
hats saluted the wondering crowd: the ærial navigators were
soon beyond the reach of discernment from the earth, but the
ball itself was seen towering towards the confines of æther. The
travellers having found their experiment successful, agreed to
descend by gradually lessening the application of air, and arrived safely in an open field at some distance from the city.[P]
The event of this experiment with rarefied air, encouraged farther
trials; Monsieur Charles, the professor of natural philosophy at
Paris, suggested the improvement of inflammable air, instead of
rarefied. In 1784 the experiment was tried in England by Mr.
Lunardi, an Italian gentleman. On the 15th of September, Ascent of
this gentleman, about five minutes after two o'clock, ascended Lunardi
from the artillery ground, before 150,000 people, who were from the
collected in the places immediately adjacent: many of the artillery
other inhabitants of London and the environs were gazing from ground.
the house tops; business of every kind appeared to be suspend- Astonished, and every ray of thought converged into one focus; in ment of the
short, Lunardi and the balloon occupied general conversation. metropolis
The sky fortunately was without a cloud, so that his ascent at this phe-
above London was clearly perceived from a distance of many nomenon
miles around. The balloon took a northerly direction: at half
past three, Lunardi arrived at South Mimms, where he descended on a common; but again raising himself, he proceeded
in the same direction, and afterwards descended at Ware.[q] Va-

[P] In an epilogue to a play exhibited at Westminster soon after this experiment, there was a verse containing the following pun on this *Gallic* invention :

    " Quis propria Gallo plus levitate valet ?"
    " Who can surpass a Frenchman in appropriate levity ?"

[q] The following passage is quoted from Lunardi's written account of his
own voyage, observations, and feelings, when from the ærial heights he
looked down upon the British metropolis :—" When the thermometer was
at fifty, the effect of the atmosphere, and the combination of circumstances
around, produced a calm delight which is inexpressible, and which no
situation on earth could give; the stillness, extent, and magnificence of
the scene rendered it highly awful; my horizon seemed a perfect circle ;
the terminating line several hundred miles in circumference. This I conjectured from the view of London, the extreme points of which formed an
angle of only a few degrees; it was so reduced on the great scale before
me, that I can find no simile to convey an idea of it. I could distinguish
St. Paul's and other churches from the houses; I saw the streets as lines,
all animated with beings whom I knew to be men and women, but which I
should otherwise had a difficulty in describing; it was an enormous bee-
hive, but the industry of it was suspended. Indeed the whole scene before

CHAP.
XXXIII.

1784.

rious balloons were afterwards launched, in Britain and other parts of the world, and many treatises were published, endeavouring to demonstrate the important advantages which might arise from this invention, but none of them have been hitherto realized.

me filled my mind with a sublime pleasure of which I never had a conception ; I had soared from the apprehensions and anxieties of the world, and felt as if I had left behind all the cares and passions that molest mankind." Of the second descent he gives the following account :—" At twenty minutes past four, I descended in a spacious meadow in the parish of Stondon, near Ware in Hertfordshire ; some labourers were at work in it, I requested their assistance ; they exclaimed they would have nothing to do with one who came in the devil's house ! and no intreaties could prevail on them to approach me. I at last owed my deliverance to the spirit and generosity of a female ; a young woman took hold of a cord which I had thrown out, and calling to the men, they yielded that assistance to her request, which they had refused to mine. A crowd of people from the neighbourhood assembled, who very willingly assisted me to disembark.

CHAP. XXXIV.

PARLIAMENT met on the 26th of January 1785, and the chief object recommended by his majesty to the attention of the legislature, was the adjustment of such points in the commercial intercourse between Great Britain and Ireland, as had not before been arranged. The success attending measures which were embraced in the last session for the suppression of smuggling, would encourage them to persevere in their application to those important concerns; they would also consider the reports suggested by the commissioners of public accounts, and make such regulations as might appear necessary in the different officers of the kingdom. Notwithstanding the dissensions on the continent, his majesty continued to receive assurances from foreign powers of their amicable disposition towards this country.

The earl of Surrey opposed the address, or rather objected to it on account of what he conceived to be wrongly omitted; especially because no mention had been made of the reduction of the army. Lord North, conceiving parliamentary reform to be intended by one recommendatory expression, declared his

CHAP.
XXXIV.

1785.

sentiments very strongly against any alteration of the constitution; and Mr. Burke blamed the total silence relative to the
affairs of India. Mr. Pitt replied to the objections; the observations on the reduction of the army were premature, until
the supplies of the year should be before the house: parliamentary reform was a subject of the highest importance, but at
this early period of the session it was impossible to state his
plans specifically: all his ideas were not yet thoroughly matured; the subject comprehended a great variety of considerations, and related to essentials and vitals of the constitution;
it therefore required considerate and delicate attention; and
though it was a path which he was determined to tread, he knew
with what tenderness and circumspection it became him to proceed. There was not a general debate, and the address was
carried without a division.

Considera-
tion of the
Westmin-
ster scru-
tiny.

The scrutiny of the Westminster election was again brought
before the house in the month of February. Mr. Fox had contended, that the election ought to be tried by Mr. Grenville's
act, and had imputed the perseverance in the scrutiny to the
persecuting spirit of the minister. Mr. Pitt argued, that Mr.
Grenville's act was for trying elections virtually made, but that
there being no return from Westminster, the law in question
was not applicable: a scrutiny had been demanded by one of
the candidates, the returning officer had complied, as official
duty required; far from having any personal motives to promote
a scrutiny, the very reverse was the case; it would have been
more convenient and easy for ministers to have suffered Mr.
Fox to take his seat without question, but instead of attending
to their own accommodation, they had consulted the rights of
the electors, and the purposes of substantial justice. The
house continued in the same opinion as to the legality of the
scrutiny; but finding in its progress that, though there were ob-
jectionable votes on both sides, a majority, nearly the same in
proportion as at the close of the poll, remained in favour of Mr.
Fox, they judged it expedient and equitable to direct the high
bailiff to make a return; and the following day that officer returned lord Hood and Mr. Fox.

Debts of
the nabob
of Arcot.

On the eighteenth of February, the nabob of Arcot's debts
to Europeans were the subject of parliamentary discussion. In
Mr. Fox's India bill the new commissioners had been instructed
to examine into the origin and justice of the claims; by Mr.
Pitt's law the examination was appointed, but referred to the
court of directors, who were to enjoin their presidencies and
servants to inquire into the case, and in concert establish a
fund from the nabob's revenue, for the discharge of the debts
which should be found just, that they might be liquidated according to the respective rights of priority of the several creditors, and consistently with the rights of the company, and
the honour and dignity of the nabob. Comformably to this
clause, the directors had prepared orders; but after inspection,

the board of control rejected them, and gave new instructions,
which admitted the greater part of the debts to be just, assigned a fund from the revenues of the Carnatic for their discharge,
and established the priority of payment among the several
classes of creditors: these directions had been publicly read at
a meeting of such creditors as were in England. Motions were
made in both houses, that copies of the letters or injunctions
issued by the court of directors might be produced; the object
of this requisition was to prove, that the board of control, in
originating the contrary order, had departed from the express
purpose of their institution, and had violated the act of parliament. Mr. Fox having opened this subject in the house of
commons, and assuming the position that was to be proved,
expatiated with copious eloquence on the arbitrary power
which was usurped by the board of control, and the mischievous
consequences that the present act must produce to the interests
of the Carnatic, and of the India company. Mr. Dundas
argued from the act of parliament, that the power exercised
was not an usurpation, since, by the strict letter of the statute,
the board was enabled to originate orders in cases of urgent
necessity, and to direct their transmission to India. In the
present exercise of that power, the board of control had acted
upon the most complete information that could be received, and
had directed the arrangement in question, on finding it the most
fair and just to all the parties concerned. It was expedient
not to keep the nabob's debts longer afloat; the final conclusion
of the business would tend to promote tranquillity and harmony,
and the debtor had concurred with the creditors in establishing
the validity of the claims. After these general observations,
he, by a particular detail of their respective circumstances, undertook to justify the several debts which were admitted by the
board.

On this subject Mr. Burke made a very long oration, which MrBurke's
displayed a most extensive knowledge of the history and state speech on
of India; but it was much more remarkable for narratives, the sub-
imagery, and philosophy, to inform, delight, and instruct a ject.
reader in his closet, than for appropriate arguments to the point
at issue, to convince a hearer in the senate, and induce him to
vote as the speaker desired. The part of his reasoning that
appeared specifically applicable to the subject before the house
was adduced, to demonstrate that the alleged debts arose from
a collusion between the nabob and certain servants of the company, who had been guilty of the most heinous fraud, oppression, and cruelty: forcibly animated and highly coloured was
the picture he drew, of tyranny and suffering, guilt and misery,
in British India, as the result of the alleged connivance; but
since, as a chain of logical deduction, the evidence did not make
out the case, the motion was negatived; and in the house of
peers a similar proposition was rejected.

CHAP.
XXXIV.

1785.

Mr. Pitt's plan of parliamentary reform,

is introduced into parliament,

On the eighteenth of April, Mr. Pitt again introduced his propositions for a reform in parliament. Desirous, as the minister professed himself, of such a change in the representation as he conceived most consistent with the principles, and conductive to the objects of the constitution, he was aware of the danger of essays of reform, unless very nicely modified and circumscribed. The general characteristics of his plan for that purpose, were caution and specification: nothing vague or indefinite was proposed; no chasm was left, which visionary imaginations might fill with their own distempered fancies; thus far shalt thou go and no farther, was obviously expressed in the extent and bounds. The leading principle was, that the choice of legislators should follow such circumstances as give an interest in their acts, and therefore ought in a great degree to be attached to property. This principle being established, it was obvious, that as many very considerable towns and bodies either had no vote in electing representatives, or had not the privilege of choosing a number proportioned to their property, it would be necessary to disfranchise certain decayed boroughs. In relations between government and subject, it was a manifest rule in jurisprudence on the one hand, that the interest of a part must give way to the interest of the whole; but on the other, that when such a sacrifice is required from a subject, the state should amply compensate individual loss incurred for the public good. Guided by these maxims of ethics, Mr. Pitt proposed to transfer the right of choosing representatives from thirty-six of such boroughs as had already fallen, or were falling into decay, to the counties, and to such chief towns and cities as were at present unrepresented; that a fund should be provided for the purpose of giving to the owners and holders of the boroughs disfranchised, an appreciated compensation; that the acceptance of this recompense should be a voluntary act of the proprietor, and, if not taken at present, should be placed out at compound interest, until it became an irresistible bait to such proprietor; he also projected to extend the right of voting for knights of the shire to copyholders as well as freeholders. The chief arguments in favour of a reform were derived from the alleged partiality of representation; an active, reforming, and regulating policy, which kept pace with the alterations in the country, was requisite to preserve the constitution in its full vigour: when any part of our system was decayed, it had ever been the wisdom of the legislature to renovate and restore it by such means as were most likely to answer the end proposed; and hence had arisen the frequent alterations that had taken place with respect to the rule of representation. From a change of circumstances, towns which once ought to have a vote in choosing a senator or senators, now behoved to have none; and towns once without any just claim to the right of such an election, were now aggrieved and injured by the want of that privilege.

The principle continued the same in both the former and the CHAP.
latter, but its application should be altered in a difference of XXXIV.
case. The opposers of reform, on the other hand, contended,
that no necessity had been shown for such a change; that 1785.
whatever inequalities theory might exhibit in the existing system, the people were all actually represented, as far as was
necessary to their rights and happiness; that no man could be
deprived of liberty, property, or life, but by his own act,
whether he had a vote for a member of parliament or not; that
under the present mode of representation, both individual and
national prosperity had risen to a very great pitch, and was
rapidly rising to a higher; that it was extremely dangerous to
alter what experience, the only sure test of political truth, had
uniformly shown to be good.ʳ The people did not want reform; the large towns that were said to be aggrieved by the
present ·state of representation, had made no complaint, or
sought any redress; those which were called rotten and decayed boroughs were frequently represented by gentlemen who
had the greatest stake in the country, and consequently were as
much concerned in its welfare as any other representatives.

ᵣ Never, perhaps, were the arguments on this side of the question more
clearly exhibited, than those which are compressed into a page of one of the
most valuable works that can be recorded in the literary history of the present reign. Paley, in his Principles of moral and political Philosophy, resting the question concerning representation, as well as every political establishment, solely on expediency, says, " We consider it (representation) so
" far only as a right at all, as it conduces to public utility; that is, as it con-
" tributes to the establishment of good laws, or as it secures to the people
" the just administration of these laws. These effects depend upon the dis-
" position and abilities of the national counsellors: wherefore, if men the
" most likely, by their qualifications, to know and to promote the public in-
" terest, be actually returned to parliament, it signifies little who return
" them. If the properest persons be elected, what matters it by whom they are
" elected ? At least no prudent statesman would subvert long established
" or even settled rules of representation, without a prospect of procuring
" wiser or better representatives. This then being well observed; let us,
" before we seek to obtain any thing more, consider duly what we already
" have. We have a house of commons composed of five hundred and forty-
" eight members, in which number are found the most considerable land-
" holders and merchants of the kingdom, the heads of the army, the navy,
" and the laws; the occupiers of great offices in the state, together with
" many private individuals, eminent by their knowledge, eloquence, or
" activity. Now, if the country be not safe in such hands, in whose may it
" confide its interest ? If such a number of such men be liable to the in-
" fluence of corrupt motives, what assembly of men will be secure from the
" same danger ? Does any new scheme of representation promise to collect
" together more wisdom or produce firmer integrity ? In this view of the
" subject, and attending not to ideas of order and proportion (of which
" many minds are much enamoured,) but to known effects alone, we may
" discover just excuses for those parts of the present representation which
" appear to a hasty observe most exceptionable and absurd." Paley, vol.
ii. p. 219.

CHAP.
XXXIV.

1785.
and nega-
tived by a
great ma-
jority.
State of
Ireland.

Mr. Pitt's propositions were negatived by a majority of two hundred and forty-eight to one hundred and seventy-four.

Parliament was this year principally occupied by forming arrangements for a commercial intercourse between Great Britain and Ireland.

We have seen that, in the year 1780, the trade of Ireland had been freed from the hurtful restrictions by which it had long been shackled. In 1782, the independence of the Irish parliament had been for ever established. It remained for the legislature of the two countries to arrange a system of commercial intercourse, which might best promote the advantage of the two parties so nearly connected. The freedom of trade had afforded to Ireland the means of improvement; of which the success must depend on the active, well directed, and persevering industry of the inhabitants; as without those exertions, the mere exemption from former restriction could be of little avail: no effectual measures had hitherto been employed for exciting and cherishing so beneficial a spirit: the manufacturers had for some years been much engaged in political speculations, which, by abstracting their attention from their own business, naturally caused great distress ; and that distress, discontent and violence. Various expedients were attempted for their relief. In 1784, Mr. Gardener brought forward a plan for protecting their own manufactures, and enforcing the consumption of them at home, by laying heavier duties on similar manufactures imported from other countries; he had therefore moved to restrict the importation of English drapery, by subjecting it to a duty of 2s. 6d. per yard. It was objected to this motion, that Great Britain would probably retaliate, and that Ireland might endanger the loss of the linen trade, the annual value of which was a million and a half, for the uncertain prospect of increasing the woollen, that did not exceed 50,000l. A proposition of such obvious impolicy was rejected by the great majority of one hundred to thirty-six. The populace having been ardently desirous that the bill should pass, were inflamed with the greatest rage at its rejection, and gave loose to excessive outrage They entered into compacts not to consume imported goods, and inflicted the most severe punishment on those who either did not subscribe or adhere to such agreements : the riotous outrages of the mob rendered the interference of military force necessary, and though the soldiers behaved with all possible moderation, still in the tumults disagreeable violence took place, and Dublin was a scene of dissension. In such a situation, regard to temporary tranquillity, as well as to general, commercial, and political interest, rendered it necessary to devise some tie, that, by connecting the interests, might combine the inclinations of both countries. Mr. Pitt, seeing so strong special reasons, and urging immediately what the general consideration required to be speedily effected, took measures for a commercial treaty with Ireland. Commissioners appoint-

ed on the part of the sister kingdom concerted with the British
cabinet a plan for regulating and finally adjusting the commercial intercourse. The result Mr. Orde stated to the Irish parliament on the 11th of February, and moved a corresponding set
of resolutions, which passed the house of commons with little Propositions of Mr.
Pitt to set-
tle trade
on the basis
of mutual
recipro-
city.
alteration. The concurrence of the house of peers being soon
after obtained, the resolutions, ten in number, were immediately
transmitted to England, as, on their part, the proposed basis
for an equitable and final adjustment. Mr. Pitt having received these assurances of the disposition of the body of the Irish
parliament to settle their commercial intercourse on the basis
of reciprocity, moved a resolution to the following effect:
" That it is highly important to the general interests of the em-
" pire that the commercial intercourse between Great Britain
" and Ireland should be finally adjusted, and that Ireland
" should be permitted to have a permanent and irrevocable
" participation of the commercial advantages of this country,
" when her parliament shall permanently and irrevocably
" secure an aid out of the surplus of the hereditary revenue of
" that kingdom towards defraying the expense of protecting
" the general commerce of the empire in time of peace." After
reviewing what had been already granted to Ireland by the
British parliament, he generalized his object: which was to
settle commercial intercourse on the firm basis of mutual reciprocity. In applying this principle, he exhibited an extensive
knowledge of the relative and absolute state of manufactures, and other materials of commerce, in both countries, and
proposed a plan, under two general heads: First, Britain was
to allow the importation of the produce of our colonies in the
West Indies and America into Ireland: secondly, There should
be established between the two countries a mutual exchange of
their respective productions and manufactures upon equal terms.
The first, he allowed, had the appearance of militating against
the navigation laws, for which England ever entertained the
greatest partiality; but as she already allowed Ireland to trade
directly with the colonies, the importation of the produce of
those settlements circuitously through Ireland into Britain,
could not injure the colonial trade of this country. Such
was the general outline of the proposed system on its first appearance. A considerable portion of the session was employed
in examining merchants and manufacturers upon the various
details which could elucidate the subject; and after fully
investigating the evidence of the traders, Mr. Pitt, on the 12th
of May, proposed twenty resolutions, containing a full explanation of the terms before proposed, and also new resolutions,
which arose from the increased knowledge that had been acquired. The chief objects of the additional propositions were
to provide, First, That whatever navigation laws the British
parliament should hereafter find it necessary to enact for the
preservation of her marine, the same should be passed by the

CHAP. debt. At present, however, he had only seen the general
XXXIV. practicability of the principle, but not having matured mea-
⌣⌣⌣ sures for such an appropriation, he chose to defer a specific
1785. plan till the following year. There remained unfunded up-
Mr. Pitt's wards of ten millions of navy bills, and ordnance debentures:
statements these were funded in the five per cents, taken at about ninety
of finance, pounds, and a million was borrowed from the bank at five per
and intima-
tion of a cent. to supply deficiencies still remaining from the expenses of
plan for the war. The new taxes were, an additional duty on male
paying the servants; a duty on female servants, increasing in a stated
national proportion according to the number, with a farther charge to
debt bachelors having such servants; a tax on attorneys, on post-
horses, on carriages, coach-makers, pawn-brokers, gloves, and
retail shops; besides one hundred and fifty thousand pounds
The ses- raised by a lottery. On the 8th of August, on a message from
sion rises. the king, parliament was adjourned to the 27th of October,
and afterwards prorogued by proclamation.

Affairs of The emperor and the Dutch still persevered in the contest
Europe. about the Scheldt, but commotions in Germany unexpectedly
arising, prevented him from bearing down upon Holland with
his whole force. Joseph was become sensible, not only that
other powers would not suffer him to open the Scheldt, but
that his present possessions in the Netherlands were precarious;
Designs of and finding one project likely to misgive, in the true spirit of
the empe- an adventurer resolved to try another, by making an exchange
ror upon with the elector of Bavaria, which should put the emperor in
Bavaria. possession of the duchy of Bavaria, with all the appendages confirmed at the peace of Teschen, and make the elector sovereign
of the Austrian Netherlands, which, more to render the proposal
palatable, was to be erected into a kingdom. This scheme
would have been very advantageous to Austria, by the accession of a large and productive country, which, surrounding
and completing the Austrian dominions, would have consolidated and compacted so great a body of power as would
overbalance the other states of Germany. A man of deep
reflection, in the very important advantages of the object,
would have discovered an unsurmountable obstacle to its attainment; that the king of Prussia and other members of the
Germanic body would not suffer the establishment of a power
that must overbear themselves; profound sagacity, however,
was no part of Joseph's character. Ambitious in design, but
fantastic in project, and light in counsel, he very superficially
investigated circumstances, and imperfectly calculated the
probabilities of success. As soon as he had formed his
scheme, he communicated it to the court of Petersburgh.
Catharine, who perfectly comprehended the character of the
Supported emperor, studiously cultivated amity with a prince whom she
by Russia could render so powerful a coadjutor to herself. She most
readily acceded to hasty and ill digested schemes for gratifying
his ambition, that thereby she might prevent his obstruction,
and secure his co-operation to the mature and well digested

plans she had formed for extending her power and dominions; CHAP.
she also joined him in making overtures to the house of Bavaria, XXXIV.
but these were peremptorily and indignantly rejected. The
king of Prussia being informed of the proposal, made very 1785.
strong remonstrances; and having concerted with the two Opposed
chief powers of Northern Germany, the electors of Saxony by Prussia
and Hanover, he effected a confederation for maintaining the ver.
indivisibility of the empire. The court of Vienna did every
thing in its power to stop the progress of the combination, but
it was joined by most of the other states, and France was
known to be favourable to its object. Besides the insuperable
impediments to the projects of Joseph from the well founded
jealousy of foreign powers, great intestine commotions prevailed in his own dominions; his numberless innovations in the
civil and religious establishments of Hungary and its appendages, had the usual effect of schemes of reform founded on
abstract principles, without regard to the character, sentiments,
and habits of the people, and produced much greater evils
than those which they professed to remedy ; by violating
customs, offending prejudices, annulling prescriptions, and
trenching on privileges, he drove his sujects to dissatisfaction,
insurrection, and rebellion: to quell the revolters required
powerful and expensive efforts, nor were they finally reduced
\till the close of the campaign ; these various causes prevented
hostilities from being commenced against the states-general.
Pacific overtures were resumed under the meditation of the
court of France, and the management of the count de Vergennes, the French prime minister . the Dutch agreed to pay Joseph a certain sum of money in lieu of his claims over Maestricht, which he renounced for ever, and also resigned his pre- Abandons
tensions to the free navigation of the Scheldt : less material dis- the naviga-
putes were compromised and adjusted, and a treaty of peace tion of the
was concluded between Austria and Holland. Before the expi- Scheldt,
ration of the year, the Dutch and France entered into a new and con-
alliance, offensive and defensive. France was internally occupi- cludes
ed in schemes of diminution of the immense debts which she Holland.
had contracted in the late war, and in the improvement of her Treaty
manufactures and commerce. A merchant, raised to be prime between
minister, contributed to the speedy elevation of the mercantile France and
profession in the opinion of Frenchmen ; and trade which before Holland.
had been considered as derogatory to the character of a gentlemen, was now highly respected. Numberless treatises in favour Internal
of agriculture, manufactures, and commerce, flowed from the state of
fertile ingenuity of their writers, which, if they did not much France.
inform or convince acute and distinguishing understandings, by
striking ductile imaginations, influenced a much more numerous
class. The lively fancies, ardent feelings, and impetuous spirits
of Frenchmen were now turned to mercantile adventures ; they
conceived themselves happily emancipated from the old prejudices which had kept many of their forefathers in proud poverty.

CHAP. On other subjects also, they fancied they had dispelled the
XXXIV clouds of ignorance, and were enlightened by the sunshine of
reason.   There was at this time a great multiplicity of ingenious
1785.   writers in France, without that patient investigation, research,
Multipli- cautious consideration, and experimental reasoning, which only
city of in- can lead to just, sound, and beneficial philosophy; to religious,
genious moral, and political wisdom.   A few eminent framers of hypo-
writers. thesis had given the tone to the rest; Helvetius, Rousseau,
and Voltaire, taught infidelity to numerous classes of disciples,
who admitted their doctrines upon the faith of their assevera-
Doctrines tions.   Their multiplying votaries, professing to disregard all
of Voltaire superstitious bigotry, were still Roman Catholics in reasoning :
and Ros- they admitted *an infallible authority*, if not in the pope, in Jean
seau impli- Jacques ; decrees from the mountains of Switzerland were re-
citl recei- ceived with no less veneration, than bulls had formerly been re-
vedy ceived from the Vatican ; infidelity was become the prominent
Prevalence feature of the French character, and occupied the principal
of infideli- share of conversation in fashionable societies.   The royal family,
ty. indeed, were not tinctured with the prevalent impiety, but the
indulgent liberality of the monarch did not watch and rigorously check such opinions with the vigilance which sound policy
required, and neither he nor his minister appeared to be aware
of the danger attending the diffusion of irreligion through a
nation.

Great and British commerce continued to increase and extend ; the
increasing flourishing state of trade, together with the announced project
prosperity of Mr. Pitt for the discharge of the national debt, raised the
of Britain. stocks in a short time from fifty-four to seventy, in the three per
cents. consolidated the barometer of the other funds.   The
Confidence mercantile and monied interest, in its various departments and
of the mo- corporations, evidently reposed in the chancellor of the ex-
nied inter- chequer a confidence which they had bestowed upon no minis-
est in the ter since the time of his father.   They conceived the highest
talents and opinion of his integrity and talents, approved the principles on
integrity of which he was proceeding, and the regulations he had actually
Mr. Pitt. proposed, and were thoroughly satisfied with the rapid advances
of trade, as well as the increasing means of enlarging their
capitals.   While ministers impressed the public with a favourable idea of their qualifications to promote the prosperity of the
country, the supporters of apposition were foremost in their
efforts to amuse and entertain ; wit and temporary satire appeared with brilliancy and force in the Rolliad, a mock heroic
poem, of which the professed hero was a respectable and worthy
gentleman, Mr. Rolle of Devonshire, a zealous friend of administration, and therefore held up by their opponents to ridicule.
The notes on the poem display considerable humour, and illustrate the feelings, sentiments, and opinions of opposition, concerning the general politics of the times.   The death of Mr.
Satirical Warton, the poet laureat, also afforded an occasion to ingenuity
literature. for exhibiting a sarcastic account of ministerial characters in

the *birth-day odes;* performances satirically inscribed with the CHAP.
names of various gentlemen and noblemen as candidates for XXXIV.
the vacant office, and, as in characteristic compositions, presenting specimens of their poetical powers by odes on the king's 1785.
birth-day. The respective essays painted the alleged foibles
of the chief supporters of the cabinet: viewed together, the
Rolliad and the birth-day odes presented ministerial men and
measures in the light in which the satirists of opposition at this
period wished them to be beheld, and are not therefore unconnected with the serious literature and politics of the anti-ministerial party.

A cause affecting literary property was this year determined Question of
by the court of session, the chief civil tribunal of Scotland. literary
The compilers of the Scottish Encyclopedia had inserted in that property.
work large extracts from Dr. Gilbert Stewart's history of Scotland, and his history of the reformation of Scotland: Mr. Stewart prosecuted them for piracy, and the transcripts being long
and continuous, the court, having a power of determining equitably as well as legally, gave sentence in favour of the prosecutor, on the ground that the defenders had quoted more, and
with less interruption, than was allowed by the rules of literary
property. The principle of the Judgment appeared to be,
that large and connected passages copied from a literary work,
tend to injure the sale of that work, and consequently lessen the
value of the property to the rightful owner.

Peace having been now completely established between the Return of
East India company and Tippoo Saib, tranquility was diffused Mr. Hast-
over British India. During the recess, Mr. Hastings, the go- ings, a
vernor-general, returned; and the periodical writings of the times ject of
teemed with attacks and vindications of his character. temporary
literature.

CHAP. On other subjects also, they fancied they had dispelled the
XXXIV clouds of ignorance, and were enlightened by the sunshine of
reason. There was at this time a great multiplicity of ingenious

1785. writers in France, without that patient investigation, research,
Multipli- cautious consideration, and experimental reasoning, which only
city of in- can lead to just, sound, and beneficial philosophy; to religious,
genious moral, and political wisdom. A few eminent framers of hypo-
writers. thesis had given the tone to the rest; Helvetius, Rousseau,
and Voltaire, taught infidelity to numerous classes of disciples,
who admitted their doctrines upon the faith of their assevera-

Doctrines tions. Their multiplying votaries, professing to disregard all
of Voltaire superstitious bigotry, were still Roman Catholics in reasoning :
and Ros- they admitted *an infallible authority*, if not in the pope, in Jean
seau impli- Jacques; decrees from the mountains of Switzerland were re-
citly recei- ceived with no less veneration, than bulls had formerly been re-
ved. ceived from the Vatican; infidelity was become the prominent

Prevalence feature of the French character, and occupied the principal
of infideli- share of conversation in fashionable societies. The royal family,
ty. indeed, were not tinctured with the prevalent impiety, but the
indulgent liberality of the monarch did not watch and rigorously check such opinions with the vigilance which sound policy
required, and neither he nor his minister appeared to be aware
of the danger attending the diffusion of irreligion through a
nation.

Great and British commerce continued to increase and extend; the
increasing flourishing state of trade, together with the announced project
prosperity of Mr. Pitt for the discharge of the national debt, raised the
of Britain. stocks in a short time from fifty-four to seventy, in the three per
cents. consolidated the barometer of the other funds. The

Confidence mercantile and monied interest, in its various departments and
of the mo- corporations, evidently reposed in the chancellor of the ex-
nied inter- chequer a confidence which they had bestowed upon no minis-
est in the ter since the time of his father. They conceived the highest
talents and opinion of his integrity and talents, approved the principles on
integrity of which he was proceeding, and the regulations he had actually
Mr. Pitt. proposed, and were thoroughly satisfied with the rapid advances
of trade, as well as the increasing means of enlarging their
capitals. While ministers impressed the public with a favourable idea of their qualifications to promote the prosperity of the
country, the supporters of opposition were foremost in their
efforts to amuse and entertain; wit and temporary satire appeared with brilliancy and force in the Rolliad, a mock heroic
poem, of which the professed hero was a respectable and worthy
gentleman, Mr. Rolle of Devonshire, a zealous friend of administration, and therefore held up by their opponents to ridicule.
The notes on the poem display considerable humour, and illustrate the feelings, sentiments, and opinions of opposition, concerning the general politics of the times. The death of Mr.
Satirical Warton, the poet laureat, also afforded an occasion to ingenuity
literature. for exhibiting a sarcastic account of ministerial characters in

the *birth-day odes;* performances satirically inscribed with the
names of various gentlemen and noblemen as candidates for
the vacant office, and, as in characteristic compositions, presenting specimens of their poetical powers by odes on the king's
birth-day. The respective essays painted the alleged foibles
of the chief supporters of the cabinet: viewed together, the
Rolliad and the birth-day odes presented ministerial men and
measures in the light in which the satirists of opposition at this
period wished them to be beheld, and are not therefore unconnected with the serious literature and politics of the anti-ministerial party.

A cause affecting literary property was this year determined Question of
by the court of session, the chief civil tribunal of Scotland. literary
The compilers of the Scottish Encyclopedia had inserted in that property.
work large extracts from Dr. Gilbert Stewart's history of Scotland, and his history of the reformation of Scotland: Mr. Stewart prosecuted them for piracy, and the transcripts being long
and continuous, the court, having a power of determining equitably as well as legally, gave sentence in favour of the prosecutor, on the ground that the defenders had quoted more, and
with less interruption, than was allowed by the rules of literary
property. The principle of the Judgment appeared to be,
that large and connected passages copied from a literary work,
tend to injure the sale of that work, and consequently lessen the
value of the property to the rightful owner.

Peace having been now completely established between the Return of
East India company and Tippoo Saib, tranquility was diffused Mr. Hast-
over British India. During the recess, Mr. Hastings, the go- ings, a
great sub-
vernor-general, returned ; and the periodical writings of the times ject of
teemed with attacks and vindications of his character. temporary
literature.

CHAP. XXXV.

CHAP.   ON the 24th January 1786, parliament was assembled.
XXXV.   The speech from the throne mentioned the amicable conclusion
of the disputes which had threatened the tranquillity of Eu-
1786.   rope, and the friendly dispositions of foreign powers towards
Meeting of this country: it expressed the royal satisfaction, that his majes-
parliament
and the   ty's subjects now experienced the growing blessings of peace
king's   in the extension of trade, improvement of revenue, and in-
speech.   crease of public credit. For the farther advancement of those important objects, the king relied on the continuance of that zeal
and industry which was manifested in the last session of parliament. The resolutions which they had laid before him, as the
basis of an adjustment of the commercial intercourse between
Great Britain and Ireland, had been by his direction recommended to the parliament of that kingdom, but no effectual step
had hitherto been taken, which could enable them to make any
farther progress in that salutary work. His majesty recommended to the house of commons the establishment of a fixed plan
for the reduction of the national debt; a measure which, he
trusted, the flourishing state of the revenue would be sufficient
to effect, with little addition to the public burthens.

The objects proposed by the sovereign for parliamentary deliberation, were evidently of such primary importance, that
the speech and corresponding address afforded little opportunity for animadversion from opposition. Without objecting to
the address, Mr. Fox expatiated into a very wide field of continental politics. He went over the state and recent transac-

tions of Russia, Germany, Holland, and France, and endeavoured to prove, that the accession of the king, as elector of
Hanover, to the Germanic confederation, would disgust the emperor with this country, and indispose him to an alliance with Britain in any future war. Viewing the interests and relations of the
various states of the continent, he deduced from them the principles of alliance which he judged most expedient for this country to adopt. From the connexion between France and Spain,
the emperor was the only power whose co-operation could occupy the exertions of France by land, and thereby prevent her
from directing to maritime contests such efforts as she had employed in the recent war. An intercouse both commercial and
political with Russia, was also an object of the highest consequence to this country; a favourable opportunity had been lost,
but still an advantageous alliance might be concluded. He understood that a treaty was on the point of being established between Britain and France; and he strongly reprobated the policy of such a measure, appealing to the experience of former
times, which (he said) proved that this nation had become powerful and flourishing, from the moment that she quitted all commercial connexion with France. With strictures on the Irish
propositions and the India bill, he concluded a speech, which,
as usual with opposition on the first day of the session, exhibited a statement of all the alleged errors and miscarriages of
ministers. In replying, Mr. Pitt made an introductory observation, deserving peculiar attention, as it very strongly exhibited
a prominent feature in the eloquence of his opponent. " Mr.
" Fox (he said) discovered most extraordinary dexterity in
" leaving out of a discussion* such parts belonging to the sub-
" ject as did not suit his purpose to be brought forward, and a
" similar dexterity of introducing, however foreign to the ques-
" tion, such matter as he expected would be favourable." By
reverting to the course of Mr. Fox's oratory during the administration of lord North, the reader will perceive this remark
of the minister not to be groundless. Mr. Fox had often allowed himself unbounded liberty of expatiation, and roamed
at large in the wide regions of invective. Lord North had
most frequently followed his adversary through the devious
tracts, and much time was spent by both orators in contentions
on subjects which were foreign to the immediate business of
the house. Forcible as Mr. Fox was in argument; dexterous,
skilful, and ingenious, as lord North was in eluding a strength
which he could not meet; the reasoning of both wanted closeness, and compacted arrangement: besides, as of two very able
combatants Mr. Fox was incomparably the superior, lord North
in his tactics naturally imitated, in order to parry his assailant.
Mr. Pitt was of a different cast, and character; he was far
from being under the necessity of shifting blows that he could

Side notes:
CHAP.
XXXV.

1786.

Views of
Mr. Fox
concerning
continental
alliances.

s See parliamentary reports for 1786, Jan. 24.

CHAP
XXXV.

1786.

Duke of
Rich-
mond's
scheme for
fortifying
the dock-
yards.

repel by equal force, and return with well directed effort. Disciplined in reflection and argumentation, as well as powerful
in talents, he thoroughly knew his own ground, and his ability
to maintain it in any mode which he judged expedient; he was
not therefore to be hurried away by the evolutions of his adversary. Mr. Pitt at this time declared an intention, to which
in the course of his parliamentary warfare he generally adhered, that let Mr. Fox range ever so wide into extraneous subjects, he should confine his answers to what he conceived relative to the purpose. In the present debate, he observed, various topics had been discussed by Mr. Fox, such as the politics
of the emperor and the German confederacy, which were not
within the control of the house: the treaty with Russia was in
considerable forwardness, but neither that proposition nor the
negotiation with France were yet proper to be discussed; objections were therefore premature, and only hypothetical concerning a subject so imperfectly known. Fox replied, by placing his former observations in a new light, without any fresh argument; and no general debate having ensued, the address was
carried without a division.

The first important object that occupied the deliberations of
parliament, was a measure which originated with the duke of
Richmond, master-general of the ordnance. Intelligent and
ardent, this nobleman had paid peculiar attention to mathematics, as a ground-work of military skill, especially gunnery and
fortification, and desired to rest a great portion of the national
defence against the approaches of an enemy, on the abilities
and exertions of an engineer. In these sentiments he was confirmed by his conception of recent events. The late war had
seen the Bourbon armadas hovering on our coasts: accident
only (he thought) secured us from the danger with which we
were menaced: our country might have been attacked, our
docks and harbours destroyed. Under this impression the duke
from the time he became master of the ordnance, had been
uniformly eager for adding to our defences a plan of fortification, and, as we have seen, had inculcated this doctrine upon
ministers. In the former session, a scheme of his grace for
fortifying the dock-yards of Portsmouth and Plymouth was in-
cidently mentioned in the house of commons, without being introduced in a regular motion: the house expressed an unwillingness to apply the public money to the execution of such a
scheme, until acquainted with the opinions of persons most
competent to decide on the wisdom and utility of such a measure. That the desired information might be obtained, his majesty appointed a board of military and naval officers to take
the project under consideration, and to meet for that purpose
at Portsmouth with the duke of Richmond as their president.
The instructions issued to this council propounded six hypothetical positions as themes for discussion, and annexed heads and
questions for directing the application of the assumptions to the

objects of inquiry.[t] The hypothesis on which the proposition CHAP.
was grounded was, that the fleet should be, absent, or for some XXXV.
other cause prevented from affording its protection to the dock-
yards. In the first and second problems, this case was assumed 1786.
and submitted to the council : the unanimous answer was, that
if the dock-yards were not defended by the fleet, fortifications
would be necessary.[u] The four subsequent heads of consultation were grounded upon this basis ; and presupposing the absence of the fleet, examined the probable force with which an
enemy might invade Britain during such absence of our navy,
the troops that might be expected to be ready, the time in which
the strength of the country could be collected, and the insufficiency of the present works to hold out until an army were assembled to oppose the invaders. Concerning these subordinate
questions, there was considerable diversity of opinion ; the
greater number, however, delivered a report, which approved
the scheme of fortification as requisite for the supposed emer-
geney, but gave no opinion on the probability that such a crisis
would arise. Lord Percy and general Burgoyne, with several
naval officers, went beyond the given case, and represented the
hypothetical event as so extremely unlikely to happen, that it
was neither wise nor expedient to provide against it by the expensive system which was proposed. Admirals Milbanke and
Graves, captains Macbride, Hotham, Jarvis, and some others,
explicitly affirmed the fortifications to be totally unnecessary.
The opinion of the majority of land officers did not amount to
an approbation of the scheme, as actually right to be executed
in the present state of the country; but was merely an assent
to the alleged necessity of fortifying the docks, if the country
afforded no other means of defence, and no more than an admission of a conditional proposition as true, in the circumstances
which its author supposed. So bounded an acquiescence was
construed by the duke of Richmond to authorize the immediate
adoption of his plan ; to which the cabinet ministers acceding, a
board of engineers was directed to make an estimate of the expense, and the requisite sum, as stated by these gentlemen,
amounted to 760,097*l* After preparatory motions for the production of papers, Mr. Pitt, on the 27th of February, introduced the
plan in the following general resolution : " It appears to this house,
" that to provide effectually for securing his majesty's dock-
" yards at Portsmouth and Plymouth by a permanent system of
" fortification, founded on the most economical principles, and
" requiring the smallest number of troops possible to answer
" the purpose of such security, is an essential object for the
" safety of the state, intimately connected with the general de-

Is submit-
ted to par-
liament.

[t] See instructions transmitted to the board of officers, dated April 13th,
1785, with extracts from the reports of the board, as laid before the house
of commons on the 27th of February, 1786.
[u] See opinion of officers on the first and second data.

"fence of the kingdom, and necessary for enabling the fleet to
" act with full vigour and effect for the protection of commerce,
" the support of our distant possessions, and the prosecution of
" offensive operations in any war in which the nation may here-
" after be engaged."

Argu-
ments for
it.

The favourers of the measure founded their arguments on
the report of the board of officers, which stated, that neither
naval nor military force, nor even both united, could afford a
security adequate to the importance of our dock-yards; fortifications were therefore absolutely necessary, in addition to both.
They represented the duke of Richmond's scheme as the most
eligible that could be adopted, since it was sufficient for the requisite defence, capable of being manned by the smallest force,
demanded the least expense to erect, and afforded an increasing
degree of security in the course of the construction. These
works, moreover, would give greater scope to our fleets: because the dock-yards being thus protected, the navy would consequently be unfettered, and left at liberty to act as occasion
might require, in whatever part of the world its presence might
be necessary; and they would also reduce the standing army.
Were an invasion threatened, and were we to trust only to our
military force, there would be a necessity for augmenting to a
most enormous degree that army on which the whole safety of
the kingdom was to rest; but, if it were assisted with fortifications, a much smaller force would answer the purpose. An
alarm had prevailed, that the measure was unconstitutional in
its tendency, by laying a foundation for a standing army. and
diverting into an useless and dangerous channel those resources
which should strengthen our navy : far from rendering an increase of troops necessary, the proposed plan would actually
tend to remove the necessity of keeping up so large a military
establishment as otherwise must be maintained.

Argu-
ments
against it.

These arguments were by no means received without opposition and controversy; but the speaker who most peculiarly
distinguished himself, was Mr. Sheridan, who was fast rising to
very high oratorial fame and political importance. On the
present question he exhibited the substance of all the reasoning
that could be adduced against the scheme, and contended, that
in itself and in its consequences, the project was dangerous and
unconstitutional; that the nature and circumstances of the report made by the board of officers did not warrant or authorize
the system ; fortifications would not reduce the standing army,
or if they did, they would still be constituents of strength to the
crown, even should it interfere with the rights and liberties of
the people. The possible existence of this case was implied

Mr. Sheri-
dan's
speech on
the forti-
fications.

in the provisions of the bill of rights, and in the salutary and
sacred reserve with which, for a short and limited period, we
annually intrusted the executive magistrate with the necessary
defence of the country. The orator first viewed the question
on the general ground of constitutional jealousy, respecting the

augmentation of military force. This sentiment, so natural to
Britons, implied no suspicion personally injurious to the individual sovereign, or even his ministers; it merely considered
kings and their counsellors as actuated by the same passions
with other men: princes were fond of power; from the constitution of the army it must obey the executive ruler, therefore
it ought to be circumscribed as much as was possibly consistent
with the public safety. Soldiers were maintained for national
defence and security, and were not to be multiplied beyond the
necessity in which only they could originate.   The minister
had endeavoured to anticipate this forcible objection to the new
plan, by persuading the house that the fortifications would lessen, instead of enlarging the standing army; but his arguments
on the subject could not stand the test of examination. If it
was proper to fortify Portmouth and Plymouth, the reasons
which justified such a measure would apply to every other
port in the kingdom, which might be of sufficient importance
to require defence. The plan, as it now stood, proceeded upon
two suppositions extremely improbable; the first was, That we
should be so much inferior on our seas, as to permit the
enemy to land: secondly, That if they did invade Britain, they
would choose to attack the only places we had fortified. Might
they not, on such a supposition, land between Plymouth and
Portsmouth; or in Sussex, Kent, or the eastern coasts, and
strike at the heart of the empire? If fortification was to be
our defence, there must be a circle of fortresses round the
coasts; the completion of such a project would require a military establishment, extensive beyond all former example. The
safety of England rested on our navy, the courage and enterprise of our people, and not upon ramparts and intrenchments.
The proposed fortifications would not be our safeguard
against an invasion; but though far from being beneficial, they
might be efficacious: the garrisons requiring such an additional number of standing troops, in the hands of an ambitious
prince or minister, might be employed against the liberties of
the people. The proposition was not only unconstitutional, unnecessary, and absurd, but unauthorized by the report of officers; mutilated as the statement was which had been submitted to the house, it did not contain grounds for justifying the
scheme. The opinion of naval officers had been withheld, but
the opinion of land officers was founded upon hypothetical and
conditional suggestions, and upon such *data* as the master-general had proposed to them; for the truth or probability of
which, the board invariably refused to make themselves responsible. In this part of his speech, Sheridan diversified his close
and poignant reasoning by an interspersion of wit most happily
appropriated to the subject. The report (he said) had been
so artfully framed, that the board of officers appeared to have
admitted the *data;* whereas they only assented to conclusions,
which in their opinion would ensue on the assumption of the

data. The master-general of the ordnance deserved the warm-est panegyrics for the striking proofs which he had given of his genius as an engineer, which appeared even in planning and constructing the report in question; the professional abi-lity of the master-general shone conspicuously there, as it would upon our coasts : he had made an argument of posts, and con-ducted his reasoning upon principles of trigonometry as well as logic. There were certain detached *data*, like advanced works to keep the enemy at a distance from the main object in debate ; strong provisions covered the flanks of his assertions; his very queries were in casemates : no impression therefore was to be made on this fortress of sophistry by desultory ob-servations, and it was necessary to sit down before it, and as-sail it by regular approaches. It was fortunate, however, he said, to observe, that notwithstanding all the skill employed by the noble and literary engineer, his mode of defence on paper was open to the same objection which had been urged against his other fortifications, that, if his adversary got possession of one of his posts, it became strength against him, and the means of subduing the whole line of his argument. No sup-porter of the bill undertook to refute the arguments of Mr. Sheridan : many who usually voted with administration, were averse to the present measure; even Mr. Pitt was believed not to be very eager for its success, and the event was certainly different from the issue of most of his propositions ; for when the question came to a division, the numbers were equal, and the casting vote of the speaker negatived the motion.

Soon after the defeat of a scheme which tended to increase military establishments, a bill was introduced for enlarging the authority of military courts, by subjecting to their jurisdiction officers who held commissions by brevet. This clause occa-sioned a stenuous opposition in both houses ; the ground of disapprobation was the arbitrary nature of martial law, which was justified only by necessity, and therefore ought to be ex-tended no farther than necessity required. Its object was to secure the discharge of duty on actual military service, there-fore it ought not to operate out of that service. The supporters of the motion contended, that such officers might be invested with command, and therefore should be made subject to a court-martial in case of professional misbehaviour ; there were also many other military officers who were not mustered, such as go-vernors and lieutenant-governors, who might eventually exer-cise command, and ought therefore to become amenable to the laws which bind other soldiers ; persons choosing to have the advantage of military rank, should hold it on the condition of complying with military rules ; and if they disliked the terms, they might ease themselves of their grievance by resigning their commissions. On these grounds the clause was carried in both houses.

On the 29th of March, Mr Pitt brought forward his plans[x] for the reduction of the national debt. A committee had been appointed early in the session, in order to investigate and exactly ascertain the public income and expenditure, and strike the balance: the result of the investigation from the income of the year 1785, was,

Income, — £. 15,379,132
Expenditure, — 14,478,181

So that a surplus of more than £. 900,000 remained; and on this basis Mr. Pitt formed his scheme. He proposed that by taxes neither numerous nor burthensome, the balance might be raised to a million: by a succinct and clear view of our finances he demonstrated, that excess of income beyond expenditure was in the present and following years likely to increase; but in making his calculations, he had contented himself with concluding that it would not decrease. This million was to be appropriated unalienably to the gradual extinction of the national debt. Several savings of expense and increases of revenue, especially through the customs from the suppression of smuggling, would add to the national income: annuities would also fall into the same fund; the accumulated compound added to these sources would, in twenty-eight years, if properly managed, produce an annual revenue of four millions to the state. For the management of this fund, commissioners were to be appointed to receive two hundred and fifty thousand pounds quarterly, with the full power of employing it in the purchase of stock. In choosing persons to be intrusted, Mr. Pitt proceeded on his general principle, which had been already exhibited in his India bill: that in circumstances requiring new delegation of executorial power, the trust should be vested in men whose official situation presumed their competency to the execution of the commission; the speaker of the house of commons, the chancellor of the exchequer, the master of the rolls, the governor and deputy-governor of the bank of England, and accountant-general, were gentlemen whose nomination he recommended. After illustrating his calculations, and the advantages of his scheme, he compressed the substance into the following motion: "That the sum of one " million be annually granted to certain commissioners, to be " by them applied to the purchase of stock, towards dis-" charging the public debt of this country; which money " shall arise out of the surplusses, excesses, and overplus " monies, composing the fund commonly called the sinking " fund." The policy of contracting expenditure within income, in order to liquidate debt, was so obviously just, that no one dissented from the principle, but various objections were

CHAP. XXXV.

1786.
Plan of Mr. Pitt for reducing the national debt.

Is submitted to parliament.

---

[x] The minister is believed to have availed himself of the financial ability of Dr. Price, who so thoroughly understood political arithmetic.

1786.

Mr Sheri-
dan takes
the most
active part
in contro-
verting the
financial
proposi-
tions of the
minister.

made to the scheme. These are reducible to two general heads: first, that the alleged excess did not exist: secondly, that admitting its existence, the proposed mode of application was not the best that might be adopted. On this subject, Mr. Sheridan took a leading part in opposition; he moved a series of resolutions, declaring there were not sufficient grounds to establish the existence of the asserted surplus; that the calculations were founded upon one year peculiarly favourable, and not upon such a number of succeeding years as could constitute a fair average; and that in the existing accounts even of that year, at least in the report of the committee, there were certain articles erroneously stated to the credit of income, and others erroneously assigned to the diminution of expenditure. He, however, neither proved the alleged errors, nor the impropriety of calculating from 1785, the first year to which any reasoning on the reduced expenditure, or growing revenue of a peace establishment and rising trade, could apply. The objections to the mode were principally adduced against the appropriation being unalienable in any circumstances: in times of war and pecuniary emergency, it might be expedient to have recourse to the present fund, instead of a loan. To modify this objection, Mr. Fox proposed, that in a future loan the commissioners might accept of as much of it as they could pay from the public money in their hands; and thus, besides a prevention of that amount of future debt which would be equivalent to the redemption of the past, the public would be gainers by the profits which would accrue from such a loan.[y] Mr. Pitt not only adopted, but highly applauded this clause: Mr. Pulteney proposed that the commissioners should continue purchasing stock for the public when at or above par, unless otherwise directed by parliament. This provision, of which the object was to attach to parliament the responsibility of giving instructions to the commissioners, if necessary in the specified circumstances, was adopted. The bill containing the original principle and plan, though with some modification of the latter, passed through both houses, and received the royal assent.

Further
measure of
Mr. Pitt
for pre-
venting
frauds a-
gainst the
revenue.
He propo-
ses to sub-
ject for-
eign wines
to the ex-
cise.

Mr. Pitt had examined the frauds against the revenue with minuteness and fullness of inquiry. In no subject of impost he found they were more prevalent than in wine: the present amount of the revenue resulting from that article was less by two hundred and eighty thousand pounds, than in the middle of the last century, yet it was manifest that the consumption was greatly increased since that period : he attributed the defalcation, first, to the fraudulent importation of large quantities of foreign wine, without paying the duties: secondly, and prin-

[y] For instance, if there were a loan of six millions, of which the commissioners contracted for one million, and there was a *bonus* of two per cent. the public would gain 20,000*l.*

cipally, to the sale of a spurious liquor under the name of that
beverage. To remedy this evil, he proposed a bill for subjecting foreign wines to the excise; by this means they could no
longer fraudulently escape the payment of the revenue, as the
excise, by its opportunities of more completely vigilant inspection, could much more effectually prevent smuggling, if attempted; and there would not be the same motives to adul-
teration, when the substitute should have to pay the same
duty as the genuine; the consequence would be, that the public would, without an additional price, procure better wine,
and the revenue would be much greater, which would produce
an increased demand for our manufactures, and thus the mass
of productive industry would be augmented. For all these
reasons, Mr. Pitt recommended the adoption of his plan. The
arguments against it rested on two grounds; first, general, on
the impolicy and unconstitutional tendency of extending the
excise laws; secondly, special, on the inexpediency of the mode.
These necessarily turned on topics often discussed, the collection of the duty by inspecting and searching private houses,
the summary proceedings against offenders. Under the second
head it was contended, that the practice of gauging, so applicable to brewers, was perfectly incompatible with respect to
such an article as wine; that continual increase and diminution of the trade stock would baffle the endeavours of the officers to keep a regular account: as these objections did not
apply more forcibly to wine than to liquors already subject to the A bill for the purpose
excise, they made little impression; the bill passed through both is passed
houses, and received the royal assent. into a law.

In consequence of a message from the king, Mr. Pitt, on the Bill for ap-
20th of June, introduced a bill for appointing commissioners to pointing
inquire into the state and condition of the woods, forests, and commis-
land revenues belonging to the crown. Against this proposi- sioners to
tion it was contended, that the powers granted to the commis- examine
sioners were contrary to the security of the subjects, whose the crown laws.
rights, founded in prescription, would be invaded. It subjected
all persons who held of the crown, or possessed estates adjoining to the crown lands, to an inquisition into their ancient boundaries and title deeds, at the mere motion of the commissioners, without any other legal or ordinary process. It was supported on the
ground of expediency, that it was proper and wise to ascertain
the condition of these lands, in order to see of what improvements they were susceptible. In the commons, the bill encountered no material opposition; in the peers, lord Loughborough argued strongly against the proposition: he and other
lords entered a protest; but it passed by a majority of twenty-
eight to eighteen. Mr. Marsham proposed a bill for extending,
to persons employed by the navy and ordnance, the disqualifi-
cations contained in Mr. Crew's bill of 1782, for preventing revenue officers from voting at elections of members of parliament.
The proposition was controverted by Mr. Pitt; the situation

CHAP. of persons intended by Mr. Crew, and of those now designed
XXXV. to be excluded, was totally different: the revenue officers were
       under the influence of government, but the persons employed
1786. in the departments in question were subject to no control;
they were at all times capable of procuring what was equal to
their present salaries in foreign services, or from our merchants
at home; the former were dependent upon the crown, the latter
totally independent; no fair argument could therefore be adduced from the defranchisement of the one set, for disqualify-
ing the other: on these grounds the proposed bill was rejected.

The con-   A discussion was now begun in the house of commons, which
duct of Mr. long occupied the attention of parliament and the public; this
Hastings a was the conduct of Warren Hastings, esq. late governor-gene-
before a
subject of ral of India. Early in the session, major John Scott, late con-
inquiry. fidential secretary to Mr. Hastings, and now a member of the
house of commons, reminded Mr. Burke of his charges against
the governor-general, said that he was now returned from
India, and called on his accuser to bring forward the allegations
of criminality, that they might undergo the inquiry and receive
the decision of the house. Major Scott was, doubtless, warmly
attached to Mr. Hastings, and perfectly confident of his innocence; nevertheless, the prudence of such a challenge is very
questionable. Many warmly approved Mr. Hasting's character and administration, and conceived him the saviour of
India from a native combination co-operating with the ambition
of France: these admirers could not estimate him more highly
than at present, though he were freed from charges which they
thought altogether unfounded, while persons of a contrary
opinion might not be convinced even by his acquittal. Mr.
Scott undoubtedly knew, that however innocent his friend might
really be, there was a great body of oral and written evidence
in the reports of the committees, which tended to establish the
opposite belief, or at any rate to leave the issue doubtful; the
multiplicity and complexity of allegations would certainly render the process extremely tedious. From all these circumstances, an inquiry and trial must involve its subject in a labyrinth
of difficulty, even where the ultimate event to be favourable.
The zeal, therefore, which produced this defiance, was evidently imprudent; by rousing charges that might have lain dormant, it actually proved highly injurious to him whom it was
Mr. Burke intended to serve. Mr. Burke did not immediately answer ma-
opens the jor Scott's summons, but within a few days opened the discus-
subject.
His intro- sion. On the 17th of February he brought the subject before
ductory the house, and in an introductory speech traced the history of
speech. the proceedings of parliament respecting the affairs of British
India, and also the alleged misconduct of the company's servants, from the period of lord Clive's government to the reports
of the secret and select committees, the resolutions moved
thereupon, and the approbation repeatedly given to these proceedings by his majesty from the throne. On the authority, the

sanction, and the encouragement thus afforded him, he rested his accusation of Mr. Hastings as a delinquent of the first magnitude. There were three species of inquisition against a state culprit: first, prosecution in the courts below, which, in the present case he thought very inadequate to the complicated nature and extent of the offence, and the enormity of the offender: secondly, a bill of pains and penalties, of which he disapproved as a hardship and injustice to the accused, by obliging him to anticipate his defence, and by imposing on the house two relations that ought ever to be kept separate, those of accusers and of judges. The only process that remained, was by the ancient and constitutional mode of impeachment. The first step in such a cause, was a general review of the evidence, to enable them to determine whether the person charged should be impeached. If the general question was carried in the affirmative, they must next appoint a committee to divide and arrange the evidence, under the heads of which the impeachment should consist. He proposed, previously to a resolution of impeachment, that the evidence should be particularly investigated by a committee of the whole house, that they might be well acquainted with the grounds of procedure before they should attempt to proceed. He eloquently described the disagreeable nature of an accuser's office, and contended that it was not imposed on him by choice, but by necessity. He moved for the production of papers, alleged to contain evidence relative to the subject, and endeavoured to show that Mr. Dundas, who in 1782 had moved the recall of Mr. Hastings, ought to have taken a lead in the present business. Mr. Dundas acknowledged that he had recommended the recall of Mr. Hastings as politically expedient, but denied that his proposition expressed, or even implied, any judicial charge of criminal conduct, which consistency would require him to support; if there was appearance of guilt, he agreed that it ought to be investigated, that if found to be real, adequate punishment might be inflicted. No objection was made to the production of the papers which were then specified; but Mr. Burke continuing at subsequent meetings to move for various other documents, Mr. Pitt, before he would agree to the requisition, proposed that the accuser should exhibit an abstract of the charges which he intended to adduce, that the house might judge whether the papers required or to be required were relevant to the elucidation of the subject. Mr. Burke read a short outline of the charges, and pointed out the matters which the writings were intended to explain and substantiate. The charges were twenty-two in number: first, the Rohilla war: second, the detention of revenues of the province of Cola Alla Habad: third, the proceedings respecting Cheyt Sing: fourth, the conduct towards the princesses of Oude: fifth and sixth, the treatment of two rajabs: seventh, extravagant contracts made by Mr. Hastings in the name of the company: eighth, illegal presents: ninth, disregard

CHAP. XXXV.

1786.

He proposes to proceed by impeachment;

and presents a summary of alleged criminal acts.

of the orders of the East India company: tenth, eleventh, and twelfth, extravagant contracts on account of the company, and enormous salaries bestowed on officers of his own institution: thirteenth, ambassadors sent to Arcot and the decan: fourteenth, the Mahratta treaty; fifteenth, the management of the revenues of Bengal; sixteenth, the ruin of the province of Oude: seventeenth, the dismissal of Mahomed Khan from the internal management of Bengal: eighteenth, treatment of the mogul; nineteenth, a libel upon the directors: twentieth, the Mahratta war: twenty-first, the suppression of correspondence: twenty-second, the treatment of Fizullakham. Of these articles, by far the most distinguished were the third and fourth: Mr. Burke employed the remainder of February and the whole of March in moving for papers and preparing his accusations. On the 4th of April he charged Warren Hastings, esquire, late governor-general of Bengal, with sundry high crimes and misdemeanors; nine of his articles he then delivered, and the other thirteen the following week. Mr. Hastings petitioned the house that he might be heard in his defence, and that he might be allowed a copy of the accusation. The first request the prosecutors granted: Mr. Burke objected to the last, at so early a stage of the prosecution; he was, however, overruled. The month of May was chiefly occupied in examining evidence: and on the first of June, Mr. Burke adduced his first charge, in the following terms: "That there are grounds suf-"ficient to charge Warren Hastings, esq. with high crimes and "misdemeanors, upon the matter of the said article." After a full discussion, it appeared to the house, that this war was unavoidable on the part of Mr. Hastings; this proposition was negatived by a majority of one hundred and nineteen to seventy-six. On the 3d of June, Mr. Fox brought forward the charge respecting Benares: he contended that Mr. Hastings had acted unjustly in his first demands; that his subsequent conduct was a continuation and increase of injustice, but that his last proceedings, when he arrived in that province, were flagrantly iniquitous and tyrannical, and had rendered the British name odious in India. On the other hand, it was argued that the demands of Mr. Hastings, were agreeable to the established conduct of superiors in India, from their tributary dependents, in situations of danger and emergency: the circumstances of affairs were extremely critical; the governor-general was reduced to the alternative of either requiring pecuniary supplies, or wanting money to pay his troops, when their most strenuous efforts were necessary for saving India against the confederacy of France, and the native powers; the rajah's refusal, combined with various parts of his conduct, manifested disaffection to the British establishment, when Mr. Hastings went to Benares; Cheyt Sing was also in actual rebellion, and intimately connected with the allied enemies of British India. His conduct was therefore justified by neces-

sity, as part of that general system of wise and comprehensive CHAP.
policy which preserved our important interests in Indostan, XXXV.
Mr. Pitt admitted that the situation of affairs at that period
was extremely critical, but considered the proceedings at 1786.
Benares beyond the exigence of the case, and necessity of the of im-
service. It was carried by a majority of one hundred and peachment
nineteen to seventy-nine, that there was a matter of impeach- ceedings
ment in the charge in question. against

During these proceedings concerning part of the transac- Cheyt
tions in India, Mr. Dundas introduced a bill for the improve- Sing.
ment of its government in future. Its principal object was to Mr. Dun-
enlarge 'the powers of the governor-general ; first, by vesting das's bill
in him the nomination of the vacant seats in the council ; se- for improv-
condly, by limiting the officers of the governor-general and ing the go-
commander in chief of the forces ; and thirdly, by authorising of British
him to decide upon every measure, even though not agreeable India.
to the council. The proposition was opposed by Mr. Burke,
as tending to introduce despotic government into India ; but
its framer insisted, that the responsibility of the governor-
general was in proportion to his power, and that abuse of his
trust was punishable by a fair and established judicature ; he
was himself satisfied, after long and attentive inquiry into the
affairs of India, that all the recent mischiefs in that country had
arisen from the parties formed in the different councils, and the
factious spirit which had almost uniformly pervaded these
bodies. By his system, the governor-general on the one hand,
would no longer by restrained by personal pique and factious
opposition, from forming and executing such plans as he
thought most conducive to the public good ; yet, on the other
hand, he was amenable to the laws of his country from any
unjust, tyrannical, or injurious exercise of his power. The authority allowed to the officer in question, was founded on the
same general principle, as that conferred on the several members of the British state, sufficiently extensive to effect the useful purposes required, and so clearly bounded as to prevent
pernicious exercise.

The supplies of the session were eighteen thousand seamen, Supplies.
and about thirty thousand soldiers. A loan was wanted,
2,500,000l. were to be raised by exchequer bills, paid as usual,
from the first aids of the following year ; about 200,000l. were
to be raised by a lottery. There were no new taxes, but a duty
of a penny per gallon on spirits, on deals, and battens, on hair
powder and pomatum, the whole being intended to make up
the sum stated to be wanted ; that the surplus of income might
be the annual income appropriated to the liquidation of the national debt.

On the 11th of July his majesty closed the session by a speech The ses-
from the throne, in which he testified the highest satisfaction sion termi-
with the measures adopted for improving the resources of the nates.
country, and reducing national debt. He continued to receive

CHAP.
XXXV.

1786.

assurances that the peace was likely to remain undisturbed; the happy effects of general tranquillity appeared in the extension of the national commerce, and he should adopt every measure tending to confirm these advantages, and to give additional encouragement to the manufactures and industry of his people.

CHAP. XXXVI.

ON the continent of Europe, no event so much distinguished the year 1786, as the death of Frederick II. king of Prussia; who, for half a century, had acted such a conspicuous part on the grand military and political theatre. Were we to estimate his conduct on the simple principle, that a long and constant series of successes must arise from the possession and steady exertion of adequate qualities, we should find grounds for concluding, that the talents of Frederick, as a soldier, a statesman, and a lawgiver, were singularly eminent. Concerning a man who has long enjoyed the uncontrolled direction of any species of affairs, we may fairly and candidly ask, in what state did he find the subject of his trust? did any material advantage assist, or difficulty retard, its improvement? has he left the professed objects of his care in a better or worse situation? When the government of Prussia devolved upon Frederick, he found a small, inconsiderable, and disjointed kingdom, without arts, industry, or riches; and without either the disposition or means of rendering the territory productive, the inhabitants prosperous, or the state respectable. The treasury was scanty, and the income inferior to the necessary expenditure; his dominions were surrounded by powerful and jealous potentates, who commanded numerous, valiant, and well disciplined armies: in such circumstances Frederick raised his country to be a great, well compacted, and flourishing empire. By teaching his subjects industry, agricultural skill, manufactures, and commerce, he bettered their condition, civilized their manners, enlightened their understandings, and enabled them to acquire the comforts and enjoyments of life. His kingdom which before occupied a small space in the geography, and still less in the politics of Europe, was by him rendered the terror of its most formidable foes, and the admiration of mankind. Great as was the result, there are more special grounds

CHAP.
XXXVI.

1786.
Continental affairs.
Death and character of Frederick of Prussia.

for estimating the character of Frederick than bare effects: his progress exhibits the operations of the most efficacious quali-ties; an understanding that grasped every object of necessary or useful consideration; an invention, rapidly fertile in resources, increased both in force and effort with the difficulties by which its exertion was required: self-possession never suffered his powers to be suspended by either peril or calamity; intrepid courage faced danger, and magnanimous fortitude, sustaining adversity, rendered misfortunes temporary, which would have overwhelmed others in destruction. Never had a leader with so small a force to contend with such a powerful combination, not of mere multitude (as when Asiatic enervation by feeble crowds impotently tried to overwhelm European strength), but of hardy, disciplined, and veteran troops, equal to his own in prowess and military skill, and quadruple in number. Frederick experienced dismal reverses of fortune; having attained the highest pinnacle of success by dint of genius, he, from incidents and circumstances, against which no wisdom could provide, was driven to the lowest abyss of disaster; the very existence of his kingdom became doubtful; his inflexible constancy, uninterrupted perseverance, and transcendent abilities, triumph-ed in calamities, and rose through adversity to victory and glory. His exertions during the seven years war demonstrated to his enemies, that all their attempts to crush Frederick were unavailing against him, and recoiled on themselves. Hostilities being terminated, he had leisure to cultivate the arts of peace, and both in planning and executing measures for that purpose, he proved that his mind was formed for excelling not only in war, but in every other great and difficult pursuit to which cir-cumstances might require the direction of his efforts. Com-plete comprehension of objects simplified plans for their attain-ment: the Prussian king was a great inventor in the military system, particularly in the mode of attack. His object was to render the assault irresistible in one or more points, so that the confusion produced there might be communicated to the whole line; the means were not merely to advance intrepidly and charge vigorously; but in the moment of onset to form such unforseen and skilful dispositions, as would enable an army, greatly inferior in number, to surpass the enemy in exertion, and wherever the action was likely to prove most decisive, to bring a greater front to act against a smaller.[z] His internal improvements proposed at once to increase the resources and meliorate the character of his subjects; to render them, both from external circumstances and personal qualities, fitter for se-curing and extending individual and national prosperity, virtue, and happiness. Addicted himself to letters, he was extremely attentive to the education of his subjects, according to their circumstances, condition, or probable and destined pursuits.

[z] See Gillies's Frederick.

Tinctured with infidelity, he was far from encouraging its general diffusion. Totally free himself from bigotted prejudice or superstition, he knew the compatibility of such errors in others with most beneficial conduct, and granted every sect full and undisturbed toleration. That there were great alloys among Frederick's excellencies, he would be a partial panegyrist, not an impartial historian, who should deny. The justice of several parts of his conduct in the early part of his reign was very questionable. One very important act in a later period admits of no dispute: the dismemberment of Poland will always remain a monument of exorbitant ambition and unjustifiable usurpation by Frederick and the other powers concerned. It would not be difficult to evince, that both the subjects thus forcibly acquired were bettered in their condition by this annexation; but shallow would be the moralist who, from eventual and contingéd good, would defend injustice. It m'ght be easily shown that the greater number of victorious commanders, in proportion to their power, have been guilty of as ambitious usurpations as Frederick, and that not many of them have by their victories done so much good. In appreciating conduct we must consider the circumstances and opportunities of the agent, and the temptations which these produced; how very few men, it may be asked, having a very desirable object within their grasp, would abstain from possessing it, even though not conformable to strict justice. The perspicacious and recollecting observer of mankind must recognise such conduct to be natural, but the just estimator of moral sentiments and actions will reprobate it as unjust. Frederick, with considerable moral defects, possessed very high moral and the very highest intellectual excellencies; he raised a small poor territory to be a great, opulent, and powerful kingdom; and rendered ignorant and uncivilized inhabitants an enlightened and civilized people. To a very great portion of mankind most momentous benefits have accrued from the efforts of the renowned Frederick.

As the power of Prussia had arisen from the counsels and exertions of Frederick, many apprehended, that, resting on his character, its stability would be endangered by his death; and supposed, that the ambitious confederation of the imperial courts, so recently thwarted by the vigilant sagacity of Frederick, would take advantage of his death, and endeavour to reduce northern Germany to dependence. But the provisions of Frederick had not been temporary, to expire with his own life: he acquired and formed such strength and power as could be protected by mediocrity of talents, that he knew was to be generally expected in sovereigns as well as others, and which only he saw his immediate successor to possess. His counsellors had been trained by himself, and were likely to continue the plan of policy which the object of their adoration had delineated and conducted with so signal success. For the pre-

CHAP.   servation of his dominions, Frederick bequeathed the most ef-
XXXVI. fectual securities to his successor which human wisdom could
        provide or devise, by leaving him a full treasury, and a formi-
1786.   dable army, wise and experienced councellors, and a people
        enthusiastically attached to the government and memory of
        their illustrious king. The imperial powers thought it by no
        means expedient to interfere with a kingdom so powerfully
        protected, and were besides maturing their preparations for
        their own principal design, in the prosecution of which it was
        their obvious interests to win Prussia to forbearance, instead of
        provoking her to war. Thus the death of Frederick made no
        immediate perceivable difference in the politics of Europe.

Revolution   In Denmark a revolution had taken place in 1784, which
in Den-   proved very beneficial to that kingdom. Ever since 1772, the
mark.   queen dowager having triumphed over the unfortunate and ill
        used Matilda, from the imbecility of the king, retained the
        supreme power which she had acquired by such unjustifiable
        means. Her sway was indeed established beyond all control,
        and beyond the probability of subversion. She had filled the
        great offices of state with her adherents and favourites; the
        son of the unhappy Matilda was a child, and the chances
        against his life at that tender age being considerable, Julia's
        son, prince Frederick, (the king's half brother,) was regarded
        as the presumtive successor to the throne: all things seemed
        to concur in securing her influence and authority for life. The
        exercise of her dominion was far from dispelling the hatred
        which the dowager queen so deservedly incurred by her means
        of elevation. Imperious and tyrannical, she sacrificed the
        national good to the interests of her supporters and minions;
        and was hateful throughout the kingdom, except to her own
        creatures. Retribution though slow was not the less sure;
        as the prince royal approached to maturity, he indicated quali-
        ties that excited the hopes of the people in general, and espe-
        cially of those, many in number, who were disgusted with the
        queen dowager's government. In the seventeenth year of his
        age, the heir of the crown, by his manly abilities and character,
        was become the universal favourite of the nation, and in a few
        months acquired such influence and power as to overwhelm the
        usurpers of his fathers's authority. With such wisdom and
        secrecy had he formed his measures, that, being declared of
Queen   age at seventeen, he was placed at the head of the council
dowager   board; when he acquainted the junto that directed the affairs
disgraced, of the kingdom under the queen dowager, that the king his
and the   father had no farther occasion for their services, before they
reigns of had conceived the most distant idea of their approaching down-
govern-   fall. Having dismissed these ministers, he published an ordi-
ment as- nance, that no orders from the council of states were in future
sumed by to be received, or considered valid, which had not been pre-
the prince
royal.   viously reported to the king, signed by him, and countersigned

by the prince royal. Having accomplished so desirable and CHAP.
beneficial a change, the prince conducted himself with tempe- XXXVI.
rate, wise, and magnanimous policy toward the junto and its
head.   He abstained from punishing the planners and most 1786.
active instruments of the revolution 1772, any farther than by
the loss of their offices.   On the queen herself he bestowed a
superb castle and extensive demesnes in Holstein, whence it
was understood she was not to return to court.   Prince Frederick had never taken any share in his mother's cabals; to
him his nephew presented great possessions, and made him
second to himself in the cabinet council.   His subsequent
conduct confirmed and increased the opinion of his countrymen;
he bestowed the closest attention on public business, and studied the political and commercial interests of Denmark. His highness planned and executed a very great and royal work, which
was finished in 1786, the formation of a short and direct junction
between the Baltic and the German ocean.   This was effected
by drawing a navigable canal from west to east across the
peninsula of Jutland.   Besides his attention to official duty, the
prince manifested a disposition to literature, and became the
patron of learning and learned men.

During this year and the two former, various parts of the Physical
world suffered dreadful calamities from physical causes. Earth- calamities,
quakes, which had so desolated Calabria and other parts of in various
Europe, raged both in Asia and America. In Europe and the parts of the
adjacent parts of Africa and Asia, there was a succession of continent.
severe and irregular seasons; violent storms of rain spread
inundations over the richest parts of Poland, Lithuania, Germany, Hungary, Italy, and France. Rigorous cold destroyed
the crops of Norway and Sweden; and the same causes prevented Livonia from affording them the usual supplies: even
the fisheries of the north did not yield their wonted stores:
the consequences were, that Norway, notwithstanding every
.effort of government, laboured under an absolute famine. In
Iceland a new kind of calamity ravaged the country; mount
Hecla, and the other volcanoes which so much distinguish that
island, although perhaps they promote the purposes of vegeta-
tion, by communicating a genial warmth to its frozen bosom,
have at all times been the terror, and at particular periods
the scourge and destroyers, of the inhabitants. The present
calamity, however, was totally new; the country with its products were now consumed by subterraneous fire. This destroyer of nature made its first appearance in June 1784, reduced
to cinders every thing which it met, and continued burning
until the month of May in the following year, having in that
time extended its devastation about twenty leagues in length,
and from four to five in breadth. The great river Skaptage,
which was from seven to eight fathoms in depth, and half a
league in width, was entirely dried up, its bed and channel

CHAP.
XXXVI.

1786.

Commer-
cial and po-
litical pur-
suits of
France.

presenting a dreadful yawning chasm.[a] A similar fire broke out about this time on the eastern side of the same range of mountains, and pursued its course in the opposite direction. The pestilence also raged with uncommon malignity over those countries which it usually pervades: from the Atlantic borders of Morocco to the extremities of Egypt, and from Palestine to the mouth of the Euxine, the African and Asiatic coasts of the Mediterranean, with those of Thrace on the opposite side, the cruelty of its ravages was severe, and the destruction of mankind greater, than at any period within the reach of memory, or perhaps within the records of history.

France persevered in her attention to maritime and commercial affairs, and endeavoured to increase the number of her naval arsenals and harbours on the ocean. The port of Cherburg, on the coast of Normandy, from its vicinity to England, and lying directly opposite to Hampshire, seemed directly calculated for this purpose. Here the French were constructing a capacious basin, with docks and other requisites necessary to a great naval arsenal; the works were stupendous. It was proposed to cover the road, being about a league and a half in length, with a series of moles, leaving only two sufficient openings, one for the passage of ships of the largest size, and the other for trading vessels. Forts, with batteries of the heaviest cannon, were to be erected on the different moles, in such situations as to be impregnable, and to render the approach of an enemy utterly impracticable. M. Calonne, the prime minister of France, in order to open the way for the introduction of foreign industry, procured the publication of a law, which might be considered as a counterpart of the noted edict of Nantz. This was a decree, which invited strangers of all christian nations and religious persuasions to settle in the country, and enabled them to purchase lands and enjoy all the rights of citizens.[b] To encourage artists and manufacturers of all countries to settle in France, another ordinance was published, allowing them the same privileges which they enjoyed in their native lands, and for a limited time granting them an im-

---

a About a fourth part of the consumed soil consisted of a lava, and of mossy bogs or marshes; the remains of the burnt earth resembled vast heaps of calcined stones; and were of the colour of vitriol. Annual Register 1786, History of Europe, p. 60.

b The judicious author of the history of Europe, in the Annual Register of 1786, observes, that it afforded a singular object of moral and political consideration, to behold fourteen vessels from North America arrive together in the harbour of Dunkirk, freighted with the families, goods, and property of a colony of quakers and baptists (the most rigid, perhaps, in their religious principles of any among the reformed,) who were to come to settle at that place, in a Roman catholic country, and under the government of the French monarch; two circumstances the most directly opposite to their ancient sentiments, whether political or religious.

munity from all duties on the importation of the raw materials that were used in their manufactures ; also exempting them and their workmen from the payment of taxes, and every per- sonal impost. On these conditions they were obliged to continue for a specified number of years in the kingdom, but at the expiration of that term, they were at liberty to depart themselves, and to move their property wherever they chose. The king and his ministry were no less disposed to favour the native protestants, as far as was consistent with the well being and security of the national church: indulgences were likewise extended this year to the peasants, who long had been grievously oppressed; they were relieved from various arbitrary exactions, both of labour and money, and their condition was in general meliorated. The great objects which the mild and benevolent Louis pursued were, the improvement of the strength and productiveness of his kingdom, the alleviation of oppressions interwoven with the government, as it had descended to him from his ancestors, and the extension of the blessings of liberty to his people.

The most remarkable domestic occurrence of the year was an Alarming attempt, originating in frenzy, that fortunately answered no other attempt against our purpose than to demonstrate the warm affection with which a Sovereign. happy, feeling, and grateful people regarded their sovereign. On Wednesday the 2d, of August, his majesty came to town to the levee; as he was alighting from his carriage at the garden gate of St. James's palace opposite to the Duke of Marlborough's wall, a woman, decently dressed, presented to the king a paper folded up in the form of a petition ; his majesty stooping to receive it, felt at his stomach a thrust, which passed between his coat and waistcoat; drawing back, he said " What does the wo- " man mean ? At that instant a yeoman of the guards laying hold of her arm, observed something fall from her hand, and called providen- out, " 'Tis a knife !" The king said, "I am not hurt ; take tially pre- " care of the woman, do not hurt her." Much affected by the vented. attempt, his majesty said, in a voice expressive of tender feelings, " I am sure I have not deserved such treatment from any " of my subjects !" On opening the paper, when he entered the royal apartments, he found written : " To the king's most " excellent majesty ?" the usual head to petitions ; but nothing more. The woman was immediately taken into custody. and Magnani- carried to the guard chamber. Being questioned how she could mous hu- make such a wicked and daring attempt ; her answer was, the king. " That when she was brought before proper persons, she would " give her reasons." From the hour of twelve to five she remained in a chamber to which she was conducted, but would not answer one word to any person. In the evening, after the levee was broken up, she was examined by the ministers, the law officers of the crown, and several magistrates. Her replies, claiming the crown as her property, and threatening the nation with bloodshed for many ages if her right was denied, indicated ah insanity, which, from appearances examination, and subsequent inquiry was soon discovered to be real : her name proved to be Margaret Nicholson. It was imagined by many, that disappointment of her own, or some near connexion, concerning a place under government, had contributed to her insanity, and given her disordered fancy such a direction ; but when her history was traced, it was found to have no relation to either the court or government. After a short consultation, it was resolved that she should be sent to Bethlehem hospital, where she has been confined ever since.

Most providential it was, that this wretched creature made use of her left hand, her other presenting the petition ; and that its position was such, that she could only aim obliquely. Had her right hand been employed, which, where she stood, could have struck directly, dismal might the consequence have been.

Even with the aim which she took, the happiness of the nation, in the safety of its revered monarch, was highly indebted to our king's presence of mind. Had his majesty been thrown into confusion by a danger so unexpected, the fatal deed might have been perpetrated, before the attempt was perceived. Next to his magnanimity, the considerate humanity of the sovereign shone most evidently conspicuous. His benevolent injunction to abstain from hurting a person who had compassed against him so atrocious an act, most probably saved the assassin from the summary and immediate vengeance of his surrounding sub-

jects. Similar conduct in similar circumstances, this history has still to record, concerning the same exalted character. Fortunately for their feelings, neither her majesty nor any of the royal offspring were present. The intelligence of the danger was accompanied by the certain information that it was escaped. The report of the aim excited horror and indignant resentment through the nation, until the state of the perpetrator's mind was made generally known, and the dreadful impression of the calamity threatened, yielded to delight that it had threatened in

vain. The exquisite pleasure that results from terrible and impending evil avoided, poured itself in addresses of ardent and heartfelt loyalty from every quarter of the kingdom. His subjects before knew that they loved and revered their king; but now only felt the full force of these affections, when the impression present to their minds was the imminent danger of their object.

CHAP. XXXVII.

Mr. Pitt's enlarged views on the relation between this country and France.
—Perceives that peace and amicable intercourse is the interest of both
countries.—Thinks past enmity not an unsurmountable bar to permanent reconciliation.—Projects a commercial intercourse, to be mutually
beneficial by a reciprocal exchange of surplus for supply.—Seeks the best
assistance, and employs the most skilful agents.—Principle and details of
the treaty.—Meeting of parliament and the king's speech. —Treaty submitted to parliament.—Mr. Fox and his coadjutors oppose the treaty.—
Arguments.—France the unalterable enemy of Great Britain.—Mutual
interest can never eradicate that sentiment.—Every commercial connexion with France has been injurious to Britain.—For the treaty denied
that there is any unalterable enmity between France and this country.—
Not always enemies.—The repeated discomfiture of France, warring
against the navy of England, at length taught her the policy of peace.—
The treaty supported by a great majority.—Convention with Spain.—
Consolidation of the customs.—Application of the dissenters for the repeal
of the test act.—Number and respectability of the dissenters as a body.—
Distinguished talents of some of their leaders. -Dissenters favourable to
Mr. Pitt, and thence expect his support of their application.—Previous
steps to prepossess the public in their favour.—Mr. Beaufoy demon-
strates their zeal for liberty and the present establishment.-Lord North,
a moderate tory, opposes their application, as inimical to the church.—
Mr. Pitt opposes it on the grounds of political expediency.—The test no
infringement of toleration, merely a condition of admissibility to certain
offices of trust.—Eminent dissenters had avowed themselves desirous of
subverting the church;—therefore not expedient to extend their power.—
Application rejected.—Bill for the relief of insolvent debtors.—Lord
Rawdon's enlightened and liberal policy.—Bill negatived.—Inquiry about
Scotch peerages.—Magnanimous sacrifice by the prince of Wales of
splendour to justice.—Situation of his highness.—Satisfactory adjust-
ments.—Proceedings respecting Mr. Hastings.—Writings in his defence.
—The nation long averse to his impeachment.—Hasting's cause generally
popular.—Eloquence gives a turn to public opinion.—Celebrated speech
of Mr. Sheridan on the Begum charge.—Its effects on the house of commons and the public.—Singular instance of its impression on a literary
defender of Mr. Hastings.—A committee appointed to prepare articles of
impeachment.—The commons impeach Warren Hastings at the bar of
the house of lords.—Supplies —Favourable state of the finances.—Mr.
Dundas brings forward the financial state of British India.—Promising
aspect of affairs.

HISTORY recorded that France and England had been
usually jealous, and often hostile: statesmen on both sides acted upon an assumption, that rivalry and enmity were unavoidable consequences of their situation; and, therefore, that the
chief objects of external policy to both, were reciprocal suspicion, and provision for probable enmity. The bold and soaring genius of Pitt was not to be trammelled by precedent: he

CHAP.
XXXVII.

1786.
Enlarged
views of
Mr. Pitt on
the rela-
tion;

CHAP.
XXXVII.

1786.
between
Britain and
France.
investigated principle, and combining generalization with the experience of political systems and events, easily traced effects, either good or bad, to their causes; and could discover in what cases and circumstances, continuance, or change of plan, or of practice, was expedient or unwise. The sagacity of this minister analyzed the history and spirit of the wars which had been carried on between Britain and France, since trade and navigation became so much the objects of European pursuits: and saw that they had commonly arisen from a desire on the side of France of equalling, and even surpassing, Britain on her peculiar element. He considered the event, as well as the origin: every endeavour of our neighbour to triumph by sea had diminished the riches and power which she sought to increase by a contest: both her commerce and naval force had been uniformly reduced by the very wars, through which she attempted their extension. The resources of Britain had risen in proportion to the power which she was compelled to combat; and all the confederacies which her rival could form, were incapable of depriving this island of her maritime pre-eminence: hence it was evident, that no state which sought opulence and strength, through commercial efforts, acted wisely in provoking to conflict the mistress of the ocean, who could so effectually destroy the trade of her foes: it was, therefore, the interest of France to desist from that hostile policy which had so much obstructed the improvements of her immense resources. Peace with France was no less beneficial to Britain, which had so far consulted her advantage, as to abstain from offensive hostility against her neighbour: within the period of great commercial enterprise in northern and western Europe, England had never gone to war, but to repel aggression, direct or circuitous. Concord being the mutual interest of the parties, Mr. Pitt conceived the noble design of changing the contentious system of policy which had so long prevailed; and the execution, though difficult, he had solid reasons not to believe impracticable. That hereditary enmity was not an unsurmountable obstacle to reconciliation and close alliance, was clearly demonstrated from the former and recent relations between France and Spain, and between France and Austria. Those powers, which had been the constant enemies of France throughout the seventeenth century, and one of them during more than one half of the eighteenth, were now her fastest friends; why might not permanent amity be established between Britain and her former rival? The most effectual means of inducing the two countries to pursue objects so conducive to their mutual benefit, he thought, would be a commercial intercourse, which should reciprocally increase the value of productive labour. The minister derived his knowledge and philosophy from the purest sources; he sought information, either particular or general, wherever it was to be found authentic and important; and was peculiarly happy in arranging details, and, from either

Perceives
that peace
and amica-
ble inter
course is
the interest
of coun-
tries.

Thinks
past enmi-
ty not an
unsur-
mountable
bar to per-
manent re-
concilia-
tion.

masses or systems, selecting and applying what was best fitted
for his purpose. Political economy and commercial science he
learned from Smith: he agreed with that illustrious writer in
his estimate of the reciprocal advantage that might accrue to
industrious and skilful nations, from an unfettered trade, which
should stipulate their respective efforts. Before he formed his
scheme for promoting an intercourse between the two chief nations of the world, he made himself thoroughly acquainted
with the state of facts, the actual productions, and the probable resources of the respective countries. The minister possessed that ability and skill in choosing coadjutors, which results from a thorough comprehension of characters, and a nice
discernment of the appropriate talents and knowledge, dispositions and conduct peculiarly adapted to any specific end. For
commercial information and science, especially the history and
actual state of modern trade, no man exceeded lord Hawkesbury: from that able statesman he derived very important as- Seeks the
sistance in preparing his scheme. Greatly did he also profit by best assist-
Mr. Eden, whose acuteness and conversancy with every sub- ance, and
ject of commerce and diplomatic experience, rendered him a the most
most valuable auxiliary in digesting and composing the plan at skilful a-
home, and the ablest agent for negotiating and concluding an gents.
advantageous agreement with France. Eden accordingly repaired to Paris; where he conducted and completed the desired arrangement with the ministers of Louis.
    The treaty in question established reciprocal liberty of com- Principle
merce between the two countries. The subjects of each pow- and details
er were to navigate and resort to the dominions of the other, of the trea-
without any disturbance or question, except for transgressing ty.
the laws. The prohibitory duties in each kingdom, by enhancing the price, had reciprocally discouraged the sale of their
principal commodies; these were now modified to the satisfaction of both by a tariff. The wines of France, to be imported
into England, were subjected to no higher duty than the productions of Portugal; the duties on brandies and various other
articles were to be lowered in proportion; and the commodities
of Britain were to be equally favoured in France. On the
same basis of reciprocity were the articles respecting disputes
between the mercantile, maritime, or other subjects of the two
countries, and various details of civil, commercial, and political intercourse were to be adjusted. In whatever related to
the lading and unlading of ships, the safety of merchandise,
goods, and effects, the succession to personal estates, as well
as the protection of individuals, their personal liberty, and the
administration of justice, the subjects of the two contracting
parties were to enjoy in their respective dominions the same
privileges, liberties, and rights, as the nation or nations most
highly favoured by each. Should, hereafter, through inadver-
tency or otherwise, any infractions, or contraventions of the
treaty be committed on either side, the friendship and good un-

CHAP. derstanding should not immediately thereupon be interrupted;
XXXVII but this treaty should subsist in all its force, and proper remedies,
should be procured for removing .the inconveniencies, as like-
1786. wise for the reparation of injuries. If the subjects of either
kingdom should be found guilty, they only should be punished
and severely chastised. The relative commercial condition
and resources, on which Mr. Pitt grounded his conclusions, he
generalized into concise propositions. At first sight it appeared, that France had the advantage in the gift of soil and climate, and in the amount of her natural produce; while Britain was on her part confessedly superior in her manufactures
and artificial productions. This was their relative condition,
and was the precise ground on which he imagined that a valuable correspondence and connexion might be established. Having each her own distinct staples; each that which the other
wanted, and no clashing in the grand outlines of their respective riches; they were like two great traders in different branches, and might enter into a traffic mutually beneficial. The respective princes reserved to themselves the right of revising
this treaty after the term of twelve years, to propose and make
such alterations as the times and circumstances should have
rendered proper or necessary for the commercial interests of
their subjects. This revision should be completed in the space
of a year, after which the present treaty should be of no effect; but in that event the good harmony and friendly correspondence between the two nations should not suffer the least
diminution.

In a treaty formed on the basis of reciprocal freedom of trade,
the advantage to the contracting parties was, and necessarily
must be, in the compound rates of their resources and skilful
industry. At first sight, from the climate and soil of France,
the balance of commercial benefit appeared in favour of that
country, and so many politicians reasoned with much plausi-
bility; but Mr. Pitt had profoundly considered the relative circumstances, and justly concluded that the French industry and
skill was much more inferior to the British industry and skill,
than the French soil and climate were superior to the British
soil and climate; and thus, that greater benefit would accrue
to this country from the freedom of trade : experience justified
his conclusions.

1787.   The commercial treaty was the chief object which occupied
Meeting of the public attention when parliament met on the 23d of Janu-
parliament
and the   ary 1787. The speech from the throne mentioned the tranquil
king's   state of Europe, and the friendly dispositions of foreign powers
speech.   to this country. His majesty informed parliament, that a treaty
of navigation and commerce had been concluded between this
country and France, and recommended it to the consideration
of the houses, under two heads ; its tendency to encourage the
industry and extension of commerce, and to promote such an
amicable intercourse as would give additional permanence to

the blessings of peace : these were also the objects which his CHAP. majesty had in view in other treaties which he was negotiating. XXXVII. A convention was formed between Britain and Spain, respecting the cutting of logwood : he farther directed their attention 1787. to plans, which had been framed by his orders, for transporting to Botany Bay, in New Holland, a number of convicts, in order to remove the inconvenience which arose from the crowded state of the gaols in different parts of the kingdom : he trusted they would also devise regulations for simplifying the public accounts in various branches of the revenue : he relied upon the uniform continuance of their exertions in pursuit of such objects, as might tend still farther to improve the national resources, and to promote and confirm the welfare and happiness of his people. In discussing the proposed answer to the speech, some general observations were made upon the treaty by Mr. Fox; but they produced no debate, as the minister and his friends reserved their reasonings until the consideration of the subject was properly before the house.

On the 4th of February the treaty was submitted to parliament. After the minister had explained and supported the object, spirit, and provisions of this treaty, numbers of the opposite side attacked it on a variety of grounds, as relative to commerce, revenue, the naval, and the political interests of Britain. The arguments derived from our manufactures were, they contended, founded on a presumption, that the French character would not admit of equal industry as the English : that opinion was asserted to be unjust : the treaty would facilitate and encourage that contraband trade, which it had been the professed object of Mr. Pitt's policy to suppress : the free access of French ships to the British shores, would be unquestionably by many employed to the purposes of smuggling, and thus the revenue would be greatly injured. By reducing the duties on French wines, we had conceded advantages to France, for which we did not receive an equivalent : we had farther interfered with the Methven treaty, and the interests of our natural ally, Portugal. Respecting the naval operation of the treaty, it was a substitution of a near for a remote market, and requiring short trips would not exercise, nor form nautical skill : but the political effects of the treaty were chiefly reprobated : one argument, often repeated, was founded upon an authority, to which many politicians would bow on the recurrence of precisely similar cases. Mr. Pitt, the elder, having found the country at war with France, had displayed the whole vigour of his genius in measures most fatally hostile to France ; therefore it was unwise in any minister to cultivate friendship with France, and particularly wrong in the son of such a father. France was the natural enemy of England, and no sincerity could be expected in any professions of friendship, no stability in any contract : nations which bordered on each other, could never thoroughly agree, for this single

The treaty is submitted to parliament.

Mr. Fox and his co-adjutors oppose the treaty.

Argu-ments.

France the
unaltera-
ble enemy
of Great
Britain.
Mutual in-
terest can
never era-
dicate that
sentiment.
Every com-
mercial
connexion
with
France has
been inju-
rious to
Britain.
Argu
ments for
the treaty.

reason, that they were neighbours: all history and experience, according to opposition, assured us of the fact. Mr. Fox in particular maintained, that France was the inveterate and unalterable enemy of Great Britain; no mutual interest could possibly eradicate what was deeply rooted in her constitution. The intercourse which this treaty would produce, must be extremely hurtful to the superior national character of England. Evil communication corrupts good manners. The nearer the two nations were drawn into contact, and the more successfully they were invited to mingle with each other, in the same proportion the remaining morals, principles, and vigour of the English national mind, would be enervated and corrupted. No commercial treaty formed between the two countries had ever been beneficial to this country: on the contrary, that which followed the peace of Utrecht would have been extremely injurious, and every mercantile connexion with France had been always injurious to England. In defence of the treaty it was maintained, that the comparative character of the English and French manufactures, and artificial productions would render the free trade more beneficial to this country than to France, notwithstanding her soil, climate, and natural produce. We had agreed by this treaty to take from France, on small duties, the luxuries of her soil, which, however, the refinement of this country had converted into necessaries. The wines of France with all their high duties, already found their way to our tables; and was it then a serious injury to admit them on easier terms? The admission of them would not supplant the wines of Portugal or of Spain, but only a useless and pernicious manufacture in our own country. The diminution on brandy was also an eligible measure, and would have a material effect in preventing the contraband trade, in an article so much used. It had been objected, that no beneficial treaty would be formed between this country and France, because no such treaty had ever been formed, and because, on the contrary, a commercial intercourse with her had always been hurtful to England: this reasoning was completely fallacious; it deduced a similar conclusion from totally dissimilar premises. For a long series of years we had no commercial connexion with France, and the relative value of the respective productions were totally changed. When a treaty was proposed at the peace of Utrecht, England was extremely deficient in those manufactures in which she now excelled, and much inferior to France in produce; by a free trade she must then have been a great loser, because she would have given much more than she would have received: now she would be a great gainer, because she would receive much more than she gave. The present treaty did not in the smallest degree affect the stipulations with Portugal. The French wines would be still much dearer, notwithstanding the diminution of the duties. In a political view it certainly

could be no argument against the adoption of a system of con- CHAP.
duct in one species of circumstances, that a contrary system XXXVII.
had been pursued with acknowledged wisdom in a different situation of affairs. Although Mr. Pitt the father had, when his 1787.
country was at war with France, employed the most energetic
and successful efforts to be victorious in war, that was no reason that Mr. Pitt the son should not endeavour equally to make
the best of existing circumstances, by promoting commerce with
the same country when at peace. The minister himself con- Denied
troverted Mr Fox's position, that France was unalterably the that there
enemy of the country. The existence of eternal enmity was is any unal-
totally inconsistent with the constitution of the human mind, terable en-
                                                               mity be-
the history of mankind, and the experience of political socie- tween
ties. Every state recorded in history had been at different France and
times in friendship or amity with its several neighbours. The Britain.
dissension between France and this country has arisen from
mistaken ambition on her side; there was no more natural an-
tipathy between an Englishman and a Frenchman, than between
a Frenchman and a Spaniard, or a Frenchman and a German.
France, after being long hostile to the house of Austria, had at
last discovered, that it was much more advantageous for both
parties to cultivate peace and harmony, than to impair their respective strength, and exhaust their resources. Hostilities had
been carried on between France and Austria, without very long
intervals of peace, for two centuries and a half. During the
greater part of the seventeenth century, profound peace had
subsisted between France and England; there was nothing
improbable in an idea that such a system might again prevail;
but should war again arise, would the treaty deprive us of our The re-
natural watchfulness, or our accustomed strength? On the peated dis-
contrary, as it must enrich the nation, it would also prove the comfiture
means of enabling her to combat her enemy with more power- of France,
ful effect: but it was now much less likely that our resources warring
should be called for such a purpose, than at former periods. If against the
                                                               navy of
ever France and her allies could have expected to overwhelm England,
England, their hopes might have been sanguine in the Ameri- at length
can war; they had united the whole maritime world to re- taught her
duce her commerce and her navy, but they had totally failed the policy
in reducing our naval power, and sunk her finances to a situa- of peace.
                                                               By the
tion of extreme embarrassment; hence, though it was always treaty both
the interest of France to avoid war with Great Britain, her parties
present circumstances rendered it more necessary than ever to procure a
abstain from hostilities, which, under her embarrassment, would more ex-
expose her to inevitable bankruptcy. On the other hand, by tensive
cultivating a connexion with this country, she must perceive market for
                                                               their re-
the means of recovering from her difficulties. From all these spective
considerations, we might safely infer the sincerity of France; produc-
no doubt that country would gain by the treaty; the French tions, than
would not yield advantages without the expectation of a return: either.
                                                               could else-
unless the other party derived benefit from the agreement, we where.

could have little hopes of its permanency; but Britain would
reap much more advantage. France gained for her wines, and
her productions, an extensive and opulent market; we did the
same to a much greater degree : she procured a market of eight
millions of people; we a market of twenty-four millions;
France gained this market for her produce, which employed
few hands in the preparation, gave small encouragement to navigation, and afforded little to the state; we gained this market for our manufactures, which employed many hundred
thousand of our countrymen in collecting the materials from
all corners of the world, advanced our maritime strength, and
in every article and stage of its progress contributed largely to
the state.

The treaty underwent many and various discussions through
its passage in both houses; and although there neither was,
nor indeed could be, much novelty of argument, as it had been
so fully canvassed, yet in both houses it called forward an
exhibition of commercial knowledge and philosophy, superior
to any that had ever appeared in the British, and consequently
in any senate. In the house of commons several young members very eminently distinguished themselves, by speeches for
and against the treaty, especially Mr. Grenville on the one side,
Mr Grey and Mr. Windham on the other. In the house of
peers, though lord Thurlow, and lord Hawkesbury, lord Loughborough, and lord Carlisle, with other peers on both sides, exerted their respective abilities upon this subject, yet the fullest
and most detailed reasonings were presented by the marquis
of Lansdown, and the bishop of Landaff. The oration of the
former noblemen in some respects coincided with the supporters, and in others with the opposers, of the treaty. He with
ministers contended on the sound policy of cultivating an amicable intercourse with France ; and with the other side, that
the reciprocity on which the treaty was said to be founded
was merely ideal, and that Britain must greatly lose by the
stipulation: these objections were weighty, if well grounded;
nevertheless he declared his warm and cordial support of the
treaty.[c] The bishop of Landaff, in his oration, manifested the

c An altercation arose from the debate between the marquis and the duke
of Richmond : the former had stated the danger of the fortifications of
Cherburg, and, while on that subject, had digressed to make a severe animadversion on his grace's plan for fortifying Portsmouth and Plymouth.
The duke observed, that the marquis's opinion declared orally in writing,
as witnesses and letters could prove, had, when himself minister, declared
his perfect approbation of the plan, to reprobate which he had now deviated from the question. It appeared, however, in investigation, that the
marquis had never expressly and explicitly either said or written, that he
concurred with the duke of Richmond; his grace and Mr. Pitt, and
other hearers, had only inferred his sentiments from his words and conduct, but could not affirm that he had plainly and categorically said, that he
approved of the plan. They thought that he had agreed to the plan, because

same vigour of mind and industry of inquiry, which rendered
him so eminent in chemistry and theology, and procured the
applause of both parties. The treaty was approved by a great
majority of both houses; and on the 8th of March an address
was presented to both houses, testifying their joint approbation
of the treaty with France.

The treaty is supported by a great majority.

The convention with Spain, to which his majesty's speech had
alluded was of very secondary and subordinate moment, when
compared with the treaty that we have been considering; nevertheless, it was by no means unimportant. The agreement in
question was concluded the 14th of July[d] 1786, and chiefly regarded the privilege of cutting logwood. The British possessions on the Musquito shore were ceded in exchange for a
tract of land on the bay of Honduras. The contract produced
little animadversion in the house of commons, but underwent
severe strictures in the house of lords; the opponents of administration contended, that we certainly could have made a better bargain, than to have ceeded to Spain a tract of land, at least
as large as the whole kingdom of Portugal, which yielded us
cotton, indigo, mahogany, and sugar, in exchange for a liberty
to cut logwood, and a scanty settlement of twelve miles in extent; it was moreover ungrateful to the British subjects who
resided there on the faith of our protection, and who had contributed every effort in their power to assist their country. Ministers replied, that the complaint respecting the value of the
cession arose from geographical and statistical inaccuracy.
The territory which we relinquished was much less extensive
and productive, than lords in opposition apprehended. On the
second subject of censure they asserted, that the number of
British subjects settled there did not amount to one hundred and
forty ; and provision was made for the security of their persons
and effects : these arguments being satisfactory to the majority
of the house, they declared their approbation of the treaty.

he spoke of it very favourably when consulted on the subject. He had, as
first lord of the treasury, included a sum for the proposed fortifications in
the estimates of expense for the year. His lordship, however, now declared, that he had always disapproved of the scheme, and challenged his
grace to produce a scrap of writing to the contrary. Although, by this
declaration, it would appear that those senators were mistaken in their
construction of his words and actions, it must be allowed, that their interpretation was, according to the usual rules of reasoning, not very unnatu-
ral The applicability, however, of a general criterion to the explanation
of a particular case, must depend in a great degree on the peculiar qualities of the subject. The duke of Richmond went so far as to charge his
lordship with insincerity; an allegation which the noble peer reprobated
with great indignation. In vindicating himself, the Marquis of Lansdown
asserted that *openness was his characteristic*, and that it was solely from
the consideration of the unguardedness of his temper, that, by the advice
of his friends, he had secluded himself from the world.

d See State Papers.

CHAP.   One of the subjects recommended to parliament by the
XXXVII. speech from the throne, was the consolidation of the customs.
         The increasing commerce of this country on the one hand, and
1787   its accumulated burthens on the other, had so widely exceed-
Consolida- ed the expectation of our ancestors, and all the grounds of cal-
tion of the culation on which they founded their system of finance, that
customs. the principles which they adopted, though sufficiently suited to
the narrow and confined scale of our former exigencies and
resources were no longer applicable. The consequence of
retaining the old principle, under the altered circumstances of
the country, had been in several points of view very detrimental
to the interest of the nation. The first institution of the subsisting duties of the customs was made by the statute of the
twelfth year of king Charles II. under the name of tonnage
and poundage; the first, an impost upon wines, measured by
the quantity imported; and the second, on the price of all
other articles. The last was therefore liable to great inaccuracies: it was not calculated according to the real value of the
commodities, but by an arbitrary estimation; perhaps the market price of the article at the time of imposing the duty : this
principle, when once adopted, was pursued in every fresh subsidy : in some instances it had operated, by imposing additional
duties calculated at so much per cent. upon the duty already
paid; in others it laid a farther impost of the same description
on a particular denomination of the commodity; almost all the
additional subsidies had been appropriated to some specific fund
for the payment of certain annuities : there must, therefore, be
a separate calculation for each made at the custom house; and
from the complexity of the whole system, it was scarcely possible that a merchant could be acquainted, by any calculations
of his own, with the exact amount of what he was to pay. To
remedy this great abuse, Mr. Pitt proposed to abolish all the
duties that now subsisted in this confused and complex manner,
and to substitute one single duty on each article, amounting, as
nearly as possible, to the aggregate of the various subsidies
now paid ; only where a fraction was found in any of the sums,
to change it for the nearest integral number, usually taking the
higher rather than the lower. This advance would produce an
increase in the revenue to the amount of 20,000l. per annum,
and lay upon the public a burthen, which must be amply compensated by the relief which the merchants were to experience
from the intended alteration. Mr. Pitt had given complete attention to this business ; and had not left one person unconsult-
ed from whom any information could be obtained ; and the
greatest diligence had been used to circulate the plan among
the most competent judges of those persons who were immediately concerned in its operation and effects. The proposed
scheme caused no debate ; the object was so evidently advantageous, and the means so well adapted, as to command the

concurrence and approbation of the whole house;[e] and a bill
for the purpose was introduced and passed. On the 26th of
April, Mr. Pitt presented to the house of commons a bill, stating, that notorious frauds had been committed in the collection
of the tax on post horses, and providing that, as a remedy to
the evil, the tax should be farmed. The several districts were
to be put to public auction at the present amount received in
each, and at the highest rate which it ever had produced ; and
it was not doubted there would be many candidates; hence the
full value might be expected. Mr. Fox opposed the bill, as
tending to enlarge the number of collectors very considerably,
and in the same proportion to increase the influence of the crown :
it was, besides, argued against the proposed mode of taxation,
that it was repugnant to the principles of our constitution, and
to the general system of our revenue ; and was the mode adopted under arbitrary governments, and one of the principal sources
of oppression in France: the precedent was in the highest
degree alarming, and required to be warmly resisted in the
outset. To these objections the minister and his friends replied,
that although farmers of the revenue contributed, under arbitrary governments, very greatly to the miseries of the people,
yet it was not from the nature of their employment, but from the
system under which it was exercised. The powers to be given
to the farmer were no greater than those at present intrusted to
collectors: after considerable discussion, the bill passed both
houses without a division.

A subject was introduced into the house of commons, which
became repeatedly the object of its consideration in succeeding
sessions: this was a proposition for the repeal of the test and
corporation acts. The dissenters from the church of England
were very considerable, both in number and opulence; and
certain classes of them derived great lustre from the learning
and genius of their leaders. Among them there were not a few
active, bold, and aspiring men ; these very naturally wished to
enjoy the sweets of power, to rise to a political superiority
over those to whom they might fancy themselves intellectually
superior. Among sectarians, the influence of their ministers is
generally greater than under an establishment. The relation
between the dissenting pastor and his flock is voluntary; whereas between a clergyman and parishioners it is created by the
law of the land. The former has, from his situation, dependent on the liberality of his employers, the strongest motives of
interest to accommodate himself to their passions, prejudices, and

*Applica-
tion of the
dissenters
for a repeal
of the test
act.*

[e] Mr. Burke, who rose immediately after the minister, professed that it
did not become him, or those who like him unfortunately felt it to be frequently their duty to oppose the measures of government, to contend themselves with a sullen acquiescence ; but on the contrary to rise manfully and
do justice to the measure, and to return their thanks to its author, on behalf
of themselves and their country. See parliamentary debates, 1787.

CHAP. humours;[f] because, if he thwart these, the proceeds of his
XXXVII. labours will be much diminished. The latter, being independent
of the bounty of those whom the constitution of the country has
1787. delegated to his spiritual care, has no interested motive to gratify
his parishioners, any farther than is consistent with wisdom and
virtue. The sectarian minister, like a tradesman, depends for
subsistence on his customers;[g] and the sure way of increasing
the number of those is obsequiousness.[h] The beneficed clergyman, as a gentleman, may cultivate the good will of his people,
and the friendship of the most deserving; but in paying his
court need not stoop beneath a dignified equality. Sectarians
also are infinitely more addicted to theological disputations,
than members of an established church. The zealous agitators
of controversy naturally regard with much veneration the chief
professor of their tenets. From these causes, the influence of
dissenting preachers over their employers was and must have
been very great. It certainly then was very easy for them to.
render the people zealous and eager to procure privileges so.
gratifying to human passions, nor were they actually wanting
in attempts to predispose the public in their favour. Many of
their preachers were literary undertakers, who would write on
any or every subject. Doctors Price, Priestley, and some
others, furnished ideas, which, by the assistance of dilation, repetition, and prolixity, sent to the world numberless books and
pamphlets on the severe policy of the British constitution,
which, in its allotment of offices, had required certain standards.
of qualification and disposition to discharge the respective duties. There were circumstances which they conceived favourable to the attainment of their object. The dissenters had
coincided with the majority of the established church, in supporting the minister of the crown and people against the leader
of a confederacy; thence they inferred that *gratitude* would.
induce him to support a cause, in the discussion of which he
was to be one of the JUDGES; that Mr. Pitt was to be guided
by private affection in deliberating on a question of public expediency. The minister was on terms of friendly intercourse
with various dissenters, especially Mr. Beaufoy: this consideration, they apprehended, would have great weight in determining the part which he, as a LAWGIVER, was to act. Mr. Fox,
from his general eagerness to diminish restraints, had often
professed, and uniformly manifested, disapprobation of tests
and subscriptions: it was not doubted he would be friendly to
the project, the whole dissenting interest, supported by the
leaders of the two parties, would, they trusted, produce the desired repeal.

Dissenters favourable to Mr. Pitt, and thence expect his support.

[f] See Hume, vol. ii p. 301. prefatory to the history of the reformation.
[g] Ibid. 302.
[h] The reader will observe, that here I merely describe the general tendency of situation to influence conduct.

Delegates were appointed to arrange and conduct their
plans; these did not directly petition parliament, but first
published and dispersed a paper which they called " the case
" of the protestant dissenters, with reference to the test and
" corporation acts."[i] This treatise exhibited the history of
the corporation and test acts; the hardships to which conscientious dissenters were exposed by those restrictory statutes; and endeavoured to demonstrate both the justice and
expediency of affording them effectual relief. When this
representation explained to the public their apprehension of
the predicament in which they stood, the dissenters engaged
Mr. Beaufoy to move, that the house should resolve itself into
a committee to consider those acts. In introducing this subject, on the 28th of March, the senator in the first place, stated, what were the exceptionable provisions of the law; and
in the next, the peculiar period and circumstances of its enactment. The test act required of every person accepting a
civil office, or a commission in the army or navy, to take the
sacrament within a limited time . and if, without qualifying
himself, he continued to occupy any office. or hold any commission, he not only incurred a large pecuniary penalty, but
was disabled thenceforth for ever from bringing any action in
course of law; from prosecuting a suit in the courts of equity;
from being the guardian of a child, or the executor of a de-
ceased person, and receiving any legacy. On the second head,
he recapitulated the history of the act, and the noted though
despicable artifice by which Charles II. defeated its repeal.[k]
He farther endeavoured to prove, that the dissenters had always been favourable to the present happy establishment, and
that their general conduct had been such as to entitle them to
the gratitude and regard of every true patriot. Lord North,
who had been lately deprived of the organs of sight, and
thereby prevented from regular and constant attendance in
parliament, came that day forward to defend the church from
apprehended encroachment. His lordship, educated at Oxford, and impressed with the sentiments which that university
has uniformly inculcated, was a strenuous supporter of episcopal
doctrines. Though too benevolent in disposition and mild in
temper for bigotry, he was the warm friend of the rights and
privileges of the ecclesiastical establishment, and had always
opposed the dissenters when applying for a change. He now
declared himself, though attached to the church, the sincere
friend of religious liberty. Far should he be from opposing
the present motion, if it sought no more than the free and entire exercise of the rights of conscience; but it prayed for the
repeal of an act, which was the great bulwark of the constitution, and to which we owed the inestimable blessings of .

CHAP.
XXXVII.

1787.
Previous
steps to
prepossess
the public
in their fa-
vour.

Mr. Beau-
foy pleads
their cause
in parlia-
ment.

Lord
North, a
moderate
tory, oppo-
ses the ap-
plication as
inimical to
the church.

i See Domestic Literature in the New Annual Review for 1787.
k Hume, vol iv.

CHAP. freedom; and recommended a proceeding contrary to the
XXXVII. happy experience of a century. It had been said, that the
test act was an indignity to the dissenters, but had we not re-
1787. solved, that no monarch should sit on the throne who refused
to comply with the test? If the throne were offered to any
prince, who, from motives of conscience, declined this condition, surely the refusal of the throne to that prince would be
no indignity. There was no complaint of ecclesiastical tyranny; universal toleration was established; let them therefore
guard against change in the church, nor confound the free
exercise of religion with admissibility to civil and military appointments. Mr. Pitt supported the same side of the question;
and began by marking the difference between civil and religious
liberty on the one hand, and political trusts on the other. The
former, every good constitution of government must secure to
all its subjects; the latter was bestowed with discrimination,
according to individual qualification and disposition, of which
the community had the right of judging by any rule that it
thought expedient. The test was merely the condition required by the employer from persons to whom he committed a
trust. Every master had an unquestionable right to declare
the conditions in which he would admit service; and none
could be aggrieved by an exclusion arising from himself. The
present therefore, was not a question of grievance and redress,
but simply of policy. On this question legislation had only
one subject of deliberation, was it expedient, in the present
circumstances, sentiments, and principles of the dissenters, for
the nation to employ them in certain specified offices? To
such an inquiry, every recapitulation of former history was extraneous: a repeal might have been wise in the time of
Charles II., and unwise in the reign of George III. The dissenters were, undoubtedly, a body of men, who were entitled
to the consideration of parliament; but there was another
class equally respectable, and more numerous, whose fears on
this occasion would be alarmed. Many members of the church
of England conceived, that the ecclesiastical part of our constitution would be seriously injured, and their apprehensions
were not to be treated lightly. If he were arguing on principles of right, he should not talk of alarm; but he had already said, he was arguing upon principles of expediency.
The church and state were united upon principles of expediency; and it concerned those, to whom the well being of
the state was intrusted, to take care that the church should not
rashly be demolished. The persons who now applied, declared, that they meant nothing political by their application;
but he must look at human actions to find out the springs.
Highly as he thought of many of the present dissenters, he
could not but observe there were persons among them, who
would not admit that any establishment was necessary; and
against such it became the legislature to be upon their guard.

Mr. Pitt
opposes it
on the
grounds
of political
expedien-
cy.

The test
no in-
fringement
of tolera-
tion;
merely a
condition.
Of admis-
sibility to
certain of-
fices.

Eminent
dissenters
avowed
themselves
hostile to
the
church.

Doctor Priestley, whose abilities and learning were very high, CHAP.
and whose opinions were received as oracles by a certain XXXVII.
class of dissenters, had proclaimed enmity against the church.
Sectarians (he said) were wisely placing as it were, grain by   1787.
grain, a train of gunpowder, to which the match would one Therefore
day be laid to blow up the fabric of error, which could never notexpedi-
be again raised upon the same foundation. When he saw pro- ent to ex-
ceedings, intended to subvert so important a part of our polity, tend their
power.
he thought circumspection and vigilance absolutely necessary:
when there was an avowed design to sap the fortress, it became the duty of the garrison to secure the outposts: the dissenters already enjoyed every mental freedom to serve God,
according to their consciences, in the most ample degree:
what they now required, was inexpedient and dangerous.
These sentiments deeply impressed the house: and on a di- The appli-
vision, the proposition of Mr. Beaufoy was negatived by a cation is re-
majority of one hundred and seventy-eight to one hun- jected.
dred.

Soon after this application, a bill was introduced for granting
indulgence to a different species of complainants; these were
insolvent debtors. The vast increase of commerce poured
opulence on the nation; but to many individuals, unavoidable
losses or injudicious speculations, brought bankruptcy and ruin.
Luxury, growing with commerce and riches, spread its influence over society; the immense fortunes that were acquired by
extortion and peculation in the east, and during the American
war, through the prodigal effusion of the public money, stock-
jobbing, and other causes, operated upon the minds of many
traders, and inspired them with a desire of rapid accumulation.
This spirit suggested various schemes, which being much more
extensive than the capital that could be employed, failure produced certain ruin. Gaming of every kind was extremely prevalent: the example of some very eminent characters, combining with their winning and impressive manners, infected their
intimate associates with this particular vice, and with general
extravagance; and that consequence extended itself to many
of their political supporters. The metropolis teemed with
gambling tradesmen; these became strenuous politicians, who
wished to have a share in directing the business of the nation,
and that they might deliberate in the tavern, they neglected
their shops; imitating those whom they admired, they followed
them to their private pastimes; and closed their exertions in the
king's bench or fleet prisons; and the number of imprisoned
debtors, through either misfortune or vice, was extremely great.
There can be no wise and just reason for confining a debtor,
but to compel payment: if there be no property concealed, confinement of the debtor cannot restore the creditor's
right: were it practicable to compel, in every case, the debtor
to give up his effects to the creditor, as from effects, not per-

son, his reimbursement must proceed, imprisonment[1] might appear no longer to answer any just purpose to the creditor. The laws of imprisonment for debt, were, by many of the most enlightened men, deemed a great blemish in the legislative code of the country. Cautious, however, not hastily to innovate, lawgivers, instead of changing the principle, had endeavoured to lessen the severity of the operation by temporary expedients. One of these was by insolvent acts, which have been usually passed at periods of various distance, when the prisons of the kingdom were so full, as to be supposed to render them absolutely necessary. The last of these had been passed in the year 1780, and bills of this kind had been repeatedly proposed, but negatived. This year a proposition to a similar effect was

Bill for the
relief of in
solvent
debtors.

made in the house of lords; the chief supporters were lord Kinnaird, the earl of Hopetoun, the duke of Norfolk,[m] but above all lord Rawdon. This accomplished nobleman we have already seen[n] distinguished as a soldier; equally excelling in the arts of peace, he was now become eminent as a member of the senate. With his many other virtues, remarkable for humanity, he directed his attention to the alleviation of misery : his lord-

Enlighten-
ed and li-
beral poli-
cy of Lord
Rawdon.

ship supported the liberation of insolvent debtors both on the ground of mercy and political expediency. Do not confine debtors, (he said) to gratify the resentment of creditors! Do not, because one individual is malignant suffer another to be miserable! By confining insolvent debtors, you prevent them from benefiting themselves, their families, and the community ; and you deprive them of every possible means of indemnifying their creditors. Clauses may be introduced, which would re-

1 Mr. Burke delivered the following opinion on this important subject, in his address to the electors of Bristol:—" There are two capital faults in our law, with relation to civil debts. One is, that every man is presumed solvent; a presumption, in innumerable cases, directly against truth; therefore the debtor is ordered, on a supposition of ability and fraud, to be coerced his liberty until he makes payment. By this means, in all cases of civil insolvency, without a pardon from his creditors, he is to be imprisoned for life; and thus a miserable mistaken invention of artificial science operates to change a civil into a criminal judgment, and to scourge misfortune or indiscretion with a punishment which the law does not inflict on very great crimes. The next fault is, that the inflicting of that punishment is not on the opinion of an equal and a public judge; but is referred to the arbitrary discretion of a private, nay interested and irritated, individual. He who formally is, and substantially ought to be, the judge, is in reality no more than ministerial, a mere executive instrument of a private man, who is at once judge and party: every idea of judical order is subverted by this procedure. If the insolvency be no crime, why is it punished with arbitrary imprisonment? If it be a crime, why is it delivered into private hands to pardon without discretion, or to punish without mercy and without measure."

m This nobleman, hitherto mentioned in the history as the earl of Surry, had, about a year before, succeeded to the dukedom by the death of his father. The present duke is the first protestant representative of the family.
n Vol. i. *passim.*

lieve misfortune, without suffering fraud to escape. Lord Thurlow had been uniformly the chief opposer of the several insolvent bills, and now maintained the same ground. His arguments on the subject have been frequently imputed to a severe unmerciful disposition; but whether conclusive or not,
when fairly canvassed, they discover no marks of such a spirit;
they manifestly arise from a policy, suggested by an extensive
view of a commercial country, and the means of encouraging
industry and frugality, and restraining idleness, and extravagance:
whatever opinion we may form of his reasoning, these were evidently his objects. His lordship, to answer theoretical ingenuity,
which expatiated on the miseries that a rigorous creditor might
inflict on an innocent though unfortunate debtor, stated a simple
and broad fact : English creditors, as a collective body, are distinguished for lenity; to support this assertion he appealed to
observation and experience; and affirmed, that lawyers and
judges, who, in the exercise of their professions, had the most
frequent opportunities of knowing the treatment of debtors by
creditors, were beyond all others the most deeply impressed with
this truth. Lord Mansfield had observed, that for twenty prodigal debtors, there scarcely appeared in the course of law one
cruel creditor; the law, as it now stood, discriminated between
misfortune and vice : the bankrupt code was instituted for the
relief of traders, who failed through unforeseen misfortunes;
they were the proper objects of generosity and protection ; while
on the other hand, those who ran in debt, knowing that they
should never be able to pay, were certainly fit subjects of that
severity, which the law, as it stood, empowered their creditors° to
exercise; besides, in the last insolvent act, the preamble had declared, that it was not likely any more such acts should be passed; and thus in a great measure pledged the public faith to
creditors: as he was inimical to the insolvent bill, he said he intended to propose several regulations for mitigating the miseries
of imprisoned debtors. The bill was negatived, on a division, by
a majority of twenty-three to twelve.

A question was this session submitted to the house of lords
concerning peers of the kingdom of Scotland who acquired
British peerages. During the preceding summer, the earl of
Abercorn, and the duke of Queensberry, of the kingdom of
Scotland, had been called to the dignity of British peers, by
the titles of viscount Hamilton, and baron Douglas, notwithstanding which, they continued to sit as representatives of the
peerage of Scotland. Lord Stormont contended, that the right
of representation was granted to Scottish peers as a recompense
for the loss of an hereditary seat in parliament ; those who no
longer suffered the loss, could therefore no longer be entitled to
a share in the compensation. Having recapitulated the history

° Lord Thurlow did not here overturn the objection to a system which
makes the party both judge and punisher.

CHAP. of the union to illustrate his positions, he moved that the earl of
XXXVII. Abercorn and the duke of Queensberry, who had been chosen in
the number of the sixteen peers, having been created peers of
1787. Great Britain, thereby ceased to sit in that house as representatives of the peerage of Scotland. His lordship rested his principal argument on a resolution of the house of lords, which was
passed in January 1709, that a peer of Scotland, sitting in the
parliament of Great Britain, by virtue of a patent passed since
the union, had no right to vote in the election of the sixteen peers
of Scotland. From this opinion of the house, declaring that such
peers could not choose representatives, his lordship inferred, that
they could not be representatives themselves. Lord Loughborough supported this constructive interpretation; lord Thurlow, on the contrary, maintained, that a resolution of either house
did not constitute the law of the land; and that they ought to
abide by that law according to its literal meaning. Another debate soon after took place on a question, nearly connected with
this, but to which the resolution of 1709 more directly applied:
whether British peers, created since the union, could vote at the
election of a Scottish representative: both sides were supported
and opposed on the same grounds as in the foregoing case; and
both motions were negatived.[p]

Magnani-   A subject equally interesting and important at this time at-
mous sacri- tracted the public attention, and underwent a discussion in the
fice by the house of commons. The prince of Wales, amiable, engaging,
prince of   and accomplished, with a vigorous understanding, possessed
Wales of   strong affections, and was not without that disposition to plea-
splendour
to justice. sure which so often accompanies the sensibility and animation
of youth, especially in such rank and circumstances as easily
afford the objects of pursuit and the means of attainment.
Attached to the fair sex, the manly beauty of his face and
person, apart from his other advantages, procured him, in the
susceptible hearts of his countrywomen, incitements, which
while it is admitted as a moral proposition that ascetic virtue
ought to have resisted, it must be allowed as an historical fact,
that such virtue is not very common in young men of twenty-
four. Generous by disposition, the prince was munificent in
bounty; social and elegant, he was sumptuous in hospitality:
much connected with the chief characters of opposition, he
partook of amusements which constituted the favourite recreation of some of the most illustrious men of the party. The
effect of so great an additional source of expenditure to his
convivial splendour and expanded generosity, was, that his income did not prove sufficient, and that he had before summer
1786 incurred a very considerable debt. Finding himself in

[p] At the election of the earl of Selkirk and lord Kinnaird, to represent
the peerage of Scotland, in the room of the duke of Queensberry and the
earl of Abercorn, the dukes of Queensberry and Gordon had given their
votes as peers of Scotland.

such circumstances, and desirous of rendering justice to his CHAP.
creditors, his highness resolved to suppress the establishment XXXVII.
of his household and every useless expense, and to save from
his income its greater portion, to be applied by trustees for the 1787.
liquidation of his incumbrances. He had hitherto, like many
other persons of rank and fortune, trained running horses for
Newmarket, and the other places of public contention. His
racers, his hunters, and even his coach-horses, were now sold
by public auction. The buildings of Carlton-house were
stopped, and some of the principal rooms shut up from use:
and the heir of the crown retired from the magnificence of his
station to do justice to his creditors. This conduct in itself did
the highest honour to the sentiments and rectitude of the prince;
but a consideration totally irrelative, entered into the estimate
which many formed of its merits. His highness had, in the
several objects of his attachment, displayed a discriminating
selection, which required the union of mental qualifications
with corporeal graces. The lady who at this time occupied Situation
the principal share of his attention, was Mrs. Fitzherbert; a of his high-
woman who, besides the charms and fascinations of beauty ness.
and accomplishments, possessed a very respectable character:
from this last circumstance a report originated, that greatly
interested the public: one relation being presumed, was justified on the part of the lady by the presumption of another.
It was currently reported, that the ceremony of marriage
between Mrs. Fitzherbert and her lover had been privately
performed; and as she was of the Roman catholic persuasion,
that the officiating clergyman was a priest of her own religion.
As a legal contract, no such marriage could have been concluded, according to the written statutes which regard the
royal family as a matter of fact, such a ceremony might have
been performed, but the belief that it actually took place, was
totally inconsistent with a just and candid estimation of the
prince's character: it proceeded on one of two suppositions: either that he disregarded his own particular station,
under its constitutional limits and prescriptions, and the recent
laws enacted respecting the royal family, or that he had consented to an appearance which he well knew could not be
valid; and thus practised deception on the other party. Improbable as the report was in its subject, and totally unsupported by any evidence, nevertheless it was very prevalent,
and created considerable alarm. The prince's friends had
expected an interference from a still higher quarter to extricate
him from his pecuniary difficulties. Finding no measure of this
kind in agitation, and from other incidents inferring disapprobation on the part of the father, many imputed the apprehended
coldness to dissatisfaction with certain portions of the son's
conduct, especially his close connexion with that party which
opposed the ministers of his majesty's choice, who had been
appointed under so very peculiar circumstances; and not a few

CHAP.
XXXVII.

1787.

attributed some share of the alleged displeasure to the above-mentioned report. From July 1786, to April 1787, these topics continued greatly to engross the thoughts and conversation of the public ; but had not been deemed fit subjects for parliamentary consideration. His highness now authorized Mr. Alderman Newnham to represent to the house of commons his embarrassed situation. On the 20th of April that gentleman opened the business: he previously asked Mr. Pitt if he had any design of bringing forward a motion for the relief of the prince; and being answered that he had received no commands from the king on the subject, the alderman give notice, that, on the 24th of May, he should make a motion to that effect. This intimation excited much anxiety in the house, as it seemed to lead to such interesting discussions. Mr. Newnham, on one of the intervening days, explained the precise nature of his motion; which was to address the king, praying him to take into his consideration the derangement of the prince's affairs; and to grant him such relief as his wisdom should deem expedient and suitable; and pledging the house to make good the same. Mr. Pitt earnestly wished that the motion should not be brought forward: there were circumstances (he said) respecting the pecuniary concerns of the prince, that would render the present proposition inimical to the object of its author: the application ought to originate elsewhere, and not in the house: a correspondence had taken place between the party principally concerned, and another personage, respecting financial embarrassments. Mr. Pitt, with his usual closeness, kept to the subject which was introduced by Mr. Newnham ; but some of the most zealous supporters of administration introduced an extraneous topic, in an allusion to the prevailing rumours. Messrs. Fox and Sheridan reprobated the report to which this insinuation referred; and, at the next meeting of the house, Mr. Fox declared he had authority from the prince to contradict the allegation. In law, as Mr. Fox observed, it could not take place; and in fact Mr. Fox pledged the veracity of his highness that it had not taken place. This public disavowal, at the instance of the heir apparent, afforded very great satisfaction to the whole house. On recurring to his pecuniary situation, Mr. Fox declared, that the prince was willing to give a general and fair account of his debts; and if any part of it was doubted, he would present a clear explanation of the particulars to the king or his ministers. He had not the smallest objection to afford the house every possible satisfaction; and there was not a circumstance of his life which he was ashamed to have known.

Satisfactorily adjusted.

Meanwhile, interviews took place between Mr. Dundas and his highness; and the following day between the minister and the prince. Mr. Newnham being made acquainted with the result, on the day on which the motion was intended to be made, declared it was no longer necessary. About a fortnight

afterwards, a message from the king was delivered to parliament, stating, that his majesty with great concern acquainted
them, that the prince had incurred a very large debt, which, if
left to be discharged out of his annual income, would render it
impossible for him to support an establishment that would be
suited to his rank and station. His majesty was induced to the
present application by his paternal affection to the prince of
Wales: he could not, however, desire the assistance of parliament, but on a well grounded conviction that the prince
would avoid contracting any debts in future. With a view to
this object, the king had directed a sum of 10,000l. to be paid
out of the civil list, in addition to his former allowance; he had
the satisfaction to observe, that the prince had given the fullest
assurance of his determination to confine his future expenses
within his income, and had settled a plan, and fixed an order
in his economy, which, it was trusted, would effectually secure
the due execution of his intentions. He farther recommended
to the commons to direct, that the works of Carleton-house
should be properly finished. In answer to this message, 161,000l.
were voted for the payment of the prince's debts, and 20,000l.
for the completion of his palace.

The conduct of Mr. Hastings continued to occupy the atten- Proceed-
tion of parliament, and produced an extraordinary display of ings re-
abilities. One charge of great importance had been decided specting
against the late governor-general: the event of the accusation Mr. Hast
respecting Cheyt Sing, had surprised and alarmed Mr. Hast- ings.
ings and his friends. Many supporters of administration regarded the conduct of the accused in a very favourable light; thence
his advocates seem to have inferred, that Mr. Pitt entertained
a similar opinion. One of the most important qualities of a
great minister is, that secrecy which avoids the communication
of sentiments or intentions, unless prudence admit or duty require that they should be manifested. This self command, the
firm mind of Mr. Pitt possesses in a very high degree; and no
artifice can discover what he resolves to conceal. In the present case he studied the charges separately, and as became a
judge, abstained from publishing his opinion, until he was prepared to deliver judgment. Mr. Hastings, therefore, saw that
the vote of the prime minister would depend entirely on the
view which he took of the respective charges; and that in cases
comprehending probable grounds both of blame and justfica-
tion, it might be doubtful what his sentence might be on some
of the subsequent accusations. The authority, he was aware,
of so highly prized talents and integrity, would be great with
those who, hesitating between contending probabilities, found a
difficulty themselves in forming a decisive opinion. Much
more anxiety and doubt now, therefore, displayed themselves in
the friends of Mr. Hastings, than when major Scott, in the ex- Writings
ultation of anticipated victory, had so eagerly invited Mr. Burke in his fa-
to the combat. The press teemed with defences of the late vour.

CHAP.   governor-general ; either the spontaneous effusions of convic-
XXXVII. tion and friendship, or the purchased productions of literary
         ability : the former were more disinterested in the motive ; the
1787.   latter more successful in the execution. Some of Mr. Hastings's
         friends, indeed, very injudiciously, as well as uncandidly, ascrib-
         ed bad or frivolous motives to the chief men on both sides of
         the house, who voted for the impeachment. They asserted,
         that Mr. Burke was actuated by resentment ; that Messrs.
         Fox, Sheridan, Windham, Adam, Anstruther, Grey, sir Gil-
         bert Elliot, and other members of opposition, merely wished
         to gratify Burke, and to attack a man whom they thought
         favoured by the court and some of the ministers ;�q and that
         leading men of administration were moved by jealousy of Mr.
         Hastings's influence. Apprehending those advocates to be con-
         vinced, that the person whose cause they so warmly espoused
         was innocent, and also able to prove his innocence, the im-
         partial reader must deem them extremely imprudent, and in-
         deed unwise in resting his defence upon extraneous grounds.
         This imputation was uncandid, because it assigned unjustifia-
         ble motives without proof, or even plausible argument. The
         motive ascribed to the principal accuser was virulent resent-
         ment, because a friend of his had been promoted by Hastings ;
         but the alleged cause is not adequate to the effect. That Mr.
         Burke or any man would undertake so laborious a task, which
         required such minuteness of investigation concerning intri-
         cate details, the materials of which were to be fetched from
         such a distance, with so great and powerful a body inimical to
         an inquiry, merely because his friend had been slighted, is hard-
         ly within the compass of credibility : the same observations will
         apply to all the other prosecutors, as far as they were concerned.
         As to the jealousy of ministers, where can we find the grounds
         for such a passion in the relative situation of these and of Mr.
         Hastings ? Fully admitting extraordinary talents and also me-
         ritorious conduct in the political saviour of India, can a reader
         discover any official situation which he was likely to fill, that
         could in the smallest degree interfere with the power and in-
         fluence of the ministers in question? But the hired pleaders
         for Mr. Hastings, being much more accustomed to reasoning,
         defended him on stronger grounds. Instead of forming hypo-
         thesis concerning the *motives of the accusers*, they adduced ar-
         guments from the CONDUCT OF THE ACCUSED, which, in detailed
         series, principle and system, they justified by the circumstances
         in which he was placed, and illustrated by the effects that his
The majo- exertions produced. These two classes of defenders had each
rity of the
nation is   considerable success; the first with the weak and undistinguish-
adverse to ing; the second with men of discernment and abilities : and the
the im-   majority of the nation was inimical to the impeachment.
peach
ment.   q. See pamphlets in favour of Mr. Hastings *passim*; also periodical
         works, especially a newspaper called the World.

Such was the state of the public opinion, when one most CHAP.
powerful effort of eloquence diffused quite different senti- XXXVII.
ments through the kingdom; and presented Mr. Hastings as
an atrocious criminal. This was the celebrated speech on the 1787.
charge of the Begums.   Eloquence

An opinion long prevailed among literary men, that though gives a con-
Britons surpass the ancients in knowledge and philosophy; to public
equal them in epic, and excel them in dramatic poetry; yet opinion.
they are inferior in eloquence. Writers of transcendent talents, British elo-
distinguished taste and profound erudition, deem this notion so quence.
evident as not to require any discussion : they take the fact for
granted, and confine their inquiries to the cause.[r] Great. ingenuity is employed in comparing the fields of ancient and modern oratory, and discovering motives that led to much more
powerful and impressive exertions among the Greeks and Romans, than any that influence British speakers: hence (say
Hume and Blair) no Demosthenes or Cicero arises in a modern
senate. A careful examiner of the eloquence which adorns
the parliamentary history of the present reign, may probably
doubt the truth of this assertion: he who peruses the orations
of the elder or younger Pitt, Burke, or Fox, may hesitate before he will determine that they are surpassed by either Cicero
or Demosthenes. It is, indeed, in the supreme excellencies of
the Roman or Grecian orator, that they are most nearly equalled
by British senators. Like Demosthenes,[s] especially, the highest of our orators are much less eminent for rhetorical flourishes,
than for clear and forcible statement of important facts; combination of whatever illustrates the question, or promotes the
measure proposed; comprehensive views of the situation,
intentions, and interests of the parties concerned; energetic
reasoning appropriated to the point at issue; and application of forcible motives to impel hearers to the counsels
and conduct which the speaker desires. Eloquence, to be
efficacious, must be adapted to the sentiments and knowledge of the persons to whom it is addressed; the same
species and mode would not suit informed and enlightened
gentlemen of the British house of commons, and the populace
which constituted so great a part of the Grecian and Roman
assemblies. The same genius and wisdom which enabled and
directed Demosthenes to perform such intellectual wonders,
empowered and guided him to adapt his oratory to the feelings
and capacity of his audience : the acuteness and ingenuity of
the Athenian meetings did not admit of much tinsel, instead of
sterling value; nevertheless, they were in many respects a

r See Hume's Essay on Eloquence; see also Blair's Lectures, lect. xxvi.;
and *Man of the Moon*, by Dr. William Thomson.

s Of British orators Mr. Fox unquestionably bears the nearest resemblance to the Athenian in materials, spirit, and expression; and equals him
in force and in fire, but is less attentive to luminous arrangement.

CHAP.
XXXVII.

1787.

mere mob; consequently, there was sometimes room for sub-
stituting impression for conviction; addressing their feelings
instead of their understandings; their weakness instead of
their strength. Demosthenes, in order to carry the most beneficial plans into execution, was often obliged to soothe and
cajole them; and for that purpose occasionally to admit into
his discourses ornaments, which his own austere, strong, and
chaste judgment would have induced him to reprobate. British
eloquence is rather unlike to ancient in some of the subordinate
instruments,ᵗ than unequal in the combination of strong reasoning, vivid imagery, and pathetic exhibition; which passing
through the head affects the heart, and influences the conduct:
the operation and result of oratory are no less vigorous and
effectual in Britain, than in Rome or Athens. These observations though somewhat digressive, will not, I trust, be accounted
foreign to the subject of our narrative, that now comes to a
display of eloquence, which has, perhaps, never been surpassed
in ancient or modern times.

Speech of
Mr. Sheri-
dan on the
conduct of
Mr. Hast-
ings to-
wards the
Begums.

On the 7th of February Mr. Sheridan opened the third
article of accusation against Mr. Hastings; which was his
conduct towards the Begums,ᵘ or dowager princesses of Oude.
The introduction attacked a ground of defence chosen by

ᵗ That, in point of action, ancient orators far surpass modern, is deemed
one of those critical observations, which it would be equally superfluous
to illustrate, as absurd to controvert; a common inference from the allowed
superiority of action is greater excellence of oratory; and the noted saying
of the Roman is often quoted to prove, that gesticulation is the primary
constituent of eloquence. One of the wisest men that has written on that
or any other subject, views the importance of action in a different light.
" It is (says Dr. Johnson) a complaint which has been made from time to
time, and which seems to have lately become more frequent, that *English*
oratory, however forcible in argument, or elegant in expression, is deficient
and inefficacious, because our speakers want the grace and energy of action.
Among the numerous projectors who are desirous to refine our manners,
and improve our faculties, some are willing to supply the deficiency of our
speakers: we have had more than one exhortation to study the neglected
art of moving the passions; and have been encouraged to believe, that our
tongues, however feeble in themselves, may, *by the help of our hands and
legs*, obtain an uncontrovertible dominion over the most stubborn audience,
animate the insensible, engage the careless, force tears from the obdurate,
and money from the avaricious. If, by slight of hand, or nimbleness of foot,
all these wonders can be performed, he that shall neglect to attain the free
use of his limbs, may be justly censured as criminally lazy: but we are
afraid that no specimen of such effects will easily be shown. If we could
once find a speaker in '*Change-Alley*, raising the price of stocks by the power of persuasive gestures, we should very zealously recommend the study
of his art; but having never seen any action by which language was much
assisted, we have been hitherto inclined to doubt whether our countrymen
are not blamed too hastily for their calm and motionless utterance." Idler,
No. 90.

ᵘ See vol. i. of this history, chap. xxix.

many advocates of Mr. Hastings, that the successful result of CHAP. his administration, amounted to a sufficient justification of his XXXVII. conduct: this principle the speaker reprobated, as contrary to every rule of natural and christian morals, which both taught, 1787. in the most unequivocal language, that wicked means were not to be employed for the purpose of accomplishing desirable ends; it was, moreover, a new and base sophism in the maxims of judicial inquiry, that crimes might be compounded, and that fortunate events were a full and complete set-off against oppression, corruption, breach of faith, peculation, and treachery. The conduct of the house of commons, during the preceding year, was guided by the soundest principles of jurisprudence; they had asserted, that there were acts of moral turpitude, which no political necessity could warrant; and proved to the world, that, however degenerate an example some of the British subjects had exhibited in India, the people of England, collectively, speaking and acting by their representatives, felt, as men should feel on such an occasion: they had demonstrated themselves superior to the presumptuous pretensions that were advanced in favour of this pillar of India, this corner-stone of our strength in the East, this talisman of the British territories in Asia, whose character was said to be above censure, and whose conduct was not within the reach of suspicion. After this conciliatory exordium, the orator proceeded to rouse the attention of his hearers, by a concise but striking outline of the nature and magnitude of the subject which he was about to submit to their consideration. The present charge he stated to be replete with criminality of the blackest die, tyranny the most vile and premeditated, corruption the most open and shameless, oppression the most severe and grinding, and cruelty the most hard and unparalleled. He professed to God, that he felt in his own bosom the strongest personal conviction on the present subject. It was upon that conviction that he believed the conduct of Mr. Hastings, in regard to the nabob of Oude, and to the begums, comprehended in it every species of human offence. He had proved himself guilty of rapacity, at once violent and insatiable; of treachery, cool and premeditated; of oppression, useless and unprovoked; of breach of faith, unwarranted and base; of cruelty unmanly and unmerciful! These were the crimes of which his soul and conscience arraigned Mr. Hastings, and which he trusted he should demonstrate to the satisfaction of every hearer. He was far from meaning to rest the charges upon assertion, or upon the warm expressions which the impulse of wounded feelings might produce: he would establish every part of the accusation by the most unanswerable proof, and the most unquestionable evidence. He would support every fact by a testimony, which few would venture to contradict, that of Mr. Hastings himself. As there were persons ready to stand up advocates for the late governor-general, he

CHAP.　challenged these to watch every particle of the accusations which
XXXVII.　he should advance; he desired credit for no fact which he did
　　　not prove beyond the possibility of refutation.

1787.　　　Mr. Hastings had endeavoured to establish, that the treasures of the begums were not private property, but belonged to
the nabob; that the real proprietor had a right to reclaim his
own property, whenever he chose; and actually had resumed
it for the purpose of liquidating his debts to the East India
company.　To controvert this assertion he quoted the mahommedan law, and decisions upon that law concerning this
very case; the amount was, that women, on the death of their
husbands, are entitled only to the property within the zenana
or harem where they lived.　This opinion had been fully admitted by the council of Calcutta; the begums retained only
the treasures which were within the harems, and relinquished
every other property to the reigning prince.　The British government of India at the time admitted, and even guaranteed
the tenure by which the begums held this residue of effects;
that property, therefore, was their own, and not the nabob's;
it might be plundered, but could not be justly reclaimed.　Mr.
Hastings, in mitigation of his own severities, mistated the
principles of mahommedan law, as if he meant to insinuate,
that there was something in the eastern codes which rendered
it impious in a son not to plunder his mother.　From these
arguments, to establish that the property was the right of the
begums, and consequently the seizure a violation of rights, the
orator proceeded to the reasons which had been adduced for
appropriating the treasures of the princesses: here, he rested
his inference on the report of the governor-general himself.
The begums had at all times given disturbance to the nabob;
they had long manifested a spirit hostile to his and to the English government; they had excited the zemindars to revolt;
and they were accessary to the insurrection at Benares.
Each of these allegations was sufficiently disproved by Mr.
Hastings himself; who made it appear, that on the contrary
they had particularly distinguished themselves by their friendship with the English, and by the various good offices which
they rendered to the government.　Mr. Hastings left Calcutta
in 1781, and proceeded to Lucknow, as he said himself, with
two great objects in his mind, Benares and Oude.　What was
the nature of these boasted resources?　They resembled the
equitable alternative of a highwayman, who, in going forth in
the evening, was held in suspense which of his resources to
prefer, Bagshot or Hounslow.　In such a state of generous irresolution did Mr. Hastings proceed to Benares and Oude: at
Benares he failed in his pecuniary object; then and not till
then, not on account of any ancient enmities shown by the
begums; not in resentment for any old disturbances; but because he had failed in one place, and had but two in prospect,
did he conceive the base expedient of plundering these aged

women. To carry his scheme into execution, Mr. Hastings,
said his eloquent accuser, formed the atrocious design of instigating a son against his m~other~, of sacrificing female dignity and distress to parricide and plunder. At Chunar was
that infamous treaty concerted: in which, among other articles, Mr. Hastings had stipulated with one whom he called an
independent prince, that, as great distress had arisen to
the nabob's government from the military power and dominion assumed by the dowager princesses he be permitted to re-assume such of their lands as he may deem to
be necessary. From the plan, the accuser proceeded to
the execution; no sooner was this foundation of inquiry
established, in violation of the pledged faith and solemn guarantee of the British government: no sooner had Mr. Hastings
determined to invade the substance of equity, than he resolved
to avail himself of judicial forms.; and accordingly despatched
a messenger for the chief justice of India, to assist him in perpetrating the violations he had projected. Sir Elijah Impey being arrived, Mr. Hastings, with much art, proposed a question
of opinion, involving an unsubstantiated fact, in order to obtain
a surreptitious approbation of the measure he had predeter-
mined to adopt; the begums being in actual rebellion, might
not the nabob confiscate their property? "Most undoubtedly!"
was the ready answer of the friendly judge. Not a syllable of
inquiry intervened, as to the existence of the imputed revolt;
not a moment's pause as to the ill purposes, to which the decision of a chief justice might be perverted. It was not the
office of a friend to mix the grave caution and cold circumspection of a judge, with an opinion taken in such circumstances;
and sir Elijah had previously declared, that he gave his advice
not as a judge, but as a friend; a character which he equally
preferred in the strange office that he undertook, of collecting
justificatory affidavits on the subject of Benares. It is, (said
the orator) curious to reflect on the whole of sir Elijah's circuit
at that perilous time: he stated his desire of relaxing from the
fatigues of office, and unbending his mind in a party of health
and pleasure; yet, wisely apprehending, that too sudden relaxation might defeat its object, he contrived to mix some concerns
of business with his amusements. In his little airing of nine
hundred miles, great part of which he travelled post, escorted
by an army, he selected those very situations where insurrection
subsisted, and rebellion was threatened; and had not only delivered his deep and curious researches into the laws of nations
and treaties, in the capacity of the oriental Grotius, whom Mr.
Hastings was to study, but also appeared in the humbler and
more practical situation of a collector of *ex parte* evidence: in
the former quality his opinion was the premature sanction for
plundering the begums; in the latter character he became the
posthumous supporter of the expulsion and pillage of the rajah
Cheyt Sing. Acting on an improved fact, on a position as ideal

CHAP.
XXXVII.

1787.

as a *datum* of the duke of Richmond, he did not hesitate, in the first instance, to lend his authority to an unlimited persecution; in the latter, he did not disdain to scud about India, like an itinerant informer, with a pedlar's pack of garbled evidence and surreptitious affidavits. With a generous oblivion of duty and honour, with a proud sense of having authorized all future rapacity, and sanctioned all past oppression, this friendly judge proceeded on his circuit, of health and ease : while the governor-general issued his orders to plunder the begums of their treasure, sir Elijah pursued his progress, and explored a country that presented a speaking picture of hunger and nakedness, in quest of objects best suited to his feelings ; in anxious search of calamities most akin to his invalid imagination : thus, at the same moment that the sword of government was turned to an assassin's dagger, the pure ermine of justice was stained and soiled with the basest contamination. Such were the circumstances, under which Mr. Hastings completed the treaty of Chunar : a treaty which may challenge all the treaties that ever existed, for containing in the smallest compass the most extensive treachery. An apology adduced by Mr. Hastings for his conduct is, that the begums resisted the resumption of the jaghires : the amount of this charge is, that these poor old women attempted to prevent robbery. Could any thing be more absurd, than to accuse persons of endeavouring to preserve their property from plunder ? But the fact is, they made no resistance ; they well knew that their feeble efforts could not restrain the force of the plunderer : but, Mr. Hastings farther added, the begums complained that they had suffered injustice. " God of " Heaven ! had they not a right to complain ? After the viola- " tion of a solemn treaty, plundered of their property, and on " the eve of the last extremity of misery, were they to be de- " prived of the ultimate resource of impotent wretchedness, la- " mentation, and regret ? Was it a crime that they should crowd " together in fluttering trepidation, like a flock of helpless birds, " on seeing the felon kite, who, having darted at one devoted " victim and missed his aim, singled out a new object, and was " springing on his prey with redoubled vigour in his wing, and " keener vengeance in his eye ?" After the eloquence of Sheridan had exhibited such a view of the acts of the accused, he proceeded to his general character. " It has (he said) been " advanced by admirers of Mr. Hastings, who are not so impli- " cit as to give unqualified applause to his crimes, that they " found an apology for their atrocity in the greatness of his " mind. To estimate the solidity of such a defence, it is suffi- " cient to consider wherein this prepossessing distinction, this cap- " tivating characteristic consists : is it not solely to be traced in " great actions directed to great ends ? In them only are we " to search for true magnanimity; to them only can we affix " the splendour and the honours of true greatness. There is, " indeed, another species of greatness, which displays itself in

" boldly conceiving a bad measure, and undauntedly pursuing
" it to its accomplishment. Had Mr. Hastings the merit of
" exhibiting either of these? There was nothing great,
" nothing magnanimous, nothing open, nothing direct, in
" his measures or his mind : on the contrary, he pursued the
" worst objects by the worst means ; his course was an eternal
" deviation from rectitude ; at one time he tyrannized over the
" will, and at another time deluded the understanding ; he was
" by turns a Dionysius and a Scapin ; as well might the writh-
" ing obliquity of the serpent be compared to the direct path of
" the arrow, as the duplicity of Mr. Hastings's ambition to the
" simple steadiness of genuine magnanimity ; in his mind all
" was shuffling, ambiguous, dark, insidious, and little ; nothing
" simple, nothing unmixed ; all affected plainness and actual
" dissimulation : he was an heterogeneous mass of contradicto-
" ry qualities, with nothing great but his crimes, and those con-
" trasted by the littleness of his motives ; which at once denoted
" his profligacy and his meanness, and marked him for a traitor
" and a juggler : his very style of writing there was the same
" mixture of vicious contrarieties ; the most grovelling ideas
" he conveyed in the most inflated language; giving mock con-
" sequence to low cavils, and uttering quibbles in heroics; so
" that his compositions disgust the taste of the understanding,
" as much as his actions excite the abhorrence of the soul. The
" same character pervaded every department of his govern-
" ment ; alike in the military and the political line, we may ob-
" serve auctioneering ambassadors, and trading generals : we
" saw a revolution brought about by an affidavit ; an army em-
" ployed in executing an arrest; a town besieged on a note of·
" hand ; and a prince dethroned for the balance of an account.
" Thus a government was exhibited, uniting the mock modesty
" of a bloody sceptre, and the little traffic of a merchant's
" counting house, wielding a truncheon with one hand, and pick-
" ing a pocket with the other." This energetic, grand, and
spledid display of eloquence was closed by the following peroration. " Factions exist in this house, and there is scarcely a
" subject on which we are not broken and divided into sects ;
" habits, connexions, parties, all lead to diversity of opinion; but
" when inhumanity presents itself to our observation, it finds
" no division in the representatives of the British people ; we
" attack it as our common enemy ; and conceiving that the cha-
" racter of the country is involved, in our zeal for the destruc-
" tion of cruelty, we quit not our undertaking till it be complete-
" ly overthrown. It is not allowed to this assembly to behold
" the objects of our compassion and benevolence in the present
" extensive inquiry : we cannot contemplate the workings of
" their hearts, the quivering lips, the trickling tears, the loud
" yet tremulous joys of the millions, whom our vote of this night
" will forever save from the cruelty of corrupted power : but,
" though we cannot directly see the effect, is not the true enjoy-

"ment of our benevolence increased, by its being conferred un-
"seen? Will not the omnipotence of Britain be demonstrated
"to the wonder of nations, by stretching its mighty arm across
"the deep, and saving by its fiat distant millions from destruc-
"tion? And will the blessings of the people dissipate in the
"empty air? No. If I may dare use the figure, they will consti-
"tute heaven itself their proxy, to receive for them the blessings
"of their pious thanksgiving, and the prayers their gratitude
"will dictate!"

Such is the outline and chief substance of this celebrated
speech, whose delivery occupied the extraordinary length of
five hours and a half; during which its excellence was uniform-
in vivid, animated, and fervid description of conduct that excited the various emotions of the human heart[x] for the alleged
sufferers, and against the alleged tyrant: filled the hearers with
contempt and scorn against exhibited meanness, detestation of
represented atrocity, and called their vengeance upon powerful
guilt overwhelming helpless innocents. Never was Mr. Sheridan surpassed by any orator in brilliant and irresistible eloquence, nor has he often been equalled in ingenuity and acuteness of deduction from the premises which he assumed. If the
governor-general had acted in the mode, and from the motives
represented with so impressive effect by Mr. Sheridan, he would
have certainly deserved to have been ranked among all the Ca-
ligulas, Neros, and Caracallas, that had ever scourged humanity by lawless power, with all the Jonathan Wilds and Scapins,
that, by fraud and imposture, supplied the want of force to per-
Its effects   petrate villainy.   The speech so manifestly astonished the
on the   house, that Mr. Pitt proposed to adjourn their meeting without
house of   coming to a deliberation until they should be sufficiently re-
commons   covered to distinguish the blaze of eloquence from the light of
and the   truth: throughout the country the impression was little less
public.   powerful; and great numbers conceived Hastings as guilty as
he was represented by transcendent genius. To the commons
there appeared so probable grounds of accusation, as to produce a vote of one hundred and seventy-five to sixty-eight, for
impeaching Mr. Hastings upon the third charge: several other
inferior charges were voted to contain grounds of impeachment. On the second of April various other accusations were
examined, and the impeachment was at length voted; when the

x The late M. Logan well known for his literary efforts, and author of a
most masterly defence of Mr Hastings, went that day to the house of
commons, prepossessed for the accused and against his accuser. At the
expiration of the first hour he said to a friend, " All this is declammatory
assertion without proof:" when the second was finished; this is a most
wonderful oration: at the close of the third; " Mr. Hastings has acted
very unjustifiably:" the fourth: " Mr. Hastings is a most atrocious criminal!" and at last; " Of all monsters of iniquity the most enormous is
Warren Hastings!" This I was told by Mr. Peter Stewart, proprietor of
the Oracle, who was present.

form in which that inquest should be carried on, became a sub- CHAP.
jeet of consideration. Mr. Fox proposed, that there should XXXVII.
be a general charge of impeachment, and that the house, on
acquainting the lords with their intention, should inform them ·1787.
that they were preparing articles which they would present with
all convenient despatch; reserving to themselves the constitutional rights of supplying more heads, after they had gone
through the whole. Mr. Pitt proposed they should separate
and analyze the charges, since the accusation consisted of a
diffuse and complicated mass; of many allegations which had
not been substantiated, and of many facts which could not be
considered as criminal; that thus each part should be tried by
its distinct and individual merits. Mr. Burke and Mr. Sheridan
coincided with the minister; and his plan was adopted Mr.
Hastings now made, through major Scott, an application to the
house, that if they resolved there was ground for impeachment,
they would vote that he should be brought to trial: he trusted
that the house of commons would not suffer his name to be
branded upon their records, without allowing him at the same
time the only legal means of effacing the stigma.

A committee was formed to prepare articles of impeachment
against Warren Hastings, esq. and empowered to send for per-
sons, papers, and records. The committee consisted of Mr.
Burke, Mr. Fox, Mr. Sheridan, Mr. Pelham, sir James Erskine,
Mr. Windham, Mr. St. John, Mr. Francis, sir Gilbert Elliot, sir
Grey Cooper, Mr. Frederick Montague, Mr. Wellbore Ellis,
general Burgoyne, colonel North, Mr. Taylor, Mr. Grey,
Mr. Anstruther, Mr. Adam, Mr. Dudley Long, and lord
Maitland.

On the 20th of May, Mr. Edmund Burke went in the name The com-
of the house of commons, and of all the commons of Great mons im-
Britain, to the bar of the house of lords, and impeached Mr. peach
Hastings of high crimes and misdemeanors; and acquainted Hastings
the lords, that the commons would, with all convenient speed, at the bar
exhibit articles against him, and make good the same. The of the
articles were eight in number: the charge of Cheyt Sing, the house of
begums, charges of Farruckahad, the contracts, Fizulla Khan, peers.
the presents, the revenues, and misdemeanors in Oude. At the
instance of Mr. Burke, Mr. Hastings was taken into custody by
the sergeant at arms; and being immediately conducted to the
bar of the house of lords, was delivered to the gentleman usher
of the black rod. Upon the motion of the lord-chancellor he
was admitted to bail, himself in 20,000l. and two sureties, Mr.
Sullivan, and Mr. Sumner, in 10,000l. each, and was ordered
to deliver in an answer to the articles of impeachment in one
month from that time, or upon the second day of the next session of parliament.[y]

y See Annual Register for 1787; British and foreign history, p. 148.

CHAP. XXXVII. — 1787. Supplies. Favourable state of the finances.

On the 20th of April the financial accounts and arrangements of the year were brought forward. The minister opened the subject by testifying the high satisfaction that he felt, and which he doubted not the house would share, when he laid before them such an account of our finances, as would justify his former statements, reasonings, and predictions. The public services were to be provided for without additional imposts, although a very bad season in the West Indies had caused a defalcation in the customs to the amount of 350,000l.

Mr. Dundas brings forward the financial state of British India.

On the 7th of May, Mr. Dundas, as president of the board of control brought forward the financial state of British India. He conceived it (he said) highly improper that any part of the empire should be in the receipt of a revenue of five millions, and maintain an army of seventy or eighty thousand men, without its being known to the house of commons how that revenue was disbursed, and why such an establishment was supported. The debt in India amounted to nine millions, the revenue of the last year afforded a surplus of 1,800,000l. and the company would be able to discharge their debt in this country in the year 1790. Having clearly and concisely stated these facts and opinions, Mr. Dundas moved resolutions respecting the revenues of India; these were carried without a division.

On the 30th of May his majesty prorogued parliament with a speech, expressing his entire approbation of the zeal and assiduity with which the houses applied themselves to the important objects recommended to their attention at the commencement of the session, and returning his majesty's particular thanks for the proofs which they had given of affection for his

Promising aspect of affairs.

person, family, and government. Satisfied as he was with the assurances which he received of the continuance, among foreign powers, of general tranquillity, he greatly regretted the internal dissensions among the states of the united provinces. He rejoiced at the progress made in the reduction of the national debt; and at the measures adopted by parliament for carrying into effect the commercial treaty with France, and for simplifying the revenue; he trusted the same patriotic dispositions would be exerted in their several counties, in promoting industry and good order; the surest sources of private and public prosperity.

CHAP. XXXVIII.

Affairs of Holland.—Ruinous effects of the war with Britain.—Complaints against the stadtholder.—Charge concerning the inaction of the fleets.—Objects of the aristocratic party at the end of the war.—They put arms into the hands of the multitude.—Effects of this measure.—Beginning of a democratic party.—Both the aristocratic and democratic parties agree in hostility to the house of Orange.—Advantages which they possessed over the stadtholderian party.—They are supported by the monied men—and sectaries.—Circumstances favourable to the prince.—He is commander of the army and fleet.—Civil power and authority.—He is governor-general of the East and West India companies.—His hereditary possessions.—Several provinces favourable to his cause.—Friendship and affinity with Prussia.—Adverse faction trusts to the protection of France. They deprive the prince of the command of the Hague.—The Orange family leave the Hague.—Temperate remonstrances of Prussia—disregarded by the faction,—who absolve the troops from their oath of fidelity.—Meeting of the states of Holland and West Friezeland,—violence of.—Remonstrance of the prince.—Frederick William sends his prime minister as ambassador to the states of Holland.—Firm memorial of.—Conduct of France—encourages the faction.—Rebellion commences at Hattem.—The insurgents are defeated.—Conciliatory interposition of Prussia—and of Britain—unavailing.—Joint mediation of Prussia and France.—Different views of these powers.—Alarming power of the democratic party—is exerted in levelling innovation—defeated in an attempt to suspend the office of stadtholder.—They try a new fabrication of votes. —The armed burghers are employed as instruments of revolution.—Fury of a revolutionary mob.—The states-general avow themselves supporters of the constitution.—Disorders at Amsterdam.—The army continues attached to the prince.—The faction becomes desperate.—Arrest of the princess on her way to the Hague.—She is compelled to return.—On this insult the king of Prussia changes his tone.—He demands satisfaction of the states of Holland—which is not granted. He determines on force.—The revolutionists rely on France.—The duke of Brunswick enters the United Provinces at the head of an army.—The revolutionists apply to France for aid.—Conduct of Britain.—The king of France intimates an intention of assisting the states of Holland.—Our king declares he will forcibly oppose such interference, and prepares an armament.—France relinquishes her design,—and the duke of Brunswick is completely victorious.—Restoration of the stadtholder.—Great and unanimous praises of the British cabinet.

THE most important events of the summer regarded the United Provinces. Their unfortunate war with Britain, and its ruinous consequences, had shaken the republic to its foundation, occasioned a departure from many of its ancient maxims and principles; and not only strengthened the old party which was friendly to France, but made way for the rise of a new faction, much more dangerous and destructive. The known

CHAP.
XXXVIII.

1787.
Affairs of Holland.

CHAP. averseness of the stadtholder to connexion with the house of
XXXVIII. Bourbon and the American colonies, his near relation and believed attachment to the British sovereign, afforded grounds for
1787. suspicion, that he could not engage very heartily in a cause so
directly opposite to opinions in which he had been nurtured.

Ruinous ef-
fects of the
war with
Britain.
The disgraceful and ruinous consequences of the war, the immense losses sustained by the capture of St. Eustatius, with
other severe blows, as well on the seas as in both the Indies,
which the republic had received during that ill sought and unfortunate conflict, not only disappointed the views of the supporters of the French interest, but produced great discontent
among many other individuals, who did not originally belong
to that party; and they imputed to the backwardness of the
stadtholder, losses which proceeded from their own folly in
courting a war with England. They commenced hostilities
unwisely and unjustly, when they had so much valuable merchandise, either on sea or in their factories, exposed to an enemy, who, notwithstanding every opposition, still retained the
command of the ocean; and were enraged that the stadtholder
did not perform impossibilities by saving them from the consequences of their iniquitous impolicy. The charges against the

Com-
plaints
against the
stadthol-
der.
stadtholder were chiefly general: it was said, that he had not
exerted the force with which he was intrusted by the state, in
that manner, or with that energy which he might have employed, and which would have been most effectual for counteracting the designs and frustrating the efforts of the enemy. On
these points, the prince in vain repeatedly challenged his adversaries to the inquiry and proof; but, aware of the futility of

Charge
concerning
the inac-
tion of the
fleet.
their charges, they did not wish for investigation. One specific object of examination was, why the Dutch fleet did not
proceed to Brest, according to compact, in the year 1782, that
the whole combined naval force of the house of Bourbon and
Holland might have descended at once on the coasts of Britain. The failure had been loudly attributed to criminal neglect, if not treachery; and a committee was speedily appointed to inquire into the causes: the result was, no discovery
was made, tending in the smallest degree to affect the stadtholder.

Objects of
the aristo-
cratic par-
ty at the
end of the
war.
At the termination of the American war, no ideas of democratic liberty, or of the admission of the whole people into a
share of the government, appear to have been entertained by
the party in opposition to the stadtholder: their design was to
strengthen the aristocracies, and to place the government in the
hands of an oligarchy, composed of their own principal leaders,
who would likewise be self elected and perpetual; and who,
not subject to the jealousy attendant on the sway of a single
person, in the nature of things would soon assume a decisive authority, which had never been possessed by the stadtholderate.
The contest with the emperor afforded a pretext for a measure
which the aristocratic faction intended for strengthening their

power, but eventually produced the total dissolution of their **CHAP**
authority; this was, the bestowal of arms on the multitude: **XXXVIII.**
the people finding arms in their hands, began at once to feel
their own importance; they awakened, as it were, from a dead   **1787.**
sleep, and wondered why they held no share in that govern- They put
ment which they were called upon to defend or support, and arms into
which it was evident without them could have no permanent the hands
of the mul-
security. The examples of Ireland and America were fresh titude.
before them; the very term of volunteers, which they assum- Effects of
ed, contributed to stamp the character of the part they were this mea-
to act. The democratic spirit being thus suddenly brought to sure.
life,. felt the possession of its faculties, and displayed all the
vigour, and, perhaps, even the wantonness of youth. The
armed burghers had been designed as a counterpoise to the
army, which was known to be generally attached to the stadtholder; and it was fondly expected, that when they had performed the service, they would have silently sunk into their
former insignificance; but without waiting for that issue, they
began to account themselves constituent members of the commonwealth, and demanded to be admitted to a share in the
legislation and government of their respective cities, by electing delegates, who were to be received as their legal representatives in the public assemblies, and thus form a popular
counterpoise to the aristocratic power. When these sentiments
were avowed, nothing could exceed the surprise and consternation which they excited. The principal leaders of the faction Beginning
were disconcerted and alarmed; they had improvidently rais- of a demo-
ed a dangerous spirit, and brought a new power into action, cratic par-
without a due consideration of the force and eccentricity of its ty.
movements; and these were evidently beyond their control or
management. This new body they saw would prove equally
inimical to the aristocratical, as to the stadtholderian authority;
but afraid, if they should then oppose the pretensions of the
democratical party, that a powerful body would go over to the
Orange adherents, and both united put an end to the sway of
the nobles, they temporized, and appeared to coincide with the
plebeian combination.   Both the
    This union of two parties, of adverse interests, but concur- aristocra-
ing in desire to humiliate the stadtholder, was very formidable tic and de-
to that prince and his friends. The states of Holland and mocratic
West Friezeland were the great and constant impugners of the parties a-
stadtholder's authority and prerogatives. They assumed a gree in ho-
superiority which was not admitted by the constitution of the stility to
the house
union, and was derived only from the circumstance of Holland of Orange.
possessing a greater share of wealth and a larger extent of terri- Advanta
tory, than any of the others. The most bitter animosity which ges which
appeared against the prince, seemed to be peculiarly lodged in they pos-
that province; and the city of Amsterdam took the lead of sessed over
the stadt-
all other places in the invariable display of enmity. The holderian
adverse faction had many and great advantages over the party.

CHAP. Orange party in this contest: for several years they pursued
XXXVIII. one common object, to which all their measures were directed;
thence they were closely united : while their antagonists having
1787. no purpose to attain, which might serve to combine their zeal
or excite their enterprise, were loose, careless, and unconnect-
They are ed. The opposite party had likewise the important advantage
supported of being favoured by the monied men; they were, besides,
by the mo- quickened by the ardour, and kept in constant exercise by the
nied men indefatigable zeal and restless spirit,[z] which is always observa-
and secta- ble in sectaries; and though the measure of arming the volun-
ries. teers had been productive of much trouble and disorder among
themselves, yet it afforded them at least the benefit of a formidable appearance.

Circum- To balance these unfavourable circumstances, the prince
stances fa- was not without considerable means, both internal and exter-
vourable to nal : as captain-general and admiral-general of the United
the prince. Provinces, he had command of the whole military and naval
He is com- force of the republic: he had the nomination of all the commander of missioned officers in either service, and was considered by
the army these as their patron and master; he had also the appoint-
and fleet. ment of most of the civil servants of the state. The landed
interest, though a much less proportion of the aristocracy of
Holland to the monied, than the corresponding class of England, was, with few exceptions, friendly to the prince in
all the provinces; even of the people great numbers (though
not amounting to a majority) were partisans of the stadtholder.
His civil But his authority and legal powers were by no means confined
power and to the fleet and army: by his office he was placed as presi-
authority. dent at the head of most, if not all of the civil departments of
the republic. He presided, either in person or by deputy, as
he chose, in all the assemblies of the several respective provinces. He had a seat, though not a vote, in the assembly of
the states-general; and it was not merely a matter of right,
but a part of his official duty, to be present at their deliberations, and to give his opinion or advice upon all matters of discussion, in which he deemed it necessary; and this had not only
a great influence upon their proceedings, but in times of harmony, and under a vigorous and successful administration of public
affairs, was generally decisive of their conduct. His right of
nomination or rejection with respect to the new members
appointed to fill up the town senates and magistracies, was
now contested, and generally overruled, but could not fail to
have given him by its past operation a great influence in those
He is gov- distinct republics. In the quality of governor-general, the
ernor gene- supreme director of the East and West India companies, the
ral of the stadtholder, likewise had an unbounded influence in those great
East and
West India commercial bodies.[a] The prince, moreover, inherited very
companies.

z Annual Register, 1786.

a See Annual Register for 1786, p. 74.

large estates and possessions which included palaces, cities, and CHAP.
castles, and endowed him with several important privileges, in- XXXVIII.
dependent of his offices under the state. Powerful as the aristocracy was, yet the party favourable to the stadtholder had 1787.
many votaries; even in Amsterdam and Rotterdam, and the His here-
greater cities of Holland, which were peculiarly hostile to the ditary pos-
house of Orange, the domineering faction had to combat nu- sessions.
merous adversaries. In the smaller towns the parties ap- Several
proached more nearly to an equality: of the provincial states, provinces
Guelderland and Utrecht were devoted to William: Overyssel, favourable
Groningen, and Zealand were fluctuating, and disposed to be cause.
mediatorial; so that Holland and West Friezeland only were
absolutely hostile to the stadtholder. The prince possessed Friendship
an external resource and support in the friendship and protec- and affini-
tion of the illustrious Frederick: policy directed a wise king ty with
of Prussia to repress the ambition of France, and prevent Prussia.
her from acquiring, under the name of alliance, the command
of those provinces, and bound him to the anti-gallican party;
while affinity cemented the bands by which he was connected
with the house of Orange. The authority of so renowned a
protector, long shielded William and his consort from any measures of extreme violence. Such was the state of affairs in the
beginning of autumn 1785. The aristocratic faction now found Adverse
themselves very potent at home, and placed unbounded confi- faction
dence in the assisting power of France. Proud of this pro- trusts to
tection, and freed of every apprehension from the emperor, tection of
they became less attentive to the admonitions of Frederick him- France.
self: they proceeded at once to show that they were no longer
disposed to observe any measures of amity with the prince
stadtholder, nor even to preserve those outward appearances
which might indicate a disposition to future conciliation. This They de-
was announced by divesting him of the government and com- prive the
mand of the garrison of the Hague; a measure not more vio- prince of
lent in the act, than it was degrading in the execution, through mand of
the unusual circumstances with which it was accompanied. the Hague.
The committee of the states issued a decree, by which they deprived the prince of his government and command, forbidding
the troops to receive the word from him, to obey his orders
in any manner, or even to pay him any of the customary military honours. To render the degradation complete, and as it
were, to add the incurable sting of a personal insult, they, at
the same time, stripped him of his own body guards, and even
the hundred Swiss, who were destined merely to civil purposes,
and to the support of state parade and magnificence. A remonstrance of the prince termed this decree a violent breach
of the constitution, an invasion of his rights, and an indignity
to his person and character; but his complaints produced no
other satisfaction than the contemptuous intimation, that the
guards were maintained for the purpose of supporting the
grandeur of the state, and not for the pageantry of the stadt-

CHAP.
XXXVIII.

1787.

The
Orange fa-
mily leave
the Hague.

Temperate
remon-
strances of
Prussia,

disregard
ed by the
faction;

who ab-
solve the
troops
from their
oath of fi-
delity.

holder. After such an open indignity, the prince and princess could no longer continue in a city, which was the seat of the court, public business, and government; as well as the residence of all foreign ministers: they therefore immediately abandoned the Hague. The prince retired to his own city of Breda, and the princess with the children repaired to West Friezeland, where, notwithstanding the implacable enmity of the states of that province, the people were generally well affected to the Orange family. The faction followed their late measure by an order for furnishing the guards with new colours, in which the arms of the house of Orange were totally omitted, and those of the province of Holland substituted in their place. The king of Prussia regarded this personal insult, and violent attack upon the authority of the stadtholder, with great but regulated indignation; he still preserved the most temperate language in his remonstrances; and while his expostulations placed in the fullest light the wrongs and undeserved injuries sustained by that prince, and sufficiently indicated that he was too much interested in his cause to permit him to become ultimately a victim to oppression; yet for the present, he appeared rather in the character of a friendly neighbour to both, and an amicable mediator, wishing to reconcile the differences and misunderstandings between the parties, than the direct advocate of either:[b] but the faction was too far advanced in violence to regard moderate remonstrances; and proceeded to still greater innovations. They issued an order, that the military honours usually bestowed on the stadtholder, in all his different capacities of captain-general, governor of the Hague, and commander of the garrison, should in future be paid only to the president of their committee, as the representative of the states, and to the grand pensionary of Holland. This was soon followed by an order to discharge all the troops of the province from their oath of fidelity to the stadtholder, and to prescribe a new oath, by which they were bound to the states only. The faction took the press entirely into their own hands, and the most scurrilous invectives were every day published against the stadtholder; and not only passed with impunity, but received high applause: while the most temperate writings in defence of his rights, or a bare statement of their nature, subjected the publishers and writers to severe and certain punishment. Such was the state of affairs at the end of the year 1785.

The prince stadtholder from Breda had repaired to Middleburgh; but finding the faction in Holland had proceeded to extremities, he concluded force would be necessary, resolved to betake himself to the province in and near which his strength chiefly lay; and, therefore fixed his residence in Guelderland: besides vicinity to his partisans, he there could easily avail himself of the co-operation of Prussia. The faction were not

b Annual Register for 1786, p. 77.

at first sensible of the advantages which must accrue to the CHAP.
prince from the residence which he had chosen, and pro-XXXVIII.
ceed in their violence. Great expectations had been formed on both sides, from the assemblage of the states of Holland 1787.
and West Friezeland, which was to take place at the Hague in Meeting of
the middle of March. When this body was convened, instead the states
of the cool impartiality of a deliberative meeting, it exhibited and West
all the violence and outrage of a mob: and the members ap-Frieze-
peared to have parted with the phlegm of Dutchmen, and to land;
have borrowed the animated virulence of enraged Frenchmen.
In the course of the session, the most important question violence of.
which was handled by the assembly, was, whether the stadtholder should be restored to the government of the Hague?
and after many vehement debates it was, on the 27th of July,
carried against the prince of Orange by a majority of only
one; the numbers being ten to nine. The equestrian order,
and the deputies of some towns, protested against this resolution as violent, illegal, and unconstitutional. William did not Remon-
fail to express the strongest reprobation of this conduct of the strance of
states : in a letter to that body he denied the legality of one the prince.
or two provinces presuming to deprive him of a power which
had been conferred by the whole confederacy ; he did not
even acknowledge the right of the whole union to dispossess
him of the dignities and powers, which were in the fullest
manner rendered hereditary in his family ; but without, for
the present, investigating that question, he argued, that at
least the retraction of the authority should be attended with
the same unanimity which prevailed in the donation. The
states of Holland, regarding this letter as a defiance, passed
a second decree confirming the first. The death of Frederick
brought to the throne of Prussia the brother of the princess of
Orange, and produced a more active interference to support
the interests of the sister, than had been employed while she
was only the niece. Soon after his accession Frederick William Frederick
sent his prime minister the count de Goertz, as ambassador William
extraordinary to the states of Holland ; and by him a long let-sends his
ter[c] to the states-general. This paper mingled temperance of nister am-
manner with vigour of substance, and was in every respect bassador
worthy of ministers formed under the wise and resolute Fre-to the
derick. Its introduction removed the objections, which might states of
be made by the states to the interference of a foreign power Holland.
in their internal affairs. The firm friendship, which for two
centuries had subsisted between his predecessors and the republic, would even have demanded his friendly and mediatorial
interposition in the present unhappy and dangerous state of
their civil dissentions : his situation as their nearest neighbour,
and the vicinity of a part of his dominions to their territories, Firm me-
must necessarily prevent him from being indifferent to any morial of.

c See State Papers of 1786, Sept. 18.

violent or essential change that was attempted to be made in the constitution of the republic: besides these causes, the near relation in which he stood with the prince stadtholder, and the affection which he bore to the princess his sister, rendered it impossible that he could be unconcerned in seeing them degraded from their high rank and authority, and the stadtholder arbitrarily deprived of his rights and prerogatives: he, therefore, urgently pressed the states-general to interpose their friendly and powerful mediation with the states of Holland and West Friezeland, that the differences between them and the stadtholder might be amicably settled, and the prince restored to his rights and dignities. The application expressed the fullest confidence that the states-general would exert themselves for the attainment of its purposes: and prudently forbore any intimation of the measures which Prussia would pursue, should the letter not produce the intended effects. This representation made a very strong impression on the states of five of the provinces; Holland and West Friezeland vehemently protested against foreign interference; but while they reprobated the interposition of a potentate hostile to their faction, they closely connected themselves with a power that was friendly to the anti-stadtholderian party. The court of Versailles skilfully fanned the flame of discontent by subordinate agents, but her public memorials were couched in so equivocal terms as to admit of different and even contrary constructions: and carefully abstained from pledging France to any specific line of conduct. The faction, however, was well assured of the support of France: and by that expectation inflamed to the most insolent violence: they seemed indeed not only to cast off all obedience to their own laws, but every regard to the law of nations. A courier from Berlin to London was stopped and narrowly escaped having his despatches examined by the populace of Woerden. This outrage obliged the count de Goertz formally to demand a passport from the states-general for a courier he was sending with despatches to his royal master. The states which were in the interest of the Orange family, strongly remonstrated against the turbulent outrages of Holland, but found their interference made no impression; the standard of rebellion at length was hoisted at Hattem and Elbourg: the states of Guelderland, at the frontiers of which these towns are situated, determined to employ force in repressing revolt: they charged the prince stadtholder, as captain-general, immediately to send a sufficient number of troops under the conduct of an experienced officer, to these scenes of disturbance, with injunctions to continue there until further orders: but that if the inhabitants were to make any resistance to the performance of this service, such officer was authorized, in spite of all obstacles to support the sovereign authority of their noble mightinesses, by proceeding to force and violence in the establishment of the

Conduct of
France

encoura-
ges the
faction.

Rebellion
commen-
ces at Hat-
tem.

garrisons. · General Spengler, with four regiments, and proper
artillery, was appointed by the stadtholder to this service,
with strict injunctions, if possible, to avoid the shedding
of blood. The armed burghers of Hattem, being re-enforced
by as many volunteers as money or party zeal could procure
from different quarters, exhibted a great parade of making a
most obstinate resistance. Their cannon were mounted on the
walls and works ; and on the approach of the stadtholder's
little army, as they called the regular forces by way of contempt,
they fired several rounds of artillery with great briskness, but
with so defective judgment in the direction, as not to produce
the smallest effect. As soon as Spengler arrived within a proper distance, in order to do the least possible mischief, he
pointed his artillery at the chimneys and tops of the houses
only ; this, however, along with the bold advance and near approach of the troops, soon produced the desired effect; the
armed burghers, with their adherents and auxiliaries, abandoned
the town; and Spengler's men entered at one gate as they The insur-
were retiring through another. Elbourg was relinquished in gents are
the same manner, and with still less trouble.[d]   The faction com- defeated.
manded all the public papers, and represented the trifling affair
at Hattem as a signal display of republican heroism, worthy of
the descendants of those bands which had risen to vindicate
their liberty from Alva and Philip ; they could have completely
routed the soldiers of Orange, but patriotic as well as valiant,
they were willing to spare the effusion of the blood of their
countrymen. In the same style of delusion, nothing could be
more shocking or deplorable than the accounts which they
published of the enormities, the plunder, and cruelties, committed by the troops who gained possession of Hattem and Elbourg.
The capture of the two towns was represented by the faction
as the actual commencement of civil war; and nothing was to
be heard but execrations, as well against the states of Gueldres,
as the prince stadtholder. In the province of Holland especially, the flames seemed to be blown up nearly to the greatest
height at which they were capable of arriving. All regard to
forms was now laid aside in completing the deposition by force,
of those magistrates, senators, and members of the respective
town councils, who were known or suspected to be of the opposite party. Towards the close of 1786, the fortune of the
house of Orange appeared to be entirely fallen; but external
efforts were made in its favour, which proved ultimately successful. The king of Prussia was incessant in his endeavours Conciliato-
to promote all such measures of conciliation, as could in any ry interpo-
degree tend to prevent those unpleasant and dangerous conse- sition of
quences, which the present state of things, and the violence of Prussia
the republican party could not otherwise fail to produce. For
the attainment of this purpose he showed himself disposed to try

[d] See Annual Register for 1786, p. 87.

CHAP.   any means, however unpromising, and to coincide with any inte-
XXXVIII. rests, however discordant, that afforded even a possibility of
         success.

1787.   The court of London offered its joint mediation with Berlin;
and of Bri- but the faction, aware of the predilection of Britain for the in-
tain, una- terest of the stadtholder, as well as the family of Orange, to-
vailing.   tally refused her mediation. The king of Prussia therefore
            proposed that France, the avowed friend, and close ally of the
            republic, should, along with himself, undertake the kind office,
            but arduous task, of settling and composing the differences by
Joint me.   which it was distracted. The court of France professed to re-
diation of ceive these overtures with the warmest cordiality; and an am-
Prussia   bassador was sent to the Hague for the purpose desired. Though
and
France.   such movements wore the appearance of returning tranquillity,
            yet it was easily seen that the actual conciliation of the con-
Different   tending parties was very improbable. France, it was conceiv-
views of   ed, would never really coincide with the king of Prussia in re-
those pow- storing the stadtholder to his power, which the faction regarded
ers.   with bitter hatred; the king of Prussia would not sacrifice to
            France the interests of the prince of Orange, by making such
            concessions as the adverse combination would require. The
            ministers, however, of France and Prussia entered upon the
            negotiation, which was carried on during the winter months;
            and though the mediators had agreed in their views and inten-
            tions, the objects and notions of the parties concerned were so
            diametrically opposite, that it would be totally impossible to sa-
Alarming   tisfy both. While contests, begun by an aristocratic faction,
power of   were thus distracting the United Provinces, the democratical
the demo-   party, which, as we have seen, the dissensions generated,
cratic
party;   was becoming extremely powerful. In Utrecht, a government
is exerted entirely democratical, was established; and in Holland the
in levelling states found that in stimulating the efforts of the populace, they
innovation; had called in an auxiliary more formidable than the adversary
            whom they desired to subdue: the violence and anarchy of
            mob government now prevailed throughout the provinces. It
            sometimes fortunately happens, that the desultory efforts of a
            domineering populace, from unskilful direction, produce effects
            diametrically opposite to the intentions. The city of Amsterdam
            from the beginning had been the bitterest and most implacable
            of the stadtholder's enemies; so that it seemed as if all the vio-
            lent measures pursued against him, had originated in the pride,
            malice, and power of those citizens: but Amsterdam suddenly
            changed sides, and declared in favour of the stadtholder. To
            detail the causes of this revolution, belongs not to a history
            which considers the affairs of the United Provinces, only as
            they affected the interests, or came to stimulate the energies of
            Britain; and it may suffice to say, that the change produced
            great alarm in the anti-stadtholderian faction, and eventually
            facilitated the re-establishment of the house of Orange. The
            defection of Amsterdam could not but excite an universal alarm

among the leaders of the revolutionary party, and urged them CHAP.
to the adoption of every measure that could possibly tend to XXXVIII.
counteract its effect : for this purpose they proceeded to very
violent conduct ; and at length resolved to propose a daring 1787.
measure, which, though they had often meditated, they had not Defeated
yet ventured to carry into execution ; this was the suspension of in an at-
the prince of Orange from his offices of stadtholder and admi- tempt to
ral-general, in the same manner they had already succeeded in suspend
suspending him from his command of captain-general. This the office
question was brought forward on the 10th of January 1787, and of stadt-
for two succeeding days occasioned the warmest and most vio- holder.
lent debates that had ever been known in the assembly. The
proposers, however, found the opposition so formidable, and the
aspect of the independent members so doubtful, that they did They try a
not choose to hazard the decision of a vote on the question. new fabri-
Defeated in this attempt, the faction attempted a new fabri- votes.
cation of votes ; but the project was treated with indignant resentment and scorn. The states of Holland, deprived of the
co-operation of Amsterdam, and thwarted in schemes of vio
lence, began in spring 1787 to assume a moderate tone, and to
adopt measures very disagreeable to the violent leaders of the
adverse faction; the cause of the stadtholder became popular,
even in the province of Holland. The aristocratic confederates hitherto, as much as possible, repressed the ambition of The armed
the democratical malcontents : but now they saw that there was burghers
no alternative but acquiescence in their claim, or submission to are em-
the stadtholder : on the former they resolved, and called in the ployed as
armed burghers as their instruments in revolutionizing the ments of
state. Such reformers proceeded with the usual fury of a de revolution.
mocratic mob. They attacked the assemblies of Rotterdam
and other towns, and to produce unanimity drove away by force
every member whom they knew or suspected to be friendly to
the house of Orange, or enemies to boundless innovation. Encouraged by their success, they carried their reforming projects Fury of a
to Amsterdam ; and effected a similar change in the metropolis. revolution-
During antecedent disorders, the states-general had observed ary mob
strict impartiality ; and it could not be discovered to which side
they inclined ; but now that an armed mob threatened confusion
and anarchy, they thought it was full time to rally round the constituted authorities, in whose downfall, their own ruin must be The states
involved. general
In May 1787, they avowed themselves the defenders of the avow
existing establishments ; and now it was no longer a contest themselves
between the house of Orange and a party of nobles, but be- of the con-
tween constitutional order and revolutionary rebellion. The stitution.
armed populace having forcibly restored the majority of malcontents in the states of Holland, that body assumed to itself
powers that could only belong to the states-general. Among
the respective partisans frequent skirmishes took place, not
without bloodshed. The revolutionary democrats did not con-

CHAP. fine themselves to personal outrage and savage cruelty, but added
XXXVIII robbery : the richest towns of that very opulent country became
scenes of pillage.[e] In the course of the summer, Amsterdam
1787. was a scene of more dreadful devastation, than any European
Disorders metropolis had exhibited during the preceding part of the
at Amster- eighteenth century ; it indeed afforded a specimen to the world
dam. of the consequences of a furious love of change, which entirely
overleaped every bound of reason and of justice. The states
of Holland were extremely anxious to obtain a command of
the troops ; and the states-general with equal activity, and
much greater effect, counteracted these efforts : this, indeed,
was the less difficult, as the disposition of the army continued
very favourable to the family of Orange ; many, both of officers
and privates, refused to obey the orders of the provincial states,
The army and ardently desired the restitution of the stadtholder. The
continues states-general very properly encouraged this repugnance to
attached usurped authority, and took the troops into immediate protec-
to the tion and pay. Colonel Balneavis, a Scottish gentleman of great
prince. ability and resolution, by his successful address was the means
of recalling the military force of Holland to the service of their
prince. Possessing the affection and confidence of the soldiers,
he carried with him two battalions to join the stadtholder, and
the other regiments immediately followed so laudable an exam-
The fac- ple. But the departure of their troops, instead of intimidating
tion be- the states of Holland, served only to drive them to more despe-
comes rate violence.
desperate. Amidst all the rage which the revolutionists vented against
Arrest of the government of the house of Orange, the persons of these
the prin princes had not hitherto been violated ; but the infatuated fury
cess on her of a mob no longer confined itself within these bounds. The
way to the consort of the stadtholder was a princess of vigorous capacity,
Hague. and intrepid spirit : from the justice of the cause, as well as
the late accessions to the party, she conceived that the hour of
restoration was approaching, and might be accellerated by a
bold and resolute effort. She accordingly determined to leave
Nimeguen, unaccompanied by her husband ; to proceed to the
Hague and show herself to the people ; she hoped, through
the states-general, and other adherents, corporate and private,
to effect the restoration of the prince. Accompanied only by
the baroness Wassanaar, count Bentick, and a field officer or
two, and attended by a few domestics, the princess arrived at
the borders of Holland, near Schoonhoven. Since the departure of the constitutional troops, the revolutionary burghers
composed the sole military force of Holland: a party of these
surrounded the carriage, and arrested the person of the princess. The commander of this notable troop was altogether
worthy of such a corps ; a vulgar and ignorant[f] burgher ; and,

e Annual Register, 1787, chap. i

f See annual Register for 1787, p 32.

by unmerited authority elated to insolence, this person and his band behaved with brutal irreverence; they conducted the il- lustrious captive as a spectacle, with all the coarse vociferation of an exulting rabble : even when their barbarous dissonance startled the horses, and almost overturned her carriage in a canal, they would not permit the gentlemen of the suite to afford her assistance. At length they arrived at an inn; the gallant captain accompanied the princess to her room : regardless of the presence of a lady, this municipal commander kept his sword drawn; but her attendants representing the impropriety of such an exhibition, he complaisantly returned it to the scabbard : after this effort of politeness, he sat down by her side, cross-legged, and at the same time ordering beer, pipes, and tobacco, enjoyed a comfortable regale, but without being seduced by such appropriate pleasure to intermit the vigilance[g] of official employment.

After being confined several hours, commissioners arrived from the town of Woerden, who expressly told the princess she would not be allowed to continue the journey, but she might retire wherever she chose; accordingly she set out on She is compelled to return. her return to Nimeguen : the prince, informed of her capture, applied to the states-general for protection to his consort, and satisfaction for so gross and outrageous an insult; and his representation was seconded by a much more powerful applicant : the conduct of the revolutionists towards the princess, was attended with very important consequences. Hitherto the king On this insult the king of Prussia changes his tone. of Prussia had acted towards the United Provinces as a mediating neighbour between the two parties : though naturally, and indeed avowedly, favourable to one, he had never intimated a design of forcible interference; but from the seizure of the princess, his relation to the provinces was changed: he was now a powerful brother demanding reparation to a sister; a mighty monarch requiring the satisfaction which he could exact. He sent a memorial to the states of Holland, wherein he He demands satisfaction of the states of Holland; insisted upon immediate and ample atonement, and also the punishment of the perpetrators: he, moreover, added, that he should estimate the value which they attached to his friendship, by their compliance with this requisition.[h] Before this memorial arrived, the states of Holland had expressed their approbation of the conduct of the persons who had seized the princess : they returned a long and laboured answer; but acknowledged no blame, and proffered no satisfaction. The which is not granted. stubborn injustice of the states of Holland was contrasted by the fair and liberal conduct of the states-general, to whom the king of Prussia had also applied: that assembly declared,

g The Annual Register mentions some very laughable instances of the assiduity with which the Dutch sentinels kept watch, to prevent female attendants from effecting their escape: see A. R p. 33.

h See State papers, August 6, 1787.

CHAP. that they had made repeated representations to the provincial
XXXVIII. meeting of Holland on this outrageous,insult; that those states
themselves must be entirely responsible for measures, in regret-
1787. ting and reprobating which, their high mightinesses perfectly
He deter- agreed with his Prussian majesty. Frederick was determined
mines on to enforce from the states of Holland the satisfaction which
force. they had refused to his requisition: meanwhile he repeated
his demand in indignant and peremptory terms, and made a
representation of their proceedings to the court of France, to
which the faction chiefly trusted. His christian majesty expressed to the states very strong disapprobation of the treatment which the princess had experienced; and declared he
thought the king of Prussia very fully justified in demanding
The revo- ample satisfaction. Notwithstanding this intimation, the re-
lutionists volutionary party persisted in their course; they had no doubt
rely on that, if affairs came to an open rupture, they would receive
France. from France an assistance proportioned to the danger by which
they might be threatened: the Prussian army they knew was
strong, but the French army they naturally conceived to be
much stronger; and they were too deeply engrossed themselves
to consider or estimate internal circumstances in the dominions
of their ally, which might prevent the employment of his usual
force.

Repeated remonstrances and replications passed between the
states of Holland and the Prussian king during the month of
August; but so little to the satisfaction of Frederick William,
that he made immediate and powerful preparations for hostilities; and in the beginning of September, an army, commanded by the duke of Brunswick was ready to enter the Low
Countries. Having in the seven years war attained a very
high character for heroism and ability, while hereditary prince,
from the peace this commander had passed his time in tranquillity, but not idleness, devoting his attention to military and political improvement. On the death of his father, becoming
reigning duke, he continued such pursuits as meliorated the
condition of his territories. From these meritorious occupations he was now called to head an armament, destined to en-
The duke force the purpose of justice. On the 13th of September he
of Bruns- entered the province of Guelderland, and there the country be-
wick en- ing all favourable to his attempts, he, without opposition,
ters the reached the confines of Holland. On the duke of Brunswick's
United
Provinces approach, the revolutionary party applied to France, for aid,
at the head and obtained a promise of support.
of an army.
The revo- Britain regarded with anxious attention the important events
lutionists that passed in the United Provinces, and perceived that the cri-
apply to sis was arrived, when it must be speedily determined, whether
France for the Dutch republic was to resume her ancient and natural con-
aid.
Conduct of
Britain. ¹ See our narrative of the campaigns of the allies in Germany, in the
first chapters of this history, *passim*.

nexion with her first protector, or to become a mere appendage
of France. Our sovereign, during the course of the disputes,
repeatedly offered his friendly mediation; but his interposition
was extremely disagreeable to the revolutionary faction, which
could not stand the award of an impartial umpire. The court
of London was confident that the internal strength of the constitutional party, seconded by the king of Prussia, was perfectly
adequate to the adjustment of disputes, and the resumption of
constitutional rights, if France did not interfere with an armed
force. Dignity, justice, and policy, called from his majesty
explicit avowals,[k] that he would not remain a quiet spectator
of such forcible interference. In these circumstances, the chief
object of British policy, concerning Holland, was to watch the
movements of the court of Versailles. A message from his
christian majesty announced to our king, that he had determined to afford to the states of Holland the assistance which they
had requested. Such an intimation demanded only one line of
conduct; our king accordingly declared to France, that if she
interposed forcibly, Britain should take an active part; and he
gave immediate directions for augmenting his fleet and army.
A powerful armament was equipped with uncommon expedition: a decisive and grand tone, worthy of mighty power supporting conscious justice, produced the desired effect; and
France made no hostile effort to support the revolutionary faction. The energetic vigour of the British cabinet being so successfully exerted towards the formidable ally of the states of
Holland, the duke of Brunswick proceeded in a rapid career of
victory. The hidden friends of the house of Orange now publicly declared themselves: the revolutionists, however, still entertaining hopes France would not yield, threw themselves
into Amsterdam, and resolved to stand a siege; but finding
their expectations entirely vanished, they at length entered into
a capitulation; the constitutional party proved completely triumphant, and the stadtholder was restored to all his rights and
dignities. The discussion which arose between Britain and
France terminated amicably, after his christian majesty had declared, that in intimating a design of active interposition in the
affairs of Holland, he had never intended forcible efforts.[l]
Such was the result of the disputes in the United Provinces,
and the measures which Britain adopted respecting the contests. This was the first occasion that displayed the genius
and energy of Pitt in foreign policy, and procured him general
admiration abroad and at home. Opposition as warmly and
loudly praised his conduct, as the rest of the nation: indeed it
is difficult to conceive that two opinions could be formed on the

Marginal notes: CHAP. XXXVIII. 1787. The king of France intimates an inten-tion of as-sisting the states of Holland. Our king declares he will forci-bly oppose such inter-ference; and pre-pares an armament. France thereupon relinquish-es her de-sign; and the duke of Brunswick is com-pletely vic-torious. Restora-tion of the stadthol-der. Great and unanimous praises of the British cabinet.

k See his majesty's speech, November 27, 1787. State papers.

l See correspondence between the respective ministers of Britain and
France on this subject, in the state papers of October 1787.

CHAP.
XXXVIII.

1787.

subject by any Britain who at once valued and understood the interests of his country. The interference was requisite, to prevent such an aggrandizement of France, as must endanger this country. The means were vigour of tone, seconded by powerful preparation, the most successful instruments which a mighty nation can employ for averting aggression, either direct or circuitous.

CHAP. XXXIX.

Meeting of parliament.—Unanimous approbation of the conduct of ministry respecting Holland.—Bishop of Landaff's speech on British interference in continental affairs.—Subsidiary treaty with the landgrave of Hesse-Cassel—Plan for the defence of the West Indies.—Complaints of a
partial promotion of flag officers.—Ministers contend that the complaint
is unfounded—Declaratory law for explaining certain parts of Mr. Pitt's
East India bill.—Origin of the doubt from which this measure proceeded.
—Regiments ordered by government to India, to be paid and subsisted
at the expense of the company—Question by Mr. Pitt's bill; had government that power? denied by the directors and by opposition in parliament.—Arguments for and against.—Passed into a law.—Extension of
the mutiny bill.—Bill against the smuggled exportation of wool—passed
into a law—Commencement of an inquiry concerning negro slavery.—
State of facts.—General and special objections to negro slavery.—Impugned as contrary to christianity, as well as justice and humanity.—Pious
and benevolent enthusiasm in favour of the negroes.—Mr Wilberforce—
character, talents, and laudable zeal—opposite arguments—Slavery an
evil great or small, according to the sentiments and circumstances of the
sufferers—The condition of the African negroes is meliorated by becoming slaves to British masters.—Slaves in our plantations generally
happy.—If Britain abolish slavery, other European states will enjoy the
benefits.—Great capitals are embarked on the public faith guaranteeing
this trade—An ample source of private opulence, and public revenue.—
Petitions for and against the abolition of the slave trade—The privy-
council institutes an inquiry into the details and alleged cruelties of the
slave trade Sir William Dolben's motion for regulating the transportation of negroes—passed into a law.—Mr. Pitt's bill for the relief and
recompense of the American loyalists.—Commencement of Hastings's
trial.—Speech of Mr. Burke—Motion for the impeachment of sir Elijah
Impey—negatived.—Mr. Grenville's bill for improving his father's law
respecting contested elections—Supplies.—Flourishing state of commerce and finance.

PARLIAMENT assembled on the 27th of November; CHAP.
and his majesty's speech exhited to the houses an outline of XXXIX.
the policy which he had adopted concerning Holland. He
had endeavoured by his good offices to restore tranquillity be- 1787.
tween the contending parties, but found his efforts unavailing: Meeting of
he also discovered a desire of forcible interference on the part parliament
of France; he expressed to his christian majesty his determination to counteract any such intention, and had armed for that
purpose; but the success of, the Prussian troops had re-esta-
plished the lawful government in Holland; an explanation had
taken place between his majesty and the king of France, which
had terminated amicably, and both parties had agreed to disarm. The necessary preparations had produced extraordinary

expenses for which he doubted not his faithful commons would provide, and also adopt proper means for the defence of his distant dominions. He rejoiced at the flourishing state of commerce and the revenue, and the zeal and unanimity which his subjects demonstrated during the late expectation of war. From the dispositions which were then manifested, in any future emergency, he should depend on a promptness and vigour of exertion, proportionate to the exigence by which it might be required.

Unanimous approbation of the conduct of ministry respecting Holland.

The conduct of Mr. Pitt respecting Holland was extremely popular among all parties throughout the kingdom; and in both houses it experienced the same unanimous commendation. Mr. Fox, Mr. Burke, and Mr. Sheridan, perfectly coincided with Mr. Pitt and his friends in the general principle of interference in continental affairs to preserve the balance of Europe. In the house of peers the bishop of Landaff, in justifying the principle, adduced reasoning at once appropriate to that specific case, and generalizing the constituents of wise and just interposition in any future circumstances. " Upon what ground

Bishop of Landaff's view of British interference in continental affairs.

" (he said) did he approve of our late interference? on the " ground of SELF PRESERVATION. *If France had gained Holland,* " *the security of Britain would have been endangered :* when " it is said that Holland and the other states of Europe are in- " dependent states, the proposition is true only on a certain " consideration, for they all depend one upon another, like the " links of a chain; and it is the business of each to watch " every other, lest any one become so weighty and powerful as " to endanger the security or political importance of the rest."

Subsidiary treaty with the landgrave of Hesse-Cassel.

During the preparations, a subsidiary treaty had been concluded with the landgrave of Hesse-Cassel; by which that prince was to receive 36,093l. to hold twelve thousand troops ready to be employed by Britain when their services should be required. This treaty was part of a general system, which it was then deemed premature to detail: the motion passed without a division. On the 10th of December an augmentation of the army was proposed, for the purpose recommended by his

Plan for the defence of the West Indies.

majesty's speech, of strengthening our distant possessions. On particular inquiry into the state of defence of our western settlements, ministers had found the force to be inadequate; this opinion had been confirmed by the reports of the officers commanding in the West Indies, who had been severally consulted upon the troops which each thought requisite for the security of the island he commanded. It was objected by some members of opposition, that the opinions of our commanders abroad did not afford satisfactory grounds for increasing our present establishments. It was obvious, that each of these officers would demand as large a force as he thought adequate to the defence of his own particular situation, and would govern himself in such requisition, merely by regard to his own responsibility; whereas, in judging of an adequate peace establish-

ment for all the possessions of Britain, the whole would depend
on a general view of its parts, and their relative exigencies ; by
the present motion the house was called on to vote an increase
of the army without sufficient grounds. It was replied, that
the opinion of the officers had not been asked on the whole
force requisite for the defence of the West Indies, but that undoubtedly in forming plans concerning remote objects, men
must proceed on information, and in seeking information must
have recourse to those by whom it can be best afforded ; officers
who had been on the spot were certainly competent to state the
separate facts, on the joint results of which ministers form their inferences.   The west India islands were, without doubt, objects
of the highest importance to Britain.   For their secure defence,
three modes might be mentioned : first, a great stationary fleet :
secondly, succours might be sent on the prospect of a rupture ;
or thirdly, such a military force as would prevent a surprise.
The experience of last war proved that a fleet could not solely
defend these possessions ; since some of the islands had been
wrested from us, when our naval strength was equal to the
strength of the enemy : respecting the second means, it might
be unsafe to detach any part of our army or navy from Europe ;
and though there should be no danger in the attempt, the succours might not arrive in time to prevent mischief ; therefore
the most eligible mode was to have a sufficient military force
upon the respective islands to secure them from surprise ;
since, from the dispersion and distance of the islands, and the
peculiarities of that climate, winds, and currents, it would sometimes be absolutely impossible for a fleet to afford that speedy
relief which the occasion might require.

After the recess, one of the first subjects of discussion before   1788.
the commons was a recent promotion of flag officers during Complaint
the preparations for war. Sixteen captains had been promoted of a partial
to the flag, and about forty passed over. This partial promo- promotion
tion had greatly displeased the officers whom it omitted. They of flag
brought forward their complaint in the house of peers, under
the patronage of Lord Rawdon, who moved for the presentment
of an address to the king ; praying, that he would be graciously
pleased to take into his royal consideration the services of such
captains of his majesty's navy, as were passed over in the last
promotion. Lord Howe, first commissioner of the admiralty, Ministers
endeavoured to justify the conduct of the board ; to execute contend
beneficially the functions of their office, the lords of the admi- that the
ralty must employ their own judgment and discretion in dele- complaint
gating an important trust : unless they were invested with the is unfound-
privilege of selection, they certainly could not undertake the ed.
burthen of responsibility. His lordship could not state in a public
assembly the particular grounds on which he had formed his
judgment ; there might be several reasons for not promoting
captains to be admirals, without impeaching the character of the
officers in question. The same persons might be fit for a

CHAP.
XXXIX.

1788.

subordinate employment, without being qualified for a higher trust: officers who had served ably and meritoriously all their lives, might not appear proper to be intrusted with the care of a fleet. So important a charge ought to be committed to men, not only of firm minds, but of such bodily strength as would enable them to endure the fatigues of the hard service which they might have to sustain. The executive government must have the choice of its own officers in the various degrees and kinds of service, otherwise it cannot be responsible for the effectual discharge of its duties. On these grounds the motion was rejected by the lords: in the commons a similar proposition was brought forward and supported by great particularity of detail, in order to illustrate individual hardships ; but as the general principle was the same, the proposed address was negatived, though by a small majority. It was afterwards moved, that the arbitrary powers which were claimed by the admiralty having in some degree received the sanction of the house, to prevent the mischievous conseqences which might ensue, they should adopt, as a rule of service, some permanent principle, to which officers might trust ; and a motion was made, that it is highly injurious to the navy, to set aside from promotion to flags, meritorious officers of approved service, who are not precluded by the orders of his majesty in council. Ministers objected to the proposition as unnecessary ; and it was negatived.

Declaratory bill for explaining Mr. Pitt's East India law.

The most important measure of this session, was a bill introduced by Mr. Pitt to explain doubts which had arisen concerning a part of the law of 1784, for the administration of British India. During the apprehensions of a rupture with France, government had formed a resolution of sending out four additional regiments to India, on board the company's ship's for the protection of our possessions in that quarter; and the proposition had been received with general approbation by

Origin of the doubts from which this measure proceeded.

the court of directors. Though apprehensions of war were dissipated, yet government was anxious for the security of distant possessions, and for that purpose proposed a permanent establishment of his majesty's troops in India ; on these grounds they adhered to the determination of sending the soldiers. A question had arisen between the directors and the board of control, concerning the expense of their conveyance, their future

Regiments ordered by government to India, to be paid and subsisted at the expense of the company,

pay and subsistence. By an act which passed in the year 1781, it was stipulated, that the company should be bound to pay for such troops only, as were sent to India upon their requisition : and upon this act the directors had refused to charge the company with the expense of the forces now about to be sent. The board of control contended, that they were invested with a power of ordering the conveyance of such troops, as circumstances might require ; and that if the directors refused, the expense should be defrayed out of the revenues which arose from their territorial possessions. The court of directors took the advice of several eminent lawyers, who concurred in their opinion. , Mr. Pitt, impressed with the contrary idea, proposed to bring in a bill for removing the doubts in question, by declaring the intention of the legislature in the act of 1784, to have been agreeable to the construction put upon it by administration. By the law of 1784 he contended, every power, which before that time was intrusted to the court of directors for administering the territorial possessions, was by that act vested in the board of control. Those commissioners had the sole direction of the military and political concerns, the collection and management of territorial revenue. His object had been to leave to the corporate proprietors, and their representatives, the direction of those commercial concerns for which their charter had been granted, but to take into the hands of the executive government territorial affairs; under the political department was evidently to be classed, the disposal of troops, and the provisions, for their maintenance. As doubts were entertained and sanctioned by legal authority highly respectable, he proposed an act declaring the meaning of the law. This motion was controverted, first, on general grounds: le-gislature ought never to have recourse to this expedient, except when either the wording of an act was evidently so ambiguous as to stand in need of. explanation, or where, in consequence of the clashing judgment of courts, or doubts expressed by judges from the bench, it became necessary for the legislature to pro-pound anew its own meaning. In all other cases, parliament by interfering would quit its legislative, and assume a judicial capacity; and in the present instance would decide, in a cause, in which it was in some respects interested as a party; since it would gain by its own decision. It was a dispute between the crown or the public, and a corporation, on a pecuniary claim. The king insists upon a certain sum of money from the company, for a specified object. The company admit a sum to be due, but not the amount demanded: here is a clear and simple question, on which an issue might be tried in a court of law. The measure proposed was liable to many serious political objections, and might be used as a precedent for the worst purposes. A minister has nothing to do but to propose, and bring in a bill for granting new powers, in doubtful and ambiguous words, under restraints indistinctly defined, and with clauses that have a double aspect. The company had been induced to consent to the act of 1784, upon pretences, which now proved to be delusive; and the minister, having obtained that consent, was resolved to put his own construction upon it, contrary to the original intention of the party concerned. In the farther progress of the bill, counsel was heard for the India company at the bar of the house, and the whole ability of opposition was exerted, to prevent its enactment.

The following was the substance of the arguments, legal and political, which were employed on each side. Its opponents

Question; Had government by Mr. Pitt's power? denied by the directors and opposition in parliament.

Arguments against the declaratory bill.

controverted it principally upon two grounds: first, that the construction attempted to be put upon the act of 1784, was not its true and just construction: and secondly, that if it admitted such interpretation, the powers it vested in the board of control were injurious to the rights and interests of the company, and of a dangerous political nature, and therefore ought not to be confirmed. To prove the former proposition, its supporters contended that, the charter granted to the company having been purchased for a valuable consideration, every statute that diminished their rights ought to be construed, like penal laws, in the mildest sense, and so as to infringe those privileges in the least possible degree; and in ambiguous cases, acts of parliament should be explained in such a sense as to be consistent with each other. In the act of 1781[m] it was expressly stipulated, that the company should defray the expense of no troops, but such as were sent to India upon their own requisition; therefore the acts of 1784 should be interpreted so as to coincide with the preceding law. But the best and safest mode of expounding a statute, was to illustrate one part of it by other clauses of the same act. By the law of 1784,[n] " the commis-
" sioners (it was admitted) are authorized and empowered from
" time to time, to superintend, direct, and control all acts,
" operations, and concerns, which in any wise relate to the
" civil or military government, or revenues of the territorial pos-
" sessions of the company, in the manner in the said act direct-
" ed :" and " the court of directors are required to pay obedi-
" ence to, and to be governed and bound by, such orders and di-
" rections as the said court shall receive from the said board."
Were these clauses taken solely, it was allowed that they would justify the construction which was intended by the declaratory act; but from subsequent passages it was argued, that the positive directorial power of the commissioners was restrained to definite circumstances; and to be exercised on specified omissions of the East India directors. The directors by the act were required to deliver to the commissioners copies of all despatches which were received from their servants in India, and all instructions proposed to be sent to the company's officers in that country: these the commissioners, within fourteen days, were to return to the directors, either approved or disapproved and amended; and the directors were bound to obey the orders so amended or altered. If within fourteen days the court of directors should neglect to yield the obedience commanded by the act, then and then only, the commissioners might originate instructions. If the board were invested with the positive power claimed by the declaratory act, it was absurd to specify certain cases in which it might be lawful for them to send orders and instructions to the company's servants in India with-

m See act of parliament 1781, respecting India.
n See act for the government of India, July, 1784.

out the consent of the company. It was evident, from the
whole tenor of the clauses taken together, that the authority
vested in the commissioners was no other than a superintend-
ency and control over the transactions of the company in their
management of their affairs in India; a power to alter and
amend their orders and instructions, and, in case of neglect in
the directors, to carry such orders so amended into execution;
but not to originate measures, in opposition to the chartered and
stipulated right of the company. It was farther contended,
that the directors had understood the power proposed to be conferred by Pitt's bill on the commissioners, to be subject to
the alleged limitations; and that even the minister' had expressly declared his coincidence in that construction; that
otherwise the directors would have opposed it as no less hostile
to the rights of the company, than the obnoxious bill of Mr.
Fox.[o] The board of control itself had not understood the act
of 1784 as investing them with the unlimited sway which they
now claimed; they had acted upon the statute of 1781 for upwards of two years after the law of 1784, and by their conduct
admitted that they had no power to send out any of his majesty's troops to India without the consent of the company.
From the general rules of interpretation, from the clauses and
tenor of the act in question, the opinions of those whom it first
affected, the declaration of its framer, and the construction of
the persons who were appointed to carry it into execution, members of opposition endeavoured to prove, that the power now
proposed to be declared did not arise from it as a law.[p]

They next objected to it as a measure of policy: the authority which was claimed annihilated the court of directors, and
even the property of the company. The territorial revenues
being in many instances unavoidably implicated in their commercial concerns, the absolute command of the former, as to
their application and expenditure, would necessarily carry with
it a control over the latter, and might be used to supersede the
efficiency of the directors in the only branch of the company's
affairs that was left to their management. The measure itself
of sending four regiments to India was not less injurious to the
rights and interests of the company, than the unlimited power
under which it was to be executed. It would have been more
economical and just, either to have suffered the company to
raise four regiments, or to have sent over the 2,400 men which
were wanting to complete the king's regiments, already in India:—more economical, because in the one case the company's
troops are, and would be maintained at infinitely less expense
than the king's; in the other, the company would be free from
the additional burthen of all the officers of the four new regiments:—more just, because in the former case, the company

o Speech of Mr. Fox on the second reading of the bill.
p See parliamentary debates, March 1788, *passim*.

CHAP. would have enjoyed the patronage of the troops which they
XXXIX. were to pay, and might provide for many of their own descrv-
        ing officers, six hundred of whom, reduced at the late peace,
1788.   were living in very distressed situations in India. It was far-
        ther impolitic, as it would create a jealousy and disgust among
        the officers in the company's service. The opponents next pro-
        ceeded to the motives of ministers, which they alleged to be a
        desire of extending their own influence and patronage, at the
        expense of the India company. The ministers had formed a
        regular progressive plan, to grasp all the patronage of India.
        The direction claimed by the board of control afforded grounds
        of jealousy in another view; it placed a revenue at the disposal
        of the king's ministers, for raising and paying an army without
        consent of parliament, and was therefore inconsistent with the
        bill of rights, and a dangerous departure from the principles of
        the British constitution.

Argu-   By the supporters of the declaratory act, it was contended,
ments for first, respecting the rule of construction, that the principle
it.   could only be admitted, so far as was consistent with the spirit
        and express objects of the statute itself; it could be no rea-
        son for an interpretation of a subsequent law, that it militated
        against a prior; it would be absurd to put a sense upon an act,
        that would defeat the main ends for which it was passed; and
        with regard to the act of 1781, such parts of it as were incon-
        sistent with the provisions of the subsequent arrangement,
        were virtually, though not expressly repealed. The object of
        the plan of 1784 was, to take the entire management of terri-
        torial possessions, and the political government of India, out of
        the hands of the company, leaving them only the direction of
        their commercial concerns. The board of control was in future
        to be responsible to the public for the prosperity, defence, and
        security, of our Indian possessions, and was therefore to be in-
        vested with all the authorities necessary for the due discharge
        of the important trusts. These powers were given in general
        terms, and the mode of exercising them in particular cases was
        specified: in some they had a negative upon the orders of the
        directors: in others, where a difference of opinion arose, the
        board might enforce the execution of its own orders   The
        act in general clauses expressed this power which was claimed,
        and without it would have been totally inadequate to its object.
        Could it be supposed that parliament intended to leave to the
        company, who, it might be expected from the short duration
        of their charter, would attend chiefly to their own immediate
        pecuniary interests, the entire disposition of their revenues,
        without enabling the board of control, who were responsible
        for the defence and security of the whole, to appropriate such
        part of them as should be thought necessary for those purposes?
        The assertion of opposition, that either Mr. Pitt or the board of
        control had understood the act in the sense, imputed, was total-
        ly unfounded in truth, and unsupported by any evidence. With

regard to the economy and policy of the measure, the company's troops might be raised and maintained at a smaller expense; but these were not sufficient for guarding India against dangers by which it was now threatened. As to the additional patronage said to accrue to the crown, it was denied : on the grand question of standing armies, there were inaccuracies in all the existing laws. The bill of rights was not very explicit; it hardly stated the illegality of a standing army within the kingdom, but was silent with respect to military force in our settlements abroad. Mr. Pitt declared, that if any danger was apprehended from the bill before the house, relative either to the augmentation of the army, or the patronage of India in general, he was ready to receive any modifications which might be offered to avert such danger. In the committee he proposed several clauses for so modifying the bill, as to remove the objections respecting patronage. The bill was carried in the house of commons by a majority of fifty-four ; and, after experiencing strong opposition in the house of peers, was\ passed into a law ; and thus it was declared that the commissioners, being instituted for the territorial administration of India by the act of 1784, possessed a directorial, as well as controlling power, in whatever was necessary to the effectual execution of the trust reposed in them by the act of 1784.

The bill is passed into a law.

In the mutiny bill of this session, a clause was proposed for incorporating with the army a new body of military artificers. It was objected to this project, that it was an unnecessary extension of the military law, and consequently inconsistent with the principles of the constitution. These artificers had served the army, hitherto, without diminution of their liberty, and no necessity was shown why their tenure of service should be changed. The great advocate for the clause was the duke of Richmond.[q] Such a corps (he said) was employed in all the armies abroad, and found to be extremely useful : he had proposed such an establishment to his majesty, who was pleased to signify his approbation of the scheme. The policy of the nation had considered it as right that all soldiers should continue in such a state of subordination ; therefore artificers, being enlisted regularly as soldiers, ought undoubtedly to become subject to the same law. Such a change was not to be accounted any hardship ; since no species of trials, however popular it might be, was more fair and candid than trials by a court martial. The clause, after a long discussion, was at length carried without a division.

Extension of the mutiny bill.

At the instance of the woollen manufactures, a bill was introduced in the house of commons, for rendering more effectual, laws against the private exportation of wool. The manufacturers asserted, that of long or combing wool, to the amount of 13,000 packs were annually smuggled to France : hence it

Bill against the smuggled exportation of wool.

q Debates of the peers, 1788.

was inferred; first, that the wool growers were by this means enabled within the kingdom to keep up the price of their commodity beyond its just standard, to the great detriment of our staple manufacture; secondly, that there ensued a loss to Britain of the surplus value of the manufactured articles over the raw materials, and of the increased population, which the employment of an additional number of manufacturers would produce; and thirdly, that the smuggled wool being an article necessary to the French manufactures, it enabled them to rival ours. In answer to these arguments, it was contended, chiefly by country gentlemen, that it was an unnecessary and unjust attack upon the landed interest. The quantity alleged to be smuggled bore no proportion to the whole produce of the country, and subtracted only about a fifteenth share even at the calculation of the proposers; but there was no evidence of the calculation being just. The price of wool was not enhanced beyond its just standard: as a proof that the manufacture was not injured by it, they demonstrated the increase of the value of woollen goods, exported from the year 1776 to the year 1787, to be in the proportion of nearly one-third. Upon the second inference it was said, that admitting the quantity of wool stated to be smuggled into France, it did not follow that our manufacturers would work up that additional quantity above what they now do merely by preventing its making its way thither; on the contrary, unless it were first proved, which had never been asserted, that, in consequence of the exportation, the manufacturers are in want of materials to work upon, it was fair to conclude, that the quantity exported was a mere surplus, and that the British manufacturers would not work a single pound more, though the whole should be kept at home: a view of the very flourishing state of our manufactures was sufficient to convince us that there was no ground of apprehension from the rivalship of France. It was replied, that the restraints proposed to be laid upon the wool growers would not materially affect their interests. The present bill was consonant to the existing laws, and was only designed to carry into more effectual execution those principles of policy, respecting the exportation of wool, by which this country for so many years had been governed, and under which both our manufacturers and our wool growers had flourished and grown rich together. The bill underwent a very minute discussion, in which party politics appeared to occupy no share; and at length was carried by a large majority.

A subject of very considerable importance, and which long occupied the attention both of parliament and the nation, was this year for the first time brought before the house of commons: this was the celebrated question concerning the trade carried on for purchasing negro slaves to cultivate our possessions in the western world.

Slavery is so evidently repugnant to the feelings of a Briton, that it may at first sight appear astonishing no means had been devised to prevent the existence of such a state in the British dominions. The mercantile character of this country predominated over the political, when, for the acquisition of wealth, she admitted the destruction of freedom; and the guardians of European liberty became the most active instruments of African slavery. This inconsistency did not appear to have impressed any of the most zealous and powerful champions of constitutional freedom, during the greater part of the eighteenth century. Planters and traders, who are the most frequent and constant observers of this state, were not likely to testify an abhorrence of a system, by which they were so considerable gainers, or even perhaps to feel the adequate detestation for oppressions, with which they were so familiar. Statesmen might overlook some rigours, through which they conceived the nation derived private and public wealth; and the people in general were too distant to consider the condition of the negroes. Nevertheless, the mild and liberal principles of British policy seemed extremely inimical to human thraldom; and the doctrines of benevolent philosophers were totally hostile to such a practice; but neither enlightened policy, nor ingenious theory, were the causes which at this period produced a prevalent enmity to slavery: a more rapidly operative principle exerted itself in favour of negro freedom: religious zeal was infused into the subject,.and, engaging the passions of many individuals, stimulated them much more powerfully than the deductions of moral science, or the dictates of political wisdom. An opinion was eagerly disseminated, that the state of slavery was incompatible with christianity. This notion seems to have been drawn from the consideration of detached passages, rather than from the general spirit of that admirable system. The religion of Jesus seeking the happiness of mankind, finds its sources in the disposition and character of the individual; and comprehending the vast variety of situation and sentiment, delivers general rules, enforced by cogent motives, for performing the various duties of social and civil life; political establishments and gradations it leaves to be formed according to the circumstances of the case, and character of the people. Philanthropy, which mingled with a piety sincere, though somewhat eccentric, distinguished many of the earliest votaries of negro freedom; and in the ardour of benignant project overlooked difficulties of execution; indeed, perhaps, rather indulged itself in fancying advantage from the change, than accurately ascertained the probability of benefit, even should their wish be accomplished. In the southern provinces of America, soon after the establishment of their independence, the quakers presented a strong. and pathetic address to the several legislative assemblies; in which they exhorted these bodies to abolish slavery; and

CHAP.
XXXIX.

1788.
State of facts.

General and special objections to slavery.

It is impugned as inimical to christianity, as well as justice and humanity.

Pious and benevolent enthusiasm in favour of the negroes.

CHAP.
XXXIX.

1788.

in many instances emancipated the negroes in their own possession. In Britain the same sect first followed the example of
their American brethren, and presented a similar petition in
1787 to parliament. The cause, embraced by the enthusiasm
of religion and benevolence, procured a great number of votaries. From sympathy and imitation, it became extremely
popular; literary ingenuity was not wanting, and no works
were read with such avidity, as compositions which decried
negro slavery. As usual in controversy, one side of the question only was considered by its supporters, and the statement
of propositions was such, as to render conclusions obvious. A
topic repeatedly employed was, DIFFERENCE OF COLOUR IS NO
REASON FOR FORFEITURE OF LIBERTY. On so trivial a truism
very popular pamphlets were founded; eminent divines embraced the cause; recommended it from the pulpit, and in
printed discourses. Churchmen and dissenters concurred
in eagerly inculcating the abolition of slavery; many were
so far transported by philanthropic feelings, as to declare
their readiness to forego all the advantages and habitual gra-
tifications which arose from our West India islands, rather than
enjoy them through the compulsory labour of their fellow creatures. With this enthusiastic zeal, hypocrisy, as usual, occasionally mingled; and there were demagogues who, without
possessing much tenderness of disposition themselves, courted
popularity by coinciding with the humane sentiments, which
were so generally diffused. For a considerable time a stranger
might have supposed, if he judged from prevalent discourse and
writing, that the African negroes monopolized misery, and therefore, that the highest duty of christian benevolence was to afford
them relief. While this fervour predominated, a society was
formed to collect information on which to ground a petition to
parliament; and a very considerable sum of money was subscribed in order to defray the expense.

Mr. Wil-
berforce;
talents,
character,
and lauda-
ble zeal of

Among those who took the most active share in endeavouring
to relieve the negroes, was Mr. Wilberforce, member of parliament for the county of York.. Of good talents, active and
indefatigable industry, and extensive knowledge, this gentleman
held a high place in the public estimation; and possessed considerable fortune and influence: these advantages he uniformly
directed to such pursuits as he thought conducive to virtue, religion, and the happiness of his fellow creatures. Conceiving the
cause of the negroes to be that of piety and humanity, he had
employed persevering labour, in order to learn the particulars
of their treatment; and viewing the subject as a British senator,
he attempted to reconcile political expediency with what he
deemed a discharge of christian and moral duty. From these
motives he was believed to have entered much more minutely
into the detail of the slave trade, than any other member of the
legislature.

While one party exerted itself so strenuously to render the abolition generally popular, and thereby prepared to facilitate its passage through parliament, another with less animation and impressiveness of eloquence, but with a considerable share of sound reasoning, laboured to prove, that the advantages alleged to be consequent upon abolition were ideal, and founded upon abstract theories of philanthropy without a knowledge of the existing case. The evil of slavery (it was said) depends on opinion : that state is universally prevalent in Africa; and the minds of the negroes are habituated to its contemplation, as one of the most common conditions of life. Having the principles of dissension and hostility in common with other men, the African tribes are often engaged in war : one consequence of war is captivity ; the usual treatment of captives is either massacre or sale. The market for slaves, independent of European purchasers, is comparatively inconsiderable in Nigritia. The chance to the individual of escaping butchery, in a great measure depends on the demand from European traders. Carried to the West Indies, the negroes are on the whole well treated : by some individual masters they may have been hardly used ; but in general, as can be proved from persons most conversant with these countries, they are contented and happy. Severity is not the interest of planters ; and if even malignant passions transport masters or their delegates to unwise cruelty, the recurrence of such acts may be prevented by judicious regulations. Narrow in their views, the negroes like other savages repose their chief happiness in the supply of animal wants : indolent and improvident, they are often deficient in the exertions requisite for their maintenance. Nothing is more frequent in Africa than famine, which destroys great numbers of the inhabitants ; whereas in the West Indies they have abundance of provisions. To a Briton, death, either by sword or famine, may be preferable to life and slavery ; but to a Nigritian the case is far different : by transporting him to a situation, in which his animal wants are fully supplied, where by personal exertions he can modify slavery, and has nothing to fear from either famine or a victorious enemy, you place him in a higher state, according to his estimate of good, than if you had suffered him to remain in Africa. The slave trade, does not on the whole violate humanity, because it does not on the whole diminish that happiness which humanity seeks to promote. The culture of the West India islands, so productive a source of private opulence and public revenue, depends upon labourers inured to such a climate. Were we to forego the advantage of such possessions, what would be the consequence? the other European states would take up the benefits which we abandoned : the slave trade would be still carried on, though Britain did not participate. It would not be real generosity, but romantic extravagance, to abstain from so advantageous a commerce, when we ourselves should lose, and our rivals only

Marginal notes:

CHAP. XXXIX.

1788.

Opposite arguments.

Slavery an evil great or small, according to the circumstances and sentiments of the sufferers. The condition of African negroes is meliorated by becoming slaves to British masters.

Slaves in our plantations generally happy.

If Britain abolish slavery, other European states will reap the benefit.

CHAP.
XXXIX.

1788.
Great capi-
tals embar-
ked in this
trade,
which is a
large
source of
riches and
revenue.
Petitions
for and
against the
slave trade.
The coun-
cil institu-
tes an in-
quiry into
the details
and alleged
cruelties.
Sir Wil-
liam Dol-
ben's mo-
tion for re-
gulating
the trans-
portation
of negroes.

Is passed
into a law.
Mr. Pitt's
bill for the
relief and
recom-
pense of
the Ameri-
can loyal-
ists.

should again by its discontinuance. Very great capitals have been embarked, both in the West India islands and African slave trade, under the sanction of the public faith, which guaranteed the commerce by many internal regulations and foreign treaties for rendering it productive. Are we to sacrifice a great and valuable property to philanthropic chimeras, totally unfounded in fact and experience?

Petitions and remonstrances containing such topics, for and against the abolition, were presented to the house of commons and privy-council. A committee of the latter was appointed for investigating facts. Mr. Pitt finding that the information hitherto collected was not sufficient to authorize parliamentary discussion, on the ninth of May proposed, that the consideration of the slave trade should be deferred till the commencement of the next session; meanwhile, the inquiry which was instituted before the privy-council would be brought to such a state of maturity, as to make it fit that the result should be laid before the house, that it might facilitate their investigation, and enable them to proceed to a decision, founded equally upon principles of humanity, justice, and sound policy.

Sir William Dolben introduced a measure of intermediate relief, in a bill for regulating the transportation of African natives to the British West Indies: the object of this proposition was to accommodate the slaves, during their passage, better than had been hitherto done. It was intended to limit the number who should be conveyed, in proportion to the tonnage of the vessel; to secure to them good and sufficient provisions, and other matters equally conducive to their health, and their accommodation. While the bill was pending, a petition was presented from the merchants and other inhabitants of Liverpool, praying to be heard by their counsel against this regulating bill: this request being granted, it was contended at the bar of the house, that the proposed reduction of number would essentially injure the trade, and that it was founded on an assertion of hardships which did not exist. The plea of the merchants was not made out to the satisfaction of the house; and the bill, though in a small degree modified, passed unanimously, without any material alteration. In the house of lords it underwent such changes, that the commons considered its original object as not attained: a new bill was accordingly introduced, which passed both houses, and received the royal assent.

About the same time, Mr. Pitt called the attention of the house to a different class of sufferers, the American loyalists, and the losses sustained by them through their adherence to the parent country during the late war. Commissioners had been appointed to inquire into the claims; and in consequence of their report, the minister divided the claimants into four classes. In the first class he ranked those who had resided in America at the commencement of the war, and who, in pursuance of their principles of loyalty and adherence to Britain,

were obliged to abandon their estates and property in the co- CHAP.
lonies; which were in consequence seized and confiscated by XXXIX.
the revolters. The mode he meant to adopt,[r] with respect to
this class of loyalists, whom he considered as having the 1788.
strongest claims of any, would be to allow the full amount[s]
to those whose demands were so small, that any deduction from
them would materially affect their means of comfortable existence. The second class of claimants were persons who, having resided in England during the war, made claims upon alleged loss of property in America: these were not sufferers in
the same degree as the first class, because they had not been
driven out of America, but had made their choice: though,
however, their option was to remain in England, still they
were entitled to expect compensation for the loss of property
in America, which they had incurred through a preference of
this country: he proposed respecting this as the former class,
that property affording only the means of comfortable subsistence should be paid in full of the established claims; but that
beyond the sum deemed requisite, the deduction should be considerably greater.[t] The third class consisted of loyalists who
had either enjoyed places or exercised professions in America,
but were driven away in consequence of their loyalty to this
country, and lost their income. With regard to these it was to
be considered, that though they had been expelled from America, they were able to obtain fresh incomes in this country, by
exercising their talents and their industry: he therefore proposed, that all whose incomes did not exceed four hundred
pounds a year, should receive half-pay; persons whose incomes
were higher, should receive forty pounds for every hundred
above four hundred, and under fifteen hundred; and beyond
that sum, at the rate of thirty per cent. The fourth class of
claimants consisted of those who had been obliged to leave
their habitations and property in consequence of the cession of
that country at the late peace: as their loss had been incurred
by a national act, without any alternative of their own, he pro-

r See Annual Register, 1788, p. 13.

s His proposition was, " that all such loyalists shall receive the full a-
mount of their losses, as far as the same do not exceed the sum of ten thousand pounds; and shall also receive, where the amount of such losses
shall be above ten thousand pounds in the whole, and not above thirty five
thousand pounds in the whole, ninety pounds per cent. of such part of the
said losses as shall exceed ten thousand pounds; and where such losses
shall be above thirty five thousand pounds, eighty five pounds per cent of
such of the said losses as shall exceed ten thousand pounds; and where the
same shall be above fifty thousand pounds, eighty pounds per cent. of such
part of the said losses as shall be above ten thousand pounds "

t That from all those claims, amounting from ten thousand pounds to
thirty thousand, a deduction should be made of twenty per cent.; and a
farther additional deduction of twenty per cent. in progression, upon every
additional fifty thousand claimed.

CHAP.   posed that they should be completely reimbursed by the pub-
XXXIX. lic. He then stated the sum to which the established claims
⌣⌣⌣   amounted. The propositions which he founded on this account
1788.   were received with great approbation, and a resolution for the
payment of the same, after some modification, was unanimously
adopted. Thus, sufferers through loyalty and patriotism to
our sovereign and country, received from the national munifi-
cence a liberal compensation for the damages which they had
sustained.

Com-   A considerable portion of parliamentary attention was di-
mence. rected to the prosecution and trial of Mr. Hastings. In con-
ment of the sequence of the order of the house of lords, near the close of
trial of Mr. the last session, to the defendant to deliver answers to the charg-
Hastings. es alleged against him by the house of commons, on the prescribed day he appeared at the bar, and presented answers.
Of these the lords sent a copy to the house, of commons; the
answers being read, Mr. Burke moved, that they should be referred to a committee which should have the conduct of the
prosecution. This measure being embraced, Mr. Pitt proposed
Mr. Burke as the first member ; the house unanimously concurring, Mr. Burke named Mr. Francis, and to support his nomi-
· nation, stated the immense advantages which would accrue to
the committee from the very extensive knowledge of that gentleman. The abilities and information of Mr. Francis were
universally allowed ; but great political differences had subsisted between him and the accused, in India, and some personal animosity was conceived to remain ; on these grounds a
great majority of the house voted against the motion. The
rest of the committee consisted of the same gentlemen who
had been delegated to present the charges to the lords; and in
addition to them, Mr. Wilbraham, Mr. Fitzpatrick, and Mr.
Courtney. To the answer of Mr. Hastings, two days after,
Mr. Burke brought from the committee a replication, averring
the charges to be true, and that they would be ready to prove
the same against him before the lords, at such convenient time
and place as should be appointed. The reply being carried by
Mr Burke to the peers, Wednesday the thirteenth of February
was fixed for proceeding upon the trial in Westminster-hall;
and the members of the recently appointed committee were
nominated managers for conducting the trial. Mr. Fox proposed that Mr. Francis should be added to the committee ; but
the majority of the house continued to oppose the insertion of
his name.[u] The committees were appointed by both houses to

* u Mr Francis at this time, in a very able speech, entered into an account of his conduct respecting Mr. Hastings, for the last thirteen years,
both in India and in England ; which, though in some degree individual
justification, contains much important statement and remark on the general subject concerning which the differences existed. Mr. Francis and
Mr Hastings having fought a duel, and the former gentleman having been
dangerously wounded, they had exchanged forgiveness ; in what sense that

search the records of parliament, for precedents relative to the
mode of proceeding in trials by impeachment; and the necessary orders were made for their accommodation in Westminster-hall, for the admission of spectators, the attendance of witnesses, and other matters respecting the regularity of their
proceeding.   On the thirteenth of February the trial commenced with the usual formalities.ˣ   Mr. Hastings being called into
court, the lord-chancellor addressed him in the following
terms:

" Warren Hastings,

"You stand at the bar of this court, charged with high crimes
" and misdemeanors; a copy of which has been delivered to
" you: you have been allowed counsel, and a long time has been
" given you for your defence; but this is not to be considered as
" a particular indulgence to you, as it arises from the necessity
" of the case; the crimes with which you are charged, being
" stated to have been committed in a distant place.   These
" charges contain the most weighty allegations, and they come
" from the highest authority: this circumstance, however,
" though it carries with it the most serious importance, is not to
" prevent you from making your defence in a firm and collected
" manner; in the confidence that, as a British subject, you are
" entitled to, and will receive, full justice from a British court."
Mr. Hastings answered:

" My lords,

" I am come to this high tribunal, equally impressed with a
" confidence in my own integrity, and in the justice of the court
" before which I stand."

forgiveness was to be interpreted, Mr. Francis explained in the following
passage:—" It was my lot to be dangerously wounded: as I concieved immediate death inevitable, I thought of nothing but to die in peace with all
men, particularly Mr. Hastings.   I called him to me, gave him my hand,
and desired him to consider in what situation my death would leave him.
By that action, and by those words, undoubtedly I meant to declare, that I
freely forgave him the insult he had offered me, and the fatal consequence
which had attended it.   I meant that we should stand in the same relation
to each other, as if the duel and the cause of it had never happened.   But
did I tell him that, if I survived, I would renounce the whole plan and principle of my public life?   That I would cease to oppose his measures?   On my
return to England, I found that a parliamentary inquiry into thel ate transac-
tionsn India was already begun, and I was almost immediately ordered to attend one of the committees employed upon that inquiry.   Could I without
treachery to the public, refuse to give evidence or information necessary
for the public service when it was demanded of me by the authority of the
house of commons?"   See parliamentary debates.

x The house of commons, about eleven o'clock, preceded by the managers of the impeachment, who were led by Mr. Burke, came from their own
house into the hall.   The lords, half an hour after, entered from the house
of peers; first, official attendants on the house in a rising series, commencing with the clerks, and terminating with the judges; afterwards the
peers, beginning with the junior barons, and ending with the prince of
Wales.

CHAP.   The two first days being employed in reading the charges,
XXXIX. the third was appointed for opening the same, stating the na-
~~~   ture and quality of the imputations, the evidence by which
1788.: they were to be supported, and the guilt which, to the defendant, if they were proved, would attach. Never had an inquiry
of more magnitude been instituted before a judicial assembly.
The question was, whether a man to whom a trust affecting the
happiness or misery of millions had been delegated, in the discharge of his office, had been a faithful or unfaithful trustee to
his employers, the protector or the scourge of the immense and
populous regions committed to his care ? The question derived
a very high additional importance from the character of the
accused, whom friends, enemies, and impartial men, concurred
in deeming a person of the most powerful and comprehensive
talents ; from the character of the accuser, whom friends, enemies, and impartial men, concurred in esteeming a person of
the most extraordinary genius, multifarious knowledge, and
splendid eloquence, that had ever graced a British senate. The
anxiety of the public to hear Mr. Burke speak upon so vast a
subject, against Mr. Hastings, brought an immense concourse of
hearers to the hall.

Speech of   The court was assembled to the number of one hundred and
Mr. Burke. sixty-four peers, and the chancellor having called the managers
to proceed, Mr. Burke rose and said, that he stood forth by
order of the commons of Great Britain, to support the charge
of high crimes and misdemeanors which they had exhibited
against Warren Hastings, esq ; and that he had a body of evidence to produce to substantiate the whole and every part of those
charges. The gentlemen who were joined with him in supporting the impeachment, had instructed him to open the cause
with an account of the grounds on which the commons had
proceeded; a general view of the nature of the crimes alleged ; and with an explanation of concomitant circumstances that were necessary to elucidate the accusation. The
dreadful disorders of our Indian government were acknowledged ; it was not till after every mode of legislative prevention had been tried without effect, till they found, during a
course of fourteen years, that inquiries, and resolutions and
laws were equally disregarded, that they had recourse to a penal
prosecution. The crimes imputed were not errors of human
frailty, nor the effects of imperious necessity ; they originated
in the worst passions, and evinced a total extinction of moral
principle; they were committed against advice, supplication,
and remonstrance, and in defiance of the direct commands of
lawful authority. The accused was the first in rank, station,
and power, under whom as the head all the peculation and
tyranny of India was embodied, disciplined, and paid ; and in
striking at whom, therefore, they would strike at the whole
corps of delinquents. The evidence, which supported the
charges, in many instances amounted to the clearness and pre-

cision required by the English law; but a considerable part
did not reach municipal accuracy. The prosecutor contended,
that it was a right of the house of commons, in an impeachment, not to be bound by the confined rules and maxims of
evidence prevalent in the lower courts ; nor by any other than
those of natural, immutable, and substantial justice.*y* This
mode of interpretation was due to suffering nations, who were
unconcerned in our technical distinctions, but on the great principle of morality wished punishment to follow guilt. It was
highly necessary to prevent the disgraceful imputation*z* which
might fall either upon that high court, as if it were corrupted
by the wealth of India, or upon the laws of England, as impotent in the means of punishing successful fraud and oppression. Descending from preliminary observations to the actual
subject of the charge, he stated the relations in which Mr.
Hastings stood, and the duties which from these he had incurred ; in order to prove his transgressions. The powers delegated to Mr. Hastings, by the India company, and which he
was charged with having abused, were derived from two sources ; the charter bestowed by the crown, under the authority of
parliament, and the grant from the mogul emperor of the
Dewannee, or high stewardship of Bengal, in the year 1766.
He exhibited an historical account of the company from its
first establishment, the powers which it had delegated to Mr.
Hastings, and which Mr. Burke charged him with having abused. He next proceeded to the rights with which the company
were invested by the mogul emperor, to the collection of the
revenue delegated by the company to Mr. Hastings, and which
he also charged him with having grossly violated. The alleged violation of duties so originating, and abuses of powers delegated for such general and specified purposes, Mr. Burke represented with an eloquence which so astonished and agitated
every hearer of fancy or sensibility, as for a considerable time
to preclude the exertion of that judgment that could distinguish
pictures from realities. Having exhibited Mr. Hastings as a
monster of flagitiousness and crimes, he concluded with a peroration which described the nature of the cause, accusation,
accused, accuser, and tribunal, in all their constituent parts,
and closed with the following words: " Therefore it was with
" confidence ordered by the commons, that I impeach Warren

y This doctrine, that the rank and dignity of the assertor constituted a
just ground of difference in the criterion of proof, is certainly not logically
accurate; neither would it be politically wise, that the quality of the accuser should affect the requisite testimony, as in a criminal case there would
be a substitution of authority for proof, which might subject liberty, pro·
perty, and life, to arbitrary caprice.

z This argument proceeded on a supposition, that the high court was to
be influenced by the fear of censure from misapprehension, instead of giving judgment according to the merits of the case.

CHAP. " Hastings, esq. of high crimes and misdemeanors: I impeach
XXXIX. " him in the name of the commons of Great Britain in par-
～～～ " liament assembled, whose parliamentary trust he has be-
1788.   " trayed:
        " I impeach him in the name of all the commons of Great
" Britain, whose national character he has dishonoured :
        " I impeach him in the name of the people of India, whose
" laws, rights, and liberties he has subverted, whose properties
" he has destroyed, whose countries he has laid waste and de-
" solate."
        Such were the grounds adduced by the orator in a speech
which occupied three hours for four days successively.   Mr.
Burke having concluded his account of the substance, Mr. Fox
addressed the court on the mode of the charges: he stated,
that the committee proposed to open and adduce evidence which
should substantiate one charge at a time; to hear the prisoner's defence and evidence upon that charge, and afterwards to
reply; and to proceed in the same manner in all the other articles.   Mr. Hastings's counsel being asked if they consented to
this mode? replied in the negative.   The manner proposed
was, they said, contrary to the practice of all courts of justice,
and was inconsistent with all principles of equity.   After some
debate it was resolved, that, according to the usual practice on
trials, the prosecutor should complete his case before the accused
commenced his defence.   Mr. Fox opened the Benares charge
which he brought down to the expulsion of Cheyt Sing; the
following part was finished by Mr. Grey: Mr. Anstruther conducted the examination of evidence, and summed up the whole
of that article.   Mr. Adam, on the fifteenth of April, opened
the second accusation respecting the begums; Mr. Sheridan
examined the witnesses and summed up the charge; the last
that came before the court during that session of parliament.

Motion for   Another accusation of Indian delinquency was brought be-
the im-   fore the commons in the conduct of sir Elijah Impey. This
peachment task was undertaken by sir Gilbert Elliot, who, in a very able
of sir Eli-
jah Impey. and eloquent speech, maintained two general principles ; that
India must be redressed or lost, and that the only means left of
reforming Indian abuse, was the punishment, in some great and
signal instances, of Indian delinquency: he stated the nature,
the occasion, and the purposes of the commission with which
sir Elijah Impey was sent out to India, as involving circumstances which were strong aggravations of his guilt, and increased the necessity of its punishment; that in the two grand
objects which were committed to his charge, the protection of
the company from the frauds of its servants, and of the natives
from the oppression of Europeans, he had, by corruptly
- changing sides, added his new powers to the very force they
were intended to control, and taken an active part in the op-
'pressions which it was his duty to have avenged.   Sir Gilbert
Elliot presented to the house six distinct articles of accusation.

The subject of the first was the trial and execution of Nundcomar; the second, the defendant's conduct in a certain Patna
cause; the third, entitled *extension of jurisdiction*, comprehended
various instances, in which the jurisdiction of the court was alleged to have been exercised illegally and oppressively, beyond
the intention of the act and charter; the fourth charge, entitled
the Cossijurah cause, though also an allegation of illegal assumption, was distinguished (according to the statement of the
accuser) by circumstances so important, as to become properly
the subject of a separate article; the fifth charge was for his
acceptance of the office of judge of the Sudder Dewannee
Adaulut, which was contrary to law, and not only repugnant
to the spirit of the act and charter, but fundamentally subversive of all its material purposes; the sixth and last charge related to his conduct in the provinces of Oude and Benares,
where the chief justice was said to have become the agent and
tool of Mr. Hastings in the alleged oppression and plunder of
the begums.

Sir Elijah Impey on his defence contended, that in the acts
which were charged he had not exceeded the powers intrusted
to him as supreme judge. Respecting the first and most important article, the trial and execution of Nundcomar for forgery, he had been accused of extrajudicial interference. Neither
Nundcomar (it was contended by sir Gilbert Elliot) nor the
person whose name was forged, were subject to the jurisdiction
of the English court. By the laws of India, forgery is not punishable capitally; and thus a man was put to death by a court
to which he was not amenable, for a crime not capital by the
laws to which he was amenable. Sir Elijah Impey argued, that
though the authority of the supreme court did not extend over
all the inhabitants of the English provinces in India, it included
the inhabitants of Calcutta. Nundcomar had not been tried as
a native of Bengal, but as an inhabitant of Calcutta, where he
resided, and where of course he was amenable to the laws of
the place. A motion being made in the house, resolved into
a committee, that the first charge exhibited against sir Elijah
Impey contained matter of impeachment, it was negatived by a
majority of seventy-three to fifty-five; and it was afterwards voted, that the other charges should not be taken into consideration.

This year Mr. Grenville proposed certain amendments and
additions to the bill brought into parliament by his father, for
the better regulation of the trials of controverted elections.
When the existing act had been proposed, Mr. Grenville said
its principal aim was to take the trial of petitions on controverted elections out of their hands, and to place them in a committee so constituted, likely to do strict justice to the parties.
That object, it was universally allowed, had been fully answered; but collateral inconveniences had been incurred, which,
intent on the main end, the author had overlooked. Ever since
the bill had passed into a law, an infinite number of petitions,

CHAP.
XXXIX.
~~~
1788.

complaining of undue elections, had been presented in the first session of every parliament; and many of them, after having taken up much of the time of the house, had proved frivolous. To prevent the interruption of public business, he proposed that the committee empowered to determine whether the election petition presented, or the defence offered in answer to it, was frivolous, should adjudge the payment of costs against the party to blame. This was merely an act of justice; yet such a regulation would save much expense to individuals, and much time and trouble to the house. The present was the most proper season for considering and determining such a subject, as there was actually no petition concerning elections before the house, and the minds of members were therefore perfectly cool and open to impartial deliberation. The bill was introduced, passed both houses without opposition, and received the royal assent.

Supplies.

On the sixth of May, the financial plan for the year was proposed by Mr. Pitt. The minister observed, that several extraordinary expenses had been necessarily incurred; in the navy there was an increase beyond the peace establishment of 446,000l.; in the army of 233,000l.; and in the ordnance of 61,000l. These augmented demands were occasioned by the circumstances of our putting the distant possessions of the country into a state of more complete defence, and were not to be considered as the permanent necessary expenses of the nation; and to these there were several sums to be added, which could not occur again, or at least could not make a part of our settled yearly expense: such was the sum for the relief of the loyalists, the expense of the late armament, and the vote for the payment of the debts of his royal highness the prince of Wales; these demands added together amounted to 1,282,000l. which was to be considered as extraordinary, and consequently to be deducted from the settled regular establishment of the country. It had been deemed wise to put every part of the British dominions into such a posture of defence as to secure the blessings of peace. Notwithstanding the extraordinary expenses incurred, the receipts of the country had fully answered even unforeseen demands, without deviating from the plan which the legislature had adopted for diminishing the national debt. When such were the savings in a year of unusual expense, as our resources were fast increasing in the extension of commerce, and the improvement of revenue, we might most fairly infer that our financial concerns were in a state of progressive melioration: it might be well argued from probable causes, that such a country as England, blessed with peace, must rapidly increase in the various constituents of prosperity; that she did so, was ascertained from fact and experience: he had formed an estimate from an average of four years; the revenue of 1783 amounted to ten millions, besides the land and malt tax: the revenue of 1787, with the same exclusion, amount-

ed to thirteen millions; the additional imposts had not exceeded a million and a half; hence the other million and a half must
have arisen from the suppression of smuggling, and extension of
trade: he was about soon to adopt farther regulations for the restrictions of fraud, and commerce was very fast rising, so that he
augured a much greater excess of receipt beyond expenditure.
Mr. Sheridan, with an ingenuity that evidently surpassed his investigation of financial details, endeavoured to controvert the ministerial statements, but did not succeed. The supplies granted this year were eighteen thousand seamen, and about twenty
thousand landmen, besides those who were on foreign service;
no new taxes were imposed, but a lottery was appointed. The
various departments of duty occupied parliament until the
eleventh of July, when the houses were prorogued by a speech
from the throne. His majesty thanked the legislature for their
uniform and diligent attention to the laborious services of the
present year. To the house of commons he expressed peculiar
gratitude for the readiness and liberality with which they had
granted the requisite supplies. Hostilities had commenced between the imperial sovereigns and Turkey, but he received the
strongest assurances from the respective powers of their amicable dispositions to this country. The security and welfare of
his own dominions, and the preservation of the general tranquillity of Europe, were the objects of engagements which he
had recently formed with the king of Prussia and the states-general.

CHAP. XL.

CHAP.
XL.

1788

Affairs of
the conti-
nent.
Objects of
the impe-
rial combi-
nation.

THE attention of Europe was at this time principally occupied by the conduct and operations of its eastern powers.
The confederacy between Austria and Russia, originating in
the causes and directed to the objects which have been already
commemorated, had been long engaged in maturing its plans.
Ever since the conquest of the Crimea, Catharine was occupied
in desultory war with the Tartar tribes, adjoining her frontiers.
Immensely superior as the Russians were in force and discipline to these hordes, yet rapid irruptions annoyed those who
could have easily repelled regular warfare. Catharine proposed
either to conciliate the hostile Tartars by proffered kindness,
to dazzle them by displayed magnificence, or to intimidate them
by manifested power.[a] The reduction, however, or pacification

a History of the Reign of Catharine, vol. ii. book x.

of these hordes was but a small part of the mighty designs, to promote which she deemed it expedient to visit her late acquisition the Cherson. This journey, planned in 1786, was executed in 1787, but before that time the Tartars produced a change in her original intention. As soon as the intended progress was known, and its believed object was reported, instead of either dazzling or terrifying the Tartars, it became a signal of general and immediate danger, to cement their union in the strongest manner, and urge them to the greatest possible excretion, and determined resistance. Catharine diminished a considerable part of her destined splendour, when not likely to answer her purpose, and a great portion of her military force, which, in the war with the Tartars, could be so much more usefully employed elsewhere ; she still had various purposes to accomplish ; by visiting the confines of her own and the Turkish empire. She had employed by her agents, very skilful incessant and extensive efforts, to seduce the christian subjects, of the Ottoman Porte. Mistress of the principal country in which the Grecian faith prevails, she had declared herself the friend and protectress of the Greek church in all parts of the world; her partisans were very numerous in the heart of the Turkish empire, and she did not doubt, by a near approach, to stimulate their zeal, and rouse them to schemes of ready cooperation.[b] Aware of the imbecility of her son and heir, she had rested the hopes of talents, similar to her own, on the puerile promise of her two grandsons. The second of these princes received the name of Constantine, was dressed and educated from his childhood according to the manner of the Greeks, and always attended by a guard of Grecian youth, who were formed into a corps for that purpose: in short, she endeavoured to excite the wishes and hopes of the Greek christians, that the empire of the east should be restored under a prince who bore the name of its founder. This youth she proposed to carry with her to the frontiers of Turkey, but indisposition prevented his attendance: she farther designed to inspect her new dominions, to estimate their value, both as actual possessions, and the means of farther acquisition. While the empress thus pursued her grand project, she was anxious to concert measures with Joseph, at once her confederate and tool; and for that purpose invited him to meet her at Cherson: the king of Poland too was present at this congress. Though Stanislaus was far from being able to yield active assistance to the confederates, yet, by the position of his kingdom he could afford the two empires important aid against the Ottomans, by enabling them to unite their force, and act in perfect concert along the whole line of frontier belonging to European Turkey. At this congress the system of aggression appears to have become completely adjusted, although farther preparations were resolved before it should actually commence.

CHAP.
XL.

1788.

Catharine prepares to visit the Crimea.

She attempts to seduce the christian subjects of Turkey.

At Cherson she meets her confederate Joseph.

b. See Annual Register, 1787.

CHAP.   Meanwhile, report had carried to Constantinople the in-
XL.   tended progress to the Cherson, and had represented with her
         usual exaggeration the superb splendour which was originally
1788.   designed. Catharine, it was said, was about to be crowned
         empress of Taurida, and to be declared protectress of auto-
         cratrix of the nations of Tartars.[c] A christian was, by osten-
         tatious triumph, to insult mussulmen, whom she had outraged
         by usurpation. Were Turks so degenerate from their anecs-
         tors, as to suffer such insolence and spoliations with impunity ;
         were those Ottomans who had kept the whole christian world
         in awe, now to be trampled by a power, till within this century
         scarcely known in Europe? These considerations influenced
         the Turks to hostilities, in which they might have appeared
         precipitate, if it had not been evident that they speedily either
         must attack or be attacked themselves. War was now un-
         doubtedly, the purpose of Catharine and Joseph : the question,
         therefore, with the Turks was, which was the wisest time for
         commencement? Various circumstances in the situation of the
States of   Turkish empire were unfavourable to war : in the northern
the Turk-   part of the grand signior's territories the influence of the Rus-
ish empire. sians was not only generally great, but conspiracies were with
         strong reason suspected to have been formed by the governors
         of the two principle provinces, Moldavia and Wallachia, to join
         the combined empires. In the east the prince of Georgia had
         renounced his allegiance, and even made successful inroads
         into Asia Minor. The Persians attempted hostilities on the side
Commo-   of Bassora. In the south the turbulent beys involved Egypt
tions in   in civil commotions. These insurrections were believed to
Egypt.   have been fomented by the Russian consul at Alexandria, and
         were headed by Murat Bey, a Mameluke chieftain. The dread-
         ful contests almost desolated that fertile country before any as-
         sistance could arrive from Constantinople. Hassan Bey, the
         grand admiral of the Turkish empire, being consulted, formed
         a project for not only crushing the present insurrection, but an-
         nihilating as a separate class, the Mamelukes whose ferocity
         and rapacity had so long oppressed and plundered Egypt ; and
         for this purpose to extinguish the orders of the beys which had
         headed and directed these outrages. When this essential reso-
         lution should be effected, he intended to divide the country into
         five distinct governments, under the immediate authority of the
         Porte, and all the officers of its new appointment. An arma-
         ment, comprehending two strong fleets, twenty thousand land
         forces with a train of artillery, plentifully supplied with stores
         and provisions, and equipt with equal secrecy and dispatch,
         arrived at Rosetta before the rebellious beys had entertained
         the smallest conception of such a design. The pacha imme-
         diately marched against the Mamelukes, waiting to receive him
         with a more numerous army. After being repeatedly superior

        c Annual Register, 1786   d See Annual Register, 1786, chap. viii

he gained one decisive victory at Grand Cairo, made himself
master of all lower Egypt, compelled the rebel chieftains to fly
into upper, and was preparing to pursue them into those regions,
with the confident expectation of completely accomplishing his
design. The situation of the beys now appeared desperate,
and another year probably would have enabled the pacha to
overthrow the Mameluke power. Should hostilities commence
with Russia and Germany, the whole force of Turkey must be
exerted against these formidable enemies; the pacha and his
army must be immediately recalled: a declaration of war,
therefore, was a necessary dereliction of the pacha's project,
when it was about to be crowned with complete success. On
this view, policy appeared to dictate that war should, if possible, be deferred ; on the other hand, besides the general advantage from striking the first blow, there were special reasons of
considerable weight for anticipating the certain intentions of
the christian empires. Catharine, conceiving the time of beginning the war to depend upon herself and her ally, had not
been hasty in preparation, and was at present chiefly occupied
in providing for her own security, in the north and west, before
she, with her confederate, proceeded to invade the security of
her neighbour in the south and east. Engaged in negotiation
with the powers in the western vicinity of her capital, and not
intending to go to war during that campaign, she had suffered
her military equipments to proceed slowly. Her finances were
by no means in a condition favourable to the increased demands
of hostilities ; she had been greatly exhausted by the former
war: and though her projects and improvements might ultimately tend to enrich her country, yet her establishments, both
for splendour and for force, together with her profuse lar-
gesses to her favourites,[e] or at their instance, were extremely
expensive; and her present expenditure actually exceeded her
present income.

The sultan had beheld with most indignant resentment the
ambitious usurpation of Russia; from her invasion of the Crimea, he appealed with success to his subjects, both as Turks and
mussulmen, on the treatment which he had received; he aroused their patriotism, and their religious enthusiasm; animated
by such incentives, he trusted that their native courage would
operate, and that the ability of the pacha, aided and supported
by other officers, would give it discipline and direction: great
western powers, he not only inferred from their policy, but
knew from their assurances, would interest themselves in a contest so materially affecting the balance of Europe, which they
had ever been so anxious to preserve. The vast accession of
treasure from the capture of Cairo, the depository of Mameluke
riches in addition to their usual revenue, placed the Turkish
finances in a flourishing state.[f] From the situation of his ene-

CHAP.
XL.

1788.

Reasons
which dis-
posed Tur-
key to
strike the
first blow.

e Memoirs of Catharine, *passim:*   f See Annual Register, 1788, chap. i.

CHAP.
XL.

1788.

Treaty of
the pacha
with the
Mame-
lukes.

Catharine
proposes
extensive
cessions by
Turkey to
Russia, as
the only
means of
securing
peace.

my, the state of his own resources, and, beyond all, the spirit
which diffused itself through his people, notwithstanding the
successes of his armies in Egypt, he resolved immediately to
withdraw them from the south, and employ them in striking
the first blow against the autocratrix of the north. The grand
pacha, hearing from Constantinople that his talents and military force might be required elsewhere, lamented the cause, but
did not repine at the order: and since he could no longer hope
to subvert the Mamelukes, endeavoured to avail himself, as
much as possible, of the advantages which they must still retain. In these circumstances he discovered political ability not
inferior to his military; he cautiously concealed both his intention of leaving Egypt and its cause, and intimated to the beys,
that, though, as they themselves must be sensible, his power
was able to effect their speedy destruction, yet his master and
he would more willingly dispense pardon than punishment.
The Mamelukes gladly listened to these overtures, and entered
into a negotiation, in which the pacha so completely wrought
upon their fears, that he compelled them to purchase, with
their still remaining treasures, the forbearance of a war which
he had previously determined to abandon. Hassan, having
thus despoiled and reduced the revolters, returned to Constantinople with such treasures as had not been brought
thither for many years, and were alone sufficient to invigorate
all the preparations for war. The conduct of the Russian ministers at the Turkish capital since the last peace, had been
haughty and imperious, without exciting any strong expressions
of resentment on the part of the Ottomans. Bulgakow, the
ambassador, having been called to attend his mistress at Cherson, on his return repeated a set of propositions g which were
laid down by the empress as the basis of a new treaty, and as
the only means of establishing on a permanent footing the tranquillity of both empires. The general principle of the proposed contract was, the most extensive and important cessions to
Russia by Turkey, without any equivalent; indeed a surrender
of a great part of a territory. So dictatorial and insolent a

g They included, besides the admission of a Russian consul at the port
of Varna, within a hundred and twenty miles of Constantinople, which had
long been an object of much solicitude, a total renunciation of the sovereignty of Georgia: which, as that ill defined denomination of territory
might be extended to all the neighbouring countries, as well as to Min-
grelia, would have afforded sanction to all the past and future encroachments of Russia on that side. Another proposed condition, and still harder
to be admitted, was a new settlement of the provinces of Moldavia and
Wallachia, by which their governors, generally called in Europe princes,
were to hold them by hereditary succession, and in a great measure independent of the Porte But the most singular claim, perhaps, of any, was
that upon Bessarabia, which, as having once belonged to the Tartar khans,
Russia now demanded; a principle of no very limited operation, and which,
if pursued to its full length, would have made the usurpation of the Crimea
a lawful title to all the conquests of Tamerlane. Annual Register,
1788, p. 9.

proposal was immediately rejected: the divan, not satisfied
with this absolute refusal, proposed a set of conditions, not
only as the basis of a treaty, but as the only means for preserving peace. The leading articles was the restoration of the Crimea, that had been usurped by Russia, with others of a similar
nature; and producing a written instrument, which contained
the proffered terms, they required the Russian to sign them on
the spot. Bulgakow declared his incapability of subscribing
any conditions, without express orders from his mistress, and
desired time for receiving instructions concerning some of the
articles: but respecting the Crimea, he avowed, that he could
not venture to mention such a proposal to his sovereign; and
that he well knew, in no fortune, and in no circumstances
whatever, could she ever be reduced to relinquish the sovereignty of that country. A barbarous custom prevailed under
Turkish ignorance and despotism, of imprisoning foreign ambassadors on a rupture with their principals; accordingly, Bulgakow was sent to a castle with seven towers, allotted to alleged offenders against the state: but he was treated with much
more indulgence than former captives in such circumstances
had there experienced. Two days after, on the eighteenth of
August 1787, war was declared against Russia. The manifesto
presented to the christian ambassadors, stated the good 'faith[h]
and the strict attention to the terms of the treaty of Kainardgi,
which the grand signior had uniformly observed; and to this
conduct contrasted the continued violation of the most solemn
conventions by Russia. The empress had instigated the prince
of Georgia to rebellion, and supported him by her troops
against the sultan his sovereign: she had deprived the inhabitants of Oczakow of the benefit of the salt mines, which not
only from time immemorial had been open to them, but which
were expressly stipulated by treaty to be held in common by
both nations. Russia, through her agents, had endeavoured to
corrupt and seduce the subjects of the Porte: she constantly
interfered in the internal policy of the Turkish empire, and
presumed to dictate to the sultan, insomuch that when the
pachas, governors, or judges, by a faithful discharge of their
duty, displeased her, she arrogantly demanded their removal
or punishment. The complaints in the manifesto respecting
commerce were equally numerous; and the whole detail endeavoured to establish, and in many cases with success, a spirit
of encroachment, rapacity, usurpation, and insolence, on the
part of Russia. The court of Petersburgh had regarded Turkey with so much contempt, as to entertain not only no apprehension, but no idea that they would commence hostilities, and
received the manifesto with astonishment. The counter manifesto[i] was expressed in that lofty style which Russia had used

Marginal notes: CHAP. XL. — 1788. — Turkey indignantly rejects those claims, and declares war against Russia. Manifesto. — Counter manifesto of Russia.

h See State Papers, August 24, 1786.
i See State Papers, Sept. 13, 1787.

CHAP. since the peace of Kainardgi; and represented Turkey as hold-
XL.   ing all which she possessed by her merciful bounty exercised
       at that treaty: it repeated her former justification of her con-
1788. duct respecting the Crimea, and, vindicating in detail her own
       acts, endeavoured on the usual tenor of such productions, or
       where argument was wanting, by bold assertion to throw the
       blame upon her adversary. As the season of 1787 was so far
       advanced before hostilities began, no very important operations
       took place. The Turks made several attemps on Russian for-
       tresses, but were not successful. The Russians contented
       themselves with defensive efforts; reserving offensive exertions
       for the next campaign. During the winter the French and
       Spanish ambassadors made several attempts to mediate between
       the belligerent powers, and to procure an armistice. The grand
       vizier declared the proposal to be totally inadmissible, from its
       affording every advantage to Russia, and none to the Porte:
       their perfidious enemy, whose rapacity and ambition were insa-
       tiable, would gladly put them off their guard, and amuse them
Joseph II with a negotiating, until her preparations were complete. The
without   Porte now demanded of the imperial ambassador, what part
provoca-   his master intended to take in the war? That minister, having
tion joins
Russia a   applied for the emperor's instructions, answered by his prince's
gainst Tur- directions, that his imperial majesty, as the friend and ally of
key.   Russia, was bound by treaty to furnish her with eighty thou-
       sand men, in case of war; that if the Porte should consider
       this engagement as an act of hostility, he was prepared to
       abide the consequence; but, on the contrary, if they should
       choose to maintain the good understanding which subsisted be-
       tween the two empires, he would with pleasure undertake the
       office of mediator, in order to prevent the effusion of blood.
His mighty Great preparations were made in all parts of the emperor's
prepara-   dominions: four armies were ordered to be assembled; one at
tions.   Carlstadt in Croatia, under the command of general de Vins;
       another at Peterwaradin in Hungary, commanded be general
       Langlois; a third on the borders of Lithuania, under general
       Febris; and the fourth in the Buccowine, headed by the prince of
       Saxe-Coburg. On the tenth of February 1788, the emperor
Manifesto declared war against Turkey; in his manifesto[k] there is not
of the em- a single sentence asserting the least ground of complaint from
peror.   Austria on her own account; the whole pretext is, that the
       Porte had not acceded to the reasonable requisitions of the
       empress of Russia, and had maltreated her envoy; that by this
       conduct the Porte had manifested hostile disposition to the
       emperor, who was in alliance with the empress of Russia.
       " The Porte (says this manifesto) were not unacquainted with
       " the strict bonds of amity and alliance which unite the courts
       " of Vienna and Petersburg: of this occurrence they were
       " informed, as well by verbal insinuation, as by a memorial

k See State Papers, Feb. 10, 1788,

" presented towards the close of the year 1783. This was
" accompanied with an energetic representation of the nature
" of this alliance, and the danger of encountering its force:
" the Ottoman court have, therefore, themselves only to blame,
" if the emperor, after being for many years employed in the
" preservation of peace, and in his endeavours to live with
" them on the best terms, and after having seized upon every
" opportunity of amicable intervention, finds himself at length
" obliged by their conduct to comply with his engagements to
" the empress, and take a part in the war into which she finds
" herself so forcibly drawn." Such were the principles of
morals exhibited in the emperor's declared reasons for a rupture with the Turks, from whom he did not allege that either
he or his subjects had received the slightest provocation. He
went to war with an unoffending nation, and plunged his own
country in all the evils of hostilities, that he might fight the
battles of the empress of Russia.

Before his declaration, he began his enmity by an ineffectu- Com-
al attempt to surprise Belgrade, which believed itself to be mence-
still in a state of peace: six chosen regiments of imperial in- ment of the
fantry were, at a season of peace, despatched in two divisions campaign.
to attack this fortress: by some failure in the time and place
of rendezvous, the one body did not arrive speedily enough to
assist the other: the first detachment formed under the fire of
the garrison and town, without any prospect of being joined
by the second. The Turkish governor was well prepared for
their reception, and with great coolness sent a polite message
to the Austrian commander, expressing his surprise at seeing,
in a season of profound peace, such an appearance of troops
on their territory, and in the precincts of a fortified city; only
requiring farther to know the cause or motive of their coming.
The Austrian leader answered, that hearing a party of Turks
was preparing to surprise the neighbouring city of Semlin, he
had advanced to counteract their scheme; but that, finding
himself mistaken, he would withdraw his troops. Though
the excuse was accepted, yet conscious of their own intentions,
and afraid that the moderation of the Turks was only affected,
the imperialists crossed the Saave with great precipitation,
and lost a considerable number of men. An attempt of the
same kind was, before the termination of the peace, made
by the Austrians upon the frontier fortress of Turkish Gradisca: this place they endeavoured to take by assault, but
were repulsed with the loss of at least five hundred men killed
and wounded.

War being now declared, both parties made dispositions for
regularly commencing the campaign. The emperor applied to
the court of Warsaw for leave to pass through the Polish dominions, if requisite, in order to form a junction with the Russians.
The king and permanent council replied, that they had no
power to grant the passage demanded, as it entirely depended

CHAP.
XL.

1788.

The empe-
ror takes
the field.

Generous
indigna-
tion of the
Ottomans
against the
imperial
aggressor.

Wise and
skilful con-
duct of the
vizier.'

on the general diet. The emperor had intended to force a passage, if refused, but found it expedient to change his resolution.
He also requested the consent of the Venetians to a Russian
fleet to be received into their harbours, but his requisition was
absolutely refused. Notwithstanding these disappointments,
the imperial troops took the field. The emperor joined his
principal army about the middle of April, being on the south
side of the Danube, and about to invest the small fortress of
Schabatz in Servia. The investment was deferred until the
emperor's arrival, that he might have his share of the military
glory that would accrue from such an achievement. The place
was obviously incapable of resistance, and was easily captured.
The triumph of this victory, however, was soon balanced by a
check which prince Lichtenstein's army received about the
same time at Dubicza. That prince having carried on his
approaches regularly against .the fortress, and made a breach,
which he deemed practicable, resolved to attempt it by storm.
The animosity of the Turks was vehemently inflamed against
the Austrians: in their estimation the emperor was an officious
intermeddler in quarrels which did not concern him or his territories; he endeavoured to take advantage of their recent misfortunes, and without provocation to insult and despoil those
whom he conceived unable to resist his power: they considered him as invading them without even any pretence of wrong,
or any other motives than those of a robber and common enemy to mankind: they were inspired with generous eagerness
to make so flagrant aggression recoil on the head of its author.
This indignant spirit, so merited by its object, pervaded all
ranks of the Turkish host; invigorated their efforts against
the imperial armies, during the whole campaign ; and turned
upon the offender that defeat and disaster, which he had
projected against those who were doing him no wrong.
The garrison of Dubicza, being re-enforced before the assault
was attempted, instead of waiting for the enemy, threw open
their gates, and rushing out, attacked the intrenchments, forced
them sword in hand, and compelled the foes to raise the siege
with the loss of two thousand men.[1] The grand vizier, who commanded the principal army in Bulgaria and Silistria, was a man
of very vigorous abilities: he knew the troops under his command,
and the enemy with which he had to cope: reviewing the history of former wars, and the relative character of the contending forces, he saw that, since the art of war in christian countries had been reduced into a regular system, the Turks, devoid
of discipline, were generally unsuccessful, though a prevalent
impolicy of hazarding pitched battles, which depended chiefly
upon tactical skill; he, therefore, resolved to pursue a plan much
more adapted to his materials: fierce as the Ottomans were in
natural courage, stimulated by strong incentives, and animated
by partial successes, he was fully aware, that they were very

I See Annual Register, 1788, chap. ii.

much inferior to German discipline; he, therefore, resolved not to hazard a general engagement, unless absolutely necessary, but to employ the energy of his forces in attacks on posts and detachments, in which the discipline of the enemy could be of little avail. This mode of warfare would give full scope to the qualities in which the Turks excelled, and prevent the effectual operation of those in which their enemy was so superior : he thus intended to train his troops to obedience, discipline, and military skill, to give them continual opportunities of signalizing their valour in encounters with the enemy ; and gradually to approach to decisive combat, as he found his forces increase in tactical knowledge and efficiency. While the inventive mind Military of the grand vizier was exerting itself in devising changes ne-reforms of cessary for his object, and thus improving the means instrusted the empe-to his direction, the visionary fancy, and flimsy understanding ror. of Joseph, was occupied in projects of reform, which tended to render his materials worse instead of better. Applying to military subjects the same general principle which distinguished his civil government, *that change is improvement*, he contrived Injudici-a variety of innovations, far from being conducive to the pur-ous and poses of war, and really inimical to success, because they dis-precipitate gusted his soldiers. After having profusely lavished his treasures they dis-in equipping mighty armies to fight the battles of another, he en-gust his deavoured to exert his economy by making hard bargains with soldiers. dealers in corn and cattle, contrived new modes of supplying his troops with necessaries; and by these reforms reduced his armies, before the close of the campaign, to the greatest scarcity, distress, and consequently discontent.[m]

The first considerable battle which took place after Dubicza, arose from an attack made by the Turks on the prince of Saxe-Coburg; and though, after a furious contest, they were repulsed by the arrival of an Austrian re-enforcement, yet they being joined by fresh troops, renewed the engagement: for several successive days they fought with various fortune ; but the Turks His opera-astonished the Austrians by their furious valour : with their tions are spears they did not fear to meet hand to hand, the enemy with ineffectual. their guns and bayonets, and showed themselves unappalled by the formidable artillery to which the Germans so much trusted. The Austrians had commenced the campaign with a thorough contempt of their adversaries, and a confident expectation, that the only difficulty they had to encounter would be from the speed of the enemy's flight, but they now underwent a total change of opinion and sentiment, and by a natural transition regarded their foes as the most terrible of mankind. Dislike to the war against an enemy who had been so much mistaken, and discontent on account of the emperor's innovations, was strongly enhanced by the resentment which they entertained against the Russians for not co-operating with the Austrian ef-

m See Annual Register, 1788.

forts: the emperor himself was irritated at the commencement of the war, so different from his sanguine hopes, and, indeed, confident declarations, and determined to venture on an exploit which had been held out as the first object of the campaign; this was the siege of Belgrade; he accordingly adopted measures for speedily carrying the project into execution. The vizier, with an army of eighty thousand men advanced to the relief of this most important fortress, and occupied a strong position covered by the Danube in front, Belgrade and the Saave on the left, the fortress of Orsova on his right, and garrisons on his rear. The imperial army, instead of persevering in their design upon Belgrade, returned to Semlin; and the invaders acted avowedly upon the defensive: various encounters took place, in which great numbers were slain on both sides; but the loss of the Austrians was the greater. Besides war, the Germans had to contend with a still more dreadful enemy in a pestilential fever, very frequent in the Danubian lower provinces, and most destructive to armies which come from higher and more healthy countries; the inactive indolence, under which the grand army languished at Semlin, added to this distemper: as the season advanced to the sickliness of autumn, the mortality became more dreadful; and before the close of the campaign, at least the half of one of the finest armies that ever marched from the Austrian dominions, without performing a single exploit of any note, perished, partly by the sword, but chiefly by disease.

On the side of the Buccovine, where the prince of Coburg commanded, the war languished in the beginning of the campaign, from the failure of the Russians in effecting a junction. The object of the confederates on that side was to invest the fortress of Choczim; and a body of Russian forces arriving, at length, in the beginning of July, preparations were made for the siege: the attempt was greatly facilitated by the governor of Moldavia, who, having been before corrupted by the Russians, treacherously surrendered the country on the first approach of the enemy. The combined generals conceived the reduction of Choczim would immediately follow the investment; but they were mistaken: the seraskier, who commanded the garrison, conducted his defence with such intrepidity and skill, that, after undergoing the severest hardships for upwards of two months, he, at last, on the 29th of September, obtained a most honourable capitulation. The capture of Choczim closed the campaign on the frontiers of Poland. The army third in force employed by the emperor, was that which acted on the side of Croatia, and had been compelled to raise the siege of Dubicza. Prince Lichtenstein's bad health having compelled him to resign the command, he was succeeded by marshal Laudohn: under this veteran officer the Austrians, dejected by the disappointment, both of the secondary and principal armies, began to recover their vigour and confidence. Laudohn made

a second attempt upon Dubicza, which after a very gallant defence he compelled to surrender: he afterwards invested the
fortress of Novi, which in the month of October capitulated.
He proposed to close the campaign by the reduction of Gradisca, after Belgrade, the principal fortress on the northwest
frontier of Turkey, but from the strength of the place, and the
autumnal rains, was compelled to raise the siege. General Fabre,
with the fourth army, contended with the Turks on the borders
of Transylvania, where, being obliged to act in the defensive,
after many bloody contests, he was so far successful as to prevent the enemy from penetrating into the country. The grand
vizier, instead of imitating the quiescent example of the emperor's army at Semlin, was active in annoying the dominions of
the invader. One of the most fertile portions of Lower Hungary is the Bannat of Temiswar, divided by the Danube from
the Turkish Servia, and the fortress of Belgrade. The vizier
made bridges over the river, and sent great detachments, that
he might either desolate and despoil so rich a tract of the enemy's country, or compel the emperor to leave Semlin for the protection of the Bannat, and thus expose his enfebled army to
the continual attacks of the Turkish cavalry, in a dry, firm, and
open country. The Bannat is a tract, which, from the strength
of its capital, and its vicinity to the strong posts in the mountains of Transylvania, is extremely difficult to be conquered;
but having no other fortress of note, besides Temiswar, it is
easy to be overrun by any army that commands the field, and is
secure on the side of the Danube: therefore the vizier wisely
resolved not to attempt the conquest, which would be operose
and ultimately unproductive, but to overrun the country, from
which the advantage to himself would be immediate, by the extreme fertility and high cultivation of the province, and the distress to the enemy would be grievous and ruinous: he accord- The Turks
ingly put his design in execution, invaded the Bannat, and spread overrun
desolation wherever he went. the Hannat

Terror and dismay pervaded the imperial armies and pro- Dismay '
vinces, and even Vienna itself, when they found that, instead of seizes the
those conquests for which the war had been undertaken, the imperial
richest dominions of the aggressor were now seized by the de- armies.
fender: they conceived that, instead of Constantinople, Vienna
might again be the scene of attack. The emperor, as the vizier had foreseen, sent troops to the relief of his province; and
a large division of the grand army was attacked by the Turks
on the eighth of August, with such fury, at Orsova, near the
northern bank of the Danube, that they were defeated, and a
dreadful slaughter ensued. The emperor now thought it necessary to quit his camp at Semlin, and march northward to cover
Temiswar, and secure his communication with his forces in
Transylvania. The vizier being re-inforced with large bodies
of troops, closely followed his enemy: several engagements
took place, in one of which the Austrians were defeated with

.CHAP. the loss of no less than five thousand men, and were obliged to
 XL.   ·abandon their camp with terror and disorder, and the ·remain-
       der of the forces took refuge in Temiswar and Transylvania.
1788. The autumnal rains having set in with· uncommon violence, the
       vizier found, that to keep the field would be ruinous to his
       troops, as little inured to the extreme cold and wet, as their ene-
       mies.were to the extremes of heat; and now that he had effected
       his purpose of doubly annoying the foe, by despoiling his rich-
       ✦est territory and defeating his strongest army, he re-crossed
       the Danube, and returned to Belgrade.   At Constantinople,
       great as was their joy for the victories of the vizier, both the
       people and the court were much displeased with the evacuation
       of the Bannat. The sultan, notwithstanding his condition, so
       very unfavourable to either intellectual or moral excellence, was
       really a· prince of sagacity, prudence, and moderation. He
       perfectly comprehended the policy ·of ·his officer, its reasons
       and motives, and did justice to both. The emperor in Novem-
       ber returned to Vienna; having, for such immense expenses,
       and losses, ·of this bloody and destructive campaign, the
       ruin of ·so valuable a province, acquired three fortresses of little
       significance. Such were to Joseph the first year's consequences
       of unprovoked aggression.·

Operations ··The preparations of the emperor had been formed, in the re-
of Russia. .liance· that a very strong force from Russia would co-operate
       ·with him on the Danube. Such had been the· plan concerted
       between the imperial courts, and such, as we have seen, the
       ·failure· of the execution. The empress of Russia, in seeking
       ·the alliance of Joseph, had considered her own advantage solely,
       without·· any regard to the interest of her confederate she
       ·deemed him a powerful tool, whom, by working on his weak-
       ness, vanity, and ambition, she could apply to her own use: she
       ·had left him to promote her views at his expense, by weaken-
       ing her enemy on one side, while she should direct her efforts to
       her own sole benefit on the other. Joseph was defeated; and
       lavished the blood and treasure of his subjects, without any
       advantage to Austria; nevertheless, he thereby effectually
       served Russia: he employed the chief Turkish force, and by
       his disasters, incurred with such struggles, facilitated her acqui-
       sitions. Her first object was to enlarge and secure her posses-
       sions on the Black Sea. and to form such a body of power as
       could not hereafter be shaken. From the immense extent of her
       dominions, much time must necessarily elapse before her armies,
       spread through the interior country, could reach the frontiers.
       She, meanwhile, equipt a powerful fleet, destined for the Medi-
Effect of terranean, and another naval armament for the Black Sea. In
the ag- the former war she had experienced no hostile opposition, from
gressive any of the maritime powers, to her ,plan of obtaining ,a footing
confede- in the Mediterranean, and was by the mistress of the ocean.se-
racy on the
neighbour- conded in that scheme. Now, a different plan of policy was
ing states. adopted; both the maritime and other powers of Europe re-

garded the confederacy between the two empires, with a jea- .CHAP.
lousy which increased as its objects unfolded themselves; but   XL.
principally directed against the member most powerful both in
resources and in personal character, and whose aggrandizement   .1788.
it tended chiefly to promote. The smaller states firmly resolved not to support a combination by which they themselves
might be eventually crushed; the greater determined, if necessary, 'to oppose a confederacy by which their own independence might be endangered: what part Prussia might take,
could not be affirmed from either the declarations or conduct of
that court, though it might be easily inferred from its interest.
Spain and France were known both to be friendly to the preservation of the Turkish empire; and internal affairs only
prevented the latter from manifesting her disposition in hostile
interference. Holland was sounded on the occasion; her conduct, it was foreseen, would be chiefly governed by the example of England. It became a subject of great political anxiety how
England was to act in the present case: some supposed, that
inspired by resentment for the hostile conduct of Russia in the
armed neutrality, and her manifest indifference to friendly intercourse more recently exhibited, she would now oppose her
naval schemes: others argued that this was the time for procuring most beneficial commercial arrangements from Russia
by seconding her favourite object. Those who were most
thoroughly acquainted with the present British government,
concluded that it would not be determined by so contemptible a
motive to public conduct as resentment, but would be guided by
policy; that not confining its political estimates to mere commercial gain, it would include ultimate security, and that Britain would resume her appropriate character of protector of
Europe, from whatever quarter its independence and security
might be endangered. England soon manifested a determination not to second Russia. The empress had employed agents
to hire British ships for serving as tenders and transports to her
fleet, and a considerable number was provided for that purpose,
when a proclamation in the London gazette, prohibiting British
seamen from entering into any foreign service, threw a fatal
damp on the design. This was attended with a notice to the
contractors for the tenders, that the engagement for shipping
must be renounced; that the ships would not be permitted to
proceed; and that government was determined to maintain the
strictest neutrality during the war. In hopes of diminishing
this great disappointment, Russia applied to the republic of
Holland for a sufficient number of transports to answer the purpose, but that government refused to comply with the request,
and also declared its resolution to maintain the strictest neutrality; and Catharine's expedition to the Mediterranean was
laid aside. On the Black Sea the prince of Nassau commanded
the Russian fleet, and the captain pacha the armament of Turkey. Prince Potemkin with an army of a hundred and fifty

CHAP. thousand men, approached the Euxine, on the banks of the
XI. Bog. The first object of this expedition was the reduction of
Oczakow, a very strong fortress near the Bog, and on the Black
1788. Sea, which, as the frontier garrison of Turkey in that quarter,
was of the highest importance in her wars with Russia, but
more indispensably necessary since her ambitious adversary had
occupied the adjacent Crimea. The preparations of attack
and defence corresponded with the value of the object. On the
twelfth of July, Potemkin invested this fortress aided by his
fleet: the Turkish troops did not exceed twenty thousand men,
nor, indeed, would the garrison have easily contained a greater
number of defenders. During five months this gallant and intrepid band resisted the whole Russian host. In the sixth, the
apparent hopelessness of effort, together with the inclemency of
winter, seemed about to force the besiegers to desist from their
attempt; when Potemkin, ashamed of making so little progress
with so great a power, on the seventeenth of December, as the
last effort, ordered a general bombardment and cannonade of the
place with red hot balls to commence. One of these fell upon
the grand powder magazine, which, being still amply provided,
blew up with so terrible an explosion, as to demolish too great a
portion of the wall to admit of the fortress being any longer ten-
The Rus- able: the Turks still made a most desperate resistance, both in
sians cap the breach and in the streets; but they were at last overpowered,
ture Ocza- and the place was taken by storm.
kow.
State of   While these hostilities were carrying on between the imperial
Sweden. powers and the Turks in the south, war suddenly broke out
against Catharine in the north. Sweden, beyond most nations,
had reason to regard Russia with resentment, since by that
power she had been driven from the high place which, during
the seventeenth century, she had held among the powers of
Europe. Fear, however, of force so enormous, had restrained
the expression of resentment, and produced an apparent connexion between the two countries; and there was always at
the court of Stockholm a strong and numerous party favourable to Russia. It was an uniform policy of the court of Petersburgh to govern by influence and intrigue foreign states,
which they could not so easily command by power: this means
of influence was carried to a much greater extent by Catharine, than by any of her predecessors. One of the chief instruments of her foreign politics, was the seduction of subjects
from allegiance to princes, from whose civil dissensions she expected to derive benefit. It was, indeed, a part of her plan to
weaken the executive authority in the countries which she
wished to direct, that from contest there might be the more
frequent occasions for her interference.[n] As the Swedish revolution, whatever its other consequences might be, strengthened the executive government, it was very disagreeable to
Catharine. Although perfectly satisfactory to the lower clas-

n See Memoirs of Catharine II. passim.

ses, it was and continued to be, as she well knew, extremely
hateful to the aristocracy, whose peculiar privileges it had entirely destroyed; 'thus there was a great faction in Sweeden ini-
imical to the measures of the king; and this party Russia very
constantly supported.   Gustavus was thoroughly acquainted
with these intrigues: the Swedish king was impressed with an
idea, that the liberties of the north were exposed to imminent
danger from the power and ambition of Russia, and the chief
object of his policy was to secure weaker neighbours against
the aspiring Catharine.   These sentiments he endeavoured to
communicate to Denmark, and incite that country to vigilance:
meanwhile he bestowed the closest attention on the internal
improvement of his own kingdom, with such effect, as justified
the apprehensions entertained by Russia from the Swedish
change of 1772.   A prompt, firm, executive government;
union and decision in the cabinet, with a tolerable degree of apparent harmony between the king and the deliberative orders
of the state succeeded to anarchy, weakness, and discord;
there was a good and amply supplied army with an excellent
fleet, and such a well regulated state of finances, as would give
energy to both in case of emergency.   A situation of affairs so
different from the wishes of Catharine, she formed various projects for embroiling, though at the same time she heaped the
strongest expressions of regard on the prince, whose government she was ardently desirous of disturbing.   She professed
a wish to assist, with her experience and counsels, such an'
illustrious pupil; invited him to Petersburgh, and actually gave
him advice to introduce among his subjects, innovations, which,
if adopted, must have rendered him unpopular.   Gustavus
had penetration to discern the motive of the empress; and
private dislike added to public jealousy.   Catharine, desirous
of swaying the counsels of Sweden by her influence, was enraged with Gustavus for successfully opposing her artifices;
and the Swedish monarch detested his neighbour for her endeavours to render him dependent.   The design of subverting
and partitioning the Ottoman empire, with the vast military
preparations for carrying the project into execution, could not
but increase in the highest degree the apprehension and alarm
of the king; he saw by the last war the inability of the Turks
to combat the power of Russia only, how then could they be
supposed capable now of resisting the immense combined force
of both empires? If Russia was already too formidable for the
repose and safety of her neighbours, how must she appear
when clothed and armed in the spoil and force of the Ottoman
empire.   Distant and heterogenous as the Swedes and Turks
were, common interest had often before united them against
Russia.   The feebleness of the Swedish government, however,
under Gustavus's father, and the revolutionary designs of the
son had prevented either from taking a part in the preceding
war.   Differently circumstanced now, the king of Sweden in

CHAP.
XL.

1788.

Intefer-
en e of
Catharine
in the in-
ternal po-
litics of
Sweden.

CHAP.   spring armed by land and sea. The empress pretended, and
XL.   to many even appeared, to disregard these preparations, and
~~~~~   did not deign to inquire into their object. She, however, re-
1788.   plenished her magazines and forts in Finland with ammunition,
troops, and provisions: she was indefatigable in exercising her
usual insidious policy to stimulate and promote dissensions between the sovereign and his subjects. She had two classes in
Sweden from whom she expected co-operation in her designs
against its prince: the first consisted of the ancient aristocracy, which, without any attachment to Russia, submitted to her
influence, in the hopes of recovering, through her, their former
constitution: the second of those who, through bribery or other inducements, had really become partisans of Russia, but pre-
She at-   tended to adopt the views of the nobility. On the former she
tempts to depended as the dupes of her schemes, which they would be-
stir up re- lieve beneficial to Sweden; the latter, she knew, would be the
volt a   willing and ready agents of her designs, without any regard to
gainst   the interest or security of their country. Through these parties
Gustavus   she constantly relied that she would be able to subvert the
present government of Sweden, and render that nation a de-
pency upon Russia. While her emissaries were active in
spreading dissatisfaction though Sweden, and Gustavus was
persevering in his equipments, the empress ordered her ambassador to deliver a memorial to the Swedish ministry, which, in
a very few pages, presents a sketch of that policy by which
Catharine endeavoured to promote discord. Its manifest object was to stir up the subject to sedition and insurrection
against the sovereign: it was not addressed to the king, to
whom only, by the laws regulating intercourse between nations
in the great European republic, it ought to have been addressed: it was directed to all ranks and classes of his subjects, with whom, by the law of nations, a foreign sovereign
could have no ground of correspondence. This document
professed the highest regard for the Swedes, represented the
interest of the people as separate from those of the king and
the promotion of the former° as one of her principal objects.
Mentioning the preparations of Gustavus, it called on the people to join with the empress in preserving the public tranquillity.
'The king A memorial so openly fomenting disobedience and disloyalty,
resents this was severely resented by Gustavus, who, in an answer expo-
conduct.   sed its intent and tendency, and signified to Razouffsky the
Russian ambassador, his majesty's wish that he should forth-
with leave the Swedish dominions. Manifestoes and counter
manifestoes were soon after published, detailing to other powers
War.   the alleged grounds of hostilities. Gustavus immediately repaired to Finland, in order to commence warlike operations:
Military   he himself commanded the army, and his brother, the duke of
and naval Suddermania, the fleet. Various engagements took place by
operations. sea between the Swedes and Russians, in which though the

o State Papers, June 13, 1788.

former displayed extraordinary valour, and gained several ad- **CHAP.**
vantages, yet the Russian squadron (the same that had been **XL.**
intended for the Mediterranean) being much greater in force,
formed, directed, and commanded by admiral Greig, a British 1788.
seaman, proved superior in the result of the campaign, and was
mistress of the Baltic. The king headed so gallant and strong
an army that he entertained well founded hopes of proving superior to all the Russian land forces that could be spared from
southern operations: but in Russian intrigue he found a more
formidable enemy. By the constitution of Sweden it was ordained that war should not be undertaken without the consent of
the states; and the present hostilities had not received that sanction. Catharine had directed her policy to the representation
and exposure of this unconstitutional deficiency, and with such
success, that though the soldiers were eagerly devoted to Gus- Refractory
tavus's pleasure, yet a great part of the officers, consisting of spirit of
the ancient nobility and gentry, declared that they could not, Gustavus's
without violating their consciences and their duty to their coun- officers.
try, draw their swords in a war undertaken contrary to their
country's laws: this refractory spirit rendered the campaign in
Finland ineffective.

To counteract the imperial confederacy of aggression, this Defensive
year a defensive alliance was concluded between the kings of confedera-
Prussia and Britain, and also these princes respectively, and cy between
the states-general, by which, besides reciprocal defence, and Britain,
the maintenance of the existing constitution of Holland, the and the
contracting parties sought the general preservation of the states-ge-
balance of power: they guaranteed each other from any hos- neral.
tile attack, and engaged in concert to preserve peace and tranquillity: if the one were menaced with aggression, the other,
without delay, should employ its good offices, and the most
efficacious means to prevent hostilities, to procure satisfaction
to the party threatened, and to settle things in a conciliatory
manner: but if these applications did not produce the desired
effect, in the space of two months, and if one of the parties
were hostilely attacked, the others undertook to defend and
maintain him in all the rights and privileges, and territories,
which he possessed at the commencement of hostilities. The Principle
general principle of this treaty was that which wise policy of this
dictated for British interference in continental affairs, security, treaty.
and the maintenance of that order and balance on which the
safety and independence of Europe rested. From the general
object of the treaty, the contracting parties had, no doubt, in
view the imperial confederacy, which if its progress were not
checked, had so strong a tendency to endanger the tranquillity
and safety of other states. The interests of England were as
essentially concerned as those of Prussia, in preventing the as- Different
cendency of Russia and Austria.   views of

Mr. Fox's project of continental alliance was to connect our- Mr. Fox
selves with Austria as in former times, that, should a war arise and

CHAP. with France, such a powerful enemy might divide her attention,
XL. and prevent it from being, as in the late war, chiefly directed
to maritime affairs. Mr. Pitt's plan was to form continental
1788. alliances according to existing situations: France was at pre-
Mr. Pitt on sent engaged in no scheme of policy, likely either to affect
this the general safety of Europe, or to provoke England to a war;
scheme of
alliance. she was, indeed, deeply occupied in plans for remedying the
evils of former ambition: what system of alliance might be
wise in circumstances not existing, nor likely to recur, was a
question of speculation rather than immediate practicable policy. The emperor was so involved in the projects of Catharine, that an alliance with him would be difficult, and indeed,
impracticable, except at the expense of adopting his partialities,
and seconding the attempts of Russia. In the formidable
combination between these two powers, that nation became
naturally the ally of Britain, which had a common interest with
Britain in watching the conduct and preventing the aggrandizement of the parties; besides, Prussia, together with England, was closely connected with the constitutional party in
Holland: however just, therefore, Mr. Fox's reasoning might
be, if it were applied to situations that very frequently occurred in our history, yet, in the present circumstances, alliance
with Prussia was more valuable to England, than with any other
great power.

Internal During the recess, that illustrious sage, who had so long pre-
occurren- sided over the judicial decisions of his country, in the eighty-
ces. fourth year of his age, thought that many years of labour,
Retire-
ment of without reproach, might be followed by a few years of rest,
lord Mans- and retired from the judicative bench. For comprehending the
field from law of this particular country, William Murray, a man of the
the king's most acute and extensive genius, had prepared himself by a
bench. profound study of history, general ethics, the philosophy of jurisprudence, investigation of human passions and conduct, and
the civil law, on which the judicial institutions of so great a
part of modern Europe are founded. On this basis he raised
his superstructure of knowledge of the English code: to the
depths of legal science, the accuracy and extent of juridical details, he added the pleasing and impressive accomplishments of
an engaging, graceful, and persuasive eloquence. From such
an union and extent of qualifications, Mr. Murray very early
Improve- rose to most distinguished practice. With such opportunities
ments un- of observing the circumstances of society, of civil actions and
der his ju- engagements, and criminal perpetrations, his penetrating and
dicative
suprema- comprehensive mind saw that the progress of social and espe-
cy, espe- cially commercial intercourse, was producing new combinations,
cially in which had not been specially foreseen when the laws applied
mercantile to such subjects were enacted; therefore he inferred, that the
laws. essential principles of justice required such a latitude of interpretation, as would render existing laws applicable to the new
cases. The intelligent reader must know that there are two

great standards of judicial interpretation; the one the authority CHAP.
of custom, decision, and statute, according to literal definition; XL.
the other, according to the general principles of equity, con-
struing particular law, unwritten or written, in such a way as 1788.
best to answer the great ends of justice. The learned reader
must recollect, that at Rome two sects of civilians arose from
the abovementioned difference; the Proculians and the Sabi-
nians,[p] taking their names from two eminent jurists. The first
of these, resting entirely on authority and definition, merely
considered the letter of the law: the second, interpreting more
freely, endeavoured to adapt it to their conceptions of justice
in the case. Each of these modes has advantages and disad- Strict and
vantages: by the former the parties may know the exact rule liberal in-
by which their dispute will be tried, but may find the literal terpreters
judge difficulted in applying his rule to their case; or entangled their re-
by precedents, forms, and definitions, unable to solve the ques- spective
tion agreeably to substantial justice: by the latter the parties advanta-
may, from a just and competent judge, expect an equitable de- ges and
termination of the question: but they depend on his individual disadvant-
understanding and integrity. By deviating from literal expla- ages.
nation, in the progress of construction the law may be changed;
and thus the judge may become a legislator. During the republican periods of the Roman law, strict and rigid interpretation of usages and decrees prevailed: during its imperial history, latitude of construction was gradually substituted. When
Tribonian and his associate civilians digested the laws into one
great body under Justinian, its constructive character predominated: hence, modern jurists, whose legal doctrines have owed
a great part of their formation to the civil law, have interpreted freely. The close precision of English reasoning has
diffused itself through municipal institutions, and combining
with the English accurate sense of justice, has, in the great
body of the law, made so specific provisions for all cases, when
the laws were enacted, likely to occur, that it may be safely
advanced as a general position, that in every question within
the knowledge, foresight, and intent of our lawgivers, the more
nearly the decision follows the letter of the law, the more fully
will the purpose of justice be answered: but when combinations of engagements and conduct arise, which lawgivers have
not specifically anticipated, and on which the judge is called to
give decision, he must apply the constructive character of the
civil law. The personage before us, partly from his education, Lord
in a great measure from having to meet subjects of judicial in- Mansfield
quiry, to which neither decisions nor decrees could precisely of the lat-
apply; and, perhaps, also partly from that powerful and com- ter kind.
prehensive genius, which in seeking its ends might less regard
customary details than adequacy of means, verged more to a
constructive than literal interpretation: but his judgments

p See account of Justinian's Code, Gibbon, vol. vi.

CHAP.
XL.

1788
Principle
of his de-
cisions in
undefined
and unpre-
cedented
cases.

He is the
Justinian
of English
commer-
cial law.

were just; they repaired injury, compensated losses, and punished crimes; they confirmed civil rights, repressed vice, supported virtue, promoted the order and tranquillity of the
society. The most fertile sources of new cases, during the
long judicial supremacy of this eminent judge, were commerce
with its subordinate arts and instruments. In considering the
various and diversified contracts of this kind, which neither
precedents nor statutes could solve, lord Mansfield recurred to a
very simple principle of ethics; that, where the terms of cove-
nants do not precisely ascertain the extent and obligations, general custom is the most equitable rule of construction. This
principle he applied to delivery of goods, insurances, wharf-
ages, bottomry, and an infinite diversity of mercantile and maritime transactions. In the great department of commercial
jurisprudence, this illustrious judge formed a code of decisions,
digested into a complete system, and may well be syled the
JUSTINIAN OF COMMERCIAL LAW. Lord Mansfield, with a sagacity almost intuitive, apprehended the scope, unravelled the
intricacies, and understood the nature of a case; discerned
whether it was common or new; and if new, by what general
principle or analogy of law its merits were to be ascertained.
In his charges to juries, he made the evidence and arguments
on both sides, and their comparative force, so very clear, and
also the reasons and rules on which he formed his judgment,
that every hearer of common understanding must be master of
the cause, and of the judge's view of the cause; and as his
principles of judgment, the result of combined knowledge and
wisdom, were uniform, by hearing one charge or decision, you
were assured of the decision which he would give in any similar case. The acute penetration of this sage was very happily exerted in eliciting truth from unwilling witnesses; and in
the course of his judicial services he was very successful in
repressing not only a great variety of individual attempts at
perjury, but in preventing the commission of that crime in
certain classes of subjects, in which it was before universally
prevalent.q This judge, thoroughly comprehending, not only,
the general object, but the special compartments of his office,
very carefully distinguished between the duties of a civil and
criminal magistrate. In the former relation he confined his con-

q Especially custom-house questions, and justification of bail. In the
former instance the incredibility of oaths was proverbial; in the latter it
was customary for persons to attend in Westminster-hall on the first day of
term, offering to bail any person who wanted their services, and to swear
themselves to have property to any amount requisite for that purpose. A
person who had not five pounds in the world, frequently bailed to the
amount of ten thousand pounds in a term. His lordship, having discovered
this practice, examined those bondsmen so closely, as to the disposal of
their alleged property, that he drove them from that kind of traffic. From
his time the perjury of fictitious bail has been discontinued, to the great
security of property, and reformation of morals.

sideration, at least so far as it dictated his charge to juries, to
the *damage sustained by the plaintiff*, without adducing the
conduct of the defendant as a reason for enhancing damages
beyond the actual injury, the reparation of which was, and
must be, the sole ground of a *civil action*.[r] He did not confound redress for a private wrong with punishment for a public
wrong ; but by keeping the adminstration of civil and criminal justice separate, as intended and prescribed by law, he
most effectually answered the purposes of both. Lord Mansfield was frequently reproached with attempting to increase
the influence and power of the crown, and was, as we have
seen, exposed to great obloquy from factious demagogues, who
directed and inflamed the populace at the time : but on investigation it was found, that his opinions on the law of libels
were those that had been received by former lawyers and
judges ; that if not precisely correct, they were by no means
of his invention, but adopted on very eminent authority.
With talents to excel in any department, professional excellence
was what lord Mansfield chiefly sought, and sought with the
greatest success. As a politician his lordship aspired not to
the eminence which his abilities could have so easily attained ;
and he never was a leader. The measures which he supported
during various periods, especially the administration of lord North
and his predecessors, were not those on which his character for
wisdom could be founded. As an orator he shone brightly, but
not unrivalled ; though equalled by few, he was by one surpassed.
The engaging and graceful persuasion of a Murray yielded to General
the commanding force of a Pitt. But as a judge he earned the character.
highest fame by combining philosophy and detail, by instantaneously and completely apprehending the case ; and by accurate
discrimination, which, though deviating somewhat from the letter of the laws, bounded his constructions by the lines of equity
and justice. In him you could not always find his precedents in
the law reports, or his rules in the statutes at large, when neither
would apply ; but you must recognise his principles and criteria
of determination in the immutable laws of reason and rectitude.
Lord Mansfield's procedure on the bench was, on the whole,
the best that could be adopted by himself, or any other judge
of consummate wisdom : how far, as a general model, it ought
to be followed by all judges, might be a matter of doubtful inquiry. Perhaps, on the whole, unless a judge be uncommonly
sagacious and able, literal interpretation, keeping as closely as

r This judge was severely blamed for having stated, in his charge to the
jury on the trial of the duke of Cumberland, at the instance of lord Gros-
venor, that the rank or condition of the defendant did not entitle the plaintiff to any increase of damages. It was alleged by party writers, that lord
Mansfield wished to screen a prince of the blood : but the real and fair interpretation is, that in a civil action the plaintiff applies for the redress of
a certain injury ; that the injury done, and that only, is to be considered
in an award of damages.

CHAP. possible to precedent and statute, if in some cases it may be an
XL. obstacle to what is completely right, yet in a much greater variety is a preventive of wrong.

1788. His lordship was succeeded by Lloyd Kenyon, who, by professional ability and industry, had risen to be master of the rolls;
and now being chief justice of the king's bench, was called to
the house of peers by the title of lord Kenyon.

CHAP. XLI.

Distemper of the king—assumes an alarming appearance.—Peers and commons assemble on the day appointed for the meeting of parliament.—Adjourn for a fortnight till the fact be ascertained.—Physicians being examined, agree that a temporary incapacity exists.—Houses meet to prepare for a supply.—Mr Pitt moves an inquiry into precedents.—Mr. Fox
declares, that in such circumstances the heir apparent has a right to exercise the executive power.—Mr Pitt contends that the right of supplying the deficiency is in the people, through their representatives.—Lord
Loughborough, with some distinctions, agrees with Mr. Fox.—Mr. Fox
explains his doctrine, which Mr. Pitt still controverts.—Question brought
to issue.—Determined that the supply of the deficiency rests with the
houses of parliament.—Mr. Pitt proposes that the chancellor shall be
empowered to put the seal to a commission for opening parliament.—After a violent debate, carried.—Frederick duke of York opposes administration.—Mr. Cornwall dying, Mr. Grenville is chosen speaker.—Mr.
Pitt's plan of regency—is submitted to the prince of Wales.—His highness expresses his disapprobation and reasons, but deems it incumbent
on him to accept the office.—Second examination of the physicians.—
Hopes of his majesty's speedy recovery—Mr. Pitt's plan of regency laid
before parliament.—Principle; that the power delegated should answer
without exceeding the purposes of the trust.—Details and restrictions.—
Scheme reprobated by opposition—Arguments for and against.—Princes
of the blood all vote on the side of opposition—Warm praise and severe
censure of, by the respective parties throughout the nation.—Impartial
estimate of its merits.—Irish parliament addresses the prince to assume
the regency of Ireland.—Favourable turn of his majesty's distemper.—
Convalescence—Complete recovery.—Universal joy throughout the nation.—His majesty goes to St. Paul's to return thanks.—Festive rejoic-
ings.—Renewed application for the repeal of the test and corporation acts.
—Chief sects and most eminent men of the dissenters.—Proposed relief
from the penal laws against nonconformists—opposed by the bishops—
Refused.—Slave trade—Mr Wilberforce's motion for the abolition—Arguments for, on the grounds of religion and humanity.—Consideration
postponed to the next session.—Mr Grenville appointed secretary of state.
—Mr. Addington speaker of the house of commons.—Financial scheme.
—A loan required (according to the minister) from a temporary cause.—
Mr. Sheridan disputes his calculations.—Bill for subjecting tobacco to an
excise.—Popular clamour against this bill.—Passed into a law.—Progres-
sive prosperity of India stated by Mr. Dundas—Slow progress of Mr.
Hastings's trial.—Motions respecting it in the commons.—Session rises.

THE close of the present year was marked by a signal calamity which befel this nation; but dreadful as was its first aspect, terrible and afflicting the fears of its continuance, proving
only temporary, grief and dismay for its existence were speedily
overwhelmed in joy for its removal.

The vigorous constitution and temperate habits of our sovereign, now in the prime of his life, appeared to promise to his

CHAP.
XLI.

1788.

Distemper
of the king.

CHAP.
XLI.

1788.

assumes an
alarming
appear-
ance.

The peers
and com-
mons as-
semble on
the day ap-
pointed for
the meet-
ing of par-
liament.
They ad-
journ for a
fortnight
till the fact
be ascer-
tained.

people the long duration of a reign directed to their happiness :
contemplating his countenance and form, with natural health,
invigorated by exercise, and secured by regularity of living, his
people confidently expected, that the paternal goodness, which
for twenty-eight years they had experienced, would, after twenty-
eight years more, be still exerting itself for their benefit, but the
prospect was now overcast.

In the latter end of autumn all ranks were alarmed by a report that his majesty was seriously indisposed. On the twenty-
fourth of October resolved, notwithstanding illness, to perform
the functions of his royal office, he held a levee; and though it
was obvious to every one present, that his majesty's health was
very materially affected, yet no symptoms indicated any definite
species of malady. On the king's return to Windsor, his distemper assumed a very alarming appearance; it was found that it
had formed itself into a brain fever, attended with a delirium,
so often resulting from that dreadful disorder.   The mental
derangement having continued to the beginning of November,
without any intermission, at length became public; and the intelligence diffused grief and consternation among his loyal and
affectionate subjects. The prince of Wales repairing to Windsor to the queen, these personages were attended by the lord-
chancellor, and concerted measures for the management of his
majesty's domestic affairs in the present emergency.   Meanwhile, all those who, by their rank and situation in the state,
were required to take a part in so new and unexpected an exigence, assembled in the capital.   Mr. Fox had spent part of
the recess in Switzerland; to him, as a man from whose extraordinary abilities most beneficial advantage was expected, an
express was immediately despatched, and he hurried to England.   The twentieth of November, was the day on which the
prorogation of parliament was to expire; and the meeting took
place as a matter of course.   The peers and the commons remained in their separate chambers; the chancellor in the upper, and Mr. Pitt in the lower house, notified the cause of their
assembling without the usual notice and summons, and stated
the impropriety of their proceeding, under such circumstances,
to the discussion of any public business; and both houses resolved unanimously to adjourn for fifteen days.   Mr. Pitt observed that, if his majesty's illness should unhappily continue
longer than the period of their adjournment, it would be indispensably necessary for the house to take into immediate consideration the means of supplying, as far as they were competent, the want of the royal presence; it was, therefore, incumbent upon them to insure a full attendance, in order to give
every possible weight an solemnity to their proceedings : for
this purpose it was ordered, that the house should be called
over on Thursday the fourth of December, and that letters
should be sent, requiring the attendance of every member:
orders to the same effect were issued by the lords.   On the day

before the appointed meeting, the physicians who had attended CHAP.
XLI. his majesty were examined by the privy-council, and the three following questions were proposed and answered : first, is his majesty's state of health such as to render him incapable of meeting parliament, or attending to public business ? the answer of all was, he certainly is incapable: the second question respected the probability of a cure, and the duration of the illness : they concurred in the probability of a cure, though they could not limit the time : the third question was, whether the physicians judged from general experience, the particular symptoms of his majesty's case, or both ? the most frequent answer was, from general experience ; but doctor Willis, who entered more minutely on the subject, in his answers, than the other physicians, stated the circumstances which he deemed favourable to a speedy recovery. It was afterwards agreed by both houses, that the physicians should be examined by committees composed, as nearly as possible, of an equal number of members from both parties. It being ascertained that a temporary incapacity existed, Mr. Pitt, in order to pave the way for a supply, moved, that a committee should be appointed to examine the journals and report precedents from similar or analogous cases. Mr. Fox objected to a committee for such a purpose, as nugatory and productive of unnecessary delay : Mr. Pitt (he said) knew there was in the journals no precedent to be found of the suspension of executive government, where there was at the same time an heir apparent of full age and capacity : he himself was fully convinced, upon the maturest consideration of the principles and practice of the constitution, and of the analogy of the common law of the land, that whenever the sovereign, from sickness, infirmity, or other incapacity, was unable to exercise the functions of his high office, the heir apparent, being of full age and capacity, had as indisputable a claim to the exercise of the executive power, in the name and on behalf of the sovereign, during the continuance of such incapacity, as in case of his natural demise:[s] the prince himself, from the peculiar delicacy of his situation, had not made the claim, but there was no doubt that it was his right to supply the place of his father. Mr. Pitt combated this doctrine, as totally inconsistent with actual history and the spirit of the constitution : there were, he admitted, no precedents applicable to this specific cause of incapacity ; but whatever disability had at any time arisen in the executive branch, as the history of the country showed, had been supplied by parliament. When the regular exercise of the powers of government was from any cause suspended, to whom could the right of providing a remedy for the existing defect devolve, but to the people, from whom all the powers of government originated ? To assert an inherent right in the prince of Wales to assume the government, was virtually to revive

1788.

Physicians
being ex-
amined,
agree that
temporary
incapacity
exists.

the houses
meet to
prepare for
a supply.
Mr. Pitt
moves an
inquiry
into pre-
cedents.

Mr Fox
declares,
that in such
circum-
stances the
heir appa-
rent has a
right to ex-
ercise the
executive
power.
Mr Pitt
contends
that the
right of
supplying
the defi-
ciency is in
the people,
through
their re-
presenta-
tives.

s See Parliamentary Debates, Dec. 10, 1788.

CHAP.
XLI
1788.

those exploded ideas of the divine and indefeasible authority of princes, which had justly sunk into contempt, and almost into oblivion. Kings and princes derive their powers from the people, and to the people alone, through the organ of their representatives, did it appertain to decide in cases for which the constitution had made no specific or positive provision. On these grounds Mr. Pitt insisted that the prince had no more RIGHT to be appointed to supply the existing deficiency, than any other subject; though he admitted that, in the present case, *expediency* dictated that parliament should offer him the regency: substitution of another to execute the office of a king, during a temporary incapacity, was merely a measure of necessary policy: it was incumbent on legislature to intrust the authority to such person or persons, as it should deem most likely to answer the purpose: after these observations the question being put, it was carried that a committee should be appointed to search for precedents.

Lord Loughbo-rough with some distinctions, agrees with Mr. Fox.

Mr Fox explains his doc-trine, which Mr. Pitt still contro-verts.

In the house of peers, lord Loughborough supported the position which Mr. Fox had advanced, and adduced great legal ingenuity and acuteness to prove, that the right ascribed to the prince was a corollary from the act of settlement, the general analogy of English law, the privileges and immunities peculiar to the prince, and belonging to no other subject. He admitted, however, that the exercise of this right ought not to commence until parliament had declared the sovereign's incapacity. Mr. Fox at the next meeting of the commons, made an explanation of his meaning, agreeable to lord Loughborough's interpretation, and said, that his expressions on a former day had been misrepresented: his position, which he was still ready to maintain, was that the houses of parliament had the right to adjudge the fact of incapacity, but on such adjudication the heir apparent had the right of holding the reins of government whilst the incapacity lasted: as, however, Mr. Pitt agreed with him, that in the present circumstances the prince was the person who ought to hold that office it would be much more prudent to abstain from discussing so nice and subtle distinctions. Mr. Pitt replied, that he differed as much from Mr. Fox respecting the question of right, now that he had explained his meaning, as before such an explanation. Mr. Fox (he said) now asserted, that the prince of Wales had a right to exercise the royal authority, under the present circumstances of the country; but that it was a right not in possession, until the prince could exercise it on what he called the adjudication of parliament. He on his part denied that the prince of Wales possessed any right whatever, and upon that point Mr. Fox and he were still at issue. This was a very important question, and must be decided before they could proceed any farther; there might be differences of opinion whether any regency was necessary as yet, and a difference of opinion might arise, if necessary, what were the powers requisite to be granted to the regent? but nothing could

be determined till the matter of right should be discussed. He
not only challenged Mr. Fox to adduce either precedent or law
to support his doctrine, but actually showed from history that
such a claim of right had been made, and had been resisted
by parliament. In the reign of Henry VI. the duke of Gloucester, next heir to the crown,[t] claimed the regency during the
minority of the king, and applied to parliament; the answer
to this claim was, that he neither had by birth, nor by the will
of his brother, any right whatever to the exercise of royal authority: they, however, appointed him regent, and intrusted
him with the care of the young king. At the revolution, parliament proceeded on the same general principle; the king had
ceased to act; to supply this deficiency, parliament acted as
legislators: they did not restrict themselves to a simple address
to the prince of Orange to accept the crown; they felt not only
that they must have a king, but they must have a king on certain terms and conditions: they did what amounted to a legislative act: they came to a resolution to settle the crown, not on
the prince of Orange and the heirs of his body, nor on the princess Mary and the heirs of her body, but on the prince and
princess jointly. Here it was evident that, whatever the necessity of the case required at that time, the lords and commons possessed the power to provide for it, and consequently,
whatever the necessity of the case demanded at present, the
power belonged to the lords and commons to supply the deficiency. Parliament could have no possible interest in acting in
any other way than as duty prompted and wisdom directed:
and, as it was agreeable to history, reason, and expediency,
that they should provide for a specific object, it became them,
in making the provisions, to extend or contract the trust to be
delegated according as they thought either necessary for its
execution. Thus, according to Mr. Pitt, precedent confirmed
the analogy of the constitution, and both concurred with the
expediency which required that the peers and the representatives of the people should provide for supplying an unforeseen
deficiency.

Having grounded his doctrine on these arguments and facts, The
concerning the right which Mr Fox had asserted to be vested question
in the heir apparent, Mr. Pitt proposed on the sixteenth of De- brought
cember three resolutions:[u] the first stating his majesty's present to issue.

t After the death of prince John of Lancaster duke of Bedford.

u The following are the resolutions: 1st, That it is the opinion of this committee. that his majesty is prevented, by his present indisposition, from
coming to parliament, and from attending to public business; and that the
personal exercise of the royal authority is thereby for the present interrupted: 2dly, That it is the opinion of this committee, that it is the right and
duty of the lords spiritual and temporal, and commons of Great Britain,
now assembled, and lawfully, fully, and freely, representing all the estates
of the public of this realm, to provide the means of supplying the defect
of the personal exercise of the royal authority arising from his majesty's

CHAP. unfitness for performing the functions of the kingly office: se-
XLI. condly, that the lords and commons had the ri ht to provide for
that case, and were in duty bound to make such provisions:
1788. thirdly, that the lords and commons should determine on the
most effectual means of exercising their right, by vesting the
powers and authority of the crown on behalf of the king
during his majesty's illness. Several amendments were proposed; without detailing these, it is sufficient to mention that
their object was to address the prince of Wales, heir apparent,
and of mature age, beseeching him to take upon himself the
administration of the civil and military government of the
country, during the indisposition of his majesty, and no longer.
The admission of this proposition would have precluded every
limitation of the kingly power, thus to be intrusted to a regent.
Its supporters contended, that every part of the royal authority
and prerogative was necessary for the discharge of kingly
duties; if the regent were not intrusted with the whole power,
he could not perform all the duties. By its opponents it was
answered, that the situation for which they were called to provide was, from the concurrent testimony of the most competent
witnesses, only temporary; the supply wanted, therefore, was
also temporary. Various parts of the royal establishment
belonged to the splendour and dignity of the crown, more than
to its power or its executive functions. So much authority as
was necessary to enable the regent to act as executive magistrate during the illness of the sovereign, should be conferred,
but no more. The bounds and circumscriptions necessary
upon this principle would be matter of cautious consideration
to parliament, according to all the circumstances of the case.
Such restrictions would be impossible if the present amendment were adopted. Parliament was to reflect on the present
as a general question that would be a guide to future ages:
they were to form measures for insuring the restitution of his
power to the principal, when a substitute was no longer necessary; and in making this provision they were to consider
men as men are generally found Cases might arise, in which,
if an heir obtained possession, he might be unwilling to return to expectancy; or, though an heir were ever so dutifully disposed himself, he might be misled by evil counsellors. No
character could be more meritorious or more worthy of confi-

said indisposition, in such manner as the exigency of the case may appear
to require: Resolved, "That for the purpose, and for maintaining entire the
constitutional authority of the king, it is necessary, that the said lords
spiritual and temporal. and commons of Great Britain, should determine
on the means whereby the royal assent may be given in parliament to such
bill as may be passed by the two houses of parliament, respecting the exercise of the powers and authorities of the crown, in the name and on the
behalf of the king, during the continuance of his majesty's present indisposition." See parliamentary reports, Dec. 1788.

dence than the present prince of Wales. Constitutional policy, CHAP.
however, proceeds not upon individual merits, but on general XLI.
expediency. Every part of the principal authority was not
wanted to the efficiency of the substitute. Why should they con- 1788.
fer on a delegate any more power than was necessary to answer
the purposes of the delegation? Our sovereign possessed as
much power as was consistent with a free government, and no
more: the regent was, by the scheme of ministers, to possess
as much as was consistent with the object of his temporary
office, and no more; there was no disrespect offered to the
regent by a circumscription applying to the particular circumstances, as there was no disrespect to our kings in the circumscription affixed to their authority by the constitution. In
both cases the principle was the same; princes are men, and
fallible like other human beings; let them be invested with all
the authority which is conducive to the public welfare, and
restrained from that which might be prejudicial. Mr. Pitt informed the house, that he intended, if the resolutions should
be adopted by the commons, and also meet the concurrence
of the lords, to propose, that the lord high-chancellor should
be empowered to put the great seal to a commission for opening the parliament in the usual form; and that as soon as a
bill should be passed by both houses for providing for the
exercise of the royal authority, under certain limitations, during his majesty's indisposition, another commission should be
sealed for giving to such act the royal assent. This project
was very strenuously opposed: first, as unnecessary; because
all parties concurring unanimously in opinion that the prince
of Wales should be invested with the regency, the procedure
by address or declaration was the most simple, and the most
consonant to the practice and constitutional functions of the
two houses: the measure was unwarrantable in fact it altered
an essential part of the state; it made the two houses KINGS.
To fix the form of a legal sanction on their proceedings, they
were to give fictitiously a royal assent, but in reality their own assent to their own acts. If the houses assumed to themselves powers which belonged to the legislature, and proceeded to legislate,
they would act in direct violation of the spirit of the constitution:
even to a positive act of parliament, the 13th of Charles II. Determin-
which expressly declared, that the two houses could not make supply of
laws without the king: after a long debate the resolutions the defici-
were voted. Having passed the house of commons, they were ency rests
introduced to the lords by the chancellor, and similar amend- with the
ments were proposed. In the debate which ensued on that houses of
occasion, the question of right was resumed: an active part parliament
was taken by their royal highnesses, the princes, and particular- Frederick
ly by his majesty's second son, Frederick duke of York. Yorkoppo,
  This illustrious youth received the first part of his education ses admi-
in his native country. Destined for the military profession he nistration.
was afterwards sent to Germany, and spent several years in his

CHAP. own bishopric at Osnaburg, and his royal father's electoral do-
XLI.   minions: thence he repaired to the court of Berlin, and com-
       pleted his military education under the system which the Prus-
1788. sian hero had established. Eminently distinguished for manly
       beauty and graces, in natural endowments and acquired quali-
       fications, he was one of the most accomplished princes of the
       age: having the strongest fraternal affection for his elder
       brother, between whom and him the closest intimacy from their
       childhood, had enhanced the sentiments of relation, on coming
       back to England he chiefly associated with the prince of Wales,
       and becoming acquainted with the companions of that exalted
       personage, he in a considerable degree adopted their political
       opinions. " No claim (said his highness) has been made by
       " my royal brother; I am confident the prince too well under-
       " stands the sacred principles which seated the house of Bruns-
       " wick on the throne of Great Britain, ever to assume or exer-
       " cise any power not derived from the will of the people, ex-
       " pressed by their representatives, and your lordships in par-
       " liament. On this ground, I hope, the house will avoid pres-
       " sing a decision which certainly was not necessary to the great
       " object expected from parliament, and which must be most
       " painful in the discussion to a family already sufficiently agita-
       " ted and afflicted: these (continued his highness) are the sen-
       " timents of an honest heart, equally influenced by duty and
       " affection to my royal father, and by attachment to the con-
       " stitutional rights of his subjects; and I am confident, that if
       " my royal brother were to address you in his place, as a peer
       " of the realm, these are the sentiments which he would dis-
       " tinctly avow." Though the peers warmly approved of the
       general sentiments expressed by his highness, and of the dig-
       nified manner in which they were delivered, yet the majority
       thought it necessary, since the question of right had once been
       started, to have it fully discussed; and the resolutions were car-
       ried by a considerable majority. A strong protest was entered
       against agreeing to these resolutions, and signed by the dukes of
       York and Cumberland, and forty-six other peers.[x] These pro-

Mr. Corn ceedings of the house occupied the greater part of December.
wall dying, On the twenty-ninth of the month Mr. Cornwall, speaker of the
Mr Gren- house of commons, was seized with a dreadful illness, which, four
ville is ap- days after, the second of January 1789, ended in his death. The
pointed house meeting on the fifth, Mr. William Grenville was proposed
speaker by the friends of ministers as his successor, and sir Gilbert Elliot
1789.   by opposition: the election was carried in favour of the former
       by a majority of two hundred and fifteen to one hundred and forty-
       four.

Mr. Pitt's The preliminary subjects having been discussed by both
plan of re- houses, Mr. Pitt, before he explained his plan of regency to
gency is parliament, submitted its outlines to the prince in a letter,
submitted
to the
prince of
Wales.   x See their names, State Papers, Dec. 29, 1788.

wherein he offered either to attend his highness, should any
farther explanation be required, or to convey such explanation,
in any other mode which the prince should signify to be most
agreeable. This letter, sent on the thirtieth of December,
stated the plan to be that which, according to the best judgment which they were able to form, his majesty's confidential
servants had conceived proper to be proposed in the present
circumstances: the outlines were, that his highness should be
empowered to exercise the royal authority, in the name and on
the behalf of his majesty, during his majesty's illness, and to
do all acts which might legally be done by his majesty. The
care of his majesty's person, the management of the household, and the direction and appointment of the officers and
servants therein should be in the queen, under such regulations
as might be thought necessary. The power to be exercised by
his highness should not extend to the disposal of either real or
personal property of the king (except in the renewal of leases,
to the bestowal of any pension, the reversion of any office, or
any appointment whatever, but during his majesty's pleasure,
except those granted by law for life; that his highness should
not be empowered to confer the dignity of the peerage on any
person except his majesty's issue who had attained the age of
twenty-one years. This plan, the letter declared, was formed
on the supposition, that his majesty's illness was only temporary, and would be of no long duration. It would be difficult
to fix beforehand the precise period for which these provisions
ought to last; but should his majesty's recovery be protracted
to a more distant period than there was then reason to expect,
the consideration of the plan, according to the exigency of the
case, would be open to the wisdom of parliament.[y]

On the first of January an answer was delivered by his royal His high-ness ex-presses his disappro-bation and reasons, but deems it incum-bent on him to ac-cept the office.
highness to the lord-chancellor to be conveyed to Mr. Pitt.
Respecting the measures already embraced by parliament, his
highness declared he would observe a total silence: no act
of his lords and commons could be a proper subject of his animadversion: but (he said) when, previously to any discussion
in parliament, the outlines of a scheme of government are sent
for his consideration, in which it is proposed that he shall be personally and principally concerned, and by which the royal authority and the public welfare may be deeply affected, the prince
would be unjustifiable were he to withhold an explicit declaration of his sentiments: his silence might be construed into a
previous approbation of a plan, the accomplishment of which,
every motive of duty to his father and sovereign, as well as of regard for the public interest, obliges him to consider as injurious
to both. The scheme communicated by Mr. Pitt is a project
for producing weakness, disorder, and insecurity, in every
branch of the administration of affairs; a project for dividing

y See State Papers, Dec. 30, 1788.

CHAP.
XLI.

1789.

the royal family from each other; for separating the court from the state; and therefore by disjoining government from its natural and accustomed support, a scheme for disconnecting the authority to command service, from the power of animating it by reward; and for allotting to the prince all the invidious duties of government, without the means of softening them to the public by any one act of grace, favour, or benignity. These positions the prince adduced detailed arguments to support: the plan (he proceeded) was not founded on any general principle but was calculated to infuse groundless jealousies and suspicions in that quarter, whose confidence it should ever be the first pride of his life to merit and obtain. With regard to the object of the limitations, his majesty's ministers had afforded him no light; they had informed him *what* powers they meant to refuse him, but not WHY they were to be withheld: he deemed it a fundamental principle of this constitution, that the powers and perogatives of the crown are vested there, as a trust for the benefit of the people; and that they are sacred only as they are necessary to the preservation of that poise and balance of the constitution, which experience has proved to the true security of the liberty of the subject: but the plea of public utility ought to be strong, manifest, and urgent, which calls for the extinction or suspension of any one of those essential rights in the supreme power or its representative. If security were wanted, that his majesty should repossess his rightful government whenever it pleased Providence to remove his present calamity, the prince would be the first to urge the adoption of measures conducive to that purpose, as the preliminary and paramount consideration of any settlement in which he would consent to share: if attention to what his majesty's feelings and wishes might be on the happy day of his recovery were the object, the prince expressed his firm conviction, that no event would be more repugnant to the feeling of his royal father, than the knowledge that the government of his son and representative had exhibited the sovereign power of the realm in a state of degradation, curtailed authority, and diminished energy; a state hurtful in practice to the prosperity and good government of his people, and injurious in its precedent to the security of the monarch, and the right of his family. The provision respecting the king's property was totally unnecessary, as that was perfectly secured, during his majesty's life, by the law of the land. The prince having discharged, as he conceived, his indispensable duty in giving his free opinion on the plan submitted to his consideration, concluded with declaring in the following terms, his reasons for accepting, notwithstanding the objections he had enumerated, the proffered trust: His[z] conviction of the evils which may arise to the king's interests, to the peace and happiness of the royal family, and to the safety and welfare of the

z The letter is written in the third person. See State Papers, January 1, 1789.

nation, from the government of the country remaining longer in its present maimed and debilitated state, outweighs, in the prince's mind, every other consideration, and will determine him to undertake the painful trust imposed upon him by the present melancholy necessity (which of all the king's subjects he deplores the most,) in full confidence, that the affection and loyalty to the king, the experienced attachment to the house of Brunswick, and the generosity which has always distinguished this nation, will carry him through the many difficulties inseparable from this critical situation, with comfort to himself, with honor to the king, and with advantage to the public.

Such was the substance of the letter written by the heir apparent on this momentous subject, and though great numbers did not assent to his highness's conclusions, concerning the inexpediency of the proposed restrictions, yet every judge of composition and argument allowed that it was a very masterly performance.

On the sixth of January, when Mr. Pitt was about to propose his plan of regency to the house of commons, Mr. Loveden, member for Abingdon, moved, that, as the intended limitations would have a reference to the state of his majesty's health, and several weeks had elapsed since that had been ascertained, the physicians should be again examined. After a very warm debate, including a considerable share of personal altercation, it was agreed that a new committee should be appointed, and that the physicians should be interrogated. The result of the examination was, that his majesty's recovery continued probable. The proceedings of the committee having occupied about a week, the report was brought up on Tuesday the thirteenth of January, and appointed to be taken into consideration the following Friday. On the sixteenth Mr. Pitt opened his plan to the house: the subject (he said) divided itself into three distinct heads: first, the nature of the king's illness; secondly, the principles upon which the two houses were authorized to act on this occasion: and thirdly, the application of those principles to the measures which he should propose, of remedying the present defect in the personal exercise of the royal authority. From the recent examination, they were confirmed in the conclusions drawn from the former, that his majesty was by his illness rendered incapable of attending to the business of his station; but that it was probable he might recover, and once more be able to resume the reigns of government. In these two points all the physicians were agreed, they were not all equally sanguine in their hopes of his majesty's recovery: it was, however, extremely satisfactory, that the expectations of the several physicians were respectively favourable, in proportion to their knowledge of that particular distemper and that individual case: the deficiency for which they were called to provide was temporary, and would probably be short. The principles by which the houses were to proceed, arose from the nature and

Marginal notes:

CHAP. XLI.

1789.

Second examination of the physicians.

Mr. Pitt's plan of regency is laid before parliament.

Principle; that the power

CHAP.
XLI.

1789.
should an-
swer with-
out ex-
ceeding
the pui po-
ses of the
trust.
Details and
restric-
tions.

probable duration of the deficiency; they were to provide for
the present necessity only, and to do no more than it required;
they were also to guard against any embarrassment in the resumption of the royal authority, and therefore to grant such
powers only as were requisite for the government of the country
with energy and effect. On these principles he had framed his
plan; of which the outlines were exhibited in his letter to the
prince of Wales. The regent was to exercise the whole royal
authority, subject to restrictions which were intended not to interfere with executive efficiency. The limitations were reducible to four heads: first, that the power of his highness
should not extend to the bestowal of the peerage, except to his
majesty's issue that had attained twenty-one years of age. To
prove the propriety of this limitation, Mr. Pitt adduced three
grounds upon which this prerogative was intrusted by the constitution to the crown: first, it was designed to enable the king
to counteract the designs of any factious cabal in the house of
lords: secondly, to enable the sovereign to reward eminent
merit: thirdly, this power was designed to provide for the fluc-
tuations of wealth and property in the country; by raising men
of great landed interest to the peerage, that branch of the legislature would be always placed upon its true and proper basis:
for none of these objects was this prerogative wanted in the
present case; there was no probability that any such cabal should now be formed to obstruct the government of
his royal highness; on the other hand, if this power were
conferred on the regent, such a number of peers might be
created, as would greatly embarrass the government of his
majesty on his restoration to health: as a reward of merit, or
a nobilitation of property, the suspension of this prerogative,
during the *temporary* incapacity which they were supplying,
could be attended with no material inconvenience: should the
unfitness prove more permanent than they expected, parliament
could extend the regent's power as far as might be then deemed
necessary for the public welfare. On the same principle was founded the second restriction, by which the regent was not empowered to grant any pension or place for life, or in reversion, except
such offices as are by law held for life, or during good behaviour:
the powers restrained were not necessary to the executive government, temporarily to be held by the regent; and their exercise
might be injurious to the government of his majesty on his recovery. The third restriction, respecting the king's personal property, he scarcely thought necessary; but as they were acting on parliamentary principles, and endeavouring to make their provisions
as comprehensive as possible, he accounted it his duty to make
this regulation a part of his plan. The fourth resolution was
intended to intrust the sovereign's person, during his illness, to
the guardianship of the queen: he proposed to put the whole
of his majesty's household under her authority, investing her
with all powers to dismiss and appoint as she should think

Argu-
ments for

proper: unless she held this control, the queen could not discharge the important trust committed to her care: a council
should be named to assist the queen with advice, but without
any power of control: trustees should be appointed to manage
the real and personal estate of the king, but should have no
power of disposing any part of it, except by lease. The propositions were very strenuously supported, both upon the arguments which the minister himself adduced, and on others.
The law officers maintained, as a fundamental doctrine, that
the king's political character was, in the eye of the law, inseparable from his personal; that it remained entire and perfect,
and would continue so to do until his natural demise; and to
this principle frequent reference was made in the course of the
debates. The senator who vindicated the plan of Mr. Pitt, in
the most extensive details, elaborate research, and accurate in-
duction, was Mr. Grenville, the new speaker: in the committee
this member took an opportunity of delivering his opinion;
and for near three hours both occupied and engaged the attention of the house. His oration on the subject stated every historical fact, explained and enforced all the arguments of precedent, law, and constitutional analogy, by which the proceedings of the ministers were justified; and also endeavoured to
combat each and all objections which they encountered. From
the constitutional history of the country he attempted to demonstrate, that the principle on which our ancestors both conferred and bounded the powers of a regent were the same that
were now applied. It was proposed on the one hand to establish a form of government capable of conducting the public
business; and on the other, to provide complete and ample security to enable the sovereign to resume the exercise of his authority, fully, freely, and without embarrassment, when the existing deficiency should terminate. Keeping this principle uniformly in view, he applied it to the various restrictions, and
contended, that the extent of the delegation was sufficient for
the energetic useful execution of the trust; and that the bounds
were necessary to the security of resumption. The propositions were opposed on the following grounds: they tended, it
was affirmed, to debilitate and humble the executive government, by stripping it of its legal prerogatives: the power of
bestowing peerages was an integral part of the royal authority,
a shield that, from its earliest days, the constitution had provided for its own defence and preservation; and which could not
be wrested from the crown without bringing destruction on our
polity. Mr. Fox, with his wonted energy, impugned the
doctrine of the law officers, concerning the inseparability of
the king's personal and political character: he wished (he said)
to hear this doctrine explained; for how that person, whose
political faculties were confessedly suspended by a severe visitation of Providence, could still exist in the full enjoyment of
his political character, was beyond his understanding to com-

CHAP. prehend; the doctrine seemed, indeed, to be founded on those
XLI.   blind and superstitious notions, by which, as they all knew
       from history, human institutions had been, as it were, deified;
1789. and which were inculcated for the purpose of impressing a
       strong and implicit reverence of authority in the minds of the
       multitude: while the supporters of this doctrine took up the
       superstitions of antiquity, they rejected their morality; they
       enveloped the sacred person of the king with a political veil,
       which was calculated to inspire awe and secure obedience;
       but laboured to enfeeble the arms of government, to cripple it
       in all its great and essential parts, to expose it to hostile attack
       and to contumely; to take from it the dignity which apper-
       tained to itself, and the use for which it was designed towards
       the people. He reprobated with peculiar severity the restric-
       tions which were proposed on the creation of peers : Mr. Pitt
       had conferred that rank upon no less than forty-two persons
       during the five years that he had been in office; and he had
       not the pretext of saying that any cabal was formed to thwart
       his measures in the house of lords, which made such a promo-
       tion necessary; and if such were the means to which he had
       been obliged to resort, surrounded with all the power and influ-
       ence of the crown, what must be the condition of those who
       should have to contend, in the crippled state to which they
       would be reduced, against an opposition armed with so large
       a portion of the usual patronage of government. He express-
       ed his indignation and abhorrence of a project that placed in a
       state of competition persons so nearly connected by blood, by
       duty, and by affection, and thereby excited that mutual jeal-
       ousy which, in some degree, is inseparable from the human
       mind : how much (he said) had they to answer for, who, with
       a perfect knowledge of this weakness of human nature, wick-
       edly and wantonly pursued a measure which might involve the
       empire in endless distractions. To these objections ministers
       replied, that though the prerogatives proposed to be withheld
       from the regent were necessary for the sovereign, they were
       not indispensably requisite to a temporary substitute : the regent
       was to possess the supreme direction of the ordnance, army,
       and navy; the power of making war, peace, and alliances;
       the choice of his ministers, and all subordinate officers; the
       appointment of bishops and judges: such authority was suffi-
       cient for a temporary exercise of the executive functions,
       though restrained from promotions and donations; the in-
       fluence of which, lasting after the trust had terminated, might
       have disturbed the government of the rightful holder. These
       were the grounds on which Mr. Pitt, his coadjutors and sup-
       porters, replied to the objections of the other party, on the
       restriction concerning peerages. The resolution, vesting in the
       queen, instead of the regent, the appointment and direction of
       the household officers, was opposed upon more special grounds :
       it withheld a power from a responsible, to confer it on an irre-

sponsible person; tended to establish in the empire a fourth estate, against which Mr. Pitt had exerted himself so successfully
a few years before; and was calculated to excite discord
between the members of the royal family. If the nomination of attendants were withheld. from the regent because it
was dangerous to trust him with such appointments, the remedy was inadequate to the disease; for the army and navy
could not be very harmless engines in the hands of a man,
to whom it would not be safe to trust the nomination of lords
and grooms of the bed-chamber.ʸ Ministerial speakers
replied, that it was unanimously agreed the royal person
should be instrusted to her majesty; the disposal of the household was necessary for her execution of that trust; besides,
the officers in question, though a proper and becoming part of
the state and splendour of a monarch reigning over a great and
opulent people, were not necessary to the energy of the executive government during its temporary delegation: on these
grounds the resolutions were supported and opposed in both
houses: they were at last carried; and it was voted, that the
prince and queen should be informed of the measures of legislation. On the thirtieth of January the resolutions were presented to these illustrious personages, by a committee of peers
and commoners. The answer of his highness was similar in
substance to the concluding parts of his letter to Mr. Pitt, which
are already embodied in this narrative. Her Majesty's answer
was to the following effect: " My lords and gentlemen, my
" duty and gratitude to the king, and the sense I must ever en-
" tertain of my great obligations to this country, will certainly
" engage my most earnest attention to the anxious and momen-
" tous trust intended to be reposed in me by parliament. It
" will be a great consolation to me to receive the aid of a coun-
" cil, of which I shall stand so much in need, in the discharge

---

y Lord North, declining in years, and afflicted with blindness, took a
very active share in opposing the plan of regency, and fully showed, that
the appropriate excellencies of his eloquence, ingenuity of argument,
promptness of reply, and brilliancy of wit, were still undiminished. Expatiating upon the arguments stated in the text, the minister (he said)
strains at a gnat, but swallows a camel: he is not afraid to delegate the
great functions of the executive power, but he startles at the small: take
the patronage, take the disposal of the civil, political, and military appointments, but keep away from the court: command the navy and army, but
abstain from the household troops: let the houses of parliament become
executive, as well as legislative; break down the barrier of the constitution, cripple the sovereign power: all this you may do, but touch not the
pages, grooms of the stole, gentlemen ushers, or lords of the bed chamber.
This, said his lordship, reminds me of the stories with which my old nurse
used to entertain me about the achievements of witches; they could ride
through the air, agitate the elements, raise the wind, bring rain, lightning,
and thunder; all this they would do without flinching, but if they came to
a *straw*, there they boggled, stumbled, and could proceed no farther.

CHAP.
XLI.

1789.

Princes of
the blood
all vote on
the side of
opposition.

Regency
bill.

Recovery
of the king.

"of a duty wherein the happiness of my future life is indeed
"deeply interested, but which a higher object, the happiness
"of a great, loyal, and affectionate people, renders still more
"important." The answers being communicated to the houses, it was moved in the house of lords, that letters patent
should be issued under the great seal, empowering certain commissioners to open and hold the king's parliaments at Westminster.[z] The arguments already adduced on this subject, by
both parties, were frequently repeated; and the names of the
proposed commissioners were read, and at their head were the
prince of Wales, the duke of York, the dukes of Gloucester and
Cumberland. The duke of York, rising, said he had not been
informed that it was intended to insert his name in the commission; he, therefore, had not been able to take steps to prevent the nomination: not wishing to stand upon record, and to
be handed to posterity as approving such a measure, he could
not sanction the proceedings with his name: his opinion of the
whole system adopted was already known: he deemed the proposition, as well as every other that had been embraced respecting the same object, to be unconstitutional and illegal: he
desired, therefore, to have no concern with any part of the business; and requested that his name, and the name of his brother, the prince of Wales, might be left out of the commission:
the duke of Cumberland desired his own name and the duke of
Gloucester's might also be omitted: accordingly the princes
were left out of the nomination. The resolution being carried,
was on the second of February adopted by the commons; the
following day the houses assembled as a regular parliament,
and, the lord-chancellor being indisposed, earl Bathurst, president of the council, opened the causes of the present meeting,
and the objects for which they were to provide. On the sixth
of February Mr. Pitt introduced his regency bill, founded on the
principles already investigated, and the resolutions already voted.
Its various clauses and provisions having undergone in detail
much opposition, it was passed on the twelfth of February,
carried to the house of lords, and read a second time without opposition.

Her majesty, knowing the anxious concern that his subjects
felt for their beloved sovereign, with the most considerate goodness gratified them by sending to St. James's daily accounts of
the state of his health, as ascertained by the opinion of his physicians. For some days these reports announced that his majesty's illness had begun to take a very favourable turn, and
aroused all ranks of his subjects with the most pleasing and
sanguine expectations. On Thursday the ninth of February
the lord-chancellor, as soon as the peers assembled in order to
go into a committee on the regency bill, informed them, that
the improvement of the king's health, already stated in the offi-

z See Parliamentary Reports.

cial reports of the physicians, was still progressive; an intelli- CHAP.
gence which certainly must prove pleasing to every man in the XLI.
kingdom: in this situation of things he conceived they could
not possibly proceed upon the bill before them; and therefore 1789.
moved, that their lordships do immediately adjourn to Tuesday next the twenty-fourth. On the day appointed the chancellor informed the house, that he had that morning attended
his majesty by his own command, and found him perfectly recovered; he therefore moved a farther adjournment, which being
again repeated, his lordship on the fifth of March informed the
peers, that his majesty would signify his farther pleasure to
both houses on Tuesday the tenth of March : and thus ended
the necessity and project of a regency.

The plan of regency received the warmest praises and se- Warm
verest censures from the supporters of the respective parties praises and
throughout the kingdom. By the one Mr. Pitt was represent- severe cen-
ed as having again saved the country from the domination of the plan of
an ambitious faction, which, if restored to power, might not regency
have been easily displaced; that the prince, intelligent and through-
well disposed as he was himself, was so much guided by these out the
counsellors as to excite apprehension, lest at their instigation nation.
he might act differently from what his own mind would prompt
and dictate. By the other it was alleged, that Mr. Pitt's object
was to restrict the regent so much, as to render it necessary for
him to come to some terms of accommodation with those who
should oppose his present favourites; that his purpose simply
was, by retaining a considerable portion of the kingly influence
in hands favourable to his measures, to secure the means of
re-establishing in office himself and his friends; that the restraints designed for the prince were inconsistent with the energetic exercise of the executorial functions; that they were justifiable on no general principle, as every part of the kingly prerogative was necessary for its constitutional purposes; that
they implied an injurious doubt and suspicion concerning the
character and probable conduct of the prince; and were personally and individually insulting as well as unjust to his highness.

Impartial observers, probably, will neither altogether agree Impartial
in the panegyric or the reproach. From history, as well as estimate.
the general principles of the constitution, it appears that it belongs to parliament, as representatives of the people, to provide
for any exigency which was not foreseen or described by the
law of the land; that parliament has exercised this power, and
that its exertions have been beneficial. Mr. Fox's first position
was a theory which neither experience nor analogy supported :
his explanatory doctrine, declaring the prince's right, on a parliamentary adjudication of the case, equally wanted the support
of experience or analogy. Concerning the competency to provide a remedy in the existing exigency, the opinion of Mr. Pitt
seems to rest on more logical and conclusive reasoning than

CHAP. the opinion of Mr. Fox: but as it was evidently expedient
XLI.   that the heir apparent should be the regent, the power to be
       conferred ought to be as much as was necessary for answering
1789. the purposes of the appointment: he was for the time to supply the want of the kingly office. It is difficult to conceive
that the acting chief magistrate could perform the official functions necessary for the good of the country, without the full prerogative, unless by a supposition totally inconsistent with the
constitution, that the crown possessed perogatives not necessary for the good of the subject. That any difficulty could arise
in the resumption of his office by the rightful holder, when it
should please heaven to restore his health, was an hypothesis
containing an union of many and great improbabilities: that
the heir apparent should desire to obstruct the resumption,
could only be apprehended on a supposition that the prince
was totally deficient of filial duty, loyalty, and patriotism; in
short, in every virtue becoming his station: such a notion had
evidently no foundation in his conduct: that, intending well
himself, he might by his advisers be misled to so great a degree,
would be impossible, unless on a supposition that he himself
was totally deficient in point of judgment and common intelligence, which was well known to be quite contrary to the truth.
Reviewers of the conduct of the party which he countenanced,
though they might disapprove of many of their acts and measures, could find nothing in the history or character of lord
Loughborough, the duke of Portland, lord North, and Mr. Fox,
that could render it likely that they would counsel such an obstruction: but if the prince and these illustrious supporters
should propose or attempt such measures, how were they to
be put into execution? were the legislature and the nation to
join in the scheme? without their concurrence, such a disloyal
and undutiful attempt would be impracticable, and would discover infatuated folly as well as desperate wickedness in its authors. Vigilant caution to guard against such improbable dangers would be a superfluous and idle exercise of deliberative
policy. In fact, from Mr. Pitt's scheme it is evident that no
such fears were seriously entertained: the most efficient engine
of power, the command of the national force, was to be put into
the regent's hands. The chief object of restriction was the bestowal of titles, the distribution of donative, either in pensions or
appointments equivalent to pensions: the subtraction of these measures of influence from the intended regent, it was morally certain, in the circumstances of the case, would be an accession of
influence to the proposer of the restrictions: unbiassed examination, therefore, without questioning Mr. Pitt's *motives* to have
been pure, loyal, and patriotic, in his project of regency, cannot avoid perceiving that the manifest *tendency* of his restric-
tive clauses was to secure considerable influence to his own
party: such an opinion is certainly no imputation on the cha-

racter of a statesman; it merely supposes that he was a lover **CHAP.** of power, and preferred an administration composed of his po- **XLI.** litical friends, to an administration composed of his political adversaries. But whatever may be the opinion formed of the 1789. restrictions designed to be imposed on the prince regent, we may safely conclude, that the principle of ministers, respecting the right of supplying a deficiency in the executive government, was the most agreeable to the history and spirit of the constitution.

The Irish parliament on this occasion exercised that inde- The Irish pendent political power which it had so recently ascertained, parliament and adopted a plan totally opposite to the project of the British addresses senate, and similar to that which had been in England propos- to assume ed by Mr. Fox. A motion, supported by Mr. Grattan, and op- the regen-posed by Mr. Fitzgibbon, with other eminent speakers, was cy of Ire-carried without a division, for presenting an address to the land. prince of Wales, requesting him to take on himself the government of Ireland, during his majesty's incapacity. A similar address was voted in the house of peers; and on the nineteenth of February, both lords and commons waited on the lord-lieutenant with their address, and requested him to transmit the same, his excellency returned for answer, that, under the impressions he felt of his official duty, and of the oath he had taken, he did not consider himself warranted to lay before the prince an address, purporting to invest his royal highness with powers to take upon him the government of that realm, before he should be enabled by law so to do, and therefore was obliged to decline transmitting their address to Great Britain. After the answer was discussed in parliament, it was resolved that, his excellency the lord-lieutenant having thought proper to decline to transmit to his royal highness George prince of Wales the address of both houses of parliament, a competent number of members should be appointed to present the said address to his royal highness: the resolution was carried in both houses: the duke of Leinster and earl Charlemont were appointed commissioners on the part of the peers; the right honourable Thomas Conolly, right honourable J. O'Neil, the right honourable W. B. Ponsonby, and J. Stuart, esqrs. were appointed commissioners on the part of the commons. These gentlemen soon after departed for England, but the auspicious recovery of our king rendered their purpose unnecessary.

On the tenth of March, the commons having attended at the bar of the house of lords, the chancellor informed them that his majesty, not thinking fit to be then present in his royal person, had caused a commission to be issued, authorizing the commissioners, who had been appointed by former letters patent, to hold the parliament, to open and declare certain farther causes for holding the same. The commission being read, the chancellor addressing the houses in the name of the commissioners, acquainted them that his majesty, being recovered

CHAP. from his late severe indisposition, and enabled to attend the
XLI.   public affairs of his kingdom, had commanded him to convey
       his warmest acknowledgments for the additional proofs which
1789. they had given of their affectionate attachment to his person,
       and of their zealous concern for the honour and interests of
       his crown, and the security and good government of his domi-
       nions. Since the close of the last session the king had conclud-
       ed a defensive alliance with Prussia, copies of which would be
       laid before the house: his majesty's endeavours were employ-
       ed, during the last summer, in conjunction with his allies, in or-
       der to prevent, as much as possible, the extension of hostilities
       in the north; and to manifest his desire of effecting a general
       pacification, no opportunity would be neglected on his part to
       promote this salutary object; and, in the mean time, he had
       the satisfaction of receiving from all foreign courts continued
       assurances of their friendly disposition towards this country.
       Addresses of congratulation and thanks were moved in both
       houses, and unanimously voted: an address to the queen was
       also proposed and carried with the same unanimity.

Joy diffus-   So great was the joy which diffused itself through the me-
ed through tropolis and the nation, that for several days scarcely any thing
the nation was attended to, but expressions of delight for the recovery of
on the re- their sovereign. Conscious as his subjects were of their affec-
covery of   tion and veneration for their king, they had never known how
their be-   dearly they loved his goodness, how highly they prized his vir-
loved mo-   tues, until grief for his calamity, and the dread of its conse-
narch.   quences, disclosed to them the poignancy of their feelings. Con-
       fident as our king was of being beloved and valued by his sub-
       jects, yet occasion had not fully manifested to him the force,
       extent, and intenseness of their affections, until they had exhi-
       bited themselves in universal delight that he was, as it were,
       risen to them from the dead. Perhaps the annals of history do
       not record a more sincere, tender, and general concern of subjects
       in the welfare of a sovereign, than displayed themselves in the
       affliction, gloom, and despondency of Britons, when his majes-
       ty's illness was known, and before the probability of recovery
       was declared, the anxious and eager hopes that sprang from
       the opinions of the physician most conversant in such mala-
       dies; and the ardent expectation that arose from the reports of
       beginning convalescence; these sentiments increasing with the
       augmented probability of approaching recovery, until the com-
       pletion of the cure turned hope and expectation into the strong-
       est joy. Nor were external testimonies wanting to correspond
       with the gladdened feelings of the people: all ranks and all in-
       dividuals vied with each other in rejoicings; invention was
       roused to devise emblems expressive of the general sympathy;
       and taste was employed in superadding grace and decoration
       to the efforts of genius which were employed to promote and
       heighten the prevalent passion. Illuminations received a new
       character, and, in addition to former mechanism, exhibited

fancy, ingenuity, and design. It was not a mere blaze of light, but in many places light exhibiting a happy resemblance of the painter and sculpture's skill, and in some even of the poet's art.

His majesty was desirous of publicly testifying his gratitude to the Supreme Being for the late signal interposition of his benignant providence in removing the illness with which he had been afflicted: with this view he appointed a thanksgiving, and resolved for the greater solemnity to go to St. Paul's cathedral, there to return thanks to Almighty God for his merciful goodness; the twenty-third of April was the day fixed for the purpose; and a more splendid exhibition has rarely met the public eye. The procession began with the commons, as representatives of the people of Britain; at eight o'clock the members set off in their carriages, followed by their speaker in his state coach; preceded by the masters in chancery and judges, next came the peers, the younger baron first, and the lord chancellor in his state coach closing this part of the procession: afterwards came the princes, escorted by parties of horse-guards. Their majesties set out from the queen's palace soon after ten o'clock, in a coach drawn by eight cream-coloured horses, followed by their royal highnesses the princesses, and proceeded along Pall Mall, and through the strand, amid the loyal acclamations of a prodigious concourse of people. At Temple-bar his majesty was met by the lord-mayor in a gown of crimson velvet, by the sheriffs in their scarlet robes, and a deputation from the aldermen and common councilmen, (being all on horseback) when the lord-mayor surrendered the city sword to the king, who having returned it to him, he carried it bare-headed before the monarch to St. Paul's. His majesty, being come to St. Paul's, was met at the west door by the peers, the bishop of London, the dean of St. Paul's (bishop of Lincoln) and the canons residentiary. The sword of state was carried before his majesty by the marquis of Stafford into the choir, when the king and queen placed themselves under a canopy of state, near the west end, opposite the altar. The peers had their seats in the area, as a house of lords; and the commons in the stalls. Divine service[a] being finished, the procession returned in the same order: the whole spectacle was extremely magnificent,

[a] The prayers and litany were read and chanted by the minor canons: the Te Deum and anthems composed for the occasion were sung by the choir, who were placed in the organ loft, and were joined in the chorus, as also in the psalms, by the charity children, in number about six thousand, who were assembled there, previous to his majesty's arrival: the communion service was read by the dean and residentiaries, and the sermon preached by the lord bishop of London, from Psalm xxvii. 16.—" O, tarry thou the Lord's leisure be strong, and he shall comfort thine heart, and put thou thy trust in the Lord" See Annual Register, 1789. Appendix to Chronicle, p. 249.

CHAP.
XLI.

and, viewed in combinations with its objects and cause, was admirably calculated to strike every beholder of feeling and reflection with mingled joy, gratitude and piety.

1789.
Festive re-
joicings.

Very splendid galas were given by many individuals on the auspicious occasion ; the most sumptuous and magnificent was exhibited by the princess royal at Windsor ; the whole disposition of the entertainment, but especially the emblematical figures, did great honour to the taste and ingenuity of its lovely and accomplished author; dresses, of which the principal characteristic was UNIFORMITY, exhibiting gracefulness and loyalty, with a beautiful VARIETY of finely fancied ornaments exemplified Hutchinson's doctrine on the constituents of beauty.

The French and Spanish ambassadors also gave entertainments on the same auspicious occasion; that which was exhibited by the former, both in magnificence and splendour, in beauty of decoration[b] and ingenuity of device, approached nearest to the princess's gala.

Parlia-
mentary
proceed-
ings.

Private and public congratulations occupied, without interruption, the first week after the re-establishment of our sovereign's health was announced: and it was the middle of the second before parliamentary business was resumed. On the eighteenth of March a plan, formed by the master-general of the ordnance, for fortifying the West India islands, was submitted to the house of commons; and after undergoing considerable discussion, on the same grounds as that of the former year, was adopted. A tax imposed upon shops some years before, at the instance of Mr. Pitt, and assessing them in proportion to the rent of the dwelling-house of which they made a part, had been found to fall heavily on the metropolis and other great commercial towns, where the rents of houses are necessarily high. It had been intended by legislature, that the tax should fall ultimately upon the customers but shopkeepers alleged this object to be impracticable: they represented it as partial and oppressive, and Mr. Fox had repeatedly on these grounds applied for a repeal. This year he renewed his motion, and the house, without admitting the grievance to the alleged extent, yet wishing to satisfy so numerous and useful a body, consented to adopt the motion: and a bill for the purpose was introduced, and passed both houses unanimously.

Renewed
applica-
tion for the
repeal of
the test and
corpora-
tion act.

On the eighth of May Mr. Beaufoy again moved for the repeal of the test and corporation act, which he supported by the same arguments that he had used two years before;

b This entertainment was given in a very large and magnificent house, which the ambassador occupied in Portman-square. Among the devices was the following : on each side of the grand saloon was a transparent painting ; that on the right of her majesty representing the genius of France congratulating the genius of England on the recovery of the king, an excellent likeness of whom the goddess of health held in her hand.

and was also opposed on grounds that had been formerly employed ; and his motion was rejected by a majority of one hundred and twenty-two to one hundred and two. One of the
principal objections to the desired repeal was, that certain classes of dissenters not only maintained principles contrary to
the fundamental tenets of our faith, but declared intentions
inimical to our establishment: there were other bodies of
dissenters that differed from the church of England merely
respecting forms: it was thought by many who belonged to
neither, that if the sectaries of the latter kind had drawn
a strong line between themselves and the sectaries of the
former, they more readily might have experienced the indulgence of legislature. The first of these classes might be compromised under the general name of calvinists or presbyterians ; they branched in a great measure from the church of
Scotland, were orthodox in all the essential articles of our religion, and well affected to our constitutional establishment :
the second may be comprehended under the general term of
unitarians or socinians, heterodox in their opinions concerning
the trinity, the divinity of Christ, the necessity of an atonement, and other important articles of christian belief : they
were, besides, inimical to our ecclesiastical establishment, and
many of them by no means friendly to our political constitution: here was a very important difference; but there were
reasons which prevented the calvinistical dissenters from exhibiting the distinction between themselves and the unitarians.
If the presbyterians had the constitutional principles, the unitarians in their number comprehended the abler men : the
great talents and learning of Drs. Price and Priestley had diffused their respective sentiments through many ingenious young
men, not only originally of their own cast, but others bred in
the strictness of presbyterian orthodoxy. It was, indeed, natural for young non-conformists, who were either really able,
or aspired at the reputation of literary talents, to follow the
admired genius of the heresiarchs, rather than associate with
the less splendid, though more useful, teachers of the orthodox
dissenters. The presbyterians possessed many respectable
and some eminent preachers, well fitted for the real business of
a clergyman to afford religious and moral instruction to a congre-
gation ;[c] but they had no Price or Priestley fitted to form great political plans, or execute great political undertakings : they did not
possess the literary activity which, by circulating arguments in
favour of the dissenters, through periodical works, tended to render their cause popular. From the general mass of sectarian liter-
ture and exertions. they expected they, in common with the rest,

c Except Drs. Price and Priestley, I do not at present recollect among
the socinian and republican schismatics any persons of transcendent genius
and profound erudition, or who could with justice be affirmed to surpass
Drs. Fordyce and Hunter, and other presbyterians who are still alive.

CHAP.
XLI.

1789.

Proposed
relief of
nonconfor-
mists
against pe-
nal laws,

would ultimately obtain their wish: separated from such coadjutors, their efforts, they knew, must be comparatively feeble,
and, therefore, concluded would be unavailing: they never tried
the experiment.

A few days after this motion, lord Stanhope proposed a bill
" for relieving members of the church of England from sundry
" penalties and disabilities, to which by the laws now in force
" they were liable, and for extending freedom in matters of re-
" ligion to all persons (papists only excepted), and for other
" purposes therein mentioned." He presented to their lordships a sketch of all the penal laws enacted upon religion, sor-
cery, and various other subjects: he insisted that it was both
unjust and disgraceful to suffer these to remain amongst our
statutes: he proposed, therefore, that they should be repealed;
that all persons (papists excepted on account of their dangerous
and persecuting principles) should possess the free exercise of
their faith, and by speaking, writing, and publishing, be permitted to investigate theological subjects; by preaching and
teaching to instruct persons in the duties of religion in such a
manner as they should judge the most conducive to promote
virtue, the happiness of society, and the eternal felicity of man-

is opposed
by the
bishops,

kind. The bill was strongly opposed by the bishops, as tending to sweep away all order and subordination in religion, and
to substitute fanaticism; to unloose the bonds of society, and,
under pretence of establishing religious liberty, to open the door
to every species of licentiousness, neglect, and even contempt
of christianity. Dr. Horsley admitted the absurdity of some
of the penal laws, and their total inapplicability to the present
circumstances of society: but he objected to the bill, as he
thought it would tear up the church of England from the root;
and as the destruction of an ally must necessarily affect the
interests and existence of the principal, it would tend to destroy

and reject-
ed.

the very being of the English constitution: the bill was rejected
at the second reading.[d]

Slave
trade.

By a vote of the last session, the consideration of the slave trade
having been prostponed to the present, the commons intended
to have resumed it early, but the unforeseen business which occupied the attention of parliament from November to March,
rendered it impossible to take it into consideration, until the
season was too far advanced for fully discussing such an extensive and complicated subject. The privy-council had persevered
in investigating the facts; from them a large and elaborate re-

d Lord Stanhope, replying to the bishops, said, that if the reverend bench
would not suffer him to load away their rubbish by cartfulls, he would endeavour to carry it off in wheel-barrows; and if that mode should be resisted, he would take it away with a spade. Having soon after soon conversation respecting the exaction of tithes from quakers, in which he differed
from the chancellor, lord Stanhope said, I shall teach the noble and learned
lord law, as I have this day taught the bench of bishops religion. See Parliamentary Debates.

port was presented to the house, and several petitions both for and against the proposed abolition of the slave trade, were submitted to their consideration. On the twelfth of May, Mr. Wilberforce introduced a set of resolutions amounting to twelve, which he deduced from the report of the privy-council. Africa (he said in his prefatory speech) was a country divided under many kings, governments, and laws · a great portion of that region was subjected to tyrannical dominion; men were considered merely as goods and property, and articles of sale and plunder like any other mercantile wares. The kings and princes had been purposely inspired with a fondness for our commodities: they waged war on each other, and ravaged their own country, in order to procure thereby the captivity and disposal of their countrymen; and in their courts of law, many poor wretches, though innocent, were condemned to servitude. To obtain a sufficient number of slaves, thousands were kidnapped and torned from their families and their country, and sentenced to misery. All these assertions (he said) were verified by every history of Africa, and now confirmed by the report of the privy-council. He considered the subject, first, as a question of humanity; and secondly of policy. From the evidence before the council it appeared that the number of slaves carried away from Africa, on an average of four years, amounted to thirty-eight thousand annually: of these by far the greater part was brought from the inland country, and at a great distance from the coasts. According to the information that had been received, the persons purchased for slaves consisted chiefly of four classes: first, prisoners taken in war: secondly, persons seized for debt, or on account of real or imputed crimes, particularly adultery and witchcraft, in which cases the whole families of the captives were frequently vended for the profit of those by whom they were condemned : thirdly. domestic slaves sold for the emolument of their masters, at the will of their owner, and in some places on being condemned by them for real or imputed crimes: fourthly, persons made slaves by various acts of oppression, violence, or fraud, committed either by the princes and chiefs of those countries on their subjects, or private individuals on each other; or by Europeans engaged in this traffic. The trade carried on for the purpose of slaves had a necessary tendency to cause frequent and cruel wars among the nations; to produce unjust convictions and aggravated punishments for pretended crimes: to encourage acts of oppression, violence, and fraud; and to obstruct the natural course of civilization and improvement in those countries. He considered the subject next on the ground of policy: the continent of Africa furnished several valuable articles peculiar to that quarter of the globe, and highly important to the trade and manufactures of this kingdom. For the slave trade, there might be substituted an extensive commerce, which would equal the profits of that trafic, and would probably increase with the civilization and

CHAP.
XLI.

1789.
Mr Wilberforce's
motion for
the abolition.

CHAP. improvement that would proceed from the abolition of such a
XII.   barbarous and depopulating merchandise. The infectious dis-
       tempers arising from the confinement of negroes rendered the
1789. slave trade more destructive to British seamen, than other kinds
of commerce on the same coasts, or in equally torrid latitudes. The
mode of conveying blacks from Africa necessarily exposed
them to many grievous sufferings, which no regulation could
prevent: on their passage, and in the West Indies, before they
were sold, great numbers perished, and proportionably diminished the value of the cargo: diseases prevailed with peculiar
severity among negroes newly imported, and the number of
deaths far exceeded the usual mortality of natives. The
natural increase of population among negroes in our plantations
was impeded by the inequality of the sexes in the importations
from Africa; the general dissoluteness of manners, and the
want of proper regulations for the encouragement of marriages,
obstructed the nourishment of healthy children: hence, he
concluded, that if we obviated the causes which had hitherto
obstructed the natural increase of negroes in the West Indies,
and established regulations respecting their food, health, and
labour, without diminishing the profits of the planter, no inconsiderable or permanent inconvenience would result from dis-
continuing the farther importation of African slaves. All impartial hearers, or readers capable of comprehending and appreciating, Mr. Wilberforce's view of the slave trade, whatever
their opinions might be concerning the evidence on which he
grounded his reasoning, agreed in esteeming the present speech
and propositions the ablest, fullest, and most masterly exhibition of the reasons for abolishing the traffic, that had been pre-
The ques-   sented on that important subject. The defenders of the traffic
tion is post did not then enter minutely into the question, but, confining
pon'd to   themselves to some general animadversions, postponed a detail-
the follow- ed answer to the following session; to which period it was set-
ing ses-   tled that farther consideration should be deferred: meanwhile,
sion.   the bill brought in by sir William Dolben for regulating the
transportation of slaves from Africa to the West India islands,
was by another act continued and amended.
Mr. Gren-   In the beginning of June, lord Sidney resigned the office of
ville is ap- secretary of state for the home department, and Mr. Grenville
pointed se- was appointed to supply his place. The speaker's chair being
cretary of thus vacant, Mr. Henry Addington, member for Berkshire,
state, and   was proposed for that office by the friends of the ministers, and
Mr. Ad   sir Gilbert Elliott by opposition: the election was carried in
dington   favour of Mr. Addington, by a majority of two hundred and
succeeds   fifteen to one hundred and forty-two. On the eleventh of June,
him as   Mr. Pitt opened to the house his financial scheme for the year:
speaker.   the permanent income declared necessary by the committee of
1786 to defray the annual demands, was 15,500,000l.; for the
last two years the income had exceeded that sum 78,000l., but
the expenses of the preceding year, the armament, the dis-

charge of the prince of Wales's debts, the sums bestowed on CHAP.
the loyalists, and other unforeseen contingencies, had greatly XLI.
exceeded the usual peace establishment: from these causes the
total amount of the supplies required for the current year 1789.
amounted to 5,730,000l., besides the annual renewal of ex- Financial
chequer bills: the minister informed the house, that to provide scheme.
this supply, in addition to the usual resources, a loan for a mil- A loan is
lion would be necessary: this sum he proposed to borrow on a required
tontine, by which means the incumbrance would in time be (according
removed without any permanent augmentation of the public to the mi-
debt. As the necessity of the loan arose, not from a defalca- from a tem-
tion of income, but from temporary increase of expenditure, porary
the minister contended, that no fair argument could be addu- cause.
ced from it, tending to discredit accounts that our finances
were flourishing, or to diminish the probability of reducing the
national incumbrances.   To pay the interest of four and a
half per cent. for the sum now borrowed, and also to supply
the deficiency of 56,000l. incurred by the repeal of the shop
tax, Mr. Pitt stated, that new taxes would be wanted to the
amount of 100,000l.; for this purpose he proposed to add one
halfpenny to the stamp duties on every newspaper, and six-
pence additional on each advertisement; fresh duties also upon
cards and dice, upon probates of wills, and upon horses and
carriages.   The ingenuity of Mr. Sheridan endeavoured to es- Mr. Sheri-
tablish the following propositions: that, for the three last dan dis-
years, the expenditure has exceeded the income two millions, putes his
and may be expected to do so for three years to come: that no tions.
progress has hitherto been made in the reduction of the public debt: that there is no ground for rational expectation that
any progress can be made without a considerable increase of
the annual income, or reduction of the expenses.   The committee had declared upon a comparison between the income and
expenditure, that the former would be adequate to the latter
without a loan: a loan had, however, taken place.   The committee had declared that the annual income would amount to a
specific sum; but on an average of three years there had been
a deficiency: that the expenditure exceeded the income he endeavoured to prove from calculating probabilities, instead of
detailing items; and adopted the same hypothetical mode of
argument to support his other positions.[e] In stating both income and expenditure, he took into the account on the one
hand the year 1786, of diminished productiveness from a temporary cause, the reduction of duties, in consequence of a commercial treaty, that so soon compensated this diminution of receipt; on the other the year of 1788, a period of expenditure
beyond the usual demands in time of peace; and thus endeavoured to make subjects specially circumstanced the foundation
of a general average.   Mr. Grenville, from plain facts and

e See Parliamentary Debates, June 11, 1789.

CHAP. authentic documents, detected, and clearly exposed the sophis-
XLI. tical reasoning of extraordinary genius, exercised in forming an
hypothesis inimical to political adversaries.[f]

1789.   To increase the revenue by the farther prevention of frauds,
Bill for Mr. Pitt proposed a bill for transferring the duties on tobacco
subjecting from the customs to the excise: tobacco, being a commodity
tobacco to of general consumption, might be rendered a productive source
an excise. of revenue, but under the present regulations and duties, was an
article of smuggling, and indeed the principal subject of contraband trade, since the late act concerning tea, wines, and spirits.
It appeared on inquiry and investigation, that one half of the tobacco consumed in the kingdom was smuggled, and that the revenue was defrauded by this means to the amount of nearly
300,000l. To remedy this evil, the most effectual means would
be to subject the greater part of the duty on tobacco to the survey of excise: the peculiar benefit of this change in the mode
of collection, as a detail of the proceeds proved, had been very
clearly exemplified in the article of wine; the manufacturers
would no doubt make objections to the present proposition, as
dealers in wine had done respecting the change in the duties upon their merchandise: but though they were to be heard
with candour, assertions affecting their own interests were to
be scrutinized with strictness, and to be no farther admitted
than they were supported with collateral proof. While the bill
affecting their commodity was pending, dealers in wine had
asserted confidently, that, under the restrictions, they could not
carry on their trade; the house at that time thought their reasoning insufficient, and tried the experiment; the result had
been, that the trade had increased to an astonishing degree.
The plan was controverted on general and special ground;
by exposing British subjects to summary inspection and summary trials, the extension of the excise laws was inconsistent
with the principles of the constitution: there was a peculiar
hardship in subjecting this manufacture to the excise, and the
total loss of the trade itself would probably be the consequence: the variations in the weight of tobacco, during the
process of its manufacture, were so inconceivably great, and
at the same time so uncertain, that it would be impossible for
the officers of the excise to take any account of stock, which
might not subject the retailer, on the one hand, to a ruinous
excess of duty, or on the other, to fines and forfeitures equally pernicious: there were, moreover, valuable secrets possessed
by manufacturers of tobacco and snuff;[g] these would be inevitably exposed to the discovery of excisemen, among whom
there might be persons capable of profiting by such an op-
Popular portunity. A loud clamour was echoed through the country,
clamour against the extension of the excise, as an unconstitutional and
against it.

f See Parliamentary Debates, June 11, 1789.
g Some of these, it was affirmed, had been purchased at upwards of 10,000l.

oppressive measure, and an infraction of British liberty; but CHAP.
such trite declamation did not influence legislature. The bill, in XLI.
its passage through the houses, underwent various modifications; after which it received the royal assent. 1789.

On the first of July Mr. Dundas presented to the house a It is passed
statement of Indian finance: from this account it appeared, that into a law.
the annual revenues, after defraying the expense of the different Progres-
settlements, amounted to 1,848,000l. that the interest of the debt perity of
was 480,700l. and the principal 7,604,000l.; the excess of the India sta-
revenue beyond the interest was 1,367,300l. to be applied to the ted by Mr.
liquidation of their debt. A petition was soon after presented Dundas.
from the company, praying that they might be permitted to add
one million to their capital stock. This application was supported by Mr. Dundas, who affirmed that, upon a supposition
of the final extinction of their charter in 1794, their effects in
Europe would overbalance their debts by the sum of 350,000l.;
and that with respect to their debts in India, they would go along
with the territory, and be very readily undertaken by those into
whosoever hands the possession of that territory might come.
A bill to enable the company to carry the prayer of their petition
into effect was brought in, and passed through both houses with
little opposition.

The trial of Mr. Hastings proceeded very slowly; it was the Slow pro-
twentieth of April before the court was resumed, and a charge gress of
was then opened by Mr. Burke, relative to the corrupt receipt Mr. Has-
of money. In the course of this accusation, having occasion tings's
to mention Nundcomar, Mr. Burke said, that Mr. Hastings had trial.
murdered Nundcomar by the hands of sir Elijah Impey. As
the proceedings concerning this rajah made no part of the
charges which the managers were appointed to conduct against
Mr. Hastings, the defendant petitioned the house either to bring
forward and prosecute the allegation in a specific article, or to
restrain their manager from assertions totally irrelevant to the
business intrusted to the prosecutors. A proposition of censure
was moved against Mr. Burke, as having exceeded the authority vested in him by the commons, and employed words which
ought not to have been used. The motion occasioned a warm
debate, in which the supporters of Mr. Burke contended, that
the complaint was made for the purpose of disgusting the managers with the office which they had undertaken; that if admitted it would so narrow their ground of procedure as to defeat the purposes of justice. Those who thought his expressions blamable, insisted that in no criminal process could the
imputation of a crime not prosecuted, and consequently by the
law presumed not to exist, tend to the attainment of justice.
The matter of the charges was definite: to them only was the
accuser to speak, and to them only could the defendant answer: an assertion of extraneous guilt without an opportunity
of denial, tended to produce an unfavourable impression that
might affect the opinion of some judges on the real matter of

CHAP.
XLI.

1789.

the charges. The proposed motion, introduced by the marquis of Graham, was carried by a majority of one hundred and thirty-five. The proceedings respecting Mr. Hastings underwent very virulent invectives in periodical journals : one of these had the hardihood to assert, that "the trial of Mr. Hastings was to be "put off to another session, unless the house of lords had spirit "enough to put an end *to so shameful a business!*" This paragraph being complained of in the house, it was unanimously agreed the attorney-general should be directed to prosecute the printer.[h] A bill was this year introduced into parliament to establish a perpetual anniversary thanksgiving to Almighty God, for having by the glorious revolution delivered this nation from arbitrary power, and to commemorate annually the confirmation of the people's rights. After passing the house of commons it was rejected by the lords, on the ground of being unnecessary, as the service of the fifth of November had been altered for the express purpose of commemorating that glorious event.

On the eleventh of August ended the longest session which the history has hitherto recorded, after having continued almost nine months without interruption. The chancellor, by his majesty's command, prorogued the houses, and delivered a short speech containing his majesty's thanks for the attention manifested to public business, and the supplies which were granted : though the good offices of his majesty and his allies had not hitherto been effectual for restoring the general tranquillity, yet the farther extension of hostilities had been prevented, and the situation of affairs abroad promised to this country the uninterrupted enjoyment of peace.

[h] In the course of the conversation to which this motion gave rise, Mr. Burke read from one of the public prints a curious paper, purporting to be a bill of charges made by the editor upon major Scott, for sundry articles inserted in the paper on his account. They chiefly consisted of speeches, letters, and paragraphs composed by him ; and amongst the rest was this singular article: *For attacking the veracity of Mr. Burke,* 3s. 6d.

CHAP. XLII.

THE summer of 1789 teemed with events of greater im- CHAP.
portance to the civilized world, than any which are recorded in XLII.
modern history. Causes that had long secretly operated and
gradually increased in force, now manifested themselves in the 1789.
most stupendous effects. Before, however, the history pro- 1789 event-
ceeds to the principal transaction which will render the year civilized
1789 for ever memorable, it is proper to carry the narrative to world.
other subjects that may illustrate the collateral and relative
state of other countries at the time in which a system commenced, that changed not only the policy but the opinion, sentiments, and character of continental Europe.

During the last thirty years a very important alteration had Changes in
taken place in the political relations of the continent. Through the rela-
a great part of the sixteenth century, and the whole of the se- tive policy
venteenth, the wars which agitated the christian world arose of France
chiefly from the contending ambition of France and of Austria. tria.
At the accession of the house of Bourbon, both the royal and

CHAP.
XLII.
1789.

Profound
policy of
Kaunitz in
the treaty
of Austria
with
France.

imperial princes of Austria had begun to decline from that
power which the family had possessed under one head. The
infatuated bigotry of Philip undid much of what the skilful policy of Charles had done : nevertheless, the dynasty, in the
dominions of both the sovereigns retained a power very formi-
dahle to their neighbours. To impair the strength of the house
of Austria was the principal object of Henry IV in his foreign
politics. His successors, as we have seen[i] throughout the seventeenth century, pursued this policy, and with such efficacy
as to render the French monarchy far superior to the combined dominions of the two Austrian branches. In the successive wars of Louis the XIII. and XIV. against Spain and Austrian Germany, France made large acquisitions; and that war,
which was more fatal to her than any which she had encountered in modern times, secured to her princes the kingdom and
dominions of Spain. This was the most disastrous blow which
France ever gave to the house of Austria, and appeared to threat-
en her rapid humiliation. But the maritime ambition of France
having driven her to pernicious contests with England, arrested the progress of her continental advantages :[k] she required
a long interval of peace after the death of Louis XIV. to recruit her strength ; and at the demise of the emperor Charles
VI. she was recovered from her losses, and sufficiently potent to
annoy her neighbours. A new co-operater now arose against
the house of Austria ; the king of Prussia on the one side aggrandized himself at the expense of Maria Theresa, while
France pressed her on the other; and at the peace of Aix-la-
Chapelle the empress-queen found her hereditary dominions
curtailed, and her strength impaired. For a century and a
half Austria had been progressively losing; her maritime ally
had been uniformly victorious : but the naval triumphs of Britain had not averted disaster from Austria. Such was the general series of policy and events when Kaunitz came to be the
minister of the empress-queen. The penetrating and comprehensive genius of that celebrated statesman saw, that in the
whole result of contention Austria was really not a match for
France : and that if she persisted in enmity to that kingdom,
she not only would be totally unable to recover her losses, but
must incur greater. He conceived a design which, he trusted,
would restore the splendour of Austria, and might permit
France to embark in projects that he knew to be agreeable to
her inclinations, but was convinced would reduce her resources,
and leave to her less strength for continental advancement.[l]
Hence arose the treaty of 1756 with France, which suffered

i See the introduction to this history.
. k The impolicy of the French contests with England is placed in a very
striking light by Soulavie, a writer now at the court of Bonaparte. See
his memoirs of Louis XVI. passim.
l See Soulavie's Memoirs of Louis XVI. vol. iii. chap. viii.

Austria, instead of acting on the defensive, to resume her offen- CHAP.
sive ambition; and though her projects were defeated for the   XLII.
time by the genius and heroism of Frederick, yet her means of
influence and aggrandizement were essentially increased by her   1789.
amity with France. The want of a continental rival encouraged France to direct her principal efforts to a favourite ob-
jcet, that she never could nor can obtain: she hoped to overpower the naval strength of the mistress of the ocean: failed
in the extravagant and impracticable attempts, and wasted at
sea that strength which might have made her irresistible by
land; and thus the diminution of the resources and power of
France was, as Kaunitz foresaw,[m] the consequence of her connexion with her ancient rival, while Austria by the exhaustion
of her neighbour was able to avail herself of the plundering
projects of Russia and Prussia; and the dismemberment of Poland was evidently one fruit of Kaunitz's scheme. By the
American war France was so much enfeebled, as in a great
degree to have lost her former efficiency on the continent of
Europe. The ancient opponent of Austrian ambition having
thus discontinued her efforts, Joseph now hoped by his co-ope- Imperial
ration with the other principal potentate of the continent, that confedera-
he would share the spoils of the Turkish empire, strip Prussia cy
of her late acquisitions, extend the Austrian influence in Germany, and raise his family to an extent of dominion and splendour unparalleled since Charles V. In this expectation he had
commenced the war, and notwithstanding the untoward events
of the preceding campaign, he still trusted that he would ultimately succeed in his projects of lawless spoliation. The principle of British interference in continental politics was uniform:
to prevent any other potentate from acquiring such an accession
of power as might endanger the independence of Europe, and
the security of these realms. The application of this princi- produces
ple led the English cabinet to inspirit measures of defence the defen-
against the imperial aggressors; and in such circumstances to sive alli-
combine with Prussia, which was the most interested, dispos- Britain,
ed, and able to repel the ambitious confederacy. Frederick Holland
William very readily assented; thence arose the defensive al- and Prus-
liance whose political counsels and efforts directed and invigo- sia.
rated the military preparations of the nations that were at war
with Austria and Russia; but the ignorance and barbarity of
one of the belligerent maintainers of national independence,
prevented her from steadily following the advice of British
wisdom.

We left the emperor returned to Vienna, with disappoint- State of
ment and disgust, because a war contrary to justice and policy the belli-
had produced disaster and disgrace; Russia profiting by his ef- gerent
forts, in employing so great a part of the strength of her ene- powers.
my, and enabled to make a powerful impression on the Turk-

m See Soulavie *passim.*

CHAP. ish dominions. Notwithstanding the loss of Oczakow, the
XLII. campaign of 1788 had been on the whole favourable to the Ottomans: the advantages on the Danube compensated the loss
1789. upon the Niester. The ability of the vizier had invigorated and
formed his troops, restored the military character of the Ottomans, and displayed itself in policy as well as in war: but the
talents and virtues of this minister were misrepresented by
envy, and misapprehended by ignorance: conduct, not only
wise but necessary, was imputed to weakness and pusillanimity. One man, however, at court was able to appreciate
Character his merit; this was the sultan himself, Abdulhamet, a prince of
of the sul- a very different character from those who usually filled the
tan. Turkish throne: far from the gross ignorance that commonly
marked the Ottoman despots, he was distinguished for intelligence and information: instead of ferocity, cruelty, and barbarity, leading features in his character were humanity and bene-
ficence: he was conversant in the languages and sciences of
several christian countries: he spoke the Italian, Spanish, and
French tongues with considerable fluency, and understood them
all perfectly; he delighted greatly in perusing European books,
and conversing with European men; and his favourite subjects
of discourse and study were history and politics. Such abilities, acquirements, and dispositions, were not the most favourable to admiration, of either the gloomy superstition or savage
despotism of his empire. As a prudent sovereign, he scrupu-
lously adhered to the established forms of his country's religion; but by persons who were well acquainted with his acuteness, he was conjectured not to be without a perception of its
absurdities: he saw and deeply lamented the dreadful vices of
the Turkish government and institutions, but knew them to be
so interwoven with the sentiments, opinions,[n] and characters of
mussulmen, that any attempt to effect a reform would be unavailing, until the people themselves should undergo a complete
revolution; what he could not correct in principle, he endeavoured to moderate in practice; to improve his subjects, and to
prepare them gradually for beneficial change, he encouraged
industry and the arts, agriculture, commerce, and manufactures.
He abhorred the janizaries, as a body of men insolent and oppressive to his subjects, and dangerous to himself; and had projected the formation of a regular army on the European model,
which might have afforded the means of internal tranquillity and
of defence from foreign attack, without enslaving the people and
endangering the sovereign. In his grand vizier he found a very
able counsellor and coadjutor: when that officer returned from
the army to the capital, a violent faction having sought his destruction, the sultan ordered him to be arrested, not with a view
to inflict summary punishment, according to the usual mode of
the Turkish emperors, but to make him stand a fair and impar-

n Annual Register, 1789.

tial trial: the result was an honourable acquittal; soon after CHAP.
which he returned to the army to make dispositions for the ap- XLII.
proaching campaign. On the seventeenth of April, 1789, the
Turkish empire experienced a misfortune, productive in its con- 1789.
sequences of the greatest calamities and humiliation; Abdul- His death.
hamet being suddenly seized with a fit in the street, dropped
down, and after languishing a few hours expired. He was Succeeded
succeeded by his nephew Selim, of whom great hopes had been by Selim.
entertained, as he was educated under the eye and direction of
his excellent uncle: but the first act of his reign by no means
confirmed the expectations in his favour; the most tyrannical
rapacity manifested itself in his conduct: its first victim was
Jussu Pacha, the illustrious grand vizier; this minister possessing wealth to the amount of about a million sterling, was seized at the head of the grand army, conveyed prisoner to Constantinople, sentenced to banishment and the forfeiture of his
treasures: on his way to his place of exile he was murdered, his
head was brought in triumph to the sultan, and by his orders
hung up to grace the gates of the seraglio. Confiscation and
execution were the daily acts of the young despot; every wise
measure of his uncle was changed, and, except the grand admiral, every able officer and wise counsellor was displaced:
the Turkish empire rising to ancient glory under the wisdom
and virtue of one ruler, was, by the vice and folly of another,
soon precipitated to a lower abyss of disgrace and disaster than
it had ever experienced. The bashaw of Widin was appoint- Change of
ed grand vizier, and soon showed how totally unqualified he counsels
was to supply the place of his predecessor. As the preceding and effects
campaign had been successful against the emperor, and unsuc- operations.
cessful against the Russians, the late vizier had proposed for
the present campaign an offensive war against the Austrians,
to improve the advantages already obtained, and a defensive
warfare against the Russians, to prevent their farther progress:
the young sultan and his minister to show that they would be
governed entirely by their own counsels, reversed the plans of
their predecessors, and by a most preposterous policy, determined to attack the conquerors, and defend themselves against
the vanquished;° and on this scheme they concerted their operations. The grand vizier promised to retrieve Oczakow, and
marched northward for that purpose: the Russians, under general Kamenskoi, being placed on the borders of Bessarabia,
not only protected Oczakow, but endangered Bender: the
grand Russian army, under the princes Potemkin, and Repnin, was stationed between the Bog and the Neister, to cover their late conquest and make farther advances. A plan
of much better concert was this year contrived and executed
between the Austrians and Russians, than in the former:

° See Annual Register, 1789, chap. vii.

CHAP.
XLII.
⁓

1789.
Successes
of the Rus-
sians and
Austrians.
the emperor prepared as before, four armies; his own health
did not admit of his taking the command in person, but he prevailed on old marshal Haddick to head his grand army, which
was destined to act in the neighbourhood of Belgrade. The
troops next in force, the scene of whose exertions was to be
the northwest frontiers of Turkey near Croatia and the river
Saave, he placed under marshal Loudohn : the prince of Saxe-
Coburg took the lead on the side of Moldavia, and co-operated
with the Russian general Suwarrow; between him and the
grand Austrian army the prince Hohenloe commanded on the
frontiers of Wallachia to carry on a war of posts and skirmishes,
and to act in concert with either the forces to his right or left,
as occasion might require; thus from Oczakow to Dalmatia,
from the northern extremity of the Euxine to the Adriatic, a
line of armies extended along the whole frontier of Turkey,
amounting to three hundred thousand brave men, well disciplined, commanded by skilful generals, and so stationed as to
act with the most perfect concert. Against such a confederacy
of force and skill had the Turks to contend : by wickedness
and infatuation, deprived of the leaders and counsellors who
could have best directed their efforts. The prince of Saxe-
Coburg first retrieved the honour of the Austrian arms in this
war : a Turkish seraskier at the head of an army of thirty
thousand men, being encamped near Focksan, a fortified town
in Wallachia, the prince of Coburg, with a much inferior force,
attacked him in his camp, and gained a complete victory; the
seraskier himself, with a number of his principal officers were
taken prisoners; above five thousand of his men were killed
or captured; the whole army was dispersed and ruined, while
the artillery and spoils of the camp, with the town of Focksan,
fell into the hands of the conquerors. In Bessarabia the Turks
engaged in a number of small and desultory battles, in which
they were generally defeated. The vizier seeing no hopes of
making good his boast respecting Oczakow, in the month of
August, with the grand Turkish army, took a western direction,
and came to the heart of Wallachia. The prince of Saxe-Coburg and marshal Suwarrow, having marched southwards with
an army consisting of near thirty thousand men, attacked the
Turkish host, that amounted to ninety thousand, near Marti-
neste, and with little difficulty or loss, gained one of the most
signal victories recorded in modern history; ten thousand were
killed on the spot, the route and dispersion was complete : cessation of pursuit from the conquerors only saved the slaughter
from being general; and the whole camp, including the grand
vizier's tent and equipage, an immense quantity of stores,
furniture, provisions, and ammunition, were among the spoils of
the conquerors. The fugitives hastened across the Danube,
execrating their general, to whose folly and misconduct they
imputed their disaster; they reminded him of his boasts, and

compared these with his actual performance.[p] The victors pursuing their advantage, captured Bucharest the capital of Wallachia, with the fortress of Cyernitz, and reduced the greater part of the province. Near Bender the Turks displayed great valour in several encounters under Hassan Bey; but engaging in a pitched battle, after a very obstinate contest, they were entirely defeated: in consequence of this victory prince Potemkin laid siege to Bender, which, after having vigorously defended itself, surrendered in the month of November. On the western frontier of the Turkish empire, the most important enterprises were undertaken on the side of Croatia; marshal Laudohn began the campaign with besieging Gradisca, which in the former year had so vigorously withstood the Austrian attacks; on the twentieth of June, instead of regularly constructing lines of circumvallation, he commenced a violent cannonade and bombardment: the Turks were so much intimidated that on the second day they evacuated the place: they had, indeed, no confidence in the present commander in chief, the grand vizier; and predestination, mingling with their dejection, on account of so many disasters, they conceived that every attempt against the Russians and Austrians would be totally useless, and that fate had decreed they were to be vanquished: this superstition had a very powerful influence on their conduct, and greatly contributed to the victories of their enemies. After his success at Gradisca, Laudohn made preparations for the siege of Belgrade: the Turks were so dismayed, that an operose attack was not necessary: the systematic and steady adherence of the Germans to precedent, however, made them employ the same time and labour in dispositions for this enterprise, that would have been wanted in quite different circumstances, and quite different sentiments of the enemy. Formerly in besieging Belgrade great numbers of boats had been employed by the Austrians in order to oppose multitudes of the boats employed by the Turks in its defence: at present the Ottomans had on the Danube no nautical force of the kind: the Germans, however, proceeded upon their general principle, both in war and politics, authority and precedent; and like other votaries of the same rules of reasoning, did not very nicely investigate the case; prince Eugene, they said, employed boats in besieging Belgrade; therefore we must use them also: in making preparations upon this principle, so much time elapsed, that it was the twelfth of September before the Austrians invested the place: the trench-

p So blindly and stupidly arrogant was this weak, headstrong, and ignorant man, that, when he took the command of the army, he caused an immense quantity of iron chains to be made, in order to manacle the legions of Austrian and Russian prisoners, whom he expected to drive before him to Constantinople, as monuments of triumph. At the close of the campaign he was beheaded. See Annual Register, 1789.

CHAP. es were speedily opened, and the batteries constructed; and
XLII. after a defence of about eighteen days the town was taken by
~~~~   assault. Thus the principal fortresses on the Turkish frontiers
1789. fell under the arms of Austria and of Russia; the Turkish
       troops were defeated, and believing themselves victims of all
       powerful destiny, were filled with consternation and dismay;
Ottoman they could no longer bear the sight of their enemy, and any
empire in small Austrian or Russian detachment was sufficient to dis-
danger. perse any number of those who attempted to form a body:
       winter only seemed to retard the subversion of the Ottoman
       empire.

Sweden.   While the Russians were making rapid stretches to the at-
       tainment of their grand objects in the south, their active, en-
       terprising, and intrepid foe in the north afforded them conside-
       rable annoyance. Gustavus, when about to commence hostili-
       ties with Russia, had employed great pains to convince the
       court of Denmark, that it was the common interest of both
       kingdoms to oppose the encroaching politics of Catharine.
       There were, however, several obstacles to a confederation be-
       tween Denmark and Sweden. The very year in which Gus-
       stavus had accomplished a revolution in his own country, great
       discontents having arisen in Norway, the king of Sweden had
       studiously fomented them, and almost succeeded in exciting an
       insurrection. Though the discovery of the design by the
       court of Copenhagen, before it was ripe for execution, prevent-
       ed it from being accomplished, yet Denmark had ever since
       regarded Sweden with a very watchful and jealous eye: Catha-
       rine, on the other hand, had cultivated the friendship of the Da-
       nish court with the closest assiduity : she had sacrificed to Den-
       mark patrimonial rights and inheritances of person in the
       duchies of Sleswick and Holstein, and thereby enabled the
       Danes to round their dominions on the side of Germany. In
       addition to the general policy by which Catharine established
       powerful partisans in the neighbouring courts, this conduct en-
       hanced the connexion that had long subsisted between Den-
       mark and Russia. The king of Sweden, by subsequent atten-
       tions, endeavoured to obliterate in Denmark his measures re-
       specting Norway. On the commencement of the Turkish war
       he paid a very unexpected visit at Copenhagen; and endea-
       voured fully to conciliate the court and nation, and to impress
       them with an opinion of the danger that must accrue to smal-
       ler powers from the ambition of Russia. The court of Den-
       mark could not perceive any of those dangers, which so deeply
       affected the Swedish king; and accordingly treated, and seem-
       ed to consider them as entirely visionary, and mere creatures of
       his imagination. They lamented that he should entertain in-
       tentions of involving himself in so unequal and ruinous a con-
       test, and endeavoured strongly to dissuade him from such an
       undertaking.q Although the king was unmoved by their argu-

q See Annual Register, 1789.

ments, yet he did not entertain the most distant idea of any CHAP.
connexion subsisting between Denmark and Russia. Catha- XLII.
rine, however, had been so successful in her intrigues at the
court of Denmark, that she prevailed on the prince regent to 1789.
conclude a treaty, by which he bound himself to assist Russia
with a certain number of forces, should she be involved in a
war with Sweden. Gustavus, having no apprehension of hostilities from Denmark, when preparing to open the campaign
in Finland, had drawn away his forces to that quarter, and
left the vicinity of Norway defenceless; when he was involved
in all the trouble and danger occasioned by the refractoriness,
or rather the revolt of his army in Finland. The court of Copenhagen issued a public notice to the foreign ministers, and
among the rest to the Swedish, who was most immediately concerned, of the conditions by which she was bound to Russia,
to supply her with a considerable auxiliary force by sea and
land, and of her own determination to fulfil those conditions.
This denunciation was soon followed by an invasion of Sweden
on the side of Norway, in September 1788. In this distressing Distresses
situation, Gustavus, surrounded by enemies, and deserted by of Gusta-
his own troops, appeared overwhelmed with ruin. The conta- vus.
gion from the army had spread through various parts of the
kingdom, and infected even the capital; while the nobility
seemed fast approaching to the recovery of their former power
and consequence in the nation. The senate was eagerly disposed to resume its ancient authority: all the circumstances of
the time, the deplorable state of the king's affairs, together
with the prevalent disposition of the nobility, rendered them
confident of success; they accordingly took measures, without
consulting the king, to assemble in diet, the states of the kingdom, under colour of considering the deranged and dangerous
state of public affairs, the discontents and disorders which prevailed in the nation. Before this design was executed, the king Effects of
arrived at Stockholm: knowing, that though the nobility were his genius
inimical to his interests, the burghers and people were warmly and cour-
attached to him, he summoned an assembly of citizens; he age for ex-
thereing declared, that reposing the most unbounded confidence trication.
in their affection, loyalty, and valour, and being himself called
to oppose an unexpected enemy, he should intrust the defence
and preservation of the capital, the protection of the queen and
family to their faithful zeal. Such an important trust, and sacred deposit, inspired the generous plebeians with an enthusiastic desire of showing themselves worthy of the royal confidence; they immediately embodied themselves, and cheerfully
performed all the duties of soldiers. Gustavus, meanwhile,
sent an answer to the intimation of Denmark: he expressed
his astonishment that, when peace and friendship had subsisted
for sixty years between the two powers, without interruption,
and he himself had employed his utmost endeavours to preserve a harmony so beneficial to both parties, his Danish ma-

CHAP. jesty should have 'commenced hostilities: he knew nothing of
XLII. the engagements subsisting between Denmark and Russia, but
‿‿‿ he now desired from the court of Copenhagen a direct expla-
1789.· nation of its intentions, whether Denmark meant only to act as
an auxiliary, by furnishing a stipulated force, or intended direct
aggression against Sweden? If the latter was their resolution,
he must consider the war as commenced, and act accordingly.
Were so unjustifiable a measure adopted, other powers, he insinuated, would, for their own security, interfere to prevent the
advances of such ambitious rapacity. The prince regent of
Denmark in reply declared, that he had no intention of interfering in the war, any farther than he was bound to Russia by
a treaty concluded in 1781, long before hostilities were in contemplation, and that he would not exceed the force therein stipulated; he expressed his earnest desire for the restoration of
peace. Meanwhile, the new treaty between Great Britain
and Prussia began to unfold its objects, to the great encouragement of all those states that wished to preserve the balance of Europe from being overturned by the imperial confederacy. France, the old ally of Sweden, being unable to afford any assistance, he now looked for support and protection
to the wise and vigorous policy of the defensive alliance, and
with confident expectations of ultimate success.

Miners of   On the confines of Norway, is the province of Dalecarlia,
Dalecarlia. memorable in Swedish history for having afforded shelter and
concealment to the celebrated Gustavus Vasa, when flying from
the Danish usurpers, and for having begun the revolution which
placed that hero on the throne of his ancestors. The inhabitants, sunk in their mines among the rocks and mountains, and
secluded from the rest of the world, are ignorant and rough;
but hardened by climate, situation, and pursuit, are strong and
valiant, and have the honesty and hospitality of generous barbarism: from their ancestors they inherit the warmest loyalty
and attachment to their sovereigns; their native courage operating upon this priciple induces them with the promptest heroism to abandon mines and forests whenever their king requires
their assistance. To these gallant rustics Gustavus had recourse;
he followed the example of his illustrious namesake, and descended to desert mines and caverns to visit the loyal heroes.
The second appearance of a king in these recesses, also a
Gustavus, and come to solicit their assistance, recalled tradi-
tionary glory to the miners of Dalecarlia: they anticipated the
application of their sovereign; eagerly proffered their services
to defend their prince, and inflict vengeance on the Danes, towards whom they cherished an hereditary hatred ever since
the time that they tyrannized over Sweden. The king having
testified his gratitude for· their loyal ·and affectionate offers,
limited his request to three thousand men. This body was
immediately equipt to attend their monarch, and though by no

means all provided with regular arms,[r] yet, furnished with such weapons as they could procure, and inspired with loyalty, with vigorous bodies and intrepid courage, they were a formidable band.

The Danes, meanwhile, entered Sweden from the east part The Danes of Norway, under prince Charles of Hesse, and marching invade along the sea-coast, captured Stramstead, and penetrated as Sweden. far as Gottenburgh, the principal port of Sweden for foreign commerce; and the governor was about to surrender by an inglorious capitulation: Gustavus was aware of the danger of this valuable city, and sensible that, before he could bring his troops to its relief, the capture might be effected, in order to inspire the inhabitants by his presence, he hastened to the place alone, and travelling night and day, arrived a few hours after the determination to surrender. The king immediately displaced the governor, and having assembled a meeting of the citizens, by the powers of his persuasive eloquence so inspirited them with courage and confidence, that they resolved to defend the city to the last extremity. The force, however, of the Danish army, and the absence of the Swedish troops, rendered the success of the defenders very improbable. In this British po- critical situation, the wise, protecting policy of Britain, that licy indu- has uniformly supported the weak against the strong, interfer- ces the ed for the preservation of Gustavus. There being no ambas- Danes to sador from either Britain or Prussia at the court of Stockholm, retreat. Mr. Elliot, envoy at Copenhagen, was sent to the Swedish king, delegate of the allied powers, and to mediate between the belligerent parties. Mr. Elliot sent a letter in his new character from Gottenburgh to prince Charles, informing him that the allied powers had sent a courier to the empress to demand a general armistice; meanwhile, he desired a particular truce, until the effect of the application to Petersburgh should be known. Prince Charles answered, that he should not suspend hostilities without the express orders of his court: Mr. Elliot, in reply, informed him, that if the army which he commanded, proceeded farther in offensive operations against Sweden, Prussia would attack Denmark by land, and England would attack her by sea; but that he hoped the prince royal, regent of Denmark, would adopt such measures as would prevent the farther effusion of blood. This notification was not without effect: the Danish general, instead of pressing the siege, sent to his court for instructions. The firm and determined remonstrances of the British ambassador, supported by the strongest and most con-

r The author of the Annual Register for 1788, in this part of his narrative observes: "They formed a grotesque appearance; some, whose families had preserved the rusty uncouth weapons of antiquity, gloried in the possession, and fancied themselves thoroughly equipt for war; but the greater number had no other resource than those rustic instruments of labour used in the mines or in husbandry, which seemed the best calculated for their purpose."

vincing arguments, manifesting the wise and·comprehensive principles of the allied powers, and the real interests of Denmark, so deeply impressed the prince regent, that he agreed to conclude a short armistice; after that a longer; and lastly for six months. The Danish army departed from Sweden; but the proffered mediation of the defensive alliance was refused by Russia. Freed by the intervention of the protecting confederacy from the invasion of the Danes, Gustavus had in winter leisure to attend to the internal affairs of his kingdom, and to make preparations for the campaign. He had still very great difficulties to encounter: his army had not only refused to fight in his cause, but actually concluded an armistice with Russia without his consent. The party of his subjects connected with his mighty enemy was extremely powerful and desirous of exerting their strength, in effecting a revolution which would totally overturn the royal authority. In this state of affairs peace must have been of all things the most desirable to the king, and the most suitable to his circumstances; but his potent enemy was too haughty, and too implacable in her resentments, to listen now to accommodation on any terms of equality: she knew his situation, and the advantages which she might derive from his embarrassments; so that personal animosity and political interest dictated the same conduct. The king saw that, desirable as peace would be on fair, equitable terms, it could then be attained only by submitting to conditions disgraceful and ruinous: of two great evils war was the smaller; he had no alternative, but either to surrender his crown to disaffected nobles, and the ambitious Catharine, or by magnanimous efforts to conquer both foreign and domestic enemies. In order to cope with Russia, Gustavus had two great objects to be previously accomplished, the subjection of the mutinous army, and the coercion of the rebellious aristocracy. There is an elasticity in vigorous minds which apportions effort to difficulty, and in pressing emergencies produces exertions beyond the previous conception of powers. In such exigencies Gustavus felt that his invention was fertile, his courage undaunted, and his magnanimity elevated; he knew that by a great majority of his subjects he was beloved and revered: in his own genius and fortitude, and in the affection of his people, he sought and found resources. Trusting to his popularity among the plebeian classes, on his return to Stockholm from Gottenburgh, he called a meeting of the magistrates and most respectable citizens of the capital; to these he gave the flattering name of a grand council of state, by whose advice he professed to be governed in all his measures: he thanked them for the care with which they had executed the important trust committed to them in his capital and family: he informed them that in the preceding campaign, instead of retrieving Swedish glory, the national honour had been blasted by the disaffection of his nobles: these had corrupted his army, had led it to the disgraceful and fatal excess of a mutiny, in the pre-

sence of their sovereign, and in the face of a foreign enemy.
Expatiating upon these subjects, he impressed his audience with
the fullest conviction, and they unanimously declared for
the continuance of the war; with a warm assurance of their
lives and fortunes being devoted to his service. Having secured the support of his capital, he waited with confidence
for the meeting of the states : determined as to the measures
which he would pursue, if they continued refractory. On the
twenty-sixth of January, the diet having met the order of the
nobles, immediately displayed their animosity to the king, and
their disregard for his authority : they grossly insulted count
Lowenhaupt, the president appointed by his majesty, and even
treated the name of Gustavus himself with great virulence and
contempt. The king having found that the three other orders,
the peasants, clergy, and burghers, were unanimous in supporting the war, disregarded the opposition of the nobles, and determined to repress their insolence. On the 17th of February
he repaired in person to the diet to demand satisfaction for the
insult that was offered to the president, his representative in
the assembly : a violent altercation here arose between the king
and nobles, in the course of which his majesty made a charge
of disaffection and treason; the nobles arose and left the assembly : the king addressing the three remaining states, most
solemnly disclaimed every intention of aspiring at absolute authority, but declared there was a faction in the kingdom inimical
to Sweden, and devoted to her enemy: that for the good of
the country the faction must be crushed. The states unanimously expressed their concurrence with his majesty, and their
determination to support any measures which he should think expedient for so desirable a purpose. On the twentieth of February, the king having communicated his plan of procedure to
the three estates, ordered twenty-five of the principal nobility to
be arrested, and the officers who had been most active in exciting mutiny, to be seized and brought to Stockholm for trial.
These vigorous measures received the general approbation of
the three remaining orders. Gustavus proceeded in his efforts,
and formed the bold measure of abolishing the senate, a council
consisting chiefly of nobles, and that had of late greatly thwarted
the king : his vigorous resolution entirely suppressed this assembly, without the least commotion or opposition, and in its
place he instituted a new council, totally dependent on himself:
the nobles were so much dismayed and intimidated by these
acts, that they suffered Gustavus to extend his changes; his
majesty to secure and confirm the remaining orders in their attachment, granted them respectively such new privileges, and
paid them such honours, as he knew they would most highly
value. To render these alterations permanent, Gustavus pro- He con-
posed an act of confederation, union, and surety, by which he firms his
and all true Swedes were to be mutually bound in the most popularity.
firm and solemn manner, not only to common defence, but to

CHAP.
XLII.

1789.

the preservation of the present constitution and laws, against all impugners, whether foreign or domestic. Though the nobles so far recovered from the consternation as to oppose this measure, yet his majesty directed the president to subscribe it in their name; and thus Gustavus effected in a few weeks a revolution, which entirely destroyed the authority that the nobles had been so long endeavouring to re-establish, and the influence which the intrigues of Russia had been so many years employed in acquiring. The trials of the officers charged with mutiny, commenced soon after the arrest; and though the necessity of obedience and military subordination required condign punishment, the executions were not numerous.

He directs his whole energies against Russia.

By the reduction of the nobles, the suppression of the mutiny, and his popularity with the other states, Gustavus was now master of the whole efficient force of his kingdom, and thereby was enabled to make a vigorous preparation for prosecuting the war with Russia: besides the supplies afforded him by the estates, he received a very considerable sum from the Ottoman Porte. Before he opened the campaign against Russia, the strong arguments, and urgent instances of Mr. Elliott, on the part of the defensive alliance, prevailed upon Denmark to consent to an absolute neutrality, and thus freed the Swedish king from that source of apprehension. Gustavus was now enabled to direct his whole attention and force to the prosecution of the war in Finland, and opened the campaign in the beginning of June.

Military and naval campaign between Sweden and Russia.

On the twenty-eighth a very fierce battle was fought between the Swedes and Russians, in which the latter had almost prevailed, when the king springing from his horse, put himself at the head of his infantry, rallied them, and compelled the enemy to fly. Various skirmishes were afterwards fought, in which the Swedish monarch displayed the most intrepid and active valour, bold and fertile genius:[s] the successes were various; but during the first part of the campaign most frequently on the side of Sweden. Encouraged by his advantages, the hero penetrated into Russian Finland, having on the coast a fleet of light galleys to co-operate with the army as occasion might require. Between this fleet and another of the same sort from Russia, a battle was fought, in which great numbers were destroyed on both sides: the Swedes were obliged to retire; and though they were not totally defeated, the superiority of the Russians was such, that it compelled Gustavus to evacuate the enemy's country.[t] The season being now too far advanced to admit military operations in those cold latitudes, both armies withdrew into winter quarters, and the king returned to Stockholm. The duke of Suddermania, the king's brother, commanded the prin-

s Gustavus depended entirely on genius and heroism; being deficient in military experience and skill, as he himself afterwards acknowledged in conversation with the marquis de Bouille. See Memoirs, p. 396.
t Annual Register, 1789, chap. viii.

.cipal fleet of Sweden, but no decisive action took place between his armament and the fleet of Russia.

While the emperor was by his preparations and expense, together with the misconduct of the enemy, obtaining victories
and conquests from which he could derive no permanent advantages, he was endangering his most productive possessions.
The Netherlands, first of all the states of modern Europe, successfully cultivated agriculture, commerce, and manufactures,
and acquired at an early period a considerable degree of liberty. They consisted of independent states, resembling one another in their pursuits, manners, character, and constitution of
government. Their polity was composed of three orders, the
nobles, clergy, and people under the limited principality of one
person denominated count: the contests between the prerogatives and privileges of the respective principalities, according
to their result, gave different modifications to the freedom which
they all possessed, and which they continued to retain under
various families of princes that happened, through intermar-
riage, to succeed to the sovereign authority. The best defined,
and most perfect of their political systems, was the constitution
of Brabant. The great charter of that country was no less venerated by the inhabitants, than the charter of Runnymede is
revered by Englishmen: from a circumstance attending its execution, it was known by the name of Joyous Entry. The inhabitants of the Austrian Netherlands were extremely devoted
to their ancient religion: this predilection probably arose, partly from their long intercourse with Spain, and, perhaps, still
more from the animosity between them and their neighbours
and countrymen the Dutch, that originated in wars in which
they were the principal sufferers: but, whatever might be the
cause, it is a certain fact, the Netherlanders were extremely
addicted to the most absurd and extravagant tenets of the Roman catholic faith: they manifested a very warm affection to
their princes, both the aboriginal sovereigns of the country,
and their descendants of the house of Austria. Upon the accession of the German branch of that house to the dominion
of these provinces, Charles VI. was received by the people with
the greatest cordiality and good will, he having first sworn at
his inauguration, as his successors have constantly done, to the
preservation of their ancient constitutions and rights. During
the distresses of the family, at the accession of Maria Theresa,
they derived the most essential benefit from the zeal and fidelity,
the loyalty, and the resources of money and of men, which
were supplied by their subjects in the Low Countries. The
free subsidies were granted with a liberality proportioned to the
emergency for which they were required: they continued during her life to manifest undiminished affection, and cherished
the same sentiments for her son Joseph. Beloved by them before, the emperor had confirmed their attachment by the flattering hopes which he raised in the Low Countries, that he

CHAP.
XLII.

1789.

would recover and open to them the navigation of the Scheldt. Blasted as their expectations were, imputing the disappointment to necessity, they had not relaxed in attachment to their sovereign; and though they did not rise in their estimation of his political and military abilities, they were grateful for the benignity of his intention. The spirit, however, of restless innovation, which so much distinguished the active, but superficial character of Joseph, soon extended to the Netherlands, and interfered with their ancient privileges and ancient religion, the two objects of which they were most peculiarly tenacious.

No position in political philosophy is more obvious, than that systems of polity, civil or ecclesiastical, must be adapted to the sentiments, habits, opinions, and even prejudices of the people:[u] such reforms, therefore, as overlook these, however abstractedly agreeable to reason and rectitude, are neither reasonable nor right in their application to those particular cases, because they do not conduce to the happiness of the subject. The clergy were alarmed and enraged; the people grieved and astonished by the suppression of religious houses, to which, however absurd in the enlightened views of an Englishman, the Netherlanders annexed an importance that a wise ruler would have regarded. It was soon seen that reform was not his only object; and that he desired change for the sake of confiscation, that he might procure the means of gratifying an extravagant and infatuated ambition. Men of abilities and enlarged minds, being totally free from bigotry and superstition, thought that some of the monasteries and convents might be very easily spared; but by no means relished suppression for the sake of plunder; the same rapacity which seized that species of property, would, they apprehended, extend to other kinds of possessions. The ecclesiastical order formed a very powerful, numerous, and opulent body in the Low Countries; and their property, of every sort, was estimated at the immense sum of twenty-five millions sterling. The states being composed of the representatives of the clergy, the nobility, and the commons: the church had likewise possessed, from time immemorial, at least a third part in the government of the country. It was apprehended, from the emperor's conduct, that he had projected to destroy the privileges of this order, as a preliminary step to the seizure of their immense wealth. All ranks were alarmed, and began to coalesce, in order to oppose an innovating system, the real purpose of which they conceived not to be reform but robbery. Those who were themselves merely anxious for the preservation of their civil rights, found it expedient to encourage the discontents of the clergy, and even to profess sympathy with the superstition and bigotry of the lower orders: these various causes coinciding, formed a compact and powerful opposition against the dangers which threatened their

Joseph's violent desire of change under the name of reform.

Innovations in the ecclesiastical establishments.

Suppression of religious orders,

and confiscation of their property.

u See Aristotle's Politics.

ancient establishments. Fortunately for his subjects and neigh- CHAP.
bours, as the objects of Joseph were wicked, his policy was XLII.
weak : he was totally deficient in that dexterity and address,
which can varnish mischievous schemes, and smooth the way 1789.
for their reception : he neither tried disguise, insinuation, nor
deceit, the usual engines of ability attempting injustice, where
the effect of force would be doubtful : his heart dictated usurpation and injury, but his head was not well fitted for insuring
success : a harsh arbitrary and imperious display of authority
appeared in all his measures : he was particularly desirous of
suppressing ancient customs, and changing ancient institutions.
There was a festival of great antiquity in the Low Countries, Suppres-
called the Kermesse, and highly venerated by the inhabitants : sion of
it was a season of mutual visiting, and of reconciling differ- ancient,
ences, not only between individuals, but villages ; it was equally venerated,
a season for contracting marriages, forming new friendships, cial cus-
and renewing and cementing the old. This innocent source of toms.
festive recreation, this laudable occasion of social virtue, was
in the emperor's innovating zeal suppressed. The disposal of
land and revenue, belonging to the abolished convents produced
great dissatisfaction and complaint: they were rendered part
of the royal domains, and merely filled the coffers of the emperor. His next attempt was upon the abbacies, the most opulent and splendid of the religious establishments. Several of
these conferred a right on the possessors of being directly inherent members of the states. In Brabant this high distinction
and privilege in favour of the abbots, was carried to a greater
extent than elsewhere; for the whole of the clergy, being the
first order of the state, were represented by abbots only. Joseph did not at first subvert the abbacies, but as the incumbents
died, placed them to be held *in commendam*, which was directly
contrary to an express article of the Joyous Entry. In the beginning of 1787 he published two edicts, which entirely absorbed the consideration of every smaller change; by these all the
tribunals,ˣ all the forms and course of civil justice, which for
so many centuries had been established and pursued in the Low
Countries, which the people had so long considered as their
glory and regarded with enthusiastic admiration, were to be
abolished in one day. The forms of process in the old courts
were fair and open : they publicly exhibited the series of evidence,
rules of interpretation ; the principles applied, and grounds

x The principal tribunals were in the villages ; a court held by the lord
of the manor, who in smaller cases delegated his authority to a set of repu-
table men within his district ; but in greater judged himself, being assisted
by two eminent counsellors to expound the laws. In the cities the jurisdiction was in the hands of their respective magistrates : there was a supreme
tribunal composed of sixteen judges and a president, in which, causes either
civil or criminal might originate ; and in civil cases an appeal lay from the
inferior courts. See Annual Register, 1789, p. 207.

CHAP.
XLII.

1789.
Change of
judicial
forms and
proceed-
ings.
Arbitrary
system in-
troduced.

of decision. New tribunals were appointed, in which the secrecy
of despotism marked the proceedings; witnesses were privately
examined, the parties were often ignorant of the evidence on
which they were tried, and the decision was left to a single
judge, who was to determine according to his discretion without
any existing law. The persons appointed to this office were
foreigners,ʸ totally unacquainted with the ancient laws of the
Netherlands, or at least altogether regardless of their spirit and
tenor. Such modes of judicial procedure, combined with the
other parts of the emperor's conduct, were considered as the
forerunners of proscription and tyranny: they excited great
alarm among the people, not without a determination to resist
acts so contrary to the compact by which Joseph held the
sovereignty of the Netherlands. But the second edict advancing
in lawless usurpation, confirmed their resolution not quietly to
submit to the destruction of their rights.

The states of the Netherlands were justly deemed by the
people the guardians of their laws, liberty, and property;
and in them was vested the power of imposing taxes on the
subjects, and granting subsides to the prince. In the exercise
of this power they had uniformly satisfied both parties, by
liberal grant without burthensome impost. The assembly of
the states met annually at Brussels, and having performed the
most material part of their business, intrusted the rest to a
select committee, whose proceedings they reviewed at the fol-

Subversion
of the esta-
blished le-
gislature.

lowing meeting. This legislative branch of the constitution
was no less valued than the judicative, but the emperor in
his second edict, proclaimed its subversion; he abolished the
old institutions and forms, and substituted an engine of state
under the name of a council of general government, which,
while it drew all public affairs within the sphere of its own
action, was to be ruled by the court minister who was placed
at its head. Without nominally annihilating the assembly of
the states, the new form of government really destroyed its
powers: it ordained, that the states might nominate a deputy, who, if approved of by the minister had his council, might
be a member of that council, and when required by the minister was to sign all the acts formerly exercised by the states,
but now to be proposed by the council. Thus the states were
really to have no other power but to subscribe imperial mandates; and their authority was to be exercised by a nominal
representative under the control of the minister and his council: the jurisdiction of this new council was farther to extend
to all cases of police and revenue: all persons even suspected,

y The baron de Martini, an Italian, was sent into the Low Countries,
with the title of Imperial Commissary, to establish and regulate the new
tribunals, and to prescribe to a nation, which had for many ages gloried in
the freedom, as well as the equity of its civil institutions, in what manner
justice should be dispensed in future.

or pretended to be suspected, were the objects of inquisitorial
procedure, by order of the council and minister from whose
decrees there lay no appeal. When the nature and extent of
this despotic usurpation was understood and comprehended,
the people very loudly expressed indignant resentment against
so daring a violation of that convention, by which only the
archduke of Austria, held the limited sovereignty of the
Netherlands. In language less mindful of his rank than de-
scriptive of his conduct, they plainly and unequivocally charged Joseph with having violated the inaugural compact and
oath, and not obscurely intimated, that a breach of a conditional contract by one of the parties absolved the other from
its obligations. Those who were most favourable to the emperor, alleged, that the obnoxious edicts proceeded from
mistaken views of the public good, and not from a design upon
their liberties : according to such advocates he had suppressed
the ancient tribunals, that the people might be enabled to obtain
justice in a less expensive and more compendious way, and
his alteration of the government was designed to give it more
simplicity and energy: the small military force in the Low
Countries was totally inadequate to the establishment of an
absolute sovereignty ; he had been deceived by partial and
false representations, and misled by evil counsellors. The
reply to this species of vindication was obvious; whether
violation of their dearest rights proceeded from the despotic
intentions, or the defective judgment of the sovereign, it was
equally incumbent on subjects to defend their constitutional
liberties: though the conduct of the emperor was, in all his
dominions, such as to evince a narrow understanding, yet in
the Netherlands, and every other part, it was so uniformly directed to one object, the invasion of property to increase his
own revenue, that misinformation and erroneous reasoning did
not account for its general tenor : *no person could be a systematic robber by mistake.*

The emperor's chief counsellor was the count. Belgiojoso,
his minister, a Milanese, a great favourite with his master ; and
who possessing all the subtlety, artifice, and crooked policy of
an Italian statesman, was extremely disagreeable to the open,
frank, and honest Flemings. The governor-general, the duke of
Saxe Teschen, and his wife, the archduchess, sister to the emperor, were extremely popular, and never suspected of promoting any unconstitutional designs; but the minister possessed
the real power of government. Belgiojoso proceeded to a violent exercise of the powers so lawlessly usurped ; indeed, if he
had conceived a design of extending and consolidating a revolt, he could not have formed a more efficacious plan for the
purpose: having excited the resentment of the civil orders, by
the overthrow of the established judicature and legislature, he
next attacked the clerical order, not as before, by suppressing
certain fraternities, the least essential to the church, but those

CHAP.
XLII.

1789.
Progress of
despotism
trampling
liberty and
franchises.

institutions which nourished its appropriate learning, preserved its most important rights, and that literature and science from which it chiefly derived its influence. The principal university of Brabant was the Louvain, one of the most celebrated schools of Roman catholic theology, distinguished for the extraordinary reverence with which it regarded the supreme pontiff, by its profound respect for the priesthood, and consequently highly prized by zealous votaries of the Romish church: all its colleges were abolished, and a general seminary was established, in which, by an edict, all youth designed for the church were required to pursue their theological studies. For this new school a German rector and professors were appointed, to the exclusion of native teachers. Such a change, violating the ecclesiastical constitution, and tending to introduce new doctrines of theology, was warmly opposed by the bishops, the university, and the people. The Low Countries, so long famous for the purity of its catholic faith ; the Louvain, the nurse of holy religion, was to be contaminated with the heresies in which Germany abounded. The minister enjoined father Godefroy, visitor of the capuchins at Brussels, to send the young students of his order to be educated in the general seminary : this clergyman refused to comply. Belgiojoso commanded him to depart from Brussels in twenty-four hours, and the emperor's dominions in three days. Such a violent act afforded a new subject of complaint to those who were zealous in religion, and strengthened the abhorrence of the new seminary; but it increased the apprehensions of the progress of arbitrary power, which were already so generally entertained.

Joseph
considers
his Flem-
ish sub-
jects mere-
ly as sour-
ces of re-
venue.

The emperor and his counsellors appeared to have adopted, respecting his richest and most productive dominions, one of the most dangerous principles that can actuate the conduct of a government, *that subjects are merely to be considered as a source of revenue*, and the expediency of political plans and acts to be estimated by their tendency to supply the coffers of the prince. The discontents and commotions in the Netherlands very greatly diminished its financial efficiency, and consequently defeated the purpose which the authors of the innovations meant chiefly to promote. The minister, pretending to impute the defalcation to contraband traffic, proceeded in a summary and arbitrary way against persons whom he professed to suspect to be engaged in such a commerce. One respectable and eminent merchant, who held a contract with government, was, after his accounts had been closed and passed, charged with a fraud : he challenged his accusers to make good their assertions by a fair and open trial, agreeably to the laws of his country; but, instead of a legal inquiry, he was seized by armed soldiers, and hurried away to Vienna. So flagrant a tyranny, joined to the general system, impressed the people with a belief, that their only alternative was subjection to foreign despotism, or vigorous and immediate resistance.

In Brabant the constitution had been the most precise, and CHAP.
its violations the most manifest; and there the resistance was XLII.
the most prompt. In Brussels the companies of arts and trades,
nine in number, chose representatives, each known by the 1789.
name of syndic: these delegates constituted a corporation, en- Remon-
titled the syndics of the nine nations: they possessed not only strances of
municipal power, but also very considerable political direction the Ne-
in the choice of members for the assembly of the states; and crs.
being composed of the chief citizens, they added extensive influence to their strength. This was the first public body
which expressed its sentiments concerning the usurpations:
they drew up a plain, bold memorial, that stated actual facts
and obvious consequences; and enumerated the conditions on
which the prince of the Low Countries held his sovereignty, as
set forth in the Joyous Entry; the representation quoted Joseph's inaugural oath to observe the prescribed stipulations,
and his actual conduct, which was a systematic violation of
his engagements; and concluded, that "if the sovereign shall
" infringe upon the articles of the Joyous Entry, his subjects
" shall be discharged from all duty and service to him, until
" such time as due reparation shall be made for such infringe-
" ments." This animated remonstrance inspirited and guided
the other cities, and also the other provinces; and the people in
general were determined to assert their rights; but before they
should commence any active exertions, they waited the meeting
of the states, that they might know how far they could trust to
their counsel and co-operation.

The assembly met, and the very first step demonstrated the Meeting of
firm and resolute part which they intended to act. An appli- the states.
cation having been made for subsidies, they totally refused to
grant supplies until grievances were redressed; they sent immediate orders to the collectors of the revenues to pay no regard to the financial officers appointed by the new council,
since they exercised an authority which was not admitted by
the Flemish constitution: they then drew up a declaration of
rights, a statement of grievances, and an exhibition of consequences, both more detailed and comprehensive than that of the
syndics, and which avowed their determination to persevere in
maintaining the constitution of their ancestors; this manifesto
they addressed to the governor-general. At the same time Mr.
Vandernoot, a counsellor of Brussels, and an eminent advocate
in the cause of liberty, published a treatise addressed to the
states, in which, from ancient documents, he traced out and
elucidated the constitution of Brabant. The states not only
ordered this treatise to be read in their presence, but decreed
public thanks to the author, for having so ably and justly vindicated the rights of the people. The states of Flanders and
Hainault concurred in the determination to resist all the unconstitutional changes. The governors-general endeavoured to
break the force of the opposition by small concessions and libe-

CHAP.   ral promises: the Italian, to his great surprise, found that the
XLII.   Flemings were not to be intimidated; and, until he could be
        supplied with an adequate force, he had recourse to the more
1789.   appropriate instruments of his country, duplicity and decep-
        tion: the attempt, however, was now too late; the patriots
        persevered in their efforts, and held out to the minister the ter-
        rors of an ancient statute of Brabant, that declared it lawful
        to apprehend and to punish any person who should obstinately
        persist in obstructing the public good: they abolished the new
        seminaries and other unconstitutional innovations; urged the
        governors-general speedily to redress their grievances; and ad-
        ded, that the people were in such a ferment, that they could
        not answer for the consequences of longer delay. The minis-
        ter had hitherto obstructed concessions on the side of the go-
        vernors-general, but now pretended no longer to oppose con-
        ciliatory measures: alarmed at the revolution in the temper
        and dispositions of a people from whom they had before expe-
        rienced the most affectionate attachment, the governors resolved,
        as far as their power extended, to restore the tranquillity and
        happiness of the provinces. They issued a decree on the thir-
        tieth of May, declaring that all arrangements contrary to the
        Joyous Entry should be entirely set aside, and that due repa-
        ration should be made for all infringements on that great char-
        ter which the people held so sacred: they hoped the empe-
        ror would ratify this declaration, and promised to exert their
        utmost influence with him to accomplish such a desirable pur-
        pose. This proclamation at first diffused general joy through
        the Netherlands: but these sentiments were interrupted by
        doubts concerning the emperor's ratification. Joseph, instead
        of sanctioning the decree, despatched a mandate to the states
        of the Low Countries, strongly expressing his astonishment,
        indignation, and displeasure, at those intemperate and violent
        measures which they had adopted, and that bold defiance
        which they had given to his authority: his edicts had not been
        intended to subvert the constitution, but to correct ancient
        abuses and to make salutary reforms. As a proof of their
        obedience, he required the states of each province to send de-
        puties to Vienna, to lay their subjects of complaint at the foot
        of the throne. As a father, he would pardon the errors and te-
        merity of his subjects, but would severely punish them, if they
        continued refractory.

             Disappointed by so imperious an order, and so unfounded
        reprehension, they did not sink under the insolent claims of
Deputies   usurped authority, but took vigorous measures for their own
are sent to security. To prevent, however, matters from coming to ex-
Vienna.   tremities, they thought it prudent to comply to a certain extent
        with his requisition: they appointed deputies, intrusted with
        very limited powers, merely to express the loyalty of the na-
        tion, and to state their grievances, but to come to no conclusions
        respecting public affairs, without the special and immediate or-

der of the states. While the deputies was on their journey,
they were informed that great bodies of imperial troops were
marching towards the Low Countries. Though this intelligence
greatly agitated, yet it did not depress the minds of the Flemings; resolved to maintain their liberties at every hazard of
their lives and fortunes, they calculated their strength and resources, and found them much superior to those with which
the Dutch had formerly resisted Spanish despotism: they hoped for the interference of the powers that were already inimical to Joseph's ambition; and that France in particular
would willingly accept of the sovereignty of the Netherland
provinces, so beneficial and commodious, upon the constitutional conditions which they would most gladly offer. The
governors-general having been called to Vienna, to be present
when the deputies should appear before the emperor; count
Murray, a nobleman of Scottish extraction commander of the
Austrian troops in the Netherlands, was appointed governor
during their absence. This officer, a man of prudence and
temper, endeavoured to accommodate matters by moderating
the fervour of the people, and the imperiousness of the sovereign. The Flemings, meanwhile, were turned with the most
anxious expectation to the reception of their deputies at Vienna: and the first accounts were very far from being satisfactory. When presented to the emperor they were received
with all that angry haughtiness which narrow understandings
and illiberal sentiments in power produce to real or supposed
inferiors, when they are the objects of displeasure. Undismayed by imperious insolence, the deputies stated their grievances; but Joseph informed them, that before he would vouchsafe to explain himself upon that subject, there were certain
preliminary articles that count Murray would communicate to
his states: the articles were, that things should be restored to
the same footing in which they had stood at the meeting of the
states; that the new tribunal council and seminaries abolished
by the Flemings should be restored, the subsidies paid, and
the volunteers dismissed: if these articles were not executed,
the Austrian army should proceed in its march to the Netherlands.

The Flemings with great indignation refused to comply, and
between volunteer corps, and parties of soldiers, quarrels and
skirmishes arose, not without the effusion of blood; every
thing, notwithstanding the conciliatory efforts of count Murray, seemed tending to hostilities, when despatches arriving
from the deputies totally changed the public sentiments; by
these it appeared, that harsh as the first reception of the deputies had been, at succeeding interviews the emperor had declared, that though he had thought it consistent with the digni- Joseph
ty of his throne to testify his displeasure at the violent proceed- pretends to
ings of his Flemish subjects, he was really favourable to their grant their
requests; and though he would not consent to the re-establish- requests.

CHAP. ment of convents, nor to restore the nomination of abbots, he
XLII. would grant all the other principal articles: he never propos-
       ed[z] to enforce his edicts by arms, and was willing to restore
1789. the Joyous Entry to its primitive vigour; he intended to visit the
       Netherlands, and to concert measures with the states for the
       welfare of his people. These agreeable declarations were ac-
       companied with an unassuming and engaging politeness, which
       manifested, if not the ability of a statesman, the versatility of
       a courtier. The deputies were so captivated with the man-
       ners and address of the emperor, that they received every as-
       surance and profession with unbounded faith: their constitu-
       ents, though not so implicit in their confidence, yet were great-
       ly pleased and at last agreed to pay the subsidies into the roy-
       al treasury, as a mark of their reliance on the emperor's pro-
       testations. The count Murray in return published a declara-
       tion from the emperor, by which the Joyous Entry of Brabant
       was to be preserved entire, as well with respect to the ecclesi-
       astical as the civil orders; the new tribunals were to be sup-
       pressed, and the ancient courts of judicature to resume their
       function. The sovereign promised, that whatever infraction
       had been made upon the Joyous Entry, he would employ
       measures for granting redress. This accommodation between
       the emperor and his subjects diffused a general joy through
       the Low Countries. But the moderate system now adopted by
       Joseph, by discerning politicians, was imputed to particular
       circumstances, and not to any deviation from his general prin-
       ciples of action. In his innovating plan he had proceeded on
       the supposition, that the Netherlanders would make no mate-
       rial opposition, and that his wishes might be accomplished
       without distracting his attention, or withdrawing his force from
       the execution of his other schemes. From the spirit and
       vigorous conduct of the Flemings he saw that they could not
       be brought to submission without a considerable army, the em-
       ployment of which in that service would weaken his efforts
       against the Turks; he therefore abandoned one unjustifiable
       project of aggression, that he might the more effectually
       promote another; and it was inferred, that really he had
       only postponed his design respecting the Low Countries to a
       more favourable opportunity. The great object[a] of Joseph
       appears to have been to establish one simple uniform military
       system of government through all the parts of his vast domi-
       nions. This purpose was obstructed in the Netherlands by the
       present concession; there were, besides, important articles left
       unsettled, which might be the ground of future dispute. His
       expressions, upon being more closely examined than during the
       first ebullitions of joy, were found to be general and vague.

       z See declaration of the emperor to the states of the Belgic Provinces;
State Papers, July 3, 1787.
       a Annual Register, 1787, chap. viii.

On reflection, the Flemings perceived that they held no pledge
from the sovereign but his promises, while in disbanding the
militia they had given the most solid and substantial security
on their part [b]   The emperor after he had expressed his approbation of the lenient and conciliatory conduct of count Murray, appointed another commander in chief, who had no local
connexions in the Netherlands; this was general Dalton, a sol- Sends gen-
dier of fortune from Ireland, brave and enterprising, but whose eral Dalton
principle of conduct was simply obedience to his master's or- to the Ne-
ders, whatever they might be, or whatever rights they might therlands.
violate. He had been employed against the rebellious moun-
taineers of Transylvania, and acquired considerable reputation
by his military efforts; but had been noted for the cruelty with
which he treated his prisoners.   Count Trautmansdorff was
appointed to the civil government, to the great satisfaction of
the Low Countries, as he was a man of very amiable dispositions, and extremely popular; but it soon was found, that in
power he was totally subordinate to Dalton. The governors-
general were by the emperor's new plan to be mere pageants
of state and splendour, without any share of the government.

The first manifestation of the emperor's perseverance in the Despotic
plan which he pretended to relinquish, was an attack upon conduct of
the university of Louvain. While the Flemings were cherish- that officer
ing the hopes of preserving their revered constitution, and
indulging the convivial festivity of the Christmas season, exhi-
larated by the flattering prospect, a peremtory order arrived
in the emperor's name to the members of Louvain university,
commanding them, without deliberation, delay, or remonstrance, immediately to enregister in their archives, and submit to, the system of reform prescribed by the sovereign.
These mandates the university peremtorily refused to obey;
they pleaded their constitutional rights, and appealed to the
laws and justice of their country for protection. The minister, in his reply to this appeal, propounded a very simple, and
comprehensive principle, *that subjects must not plead rights,
laws, justice, or their constitution, against the will of the sovereign.* Declarations were issued, commanding them to conform
to the mandates of the emperor, and threatening the severest
vengeance against all persons who should dare to assert a
right contrary to the will of his imperial majesty. These dictatorial menaces were totally disregarded by the university,
which was determined to assert its freedom. Count Trautmansdorff was now become entirely subservient to Dalton, and
in his conduct showed, that the amiable dispositions and pleasing manners which had rendered him so popular, were not
fortified by vigour, or secured by virtuous principles. This
minister, by the direction of Dalton, sent a letter to the grand
council of Brabant, requiring their efforts to reduce to obe-

b Annual Register, 1789, p. 38.

CHAP. dience the refractory university, and specifying the time before
XLII. which the mandate was to be executed: the council, with a
dignified indignation replied, that the letter was founded in
1789. ignorance of their laws, tended to despotism, and must be revoked. The minister replied, that it was his majesty's absolute determination that *on whatever subject he signified his
will, obedience must follow;* and he gave them twenty-four
hours for publishing the decree. His commination being still
disregarded, the following day he sent a notice, that if the decrees were not published within two hours, he should have
recourse to the dire expedient of cannon and bayonets, which
his majesty had most expressly prescribed. The council still
paid not the smallest attention to those insolent threats; Dalton drew up a regiment of infantry near the council house,
and ordered an ensign with a party of troops to patrole the
streets. This officer, young, inexperienced, and desirous of
showing power, on some trifling disturbance, ordered his men
to fire a platoon among the multitude, killed six of the people,
and wounded many more: the juvenile instrument of military
despotism and murder, dreading the just vengeance of the
people, hastily fled with his party to the main body of soldiers.
The emperor informed of this achievement, highly applauded
the ensign's conduct, and desired Dalton to inform him he
might expect promotion on the first vacancy: he also expressed
his warmest gratitude to Dalton for *supporting the dignity of
the military character, and impressing the people with a due
dread of the soldiers.* This massacre, *unimportant* (THE EMPE-
ROR SAID) *as it was in itself*, might produce a salutary effect;
but to insure obedience it was necessary for Dalton *to persevere
in the same meritorious conduct.*[c] The army being once employed against the people, constant insolence and frequent
bloodshed were the result. The people expressed their indignation in riots and tumults: one of these being quelled without firing a shot, the emperor in a letter to his ministers, testified his disapprobation of such forbearance, and desired it might
not be repeated. Trautmansdorff declared, that if the troops
serving in the Netherlands were not sufficient, forty thousand
men would immediately enter the Low Countries: this assertion his hearers well knew to be a boasting bravado, as the
emperor's troops were elsewhere fully employed. It is frequently difficult to discover the precise motive for conduct
which is dictated by unprincipled wickedness, and guided by
extreme folly. As Joseph's armies were engaged in the Turkish war, policy obviously dictated forbearance of injustice
and tyranny in the west, that he might effectually promote
aggression and spoliation in the east. His force in the Low
Countries was very inadequate to his despotic purposes, or
to the cruel intentions of his deputy. At the very time that

c Annual Register, 1789.

the emperor was enjoining perseverance in military despotism
to his willing and prompt underling, he, through the governors-
general, issued a declaration, setting forth his tender affection
to his subjects, his desire of satisfying their wishes, the com-   1789.
plete return of his favour, and his determination to give the
Low Countries most convincing proofs of his benevolence and
confidence. Flagrant as the duplicity of these professions
were, their uselessness was no less obvious : force, not deception
was his instrument of government ; the soldiers could not the
more easily massacre one man by proclaiming to him the *tender feelings* of their employers: it was a mere waste of falsehood, which could answer none of the assertor's purposes ;
more resembling the capricious versatility of a froward child,
than the steady policy of a firm man, resolute in wicked designs.

The interpreter of the emperor's tenderness was Dalton:
among the sources of Dalton's fame acquired in Transylvania
was a *gallows*[d] of an extraordinary height for hanging insurgents, and he declared his determination to erect an edifice of a
like construction in the great square at Brussels. He now went
to establish at Louvain the new professors of divinity ; and to
reform the errors of theological schools, the argument employed was the bayonet: the rector and professors were ejected
by a file of musketeers, and the new teachers were established
by the same authority. To celebrate the admission of the im- Effects of
perial instructors in theology, the soldiers murdered a great his tyran-
number of the inhabitants,[e] who could not refrain from as- ny.
sembling to pay the last tribute of grief at the overthrow of an
institution, which had for so many ages been the pride and
support of their city. But although soldiers could inaugurate
persons appointed to *teach* the christian system according to the
imperial canons of orthodoxy, they could not compel students
to *learn ;* the pupils had universally abandoned the colleges,
and the masters were left to deliver their lessons, either in
empty halls, or without any hearers, but their military coadjutors. At Malines and Antwerp the massacre was much more
extensive than even at Louvain ; and personal security was deemed
so precarious in the Netherlands, that some of the nobility, and
a great number of other inhabitants of distinction, and property
sought refuge in exile. The cruel executions committed upon
a defenceless people by their rulers, in a season of peace and
most profound tranquillity, excited the abhorrence of the neighbouring nations, and procured asylums for the unfortunate
sufferers. Confiscation, despotism, and military execution being once established, property, liberty, and life being insecure
those that still remained in the country withdrew their capitals
from manufactures and commerce, and vested them in foreign

d Annual Register, 1789, chap. ii.
e Annual Register, 1789, chap. ii.

CHAP.
XLII.

1789.

funds, as a provision for their own flights, and repositories which Dalton's bayonets could not reach. In a country so recently eminent for industry and the arts, trade was entirely stagnant, and every occupation ceased, except those which minister to the necessity of life: revenue proportionably declined: fiscal productiveness, the great object of the emperor's tyranny, experienced a most important diminution: the states of Brabant announced a determination, under the present outrageous tyranny, to withhold the supplies. Such was the state of affairs at the close of 1788.

Farther cruelty and robbery by Joseph.

The emperor published an edict annulling all his former concessions, even recalling his inaugural oath to maintain the Joyous Entry; and all the obnoxious establishments of 1787 were to be speedily restored. The grand council of Brabant having refused to sanction so despotic an edict, that constitutional tribunal was suppressed; the management of the revenue, which had formed one of its delegated departments, was vested in a commission nominated by the emperor: no abbots were thenceforth to be appointed in Brabant, and thus the clerical order was about to be suppressed; the commons were to be new modelled according to the emperor's pleasure: the right of granting subsidies was to be no longer vested in the states, but in a council appointed by the emperor; the Joyous Entry was to be abolished; the whole government and all its parts were to be modelled according to the imperial will. A considerable part of the year 1789 was employed in executing these nefarious projects of infatuated ambition. The enmity to the clergy, and rapacity for money, two predominant features in the emperor's character, combined in dictating his most extensive and systematic schemes of robbery. By one decree he sequestered all the abbeys of Brabant, and appointed civil officers to manage their revenues for his use. [f]

The Flemings resolve on forcible resistance.

Such a seizure of property, in a country which had so long enjoyed the blessings of a free constitution, and of ecclesiastical possessions, among a people so devoutly attached to the priesthood, excited very general resentment, and open remonstrances from men, who already indignantly brooded over their fallen constitution, and meditated the re-assertion of their rights: they resolved no longer to yield even the appearance of submission, either to subordinate tyranny, or the imperial despot himself. Stimulated to resistance by the strongest motives which can inspirit generous breasts; considering death as preferable to slavery; and recalling to their minds those gallant exertions by

[f] The author of Dodsley's Annual Register 1791, having attentively considered the detail of the spoilations, says, that he suppressed no less than a hundred and sixty monastic establishments, and that the only precaution he appears to have used, was, that in this great suppression the men were more favoured than the women: of the male convents, only forty were sequestered; of the nunneries, one hundred and twenty.

which a kindred people had emancipated themselves from an Austrian despot in the sixteenth century, they trusted that with much greater resources, against a foe less powerful, they would be no less successful in resisting an Austrian despot of the eigh- teenth;g besides their own resources, so valuable and effica- cious, in the riches, population, and spirit of the people, and nature of the country, they might reasonably expect support from the arms of Prussia, and even of her maritime confede- rates. The emperor was engaged in the Turkish war, and his force greatly impaired by the disastrous events which it had produced : though emigration was very prevalent, yet the re- fugees chiefly sought shelter in the most adjacent states, and had greatly promoted the cause of their countrymen by describ- ing the dreadful oppressions from which they had fled. With the emigrants the Flemish patriots maintained a very close cor- respondence, and concerted with them the plan and commence- ment of open resistance. Dalton, meanwhile, despatched part of his troops to seize every person suspected of disaffection, and carried the system of proscription and murder to a more enormous extent than at any former period of his tyranny, while Trautmansdorff acted as the civil instrument of oppression. A conspiracy was formed to blow up the houses of these tyrants with gunpowder; during the confusion to seize the gates of Brussels and the arsenal, and admit bodies of emigrants, who were prepared, and to be ready at hand for that purpose : the execution of this plot was fixed for August 1789; but being discovered, a great number of suspected persons were appre- hended. While the ministers were inflicting summary punish- ments, the vigorous proceedings of the patriots called their at- tention to more formidable objects. About the middle of Sep- tember 1789, the duke of Ursel, and the prince of Aremburg, count of la Mark, his son, with the other nobles who had retired to Breda, were joined by the archbishop of Malines or Mechlin, primate of the catholic provinces of the Netherlands, and by

g There was a considerable resemblance between the conduct of Jo- seph II. and his ancestor Philip II. of Spain ; though the former was the professed champion of toleration, the latter of intolerance, the principle of both was much more nearly allied than would appear from a superficial view of their respective objects. Each sought to model the opinions of mankind according to his will ; each endeavoured to effect his purpose by violence; each was cruel in persecuting all those who opposed his system ; each was imperious and despotical; both were ambitious without ability, restless without enterprise, aggressive and usurping in intention, mighty in project, but futile in execution, and unsuccessful in event. Philip, the creature of imitation, was the implicit votary of priestcraft : Joseph, the creature of imitation, was the implicit votary of infidelity : neither of them were guided by sound reasoning and original reflection ; both, in support- ing their favorite tenets, and gratifying malignant passions, did much mis- chief; but attempted much more than their incapacity suffered them to perpetrate.

CHAP.   most if not all the states of Brabant, both civil and ecclesi-
XLII   astical, were constituted and declared to be the regular and le-
        gal assembly of the states of that province: they framed and
1789.   unanimously passed a remonstrance to the emperor, declaring
Declara- their rights and their resolutions to maintain them against every
tion of violater: they were prepared to sacrifice their lives and for-
rights. tunes for a sovereign who should govern them constitutionally,
        but they would not surrender those privileges which they held
        in trust for their fellow citizens, and for posterity: they adjured
        him to spare them the cruel necessity of appealing to God and
        their swords.

 The declaration of the states, so contrary to his despotic sentiments and views, highly enraged the emperor, and he gave
orders for increased severity and violence of military execution. The Belgians saw no hopes of redress, but by their
swords, and in October 1789, they hoisted the standard of revolt: a body of insurgents took the two small forts of Lillo
and Liefenshock on the Scheldt: in fort Lillo, besides the military stores, they found a considerable sum of money. Dalton
sent general Schroeder against the invaders, at the head of four
thousand troops, well disciplined On the advance of this
force the insurgents abandoned the two forts and retreated
towards Furnhout, a small town about eight miles from the
forts: the imperialists pursued them to the gates, and forcing
these open, entered the town: the Brabanters retreating from
the main street, drew the Austrians after them until they were
inclosed in the market place; there the patriots firing from
the adjoining houses, windows, and lanes, did great execution;
the regulars being thus ensnared. and unable to extricate themselves, were broken and defeated, and compelled to retreat
with the loss of seven hundred men. Hope, encouraged by
success, roused all the patriotic and martial ardour of the Belgians: assuming the name of the patriotic army, they penetrated into the heart of the country: in the other provinces, as
well as Brabant, the votaries of freedom flocked to the standard erected for its preservation, and burned with impatience to
join their brethren in the field, that they might contribute their
efforts to deliver their country from foreign tyrants. In the beginning of November a battle was fought at Tirlemont: a body of patriots having been pursued by Bender, an Austrian general, had taken refuge in this place, and were warmly supported by its patriotic inhabitants. Bender having entered the
town, was very vigorously received by the Flemings, and after
an obstinate contest compelled to retreat. The Netherlanders
The patri- now ventured to meet their adversaries in an open field, and
ots defeat having gained a complete victory, took possession of Ostend,
the Austri- Bruges, and Louvain. Animated by these successes they had
an troops. the boldness to attack the strong city of Ghent: having enter-

h See Annual Register for 1791, p 32.

ed the town, they assailed and defeated the enemy in the
streets; and compelled one part of them to fly for refuge
to the barracks, while another sought shelter in the citadel.
The third day of the siege the barracks surrendered; the de-
fendants of the citadel finding they could no longer retain the
place, committed the most infamous enormities in the streets,
but soon evacuated the garrison: the defence of Ghent was by
no means adequate in either vigour or skill to the force by which
it was guarded. Joseph, desirous of winning his soldiers, had
given directions for allowing them great laxity; the troops who
were in the Netherlands, besides being recently freebooters,
and accustomed to trample on the defenceless inhabitants, conceived a most thorough contempt for the Flemings; but when
they came to battle, and were compelled to face the enemy on
equal terms, they showed themselves to have totally deviated
from the characters of Austrian soldiers, and to be as dastardly
as they were profligate. The reduction of Ghent was of the
greatest consequence to the Flemish patriots; and the more
especially as it enabled the states of Flanders to assemble in
that capital of the province, for the purpose of legalizing their
public proceedings, giving a form to their intended new constitution, and concluding a league and federal union with the
other provinces. The emperor informed of the great successes
of the Flemish patriots, descended from his despotic haughtiness, and endeavoured by amicable promises to conciliate his
late subjects; he exhorted the malcontents to lay down their
arms, and to trust for the redress of real grievances to his clemency and paternal affection: dreadful consequences (he said)
would ensue if they compelled him to relinquish the conquests
which he was now prosecuting, and pour into the Netherlands
armies that were now gathering laurels from a foreign enemy.
Endeavouring partly to justify, and partly to explain his most
obnoxious acts, he offered to revoke the offensive edicts, to
comply with all their former demands, and to grant a general,
full, and perpetual amnesty to all who should return to their
duty within a specified but distant time, the leaders of the revolt alone excepted: but the Flemings had been too often deceived by Joseph to repose any confidence in his professions;
and they now paid the less attention to his overtures, than from
their successes they began to deem themselves no longer dependent on his power. On the twentieth of November the
states of Flanders seized on the sovereign authority in their
province, and, in imitation of their Dutch neighbours, assumed
the title of high and mighty states: they passed resolutions, declaring the emperor to have forfeited all title to the sovereignty of the Netherlands; for raising, organizing, and disciplining
an army, and uniting themselves with the states of Brabant.
The ardour and success of their countrymen inspired the inhabitants of Brussels with the desire and hope of rescuing their
capital from the despotic ministers of Joseph. Intimidated by

They form
themselves
into a fede-
ral repub-
lic.

CHAP. the victories of the Flemings, Dalton confined himself within
XLII. the walls, and ordered the gates to be strictly guarded: his
       force consisted of about six thousand men, whereas the patri-
1789. otic band did not exceed one thousand: the soldiers were,
however, dispersed through different parts of the city; their
adversaries were at a fixed rendezvous to form a compact body,
which assailing the scattered enemy, by throwing them into
partial confusion might cause general disorder, and animate
the other citizens to join in the conflict. This gallant design
was executed: the Flemish band defeated an Austrian detachment in one of the streets; the battle became general, and the
insurgents got possession of the barracks, with two thousand
muskets, and plenty of ammunition. Dalton retreated to the
great square, where, attempting to defend himself, he was obliged to capitulate, and to give up Brussels, on being allowed to
escape with his garrison: he accordingly retired to Luxemburg: Trautmansdorff, with the other chief members of the
government, withdrew to Liege. The governors-general, from
their popularity were not afraid of any violence, yet, as the
emperor's sovereignty was no longer acknowledged, they betook themselves into Germany. The Flemings, in their victories, far from imitating the brutal cruelty of the imperial despot's soldiers, killed no one but in battle. Having thus made
themselves masters of the chief towns, after celebrating the
most solemn institution of religion, they restored the ancient
courts of justice, rescinded all the emperor's innovating edicts,
settled the exercise of the sovereign power and completely rees-
tablished tranquillity. The states of Brabant being assembled at
Brussels, on the last day of the year 1789, bound themselves
by oath, in the presence of the citizens, to preserve the rights,
privileges, and constitution of their country, and then proceeded
to administer the same oath to the members of the sovereign
council of Brabant amidst the general acclamations of the people. The other provinces, except Limburgh, having concluded
similar engagements concerning their respective internal constitutions, all the Austrian Netherlands, Limburgh excepted,
formed themselves into a federal republic, to be distinguished
by the title of the United Belgic States. Such was the result
of the restless changes, rapacity, and usurpations of the emperor Joseph.

CHAP. XLIII.

Retrospective view of France.—Old government.—Character and spirit of
France under Louis XIV.—Sources of submission to arbitrary power—
commencing and progressive change under Louis XV.—Beginning of infidelity.—Voltaire and his disciples.—Beginning of anti-monarchism—
Rousseau supposes man a perfectable being.—Progress of his doctrines
through the efforts of literature.—Co-operating political causes.— general impolicy and burthensome expense of the French wars against Great
Britain.— Enormous expenditure and distressful consequences of the war
to support our revolted colonies.—Pecuniary embarrassments.—Various
schemes of alleviation.—Convention of the notables.—Calonne unfolds
the dreadful state of the finances.—Calonne proposes an equalization of
public burthens—incenses the privileged orders.—Outcry against the
minister—disgraced—retires into banishment.—Brienne minister.—Trifling and inefficient reforms.—Contests with parliaments.—Attempts of
the crown to overawe the refractory—unsuccessful.— Arbitrary suspension
of parliaments.—National ferment.—Distressed situation of the king—
abandoned by many of his courtiers—resolves to recall Mr. Neckar—
who consults the convocation of the states-general.—Question concerning the consolidation of the orders.—Meeting of the states.—Commons
propose to meet in one chamber—opposed by the crown.—Commons constitute themselves a national assembly, without regard to the other orders.—Violence of demagogues.—Soldiers infected with the popular enthusiasm—insubordination and licentiousness.—King orders troops to
approach to Paris.—Popular leaders prepare to defend the capital.—An
army of volunteers immediately raise—attack the royal magazines to
procure arms—assail the Bastile.—Subversion of the old government.—
Declaration of rights—fundamental principle the RIGHTS OF MAN.—First
acts of the revolutionists—power—great and general object to subvert
establishment—to that object all the whole energies of the French genius
and character exerted.—Licentiousness of the press.—Twenty thousand
literary men employ themselves in stimulating the mob to outrage.—An
engine of government new in the history of political establishments.—
CLUBS—influence of—extended by association—doctrines—influence and
operation.—Lawless violence in the country.— Peasants turn upon the
proprietors.—Some of the nobility propose to sacrifice a large portion of
their privileges and property—their example imitated and emulated.—
Sacrifices of the nobles and clergy.— Admiration of the commons.—Proposition for the seizure of church property—remonstrances of the clergy
—disregarded.—Parliaments annihilated.—Immunities sacrificed.—The
law and policy of the kingdom overturned.—Scheme for voluntary contributions.—Gold and silver sent to the mint.—Preparations for the new
constitution—the authority to be possessed by the king.—Suspensive
VETO—Question, if the assembly was to be composed of one or two
chambers—carried, that there should be only one.—English constitution
proposed as a model—rejected.—French commons inimical to mixed
government—settlement of the succession.—Ferocity of the people—in-

flamed by scarcity.—Additional troops arrive at Versailles—entertainment given by the officers in the palace to the new comers—The royal
family visit the banqueting room.—Music describes the sufferings of a
captive prince .—The queen having in her arms the infant dauphin presents him to the officers—the ladies of the court accompany her.—Effects
of beauty, music, and wine, combined.—Unguarded enthusiasm of the
loyal soldiers—trample on the national cockade.—Report of this entertainment at Paris.—Rage and indignation of the revolutionists.—Activity
and influence of the fish-women and courtezans.—The mob determines
to bring the king to Paris—expedition of the women for that purpose—
hang priests and aristocrats—march to Versailles—overawe the legislature—break into the assembly and take possession of the speaker's
chair.—Mob assault the palace—attempt to murder the queen—prevented by the heroism of her defenders.—King and queen agree to depart
for Paris.—Mournful procession of a degraded monarch.—Farther proceedings at Paris.—The existing government endeavoured to quell the
mob—severe prosecutions for that purpose.—Effects of the French revolution in Britain.—Detesting the old French government and not acquainted with the new, Britons approve of the revolution as friendly to
liberty.—Sentiments of various classes—respectively differing, concur in
favouring the French revolution.

CHAP.
XLIII.

1789.
Old go-
vernment
of France.

THE event which rendered the year 1789 most important
to Britons and all the civilized world, was the French revolution, the causes and means of which extraordinary change it
requires a retrospective view of the scence of operation to investigate and comprehend. The government of France was,
in the earlier ages, one of those feudal aristocracies, which the
northern conquerors established over Europe. The degree of
civil and political liberty that extended to the commons was
very inconsiderable in France, as in most other countries, except England and the Netherlands. The power of the king in
the middle ages was extremely limited; the country consisted
of a collection of principalities, in each of which the lord superior enjoyed an arbitrary sway, and held the people in a condition of abject vassalage. This state of relative power in the
vicissitudes of human affairs underwent material changes. The
kings had one general object, diminution of baronial authority;
prudence required the barons to unite for their common advantage, yet they had respectively separate interests which much
more constantly occupied their attention. By sowing discord
between these turbulent chieftains, the sovereigns rendered
their aggregate force less formidable. Conquests, escheats, or
treaties, united several fiefs to the crown : Louis XI. considerably reduced the power of the nobility, the feudal aristocracy
was entirely destroyed by cardinal Richelieu, and the separate
sovereignties were consolidated into one entire mass.[i] As the
people had been without liberty under feudal lords, they continued to be in servitude under the monarch : before the total
reduction of the aristocracy, they had indeed possessed an assembly of states, but so modelled, that the commons had little real

i See introduction to this history.

share of the power: the nobles and clergy were closely connected by immunities and other privileges, and could easily
overpower the third estate. From the administration of Richelieu, France had been without even the appearance of a legislative voice: every privilege of the subject was under the control of a government habitually corrupt and tyrannical. The
men of wealth and distinction were purchased either by courtly
honours, presents, pensions, or a lavish waste of the public revenue, which was endeavoured to be exclusively wrung from
the grasp of the poor, the weak, and the laborious. Liberty and
even life were insecure, if either interfered with the will of the
prince. Instead of making a part subservient to the whole;
estimating either permanent regulations, or temporary measures,
by the aggregate of happiness which they were calculated to
produce; the old government of France administered the
whole according to the pleasure and caprice of a very small
part; the comfort and welfare of twenty-four millions was of
little account when compared with the freak or fancy of the
prince, the interest or inclination of his favourites. The suggestion of a priest or a prostitute would desolate a whole province,[k] and drive from that country its most industrious inhabitants. The nobility and clergy, and also the magistrates, were
exempted from their share of the public burthens; the taxes,
instead of being paid by the rich and the great, fell upon the
poor. These tyrannical exactions were rendered more cruelly
oppressive by the established mode of extortion; the revenue
was farmed, and farther leased by the principal undertakers to
others, and by these to subordinate collectors with advance of
rent; in the various steps of intermediation between the payer
of the impost and the government, much greater sums were
squeezed from the commons than ever found their way to the
public treasury. The farmers of the revenue principally constituted the monied class, or at least, were the greatest capitalists;[l]
in them government had its chief resource for loans to carry on
the projects of extravagant ambition, and infatuated aggression. Many of the nobility from their prodigality were poor
notwithstanding their immunities and donatives, and from these
men had the means of supply; the court, therefore, very readily connived at most flagrant extortions in the administration
of the revenue, as the commons only were to offer by the spoliation.

The old government of France, was, no doubt, liable to these
and other objections, both in its principles and practice; and
in the reigns of Louis XIV. and XV. it was a very arbitrary
and oppressive system. Its vices appeared the more glaring to
political observers, by being contrasted with the constitution of

k See in Render's Tour through Germany, an account of the devastation
of the Palatinate.
l Annual Register, 1787 and 1789.

the neighbour and rival of France. Perhaps, indeed, this cir-
cumstance· produced to that system, still less·estimation than it
really deserved. ·, To Britons it would have been an intolerable
scheme of policy, and must have crushed the energy of the
British character, which in a great measure results from civil
and political liberty ; but a greater or less degree of restraint is
necessary according to the knowledge and dispositions of a nation as was as an individual. The French minds, sentiments,
and habits, appeared to require a stronger curb than the British ; but on the other hand the authorities which were to control the violence, regulate the vivacity, and guide the versatile
instability of the Gallic character, were by no means well placed. The power was not exerted for rendering the greatest
benefit to the subjects which even their tempers would admit ;
it was much more arbitrary than was expedient for a civilized
people to tolerate. The great mass of the commons were in a
state of slavery to the priests, the nobles, and the officers of the
crown ;[m] such a condition only profound ignorance, fear, or infatuation could suffer. It was natural for intelligent and ingenious men to see the imperfections of the arbitrary government,
and to wish for a reform of various abuses. The splendid actions of Louis XIV. notwithstanding their real impolicy, daz-
zled his subjects ; his ostentatious displays to other nations of
his superiority, so flattering to the predominant vanity of the
French character, rendered them eager partisans of their
great monarch. Instrumental to the glory of the sovereign,
they thought they were promoting their own ! Vanity assumed
the disguise of honour ; and in gratifying the prince, and courting his approbation, they overlooked their own conditions; they
forgot they were bearing slavery, encountering war, poverty,
and starvation, merely as puppets in the hands of a vain-glori-
ous tyrant.[n]   Under Louis XIV. their subserviency was very
abject, but it arose from causes that could not be permanent,
and, indeed, from a certain operation of passions and energies,
which, in another direction, might readily attempt, and powerfully affect the dissolution of their fetters. Submission to arbitrary power arises from various causes, and operates differently
according to the diversities of national characters ; often it may
proceed from barbarous ignorance and intellectual debasement,
which mindful of only animal wants thinks not of any higher
enjoyments than the supply of these ;[o] a phlegmatic temper,
that does not feel injustice and oppression; or from relaxation,
indolence, and timidity, which, notwithstanding a knowledge of
right, and a feeling of wrong, prevents strenuous efforts for
vindication and redress ; servitude in these cases is a *passive
principle.* The French were very far from being void of know-

m New Annual Register, 1789.
n Smollett's Continuation of Hume, vol. i.
o As in the case of the negroes, see Park's Travels, *passim.*

ledge, sensibility, courage, or active exertion: on the contrary, CHAP.
they were intelligent, ardent, bold, and enterprising, but their ·XLIII.
passions engaged their ingenuity and their force in supporting
and aggrandizing their absolute monarch. Submission to arbi-   1789.
trary power was, in them love for the sovereign, a STRONGLY
ACTIVE PRINCIPLE; theirs was implicit obedience yielded by
strength, not despotism forced upon weakness. The French
animation was extremely eager in the pursuit of pleasure as its
levity was very fond of pageantry and show. The magnificent
profusion of Louis and his court was well adapted for increasing the popularity acquired by political and military achievements; the high admiration, or rather the adoration with which
his subjects regarded this monarch, soon excited in their warm
and enthusiastic minds an ardent affection for the whole royal
family, and indeed all the princes of the blood; they associated the ideas of estimation for royalty with military prowess.
These effects were, as long as they lasted, very favourable to
the continuance and extension of absolute sway, but the causes
were perfectly compatible with totally different sentiments.
Under Louis XV. the French long continued ardent in loyalty,
and manifested their affection and reverence for the kingly name
in implicit obedience to the mandates of his most christian majesty; but while energy was exerting itself in the boldest enterprise for promoting the great monarch's glory, props of his Commen-
power were beginning to be impaired. From the middle of his cing and
reign the Roman catholic faith commenced its decline, and progres-
towards the close, the political power of the sovereign received sive
change un-
a considerable shake. der Louis
The abandoned debauchery of the court under the duke of XV.
Orleans's regency had prepared the higher ranks for the infusion Begin-
of infidelity which was afterwards so extensively received. nings of in-
The first movers of this scheme of irreligion were certain vota-fidelity.
ries of literature, who employed men of high rank as their instruments. Learning became daily more prevalent in Europe,
and having been fostered in France, by the ostentatious vanity
of Louis XIV. though limited during his reign to subjects of
taste, sentiment, and natural philosophy, afterwards extended
to theology, ethics, and politics. Voltaire was admirably fitted Voltaire,
for impressing the susceptibility, gratifying the taste, amusing
the fancy, inflaming the passions, and so misleading the judgment of lively, refined, ingenious, ardent, and volatile readers
and hearers: he, therefore, was thoroughly skilled in the most
effectual means of attacking the faith of Frenchmen. Vanity
materially assisted the infidel's operations: the nobility having
imbibed under Louis XIV. a relish for literature and still more
for literary patronage, were desirous of cultivating, or appearing to cultivate, intimacy with a man of so high rank in letters,
repeated his doctrines and witticisms, and abandoned their
religion to pass for philosophers. Besides, the debauchery of
Louis XIV., carried by his pupil the duke of Orleans to a much

more profligate excess, and not much corrected under the mature age of Louis XV., established in the morals of courtiers a powerful auxiliary for spreading infidelity. The ridiculous absurdity of many of the popish doctrines was easily discernible to French sagacity when turned to such animadversions: and their various mummeries afforded scope to the French wit and satire, when permitted to take such a range. Gallic ingenuity could easily find arguments to expose the frivolity and folly of many of their priestly doctrines, rites, and observances; but as ardent as versatile, leaving their superstitions, they took the opposite and much more dangerous extreme. Some of the king's ministers, pleased with the theories of the Voltaire school, and converted by his jokes, became deists, made the king inimical to various parts of the ecclesiastical establishment, and inspired him with a desire of reforming the church. This reform both in France and other countries arose partly from a diminished regard for the established church, but principally from the love of plunder: its consequences were a degradation of the clerical character to a much lower state than was requisite for the purposes of spiritual and moral instruction. The suppression of the religious orders, and the general system of policy towards the church, from the peace of Paris to the end of the duke de Choiseul's administration, tended very powerfully to second the efforts of deistical writers against the church. Indeed the acts of Louis XV. at the instigation of his favourites, were powerfully efficient causes, though not the proximate, of the downfall of religion in the reign of his successor. It is by no means a difficult undertaking for a man of genius to-establish a new sect in religion or politics; if he mean to mislead the judgment, he has only by animated description to impress the imagination, or by impassioned eloquence to impel the affections.[p] Voltaire was very successful in the use of these instruments: other literary adventurers readily pursued a tract leading so directly to esteem and patronage. Under such influence, projects and institutions were formed for circulating their doctrines. By such influence, projects, and institutions,[q] infidelity made very rapid advances: except in the lower classes of people, in the latter period of the reign of Louis XV. the majority of laity in France were deists. Opinions and sentiments so inimical not only to absolute monarchy, but to every form of regular government, are indebted for their disseminations to the imbecility of Louis XV., and the narrow views of his ministers. The same spirit of free inquiry not being properly understood or wisely modified by the court of France, from exposing the absurdities of many

p Whitfield, Wesley, and other adventurers of a more recent date clearly and strongly illustrate the facility with which ingenuity fashioning itself to the fancies and passions of men, may impress a new hypothesis of religion.

q See Barruel on Jacobinism, vol. i. passim.

popish observances preceded to attack christianity itself, and soon extended to politics. In their efforts against superstition, the philosophists, in the violent ardour of the French character, rushing to the opposite extreme, pulled up the wheat as well as the tares; the same operators, employed on the same materials, using a similar process in politics, produced similar effects; and in both, seeking to avoid one evil, without discriminating it from the good in which it was mixed, they incurred a greater. Speculating upon the rights and happiness of man, they easily saw that the government of France was very far from being well adapted to the security of rights or the diffusion of happiness. The ingenuity of Frenchmen has, in most subjects of study, exhibited itself much more frequently in framing hypotheses than in collecting facts, investigating principles, and deducing consequences from actually established premises. This mode of procedure, well adapted to the poet's invention, was employed in cases which required the reasoning of the philosopher, and the wisdom of the sage. A position was assumed by Helvetius and many others, but above all by Rousseau, that man was a perfectible being, and that every change of system was to be adapted to the perfection which he might attain. While Voltaire and his sect were labouring to undermine existing establishments, Helvetius, Rousseau, and their sects, besides rendering a helping hand to the scheme of demolition, were very active in proposing new models totally impracticable, because to consist of perfect men, materials no where found to exist. The French statesmen were equally blind to the probable consequences of the political as of the theological theories so prevalent towards the close of Louis XV.'s reign. Then was the time[r] to have prevented their destructive effects by gradual and progressive melioration of church and state, which both demanded correction. The systematic impolicy of France in seeking commercial and maritime aggrandizement by provoking that nation that can always ruin her trade and crush her navy, tended very powerfully to give a practical operation to the spirit of liberty. The immense expense incurred in the seven years war, causing fiscal derangements, was the chief source of those contentions with the provincial parliaments that principally distinguished the last years of Louis XV. The actual opposition of these political bodies was perfectly justifiable, but called into action the prevailing theories, and paved the way for much more unrestrained efforts against the prince's power. Louis XVI., kind and liberal by nature, was disposed

CHAP.
XLIII.

1789.
Commencement of anti-monarchical doctrines.

Rousseau supposes man a perfectible being.

Co-operating political causes.

General impolicy and burthensome expense of the French wars against Britain.

r So early as the year 1772, Edmund Burke, in the theological scepticism and political hypotheses of the French writers, saw the probable overthrow of religion and government; and even in the house of commons mentioned his apprehension of the danger, and proposed to form an alliance among believers against (he said) those ministers of rebellious darkness who are endeavouring to shake all the works of God established in beauty and order.

CHAP.
XLIII

1789.

to moderate in its exercise the regour of his absolute power, and to accommodate his government to the sentiments which, without comprehending their precise nature or extent, he in general saw become prevalent among his subjects. The first years of his reign promised popularity to the prince with increasing happiness to his people. Repetition, however, of the same preposterous policy which had cost France so much blood and treasure, not only drove him to an unprovoked war with England, but to a war in which he was to support revolting subjects against their sovereign in which every argument that he could adduce in favour of the Americans might be employed with much greater force to vindicate a revolt of his own subjects. The intercourse of the French with the defenders of a republican constitution very rapidly increased an anti-monarchical spirit in a country predisposed for its reception. The enormous expenses incurred in nourishing America, and endeavouring to injure Britain, plunged France into unexampled distress, and the aggression recoiled on the aggressor. An immense new debt was added to the old, the accumulation became intolerable. The multitude of the distinct loans which altogether composed this vast mass of debt, and the diversity of the conditions upon which, according to the genius of the respective projectors, they had been raised, the numberless appropriations of specific revenues to particular funds, and the frequent infractions of these to supply the immediate necessities of the state, occasioned such voluminous detailed accounts, such endless references,* explanations, and deficiencies, with such eternal crowds of figures, that the whole presented a choas of confusion, in which the financiers themselves seemed scarcely less bewildered than the public. The taxes, numerous as they were, and ruinous in the last degree to the people, were totally unequal to the supply of the current expenses of the state and to the discharge of the interest or annuities arising on the various funds; new funds could not be raised, but the exigencies of the state must be supplied. No effectual means were devised but by withholding the annuities due to the public creditors to the amount of the deficiency. This measure involved numbers in distress and calamity, and caused loud clamours: in a situation so disastrous, projects and projectors of relief multiplied. The wealth of France was certainly very great, but the principal was in the private repositories of ministers, contractors, commissioners, stock-jobbers, farmers-general, and the minions of the court.

Vergennes died in 1786, and was succeeded by Monsieur de Calonne, who having in vain tried the experiment of new loans, the king proposed to assemble the states, but was dissuaded by the court and ministry. If the states were assembled, they might, instead of granting supplies, begin their deliberations

Enormous expenses and distressful consequences of the war to support the Americans

Pecuniary embarrassments.

Schemes of extrication

a See Annual Register, 1787, chap. vii.

with demanding a redress of grievances. Monsieur de Ca- CHAP.
lonne wished to convene the 'notables, an assembly deriving its XLIII.
name from the members being men of rank and respectability.
The ministers had endeavoured to prevail on the nobility and   1789.
clergy to contribute a share spontaneously of those immense Conven-
sums, which through their exemptions they were presumed to tion of the
have accumulated. The same influence, it was also hoped, notables.
would be successfully used in prevailing on the great monied
capitalists to bring forward part of their stores for the relief of
the nation. A proclamation was accordingly issued the 16th
of December for holding this assembly.t

In an introductory speech Calonne contended that the pub- Calonne.
lic' embarrassment arose from causes which were highly honourable to France, and the present reign, and, notwithstanding the immediate exigency, ultimately beneficial as well as
glorious. A marine had been formed infinitely more powerful
than any ever known in France, his majesty's fleets had sailed triumphant over the ocean, he had humbled the rival, and
terminated an honourable war by a solid and permanent peace:
devoting his attention to the public welfare, he had, since
peace was established, invariably pursued extensive commerce
abroad and good administration at home. The minister had He unfolds
found the finances, when he was intrusted with their manage- the dread-
ment, in a deplorable state; a vast unfunded debt, all annui- ful state of
ties and interest greatly in arrear; all the coffers empty, the es;
public stocks fallen to the lowest point, circulation interrupted,
and all credit and confidence destroyed. He then showed the
measures which he had pursued, and the happy effects they had
produced (so far as his measures could reach) in remedying
these complicated evils. He had, he said, re-established public credit upon a sound basis, had undertaken great and expensive works of the highest national importance; but notwithstanding all those favourable appearances of prosperity, there was an
evil every year increasing in magnitude, this was the great annual deficiency of the public revenue, and its inadequacy to
the national expense; to eradicate this evil was beyond the
reach of ministers; additional taxes would oppress the people,
whom the king wished of all things to relieve; anticipation on
the revenue of subsequent years had already been practised to
a ruinous extent; and the reduction of expense had been carried as far as was possible without weakening the state and government. In the reform of abuses, the king and his minister
chiefly trusted to find a remedy for the evil. One of the most

t It consisted of seven princes of the blood, nine dukes and peers of
France, eight field marshals, twenty two nobles, eight counsellors of state,
four masters of requests, eleven archbishops and bishops, thirty-seven
judges parliament, twelve deputies of the pays d'etat, the lieutenant civil,
and twenty five magistrates of different towns; in all, one hundred and forty-four. See Macfarlane's history of George III. vol. iii. p. 345.

CHAP. intolerable grievances which then prevailed, was the immunity
XLIII. of the most opulent classes from taxation; Calonne therefore
      proposed to equalize public burthens, by rendering the taxes
1789. general; to accomplish this purpose, the nobility, clergy, and
He propo- magistracies should be no longer exempted, but contribute
ses an   their share to the exigencies of the state; the officers un-
equaliza- der the crown were to be assessed; and there should be a ge-
tion of   neral impost on land, without excepting the possessions of any
public bur-
thens.   order or individual. Such a project, in whatsoever motives it
originated, was certainly just in its principle, and efficient in its
object, as a scheme of finance: as a measure of policy it was
wise and equitable, since it proposed to restore to the commons
so great a part of their usurped rights: but the minister did
not show much judgment and prudence in the means which he
chose for carrying his plan into execution. It was very improbable that the aristocratical corporations, to influence whom
he had called the council of notables, would willingly recede
from such lucrative immunities; indeed, the notables themselves consisted of members of the privileged orders, and might
as a body be presumed unfavourable to a project tending so
He incen- much to diminish their corporate advantages. They actually
ses the   proved very inimical to the plan, which they represented as
privileged merely a new expedient for getting immense sums of money
orders.   into the hands of government, to supply its extravagance and
corruption; they refused to concur in the territorial impost,
unless they were suffered to investigate the past expenses and
accounts, and future estimates, as thereby only they could know
how far public money had been, or was likely to be, applied
Outcry   for the national good. The privileged orders raised a general
against the outcry against the man who had proposed to abolish their im-
minister. munities: they even persuaded the other classes, that the sole
object of the minister was rapacity, for the purposes of embez-
zlement and peculation; that, so far from intending to lighten
their burthens by his new system of impost, he designed to load
them with fresh taxes, and thus the aristocrats excited the hatred of the people against the minister, whose plan, if adopted
and fairly executed, would have rendered to the people themselves so essential a service. Moreover, the queen was a great
enemy to the minister, because he attacked one of her favourites. The mild and compliant Louis readily imbibed the prevailing sentiment, and withdrew his confidence and regard from
a man whom he saw distrusted and hated by so many others.
Disgraced: Calonne, fearing a judicial prosecution while the minds of all
he retires ranks were so biassed against him, retired into England.[u]
into ban-
ishment.

    u This minister has been charged with having amassed immense riches
by plundering the public. He certainly lived in London, for several years,
in magnificent splendour; but what his funds were, or how acquired, was
never ascertained.

Meanwhile, monsieur de Brienne,[x] archbishop of Thoulouse, a CHAP.
leading member of the notables, was appointed prime minis- XLIII.
ter, and without attempting the radical reform which the exigency required, he proposed and executed various partial im- 1789.
provements in the collection of taxes, and the management of Brienne
the public money. It was manifest that a change so confined minister
in principle and operation, could not extricate the country from Trifling
its present evils. By the new minister the assembly of notables and ineffi-
was dissolved,[y] and he thought himself obliged to have re- cient recourse to the usual mode of raising money by edicts. Among the form.
measures was a double poll tax, and a heavy stamp duty. The Contests
parliament of Paris remonstrated against the first subsidy, in with the
terms very unlike the former language of their assemblies, parlia-
even when they opposed the will of the king. Before they should ment
concur in raising money, they required to be informed of the real of Paris
state of the finances, and the purposes to which the new imposts
were to be applied; and they particularly objected to the
stamp duty; their requisition not having been admitted, they
refused to enregister the edict. The king finding them inflexible to persuasion, held a bed of justice, to compel them to registration. This procedure, hateful in the reign of Louis XV. Attempts
was infinitely more odious at present, when the spirit of liberty of the
was so much stronger and more generally diffused. The edict crown to
having been forcibly registered, the parliament PROTESTED, that overawe
not having been obtained by their approbation and consent, IT the refrac-
SHOULD NOT BE VALID; and that whoever attempted to put it in tory, un-
execution should be doomed to the galleys as a traitor. This successful.
resolute opposition was imitated by all the other parliaments.
Matters now appeared to draw to a crisis; the alternative of
the crown seemed to be, either to proceed to coercion, or to
relinquish for ever the long usurped power of raising money
by its own authority. On the other hand, the judicative
bodies were determined to show that they would not, without
resistance, any longer permit an arbitrary invasion of property,
however supported by precedent. On the 24th of July the Remon-
parliament of Paris published a remonstrance,[z] highly cele- strance of
brated for a forcible reasoning, a bold and animated eloquence, the parlia-
which clearly demonstrated and strongly impressed awful ment of
truths. After a happy peace that had lasted five years, they, Paris.
from the revenue before possessed by the crown, had trusted
that no fresh imposts would have been proposed; great, then
was their surprise at the requisition of an additional tax so
extensive, and generally odious. Ministers had never approached the throne with a voice of truth, but had disguised
from the king the actual state of his dominions, and the sentiments of his subjects. The council of the notables had been

x Bouille on the French Revolution, p. 50.
y In the opinion of Bouille, very unwisely, p. 51.
z See remonstrance, State Papers, July 24, 1787.

CHAP.
XLIII.

1789.

the occasion of discovering to the public the dreadful situation of affairs, and the progressive steps of error, corruption, and vice, by which courtiers had reduced France to such a condition. Taxes were the contributions of citizens for their own private security and the public safety; if they exceeded those purposes, they were inconsistent with justice and the good of the people, the sole objects of legitimate government. Neither parliaments, nor any other authority but the whole nation assembled, could sanction a new impost. The nation only, being convened and instructed in the true state of the finances could extirpate the abuses that actually existed, and offer resources to obviate such evils in future. If this remonstrance be considered in relation to the rights of a free people, and to the actual abuses under the French government; it was firm, yet perfectly temperate and respectful. Addressed, however, to a monarch who had inherited arbitrary power, it appeared a presumptuous encroachment. It was extremely natural for Louis to think himself rightfully entitled to the sway of his ancestors; to overlook the injustice in which that dominion was founded, and the great change of popular sentiment from the time even of his last predecessor. Like Charles I. he presumed a divine right to what his ancestors and he had possessed only by human sufferance; and, like Charles I. he did not discern that the opinions and sentiments which had permitted thraldom, no longer existed among his subjects. Louis, however, had a much more formidable force than Charles, in which he conceived he might repose secure confidence. He therefore determined on coercion; collected great bodies of troops round the metropolis; and sent parties of soldiers to the house of every individual member of the parliament of Paris, to carry him in banishment to Troyes, about seventy miles from the capitol and not to suffer him to write or speak to any person of his own family before his departure. These orders were executed at the same instant on the 18th of August, and by force the judicial body was prevented from proceeding in its official business. In the following month the president was despatched by the exiles to Varsailles, to represent to his majesty the pernicious effects of the compulsory measures which he was then pursuing. After several audiences, instead of adhering to the hereditary maxims of arbitrary power, the king yielded to the dicdates of his individual benignity and patriotism; he consented to abandon the obnoxious attacks, and to suffer parliament to resume its functions. Meanwhile the flame of liberty was bursting forth in various parts of the kingdom.[a] Other parliaments not only emulated, but surpassed the generous boldness of Paris, and with the right of property asserted the claims of personal security. The parliament of Grenoble declared

a Annual Register, 1787, chap. vii. passim.

lèttres de cachet, or arbitrary imprisonment, to be totally un- CHAP.
constitutional; and pronounced a decree, rendering it capital XLIII.
for any person, under ANY authority, to attempt such an act
within that province. In all the populous towns, where there 1789.
was the most ready and extensive interchange of opinion and
sentiment; the conduct of government, once so sacred in
France, was openly discussed, and most severely reprobated,
both in discourse and publications.[b] The king, in November,
appeared to have changed his disposition and intentions: meeting the parliament of Paris, he said he had come to hear their
opinions; but before they delivered them, to signify his own.[c]
They ought to confine themselves to the functions intrusted by
the king to their predecessors: the expediency of calling public assemblies was a measure of which he was the sole judge.
He was about to issue an edict, creating for five successive years
a loan that would require no new impost. Permission being
given for every member to speak without restraint, a warm debate on the registration of the edict ensued in the presence of
the king; but at last his majesty, suddenly rising, commanded
the decree to be registered without delay. The duke of Orleans, first prince of the blood after the king's brothers, warmly
opposed this order, as a direct infringement of parliamentary
right; and protested against all the acts of the day, as thereby
rendered void. His majesty, astonished at a proceeding so new
to an absolute prince, repeated his order, and quitted the assembly. The next day he banished the duke and two of his most Banish-
active supporters. The parliament, far from tamely submitting ment of
to this act of power, published a very strong address, which the active.
justified the exiled members, avowed the highest approbation ists.
opposition-
of their conduct, and represented the dangerous consequences
of such a restriction on the necessary freedom of speech. The
king answered, that he had strong reasons for the banishment
of those members; with this assurance parliament ought to
rest satisfied; the more goodness he was disposed to show to
his parliaments, the more firmly he would approve himself if
he saw his goodness abused. Parliament replied in the bold Bold tone
tone of men determined to assert their freedom; "your par- of parlia-
" liament does not *solicit* favour, it DEMANDS justice. No man forcible
ment, and
" ought to be condemned without a fair trial: arbitrary ba- address.
" nishments, arrests, or imprisonments, constitute no part of
" the legal prerogative of the French crown. It is in the name
" of those laws which preserve the empire, in the name of that
" liberty of which we are the respectful interpreters and law-
" ful mediators, in the name of your authority, of which we are
" the first and most confidential ministers, that we dare demand
" either the trial or the release of the duke of Orleans and the
" exiled magistrates." This attack on a prerogative so long
exercised by the court, and essential to the maintenance of arbitrary monarchy, was resisted by the king; and he told them, that

b Bertrand de Moleville, introduction. c State Papers, Nov. 19, 1787.

what they demanded of his justice depended on his will. This
principle that would subject the freedom and happiness of millions to the will of an individual, though the foundation of
French absolute monarchy, the enlightened parliament totally
condemned; they refused to purchase justice by concession;
declared parliament would never cease to demand the impeachment or liberty of the persons in question, and would employ
the same zeal and perseverance to ensure to every Frenchman
the personal security promised by the laws, and due by the principles of the constitution. This patriotic assembly supported
the claim in question, and urged new assertions, not for their
own body alone, but for the whole nation. They published a
remonstrance,[d] declaring that no taxes could be granted but by
the consent of the people; they extended the same doctrine
to the whole body of legislative power, insisting that no man
ought to be imprisoned, dispossessed of his property or liberty,
outlawed or banished, or in any way hurt or injured, unless
through his own act, his representatives, or the law of the land.[e]
The parliament[f] of Paris vindicated those fundamental rights,
which no time, nor precedent, nor statute, nor positive institution can abolish, which men always may reclaim when they
will. They endeavoured from history and authority to prove
this popular consent to have been the foundation of laws in
former times, before the subversion of the constitution under
the house of Bourbon The precedents which they quoted did
not apply to the present situation, and indeed obscured instead
of illustrating their claims. But as neither the justice or expediency of the doctrine rested upon former usage or authority,
the irrelevancy of their citations affected neither the truth of
their positions, nor the wisdom of their conduct.

The parlia-
ment of
Paris as-
serts the
rights of
a free peo
ple.

d State Papers, Nov. 23d, 1787.
  e See this doctrine stated by Hume in his remarks on the great charter
of England, Hist. vol. i. p 415.
  f The provincial parliaments of France were originally courts of justice,
possessing no share in the legislation, either as an order or as representatives of the people From the time of cardinal Richelieu, the legislative as
well as the executive authority was vested entirely in the crown The practice of employing the parliaments to enregister the king's edicts, was never
intended to convey any authority or force through these bodies; they were
considered merely as notaries, to record and authenticate their existence,
and thereby as well to promulgate them, as to prevent any doubts being
entertained by the public of their reality The parliament, however, as
their popularity and power increased, and times and circumstances proved
favourable to the design, assumed a right of judging whether these edicts
were injurious to the public. If they determined them to be hurtful, they
by a legal fiction pretended that being contrary to the welfare of the people,
and contrary to the king's wisdom, justice, or clemency, they did not believe them to be the king's real acts, but considered them as an imposition
practised by his ministers; and on this ground they presented memorials
or remonstrances to the king, placing in the strongest colours they could
all the evil consequences which they presumed would attend their being
passed into laws. See Annual Register, 1789.

CHAP.
XLIII.

1789.
Spirit of
boundless
innovation.

The spirit of liberty and reform, operating on the ingenious and volatile character of Frenchmen, and tinctured by the peculiar doctrines of late political philosophers, produced a disposition to innovation. Even at this period many reformers assumed a position, that every existing establishment was bad, and therefore that melioration consisted in a total change. The court imputed to parliaments the prevailing spirit, which these bodies rather expressed than incited; and, confounding the organs with the cause, formed a project for annulling the authority which was recently assumed by these bodies. Professing to gratify the popular passion for reform, ministers proposed a general amendment in the codes both of civil and criminal justice. For this purpose, a tribunal was to be instituted, endowed with such powers as would carry back the parliaments to the original principles of their institution, and reduce them to the condition of mere courts of justice.[g] The members of this body were all to be chosen by the king:[h] their number and every circumstance relative to their meeting, was to depend on the royal will. Profound secrecy was observed in conducting this project: the edicts were privately printed at the royal press, and intended to be presented, on the same day to all the parliaments in France, and the registration was to be enforced by soldiers. The scheme, however, being discovered before it was ripe for execution, by M. d'Epresmenil, was by him communicated to the parliament of Paris, of which he was a member. This body meeting on the 3d of May 1788, issued a declaration, stating a report of a conspiracy, by the court, against the authority of parliaments, the interests and liberties of the nation. Detailing the alleged rights of parliaments, and the purposes both of their general bestowal and recent exercise, they declared their resolution of surrendering their privileges, not to ministers, or any new courts established by their influence, but to the king himself, and the states-general. Though Louis had, as an act of grace, liberated Orleans and the magistrates, he still determined to support the principle of arbitrary imprisonment. Agreeably to this resolution, he ordered M. d'Epresmenil, and M. De Monsambert, two of the most active members of the parliament to be arrested in their houses. Though these patriots evaded immediate caption, by concealing themselves from the soldiers, they disdained to abstain from their duty in parliament. That body, informed of the attempt, sent a deputation to remonstrate with the king; but the delegates were not admitted. A regiment of guards surrounded the court of parliament; its commander entering the assembly, demanded the two magistrates whom the king had ordered to be arrested:

g Bouille, p. 54.
h They were to have consisted of princes of the blood; of peers of the realm; of great officers of state; of marshals of France; of governors of provinces; of knights of different orders; of members of council; and of a deputation of one member from each parliament of the kingdom, and two from the chamber of accounts and supply. Annual Register, 1789, c. i.

CHAP. a profound silence for some time ensued; at last, the president
XLIII. rising, with the acclamations of the whole body, replied, every
member here, is a d'Epresmenil, and a Monsambert.[i] These
1789. magistrates, however, surrendered themselves, and were led
off to prison amidst the loud execrations of the people. The
king, on the 8th of May, held a bed of justice to introduce the
intended reforms : he inveighed against the undutiful behaviour
of parliament, and declared his determination to suppress such
excesses, in a few of the magistrates; yet in general he preferred prevention to penal animadversion; he then announced the
heads of the new constitution which his chancellor fully detailed.[k] Parliament the following day entered against these proceedings a protest, repeating the substance of their former
remonstrances and declaring individually and aggregately
that they would accept of no employment under the projected
establishment. This protestation was seconded by a great
body of the members; and so generally was the new spirit
now disseminated, that even many of the clergy declared concurrence in their sentiments and resolution. Thus encouraged,
parliament published a still stronger memorial than any which
they had before issued; peremptorily declaring their inflexible
determination to persevere in their past measures. Through
all the kingdom, public bodies, spontaneous associations, and
private individuals, appeared agitated by the same spirit.
The court on the other hand, proceeded to coercive measures;
the governor of Paris entering the parliament house, took possession of all the papers and archives; having locked the doors,
and stamped them with the king's seal, he carried away the
Arbitrary keys. All the other parliaments in the kingdom were suspend-
suspension ed from their functions, and forbidden under the severest
of the par- penalties to hold any meetings. In this crisis the question now
liaments. evidently lay between the establishment of liberty, or of com-
National plete despotism.[l] Brienne was by no means capable of con-
ferment. ducting affairs in so difficult a situation; he possessed neither the
Unfitness sagacity which could have discovered the force of a general
of Brienne spirit diffused through a people of such boldness and energy,
for his nor the wisdom which, to a certain extent, would have grati-
office. fied the national desire, in order to prevent the national violence; and moderated the regal power to preserve its essential
and useful prerogative. He was no less deficient in that boldness of design and vigour of execution, which only could
have overborne the determination of the people, and crushed
their rights. The ready and willing tool of arbitrary power
in its usual and established exercise, he possessed neither invention nor courage to be its counsellor or champion in
untried dangers. The conduct of government was a motley
mixture of outrage and irresolution, violence, and feebleness:
for a short time the court persisted in coercive efforts, both in

i Annual Register, 1789, chap. i.   Mackintosh's Vindiciæ Galliciæ.
k State Papers, May 8th.   l Bouille, passim.

Paris and other provinces; and in Dauphiny, Languedoc, and CHAP. Brittany, the parliaments were exiled, but the rage of the XLIII. people broke out in riots which produced disorder and blood- shed. In some instances it appeared, that the soldiers being com- 1789. manded to quell the disturbances, manifested an extreme un- willingness to act against their countrymen. The king was at Distressed this time in the greatest pecuniary distress, which he saw the situation of people would not voluntarily relieve: nothing, he perceived, the king. short of military execution would enforce the obnoxious edicts. Destitute of money, he lost a great part of the influence which through donative he had possessed; many of the nobility, from the extravagance of their ancestors, their own, or both, were mere dependents on the bounty of the crown; and in the poverty of the king they saw themselves precluded from the usual resource of titled insignificance and beggary; accus- tomed to luxury and splendour, and eleemosynary fountain of their prodigality and ostentation no longer flowing, they from a special cause became infected with the general dis- content;. poor lords, who had subsisted by the royal dole, forsook the king when he had no dole to bestow.[m] The household of the monarch, extremely magnificent and expen- sive, had supported vast numbers of officers and attendants; in the king's distresses four hundred of these were necessarily dis- missed; many of them, no longer maintained in idleness and pomp, turned against the hand which had given them food while it had food to give, and from the most despicable and unworthy motives added to the number of those who opposed the king's government from generous and patriotic principles. The dis- contents rising from political causes were enhanced by a phy- sical calamity; a dreadful hurricane of wind, rain, hail, thun- der, and lightning, on the 13th of July, assailing the land, de- stroyed the fruits and corn. Want and misery were soon felt through the kingdom; and the capital itself was apprehensive of a famine. The dearness of provisions induced or compelled many families to dismiss their servants, and thus increased the number of the idle, distressed, and dissatisfied. To aggravate the danger which menaced the court from so many concurring causes, the wild theories of sophistical projectors, equally inimi- cal to religion as to regular government, to beneficial liberty as to absolute monarchy, were fast gaining ground. In the latter end of 1788, the opponents of the king consisted of two great classes:—first, the champions of rational liberty, determined not only to prevent future encroachments, but to correct past usurpations; to change the government from an absolute to a limited monarchy; to render its object the general happiness, instead of the pleasure of individuals, its rule the national voice, instead of the monarch's will. The other class consist- ed of those who, not contented with an alteration of measures, sought an utter subversion of the establishment, and promoted

m Annual Register, 1789.

CHAP. doctrines and schemes, which would destroy all government:
XLIII. between these two extremes there were various gradations,
from the supporters of limited monarchy to the levellers of all
1789. ranks and orders. The principal actors were at this time
chiefly of the former division, or at least more nearly allied to
it than to the latter; but subordinate agents, especially many
of the literary men employed as efficacious instruments by the
leaders, were closely connected with the votaries of boundless
revolution. Many of the writers, in combating absolute power
to assist parliaments and vindicate the rights of the people, attacked all existing forms and establishments, and loosened the
great cements of society.[n]

. The minister seeing his sovereign in such calamitous circumstances, was more mindful of his own safety, than gratitude to
his master; he resigned his office, and sought refuge in Italy.
Louis finding his own distresses, and those of his kingdom,
multiplying, and that the arbitrary measures which were suggested by his ministers were producing effects so different from
their predictions, and his wishes, resolved to adopt a new plan,
He resol- more consistent with his own benignant character. To gratify
ves to recal the nation, and procure a counsellor likely to relieve the coun-
Mr. Neck- try and himself, he determined to recall the celebrated Mr:
ar. Neckar. From this gentleman, so universally popular, and,
indeed, the idol of their adoration, the warm fancies of Frenchmen expected impossibilities. They seemed to have conceived
that he possessed a kind of magical power, which could pay
off an immense public debt without money, and supply twenty-five millions of people with corn and bread. But Neckar
by no means possessed those extraordinary talents which were
once imputed to him by the grateful subjects of Louis, and by
that monarch himself. Strict morals and integrity even his
adversaries[o] ascribed to this celebrated economist; but the impartial philosopher[p] readily discovered that he was a mere man
of detail; a skilful and upright steward, but not a profound
statesman. " Neckar (says Bouillé) viewed France with the
" eyes of a citizen of Geneva." Native of a republic, he was
warmly attached to the rights and interests of the people; of
plebeian extraction, he too little regarded the distinctions of
rank and of birth, and estimated them by the abstract princi-
ciples of equality, instead of the actual institutions of an established government in a great and powerful nation: his sentiments and habits of thinking were inimical to the privileged
orders. Neckar was, individually, a man of immense riches,
during a considerable part of his life, he had been chiefly conversant with monied capitalists, and naturally attributed more
than its due share of importance to the distinction of wealth:
hence, in every regulation which he should desire to frame,
farmers of the revenue, contractors, bankers, and merchants,

n Bertrand de Moleville on the French Revolution, v. i. c. 1.
o Bouille, page 70.   p Adam Smith.

were likely to be more considered than the clergy or nobility:
and from these various causes Neckar was chiefly attached to
the third estate. With such notions and predilections he came
to the administration of France, at a season which required a
statesman and lawgiver that could survey the whole circumstances and interests of the empire without leaning either to
clergy or laity, nobility or plebeians, to riches or to birth; and
would provide impartially and effectually for the welfare of the
whole.

On Mr. Neckar's appointment, the chief persons of Brienne's
party were dismissed from office. The parliament of Paris was
restored to its functions, met in the middle of September, and
caused all the king's late decrees, which they represented as
unconstitutional, to be publicly burnt. Mr. Neckar found the who coun-.
seis the
convoca-
tion of the
states-ge-
neral.
finances in so disordered a condition, that he advised a convocation of the states-general as the only effectual measure for
relief. He proposed, however, as a preliminary, to summon a
new convocation of notables, who should deliver their opinion
concerning the composition of the states-general, the qualifications of the electors, and of the elected; the mode of election, the proportion of delegates to the wealth and populousness of the several districts; also, the amount and relation of
members to be sent by the different orders, and the instructions
which they were to receive from their constituents; and the 1st
of May, 1789, was the day appointed for the meeting of the states-
general.

Two great questions existed between the three orders, the
nobles, the clergy, and the commons; first, whether all the deputies should meet in one assembly, wherein the concentrated
power of the states-general should reside, or whether they
should be divided as they had been at the last meeting in 1614,
into three chambers, through which a resolution must be carried (at least two of them) before it became the acknowledged
act of the states.[q] Secondly, whether the number of deputies
from each of the orders should be three hundred, as in 1614, or
the clergy and nobles should retain their former numbers, and
the commons send six hundred, so as to equal the amount of
the other two estates : this was called the double representation of the people. These two questions agitated the public
with great violence; if they voted by orders, a double representation would be of no effect, as the two estates could out-
vote the three; therefore, the double representation was proposed on the supposition that they were to vote by numbers.
The arguments for three assemblies were founded on ancient
usage; for one, upon justice and expediency. By the supporters of the last it was contended, that unless there was but
one assembly, the power of the commons would really be nugatory. The clergy and nobles would coalesce together to defend their immunities against the commons, who, in their own,

q Voting *by heads* was the term applied to the first of these alternatives,
and voting *by orders* to the second.

CHAP.
XLIII.

1789.
and the
double re-
presenta-
tion.

maintained the general interests of the people. If their numbers were not equal to those of the other two orders, they
could effect no purpose of important improvement.   The aristocratical estates prevailing among the notables, that council
voted for separate chambers.   In their opinion concurred the
parliament of Paris, which, though desirous of repressing the
power of the crown, was inimical to the exaltation of the commons.   Mr. Neckar inclined to the third estate, but at the same
time professed a desire to preserve the necessary and useful prerogatives of the crown; but the means were not wisely adapted to the end.   Neckar reasoned like an accountant rather
than a statesman, and treated a question for constituting the legislation of a mighty nation, as if he had been summing up the
items of a day book in order to make an entry into a ledger:
he thought that by equalizing the *numbers* of the commons and
the two privileged orders, the one would balance the other;
the states-general, like the parliament of England, would consist of two great branches of lawgivers, which, together with
the king, might produce mutual support and reciprocal control;
therefore he promoted the double representation.   But though
there would be thus an *arithmetical* equality between the two
first orders and the third, perfectly satisfactory to an auditor of
accounts, there was by no means that POLITICAL equality,
which would have satisfied a wise lawgiver, who proposed to
establish an effectual balance in a constitution   If Neckar had
discerned the actual state and party, he would have found that
the partisans of the privileged orders among the commons
were very few, that the partisans of the commons among the
privileged orders were very many,[r] and therefore, that if they
were equal in number, the commons would engross the power
which he proposed to be separated.   Intending that the aristocracy and democracy should be a mutual equipoise, Mr.
Neckar, to whose opinion the king implicitly resigned himself,
in no small degree contributed to the destruction of the one and
predominancy of the other.   The minister entirely neglected
the question concerning the consolidation of the orders; an
omission which prevented a corrective of the power which the
commons were to obtain by the double representation.   The
parliament of Paris found they had lost their popularity by
taking the side of the other privileged orders, and that they
might regain the favour of the commons, published a decree
which vindicated as the rights of a Frenchman, all the leading
objects that have been attained, or indeed sought, by the best
and most admired constitutions.   The rights claimed, nearly
the same as those secured to Englishmen, were such as must
have contented all who understood both the extent and bounds
of useful liberty.   The chief heads of the decree were, that
no assembly could be considered as national, unless it ascertained the following points in favour of the people: the periodical returns of the states-general; no subsidy to be allowed,

r See Annual Register, 1789.

unless granted by the states; no law to be executed by the
courts of justice, unless ratified by the states; the suppression
of all taxes which marked the exemption of certain orders;
equalization of imposts, the responsibility of ministers; the
rights of the states-general to bring accusations before the
courts of justice for crimes; the abolition of arbitrary imprisonment, by bringing before the proper judges every man who
was detained; and confirming the lawful freedom of the
press. These claims were far from answering the ideas of liberty now spread through France. The decree was regarded
with indifference; and the parliament henceforward dwindled
into insignificance. The year 1789 began with very great
dissensions between the orders. The nobility and clergy,
which, in 1787, had refused to part with their immunities, now
expressed their willingness to take an equal share of the public
burthens. The commons, far from being satisfied with this sub- The commission, proposed to overthrow all privileges whatsoever; to mons of
reject every claim founded on ancient usage, or on compact; to France al-
make general equality the standard of private or public right. ready d
The writers of the time employed their separate and joint inge- sire a li⸗
nuity in attacking the rank and titles of the nobles, and the great for
tenure by which many of them held their estates; and French useful
liberty, in the beginning of 1789, was mingled with principles liberty.
subversive of rank and of property. Until the meeting of the
states, the question concerning the amalgamation of the orders,
agitated the nobles and commons, while the clergy appeared
undecided, and ready to join the party which should prevail.
It had been customary in France, in former times, when the
states-general met, for the orders in each district to deliver instructions to their respective delegates. This practice being Instruc-
now revived, the directions given to the deputies of the nobles, tions from
and to the deputies of the commons, by their respective constitu-
constituents, very fully manifested the diversity of the spi- ents to de-
rit which actuated the three bodies. The instructions of the legates.
nobility enjoined their representatives to urge a reform of the
constitution: to strengthen the securities for property, liberty,
and life; and to surrender their pecuniary exemptions, but not
resign their feudal rights, nor to consent to a consolidation of
the orders. The commons, in their mandates to their commissioners, instructed them to insist on the abolition of all distinctions, the abandonment of feudal rights, and the resolution
of the different states into one mass. The injunctions of the
nobility tended, if followed, to establish a moderate and limited
government, securing civil rights to all classes of subjects, but
preserving a distinction of orders and a subordination of ranks.
The injunctions of the commons, previous to their first assembly, tended to overturn the other states under the weight of a
democracy.[s]

s Mr. Lally Tollendal, in exhibiting the different views of the parties of
this time, observes, the commons wished to conquer, the nobles wished to

CHAP.   On the first of May 1789, after a cessation of 175 years,
XLIII.   the states-general of France met for the first time. The par-
         ties which had prevailed throughout the kingdom appeared in
1789.   the states-general, and ranged themselves into three great di-
Meeting of visions. The first was the aristocratic party, determined to sup-
the states. port the ancient form and mode of procedure, by a separation
         of the states into three chambers. This class was considerable
         from the rank, talents, and situation of its members. The
         second division was that of the moderate party; its members
         were, on the one hand, averse to assemblies of three separate
         orders, as tending to throw the legislative power too much into
         the hands of the privileged states, and, instead of an unlimited
         monarchy, to establish an uncontroled aristocracy; on the
         other, they were inimical to the confusion of the orders, as
         tending, instead of reforming, to subvert the government.
         These were desirous of forming the nobles and clergy into
         one house, upon a principle of reciprocal control, analogous
         to the British constitution. The third division was the great
         and formidable democratic party, seeking and tending to
         overbear all rank and distinctions. In this class were to be
         numbered some of the most conspicuous men of the other
         orders. The extraordinary abilities of Mirabeau were em-
         ployed against that estate to which he himself belonged. The
         first prince of the blood was active in promoting factions tend-
         ing to subvert the monarchy from which he derived his elevated
         rank and immense possessions.[†] Against the clergy appeared
         the bishop of Autun, carrying with him a great body of his
         brethren, and prepared to join the most violent commons in
         their democratic excesses. The Abbe Sieyes, an eminent disci-
         ple of the new philosophy, penetrating, crafty, and versatile,
         brought all his ability and address to support the faction which
         his discernment easily perceived about to be paramount. The
         literary men, a great and powerful class in circumstances that
         so much depended on public opinion, ranged themselves under
         the standard of the commons, pursuing measures so inimical to
         that tranquillity and prosperity which best nourish the pursuits
         of literature. The monied capitalists, proud of their wealth,
         and envious of the rank which their opulence could not attain,
         were foremost in instigating measures tending to the destruc-

preserve what they already possessed; the clergy waited to see which side
would be victorious, in order to join the conquerors.

    † The yearly income of the Duke of Orleans was estimated at half a mil-
lion sterling. A considerable part of this revenue was employed in acquiring popularity, and forming, from the idle and profligate rabble through
the provinces, but especially in the city of Paris, a numerous body of retainers, ready to undertake any service, however desperate, at his instance.
If his views, as has been often asserted, were directed to the highest pinnacle of ambition, by a fatality which often accompanies wickedness, the
measures which he pursued for the destruction of another, destroyed
himself.

tion of that property which only could prevent them from insignificance. Besides these classes, the third division included numbers of profligate spendthrifts, abounding in France, as in all luxurious countries, who wished for a change by which they hoped to be better, and knew they could not be worse.

The states being met, his majesty, in a speech from the throne, mentioned his reasons for convoking the assembly: he notices the restless spirit of innovation, and the general discontent which prevailed among his people. A great object of the states he trusted, would be to remove those evils; and they would manifest in their proceedings that loyalty and attachment to the monarchy from which France derived such glory and benefit. The chancellor spoke of the advantages which accompanied a limited government, equally distant from despotism and anarchy. Mr. Neckar then rising, excited in the audience the highest expectation. From him all parties trusted for the most full and accurate information concerning every important department of public affairs; strong practical reasoning, which would demonstrate what was wise and right to be done at such a crisis; with manly eloquence to inculcate the necessity of correspondent conduct: but all were totally disappointed: his speech was loose and declamatory, abounding in general maxims of morality and politics, which were obviously true, but in no way illustrated the momentous subjects of deliberation; and sentimental effusions, that asserted the wishes of the speaker for the happiness of France, without explaining any means for its attainment. On the great subject of consolidation he said nothing decisive, he merely expressed a desire that the matter might be accommodated. Appointed by his sovereign to address the national representatives, who were assembled to deliberate on great public difficulties, he neither stated facts, nor proposed means leading to extrication; his harangue was totally inadequate to the office which he was chosen to discharge. The ministry were no less feeble and indecisive in their conduct than their language. The king at this time possessed all the legal authority of the kingdom; and though the states were met, they were not yet constituted, as the writs of election had not been examined. He, by his established authority might have instituted concerning their sessions, any regulations which should be conformable to ancient precedent and usage; and to have refused compliance with his directions would have been rebellion. Notwithstanding his possession of this power, his ministers most impolitically neglected the exercise of it to prevent the confusion of the orders, and thereby suffered the states to become a democratical assembly. The verification of their powers[u] afforded the first

---

u Each member was obliged, before the commencement of public business, to present his writ of election upon the table of the chamber to which he belonged. Commissaries were then appointed by each order to examine the authenticity of all the writs immediately belonging to itself; and until

CHAP.
XLIII.

1789.

Disunion
and inde-
cision of
the nobles
and clergy.

The com-
mons de-
clare them
selves a
national
assembly.

occasion to the commons of insisting that they should meet in one chamber. Encouraged by their own strength, and the backwardness of the ministers, they very boldly asserted, that unless the writs were verified in their presence, they could not admit their holders to a seat in the assembly, and that both nobles and clergy would be illegal meetings. The clergy wavered; many of the nobility were firm in maintaining the rights of a separate verification, but there were great dissensions in that body. The commons, on the other hand were united. Mr. Neckar proposed conciliatory measures, which, from their indecisiveness, satisfied neither party. The nobles remaining inflexible, the commons, by a still bolder stretch of their power and influence, declared that they would constitute themselves into an active assembly, and proceed to legislative business. Many of the clergy, seeing the commons prevalent, flocked to their hall, and were most joyfully received. The commons executed the bold design which they had formed, and constituted themselves into a meeting which they denominated the NATIONAL ASSEMBLY. This body so formed by its own act, rapidly advanced in the assumption of power. On the 17th of June, they published a decree, intimating that they possessed the sovereign authority, and exercised the same by a very popular act, declaring all existing taxes to be illegal.[x] The king was alarmed at proceedings which changed the constitution, and tended speedily to draw the supreme authority into this democratic vortex: and began to be dissatisfied with his ministers, to whose irresolution and inaction, he now imputed the progress of ambitious violence. The princes and other votaries of the old government, exhorted him to vigorous measures;[y] they advised him to hold a royal session in the hall of the states-general, which by assembling would suspend the meeting of that body. The king agreed to follow the advice, and on the 20th of June he issued a proclamation appointing the 22d for that purpose. The majority of the clergy having now agreed to join the commons, the members of the third estate repaired to the hall. The king having appointed the same day for the royal session, the guards were ordered to keep that apartment clear until the arrival of his majesty. As the members of the assembly came to the door, they were refused admittance by the soldiers; the commons, from so violent an act, apprehending an immediate dissolution, retired to an old tennis court, where they bound themselves by a solemn oath never to part until the constitution was completed. The majority of the clergy now joined the commons, and met them in St. Louis's church, on the

this business was finished, which usually took up several days, the states-general were destitute of all legal authority whatsoever. The sanctions of these commissaries to the authenticity of the writs, afforded what was called the *verifications of powers.*

x Bertrand, vol. i. 69.   y Bertrand, chap. ii.

23d. The royal session being opened, his majesty proposed the outlines of a new constitution : he engaged to establish no fresh tax, nor to prolong an old impost beyond the term assigned by the laws, without the consent of the represent- atives of the nation ; he renounced the right of borrowing money, unless with the approbation of the states ; there should be an end of pecuniary exemptions; and *lettres de cachet* should cease with some modifications. He condemned the late decree of the commons, which assumed by their own sole act, the whole legislative power of the kingdom ; and concluded that none of the laws established in the present states-general could ever be altered, but by the free consent of future states general, and that they should be considered as equally sacred with all other national properties. On the other hand he declared that all tithes and feudal rents should be accounted property, and therefore sacred ; and that the states should be assembled in three chambers instead of one. The manner of the address by no means suited the conciliatory professions, nor indeed the substance of the proposition. It frequently introduced the king's will as the foundation of grants which in a government intended to be free were RIGHTS, not *favours*. In themselves, however, the propositions were such as a few years before, political sagacity could have not conceived that a king of France would offer to his subjects. His majesty commanded them to separate, and to meet the next day in the halls of their respective orders. Equitable as the plan was in itself, it required little penetration to perceive, that it would by no means meet the ideas of the commons; that the magisterial expressions would render it still more unpalatable, and were therefore extremely unwise. The commons listened in haughty silence, while the plan was reading; and as soon as the king departed, absolutely refused to break up their session. The king's attendants having reminded them of his majesty's order, the president answered, THE NATION ASSEMBLED HAS NO ORDERS TO RECEIVE.[z] They passed a resolution declaring the adherence of the assembly to its former decree: and another pronouncing the persons of the deputies sacred and inviolable. The populace at Versailles became violent in behalf of the commons. At Paris the ferment was still more Popular outrageous,[a] and increased in proportion to the attempts of violence.

z Mirabeau, who through some acts and some suspicions had nearly lost his popularity, had the fortune upon this occasion to recover it with increase, by the impetuosity with which he told the king's attendants, that nothing but the points of bayonets should force them out of their chamber.

a No class of rioters was more active in the French capital than the (poissardes) fish-women; who in addition to the violence of their sisters in our own metropolis, possessed all the Gallic vivacity. Far exceeding the Billingsgate fair, instead of confining themselves to volubility of invective, from time immemorial they had acted a distinguished part in Pa-

CHAP.
XLIII.

· 1789.

Firmness
in the no-
bles.

either the nobles or the court, to oppose or control the pretensions of the third estate. The commons now found themselves so strong in the public support, that they affected to treat
the king's system and declaration as too insignificant to merit
consideration or answer. On the 24th of June, the count de
Clermont moved, that the nobles should unite with the commons, and was ably joined by monsieur de Lally Tollendal;
but the majority of nobles would not bend to a proposal which
the natural prepossession of birth, rank, and custom, taught
them to deem humiliating. Many of that body, however,
were either connected with the popular party, or convinced
that inflexibility would answer no purpose; and therefore
joined the assembly. The people became hourly more violent
against the majority of the nobles, whom they deemed refractory: outrage and bloodshed were expected. The members of
this self created assembly had far exceeded the instructions
of their constituents; in assuming the legislative power, they
were not the representatives of the people ; they were a strong
and numerous faction, that usurped the office of lawgivers
by force ; by force only could usurpation have been opposed.
Concession never did nor can avert the encroachments of determined ambition. This was the language which the princes
of the blood,[b] and all the firmest friends of the monarchy held ;
it was indeed not the language of choice, but necessity.
From the attempt of the popular faction to seize the direction
of the empire, the simple question with the votaries of monarchy was, shall we defend ourselves or be overwhelmed ? There
was no alternative. The king was uniformly impelled by humanity, and in the mildness of his disposition, seeking the
good of his people, he deviated from that firmness by which
only their welfare could have been effectually secured. To
avert the dangers which he conceived to impend over the
unyielding nobles, he entreated that order to give up their
judgment and determination to the wishes of the governing
faction. On the 27th of June he sent the following message
to the nobles, by their president the duke of Luxemburgh:
"From the fidelity and affection of the order of which you
"are president, I expect its union with the other two. I have
" reflected upon it, and am determined to make every sacrifice
" *rather than that a single man should perish on my account.*

The king
exhorts
them to
yield.

risian mobs, and were noted for their ferocious actions. On so great an occasion they were not slow in displaying their zeal and their talents. The
sex likewise afforded another class of auxiliaries, more insinuating, less
savage in appearance, but not less effective. These were the courtezans,
whose numbers were immense in that profligate city. One of the chief
scenes of disorder and enormity was the garden of the duke of Orleans,
whither the mob daily resorted, where hired orators inflamed them to every
act of atrocious violence.

b See Bertrand.

" Tell the order of the nobility, therefore, that I entreat them to
" join the other two estates ; and if this be not enough, I com-
" mand them to do it as their king—it is my will. If there be
" one of its members who believes himself bound by his instruc-
" tions, his oath, or his honour, to remain in the chamber, let me
" know: I will go and sit by him, and die with him if it be ne-
" cessary !" A long and violent debate took place, in which the
duke of Luxemburgh read a letter from the count d'Artois, intimating that the king's person might be exposed to immediate
danger, if the popular fury was roused by their refusal. The
question of union was at last carried in the affirmative, and the
nobles repaired to the hall of the commons that evening. The
proposed meeting of the orders became a popular convention ;
and, from this moment, the constitution of France may be considered as actually changed, although the commencement of the
revolution be dated from a subsequent period. The popular
leaders now saw that imperious demand would extort concession ;
and on this discovery they formed their judgment, and regulated
their conduct.

CHAP.
XLIII.

1789.

At his ma-
jesty's in-
stance
they unite
with the
commons.

The people, seeing the orders united, believed the happiness
of France on the eve of completion. All parties agreed on the
necessity of correcting the ancient government ; the only difference appeared to be respecting the extent to which the reform should be carried, and the means that should be employed. It was hoped that the presence of the nobility and clergy,
containing, besides rank, so much of talents and of learning,
might restrain the intemperate heat of republicans, while the
ardent zeal and bold freedom of the commons might inspire
and invigorate the other states; and that thus they should establish liberty without licentiousness; but these expectations
were entirely disappointed. The conduct of the court, having
before exhibited such a mixture of rashness and timidity, violence and irresolution, consistent in weakness and fluctuation
only, soon presented appearances that excited considerable
alarm, but much greater suspicion. The states-general, since
their consolidation, had been more moderate than at any other
period of their session. They had already appointed a committee to prepare materials for the new constitution : monsieurs
Lally Tollendal, and Mounier, two of the most able and temperate leaders, were of this committee ; and entertained flattering hopes that the moderation would prove general. The demagogues very early endeavoured to cultivate a close connexion
between their votaries and the soldiers, and successfully instilled
the popular doctrines into these troops. In seducing the army
from obedience to their king, the democrats very liberally, employed wine, gold, and women, of which last article they had
an abundant supply by their alliance with the harlots of Paris.
The soldiers now having their professional daringness and debauchery, without the professional restraints of subordination
and military discipline, totally disregarded their officers ; left

The sol-
diers are
infected
with the
popular
enthu-
siasm.

CHAP.
XLIII.

1789.

Insubordi-
nation and
licenti-
ous-
ness.

their barracks without leave, repaired to the Palais Royal, joined and even headed the mob in their most enormous excesses, while hand bills and ballads were composed and dispersed, to spread the flames. The soldiers vied with the populace in their democratic exclamations and other excesses: the most daring and refractory being committed to prison, the people flew in crowds to the jail, forced the gates, liberated the captives, and demanded for them a free pardon. The national assembly endeavoured to accommodate the matter by exhorting the Parisians to tranquillity, and the king to clemency. His majesty having no efficient force at hand was obliged to comply, and thus ended military discipline and civil government at Paris.

The king orders troops to approach Paris.

The disorderly state of the metropolis, and the unfitness of the guards for re-establishing tranquillity were ostensible reasons for bringing a great armed force from the different provinces. In the beginning of July about thirty-five thousand men drew near Paris and Versailles. On the tenth of the month the national assembly presented very strong remonstrances to the king on the approach of the forces. He answered that he had no other motive for his conduct, than the necessity of establishing and maintaining good order in the capital. He was so far from intending to interrupt the proceedings of the assembly, that if the presence of the soldiery gave them umbrage, he was ready to transfer the states-general to Noyon, or Soissons, and repair himself to some place in its vicinity, where he could maintain a ready communication with the legislative body. The moderate members were willing to accede to this proposal; but the popular leaders were aware of the strength which they derived from the capital, and would not leave its vicinity. They either reposed, or professed to repose, no confidence in the king's assurances, and gave out that a plot was formed by the court to crush the nascent liberties of Frenchmen. The king now appeared evidently to listen to the supporters of the old government, and withdrew his confidence from those counsellors who had been favourable to popular measures. The partisans of the ancient monarchy severely reprobated the conduct of Neckar, to whose republican sentiments and counsels they imputed the degraded state of royal authority; and strongly urged the king to discharge a servant who from either design or imprudence[e] had endangered the mo-

M. Neckar
dismissed.

narchy. Accordingly on the 11th of July, Mr. Neckar was dismissed[d] from administration, and ordered to quit the kingdom,

c Bertrand, vol. i p. 191.

d Mr. *Neckar* kept his disgrace a profound secret, even from his wife, and received company that day at dinner, as usual. Those who dined with him did not perceive the least alteration in his countenance. After dinner his wife and daughter invited him to take a ride to the Val, a country house situated in the forest of *St Germain* belonging to madame *de Beauvais*, an intimate friend of Mrs. Neckar's. He consented, and went into the carriage and with him the other members of the cabinet were also discharged from their employments. Mr. de Breteuil, a zealous friend of the old government, was appointed prime minister, and marshal Broglio, who maintained the same sentiments, commander in chief. On Sunday the 12th of July, these changes being reported at Paris, caused the greatest despair and fury, and riots prevailed in every quarter. The rashness of the prince de Lambese, who, endeavouring to disperse a riotous body of populace, wounded with his own hand, one who was said to be only a spectator, not only increased the tumult, but hastened the general insurrection for which the people were so ripe. The mob, with clubs, spits, and such weapons as they could procure, rushed upon Lambese's troops, and put them to flight, not without killing some of the number.[e] The following night Paris was filled with a dread of slaughter from the army, and of general plunder from the multitudes of miscreants with which that vast metropolis abounded ; but prompt in expedient, they next day. generally armed, formed themselves into one great body with the professed intention of securing internal order, and defending themselves against external enemies. They adopted a peculiar cockade for the purpose; and thirty thousand citizens totally unaccustomed to arms, were soon seen completely accoutred, and in a few hours assumed the appearance of order and discipline. The national volunteers came in a body to proffer to the people their service, which was most joyfully accepted. Directed by the popular leaders, and instructed by their military auxiliaries, the armed citizens prepared to defend the capital against the approaching troops. They threw up intrenchments, and formed barricadoes in different parts of the suburbs. A permanent council was appointed to sit night and day at the Hotel de Ville ; and a communication was established between this body and the national assembly.

An army of volunteers is immediately raised.

The national cockade.

with his wife, but instead of going to the Val, he took the road to Brussels, in order to be the sooner out of the kingdom.

e This transaction of Lambese's appears to have been without any orders from the ministers, or any concert with the other military commanders. Though there were several regiments of foot stationed close to Paris, none of them stirred to assist and protect Lambese's corps. The total inaction of the troops, both on the succeeding day and night, during all which time, critical as the season was, and notwithstanding the preparations they knew to be making in Paris, they never attempted to enter the city, seems to exculpate the court and ministers from. the bloody designs imputed to them by the popular party. If such a scheme had been proposed, this would have been the season for its execution, when prevalent confusion and terror would have prevented any effectual plan of resistance Weakness and folly, indeed, chiefly characterized the ministerial councils of the time. Knowing that in former periods the very appearance of troops had intimidated the Parisian populace, they without adverting to the total change of sentiments and circumstances, seem vainly to have expected the same effect at present.

CHAP. In the course of this day various robberies being committed, the
XLIII. multitude seizing some of the thieves in the fact, dragged them
~~~~~~ instantly to the Greve, the common place of execution, and
1789.   hanged them by the ropes which were used to fasten the lan-
therns. Hence originated that most horrid practice of the French
mob, making themselves judges and executioners in the same
instant, without the smallest regard to law or justice, rank, age,
or sex.

They at-   The next day was the celebrated 14th of July. The new
tack the   army, early in the morning, attacked the Hotel des Invalids,
royal mag- and taking it by surprise, seized a large magazine of arms and
azines to ammunition; thence they proceeded to the *Garde Meuble*, or
procure
arms.   ancient armoury, forced it open, and distributing the contents
among their own body, completed their means for defensive and
offensive operations. They now conceived a much bolder design, which was to seize the Bastile; but aware that this fortress was very strong, and amply supplied with provisions for
standing a siege, they bethought themselves of attempting stratagem; they accordingly negotiated with the marquis de Launay, and coming to the gates, demanded arms and ammunition.
The governor appearing to comply with this requisition, the
gates were opened; a great number being admitted over the
first bridge, the bridges were drawn up; in a short time a discharge of musketry was heard; but whether from a precon-
certed scheme of De Launay, or provoked by the intemperate
violence of the citizens, has never been ascertained.[f] But
whoever might be the aggressors, when the firing was heard,
the passions of the populace were inflamed to such enthusiasm

[f] The testimonies on this subject are so extremely contradictory, that an
impartial judge would find very great difficulty in developing truth, amidst
the exaggerations of infuriated passions. Where we can place no reliance
on the declarations of witnesses, our opinions must be formed from probability. De Launay could expect no advantage to the royal cause from this
partial massacre. Instead of intimidating, he must have seen that it would
inflame the Parisians to still more violent outrages. The cruelty imputed
by the popular hypothesis was not found in any one authenticated instance
to be a part of the royal policy. What purpose could it serve, from what
motive could it spring? On the part of De Launay, this hypothesis implies,
that from mere wanton barbarity he perpetrated mischief tending most powerfully to ruin himself, and injure his master's cause. Such a supposition
is, no doubt, within the verge of possibility, but another view appears much
more probable. The Parisians were in a state of the most violent rage and
indignation against every supporter of government, and gave full vent to
their passions both in words and actions. The Bastile they considered as a
great bulwark of despotism, and the receptacle of its most miserable victims; entered into that gloomy mansion, whose horrors had so much occupied their imaginations, and stimulated their passions: and viewing its
guards, whom they considered as the minions of atrocious tyranny, nothing
could be more likely than that their conduct to the soldiers would be abu-
sive, insulting, and furiously intemperate, and that thence quarrels might
arise leading to a bloody catastrophe.

and fury, that the Bastile, the citadel of Paris, with its seemingly impassable ditches, and its inaccessible towers and ramparts, covered with a powerful artillery, was, after an attack of
two hours, carried by storm. De Launay was immediately
dragged to the Place de Greve, and miserably murdered. M.
de Losme, the major of the Bastile, met with a similar fate,
and equal cruelty. When the place was captured, the Parisians loudly exclaimed, let us hang the whole garrison; but the
prisoners were saved by the intercession of the national troops.
The popular rage now manifested itself in a species of savageness long unknown in civilized Europe. They insulted and
mutilated the remains of the dead, and exhibited their heads
upon pikes to applauding multitudes; so dreadful were the in-
gredients already mingled with Gallic liberty. The victorious
Parisians, exploring the gloomy dungeons or oppression, in expectation of delivering numbers of unfortunate victims, to their
great surprise and disappointment, found only seven captives,
four of whom were confined on charges of forgery, and three
only were state criminals. So little was this engine of tyranny employed under the mild and humane Louis XVI. When
the capture of the Bastile was reported at Versailles, the ministers at first treated it as an extravagant fiction of the democratic party, but they were soon too well assured of the fatal
truth. In this situation they formed the absurd resolution of
keeping the king in ignorance of what had passed, and urged
Broglio to proceed immediately to the reduction of Paris; but
he answered, that his troops were infected with the popular
spirit, and that he could not rely on their efforts. The ministers
and the princes were soon convinced that opposition would be
ineffectual, and began to provide for their own safety. The
count de Artois had hitherto used every effort to inspirit the
king, and to prevent the downfall of the whole fabric; but he
now saw that the attempt was hopeless. At midnight, the
duke de Liencourt, who was master of the wardrobe, forced
his way into his majesty's apartment, and informed him of the
whole. The king resolved on the most unconditional submission
to the national assembly; and repairing thither without guards,
early in the morning, he declared he resigned himself into their
hands; and thus, deserted by its most efficacious supporters, attacked by the combined efforts of the people, and relinquished
by its possessor, fell the absolute monarchy of France; and
here the historical reader may date the commencement of the
French revolution.[g]

Louis arrived in the national assembly, and having declared
that his sole reliance was on their wisdom and patriotism, entreated them to use their power for the salvation of the state.

g The susceptibility of the French character renders that people very
easily impressed by any address to their senses, imagination, or passions.
A song that was composed about this time had a still stronger effect than
even that which is ascribed by our historian to the celebrated air Lillibul-

CHAP.   He informed them, that he had ordered all the troops to quit
XLIII. the neighbourhood of Paris and Versailles: the Parisians how-
        ever being still afraid of sieges and blockades, proceeded with
1789.   preparations for defence., They appointed M. La Fayette
commander of their armed corps, to which they gave the name
of National Guards. The capital was now a great republic,
and it soon was so sensible of its power, as to give the law, not
only to the unfortunate sovereign, but to the national assembly
and the whole kingdom. The national assembly sent a deputation, consisting of eighty-four members, with a view of restoring tranquillity. The Parisians received the deputies with
every mark of respect and applause, but expressed a desire
that the king himself should visit the city of Paris. This
humiliating measure Louis carried into execution on Friday
the 17th of July, under a full conviction that he thereby encountered the peril of instant assassination. He was received
by a body of twenty-five thousand national guards; and thus
led in a melancholy procession, amidst the loud and continual
acclamations of *Vive la nation*, while the ancient favourite cry
of *Vive le roi* was not once heard. Being conducted to the
hotel, he was obliged to accept the new cockade, and to hear
an harangue from the popular leaders, charging the court with
all the cruel designs that were reported to have been formed
against the city of Paris. Having so clearly and positively
denied this imputation, as to impress conviction on the most democratical of his hearers, he returned safely to Versailles, to the
great joy of his friends, many of whom never expected to see
him again. Meanwhile the princes, and some of the chief nobility, with many of the inferior courtiers, perceiving the popular party paramount, sought safety in flight. The national assembly having signified a wish that Mr. Neckar[i] should be recalled, that minister was invited to return to Paris, and other
popular ministers were appointed. Some degree of tranquillity having been re-established at Paris, the national assembly
proceeded to the formation of a new constitution. As the
groundwork on which they were to build a fabric, they began
with forming a declaration of rights. This manifesto was introduced by a remark tending to show, that the ignorance, neglect, or contempt of human rights, are the sole causes of public misfortunes, and to avoid these evils, that it was necessary

lero:[*] this was the famous *Ca Jra*, both in the words and music skilfully
adapted to the impetuous ardour of impassioned Frenchmen: in rapid
strains and expressions, it announced the immediate downfall of existing
establishments
                    [*] See Hume, vol. iv. chap lxxi.
   i Mr. Neckar was welcomed both at Versailles and Paris, with such de-
monstrations of general and excessive joy, that democratic writers compared it to the transports of the Romans on the return of Cicero from banishment.

to define and explain those rights. The declaration contains the outlines of the doctrines afterwards held out by the various revolutionists, and, indeed, is the text that has given rise to the principal class of the comments so long the subject of literary and political discussion. Here was the noted principle brought forward which founded legitimate government upon the NATURAL RIGHTS OF MAN. This theory, however, supposing mankind susceptible of perfection, deduces its inferences from an assumption which it neither did nor could prove, and which daily experience disproved. Many of the remarks are, no doubt, abstractly true ; but they are useless, because they do not apply to circumstances either existing or likely to exist:^k on this basis they proceeded to raise the new constitution.

1789.

Declara-
tion of
rights :

its funda-
mental
principle
the Rights
of Man.

k The following is a copy of the declaration of rights, consisting of seventeen articles:

I. Men were born, and always continue, equal in respect of their rights ; civil distinctions, therefore, can be founded only on public utility.

II. The end of all political associations is the preservation of the natural and imprescriptible rights of man; and these rights are liberty, property, security, and resistance of oppression.

III. The nation is essentially the source of all sovereignty ; nor can any individual, or any body of men, be entitled to any authority which is not expressly derived from it.

IV. Political Liberty consists in the power of doing whatever does not injure another. The exercise of the natural rights of every man has no other limits than those which are necessary to secure to every other man the free exercise of the same rights; and these limits are determinable only by the law.

V. The law ought to prohibit only actions hurtful to society. What is not prohibited by the law should not be hindered; nor should any one be compelled to that which the law does not require.

VI. The law is an expression of the will of the community. All citizens have a right to concur, either personally, or by their representatives, in its formation. It should be the same to all, whether it protects or punishes; and all being equal in its sight, are equally eligible to all honours, places, and employments, according to their different abilities, without any other distinction than that created by their virtues and talents.

VII. No man should be accused, arrested, or held in confinement, except in cases determined by the law, and according to the forms which it has prescribed. All who promote, solicit, execute, or cause to be executed, arbitrary orders, ought to be punished : and every citizen called upon or apprehended by virtue of the law, ought immediately to obey, and renders himself culpable by resistance.

VIII. The law ought to impose no other penalties than such as are absolutely and evidently necessary ; and no one ought to be punished, but in virtue of a law promulgated before the offence, and legally applied.

IX. Every man being presumed innocent till he has been convicted, whenever his detention becomes indispensable, all rigour to him, more than is necessary to secure his person, ought to be provided against by the law.

CHAP.
XLIII.

1789.

First acts of the French revolutionists.

Great object to subvert establishment.

Licentiousness of the press.

Twenty thousand literary men stimulate the mob to outrage.

The practical operation of the principles immediately manifested itself in the acts and proceedings of the national assembly, and the various classes of the French revolutionists. Manifold were the subjects of consideration; but the great and general object was subversion of establishment. In prosecuting this purpose, the energy, susceptibility, and violence of the French character, were clearly displayed. Freed from all the restraints which not only superstition and despotism, but religious and salutary control, had formerly imposed, they now gave full vent to their dispositions. Their natural ardour was farther goaded to fury by demagogues. The licentiousness of the press even exceeded the licentiousness of the mob, and most powerfully prompted its atrocity. Twenty thousand literary men were daily and hourly employed, not as became superior ability and knowledge, in restraining vicious passions, and in teaching the ignorant the way to virtue and happiness, but in exhorting and stimulating them to outrageous actions. Never was intellectual superiority more disgracefully debased by the venal panegyrist of corrupted courts, or the hired encomiast of titled stupidity and insignificance, than by these adulators of an infuriate populace. But even in scheming and promoting anarchy and disorder, the inventive, bold, and ready genius of Frenchmen appeared. A confederacy was framed which in its institution and effects, exhibited a new phenomenon in the history of political organs. A combination was first formed of literary men, to associate under the name of a *club*, at their meetings to concert measures which might give the tone to the

X. No man ought to be molested on account of his opinions, not even on account of his religious opinions, provided his avowal of them does not disturb the public order established by the law.

XI. The unrestrained communication of thoughts and opinions, being one of the most precious rights of man, every citizen may speak, write, or publish freely, provided he is responsible for the use of his liberty in cases determined by law.

XII. A public force being necessary to give security to the rights of men and of citizens, that force is instituted for the benefit of the community, and not for the particular benefit of the persons to whom it is intrusted.

XIII. A common contribution being necessary for the support of the public force, and for defraying the other expenses of government, it ought to be divided equally among the members of the community, according to their abilities.

XIV. Every citizen has a right, either by himself or his representatives, to a free voice in determining the necessity of public contributions, the appropriation of them, and of their amount, modes of assessment, and duration.

XV Every community has a right to demand of all its agents, an account of their conduct.

XVI. Every community in which a separation of powers and a security of rights is not provided for, wants a constitution.

XVII. The right to property being inviolable and sacred, no one ought to be deprived of it, except in cases of evident public necessity, legally ascertained, and on the condition of a previous just indemnity.

mob, and through their overbearing influence direct the decrees
of the national assembly, and the acts of all municipal, judicial,
and executive bodies, and thus make the whole power of
France ultimately depend upon their resolves. These demagogues invited into their society such of the populace as they
conceived likely to become useful instruments, and exhorted
them to construct other clubs, both in Paris, and through all the
provinces; and that such meetings should be connected, or to
use a new revolutionary metaphor, *affiliated* together. These
conventicles consisted first of literary votaries of the new philosophy, who promulgated and inculcated suitable doctrines, sentiments, and conduct. One of the clubs meeting in a convent
formerly belonging to the jacobins, assumed the name of Jacobin Club,[1] which afterwards extending to appendant societies,
gained a superiority over the rest, and became so noted throughout the world. In the first deliberations of the national assembly,
these societies, guided by literary demagogues, and directing the
populace, had a powerful influence. Many of the lawgivers
were indeed members of the new institutions; and those who
were most inimical to the existing establishments, and to rank
and property, were held in the highest estimation, and were really
the directors of the revolutionists. Various in detail as were the
precepts of these innovators; in principle and object they were
simple and uniform. Their lessons of instruction, or exhortations to practice, may be compressed in a few words. Religion
is all folly: disregard religion and its ministers. Every establishment is contrary to natural right; pull down establishments.
Order is an encroachment upon natural freedom; overturn all
order. Property is an infringement upon natural equality; confiscate all property.[m] Such was the system generally received
in the enthusiasm of reform, through a most extensive and populous nation, distinguish for promptness and fertility of genius,
for boldness and activity of character, and by its very virtues
rendering its errors more extensively pernicious. To follow
through the various and manifold details, the doctrines and objects which guided the national assembly, would be foreign to
our history; but assuredly it belongs to our subject to sketch the
spirit and principal operations of a revolutionary system by which
Britain was so essentially affected.

The licentiousness of Paris spread through the provinces;
and the peasants, having been long severely oppressed by seig-
norial tenures and privileges, conceived themselves now emancipated, and turned upon the proprietors with the most outrageous violence.[n] Reports of robberies, rapes, and murders,
daily reached the assembly. Landed proprietors apprehended
the plunder of their property; and some of the nobility, whose

An engine
of govern-
ment new
in the his-
tory of po-
litical es-
tablish-
ments.
CLUBS.
Their in-
fluence ex-
tended by
affiliation.

Lawless
violence in
the coun-
try.

The peas-
ants turn
on the pro-
prietors.

1 Annual Register, 1790, chap. i.
m See revolutionary publications at Paris, 1789, passim.
n Bertrand, vol. i. c. xi.

CHAP. possessions were very great, were seized with a sudden im-
XLIII. pulse of sacrificing a large portion to secure the rest. On the
1789. 4th of August the viscount de Noailles, and the duke d'Agui-
Some of lon, proposed an equalization of taxes, and an abolition of feudal
the nobili services. This offer striking the assembly and galleries with
ty propose the warmest admiration, excited in the other proprietors a wish
to sacrifice to emulate conduct which was so highly applauded. The nobles
a large por- and clergy vied with each other in surrendering privileges of
tion of their orders, and both these estates concluded with sacrificing
their pri- their manerial jurisdictions. So far there was nothing but vo-
vileges and luntary cession, directed by preventive policy, and stimulated
property. by praise, or flowing from enthusiasm. The next day it was
Admira- proposed that tithes should be abolished, and church property
tion of the should be seized by the state. This proposition the clergy
commons. eagerly combated, but their remonstrances were ineffectual;
Proposi- and at one blow all the immense property of such a numerous
tion for the body was confiscated, without the least allegation of delinquency.
seizure of The Abbe Sieyes, though a friend to the revolution, strongly
church remonstrated against this forfeiture, as commencing freedom
property. with iniquity.[o] But the sound reasoning, even of a partisan,
Remon- was unavailing against determined rapacity. Equality being
strances of the professed object of the revolutionists, it was proposed that
the clergy all the provincial distinctions, the peculiar rights and privileges
disregard- of each district should be abolished, and that, without any local
ed. diversity and immunity, or any regard to particular customs,
usages, and prescriptions, the whole nation should be consolidated into one compact body. The deputies of privileged
towns and districts surrendered the immunities of their constituents, all exclusive claims in every part of France were resigned; and the provinces which had possessed the right of taxing
Parlia- themselves, renounced the power of taxation. The parliaments are ments, which had so long held the judicial authority of France,
annihilat- and had been considered as the able, upright, and intrepid
ed. guardians of the public welfare, were annihilated. All the
Immuni- canon, ecclesiastical, and political codes of law, all the claims
ties are sa- of the court of Rome, all the fees or taxes which it heretofore
crificed. received, were abolished. Even the very systems of theology
The law and metaphysics, which had prevailed for so many ages, fell,
and policy not under the regular and well conducted force of reason, but
of the king- the furious rage of innovation. In a few days the whole law
dom are and policy of the nation were changed, a great part of its pro-
overturn- perty was disarranged; and every thing had altered its ancient
ed. form and aspect. A revolution more comprehensive and com-
piete in its objects, as well as more minute and particular in its
details, than any which is recorded in the annuals of mankind,
was carried into effect by an assembly of men professing to
deliberate, with little more reflection or discussion, than in a
senate of prudent lawgivers and statesmen, would have been

o Bertrand, vol. i. chap. xii. and xiii.

bestowed on the most ordinary municipal or local regulation.
The nobility and clergy in the provinces, not having been impressed with the impassioned enthusiasm, from which their delegates in the national assembly had so lavishly surrendered
their rights of tithe, without their concurrence, very generally
condemned a bounty that bestowed what did not belong to the
donors. They were greatly enraged and grieved at the confiscation of their property, and could not think highly of a new
system of government, the first specimens of whose character
were irreligion and robbery. Resistance, however, they saw
would be vain ; and they were therefore compelled to acquiesce
in the humiliating and plundering decrees. But the pecuniary
pressure, the proximate cause of the present crisis, still continued. The peasants considered taxes as an infringement upon
liberty, and refused payment; others followed their example,
and there was no money to support government, or carry on
the public business. After stating the national wants, Mr.
Neckar asked for a loan of thirty millions of livres, but the sub-
scription was not filled. A scheme for voluntary contributions **Scheme of voluntary contributions.**
was adopted, and from its novelty eagerly embraced by this
volatile people. All ranks vied in bringing their silver and
gold to the public treasury, nor was coin only produced, but
also plate, and the minutest articles of dress. The members
of the assembly themselves, in their bountiful patriotism, agreed
to sacrifice their shoe-buckles to the exigencies of the commu-
nity. The king and queen sent their gold and silver plate to **Gold and silver uten-sils carried to the mint.**
the mint for coinage. These offerings, however, were very
inadequate to the supply of the public wants. A scheme was
proposed by Mr. Neckar, and after many strong objections and
remonstrances, embraced by the national assembly, for applying
one FOURTH of every man's annual income to the wants of the
state.[p]

Having made these very momentous changes respecting **Prepara-tions for the new constitu-tion.**
corporate and private property, they proceeded now to new
model their constitution, according to the declaration of rights.
The assembly was divided into sections and committees ;[q] to
each of which was assigned a specific part of the new polity,
to be prepared, and grooved with the rest. The first question
considered respecting the constitution was of the very highest
importance ; what share of authority the king should possess **Authority to be pos-sessed by the king.**
in the new legislature ? On the solution of this problem it was
to depend whether the royal power should be strong enough
to restrain the violence of democracy. On the one hand, it
was proposed that the king should possess a veto, or negative
in the passing of a law ; on the other, that he should be merely the chief executorial magistrate, without any voice in the
legislation. For the negative voice were ranged, not only all

p Annual Register, 1790, chap. i.   q Bertrand, vol. i. chap. xiii.

CHAP. the friends of the ancient monarchy, but the majority of the
XLIII. nobility and clergy; now sensible that they had conceded
        too much; apprehensive that their total ruin was intended,
1789.   and desirous in the kingly prerogative to preserve a bulwark
        which might afford some defence to the remaining rights, to
        resist the torrent of democracy. Against it was opposed the
        whole body of the commons, who containing many subordi-
        nate divisions, agreed in the general desire of reducing the
        monarchy. The question was agitated with great force and
        violence on both sides. The opposition of the privileged
        orders was represented by demagogues to arise from an in-
        tention of attempting a counter revolution; and the people
        were transported into fury and alarm. Louis himself, ever
        desirous of accommodating differences, satisfying all par-
        ties, and maintaining tranquillity, made a proposal of a com-
        promise, by which he should have a power of suspending a law
        during two legislatures; but that if the third assembly persist-
        ed in its support, he should be obliged to give it his sanction.
        This proposal proving satisfactory to both parties, a decree
        passed, conferring these prerogatives on the king, under the

Suspensive denomination of *a suspensive veto.*[r] Another question was now
veto.   discussed, also of very great importance. Whether the na-
Question if   tional assembly should be composed of one or of two cham-
the assem-   bers. Lally Tollendal, Clermont, Mounier, and other leaders
bly was to   of the moderate reformers, were equally zealous, with the
be compos-   republicans for the establishment of a free government; but
ed of one   considering a limited monarchy as affording the fairest pro-
or two   spect of beneficial and permanent liberty, they ardently recom-
chambers.   mended a senate and a house of representatives, which should
              control the proceedings of each other, agreeably to the princi-
              ple, and nearly after the model of the British constitution.
              From the narrow and interested impolicy of many of the
              nobles and clergy, who vainly hoped for the re-establishment
              of the three chambers, together with the predominance of the

Carried   republicans, this proposal was entirely overruled. The com-
that there   mons reprobated every species of mixed government, and
should be   steadily abstaining from imitation of England, proposed, and
only one.   carried, that the duration of the French legislative assembly
The com-   should be only two years. Notwithstanding the rage for inno-
mons re-   vation, they confirmed the hereditary succession of the crown
probate   according to the Salic law. The friends of the duke of Or-
the exam-   leans eagerly contended that the assembly, by confirming the
ple of   renunciation of the first Bourbon king of Spain,[s] should render
Britain.   their patron next heir after the king, his son and brothers.
Settlement   But the assembly, however violent and precipitate in what
of the suc-   concerned France only, cautiously refrained from giving um-
cession.   brage to other powers; and avoided the discussion. Mean-

r Bertrand, vol. ii. chap. xiv.   s Bertrand, vol. ii. chap. xiv.

while the furious republicans, both in the clubs and the national
assembly, resolved that the residence of the royal family, and the
legislature, should be changed from Versailles to the capital,
where they would be still more completely under the control of
democratic direction. The court, and especially the queen, conceived the greatest horror at the idea of a compulsory abode,
among so tumultuous, bloody, and ferocious a people. A transaction which took place in the beginning of October, accelerated
the removal of the king and his family to a scene which they
had so much reason to dread.

Among other causes of popular violence, famine still raged
throughout France, but particularly in Paris and Versailles.
To repress the tumults additional troops were ordered to march
to the royal habitation. The king himself was still allowed
to have about his person a regiment of his own life-guards;
and the newly arrived corps was the regiment of Flanders.
The gentlemen of the stationary forces, on the arrival of the
strangers, according to the established custom of military hospitality, gave their brother officers an entertainment. In the
course of their festivity, when both hosts and guests were heat-
ed by wine, the king and queen, with the infant dauphin, visited
the banquetting room. The royal mother carried the infant
prince completely round the table. Meanwhile the music played an air[t] which the ladies of the court accompanied with the
appropriate stanzas pathetically describing the feelings and sufferings of a captive king.[u] The power of music and the charms
of beauty combining with inherent loyalty, inspired the company with an enthusiasm which wine drove beyond all bounds of
caution. Drawing their swords, they drank copious bumpers
to the august health of their illustrious visitors and their family,
successively,[x] while the chief personages, having expressed
their warmest gratitude, retired. In such a disposition of
mind, no moderation could be expected. A scene of complete
intoxication ensued, and exhibited without disguise, and with

CHAP
XLIII.

1789.

Ferocity of
the people,

inflamed
by scarcity.

Additional
troobs ar-
rive at
Versailles.

Entertain-
ment given
by the offi-
cers in the
palace to
the new
comers.

The royal
family visit
he pan-
quetting
room.

The queen
presents
the infant
dauphin to
the officers.

Music de-
scribes the
sufferings
of a captive
king.

Effects of
beauty,
music, and
wine.

t Bertrand, vol ii. chap. xiv.
u Taken from a dramatic work founded on the story of Richard Cœur de
Lion's captivity when returning from the Holy Land, and beginning, " O
Richard, O mon Roi."

x Bertrand, who gives a very particular account of this entertainment,
mentions the following circumstance, which I do not recollect to have seen
in any other publication, "I have (he says) been assured by two persons
who were present at this entertainment, that the words *to the health of the
nation* were also pronounced feebly by one of the guests, or one of the
spectators, and that the not repeating or seconding this toast, was attended with no consequences. The custom of drinking to the health of the
nation had not been then established, and one may be allowed, without a
crime, to think that was not the moment for introducing such an innovation ; yet one of the greatest crimes imputed to the *gardes-du corps*, was
their not being willing to drink to the health of the nation, that is to say, to
their own health, for they were indisputably a part of the nation."

CHAP. augmented fervour, the sentiments with which it commenced.
XLIII. All the extravagance followed which wine could produce on
~~~~~ romantic fancies and impassioned hearts. The national cock-
1789. ades were by the officers of Flanders torn from their hats, and
The offi- trampled under foot;[y] and in their place were substituted old
cers tram- royal cockades, supplied by the ladies of the court, who took
ple the na- white ribbands, from their own head dresses, to decorate the
tional
cockade. loyal officers, while the three coloured cockade was treated
Report of with contempt and scorn. This banquet was really no more
the enter- than an excess of conviviality, at a season when prudence would
tainment have dictated reserve; but being exaggerated by all the cir-
at Paris.
Rage and cumstances which malicious invention could devise, filled Paris
indigna- with the most violent rage. The innovating leaders pretended
tion of the that the conduct of the officers and courtiers arose from
revolution- counter revolutionary projects, with exulting joy from the con-
ists.   fident expectations of success: a conspiracy, they affirmed,
was matured for the restoration of despotism, and that the
queen was at its head. The carousal of the royalists, at the
time that the people wanted bread, was a flagrant insult to the
nation. These sentiments were disseminated by the various
classes and factions that were friendly to innovation; but
were spread with peculiar activity by the adherents of the duke
of Orleans.

Character Louis Philip Bourbon, duke of Orleans, was the descendant
and pro- and representative of the only brother of Louis XIV., and
jects of the after the posterity of that monarch, next heir to the throne of
duke of
Orleans. France. In such an elevated rank, with riches far beyond the
measure of any other European subject, he had devoted his
youth to the most profligate debauchery: his vices, by their
coarseness, excited the indignant contempt of a gentleman almost as much as the enormity of his crimes called on him the
detestation of every virtuous man. His wealth affording him
the means of very extensive depravity, enabled him to corrupt
great numbers of the youth, and even to make considerable advances in vitiating the metropolis; and his habitation at the
Palais Royal, far exceeded any other part of the French capital
in variety, extent, and flagrancy of wickedness. Such was the
mode of life by which this prince was distinguished by the time
he had reached his fortieth year. His reputation, however, did
not rest solely on uniform and habitual debauchery: other species of turpitude concurred in rendering him at once flagitious
and execrable. Opulent as Orleans was, he was boundless in
avarice. The duc de Penthiévre, high-admiral of France, was
one of the wealthiest noblemen of his country. Orleans cast
his eyes on the daughter of this minister, but the son Lamballe
intervened: with this youth he cultivated a close intimacy, and
according to the concurrent accounts of various writers,[z] was the

y Annual Register, 1789.
z See Playfair on Jacobinism.—Adolphus's Memoirs.—Picture of
Paris, &c.

means of shortening the brother's life, after which he married the sister, now heir of her father's possessions. He moreover proposed to secure the reversion of Penthiévre's very lucrative post. With this view he entered the navy, and the first time he saw an enemy, a descendant of Henry IV. betrayed the despicable degeneracy of personal cowardice.[a] Such an exhibition effectually destroyed all his pretensions to naval promotion; and he conceived the blackest vengeance against the royal family, because the king would not intrust the supreme direction of his navy to a person who was afraid to fight: various circumstances also rendered the queen, the peculiar object of his hatred. The commencing discontents in France opened to him prospects not only of revenge, but ambition: he hoped by fomenting disaffection to pave the way for the overthrow of the royal family, and his own advancement to the regency, if not to the throne. Weak as well as wicked, in seeking the downfall of the reigning sovereign, he promoted and headed attacks upon the monarchical authority; and what he sought by villany, by folly laboured to impair. He did not reflect that the doctrines which he promoted tended to overturn the crown which he pursued. He was so infatuated as to suppose that the bold and able leaders of a revolution which annihilated all adventitious distinctions, would labour to exalt a person, who, destitute of genius and of courage, had none but adventitious distinctions to boast. Since the subversion of the old government, he had abetted the most violent and licentious proceedings of the revolutionary mobs. Sagacious agitators at once saw his designs, and their futility, and professsing to be his agents, used him as their dupe. The most eminent of his declared partisans at this time was Mirabeau, who at certain periods appears to have desired the promotion of Orleans to be regent of the kingdom, in the expectation of being the supreme director himself. Mirabeau very actively promoted the rage of the Parisians: he and his agents pretended to impute the scarcity to the machinations of the aristocrats, and the absence of the royal family, and encouraged the popular cry for the removal of the king to Paris. He promoted the belief of a conspiracy by the queen, and even intimated an intention of impeaching her majesty,[b] as a conspirator for destroying the freedom of the people, and keeping bread from the Parisians. These topics being repeated in the capital, the malignity of the Orleans faction, revolutionary enthusiasm, and popular licentiousness, concurred with the scarcity in producing a determination to hasten to Versailles to demand of the king bread, punishment of the aristocrats, and especially the guards. A multitude of the lowest women undertook this expedition;

a In D'Orvillier's running fight with admiral Keppel. See this History, vol. i. p. 583.

b Bertrand, vol. ii. chap. xvii.

CHAP.
XLIII.

1789.
They hang
priests and
aristo-
crats.

Expedi-
tion to Ver-
sailles.

these amazons broke open the town-house, seized the arms there deposited, and meeting on the stairs a priest, required no farther proofs of his guilt than his dress ; and commenced their orgies by hanging him to a lamp-post. With the yell of infuriate savages they set out for Versailles, joined by Maillard, a creature of Orleans, and a favourite spokesman in the Palais Royal, with a few of his associates. They proceeded on their march : and meeting two travellers in the dress of gentlemen, they concluded them to be aristocrats, and hanged them without further inquiry. Arriving at Versailles, they sent Maillard to the national assembly, to demand the immediate punishment of the aristocrats and the life-guards. The assembly sent their own president with a deputation of the women to wait upon the king. The deputies being thus employed, their constituents set about drinking—an operation for which their hasty departure in the morning had not allowed them time, and the road had not afforded materials. In half an hour the greater number of them were completely intoxicated. Thus prepared they broke into the national assembly, not only filled the galleries, but took their seats among the lawgivers, overwhelmed them with the grossest and loudest obscenity and imprecations. At last two of them, observing the president's chair to be empty, took possession of it themselves, and dictated the subjects of discussion. Such, even then, was French liberty ; such were the assessors who controled the deliberations of men assembled on the most momentous business that could occupy legislators. While the female army was thus employed at Versailles, the fermentation at Paris rose to an extraordinary pitch, and all classes of the populace burned with anxiety to know the result of the expedition. The national guards became so impatient, that they compelled their officers to lead them to Versailles, and declared their resolution to join in obliging the king to repair to Paris. La Fayette, the commander, though a friend to the new constitution was favourably disposed to the person of Louis,[c] as well as to the authority[d] which the new system had conferred on the sovereign, and was the adversary of violent republicans on the one hand, and of the Orleans faction on the other. He endeavoured to dissuade his soldiers from this expedition but found that the attempt would be impracticable ; he therefore tried to moderate its operation. As the guards made no scruple of publicly proclaiming their opinions and sentiments on national affairs, La Fayette and his officers easily discovered whence their present thoughts and intentions originated. The grenadiers informed the general, without reserve, they understood the king to be an ideot, therefore they (the grenadiers) would not hesitate to declare, that matters must go on much better by the appointment of a regent. As this was the peculiar language and doctrine of Mirabeau and

The women over-awe the legislature, break into the assembly, and take the president's chair.

c Bertrand, chap. xvi.   d Bouille's Memoirs.

other directors of the Orleans faction, there could be little doubt CHAP.
where either the politics or the march of the guards originat- XLIII.
ed.[e] Many of the soldiers also declared an intention of massacreing the queen. The Parisian guards arrived at Versailles 1789.
late in the evening, and were most cordially received by the national guards at Versailles, the mob of the same place, and the
amazons of Maillard.[f] The most ferocious of the guards and other
mob in the morning surrounded the palace, and, with dreadful
howlings, denounced the murder of the queen, and the palace
was filled with consternation. But Marie Antoinette was not
frightened. Amid crimes, (says Bertrand) alarms, confusion,
and general stupor, the queen majestically displayed the sub-
limest and most heroic character. Her constant serenity,
her countenance, firm and ever full of dignity, transfused her
own courage into the soul of all who approached her. On
that day she received a great deal of company. To some who
expressed uneasiness she replied, " I know they are come
" from Paris to demand my head; but I learned of my
" mother not to fear death, and I will wait for it with firmness."
Her answer to the advice given to her, to fly from the dangers
that threatened her, does not less deserve to be recorded—
" No, no," said she; " never will I desert the king and my
" children : I will share whatever fate awaits them." Some
hours of sleep happily came to repair her exhausted strength,
and to enable her to encounter on the next day, with equal
magnanimity, dangers still more horrid. About half past five
in the morning the repose of the princess received a frightful
disturbance. An immense crowd endeavoured to break down
the palace gate, and after murdering two of the life guards, effected their purpose. Dreadful howlings announced their
entrance into the palace : they soon arrived at the foot of the
great staircase, and ran up in crowds, uttering imprecations and
the most sanguinary threats against the queen.[g] Before six The mob
they forced their way to the apartments of the royal con- assault the
sort. The sentinel, monsieur de Miomandre, perceiving the palace;
ruffians, called out, " Save the queen ; her life is sought: I
" stand alone against two thousand tigers." Her majesty escaped by a private passage into the king's apartment. Louis, fly- attempt to
ing to her relief, was met by his own guards, who escorted him murder the
back to his apartments, where he found his queen and children queen; pre-
arrived. The ruffians now endeavoured to force the anti- vented by
chamber, which a body of loyal guards defended with heroic the hero-
courage; but their number was decreasing under the murder- ism of her
ing hands of the banditti. The assassins had almost entered defenders.

e Annual Register, 1790, page 48.
f Bertrand informs us, that this man was rather turbulent than malignant,
and even tried to preserve some degree of moderation among his troop ;
which was certainly, in their present condition, no easy task.
g Bertrand, vol. ii. p. 112.

CHAP.
XLIII.

1789.

The king
and queen
agree to
depart for
Paris.

the apartment when the persuasions and supplications of Fayette and his officers induced them to desist. Meanwhile, the
furious mob in the outer court demanded the appearance of
the king and queen : the royal pair was persuaded to present
themselves on the balcony. An universal cry arose, To Paris,
to Paris. Refusal or remonstrance would have been instant
death : the king's assent was immediately notified, and the
furious rage converted into the most tumultuous joy. Within
an hour began the procession, more melancholy and humiliating
to the king and queen than any which history records of captive princes exhibited as spectacles to triumphant enemies. The
sovereign of a mighty and splendid monarchy ; so long and so
recently famed for learning, arts, sciences, and civilization :
renowned for the generosity, honour, and valour of its nobility ;
the courage and discipline of its numerous and formidable armies ;
Mournful
procession
of a degra-
ded mon-
arch.
their zealous and enthusiastic affection for their king and his
family ; the ardent loyalty of the whole people ; was now, without foreign invasion or war; without any avowed competitor
for his throne ; even without any acknowledged rebellion of his
subjects, with his queen and family, dragged from his palace,
and led in triumph by the off-scourings of his metropolis, the
lowest and most despicable of ruffians, the meanest and most
abandoned trulls.

Farther
proceed-
ings at
Paris.
From the 6th of October 1789, the king is to be considered
as a prisoner at Paris. Mounier, equally the friend of liberty
and of monarchy, from these horrid transactions augured the
downfall of both. He and other penetrating observers saw that
the outrages were not the mere accidental ebullitions of a temporary and local frenzy, but the effects of a general cause.
He, Lally Tollendal, and others of the moderate party, who
had been the vigorous and ardent advocates of a limited monarchy, now seeing their efforts unavailing, seceded from the
assembly. But the just and virtuous Mounier, before his retirement, established an inquiry into the recent massacres. The
national assembly followed the king to Paris. The republican
party now began to express suspicions of the duke of Orleans,
which they had before entertained ; though finding him and
his creatures instrumental to their designs, they had made use
of his agency as long as it was wanted. Become now so
powerful, they thought proper to drop the mask, and intimated to him through Fayette, that his presence in France was
incompatible with the public good : he was accordingly compelled to retire into England. At this time the Parisian mob
The exist-
ing govern-
ment en-
deavours
to quell
the mob.
promulgated its resolution to take the administration of justice
into its own hands : and accordingly hanged[h] several aristocrats (especially bakers) at the lamp-post. The assembly,
from regard to its own safety, resolved to prevent so summary
proceedings. They passed a very effective decree, by which

h Annual Register, 1790.

the municipal magistrates were obliged to proclaim martial law whenever the mob proceeded to outrage. They instituted a criminal inquiry into the late murders; several ringleaders were hanged, and terror thus was struck into the rest. Some degree of tranquillity was established in the metropolis; and the assembly proceeded with less interruption and greater security in its schemes of legislation.

CHAP. XLIII.

1789. Severe prosecutions for that purpose.

Such were the leading features and principal acts of the French revolution in 1789. Britons rejoiced at the overthrow of the old French government because so contrary to the liberty which they themselves enjoyed. A change from such a system they concluded must certainly be an improvement. They trusted that the alterations in France would generate a government similar to the British constitution. Presuming beneficial effects from the French revolution, the greatest part of the people rejoiced at this event. The generous feelings of Englishmen sympathised with the assertors of liberty, before they had time and opportunity to ascertain its effects on the situation and characters of its new votaries. Men whose classical erudition had a greater influence in forming their opinions than experience and reason ; who judged of political wisdom more from the practice of the ancient republics than from history, investigation of character, and circumstances, admired what they conceived to be approaches to the democratic institutions of Greece and Rome. Scholars, chiefly eminent for philology, were, with very few exceptions, admirers of a system[i] that they supposed similar to those which they found delineated and praised in their favourite languages. Literary men of a higher class than mere linguists; persons of profound metaphysical and moral philosophy, but of more genius and speculative learning than conversancy with practical affairs, commended the lawgivers of France for taking for their guide the " polarity of reason, in-" stead of following the narrow and dastardly[k] coastings of " usage, precedent, and authority." There were many who, forming their ideas of civil and political liberty from their own abstractions more than from experience, admired the French for declaring the equality of mankind, and making that principle the basis of government, instead of modifying it according to expediency. This latter class comprehended the greater number of eminent projectors of civil and ecclesiastical reform, who long had considered even Britain herself deficient in the liberty which their fancies represented as deducible from the rights of man. Various political societies had been constituted for different purposes of reform, but of late years the most active of them had manifested principles too abstract and visiona-

Effects of the French revolution in Britain. Detesting the old government, and not acquainted with the new, Britons approve the change as friendly to liberty. Sentiments of various classes.

i The instances are numerous, as the observing reader can easily recollect without particularization.

k See Vindiciæ Gallicæ.

ry[1] to be practicably consistent with the British constitution, or indeed any form of government founded upon an opinion that human nature is imperfect, and requires controls proportioned to the prevalence of passion. These societies[m] praised the French revolutionists, and recommended their example as a glorious pattern for the human race. They sent congratulations to the French leaders. A regular official correspondence was carried on between the members of private clubs in England, and the leaders of the republican revolution in France. Statesmen of high rank, and of the highest talents,[n] venerating liberty in general, presumed French liberty would render its votaries happy ; and imputing the aggressions of France on this and other nations to the corrupt ambition of her court, anticipated tranquillity from her renovated state, and rejoiced at a change that appeared to them to forebode peace to Britain and to Europe. These admirers of the French revolution were stimulated by British patriotism as well as love of freedom. The excesses they saw and lamented, but tracing them to their source, they imputed them to enthusiasm ; which, reasoning from experience, they trusted, though furiously violent in its operation on such characters, would gradually subside, and leave only the ardour of useful reform and improvement. The ablest men on the side of administration, abstained[l] from delivering any opinion concerning the internal proceedings of a foreign state which had not then interfered with ours. At the end of 1789, by far the greater number of all classes and parties in Britain was friendly to the French revolution ; and its favourers included a very great portion of genius and learning, while none was hitherto exerted by our countrymen on the opposite side. Such was the impression which this extraordinary change of Gallic polity produced in the most liberal and enlightened of neighbouring nations.

l See Price's Discourse of the love of our country, November 4, 1789, in Priestley, passim ; also, Writings of their votaries, passim.
m Revolution Club and Society for Constitutional Information.
n See Speeches of Messrs. Fox and Sheridan in session 1790.

CHAP. XLIV.

Meeting of Parliament.—At the beginning of the session little debate or discussion.—Mr. Fox takes an opportunity of praising the French revolution—commends the conduct of the French army in supporting the cause of the people against an arbitrary court—likens them to the English army supporting the prince of Orange—deems the French revolution in many respects, similar to the deliverance of England.—His friend and political associate Mr. Burke, manifests a different opinion —unfolds his view of the French revolution—considers its principles, and the characters on which they are operating—points out its first effects, and deduces the outrageous excesses from its nature and doctrines—deprecates the French system as a model for England—denies the allegations of similarity between the French and British revolution —praises the excellence of the British constitution, as contrasted with the French system.—Mr. Sheridan concurs in Mr. Fox's praises of the French revolution—Mr. Pitt, praising the British constitution, delivers no opinion on the French system.—Dissenters again propose to seek the repeal of the test act.—Circumstances apparently favourable to the hopes of the dissenters—they are strenuously opposed by the members of the church.—Work entitled, Review of the case of the Protestant dissenters— Dissenters trust their cause to the transcendent talents of Mr. Fox—his view of the subject, and answers to objections.—Mr. Pitt continues to treat admissibility to offices as a mere question of expediency—deems the leaders of the dissenters inimical to our establishment—adduces from the conduct of the dissenters, and the situation of political affairs, arguments against the repeal.—Mr. Burke speaks on the same side.— Majority against the proposed repeal.—Mr. Flood proposes a plan for a parliamentary reform—his subtile theory is controverted by Mr. Windham—withdraws his motion—Petitions from manufacturers of tobacco, praying to repeal the law subjecting them to excise.—A motion to that effect by Mr. Sheridan —is negatived —Financial statements.—Prosperous situation of the country.—Mr. Dundas presents an account of our East India possessions.—Libels against the commons on account of the management of Hastings's trial—censured.—Dispute with Spain.— Nootka Sound.—Insult offered by Spain— satisfaction demanded.—Conduct of Spain.—King's message to parliament.—Parliament unanimously pledge their support of the king in vindicating the rights of Britain.—Dissolution of parliament—Warlike preparations.—Diplomatic discussion between Britain and Spain —Spain attempts to interest France.—The French nation is inimical to war with England.—Spain, hopeless of aid, yields to the demands of Britain.—The disputes are adjusted in a convention.

THE British parliament had sitten so late in the preceding year, that it did not meet till the 21st of January, 1790. In the opening speech, his majesty mentioned the continuance of the war in the North and East of Europe, and inform the house that the internal situation of different parts of the continent engaged his majesty's most serious attention. Concerned as he was at the interruption of tranquillity, he was per-

CHAP.
XLIV.

~~~

- 1790.

suaded his parliament would join him in entertaining a deep
and grateful sense of the favour of providence, which continued to his subjects the increasing advantages of peace, and
the uninterrupted enjoyment of those invaluable blessings
which they had so long derived from our excellent constitution. His majesty informed them, that during the recess of
parliament, he had been under the necessity of adopting measures for preventing the exportation, and facilitating the importation, of corn. The addresses were voted without opposition
or debate; an act of indemnity was proposed, and unanimously
carried, respecting the order of council about grain.

At the be-
ginning of
the session
there is lit-
tle debate
or discus-
sion. Mr.
Fox takes
an oppor-
tunity of
praising
the French
revolution;

During the first weeks of the session, there was scarcely any
parliamentary discussion, but afterwards some of the most
striking efforts of eloquence arose from a subject which was not
properly before the house. Such a momentous event as the
French revolution, interesting all enlightened men, had very
early engaged the ardent mind of Mr. Fox. This illustrious
senator venerated and admired liberty; and contemplating the
Gallic change, estimated its nature and value by the happiness,
which, he conceived, from overturning an arbitrary government,
it would bestow upon many millions. He spoke with transport and exultation of a great people breaking their chains on
the heads of their oppressors, and celebrated the particular
acts, both civil and military, that had been most instrumental
in effecting the change. As a man, he rejoiced in the subversion of despotism, and as a Briton, in a state from which he
foreboded tranquillity to this country. When the army estimates were under consideration,[o] this distinguished orator first
promulgated to parliament his opinions concerning the French
revolution. The military establishments proposed were nearly
the same as in the former year. Messrs. Pitt and Grenville
contended, that though there was no reason to apprehend hostilities from any foreign power, yet the unsettled state of Europe, and the internal situation of several parts of it made it
necessary for us to keep ourselves in such a condition as might
enable us to act with vigour and effect, if occasion should require our exertions. It was (they argued) a preposterous economy to tempt an attack by our weakness, and for a miserable present saving to hazard a great future expense. Our foreign alliances had been approved by all parties, as necessary
for the preservation of that balance of power in Europe, upon
which the permanence of its tranquillity depended; but they
could only be rendered effectual for their purpose by our ability
to support them with an adequate force. Mr. Fox argued,
that our ancient rival and enemy, by her internal disturbances,
probably would be disabled from offering us any molestation for
a long course of years; and the new form that the government

· o February 9th, 1790. See parliamentary reports.

of France was likely to assume would make her a better neighbour, and less propense to hostility, than when she was subject
to the cabal and intrigues of ambitious and interested statesmen.[p] He applauded the conduct of the French soldiers during
the late commotions: by refusing to obey the dictates of the
court, that army had set a glorious example to all the military
bodies of Europe, and had shown, that men, by becoming
soldiers, did not cease to be citizens. Their conduct (he said)
resembled the behaviour of the patriotic soldiers of England,
when the prince of Orange landed to assist in preserving our
civil and religious liberties: the French revolution, indeed, in
many respects, was like to the glorious event which established
and secured the liberties of England.

To these doctrines Mr. Fox found an opponent in a very
eminent senator, with whom he had coincided during the greater part of his parliamentary life. Habituated to profound meditation on important questions in political philosophy, and
thoroughly conversant with history, Mr. Burke had applied
himself, with the most watchful attention, to observe the details, and to study the principles, of this extraordinary change.
He had reprobated the old government of France; and although
he thought it, in the reign of Louis XVI. softened in its exercise by the progress of civilization, and the personal character
of the monarch, still he deemed the welfare of the people to
rest on an unstable basis, and to require very considerable reform before it could be a beneficial system. But esteeming arbitrary power a great evil, he knew that unwise efforts to
shake it off might produce more terrible calamities. He venerated the spirit of liberty as, when well directed and regulated, a means of human happiness; his respect for it, in every
individual case, was proportionate to his opinion of its probable tendency to produce that end, where he had not actual
experience to ascertain its effects. It was not merely the possession of it that constituted it a blessing, but the enjoyment
of it to such an extent, and with such regulations as could
make it subsidiary to virtue and happiness. Its operation, as a
blessing or a curse, depended, he thought, on its intrinsic nature, compounded with the character of his subjects, and, in a
certain degree, extrinsic causes; and he uniformly controvert-

CHAP.
XLIV.

1790.
commends
the con-
duct of the
French ar-
my in sup-
porting the
people
against an
arbitrary
court.
Likens
them to the
English ar-
my sup-
porting the
prince of
Orange.
His friend
and politi-
cal associ-
ate Mr.
Burke,
manifests
a different
opinion;

---

p Mr. Fox's expectation of tranquillity to other states from the prevalence
of freedom in France, even had there been nothing peculiar in the nature of
that freedom, and the habits and dispositions of its votaries, seems to have
arisen more from theory than from the actual review of the history of free
countries. Had the comprehensive and full mind of this philosophical
politician called before him his own extensive knowledge of the actions of
mankind, he would have immediately perceived that free nations have been
as propense to hostility as the subjects of an arbitrary prince. See the several histories of the ancient republics in the Greek, Latin, or modern languages: in our own tongue, Ferguson, Gillies, and Mitford.

CHAP.
XLIV.

1790.

ed^q those doctrines of the rights of man which would allow the same freedom to all persons, and in all circumstances. Neither did he conceive, that every one state, though refined, was equally fit for the beneficial exercise of liberty as every other state, which was not more refined. The control, he thought, must be strong in the direct ratio of passion, as well as the inverse ratio of knowledge and reason. Having long viewed, with anxiety, the new philosophy become fashionable in France, he bestowed the most accurate attention on the designs of its votaries, as they gradually unfolded themselves. A sagacity, as penetrating as his views were comprehensive, discovered to him the nature of those principles which guided the revolutionists, as well as the characters on which they were operating. The notions of liberty that were cherished by the French philosophy he accounted speculative and visionary, and in no country reducible to salutary practice: he thought they proposed much less restraint than was necessary to govern any community, however small, consisting of men as they are known from experience; he conceived also that the volatile, impetuous, and violent character of the French, demanded in so great a nation much closer restraints than were requisite in many other states. From the same philosophy which generated their extravagant notions of freedom proceeded also infidelity. He had many years before[r] predicted that the joint operation of these causes, unless watchfully and steadily opposed, would overturn civil and religious establishments, and destroy all social order. The composition of the national assembly, the degradation of the nobility, the abolition of the orders, the confiscation of the property of the church, and many other acts, tended to confirm the opinion which he had formed. Much as he detested the outrages, he reprobated the principles more, and foresaw that in their unavoidable operation, they would lead to far greater enormities: in the spirit and details of the new constitution, he did not expect either happiness, or even permanent existence. The vicinity of France to England made him apprehensive lest the speculations of that country should make their way into this, and produce attempts against a constitution founded on observation and experience, and not on visionary theories. The approbation manifested by many Britons, both of the doctrines and proceedings of the French revolutionists, increased his apprehension. When he found that his friend, of whose wisdom and genius he enter-

Marginal notes:
unfolds his view of the French revolution; considers its principles, and the characters on which they were operating,

points out its effects,

and deduces its outrageous excesses from its nature and doctrines.

He reprobates it as an example to England.

q See life of Burke, passim.
r This was the opinion which he had maintained of infidelity and speculative politics in general, in his vindication of natural society, and in his letter to the sheriffs of Bristol, and of French infidelity and speculative politics in particular, in his speech after returning from France in 1773;* and in all his speeches and writings, whenever the occasion required his admonition.

* Life of Burke, p. 161.

tained so very exalted an opinion, was among the admirers of
the recent changes in France; he was anxious lest a statesman
to whose authority so much weight was due, should be misunderstood to hold up the transactions in that country as a fit object of our imitation. Our patriotic ancestors had with cautious wisdom guarded against the contagion of French despotism, which had not only infected our sovereigns Charles and
James, but also made some impression on many of their subjects.
The danger in the last ages, he observed, was from an example of tyranny in government, and intolerance in religion. The
disease was now altered, but far more likely to be infectious.
Our present danger arose from atheism, instead of bigotry, anarchy instead of arbitrary power. Through an admiration of
men professing to be the votaries of liberty, those who did not
thoroughly examine the real features of the French revolution,
might be led to imitate the excesses of an irrational, unprincipled, proscribing, confiscating, plundering, ferocious, bloody, and
tyrannical democracy.[t] He severely reprobated the conduct of
the army: the abstract proposition that soldiers ought not to
forget they were citizens, he did not combat; but applied to
any particular case, it depended entirely on the circumstances:
in the recent conduct of the French guards, it was not an army
embodied under the respectable patriot citizens of the state, in
resisting tyranny; it was the case of common soldiers deserting
from their officers, to join a furious and licentious populace.
The conduct of the British soldiery in 1688, was totally different from the conduct of the French soldiery in 1789. William
of Orange, a prince of the blood royal of England, was called
in by the flower of the English aristocracy to defend its ancient
constitution, and not to level all distinctions. To this prince, so
warmly invited, the aristocratic leaders who commanded the
troops, went over with their several corps, as to the deliverer
of their country: military obedience changed its object; but
military discipline was not for a moment interrupted in its prin- He contro-
ciple. After enumerating the constituents and acts of the French verts the
revolution, he contended that in almost every particular, and in allegation
the whole spirit of the transaction, that change differed from ty between
the alteration effected by Britain. "We," said Mr. Burke, the French
"took solid securities: settled doubtful questions; and cor- and British
"rected anomalies in our law. In the stable fundamental parts revolu-
"of our constitution, we made no revolution; no, not any al- tions,
"teration at all; we did not weaken the monarchy; perhaps the British
"it might be shown that we strengthened it very considerably. constitu-
"The church was not impaired; the nation kept the same ranks, tion as
"the same privileges, the same franchises, the same rules for contrasted
"property. The church and state were the same after the French
"revolution that they were before, but better secured in every system:
"part."

t See Parliamentary Debates, Feb. 9, 1790.

CHAP.   Mr. Sheridan declared that he entirely disagreed from Mr.
XLIV.   Burke concerning the French revolution, and expressed his sur-
         prise that a senator whose general principles had been uniformly
1790.   so friendly to liberty, and to the British constitution, could de-
Mr. Sheri- clare or feel an indignant and unqualified detestation of all the
dan con- acts of the patriotic party in France. He conceived theirs to
curs in Mr.
Fox's   be as just a revolution as ours; proceeding upon as sound a
views of principle, and a greater provocation. Abhorring their excesses,
the French he imputed them to the depravity of the old goverment, the
revolution. sentiments and characters which despotism formed. He him-
         self regarded the French revolution as a glorious struggle for
         liberty, and wished its supporters the fullest success. Concern-
         ing the British revolution, he no less differed from Mr. Burke.
         That event was founded on the same principle with the French
         change; regard for the rights of man. It overturned tyranny,
         gave real efficient freedom to this country, which he would wish
         to see diffused throughout the world.ʷ Mr. Pitt testified his high
         approbation of the principles laid down concerning our excel-
         lent constitution : for these he declared this country to the latest
Mr. Pitt, posterity ought gratefully to revere the name of Mr. Burke.
praising With that caution which, advancing all that was necessary, ab-
the British stained from declarations not required by the occasion, Mr. Pitt
constitu- confined his applause to that part of Mr. Burke's speech which
tion, deli- referred to the constitution of Britain. That was a subject of
vers no
opinion on discussion that could never be foreign to a British parliament :
the French concerning the French revolution, as affecting, or likely to af-
system. fect France itself, he delivered no opinion.
         Colonel Phipps and sir George Howard, as military men,
         strongly objected to the panegyric pronounced by Mr. Fox, on
         the French guards, as a model of military conduct, and con-
         trasted their desertion of their master, and junction with riot-
         ers, with the behaviour of the British troops, during the disturb-
         ances of 1780. Our soldiers did not, in violation of their oaths,
         and of their allegiance, join anarchy and rebellion, but feeling
         as citizens and soldiers, patiently submitted to the insults of the

         w Mr. Sheridan's admiration of the French revolution appears to have
         arisen first from considering it as a triumph of liberty over despotism, in
         which estimate he had not paid an adequate attention to its peculiar nature
         and principles ; and secondly, from an idea that in principle it resembled
         our revolution, though dissimilarity had been very clearly and strongly
         stated by Mr. Burke, and that statement, though not admitted, had not
         been overturned by Mr. Sheridan, or any of his supporters.* His ardent
         wish for the diffusion of a liberty producing the greatest blessings
         to Britain, overlooked the diversities of national characters in different
         countries. From a partial consideration of the case instead of an accurate
         and complete view of every circumstance, and its whole character, appear-
         ed to arise the prepossessions of many men of genius and patriotism in fa-
         vour of the French revolution.

                  * See Parliamentary Debates, February, 1790.

populace; in spite of provocation, maintained the laws, and acted under the constituted authorities of the realm.

The dissenters, encouraged by the smallness of the majority which had rejected Mr. Beaufoy's motion of the former year, persevered in their application to parliament, and spared no efforts, either by general appeals to the public, or by canvassing particular members of the legislature; nor were grounds wanting to excite their sanguine hopes of success. The French revolution was favoured by a considerable number of Britons, who venerating the principles of liberty that were enjoyed by themselves, regarded with pleasure the supposed diffusion of freedom to their neighbours. This approbation of the Gallic system, in many was not without a tinge of their peculiar doctrines; and they began to think that the highest perfection of a free government, consisted in exemption from restraint. Hence great numbers totally unconnected with the dissenters, and before quite indifferent about their peculiar views and interests, became zealous advocates for the repeal of the test and corporation acts, as inimical to the rights of man, lately promulgated in the neighbouring nation. On these visionary theories the claims of the dissenters were maintained in periodical publications,[y] which were employed in promoting their cause, and in other occasional works produced for their service. The leaders of the non-conformists having declared their enmity to the national religion, found ready and willing auxiliaries among those who had no religion at all. The deists, encouraged by the aspect of affairs in France to hope for the speedy diffusion of infidelity, or as they phrased it, *light*, eagerly joined in a measure tending to weaken the great bulwark of national faith. From the time of the French revolution, we may date a coalition between the deists and the Socinian dissenters, which, in its political or religious effects, afterwards extended to many others. Republicans aware of the close connexion between the church and monarchy, most readily joined a class of men who were alleged to seek the downfall of our ecclesiastical establishment; a change, which they well knew, would tend to the overthrow of the monarchy. Besides this new accession of strength, the circumstance of an approaching election appeared also favourable to the attempt of the dissenters, on account of their great weight and influence in many counties and corporations, and their avowed determination to exert them on the ensuing occasion, in the support of such candidates only as were known, or should promise to be their supporters.[z] Farther to strengthen their cause, they proposed to consolidate with their own, the interests of the Roman catholic dissenters, and from

CHAP.
XLIV.

1790.

Dissenters again propose to seek the repeal of the test act.

Circumstances apparently favourable to it.

y See Analytical Review, passim.

z This mode of proceeding is much blamed by eminent, but moderate members of their own body, whose opinion I have heard very lately in personal conversation.

CHAP.
XLIV.

1790.
They are
strenuous
ly opposed
by mem-
bers of the
church.
Work en
titled *Re-
view of the
case of pro-
testant dis-
senters.*

the various constituents of their force, they had sanguine expectations of success.

On the other hand, the friends of the church, though not so
early in their preparations, were fully as vigorous when they
did commence. Less numerous, but more forcible, literary efforts were made in defence of our ecclesiastical establishments.
The case was argued from the probable tendency of dissent,
from actual experience of the general conduct of dissenters,
and from the present state of political affairs. On the first
head it was observed, that ill will to the establishment[a] must in
all governments belong to the character of the dissenter, if he
be an honest man, however it may be softened by his natural
good disposition, or restrained by political sagacity. A dissenter may occasionally support an establishment which he hates,
if he foresee that its ruin would raise another from which his
party would meet with less indulgence.[b] But a preference to
his own sect is in itself a virtuous principle; every dissenter
must be inclined to use any influence or authority with which
an imprudent government may intrust him, to advance his sect
in the popular esteem, and to increase its numbers. He will
employ all means that appear to himself fair and justifiable, to
undermine the church, if he hope that its fall may facilitate the
establishment of his own party, or some other more congenial
to his own. In all this, the crime is not in the man, but in the
government intrusting him with a power, which he cannot but
misuse. The man himself, all the while, supposes he is doing
good, and his country service; and the harm which he may effect under the notion of doing good, will be the greater in proportion to his abilities and virtues; on these undeniable principles the policy of a test is founded To confirm arguments
from probable tendency, appeals were made to facts; and the
history of dissenters was traced from the first germs of purita-
nism to the present time. Under certain restrictions, they had
been beneficial to the community, but without these restrictions
they had been hurtful. This position was illustrated by views
of their proceedings during the last century; from the attainment of partial advantage, to the overthrow of the church and
monarchy, the destruction of rank, confiscation of property,
cruel persecutions and massacres. The principles which had
produced such enormities were now cherished and supported,
and wanted only predominant power to give them effect. Dr.
Priestley, followed by a numerous tribe of votaries, had published his enmity to the church; while Dr. Price had no less
publicly proclaimed his enmity to monarchy. They and their
disciples had, from the downfall of the orders in France, be-

a See *Review of the case of protestant dissenters ;* a celebrated pamphlet
imputed to Dr Horsley.
b The dissenters often cited their fidelity to the house of Hanover, and
enmity to the Stuarts. This remark was probably intended to account for
their zeal.

come more eager in their expectations, more confident in their
boasts, and more incessant in their efforts. For these and
other reasons founded on the same principles, the most eminent
of the prelates, the body of the clergy and the friends of the
church, called to the people to assist them in defending the ecclesiastical establishment. The dissenters, to have an advocate Dissenters
of abilities proportioned to their conception of the importance intrust
of the question, intrusted the discussion of their cause to the their cause
brilliant and powerful talents of Mr. Fox; and on the 2d of transcend-
March, the orator brought the subject before the house of com- ent talents
mons. Acquainted with the arguments employed by Dr. Hors- of Mr. Fox.
ley, and other champions of the church, he directed his reasoning chiefly to impugn their allegations, and pursued nearly the
order of those whom he wished to confute. It was, he contended, unwarrantable to infer *a priori*, and contrary to the
professions and declarations, of the persons holding such opinions, that their doctrines would produce acts injurious to the
common weal. Men ought not to be judged by their opinions,
but by their actions. Speculative notions ought never to dis-
qualify a man for executing an office, the performance of whose
duties depends upon practical abilities, dispositions, and habits.
The object of the test laws at first had been to exclude anti- His view of
monarchical men from civil offices; but such conduct proceeded the sub-
upon false pretences, it tended to hypocrisy, and served as a ject.
restraint on the good and conscientious only. Instead of a
formal and direct oath of allegiance, they resorted, by means
of a religious test, to an indirect political standard. The danger of the church arose only from the supine negligence of the
clergy, and the superior activity and zeal of the dissenters, in
discharging the duties of their sacred functions. History exhibited the dissenters supporting the principles of the British constitution, while the high church promoted arbitrary power.
When this country had been distracted with internal troubles
and insurrections, the dissenters had with their lives and properties stood forward in its defence. Their exertions had powerfully contributed to defeat the rebellions in 1715 and 174 , to
maintain the constitution, and establish the Brunswick family
on the throne: in those times every high churchman was a
jacobite, and as inimical to the family of Hanover, as the dissenters were earnest in their support. An attempt had recently
been made, with too great success, to raise a high church
party: the discipline of the church, and the abstract duties
which she prescribed, he admired and revered, as she avoided
all that was superstitious, and retained all that was essential:
he therefore declared himself her warm friend. Individual
members of the body he esteemed for their talents, learning, and
conduct; but as a political party, the church never acted but
for mischief. Objections had been raised for the repeal, from and an-
the French revolution; but this great event was totally irrele- swer to ob-
vant, as an argument against the claims of the dissenters: it jections.

CHAP. had, indeed, a contrary tendency; the French church was now
XLIV· paying the penalty of former intolerance. Though far from
       approving of the summary and indiscriminate forfeiture of
1790. church property, in that country, he could not but see that its
       cause was ecclesiastical oppression. This should operate as a
       warning to the church of England; persecution may prevail
       for a time; but ultimately terminates in the punishment of its
       abettors. He was aware that the cause which he had underta-
       ken, was not at present popular; some of those whom he most
       highly valued differed with him upon this subject. So far was
       he individually from having any connexion with the dissenters,
       that in them he had experienced the most violent political ad-
       versaries; but regarding their cause as the cause of truth and
       liberty, he should give it his warmest support both on the present
       and every future occasion. He concluded with proposing a
       more specific motion for the revision of the test act, than any
       which was formerly made.

Mr. Pitt   Mr. Pitt, after arguing that eligibility to offices in any com-
continues munity, was a question not of right but expediency, considered
to treat ad· the test act upon that ground. Presuming the utility of the ec-
missibility
to offices clesiastical establishment to be generally granted, he inquired
as a mere whether the principles of the dissenters did not aspire at the
question of subversion of the church, and whether their conduct did not
expedien- manifest an intention of carrying these principles into practice.
cy,   Mr. Fox had proposed to judge men, not by their opinions,
       but by their actions. This was certainly the ground for proce-
       dure in judicial cases; but in deliberative, the policy of pre-
       vention was often not only wise but necessary; opinions produ-
       ced actions, therefore provident lawgivers and statesmen must
       often investigate opinions, in order to infer probable conduct.
       Leading dissenters, from their principles inimical to the church,
and deems had indicated intentions immediately hostile; and favorite ar-
the leaders guments in their works were the uselessness of an establish-
of the di -
senters in- ment, and the probability that by vigour and unanimity it might
imical to be overthrown. Against such avowed designs, it became all
our esta- those who desired the preservation of the church, firmly to
blishment. guard. Admissibility into offices of great trust would obviously
       increase the power of the dissenters; the assertions of their
       advocates, that their theological opinions had no influence on
       their political conduct, were most effectually confuted by their
       own declarations. At a general meeting they had subscribed
       resolutions recommending to voters to support, at the election,
       such members only as favoured the repeal. Thus while they
       themselves reprobated a religious test established by the con-
       stituted authorities of the kingdom, they wished to enforce a
       political test by their own sole authority. Perceiving their
       general principles practically operating in conduct hostile to the
       church, he should vote against a repeal, which in the present
       circumstances he deemed injurious to our establishment.

Mr. Burke, from various details and documents, endeavoured
to prove, that the dissenters anxiously desired, and confidently
expected, the abolition of tithes and the liturgy; and that they
were bent on the subversion of the church [c] The arguments
recently and now employed in the writings and speeches of the
friends of the church, the conduct of the dissenters, and the
downfall of the French hierarchy, placed in the most striking
light by Mr. Burke, added powerfully to the effect of Mr. Pitt's
reasoning, and made a deep impression on members of parliament.   In a meeting consisting of about four hundred,
there was a majority of near three to one against the projected
repeal.

The spirit of change extended itself to our political constitution; two days after the rejection of Mr. Fox's motion, Mr.
Flood proposed a reform in the representation of the people in
parliament. This proposition, like the reasoning for the eligibility of dissenters, was grounded upon abstract theories concerning the rights of men.   In a speech replete with metaphysical subtlety, he endeavoured to prove, that in the popular
branch of our government, the constituent body was inadequate
to the purpose of elections.   Electoral franchises ought to be
formed on principles both of property and number.   Electors
should be numerous, because numbers are necessary to the spirit
of liberty; possessed of property, because property is conducive to the spirit of order.   Pursuing these principles through
various theoretical niceties, and applying them to the actual
state of representation, he endeavoured to evince the necessity
of a reform, which should extend electoral franchise to every
householder.   In answer to this theory, Mr. Windham urged
from plain fact and experience, Mr. Flood had proved by an
arithmetical statement, what no one denied, that the representation was unequal, but he had not proved from political history
and reasoning, that it was inadequate.   Statesmen and lawgivers should argue from experience, and not from visionary theories; we had no *data* to ascertain the operation of such fanciful
projects.   Our representation as it stood, answered its purpose,
as appeared in the welfare of the people, and the prosperity
of the country.   According to the present system, it was evident that the influence of the people was very extensive and
powerful.   It was their voice that sanctioning, permitted the
most important acts of the executorial government; the commencement and continuance of war; the conclusion of peace,
aud the appointment of ministers were most frequently dictated
by the people.   Their weight was fully as great as expediency,
their own security, and happiness admitted.   Besides, were
parliamentary reform generally desirable, the present æra of

CHAP.
XLIV.

1790.

The argu-
ments
against the
applica-
tion.

Great ma-
jority
against
the repeal.

Mr. Flood
proposes a
reform in
parlia-
ment;

his subtle
theory

is contro-
verted by
Mr. Wind-
ham.

c To establish these positions, he quoted passages from the resolutions
at the public meetings; their catechisms; the writings of doctors Price
and Priestly, and other supporters of the cause.

CHAP.
XLIV.

~~~~~~

1790.
He with-
draws his
motion.

Petitions
from deal-
ers in to-
bacco,
praying to
repeal the
law sub-
jecting
them to
the excise
A motion
to that ef-
fect by Mr
Sheridan.

is nega-
tived.

Financial
statements

speculation, change, and ferment, was totally unfit for the purpose. Messrs. Burke, Pitt, and others, maintaining the same
ground, and a great majority appearing inimical to Mr. Flood's
plan, he withdrew his motion. These were the only great political questions which engaged the house of commons that season; and there they rested without extending to the peers.

Subjects of revenue occupied the chief attention of parliament, during the remainder of the session. Dealers in tobacco
presented a great number of petitions, praying for the repeal
of the act which subjected that commodity to the excise. Mr.
Sheridan took the lead in this subject, and, having in a splendid
speech directed his eloquence against the whole system of excise laws, by the fertility of his genius, in his illustrations, he
gave an appearance of novelty to so very trite a subject. He
came at last to the peculiar hardships of the tobacco bill, enforced the objections made the preceding year, and proposed a
resolution, that the survey of the excise is inapplicable to the
manufactory of tobacco. It was contended by ministers, that
the arguments against this application of excise, rested on the
testimony of dealers, who had derived a great profit from
fraudulent traffic, of which they were now deprived by the
new mode of collection. It could be no just argument against
a plan for the prevention of illicit trade, that it was not sanctioned by the approbation of contraband dealers. Was it
unfair or illiberal to doubt the veracity and honour of a smuggler, when he gives testimony concerning his forbidden articles.
The extent of former frauds was obvious in the productiveness
of the late preventive means. Since its subjection to the excise,
the revenue from tobacco had increased upwards of three hundred thousand pounds a year.[d] For these reasons, Mr. Sheridan's motion was negatived by a majority of a hundred and
ninety one to a hundred and forty-seven.

In the month of April, Mr. Pitt opened his scheme of finance
for the year; having in general stated the prosperous situation
of the country, to prove and illustrate his position, he recapitulated the extraordinary expenses, defrayed in 1789, in addition to the regular establishment. Notwithstanding these unforeseen
demands, though we had borrowed only one million, we had
paid six millions of debt. The increase of revenue, which had
thus liquidated so many and great charges, originated in two
permanent causes, the suppression of smuggling, and the in-

---

d From the statement of the tobacconists, it appeared, that the manufacturers were about four hundred in number; eight millions of pounds were
annually smuggled. The revenue of which amounted to four hundred
thousand pounds sterling; this sum purloining from the public they divided
among themselves so that each manufacturer on an average gained a thousand a year, by cheating the public.

crease of commerce.[e] Our navigation[f] had increased in proportion to our commerce. This prosperity arose from the
industry, and enterprise, and capital, which are formed and protected under the British constitution. A system productive of
so momentous benefits, it was our most sacred duty to defend
against all innovations. Mr. Sheridan endeavoured, as in the
preceding year, to controvert the minister's calculations, and
through the same means, by including in a general average, the
year 1786, that had been unproductive from causes peculiar to
itself. The supplies for the army, navy, and ordnance, were
nearly the same as in the former year: no new taxes were imposed ; but there was a lottery as usual.

Mr. Dundas about the same time, presented an account of
the financial state of India. The result of his statement was,
that the revenue considerably exceeded the product of the former year ;[g] and that the increase, though in some particulars,
owing to temporary circumstances, was chiefly the effect of
permanent causes. The system of justice and moderation
adopted from the time that the territorial possessions were sub-

e The exports for the year 1789, as valued by the custom-house en-
tries, amounted to no less a sum than 18,513,000*l.* of which the British
manufactured goods exported, amounted to 13,490,000*l.* Upon an average of the exports six years prior to the American war, which average
he took on account of those years being the period in which our commerce flourished most, it appeared, that the British manufactured goods
exported, amounted to no more than 10,343,000*l.* The imports for that
year, amounted to a higher sum than was ever before known, being valued
at 17,828,000*l.* This increase of import, which might at first appear disadvantageous, as it might seem to lessen the balance of trade in favour of
the country, Mr. Pitt having traced to its real source, showed to arise from
circumstances demonstrating the wealth and prosperity of the nation. It
issued in remitted property from the East and West Indies, from the increased products of Ireland showing the growing prosperity of the sister
kingdom, from the Greenland and South Wales fisheries, being wealth
poured in from the ocean.

f In the year 1773, there belonged to British ports, 9,224 vessels, and
63,000 seamen; and in the year 1785, 11,085 vessels, and 83,000 seamen,
showing an increase of seamen in 1788, above the number in 1773, of no
less than one-third.

g The revenues of Bengal amounted to   -   -   -   5,619,999*l.*
— of Madras   -   -   -   -   -   -   1,213,229
— of Bombay   -   -   -   -   -   -   138,228

Charges of Bengal	3,183,250*l.*		6,971,456*l.*
of Madras	1,302,037		
of Bombay	568,710		5,053,997*l.*
	5,053,997*l.*		1,917,459*l.*

To this amount of the net revenue was to be added 230,361*l.* for exports ;
and the sum of 65,000*l.* charges for Bencoolen and the prince of Wales'
Island; leaving on the whole, a net sum of 2,147,815*l.* applicable to the
discharge of debts, and the purchase of investments.

CHAP. jected to the control of the British government, had produced
XLIV. the most beneficial consequences both to the natives and to this
country. The landed revenues being much more willingly paid,
1790. were much more easily collected. The friendly intercourse between the Hindoos and the British, had suggested various improvements in the collection. Fostered by a humane and equitable administration, the internal commerce of our India settlements had greatly increased. Observing rigid faith with the
Indian natives, we had to encounter no formidable confederacies, which should at once diminish territorial improvement,
and cause enormous expenses. Prosperity, arising from a general scheme of policy at once wise and liberal, must increase
with accelerated rapidity. In a few years the company would
be enabled to pay off their arrears:[h] British India would be
more flourishing in wealth, in commerce, manufactures, and in
every enjoyment, than any other part of the whole continent of
Hindostan. In the present state of our power, we certainly
had no danger to apprehend from any European nation. Holland was in alliance with us, and the French were not in a situation to disturb British India. We had still one enemy in the
country, but without European auxiliaries, unsupported by
the other native powers, Tippoo Saib could not be formidable
to the British force. Mr. Francis endeavoured to controvert
Mr. Dundas's allegations respecting both the territorial and
commercial situation of affairs, and rested his objections chiefly
upon extracts from letters. These Mr. Dundas insisted, being
garbled, were partial and incomplete evidence; and resolutions
formed on Mr. Dundas's statement, were proposed and adopted.
The house voted several sums as a recompense for service, and
an indemnification for losses sustained in the cause of the public.
On a message from his majesty, parliament bestowed an annuity of a thousand pounds for twenty years, on Dr. Willis, who,
under providence, had been so instrumental in restoring to the
country so valuable a blessing.[i] The salary of the speaker
was augmented from three thousand to six thousand a year.
In a committee upon American claims, Mr. Pitt represented to
the house the losses sustained by the family of Penn; their case
was different from that of any of the other American loyalists,
and therefore could not be governed by the rules which the house
had established respecting the generality of cases. He proposed to grant to them and their heirs four thousand per annum
out of the consolidated fund. Mr. Wilberforce moved for the
consideration of the slave trade'; most of the time allotted to
that subject was occupied in hearing evidence, and no bill was
introduced during this session.

h The debts of the company for the last year were 7,604,754l. those of
the present year 6,501,385l. giving a decrease of 1,103,369l.

i See this vol. chap. xli.

‎The trial of Mr. Hastings made but little progress during the present session. The court sat but thirteen days, in which the managers of the house of commons went through the charge relative to the receipt of presents, which was opened by Mr. Anstruther, and summed up by Mr. Fox, in a speech which lasted two days. Mr. Burke detailed the circumstances which retarded the trial: the appointed mode of procedure had increased the difficulties and delays; the managers had proposed in the written evidence, to confine recital of letters and papers to such extracts as related to the charges; but the counsel for Mr. Hastings insisted on reading the whole of such documents, though many of them were extremely long; and the lords had agreed that no partial quotation from any paper could be received as evidence; that either the whole contents, or no part should be adduced; and the resolution evidently tending to promote impartial and complete inquiry, Mr. Burke complained of as an obstacle to the prosecution. It was however, he contended, the duty of the house of commons, and their managers, to persevere in the trial, without regarding any hindrances which might occur. He moved two resolutions to that effect and the motions were both carried. Mr Hastings continued to have a most zealous and ardent advocate in major Scott, who very frequently employed not only his tongue but his pen in the cause. Scott had indeed a great propensity to literary exhibitions; and sundry letters to editors of newspapers, and several pamphlets, manifested his zeal as a pleader, and his fruitfulness as an author. Among his other effusions was a letter subscribed with his own name, in a newspaper called the Diary; this essay contained many injurious assertions against the managers, and also blamed the house of commons for supporting the impeachment. On the 17th of May, general Burgoyne complained of the letter as a gross libel. Major Scott avowed himself the author; but declared that he meant no offence to the house. If he had been guilty of an error, he had been misled by great examples; Messrs. Burke and Sheridan had published *stronger*[k] libels than ever he had written. After offering this defence, Scott withdrew from the house; several motions of censure were made, and various modifications were offered. Mr. Burke was very urgent that an exemplary punishment should be inflicted; the conduct of Mr. Scott, he averred, had been extremely reprehensible: from the commencement of the prosecution he promoted libels against the managers, and their constituents.[l] After a long consideration it was agreed,

CHAP XLIV.

1790.
Libels against the commons on account of Hastings' trial.

k If either of these gentlemen published libels, few will controvert the major's opinion that they must be *stronger* than any which he wrote.

l Mr. Burke said, he was well assured, that not less than twenty thousand pounds had been expended in libels supporting Mr. Hastings; that major Scott was his agent in all these cases, and the common libeller of the house.

CHAP.
XLIV.

1790.
Dispute
with Spain
about
Nootka
Sound.

Insult of-
fered by
Spain.

that the letter should be voted a gross libel, and that the author should be censured in his place.

While the nation flourished in the enjoyment of peace, an alarm arose that so beneficial a tranquility would be speedily interrupted. On the 5th of May, Mr. Pitt delivered a message from his majesty to the commons, and the duke of Leeds to the peers; intimating an apprehension that the peace, during which Britain had so greatly prospered, might be broken. The following were the circumstances in which the message originated. During the last voyage of the celebrated Cook, the Resolution and Discovery having touched at Nootka (or Prince William's) Sound, the crews purchased a considerable number of valuable furs, which they afterwards disposed of to very great advantage in China; and captain King, who published the last volume of Cook's voyages, recommended the traffic with those northern coasts, as very lucrative. In consequence of this advice, some mercantile adventurers settled in the East Indies m and having consulted sir John Macpherson, the gover-nor-general, with his consent they undertook to supply the Chinese with furs from those regions, and also ginseng, an arti-cle that was likewise plentiful : for this purpose they fitted out two small vessels. The trade proved so advantageous, that in the year 1788 the adventurers determined to form a permanent settlement. With this view Mr. Mears, the gentleman princi-pally concerned, purchased ground from the natives, and built a house which he secured and fortified, as a repository for his merchandise. The following year the settlement was enlarg-ed; more land was bought from the country proprietors, and about seventy Chinese, with several artificers, constituted the establishment. In the month of May, two Spanish ships of war arrived in the sound; for some days they made no hostile attempt, but on the fourteenth, one of the captains seized an English vessel, conveyed the officers and men on board the Spa-nish ships, and afterwards sent them prisoners to a Spanish port. He also took possession of the lands and buildings be-longing to the new factory, removed the British flag, and de-clared that all the lands between Cape Horn, and the sixtieth degree of north latitude, on the western coast of America, were the undoubted property of the Spanish king. Another vessel was captured afterwards under the same pretence; the crews of both were thrown into prison, and the cargoes were sold for the captors, without the form either of condemnation or ju-dicature. The Spanish ambassador first informed the court of London that the ships had been seized; and at the same time expressed his master's desire, that means might be taken for preventing his Britannic majesty's subjects from frequenting

m The statement of the grounds of the dispute is compressed from the memorial of lieutenant Mears, presented to Mr. Secretary Grenville, which see in State Papers, 1790.

those coasts, which he alleged to have been previously occu- CHAP.
pied by the subjects of the catholic king. He also complain- XLIV.
ed of the fisheries carried on by the British subjects in the seas
adjoining to the Spanish continent, as being contrary to the 1790.
rights of the crown of Spain. His Britannic majesty immedi- Satisfac-
ately demanded adequate satisfaction to the individuals injured, tion de-
and to the British nation for the insult which had been offered. manded.
The viceroy of Mexico had restored one of the vessels,[n] but had Conduct of
not thereby satisfied the nation; on the contrary, the court of Spain.
Spain professed to give up the ships as a favour, not as a right,
and asserted a direct claim to exclusive sovereignty, navigation, and commerce, in the territories, coasts, and seas in that
part of the world. His majesty, far from admitting this allegation, made a fresh demand for satisfaction, and having also received intelligence that considerable armaments were equipping
in the ports of Spain, he judged it necessary to prepare on his
side for acting with vigour and effect in supporting the rights
and interests of Britain. The message from the king stated The king's
the injury and insult, the satisfaction demanded, the reply, the message to
second demand, the subsequent conduct of Spain, and the mea- parlia-
sures of Britain arising from that conduct: it farther recom- ment.
mended to his faithful commons, to enable him to make such
augmentations to his forces as might be eventually necessary.
His majesty earnestly wished that the wisdom and equity of
the catholic king might render that satisfaction which was unquestionably due, and that this affair might so terminate as to
prevent future misunderstanding, continue and confirm harmony and friendship between the two nations, which his majesty would ever endeavour to maintain and improve by all means
consistent with the dignity of the crown, and essential interests
of his subjects.[o]

The message being taken into consideration, Mr. Pitt declared, whatever the house must feel on the subject of his majesty's communication, he was too well assured of the public
spirit of every member, to conceive that any difference of
opinion could arise as to the measures which such circumstances would make it necessary to adopt. From the facts stated
in the message, it appeared that British subjects had been forcibly interrupted in a traffic which they had carried on for years
without molestation, in parts of America where they had an
incontrovertible right of trading, and in places to which no
country could claim an exclusive right of commerce and navigation. Ships had been seized, restitution and satisfaction demanded, but without effect: the court of Madrid had advanc-

n The ship and crew (they said) had been released by the viceroy of
Mexico, on the supposition, as he declared, that nothing but ignorance of
the rights of Spain could have induced the merchants in question to attempt any establishment on that coast.

o See State Papers, May 25, 1790.

CHAP. ed a claim to the exclusive rights of navigation in those seas,
XLIV. that was unfounded, exorbitant, and indefinite : in its conse-
〰〰〰 quences aiming destruction at our valuable fisheries in the
1790. southern ocean, and tending to the annihilation of a commerce,
which we were just beginning to carry on to the profit of
the country, in hitherto unfrequented parts of the globe;
it was therefore necessary and incumbent upon the nation to
adopt measures which might in future prevent any such disputes.   Much as we wished for peace, we must be prepared for
war, if Spain continued to refuse satisfaction for the aggression, and to assert claims totally inconsistent with the rights
of independent navigators, to lands which being before un-
appropriated, they should make their own by occupancy and
labour.   He therefore moved an address conformable to the
message.

On a subject which involved both the interest and honour
of the country, there was but one sentiment in both houses of
parliament.   No British senator could bear without indignant
resentment, such an imperious assumption by any foreign
power; and in the commons, the first to declare his cordial
support was Mr. Fox; he however blamed the minister for
having so very lately afforded such a flattering prospect of
the continuance of peace, when before that time he had
known from the Spanish ambassador, the principal grounds
of his majesty's message.   It was replied that this animadversion was founded on a misapprehension of fact : at the
period mentioned, government did not know the extent of
the Spanish claims, nor the preparations that were carried on
in the Spanish ports.   An unanimous address was presented
by parliament, assuring his majesty of their determination to
afford him the most zealous and effectual support for maintaining the dignity of his crown, and the essential interests
of his dominions.[p]   This address was soon followed by a vote
of credit of a million for the purpose of carrying into effect the
warlike preparations that might be necessary.   Motions were
afterwards made in both houses, for papers that might illustrate the grounds for the dispute, but they were resisted upon an
established rule, founded in wise policy, and sanctioned by uniform precedent, that no papers relating to a negotiation with a
foreign power should be produced while such negotiation is
pending.

On the 10th of June, his majesty closed the session with a
speech, in which he acquainted the two houses that he had
yet received no satisfactory answer from Madrid, and was
therefore under the necessity of continuing to proceed with
expedition and vigour in preparations for war, in the prosecution of which he had received the strongest assurances from his
allies, of their determination to fulfil the engagements of the

Parlia-
ment un-
animously
pledge
their sup-
port of the
king in vin-
dicating
the rights
of Britain.

p See State Papers, May 26, 1790.

existing treaties. His majesty announced his intention of immediately dissolving the present parliament; and in signifying
this determination, he thanked them for the proofs they had
given of affectionate and unshaken loyalty to his person, their
uniform and zealous regard for the true principles of our invaluable constitution, and their unremitting attention to the happiness and prosperity of the country. In a very concise, but
comprehensive and strong summary, his majesty exhibited
the effects of their exertions. " The rapid increase (he said)
" of our manufactures commerce, and navigation, the addition-
" al protection and security afforded to the distant possessions
" of the empire, the provisions for the good government of
" India, the improvement of the public revenue, and the esta-
" blishment of a permanent system for the gradual reduction
" of the national debt, have furnished the best proofs of your
" resolution in encountering the difficulties with which you
" had to contend, and of your steadiness and perseverance in
" those measures which were best adapted to promote the es-
" sential and lasting interests of my dominions." His majesty
farther emphatically added, " The loyalty and public spirit,
" the industry and enterprise of my subjects, have seconded
" your exertions. On their sense of the advantages which
" they at present experience, as well as on their uniform and
" affectionate attachment to my person and government, I
" rely for the continuance of that harmony and confidence, the
" happy effects of which have so manifestly appeared during
" the present parliament, and which must at all times afford
" the surest means of meeting the exigencies of war, or of cul-
"tivating with increasing benefit the blessings of peace." The Dissolu-
parliament was dissolved the following day by proclamation.   tion of par-

The preparations for maintaining our rights against the aggres- liament.
sion were carried on with vigour and expedition, proportioned Warlike
to the resources of so potent a nation. But it being the inten- preparation of the British government to avoid hostilities, unless abso- tions.
lutely necessary for the national honour and security, Mr. Fitzherbert was sent to Madrid with full powers to settle the disputes between the Spanish and British nations, in a decisive
manner. The grounds of the Spanish claims were set forth in Diploma-
a declaration to all the European courts, dated the 4th of June, tic discus-
1790,q and more specifically detailed in a memorial delivered sion be-
the 13th of June, to Mr. Fitzherbert, the British ambassador.r tween Bri-
According to these statements, Spain had a prescriptive right Spain.
to the exclusive navigation, commerce, and property of Spanish
America and the Spanish West Indies. The various treaties
with England had recognised that right: in the treaty of
Utrecht, which was still in force, Spain and England had agreed,
that the navigation and commerce of the West Indies, under
the dominion of Spain, should remain in the precise situation

q State Papers, 1790.   r State Papers, 1790.

CHAP.   in which they stood in the reign of his catholic majesty Charles
XLIV.   II. It was stipulated that Spain should never grant to any na-
         tion, permission to trade with her American dominions, nor cede
1790.   to any other power any part of these territories.* These rights
         extended to Nootka Sound; and though Spain had not planted
         colonies in every part of these dominions, still they were within
         the line of demarkation that had been always admitted. On
         the part of England it was answered,† that though the treaty
         of Utrecht, and subsequent conventions recognised the rights
         of Spain to her dominions in America, and in the West Indies,
         to be on the same footing as in the reign of Charles II. and we
         were still willing to adhere to that recognition, the admission
         by no means proved that Nootka Sound made part of those ter-
         ritories. By the plainest maxims of jurisprudence, whatever is
         common belongs to the first occupier; but the right co-exten-
         sive with occupancy is by occupancy determined : every nation,
         like every individual, has a right to appropriate whatever they
         can acquire without trespassing on the previous appropriations
         of others. The English had a right to possess as much of the
         desert coast of America as they could occupy or cultivate. The
         Spaniards not having established their claims by either occu-
         pancy or labour, proved no right to the exclusive property of
         Nootka Sound. The seizure, therefore, of the British vessels
         and British effects, was an injury and an insult for which Britain
         demanded restitution and satisfaction. The language of British
         justice demanding what British power could so easily enforce
         from any aggressor that dared to provoke its vengeance, was
         represented by Spain as haughty and menacing; and various
         difficulties occurred before matters were brought to a decision.
Spain at- The Spaniards professed a desire of conciliation, but were
tempts to really endeavouring to interest the French government in their
interest behalf; and the royal family of France was sufficiently disposed
France. to support the Bourbon compact; but the king had now lost the
         power of giving effect to this agreement. The national assem-
         bly decreed an armament of fourteen ships of the line, but
         avowedly to protect their own commerce and colonies, and to
         embrace no measures that were not purely defensive; and this
The   resolution highly gratified the people, who were not then dis-
French   posed to go to war with England. Though the preparation,
nation is of Spain were vigorous as far as her power and resources ad-
adverse to mitted, yet her fleets consisting of seventy ships of the line,
war with manned by such sailors as she could collect, was little able to
England. cope with the navy of England, amounting to one hundred and
Spain   fifty eight ships of the line, manned by British seamen. Find-
hopeless ing no prospect of effectual assistance from France, and con-
of aid,
yields.

         s The object of this stipulation was, to exclude France, which was be-
         come so closely connected with Spain, from any share in her American
         trade or possessions.

         t State Papers, 1790; Mr. Fitzherbert's answer to the Spanish memorial.

scious of her own inability to contend with England, Spain began to mingle proffers of concession with her former declarations of pacific intention. Mr Fitzherbert having persisted in
his demands, without relaxing the claims, the Spanish court on
the 24th of July, issued a declaration testifying their willingness
to comply fully with the demands of his Britannic majesty, by
rendering satisfaction and compensation. In order to mitigate
to the people of Spain the bitterness of a just concession, extorted by fear, the declaration[u] set forth that his catholic majesty was fully persuaded the king of Britain would act to him
in the same manner, under similar circumstances. Mr. Fitzherbert having accepted the declaration, all differences between
the courts of Madrid and London were terminated with proper
formality and precision, by a convention[x] between his Britannic
majesty and the king of Spain, signed at the Escurial, on the
28th of October, 1790. This settlement at Nootka Sound was
restored, a full liberty of trade to all the northwest coasts of
America, and navigation and fishery in the southern pacific
were confirmed to England. Both nations were equally restricted
from attempting any settlement nearer to Cape Horn than the
most southerly plantations already established by Spain. It was
agreed, that should any ground of complaint thereafter arise, no
violence should be committed, but the case should be reported to
the respective courts, who would bring it to an amicable termination.

The declaration of the 24th of July having been received in
England, and the result communicated by the duke of Leeds,
secretary of state, to the lord-mayor, and published in the Gazette extraordinary, afforded great pleasure to the nation; but
the convention completed the satisfaction of the people, who
'deemed it equally honourable and advantageous to Britain; as
the minister without involving the country in a war, had obtained every compensation which justice could demand; and had
shown to other powers, that BRITISH SUBJECTS WERE NOT TO BE
MOLESTED WITH IMPUNITY.

CHAP.
XLIV.

1790.
to the de-
mands of
Britain.
The dis-
putes are
adjusted in
a conven-
tion.

u State Papers, July 24, 1790.   x State Papers, October 28, 1790.

CHAP. XLV.

CHAP.
XLV.

1790
Continent-
al affairs.
Measures
of Britain
and her al-
lies for
counter-
acting the
ambition of
Joseph,and
Catharine.

WHILE Britain was thus successfully employed in securing the blessings of peace to herself, she was desirous of also
extending them to others. The grand scheme of confederacy
which was formed by Kaunitz for uniting the great continental
powers, had been discomfited· by the co-operating talents of
William Pitt the English minister, and Frederick the Prussian
king. The alliance having since been renewed between the
two empires, and endangering the balance of power, had stimulated the son of Pitt, and Frederick's counsellors, to form a
new plan of defensive confederation, to counteract the ambi-

tious designs of Russia and Austria.y Their project was so extended as to embrace all those states which were likely to be
affected by the imperial aggressors. Poland, Sweden, and
Turkey, were equally interested in forming a part of this confederacy. Mr. Ewart, British ambassador at Berlin, a man of
great abilities, and extensive political knowledge, having attained very considerable influence with the Prussian court, employed it in promoting the purposes of the defensive alliance.
This minister, viewing the situation and productiveness of Poland, saw that it might be rendered the source of immense political benefit to the confederacy, and might ultimately produce
important commercial advantages to Great Britain. Poland
might be rendered a formidable barrier to the designs of Russia;
and the acquisitions which Prussia might obtain by another
dismemberment of Poland, would not contribute so essentially
to her security as the independence of the Polish monarchy;
it was, therefore, the interest of Prussia to support and strengthen
that neighbour.z The Poles themselves were made sensible
that it would be mutually beneficial to Prussia and their country
to be closely connected. Having long nourished the most indignant resentment against the Russians, their rage was recently
inflamed by the insolence of the imperial confederates, who,
without asking their consent, had stationed large bodies of
troops in their territories, and even urged them to enter into an
alliance against Turkey, a power which had been always
friendly to Poland; induced by these considerations, they readily
acceded to the defensive union, and made vigorous preparations. Poland
This confederacy, when joined to the belligerent opposers of friendly to
the two empires, constituted a sextuple alliance, comprehend- the defen-
ing Great Britain, Prussia, Holland, Sweden, Poland, and Tur- sive alli-
key. Its first and principal object was to save the Ottomon ance.
empire from the grasp of the imperial confederates; and to
afford to the contracting parties reciprocal protection from the
boundless ambition of the combined aggressors. Not only to
liberate Poland from its subjection to Catharine, but to draw to
the English ports the numerous productions, naval and commercial, of that extensive and fertile country, formed a secondary, but essential object of British policy. As negotiation was
the first purpose of the powers which were not actually engaged,
they made overtures for a congress, which, though rejected by
Russia, they, from a recent change in the sovereignty of Austria, expected to meet with a more favorable reception from
that power.

Joseph II. emperor of Germany, whose life had been chiefly Death of
distinguished for extent and variety of project terminating in Joseph II.
disappointment, had long laboured under bodily distemper; if emperor of
Germany.

y Segur's History of Frederick William, vol. ii. p. 156.
z Otridge's Annual Register, 1791.— Segur; vol. ii. passim.
a Otridge's Annual Register, 1791, chap. 1.

CHAP. not caused in its origin, increased in its operation, and accele-
XLV. rated in its effects, by the distresses of a mind impatient of crosses
encountered from its own injustice, precipitancy and folly. The
1790. gleam of success from Turkey was soon forgotten in the gloomy
prospect which opened from the Netherlands. The unbounded
spirit of reform had produced subversion; the attempt to govern without control had, in the most valuable part of his dominions, left him no subjects to command. In Hungary also,
his innovations generated discontent, discontent demands of
redress; demands of redress were first haughtily refused, but
at length extorted concession. Indeed, his imperious severity
appeared softened, and his ambition weakened as he approached
that period when earthly power and glory could no longer avail.
In his last illness, he sought consolation in that religion which
for so great a part of his life he had disregarded, and learned
on his death bed, how absurd and pernicious the attempt was
to suppress in his subjects that principle which only could restrain turbulent passion, and heal a wounded breast. In the
langour of illness, and the awful hour of dissolution, he saw
that his policy had been as unwise as unjust; and that disgrace
and disaster awaits the prince who attempts to enslave a free
and gallant people. Being now weaned from the ambition
which had so much agitated his life, he acquired tranquillity,
and preserved it to the last. On the 20th of February he expired, in the forty-ninth year of his age, the twenty-fifth of his imperial reign as the successor of his father, and the ninth of his sovereignty over the Austrian dominions as the heir of his mother.

Joseph II. was by nature ardent in spirit, active in disposi-
and cha- tion, and fond of distinction. His situation cherished in such
racter. a mind the love of power which he had so much the means of
gratifying. With lively feeling, but without strength of understanding and originality of genius, in his objects and undertakings he was the creature of imitation. From the splendour of
Frederick's character, his illustrious exploits, and his immense
improvement in his dominions, as well as the vicinity of their
situation, and personal and political intercourse, he chose for a
model the Prussian king, without discrimination to understand
the peculiar features of his supposed archetype; acuteness to
discern the principles and rules of that monarch's conduct, or
compass of mind to comprehend the general system of his
measures and actions. He also was an admiring imitator of
Catharine, and supposed himself the confident of her counsels
when he was only the tool of her schemes. From both he
copied infidelity,b but did not copy from them that prudent policy which cherished religion in their subjects, adapted themselves
in appearance to the popular prepossessions, and made their
respective churches engines of state. He imitated their ambitious projects without possessing the wisdom of plan, or the

b See Abbe Barruel, vol. i.

consistent and well directed vigour of execution, which accomplished their designs. Springing from a variety of causes, and encouraged to a certain extent by these sovereigns, there prevailed in Europe a great disposition to reform. Frederick clearly apprehending what was right or wrong, innovated wherever change was improvement. Joseph was a reformist because innovation was the favourite pursuit of the times; and on the same principles, by which private votaries of some favourite fashion are often actuated, sought distinction by being a leader of the reigning mode, without considering how far it was wise, prudent, or suited to the circumstances in which he was placed. His pursuit of reform being neither accommodated to the habits nor to the sentiments of its objects, was the primary end of his conduct; and from the violence of his temper, and the total want of moderation, the principal source of his manifold disasters. In his wars, as well as in his internal politics, Joseph was a factitious and imitative character. Without military talents or inclinations, without well founded prospects of advantage, he appears to have sought hostilities from the desire of rivalling his warlike neighbours. Joseph's misfortunes arose entirely from his incapacity of directing himself, and from not being counselled by able and upright men. Without sound judgment himself, he wanted wise and faithful advisers[c] to oppose projects which were evidently hurtful to the projector. Qualities apparently contrary, indecision with precipitation, obstinacy with fickleness and inconstancy, openness, and benignity of manner and countenance, with duplicity and faithlessness, arose from the same source; an understanding which judged without examination; and a will directed by temporary impulse, without any fixed principles of conduct. The character of Joseph, from his condition, was very conspicuous in its operation, and very pernicious in its effects; but instead of being, as has been often represented, *singular*, is, in its springs and constituents, EXTREMELY COMMON. Whoever observes, in private life, vivacity of fancy without soundness of judgment; ardour of disposition and eagerness of pursuit, without just appreciation of end, or skilful selection of means; emulation in mere fashion; multiplicity of project formed without wisdom, and carried on without constancy, beholds, in a confined scene, the same character exhibited which the world contemplated on the great European theatre, performed by Joseph II. emperor of Germany.

Joseph was succeeded by his brother Leopold, grand duke of Tuscany, a prince of a very different character. Accustomed to the pleasurable regions of Italy, and the enervating refine-

---

c The ruling principle of Kaunitz being the elevation of the house of Austria, successful as he had been as the counsellor of the prudent Maria Theresa, yet he soothed and abetted the impetuous Joseph, in projects that eventually tended to its depression.

CHAP.
XLV.

1790.

ment of Italian manners, Leopold, presiding at Florence, was chiefly distinguished for luxurious softness; and having no incentives to war, or opportunities of ambition, was habitually pacific, and actually indolent. Both from nature and circumstances, and perhaps also from contemplating the effects of his brother's violence, he was remarkable for moderation. When, instead of being an Italian prince, he became head of the house of Austria, he demonstrated that his apparent indolence arose from the want of motives to action, and not from an inherent inertness of character; he showed himself firm and efficient, but retained his moderation and pacific disposition; and though he did not possess superior talents, was, by his mixed steadiness and prudence,[d] well qualified to remedy the evils which had proceeded from the capricious and violent Joseph. Averse himself from war as an *adventure of ambition*, he saw, in the circumstances of his affairs, and his relation to foreign powers, strong reasons for promoting his disposition to peace. He was involved in hostilities with his own subjects : at variance with the principal electors, he was in danger of being excluded from the imperial throne : the conquests on the desolated borders of Turkey, obtained at an immense expense, were of little value. The supplies for carrying on the war had lost, in the Netherlands, their most productive source. A hundred thousand disciplined Prussians hovered over the frontiers of Bohemia, while three other armies were prepared to act in different quarters. England would pour her wealth, and Prussia her troops, to support the revolted Netherlands. From war

He agrees to open a congress at Reichenbach.

Austria had little to gain and much to lose. For these reasons Leopold was disposed to pacification, and acceded to, a proposal for opening a congress at Reichenbach in Silesia. Meanwhile the campaign was opened on the frontiers of Turkey. Selim, to compensate the impolicy, and consequent losses of the former year, chose for his vizier Hassan Aly, a man of great

Military operations between the Austrians and Turks;

ability. The Turks, who imputed the adverse events of the last campaign, to the misconduct of the late vizier, were ready and eager to renew the contest, and a great army was prepared. The sultan spared no aid, which superstition could afford, to inspirit his troops. He clad them in black, to denote their readiness to meet death in defence of their cause; and, in concurrence with his chief priests, proclaimed a remission of their sins to all who should die in battle : these incentives, cooperating with the native valour of the Turks, early in the season he had four hundred thousand men ready to take the field. The campaign on the Danube was opened by the capture of Orsova, which having been blockaded during the whole winter by the Austrians, was suddenly reduced through the misapprehension of the garrison. The Turks, conceiving a

: d. See Otridge's Annual Registers for 1791 and 1792, passim; also Segur, vol. ii.

shock of an earthquake to be the explosion of a mine, were struck CHAP.
with a panic, and supposing themselves about to be blown up, XLV.
immediately surrendered. A detachment of the Austrians besieged Guirgewo, but the Ottomans, resuming their wonted 1790.
courage, marched to its relief. Encountering the Austrians,
they fought with the most desperate valour, threw those
brave and disciplined troops into confusion, and defeated them
with the loss of three thousand men. Among the killed was
count Thorn the general, whose head the Turks, agreeably to
the custom of those ferocious barbarians, displayed in triumph
through the army. This was the last act of hostilities carried on bloody but
between the Turks and the Austrians.   indecisive.

At Reichenbach the ambition of Raunitz, which, for forty Habitual
years, had been chiefly directed to aggrandize the house of preposses-
Austria, still entertained hopes of acquiring advantages from sions of
the Russian confederacy, and the prosecution of the Turkish Kaunitz
war, and was averse to the peace. Count Hertsberg, the Prus- berg.
sian minister, formed under Frederick, and considering every
maxim of that illustrious monarch's policy as the rule of conduct, without adverting to the change of circumstances, desired to attack Austria when weak and exhausted; dispossess
her of the rest of Silesia, abet the revolt in the Netherlands,
and prevent the elevation of Leopold to the imperial throne.
A more comprehensive and liberal policy, however, originating Liberal and
in the wise councils of Britain, and urged by Mr. Ewart, incul- wise policy
cated the necessity of sacrificing hereditary enmity to solid in- of Britain,
terest, and influenced the Prussian king. Leopold being no and ability
less disposed to conciliation, tranquillity was, without difficulty, of Ewart.
established; and on the 27th of July, a convention was concluded. The king of Hungary agreed to open a negotiation
for peace, on the basis of reciprocal restitution under the um-
pirage of the defensive alliance.[e] The empress of Russia was Peace be-
to be invited to accede to these conditions; but if she should tween Aus-
refuse, Leopold was to observe a perfect neutrality between tria and
the contending potentates. The king of Prussia would co-operate under the
with the maritime powers to allay the troubles in the low coun- guarantee
tries, and restore them to the Austrian dominions, on condition of the de-
that their ancient privileges and constitution were re-established. fensive alli-
The English and Dutch ministers engaged in behalf of the re- ance.
spective courts, to guarantee those stipulations; and an armistice
for nine months was, not long after, concluded between Leopold
and the Turks, which, notwithstanding various obstacles, arising
from the artifices of Catharine, terminated in a peace. The war
between Russia and Turkey was this year languid in its operations, as Catharine's attention was chiefly directed to the congress in Silesia, and also to schemes of policy in various quarters:

e Segur, who shows himself well acquainted with continental politics,
betrays gross ignorance of the views of Britain, when he deems this league
to spring from offensive ambition. See vol. ii. chap. i.

CHAP.
XLV.

1790.

Operations
between
Russia and
Turkey.

Siege of Is-
mail.

some desultory engagements took place, both by land and on the Black Sea, but without any important event. To facilitate her favourite objects of driving the Turks from Europe, and raising her grandson to the Byzantine throne, the empress persevered in a plan of detaching the Greek subjects of Turkey from their obedience. By her encouragement, and pecuniary assistance, a rebellion was fomented in Albania: the leader of the insurgents defeated a Turkish governor; and acquired such power and confidence as to form a regular and extensive plan for emancipating themselves from the Turkish yoke, and offering the sovereignty of Greece to the Russian prince. A memorial,[f] not unworthy of the descendants of ancient Greeks, stating both the object and plan, was presented to Catharine, and very graciously received; but before it could be matured, Russia had been induced, if not to relinquish, to postpone her plan of subjugating Turkey. It was the latter end of autumn before prince Potemkin was in motion: his tardy commencement of the campaign was not without policy and design. The Russian troops, inured to the colds of the north, were much less adapted to the summer heats even of their own southern frontiers. The Asiatic Turks, on the contrary, could easily bear the solstitial season in countries so much colder than their own as the banks of the Danube and the confines of Tartary: but even the autumnal cold of those countries they could not endure: and on the approach of winter it was their uniform practice to leave the army and return to warmer latitudes. Potemkin knowing the number and valour of those troops, deferred his military operations until they had taken their departure. His plan was, first to reduce Ismail, then Braicklow, which would complete the Russian conquest to the Danube; passing that river, to place himself between the Turkish army and Constantinople, and thus compel the vizier either to risk an engagement, or to accept of a peace on terms prescribed by Russia. Abandoned by the Asiatics, the Turkish army did not exceed forty thousand men. Dissensions and conspiracies prevailed in Constantinople, and the affairs of the Turks were in the most critical and dangerous state; but the divan, unbroken by these distressing circumstances, had resolved to maintain the Ottoman independence to the last extremity; and for the accomplishment of his purpose, Selim trusting not only to the resources which still remained, but to the vigorous mediation of the defensive alliance, cherished and supported the firmness of his council. The town of Ismail had always been deemed the key of the lower Danube: it was surrounded by two walls, covered by their respective ditches, of considerable depth and breadth, and capable of being filled with the waters of the Danube. A select and numerous garrison had been

f The reader will find a translation of this ingenious and eloquent performance in Otridge's Annual Register for 1791, page 273.

early appointed, with an artillery amounting to more than three hundred pieces, and lately re-enforced by thirty thousand men. The Russian forces on the Danube were formed into three divisions; one commanded by prince Potemkin, a second by prince Repnin, the third by general Suwaroff. To this last body, covered and supported by the two others, the siege of Ismail was intrusted. Suwaroff surrounded the place with batteries constructed on every spot of ground which would answer the purpose: and these were loaded with forges for heating the balls, with the heaviest battering artillery and mortars and every other engine of destruction hitherto invented. On the 22d of December the besiegers made a general assault in eight columns: the Turks received them with intrepid valour. Five times were the Russians repulsed: five times they renewed the attack; and at the last onset were discomfited with a slaughter which seemed to render all farther effort hopeless. The besiegers now began to think of nothing but to sell their lives as dearly as possible, when Suwaroff, having dismounted his cavalry to supply the slain infantry, snatched a standard, and running up a scaling ladder, planted it with his own hand on a Turkish battery. Re-animated to enthusiasm by the personal prowess of their general, the Russians not only withstood the attack of the pursuing enemy, but repulsed them, and again became the assailants. The Turks disputed every inch of ground; but the Russians being re-enforced by fresh troops from the covering armies, by numbers overpowered the valiant defenders of Ismail; carried post after post till they reduced the whole. With the fury of enraged barbarians, they effected a merciless, horrid, and undistinguishing slaughter, which spared neither age nor sex. The annals of Attila or of Gesneric, in the benighted ages of northern Europe, furnish no record of savage butchery which surpasses the carnage at Ismail, by troops employed, according to their mistress's professions, to expel barbarism from this quarter of the globe, and instead of the bloody superstition of Mahomed, to establish the mild and peaceful religion of the meek and benevolent Jesus: such was the Russian mode of making converts to the Greek church, and extending christianity. The inflexible endurance[g] of the vanquished was as great as the inflicting cruelty of the conquerors; as the Russians would give, the Turks would receive no quarter: they either rushed on the bayonet, plunged into the Danube, or sought death by some means equally efficacious. Twenty-four thousand of the Turkish soldiers perished in this bloody contest: the governor of Ismail was found covered with wounds; the whole number of massacred Turks, including inhabitants of all ages, sexes, and conditions, amounted nearly to thir-

CHAP. XLV.

1790.

Desperate, valiant defence.

Stormed.

Cruel and dreadful slaughter.

[g] The suffering fortitude of the Turks illustrates the very ingenious reasoning of Dr. Smith, in his Theory of Moral Sentiments, wherein he accounts for the unconquerable firmness of savages.

CHAP.
XLV

1790.
Campaign
between
Sweden
and Rus-
sia.

ty-one thousand.[h] The slain on the side of the Russians exceeded ten thousand men, among whom were many of their officers.
The king of Sweden, having entirely conciliated the affections of his people, and excited their admiration, by his conduct in the preceding year, was, through their unanimous efforts, enabled to open the campaign of 1790 early in the season. In the beginning of April, putting himself at the head of
three thousand forces in Finland, he penetrated into the Sava-
lax, a district of Russia not far from Wiborg. Alarmed by the
approach of the enemy within a hundred miles of Petersburgh,
Catharine sent ten thousand troops to obstruct his progress.
They found their enemy intrenched in a very strong position.
Trusting to their superior numbers, the Russians attacked the
Swedish lines; but the cool intrepid courage of the Swedes,
headed by the personal valour and genius of their sovereign,
repelled the attack: it was soon, however, renewed by the
impulse of national pride, rivalry, indignation, and shame of
being defeated by such a handful of men. The engagement,
for about two hours, was most desperate, obstinate, and bloody;
but rage, fury, and superior numbers, gave way at last, to calm
and determined valour. The Russians left about two thousand
dead upon the spot, and Gustavus, encouraged by this success,
advanced farther into Russia. Meanwhile, the fleet under the
duke of Suddermania sailed up the gulf of Finland. The
prince projected the destruction of the Russian squadron lying
in the port of Revel, the great naval arsenal, along with its
docks and magazines. The ships were, eleven of the line,
three of which carried a hundred guns each, and five frigates;
and they were protected by numerous batteries. The Swedish
fleet, notwithstanding all these obstacles, on the 13th of May
penetrated into the harbour, and in the midst of the hostile
fire maintained for four hours a doubtful conflict; but towards
the evening a violent storm arose, which obliged the Swedes to
retreat. They afterwards fell in with a Russian fleet from
Cronstadt, and an engagement ensued, in which the Swedes
at first appeared superior, when night intervening interrupted
the contest. The next day battle being renewed, while the
Swedish fleet was engaged with the enemy in front, the squadron from Revel appearing in the rear, the duke was in extreme
danger of being surrounded, but by judicious manœuvres and
bold exertions, assisted by a favourable wind, he extricated
himself from the danger, and joined his royal brother not far

h About three hundred Circassian women, consisting partly of those belonging to the governor's haram, and partly of others who had fled thither
for refuge from other harams, were preserved and protected by an English
gentleman, in the Russian service, colonel Cobley, who commanded the dismounted cavalry, when they were on the point of throwing themselves into
the Danube to escape violation from the Cossack and Russian soldiers. See
Otridge's Annual Register for 1791, page 101.

from Wiborg. Against this city the land and naval force of CHAP.
Sweden directed their efforts; but while they were making XLV.
dispositions for the purpose, the Russian fleet came in sight.
The Swedes were now hemmed in between the united squa- 1790.
drons of Russia and the garrison of Wiborg. His majesty and
his army were accompanied by a fleet of galleys, which were
likewise enclosed; the only alternative, therefore, was, to
force their way through the enemy or to surrender: the former was of course chosen: they effected their escape, but not
without incurring very great loss of ships and troops, that
were either taken or sunk: the whole number of men either
killed or captured, amounted to seven thousand. The genius
of Gustavus, stimulated by difficulty, soon refitted his shattered
fleet, and recruited his diminished army. On the 9th of July,
with his armament, he encountered a large Russian fleet,
commanding his own squadron in person, he immediately offered them battle, and conducted his operations with so masterly
skill, that, after a very obstinate conflict, he gained a decisive
victory. The loss of the Russians amounted to four thousand
five hundred prisoners, and nearly as many killed and wounded.
This defeat astonished and alarmed Catharine: in the great
talents of Gustavus, she was at last convinced, she had to encounter a formidable foe, which she had not apprehended in a
contest with Sweden. Such an antagonist was not to be subdued either by overwhelming numbers, or the adversity of fortune. Being now abandoned by the Austrians, and threatened
by the English and Prussians, she saw her projects respecting
Turkey had little chance of being accomplished, if she continued at war with Sweden: she therefore directed the chief
efforts of her policy to the attainment of a peace; she accordingly signified to Gustavus a pacific disposition. The Swedish
king, finding his country greatly exhausted by her extraordinary efforts, and not doubting that the defensive alliance would
repress the ambitious projects of Russia as far as general security required, was not averse to these overtures of amity.
Neither Catharine nor Gustavus communicated to their allies Peace be-
their pacific intentions, but concluded between themselves tween Rus-
an armistice, which in the middle of August terminated in sia and
a peace. Sweden.

Freed from a Turkish war, Leopold had leisure to turn his State of af-
chief attention to the affairs of the Netherlands. The Fle- fairs in the
mings had begun their opposition to Joseph from a desire of Nether-
preserving existing establishments. They limited their wishes lands.
and designs to the maintenance of that constitutional liberty,
which they inherited from their ancestors. Their principle of
conduct was totally different from that of the French. Dislike
of innovation, ecclesiastical, civil, and political, was the leading
feature of the Flemish character at the time they renounced
their allegiance to Joseph of Austria. But the vicinity of the
Netherlands to France produced a close intercourse between

CHAP. the two countries, and opened the way to the French doctrines,
. XL· which various causes now co-operated to disseminate. Since
 the revolt the states-general had exercised the supreme authori-
1790. ty : the composition of that body was, in a considerable degree, aristocratical, as the states of the nobility and clergy had
a greater share in the representation than the commons: this
inequality was very soon remarked by the members of the third
estate, and strongly reprobated by those who either had imbibed democratical notions; or from ambition, by raising the
Rise of a commons proposed to aggrandize themselves. So early as
democrati- January 1790, a number of individuals, professing such senti-
cal spirit. ments. formed themselves into an association, which they called a patriotic assembly. After passing various resolutions of
partial and subordinate reform, they framed a general and comprehensive system of revolution, which, subscribed by two
thousand persons, they published as an address to the states. in
the name of the people. They therein decreed the permanent
exercise of sovereign authority, an aristocratical despotism,
equally contrary to the rights of the people as the imperial tyranny of Joseph. The states-general they allowed with propriety, exercised the sovereign power on the *dismission* of the
emperor, and the declared independence of the Belgic provinces. But his authority, arising from a temporary cause,
could only endure until a legitimate constitution, formed and
ratified by the people, could be established. The ancient con-
Its votaries stitution of the Austrian Netherlands was no more. It fell by
propose to the stroke that cut off its head Joseph II. of Austria, represen-
subvert all tative of the dukes of Burgundy, in whom the functions of the
the consti-
uted au- other branches of the legislature centered: they were not ori-
thorities ginal and absolute, but relative and conditional. The states-
general were therefore responsible to the people for all which
they had done since the deposition of the emperor: a national
assembly only could insure tranquillity and security to the commonwealth. These principles and claims were very offensive
to the two higher orders, as they were totally inimical to the
power which they wished to retain without control. Knowing
the influence of the parish priests among the people, they attempted to employ these in persuading their respective parishioners to sign a counter address, requesting the states to seize
and punish all those disturbers who wished to introduce innovations in their religion and constitution. Those clergymen,
however, connected by the closest intimacy and friendship
with their flocks, were by no means zealous and active in recommending a measure so very unpopular. The states farther
endeavoured to prevent the sentiments which they wished to ·
inculcate from being counteracted through the press. They issued a decree, that this great engine of public opinion should
be limited to the same restrictions as under the sovereignty of
the emperor; that all literary works should be subject to the ·
scrutiny of censors, before they were republished; and that all

publishers should be responsible for the contents of the books
which they presented to the world. These attempts to restrain the actions, and even control the thoughts, of the people,
gave great dissatisfaction to those who wished for a larger portion of democracy in the constitution. The two higher orders,
joined by a common opposition to the democratical schemes,
formed one party, while the third, and all those who were inimical to privileged orders, formed another party. The nobility,
on their side, possessed great inheritances, and were reverenced
on account of their ancient families, and many of them highly
esteemed for their personal characters: but the clergy, in a country distinguished for extreme bigotry, possessed peculiar influence: these circumstances prevented democratic turbulence from
rising to the pitch which it would have otherwise attained. But
the discontented restlessness of innovation soon triumphed in the
minds of the populace over the submissive acquiescence of superstition. The higher orders attempted to awe the multitude
by force, but soon found that here, as in France, the army had
embraced the popular side. The commander of the Flemish
troops was general Vandermersch, who, after having long served
under the emperor, on the first dawnings of the revolution had
returned to his native country. This gentleman was distinguished for his military talents and recent successes: he embraced the popular side, and spread his sentiments through the
army. In March an attempt was made by the aristocratical
party to remove the commander from his office, and deputies
were sent by the states for this purpose. In this situation the
general adopted very bold measures: being nominated by the
army commander in chief of the Belgic forces, in defiance of
the states, he ordered the deputies to be committed to prison.
He issued a proclamation, declaring that he was placed at the
head of an army for the purpose of defending the civil and religious rights of the people, which he was determined to protect from all invasion. Officers of similar sentiments were
placed at the head of the war departments; and next to Vander-
mesch in the command of the army were the duke of Ursel
and the prince of Arenberg. The states ordered the troops
which were stationed at Brussels to march against the general.
A civil war appeared on the eve of commencement between
the aristocratic and democratic parties; but the army, by some
sudden impulse of passion, the causes of which have never been
ascertained, abandoned that general whom they had so highly
valued and recently exalted, and gave him up to the rage of his
enemies. The congress of the states at this time was chiefly
directed by Vandernoot and Van Eupen; the former a lay nobleman, the latter an ecclesiastic. Under their direction,
charges were drawn up against the general; and also against
the duke of Ursel, hereditary chief of the nobles in Brabant,
a man of large fortune and popular character. Vandermersch
was doomed to a dungeon at Antwerp: Ursel was arrested and

confined for five weeks, without any form of justice : but being tried and acquitted, he was still retained in confinement until a strong body of volunteers forcibly rescued him from this tyranny. These unjust and violent proceedings of the aristocratic party excited the severest reprobation of their adversaries. Priests and feudal tyrants (they said) had seized the sceptre and sword, and used them as instruments of injustice and cruelty against the most patriotic and exalted characters.

A government which had, in a few months from its formation, manifested such discord, was not likely to be permanent. The army having lost its honour as well as its general, became disheartened, and was now not unfrequently defeated. Great supplies were wanted for maintaining and paying the troops ; but the congress had so disgusted the principal cities, that their applications for a loan were totally unsuccessful. Attempts were made in Holland and in England, but to no purpose ; and it was evident that the Belgic states were every day, from their internal dissensions, becoming weaker in power, and less important in the estimation of foreign countries.

Leopold, aware of these circumstances, sent a memorial to the people of the Netherlands, which professed sincere regret for the despotic proceedings of the Austrian government; and declared the disposition of the prince to redress all their real grievances, but vindicated his undoubted right to the sovereignty of the Netherlands, and announced his resolution to maintain his claim. This address, together with the situation of affairs, revived the loyalists, or friends of the house of Austria ; who, before overawed by the prevailing power, had made no efforts to resist. As the folly and violence of the present government became more evident and more hateful, this party increased : many moderate men, who had at first favoured the revolution, compared the present miserable situation with the tranquillity and contentment enjoyed under Maria Theresa. A coalition of priests and nobles (they observed) was formed, obviously for the purposes of self interest and ambition. If the states-general should continue to govern, the Belgic nation must groan under a two-fold aristocracy. If a republic were attempted on democratical principles, the first probable consequence would be anarchy; which, after producing all its horrible evils, would terminate in a single despotism. An hereditary monarchy, properly limited and modified, appeared most suitable to the character and habits of the Flemings. These considerations induced many considerate men to favour a reconciliation with Leopold. The populace, without examining matters so deeply, but actuated by the impulse of resentment and indignation, against the usurpers of sovereignty, very readily joined the loyalists. That party now displayed a force which, even without the assistance of Austrian troops, was formidable and rapidly increasing. The king of Prussia, intimating that he

Leopold
prepares to
avail himself of
their dissensions.

He offers
to redress
their real
grievances, but
vindicates
his right to
the sovereignty.

had acknowledged Leopold as duke of Brabant, the aristocra- CHAP.
tical party saw their hopes of foreign assistance totally vanish- XLV.
ed, whilst their internal power was fast declining: Leopold,
now emperor of Germany, immediately after his coronation, is- 1790.
sued a manifesto, engaging himself, under an inaugural oath, Britain and
and the guarantee of Britain, Prussia, and the United Provinces, her allies
to govern the Belgic Netherlands according to the constitution, mediate
charters, and privileges, which were in force during the reign the Flem-
of Maria Theresa. He offered a general amnesty to all who, ings and
before the 1st of November, should return to their duty. The Leopold.
mediating powers notified to the Belgic states their approval of Under
these terms; but that body still refused to acquiesce, and pub- their gua-
lished a counter manifesto, denying Leopold's right to the so- Nether-
vereignty of that country, derived from his ancestors; and as- landers are
serted, that though many of them had enjoyed the sovereignty restored to
of the Netherlands, they owed it entirely to the free choice of their an-
the people, who had a right to choose for their governors cient privi-
whomsoever they pleased. This doctrine, inimical to hereditary leges.
right, and favourable to popular election of sovereigns, combined with their enmity to monarchical power, to bring back the
democratical party to some concert with the other revolutionists.
The congress used various endeavours to animate the people to
a general combination, but without effect. Willing to catch at
every twig to save their sinking power, they proposed to confer
the sovereignty on the archduke Charles of Austria, and his
heirs of that family, but with the perpetual exclusion of its
head: these terms were rejected. Various engagements uniformly unsuccessful, intimated that resistance was hopeless.
The allied powers represented to them the futility of their efforts, and in its uselessness the cruelty of their warfare. The
Austrian troops pressed on all sides, the Flemish people without
exception acknowledged the authority of the Austrian prince,
heir and representative of their ancient rulers. The members
of the congress, and other leading partisans of the revolt apprehending severe resentment from the emperor, especially after the refusal of his recent offers, sought safety in flight. The
Austrians used their success with wise moderation; the general,
by observing the strictest discipline among his victorious troops,
protected the persons and property of all men. In a conven- They ob-
tion guaranteed by the defensive alliance, and executed at the tain fur-
Hague, the 10th of December 1790, the Belgic provinces were ther con-
not only restored to the rights and privileges which they enjoy- cessions
ed at the death of Maria Theresa, but obtained several advan- pold.
tages tending to render them more secure in the enjoyment of from Leo-
their ancient constitution. Thus the catholic Netherlands They find
having with reason and justice, to preserve their constitutional their secu-
rights, resisted Joseph's tyranny, after they had experienced rity in their
within two years despotical oppression, aristocratic usurpation, mixed go-
and democratic violence, at last found refuge and tranquillity vernment.

CHAP.
XLV.

1790
Proceed-
ings of the
French re-
volution-
ists in
fo. ming
the new
constitu-
tion.

Qualifica-
tions of ac-
tive citi-
zens,

precludes
universal
suffrage.

Division
into de-
partments.

in the mixed government that had descended to them from their
ancestors.

We left the national assembly on the establishment of some
degree of tranquillity, proceeding in the formation of the new
constitution. Operose as this object must have appeared to
persons who intended to frame a system of legislation on principles justified by experience, a knowledge of human nature,
and an accurate acquaintance with the character of the people
for whom the constitution was intended, these revolutionists
found the attainment of their purpose neither tedious nor difficult. Their system was free from complexity; equality was to
be the basis of the polity to be formed; the means were simple
and expeditious, perseverance in the course which they had so
effectually begun, by reducing every inequality. In the application of this simple maxim they struck a very effectual
blow, by a decree, announcing that there was no longer any distinction of orders in France, and thus crushed the nobility and
clergy. Having equalized rank, the next business was to model
elections agreeably to this new system. The choice of representatives was ultimately vested in primary assemblies, composed of men to be distinguished by the appellation of active citizens. The activity was to consist in contributing to the public
exigencies, an annual sum not less than half a crown. By requiring this qualification in electors, they contravened their own
principles of equality, and precluded universal suffrage; they
excluded from legislation, beggars and many other citizens, not
only effectually active in their respective vocations, but active
by their tumults in the streets and galleries, in controling the national assembly itself. It farther debarred from the legislation,
the deliberative wisdom of fish-women and prostitutes, whose executorial efforts had so powerfully promoted the revolutionary
schemes. The primary assemblies, constituted with these exceptions to equality, were to choose electoral assemblies: the
electoral assemblies delegates to the legislative, judges, and executive administrators. That no vestige of antiquity might remain, they proceeded in the abolition of provincial distinctions;
and dividing the whole kingdom into eighty-three departments,
consolidated the diversities into one mass: as a geographical arrangement, this change was executed with great skill and ability, the departments chiefly took their names from mountains,
rivers, and seas, which shape and bound countries; and as a
political alteration, it certainly tended to render the government
more uniform. A plan was established of municipal jurisdictions, to constitute a fourth arsembly, to be chosen by the same
electoral assembly which, constituted by the primary, appointed
the members of the legislature. Financial legislation next occupying their attention, they began this branch of politics as
they had begun others, by establishing a simple and comprehensive principle, which would apply to every possible case.
They enunciated a theorem totally new in jurisprudence, that

all property belongs to the nation. Having declared their sovereign power over property, the next question was, how private
and corporate wealth was to be forth coming. They saw it
would be prudent to augment the pay of the army which was
so very serviceable to the revolutionists, and which would be- New and
come more and more attached to systems of confiscation, by compre-
sharing in the proceeds. There were many and numerous de- hensive
mands upon the public, and it was farther expedient to have a principle
governmental bank, which would be able to accommodate the legisla-
nation by advances, but a capital was wanting. Whatever tion.
their lawgivers were in wisdom and virtue, they certainly manifested the national ingenuity in fertile invention and prompt expedient. They soon discovered a very efficient fund for the
exigency, in the landed estates of the clergy ; some politicians
opposed the seizure of clerical property, not as unjust, because
they knew its justice had been already established in the new
code of ethics ; but as impolitic. The appropriation would en-
rage the clergy, who still retained great influence among the
less enlightened people ; and would also displease and alarm
foreign powers, who might not only reprobate a confiscation,
but dread the principle : these admonitions, however, were of
little avail. A decree was passed declaring the ecclesiastical Confisca-
estates to be at the disposal of the nation. The clergy expos- tion of cle-
tulated on the robbery, and excited great discontents among rical pro-
their votaries, which were farther increased by the nobility in- perty
dignant at their own degradation. To counteract the growing
disaffection, the assembly spread reports of plots and conspiracies, and thus by alarming their fears, diverted the attention of
the people from the iniquities of government. Rumours were
spread that the princes were now in exile at Turin, and the
aristocrats both in and out of the kingdom were confederating
with foreign princes to effect a counter revolution. Aware that
the king was considered by their adversaries as a prisoner, and
that his acts could in that supposition be no longer binding, than
the compulsion lasted, they endeavored to procure from him
an approbation of their proceedings which should appear voluntary ; they attempted to prevail on his mild and compliant disposition, to come to the assembly and explicitly declare himself
the head of the revolution, and satisfied with all their proceedings ; but this application his majesty resolutely refused.—
Finding the king inflexible, the republicans disseminated reports
of new plots and conspiracies, for rescuing Louis from his present situation. To deter aristocrats and loyalists from such an
attempt, it was very frequently declared in common conversation, and in the clubs, that an endeavour to extricate the king
would certainly produce his death. The queen was very openly and loudly threatened as the instigator of his majesty's refusal ;
the benignant Louis from tenderness for his wife and children,
was induced to make a concession, which no apprehension for
his personal safety could have extorted ; and he repaired to the

CHAP.
XLV.

1790.
Civic oath.

national assembly, and spoke to the purport desired by the republicans. The democratic party seeing the anti-republicans
overwhelmed with dismay by the acquiescence of the king, resolved to take advantage of the consternation, and issued a decree obliging every member to take a newly devised civic oath
under the penalty of exclusion from voting in the assembly.
They now published a general address to the nation, stating
their acts and measures for the sake of public liberty, and their
farther intentions in order to complete the great work of regenerating France. Various tumults having arisen, and murders and other outrages having been committed both at Paris
and Versailles, the ringleaders were seized and punished by the
assembly, which with considerable vigour chastised such riots
and disorders, as did not promote its own purposes. Having
again re-established nearly as much quietness as they wanted,
and attained their object from the king, they resumed the affairs
of the clergy. In February they suppressed all monastic es-

Scheme for
converting
the spoils
of the cler-
gy into
ready mo-
ney.

tablishments, and forever confiscated the lands. By another
decree in April, they forfeited all the territorial possessions of
the church, for the payment of the public debts, but generously
allowed the plundered proprietors a small annual pittance from
the booty. As the spoils were not immediately convertible into
ready money, they employed them as *pledges*. They issued
out a species of notes under the name of *assignats*, being as-
signments to the public creditor of confiscated property; and
payable to bearer, that they might serve the purpose of a bank
paper currency. About this time they began to affect an imitation of the Roman republic, and adopting its phraseology
with one of its customs, decreed that mural crowns should be
publicly presented to the conquerors of the Bastile.

Boundless
power of
the mob.

The legislature were not without experiencing inconveniences
from the diffusion of their own doctrines. They had found it
necessary to idolize the mob; to talk of the majesty of the
people; their supreme authority; their uncontrolable sway to
which all things must bend. These ideas with the experience
of their own force, operating on the ardent fancies and com-
bustible passions of the French populace, meetings, clubs, parties, and individuals considered themselves as collectively and
separately, rulers of the empire. They indeed regarded the
national assembly as a necessary, legislative, and executive organ, but subject to their own general and supreme control. As
force was the great spring of government, the soldiers with reason claimed an important share in the direction of affairs; and
by the laws of equality deemed themselves exempted from
every degree of subordination and obedience, excepting, so far

The multi-
tude civil
and milita-
ry desti-
tute of reli-
gion.

as suited their wishes or convenience. Both the populace and
soldiers conceived, that by their political regeneration, they
were entitled without restraint to gratify every passion. The
most active of the revolutionary leaders had spared no pains
to banish from the people, that salutary moderator of passion,

the christian religion.[i] In extent of despotic power, the French
mob equalled the Turkish sultan ; the army the janissaries ; and
the national assembly the divan, despotic under the despot and
his soldiers, but totally dependent upon these for its own sway.
But the horrible tyranny of Turkish rule was mitigated by the
Alcoran, whereas the despotic license of France was devoid of
any such corrective. A great portion of the vulgar both civil
and military were rank infidels. Thus destitute of moral restraint, all the energy of a most ingenious people, all the
French force and versatility of intellect and temperament, were
the instruments of moral depravity. A great object of the republicans in the assembly had uniformly been to identify in the
opinion of the civil and military vulgar, their interests and views
with their own; and like other demagogues, while they professed to admit the rabble as their associates, really to employ
them as their tools, and they in a great measure accomplished
their purpose. There was under the direction of the national
assembly, an army much more numerous than ever had been
commanded by the French monarchs.

Many of the nobility, as we have seen, had been the zealous
votaries of reform, while they conceived it tending to limited
freedom and limited monarchy. But they had always been deficient in point of concert, by suffering separate and subordinate
views to occupy their attention, they had facilitated the progress of republicanism. They had already felt the fatal effects
of disunion, among the opponents of jacobinism militant, they
were destined to feel them more severely from jacobinism triumphant. There was in the proceedings of the French democrats, a strange mixture of ridiculous levity with the most serious iniquity. Paris at this time overflowed with adventurers
from all countries. Among these was a Prussian of the name
of Clootz,[k] who having left his own country for reasons recorded
in the journals of the police, had resorted to Paris, and assuming the name of the ancient Scythian sage, Anarcharsis, set up as
a philosopher, and by his lectures instructed the Parisians. But
not having hitherto attained notoriety equal to his ambition, he
bethought himself of the following expedient to become conspicuous : collecting a great number of his companions and
other vagabonds who swarmed about the streets, and hiring all
the foreign and grotesque dresses from the opera, and play-
houses, he bedecked his retinue ; and proceeding to the national
assembly, he introduced his followers, as strangers arrived from
all countries of the globe, being the virtual ambassadors of all
those enslaved nations who wished to be free, and were there-

CHAP.
XLV.

1790.

Mixture of
ridiculous
levity and
serious
iniquity.

Anarchar-
sis Clootz,
ambassa-
dor from
the whole
human
race.

i Mirabeau laid it down as an axiom in the science of politics, that if they
would have an effectual reform, they must begin by expelling christianity
from the kingdom. This maxim was loudly praised, and generally followed by the republican partisans.

k Otridge's Annual Register, p. 148.

CHAP.
XLV·

1790.

Abolition of titles and hereditary nobility.

Summary of changes within the year.

Anniversary celebration of the 14th of July in the field of Mars.

Federal oath.

Violent proceedings against those who refused it.

Britain.

fore disposed to enter into fraternity with France, for the glorious purpose of establishing universal liberty. This deputation was most graciously received by the assembly, of which it being evening sitting, many of the members were in a condition[1] suited to a frolic. The legislature after some decrees and resolutions suitable to this contemptible farce, followed their deliberative levity by a very serious act. A decree was proposed for the abolition of titles, and hereditary nobility, with all the heraldic monuments, which would recall to descendants the distinctions and merits of their ancestors. In vain the nobles opposed so hasty and violent a proposition, it was immediately passed into a decree. Thus in one year, the national assembly crushed rank and distinction, confiscated property, annihilated hierarchy and aristocracy, left monarchy only an empty name, and perfected their levelling efforts; they now proposed that the 14th of July, the anniversary of the captured Bastile, and of the birth of liberty, should be solemnized by a general confederation of Frenchmen, pledging themselves to maintain the new constitution, and to bind the king, the assembly, and the people civil and military in one general fraternity. This spectacle was exhibited in the field of Mars, appointed to be called ever after, the field of confederation. The king, the assembly, the people, and the army, were reciprocally sworn. The same oath was taken the same day through the whole kingdom.

Mr. Neckar friendly as he had been to the popular side, disapproved very highly of the late democratical proceedings, and especially the confiscations. Being now received with great neglect and displeasure, and being apprehensive of his personal safety, he quitted the kingdom, and retired to Switzerland. In prosecuting their system of reform, the assembly thought it expedient to render the clergy still more dependent on their will. They accordingly passed a decree, imposing on clergymen a new oath, by which they were bound to submit to the constitution as decreed by the assembly, in all cases whatever. This oath was a direct breach of the oath taken at ordination; and great numbers of the clergy refused to swear contrary to their engagements and principles. All the recusants were immediately ejected from their benefices; and their livings filled by others. Thus a republican assembly endeavoured to force men's consciences to be guided by its decrees, and not satisfied with exercising tyranny over persons and property, attempted by the same despotism to enchain their minds.

This year the French revolution began to be better understood in Britain, and to produce more definite and specific opinions, either of approbation or censure, or of a mixture of both. Many Britons still continued upon British principles to admire

1 Drunkenness, a vice formerly so little known in France, was since the revolution become extremely prevalent even among the lawgivers. Annual Register.

the French revolution, and though they regretted the excesses
which had accompanied its operations, yet expected that the
violence would subside, and that a system of rational and beneficial liberty would be established. They saw that the plan
of polity would considerably deviate from the British constitution. The greater number of literary men continued to favour
the changes, and imputed the enormities to the vitiating system of government under which the French had so long lived,
joined with the enthusiasm of new liberty. But the most ex- The
perienced and discriminating of philosophical politicians per- French received that the Gallic revolution in its nature, principles, and volution is
effects, was different from any former case, and avoided un- derstood.
qualified opinions concerning either its merits, or probable duration. They considered it as a composition of extraordinary
phenomena, not yet sufficiently investigated to become the foundation of a just theory; but they saw that the rapidity of
French change far exceeded the progressive variations of circumstances, and the human character.[m] Writers of genius and Majority
erudition attached to certain visionary principles and doctrines, of literary
prized the French revolution more for its particular acts and men favour
innovations, than for the general assertion of liberty; and cele- the new
brated most highly those measures which overthrew hierarchy, though
reduced monarchy, and degraded aristocracy. Dissenters of they cen-
very high literary reputation, and unimpeached private cha- sure its
racter, were so transported by their peculiar doctrines and sen- excesses.
timents, as to praise the lawless violence of the Parisian mob,
and the abduction of the royal family in triumph, because these
acts tended to overthrow the existing orders : and even recommended the example of the French to the imitation of the
English. The able and eminent Dr. Price, and his many votaries in civil and religious dissent, manifested in 1790, an unqualified admiration of the French changes, and proposed a
close connexion between the revolutionists of France, and the
people of England. Certain members of parliament, at the
head of whom was Mr. Fox, continued to admire the principles of the French revolution, as tending eventually to produce
a moderate and rational liberty, that would in time fit the circumstances and character of the people, and promote the tranquillity of Europe. The great ministerial leaders, cherishing Mr. Pitt
the principles of constitutional liberty, could not reprobate in and his
another country an attempt to procure that blessing, the enjoy- friends for-
ment of which made this nation prosperous and happy; and bear dis-
when they discerned the peculiar nature and tendency of the its merits.
new system, conceiving that it became statesmen less to specu-
late than to provide, instead of delivering judgment on the
measures of the French, vigilantly watched the conduct of
Britons. The sentiments of the minister and his principal supporters concerning the affairs of France, were not hitherto de

[m] See Dr. William Thomson's letter to Dr. Parr.

CHAP.   clared.   The first open censurers of the French revolution, were
XLV.   courtiers, who being the votaries of pageantry and show, under
        a kingly government, regarded the pomp and ceremony of the
1790.   palace more than the vigour and efficacy of the monarchy ;
        who regretted Louis's loss of royal trappings and appenda ჻es,
        more than the seizure of his power; who considering the king's
        friends and attendants as no longer enjoying the balls and pro-
        cessions of Versailles, saw grievances which being thoroughly
        conceived by their fancies, could attract their sympathetic feel-
        ings.   But a ferocious confiscating democracy, overturning reli-
        gion and property, did not equally affect their sensibility, be-
        cause they by no means so clearly understood the nature, or
        comprehended the extent of the evil.   One class, indeed, emi-
        nent for ability and learning, venerable for profession and ag-
        gregate character, in the early stages of the French revolution,
The cler- observed its leading principles with horror, and its conduct with
gy are   dread.   The clergy augured ill from a system guided by pro-
alarmed by fessed infidels, and sympathizing with plundered brethren, be-
the infide- held not without apprehension, the contagion of confiscation so
lity and very near themselves.   In this country, they knew there were
confisca- men as willing to plunder the church as the most rapacious re-
tion of the volutionists of Paris.   But though they disapproved of the
revolution- French system, they did not deem it expedient to declare an
ary sys.   alarm.   Such an avowal, they thought, might imply an impu-
tem.   tation of disloyalty, and enmity to the church, which could not
          be justly charged to the majority of Britons.   English clergy-
          men, therefore, did not decry the revolution, which many other
          literary men praised.   In autumn 1790, the declared sentiments
Burke's   of Britons, with several modifications, were on the whole fa-
work on   vourable to the French revolution.   One man, however, was
the sub- destined to effect a speedy and important change.   Edmund
ject,   Burke having formed and delivered in parliament the opinions
          already recorded, with increasing anxiety continued to bestow
          the closest attention on revolutionary proceedings.   He had
          many correspondents at Paris, of different nations, abilities, and
          sentiments.   Through them he completed his acquaintance with
          the French system.   While attending to its progress, and its
          operation within the country which it immediately affected, he
          carried his views to the impressions that it had made in his own
          country.   Penetrating into the various grounds of the praise
          which it had procured in England, his sagacity perfectly dis-
          tinguished between those who rejoiced at what they conceived
          the emancipation of France, and those who in the destruction
          of the orders, and forfeiture of property, found a model which
          they wished to be copied in England.   In considering the ad-
          mirers and supporters of the French revolution, he from the au-
          thority of Dr. Price among his votaries, apprehended that the
          late promulgation of that gentleman's political opinions in a ser-
          mon, might be very hurtful, unless precautions were used to
          expose the tendency of his doctrines.   To convince mankind,

especially Britons, that the French revolution did not tend to **CHAP.** meliorate but to deprave the human character, to promote hap- **XLV.** piness, but to produce misery, to be imitated and copied, but to be reprobated and abhorred, Mr. Burke composed and published **1790.** his work. To establish his position, he analyzed the intellectual principles by which the revolutionists reasoned: the religious, moral, and political principles by which the revolutionists acted; and contended that the effects, which had proceeded, and were proceeding, were natural and necessary consequences of the principles and doctrines. He predicted the completion of an- archy and misery from the progressive enormity of the French system. Profound wisdom, solid and beneficial philosophy, en- forced by all the powers of Mr. Burke's eloquence, produced a very great change in public opinion. From this time many men of talents, learning, and political consideration, openly declared sentiments unfavourable to the French revolution. The nobility, with few exceptions, were apprehensive of the danger which awaited their order if French principles became prevalent in Great Britain. The clergy publicly testified the opinion which they before held. Ministers, cautious as they were in avowing and ef- any sentiments concerning the French revolution, did not con- fects. ceal the high estimation in which they held Mr. Burke's produc- tion. The public opinion, which at first had been so extremely favourable to the French revolution, was at the end of 1790 greatly divided.

The most important transactions belonging to the internal his- tory of Britain in the recess of 1790, was the general election. The contests were not, however, carried on with the violence of former times. The country was in a state of progressive, and rapidly augmenting prosperity; the minister possessed the pub- lic confidence, and no great political question agitated the public mind. The election, which was most warmly disputed, did not General owe the contest to the contention of parties. Of the elective election. bodies in Great Britain, none is of importance equal to West- minister; the seat of government, the royal family, and for half the year the principal nobility and gentry: hence there had usually been a very warm competition in this city. The dispute in 1788 between lord Hood and lord John Townsend, had been carried on with extreme eagerness on both sides; and with an expense calculated to have exceeded even the costly election of 1784. It was tacitly understood between the two parties, that at the general election there should be no contest, but that lord Hood and Mr. Fox should be jointly chosen. This apparent de- termination was represented to many electors of Westminster, as a coalition between the candidates to insure themselves the choice, and thus deceive the inhabitants. Mr. Horne Tooke a gentleman of great and deserved literary eminence, and also of very conspicuous political conduct, which was variously inter- preted, proposed himself as the representative; he disavowed all connexion with any party, and assuming an independent tone,

CHAP.   procured a respectable number of supporters ; he every day ex-
XLV.   hibited from the hustings a series of acute and poignant observa-
        tion; clear, direct, and vigorous reasoning, not unworthy of be-
1790.   ing opposed to the vehement and forcible oratory of his illustrious
        competitor ; his efforts however were unsuccessful.   Though
        there were several disputed elections, yet there was none that
        attracted so much attention as the poll for Westminster, in which
        Horne Tooke was pitched against Charles James Fox.

CHAP. XLVI.

Meeting of the new parliament.—Convention of Spain is approved by parliament—Expenses of the late armament.—Unclaimed dividends.—Measures of Britain for repressing the ambition of Russia—submitted to parliament—Mr. Fox opposes hostilities with Russia—argument of Mr. Pitt on the importance of Oczakow—principle of British interference in continental politics—hostilities with Russia unpopular through the nation—war with Russia avoided.—New constitution of Canada—political principles introduced into the discussion.—Mr. Fox incidentally mentions the French revolution—Mr. Burke enveighs against that event, and the new constitution—Mr. Fox explains the extent and bounds of his approbation—declares the British constitution the best for this country—quotes Mr. Burke's speeches and writings favorable to liberty—rupture between these friends, and their final separation.—Question whether impeachments by the commons before the lords, abate with the dissolution of parliament—precedents and arguments for and against—determination of the house that impeachments do not abate by a dissolution.—Liberty of the press—motion of Mr. Fox for ascertaining and declaring the law of libels, and bill for that purpose—arguments for and against—postponed for the present but is afterwards passed into a law.—State and conduct of the English catholics—they renounce the most dangerous moral and political doctrines of popery—motion of their relief—modified and corrected by Dr Horsley, it is passed into a law.—Petition of the church of Scotland respecting the 'test act—is rejected.—Full discussion of the slave trade—motion of Mr. Wilberforce for the abolition—arguments for and against—continuance of the trade defended on the grounds of humanity, justice, and expediency—Messrs. Pitt and Fox agree in supporting the abolition—the motion is negatived.—Settlement at Sierra Leone—Finance.—Supplies.—Indian finance.—Trial of Hastings, evidence for the prosecution closed—impressive speech of the defendant—Session rises.

THE British parliament opened the 26th of November; and his majesty stated that the dispute between this country and Spain had been brought to an amicable termination. The first subject of parliamentary consideration was the convention[n] with the catholic king. In a question concerning an injury, the great objects to be regarded were reparation for the past, and prevention of future aggression. In the present case, according to opposition, the restitution promised was incomplete, and the promises were not performed. Before the commencement of the dispute, we had possessed and exercised the free navigation of the Pacific Ocean, as well as the right of fishing in the South Seas, without restriction. But the admission of Spain to a part only of these rights was all that had been obtained by the convention. Formerly we had claimed the privileges of

CHAP.
XLVI.

1790.
Meeting of the new parliament.

Convention with Spain is approved by parliament.

n See page 295 of this volume.

CHAP. settling in any part of south or northwest America, from which
XLVI. we were not precluded by previous occupancy. Now, we
consented to limit our right of settlement to certain places
1790.   only, and even in these under various restrictions. What we
had retained was vague and undefined, and consequently liable
to be again disputed. We had reserved what was insignificant to ourselves, and resigned what was very beneficial to
Spain. To these arguments ministers answered, if we had not
acquired new rights, we had obtained new advantages. Before the convention, Spain had denied our right to the
southern whale fishery, and to navigate the Pacific Ocean;
but now she had ratified those claims. In the convention,
the wisdom and energy of ministers had vindicated the honour
of the British flag, preserved the rights of private citizens, and
established the glory of the British name over all the world,
without shedding a drop of blood. On these grounds the majority in both houses approved of the terms of the adjustment.

Expenses The liquidation of the expenses incurred by the late armament,
of the late the minister proposed to separate from the general financial
armament. arrangements for the season; and to pay off in four years the
incumbrances now incurred, by a distinct plan of finance. The
first resource was the balance of the public money, which had
accumulated in the hands of the bank of England from *unclaimed dividends*.o The bank was agent for the public; received an adequate allowance for its services, and was there-
Unclaimed fore not entitled to retain a balance greater than the probable
dividends. demand. Since public creditors forbore punctually demand-
iug their interest, not the bank, who were agents for the payment of that interest, but the nation, their employers, should
profit by that forbearance. The balance had been gradually
increasing from the year 1727, and now amounted to 660,000*l*.
Of this sum the minister moved that 500,000*l*. should be applied
to the public service, and that the creditors should have securities in the consolidate fund for payment, whenever the demand should be made. In addition to this sum, he proposed
temporary duties upon sugar, British spirits, brandy, rum, malt,
assessed taxes, and bills of exchange. Mr. Fox, and some
other members, objected to the minister's proposition as unjust
to public creditors, and also unfair to the bank. But it appearing to the majority of both houses that the creditors possessed
the same security of prompt payment as before, and that no
injury could accrue to an agent from his employer withholding
money which was not necessary to the transactions which he
was appointed to manage: notwithstanding various petitions
from the bank, deprecating the application, a bill agreeable to
the minister's project was passed into a law.

o Many of the public creditors had omitted to demand their dividends
when due; the money, therefore, issued for their payment, was used by the
bank until the proprietors should demand the payment.

The contest with Spain being thus concluded, another very CHAP.
important subject of foreign politics occupied the attention of XLVI.
parliament. At the Congress of Reichenbach, the defensive alliance had proposed to Russia to accede to the peace which 1791.
Austria was concluding, and that all conquests should be re- Measures
stored; but Catharine constantly replied, that she would admit of Britain
of no interference between her and the Turks. Deprived, for repres-
however, of the assistance of Austria in the strength and ambition
determination of the allies she saw the impracticability of of Russia,
subjugating Turkey for the present, and now offered to restore
all her acquisitions by the war, except the town and dependencies of Oczakow. This possession, she conceived, would on
the one hand secure her dominions against the irruptions of
the Tartars, and on the other command an entrance into Turkey, whenever circumstances should prove more favorable to
the execution of her ambitious designs. The allied powers
perfectly comprehended the objects of Catharine, and deemed
them incompatible with that tranquility which it was the purpose of the confederacy to insure. There was, besides, an
unfriendly disposition long manifested by Russia towards
Great Britain. During our difficulties, she had headed a confederation for the express purpose of reducing the naval power
of this country. When the commercial treaty between England and Russia was expired, Catharine not only declined
renewal, but obliged our merchants to pay in duties twenty-
five per cent. more than she exacted from other countries,
though they gave half a year's credit for their exports, and
were always a whole year in advance for their imports. At
the same time she concluded commercial treaties with France[p]
and Spain, on terms that were advantageous to both these
countries. Such indications of enmity to this country, joined
to her ambitious projects, strongly impelled the British government to prevent the encroachments of the empress's court.
Britain and her allies still adhered to their purpose, of inducing
or compelling Catharine to restore the conquest. Finding pacific negociations unavailing, the defensive alliance projected
more effectual interference. Having concerted forcible media- submitted
tion for the security of Europe, his majesty, on the 24th of to parlia-
March, sent a message to both houses, stating his unsuccessful ment.
efforts for the establishment of peace, and that from the progress of the war, consequences so important might arise, as to
render it necessary for this country to be prepared to meet
them by an augmentation of our naval force. The message Mr Fox
coming under consideration of parliament, Mr. Fox opposed opposes
hostile interference on the following grounds: all wars were to hostilities
Britain unwise, as well as unjust, that did not originate in with Rus-
self defence. Too much latitude was given to the construction sia.
of defensive alliances, and treaties comprehended under that

[p] See State Papers, and Segur's history of Frederick William.

CHAP. XLVI. 1791.

denomination had at present a very offensive tendency. By including in the objects of defensive resistance not only actual, and even probable, but possible injury, the professed defenders of Europe proposed to carry on war wherever they thought it expedient to any of the confederates. We had received no injury from Russia that could justify hostilities: her demands upon Turkey could not so materially affect Great Britain as to render a bloody and expensive war prudent to prevent their attainment; expediency as well as justice, forbade war with a power which neither directly attacked Britain, nor pursued any other object by which she could be endangered: the present plan of ministers tended merely to second the ambitious policy of Prussia, in whose intrigues and projects we were lately become too much involved: Was the protection of a barren district in the barbarous recesses of Tartary, a reason for exposing Great Britain to the evils of war? Was our trade with Russia, which employed eight hundred and fifty ships, trained in that hardening service thousands of seamen, afforded materials for our manufactures to the amount of two millions sterling, received our manufactured goods of more than a million, and yielded two hundred thousand pounds to our revenue, to be all foregone for the sake of a Turkish fortress? Even were Russia to succeed in conquering Turkey, instead of becoming more formidable to her neighbours, she would become weaker, and spread over a more extensive surface. Could wisdom and policy justify Britain in going to war, for preserving an empire inhabited by a barbarous and savage race, habitually connected with our rival; a race that for the sake of religion, humanity, civilization, and commerce, ought to be exterminated from the continent of Europe.[q]

Arguments of Mr. Pitt the importance of Oczakow.

Ministers argued that the aggrandizement of Russia, and the depression of Turkey, would injure both our commercial and political interests. While Russia was confined to the Baltic, her naval exertions would be inconsiderable; but if her fleet were suffered to range through the Mediterranean, she would become a great maritime power, and a formidable rival. The possession of Oczakow would facilitate not only the acquisition of Constantinople, but of Alexandria and all lower Egypt. The object of Britain in opposing Russia was conformable to her general policy in continental interference. Britain had herself no ambitious end to pursue; we had nothing to gain; we wished only to remain as we were; our alliances could only have the tendency of maintaining the balance of power. It was known to Europe, that our principles were pacific.[r] Standing on the high eminence which we occupied, we exerted our power only for the maintenance of peace. It was a glorious distinction for England, that, placed on a pin-

Principle of British interference in continental politics.

q See parliamentary reports, 1791.

r See speeches of Mr. Pitt and Mr. Grenville. Parliamentary reports.

naele of prosperity, having in her resources and power such CHAP.
motives to ambition, she exerted her strength not as the dis- XLVI.
turber, but the protector of her neighbours :[s] this had ever been
her character and principle. In endeavouring to repress 1791.
Russia, she pursued the same line of conduct which she had
always chosen

The supreme director of a free country, and especially of
Great Britain, is PUBLIC OPINION. The forcible eloquence of Hostilities
Mr. Fox, coinciding with the immediate interests of merchants with Rus-
and manufacturers, impressed those bodies of men very power- pular
fully. Their sentiments were rapidly and widely diffused through
through the nation, and rendered the people in general inimi- the nation.
cal to a Russian war. Ministers, feeling the due and constitu- War with
tional reverence for the voice of the people, sacrificed their Russia
own counsels and measures to dictates so deservedly authorita- avoided.
tive. Although Britain was thus prevented from compelling
Russia to restore the key of Turkey, yet it was the energy of
the defensive alliance which induced Catharine to relinquish all
the other acquisitions of the war.

The circumstances of one of our provinces called on parlia- New con-
ment to frame a new constitutional code, that required discus- stitution of
sions at all times important, but peculiarly momentous when Canada.
they were combined with the questions which from the French
revolution agitated the public mind. After the acquisition of
Canada, a proclamation, as we have seen,[t] had been issued by
his majesty, promising that measures should be adopted for extending to that country the benefit of the British constitution.
Encouraged by this assurance, many British subjects had settled in the new province ; and in consequence of the American
revolution, great numbers of royalists had emigrated into a
country so near to their own, and which contained inhabitants
of congenial principles and sentiments ; these readily coalesced
with the British settlers, and joined them in frequent applications to remind government of the royal promise. The native
Canadians readily admitted the excellence of the British constitution ; but deprecated its unqualified extension to themselves, as tending to interfere with privileges which they had
inherited from their ancestors. The Canadian noblesse, especially, enjoyed many feudal rights and immunities, which they
feared the introduction of a new form of government might infringe or abolish. The minister, considering the diversity of
character, sentiment, customs, and privileges, between the
French Canadians on the one hand, the British and Anglo-
American colonists on the other, proposed a separate legislature
to each, that might be best suited to their respective interests,
and social situation. With this view he purposed to divide
Canada into two distinct provinces, upper and lower ; and introduced a bill for this arrangement, and for the establishment

s Speech of Mr. Grenville.   t. See. vol. ii.

of distinct legislatures. The division was to separate the parts which were chiefly inhabited by French Canadians, from recent settlers. For each of the provinces, a legislative council was to be hereditary, or for life, at the option of the king; and a provincial assembly was to be chosen by freeholders possessing lands worth forty shillings of yearly rent, or renters of houses paying ten pounds in six months. The provincial parliament was to be septennial, to assemble at least once in a year: the governor, representing the sovereign, might refuse his sanction to any proposed law, until the final determination of Britain were known. The British government renounced the right of taxation, and though it asserted the right of regulating external commerce, yet left the imposts to the provincial legislatures. All laws and ordinances of the whole province of Canada at present in force, were to remain valid until they should be altered by the new legislature. The bill passed through both

houses without any material alterations. But in the house of commons its discussion gave rise to a debate concerning the French revolution between Messrs. Burke and Fox, who respectively delivered their principles, sentiments, and doctrines on this momentous subject, more clearly, specifically, and categorically, than in the disquisition of the former year. In considering the constitution which the legislature was preparing for Canada, Mr. Fox proposed to confer as much freedom as was possibly consistent with the ends of political establishments, instead of mere suitableness to any existing form. The scheme for the government of Canada adhered, he conceived, too closely to the British constitution, which though the most perfectly adapted to the character, habit, and circumstances of Britons, was not the best that possibly could be framed for any case. The United States in North America would have afforded a better model, more fitted both to the character and social situation of the Canadians, than the model which had been followed. Hereditary distinctions, possessions, and powers, ought not to be abolished where they had been long establish ed; and were interwoven with the manners and sentiments o the people, as well as the laws;[u] but it was unwise to create them in countries not fit for their establishment. There was not in Canada either property or respectability sufficient to support an hereditary nobility. Mr. Pitt, in defending his own plan, confined himself to its adaptation to the proposed ends, and without entering into abstract speculations upon government, contended that a polity formed for any part of the Bri-

[u] These were nearly the words of Mr Fox, at least this was certainly the substance, as appears after a careful comparison of the several reports of parliamentary debates. Yet he was misrepresented as having declared himself, without qualification, the enemy of hereditary rank and distinction. Far was he from asserting that an order of nobility was useless in any circumstances; he merely declared his opinion, that in its present state it did not suit Canada.

tish dominions, should be as nearly as possible modelled ac- CHAP.
cording to the British constitution; that such being his object, XLVI.
he conceived it effected by the present system for the government of Canada. In the reciprocation of debate, Mr. Fox 1791.
still reprobated the council of nobles; said he could not account Mr. Fox
for the zeal in its favour, unless by the supposition that an op- incidental-
portunity was eagerly embraced of reviving in Canada, former- ly men-
ly a French colony, those titles and honours, the extinction of French re-
which some gentlemen so much deplored, and of awakening in volution.
the west that *spirit of chivalry* which had so completely fallen
into disgrace in a neighbouring country. Mr. Burke, by these Mr Burke
expressions, conceived that his opinions, and indeed his writings inveighs
on the French revolution were attacked; he also heard doc- against
trines advanced which he deemed repugnant to the British that event,
constitution; to controvert such opinions, he drew a contrast new consti-
between that admirable system, and the new order of things tution.
in France. The Canada bill (he said) called forth principles
analogous to those which had produced the French revolution.
There was a faction in this country inimical to our constitution
of church and state. It became parliament to watch the conduct of individuals or societies, which were evidently disposed
to encourage innovations. Mr Burke conceiving that Mr. Burke Mr. Fox
intended to implicate him in the censure passed on the admirers explains
of the French revolution, replied to his animadversions. Mr. the extent
Burke's object appeared to be (Mr. Fox said) to stigmatize and bounds
those who thought differently from himself on the French re- of his ap-
volution, and who had expressed their opinions in parliament; probation;
and to represent them as the supporters of republican tenets.
To vindicate himself from this charge, he distinctly and explicitly declared his own sentiments. The praise that he had
bestowed, was given to the French revolution, which had abolished the old arbitrary government; and not to the system
which was substituted in its stead. As a subverter of a tyranny that had enthralled twenty-five millions of people, he still
would maintain that it was one of the most glorious events in
the whole history of mankind. The new polity remained to
be improved by experience, and accommodated to circumstances. The excellence of forms of government was relative,
and depended on the situation, sentiments, and habits of the
people :[x] the British constitution he thought the best and fit- declares
test for this country, and would to the utmost of his power op- the British
pose republicanism among Britons; but it was contrary to sound constitu-
logic to infer, that because British liberty was most effectually best for
secured by a government of three estates, therefore such an ar- this coun-
rangement must be the fittest for France. He considered the try;
late great change as the precursor of freedom and happiness to
twenty-five millions, and therefore rejoiced at its success.

[x] These observations are conformable to Aristotle, as the English reader
will see in his Politics, translated by Dr. Gillies, book iv.

CHAP.
XLVI.

1791.
Quotes Mr.
Burke's
speeches
and wri
tings fa-
vourable to
liberty.
Rupture
between
these
friends and
their final
ship and party support, and separated from those he esteemed
separation.

From Mr. Burke himself he derived those principles, and imbibed those sentiments which Mr Burke now censured: he quoted various passages from the speeches and writings of that eloquent and philosophical senator, and referred to measures which he had either proposed or promoted, and comparing them with the sentiments now or recently delivered, endeavoured to fix on him a charge of inconsistency. Mr. Burke complained of this allegation, and declared it to be unfounded: his opinions on government, he said, had been the same during all his political life. His conduct would evince the truth of his assertions: his friendship with Mr. Fox was now at an end; deep must be his impression of truths which caused such a sacrifice to the safety of his country; he gave up private friendship and party support, and separated from those he esteemed most highly. His country, he trusted, would measure the sincerity of his avowals, and the importance of his warnings, by the price which they had cost himself. He was far from imputing to Mr. Fox a wish for the practical adoption in this country of the revolutionary doctrines; but thinking and feeling as Mr. Fox and he now did, their intercourse must terminate. With great emotion, Mr. Fox deprecated the renunciation of Mr. Burke's friendship; and tears for several minutes interrupted his utterance.[y] When the first ebullitions of sensibility had subsided, he expressed the highest esteem, affection, and gratitude for Mr. Burke, whom, notwithstanding his harshness, he must still continue to love. Proceeding for some time in a strain of plaintive tenderness, he gradually recovered his usual firmness, and afterwards contracted no small degree of severity, when having vindicated the resistance of France, on whig principles, he renewed his charge of inconsistency against Mr. Burke for deviating from those principles. This repetition of the charge of inconsistency, prevented the impression which the affectionate and respectful language and behaviour, and the conciliatory apologies might have probably made: the breach was irreparable; and from this time Mr. Fox and Mr. Burke never resumed their former friendship. In this discussion the impartial examiner cannot find a single sentence, or even phrase, of Mr. Fox, which was not highly favourable to the British constitution; so that the political difference between these illustrious men, arose entirely from their opposite apprehensions concerning the French revolution, which hitherto was to a British senator a question of speculative reasoning, and not of practical contention; but Burke had already conceived such an abhorrence of the Gallic system, that he could not bear any expression of approbation respecting a change which he deemed destructive to the best interests of society.

y This account is chiefly compressed from parliamentary debates, and partly taken from a gentleman who was present.

With colonial policy, parliament this year considered also
important questions of domestic law. One of these arose from
the trial of Mr Hastings: it was doubted whether an impeachment brought by the commons of England abated by the dissolution of parliament. Several members of high note in the
profession of the law, and among the rest sir John Scott, the
solicitor-general, were of opinion that the renewal of the impeachment was neither justified by law, precedent, nor equity.
It was a question, they said, concerning which there was no
statute; we must therefore be governed by the law of parliament, that is by the orders of the lords, and by usage. The
lords in 1678, had affirmed, that dissolution did not preclude
the renewal of an impeachment; but that order was not sanctioned by former practice. They had suffered the impeachment of lords Danby and Stafford to proceed from the stage in
which they had been left by the old parliament; but at that
time the nation was in a ferment about the popish plot; detested Stafford as a catholic, and execrated Danby as the supposed
promoter of arbitrary power and a connexion between the
king and Louis XIV. Both peers and commons were seized
with the same enthusiasm against popery and France, and under its influence continued the impeachment, contrary to law
and usage. From these cases, therefore, which were peculiarly
circumstanced, no precedent could be drawn. In 1685 lord
Danby was by the house of lords freed from the impeachment,
which in fact reversed the precedent of 1678. Lords Salisbury
and Peterborough being accused of high treason, pleaded a
dissolution, and in 1690 were liberated. On the same grounds
the lords Somers and Halifax, sir Adam Blair, and others were
released. To support their position, they also adduced several
analogies, and concluded with arguments from equity: by
continuation of an impeachment the accusers might be changed, and even not a few of the judges. If a trial is to last beyond one parliament, may it not be prolonged to an indefinite
term, or even during life; a court of justice should be free
from bias and prejudice; but how could this be the case with
a tribunal in which there were so many new judges; and some
of them even accusers from the lower house. The supporters
of continued impeachment reasoned in the following manner.
If the alledged precedents existed, they would be extremely prejudicial, because they would enable the sovereign to save a
favourite servant, and to defeat the purposes of national justice; and it would become the legislature speedily to remedy
such an evil, by a law enacted for the purpose. This remedy,
however, could only be applied to future cases, without including present or past; but such a series of usages does not exist.[z] There is no evidence of parliamentary practice to justify
the cessation of a trial before the truth or falsehood of the

CHAP.
XLVI.

1791.

Question
whether
impeach-
ment by
the com-
mons be-
fore the
lords abate
with the
dissolution
of parlia-
ment.
Prece-
dents and
arguments
for and
against.

z See speeches of Mr. Pitt and Mr. Fox.

CHAP.
XLVI.

1791.

charges be ascertained. Parliamentary records demonstrate that in ancient times impeachments were continued after dissolution. But without searching into remote monuments, in the reign of Charles II. in 1673, when there was no ferment either on the one side or the other, the house of lords declared their writs of error, petitions of appeal, and other judicial proceedings, should be narrowed as to the portion of time which they were to occupy during a session, but should extend from parliament to parliament, if they were not decided. The reason of this order evidently was, that on the one hand judicial proceedings might not employ any part of the time which was required by legislative, on the other, that the objects either of civil or criminal justice might not be defeated by discontinuance of process. The precedents, it was contended, did not apply: and in the various cases alleged, the proceedings had been discontinued by a general pardon, admission to bail, or some other cause, and not from the dissolution of parliament. These positions their supporters endeavoured to evince by a consideration of the very cases that were quoted by the advocates of the opposite doctrine. They further argued, that decisions of courts of law, and the authority of judges, with few exceptions, sanctioned the same opinion; and cited cases to prove their position: the general analogy of judicial proceedings illustrated the conformity of their conception of the law of parliament with the established modes of process before subordinate tribunals: the commons are the public prosecutors, and in this respect analogous to the attorney or solicitor-general in ordinary cases of criminal prosecutions. The removal of an attorney-general does not quash an information or indictment; and the process is carried on by his successor. The public prosecutors before the house of peers, are the successive houses of commons, as before the inferior courts, they are the successive attorneys-general. The house of peers are the judges in causes carried on at the instance of the house of commons; the peers may be not all the same in successive parliaments, as the judges of the inferior courts may be changed while the trial is pending. Equity and expediency coincide with analogy; impeachments are calculated for bringing to condign punishment criminals too exalted for the inferior courts; criminals, who to secure themselves or their friends from all responsibility as ministers of the crown, might advise a dissolution, as often as it should be required for their safety. Hence parliament would be no longer able to control either the civil or judicial administration of the kingdom. The cabinet and courts of law would remain equally without a check; it is therefore clear from the weight of precedents, the authority of the greatest luminaries of the law, the principles of the constitution, the analogy of public trials, the immutable rules of equal justice, and the dictates of expediency and common sense, that impeachments continue notwithstanding the dissolution of parliament. On these grounds a great majority in both houses voted that the impeachment of Warren Hastings was still depending.

An inquiry concerning the judicial power of parliament was soon followed by a discussion of the powers of juries. One of the chief engines of that moral and political knowledge, of those sentiments and privileges of rational and beneficial liberty which prevail in Britain, is a FREE PRESS. By this vehicle, a writer may communicate to the public his observations, thoughts, and feelings, and according to his talents, learning, and dispositions, may inform and instruct mankind: and thus the press bestows all the knowledge and wisdom which cannot be imparted by oral delivery. But as all persons who address the public through this vehicle are not both capable and disposed to inform and instruct society, an instrument of general good is frequently productive of considerable, though partial evil. The liberty of the press has often permitted seditious, treasonable, immoral, and blasphemous libels: and generated mischiefs that were followed by very pernicious consequences. For a considerable time after the invention of printing, government possessed the means of preventing noxious publications, as the press was liable to the inspection of a licenser; but the preventive was much worse than the evil; and the subjection of writings to a previous examination being found totally incompatible with the purposes of beneficial freedom, ceased soon after the revolution. Precluded by the law from preventing the publication of hurtful works, certain judges endeavoured to deter writers by increasing the punishment: to avoid one extreme running into its opposite, they attempted to attach criminality to productions, that before would have been reckoned innocent; and to supply the supposed deficiency of preventive justice, they tried to enlarge the precincts of penal law. They also endeavoured to change the judicial rules established by the constitution. For a series of years it had been maintained by very high legal authority, as we have already seen,[a] that the truth of an allegation could not be pleaded in bar of an indictment for a libel, and also that in cases of libel juries were to investigate the fact only; to return a verdict relative to the proof of the allegations, but to leave the criminality to the judge; and though these doctrines had been questioned by very high legal authority,[b] yet they were most frequently followed in recent practice. Various cases occurred in which guilt had been found on grounds, that in the popular estimation were inadequate, or punishment had far exceeded the criminality that was evinced. Mr. Fox having adopted the same sentiments respecting some late decisions, and disapproving of the interposition of crown lawyers, introduced a bill declaring the power of juries to decide upon the law as well as the fact in trials of libels. Where any special matter of law is pleaded (said Mr. Fox) the judge and not the jury is to decide; but that

1791.

Determination of the house, that impeachments do not abate by dissolution.

Liberty of the Press.

Motion of Mr Fox for ascertaining and declaring the law of libels, and bill for that purpose.

a See volume i. chap. ix.   b Ibid.

CHAP.
XLVI.

1791·

Arguments for and against.

where a general issue is joined, and the law is so implicated with the fact that they cannot be separated, the jury must, as in all other criminal processes, bring in a general verdict of guilty or not guilty. The decision of this important question greatly depended on the import of the word *meaning*, used in all indictments for libels. The different senses annexed to this term Mr. Fox explained, and marked with discriminating precision. The term to *mean* might, he observed, be understood to imply a proposition according to strict *grammatical and logical construction*, or to express the MORAL INTENTION of a writer or speaker. In the former sense it had been received for many years by judges and crown lawyers; in the latter it ought to be interpreted by a candid and impartial English jury, who were to investigate the intention of the accused, as a part of the fact to be proved or disproved. It is the intention that must constitute guilt, if any guilt existed. The bill was opposed as an innovation on the laws of the kingdom, that was agitated at present by the dangerous maxims which were embroiling our neighbours. In such circumstances we ought to avoid novelties, civil and political. The present process had been the practice for a long course of years, without producing any oppression to the subject; the judges were independent of the crown, and could have no motive to unfair and partial decisions. This bill was not debated as a party question, but as a subject of existing law, justice, and constitutional right. Mr. Pitt was no less vigorous in its support than Mr. Fox, or Mr. Erskine. In the house of lords, lord Grenville supported the motion with no less zeal than lord Loughborough, and lord Camden took the lead

Postponed for the present; is afterwards passed into a law.

in promoting its success. After passing the commons by a great majority, it was rejected by the peers; but the following session, being again proposed, it passed into a law.

Mr. Fox also proposed a law for depriving the attorney-general in right of the crown, and every other person in his own right, of a power to disturb the possessor of a franchise in a corporation, after having quietly exercised it for six years. The end of this proposition was, to secure the rights of election, and prevent vexatious prosecutions for political purposes: the bill was passed into a law.

State and conduct of the English catholics.

Parliament, endeavouring to remove all restrictions upon natural freedom, as far as was consistent with security, directed its attention to the catholics. The English catholics were now totally changed, and no longer resembled the Romanists of the seventeenth century; nor even those who, at a later period, wished to exalt a popish pretender to the throne. They were now quiet and peaceable subjects, friends to the present government, and favourable to our constitution of church and state, which was so mild and tolerant to every religious sect that worshipped God according to their own conscience, without disturbing the public tranquillity. Many of the catholics, as they mingled with protestants, imbibed a great share of their mild-

ness and moderation; and, without relinquishing the sensible
rituals, prescribed observances, or the metaphysical theology of
the popish church, were really protestants in their moral and
political principles and conduct. A considerable body of them 1791.
had recently protested in express terms against doctrines impu- They re-
ted for near three centuries to papists. They denied the autho- nounce the
rity of the pope in temporal concerns, his right to excommuni- gerous mo-
cate princes, and to absolve their subjects from their oaths of ral and po-
allegiance. They disavowed the lawfulness of breaking faith litical doc-
with heretics; and denied that any clerical power could ex- trines of
empt man from moral obligations. The penal laws against popery.
catholics arising from circumstances and conduct so totally different from the present, were still extremely severe. To render
the law more suitable to their present sentiments and character,
Mr. Mitford proposed to repeal the statutes in question, so far Motion for
as to exempt from their penal operations those who had re- their renounced the hurtful doctrines abovementioned, under the de- lief:
nomination of the PROTESTING CATHOLIC DISSENTERS, upon these
catholics taking an oath conformable to the protest. The principle of the bill was generally approved; and the bench of
bishops displayed the most liberal zeal in its favor. Dr. Horsley especially exerted his great abilities, not only in promoting modified
its success, but in removing a clause which was neither agreea- and cor-
ble to its principles nor conducive to its objects. In the pro- rected by
posed oath, the doctrine that princes excommunicated by the ley, it is
pope might be deposed and murdered by their subjects, was passed into
declared to be impious, heretical, and damnable. The catho- a law.
lies felt no reluctance to express their own rejection and disapprobation of such doctrine; but from scruples founded on a
tender regard for the memory of their progenitors, they could
not induce themselves to brand it with the terms which the oath
prescribed. To remove this objection, he proposed the oath
which had been adopted in 1778: this alteration was admitted,
and the bill was passed into a law.

The church of Scotland perceiving a disposition in parliament to grant relief to non-comformists, transmitted from the Petition of
general assembly a petition praying for the repeal of the test of Scotland
act as far as it applied to Scotland; and on the 10th of May respecting
sir Gilbert Elliot made a motion conformably to the petition. the test
The supporters of the motion endeavored to prove that the act.
law as it now stood, was inconsistent with the articles of the
union. Scotland, by her constitution, and by treaty, had a separate church, and a separate form of religion. By the treaty
of union she was to have a free communication of civil rights;
but a test which, as a condition for attaining those civil rights,
imposed on her a necessity of departing from her own established theology, and submitting to the system of England, either
abridged her religious liberty by means of the civil attainments,
or obstructed the civil attainments through the religious obligations. When the two kingdoms entered into a treaty of union,

CHAP.   being independent nations, they meant to stipulate and contract
XLVI.   on terms of perfect equality. Was it not an infringement of
~~~~~   that equality, that a Scotchman entering into any British office
1791.   in England should solemnly profess his attachment to the church
        of England, which a scrupulous man might deem a dereliction
        of his native church; while an Englishman appointed to an
        office in Scotland incurred no similar obligation. The opposers
        of the motion argued, that the test must have been understood
        as a stipulation at the time of the union, and had never been
        represented as an hardship till the present time. The grievance
        was merely imaginary; the test was not a dereliction of the
        church of Scotland, but a pledge of amity with the church of
        England. The general sentiment of members of the Scottish
        church was affection and respect for the sister establishment:
        but in Scotland there were as in England, sectaries of various
        denominations, whose sentiments were less liberal. Against
        such sectaries it was just as well as expedient, that the test
        should operate; otherwise the church of England would incur
        a danger from them, to which from the sectaries of England she
        was not exposed. Since there was no test in Scotland, the pro-
        posed exemption would let in upon the church of England dis-
        senters and sectaries of every denomination; and thus break
        down the fence which the wisdom and justice of parliament
        had so often and so recently confirmed. This petition, in real-
        ity, arose ultimately from the English dissenters. These had
        operated in the church of Scotland by representing themselves
        as presbyterian brethren. Many of the Scottish clergymen, not
        discovering the total diversity of political sentiments that sub-
        sisted between them and many of the English dissenters, were,
        from supposed religious sympathy, induced to give them their
is rejected. support. The majority of the house being impressed by these
        arguments, voted against the proposition.

Full dis-   The slave trade underwent this year a much more complete
cussion of discussion than when it was formerly agitated. The facts on
the slave   both sides had now been very thoroughly examined: there
trade.   was fulness of information; so that the public and parliament
            had the amplest means of viewing the subject in every light.
Motion of   Mr. Wilberforce, on the 18th of April, proposed a bill for
Mr. Wil-   preventing the farther importation of slaves into the British
berforce   colonies in the West Indies. In his prefatory speech he
for the   considered, as he had done two years before, first humanity,
abolition. and secondly policy. He traced the condition of the Africans
            from their native country to the West India plantations; and,
Argu-   according to the information which he had collected, in more
ments for   copious detail, with more numerous instances, repeated his
            former statements of the causes of slavery, the treatment of
            the negroes on their passage, and their sufferings under the
            planters. On the ground of policy he strongly argued that the
            abolition of the slave trade was expedient for the West India
            planters and the British nation. Compelled to promote multi-

plication among the slaves, the planters would soon find that CHAP.
their present negroes, in a climate so congenial to their native XLVI.
Africa, would, if well treated, people the plantations; and if
allowed to acquire some little interests in the soil, would be   1791.
stimulated to much greater exertions. The loss of seamen
which Britons sustained in the negro trade was immense.
From Liverpool, in one year, three hundred and fifty ships,
having on board twelve thousand two hundred and fifty men,
lost two thousand four hundred and fifty, being one-fifth. The
commercial profits were to be totally disregarded, when acquired by such a violation of humanity, and at the expense of so
many valuable lives of British sailors.

The continuance of this trade was defended on the grounds and against
of justice, policy, and even humanity. Slavery had been es- it.
tablished time immemorial in various parts of the earth,
especially in Africa and the adjacent countries. So far was
it from being reckoned a crime, that the old Testament frequently mentions male and female slaves under the names of
bondsmen, handmaids, and others of similar import, and never
censures mancipation, but speaks of all its offices as just employments. The characters held up to imitation had slaves
themselves, and endeavoured to acquire slaves to others.[e] The
habits and sentiments of Africans render this condition by no
means so grievous to them as it would be to the people unaccustomed to the daily contemplation of slavery. The assertion of the abolitionists, that the hope of acquiring prisoners
to be sold to Europeans is the chief cause of war, is far
from being generally true. Wars in Africa, as well as wars in
Europe arise from pride, resentment, envy, jealousy, emulation,
ambition, and other passions, besides avarice alone. As an
accurate knowledge of the interior country increased, it was
more clearly comprehended that captives, though a consequence of war, were far from being its most frequent objects.
The purchaser of slaves taken in war preserves the lives of
captives that would be otherwise butchered. Their ferocious
conquerors would give way to the savage gratification of rage
and cruelty, if the thirst of blood were not changed into the
thirst of gain. The extreme indolence of the Africans, notwithstanding the fertility and even spontaneous productiveness of
the soil, renders their supplies of the necessaries of life very
scanty. Prisoners taken in war, therefore, are great burthens
upon the captors; and unless there was a market for vending
them, they would be immediately massacred, not merely from
cruelty, but from the savage economy of those barbarians; and

e Joseph, a patriarch so highly favoured by God, when he became prime
minister to Pharoah in consequence of the foresight conferred on him by the
divine gift, having laid up stores of provisions against the season of scarcity, purchased with the king's corn the liberties of his subjects; and nothing in this procedure is blamed by the sacred historian. It appeared, indeed, perfectly fair and reasonable to the subjects of an African prince.

the European traders saved many a life. Our merchants, on the faith of parliament, had embarked property to a great amount in this trade ; the total loss of which would immediate-ly follow the abolition. The legislature had invited them to engage in the traffic, that Britain might be furnished from their plantations with those commodities which habit has now ren-dered universally necessary, and if not supplied by them, must be purchased from other countries. It invited them also to engage in this commerce, that the carriage of their pro-ductions might rear up a navy ; yet now, when they have a capital of seventy millions embarked, when several islands lately occupied, and therefore thinly peopled, require a con-stant succession of fresh supplies ; and when twenty millions of debt in mortgages and deeds of consignment, press heavily on the West India proprietors, the abolition is proposed in con-tradiction to so many acts of parliament, and without compen-sation of the only means by which they can be relieved from the enormous load. Is it consistent with British justice to depreciate, and even destroy, property, engaged in a commerce which the legislature pledged itself to protect, and repeatedly declared its disposition to improve ? But private property would not alone be affected : from this trade the revenue would suffer a very material diminution. The evidences adduced to prove the horrid cruelties practised upon slaves were represented to be in some instances false, in many par-tial, in almost all exaggerated. It is the interest both of the transporting owners of slaves, and their purchasers in the West Indies, to treat them humanely, and easy to devise regu-lations for enforcing this treatment, and punishing the contrary. But were Britain from an impulse of benevolent enthusiasm to abolish the slave trade, under a supposition that it subjected the Africans to the most poignant misery, would not other European nations engaged in the trade, supply the vacan-cy left by our relinquishment of a traffic necessary for raising commodities naturalized to the European palates ? Would the purchasers, the venders, or the subjects sold, be less numerous ? Would fewer slaves be exported from Africa ? Respecting the effects of this commerce on our navy, the friends of the aboli-tion were totally misinformed. A naval commander of the very highest eminence, lord Rodney, had declared that the power of obtaining from Guinea ships, so numerous a body of men inured to the climate, whenever he wished to send a fleet to the West Indies on the breaking out of a war, was, in his opinion, a consideration of great moment. His lordship's opinion was illustrated, and his authority confirmed, by concurring testimonies of other officers, both of the army and navy. The abolition would be equally contrary to the commercial and political interests of the public, as to the rights and well founded expectations of private individuals. On this question Messrs. Pitt and Fox took the same side, and

Continu-
ance of the
slave trade
defended
on the
grounds of
humanity,
justice, and
expedien-
cy.

supported the abolition with every argument that genius could
invent; but their united eloquence was not effectual: on a division it was carried in the negative by a majority of one hundred
and sixty-three to eighty-eight.	The benevolent spirit which
prompted the abolition of the slave trade directly, produced an
attempt gradually to demonstrate its inefficacy and inutility.	For
this purpose its impugners projected to try an experiment whether
Africa could not be civilized, and rendered more lucrative as a
vent for manufactures, than as a nursery for slaves.	Mr. De-
vaynes, who had long resided at Sierra Leone, on the coast of
Africa, in the eighth degree of north latitude, attested that the
soil is excellent, and produces cotton, coffee, and sugar, with the
slightest cultivation.	There a society proposed to establish a
colony in hopes of effecting the desired change in the character
and condition of the Africans.	A bill for the establishment of
such a company was introduced by Mr. Henry Thornton, and
passed through both houses without opposition.

Previous to the reduction of his financial plan, Mr. Pitt proposed to appoint a committee to consider and report the amount
of the public income and expenditure during the last five years;
also, to inquire what they might respectively be in future, and
what alterations had taken place in the amount of the national
debt since January 5th, 1786.	The report stated that the annual
income, on the average of the three last years was sixteen millions, thirty thousand, two hundred and eighty-six pounds; and
the annual expenditure fifteen millions, nine hundred and sixty-
nine thousand, one hundred and seventy-eight pounds, including
the annual million for liquidating the national debt; the balance,
therefore, in favour of the country, was sixty-one thousand one
hundred and eight pounds.[d]	Mr. Sheridan as usual, took the
lead in combatting the financial conclusions of Mr. Pitt, and
moved no less than forty resolutions, which were intended to
show that the past revenue had been considerably inferior to ministerial calculations: and that in calculating the future income,
the minister had overlooked contingencies which recent expe-
rience demonstrated to be probable.	The greater number of
these propositions were negatived, and others were amended.
Various resolutions were framed by ministers, confirming, in
detail, the report of the new committee, and maintaining the cal-
culations which were founded on their inquiry.	The supplies
were nearly the same as in the usual peace establishment, and no
fresh taxes were imposed.	Mr. Dundas produced his annual
statement of Indian finance, which had been in a state of so progressive prosperity ever since the establishment of Mr. Pitt's
plan of territorial government, and the commencement of Mr.
Dundas's executive direction.	It appeared from the documents

CHAP.
XLVI.

1791.

agree in
supporting
the aboli-
tion.	The
motion is
negatived.

Settlement
at Sierra
Leone.

Finance.

Supplies.

Indian
finance.

d 16,030,286
  15,969,178
  ─────────
    61,108*l.*

CHAP. XLVI.

1791.

which he presented, that the British revenues in the East Indies, amounting to seven millions, after defraying all the expenses of government, left a clear surplus of near a million and a half, either to be laid out in investments, or applied to contingent ser- vices. Among the pecuniary grants of this year was an annuity of twelve thousand pounds, bestowed on his majesty's third son prince William Henry, created about two years before duke of Clarence.

Trial of Hastings. The evi- dence for the prose- cution closed.

This year the prosecution of Mr. Hastings closed its evidence (May 30). The managers proposed an address to the king, praying him not to prorogue the parliament until the trial was finished; but this address was negatived. Mr. Hastings, when the prosecution was closed. addressed the court in a speech of singular acuteness, force, and eloquence, exhibiting his view of the result of the prosecutor's evidence, contrasting the situation in which he found with the situation in which he left British India; explicitly, but not arrogantly, detailing the counsels and conduct by which he had effected these great ends: he appealed to the commons, his accusers, in the following dignified and

Impressive speech of the de- fendant.

striking peroration. " To the commons of England, in whose " name I am arraigned for desolating the provinces of their do- " minions in India, I dare to reply, that they are, and their repre- " sentatives persist in telling them so, the most flourishing of all " the states of India. It was I that made them so: the value of " what others acquired I enlarged, and gave shape and consis- " tency to the dominions which you hold there: I preserved it: " I sent forth its armies with an effectual but economical hand, " through unknown and hostile regions, to the support of your " other possessions; to the retrieval of one from degradation and " dishonour, and of another from utter loss and subjection. I " maintained the wars which were of your formation, or that of " others, not of mine: I won one member of the great Indian " confederacy from it by an act of seasonable restitution; with " another I maintained a secret intercourse, and converted him " into a friend: a third I drew off by diversion and negotiation, " and employed him as the instrument of peace. I gave you " all, and you have rewarded me with confiscation, disgrace, and " a life of impeachment." Of Mr. Hastings's hearers, even those who could not admit a plea of merit as an abatement of special charges, were very forcibly impressed by this energetic

Session rises.

representation. The defence of the accused was, by the direc- tion of the court, postponed till the following session, and on June 10th the parliament was prorogued.

CHAP. XLVII.

Peace between Russia and Turkey—on moderate terms.—Reasons of Catharine's apparent moderation.—Poland attempts to recover liberty and
independence—Wise, moderate, and patriotic efforts for that purpose.—
New constitution, an hereditary, mixed, and limited monarchy—effected
without bloodshed.—Rage of Catharine at the emancipation of Poland—
She hopes to crush the new system of Poland.—Impression made by the
French revolution—on other countries—on sovereigns.—Circular letter
of the emperor to other princes.—Equitable and prudent principle of
British policy respecting the French revolution.—Paris—ejectment and
banishment of the clergy who refused the civic oath.—Progress of confiscation.—Forfeiture of the estates of emigrants—Abolition of primogeniture.—Invasion of the rights of German princes—The emperor remonstrates against this violation of national engagements.—Proposed
jaunt of the king to St. Cloud—is prevented by the populace—Memorial
of Louis delivered to foreign powers.—Flight of the king—He is arrested at Varennes—Proceedings of the legislature during his absence—
He is brought back to Paris—The monarchical party adopts a vigorous
system, but too late—State of parties.—The king's friends advise him
to accept the constitutional code.—He accepts it in the national assembly.—Honours paid to infidel philosophers—Want of money.—Inspection of accounts—Dissolution of the national assembly.—Review of the
principal changes effected by this body.—How it found and left France.—
In all its excesses it manifested the genius and energy of the French
character—Progress of political enthusiasm.—Britain—Certain ingenious visionaries expect a political millenium—Thomas Paine—Rights of
man.—Dexterous adaptation of to the sentiments and passions of the vulgar—astonishing popularity of among the lower ranks. - Commemoration
of the French revolution at Birmingham.—Riots—Destruction of Dr.
Priestley's library—the doctor's conduct.—Comparison between Priestley
and Paine—Rapid and extensive diffusion of democratic principles—
Wide diffusion of superficial literature—favourable to revolutionary projects—Mary Anne Wollstonecraft.—Debating Societies—Cheap editions
of Tom Paine's works—One able and profound work in favour of the
French revolution—Vindiciæ Galliæ.—Marriage of the duke of York to
the princess of Prussia.

CATHARINE perceived her grand object of subjugating
the Ottomans, for the present to be impracticable, and now
satisfied herself with endeavouring to compel the sultan to a
peace, before the interference of the confederates could prevent
her from dictating the terms. With this view her armies
took the field early in spring, repeatedly defeated the enemy,
and compelled them to retire nearer to Constantinople; and to
enhance their danger, several symptoms began to appear in
Asiatic Turkey of a disposition to revolt: menaced by most imminent perils both in Asia and Europe, and apprized that the

CHAP. XLVII. 1791. Peace between Russia and Turkey,

CHAP.
XI.VII.

1791.

on mode-
rate terms.

Reasons of
Catha
rine's ap-
parent mo-
deration.

Poland at-
tempts to
recover li-
berty and
indepen-
dence;

wise, mo-
derate, and
patriotic
efforts for
that pur-
pose.

co-operation of Prussia and of Britain, was now obstructed,
Selim began to. listen to the proposals of the empress; the negotiation was not tedious; and a peace was concluded on the
11th of August at Galatz. by which Russia retained Oczakow,
and the country between the Bog and the Dnieper, which had
belonged to Turkey before the war. The latter of these rivers
was to be the boundary of both powers: each to be equally
entitled to the free navigation of the river; and each to erect
fortifications on its respective shores. However important this
acquisition might be to Russia, it was certainly much inferior
to the expectations which she entertained at the commencement
of the war; and during its successful progress: but other circumstances combined with the exertions of the defensive alliance to induce Catharine to content herself, for the present,
with Oczakow and its dependencies. Frederick William agreeably to the general objects of. the confederacy, as well as his
own particular interest, cultivated the friendship of Poland.
Encouraged by their connexion with this powerful prince, and
beginning once more to conceive themselves of weight in the
scale of Europe, reviving self estimation rekindled in the Poles
that courage and patriotism, which though smothered, had not
been extinguished. and thus once more they entertained hopes
of freeing themselves from the thraldom in which they were
held by the imperious Catharine. In 1788 and 1789, various
efforts were made to establish the independent interest of Poland in the diet, and to overturn the power which Russia. had
assumed. A party of generous patriots stimulated their countrymen to emancipate themselves from a foreign yoke; the spirit of liberty was studiously diffused through all classes of the
community; and in 1790 had risen very high. Its leading votaries saw, that the only method of securing the attachment and
fidelity of the people to those who were projecting such alterations, was to accompany them with such benefits to the middling,
and even to the inferior classes, as might deeply interest
them in their support. But though desirous of changes, which
would terminate the oppressive power of the great, the Poles
were sincerely inclined to be satisfied with a moderate degree
of freedom; and at present bounded their wishes to deliverance
from the personal thraldom in which, for so many ages, they
had been tyrannically held. Conformably to this disposition,
the popular leaders exerted their influence, with so much wisdom and prudence among the commons, that they made no
claims but those that were strictly equitable and consistent with
legal subordination. On these moderate principles of freedom,
the people of Poland drew up an address to the diet, amounting to a declaration of rights. This representation, instead of
recurring to the *natural rights of man*, antecedent to political
establishment, considered *what was most expedient for the character and circumstances of the Polish people.* The constitution
of Poland having been extremely defective in various constitu-

ents of liberty and security, the address in its claims, proposed
such changes only as would remedy the defects, without subverting the existing orders. The nobles, clergy, and commons,
should continue distinct, and the nobility retain their rank, dignity, and all the privileges which were compatible with public
freedom ; they should only be deprived of the power of oppression and tyranny. The commons should not only be exempted
from civil thraldom, but have all the political power that was
consistent with the balance of the estates.   Requisitions so
discriminately moderate, tending to produce the balance of the
parts, as well as the welfare of the whole, were most graciously received by the Polish nobility, who showed themselves desirous of promoting a new system, conformable to the wishes
of the people. The Polish patriots were eager to complete
their reform, before Russia should be in a condition to give
them any effectual interruption. Reports were spread and suspicions entertained, that there was a new partition in contemplation : the only way to prevent such a calamity and disgrace,
was without delay to establish a system of polity, which should
produce an union of the whole strength and energy of the Polish nation, resist the interference of foreigners in its domestic
affairs, and preserve its natural independence and dignity. With
these views the patriots formed a system, which had for its basis, the rights claimed in the address of the people ; and they
presented their plan to the diet at Warsaw. The new constitution proposed two objects ; the external independence, and
internal liberty of the nation.   The Roman catholic religion
was to continue to be the national faith, with a toleration of
every other which should peaceably submit to the established
government.   The clergy should retain their privileges and
authority ; the nobility their pre-eminence and perogatives ; the
commons including the citizens and peasants, should participate
of the general liberty ; and the peasants were to be exempted
from the predial servitude, under which they so long
groaned. Stipulations between the landholders and the peasants should be equally binding on both parties and on their respective successors, either by inheritance or acquisition; all
property of every rank, order, or individual should be sacred,
even from the encroachments of the supreme national power.
To encourage the population of the country, all people, either
strangers who should come to settle, or natives who having
emigrated should return to their country, might become citizens
of Poland, on conforming to its laws. The constitution should New con-
be composed of three distinct powers, the legislative power in stitution,
the states assembled; executive power in the king and council ; an heredi-
and judicial power in the jurisdictions existing, or to be establish- tary, mixed. The crown was declared to be elective in point of fami- ed, and li-
lies, but hereditary in the family which should be chosen. The mited mo-
proposed dynasty of future kings, was to begin with the elector narchy:
of Saxony, and to descend to his heirs. The king at his acces-

CHAP. sion must engage to support the new constitution, and was to
XLVII. command the army, and preside in the legislature; the legisla-
       tion was to be vested in two houses, the nobility and commons,
1791. meeting by their representatives; and the judicial power was to
       be vested in a gradation of courts, rising to one general and
       national tribunal. Such are the outlines[e] of the constitution of
       Poland, which appeared to steer a middle course between aris-
       tocratic tyranny, and democratic violence. It seemed well
       calculated to maintain internal liberty, encourage the industry
       of the great mass of the people, improve the immense advan-
       tages of their soil and situation, and invigorate their energy by
       the newly infused spirit of personal freedom; to confirm subor-
       dination of rank, which best guides the efforts of the people,
       and by diffusing harmony and force throughout the nation, to
       afford the disposition and means of maintaining the independ-
       ence of Poland. There were members of the diet, who not only
       opposed these proceedings, but drew up a protest against them
       in the form of a manifesto. Their conduct excited universal
       dissatisfaction, and though the moderation of the patriotic par-
       ty offered no insult to their persons, yet the people could not
       forbear to view them with indignation. The king and the other
       leaders of the popular party were extremely vigilant in restrain-
       ing every appearance of violence. Indeed a singular and hap-
       py circumstance of this revolution, was the peaceable manner
effected in which it was, effected: Poland attained the end which it
without proposed, without the loss of a single life. In framing this sys-
bloodshed. tem, Stanislaus himself had displayed great ability: he had
       consulted the English and American constitutions, and with
       accute discrimination had selected such parts as were best adapt-
       ed to the circumstances of Poland. The Polish patriots aware
       of the disposition of Catharine, and apprehending other
       neighboring states to regard the project with a jealous eye,
       urged the speedy adoption of the new constitution; and they
       exerted themselves so strenuously, that on the 3d of May 1791,
       it was accepted by the estates, and all orders and classes of
       men, and ratified by suitable oaths, and inaugural solemni-
       ties.

Rage of   The situation of Poland, freed from the Russian yoke, and
Catharine rising to independence and respectability, galled the pride, and
at the   alarmed the ambition of Catharine; she was enraged, that the
emancipa- Poles, over whom she for many years had imperiously domi-
tion of Po- neered, now asserted a right of managing their own affairs:
land.   she saw in the power of Poland, if allowed to be confirmed,
       under her present constitution, a bar to the accomplishment
       of her vast projects: she was therefore eager to conclude the
       peace of Galatz, on terms less humiliating to the vanquished
       Ottoman, than from her successes she might have expected.

       e See Otridge's Annual Register for 1791. Appendix to Chronicle,
       p. 88.

There were circumstances which afforded her hopes of not only resuming her dictation in Poland, but also rendering her power over that country more arbitrary than ever.

At the commencement of the French revolution, the other great powers of the continent were so much engaged in their own several projects, as not to bestow an adequate attention on the character and spirit of the Gallic proceedings. Spain was by far too feeble to entertain any hopes of interfering with effect in favour of fallen monarchy. The king of Sardinia afforded refuge to the exiled princes and nobility, but could supply no important aid. The refugee princes and their party, though anxiously eager to interest foreign powers in the cause of the privileged orders, yet during the year 1790, had little success; but when Leopold had restored tranquillity in the Low Countries, after having concluded peace with Turkey, and being on terms of amity with the defensive alliance, he turned his attention[f] to the situation of France. Though moved by consanguinity, he was yet more deeply impressed by kingly sympathy: he considered the present ruling party in France as inimical to all monarchy, and holding up an example which he apprehended the subjects of neighbouring sovereigns might imitate: and in these sentiments other princes of Germany coincided. Leopold however was aware of the danger which would attend speedy hostilities, unless he should have more effectual auxiliaries than the petty princes of the Germanic empire. His own resources were impaired by the war from which he had so recently extricated himself. France under her monarchical government had been always too powerful for the German empire; the present system would afford her additional energy From these considerations, so early as the spring of 1791, he endeavoured to interest other potentates in his objects; and with his own hands wrote a letter to the empress of Russia, the king of England, and the king of Prussia, also to the king of Spain, the states-general, the kings of Sardinia and Naples; proposing to form an union and concert of counsels and plans, for the purposes of asserting the honour and liberty of the king and royal family of France, and setting bounds to the dangerous excesses of the French revolution; to instruct their ministers at Paris to declare the concert which should be so formed; and recommend to the respective princes to support their declarations, by preparing a sufficient force. Should the French refuse to comply with the joint requisition of the crowned heads, the confederated powers would suspend all intercourse with France, collect a considerable army on the frontiers, and thereby compel the national assembly to raise and maintain a great military force at a heavy expense. The interruption of trade, and general industry, would

1791.
She hopes to crush the new system of Poland.

Impression made by the French revolution on other countries; on sovereigns.

Circular letter of the emperor to other princes.

f See Annual Register, 1791. ch. iv.
g Annual Register as above.

CHAP.   bring the people of France to more sober thoughts; and might
XLVII.   tend to the evaporation of their present enthusiasm. On so
          great an undertaking, the emperor could not venture alone;
1791.   the concurrence of the other great powers, especially Prussia
          and Great Britain, was necessary to give efficacy to the pro-
          ject.

Equitable   Whatever effect this application might have on the powers
and pru-   severally, to whom it was addressed, it did not succeed in pro-
dent prin- ducing the proposed concert. The principle of Britain mani-
ciple of   fested not only in her declarations, but uniform conduct, was
British po- that an internal change in the political system of any country
licy re-   did not justify the interference of neighbouring nations, unless
specting   that internal change led its votaries to aggression: that it did
the French not belong to England to determine whether the government of
revolution. France should be monarchical or republican; and that in changing
          her constitution, humbling her monarch, degrading her nobility,
          plundering her church, and even committing various acts of
          atrocity, in her own provinces or metropolis, she did no act
          which it belonged to Britain to avenge: she inflicted no injury
          on Britain. As impartial observers, Britons might individually
          censure French proceedings, as unwise, unjust, or impious; but
          the British nation neither possessed nor asserted a right of dicta-
          tion to the French concerning the management of their own in-
          ternal affairs, so long as their conduct did not produce aggression
          against this country.

Paris—   While symptoms of enmity against the French revolution
ejectment were manifesting themselves in some of the neighbouring coun-
and banish- tries, its votaries were proceeding in their career. With great
ment of the expedition they ejected from their livings the refractory priests
clergy who who would not swear contrary to their belief and conscience,
refused the and filled their places with more complaisant pastors, who were
civic oath. willing to submit to the powers that be; and in a few months
          there was a new set of spiritual teachers, most eagerly attached
          to the revolution to which they were indebted for their benefi-
          ces. Besides this body of staunch auxiliaries, the national as-
          sembly, by robbing the church, procured another set of very
          active assistants in the holders of the assignments. These were,
          indeed, a kind of revolutionary pawn-brokers, who advanced
          money on plundered effects, and depended on the stability of
          the new system for payment. By the spiritual influence of the
          new priests, and the temporal influence of the new brokers,
          who consisted of great monied capitalists, the people became
          still more attached to the revolution, and its engine the nation-
Progress   al assembly. This body of legislators, finding confiscation so
of confis- productive a source of revenue, deemed it unwise to confine it
cation.   to the property of the church. A new fund they provided in
Forfeiture the estates of the refugee princes and nobility;[h] and with their
of the es- usual despatch they passed a decree sequestering the principal
tates of
emigrants.

          h See proceedings of the national assembly.

estates, and threatening to confiscate them all if the proprietors
did not immediately return. Farther to equalize property, they
passed a decree abolishing primogeniture, and ordaining that
the property of parents should be equally divided among their
children. But the national assembly now extended its system
of confiscation to the properties of foreigners. Several German
princes, secular and ecclesiastical, held great possessions in
Alsace, by tenures repeatedly ratified under the most solemn
treaties; and guaranteed by the great neighbouring powers.
Yet these rights the national assembly overthrow by a mere act
of lawless robbery.[i] This flagrant aggression on the rights of
independent powers, not only excited the indignant resentment
of the princes who were actually despoiled, but the displeasure
and apprehensions of others. The confiscation of French property by the government was an invasion of the rights of French
subjects. But the invasion of foreign property was a declaration of intended hostilities against all nations to which their
plundering arms could reach. The emperor remonstrated on
this violation of existing treaties, requiring compensation for
the past, and security against future attacks on the rights of
princes of the empire. The national assembly imputed this requisition to hostile intentions, and affirmed that there was a
concert of foreign sovereigns, French princes, and aristocrats, to effect a counter revolution: Louis, they said, had acceded to this confederation, and was preparing to escape from
France.

His majesty at Easter had taken the sacrament from the
hands of a refractory[k] priest, and had thereby given great offence and alarm to the Parisians. It was also remarked that he
had recently promoted officers inimical to the revolution. On
the 18th of April, being Easter monday, his majesty and family
intended to repair to St. Cloud, a palace about three miles from
the city, there to spend the holidays. In the morning, as the
family was stepping into their coaches, an immense crowd surrounding the carriages, refused to suffer them to proceed, and
insisted that they should remain at Paris. The national guards,
joining the multitude, exclaimed that the king should not be
suffered to depart; and the sovereign found it necessary to
comply with the requisition of the populace. After several discussions, the Parisians represented their apprehension of dangers assailing them from various quarters, and especially the
king's intimate counsellors. His majesty, to gratify the populace, dismissed various royalists from their places at court, and
employed other means to remove the popular dissatisfaction.
One step which he took for this purpose, was to send a memorial to the French ministers in foreign countries, with orders to
deliver a copy at each court where they respectively resided.

Margin notes:
CHAP. XLVII.

1791.

Abolition of primogeniture.

Invasion of the rights of German princes.

The emperor remonstrates against this violation of national engagements.

Proposed jaunt of the king to St. Cloud, is prevented by the populace.

Memorial of Louis delivered to foreign powers.

i See proceedings of the national assembly.
k Those clergymen who would not take the prescribed oath were, by the
revolutionists styled refractory priests.

CHAP. XLVII.

1791.

This document recapitulated the events which produced and followed the revolution, and described that great change as having importantly improved the condition both of the monarch and the people. It extolled the new constitution, reprobated the efforts employed to overthrow that beneficial fabric, most clearly and unequivocally expressed the royal approbation of the present system, and declared that the assertions of those Frenchmen in foreign parts, who complained that he was obliged to disguise his sentiments, were unfounded in truth. This despatch being communicated on the 23d of April to the national assembly, was received with the loudest applause, and ordered to be posted up in the most conspicuous places of every municipality in the kingdom, to be read at the head of every regiment and company in the army, and on board of every ship in the navy. For several weeks the greatest harmony appeared to prevail between the king and the assembly. Meanwhile the royalists, without being dismayed by the power of the revolutionists, expressed their sentiments with an asperity, which increased the more that in oppression, they saw the injustice of the predominant principles, and felt the misery of their effects. Attachment however to the king's person and family deterred them from measures which they had reason to conclude, would endanger his safety; should they make any decisive movement towards a counter revolution, they did not doubt, a massacre of the royal captives, would be the sacrifice to popular fury. The deliverance of their majesties and the family from a state of real captivity, by whatever na.. e it might be called, would enable them to begin their attempts without hazarding the royal safety. They believed that the majority of the nation secretly cherished the same sentiments with themselves, and would readily co-operate in attempting the restoration of royalty, when they saw hopes of support and success. Under this conviction, his majesty's friends employed their utmost dexterity to effect his escape from Paris. The enterprise appeared arduous, but not impracticable; his majesty was accompanied by a national guard, and also by a Swiss guard; the latter corps was warmly attached to the king and his family. The marquis de Bouillé at different times strongly exhorted the king to fly from his oppressors, and join his friends.[1] After the obstruction of his visit to St. Cloud, he represented to him that by flight, with the countenance of foreign powers, he might be able to head all those friends of moderate liberty, and mixed monarchy, that should be inimical to democratic despotism, and to save his country from the evils by which she was now threatened. At length the marquis prevailed;[m] and it was concerted that the royal family should direct their course to Luxemburgh, the nearest part of the em-

Flight of the king.

l See Bouillé's memoirs.

m The narrative of the king's flight is chiefly compressed from Bouillé's memoirs.

peror's dominions, and to which the road lay through the northern borders of Lorraine, where de Boullé being governor of
Metz, and having the command of the troops, of whom many
were well affected to the king, could facilitate and protect their
progress. On the 18th of June the Russian ambassador procured a passport for a Russian lady about (he said) to set out
for Germany, with a specified number of attendants and two
children. On the 20th, the royal party left Paris about mid- He is ar-
night : at St. Menehoud, a postillion recognising Louis from his rested at
picture, informed the postmaster; this person without ventur- Varennes,
ing to stop the king himself, despatched his son to Varennes,
the next stage, to warn the magistrates. Apprized of his majesty's approach, the magistrates of Varennes were prepared to
seize the monarch; they accordingly took him prisoner, and
sent him and his family, escorted by a strong guard, to Paris.[n]
Meanwhile the king's flight being discovered about eight in
the morning, filled the city with the greatest consternation.
To overtake him was impracticable, as Paris was not two
hundred miles from the frontiers, and he must have already effected one-third of his journey. It was universally believed
that hostilities had been concerted between the king and his
partisans awaiting him on the frontiers of the kingdom, and
that there he was to collect all the force which he could assemble, and invade France. The national assembly having met, Proceed-
gave orders that all people should take up arms to repel the ings of the
attempts expected to be made by the king's party. Louis had during his
left particular directions that no use should be made of the seals absence.
of office till his farther commands; but the assembly decreed
that the king having absented himself, the business of the nation, ought nevertheless to proceed ; for which reason the seals
of the state should, in virtue of their authority as representatives of the nation, be affixed as usual to their decrees, by the
chief minister. The following day, news arriving of the capture of the king, turned their fears into exulting joy. On the He is
22d, the unfortunate prince, amidst the most insulting and tri- back to
umphant acclamations, was conducted to the former place of Paris.
his confinement. After investigating the conduct of various
suspected persons, they at last determined to subject their sovereign himself to a judicial examination; and to manifest their
sentiments respecting kings, quoted the trial of Charles I. of
England. A deputation of three members was appointed to receive the king's deposition: his majesty refused to answer any
interrogatories, but avowed his willingness to make known the
motives for his late departure. His intention (he said) was not
to leave the kingdom, but to repair to Montmedi, a fortified
town on the frontiers, where his personal liberty would be secure, and his public conduct under no restraint; and where he
could have transacted business, together with the assembly,

n See the detail in Bouille's memoirs.

CHAP.
XLVII.

1791.

The mo-
narchical
party, a-
dopt a vi-
gorous sys-
tem, but
too late.

State of
parties.

without the imputation of force. He did not object to the constitution, but only to the small degree of liberty allowed to himself, which so impaired the sanction of his voice, as to give it the appearance of compulsion. A memorial which he left at his departure, more fully detailed the various grounds of his dissatisfaction with the national assembly; recapitulated their various acts, and very ably exposed the despotic usurpation of the revolutionary party. The assembly answered this memorial by a manifesto which was intended to prove that their conduct had been directed by regard to the public good, that its effect was internal prosperity, and a strength that would resist every attempt at a counter revolution. From the unsuccessful effort of the king to escape from thraldom, the republicans derived a great accession of strength. They, however, thought it prudent to assume in the assembly the appearance of moderation, while their emissaries and associates in the clubs were occupied in increasing among the people the prevailing hatred of monarchy. No faith could be reposed, they affirmed, in the king or any of his adherents, who were all plotting a counter revolution. Under pretence of guarding against the designs of the royalists, the assembly assumed the organization of the army, and, indeed, the chief part of the executive power, which, at the confederation, they and the people had sworn to leave in the hands of the king. The monarchical party now adopted a system of open, resolute, and vigorous opposition, which, if chosen at a less advanced stage, might have saved their country from the despotism of paramount democracy. They declared that they never would relinquish the defence of the monarchy: no less than two hundred and eighty joined in a bold and explicit protest against the decrees by which the assembly acted independently of the crown; but now their firm boldness was too late. The national assembly, to guard against foreign invasion, gave directions for fortifying the frontiers. Meanwhile they proceeded with the constitutional code; and the king's late attempt caused the insertion of several articles which had not been before proposed. It was decreed by a great majority, that a king putting himself at the head of an armed force, hostile to the state, should be considered as having abdicated the crown. The same penalty was denounced against him were he to retract his oath of fidelity to the constitution, or incur the guilt of conspiracy against it by a criminal correspondence with the enemies of the nation. It was farther decreed, that after such abdication he should be treated as a simple citizen, and subjected, like all other individuals, to the common course of law. There was a very warm debate about the inviolability of the king's person. At this time there were four parties in the national assembly, and throughout the French empire: the royalists, whose object was the restoration of the monarchy in its former power and splendour; the moderates, who wished a mixed kingly government consisting of different estates, uniting

security and liberty with social order, and subordination: 'the CHAP.
third was the constitutionalists, the supporters of the existing XLVII.
polity, which, levelling all ranks and distinctions of subjects,
still retained the name of king, and were by far the most 1791.
numerous : fourthly, the republicans. who were gaining ground
in number and strength. The royalists and moderates were
eager for the inviolability of the royal person; the constitutionalists were divided: the republicans were strenuously inimical to the proposition; but after a long and animated contest,
perceiving that by persisting in their opposition in this point,
they would lose the support of many constitutionalists, in order
to conciliate the different parties, they proposed certain provisional modifications to accompany the inviolability of the royal
person. Their opponents thought it expedient to accede to a
compromise; and it was accordingly decreed, that the king's Inviolabili-
person, with certain restrictions and limitations, should be in- ty of the
violable. A decree was passed, intrusting the education of the king's per-
dauphin to a governor appointed by the national assembly, in ried in the
order to form him to constitutional principles. The moderate assembly.
party endeavoured again to introduce two separate chambers,
and enlarged on the blessings of the British constitution, but
their propositions were rejected. The constitutional code being
finished, sixty members were appointed to present it to the
king : these waited on his majesty with great solemnity, and
were very graciously received. When they presented the code,
he informed them, that the importance of the subject required
his most attentive and serious examination; and that as soon as
he had acquitted himself of this duty, he would apprize the assembly of his intentions. The violent republicans hoped that
the king would. refuse the constitution. and thereby justify a
different system. The king and his friends were well informed
of their wishes and schemes: the people in general, however,
were not yet disposed to establish a commonwealth. and the
greater number of them were most strenuous constitutionalists.
His friends, aware of the designs of the republicans, advised The king's
the king to accept the constitutional code. Being prevailed vise him to
upon, he on the 13th of September, wrote a letter[o] announcing accept the
his acceptance, and declaring the motives of his former, recent, constitu-
and present conduct. The following day, repairing to the na- tional
tional assembly, he verbally declared his acceptance of the code.
constitution ; and in presence of the assembly,. signed his de- He accepts
claration He was received with great respect, and attended by it in the
the whole assembly on his return to the Thuilleries. amidst national
the acclamations of all Paris. On the 28th of September, the assembly.
constitution was formally proclaimed at Paris. The substance
of the proclamation was, that the important work of the constitution being at length perfected by the assembly, and accepted by the king, it was now intrusted to the protection of

o See State Papers, September 13th, 1791.

CHAP.
XLVII.

1791.

Honours
paid to in-
fidel philo-
sophers.

the legislature, the crown, and the law : to the affection and
fidelity of fathers of families, wives, and mothers ; to the zeal
and attachment of the young citizens, and to the spirit of the
French nation.p While the assembly had been thus engaged in
completing the new constitutional code, it bestowed the highest
honors on the memory of those revolutionizing philosophers
who had contributed so powerfully to the change. As Voltaire
had been so efficacious an enemy to christianity and the church,
the assembly conferred signal honours on his remains, which
they ordered to be transported from his burial place, and deposited in the church of St. Genevive, the place appointed for
receiving the ashes, and perpetuating the memory. of those
who had deserved well of the French nation. Equal honours
were decreed to Rousseau : he had been the object of almost
constant persecution by priests and their votaries. France,
that had now dispelled the clouds of superstition, and broken
the fetters of tyranny, after having profited so much by his labours ought to pay that veneration to his memory when dead,
which ignorance and superstition had denied him while he
was alive. The public joined with the assembly in doing
homage to the characters of these writers, and also to Helvetius
and others, who had distinguished themselves by their exertions
against christianity. To gratify the prevailing sentiment, the
theatres were, as usual, accommodated ; plays were represented in which infidel writers and doctrines were held up to admiration : religion, and the various establishments and orders by
which it had been maintained, were exposed to ridicule and
contempt. That they might contribute as much as possible to
the perpetuation of their system, the revolutionists endeavoured
to instil such sentiments concerning the relations of domestic and
private life, as would best correspond with their political esta-
blishments.q

Want of
money.

Amidst the many plans for regenerating France, there was
one evil which ingenuity could not remedy, this was the scarcity of money. Notwithstanding the immense forfeitures,
there was still a great deficiency of income compared with
expenditure. The army required to support the new liberty
was more numerous and much more expensive, than the armies
of the old monarchy had been at the most extravagant periods.
The populace considered exemption from taxes as one of the
sacred rights which they ought to enjoy, and therefore paid
very sparingly and reluctantly. The boldest and most ardent
champions of religious, moral, civil, and political regeneration,
neglected no opportunity *of committing theft.* The assembly
had declared that all property belonged to the state : from
this comprehensive theorem they deduced a corollary,r that

p See State Papers, September 28th. 1791.
q See Burke's Letter to a member of the National Assembly.
r See Playfair's history of Jacobinism.

whatever was thus acquired by the state belonged to any CHAP.
lawgiver or statesman that could get it into his possession. XLVII.
Though these peculators publicly celebrated the credit of the
national paper, in their own accumulations they gave the pre- 1791.
ference to gold and silver. Many other monied men who
had amassed their riches by fair means, being doubtful concerning the stability of the new government, hoarded the greater
part of their cash. All who were disaffected to the revolutionary system, to discourage assignats as well as to secure their
own property, concealed as much as possible their gold and
silver. A great part of the hidden treasures was lodged in
foreign countries, especially the British funds, which even the
French patriots practically acknowledged to afford the best
security for property.[s] As silver and gold disappeared, the
paper money was proportionably depreciated; and great pecuniary distress prevailed. The indigent now became a more
numerous body than ever, and made desperate through want,
broke into every recess where they thought money was hoarded,
and exercised their depredations with such dexterity, that numbers of individuals lost immense sums, notwithstanding the care-
fulness and extraordinary precautions with which they had been
concealed.[t] As a considerable part of pecuniary distress was
imputed to the administrators of the revenue who were the most
zealous members of the popular party, the aristocrats very minutely investigated and severely scrutinized their conduct; and
when the accounts were presented for inspection, declared open- Inspection
ly that they conceived them false, and the documents and of ac-
vouchers by which they were supported fabricated for the pur- counts.
pose of covering fraud and depredation. The arguments and
statements were very strong and clear, but the assembly overthrew arithmetical results by a majority of votes; and *so far* the
patriots were cleared from the charges. The purgation of these
patriotic financiers was the last important act of the national assembly: on the 30th of September, 1791, this body was dis- Dissolu-
solved by a speech from the king, in which he solemnly repeated tion of the
his promises to maintain the constitution. national as-
Thus terminated the first national assembly of France, which sembly.
in little more than two years had effected a more complete Revision of
change in the government, ranks, orders, laws, religion, doc- pal chan-
trines, opinions, sentiments, and manners of the people, than ges effect-
any legislative body ever before effected in a series of ages. ed by this
It found an absolute monarchy; left an uncontroled popular body.
legislature, with a king nominally limited, actually subdued. found and
It found the laws, which emanating from the Roman code, and left France.
intermingled with the feudal institutions, had spread over the

s So great was the influx of French money into England during the year
1791, that whereas seventy-five had been the average price of the consolidated annuities of three per cent. during the five preceding years of peace
and prosperity, from midsummer 1791 the average price was about eighty-
eight.
t See Playfair on Jacobinism.

CHAP.
XLVII.

1791.

In all its
excesses it
manifested
the genius
and energy
of the
French
character.

Progress of
political
enthu-
siasm.

greater part of Europe, and subsisted in France for twelve centuries; it left a new, code, which originated in a metaphy- sical fiction of universal equality; vindicated to man, when member of a community, all the rights which might belong, to him in a state of separation from his fellow men, and appli- ed to a constituted society principles that presuppose no socie- ty to exist. It found disparity of rank, a political result from inequality of ability and character, extending itself to descend- ants: it left all rank and eminence levelled with meanness and obscurity; seeing that in the progress of hereditary transmis- sion there might be degeneracy, instead of correcting the abuse, it abolished the establishment. It took away one of the strongest incentives to splendid and beneficial actions, in the desire of a parent to acquire, maintain, or extend, honour or dignity, which he may not only enjoy himself, but transmit to his children. It found the people, though turbulent and reluctantly submitting to arbitrary power, well inclined to a free system, which should include order and subordination. Expelling monarchical despotism, instead of stopping at the middle stage, which wisdom dictated, it carried the people to the opposite extreme of democratic anarchy. Impressing the multitude with an opinion that the general will was the sole rule of government, it induced them to suppose that their wills jointly and individually were to be exempt from restraint; and that the subjection of passion to the control of reason and virtue, was an infringement of liberty. It found pro- perty secure, and left arbitrary confiscation predominant. It found the people christians; left them infidels. But whatever opinion impartial posterity may entertain of this legislative body, either in the revolution which they effected, or the new system which they established, it must be admitted that un- common ingenuity, skill, vigour, and perseverance, were dis- played in the means adopted to give to the projected changes the desired effect. Their great and fundamental principle was, to revolutionize the minds of their countrymen, as the only sure means of civil and political revolution. In the clubs, the populace, and the army, modelled by their pleasure, they formed most effectual instruments for carrying their schemes into execution, and rendering their will the paramount law. The first national assembly manifested ability and genius, which, unfortunately for their country, were neither guided by wisdom nor prompted by virtue.

The revolutionary leaders did not confine their efforts to their own country. They employed emissaries in other nations to disseminate their principles and co-operate with champions in the same cause. A spirit of political enthusiasm had, in- deed been spread through a great part of Europe. In Germany, and particularly in the Prussian dominions, a set arose, though under different denominations, who, ascribing the greater part of human calamities to bigotry, superstition, arbitrary power,

and error, endeavoured to awaken their cotemporaries to the
most animated hopes, of the advantages that were to flow from
political improvement, philosophical education, and, in all
things, a vigorous exercise of reason. They professed, at
the same time, the warmest sentiments of humanity, and a
spirit of universal philanthropy. In Britain, as we have seen, Britain.
the leading doctrines of the French revolution were maintained
from various causes, and to different extents, by numbers of
writers, more especially by those of the unitarian dissenters.
In the beginning of this year Dr. Priestley employed his rapid
and indefatigable pen in answering Mr. Burke. After repeating his usual arguments against the existing establishments,
the doctor confined himself to a prophetic vision of the manifold blessings which *were to flow* through the world from the
glorious French revolution. This event was to diffuse liberty,
to meliorate society, and to increase *virtue and happiness.* A Certain in-
political millennium was about to be established, when men genious vi-
should be governed by the purity of their own minds, and the sionaries
moderation of their own desires, without external coercion, expect a
when no authority should exist but that of reason, and no le- political
gislators but philosophers and disseminators of truth. But a millen-
work soon after made its appearance, which however little nium.
entitled to historical record for its own intrinsic merits, is well
worthy of mention as the cause of very important and alarming effects; this was a treatise entitled, *The rights of man*,
by Thomas Paine; already mentioned as the author of a
violent pamphlet written to prevent re-union between Britain
and her colonies. Paine having gone to Paris soon after the Thomas
commencement of the revolution, and thoroughly imbibed its doc- Paine.
trines and sentiments, undertook to induce the English to copy
so glorious a model. Perhaps, indeed, there never was a writer who more completely attained the art of imposing and
impressing nonsense on ignorant and undistinguishing minds,
as sense and sound reasoning, more fitted for playing on the
passions of the vulgar; for gaining their affections by gratifying their prejudices, and through those affections procuring
their assent to any assertions which he chose to advance. His
manner was peculiarly calculated to impress and effect such
objects. The coarse familiarity of his language was in unison Rights of
with vulgar taste; the directness of his efforts and boldness Man—
of his assertions passed with ignorance for the confidence of dexterous
undoubted truth. It was not only the manner of his communi- adaptation
cation, but the substance of his doctrine, that was peculiarly of to the
pleasing to the lower ranks. Vanity, pride, and ambition, are sentiments
passions which exist with as much force in the tap room of an and pas-
alehouse as in a senate. When peasants, labourers, and sions of the
journeymen mechanics, were told that they were as fit for go- vulgar.
verning the country as any man in parliament, it was a very
pleasing idea; it gave an agreeable swell to their self importance: when farther informed, that they were not only quali-

CHAP. fied for such high appointments, but also, if they exerted them-
XLVII. selves that they were within the reach, they were still more
delighted. Through a book so popular, very great addi-
1791   tions were made to the English admirers of the French revo-
Astonish- lution. Societies and clubs, in imitation of the French jaco-
ing popu-
larity of bins, fast increasing in number and divisions, testified the
among the highest approbation of Paine's *Rights of man ;* and very in-
lower   dustriously, through their affiliations, spread cheap editions
ranks. of it among the common people, in all parts of the kingdom.
Com-   On the 14th of July a party of the admirers of the French
memora- revolution met at Birmingham to commemorate its commence-
tion of the ment, under the auspices of its great champion, Dr Priestley.
French re- Previous to the meeting, a handbill[u] was circulated outrage-
volution at ously seditious, stigmatizing all the established orders, and
Birming- urging insurrection against church and state. As the majority
ham.
of the inhabitants were warmly attached to the constitution,
this mischievous production excited very great alarm and rage.
The celebrators having assembled, the populace surrounded the
tavern where they were met ; and as Dr. Priestley had so often and
openly avowed his enmity to the church, they very unfortunately supposed that the present paper, dooming our establishment
to destruction, was composed and dispersed by him and his
Riots. votaries. Under this apprehension they became extremely riotous, burnt one of the conventicles, destroyed several private
Destruc- houses, and, among the rest, the library of Dr. Priestley, con-
tion of Dr. taining a most valuable apparatus for philosophical experiments,
Priestley's and also many manuscripts. The tumults raged for two days
library. so violently that the civil magistrates were inadequate to their
suppression. A military force arriving the third day, dispersed
the mob; and the magistrates, thus assisted, re-established
tranquillity. All friends to our king and constitution sincerely
regretted these lawless proceedings, though evidently originating in a zealous attachment to our establishment. Men of
science lamented the destruction of Dr. Priestley's library, of his
collection, machinery, and compositions on physical subjects,
in which department the exertions of his talents and learning were
supremely valuable.
The doc-   The conduct of Dr. Priestley himself upon this occasion,
tor's con- though it could not diminish the public abhorrence of such
duct, outrageous violence, by no means increased sympathy in the
sufferings of its principal object. Hastening to London, he
wrote an address to the inhabitants of Birmingham, in which,
though he justly exposed the lawless disorder of the insurgents,
and naturally complained of the mischiefs that they had perpetrated, yet the main scope of his letter was to attack the
church, and impute the riots to its principal supporters in the
vicinity. The tumultuous excesses he illogically and falsely

u See Gentleman's Magazine for July, 1791, and Chronicle of Annual Register for the same month.

ascribed to the badness of the cause; as if the intrinsic merits of any system could be lessened by the madness or folly of its defenders. Various addresses of condolence sent to Dr. Priestley by societies of dissenters, and other clubs, very clearly demonstrated the sanguine hopes of the writers, that the downfall of our establishments was approaching. Mr. Benjamin Cooper, secretary of the revolution society, hoped that the church which he (Mr. Benjamin Cooper) pronounced *an ignorant and interested intolerance*, was near its end. Dr. Priestley's reply chimed with this Mr. Benjamin Cooper's tune. The young students at Hackney college, expressed their conviction of the folly of existing establishments. Priestley's answer[x] to their letter may be considered as a *recitation of his political creed.* The hierarchy (he said) equally the bane of christianity and of rational liberty, was about to fall: he exhorted these young men strenuously to use their efforts in so glorious a cause, and to show by the *ardour* and *force* of their exertions against the constituted authorities, how much more *enlightened* understandings, and liberal sentiments were formed by the plan and instructions of their academy, than those that were imbibed in national institutions, fettering and depressing the mind. The doctrines so earnestly inculcated by Priestley and his class of enemies to our establishments, tended to promote the success of Paine's political lessons. Priestley was more fitted for forming visionary and sophistical speculatists among men of superficial literature, whereas Paine was best qualified for effecting a change on the vulgar and ignorant. Priestley dealt chiefly in prescription; his nostrum to be applied to every case was *alterative:* Paine was operatical and proposed *immediate incision.* From Priestley proceeded such philosophers as Godwin and Holcroft, from Paine such practical reformers as Watt and Thelwall. Priestley, to use his own words, had laid the train, Paine's desire was to light the match. Republican, and even democratic principles, continued to make a rapid progress during the remainder of the year. It would be extremely unjust and illiberal to impute to unitarian dissenters indiscriminately, the principles and intentions so obvious in the heresiarch. It is however well known, that if not all, very many of that class of dissenters were at this time inimical to the British constitution of church and state. Besides the dissenters, there were other sets of men who regarded the French revolution as a model for imitation. From causes purely political, without any mixture of theology, some of the votaries of a change in parliament, and other departments of the state, conceived the diffusion of French principles highly favourable to their plans of reform. In the metropolis, besides men of genius and learning, well affected to the French revolution, there was another

x See Gentleman's Magazine, for November, 1791, p. 1024, and Annual Register, 1791. Appendix to Chronicle, p. 86.

CHAP. set of adventurers in literature and politics, very eager in main-
XLVII. taining and spreading its doctrines. If learning be not more
profound in the present than in former ages, it is certainly spread
1791. over a much wider surface. The commercial opulence of the
Wide dif- country encourages the manufacture and sale of literary com-
fusion of modities of every value and denomination. The demand ex-
superficial
literature, tending to a vast variety of productions, which require neither
favourable deep learning nor vigorous genius, the number of authors mul-·
to revolu- tiplies in proportion to the moderate qualifications that are ne-
tionary no- cessary. All these, down to translators of German novels, and
tions.
collectors of paragraphs for daily papers, deem themselves
*persons of genius and erudition, and members of the republic of
letters.* In France, literary men possessed great direction;
many of this class in England conceived, that if the same system were established here, they might rise to be directors in the
new order of things. There were in the literary class, as in
other bodies, persons who, from a benevolent enthusiasm, hoped
that the French constitution would extirpate vice and misery,
and diffuse over the world philanthropy and happiness. Among
the literary producers, there was one set who thought the highest perfection of the human character was sensibility; and
that the restraints of religious and moral precepts, as well as
of political establishments, were harsh and tyrannical, because
they so often contradicted the impulse of sentimental feeling;
these praised the French revolution in the belief that it was
inimical to austere restrictions. Under this class were to be
ranked various female votaries of literature, and at their head
Mary Ann Mary Ann Wollstonecraft, who produced, as a counterpart to
Wollstone- the Rights of Man, a performance entitled the Rights of Woman;
craft.
vindicating to the sex an exemption from various restrictions
to which women had been hitherto subjected from the tyranny
and aristocracy of men; but first and principally from the restraint of chastity; and claiming the free and full indulgence of
every gratification which fancy could suggest, or passion stimu-
Debating late. Besides these classes, there was a great and multiplying
societies. variety of clubs for political discussion and debate. To these
resorted many mechanics, tradesmen, and others, from a desire
extremely prevalent among the lower English, of distinguishing
themselves as *spokesmen.* By degrees, from hearing speeches
and reading pamphlets, they supposed themselves politicians and
philosophers, and thought it incumbent on so enlightened men,
to drop the prejudices of education; and sacrificed religion,
patriotism, and loyalty, at the shrine of vanity. From so many
causes, and through so many agents, the revolutionary doctrines
Cheap edi- were dissembled very widely. To facilitate circulation, opulent
tions of
Tom   votaries published cheap editions of the most inflammatory works,
Paine's   especially Paine's *Rights of Man,* which contained the essence
works.   of all the rest.
But men of high rank, and of the highest ability and character, still admired the French revolution as likely to produce,

when corrected by time and experience, the extension of mode- CHAP.
rate and rational liberty; and besides Dr. Priestley, a few others XLVII.
of eminent genius celebrated the French changes, in literary
works. Of these, by far the most distinguished production that   1791.
appeared in England in vindication of the French revolution was One able
Mr. Mackintosh's answer to Mr. Burke. The obvious purpose and proof this learned and philosophical writer is the melioration of the in favour of
condition of man; convinced that men habitually guided by the French
reason, and determined by virtue, would be happier under small revolution.
than considerable restraints, he proposed a control too feeble for Vindiciæ
the actual state of men now existing; much more of a people Galliciæ.
whose national character, from the old despotism, and other
causes, required a greater degree of control than some of their
neighbours. The erroneous conclusions of this forcible and
profound writer, appear to have arisen from two sources; first
he argued from a supposition of an attainable perfection in the
human character, instead of an accurate estimate of·the degree
of perfection which it had actually attained. Secondly, he appears'to have been misinformed concerning the principles, spirit,
and character of the French revolutionists.

Great and important as the progressions of public opinions Marriage
were in 1791, to arrest the attention of the philosophical ob- of the duke
server, the actual events in England to employ the pen of the of York to
annalist, were not numerous. His highness the duke of York, cess of
in the close of the year 1791, married the eldest princess of Prussia.
Prussia, between whom and the English prince a mutual affection had subsisted ever since the royal youth's residence at the
court of Berlin. The arrival· of the fair stranger, the many
festivities that ensued on so auspicious an occasion, and the appearance of the new married couple in public, agreeably relieved the political discussions which had long absorbed the attention of the public.

CHAP. XLVIII.

Meeting of parliament.—Opposition, censure the conduct of ministry respecting Russia.—Incidental but interesting debates about the French
revolution.—Real difference between.Messrs. Burke and Fox.—Motion of
Mr. Whitbread respecting the riots at Birmingham.—Petition of the
unitarian dissenters—rejected.—Multiplication of political clubs.—Society of the friends of the people—rank, character, and property of the
members.—Mr. Grey—The earl of Lauderdale.—Address of the society
to the people of Great Britain.—Intention good, but tendency dangerous.
—Mr Pitt opposes this engine of change.—Rise and progress of corresponding societies.—Second part of Thomas Paine's Rights of Man.
—Ferment among the populace.—The lower classes become politicians
and statesmen — Proclamation against seditious writings—discussed in
parliament.—Schism among the members of opposition.—The heir apparent testifies his zeal for supporting the British constitution.—General
satisfaction from the manifestation of the prince's sentiments.—Bill for
the amendment of the London police—Humane and discriminate propositions of lord Rawdon for the relief of debtors and benefit of creditors. Abolition of the slave trade is carried in the house of commons.
—Subject discussed in the house of lords.—Duke of Clarence opposes
the abolition.—His highness exhibits a masterly view of the various arguments—The question postponed—State of the crown lands—especially forests.—Mr. Pitt's bill for enclosing parts of the New Forest—disapproved—rejected by the peers—Mr. Dundas's bill for facilitating the
payment of wages and prize money to sailors—passed.—Finances—
Prosperous state of commerce and revenue.—Prospect of farther reducing the debt, and diminishing the taxes.—Flourishing state of India finances—Political state and transactions in India.—Beneficial effects of Mr.
Pitt's legislative measures, and Mr. Dundas's executive management.—
Sir John Macpherson, governor-general.—Able and successful administration—succeeded by lord Cornwallis.—Wise plans of comprehensive improvement—Tippoo Saib recruits his strength.—His ambitious projects
revive—attacks our ally the rajah of Travancore—The British council
remonstrates to no purpose.—The English armies invade.Mysore from
the east and west coasts—Campaign of 1790—indecisive.—1791 lord
Cornwallis himself takes the field—reduces the greater part of Mysore
—comes within sight of Seringapatam—prevented by the overflow of the
Cavery from investing the metropolis of Mysore.—In 1792 besieges Seringapatam.—Tippoo Saib sues for peace, and obtains it at the dictation
of lord Cornwallis.—Generous conduct of his lordship respecting the
prize money.—Measures for the improvement of British India.

CHAP.   PARLIAMENT met January 31st, 1792. His majesty's
XLVIII.   speech mentioned the marriage of his son, and the peace con-
1792.   cluded between Russia and Turkey; but dwelt chiefly on the
         rapidly increasing prosperity of the British nation, which
         must confirm steady and zealous attachment to a constitution
         that we have found, from long experience, to unite the inestima-
         ble blessings of liberty and order; and to which, under the

favour of providence, all our advantages are principally to be ascribed. Members of opposition arraigned the conduct of ministers concerning Russia. Both the accusation and defence necessarily repeated former arguments. The British government thought interference necessary for the balance of power: and though they had sacrificed their own counsels to the voice of the public, the armament prepared upon that occasion had not been useless, as it had prevented the Turks from being obliged to make such concessions as would have been otherwise extorted.[y] Mr. Fox, conceiving himself, and those who coincided in his sentiments respecting the French revolution, indirectly censured by the praises of the British polity, clearly and forcibly demonstrated the compatibility of satisfaction at the downfall of French despotism, so inimical to human rights, and destructive to human happiness, with the highest veneration and warmest attachment to the British constitution, the preserver of rights, and promoters of happiness. He rejoiced at the overthrow of the French despotism because it was bad, but would use every effort to support the British constitution because it was good. In subsequent discussions Mr. Fox, more explicitly than ever, exhibited to the house his sentiments and views on this momentous subject. The French, with characters formed by the old despotism, now emancipated from slavery, are actuated by a most impetuous enthusiasm, which drives them, as it has driven every other votary, to violent excesses. But enthusiasm like every ardent passion, must, as knowledge of human nature and history inform us, ere long subside. It is illogical to impute to the principles of the French revolution the excesses which really arise from a sublimated state of passion that cannot last. Enthusiasm accompanied the reformation; enthusiasm marked the efforts of the puritans, which vindicated British liberty from kingly and priestly tyranny. But the free principles and beneficial establishments subsist many ages after the passion subsided. Do not therefore proscribe the French revolution because a fury that must be temporary has inspired many of its votaries. Let the noxious fumes evaporate, you will retain the genuine spirit of liberty salutary to mankind. Such was the opinion of one personage, not less profound as a political philosopher than forcible as an orator, decisive and energetic as a statesman. Many and various in detail as were the subjects of difference between him and Mr. Burke upon French affairs, the principle was simple. Fox esteemed the outrages incidental effects of an enthusiasm which must be temporary, and which formed no part of the essential character of the revolution: Burke reckoned the execsses necessary and essential parts of the revolution, which legitimately descended from its nature and principles; and increased as they advanced, and which could never cease to operate

CHAP. XLVIII.

1792.

Incidental but interesting debates about the French revolution.

Real difference between Messrs. Burke and Fox.

y See Parliamentary Debates, January 31st, 1792.

CHAP.   until the revolutionary system ceased to exist. Fox thought
XLVIII. the French to be men in the ardent pursuit of what was good,
        and transported by passion beyond the bounds of moderation
1792.   and wisdom; as men pursuing what was really good have often
        been transported: Burke considered the whole nation as actua-
        ted by a spirit of diabolism, eagerly bent on perpetrating all
        possible mischief; a phenomenon never before known in the
        history of mankind; and therefore, if true in that particular
        case, requiring, from its contravention to probability, the strong-
        er evidence. From the opposite theories which they formed
        as political philosophers, these illustrious men deduced very
        opposite practical systems, which they recommended as states-
        men. Burke very early[z] recommended and inculcated a confe-
        deracy, which, upon his hypothesis, was not only wise, but ab-
        solutely necessary. If the French were devils incarnate, to
        prevent the diabolical spirit from operation, neighbouring na-
        tions must overwhelm the power of beings so possessed, or
        perish themselves from the frenzy. Fox, not regarding them
        as a multitude of demons, but as the votaries of enthusiasm,
        recommended to encourage their spirit of liberty, and suffer
        their passions to subside through time, the surest corrector.
        Hostile interference in their internal concerns, would support
        instead of extinguishing their enthusiasm, turn its efforts to ex-
        ternal defence, and give them an energy that would prove
        fatal to those who had roused it into action. These were the
        leading diversities in the theoretical and practical systems of
        Messrs. Fox and Burke, which account for the whole series of
        their respective counsels and conduct concerning France.
        Ministers still avoided the delivery of opinions on events and
        systems which had not interfered with the interest of Great
        Britain. Though the French revolution was never directly
        before the house, yet many of its proceedings arose from ques-
        tions of liberty and reform which that great event was instru-

Motion of   mental in suggesting. Mr. Whitbread, a new member, of good
Mr Whit-   talents, respectable character, and immense fortune, who had
bread re-   joined the party of Mr. Fox, reviewing the riots at Birmingham,
specting   imputed these outrages to the encouragement given by govern-
the riots at
Birming-   ment to persecutors of the dissenters, because they were inimi-
ham.   cal to civil and ecclesiastical tyranny. The magistrates were
        not sufficiently active; the government had been dilatory in
        sending troops; and several rioters had been acquitted: some
        after being condemned, were pardoned. Mr. Dundas, now se-
        cretary of state, said, that on inquiry by the attorney-general,
        there appeared no grounds for censuring the magistrates. From
        a detail of dates, and military stations, he proved that no time
        had been lost in despatching troops to Birmingham. The rioters
        pardoned, had experienced the royal mercy on the recommenda-
        tion of the judges.

        z See his hints for a memorial to be delivered to the French ambassador;
        and Thoughts on French affairs, both written in 1791.

The Scotch episcopalians perceiving a disposition in parliament to extend toleration as far as political security would admit, petitioned for a more ample and unrestrained indulgence,
than that which they had hitherto enjoyed. The former motives for laying them under legal discouragements, subsisted no
longer: the house of Stuart, to which their attachment was
known, was extinct; and their fidelity to the actual government
was not liable, on that account, to be suspected. A petition for
exemption from restraints, the reasons of which no longer existed, was favourably received by a legislature at once indulgent
and discriminating. A bill was accordingly introduced into the
house of lords, and passed both houses. The unitarians alleging Petition of
this law as a precedent, applied for a repeal of the penal statutes; the unita-
and in addition to the usual reasons for refusing their application, rian dis-
their recent practices were stated as inimical to church and state, senters, re-
especially their active dissemination of Paine's works, and other jected.
democratical performances, and their formation of political clubs
and societies.

While various subjects of alleged defect, or projected amend- Multipli-
ment, either in measures of government, or the existing laws cation of
were agitated, a project was formed by a society of gentlemen, political
for making an important change in the composition of the legis- clubs.
lature; this association, consisting of men eminent for talents,
for character, for political, literary, and professional ability;
for landed and mercantile property, for rank and importance
in the community, took to themselves the name of the *friends* Society of
of the people. The following were the general objects which the friends
they professed to seek:—To restore the freedom of election, of the peo-
and to secure to the people a more frequent exercise of their ple,
right of electing their representatives. For the purpose of
these reforms in parliament and the country, they instituted
their society, but though determined to promote them, resolved
to confine their pursuit rigorously to such means, as should be
consistent with the existing constitution. A short declaration
of these objects and means, was framed by a committee, and
signed by the society, with an address to the people of England
tending to prove; first, that reform was wanted; secondly,
that the present, a season of peace and prosperity, was the best
fitted for commencing and establishing that reform; and that
if there existed some degree of discontent, the proposed reform
was well fitted for its removal: that the projected means were
calculated to promote the good without incurring any danger;
thirdly, the objection arising from recent events in France,
could not apply to a case so very different, as the British constitution, with some abuses, was from the old despotism of
France. The object of the society was to recover and preserve
the true balance of the constitution. They announced the determination of the society, to move a reform in parliament early
the ensuing session. On these avowed principles of their union,
they looked with confidence for the co-operation of the British

CHAP.
XLVIII.

1792.

rank, cha-
racter. and
property of
the mem
bers.

The earl of
Lauder-
dale.
Mr. Grey.

Address of
the society
to the peo-
ple of
Great
Britain.

Intention
good, but
.tendency
dangerous.

nation: these are the outlines of an address which may be considered as the manifesto of the *only* respectable body, which, since the commencement of the French revolution, un-- dertook the cause of parliamentary reform. The society in- cluded the greater number of eminent oppositionists in the house of commons with one member of the house of lords: This was James earl of Lauderdale, a nobleman of every consi- derable abilities, and deeply conversant in moral and political philosophy and. history, who had distinguished himself, first as lord Maitland in the house of commons, and afterwards made a no less conspicuous figure in the house of peers. Mr. Grey was appointed to take the leading part for the society in the house of commons. Mr. Grey had been educated an English whig, and considered the opposition party as the supporters of whig principles; and in his present measure conceived himself paving the way for a truly whig parliament. The rank and fortune of this peer and commoner, independent of their re- spective characters, and also the talents, character, and situa- tion of other members, afford very satisfactory grounds for be- lieving them actuated by constitutional motives. It is indeed not impossible to suppose, that subordinate to patriotism mere anti-ministerial considerations might have some weight, and that, as Mr. Pitt had once been the advocate of reform, and was not likely to be so in the present circumstances, they might hope to reduce him to some embarrassment, and expose him to the charge of inconsistency. But though such intentions perhaps operated in some degree with some of the members, there is much reason to be convinced that the friends of the people, as a society, desired only what they conceived to be moderate reform, without having the least design to invade the fundamental parts of the constitution. Their association how- ever was liable to weighty objections : these were not incidental, but resulted from the nature, constitution, and proceedings of the society, combined with the circumstances of the country; their two declared objects, extension of suffrage, and abridg- ment of the duration of parliament, were both expressed in vague terms; so that they might be, and in fact actually were, construed differently by the different votaries of reform : By very many they were interpreted with so great latitude, as to comprehend universal suffrage and annual parliaments. An address to the people of Great Britain, severally or aggregately respectable, as they were desiring them to co-operate in produc- ing an undefined change in the legislature, was a measure, however pure in its motives, very doubtful in its tendency. Presuming the existence of great and radical abuses, it either supposed the incompetency of parliament to remedy evils, and consequently its insufficiency for its constitutional purposes; or was futile in desiring from the people a co-operation which was not wanted. It afterwards appeared that this society proposed to the people, to form themselves into associations to petition

parliament for reform. They thereby afforded a colourable CHAP.
pretext for framing associations composed of very different XLVIII.
members, and entertaining very different sentiments: the friends
of the people eventually produced the affiliated political clubs, 1792.
which are since so well known under the name of the Corresponding Society, and proved so dangerous in their operations.

To sound the disposition of parliament, Mr. Grey, intimated
his intention of urging parliamentary reform early in the next
session. Mr. Pitt totally regardless of the imputations which Mr. Pitt
might be made against himself personally, most unequivocally, this en-
reprobated the design of the society; he was friendly to reform, gine of
peaceably obtained and by general concurrence, but deemed change.
the present season altogether improper; and was therefore
inimical to the attempt. The object of the society was to effect a change by the impulse of the people: he would strenuously oppose the movement of so formidable an engine; the operations and consequences of which was so much calculated to
outgo the intentions of the mover. Mr. Fox did not join a society whose objects and proposed means were so extremely indefinite; and the notice was received with very strong and
general disapprobation. The affiliated clubs now imitating Rise and
the French jacobins, rapidly multiplied; the principal assem- progress
blage of this sort, was the *London Corresponding Society;* the of corres-
secretary of these politicians was one Thomas Hardy, a shoe- societies.
maker, their ostensible plan was under the auspices of this shoemaker, and others of equal political ability, and importance in Second
the community, to effect a change in parliament. The great part of
preceptor of these disciples was Thomas Paine, whose second Thomas
part was now published, and strenuously exhorted the practical Paine's
application of the doctrines, which he had promulgated in his Rights
first; it directed his votaries to pull down every establishment, of Man.
and level all distinctions, in order to enjoy the Rights of Man; Ferment
by far the greater number of the lower ranks and a considerable among the
portion of the middling classes were infected with the revolu- populace.
tionary fever which operated in the wildest and most extravagant ravings. Thomas Paine was represented as the minister
of God, dispensing light to a darkened world:[a] the most indus- The lower
trious and useful classes of the state were seized with a furious classes be-
desire of abandoning their own course of beneficial and pro- come poli-
ductive labour, and taking the management of public affairs ticians and
into their own hands. All the levelling notions of John Ball, statesmen.
John Cade, and the fifth monarchy men appeared to revive
with an immense addition of new extravagance. Government
had considered the theories of Thomas Paine's first part, as
such deviations from common sense, that they expected their
intrinsic absurdity would prevent them from doing any actual
mischief, and had therefore forborne a judicial animadversion

a See a seditious morning paper of those days, called the Argus; also
democratical pamphlets, and the Analytical Review for 1791 and 1792,
passim

CHAP.
XLVIII.

1792.

Proclama-
tion
against
seditious
writings.

Discus-
sions in
parlia-
ment.

Schism
among
members
of opposi-
tion.

which might have given them adventitious importance. But'
when they found, that attempts were made to reduce the theories into practice, and that a second part of the speculative
jargon. added direct exhortation to subvert the constitution,
that they were very generally read by the vulgar and ignorant
classes, and producing other works of a similar tendency, they
adopted means both for a penal retrospect and for future prevention. A prosecution was commenced against Paine; and a
proclamation issued May 21st, warning the people against such
writings and also such correspondencies with foreign parts, as
might produce the same or similar effects; and enjoining all.
magistrates to exert their utmost efforts to discover the authors,
printers, and publishers of such pernicious works. A copy of
the proclamation being laid before the houses of parliament
was taken into consideration on the 25th of May: and the discussion which it underwent showed that a very considerable
schism had taken place among members of opposition. Mr.
Grey and the friends of the people, took the most active share
in censuring the proclamation as neither necessary nor useful
for its ostensible purpose. Their arguments were that the seditious writings which it professed an intention to restrain had
prevailed for more than a year, and if they were so noxious
ought to have been prosecuted at common law: and on their
own hypothesis that the works in question were dangerous,
ministers deserved severe censure for not having before employed proper means to remove this danger. But the prevention
of seditious writings, was not the real object of the proclamation : its purpose was to disparage the friends of the people, to
prevent parliamentary reform, and to disunite the whigs; and
it was farther intended to increase the influence of government
by subjecting to spies and informers, all who should differ from
administration. These sentiments were by no means general,
even among the usual adversaries of Mr. Pitt : in both houses,
many members accustomed to vote with opposition joined the
minister upon this occasion.[b] Considering precaution against
the present rage of innovation as necessary to preserve the
constitution, and their respective rank, property, and distinctions, they joined in supporting a measure calculated, they
conceived, to repress so alarming a spirit. The overthrow of
the aristocracy, abasement of rank, and confiscation of property
under the new French system, impressed on their minds by the
glowing eloquence of Mr. Burke, had alarmed many of the
chief nobility and great landed proprietors for their own privileges and possessions. These with their friends and adherents,
and others who entertained or pretended to entertain similar
sentiments without forming a junction with the ministers, voted
on the same side, on subjects that respected the French revolu-

b See Parliamentary Debates of May 25th, 1792.

'tion or any of its doctrines. In the house of peers, the earl of CHAP.
Lauderdale and the marquis of Lansdown only spoke against XLV II.
the proclamation : from this time ceased the great whig confederacy, which during the principal part of the two former 1792.'
reigns had been predominant; and during the present was so
powerful as to have repeatedly ejected the ministers agreeable
to the crown.

On this occasion the heir apparent for the first time delivered The heir
his sentiments in parliament. His highness considering the apparent
critical state of affairs, as requiring from every friend to his testifies his
country, a manifestation of the principles which he was resolv- zeal for
supporting
ed to support, and the more strongly in proportion to his rank the British
and consequence in the country, spoke to the following effect :— constitu-
" When a subject of such magnitude is before the house, I tion.
" should be deficient in my duty as a member of parliament,
" unmindful of that respect which I owe to the constitution,
" and inattentive to the welfare, the peace, and the happiness
" of the people if I did not state to the world my opinion on
" the present subject of deliberation. I was educated in the
" principles of the British constitution, and shall ever preserve
" its maxims : I shall ever cherish a reverence for the constitu-
" tional liberties of the people; as on those constitutional prin-
" ciples carried uniformly into practice, the happiness of these
" realms depends, I am determined as far as my interest can
" have any force, to give them my firm and constant support.
" The question at issue is in fact, whether the constitution
" is or is not to be maintained ; whether the wild ideas of un-
" tried theory are to conquer the wholesome maxims of esta-
" blished practice ; whether those laws under which we have
" flourished for such a series of years, are to be subverted by a
" reform unsanctioned by the people. As a person nearly and
" dearly interested in the welfare, and I shall emphatically add
" the happiness of the people, it would be treason to the principles
" of my own mind, if I did not come forward and declare my dis-
" approbation of the seditious writings, which have occasioned
" the motion before your lordships My interest is connect-
" ed with the interest of the people; they are so inseparable,
" that unless both parties concurred, the happiness of neither
" could exist. On this great and this solid basis, I ground my
" vote for joining in the address which approves of the procla-
' mation. I exist by the love, the friendship, and the benevo-
" lence of the people, and their cause I will never forsake so
" long as I live." The patriotic sentiments, so forcibly and General sa-
impressively declared in the manly and dignified eloquence of tisfaction
the royal speaker, conveyed very great and general satisfaction from the
manifesta-
to all his hearers, who loved their country, to whatever party tion of the
they might adhere. prince's

Among the applicants for reform this year were the royal sentiments.
boroughs of Scotland, from which certain petitioners stated
flagrant abuses in the administration of the revenues, and also

other grievances, that, if proved, would have demanded redress; but the allegations not having been supported by proof,
the motions arising from the petitions were negatived by a
great majority.

State of the
police in
the metro-
polis.
Great complaints very generally and justly prevailed at this
time of the police of London. The British capital surpasses
in populousness all European cities; in opulence any city
throughout the known world. With wealth comes luxury,
which frequently extends beyond the possessors of riches, pervades many of the poorer classes, and produces habitual
wants, that cannot be supplied but by criminal means. In
a city abounding with every pleasure that can captivate the
human heart, excess and debauchery naturally exist. The
freedom of the country does not permit the same means of
prevention as under absolute governments; hence dissipation
ripens into profligacy, profligacy rises into criminal enormity.
In London the temptations are powerful and seductive to those
indulgencies which corrupt principle, vitiate character, and
waste property. Thence arises the desire of seizing by fraud,
theft, or force, the substance of others as the means of vice.
The practicability of plunder is much greater, and the materials of depredation much more numerous, valuable, and accessible,[e] than in any other city known in the history of mankind. Besides the profligate of our own country, London, like ancient
Rome,[d] is the receptacle of exotic wickedness. Every adventurer,
who, from the poverty of his own country, personal incapacity,
idleness or dissipation, cannot earn a competent subsistence
at home, flocks into England, and preys upon the metropolis.
Hence arises a very great increase of vice and depredation,
in their various departments, but, above all, in that parent of
crime, gaming. This destructive propensity within thirty
years far surpassed the most-extravagant excesses of former
times: descending from the great it pervaded the middle and
lower conditions of life, and generated many enormities. A kin
to this propensity, and originating in the same desire of
acquisition without industry, is the spirit of chimerical adventure in lotteries, funds, and other subjects of hazardous project. Though this spirit enriched several votaries, it empover-
ished many more; and sent them, with the habits of indulgence
which had been cherished during the season of temporary success and aerial hopes, to increase the number of those who find
in fraud and rapine the means of luxurious enjoyments. From
these and many collateral causes, sprang a vast and increasing variety of crimes against the police of the country; against
the persons, habitations, and property of the inhabitants. A
multiplicity of rules and ordinances had been enacted at divers
periods and different occasions, but had experimentally proved

c See Mr. Colquhoun's Treatise on the police, passim.
d See Juvenal, satire iii,

unequal to the ends proposed, for want of sufficient powers CHAP. being lodged in the magistracy and its agents, to discover and XLVIII. suppress in a summary and expeditious manner, whatever had a visible tendency to disturb the public tranquillity. The 1792. justices of the peace were formerly men of rank, property, Justices of character, and consideration in the country where they were the peace. commissioned to act: such gentlemen gratuitously administered justice. The simplicity of life and manners prevalent among our ancestors did not afford that complication of misbehaviour and of transgressions for which such a multiplicity of. laws in modern times, have been provided. But with the modes of artificial life, and the improvements of civilized society, the modes of crime also multiplied; and the once venerable office of justice of the peace became at last too fatiguing and burthensome for people of opulence and distinction. Their unwillingness to accept of so heavy a charge. obliged the ruling powers to apply to individuals of inferior character, who, in accepting of it, had an eye to the profits and emoluments arising from the exercise of their judicial powers. From the period when that honourable and weighty office was thus degraded, it lost, by degrees, the reverence in which it had been held. Venal and mercenary persons were appointed, whose base practices became so notorious, that they drew general odium and contempt both upon themselves and their functions. Hence the vilifying appellation of *a trading justice* was at last applied with too much reason, to many of those who exercised that office. To rectify the abuses imputed to these, and to place the office itself on a footing of respectability proportionate to its importance, in the beginning of March a bill was introduced, with the countenance and Bill for the approbation of government, into the lower house. Different amendment of offices were to be established in the metropolis, at a convenient the London distance from each other for the prompt administration of those police. parts of justice which are within the cognisance of justices of the peace. Three justices were to sit in each of these offices, with a salary of 300*l.* a year to each: they were to be prohibited from taking fees individually; and the money from the fees paid into all the offices, was to be collected and applied to the payment of their salaries and official expenses. That the law might have a preventive operation as well as a penal, a clause was inserted vesting in constables a power to apprehend people who did not give a satisfactory account of themselves, and empowering the justices to commit them as vagabonds. There were, it appeared from evidence, large gangs of the most desperate villains, who were notorious thieves, lived by no other means than plunder, infested every street of the metropolis, and put the person and property of every individual passenger in danger every hour of the day and night. Various objections were made to the bill as an intrenchment on the liberty of the subject, and an increase of

CHAP.
XLVIII
1792.

Humane
and discri-
minate
proposi-
tions of
lord Raw-
don for the
relief of'
debtors
and benefit
of credi-
tors,

is postpo-
ned.

Abolition
of the
slave trade
is carried
in the
commons;

is opposed
in the
lords.
The duke
of Clarence
exhibits a
masterly
view of the
various ar-
guments,
a'd op-
poses the
abolition.

State of
the crown-
lands, es-.
pecially
forests.

the power of the crown ; but on investigation and inquiry, the necessity of it was found so strong as to overrule the arguments of its opponents, and it was passed by a considerable majority.

While these measures were adopted to secure the innocent and industrious against the profligate and atrocious, the wisely generous Rawdon resumed his efforts for affording relief to the unfortunate, by a revision of the laws relating to debtors and creditors. His lordship's general object was, on one hand to compel the debtor to give up all that he possessed, on the other to prevent the creditor, after such a cession of effects, from confining the debtor in jail for life. His lordship, with discriminating justice equal to the benevolence of his spirit, sought the reciprocal benefit of both debtor and creditor. He proposed that no man, to gratify a malignant disposition, should have it in his power to keep his fellow creature in perpetual imprisonment, merely on choosing to pay him four-pence a day ; and that no man should continue in prison to the injury of his creditor, to revel in luxury on property which might pay his debts. As the subject was of very great importance, and required a full and minute discussion of principles, and a very nice discrimination of circumstances and cases, it was recommended to his lordship to postpone its introduction till the following session, by which time it might be maturely weighed; his lordship consenting, for the present withdrew the bill.

The slave trade this session again occupied the commons, and was also considered by the lords. In the lower house, the abolitionists having succeeded in the main question, were divided as to the time when the suppression should take place. At last, at the instance of Messrs. Dundas and Addington, it was agreed that the trade should cease from the 1st of January, 1796. In the house of lords, the same arguments were used that had been employed on both sides by the commons. The duke of Clarence, who now, for the first time, spoke in the house of peers, made a very able, comprehensive, and impressive speech, against the abolition of the slave trade. This royal senator rejected all fanciful theories, argued from plain and stubborn facts, and took for his guide experience, the only unerring director of the statesman and lawgiver. Indeed his repeated orations on this subject exhibited and enforced every argument, from either humanity, justice, political and commercial expediency, that could be adduced; and his clear and manly reasonings constitute the most satisfactory and complete treatise which has hitherto appeared on that side of the question. The majority of the peers concurred with his highness in opposing the abolition, but the final determination of the question was postponed to the succeeding year.

Among the national objects which engrossed this session of parliament, was the state of our forests. Commissioners appointed to inspect the crown lands reported that the principal

reservoir of materials for our navy, the New Forest in Hamp- CH\P.
shire, was in such a condition, that unless proper attention XLVIII.
were bestowed immediately, there would be no timber fit for
public service for many years; but that if adequate care were 1792.
employed, in a short time it might yield a considerable quantity.
Impressed by their representations, Mr. Pitt proposed a bill to Mr. Pitt's
enclose certain parts of the New Forest, for promoting the bill for en-
growth of timber Very strong objections were made to this closing the
proposition in the house of commons, of which many of the New Fo-
members professed to think it a job for the private emolument rest is re-
of Mr. Rose, secretary to the treasury, instead of a national jected by
object. In the house of peers it was strongly reprobated, the peers.
particularly by the lord-chancellor, and was finally relinquished.

Mr. Dundas having in his official capacity, as treasurer of Bill of Mr.
the navy, learned the many difficulties which, through their Dundas for
thoughtlessness and ignorance of business, our gallant support- facilitating
ers often experience in the recovery of their wages and prize the pay-
money, introduced a bill to remove the obstacles, and prevent ment of
the frauds. When the bill was passed, Mr. Dundas sent a wages and
printed account of the spirit, tendency, and provisions of this prize mo-
new act, to all the parochial clergy in Britain, to be read from ney to sai-
the pulpits, and explained to sailors and their connexions. lors.
Since that time the impostures which before were so frequently
practised by personating individuals, forging wills, and other
criminal artifices, are very rarely attempted.

In bringing forward his plan[e] of finance, Mr. Pitt showed Finance.
the national revenue to be in such a favourable state, that a
diminution of the public burthens might be reasonably expected.
The taxes for the year 1791 had produced £16,730,000, exceeding the average of the last four years £500,000; after
subtracting from which the sum total of the expenditures, which
amounted by the reductions proposed to £15,811,000, the permanent income would exceed the permanent expense, including
the million annually appropriated to the extinction of the national debt, by no less than £400,000. The supplies wanted Prosper-
for the present year would amount to £5,654,000, for which ous state of
the means provided constituted a sum that exceeded the former commerce
by £37,000. From the foregoing statement, Mr. Pitt was of opi- and reve-
nion, that the surplus would enable government to take off such nue.
taxes as bore chiefly on the poorer classes, to the amount of
one half of that sum; and to appropriate the other half to the Prospect of
diminution of the public debts. By the methods projected for farther re-
the redemption of this debt, £25,000,000 would be paid off in ducing the
the space of fifteen years; towards which the interest of the debt and
sums annually redeemed would be carried to the sinking fund, taxes.
till the annual sum to be applied to the redemption of that debt
amounted to £4,000,000. This favourable state of the finances

e February 17th.

1792.

Flourish-
ing state of
India finan-
ces.

Political
transac-
tions in In-
dia.

Beneficial
effects of
Mr. Pitt's
legislative
measures,

arose from the actual prosperity of the nation, which, though arrived at an eminent degree, had not yet attained that summit of grandeur and felicity that lay within the reach of its industry and manifold abilities. During the discussion on the ways and means, several severe strictures were made on the mischiefs of lotteries, in wasting the property and corrupting the morals of the lower classes. Ministers replied, that the lottery was a tax upon adventure, which would exist though it were not taxed, it was no reason to forbear a productive source of revenue, that its subject might be abused. Near the close of the session Mr. Dundas laid before the house his annual statement of the income and expenditure of British India. In the preceding session the surplus, after deducting all charges, was £1,409,000, applicable to the reduction of the company's debt, and to purchase an investment. The actual revenues of Bengal, Madras, and Bombay, he stated at £7,350,000; the sum remaining, together with that which arose from the sale of imported goods, amounted to £591,000, from which deducting the interest paid at Bengal, Madras, and Bombay, the surplus of the whole was between three and £400,000. From a general review it appeared, that war with Tippoo Saib, and the interest of the debt had nearly exhausted the whole revenue of India and the profits of the sales; and that a debt had been contracted of £1,782,328, arising from the purchase of investments. Notwithstanding the increase of the India debt, Mr. Dundas stated the affairs of the company to be on no worse a footing at the commencement of 1792, than at the commencement of 1791; and they had been improved at home by the payment of debts to the amount of £694,000, and by an increase of money in their treasury, amounting to £541,400. Thus after a war of eight months, the company's finances were only the worse by £276,000. On the 15th of June, the session terminated with a speech from the throne, in which his majesty, mentioning the state of affairs in Europe, declared his own intention to observe a strict neutrality.

While so many important concerns both internal and continental interested the British nation, a war breaking out in India, engaged a considerable share of the public attention. The peace of Mangalore, caused by the reduction of Tippoo Saib's strength, endured no longer than his deficiencies lasted. Inheriting the views and passions of his father, he sought the empire of India, and as a step to its attainment, the expulsion of the English, his most powerful rivals. For several years he had been collecting and disciplining large armies; and though hopeless of assistance, either from France or the native powers, was not afraid singly to provoke England to war. The English government in India, well informed of his designs, was sufficiently prepared for counteraction. Mr. Pitt's plan for the administration of the Indian territories, executed under the direction of Mr. Dundas, had corrected abuses, restored pro-

sperity and extended revenue through British India. Sir John
Macpherson succeeded Mr. Hastings as governor-general, and
imitated in peace the plans of economy which his predecessor
had concerted and executed, as firmly and constantly as was
possibly consistent with the necessary expenditure of multiplied
wars: he thereby surmounted the pecuniary difficulties in which
the executive government was unavoidably involved. He liquidated the civil and military debts which had been incurred, and
established such a system for reducing expenditure and improving income, as greatly facilitated the beneficial administration
of the board of control. Lord Cornwallis being sent out to India, in spring 1786, and with the double appointment of governor-general and commander in chief, arrived at Calcutta in September, and found the different presidencies in rising prosperity.
He availed himself with moderation, firmness, and temper, of
the best arrangements of his predecessors, and introduced several new regulations that contributed farther to the public welfare, including the security and happiness of the natives. In
Madras and Bombay, affairs were proportionably flourishing;
the British presidencies were also secured by a very powerful
military force. The Nizam and the Mahrattas, as well as less
considerable powers in the southern parts of the peninsula, were
in alliance with the English. Such was the state of India when
Tippoo Saib commenced hostilities by attacking our ally the
rajah of Travancore, whose dominions the English had guaranteed with Tippoo's consent, at the late peace. The council
of Madras remonstrated, and attempted amicable mediation,
but to no purpose. Bound in honour and justice to protect our
ally, the supreme government of Bengal declared war against
the sultan of Mysore. In June 1790, general Meadows from
the Carnatic, invaded Tippoo's dominions, while general Abercrombie from the west, having conquered Cannamore, advanced towards Seringapatam. Tippoo, with masterly skill,
eluded all Meadow's ablest efforts to bring him to battle, and
after a long and tiresome succession of marches and counter-
marches, with several skirmishes, the English general was obliged by the rainy season to return to Madras. Nor were Abercrombie's exertions after the reduction of Cannamore during
the first campaign, attended with any decisive efforts. Though
the campaign in all its operations, very honourably displayed
British valour and conduct, yet it did not answer expectations,
and lord Cornwallis himself judged it expedient to take the
field the following year. In March 1791, he proceeded to Mysore by the Eastern Ghauts; and having surmounted the passes,
he attacked Bangalore, the second city of the Mysorean empire.
Tippoo marched to its relief: for so important an object ventured a pitched battle, was defeated, and the town was taken
by storm. Lord Cornwallis now proceeded towards the capital of Mysore, whither Abercrombie was also advancing with
the western army. In the month of May he arrived in the

CHAP.
XLVIII.

1792.
and Mr.
Dundas's
executive
manage-
ment.
Sir John
Macpher-
son govern-
or-general,
able and
successful
adminis-
tration of.
He is suc-
ceeded by
lord Corn-
wallis, who
proceeds in
plans of
compre-
hensive im-
provement,
Tippoo Saib
recruits his
strength.
He attacks
the rajah of
Travan-
core.

War and
invasion of
Mysore.

Campaign
of 1790,
indecisive.

1791, lord
Cornwallis
invades
Mysore,
a'd com'es
within
sight of
Seringa-
patam;

CHAP.   neighbourhood of Seringapatam, where he found Tippoo very
XLVIII. strongly posted, and protected in front and flank by swamps and
         mountains : not deterred by these difficulties, the British general
1792.   attacked the enemy, and though the Mysoreans made a very
gallant resistance, entirely defeated them, and compelled them to
seek shelter under the guns of the capital.   The sun was about
to set when the victorious English, pursuing the enemy, first
beheld Seringapatam rising upon an island, in all the splendour
of Asiatic magnificence, decorated with sumptuous buildings,
encircled by most beautiful gardens, and defended by strong
and extensive fortifications.   The grand object of their pursuit
now appeared to the English within their immediate grasp :
but disasters which no foresight could have anticipated, and no
wisdom could have prevented, now obstructed its attainment.
A covering army was necessary while they were carrying on
the siege, both for supporting their operations, and for commanding the country, to secure the conveyance of provisions.
When lord Cornwallis set out on this expedition, he had trusted
to the co-operation of the Mahrattas, but was disappointed.
is prevent- Still expecting general Abercrombie, he marched up the Cave-
ed by the ry, to secure and facilitate the advance of the western army;
floods of but the river suddenly swelling, rendered the junction of the
the Cavery two armies impracticable.   The troops from Bombay reluc-
from in- tautly yielding to necessity, departed for the western coast,
vesting the
metropolis exposed to all the fury of the monsoon which was then raging
of Mysore. on the Malabar side of the mountains.   Cornwallis having halted some days to cover the retreat of the other army, deemed
it expedient to defer the siege of Seringapatam till the following campaign, and spent the remainder of the season in reducing the interjacent country and forts, securing communication
with the allies, preparing plentiful supplies of provision, and
making other dispositions for commencing the investment as
soon as the monsoon should be over.   The most difficult and
most important acquisitions during the remainder of this campaign, were Nundydroog, the capital of a rich district, and
Savendroog, or the Rock of Death, a fortress which commanded a great part of the country between Bangalore and Seringa-
In 1792, he patam.   Early in 1792, the Nizam and the Mahrattas joined
besieges the British army, now on its march; and on the 5th of February,
Seringapa- the British host once more appeared before Tippoo's capi-
tam. tal.   On the 7th, soon after midnight, they attacked the sultan's lines, forced his camp, gained a complete victory, and
compelled him to confine himself within the city.   The Bombay army now arriving, a junction was effected between Abercrombie and the commander in chief, and the city was invested on every side.   Seringapatam has the form of a triangle
almost isoskeles : two sides are washed by the river, while the
third is joined to the country.   On this, the western side, as
naturally the most accessible, the fortifications are the strongest : aware of this circumstance, the British general instead of

directing his main attack from the island, resolved to make his **CHAP.** assault across the river. The trenches were open, the siege was **XLVIII.** advancing with great rapidity, and dispositions were made for commencing an immediate assault. The sultan seeing himself 1792. hemmed in on every side, importuned by the people to terminate Tippoo the war, and fearing sedition if he refused, at last sued for peace, sues for which was granted him on the following conditions : first, that he obtains it should cede one half of his dominions to the allied powers; at the dicsecondly, that he should pay three crores, and thirty lacks of tation of rupees;[f] thirdly, that he should unequivocally restore all the lord Cornprisoners which had been taken by the Mysoreans from the time wallis. of Hyder Ally; and fourthly, that two of his three eldest sons should be delivered up as hostages for the due performance of the treaty. Agreeably to these terms, the treasure began to be carried to the British camp, and on the 26th, the young princes were conducted to lord Cornwallis. This ceremony was performed with great pomp: meanwhile Tippoo made some attempts to retard the execution of the treaty, but lord Cornwallis issuing orders for recommencing the siege, he submitted to all the British demands; and the peace was finally concluded on the 19th of March. Thus ended a war which delivered the company from the dangers to which it was exposed, by the inveterate hostility of the most powerful of its neighbours; constantly inclined from interest and connexion, to unite with France. The territories of which Tippoo was divested, were divided between the three allied powers, in three equal portions. This act of good faith to our allies, and the separate arrangements made by lord Cornwallis with the nabobs of Oude and the Carnatic, as well as the principal native rajahs, left a very honourable and advantageous impression of British justice on the memory of the natives. Lord Cornwallis and general Meadows, with great Generous generosity, resigned their share of the plunder to the rest of the conduct of army. His lordship having reduced this potent enemy, turned his lord-his attention to the improvement of the territory which had been specting ceded by the sultan of Mysore. Several British gentlemen had prize moapplied themselves to the study of the oriental languages, and by ney. this means had become acquainted with the history and customs Measures of the natives. Among other valuable information, they had of for the learned the ancient mode of collecting the revenues throughout ment of India. By conversancy in the Persian and Indostan tongues, India. both civil and military officers discovered that the system of collection in Mysore was extremely productive, without oppressing the inhabitants ; and that its chief advantage arose from the imposts being fixed, so that accounts were simplified, and the oppressions of intermediate agents were not suffered to exist. His lordship, from the knowledge which he had acquired concerning Indian systems of finance, extended his improvements to Bengal, and other settlements in India.[g]

f About 4,125,000*l*.   g See Annual Register, 1792.

· CHAP. XLIX. ·

The French revolution chiefly engages the attention of the continent and of Britain.—The British government still resolved not to interfere in the internal affairs of France —Catharine's views respecting Poland—she desires to embroil her powerful neighbors in war with France —Cautious prudence of Leopold.—Convention at Pilnitz between the chief powers of Germany.—The parties disavow hostile intentions against France.—The French king notifies to foreign princes his acceptance of the new constitution—answers of the different powers —Circular note of the emperor.—·weden and Russia urge the German-powers to active hostilities, but without effect.—Proceedings in France - Meeting of the second national assembly—they conceive internal revolution a reason for changing the law of nations —Seizure of Avignon—Operations of the French exiles at Coblentz —The king urges them to return—rapid diminution of the king's power —General character of the French nation,—violent passions, ardour of pursuit, and energy of action—the same character appears in their religious, loyal, and democratical enthusiasm—progress of republicanism.—Intrigues between the loyalists and republican leaders —from the emptiness of the royal coffers are unavailing —The king refuses to attempt his escape —Different views of the emigrant princes and of the nobles—of foreign potentates.—Disputes between the French government and the elector of Treves.—The princes of the empire headed by the emperor and supported by Prussia form a confederacy for defending their rights —Sudden death of the emperor —Preparations of the king of Sweden.— Assassination of that heroic prince.— The French government demands of Austria and Prussia the disavowal of a concert hostile to France - Basis of tranquility proposed by Francis and Frederick William —French declare war against Austria and Prussia —Counter declarations —The duke of Brunswick is appointed general of the combined armies of Germany —Preparations of France and distribution of the armies —The French invade the Austrian Netherlands—their first operations are desultory and unsuccessful—unprovided state of their armies—is imputed to treachery —Dispositions of government to remedy this defect.—The duke of Brunswick arrives at Coblentz —The allied powers misinformed concerning the disposition of the French nation—under this misinformation they concert the plan of the campaign—they propose to invade France and restore monarchy—manifesto of the duke of Brunswick - threatens more than its authors can execute—unwise and hurtful to the cause - State of parties in France - 'the manifesto combines diversity of sentiment into unanimous determination to resist foreign interference—hurries the downfall of kingly power—and completely defeats the purpose of its framers.—Proceedings at Paris—power of the jacobins—the sansculottes—decrees for raising a jacobin army and punishing refractory priests- the king refuses his sanction —La Fayette repairs to Paris - but is obliged to fly—he leaves the French army and surrenders to the Austrians.—French enthusiasm on the approach of the combined armies —Anniversary of July 14th.—The Marseillois— passive citizens.— The mayor of Paris in the name of his constituents demands the deposition of the king —Proceedings of the 10th of August—a banditti assault the Thuilleries —valour of the Swiss guards—they are overpowered and massacred by the savage mob.—

The royal family carried prisoners to the temple—deposition of the king
—plan of provisionary government drawn up by Brissot—manifestoes to
the French and to foreign powers—plan of a convention—persecution of
the unyielding priests.—Church plate is sent to the mint and the bells
are turned into cannon.—Domiciliary visits.—Massacres of September-
atrocious barbarity towards the princess Lamballe.—Meeting of the national convention.—English societies address the convention with congratulations and praise—accompany their commendations with a gift of
shoes.—The corresponding society by its secretary Thomas Hardy, shoemaker, invites the French republic to fraternity with Britain —The convention believes the boasts of such reformers, that they speak the voice of
the British nation—this belief influences their political conduct.—
Schemes of the convention for procuring the property of other countries.
Proceedings of the duke of Brunswick. —He enters France and advances
towards Champaign.—Dumourier the French general, occupies a strong
position.—The duke of Brunswick retreats —Elation of the French.—
Dumourier enters the Netherlands, defeats his enemy at Jemappe, and
reduces the country —The French propose to conquer and revolutionize
all neighboring states.—Noted decree of November 19th, encouraging
foreign nations to revolution.—The French open the Scheldt, contrary
to treaties with Britain.—Effects in Britain from French doctrines and
proceedings.—Anti-constitutional ferment during the recess of 1792.—
English republicans confidently hope for a change.—Alarm of many
friends of the constitution.—Mr Reeve's association against republicans
and levellers—is very generally joined—and gives an important turn to
public opinion.—The king embodies the militia—and at such a crisis summons parliament before the appointed time.

WHILE lord Cornwallis thus effected so great a change
in Indostan the eyes of all Europe were fixed on the revolutions of Poland and France. From the admiration of virtue, or
from the enmity of ambition princes and sujects were warmly interested in the concerns of the gallant, moderate, and discriminating votaries of rational liberty in Poland, but they were
still more universally and vigilantly attentive to the furious
proceedings of democratical and anarchical license in France.
Every friend of human rights regarded the Polish establishment of diffused freedom with complacency and satisfaction;
but he rejoiced at it on account of the Poles themselves, without considering his own security or interest as likely to be affected by the acts of men who confined their views to their
own country. In contemplating France, whether with a
friendly, hostile, or impartial regard, every neighboring beholder saw that the conduct of the Gallic revolutionists would
and must influence other nations. The principles and proceedings, whether deserving praise, reprobation, or a mixture
of both, were general in their object, and energetic in their
operation ; and their effects, happy or miserable, evidently
must be extensive. The monarchs of the continent, conscious
that even moderate and rational liberty was by no means consistent with their own respective governments, regarded with
alarm a system, tending not merely to restrain, but to crush
and annihilate monarchy. Britain declared her resolution not

CHAP.
XLIX.

1792.
The
French re-
volution
chiefly en-
gages the
attention
of the con-
tinent and
of Britain.

CHAP.
XLVIII.

1792.
The Bri
tish go-
vernment
still resol-
ved not to
interfere in
the inter-
nal affairs
of France.
Catha-
rine's
views re-
specting
Poland.

to interfere in the internal affairs of France; but the other sovereigns by no means concurred in disclaiming such intentions;
indeed some of them were severally predisposed to a very contrary policy.   Since the peace of Werela, a close intercourse
had subsisted between Catharine and Gustavus.   The ambitious
empress foiled in the expectations with which she had begun
the Turkish war, saw a fresh barrier rising against her power
in the establishment of Polish independence, which, if suffered
to acquire strength and stability, would counteract her future
projects : she therefore resolved to crush the new-born freedom.
Austria and Prussia only possessed the power of obstructing
her designs; and though they were at present upon amicable
terms, yet she wished to have a stronger security for the forbearance of their inteference : the most effectual she well
knew, would be, if she could occupy them in another quarter.
As a sovereign she was, no doubt, inimical to doctrines so
unpalatable to crowned heads, and in some degree entered
into the sympathies of her neighbours.   But the prevention of
republicanism, not very likely to make its way among the slavish boors of Russia, was by no means her principal or immediate object.   Concealing, however, her real intentions, she expressed not only the strongest indignation against the French
revolutionists, but openly and publicly was the first to declare
herself determined to protect and restore the ancient govern-

She de-
sires to
broil her
powerful
neigh-
bours in
war with
France.

Cautious
prudence
of Leo-
pold.
Conven-
tion at Pil
nitz be-
tween the
chief
power of
Germany.

ment of France.   She applied to the king of Sweden, who very
readily listened to her suggestion, and promised to co-operate.
Catharine and Gustavus expressed the warmest approbation
of the emperor's letter.[a]   The empress despatched a minister
to the French princes at Goblentz, assisted them with money,
and pressed them to enter on their expedition.   Though determined to avoid all active interference herself, she assumed the[b]
appearance of the most ardent zeal against the French revolutionists.   Leopold proceeded in his plans with a caution and
coolness which the more ardent advocates of a counter revolution considered as dilatory.   In August, 1791, a convention was
held at Pilnitz between the emperor, the king of Prussia, and
the elector of Saxony.   The friends of the French revolution
formed an hypothesis that at this meeting a treaty was concluded for two great purposes; the restoration of absolute
monarchy, and the dismemberment of the French empire.[e]

---

a See chapter xlvii.   b Bouille's Memoirs, 457.

e On this fiction the vindicators of France in the other countries, and
especially in Britain, in conversation, speeches, and writings, during the
first five years of the war, rested their principal arguments to prove, that
innocent and unoffending friends of liberty and of the human race, were
driven by necessity to defend themselves against the confederation of
despots which met at Pilnitz A paper was actually published as an authentic copy of this treaty of Pilnitz, not only supported by no evidence,
but carrying, in its intrinsic absurdity, the clearest proofs that it was a forgery. Another fabrication of the same kind was also published as a state

The real object of this convention is now found to have been CHAP.
to preserve the public tranquillity of Europe, and for that pur- XLIX.
pose to endeavour, by combined influence, to effectuate the establishment of a moderate and limited monarchy in France. 1792.
The conference at Pilnitz was attended by the count d'Artois,
the marquis de Bouillé, and Mr. de Calonne. These illustrious
exiles and the contracting sovereigns, stipulated that they would The par-
support the establishment of order and moderate liberty; and ties disa-
that if the king of France would concur, and other potentates intentions
accede to their designs, they would exert their influence and against
power to obtain to his christian majesty freedom of action: France.
Leopold, publishing this engagement, disavowed hostile intentions towards France.

In the month of September a notification was sent by the The
French king to all the crowned heads in Europe, that he had French
accepted the new constitution. Britain sent a very friendly king noti-
answer: in his reply, Leopold expressed his hopes that this fies to fo-
measure might promote the general welfare, remove the fears princes his
for the common cause of sovereigns, and prevent the necessity acceptance
of employing serious precautions against the renewal of licen- of the new
tiousness. The answers of some of the other powers expressed constitu-
their disbelief of the king's freedom, and therefore forebore any tion.
opinion concerning the notification; but the greater number sent of the dif-
friendly replies.[d] In November the emperor sent a note to the ferent pow-
different powers of Europe, declaring that he considered the ers.
French king as free, and the prevailing party to be disposed to Circular
moderate counsels, from which his majesty augured the proba- note of the
ble establishment of a regular and just government, and the con- emperor.
tinuance of tranquillity. But lest the licentious disorders should
be renewed, the emperor thought the other powers should hold
themselves in a state of observation, and cause to be declared
by their respective ministers at Paris, that they would always be
ready to support in concert, on the first emergency, the rights
of the king and the French monarchy.[e] About the end of November his imperial majesty wrote a note to the king of France,
declaring that he had no intention to interfere with the affairs
of his kingdom as long as the French should leave to their king
all the powers[f] which they had voluntarily stipulated, and those
which he had voluntarily accepted, in the new constitutional
contract. Leopold, indeed, manifested in every part of his
proceedings a disposition to maintain peace with the French
nation. He discouraged the emigrants from assembling within

paper, and long referred to under the title of the treaty of Pavia. These
forgeries are very fully and ably exposed in the anti-jacobin newspaper, by
a writer under the signature of D·TECTOR.
    d See in State Papers of October and November 1791, the respective an-
swers.
    e State Papers, November 19th, 1791.
    f This declaration certainly was an interference, as it prescribed bounds
beyond which they were not to go in the arrangement of their own affairs.

CHAP.
XLIX.

1792.
Sweden
and Russia
urge the
German
powers to
active hos-
tilities, but
without ef-
fect.
Proceed-
ings in
France.
Meeting of
the second
national as-
sembly.
They con-
ceive inter-
nal revolu-
tion a rea-
son for
changing
the law of
nations.
Seizure of
Avignon.

Operations
of the
French ex-
iles at Co-
blentz.

The king
urges them
to return.

his territories to concert projects inimical to the revolutionary
government. This conduct was by no means agreeable to the
French 'princes, who strongly expostulated with him on the
measures which he was pursuing. The king of Sweden and
the empress of Russia strenuously urged both the German pò-
tentates to active hostilities,ᵍ but without effect: and long after
the meeting at Pilnitz. the princes who conferred proved themselves inclined to peace.

Meanwhile the second national assembly met in October
1791 : having sworn to maintain the constitution of the kingdom decreed by the constituent assembly, they immediately exhibited a specimen of their legislative justice by passing a law
to rob the pope of the territory of Avignon, which had been
ceded to that prince by the most solemn treaties. This act
was a farther illustration of the principle already exemplified
by the revolutionists in their aggressions on the German sovereigns, that because France had made a change in her internal
constitution,' she was also to alter the law of nations according
to her convenience or pleasure, and to violate the rights of independent states. Their next project of rapacious injustice
was against the bishopric of Basle.ʰ Thither they sent commissioners to settle certain differences which they pretended to
have arisen amongst the inhabitants, and between Avignon and
Carpentras. They began the system of their operations by in-
stituting a club, and gaining partisans among the people; after
massacreing the most peaceable and respectable inhabitants,
they compelled the remainder to meet, and vote their union
with the kingdom of France. The French royalists were forming an army under the prince of Condé ; and, from the continued junction of the nobles and their adherents, they were become very numerous. On the 14th of October, the assembly
decreed, that emigrants thus collected should be from that time
considered as traitors against their country ; and that, from the
1st of January 1792, such as should be known to be assembled
should be punished with death; that all the French princes
and public functionaries who should not return before the 1st of
January, should be adjudged guilty of the same crimes, and
suffer confiscation of their property. The king refused to ratify
this decree, but endeavoured to reconcile the exiles to the
French government by admonition and persuasion : he repeatedly despatched letters to all the princes, earnestly entreating

g The marquis de Bouille, who was in the confidence of the king of
Sweden, quotes several letters which prove Gustavus to have been very
anxious to take an active part in the restoration of monarchy ; but the zeal
of Catharine, he says, never extended beyond professions. Page 457.

h See French journals of the proceedings of the assembly, which the
English reader will find with considerable accuracy, in the Gentleman's
Magazine, and the historical substance in the Annual Registers ; but in
fuller and more minute detail in the Moniteurs.

them to return: he used his endeavours by a public proclamation, as well as all the private influence he possessed, to recall
the emigrants to the bosom of their country, and to retain those
who were inclined to emigrate. The French princes, in answer
to the king's repeated letters, persisted in their refusal to acknowledge the constitution accepted by the king, and declared
their views to be the re-establishment of the Roman catholic
religion, and the restoration to the king of his liberty and legislative authority. The republican party, professing to think
that the king secretly instigated the princes, endeavoured to
excite in the nation a general mistrust of his intentions; and
found their efforts so successful, that they were encouraged to
proceed in executing their design of lessening the power of the
king, and exalting their own on its ruins. The first step they Rapid di-
took for the accomplishment of this end was, by all means to minution of
get rid of the usual marks of respect to his majesty's person. the king's
On the 6th February 1792, Condorcet, appointed president, power.
was ordered to write a letter to the king, in which he was directed to lay aside the title of " your majesty." The lowest rabble were permitted, and even encouraged, to resort to the palace, and revile the royal family in the most gross and profligate
terms.

The national character of Frenchmen appeared totally General
changed: that people which for so many ages had been distin- character
guished for loyalty and religious zeal, now eagerly trampled on of the
every remnant of monarchy or hierarchy. But the change was French na-
really much less in the constituents than in the direction of lent pas-
their character. The French nation has ever been distinguish- sions, ar-
ed for ardour of sensibility to the passion of the times: whatever dour of
objects, prevailing opinions, or sentiments proposed, they pur- pursuit,
sued with an energy, rapidity, and impetuosity, which naturally of action.
and necessarily produced excess. In whatever they sought, The same
eager for pre-eminence, they ran into extremes: the same spe- character
cies of character which, in the sixteenth century, took the lead appears in
in augmenting the domination of priests, in the seventeenth their reli-
century in extending the power of kings, in the eighteenth was al, and de-
pre-eminent in enlarging the sway of atheists and levellers. mocratical
Prompt in invention, and powerful in intelligence; fertile in re- enthusi-
sources, and energetic in execution, the efforts of the French, asm.
whithersoever directed, never failed to be efficacious Readily
susceptible of impression, they were alive to sympathy. Sentiments and opinions were very rapidly communicated: what
Frenchmen seek, they seek in a body. The same national character which supported the catholic league, and spread the
glory and power of Louis XIV. now overthrew the monarchy.
To render the king obnoxious, as well as to increase the means
of force, the republicans repeated the reports of a confederacy
of despots, declared their disbelief of Leopold's pacific professions, and procured a decree of the assembly, demanding satisfaction for the alleged treaty of Pilnitz. The Jacobin clubs,

CHAP. their pamphleteers; journalists, and other agents of confusion
XLIX. and anarchy, rang the changes on the treaty of Pilnitz, and affirmed that there was in the palace a junto, which they called
1792. an Austrian committee, and of which De Gessan, the king's
Progress minister for foreign affairs was alleged to be a leading member.
of republi- At a public trial of one of the journalists for asserting the exist-
canism. ence of such a committee, he could bring no proof to support
his assertion; nor was there ever any evidence adduced to give
the smallest colour to the allegation. The royalists now counteracted the designs of the republicans with openness and bold-
Intrigues ness; they formed several projects for rescuing the king through
between the agency of Danton, and some other outrageous democrats,
the roy who manifested a disposition to betray their cause, if they
alists and found treachery more lucrative than their present violent adhe-
republican
leaders, rence. Danton, that furious republican, received a hundred
from the thousand crowns[i] for supporting motions really favourable to
emptiness the king, though professedly inimical; but finding the resources
of the royal of the court inadequate to his desires, resumed his republican-
ooff rs are ism. It is also affirmed that Brissot offered to betray his cause
unavailing. for a large sum of money, but that the court being either unwilling or unable to afford the bribe required[k] by this patriot,
he persevered in his republican career.[l] A plan was concerted
for effecting the king's escape to the coast of Normandy, which
province was attached to his majesty. His flight, it is believed,
would have been practicable; but the character of the king,
mild and benevolent, without active enterprise, was little fitted
to profit by these opportunities. His departure from Paris
would, he thought, annihilate the monarchical constitution
which he had sworn to protect; and expose all his adherents,
declared or even suspected throughout France, to the infuriate
The king cruelty of dominate licentiousness. From these considerations
refuses to the king refused to attempt his escape. Understanding reports
attempt his to have been circulated that he was projecting to leave Paris;
escape. to contradict these he wrote a letter to the national assembly,
in which he fully explained his sentiments, views, and intentions.[m] The friends of the king, and even of limited monarchy, regretted his unwillingness to venture any step that might
rescue him from a situation in which he was so degraded and
insulted. They conceived that the object was well worthy of
the risk; and that the danger of flight was only doubtful,
whereas the danger of continuance was, if not immediate, at
Different least certain. Of the emigrants, the princes desired the restitu-
views of tion of the old government, but the majority of the exiled nobles
the emi-
grant prin- i See Playfair's History of Jacobinism. k Ibid.
ces and of l Persons thoroughly acquainted with Brissot, declare that avarice was no
the nobles; part of his character; and as Mr. Playfair brings no proofs of his assertion,
disbelieve it as improbable.
m State Papers, February 17th, 1792.

and gentry desired the establishment of a moderate and limited monarchy. Foreign powers were also divided on this subject. Russia, Spain, and Sweden, proposed to restore the ancient monarch. Prussia was somewhat favourable to this opinion, but would not interfere actively, without the co-operation of Leopold. The emperor continued friendly to peace until the conduct of the French government proved to him its determination to disturb tranquillity. They still withheld satisfaction for their usurpation in Lorraine and Alsace. They threatened with hostility the elector of Treves, and alleged various pretexts for their displeasure; but chiefly, his expression of doubts respecting the freedom of the king, and permission given to French emigrants to assemble in his dominions. French troops having approached the frontiers of Treves, and menacing his territories, the elector applied for protection to the emperor. This prince, as head of the Germanic body, proposed to the other princes of the empire, an extensive plan of defensive confederation, for mutual and reciprocal security against French aggression, and ordered marshal Bender to march to the defence of Treves. The French government in a style rather menacing than conciliatory, demanded an explanation of the emperor's intentions. The answer of Leopold, though firm, was still pacific, and disavowed every intention of aggressive hostility. Meanwhile the emperor died very suddenly[n] at Vienna. Francis, his son and successor, declared his intention to persevere in the pacific plan of his father, but to be prepared for defensive war. The French government categorically demanded a declaration of Francis's intentions, and received a reply announcing the existence of a concert for the purposes of defence, but not invasion. As the discussion proceeded, it became progressively more hostile,[o] and both sides prepared for war. Catharine, operating on the heroic mind of the Swedish king Gustavus, had induced him, so early as the summer of 1791, to join in a project for the relief of Louis, even if the emperor and Prussia kept aloof; and Spain soon after had acceded to this design. Gustavus betaking himself to Coblentz, conferred with the exiled princes and nobility; and, encouraged by Catharine, prepared an army which he was to head. He consulted Leopold and Frederick William, but found both unwilling to embark in so very hazardous a project. He however, made dispositions for proceeding in his undertaking without their cooperation, and was preparing to conduct an armament which should make a descent on the coast of France; and co-operate[p]

CHAP. XLIX.

1792. of foreign potentates.

Disputes between the French government and the elector of Treves.

The princes of the empire, headed by the emperor, and supported by Prussia, form a confederacy for defending their rights.

Sudden death of the emperor.

Preparation of the king of Sweden.

n After an illness of two days, which by many was ascribed to poison; but there was never any proof of this assertion.

o See State Papers, from January to March, 1792. Correspondence between the ambassadors and ministers of France and Austria, at Paris and Vienna: especially the letters to and from count Kaunitz.

p Bouillé, chapters xii. and xiii.

CHAP.
XLIX.

1792.
Assassina
tion of that
heroic
prince.

with the royalists, when on the 16th of March 1792, being at a masquerade in his capital, from the hands of Ankerstroem, a disaffected nobleman, who, with others, had plotted against his life, he received a wound which proved mortal. He for twelve days languished in agonizing pain; but retaining the use of his faculties, very ably and completely arranged his affairs; left wise and beneficial directions to his youthful son, and breathed his last on the 28th of March, in the forty-eighth year of his age, and twenty-first of his reign;[q] a prince for genius and heroism rarely surpassed, and not often equalled, even in the glorious annals of Swedish kings. The confederacy of princes which Gustavus and Catharine first proposed for modelling the government of France, without regard to the voice of the people, did not actually take place, yet a different concert, originating chiefly in the imperious and violent conduct of France herself, was unavoidably formed. Dumourier, now foreign minister, in dictatorial terms required both from the courts of Berlin and Vienna the disavowal of any concert inimical to France, and the discontinuance of protection to the French emigrants. The answers of Prussia and Austria proposed a general principle as the basis of tranquillity; *that the French should not consider themselves, as from the revolution, entitled to violate the rights of other powers.* They therefore stated three subjects, on which they demanded satisfaction; first, that a compensation should be given to the princes possessioned in Lorraine and Alsace. Secondly, that satisfaction should be rendered to the pope for the county of Avignon. Thirdly, that the government of France should have a sufficient power to repress whatever might give uneasiness to other states.[r] Dumourier replied that the king of Hungary had no concern in these discussions, repeated in still stronger terms the demand of the French government, and denounced war unless the answer was categorical and speedy. The two German potentates adhering to their former replies, the national assembly, on the 20th of April, declared war against the king of Hungary and Bohemia,[s] and soon after against the king of Prussia. In the decree denouncing hostilities. the national assembly repeated the imputation of a hostile confederacy against the liberties of France. The court of Vienna, in its counter manifesto,[t] disavowed as before, all offensive intentions. The princes of the German empire had formed a concert for reciprocal protection against the unjust pretensions of France, which had considered her internal changes as reasons for deviations from the faith of foreign treaties. The king of Prussia, as member of the confederation for se-

The
French go-
vernment
demands of
Austria
and Prus-
sia the dis-
avowal of a
concert
hostile to
France.
Basis of
tranquilli-
ty propos-
ed by Fran-
cis and
Frederick
William

French de-
clare war
against
Austria
and Prus-
sia.

Counter
declara-
tion.

q On the sudden fall of these two princes, Tom Paine exultingly observed, " See how kings are melting away!"
r See State Papers, April 5th, 1792.
s State Papers, April 20th, 1792.
t State Papers, July 5th 1792.

curing Germany against the aggressions of France, declared himself compelled to take an active share in the war. But besides the defensive objects avowed by Francis, the king of Prussia's manifesto declared, that one of his purposes was to put an end to anarchy in France, to establish a legal power on the essential basis of a monarchical form, and thus give security to other governments against the incendiary attempts and efforts of a frantic troop.[u] Thus the repression of French principles was the chief object which, by his own avowal, induced the king of Prussia to join in hostilities against France; while the protection of the Germanic empire was ostensibly the principal motive of Francis. From the time that Leopold and Frederick William had concluded their alliance, they had joined in deeming the duke of Brunswick, the fittest general for directing the force of the defensive confederacy. An intercourse had been opened between them confidentially on this subject; and the duke was fully apprized, and approved of the enterprize of Leopold. When, from the aggression and declaration of France, war was become absolutely necessary, his serene highness accepted the command, and preparations were made for opening the campaign with the combined forces.

Immediately after the declaration of war by France, the French forces were set in motion. The king had established four armies, in orders to protect and cover his country, and to be in readiness to act as the existing circumstances might direct. The first army was assembled on the northern confines of France, under the command of the marshal de Rochambeau, an experienced officer, who had served in the French armies during the American war. This force was destined to cover the frontier towards the Austrian Netherlands, from the German Ocean at Dunkirk, to Maubeuge, in French Hainault, with their right extending to the Meuse. The marquis de la Fayette, appointed to command the second army, fixed his head-quarters at Metz, and occupied Nancy, Thionville, and Luneville. By this means was the cordon extended from the banks of the Meuse to the Moselle, and retained in check the important fortress of Luxemburg. The third army was formed on the Rhine, under Luckner, and extended from Landau, by Strasburg, towards Montbeliard, and the pass of Porentrui into Switzerland. The possession of this important defile, aided by the favourable position of the mountains of Jura, rendered the extensive frontier of Franche Compte entirely safe. A fourth army was assembled on the side of Savoy, to watch the motions of the king of Sardinia who was expected to join the hostile confederacy. The army of the north, commanded by Rochambeau, amounted to above fifteen thousand men; the centre army commanded by La Fayette, to seventeen thousand; the army of the Rhine, to about twenty-two thousand; the

u See State Papers, July 24th, 1792.

CHAP. fourth, to twelve thousand men. The reduction-of the Low
XLIX. Countries was the object of this campaign ; and the disaffection
to the house of Austria still subsisting in the provinces, afforded
1792. probable expectations of success. The army under Rocham-
The beau occupied the direct road to Brussels, without any impedi-
French in- ment but the garrison of Mons. Fayette commanded the
vade the county of Namur, and the navigation of the Meuse ; but the
Austrian armies were found very imperfectly provided and disciplined :
Nether- the French soldiers were deficient in military experience, in
lands. ammunition, and stores of every sort. Many of the officers
Their first warmly attached to the king were not eager in promoting a
operations cause which they by no means deemed the cause of their sove-
are desul- reign. The war was begun with an attack on the cities of
tory and Mons and Tournay ; but the soldiers being impressed with an
unsuccess- idea that they were betrayed by their generals, retreated in
ful. great confusion ; in their savage rage they murdered several
officers ; and among the rest Dillon, the lieutenant-general.
They trampled upon his body, and having lighted a fire,
threw the corpse into the flames. The infuriated soldiers danced
round the remains of their commander : so ferocious and hardened had they become from the influence of the revolutionary
Unprovid- enthusiasm. Rochambeau, finding the army totally loosened
ed state of from subordination and all honourable principles of duty,
their ar- resigned in the highest disgust. Luckner, appointed com-
mies, mander of the army of the north, found the troops in a much
worse situation than even his predecessor had represented.
La Fayette made the same complaints of the unprovided state
of the force intrusted to his command, as deficient in camp
equipage, artillery, ammunition, and stores of every kind :
is imputed in short, at the commencement of the war the armies of the
to treache- French government were in so very unprovided a state, as
ry. could hardly arise even from negligence, without the co-ope-
Disposi- ration of treachery. In such a condition of the forces it was
tions of go- found necessary, if not to abandon, to postpone the invasion of
vernment the Austrian Netherlands, until discipline were better establish-
to remedy ed, magazines formed, and other dispositions made, proper for a
this defect. campaign.
The Austrian force then in the Netherlands was not very
considerable ; and during the months of May and June the
operations of both sides were desultory and unimportant.
The duke On the 3d of July, the duke of Brunswick arrived at Coblentz,
of Bruns- with the first division of the Prussian army, and in the course
wick ar- of the month being joined by fresh troops, he prepared to
rives at commence the campaign. His serene highness, with very
Coblentz. great talents, the deepest military skill, and eminent political
abilities, is extremely diffident.[x] From that cause, joined to
a gentle and delicate disposition, he frequently treated very in-

x This is the account given of him by various gentlemen who have visited Germany.

ferior capacities with excessive deference, and did not with
sufficient vigor maintain in deliberation the dictates of his
own excellent understanding. Fitted to lead in council and
in war, in the former the duke of Brunswick too frequently
followed. In concerting the plan of the campaign 1792, he
left the formation chiefly to Francis and Frederick William.
These princes were impressed with an opinion, so naturally
adopted, and studiously spread by the emigrants, that the
greater number of Frenchmen were attached to the old government, and would join the standard of monarchy if they
found themselves properly supported; and on this supposition
they formed the plan of the campaign. It was proposed that
the duke of Brunswick should set out from Coblentz with an
army of Prussians; fifty thousand strong, and march by Treves
and Luxemburg to Longvy. After reducing this fortress, and
also if possible Montmedi, the next object was to establish
magazines, continue the march, and invest Verdun. In support
of these, as well as of subsequent operations, the court of
Vienna engaged to bring into the field two armies; the one
to act between the Rhine and the Moselle, and to be of sufficient strength for the purpose of at once menacing Landau
and Saar Louis, and carrying on the siege of Thionville; while
the other, of much superior force, should be engaged in the
Low Countries: their positions were to be as near the Meuse as
possible. Should the expectations of a general rise in France
be disappointed, the duke of Brunswick was not to cross the
river with his main body, but to detach a considerable portion
of his army to co-operate with the Austrians in French Hainault, in reducing Verdun, Sédan, and Meziers. Thus the allies establishing themselves upon the French frontier, would
be able to winter in security, and commence the following campaign with great advantage. To oppose this invading force,
the intrenched camp at Manbeuge, and another at Maulde,
with the strong fortress of Valenciennes, formed the principal
points of defence on the part of the French. Previous to the
march of the duke of Brunswick, a manifesto was composed
under the authority, and according to the sentiments of Francis, now emperor of Germany, and the king of Prussia;
proclaiming the objects of these two princes in their projected
invasion, and issued in the name of the duke of Brunswick,
commander in chief of the expedition. This celebrated manifesto was founded on the same misinformation concerning the
disposition of the French themselves, in which the plan of the
campaign had originated. The proclamation declared, that
the intention of the combined princes was neither to conquer
any part of France, nor to interfere with the internal government of that kingdom, but simply to deliver the king and queen
from captivity. It invited all the French soldiers and other
Frenchmen, to join the combined army in executing this design, promised protection and security to all who should accept

CHAP.
XLIX.

1792.
The allied
powers
misinform-
ed con-
cerning
the dispo-
sition of
the French
nation.
Under this
misinfor-
mation
they con-
cert the
plan of the
campaign.
They pro-
pose to
invade
France and
restore
monarchy.

Manifesto
of the duke
of Bruns-
wick,

threatens
more than
its authors
can exe-.
cute

these proffers : and denounced vengeance against the persons
and property of all who should oppose the efforts of the confederates. It declared the present governors responsible for
every evil that should accrue to the country from their refractory resistance; called on the people to submit to their sovereign, and promised to intercede with the king to grant his
gracious pardon to penitent offenders. It warned other towns,
but especially the city of Paris, that if they refused to comply,
they should be delivered up to military execution. This proclamation was extremely unwise in its principles and tenor,
and no less hurtful in its effects. The hopes of co-operation
which the invaders might reasonably entertain, rested on the
divisions which subsisted in France. The parties continued
reducible for four general classes: first the royalists or abettors of the old government, votaries of an absolute power,
much more slavish than the most bigoted English tory of the
seventeenth century would practically endure. Secondly, the
feuillants, votaries of limited monarchy, desiring a mixture
of liberty and order, and not much differing from English
whigs. Thirdly, the constitutionalist, a still numerous, though
decreasing body, friendly to the system which had been established by the late national assembly. Fourthly, the republicans, with great diversity of particular scheme, but concurring in desiring the total abolition of monarchy. If skilful
means had been employed to unite the three former parties in
defence of monarchy, perhaps the republicans and jacobins
might have been repressed. The proclamation tended to unite
those who were before divided; and by requiring implicit
submission to the king, and declaring that all constitutional
changes should originate in his will, it inculcated principles which only the slavish class would admit; and which
every monarchical votary of liberty must reject as indignantly
as the most outrageous jacobin; besides, it not only was contrary to the sentiments of every French friend of liberty, but
of every French supporter of national independence. Two
foreign sovereigns declared themselves judges between the
members of the French internal government. It could not
be reasonably expected that the national spirit of a Frenchman would suffer such an assumption of power by Germans.
This manifesto in its effects most materially injured the cause
which its framers professed to promote: it afforded a simple
and comprehensive principle of union in the abhorrence of despotism to be imposed by foreign powers : and combined the
friends of moderate and rational liberty, with the most furious
partisans of uncontroled licentiousness. By inducing many
to believe that the king approved its sentiments and principles,
it rendered his personal safety insecure; and hurried the
downfall of the kingly power in France. It totally deviated
from the defensive system which the emperor had professed
to support, and appeared to justify the imputation of a concert

Unwise
and hurt-
ful to the
cause.

State of
of parties
in France.

The ma-
nifesto
combines
diversity
of senti-
ments into
unanimous
determina-
tion to re-
sist foreign
interfe-
rence;

hurries the
downfall of
kingly
power

of kings to crush Gallic liberty. Instead of intimidating, it enraged the French nation : threats, without the power of execution, recoiled in indignant scorn upon the menacers. The apprehension of a confederacy formed to dictate to an independent nation the plan of internal government which it should adopt, roused the pride of Frenchmen, and turned the energy of their character to military efforts, invincible in defence, and, as it afterwards proved, irresistible in attack.

Meanwhile proceedings at Paris were hastening the destruction of monarchy, and in effect co-operating with the dictatorial menaces of the confederated invaders. The friends of monarchy absolute or limited, fast continued to emigrate : the king was forced to dismiss ministers of his own choice, and to receive republicans[y] in their place. The principal direction was possessed by the jacobin clubs : their system of government was simple and obvious, to overawe and overrule the legislative assembly by the national guards, and the mob of Paris, nor did they seem to have any greater or more fixed object in the exercise of their power, than the subversion of all order, and the confusion of all property. There still remained a diversity of condition, notwithstanding all their advances in the levelling system. The proprietors of estates, the merchants, and the manufacturers, were in a better situation than their respective day labourers, and also than many others, who though possessing no property, did not choose to be labourers. The disposition to idleness was greatly increased by the revolution; many of the inhabitants of Paris had chiefly subsisted by the employment which they received from the nobility and other landed proprietors. These sources no longer flowing, numbers became idle from want of industrious occupation. The sovereignty of the mob was not friendly to productive industry; it could not reasonably be expected, that men taught to conceive themselves kings would vouchsafe to dig ditches or pave the streets. Besides, these sovereigns, even if disposed to manual labour, had no time to spare. They were engaged in politics: hence a very numerous body of citizens, who before their elevation had been useful handicraftsmen, were now in their sovereign capacity extremely idle, and extremely poor; and as the new liberty included an exemption from moral and religious restraint, they were also extremely profligate. To the poverty of the idle and profligate, order and tranquillity, which preclude them from their principal means of subsistence, are naturally obnoxious. The meanest and most beggarly citizens sought a more general equalization of property, and assumed the supreme executive authority. A ragged coat was deemed

Marginal notes: CHAP. XLIX. 1792. and completely defeats the purposes of its framers. Proceedings at Paris.

y They consisted of members of a party known by the name of Girondists, from the Girond department, along the banks of the Garonne, which district the principal members of this party represented. They had been constitutionalists, but were now become republicans, though less violent in their professions than the jacobins. Among the Girondists were the chief literary men in France.

an honourable testimony of the wearer's political principles; the lowest rabble, denominated from their dress sansculottes, or ragamuffins, took a lead in public affairs. The national guards were now become somewhat moderate; the jacobin club, the sansculottes, and the violent republicans of every kind, determined that an army should be formed, composed of twenty thousand men, under the control of the republicans.

Decrees for raising a jacobin army, and punishing refractory priests. The king refuses his sanction.

Without any order from the king, the war minister proposed that the desired force should be raised and encamped under the walls of Paris. The assembly, to gratify the sansculottes, passed the decree : under the same influcnee they also enacted another law against refractory priests. The king firmly refused to sanction these laws, which were respectively inimical to his executive authority, and to justice. The republican ministers urged their master, not without threats, to comply with the desire of the people; but his majesty with becoming dignity dismissed these insolent servants. These and other republicans, as the decree was not passed, embodied a jacobin army for themselves. An immense multitude assembled from different quarters of Paris, and, armed with pikes, axes, swords, muskets, and artillery, marched in a body, on the 20th of June, towards the Thuilleries, that they might force the king to sanction the two decrees. Appearing before the palace they demanded admittance, and the gates being thrown open, the rabble violently entered into the apartment of their king. His majesty received this banditti with calmness and moderation; but though not without a dread of being assassinated, he firmly refused to comply with their insolent demands. The fury of the mob at length subsided, and they departed without effecting their purposes. Numbers of the populace who had not been engaged in the outrage, expressed their indignation against the rioters, and their admiration of the king's courage and conduct ; and the various other parties were extremely incensed against the jacobins. The new minister for the home department taking advantage of this disposition, published a proclamation on the subject of the recent tumult, which gave such satisfaction, that many of the departments sent addresses to the king and to the national assembly, demanding that the authors and abettors of the insurrection might be punished with the utmost severity. It appeared on inquiry that Petion the mayor, and Manuel the procurator, might have easily either prevented or quelled this insurrection ; they were therefore both suspended from their offices. The constitutionalists highly approved of this sentence, which the royalists thought too moderate, while the jacobins breathed vengeance against the punishers of a magistrate who instigated insurrection.' La Fayette, finding the tide of popular opinion to run somewhat less against monarchy, repaired to Paris to remonstrate concerning the late outrages; but he possessed neither ability, decision, nor intrepidity to intimidate his enemies; firmness or consistency to give confidence to his

La Fayette repairs to Paris,

friends. After being favourably received by the constitutionalists, he was severely censured by the Girondists and jacobins,
for leaving the army without permission, and attempting to
govern the assembly by intimidation. He left Paris privately;   1792.
commissaries were sent from the assembly to arrest the general ; but is obli-
he gave orders to have these deputies apprehended ; finding ged to fly :,
however, no disposition in his army to afford him support, he the French
withdrew in the night to Liege ; there falling into the hands of army and
the enemy, and refusing to join the standard of the French surrenders
princes, he was sent a prisoner to Namur.   :   to the Aus-
   Intelligence now reached Paris, that the combined armies trians.
were preparing to take the field ; the national assembly endeavoured to inspire the people with an enthusiastic eagerness
to oppose a confederation of despots ; and with the assistance
of the jacobin clubs they were successful. They decreed the French en-
country to be in danger, and published two addresses,[z] the one thusiasm
to the people of France, the other to the army, which were on the ap-
skilfully adapted to their respective objects, powerfully stimu- the com-
lated the enthusiasm of both ; and demonstrated that however bined ar-
deficient the republican leaders might be in virtuous principles, mies.
they could ably call into action the passions and energies of
men. They soon issued a decree, declaring that all citizens
qualified to bear arms, should be in a state of perfect activity.
By this measure the whole order of things was completely
changed ; and the French became a nation of soldiers. The
German potentates threatening the subjugation of a powerful
people, drove the objects of their invasion, to the ferocious
energy of a military democracy. On the 14th of July, vast Anniversa-
bodies of federates arrived in the metropolis, at the invitation ry of the
of the jacobin leaders, to celebrate the third anniversary of the 14th of Ju-
revolution. Among others a troop from Marseilles repaired to ly.
Paris, to participate of the uproar and confusion, which they The Mar-
expected to arise from the celebration. They happened to seillois.
arrive too late for the anniversary, but in sufficient time to produce disorder and tumult. They rendered their first homage
to Petion who was now restored to his office, and were received
with great kindness by that magistrate, whose duty it was to
drive them from the metropolis. They commenced their operations with attacking a party of national guards who were dining
at a tavern, and whom they supposed to be attached to the
king; killing one and wounding five, they paid their respects
to the national assembly ;[a] and were very graciously received
by the republicans. Visiting the jacobins they partook of the
fraternal embrace, and were admitted members of the club.
Small as the qualification of voters denominated active citizens
was, yet the number of those who were not included was very
great, and fast increasing from prevalent idleness and profliga-

   z See State Papers, July, 1792.
   a Ouridge's Annual Register, 1792, chap. xi,

CHAP. cy. These consisting of beggars, vagabonds, and the meanest
XLIX. classes of ruffians, thieves, robbers, and assassins, under the
name of *passive citizens*, assumed to themselves the chief por-
1792. tion of the executive power, in the exercise of which they were
Passive instigated and guided by their friends of the jacobin clubs.
citizens. The passive citizens most joyfully received the Marseillois
strangers, as a co-ordinate estate, but which was soon consolidated into one body with themselves, and their supporters,
while the jacobins by their affiliations and adherents, governed
the whole mass. The republicans now denominated the
Mountain, because they occupied the higher benches in the
assembly room, began to govern the legislature, and from this
time the acts of the national assembly are to be considered as
the acts of the jacobins. They proceeded in their efforts for destroying regal power; they imputed the king's refusal to sanction the two decress, to a correspondence with the exiles and
the enemy. His majesty having in a letter expressed his reprobation of the duke of Brunswick's manifesto, the assembly would
not suffer this expression of his sentiments to be communicated
The mayor to the public. On the 3d of August, Petion demanded, in the
of Paris in name of the forty-eight sections into which Paris was divided,
the name of that the king should be excluded from the throne, and that the
his consti-
tuents, de management of affairs should be intrusted to responsible mini-
mands the sters, until a new king should be chosen, by a national con-
deposition vention; and on the 7th of August, Collot d'Herbois a play-
of the king. actor headed a great body of passive citizens, who made the
same demand to the national assembly. They were answered
that the assembly would take the requisition into consideration.
The king informed of these proceedings addressed a proclamation to the people of France, stating his own conduct and its
reasons; the malicious artifices by which it was misrepresented;
the situation of affairs; the union and vigour required at the
present crisis;[b] but the assembly studiously prevented the
proclamation from being dispersed. On the 9th of August,[c]
the day appointed for considering the proposed deposition of
the king, bodies of armed men surrounded the assembly hall,
menaced[d] and insulted the members whom they conceived inimical to the republican proposition. As an insurrection was
threatened, the constitutional party urged Petion to employ the
municipal force in preventing tumult, but no precautions were
Proceed- adopted. At midnight the tocsin sounded, the Marseillois join-
ings of the ed by other insurgents marched with such arms, as they could
10th of Au- collect, towards the Thuilleries. The council of state made
gust,
vigorous and prudent dispositions for repelling the attack.
The Swiss guards amounting to about a thousand, joined by
other loyal and gallant men, formed themselves to resist the

b State Papers, 17th of August, 1792.
c Annual Register 1792, chap. xi.
d Clery, page 4.

insurgents. In the morning the banditti broke in; [e] and the officers of the household encouraged the valiant defenders of the king : at first the brave champions of their sovereign repulsed the insurgents, but the rebels having corrupted the national guards, the gallant Swiss were overpowered and fell under the murderous hands of the banditti. The king was strongly 'importuned to send for a large body of Swiss guards stationed near Paris, which, joining their heroic countrymen, by steady and disciplined valour might have repelled the infuriate assassins. But the virtues of Louis were not those that were most fitted for encountering the very arduous situations in which he was placed. His gentle disposition was averse to the employment of greater force, as it must cause the farther effusion of blood. In his case wisdom dictated and self-preservation required stern and unyielding firmness ; desperate resolution might perhaps have extricated him from his humiliating state ; concession to so infuriate atrocity, was certain destruction. Louis still hoping to preserve his family sought refuge from the national assembly, the rulers of which, he well knew were seeking his ruin. The royal captives were now confined in the Temple ; the palace which they had left, became a scene of pillage, carnage, and desolation. The jacobins elated with their victory, proceeded to the deposition of the king ; and on the 10th of August a decree was passed, suspending him from his royal functions, and retaining him as an hostage in the hands of the nation. Brissot one of the chief supporters of this revolution, proposed a provisional government until a national convention assembling should determine whether the king was to be restored or dethroned. The executive power was to be lodged in a council of the jacobin ministers lately displaced. Brissot wrote a manifesto addressed to citizens, and a declaration addressed to foreign powers, justifying the decree of the 10th of August; these papers were dexterously executed, and conveyed a high idea of the ingenuity of the author ; skilfully various in its efforts; the declaration to his own countrymen appealed to all their prejudices, and feelings, and passions ; and through the very susceptibility of their minds, imposed on their judgment; his memorial to foreign nations employed plausible sophistry to mislead their understandings, as he could hope for less sympathy from their hearts. The first manifesto is misrepresentation in the shape of impressive eloquence; the second in the form of logical deduction ; and both show the author to have in a high degree united declamation and subtlety. While thus exerting himself for the dethronement and imprisonment of the king, this patriot was said to be carrying on a correspondence for betraying the republican party, by suffering the king to escape; but it was

Marginal notes:
CHAP.
XLIX.

1792.
a banditti
assault the
Thuilleries.

Valour of
the Swiss
guards ;
they are
overpowered and
massacred
by the savage mob ;

the royal
family carried prisoners to
the temple.

Deposition
of the king.
Plan of provisionary
government
drawn by
Brissot.

Manifestoes to the
French
people, and
to foreign
powers.

e See a very interesting and pathetic detail of these dreadful atrocities in Clery's journal, page 2 to 16.

CHAP.
XLIX

1792.

alleged that the bribe which he required, half a million sterling, was more than the royal coffers could afford.[f]

The municipality or common council of Paris, which had been lately constituted and was composed of the very dregs of the people, assumed a large share of the direction of public affairs. By their influence the chief acts of the deliberative body were determined, and through their protection and operation the executive government in a considerable degree was administered. A party of these appearing as the deputies of the people, at the bar of the assembly, demanded in the name of the people, that a national convention should be immediately called. The assembly received these counsellors very graciously, and in obedience to their mandates, resolved to invite the French to form a national convention.

Plan of a convention.

A plan of a convention drawn up by the Brissotines, was disseminated and recommended through the nation. Meanwhile the jacobins and the sansculotte rabble proceeded in their operations. Hitherto they had not entirely crushed the ecclesiastics, or eradicated christianity, but they rapidly proceeded in the attempt. All who continued to refuse perjury were by an act of the assembly ordered to quit the kingdom. The council general next ordered, that all the vessels, images, and other moveables in the churches of Paris, whether gold or silver, should be sent to the mint; the church bells were turned into cannon. From monuments of religion they proceeded to monuments of monarchy: the brazen statues of the princes were converted into ordnance, and thus, it was said, were drawn over from the cause of tyranny to the cause of liberty. The next object after religion and monarchy was property. Confiscation hitherto grasping lands had not extended its rapacity in an equal degree to moveables. To supply this deficiency, they instituted what they called *domiciliary visits*, officers employed by the municipality, and accompanied by *passive citizens*, visited private houses, to search for arms; for refractory priests, or other aristocrats. According to their good pleasure they plundered the houses, arrested or even hanged the owners. Brissot in his professional capacity as editor of a newspaper, very strongly recommended and ardently promoted these *domiciliary visits*; Petion as mayor was still more effectually active; nor was Danton as minister of justice wanting with his assistance. He proposed, and by threats extorted a decree, for *walking commissaries*, who were to co-operate with the domiciliary visitors. Whoever should refuse to give up his arms, or to serve in the army at the requisition of the said commissaries, was to be declared a traitor and punished with death, without any further inquiry. The visitors and commissaries did not murder all those whose houses they inspected; but in many instances contented themselves with sending the owners

Persecution of the unyielding priests. Church plate is sent to the mint, and the bells are turned into cannon.

Domiciliary visits.

Walking commissaries.

f See Playfair's Jacobinism.

to dungeons. The prisons were become extremely full; the rulers thought it expedient to rid themselves of the captives by stirring the populace to another insurrection and massacre. For this purpose it was alleged, that as the duke of Bruns- wick's approach would compel the majority of the inhabitants to take the field, it would be. dangerous to leave the prisons so full of aristocrats and suspected persons.' By these representa- tions the murderous rabble was easily excited to assassination. On the 2d of September the ·oscin was sounded, the cannon of alarm were fired; and bands of ruffians were sent to the dif- ferent prisons. They commenced their carnage with priests; two. hundred and forty-four clergymen were murdered before the evening. The assassins from the ministers of religion, pro- ceeded to the gallant defenders of fallen.monarchy, and mur- dered the Swiss officers, that having been spared at the last massacre were now in prison. From these murders the sava- ges betook themselves to more indiscriminate barbarity, search¬ ed the common prisons and even hospitals, butchered felons, sick, and lunatics,[g] as well as those who were charged with disaffection to government. Among the cases which mòst strongly mark the enormous depravity of those brutalized ·har- barians, none can exceed the massacre of the princess Lam- balle: this lady sprung from the house of Savoy, was dis- tinguished for personal charms, and a character at once amiable and estimable, and had been superintendant of the queen's household. Married to a man whom she loved, she had been deprived of her husband, through the duke of Orleans;[h] and was now principally distinguished for her ardent and invincible attachment to her royal mistress, and her detestation of her husband's murderer. She with other attendants on her queen had been sent to prison on the 10th of August; the murderers about eight in the morning of the 3d of September, entered the apartment in which this unfortunate lady was immured. They offered to save her life, if she would fabricate charges against the queen. The heroic princess returned a resolute negative: they demanded that she should take the oath of liberty and equality, also an oath of hatred to the king, to the queen, and to royalty; the first she consented to take, but refused the last: an assassin said, swear or you are a dead woman; she looked in his face but made no reply. In an instant she was assassina- ted with pikes and bayonets; her clothes were torn off, and the naked corpse exposed to the most abominable insults. With religion, justice, order, and humanity, decency and modesty fled. The head and body of the massacred lady were exposed before the windows of the royal captives, with every circum- stance of brutalism, that diabolical malignity, maddened· to frenzy could suggest.[i] The murders continued for a week; in

g See Annual Register for 1792, chap. iii.   h See this volume, p. 268.
i See Otridge's Register, 1792.

CHAP. which time the numbers of the massacred exceeded five thou-
XLIX. sand. Meanwhile.the elections of the national convention were
carried on under the influence of this terrible system. A cir-
1792. cular letter from the municipality of Paris, countersigned by
Danton, was sent to all the other municipalities, required the
approbation of the whole people to the massacres, and even recommended them to imitation; and under such control the
election proceeded. The clergy were banished; the higher
and the most honourable of the nobility had fled, or fallen by the
hands of the assassins; the royal family in prison expected
their fate; all who favoured royalty or distinction of rank were
held in abhorrence, and those who had been called passive as
well as the active citizens had been declared to be eligible to all
honours and offices of the state. The convention was chiefly
chosen from the most violent and desperate republicans in the
Meeting of kingdom. The members assembled on the 20th of September;
the nation- and the next day they sanctioned the law for abolishing royalty.
al conven- Having thus proscribed monarchy, and established what they
tion. termed the French republic, their next object was, to prepare
for the murder of their dethroned king.

While the French were thus occupied, their proceedings
and projects afforded the highest satisfaction to democratic
republicans in other countries. From England many individuals flocked to Paris as the centre of liberty and happiness.
English so The societies eagerly transmitted their approbation of the
cieties ad- French revolutionists; during the successive degradations of
dress the monarchy they had in their own country published their ap-
convention plause of its invaders, but when the acts of the 10th of August
with con- had deposed and imprisoned the king, murdered his defenders,
gratula- and prostrated his power; when the busy week of September
tions of extending the massacre of aristocrats, shed the blood of the
praise; nobility, gentry, and clergy; when the national convention
doing honour to its own composition, had abolished the kingly office, the English societies eagerly testified their joy and
congratulations on the success of those with whose principles
they declared their own to coincide, and with whose feelings
they avowed the most cordial sympathy. The chief democratical clubs of England, were then the revolution club; the
society for constitutional information, both in London; and the
London corresponding society affiliated with divers places through
the kingdom. The address of the first to the national convention, the shortest of the three, restricted its applause to the
10th of August; augured happiness from the establishment of
a republic on the downfall of monarchy; repeated the opinions of the late Dr. Price; to refresh the memory of revolutionists concerning the treatment of dethroned kings, alluded to
the history of Charles I.; and expressed their hopes that peace
and constant alliance should be established between Britain
and the French republic. The address of the society for
constitutional information approved of the deposition of the

king; expressed hopes that the *same doctrines would be receiv-* CHAP.
ed, and the same example generally followed in other countries. XLIX.
Having declared their sentiments in the most pompous phraseology, they accompanied their eloquence with a donation of ·1792.
shoes;[k] but the most explicit of the address was the pro- accompany
duction of the London corresponding society and its affiliated their com-
friends; which praising the successive and various proceed- menda-
ings of the French republicans, reprobated the policy and tions with
constitution of Britain.[l] This address subscribed by Thomas shoes.
Hardy, shoemaker; and Maurice Margarot, knife-grinder; sta- The cor-
ted divers and manifold blessings which Britons might attain responding
by following the counsels of the said Thomas Hardy, shoe- society by
maker; Maurice Margarot, knife-grinder; and other politi- its secreta-
ciaus equally enlightened, instead of being guided by those Hardy,
who had so long governed Britain: the sentiments of the cor- shoe-
responding society devoted openly to the causes of mankind, maker, in-
existed, they were convinced, in the hearts of all the freemen vites the
of England; they enjoyed by anticipation and with a com- French re-
mon hope, that epoch (not far distant), when the interests of fraternity
Europe and of mankind should invite the two nations to with Bri-
stretch out the hand of fraternity. The convention received tain
the address with very great satisfaction, and strongly expres- The con-
sed their expectations of a similar change in England, and vention be-
their confident hopes, that they speedily would have an opportu- lieves the
nity of congratulating the corresponding friends, on a national such re-
convention established in England: the convention conferred the formers,
honour of citizenship on various individuals belonging to other that they
countries, and some of the departments chose for their repre- speak the
sentatives such Englishmen as they conceived proper delegates the British
for expressing their doctrines and sentiments. Of these the nation.
most noted was Thomas Paine, and the most eminent was Dr.
Priestly; this gentleman was so greatly pleased with the two-
fold honours, conferred on him, by being thus naturalized by
the anarchists, and even deemed worthy of a place in their
convention, that he wrote letters both to the convention and
individual members, manifesting and declaring the warmest
approbation of their principles, as displayed in the suppression
of monarchy and the privileged orders, and the whole series
of revolutianary proceedings : though his age and other circumstances prevented him from accepting a seat himself, he
with the greatest thankfulness and joy accepted it for his son.
The convention flattered with the approbation of one whom
they conceived to be as great in political philosophy as he
really was in physical, ordered his letter to be transcribed into

k The conveyance of these shoes was intrusted to Mr John Frost attorney, who having attained notoriety by professional achievements, had become a very zealous reformer.

l See the respective addresses, Appendix of Otridge's Annual Register
1792, pages, 70, 72, 73.

CHAP. their records, as a testimony of the applause bestowed by
XLIX. foreign illumination on their powerful efforts for the destruction of establishments; they charged their president to inform
1792. their panegyrists that they would with pleasure receive any
This belief reflections which he, from the stores of his wisdom, might trans-
influences mit to an assembly whose sentiments coincided with his own.
their poli- With these testimonies of approbation from British democrats,
tical con- the convention fancied, as indeed did many of the democrats
duct. themselves, that the voice of the British nation was in their
favour, and that Joseph Priestly, dissenting minister; Thomas
Hardy, dissenting shoemaker; Thomas Paine, cashiered ex-
ciseman and deist; Maurice Margarot, knife-grinder and deist; in conveying their own praises of the destruction of rank,
property, and monarchy, including the massacres of August
and September, echoed the feelings of all free Britons, and
that they might soon expect through the British people, the
co-operation of the British force. Pleased with attestations,
of which they so much overrated the value, the convention
proceeded in a series of measures no less conformable to their
own sentiments, than those of their panegyrists. Their operations were directed principally to two objects, plunder and
regicide.

The first head comprehended the farther extension of confiscation, and also the convertibility of the objects thus seized
into gold and silver; which they found much more current
than the assignats. The second consisted of resolutions, decrees, charges, and witnesses, which they were preparing, that
in the eyes of their deluded votaries they might give some
Schemes colour of legality to the murder of their king. In order to
of the con- accumulate gold and silver, they saw other countries might be
vention rendered extremely productive; for that purpose it was deemed
for procu- expedient to combine fraud with robbery. Agents were sent
ring the to London, Amsterdam, Madrid, and other opulent cities, with
property of orders to negociate bills on Paris, payable in assignats. Those
other coun- bills being discounted in foreign countries, the value in specie
tries. was remitted to France: when they became due they were
paid according to the course of exchange; but before this
could be converted into cash, assassins were hired to patrole
the streets and threaten all those who sold gold and silver;[m]
thus the payers were either obliged to take their paper money
or a much less sum in coin than that which had been remitted
from the discount; and by every operation of this kind the
quantity of specie of France was increased. In managing
this traffic, the jacobins, proceeding with their usual energy
and rapidity, rendered it extremely extensive and productive,
before merchants and their bill-brokers discovered its hurtful

m The gold and silver were sold by porters in the streets, some of whom
sold for their own account, but most of them for monied men, who did not
appear. See Playfair's history of Jacobinism.

result, and before political causes put an end to the neutrality
through which it was effected. The convention, with much ease
amassed immense quantities of gold and silver, both into the
public treasury, and into the private coffers of the leaders. The 1792.
other chief object, the murder of the king, they pursued with the
most iniquitous vigour and perseverance.

Meanwhile the Prussian army advanced on the left towards Progress of
Thionville, and the Austrian army on the right through Lux- the duke of
emburgh, in order to join it on the confines of France. The Brunswick.
Austrian general reduced Longvy: the armies, after their junction, captured Verdun, and besieged Thionville. The French
executive government displayed great vigour and judgment in
its exertions and dispositions for resisting and repelling the invasion. The frontier fortresses, which, not without probable
reason, they deemed purposely neglected by the royal officers, they strengthened as well as time and circumstances
would permit, but trusted their principal defence to more inland
posts. Dumourier being appointed general, undertook to defend the passes between Lorraine and Champaign, with a force
much inferior to the German host. Roland, minister for the
home department, issued a proclamation for carrying off provision and forage, cutting down trees, and forming abbatis to
impede the march of the enemy. Leaving the seiges to de- He enters
tachments, the combined troops advanced towards Champaign, France,
and found that the people, far from co-operating, were unani- and advan-
mous and zealous in annoying the invaders. Sickness and wards
want of provisions began to pervade the combined armies: Cham-
still, however, they persevered in advancing. They found paign.
Dumourier posted at St. Menehoud, a strong defile in Cham- Dumourier,
paign. They attacked his front division, but were repulsed. the French
A negotiation was opened on the 22d of September, between occupies a
Dumourier and the king of Prussia, but news arriving of the strong po-
abolition of monarchy, it was broken off. Dumourier now sition.
received daily re-enforcements. The duke of Brunswick and The duke
the king of Prussia perceiving the strength of the enemy before of Bruns-
them, and knowing every thing behind them was hostile, treats.
fearing to be hemmed in, proposed to retreat. The Austrian
general deprecated this movement, but as his command was
only subordinate, he was obliged to comply. On the 30th of
September these denouncers of conquest were compelled to
measure back their steps; and on their route, being annoyed
by the French army, lost numbers of their men, and a great
part of their baggage. Abandoning their conquests, by the
18th of October they completely evacuated France. Thus
ended the confederate invasion, which excited great hopes,
poured out splendid promises and imperious threats, but per- Elation of
formed nothing. It was soon found to have materially injured the French.
the cause of the allies: the flight of the enemy after such
boasts, operating on the susceptibility of the French character,
elevated their spirits, and turned the military energy which de-

CHAP.
XLIX

1792.
Dumourier
enters the
Nether-
lands, de-
feats his
enemy at
Jemappe,
and redu-
ces the
country.

fence had excited to offence and invasion. It was speedily resolved to enter Belgium. Dumourier made rapid and effective
preparations in provisions, artillery, and troops elated with
recent success. In the beginning of November he entered the
Austrian Netherlands; on the fifth of the month attacked the
Austrian army in its camp at Jemappe, gained a complete and
decisive victory. He successively reduced the various cities of
Flanders and Brabant; before the middle of the month was
master of Brussels; and in less than another month had totally
subdued the Austrian Netherlands, except Luxemburgh. General Custine having invaded Germany, captured the cities of
Worms, Spires, and Mentz; subjugated all the country between
the Rhine and the Moselle, except Coblentz; crossing the Rhine,
he also reduced Frankfort.

The
French
propose to
conquer
and revolu-
tionize all
neighbour-
ing states.

These rapid acquisitions operating upon the volatile minds
of the French, inspired them immediately with the desire of
unbounded conquest. They became as eager to sacrifice the
rights and properties of other nations to their ambition and rapacity, as they were to seize the rights and properties of their
fellow-subjects. They resolved to preserve or annul treaties,
without regard to national faith or to justice, as best suited the
boundless advancement of their power. Such being their end,
their means were at once simple and comprehensive: with their
own immense force, to employ in their service the disaffection,
caprice, and folly of individuals and bodies in other countries.
The susceptibility so often remarked in the French character,
appeared in credulity, or the ready admission of assertions and
allegations, as well as in sympathetic accessibility to sentiments
and doctrines. A desire of indefinite change had gone abroad
through the world; and prevalent as this passion really was,
the French both conceived and believed it to be universal. In
Germany and the Netherlands, where it was actually frequent,
they supposed it paramount and irresistible, from hatred to arbitrary power and oppression: in England they apprehended
it to be equally dominant as an emanation from the national
spirit of liberty. The praises bestowed by eminent statesmen
on their efforts to overthrow despotism, they construed into an
unqualified approbation of their levelling system. Hearing of
the rapid dissemination of the work of Paine, they imputed the
reception of these new theories to a desire of applying them to
practice. The addresses which they received from obscure
clubs, they, on the authority of the addressers believed to
speak the voice of the British people. The three last panegyrics of the reforming societies, more specifically expressing a
desire of copying the example of France, strengthened their assurance of British sympathy. The last and strongest of these
banished all doubts that Britain desired to fraternize with
France, in establishing democracy, and levelling ranks and distinctions. So little proportion is there often found in political
history between the importance of instruments and effects, that

a great scheme of French policy, directly hostile to all esta- **CHAP.** blished governments, and one of the chief causes which involved **XLIX.** Britain in a continental war, is to be traced to the ignorant vanity of the meanest mechanics, seeking importance out of 1792. their respective spheres. Believing that Thomas Hardy, a shoemaker, and other worthies of equal political consequence, represented the people of Great Britain, and that the people of other nations concurred to encourage and stimulate subversion of establishment, on the 19th of November 1792, in direct and Noted de- open contradiction to their former professions, not to interfere cree of No- in the internal government of other states, the convention pass- vember ed, by *acclamation*, a decree,[n] " That the national convention 19th, en- " declare, in the name of the French nation, that they will foreign na- " grant fraternity and assistance to all those people who wish tions to re- " to procure liberty ; and that they charge the executive power volu- " to send orders to their generals to give assistance to such tionize. " people as have suffered, or are now suffering, in the cause " of liberty." This decree confirmed a suspicion which had been entertained from their preceding conduct, that the fomen- tation of sedition and insurrection in foreign countries, was a systematic principle[o] of the French republic, immediately produced jealousy and caution in neighbouring nations, and determined most of them to prohibit all intercourse with the French revolutionists. The course of French conquests having led Dumourier to the Scheldt, soon manifested their principles of justice. Their first act, after the reduction of the Austrian The Netherlands, was to open the navigation of the Scheldt, in con- French travention to the most sacred treaties, guaranteed by Britain, open the France herself, and the neighbouring powers. As Holland was so contrary to intimately connected with Britain, their conduct was a peculiar treaties attack upon this country, and showed that they were resolved with to include Britain in a general system of aggressive hostility. Britain. With the designs of France, so inimical to the English govern- Effects in ment, a spirit of disaffection and innovation at home powerfully Britain co-operated. from

During the recess of 1792, the public ferment greatly in- French creased in this country. The efforts of the revolutionary emis- and pro- saries became more strenuous in London, and in the other great ceedings. cities of England. Government had been so completely over- Anti con- turned in France, and the possession of power and property had ferment been so entirely attained by the revolutionary banditti, that their during the courage and audacity were beyond all bounds. The retreat of recess of the duke of Brunswick ; a retreat not displeasing to some even 1792. of the moderate friends of freedom, to those, at least, who con-

n See proceedings of the national convention, November 19th, 1792.
o Most of our readers will probably recollect the noted saying of Brissot, that they must set fire to the four quarters of the globe. I am assured by a gentleman who was then at Paris, and very intimate with the Girondists, that this was the general language and intent.

CHAP. XLIX.

1792.

English republicans confidently hope, for a change.

Alarm of many friends of the constitution.

Mr. Reeves' association against republicans and levellers,

is very generally joined, and gives an important turn to public opinion.

sidered the good of real liberty more than the phantom that had assumed its name in France, greatly emboldened the democratical republicans of England, who admired that phantom. About the capital the approaching downfall of the British constitution became a subject of common talk: kings, lords, and commons, church and state, were described as on the eve of dissolution. The garrulous vanity of some of the weak and ignorat members of the democratic societies boasted of the situations they were to attain under the new order which was to be speedily established. From a multiplicity of circumstances it was evident, that a design was formed to overthrow the constitution, and that there was great confidence of its success. That such proceedings required to be checked, controled, and punished, could not be denied by any who possessed just notions of the nature of man in his social state: government employed such measures as appeared to be the best calculated to correct this growing and threatening mischief. But though the arm of law be sufficiently strong to restrain the open invader of the constitution, it was not altogether able to ferret all the secret arts of its enemies. It became necessary, therefore, to aid the efforts of law by employing their own weapons against the adversaries of our establishments. As the approaches were carried on by societies, clubs, and familiar books, suited to the meanest capacities, it became a public duty to establish associations, and prepare literary works, which might oppose these hostile attacks. An association was accordingly instituted in November, by a gentleman of the law named Mr. Reeves, for the avowed purpose of protecting liberty and property against republicans and levellers. The framer's address, stating with great perspicuity and force the multiplied and pernicious efforts of enemies to our laws and constitution, and calling on all loyal and patriotic men to unite in the defence of every thing that could be dear to Britons, made a very deep and rapid impression, and spread a general alarm. Associations for preserving the constitution multiplied in every part of the kingdom, and were joined by far the greater number of respectable Britons. These associations had a most powerful effect in counteracting the seditious societies ; they recalled the well meaning but misguided votaries of innovation to the recollection of the blessings that were ascertained by experience, diffused a spirit of constitutional loyalty through the country, and brought back the stream of popular opinion into the old and useful channel. Mr. Reeves's exhortations to patriotic and loyal union were accompanied with books explaining the hurtful effects of the Gallic changes ; and though some of these, in reprobating levelling democracy, may have urged to the contrary extreme, yet the main operation was highly salutary : [p] the

---

p For instance, *a letter from Thomas Bull to his brother John,* though it employed some of the exploded sentiments and phraseology of tory bigotry, yet

whole measures prevented or recovered great numbers of Britons
from Jacobinism, which was then the impending danger; and its
certain consequence if allowed to flourish, the subversion of the
British constitution.   Before public opinion had received so salutary a bias, the seditious practices had, in various parts, produced
such disorders as to render the interference of the executive government necessary.   The king availed himself of his legal power The king
to embody the militia, and to convene the parliament before the embodies
time to which it had been prorogued, and to call on the represent- the militia;
ative wisdom of the people for counsel and aid at so momentous and, at
a crisis.   At this eventful period some of the most distinguished such a cri-
supporters of opposition, deeming the present a season of alarm sis, sum-
and danger when all party spirit should subside, when all party liament
contentions should cease, and when all men of all parties should before the
unite to support the constitutional government of the country appointed
considered our external as well as internal enemies to be of a spe- time.
cies which never yet had been encountered; and that no weapon
could so effectually oppose their diabolical designs as an unanimous and determined spirit of resistance : they therefore supported the present measures of administration.

taught the common people the mischiefs of innovating speculations ; and
that their respectability and happiness depended not upon political theories,
but on their practical performance of their professional, moral, and religious duties.

CHAP. L.

Meeting of parliament.—The king states his reasons for this extraordinary
convocation —The chief subjects of consideration the progress of jacobinical principles – The greater number of peers and commoners conceive
there is a design to revolutionize Britain.—A small but able band think
this alarm unfounded —Conduct of France comes before parliament.—
Peace, the interest and wish of Britain, if it could be preserved with security —Commercial policy of the minister, and unprecedented prosperity
of the country —The British government observed a strict neutrality
during the hostilities between France and Germany.—Communication
between lord Grenville and the French ambassador in summer 1792.—
On the deposition of the king of the French, our ambassador to
leave Paris.—This order a necessary consequence of our
king's determination of neutrality.—Careful avoidance of interference in
the internal affairs of France —Application of the emperor and king of
Naples to his Britanic majesty to refuse shelter to murderers.—Strict
adherence to neutrality by Britain —Aggressions on the part of France.
—Chauvelin opens an explanatory negotiation.—Marat, the French secretary comes to London to confer with Mr. Pitt.—Marat justifies, on revolutionary principles, the opening of the Scheldt, though contrary to
the established law of nations.—Mr. Chauvelin supports the same doctrine in his correspondence with lord Grenville—professes the decree of
November 19th not intended against Britain.—Reply of the British minister.—He declares Britain will not suffer France to annul at pleasure
the established law of nations.—Britain requires France to forego her
projects of invading and revolutionizing other countries.—Alien bill—is
passed into a law.—Augmentation of the army and navy —Proceedings
at Paris.—Gironde party—their literary ability. boundless ambition, and
wild projects.—The Mountain blood-thirsty and ferocious.—Robespierre,
Danton, and Marat.—The Girondists desire to spare the king's life —The
Mountain and the mob desire regicide.— Pusillanimity of Brissot and the
other Girondists —A decree is passed for bringing the king to trial.—
Attempts to break the spirit of Louis—trial—not the smallest proof of
guilt.—Complicated iniquity of the process in principle, substance, and
mode.— Self possession and magnanimity of the persecuted monarch.—
Sentence —Last interview of Louis with his family.—Execution—an awful monument of the doctrines and sentiments that governed France.—
Chauvelin demands from the British minister the recognition of the
French republic—and the admission of its ambassador.—The British government refuses a recognition which would be an interference in the
internal affairs of France.—Chauvelin remonstrates against the alien bill
and the preparations of Britain—on the massacre of Louis ordered to
leave the country ·· France declares war against Britain and Holland —
Review of the conduct of both parties.—Opinions of Messrs. Burke,
Fox, and Pitt respectively, on the French revolution— the justice and policy of a war —Messrs. Burke and Pitt support the war on different
grounds.— Mr. Pitt proposes the security of Britain Mr. Burke the restoration of monarchy in France.—Violent party censures —Impartial
history finds in the conduct of neither just grounds for their reciprocal
reproach.—Public opinion favourable to war with France.—In declaring
war against France our king spoke the voice of a great majority of his
people.

ON the 13th of December parliament was assembled; and the king stated his various reasons for his present measures. Notwithstanding the strict neutrality which he had uniformly observed in the war now raging on the continent, he could not, without concern, observe the strong indications of an intention in the French to excite disturbances in other countries; to pursue views of conquest and aggrandizement inconsistent with the balance of Europe: to disregard the rights of neutral powers; and to adopt towards his allies the states-general measures neither conformable to the public law, nor to the positive articles of existing treaties. He had, therefore, found it necessary to make some augmentation of his army and navy: these exertions were demanded by the present state of affairs, to maintain internal tranquillity, and render a temperate and firm conduct effectual for preserving the blessings of peace.

CHAP. L.

1792.

Meeting of parliament

The king states his reasons for this extraordinary convocation.

Never did more momentous objects engage the attention of a British legislature than in the present session of parliament. Its many and complicated subjects of deliberation, however, chiefly resulted from two subjects which were interwoven together, the operation of jacobinical principles, and the advances of French power. Ministers, supported not only by those members who for many years approved of their measures, but by most of the principal nobility of the old whig interest, Mr. Burke, the veteran champion of that party, and many other gentlemen of the house of commons, also, many members of the North part of the coalition, especially lord Loughborough, now chancellor, declared their conviction that a design existed to revolutionize this country; and that notwithstanding the precautions which were already employed, still constant vigilance, prudence, firmness, and energy, was necessary to prevent its success. It had not hitherto, they admitted, produced such overt acts as to afford grounds for judicial process; but had discovered and even manifested, such objects and tendencies as demanded the counteraction of deliberative wisdom. There were intentions and schemes openly avowed, with many more reasonably suspected, for effecting the downfall of the existing establishments; although no specific treasonable plot had been actually brought to light, the evidence for the existence of such projects consisted of conversations, writings, specific proceedings, and general conduct. To repress such views and attempts, preventive and prospective measures were proposed, and not retrospective or penal.

Chief subjects of deliberation, the progress of jacobinical principles and French power.

The greater number of peers and commoners conceive there is a design to revolutionize Britain.

A small but very able band, headed by Mr. Fox, ridiculed and reprobated this apprehension; they said it was a mere chimera, like the popish plot of Titus Oates; that it sprang from the eloquent misrepresentations of Mr. Burke's invectives against the French revolution, and was supported by ministers to promote an alarm; divide the whigs; oppose the spirit of liberty and the reform of parliament, and facilitate hostility with France. These were the respective positions of the bodies

A small but able band think this alarm unfounded.

CHAP. 'which now differed in parliament on the subject of internal
L.   danger., Mr. Fox and his adherents called for specific instances,
       of conspiracy; and alleged, that since none were produced,
1792. the pretended schemes and projects did not exist; that every
       general imputation must be an aggregate of particular facts, or
       must be false; 'that the deduction of probable practice from
       speculative theories was inconsistent with sound reason and ex-
       perience, and totally unworthy of a legislature. Must parlia-
       ment interfere whenever a hot-brained enthusiast writes or
       speaks nonsense ? for the ostensible purposes of ministry, their
       arguments were futile; but for their real purposes their asser-
       tions and actions were well adapted. At the commencement
       of the session, Mr. Pitt was absent, his seat being vacated by
       his acceptancy of the Cinque Ports. The chief impugner of
       these arguments of Mr. Fox and his friends was Mr. Burke,
       who showing the connexion between opinion and conduct, in-
       sisted that the strongest preventive policy was necessary to the
       salvation of Britain.

Conduct of   Meanwhile the conduct of France towards this country, with
France   the part which Britain should act in the present emergency,
comes be-   was a subject of anxious concern to the parliament and nation.
fore parlia-
ment   To a commercial country, deriving its prosperity from its in-
Peace the dustry and arts, cherished by peace, war was an evil to be in-
interest   curred from no motive but necessity. The extension of com-
and wish   merce, manufactures, and every other source of private wealth
of Britain,   and public revenue, though very far from exclusively occupying
if it could
be preserv. the official talents of Mr. Pitt, had hitherto been the most con-
ed with   stantly prominent objects of his administration. He had pro-
security.   moted trade by the wisest and most efficacious means, removal
Commer-   of restraint, and reciprocation of profit. His exertions had been
cial policy   eminently successful where legislative or ministerial effort was
of the min-
ister, and   necessary, and when no political interference was wanted, the
unprece-   national capital, enterprise, and skill, nourished by freedom. and
dented   secured by peace, had done the rest. The prosperity of the
prosperity   country was beyond the precedent of any former time, and was
of the
country.   evidently more abundant from the advantages of neutrality in
The Bri-   the midst of surrounding war. The British government was
tish go-   fully aware of the blessings of peace, and the British sovereign
vernment   had uniformly adhered to the strictest neutrality, and also to a
observed a rigid forbearance from any interference in the internal affairs of
strict neu-   France. As soon as the king of France had announced to
trality dur-
ing the   Britain the commencement of a war between the German pow-
hostilities   ers and his dominions, the court of London issued a proclama-
between   tion, enjoining his majesty's subjects to receive no commission
France and from any enemy of the French king; and in no way to act
Germany.   hostilely to him or his people, under the severest penalties.q
       His majesty's subjects observed these injunctions, and no com-
       plaint of aggression was alleged either by the French king or

q See Debrett's State-Papers, 25th May, 1792.

nation. Chauvelin, the French ambassador, applied to the British secretary on the 24th of May, stating, that the proclamation published a few days before against seditious writings, contained expressions which might, contrary to the intentions of the British ministry, encourage an idea that France was considered as inimical to the internal tranquillity of England, and requested his application might be communicated to parliament. Lord Grenville's reply represented that Mr. Chauvelin had deviated (he was convinced unintentionally) from the rules of this kingdom in applying to the British minister to communicate to parliament any subject of diplomatic discussion; but assured the French minister of the cordiality of the British sovereign. Chauvelin acknowledged his mistake, and expressed his satisfaction at the assurances of amity which the British minister's answers had conveyed. On the 18th of June, Mr. Chauvelin delivered a note, stating that by the proceedings of the German potentates, the balance of Europe, the independence of the different powers, the general peace, every consideration which at all times has fixed the attention of the English government, was at once exposed and threatened; and inviting his Britannic majesty, for the general security, to interfere with his mediation. His majesty adhering rigidly to the neutrality, replied, that consistently with his impartial determination, he could not propose an intervention when not solicited by both parties.[r] On the 11th of July 1792, a small fleet sailed from Portsmouth, under the command of admiral lord Hood, to perform naval evolutions in the channel. The whole squadron consisted only of five ships of the line, besides frigates and sloops: it had but a fortnight's provision on board, and had manifestly no other destination than a sea review. The matter, however, was so magnified in France, and was represented in such a false light, that on the 26th of July, an immediate armament of thirty ships of the line was proposed in the national assembly, and the marine committee was ordered to draw up a report on the subject, and, present it within a few days.[s] But Mr. Chauvelin having inquired into the object and circumstances of this squadron, was satisfied that its purpose was not hostile; and the French government and nation were convinced that Britain had no design of taking any part with their enemies.[t] His Britannic majesty being informed of the suspension of the king's executive power by the decree of the 10th of August, directed his secretary of state,[u] Mr. Dundas, to write

CHAP.
L.

1792.

Communications between lord Grenville and the French ambassador in summer, 1792.

On the deposition of the king of the French, our sovereign orders his ambassador to leave Paris.

r See the series of correspondence between lord Grenville and Mr. Chauvelin, in Debrett's State Papers, from May 24, to July 8th, 1792.

s See the Moniteur, 28th July, 1792.

t See Moniteurs of July 1792, and Marsh's History of the Politics of Great Britain and France, chapter viii.

u Lord Grenville happening to be out of town when this intelligence arrived, that part of his official business was performed by his colleague.

CHAP.
L.

1792.

This order a necessary consequence of our determination of neutrality.

Careful avoidance of interfe- rence in the inter- nal affairs of France.

to lord Gower the British ambassador at Paris, that the exercise of the executive power having been withdrawn from his chris- tian majesty, the credentials of the ambassador were no longer valid, and that he should return to England. This order his majesty deemed a necessary consequence from his determination of neutrality ;[x] because the continuance of his representative at Paris, treating as the sovereign power that party which had overturned, the constitution recently established, would have been an interference in the internal affairs of France, by an acknowledgment of the republican party, in preference to the loyalists and constitutionalists. Our king, conformably to the same cautious and discriminating policy, which would not pledge to the one side his virtual support, repeated his declara- tions, that he would not support the other, or in any way inter- fere in the internal arrangements of France.[y] Lord Gower having communicated his royal master's orders, and the reasons wherein they were founded, to Mr. Le Brun, minister for foreign affairs, he expressed the regret of the executive council that the ambassador was to be withdrawn, but its satisfaction at his majesty's continued assurance of neutrality, and determination not to interfere in the internal affairs of France.[z] In the month of September, the emperor and king of Naples stated to his Britannic majesty their apprehensions, that the atrocities of Paris would extend to the lives of the royal family, and expres- sed their hopes, that should such a nefarious crime be commit- ted, his majesty would grant, no asylum to the perpetrators.[a] With a request so conformable to justice, humanity, a sense of moral obligation, and an abhorrence of enormous wickedness, the king complied, and induced his allies the states-general to form the same resolution. Here there was certainly no devia- tion from neutrality, no interference in the constitution of the French polity, unless a declared purpose to refuse shelter to a party that shall commit an atrocious murder, be an interference in that party's private concerns. When the theatre of advancing conquest approached so near the united Netherlands, the king declared his resolution to adhere to their mutual alliance, and at the same time expressed his conviction that the belligerent parties would not violate the neutrality of the states-general. From the time of the deposition of the king, Chauvelin could not properly be considered as ambassador from the monarch of France. Nevertheless the British government not only permit- ted him to reside in London, but even negotiated with him when he was agent for the executive council ; and lord Gren-

Applica- tion of the emperor and king of Naples to his Britan- nic majesty to refuse shelter to murderers.

Strict ad- herence to neutrality by Britain.

x The reader will see the arguments on this subject minutely and accu- rately detailed in Marsh's History of the Politics of Great Britain and France.
y See Debrett's State Papers, 17th August, 1792.
z Brissot and his party deemed the recall of the ambassador a hostile step; but admitted there had been none before. See Marsh, chap. ix.
a Debrett's State Papers, September 20th.

ville assured him "that outward forms would be no hindrance
"to his Britannic majesty, whenever the question related to ex-
"planations, which might be satisfactory and advantageous to
"both parties;" and Mr. Pitt declared to the same gentleman,
that it was his desire to avoid a war, and to receive a proof of
the same sentiments from the French ministry.[b] MR. PITT
AND HIS COADJUTORS WERE UNIFORMLY CON-
SISTENT IN MAINTAINING ONE PRINCIPLE, THAT
THE INTERNAL CHANGES OF FRANCE DID NOT
PRECLUDE AMITY WITH ENGLAND; and therein totally differed from Mr. Burke and his followers. No communications material to the question of aggression passed between
Mr. Chauvelin and the Britsh minister, until the decree of the
19th of November, the invasion of the rights of our allies, and
the rapid advances of French conquest, aroused and alarmed
Britain. There had hitherto been strict neutrality, as we have
seen, on the part of England, while there had been aggression
on the part of France; for that aggression satisfaction was due,
and the French professed to wish a pacific adjustment. Chauvelin was instructed to open an explanatory negotiation, conformable to those professions. Ostensibly to promote this purpose, Mr. Marat, now foreign minister of France, came himself
to England, to confer with Mr. Pitt. In the uniform spirit of
neutrality which Britain observed, his majesty avoided discussing the diplomatic capacity of the ministers who were sent by
the executive council of France; because an admission of their
official character would import the admission of the executorial
competency of their employers; would have been a declaration
in favour of a party, and consequently an interference in the
internal arrangements of France. Mr. Pitt therefore did not
meet Mr. Marat as the minister of England the minister of
France; however they did meet, and their conversation, as
detailed from Mr. Marat's communication,[e] showed on the one
hand, that MR. PITT EARNESTLY DESIRED TO PRESERVE PEACE
WITH FRANCE; and on the other, that the French agent endeavoured to explain the obnoxious decree as not intended to apply to Britain. On the subject of the Scheldt, Marat stated
that the order of the council, and the decree of the national
convention concerning that navigation, founded on the most sacred principles of Gallic liberty, were irrevocable, and thus admitted that the internal change in France was by its votaries
considered as authorizing them to violate the rights of foreign
and independent nations; and that they were resolved to make
no satisfaction for an injury inflicted, in conformity to this prin-

Aggression on the part of France. Chauvelin opens an explanatory negotiation.

Marat, the French secretary, comes to London, to confer with Mr. Pitt.

Marat justifies on revolutionary principles the opening of the Scheldt, though contrary to the established law of nations.

b These declarations of our two ministers are acknowledged by Brissot, in
his report to the convention of the 12th of January 1793; and in the official revolutionary journal, the Moniteur of 15th January, 1793.
c By Mr Miles, in a work entitled *Authentic correspondence.* Mr. Miles
was the intimate and confidential friend of Mr. Marat.

CHAP.
L.

1792.

Mr. Chauvelin supports the
same doctrine in his
correspondence with
lord Grenville,

and professes the
decree of
19th Nov.
not intended against
Britain.

Reply of
the British
minister.

He declares Britain will
not suffer
France to
annul at
pleasure
the established law
of nations.

Britain
requires
France to
forego her
projects of
invading
and revolutionizing
other
countries.

ciple.[d] The same questions were agitated with much greater
particularity of detail, and reciprocation of argument, between
monsieur Chauvelin and lord Grenville, in the latter end of November, and during the month of December. Chauvelin maintained the right of the French to open the navigation of the
Scheldt: he however declared, by order of the executive council, that if at the end of the war the Belgians were unfettered,
and in full possession of their liberty relinquished this navigation, the French would decline all opposition. This answer
evinced a firm and unalterable resolution of adhering not only
to the infraction of the treaty of Utrecht, but also of dismembering the Netherlands from the Austrian dominions, and making them dependant on France: he obstinately contended
that the decree of the 19th of November, could have no reference to Great Britain, and declared that if Holland continued
to observe neutrality, France would not invade her dominions.
These professions the British minister would not believe, because
they were totally contradicted by actual conduct. Concerning
the decree of the convention, the application of these principles to the British king's dominions was unequivocally shown,
by the public reception given to the promoters of sedition in
this country, and by the speeches made to them precisely at
the time of this decree, and since on several different occasions.
At the very time France declared she would not invade Holland, she had already attacked that nation by opening the
Scheldt. France, (said the British minister) can have no right
to annul the stipulations relative to the Scheldt, unless she have
also the right to set aside equally all the other treaties, between
all the powers of Europe, and all the other rights of England,
or of her allies. She can even have no pretence to interfere in
the question of opening the Scheldt, unless she were the sovereign of the Low Countries, or had the right to dictate laws to
all Europe. England will never consent that France shall arrogate the power of annulling at her pleasure, and under the
pretence of a pretended natural right, of which she makes herself the only judge, the political system of Europe, established
by solemn treaties, and guaranteed by the consent of all the
powers. This government, adhering to the maxims which it
has followed for more than a century, will also never see with
indifference that France shall make herself, either directly or
indirectly, sovereign of the Low Countries, or general arbitress
of the rights and liberties of Europe. If France is really desirous of maintaining friendship and peace with England, she
must show herself disposed to renounce her views of aggression and aggrandizement, and to confine herself within her
own territory, without insulting other governments, disturbing

[d] See Marat's letter to his colleague. Debrett's State Papers, 2d December, 1792.

their tranquillity, and violating their rights;[e] but the French CHAP.
government positively refused to satisfy Britain for the violation L.
of treaties.[f]

1792.

In the consideration of peace or war with the French republic, the proceedings of the French rulers, the negotiation between their agents and British ministers, and the conduct of our executive and legislative government, are so much interwoven, that it is frequently necessary to change the scene to review their process of action and reaction, and exhibit cause and effect. Before we follow this negotiation to its close, it is necessary to present to our readers, both internal legislative proceedings, and foreign acts, by which the negotiation was effected. The great objects of alarm, both to the British government, and to the principal part of the British nation, were the rapid advances of French principles, and the rapid progress of French power. The number of aliens at this time in Britain far surpassed the usual influx. Of these, many so conducted themselves as to justify a suspicion of their evil intentions towards this country. Agreeably to the system of Alien bill, preventive policy already recorded, the attorney-general proposed to parliament to provide for the public tranquillity by subjecting the resort and residence of aliens to certain regulations. All foreigners arriving in the kingdom were, by the plan of ministers, to explain their reasons for coming into this country, to give up all arms except those commonly used for defence or dress. In their several removals through the country, they were to use passports, by which their actual residence, or occasional movements might be manifest, and their conduct easily observed. Those who received eleemosynary support, were to be distributed in districts where they would be more liable to the vigilance of the civil power. Particular attention was to be paid to foreigners who had visited this kingdom within the present year, who should hereafter come without obvious reasons, and be thus more obnoxious to prudent suspicion. Such were the objects and chief provisions of the law known is passed by the name of the *alien bill*. Those members of both houses into a law. who had denied the existence of the dangerous doctrines, consistently with their opinions, opposed a measure, which upon their hypothesis was certainly not necessary. Admitting, how- Augment-ever, that there was external danger from abroad, they unani- ation of the mously agreed to ministerial motions for the augmentation of army and the army and navy.

While the British legislature was making these dispositions Proceed-against internal and foreign danger, an event took place in ings at France, the flagrant injustice and ferocious cruelty of which Paris. most fatally manifested the pitch of infuriate wickedness at

e See correspondence between lord Grenville and Mr. Chauvelin, in December 1792. State papers for that period.

f See Chauvelin's note to lord Grenville, Dec. 27th.

CHAP. which the jacobins were arrived. The republicans now con-
L.   sisted of two parties, the Girondists and the Mountain. The
     former contained the principal part of the literary class, in-
1792. genious, and eloquent enemies of monarchy; the latter, the
     most daring and blood-thirsty directors of the murderous mobs,
Gironde the votaries of anarchy. Though men of genius, the leaders
party: of the Gironde were much more brilliant than solid.[g] Form-
     ed to the metaphysical theories long so prevalent in France,
     they carried their visionary abstractions to practical life. To
     subtle paradox and ingenious hypothesis, which are commonly
     the effusions of literary retirement, many of them joined profli-
     gate corruption and rapacity, that would grasp all the wealth
     and power which stimulate injustice in the active world, with
     an excessive vanity, which represented all the objects of their
     cupidity as within the reach of their invention and enterprise.
their lite- This wildness of speculative sciolism, this depravity of prin-
rary abili- ciple and pursuit, and this overweening self estimation dictat-
ty, bound- ed their internal and external politics: impelled them to seek
less ambi- a republic not suitable to the human character; in which
tion and levelling others, they might themselves enjoy boundless riches
wild pro- and unlimited sway; and to fancy that their talents and ad-
jects. dress could employ both the weakness and strength of various
     parties, in their own and other countries as instruments for
     the execution of their designs. To extend the circle of their
     proposed dominion, and also that pre-eminence which French-
     men have always sought, they formed their boundless schemes
     of national aggrandizement;[h] of embroiling mankind in war;
     subjugating all countries by French principles and French
     power, and thus subjecting the whole to themselves; new as
     these men were in some part of the composition of their cha-
     racters, yet in others as old as vanity avarice, and profligacy,
     they transcended every bound of morality or religion. Pos-
     sessing great energy they in a considerable degree attained,
     and for a short time preserved the objects of their desire ; but
     wanting profound wisdom and overrating their own talents of
     managing tools, they ultimately fell by the instruments of their
     exaltation. As the great operators in the several changes
     of the revolution were the Parisian rabble, the demagogues
     who could most readily and effectually direct the mob, posses-
     sed a formidable power either instrumental or supreme accord-
     ing to the ability and skill of its possessors. The members of
     the legislature, most ferociously violent against the king, were
The Moun- the Mountain. These, less literary in their acquirements, less
tain blood- metaphysical in their harangues, exhibited in their manners a
thirsty and coarseness which the others, educated as gentlemen, had not
ferocious. been able completely to attain, and were much more popular

g The chief philosophical scholar among them was Condorcet. Brissot
was animated, enthusiastic, and operative, but by no means profound.
h See Brissot's works passim; also the writings of other Girondists.

among the governing sansculottes. The head of this party CHAP.
was Robespierre, a man much inferior to the Girondists in   L
cultivated understanding, polished eloquence, and those talents
which would have had weight with an ingenious and refined   1792.
audience; but by the uncouth plainness of his speeches, and the Robes-
energy of his invectives, he was well fitted to govern a mob at pierre,
Danton,
any time; and by his stern and sanguinary disposition pecu-
and Ma-
liarly suited to the Parisian mob, panting for regicide. Next rat.
in power was Danton, equally blood-thirsty and ambitious,
less strong and direct in his means, but more dexterous. Subordinate to these was Marat; a half lettered editor of a newspaper, hideous in appearance, loathsome by disease,[i] and squa-
lid in attire; he was pasionately desirous of reducing all
eminence and distinction to the same low level with himself;
and long the hireling of Orleans, he imbibed against the king
that rancorous gall which he had been paid for disseminating
through the populace. Bloody in his disposition, ardent in his
cruel exhortations; he was the delight of the murderous mob,
because in so many points coinciding with themselves. By
these leaders chiefly, assisted by many others of the Mountain members, the Parisian rabble was directed. The Gironde
party saw the character of these demagogues, but in their
eager efforts to subdue the constitutionalist, and overthrow
kingly power, had co-operated with the Mountain; intending,
and for a considerable time appearing, to use them as tools.
The insurrection of the 10th of August was the work of the
Girondists for the subversion of monarchy : Danton was a most
powerful auxiliary in the massacres of that bloody day. So
effectually instrumental to the execution of the Girondist designs, the mob and the leaders of the Mountain, more sensibly
felt their own resistless power. The Gironde party were totally unrestrained by conscience from seeking their ends through
means however wicked; yet they do not appear to have had
a desire of shedding blood merely for pleasure. Blood they
would not spare where they conceived it to answer their purpose; the butchery of their fellow creatures, however, they
did not seek as a *pastime*. Not so the sansculottes, who manifestly sought massacre for its own sake.[k] Before the beginning of September the power of the mountain was very greatly increased. Marat and his associates under Danton and Robespierre, were the ring-leaders in the September carnage.
Brissot had formed the plan of a national convention, and a
republic: the leaders of the Mountain were contriving that the
republic, which they had been instrumental in creating should
be directed by themselves, and that the national convention
should contain a majority of their creatures. When the assem-

i See Adolphus's Memoirs. Life of Marat.
k What but the mere delight in human carnage could have prompted
the greater part of the September massacres? See details in Playfair's Jacobinism.

CHAP.
.L.

1792.

The Giron-
dists wish
to spare
the life of
the king.

'The
Mountain
and the
mob desire
his massa-
cre.

Pusillani-
mity of
Brissot and
the other
Girondists

A decree
is passed
for bring-
ing the
king to
trial.

bly which he had projected met, Brissot found, that the Mountain was becoming very strong. The executive council, however, still consisted of Girondists, and, the army being commanded by officers of that party, they remained formidable.
The Gironde party, desirous of establishing democracy, appeared to have had no intention of attacking the life of their
sovereign, unless they conceived it to interfere with the preservation of the republic and their own power. From the German retreat, and the subsequent success of the French arms,
they entertained no apprehensions of the restoration of monarchy, and wished to save the king's life: the opposite party,
not merely murderers from policy, but sanguinary from the infuriate disposition of the multitude, desired the blood of Louis.
The jacobin clubs, now leagued with the Mountain, promoted
the savage barbarity. Their leaders, especially Robespierre,
had formed views of the most unbounded ambition, and conceived that, by involving the people in the guilt of regicide,
they would bind them entirely to their system, and overpower
their adversaries the Gironde and all other parties. The
Girondists, superior as they were in genius and literature to
the Mountain were less daring and intrepid, and besides, had
more to dread, as their adversaries were supported by the governing mob.[1] There were, however, still great numbers
throughout the provinces, and even in Paris itself, who ardently desired to spare the blood of their king. By firmness and
magnanimity, the Girondists, possessing the executorial functions, might have rallied round the metropolis a sufficient force
for saving innocent blood ; but they did not display the courage
of resolute determination, without which lawless ambition will
not retain newly usurped power. The proceedings were pu-
sillanimous half measures, more contemptible in their inefficacy
than the diabolical conduct of their adversaries; and though
less detestible in their operation, equally noxious in the result.
The Mountain persuaded the populace that Louis had betrayed
his country, and conspired against France with its enemies :
on these grounds they instigated the mob to demand his trial.[m]
After various preliminary discussions, the Girondists being
afraid to express their sentiments, a decree was passed for
bringing to trial a personage whose life, by every principle of
expediency and policy, ought to have been sacred under any
well regulated constitution ; and whose person was inviolable
according to the polity existing in France at the time when the
acts charged were alleged to have been committed. To prevent the public mind from hearing innocence calling for justice,
they suffered not the king to know that his life was sought.
From the fidelity of a zealous domestic[n] Louis of France first
learned that a perjured banditti prepared publicly to destroy
their monarch's life, which every federate Frenchman had

1 Segur, vol. iii p. 6.   m Ibid, p. 7.   n See Clery.

sworn to protect. To break down the soul of their sove- CHAP.
reign by accumulated misery, they debarred him from the   L
sight and converse of his wife and children. They hoped
that the strength of his benevolent affections, thus deprived   1792.
of their dearest objects, would crush the faculties of his Attempts
mind, and would disable him from vindicating his inno- to break
cence, and exposing the enormity of their blood thirsty the spirit
guilt; but their purpose was frustrated. The dreadful situa- of Louis.
tion in which their wickedness had placed him, roused the energies of a mind which manifested itself not unworthy of the
descendant of Henry. With every circumstance of degrada- Trial.
tion that the upstart insolence of unmerited power could bestow, he was brought to the bar, and his charges were read.
They consisted of two general heads; first, of crimes committed before his acceptance of the constitution; secondly, of
crimes committed after his acceptance of the constitution. The
evidence was composed of interrogatories put to the accused
himself, and of documents charged to have been written with
his privity and concurrence. The charges before his acceptance of the constitution he successively answered, by declaring
what every hearer well knew, that the power then vested in
him authorized the several acts, and consequently could now
be no subject of question: the accusations for conduct subsequent to the acceptance he either showed to be agreeable to
his constitutional powers, or denied to be such as were represented. In every particular case he protested he had acted
according to the best of his judgment for the good of his
subjects. The allegation of conspiracy with the enemies of his
country he firmly denied. The written evidence on which he Not the
was accused contained neither proof nor grounds for probable slightest
presumption that he was culpable, much less guilty: the asser- proof of
tions rested upon no evidence.[o] When the charge for the prose- guilt.
cution was finished, the king applied for permission to be allowed counsel. Various emigrants[p] informed of the charges,
proffered exculpatory testimony: Louis's judges would hear
no evidence but on one side: the accusation was totally unsupported by proof. His defence was conducted, first by himself, with great magnanimity and ability, and afterwards by his
counsel. It was glaringly manifest, that his accusers had totally
failed in making out their case; that there was not a shadow of
foundation to justify an arraignment, much less evidence to authorize a penal sentence, even against the meanest subject. Before judgment was passed, it was proposed to appeal to the people. The national convention, it was said, was not a tribunal

o For the proof of this assertion we refer to the reports of the trial.
p Lally, Tollendal, Bertrand, Narbon, Cazales, and Bouille offered, at
the risk of their lives, to go to Paris, and bear testimony to the falsity of the
principal charges against the king, wherein they respectively were said to
have been agents Otridge's Annual Register, 1793.

CHAP. of judges; but an assembly of lawgivers; and in assuming a
L.   judicial power they were usurpers. The people, their con-
     stituents, had not delegated to the national convention the
1793. power of trying causes. This objection, though unanswerably
     valid, had no weight with men determined to commit murder:
     for the appeal there were two hundred and eighty-three,
     against it four hundred and twenty-four. It being resolved by
     such a majority that the king should suffer punishment, it was
     strenuously contended by one party that he should be confined,
Condemna- by the other that he should be put to death. In a meeting of
tion and seven hundred the bloody verdict was passed by a majority of
sentence. five! The iniquitous sentence being delivered after midnight, on
     the 20th of January, it was that day, at two o'clock, announced
     to the king, that the following day he was to be executed.
Self-pos- With unmoved countenance hearing the decree read, he re-
session and quested permission to see his family. The hardened hearts of
magnanim- his murderers did not refuse him this last boon.[q] He himself
ity of the first conveyed to his queen, sister, and children, the agonizing
persecuted intelligence. During the dismal interview, retaining his firm-
monarch. ness, he inculcated on his son the transient nature of sublunary
Last inter- grandeur; called to his mind what his father had been, and
view of   then was; bid him trust for happiness to that virtue and reli-
Louis with gion which no human efforts could efface. Late in the evening
his family. his family left him, trusting[r] to see him the next morning
     once more. Prepared by conscious innocence, uprightness,
     and piety, for meeting death, neither guilt nor fear disturbed
     his rest. He slept soundly[s] till five o'clock, the hour at which
     he ordered his faithful valet to awaken him for the last time.[t]
     His family he now resolved to forbear again pressing to his
     arms. The bitterness of death the tranquil resignation of the
     christian regarded with complacency; the bitterness of parting
     grief the brother, father, and husband could not endure. He
     sought from religion, in his last hours, that consolation which,
     in the zenith of power, splendour, and magnificence, as well as
     in humiliation and captivity, she had never failed to afford.
     The attendance of a clergyman, a favour refused him ever since
     his imprisonment in the Temple by his atheistical oppressors,
     was, at his earnest entreaty, granted him on the day of his mas-
     sacre. Being now assisted in the external rights, as well as en-
     couraged in the internal sentiments of devotion, and having
     opened his soul to a priest whose sanctity he revered, he for a
     short interval, returned to the concerns of this world; deliver-
     ed to his faithful servant his last charges and commissions[u] to

q Clery's Journal, 235.   r Ibid. 239.   s Ibid. 242.   t Ibid.
u At seven o'clock (says Clery), the king, coming out of his closet, called
to me, and taking me within the recess of the window, said, "You will
give this seal to my son, this ring to the queen, and assure her that it is
with pain I part with it: this little packet contains the hair of all my family;
you will give her that too. Tell the queen, my dear children, and my sister,

be conveyed to his family and friends. The messengers of murder arrived; and he was conducted from the Temple. When he was ascending the scaffold his executioners seized his hands in order to tie them behind his back: as he was not prepared for this last insult, he appeared disposed to repel it, and his countenance already beamed with indignation. Mr. Edgeworth, his clerical attendant, sensible that resistance would be vain, and might expose the royal sufferer to outrages more violent, entreated his sovereign to submit.[x] He presented his hands to the ministers of blood: they tied them with so much force as to call forth another remonstrance. He now mounted the scaffold amidst the noise of drums: bound and disfigured as he was, he advanced with a firm step, and requesting the drums to cease, was obeyed. He then, with a steady voice and in a distinct tone, addressed the people to the following purport. "Frenchmen, I die innocent of all the crimes which "have been imputed to me; and I forgive my enemies. I im- "plore God, from the bottom of my heart, to pardon them, "and not take vengeance on the French nation for the blood "about to be shed." As he was proceeding, the inhuman Santerre,[y] who presided at the execution, ordered the drums to beat, and the executioners to perform their office. The king's voice was drowned in the noise of drums, and the clamours of the soldiery. As the fatal guillotine descended on his head, the confessor exclaimed, "Son of St. Louis, ascend into hea- "ven!" The bleeding head was exhibited to the populace, some of whom shouted, *Vive la republique!* but the majority appeared to be struck dumb with horror, while the affection of many led them to bathe their handkerchiefs in his blood. That every barbarous insult might be offered to the remains of the murdered prince, the body was conveyed in a cart to the church-yard of St. Madelaine, and thrown into a grave, which was instantly filled with quick lime, and a guard placed over it till the corps was consumed.

The execution of Louis XVI. violated every principle of justice, and every rule of law, which affords security to men bound together in society. By the established constitution, and which subsisted during all the time that he had any power to act, his person was inviolable.[z] By the law of the land he was amenable to no criminal court: the most tyrannical of all decrees only, a law passed after the alleged guilt could subject him to

that although I promised to see them this morning, I have resolved to spare them the pangs of so cruel a separation: Tell them how much it costs me to go without receiving their embraces once more!" Clery 249.

x The words of the priest were, "Sire, this added humiliation is another circumstance in which your majesty's sufferings resemble those of that Saviour who will soon be your recompense."

y Annual Register, 1793.

z Chap. xlvii.

CHAP. penal inquiry, whatever might have been his crime. But if his
L. person had not been by law inviolable, the assembly which presumed to try him was not a competent court. The national
1793. convention, even though admitted to be the delegates of the
people fairly chosen, were not delegates beyond the extent of
their commissions : they were chosen by the people as their legislative representatives only. In exercising a judicial power,
they were not a lawful tribunal, but a banditti of usurpers.[a] If
the national convention had been a competent court, the charges adduced were principally irrevelent ; some of the acts alleged referred to a period in which the constitution had been
different, and in which Louis had simply exercised the powers
which were then vested in the king : his former conduct they
had sanctioned by conferring on him the supreme executive
authority by the new constitution. Most of the accusations
against him subsequent to his acceptance were constitutional
exertions of his prerogative. The charges of corresponding
with emigrants and foreign powers for the purpose of overturning the liberties of France, were supported by no authentic evi-
Complica- dence. Thus a personage criminally responsible to no French
ted iniqui- tribunal, was tried by a set of men that were not a legal court,
ty of the for charges not criminal by the law of the land, if proved ; or
process in charges which, if criminal, were not proved. Condemned and
principle,
substance, executed in those circumstances, he presented to France an
and mode. awful monument of the ferocious disposition by which it was now
An awful governed. The massacre of Louis demonstrated that liberty,
monument law, and justice, were vanished ; and exhibited the prevalence of
of the doc- a system which terror only could maintain.
trines and
sentiments   While the French government was preparing this dreadful
that go- catastrophe, it instructed its agent in London to demand the
verned virtual recognition of its establishment and authority, in the
France. acceptance of an accredited ambassador. His Britannic ma-
Chauvelin jesty, considering the present rulers as only one party, and
demands
from Bri- from the rapid vicissitudes of sway, a temporary and shortlived
tain the party, in conformity with his principles of neutrality, would not
recognition receive an ambassador, because such admission would have
of the acknowledged as the rulers of France a particular junto ; and
French
republic, violated his resolution and promise not to interfere in the inter-
and the nal affairs of France. But though he would not recognise the
admission paramount faction of the day, as the firmly established and per-
of its am- manent rulers of France, yet while these powers did exist, and
bassador. menaced England with hostility, he did not forbear to repeat
The Bri- his statements of the injuries which he had received, and the
tish go-
vernment satisfaction he demanded ; and since that continued to be re-
refuses. fused, to prepare the means of enforcing redress. Chauvelin,
by the instructions of the executive council, still persisted to

a This argument was very forcibly and eloquently employed by the constitutionalists and Girondists against the murderous Mountain. See speeches of the convention, passim.

refuse satisfaction for their aggressions, demanding the recog- CHAP.
nition of the republic, and the acceptance of an ambassador. L.
He farther remonstrated against the alien bill, and the naval
and military preparations, imputed hostile intentions to Eng- 1793.
land, and notified that if the preparations continued, France Chauvelin
would prepare for war. In conformity to the principles and remon-
objects of the decree of the 19th of November, he intimated an trates
intention to appeal to the people of England against the govern- against the
alien bill.
ment. His Brittanic majesty, persevering in his former conduct, declared he would continue his preparations until France
should relinquish her ambitious aggression.[b] On the 24th of On the
January, 1793, intelligence arrived in London of the melancholy massacre
catastrophe of Louis XVI. His majesty immediately directed of the king
a notification to be sent to Mr. Chauvelin, that the character he is ordered to
with which he had been invested at the British court, and of leave Bri-
which the functions had been so long suspended, being now tain.
entirely terminated by the fatal death of his most christian
majesty, he had no longer any public character here. The
king, after such an event, could permit his residence here no
longer : within eight days he must quit the kingdom, but every
attention should be paid him that was due to the character of
the ambassador of his most christian majesty, which he had
exercised at this court. A negotiation was still open on the
frontiers of Holland, between lord Aukland and general Dumourier, but the French persisted in refusing to relinquish their
invasion of our allies, and in demanding the recognition of the
republic ; which requisitions being totally inadmissible, matters
were not accommodated. The French rulers, finding Britain France de-
inflexibly determined on adherence to the rights of independent clares war
against
nations, by a decree of the convention, declared war against Britain and
Great Britain with acclamations, and soon after against Hol- Holland.
land, which their forces were ready to invade. Britain and
Holland, in their own defence, returned a declaration of hostilities ; and thus commenced the war between Great Britain
and the French republic.

The hostile advances of France, and the refused satisfaction France the
for an aggression totally inconsistent with the law of nations, aggressor.
and existing treaties upon rights which we were bound to protect, combined with their attempts to excite insurrection in
our own country, and followed by their declaration of war,
render it evident that the French were the aggressors, and
that Britain had a just RIGHT to go to war. The EXPEDIENCY
of that measure, however, is a different question, and perhaps
few subjects have occurred in political history, which have
produced stronger arguments on both sides ; in which men of
the most patriotic hearts and wisest heads, drew more opposite

b See series of correspondence between Mr. Chauvelin and lord Grenville. Debrett's State Papers of 27th December 1792, to 27th January
1793, both inclusive.

CHAP.
L.

1793.

Opinions
and senti-
ments of
different
parties.

Views of
Messrs.
Burke,
Fox, and
Pitt re-
spectively
on the
French re-
volution,
and the
war with
France.

Messrs.
Burke and
Pitt sup-
port the
war on dif-
ferent
grounds.

conclusions, according to the light in which they viewed this
immense and complicated subject. Never was there a question
in which candour, founded on cool and comprehensive reflection, examining the mass of evidence and reasoning on both
sides, would more readily allow laudable and meritorious motives to total diversity of opinion and conduct. Yet never did
there occur a contest in which party zeal generated more
illiberal constructions and more malignant interpretation of
intentions.

The sentiments of Britons on the subject of the French revolution, may be divided into two classes ; those who wished the
establishment in England of a system resembling the French
republic, to the utter subversion of the British constitution ;
and those who, varying in their plans and measures, desired
the preservation of the British constitution. Most of the British
democrats and jacobins were inimical to a war with France,
because it interrupted the communication by which they expected to establish their favourite system ; but some of them
were said to have rejoiced at the hostilities, because they conceived war would excite such discontent as would lead to a
revolution. But far was the opposition to the war from being
confined to democrats, jacobins, and the enemies of our polity.
Of those who disapproved of hostilities, many, in the general
tenor of their conduct, evinced themselves the firm friends of
constitutional liberty, and monarchy. They sought the same
ends, the preservation of the British constitution, and the maintenance of the British security, but deemed them attainable by
peace instead of war. The friends of the British constitution,
both without and within parliament, for and against the war,
in a great measure took the tone of opinions advanced and
maintained by three of the highest parliamentary characters ;
Edmund Burke, Charles James Fox, and William Pitt. Burke
continued to deem the French revolutionists, of every opinion,
kind, and succession, the determined and inveterate enemies of
religion, virtue, civilization, manners, rank, order, property,
throughout the world ; and eagerly and resolutely bent on disseminating disorder, vice and misery ; to regard them as pursuing these ends, not only in the ardent violence of infuriate
passion, but also in the principled and systematic constancy of
depraved, but energetic and powerful reason. He reckoned
them totally incorrigible by any internal means ; and therefore
strenuously inculcated an external force to overwhelm an assemblage of beings, who in his estimation, unless conquered,
would destroy and devastate mankind. Long before[c] the commencement of hostilities between France and Germany, he
had suggested a confederation of the European powers for the
subjugation of men whom he thought revolutionary monsters;
and had uniformly written and spoken to the same purport.
He eagerly promoted war, not merely for the purpose of pro.

c See his posthumous works, memorial written in autumn, 1791,

curing satisfaction for a specific aggression, which, in both plain and figurative language, he described as comparatively insignificant, but for the restoration in France of the hierarchy, aristocracy, and monarchy, the downfall of which, was, he thought, the cause of French ambition and encroachment, menacing the destruction of all Europe. Mr. Burke desired war with the French revolutionists, to overthrow the new system, and to crush the new principles. Mr. Fox continuing to impute the increasing outrages of the new votaries of liberty to glowing enthusiasm, still conceived that the enthusiasm would subside if left to its own operation. External force, he predicted, would not only preserve, but increase the vehement heat, which might otherwise cool. The recent experience of the effects of the German invasion, confirmed him in this opinion. He thought that an attempt to force the establishment of monarchy, would drive France to become a military democracy: the project was unwise, because it was impracticable in its object, as well as pernicious in its means. Criminal, Mr. Fox said, as the French republicans were in their various confiscations and massacres, and in the murder of their king, their acts were no crimes against England; if the French nation choose to abolish existing orders, and to annihilate monarchy, they were not invading the rights of England; such a purpose of going to war was totally unjust; our efforts would spill the blood of our brave countrymen, would overwhelm us with additional debts; we might wage war year after year against France, as against America: we should make no progress, we should in the end be obliged to conclude a peace, recognizing the form of government which should then be established in France. The aggressions alleged against the French were too inconsiderable to justify war as a prudent measure, and if these were the sole causes of contest, they might be easily compromised, were Britain in earnest. We ought to receive an ambassador from the ruling powers of France, because they were the ruling powers.[d] With all foreign nations we considered neither the history of the establishment, nor the justice of the tenure, but the simple fact that the government with which we treated was established; such also was the conduct of other nations respecting England; France, Spain, and other monarchies, negotiated with Cromwell; England ought now to pursue the same course: we ought to treat with those who possessed the power of doing what we wanted, as for the same reasons we frequently negotiated with Algiers, Turkey, and Morocco, however much we reprobated their respective governments. Mr. Pitt was far from coinciding[e] with Mr. Burke, in proposing to carry

d See speeches of Mr. Fox on war with France, in January and February 1793. Parliamentary Debates.

e See Mr. Burke's two memorials written respectively in November 1792, and October 1793, published in his posthumous works; and also his regicide peace, wherein he severely censures the objects of the allies, and the little confidence they reposed in the emigrants.

on a war for the restoration of the monarchical government.
France had manifested schemes of ·unbounded aggrandizement,
actually invaded our allies, and declared her resolution to encourage revolt in other countries. By the reciprocal action and
reaction of her principles and power, she sought the unlimited
extension of both. A$_t$^{t}a$_c$k$_i$ng us in such a disposition, and with
such views, she compelled us to go to war for the repression of
principles, and the reduction of power endangering our security.
We ought not to recognize a government consisting merely of a
faction, and not having the marks of probable stability, in the
cool and deliberate approbation of the people. From a party so
uncertain and changeable, we did not choose to receive a regular
ambassador, as if it were firmly fixed in the supreme power; but
we did treat with the existing government. The source of war
was not our refusal to treat, as many believed, or pretended to
believe, but the refusal of the French leaders to make satisfaction

The ob-
j cts both
of the min-
isterial
party and
opposition
in parlia-
ment con-
stitutional,
though
sought un-
der differ-
ent impres-
sions, and
by different
means.

for injuries and insults. Not the restoration of monarchy in
France, but the security of Britain, being our reason for going
to war, we should carry on hostilities no longer than we were
in danger from the conduct and dispositions of France. As the
republicans and democrats in opposing the war, coincided with
Messrs. Fox, Erskine, Sheridan, and other able men who were
inimical to hostilities, on patriotic and constitutional grounds,
many of the other party classed them, and more affected to class
them, with democrats and jacobins. As on the other hand, the
votaries of war were presumed, by its opponents, to seek the re-
establishment of despotism in France, they were called crusaders
against liberty. On the one side party zeal represented Messrs.
Burke and Pitt, and their respective adherents, as the abettors of
tyranny; on the other, Mr. Fox and his adherents as the abettors
of jacobinism and anarchy. Impartial history, viewing the individual acts and chain of conduct of these three illustrious men,
finds no grounds to justify so injurious an opinion; but the strong-·
est reasons for concluding that they and their supporters and adherents, through different means, sought the same end, the constitutional welfare of their country.

Many as were averse to war, both on the constitutional grounds
of Mr. Fox, and on the unconstitutional grounds of democrats
and jacobins, that great engine of politics in a free country, public
opinion, was on the whole favourable to hostilities. A sense of
the actual aggression of the French republic; but much more
the alarming apprehension of French principles, rendered the

In declar-
ing war
against
France, the
king spoke
·the voice of
the nation.

country desirous of a total interruption of communication with
France. It was not the war of the court, of the ministers, of the
privileged orders; it was A WAR OF THE GREAT MAJORITY OF THE
PEOPLE OF BRITAIN. IN DECLARING WAR AGAINST FRANCE IN
FEBRUARY 1793, HIS BRITANNIC MAJESTY SPOKE THE VOICE OF
THE BRITISH NATION.

CHAP. LI.

Objects of Britain—the repression of French principles, and the prevention of French aggrandizement.—Sir John Scott the attorney-general introduces a bill for preventing traitorous correspondence—arguments for and against—modified, passed into a law.—Motion for peace.—Reasonings of Mr. Fox respecting the war and its probable effects.—The propositions are negatived by unprecedented majorities.—Mr. Sheridan proposes an inquiry in to the alleged sedition.—His motion rejected.—Motion for parliamentary reform by Mr. Grey—arguments for.—Mr. Whitbread.—Arguments against.—Proposition reprobated as peculiarly unseasonable at such a period—and rejected.—State of commercial credit, and causes of its being affected.—Mr. Pitt proposes an advance of public money on the security of mercantile commodities.—The proposition is adopted, and revives mercantile credit.—East India company's charter on the eve of expiration.—Mr. Dundas presents a masterly view of the prosperity of India under the present system.—He proposes the renewal of the charter.—His plan is passed into a law.—Measures adopted to render British India farther productive.—Plan of agricultural improvement —Sir John Sinclair—inquiries of in Scotland and England.—Result, that agriculture is not understood and practised in proportion to the capability of the country—proposes the establishment of a board of agriculture—the proposal adopted.—Lord Rawdon's motion respecting debtors.—Increase of the army and navy.—National supplies.—A loan.—Taxes.—Session closes.—Commencement of campaign, 1793.—French invade Holland—reduce Breda.—Hundart and Gertruydenburgh surrender.—Dumourier besieg s Williamstadt and Maestreicht.—The British forces arrive in Holland.—The French raise the siege of Williamstadt.—Attacked by the Austrians at Winden—defeated—French generals accuse each other.—Dumourier evacuates the Netherlands—disapproved by the convention—privately proposes to make peace with the allies and restore monarchy—suspected by the French government—summoned to return to Paris to answer for his conduct—sounds the dispositions of the army —finding them unfavourable, deserts to the Austrians.

THE grand purposes of the British government in its conduct respecting France were to repress the operation of revolutionary principles in this country, and to prevent the French system of aggression and aggrandizement from being longer carried into successful execution on the continent. In this twofold object originated the measures of external policy adopted by parliament during the remainder of the session, and also some of those that were confined to internal regulation.

War having been declared against a foreign country, it was obviously expedient to prevent correspondence between British subjects and the hostile party. To render this prohibition effectual, Sir John Scott, attorney-general, on the 15th of March introduced a bill for preventing, during the war, all traitorous

CHAP.
LI.

1793.

Objects of Great Britain—the repression of French principles and the prevention of French aggrandizement. Sir John Scott, the

CHAP.
LI.

1793.
attorney-
general,
troduces a
bill for
preventing
traitorous
correspon-
dence.

Argu-
men for
and ts
against,

correspondence with the king's enemies. The law of treason
was founded upon a statute of the 25th of Edward III. which
had been the subject of legislative exposition in different laws,
enacted since that period. The acts declared treasonable in
that statute were principally reducible to two heads;[f] to compass, that is, to intend or project the king's death; to levy war
against the king, and to abet or assist his enemies. Since that
period, during wars, parliament had repeatedly passed laws
which applied the general principle to the existing case; by
specifically prohibiting adherence or assistance to nations at
enmity with our sovereign.[g] Agreeably to the original statute,
and the consequent explanatory acts the present bill was framed.
Former laws had, in such circumstances, prohibited British
subjects from sending military stores, arms, amunition, and
provision, of various enumerated kinds. The present bill, besides interdicting these articles, prohibited purchases of French
funds or French lands. The reason of this prohibition was,
that, as the French government proposed to carry on war
against this country by the sale of lands, British subjects if
allowed to purchase such land would not only feel an interest
in the property which they had thus acquired, but furnish the
enemy with the means of carrying on war against ourselves. It
was further proposed that no person should be allowed to go
from this country into France, without a licence under his majesty's great seal; and that their neglect of this clause should be
deemed a misdemeanour; and that no persons, though subjects
of this country, coming from France should be allowed to enter
this kingdom without a passport or license, or giving to a magistrate such security as he should require. The last regulation
was to prevent the insurance of vessels which should traffic with
France.

The bill was opposed as inconsistent with the treason laws
of Edward III. the principles of the British constitution, with
justice and commercial policy. The provision against Englishmen returning to the country, was the bestowal of a power on
the king to banish, during the war, every British subject now
in France. Though he might return, in certain cases, by
giving security, who were to be the judges of the amount of
that security? This was to be left to a magistrate: here one
man was to be put under the discretion of another, who might
render his return impossible, by exacting security to an amount

f See vol. i. 667.

g An act had passed in the reign of queen Anne to prevent all traitorous
correspondence which prohibited any person from supplying the enemies
with arms, naval or military stores, or from going out of the kingdom to
the enemy's country without license. A similar act of William and Mary
had carried the regulation farther; it prohibited goods and merchandize of
every sort. See Statutes at large.

that could not be given.[h] The restriction upon the purchase
of lands was represented as extremely impolitic : it was alleged
to be founded upon an absurd supposition, that Britons having
here the most permanent security for their money, would send
their capital to France, where they could have no security.
Frenchmen, on the other hand, found property exposed to the
revolutionary grasp in their own country; and, to escape spoliation, had sent many and large sums of money to Britain to be
vested in our funds, and also great quantities of other precious
moveables : as proscription advanced they must wish to send
more . to the place of safety. If the present regulation were
adopted, France would no doubt follow the example : we
should render her government the most essential service, by
forcing Frenchmen to employ their money in their own funds.
Instead, therefore, of preventing, as proposed, the efflux of
money to the country of our enemies, we would prevent its
influx into our own; and by the project of withholding resources
from the enemy, we should add to his strength. The bill was
defended as conformable both to the general law, and to special
acts passed in periods of war. The particular provisions most
strongly combatted were supported as necessary in the precise
and specific nature of the present war; the circumstances in
which it was founded, and the projected resources of the enemy.
After many debates, the two clauses most severely reprobated,
concerning the return of British subjects, and the purchase of
property in France, were abandoned. Undergoing these import- Modified,
ant changes, and several much less material modifications, the it passes
proposed bill was passed into a law.   into a law.

Repeated motions were made in the houses of parliament in Motions for
order to procure peace. Of these the most important was a peace.
proposition of Mr. Fox, after the first successes of the allies,
and the retreat of the French armies from the Netherlands.[i]
Intelligence having arrived, that the French, leaving the scenes
of recent invasion and aggression, had retired within their
ancient frontiers ; Mr. Fox, professing to consider the avowed
objects of the war as now attained, proposed an inquiry into the
reason of its continuance ; and moved an address to his majesty
praying him to make peace. Supposing, for the sake of argu- Reasonings
ment, the present a just, prudent, and necessary war at the of Mr. Fox
beginning, he contended that the alleged reasons no longer on the inex-
existed. Holland, our ally, was not now exposed to any attack : the war,
France would willingly purchase peace by insuring the continu- and pre-
ance of that safety, whereas he was afraid perseverance in dicting its
carrying on war along with the combined powers, would again effects.
expose her to danger. The French had, no doubt, manifested
designs of aggrandizement, but these had arisen from the suc-

h See speeches of Messrs. Erskine and Fox. Parliamentary debates, 1793.
i The historical narrative of these events is somewhat subsequent: I here
only mention a result on which Mr. Fox founded part of his reasoning.

cessful repulsion of confederate attack. Besides, must England
go to war with every continental power that perpetrates injustice? Was not the conduct of the partitioners of Poland equal
in infamy and iniquity to the aggressions of France? Were the
people of England to suffer all the miseries of war because the
people of France were unjust, when that injustice, be it ever so
atrocious, was violating no right of Englishmen? They had,
indeed, threatened the security of his majesty's allies; but now
confined within their own territories, they were occupied in
defending their frontiers against the combined powers. The
danger apprehended from their former conquest was no longer
a subject of just uneasiness and alarm. The French were, at
present, in great internal confusion and distress; and Britain
could form no views of aggrandizement from the situation of
her adversary. Even were justice and humanity out of the
question, would policy and prudence authorize this country to seize the possessions of France? What advantage
could we derive from promoting the conquering and encroach-
ing plans of other powers? Having driven France from the
territories of her neighbours, for what purpose were we to
persevere in a war, unless to invade her dominions? If we did
make an inroad into her territories, could such a movement be
to attain our professed objects, security and defence? By continuing the war we should manifest an intention of either dismembering her empire, or interfering with the government
which her people chose to establish. These objects our government had uniformly disavowed, and the declared ends of hostilities had been compassed. The most favourable season for
offering peace was in the midst of success; when the enemy
were sufficiently humbled to feel the evils of war, without being
driven by the haughtiness of the conquerors, to desperate efforts,
which might turn the tide of victory. Those, who calculated
probable exertions of men fighting for conceived liberty and
independence by the usual course of military events, fundamentally erred in expecting similar effects from totally dissimilar
causes. Inspired by such animating motives, men had, in all
ages and countries, displayed valour, prowess, and policy,
astonishing to the rest of mankind. Pressed by continued and
invading war, which excited such motives, the ardent spirit and
inventive genius of the French would, Mr. Fox predicted, no
less exert themselves; WE SHOULD DRIVE THEM TO BECOME
A MILITARY REPUBLIC. Let us therefore endeavour, while opportunity was favourable, to procure an honourable and secure
peace. To this a common objection is, with whom shall we
treat? The answer is obvious; with any men who possess the
power of doing what we want: the French are desirous of
peace, and the present rulers are as competent to conclude
peace as to carry on war. Shall we be at peace with none
whose form of government we shall not have previously approved? We had formerly made peace with tyrants; not

because we approved their maxims and constitution of government, but because they had the power of making and observing.
conventions.   Peace with any ruler or rulers implies approbation
of their character no more than of their government. The French
republicans have been guilty of cruelty and atrocious murders;
so was Louis XIV.   No British statesman refused to treat with
the bigotted banisher of his most valuable subjects, nor with
the sanguinary devastator of unoffending provinces.   The
statesman treats not with the virtue[k] but with the power of
another party; and in expecting performance, looks for his best
security, not in the integrity but the interest of the contractor.
These were the arguments by which Mr. Fox inculcated the
restoration of peace; and this was the strain of reasoning which
he and other votaries of amity employed repeatedly at various
stages of the contest.[l]

In opposing the address, Messrs. Burke and Pitt argued
conformably to the different views which they had respectively
adopted concerning the French revolution and the war. Mr.
Pitt persevered in urging the impracticability of any treaty with
the persons that at present exercised the government of France;
and in supporting his position, exhibited a very eloquent view
of their individual and collective atrocities: therefore he would
not treat with them *now*.   Reprobating the French principles
as manifested in their present operation, he still disavowed every design of forcible interference in the internal government of
France: he sought only security.   This security was to be
effected in one of three modes: first, by obtaining an assurance
that the principles should no longer predominate; secondly,
that those who were now engaged in them should be taught
that they were impracticable, and convinced of their own want
of power to carry them into execution; or, thirdly, that the
issue of the present war should be such as, by weakening
their power of attack, should strengthen our power of resistance.   Without these we might indeed have an armed truce,
a temporary suspension of hostilities, but no permanent peace;
no solid security to guard us against the repetition of injury
and the renewal of attack. The present situation of affairs not
being such, in Mr. Pitt's estimation, as to admit these means of
obtaining security, he and his votaries opposed the address for
the discontinuance of the war.   Mr. Burke clearly and expressly
combatted the principle asserted by Mr. Fox, that England had
no right to interfere with the internal government of France.
If (he said) by the subversion of all law and religion, a nation
adopts a malignant spirit to produce anarchy and mischief in
other countries, it is the right of all nations to go to war with
the authors of such attempts.   In support of this doctrine he
quoted the authority of Vattal, who lays down a position,

k Parliamentary debates, 17th June, 1793.
l See also his letter to the electors of Westminster.

CHAP. " that if any nation adopt principles maleficient to all govern-
LI. " ment and order, such a nation is to be opposed from princi-
〜〜〜 " ples of common safety." This was the spirit of France; and
1793. what was to keep the effects of it from England? War, and
nothing else: therefore, war with the French republic, *on
account of her system and principles*, Mr. Burke recommended;
and explicitly declared his opinion, that while the existing
system continued, peace with France was totally inadmissible.

The propo- The proposed address to the king was negatived by a majority
sitions are equally great as that which had voted for the war; and
negatived throughout the nation perseverance in hostilities was as generally
by unpre- popular.
cedented
majorities.   Ministers, and many others who had been formerly inimical
to their measures, having expressed their conviction that there
existed in the country dispositions and designs to subvert the
constitution, and to follow the example of the French innova-
Mr. Sheri- tors, Mr. Sheridan proposed that an inquiry should be insti-
dan propo- tuted into the alleged sedition. He declared his disbelief of
ses an in- the ministerial representations upon any evidence that had been
quiry into adduced, but avowed himself open to proofs, if such should be
the alleged
sedition: established: he therefore proposed a committee of the whole
house to investigate the assertions, that it might be ascertained
whether there was really a plot against the country, or if it
was merely a false and mischievous report to impose on the
credulity of the nation; to attach obloquy to the opponents of
administration, and to facilitate the continuance of the war.
In answer to Mr. Sheridan's requisition it was argued, that
government had not asserted the existence of plots to be established by proof for judicial animadversion, but of a seditious
spirit and operations, which required deliberative precaution
and the most vigilant care to prevent them from maturing into
plots and insurrections. From a combination of various and
disconnected circumstances a man might receive a moral certainty of a general fact which ought to regulate his conduct,
though he might have no proof of such a fact[m] sufficient to
establish it before a magistrate. The active circulation of seditious writings, the proceedings and declarations of the innovating societies;[n] the public and avowed sentiments[o] of great
numbers in favour of the French system as a model for this
country, concurred in manifesting the existence of a spirit
which it became the legislature and government to repress;
his motion and Mr. Sheridan's motion was negatived by a very numerous
is rejected. majority.

Great and powerful as the body was which now supported
administration in both houses, the small band which in parlia-

m Mr. Windham's speech on Mr. Sheridan's motion, 4th March 1793.
See Parliamentary debates.
n Ib. see ib.
o Speech of sir James Sanderson the lord-mayor. See ib.

ment abetted contrary measures was not discouraged from persevering in an opposition which appeared very unlikely to attain any of their objects in parliament; and out of parliament was not gratified by that popularity which has so often encouraged and elevated parliamentary minorities. Mr. Grey, agreeably to the intimation which he had given the preceding year in the house, and to the promise which he had made to the friends of the people, proceeded in his resolution to move a reform in parliament. Various petitions were presented to the house from inhabitants of towns, villages, and districts, both in England and Scotland, who joined for that purpose. Of these, some were moderate and respectful, but others wild and violent. One petition, of a very great length, was read from persons calling themselves *friends of the people*;[p] this representatation, repeating the usual arguments, endeavoured to illustrate them by facts and instances;[q] and earnestly, though temperately, urged a change. Mr. Grey, having presented this petition, seconded its prayer by a proposition of parliamentary reform. Besides the usual arguments which, on a subject discussed so often in parliament, must necessarily be repetitions, and personal animadversions on the affirmed change of Mr. Pitt's conduct, Mr. Grey endeavoured to obviate objections to the seasonableness of the requisition. Forcibly urging the vast mass of influence which, though before known as a general fact, had never been so explicitly demonstrated by particular enumeration, he contended that the greater part of the influence in question was under the control of ministers; that thence they had been enabled, at different periods of history, to establish systems and execute measures which were totally inconsistent with the country's good. Whatever evils did or might threaten our country, there was no preventive so certain, no safeguard so powerful, as a pure and uncorrupted house of commons, emanating fairly and freely from the people. The national debt, in its present accumulation, was owing to the corruption of parliament: had a reform in the representation of the people taken place at the conclusion of the peace of 1763, this country would, in all likelihood, have escaped the American war: if it had been accomplished last year, probably,

CHAP. LI.

1793.

Motion by Mr Grey for parliamentary reform.

Arguments for.

p Not the association of which Mr. Grey was at the head, but a society that appears to have sprung from the addresses of that body.

q A work was published about this time, presenting an abstract of counties and boroughs, especially the latter, asserted to be in the nomination of peers, commoners, and the treasury, and not of the ostensible electors. The alleged result was, that seventy one peers nominate eighty-eight, influence seventy-five; that the treasury nominate two, influence five; that ninety-one commoners nominate eighty-two, influence fifty-seven; that in England and Wales the whole number of members returned by private patronage amounted to three hundred and nine. See *Report on the state of the representation, published by the society of friends of the people.*

it would have saved us from our present distress. If ever there was danger to be apprehended by this country from the propagation of French principles, the danger was now completely at an end. No set of Britons, without being bereft of their senses, could after recent events propose the French revolution as a model for British imitation. But were such principles ever to threaten danger, the surest way of preventing it from being serious was, by promoting the comfort and happiness of the people,[r] to gratify their reasonable wishes, and to grant a parliamentary reform, which was so essentially necessary, and so ardently desired: the effectual preventative of violent and forcible alteration was timely reform. This last position was still more warmly urged by Mr. Whitbread. Metaphysical opinions (he said) have never, in any instance, produced a revolution: the engine with which Providence has thought fit to compass those mighty events has been of a different description: the feelings of the governed, rendered desperate by the grinding oppression of their governors. What brought about that great event the reformation? Not the theories or speculations of philosophers, but the impolitic avarice and injustice of the church of Rome. What produced the catastrophe of Charles the First? What produced the revolution in this country? The oppressions of the executive government; and to the same cause America owes her freedom. Lastly, what produced the revolution in France? The misery of the people; the pride, injustice, avarice, and cruelty of the court.[s] The great characters who acted in these different scenes had but little power in producing their occasions. Luther, Cromwell, or Washington, the illustrious persons who appeared at the æra of the English revolution, or the wild visionaries of France could never have persuaded the people to rise, if they had been unassisted by their own miseries and the usurpations of power. When the feelings of men are roused by injury, then they attempt innovation; then the doctrines of enthusiasts' find ready access to their minds. This general reasoning was not controverted by the opposers of parliamentary change in the present circumstances. No one pretended to assert that seasonable reform was not better than perseverance in profligate corruption and tyrannical oppression; but the existence of these mischiefs was denied: no evil had been demonstrated that called for such a corrective. The persons associated to petition for a reform in parliament (their opponents said,) after a year's consideration, and, as it appears, repeated meetings, do not produce any specific plan whatever; it is therefore reasonable to infer, that they have not been able to ascertain the evil, much less to produce a remedy. The supporters of reform have asserted that the national debt originated in the corruption of parliament;

r Mr. Grey's speech on reform, 6th May, 1793. See parliamentary debates

s Mr. Whitbread's speech on reform. See parliamentary debates.

and that a reform would have prevented the many burthensome wars in which this country has been engaged since the revolution. Instead of theory examine fact: all these wars have been agreeable to the people; the proposers and supporters of them spoke in unison with the sentiments of the people. Was not a great majority of the nation favourable to the wars of William and Anne, for humbling the pride and reducing the power of Louis XIV.? Was not the Spanish war of 1739 popular? undertaken at the express requisition of the people, and even contrary to the known opinion of the government? Consider the war of 1756: was that unpopular? Never was any country engaged in a war more universally popular. The American war was equally approved by public opinion until within a year and a half of its conclusion: nothing could be more marked than the approbation which the public gave of that measure. No new system of representation could have spoken the voice of the people more plainly and strongly than the house of commons expressed it in approving these wars. That there might be improper influence in elections could not be denied; such influence, however, arose not from the political constitution, but from the imperfections, prejudices, and passions of human nature. If you are to reform, begin with moral reform:[t] but if political reform be wanted, this certainly is not the time to agitate subjects so likely to inflame the passions of the people, and to excite a public ferment. Though there may be some defects, abide by the constitution rather than hazard a change with all the dreadful train of consequences with which we have seen it attended in a neighbouring kingdom. These arguments made a deep impression, and the proposition of Mr. Grey was rejected by a very great majority, as totally inadmissible in the present state of affairs, opinions, and sentiments.

The proposition is reprobated as peculiarly unseasonable at such a period, and is rejected.

One of the most important objects of parliamentary consideration during the present session was the state of mercantile credit. A spirit of commercial speculation and enterprise had been for some years increasing in every part of the kingdom, and was now risen to such an height, as to threaten public credit with very serious danger The circulating specie being by no means sufficient to answer the very greatly augmented demands of trade, the quantity of paper currency which was brought into circulation as a supplying medium, was so large and disproportionate, that a scarcity of cash was produced which threatened a general stagnation in the commercial world. In consequence of the distress and alarm which this stagnation had caused, Mr. Pitt proposed that a select committee should be appointed to inquire into facts, and explore their causes; and the subject being investigated, it was found that the embarrassments arose from the precipitation, and not the inability

State of commercial credit, and causes of its being affected.

t The reasoning in the text is in substance taken from the speech of Mr. Jenkinson. See parliamentary debates, May 6th, 1793.

Mr Pitt
proposes
an advance
of public
money on
the securi-
ty of mer-
cantile
commodi-
ties.

The propo-
sition is
adopted,
and revive
mercantile
credit

East India
company's
charter on
the ere of
expiration.

Mr. Dun-
das pre-
sents a
masterly
view of the
prosperous
state of In-
dia under
the present
system.

of British merchants. The multiplication of paper currency, and
scarcity of coin, induced banks and bankers to suspend the usual
discounts in expectation of which, merchants had formed engagements that were far from exceeding their property, but in
the present state of pecuniary negotiation, surpassed their convertible effects. To extricate commercial men from these difficulties, Mr. Pitt proposed that government should advance money on the security of mercantile commodities, by issuing exchequer bills, to be granted to merchants, on the requisite security, for a limited time, and bearing legal interest. Opposition
expressed their apprehensions that the proposed mode would be
ineffectual, that the failures arose from the present ruinous war,
and that every remedy but peace would be futile. The projected
plan, besides, would open a path to the most dangerous patronage, since government could afford or withhold the accommodation according to the political conduct of the applicant. These
objections being overruled, the bill was passed into a law: the
temporary embarrassment was removed; and manufactures and
trade again become flourishing.

Another subject, of the highest commercial magnitude, at
the same time occupied legislature. The charter of the East
India company being on the eve of expiration, a petition for
its renewal was presented to parliament; and on the 23d of
April the subject was taken into consideration. The very general reception of Smith's commercial philosophy especially his
doctrine of free trade, and the known admiration in which Mr.
Pitt, and many of his coadjutors and votaries held the popular
system of political economy, had given rise to expectations and
apprehensions that the exclusive privileges of the East India
merchants would last no longer than the period which was
pledged by the public faith. Many supposed the commercial monopoly would be forever destroyed, and that the trade
to India would be opened to the whole energy of British enterprise. To scrutinize this subject was the peculiar department
of Mr. Dundas; and though thoroughly acquainted with the
views of theoretical economists, that able minister regarded the
question as a practical statesman. Without undertaking to
controvert the doctrines of speculative writers concerning the
productive efficacy of a free trade, or even denying the probability of its profitable effects, if extended to our intercourse
with India, he laid down a sound and prudent proposition, that
legislators ought not rashly to relinquish a positive good in possession for a probable good in anticipation. The advantages
which experience had proved to accrue from the present system were immense, varied, and momentous. The shipping
employed by the East India company amounted to 81,000 tons;
the seamen navigating those ships were about seven thousand
men, who had constant employment: the raw materials imported from India, for the use of the home manufactures, amounted

annually to about £700,000. British commodities annually
exported to India and China, in the company's ships exceeded
a million and a half sterling, including the exports in private
trade which were allowed to individuals. The fortunes of individuals annually remitted from India amounted to a million.
" The industry of Britain thus, (said Mr. Dundas) on the one
" hand is increased by the export of produce,and manufactures,
" and the consumption of those manufactures enlarged by the
" number of persons returning with fortunes from India, or
" who are supported by the trade and revenues of India ; and
" on the other, it is fostered and encouraged by the import of
" the raw materials from India, upon which many of our most
" valuable manufactures depend. So that, on the whole, the
" trade adds between six and seven millions to the circulation
" of the country. Such is the benefit accruing from the mono-
" poly of the company, exercised under the control of the legis-
" lature. The experience of nine years has justified this system !
" British India is in a state of prosperity which it never knew
" under the most wise and politic of its ancient sovereigns.
" The British possessions compared to those of the neighbour-
" ing states in the peninsula, are like a cultivated garden con-
" trasted with the field of the sluggard.[u] The revenues of In-
" dia have been increased, and the trade connected with them
" is in a state of progressive improvement. A necessary war
" has been conducted with vigour, and brought to an honour-
" able and advantageous conclusion. A system so effectually
" conducive to all its important purposes ; the prosperity of
" Britain, the welfare of India, its internal good government,
" and security from foreign aggressors, ought still to be sup-
" ported. The benefits to be derived from a free trade may be
" still greater ; but they must be contingent, whereas the pre-
" sent are certain. Before a change can be digested and exe-
" cuted many great difficulties are to be surmounted. Would
" it not create an interruption in the discharge or liquidation of
" the company's debts ? Would it not derange the regular pro-
" gress of their increasing commerce ? and would there not be
" a serious danger, that while these innovations were proceed-
" ing, rival European powers might seize the occasion, renew
" their commercial efforts, and divert into a new channel those
" streams of commerce which render London the emporium of
" the eastern trade ? On these principles, illustrated through
" a vast variety of important detail, he moved that the compa-
" ny's monopoly should be continued, under the present limits,
" for twenty years. He farther proposed regulations tending
" to promote a free trade, which should not interfere with the
" company's charter, and should embrace only such articles as
" did not employ the capital and enterprise of the East India
" company, that should bring this surplus commerce into the

u See parliamentary debates, April 23, 1793.

CHAP.
LI.

1793.

This plan
is passed
into a law.

Measures
adopted to
render
India far-
ther pro-
ductive.

Plan of
agricultur-
al improve-
ment.

Sir John
Sinclair.

Inquiries of
in Scot-
land.

"ports of London instead of the continent of Europe, to which
"it had been chiefly diverted.[x] The most important measure
"which he proposed for this purpose was, that the company
"should annually provide three thousand tons of shipping for
"conveying to and from India such exports and imports as it
"did not suit themselves to include in their own commercial
"adventures, that thus British sailors might be employed in
"this private trade instead of foreign sailors; and British sub-
"jects might be enriched by this employment of British capital
"instead of aliens." After considerable discussion, the plan
of Mr. Dundas was digested into a law; the charter was renewed, and the clauses respecting the promotion of free trade
inserted into the act.

While commercial arrangements so much occupied the attention of our statesmen and lawgivers, a kindred subject was
submitted to their consideration. Agriculture has never occupied a share of legislative attention proportioned to its momentous value as a branch of political economy, since Britain became so eminent for manufactures and commerce. This is an
omission the consequences of which have been often fatally experienced from recurring scarcity, in a country, by the fertility
of its soil and the talents of its people, so adapted for securing
plenty. An evil so frequent was naturally the subject of reiterated complaint; but no effectual measures were employed to
prevent it from often occurring again. Among the many ardent
inquirers into political economy, one of the most active and
indefatigable whom an age supremely addicted to such studies
has produced, is sir John Sinclair. This gentleman, of a vigorous and acute understanding, enriched with knowledge and
methodized by erudition, had bestowed great industry of research on various branches of political philosophy. He had
traced, investigated, and presented to the public, the history
of revenue. In the progress of his pursuits, agriculture presented itself to him as an object most deserving of promotion.
He saw that very much remained to be done; but before he
could set about propositions of improvement, he thought it
wisest and most expedient to ascertain the facts; and therefore
sought information where useful information was most likely to
be found. In Scotland, his native country, he applied himself
to the clergy, the best informed of any class of men of fixed
rural[y] residence, and addressed certain queries to the mem-

[x] See sir George Dallas's letter to sir William Pulteney, in which the
origin, history, and nature of this free trade is very ably explained; and the
means of making it to centre in British ports is clearly demonstrated

[y] From the towns also the reports were extremely valuable; but these
were not all executed by clergymen. The most important—the account of
the city of Edinburgh, came from the pen of Mr. Creech; and with the
state of the metropolis, very happily united the progress and variation of
national manners.

bers of that numerous and respectable body. These queries,
embracing the physical, moral, religious, and political situation of the respective parishes, in the result of the answers
produced an immense body of statistical knowledge; especially
on pastoral and agricultural subjects. He afterwards, less & England.
systematically and extensively executed, through different
means, a similar plan in England. He advanced, however, Result,
so far as to ascertain a general fact, of the very highest im- that agri-
portance; that though in some particular districts improved culture is
methods of cultivating the soil are practised, yet, in the great- not under-
er part of these kingdoms, the principles of agriculture are not practised
yet sufficiently understood; nor are the implements of husband- in propor-
ry, or the stock of the farmer, brought to that perfection of tion to the
which they are capable. To promote so desirable a purpose, of the coun-
sir John Sinclair projected the establishment of a board of ag- try—
riculture, to be composed of gentlemen perfectly acquainted proposes
with the subject, and considerably interested in the success of the esta-
the scheme, and who should act without any reward or emolu- blishment
ment. An address was proposed to the king, praying him to of a board
take into his royal consideration the advantages that might ac- ture.
crue from such an institution. His majesty directing the esta- The propo-
blishment of the board; the commons voted the necessary sums sal is a-
for defraying the expenses, and the board of agriculture was dopted.
accordingly established.[z]

Certain districts of Scotland, on the coast, were molested
with heavier duties upon coals than other parts of the country.
This evil had been often and strongly stated in the statistical
reports; and the duty actually amounted to a prohibition. In
the north of Scotland, from the high price of coals, the people
were obliged to trust almost entirely to their peat mosses for a
supply of fuel. In preparing this article a large portion of the
labour of that part of the country was expended, which might
be beneficially employed in fisheries and manufactures, and by
this means a great part was lost to the revenue, which would
have arisen from the industry of the inhabitants. For these
reasons Mr. Dundas proposed the repeal of the duties in question: and that the revenue might not suffer, he moved certain
imposts upon distilled spirits, which, enhancing the price of
the article, would benefit health and preserve morals. A petition was presented by the cities of London and Westminster,
praying for a repeal of a duty upon coals: in the reign of queen
Anne a tax of three shillings per chaldron had been imposed
upon imported coals, and the amount was to be applied to the
building of fifty-two churches.[a] The duty afterwards had been
employed in the maintenance of the clergymen of those churches; and lastly, was made a part of the consolidated fund; and

z See Otridge's Annual Register, 1793, chap. iv.
a This was a quite different impost from that of Charles II. of five shillings per chaldron, now enjoyed by the duke of Richmond.

CHAP.
LI.

1793.
Law for the
relief of
Scottish
catholics.

ministers alleging it was no longer a local tax, prevailed on the
house to reject the petition. Among the classes of subjects
who applied for relief this season were the catholics of Scotland:
the lord-advocate stated on their behalf, that his majesty's catholic subjects in Scotland were at present incapacitated by law
either from holding or transmitting landed property, and were
liable to other very severe restrictions, which could not now be
justified by any necessity or expediency. He therefore proposed a bill to relieve persons professing the catholic religion from
certain penalties and disabilities imposed on them by acts of
parliament in Scotland, and particularly by an act of the 8th
of king William : the bill being introduced, was, without opposition, passed into a law.[b]

Motion of
lord Raw-
don for the
relief of
debtors
and satis-
faction of
creditors.

Lord Rawdon this year presented a bill for the relief of insolvent debtors, and for amending and regulating the practice
with regard to imprisonment for debt. The bill was a compound of that humanity and discrimination which has been
already noticed in this benevolent and able character. His
lordship deemed the law of imprisonment for debt to be founded in principles at once rigorous and absurd: it was rigorous,
because it exacted from the victims of its operation, while
doomed to inaction, that which, in the free exercise of their
faculties, they were not able to perform; and was absurd, because ineffectual to its avowed purpose; for it was calculated
to defeat, not to attain its object. If the debtor be guilty of a
fraud, said his lordship, punish him as a fraudulent agent; if
not guilty of a fraud, do not punish insolvency as a crime,
which should rather be commiserated as a misfortune: to punish insolvency as criminal, and to doom fraud to the same punishment as mere insolvency, is to confound all moral distinctions. As the law now stands between debtor and creditor, in
the very commencement of an action the fundamental principle
of justice is violated. What is the great object of the institution of government, but to prevent individuals from being even
the judges, far more the avengers, of their own wrong? Yet,
by the existing laws of the land, the creditor is enabled to deprive the debtor of his liberty upon a simple swearing to the
debt. The proposed bill, however, for the present, did not
intend a general change of the law which he reprobated as so
severe and unjust: what he now desired, was a modification
of arrests and of bail, so as to prevent oppression and distress
for inconsiderable sums. The bill was opposed by lord Thurlow and by others, as striking at the whole system of the
law of England, and the lord-chancellor proposed that it
should be referred to the judges to examine the state of the
debtor and creditor laws, to consider the subject, and prepare a
bill to be introduced early the next session: Lord Rawdon agreeing, it was, for the present, withdrawn.

b Acts of parliament, 33 of Geo. III.

These were the principal subjects that came before parliament this session, except the supplies. The army and navy
were increased to a war establishment, and a considerable body
of Hanoverian troops was employed in the service of Britain.
Besides the ordinary national funds, a loan of four millions five Increase of
hundred thousand pounds was required. The high estimation the army
in which the minister stood with the monied capitalists indu- National
ced the public to expect that the loan would have been negoti- supplies.
ated on very favourable terms: but the stagnation of mercantile Loan and
credit was felt by the minister as well as others who had occa- taxes.
sion to borrow money. There was actually a great scarcity of
cash, and the public was obliged to pay a premium of eight per
cent. For defraying the interest of the loan the provisions were,
ten per cent. on assessed taxes; an additional duty upon British
spirits, on bills, receipts, and on game licenses. On the 21st of Session
June the session was closed by a speech in which his majesty closes.
expressed the highest satisfaction with the firmness, wisdom, and
public spirit which had distinguished the houses during so very
important a session and testified his approbation of the successive measures which they had adopted for the internal repose and
tranquility of the kingdom; for the protection and extension of
our commercial interests both at home and in our foreign dependencies, and for their liberal contributions towards those exertions by which only we could attain the great objects of our
pursuit. the restoration of peace on terms consistent with our
permanent security, and the general tranquility of Europe. The
signal success with which the war had begun. and the measures
that were concerted with other powers, afforded the most favourable prospect of a happy termination to the important contest in
which we were engaged.[c]

Having brought the parliamentary history of this session to a Campaign
close, the narrative now proceeds to military transactions, some of 1793.
part of which passed at the same period; including certain events
to which allusion has already been necessarily made.

From the disposition of their forces the French were enabled
first to commence hostilities: and as soon as war was declared
against Great Britain and the states-general, Dumourier proposed to invade the United Provinces. There the democratic
party, which, as we have seen, the aristocratical faction had
cherished and abetted to co-operate in their enmity to
the house of Orange, still subsisted. Though cautious in
their proceedings since the re-establishment of the stadtholder, they were increasing in number and force from the Belgian
commotions, and still more from the French revolution: especially after the republicans had become masters of the Netherlands. With the disaffected Dutch, Dumourier maintained a
close correspondence, carried on chiefly by emigrant Hollanders
assembled at Antwerp: these, formed into a kind of Batavia

c State Papers, June 21st, 1793,

CHAP.
LI.

1793.

committee, were the channels of communication between the Gallic leaders and the malcontents residing within the united provinces. The malcontents recommended irruption into Zealand, but the general himself thought it more adviseable to advance with a body of troops posted at Mordyck, 'and masking Breda and Gertruydenburg on the right, and Bergen-op-Zoom, Steenberg, Klundert, and Williamstadt, on the left, to effect a passage over an arm of the sea to Dort, and thus penetrate into the very heart of Holland.[d] The design was adventurous, but not unlikely to succeed, if executed with such rapidity as to anticipate the arrival of assistance from England. The army which Dumourier commanded on this occasion consisted of twenty-one battallions, which, including cavalry and light troops, amounted to about thirteen thousand men. He was accompanied by the skilful engineer D'Arcon, who had invented the floating batteries at the siege of Gibraltar, and a considerable number of Dutch emigrants. A proclamation was published, inveighing against the English government and the conduct of the stadtholder, and calling upon the Dutch to assist their democratic brethren in destroying the power of their aristocratic tyrants.[e] On the 17th of February the French army entered the territories of the states-general. Breda being invested surrendered by a capitulation, in which it was stipulated, that the garrison should retain their arms, and continue to fight for their country during the war. On the 26th, Klundart opened its gates to the French army; and on the 4th of March, Gertruydenburg having stood a bombardment of three days, surrendered. The same terms were granted to these two fortresses as to Breda. The strength of the captured towns was so great, that military critics, convinced they might have resisted much more effectually, did not hesitate to conclude that their easy submission arose from treachery. Dumourier now proceeded towards Williamstadt. While he was himself making such progress on the left, general Miranda, advancing on the right, invested Maestreicht with an army of twenty thousand men. Having completed his works, he summoned the garrison to surrender; but the prince of Hesse, commander of the fortress, refused to capitulate, and avowed his determination to defend such an important post to the last extremity. The French general bombarded as well as cannonaded the town; while, on the other hand the beseiged made two sallies, though without material success. General Miranda continued his investment of Maestreicht: and a covering army of French was encamped at Herve under the command of general Valence. Meanwhile general Clairfait, with the Austrian army, having crossed the Roer, attacked the French posts on the 1st of March, and compelled the army to retreat as far as Alder-

The French invade Holland.

Breda, Klundart, and Gertruydenburg surrender.

Dumourier besieges Williamstadt and Maestreicht.

d Memoirs of Dumourier.
e State Papers, February, 1793.

haven, with the loss of two thousand men, twelve pieces of cannon, thirteen ammunition waggons, and the military chest: the following day the archduke attacked several French batteries, and took nine pieces of cannon. On the 3d of March the prince of Saxe-Cobourg obtained a signal victory over the French,[f] and drove them from Aix-la-Chapelle even to the vicinity of Liege, with the loss of four thousand killed, one thousand six hundred prisoners, and twenty pieces of cannon. In consequence of this defeat of the covering army general Miranda raised the siege of Maestreicht. Dumourier, following the career of his successes in the west, laid siege to Williamstadt, and to Bergen-op-Zoom;[g] but the course of his victory was arrested; for now he had a new enemy to encounter in the British army.

The first object of the British military plans for this campaign was the defence of Holland, and a body of troops was in February sent, consisting of about six thousand British, commanded by the duke of York. A brigade of British guards was thrown into Williamstadt, who animating the Dutch to vigorous defence, and leading their efforts, made so gallant a resistance, that Dumourier saw that perseverance would be unavailing; he therefore raised the siege, ordered his troops to retire from Bergen-op-Zoom, evacuated the towns and forts which had surrendered, and returned to take the command in the eastern Netherlands, where the declining fortunes of the French required the presence of an able general. The Austrians had continued advancing to Brabant; and several skirmishes of posts had taken place, in which the Germans were generally superior. On the morning of the 18th of March, an engagement commenced at Neer Winden, on the confines of Brabant and Liege. General Dumourier attacked the centre of the imperial army with great vigour, but suffered a repulse; and he yielded to the same superior efforts from the imperial right wing. In the afternoon, however, the French right wing gained some advantage; but the corps de reserve, commanded by general Clairfait, decided the day. The army of Dumourier retreated for some time in good order, but were at length entirely routed by the Austrian cavalry. The slaughter was great; the French lost four thousand men, and soon after six thousand deserted to the enemy. The French generals, by mutual crimination, endeavoured respectively to remove from themselves the blame of the disaster. Dumourier imputed the defeat to general Miranda, who, he asserted, both fought feebly, and fled unnecessarily. In his memoirs, indeed, he admits that general La Marche committed the first error, by an injudicious movement which threw his troops into confusion; but Miranda is the subject of his principal censure.[h] Miranda, on the other

CHAP. LI.

1793.

The British forces arrive in Holland.

The French raise the siege of Williamstadt.

They are attacked by the Austrians at Neer Winden, and defeated.

French generals accuse each other.

f New Annual Register, 1793, p. 159.　　g See Dumourier's Memoirs.
h See Dumourier's Memoirs.

·CHAP. hand, imputes the discomfiture to treachery on the part of
LI· Dumourier.[i] But wherever the blame lay, if there was any,
the battle of Neer Winden decided the fate of the Belgian
1793. Netherlands. The Austrians continued to pursue the republi-
Dumourier cans; on the 21st, Dumourier judged it proper to take post
evacuates near Louvain, and on the following day he was attacked by the
the Neth enemy. The action was bloody, and lasted the whole day;
erlands. but the imperialists were compelled to retreat with great loss:
the Austrians, however, rapidly advancing in other quarters,
the French general judged it expedient to evacuate all his con-
He private- quests and re-enter France. Dumourier thoroughly knew the
ly proposes disposition of the convention, and foreseeing the fate which the
to make suspicious republicans prepared for a vanquished general, he
peace with resolved to make his peace with the allies, to march with his
the allies, troops against Paris, there to effect a counter revolution, and
and restore re-establish monarchy. On this subject he conversed with
monarchy. colonel Mack, an Austrian officer of great eminence; and it
was agreed that the imperial troops should act merely as auxiliaries for the attainment of this object; and should remain on
the frontiers, unless he wanted their assistance. If Dumourier
should find it impracticable to effect a counter revolution without the aid of the Austrians, then he should indicate the number and kind of troops of which he should stand in need to
execute his design. The Austrian forces to be furnished in
that event, should be entirely under the direction of Dumourier.
He is sus- The executive government suspecting the dispositions of Du-
pected by mourier, sent deputies to investigate his conduct. Confident
the French of the assistance of his army, he did not disguise from them his
govern- project to annihilate the national convention, and fix a king
ment, and upon the throne. Informed of his design the convention sent
summoned commissioners to supersede his command, and summoned him
to return to appear at Paris to answer for his conduct. Dumourier or-
to Paris, to dered these delegates to be seized, and conveyed to general
answer for Clairfait's head-quarters, to be kept as hostages for the safety
his con- of the royal family. But the army soon showed the vanity
duct. of Dumourier's expectations; they not only refused to follow
He sounds him to Paris, but gave him reason to doubt his personal securi-
the dispo- ty, and he was compelled to seek safety by flight. Having
sition of reached the imperial territories, he had an interview with
the army; colonel Mack, and with the prince of Saxe-Cobourg. Two
but finding proclamations were digested, one by Dumourier bimself, the
them unfa- other by the prince of Saxe-Cobourg. The manifesto of gene-
vourable, ral Dumourier contained a recapitulation of his services to the
deserts to French republic; a statement of the cruel neglect which his
the Aus- army had experienced in the preceding winter, and of the out-
·trians rages which were practised by the jacobins towards the generals of the republic, and particularly himself. It states the
reasons why he arrested the commissioners; exhibits a vivid

i In a letter to Petion, dated 21st March, 1793.

picture of the evils which might be apprehended from the continuance of the anarchical system in France; and expresses his confident expectations, that as soon as the imperialists entered the territory of France, not as vanquishers, and as wishing to dictate laws, but as generous allies, come to assist in re-establishing the constitution of 1790, great numbers of the French troops would join in promoting so necessary a purpose. He protested upon oath, that his sole design was to re-establish constitutional royalty; and that he and his companions would not lay down their arms until they had succeeded in their enterprise. These protestations, interspersed with a considerable portion of gasconading promises which he could not perform, and threats which he could not execute,[k] constituted the declaration. A manifesto[l] was also published by the prince of Saxe-Cobourg, announcing that the allied powers were no longer to be considered as principals, but merely as auxiliaries in the war; that they had no other object but to co-operate with general Dumourier, in giving to France her constitutional king, and the constitution she formed for herself. He pledged himself that he and his army would not enter the French territory to make conquests, but solely for the end now specified. He declared farther, that any strong places which should be put into his hands, should be considered as sacred deposits to be delivered up as soon as the constitutional government should be established in France, or as soon as general Dumourier should demand them to be ceded. It was at this period that Mr. Fox[m] and many others thought that the combined powers might have proposed such terms of peace to France, as would have been accepted with equal readiness and gratitude. The allies, it was alleged by the votaries of peace, ought to have declared themselves to the national convention to the following purport.

k In the last paragraph, in which he introduces his oath under the head " *I swear* (he says) that we will not lay down our arms until we shall have succeeded in our enterprise; and our sole design is to re-establish the constitution, and constitutional royalty; that no resentment, no thirst after vengeance, no ambitious motive, sways our purposes; that no foreign power shall influence our opinions; that wherever anarchy shall cease at the appearance of our arms, and those of the combined armies, we will conduct ourselves as friends and brothers; that wherever we shall meet with resistance, we shall know to select the culpable and spare the peaceable inhabitants, the victims of the infamous wiles of the jacobins of Paris, from whom have arisen the horrors and calamities of the war; that we shall in no way dread the poignards of Marat and the jacobins;—that we will destroy the manufacture of these poignards, as well as that of the scandalous writings by which an attempt is made to pervert the noble and generous character of the French nation;—and finally, in the name of my companions in arms, I repeat the oath, that we will live and die free. The general in chief of the French army, Dumourier." See State Papers, 1793.

l See State Papers, April 5th, 1793.

m It was in consequence of the present posture of affairs, that he made the motion for peace, which has been already mentioned in the parliamentary history.

CHAP.   Arrange your internal government according to your own in-
LI.   clinations: the present confederacy is formed for purposes of
        defence, not of aggression; we shall not therefore interfere in
1793·   the constitution of France. We only desire you to re-establish
        the ancient boundaries of the Netherlands, to restore your other
        conquests; to liberate the queen and the royal family; and to
        allow the emigrants a moiety of their property : we will then
        withdraw our forces, and be your friends. Had such proposi-
        tions been made, these politicians affirmed that a stop might
        have been immediately put to the effusion of blood; and that
        France would at this time have been under a regular and
        established government, and Europe would have been at peace.

Hypotheti- It is difficult to say with any degree of probability, what would
cal reason- have been the result in a very problematical question, of an ex-
ings on the periment that never was tried. The probable success of such
practicabi
lity and ex- an attempt proceeded upon an assumption that either the French
pediency of were not originally the aggressors; or, if the beginners of the
peace at   war, were from recent discomfiture tired of its continuance.
this period Perhaps if the offer had been made, in their present circum-
of victory stances they might have received it with delight : and for a
to the con-
federates. time have continued pacific; but afterwards might have re-
        sumed invasion. when the confederation was broken. But it
        belongs not to history to state possible, or even probable con-
        sequences, which might flow from measures that were not
        adopted. If as some able statesmen argued, the hour of vic-
        tory was the hour of offering peace, the confederates against
        France were of a totally different opinion. They conceived
        France to have been the aggressor: to have manifested views
        of ambitious aggrandizement; that it was the policy of her
        neighbours to prevent her encroachments, and in her present
        condition to reduce her strength so as effectually to prevent the
        future accomplishment of her projects: that therefore they
        ought now to press upon her in her weakened state. On this
        view they regulated their policy, and formed the plan of the
        rest of the campaign. A congress was held at Antwerp,
        wherein representatives attended from the several powers that
        formed the combination, which had now been joined by Spain
        and Naples. At this congress were present the prince of Saxe-
        Cobourg, counts Metternich, Starenberg, and Mercy d'Argen-
        teau, with the Prussian, Spanish, and Neapolitan envoys. It
        was determined that the fortresses on the frontiers of France
        should be invested by the armies of the confederates, that the
        enemy's coats should be beset on every side by the fleets of
        the maritime powers, and that every encouragement and prac-
        ticable assistance should be afforded to the royalists within
        France.[n] A second proclamation was now published by the
        prince of Saxe-Cobourg, annulling the first, and declaring a
        design of keeping whatever places he should capture, for the.

n New Annual Register, 1793

indemnification of his sovereign. Dumourier, when he was CHAP.
informed of this change in the imperial system of military ope-   LI
rations, declared to the prince de Coburg, that he could not
with honour serve against France. Receiving a passport, he   1793.
therefore retired into Germany.[o]

By the plan of operations concerted for attacking the frontiers
of France, the British, Dutch, Austrian, and Prussian troops
were to press on to the Netherlands ; an army of Prussians and
other Germans from the Rhine. Joined to the confederate armies were great bodies of emigrants, commanded by the princes
of the blood, and other refugees of high rank and distinction.
The chief part of the exiles was attached to the army of the
Netherlands ; and on all sides dispositions were made for invading the French dominions.

o He first came over into Britain, but was desired by ministers to quit
the kingdom ; and in his visit nothing passed of any historical importance.
See Annual Register, 1793.

CHAP. LII.

CHAP.
LII

1793
Overtures
for peace
by Le Brun,
the French
minister.

ABOUT the time that Dumourier engaged in a negotiation with Cobourg for the re-establishment of monarchy, the existing government of France made an attempt to procure the restoration of peace. The proposals were conveyed through a very unusual channel: Le Brun, the French minister, employed Mr. James Matthews, an Englishman of whom he had no knowledge but what Matthews gave himself, to carry to London two letters[q] addressed to lord Grenville, and a third to Mr. John Salter, attorney, then a vestry clerk to the parish, since a notary public in Penny's Fields, Poplar, recommended by Mat-

q Dated at Paris, April 2d, 1793, and delivered to lord Grenville 26th April 1793. See State Papers.

thews, requesting him to deliver the two letters to the British
secretary. The purport of the first was, that the French republic desired to terminate all differences with Great Britain,
and that he demanded a passport for a person to repair from 1793.
France to Britain for that purpose. The second mentioned He propo-
Mr. Marat as the person who was to be deputed, and claimed ses to send
a safe conduct for him and his necessary attendants. Mr. Sal- sador to
ter accepted the commission, as he had probably agreed with Britain.
Matthews; and on the 26th of April 1793, delivered the two Letters
letters to Lord Grenville, at his office, Whitehall. The letters from him
procured no attention, and produced no effect: they never, are deliver-
like other overtures for negotiation, were the subjects of par- Grenville,
liamentary discussion; and the literary notice which they ex- but receive
cited was inconsiderable. The partisans of war regarded the no answer.
uncommonness of the agency as a sufficient reason for over-
looking the propositions.[r] The votaries of peace did not view
the advances in that light, but from their general and cursory
account, appear to have thought the transaction of little importance,[s] and are totally unacquainted with the causes and circumstances of a mode of conveyance so different from the established etiquettes of diplomatic communication. The real
history of this mission the kind information of Mr. David Williams has enabled me to lay before the reader.

    The literary celebrity of Mr. Williams, and the use which Circum-
the French reformers had made of his " Letters on political stances and
" liberty," induced the Girondists to invite him to France, these prof-
that he might assist them in the formation of a constitution.[t] fers of con-
Brissot, whom he describes as an honest but a weak man, he ciliation.
had known in England, had corresponded with him, and warned him of the danger which he was incurring by his violence.
Repairing to Paris, he became intimate with Condorcet, Roland, and other political leaders of the times. He continued
to admonish them of the evils which they would encounter, unless they could moderate the licentiousness of the populace,
and suppress the faction of the jacobins. He saw the wildness
and extravagance of the Girondists themselves, and strongly
represented to Brissot the impracticability and madness of rousing and uniting the nation by war. He powerfully inculcated
the necessity of peace and moderation, to the welfare of the
people, and the security of any constitution which might be
formed for that purpose: he particularly recommended the
maintenance of peace with England, and strongly reprobated
the prosecution and death of the king, as giving the populace a

r See Otridge's Annual Register for 1793; a volume which, having evidently taken a side, I prize less as an authority than any of the other
volumes of the same work, which loyally and patriotically supporting our
constitution, record and estimate measures with the dignified impartiality
of authentic history.
    s See Belsham's History, vol. v. p. 47.
    t See Madame Roland's Appeal, and Public Characters for 1798, p. 472.

CHAP.
LII.

1793..

taste of blood. Eager as the Brissotines were for war, yet
they were conscious that France was not prepared for hostilities with England: patriotic policy sometimes overcame revolutionary fury; and then they would listen to the pacific counsels of Mr. Williams. When the discussions between Mr.
Chauvelin and lord Grenville were evidently tending to hostility, they asked Mr. Williams to undertake a mission to the British court, in order to effect an accommodation. Regarding
such an office as not altogether suitable to a British subject,
especially in the fluctuation of sentiment which the French
government exhibited on the question of peace and war, he
declined the mission. Still, however, he conceived that peace
might be preserved: the same opinion was expressed to him by
members of the Gironde; and it was with great surprise, on the
1st of February, that he heard the convention declare war by
acclamation against Britain and Holland. Mr. Williams now
resolved to return to his country: still Le Brun and other members of the French government professed to him their wishes
for the restoration of peace; and since he would not himself
undertake a mission, that minister asked him to bear a letter to
lord Grenville, which requested the British government to open
the ports of Dover and Calais; in the postscript declared the
French government to desire the re-establishment of peace,
proposed to send a minister. and stated that Mr. Williams was
empowered to explain their principle and project of conciliation, so as to be satisfactory to the British government. Mr.
Williams returned to Britain, repaired to the secretary of state's
office, delivered his letter,[u] and mentioned his readiness to wait
on lord Grenville whenever his lordship should appoint: but he
was never sent for by the secretary, and there his commission
ended. Mr. Williams himself appears to me to think that the
French were already convinced of their precipitation in declaring war, and would have willingly agreed to the terms which
lord Grenville had required from Chauvelin, if they found the
British government equally disposed to return to amity; but as
no opportunity was afforded him of an audience from lord
Grenville, neither his statements nor deductions could be of
any avail to the purpose of the commission with which he was
charged.

Correspondence between Britain and France being now precluded, Le Brun heard nothing from Mr. Williams. While Mr.
Williams had been at Paris, there went thither a Mr. James
Matthews, who professed great regard and veneration for Mr.
Williams, was frequently in his company, and had thereby opportunities of knowing the names and persons of some members of the French government, but was not introduced to any
of these rulers. The inauspicious commencement of the campaign between France and the allies disappointed the republi-

u See State Papers.

cans; and the desertion of Dumourier added treachery as a
fresh ground of alarm to.the apprehensions that were entertained from the British and Austrians. Perhaps these considerations rendered.the French government more anxious for
peace, or perhaps they might profess anxiety without being
sincere: whatever was the motive, they certainly did repeat
the attempt; and this Mr. Matthews was the person, on the
mere pretence of being Mr. William's confident, that was appointed to carry the second overtures to England. Why . Mr.
Le Brun chose Mr. Salter to be the deliverer of the despatches
sent by Mr. Matthews I have not learned, or why Mr. Matthews
did not deliver them himself, he not being in a state of mind to
answer such questions. Indeed, the whole transaction; Mr.
Matthew's application to Le Brun as the confident of Mr. Williams; the appointment of Mr. Salter, then vestry clerk of the
parish of Poplar, to convey the letters to Grenville; and the
assurances of Matthews, who brought the letters, that he should
instantly make peace, and provide for all his friends (in which,
however, Mr. Williams was not mentioned), can be accounted
for only from an incipient derangement of mind, the symptoms '
of which soon appeared, and for which he has been ever since
confined. Mr. Matthews was chosen to be the bearer not as
an obscure and unconnected individual, but from being conceived by the French government to have the confidence of Mr.
Williams. Mr. Williams they had first wished, in their extravagant manner, to be, in effect, an ambassador; and finding he
would not accept that general mission, they prevailed on him
to be the bearer of specific proposals, which they professed to
think conducive to peace. Thence came Mr. Matthews to be
employed in the SECOND application which the French government, within the first three months of the war, made for the
re-establishment of peace. That the republicans were sincere
in these proffers it would be very rash to affirm. Against their
sincerity there were the series of Brissotine menaces of universal warfare; the tendency and character of the revolutionary
enthusiasm: for their sincerity there were the actual disappointments which they were experiencing, and the farther
disasters which they *then* appeared likely to suffer. Perhaps
they might be sincere in desiring peace with Britain, in order to
facilitate their schemes of ambition against other countries;
but those schemes of ambition had been formed in the exultation of unexpected success, and might not be cherished at the
season of discomfiture and retreat. From the correspondence
between Grenville and Chauvelin, they well knew that no proposal would be admitted by Britain which did not renounce the
navigation of Scheldt, forbear interference with the internal
affairs of other countries, and forego their projects of aggrandizement: if they intended to offer less, their overtures, there-

CHAP.
LII.

1793.

Alarming
state of
France;
at war
with all
her neigh-
bours.

fore, would have been futile; but it cannot[x] be ascertained
whether their offers would or would not have been satisfactory
according to our requisition of satisfaction, since they were not
heard. The intervention of a vestry clerk has been stated as
ridiculous; but Le Brun did not propose Mr. Salter as a negotiator, he employed him as a courier for carrying an offer of
sending as ambassador Mr. Marat, who had a few months before
conferred and negotiated with Mr. Pitt.

The situation of France was at this time extremely alarming;
she was at war with her three most powerful neighbours, Prussia, Austria, and Britain. A body of her bravest sons, stimulated by the strongest resentment, was joined to her formidable
enemies. The states of Holland, and principalities of Germany, though not very important in their separate force, yet added to the impulse which was already so great. Sardinia,
Naples, and Spain, were embarked in the same cause. From
the Texel to the straits of Gibraltar, from Gibraltar to Shet-
land there was a circle of enemies encompassing France.[y]
Within her territories there were numerous bodies eagerly desirous of co-operating with her foes from without: a formidable
rebellion was broken out in La Vendee, and the French government divided into two violent factions, appeared on the eve of
destruction by an intestine war. These concurring circumstances seemed to justify the hopes of the confederacy, that
France, surrounded by so many enemies, and rent by such con-
vulsions, would be unable to resist their separate and united efforts: but the French republicans were not overwhelmed by the
multiplicity of dangers. The national convention informed
of the arrestation of their commissioners, and the defection of
Dumourier, manifested that rapid energy which ever distinguished the French revolutionists in emergency and danger, and
adopted efficient measures to preserve the tranquility of the
metropolis, and defend the frontiers against the invading host.
The northern army was re-organized, and general Dampierre

x On this part of my inquiries Mr W declined any particular explanation. He is writing on the subject himself.

y The people, from having such a multiplicity of enemies, conceived
themselves at war with the whole world: the following incident that occurred to a captain of the navy, a near relation of mine, is a curious illustration of these sentiments. On the 22d of March arrived at Portsmouth
from Jamaica, the Falcon sloop of war, captain Bisset, having captured off
Ushant a French privateer. Captain Bisset was not apprized of a war between this country and France, till he fell in with the above privateer, who
bore down upon the Falcon, but perceiving her to be a sloop of war, she
immediately hauled her wind, and fired her stern. Captain Bisset, astonished at this conduct, instantly stood after her, and coming up with her,
demanded the reason of such conduct; when he was told by the commander of the privateer, *"that France had declared war against all the world."*
The Falcon then fired a few guns, and the French ship struck her colours,
and was taken possession of by the Falcon.

being re-appointed provisional commander in chief, re-occupied the camp at Famars in French Hainault, near the right bank of the Scheldt. The confederate army was posted at Kieverain on the frontiers of Austrian Hainault, with their right extending to St. Amand, and their left to Bavie, so as to blockade Condé, threaten Valenciennes, and even to overawe Maubeuge.. The French general proposed to drive the allies from so advantageous a position, and to relieve Condé. On the 1st of May he began the execution of this design, by attempting to dislodge the Austrians from several villages which they possessed, but was repulsed with the loss of near a thousand killed and wounded. Dampierre undismayed by this check, and encouraged by re-enforcements which were just arrived, marched on a second time, with three formidable columns against the Prussian lines at St. Amand, and maintained a long, severe, and bloody contest, till succours from the Austrians under Clairfait, obliged him to make a precipitate retreat, after leaving two thousand men on the field of battle. His immediate object being to relieve Condé, he still threatened the Prussians, who were now joined by the British troops under the duke of York. Intending to confine his attack to the right wing, he feigned an intention of assailing the whole line; and advancing to the wood of Vicoigne, he began the charge. On his left were constructed several strong batteries, where were posted ten thousand men drawn from the garrison of Lisle. Against this numerous force the Coldstream guards, with some other British troops, were despatched. This heroic band, regardless of numbers, checked the enemy's batteries with their field-pieces; and after one discharge of musketry, rushed forward with fixed bayonets. Terrible in every species of warfare, British soldiers are irresistible in close fight; when no dexterity can elude the force of personal prowess; and hence the opportunity of charging bayonets has rarely failed to assure victory to our countrymen. Our combatants made an impression on their antagonists, which the French soon saw they could not withstand man to man; they had, therefore, recourse to their chief excellence, missiles; with rapid activity they wheeled round artillery from the front to the flank, and opened with grape shot upon the gallant English. Dreadfully annoyed, the British forces disdained to fly: they kept their ground, repulsed the multitudes of the enemy, and in the conflict mortally wounded Dampierre.[z] The French had gone forth to battle in the most assured confidence, thinking they had only Prussian tactics and intrepidity to oppose their rapidly active genius and valour; but finding it was a very different undertaking to combat the energy of British heroism, they retreated within their lines, nor afterwards attempted offensive operations in a quarter secured by so formidable champions. From this period to the 23d of May, the

British soldiers supremely excellent in close fight, in spite of French numbers and artillery, by the bayonet decide the fate of the day.

French did not venture out of their lines; the allies, on the other hand, encouraged by the impression which was made by the action of the 8th, resolved to make a general attack on the camp at Famars, that covered the approaches to Valenciennes. The dispositions for this grand object being finished, the 23d of May was fixed for executing the design. At day-break the British and Hanoverians assembled under the command of the duke of York, and the Austrians and German auxilliaries under the prince of Cobourg and general Clairfait. Great pains had been employed to conceal the projected attack, until its execution should be commenced. A fog somewhat retarded the advance of the troops, but at the same time concealed their approaches; until the sun penetrating through the mist, displayed to the astonished French the allies in four columns, proceeding

Battle of Famars. towards their camp. A tremendous fire of artillery began the action on both sides: the contest soon became closer; and one of the Austrian columns was nearly overpowered, when the Hanoverians and British repulsed its assailants: at length the combined troops, led by the British, and headed by the duke of York and general Abercrombie, entirely defeated the French army. During night the duke of York refreshed his forces, resolved to attack the enemy's fortifications the next morning; but in the night the republicans abandoned the intrenchments which they had formed with such pains and expense, and left the way open to Valenciennes. About the same time bodies of Dutch and Austrian troops employed in the maritime Netherlands, drove the French invaders on that side within their frontiers.

Blockade and surrender of Conde. Condé, as we have seen, was in a state of blockade: the town was not provided with a sufficient quantity of provisions to sustain a long siege: the governor (general Chancel,) therefore, about this period ordered the women and children to quit the place. As the diminution of consumers tended to prolong a blockade, the prince of Wirtemberg, who commanded on that service, would not suffer their departure; opposed and prevented repeated attempts. The besieged, after a very brave and obstinate resistance, and enduring with the most persevering fortitude all the rigours of famine, were, on the 10th of July,

Siege of Valenciennes. obliged to surrender at discretion. But a much more arduous enterprise, undertaken by the allies, was the siege of Valenciennes; and the victory at Famars having enabled them to approach, they formed a regular investment. Valenciennes is situate on the left bank of the Scheldt, opposite to the camp

Strength of the fortress. which the French had recently occupied. Its fortifications, among the chief efforts of Vauban's genius, rendered it a post of extraordinary strength. The garrison consisted of about eleven thousand men: Custine, appointed on the death of Dampierre to take the command of the northern army, found it impossible to relieve the fortress, which was therefore obliged to depend on its own strength. The allies, conscious of their fôrce, and confident of ultimate success, summoned the fortress **CHAP.** to surrender: the summons was disregarded; and being repeat- **LII.** ed, was still unavailing: the allies,. therefore, proceeded with their approaches. A difference of opinion prevailed between 1793. the two chief engineers of Britain and of the emperor respectively, colonel Moncrief and monsieur Fcrasis. The British officer, less regarding customary modes than efficient means, proposed to plant batteries immediately under the walls of the city, instead of. approaching it by regular parallels.[a] The German officer, adhering closely to experimental tactics, proposed to proceed in the manner which had been so long in use; and his opinion was adopted by the council of war. On the Operamorning of the 14th of June the trenches were opened; and tions. Ferasis directed the siege under the superintending command of the duke of York. The successive parallels were conducted with distinguished skill, and finished with uncommon expedition; this despatch being powerfully promoted by the British guards; who, from their habits of working in the coal barges on the Thames, were enabled to do more work in a given time than an equal number of any other soldiers.[b] In the beginning of July the besiegers were able to bring two hundred pieces of heavy artillery to play without intermission on the town, and the greater. part of it was reduced to ashes. The smallness of the garrison, compared with the extent of the fortifications to be defended, prevented general Ferrand, the commander, from attempting frequent sorties: in one which the garrison made on the 5th of July, however, they were very successful, killed several of the enemy, and spiked some cannon. ᐧA considerable part of the war was carried onᐧ under ground, by numerous mines andᐧ countermines, which both besiegers and besieged constructed. The chief of these were, one which the besiegers formed under the glacis, and one under the horn-work of the fortress.[c] These mines were completed and charged on the 25th of July, and in the night, between nine and ten o'clock, were sprung with complete success. The English and Austrians immediately embraced the opportunity to throw themselves into the covered way, of which they made themselves masters. The duke of York now, for the third time, summoned the place to surrender; and the governor seeing no hopes from farther Captured defence, capitulated; by the capitulation the troops taken in the after a garrison were allowed to retire into France, on swearing that siege of six they would not, during the war, serve against any of the allied weeks, in powers; and the duke of York took possession of Valenciennes of the emin the name of the emperor of Germany. peror.

Those promoters of war with the French republicans who Sentiments desired the restoration of monarchy as the chief object of hos- of Burke and his votaries on this subject.

a New Annual Register, 1793, page 187.
b See Macfarlane, vol. iv, page 390.
c New Annual Register, 1793, page 190.

tilities, disapproved of various circumstances in the capture of Valenciennes, and indeed in the principle on which the campaign was conducted; as, according to their hypothesis, the legitimate object of the war in which the confederacy was engaged was the re-establishment of monarchy, the emigrant princes and other exiles ought have had the chief direction in its councils and conduct; whereas these were really employed as mercenaries. On the same hypothesis Valencinnes and other towns captured, or to be captured, ought to be possessed in the name of Louis XVII as king of France, and of his uncle the count of Provence, as lawful regent during the young king's minority; and troops capitulating ought to be restricted from serving against French royalists, as well as the allied powers. These observations were fair and consistent inferences, if it had been admitted that the combined powers were actually, as the English opposition asserted, fighting for the restoration of the monarchical constitution :[d] but according to British ministers, and the greater number of their parliamentary votaries, the purpose of the war was not a counter revolution in France, but the attainment of security against the French projects of aggrandizement, and dissemination of revolt; that the most effectual means for this purpose was the reduction of her power, without any regard to her internal government; that we were to reduce her strength in the present as in former wars, by capturing, according to our respective force, her towns and possessions. Indeed, the confederates at present seemed to proceed on the same principle of conquering warfare which had been practised by the grand alliance for humbling the power of Louis XIV. To adopt the language of works less specially devoted to the support of ministerial politics, than to the restoration of monarchy in France; they were rather *anti-gallicans*, warring against physical France, on the general principles of former times, than *anti-jacobins*, warring against moral France, on the peculiarly requisite principles of present times. On the one hand, the object of Mr. Burke, however impolitic and impracticable it may have been deemed, was much more definite than the objects of Mr. Pitt, as far as these were explained: on the other, the objects of Mr. Pitt being conceived to be merely anti-gallican, were much more agreeable to the prevailing sentiments of Britons than the avowal of a combination would have been, for interfering in the internal polity of France, and re-establishing a government which, in its former exercise, Britain so very much disapproved. The capture of French towns in the name of the young prince, as sovereign of a country that had renounced its authority, would have been an avowal of a counter revolutionary project, which the British government.

are differ-
ent from
those of
Mr. Pitt
and his co-
adjutors.

d The most eloquent and illustrious advocate of this doctrine, Mr. Burke, exhibits this theory in his remarks on the policy of the allies, begun in October, 1793.

disavowed, and which the majority of the British nation would have censured. The appropriation and capitulation of Valenciennes were therefore perfectly consonant to the professed views with which the allies, having completed the purposes of defence and recovery, had invaded the French Netherlands. While the allies were thus engaged in the Netherlands in strengthening the power of the emperor on the Rhine, they were occupied in recovering the captures of the French. On Successes the 20th of June the Prussian army invested Mentz; and after of the a regular and vigorous siege, and a very gallant defence, it Prussians. capitulated on the 22d of July. Mentz is taken.

While the confederates were making such advances on the France is frontiers of France, the republic was entirely torn with dissen-torn by dissions. The Girondists, who had been long declining in authori-sensions. ty, and who were more than ever abhorred by the Mountain, since their desire to save the king, had constantly supported Dumourier against the invectives of Marat and the jacobins. As soon as Dumourier was driven into exile, the Mountain rais-The Moun- ed an outcry against his late protectors the Girondists. They tain excite were represented to the furious multitude as a band of traitors a clamour and counter revolutionists. The municipality of Paris, and the against the jacobin clubs, resounded with complaints, threats, and impre-Girondists. cations, against the party in the convention which retained some sentiments of humanity, some love of order, and some regard for justice. The Gironde party still possessed considerable influence in the convention; but the Mountain, gratifying the Parisian rabble with blood and plunder, exercised the supreme command in the city. In March was established the Establish- revolutionary tribunal for trying offences against the state. ment of the This celebrated and dreadful court, consisting of six judges, revolution- was wholly without appeal. The crimes on which it was ary tribu- to pronounce were vague, undefined, and undefinable; ex-nal. tending not merely to actions, but to most secret thoughts. On the 1st of April a decree was passed abolishing the inviolability of members of the convention when accused of crimes against the state.

The chiefs of the Brissotines appeared to be astonished and confounded at these daring and desperate measures of their inveterate adversaries, confident in their power and popularity; The Giron- and made no vigorous opposition to decrees which were evi-dists pos- dently intended to pave the way to their destruction.[e] It was sessed a now manifest that the Girondists were inferior to their antago-tive inge- nists in vigour and decision; and, notwithstanding the intel-nuity, but lectual and literary accomplishments of the leaders of the wanted party, grossly deficient in practical talents for government; practical that, therefore, they must finally sink under the contest of ability. which they were unequal to the management. The Mountain tain superi- had not only in its favour the jacobin club and the dregs of the or in deci- sion and daring atrocity.

e See Belsham's history, vol. v. p. 62.

people of Paris, but it knew that the triumphant party in that
immense city, from terror or obedience, was able to command,
throughout the whole extent of the republic; and whilst the
Girondists were reasoning, deliberating, and menacing, the
Mountain conspired, struck, and reigned. On the 31st of May,
early in the morning, the tocsin was sounded; the barriers
were shut; Brissot, Roland, and many others of the most distinguished Girondists were seized and committed to prison by
a force devoted to Robespierre. Terror quickly seized all
minds; and the theoretic republic of ingenious, but unwise
and unprincipled innovators, became subject to a detestable
and bloody tyranny. Robespierre, Danton, Marat, Collot
d'Herbois, Billaud, and Couthon, became rulers of France.
They associated with themselves ferocious individuals whose
talents were necessary to the administration, and who consented to serve them through fear, ambition, or policy.[f] They
hastily drew up the celebrated constitution of 1793; and no
policy ever existed more absurd, or more favourable to anarchy. Legislation was confined to a single council, the members of which were elected without any qualification of property: the executive power was among twenty-four ministers,
appointed by the convention, and dismissed at their pleasure.
This government, the most absolute and the most ferocious
of which there has ever been an example, was confined to
two sections, consisting of twelve deputies. The one was
called the *Committee of public safety*, and the other the *Committee of general safety*. They were to be renewed every
month; but by one of the incalculable effects of fear, which
blinds those whom it governs, the convention, divesting itself
of its inviolability, intrusted the committees with the formidable right of imprisoning its members: and thus rendered the
power of the government as solid as it was extensive. Meanwhile, some of the Girondist deputies who escaped the proscription excited insurrection. Several departments indicated
a disposition to avenge themselves, and resist oppression:
some of them took up arms. By far the most formidable resistance to the reigning usurpers arose in the south, where the
three principal cities, Lyons, Marseilles, and Toulon, formed
a combination for overturning the existing tyranny. Toulon
opened a negotiation with lord Hood, who commanded the
British fleet in the Mediterranean. The English admiral,
at the instance of the inhabitants took possession of the town
and shipping, in the name of Louis XVII. The Spaniards
advanced into Languedoc, proffering assistance to all those
Frenchmen who wished to resist the horrid tyranny of the jacobin
faction.

In comprehensive tyranny, efficacious malignity, deliberative iniquity, affecting the persons, liberties, properties, and

f See Segur's History of Frederick William, v. iii.

minds of their countrymen, the junto which now governed
France surpassed all the wickedness ever recorded in history.
Their predecessors had progressively promoted infidelity, confiscation, destruction of rank and order; but still their remain- 1793.
ed a considerable degree of religion, and great masses of pro- malignity
perty, with a small share of subordination. Robespierre and of the go-
his band abolished christianity; publicly and nationally abjur- verning
ed the Supreme Being. They proscribed genius, lest its efforts Robes-
might overthrow their horrible system. They ruined com- pierre and
merce to stimulate the multitude to plunder; and they seized his hand
all property. Totally free from every principle of religion and abolish
virtue; without humanity, pity, or remorse, they proscribed, ty and ab-
they murdered, they plundered; they deemed all mankind jure the
merely instruments for gratifying their diabolical passions.[g] Supreme
The means by which they were enabled to exercise such a Being; at-
complication of tyranny was the multitude. By the populace tempt to
conjunctly and aggregately they were able to exercise des- civil, polit-
potism over the populace themselves severally.[h] The war fa- ical, and
cilitated the extension of their power, because it enabled them moral dis-
to accuse all persons obnoxious to themselves as traitorous cor- tinctions.
respondents with foreign enemies. The war also, so much
engaged the anxious attention of the people, that they had
less time to brood over the internal sufferings of their country.
Pressed on all sides by invaders, who they conceived were
desirous of dictating to them in the arrangement of their own
government, an ardent zeal to maintain national independence
drew off their thoughts from internal despotism. The same
patriotic spirit was inflamed, not only by the fears of foreign
interference in their government, but by the belief that the dismemberment of their country was intended.

The pressure of the confederates, and their supposed de- The pres-
signs, cherished the ferocious tyranny of Robespierre. Detest- sure of the
able as this relentless tyrant was, yet, in one momentous ob- war facili-
ject, he promoted the first wish of Frenchmen; not to be con- tates their
troled by foreign invaders. In opposing the confederacy of atrocities.
princes, the revolutionary government displayed an energy
that triumphed over all obstacles. Much of this energy, no
doubt, is imputable to the very wickedness of the system.
The understanding, employing its invention and foresight in
seeking means for gratifying passions, without the least restraint from conscience, may certainly be more efficacious, than
if repressed in its devices by religion and virtue. The extinction of every pious and moral sentiment, and the removal of
the sanctions of a future state prepared minds for every enormity. It paved the way for bearing down all opposition to
the executive power proceeding by massacre or any other
crime that might most expeditiously effect its purposes. The
revolutionary government, in its total violation of justice,

g See Otridge's Annual Register, 1793.   h See Burke on Regicide peace.

CHAP.
LII.

1793.
Forced
loan
Requisi-
tions.
Bold
scheme of
the war
minister to
raise the
nation en
mass.

found ample resources for military supply. *The terrible system* wanted money: a forced loan placed the fortunes of all men at its disposal. It wanted provisions, ammunition, arms: it put all physical resources under REQUISITION [i] It wanted men: its war minister, bold in conception as unrestrained by humanity and justice, said, " let us confound all the calculations of " experienced warriors : ours is a new case ; raise the whole " nation in MASSE : overpower discipline by multitude; bear " down tactical skill and experience ; and tire out their efforts " by fresh and incessant relays : consume your enemies by the " fatigue of exertion." Scarcely were the orders given when twelve hundred thousand men[k] marched out to meet the enemy. Of these, great numbers, no doubt, were propelled by fear, and the assured alternative of massacre if they refused ; but whatever might have been the motive, the effect was prodigious. To hasten the operation of such a multitude, vehicles were contrived for carrying both men and cannon with

Efficacy of
this sys-
tem.
It over-
comes the
insurgents
of La Ven-
dee.

extraordinary despatch against the enemy. Immense bodies were sent to quell the insurgents of La Vendee, and succeeded in repressing the attempts of these royalists. Marseilles yielded with little contest to the revolutionary arms. Lyons, instead of following the example of Marseilles, made a most resolute resistance, and for two months heroically withstood an active siege. General Kellerman, who commanded the army of the Alps, was ordered to besiege that city; but not answering to the impatience of the convention, he was removed, and general Doppet appointed to succeed him; to whom the inhabitants, who were not only unused to arms, but very ill provided with the means of defence, as well as the necessaries of life, on the 8th of October, were obliged to surrender. A great part of the city was reduced to ashes by a continual bombardment. The victors, who had sustained considerable

Murderous
cruelties.

loss during the siege, were filled with furious resentment, and gratified their revenge by the most savage and atrocious cruelty. The wretched victims, too numerous for the individual operation of the guillotine, were driven in large bodies, with the most brutal and blasphemous ceremonies, into the Rhone; or hurried in crowds to the squares to be massacred by musketry and artillery.[l] Immense bodies of troops under general Cartaux, proceeded to Toulon: an advanced corps having arrived in the neighbourhood of that city, captain Keith Elphinstone, of the navy, landing from the fleet, and joining a body of English and Spanish infantry, attacked and routed

---

i See decree of August 15th, 1793, requiring all Frenchmen to be in permanent readiness for the service of the armies with every kind of warlike stores, and even every material for making arms, powder, ball, and all other kinds of ammunition or provision for military service.

k See New Annual Register, 1793

l See Otridge's Annual Register for the year 1793, p. 275.

the enemy with considerable loss. Soon after, general O'Hara, CHAP. LII.' arriving from Gibraltar, took the command of the British forces. Attacking the enemy, he defeated and put them to flight; but pursuing the fugitives very eagerly, he unexpectedly encountered a large force entirely fresh. In endeavouring to draw off his soldiers safely to Toulon, he was unavoidably engaged in a conflict with superior numbers; and after an obstinate contest he was wounded and taken prisoner. Near a thousand of the British and their allies were either killed or captured. As an immense mass of French was now approaching, against which to defend the town the remaining handful was totally incompetent, it was judged expedient to evacuate the place with all possible despatch Accordingly, the allies made dispositions for withdrawing and saving as many of the inhabitants as could be removed : and for destroying all the shipping, stores, and provisions, that could not be preserved by any other expedient from falling into the hands of the enemy. This service was performed very completely ; the troops were carried off without the loss of a man ; and several thousands of the loyal inhabitants of Toulon were sheltered in the British ships. Sir Sidney Smith, to whose active intrepidity was intrusted the conflagration of the magazines, storehouses, and arsenals, with the ships in the harbour, most effectually performed this hazardous and extraordinary duty. On this occasion, fifteen ships of the line, with many frigates and smaller vessels, were destroyed, and an immense quantity of naval stores. Three ships of the line, and several frigates accompanied the British fleet. By this destruction the French navy received a blow very difficult to be retrieved.

1793.

The French force the English to evacuate Toulon.

While the French, rising in a mass, crushed revolt and expelled foreign enemies in the south, their gigantic efforts effected in the north a momentous change in the events of the campaign. After the reduction of Valenciennes, the French were compelled to abandon a very strong position which Custine occupied behind the Scheldt, denominated Cæsar's camp. A council of war was now held by the allies to consider the most effectual plans of pursuing their successes. Generals Cobourg and Clairfait proposed,[m] while the French were under an alarm from the disasters in the Netherlands, to penetrate towards Paris, while a force should be sent under cover of the British fleets, to co-operate with the loyalists in Britanny : the duke of York was of opinion that it would be much more adviseable to extend their conquests upon the frontiers. He proposed that the army should divide; that he, at the head of his countrymen, the Dutch and Hanoverians should attack the enemy on the side of West Flanders, while the allies continued their operations in the Eastern Netherlands. It was concerted that the allies should besiege Quesnoy, and that the

Netherlands.

Progress of the duke of York and the British troops.

m Annual Register, 1793.

CHAP.
LII.

1793.

Victory at
Lincelles.

His high-
ness in-
vests Dun-
kirk with
reasonable
hopes of
success.
Late arri-
val of the
artillery
and naval
force.
Progress of
the siege
notwith-
standing.
An im-
mense
mass of
French ar-
rives.

The Bri-
tish prince
is obliged
to abandon
the at-
tempt.

duke of York marching to the coast where he could receive maritime co-operation, should invest Dunkirk. This port has ever been, in time of war, a very great receptacle for privateers, and extremely troublesome to the English trade in its approach to the Downs. Therefore the British cabinet, as well as the commander in chief, were eager to wrest from the enemy such means of annoyance. Separating from the allies, his highness marched towards Dunkirk; and on the 18th of August he reached Menin.[n] The Dutch under the hereditary prince of Orange, attacked a French post at Lincelles in that neigh- bourhood, and were repulsed; but the British troops, though very inferior in force, carried the post with fixed bayonets, and defeated the enemy. The French no longer venturing to ob- struct his advances, on the 22d his highness arrived before Dunkirk. On the 24th he attacked the French outposts, and compelled them to take refuge within the town.[o] In this engagement, however, he incurred some loss both of men and officers; and among the latter the Austrian general Dalton, so noted, as we have seen during the revolt of the Netherlands from the emperor Joseph. On the 28th of August the siege was regularly commenced by the duke of York, while general. Freytag with an army of auxiliaries, was posted to cover the besiegers. A considerable naval armament from Great Britain, intended to co-operate with a military force, by some unac- countable delay did not arrive nearly so soon as was appointed and expected. His highness nevertheless carried on the siege with great vigour and skill. Meanwhile the republican troops, commanded by general Houchard poured from all quarters, in an enormous mass. Attacking the army of Freytag the 7th of September, after several severe actions, in which the Ger- mans made a most vigorous resistance, the French at last over- powered them by numbers, defeated them, and compelled them to make a very precipitate retreat. In this route Freytag him- self, and prince Adolphus of England, youngest son of his Britannic majesty, were taken prisoners, but in a short time rescued. The duke of York, from the defeat of the covering army, found it necessary to raise the siege. Before he had departed, the garrison, informed of Houchard's success, made a sally, in which they were repulsed with great loss; while the besiegers also suffered considerably, and among other officers were deprived of the celebrated engineer colonel Moncrief, who was killed by a cannon ball. Houchard now attacked a second time all that remained of the covering army, gained a complete and decisive victory, and with his daily increasing mass hastened against the duke of York. The British com- mander found it absolutely necessary to withdraw from Dunkirk, to prevent his gallant band from being totally over- powered by such an infinite multitude of enemies. The una-

n Otridge's Annual Register, 1793, p. 272.   o Ibid. 273.

voidable hurry of his retreat compelled our prince to leave his CHAP.
heavy artillery, and a great quantity of ammunition, which fell LII
into the hands of the enemy. The military chest was preserved
by being hastily put on board a frigate. 1793.

The miscarriage of this enterprize produced great censure
among those who judge of plans by events; but at the time
that the enterprize was concerted, there were reasonable hopes of
success; and the attainment of the object would have been extremely advantageous to Britain. The delay of the gun boats
and artillery, must certainly have retarded the execution of the
design; but the final disappointment was owing to causes which
no man judging from military experience could have possibly
anticipated. The new French expedient of arming in mass had
not yet been known to the allies, and the rapid means of bringing
forward their immense multitudes were no less extraordinary and
astonishing. The prodigious hordes thus carried to the scene
of warfare, must have discomfited the British project, however
wise the undertaking, well concerted the plan, seasonable and efficient the preparations. Ends were to be sought, and means to
be employed according to probabilities, founded in the experience that then existed. From so unprecedented a collection of
armed multitudes, escape without very considerable loss was a
great achievement; so great indeed, that the enemy conceived
it impracticable: they apprehended that if general Houchard
had discharged his duty, he might have effectually cut off the
British retreat. Under this impression the French general was
afterwards denounced, and suffered by the sentence of the revolutionary tribunal.

While the duke of York was engaged before Dunkirk, the The
allies invested Cambray, Bouchain, and Quesnoy; the two French
former they found impracticable, the latter they executed. mass com-
Prince Cobourg having repulsed a detachment sent to the re- pels the
lief of Quesnoy, the fortress surrendered to general Clairfait on to retire
the 11th of September. Soon after this capture the duke of behind the
York rejoined the confederates. The French army of the Sambre.
north, after raising the siege of Dunkirk, took a strong position
in the neighbourhood of Maubeuge, where they were immediately blockaded by the whole united force of the allies, collected under the prince of Cobourg. The republican armies, after
the accusation of Houchard, were intrusted to the command of
Jourdain, who having formerly served in the French army in
a humble rank, and afterwards became a shop-keeper in a petty village,[o] but having resumed the military profession, was
by the French government deemed worthy of the supreme
command; and, as the allies experienced, did signal honour
to the penetration of his employers. Jourdain, on the 15th
and 16th of October, attacked prince Cobourg with such numbers, vigour, and effect, as to compel him to abandon his posi-

o See New Annual Register for 1793. It is there said he was a haber-
dasher.

CHAP.
LII.

1793.

tion, and repass the Sambre. The French general now freed from blockade, was at liberty to employ offensive operations. Detachments were accordingly sent to make inroads into maritime Flanders. They took possession of Werwick and Menin, from whence they advanced to Furnes: they proceeded to Nieuport, which they besieged and greatly damaged; but the place was saved by having recourse to inundation. It was some time before the allied forces were able to stop the progress of the republicans, and their generals even trembled for the fate of Ostend. A considerable armament from England, however, being at that time preparing for the West Indies, under sir Charles Grey, their destination was altered; and by arriving at this fortunate moment at Ostend, they saved the Low Countries for the present campaign.

They force the Prussians to retreat.

On the Rhine, after the capture of Mentz, a number of petty actions took place, in which the French were generally successful; but no event of importance ensued.[p] During the month of September, the duke of Brunswick gained several advantages, and the allies invested Landau. the siege of which occupied the remainder of the campaign. A French army commanded by general Landremont, strongly posted on the Lauter, covered and protected this important fortress. On the 14th of October general Wurmser forced the strong lines of the enemy; and Lautreburg surrendered at discretion, after being evacuated by the republicans. The town of Weissembourg made a longer resistance; part of it, however, was unfortunately burned, and the French before they retreated, set fire to their magazines within the walls, as well as those at Alstade. The French, not disheartened by these losses, made repeated attacks on the enemy's lines, and at last were so successful, that the duke of Brunswick deemed it expedient to raise the siege of Landau, and retire into winter quarters. The armies of the Netherlands finished the campaign about the same time.

The campaign terminates much less favourably than its commencement promised.

Although the continental campaign of 1793 was on the whole successful on the side of the allies, yet its termination was by no means equally auspicious as its preceding periods. From its commencement to the month of August, it had been progressively successful; then, however, the career of victory was arrested. In point of actual possession, the allies had preserved Holland, and recovered the Netherlands; had retaken Mentz, captured Condé, Quesnoy, and Valencinnes. But it required little discernment to see that the prospect was not now favourable to the confederates, and that the tide of success was turned. The allies never appeared to have established that concert of ends, and consistency of means, without which alliances cannot hope to succeed against a single and well compacted powerful opponent. If it was wise and expedient ts seek the restoration of monarchy, their efforts should have been direct-

Gigantic efforts of France and want of concert among the allies.

ed to that sole object. Separate aggrandizement, even were
it in itself justifiable, necessarily created jealousy and distrust.
The king of Prussia began to conceive that the successes of
the campaign were advancing the power of Austria, while he
had a share only in its expense and disasters.

From the dismemberment of France he could look for no Catharine prosecutes
accession, and was, besides, intent upon dismemberment in her designs
another quarter. Catharine having attained her wish of en- against
gaging the German powers in a war with France, had executed Poland;
her intentions, of destroying the new constitution of Poland,
which had tended to extricate that country from its dependence
on herself. She invaded Poland with an army of a hundred proposes a second
thousand men, forcibly annulled the constitution at the diet, partition
and to secure the concurrence of the king of Prussia, as well of that ter-
as gratify her own ambition, she proposed a second partition ritory, and
of the Polish territories; that the king of Prussia should for invites the
his share receive the cities of Dantzick and Thorn with Great king of
Poland, while her own portion of the spoliation was nearly partici-
half the remainder more contiguous to Russia. The Prussian pate.
king was more occupied in securing his spoils in Poland, which Frederick
a band of patriotic heroes still endangered, than in seconding William
the emperor. On the other hand, the emperor was extremely intent on
jealous of the acquisitions of his Prussian ally; and the bands of the spoils
the confederacy were evidently loosening. of Poland.

On her own element, Britain unincumbered by allies, began Rapid suc-
the war with signal success. In the West Indies, the valuable cess of the
island of Tobago was captured by a British squadron under where they
admiral Laforey, about the beginning of April. From an early fought
period of the French revolution, the West India Islands belong- alone.
ing to France, and particularly St. Domingo, had been agitated
and convulsed by the revolutionary spirit, and by premature and
injudicious attempts to confer the right of free citizens, in that
part of the globe, upon the " people of colour," who constitute
a large proportion of the inhabitants.q From the dreadful inter- Conquests
nal commotions, St. Domingo was a scene of devastation and in the West
bloodshed. In July, fort Jeremie, and Cape Nicola Mole, be- and East
ing attacked by the British squadron, surrendered themselves. Indies.
In the gulf of St. Lawrence, the islands of St. Pierre and
Miquelon, were captured. In the East Indies, the company's
troops in the first campaign of the war, reduced Pondicherry,
and all the settlements of the French on the coasts of Malabar
and Coromandel.

q See Belsham's History, vol. v. page 101.

CHAP. LIII.

CHAP.
LIII.

1793.

THE chief internal occurrences of this year regarded
projects of political reform. In Ireland a society was establish-

ed for promoting a complete emancipation of the catholics; that CHAP.
is a thorough exemption from all legal disabilities, and a *radical* LIII.
reform of parliament on the principles of universal suffrage and
annual elections. This club, constructed on the model of the 1793.
affiliated jacobins, took the name of the *United Irishmen*, which Project of
was afterwards productive of such dangerous consequences. In political
the Irish parliament an act had been passed, granting relief to reform. Club of
the catholics, but by no means so extensive as their supporters in United
and out of parliament desired. They were allowed to exercise Irishmen.
all civil and military offices under the crown, except in the very
highest departments of the law and state; and they were prohibited from sitting in parliament. The executive government Institution
appeared well inclined to extend the relief, but the apprehensions and ob-
of the protestant party were so deeply rooted, as to render it in-jects.
expedient in the legislature to proceed any farther at that period.
The united Irishmen, as a party, were not particularly connected
with the catholics, but consisted of the votaries of innovation[r] in
general; held assemblies for concerting and preparing means
to promote their schemes of change. These meetings being Conven-
considered as dangerous in the present ferment, a law was pass- tion bill.
ed by the Irish parliament for preventing such assemblies;
being specifically described, both in nature and purpose, so as
to restrain innovating cabals: the new act was known by the title
of the convention bill. While the legislature endeavoured to
prevent pernicious assemblies in Ireland, projects were formed
in Britain by bodies of individuals for holding a convention,
which should speak the national voice, and effect such changes
as in the judgments of these politicians should appear necessary
for the regeneration of Britain:

The revolutionary doctrines of France spreading into this island, Britain.
produced a desire of change, which was different in object and Great num-
extent according to the circumstances, knowledge, and character bers are in- fected with
of their votaries. Men of desperate fortune or reputation might the desire
desire a subversion of government, in hopes of profiting by the of change.
general confusion, and no doubt there were such men in the
clubs which were supposed to seek revolution. These were a
kind of associates that revolutionary leaders might be sure to
acquire, according to the believed probability of success. But, Causes—
if their conduct be candidly reviewed, by far the greater num- ignorance,
ber of the associated votaries of indefinite change will appear to vanity, and visionary
have been misled by folly, ignorance, or visionary enthusiasm, enthusi-
rather than prompted by malignant intentions. A passion asm, more
which produced the addition of many members to these clubs, than ma-
was vanity. They wished to make a figure in spheres for which lignant in-
their education and condition rendered them totally unfit. The tentions.
supposed exaltation of the people in France, inspired many
well disposed manufacturers, mechanics, tradesmen, and peasants with a desire of reaching the same distinction, and stimu-

[r] See Reports of Irish Committees in 1797 and 1798,

CHAP.   lated them to exercise their talents as orators and lawgivers.
LIII.   There is, indeed, in the lower orders of our countrymen a pe-
        culiar propensity to oratory: the free constitution under which
1793.   they live empowers them to utter their sentiments and opinions
Propensity with open boldness; the love of social and convivial intercourse
in the low- very naturally following an unrestrained interchange of thoughts
er orders to and feelings, produces clubs, which at this period were very
be spokes- numerous.   These requiring some kind of methodical arrange-
men; arises
from the   ment, introduced some kind of order and system in addresses
free inter- and replies beyond the desultory irregularity of conversation.
change of Hence arose debate, which generated emulation to distinguish
opinion
which Bri   themselves in their circle of companions; the members respec-
tons enjoy: tively tried to be spokesmen.   As their oratorial talents, in their
           own apprehension, increased, they wished for a wider field of
           exercise; this they found in vestries or other meetings of local
           arrangement; or sometimes betook themselves to debating so-
           cieties, where they could exhibit their eloquence and wisdom
           on subjects of erudition, philosophy, and politics. , From these
           causes there was, especially through the great towns, a pre-
           disposition in people of low rank, without education and litera-
           ture, to recreate themselves with speeches and dissertations.[s]
           The visions of French equality held out to their fancies and
           passions pleasing images and powerful incentives; increased
           the objects of their eloquence and political exertions, proposed
           so wide fields for exercise, and promised such rewards as stimu-
           lated great numbers to seek change, less from dissatisfaction
at this   with the present than from sanguine expectations of the future;
time is   and rendered them desirous of reforming assemblies, not so
abused.   much with a view to overthrow the established constitution, to
           crush king, lords, and commons, as to distinguish themselves
           in the proposed conventions.   That some of the ringleaders
           desired the subversion of our existing establishments admits
           very little doubt; but that a total misconception of the purpo-
           ses of their leaders, vanity and the love of distinction, and not
           treasonable motives, actuated the chief portion of their votaries
Dangerous we may candidly and fairly presume.   But, whatever might be
tendency of the intention of the individuals respectively, the tendency of
certain   such assemblages collectively, in a season of revolutionary en-
political thusiasm, was evidently dangerous; and required the unremitting
associa-
tions and vigilance of government, to restrain and correct delusion and to
senti-   chastise mischievous deluders.
ments.   In Scotland, two active agitators of political change, Messrs.
Scotland. Muir and Palmer, the former an advocate, the latter a dissent-
Mess. Muir ing clergyman, were tried for sedition, charged to have been
and Pal-
mer,

          s At the trial of Hardy, the shoemaker, one Wills a dancing-master, who
          had accompained the defendant to the corresponding society, being inter-
          rogated as to his own motives for resorting to that meeting, replied that he
          had a pleasure in hearing the conversation of *clever* men. See State Trials
          in 1794.

committed in writing and other acts. The following facts were CHAP. LIII.
established against Mr. Muir at his trial: he had actively dispersed in and about Paisley and Glasgow, Paine's Rights of
Man and other books and pamphlets of a similar tendency; in 1793.
conversation expressed his wishes and hopes of changes on the trials of,
model of France; and purchased works hostile to the British for sedition.
constitution, especially Paine, for people too poor to buy them
themselves.[t] It was farther proved that he was an active and
leading member in societies for promoting such doctrines and
conduct as Thomas Paine inculcates, and that his rank and
situation afforded great weight and influence to his exhortations. Mr. Palmer, an unitarian preacher at Dundee, had
been no less active in the east than Mr. Muir in the west, and
indeed much more violent. He had either composed or promoted addresses, which stimulated his votaries to enmity against
the house of commons and the existing orders, and declared
the highest privilege of man to be universal suffrage; inveighed
against the constituted authorities, their counsels and measures,
as oppressive and tyrannical; called on the people to join in
resisting these oppressions, and adjured them by every thing
that was dear to them, to combine for the preservation of their
perishing liberty and the recovery of their long lost rights.
These and other publications similar in inflammatory rhapsody,
were dispersed with ardent activity by Mr. Palmer, and by a
very strenuous agent, George Mealmaker, weaver.[u] There
could be no doubt that such conduct was seditious, and no
valid objection could be made to the evidence. The jury were
therefore bound to bring in a verdict *guilty* in each of these
cases. In Scotland the sentence in cases of sedition, rests with They are sentenced
the judges; and in both these cases the punishment was, that to transportation.
they should be transported for the space of fourteen years beyond the seas, to such place as his majesty, with the advice
of his privy council, should think proper. Both these gentlemen possessed fair and unimpeached moral characters, and
were deemed enthusiasts in what they conceived to be right,
and not intentionally malignant incendiaries. Though this
circumstance did not diminish the mischievous tendency of
their conduct, yet lessening their moral guilt, it excited a considerable degree of compassion for their destiny. The punishment, indeed, was by very eminent members of the law of The punishment is represented as excessive, and even illegal,
Scotland deemed and represented as an assumption of power
by the court, which was not allowed by the statute enacting
the penalties consequent on the species of sedition charged in
the indictment. They were tried on an accusation of *leasing*[x]

---

t Such as Thomas Wilson, barber, Ann Fisher, servant maid, and others
in equally humble stations. See Muir's Trial.
u See Trial of Palmer, at the Autumn Circuit at Perth 1793.
x *Leasing,* a Scotch word, in its general import signifies a *lie;* in law it is
applied to the particular species of falsehood described in the text.

CHAP.
LIII.

1793.

making, a term, which in the Scotch law means stirring up se‑
dition, by spreading false reports between the king and his sub‑
jects. It was asserted by Mr. Henry Erskine and others that the
punishment annexed by the law of Scotland to this crime, was
outlawry,[y] and not transportation ; that the judges might sentence
the convicts to be exiled from Scotland, but that their judgment
could not extend to their conveyance to any other place. Others
who were neither disposed nor competent to such legal disquisi‑
tion, censured the judges for adopting the most rigorous mode
that even by their own hypothesis could be chosen. Many, how‑
ever, deemed the castigation wholesome in example, and benefi‑
cial in tendency.

Scotch
convention
for new
modelling
the consti‑
tution, con‑
sists chiefly
of persons
of low con‑
dition,

In the end of October, 1793, a club of persons entertaining
similar extravagant ideas of reform as Messrs. Muir and Palmer,
meeting at Edinburgh, denominated themselves *the Scotch con‑
vention of delegates* for obtaining annual parliaments and uni‑
versal suffrage   This notable assembly consisted chiefly of
tradesmen and mechanics, a few farmers, many of lower situa‑
tion, and one or two men of abilities and knowledge, who were
unfortunately smitten with the revolutionary contagion. These
persons having met, adopted the modes and phraseology of the
French convention, accosted each other by the term of *citizen,*
divided themselves into *sections*, granted the honour of *sittings*,
in humble imitation of their model ; and proposed to concert
measures with the innovating clubs, especially the London
corresponding society, for the attainment of their object. It is
remarkable that those who sought universal equality of politi‑
cal privileges, claimed this equality as *an inherent right*, and
upon this assumption founded all their theories. Now political
power is the inherent right of no individual: every man has a
natural right to govern himself, but has no natural right to
govern others:[z] government is the creature of expediency. In
every society those ought to govern who are most fit for pro‑
moting the general good. All men are not equally qualified
for legislation, therefore it is not expedient that all men should
have an equal suffrage, either in legislation or in constituting a
legislature : the political inequality which these visionary inno‑
vators sought to reduce, arose from unequal means of advan‑
cing the general welfare which these levellers professed to pur‑
sue. On this absurd theory of human rights, without any proof
of expediency, these agitators proceeded ; but before they had
brought their deliberations to a conclusion, they were inter‑

dispersed
by the ci‑
vil power.

y The punishments are three, fine, imprisonment or banishment : the
question respecting the last was whether it meant merely the *exilium* of the
civil law (outlawry), or the *deportatio*, (transportation). There were very
respectable authorities on both sides.
z See this doctrine very ably explained by the learned and profound Fer‑
gusson's principles of moral and political science, vol ii. p. 471, on the ex‑
ercise of legislative power.

vupted by the civil power,[a] and dispersed. Skirving, Marga- CHAP.
rot, and Gerald, three of their most active members were tried LIII
for sedition, and received sentence for transportation; which
judgment incurred the same censure as the punishment that 1793.
was appointed for Muir and Palmer. The conduct of the Their lea-
judges who passed the sentence was very much blamed, not ders are
only by democrats, but by the constitutional opponents of tried and
government; and was not completely approved by many to trans-
others who were well affected to ministers; but the merits portation.
of the judgments afterwards underwent a discussion in parliament.

The session opened on the 21st of January, 1794; and the 1794.
diversities of political opinion continued to resolve themselves Meeting of
into three classes, the same in principle as before, though parlia-
somewhat varied in detail, from the course of events. A few, ment.
at the head of whom was Mr. Burke, deemed war against
regicides indispensably necessary, until monarchy should be
restored. A small, but greater number, reckoned the war unwise from the commencement, and a peace conducive to its
professed purposes, to be at present attainable. The season Mr. Fox
of important victory, (according to Mr. Fox and others) all and his
wise politicians thought the best opportunity for concluding support-
a peace. The continuance of war, instead of subjugating mend
France, tended to drive her to desperate efforts.[b] We had peace.
seen in her recent exertions arming her people in mass, and
hurrying them on to the scene of war with unheard of rapidity,
the consequences of invading her territories. Continued at- Argu-
tempts to trench upon her dominions, would only drive her to ments
still more extraordinary efforts. Besides to what purpose was and for.
the continuance of war; the professed objects of the British
government had been attained in the delivery of Holland, and
the expulsion of the French from the Netherlands. Unless
we propose to restore monarchy, which ministers said we did
not, we were now fighting without an object. A very nu- Mr. Pitt's
merous body, at the head of which was Mr. Pitt, maintained reasoning
that the object of the war was and uniformly had been the and the in-
same; the SECURITY of Britain, and general traquility.[c] The ternal sys-
present terrible system of France was totally incompatible with tem of
these objects: in its dreadful nature it could not last. The France,
people, if properly seconded and supported, would generally
revolt against such an oppressive, rapacious, and desolating
government. With the present rulers we could not make
peace; but we might expect that their sway would be of short
duration: the efforts of the terrible system had far exceeded
any reasonable or probable expectation; but the resources from

a On this occasion Mr Elder, the lord provost, peculiarly distinguished
himself by his activity, resolution, and prompt decision.

b See parliamentary debates, 21st January, 1794.

c Ibid.

which they arose, so desparate and iniquitous, afforded in themselves the most certain symptoms and indications of the approaching decay of that fabric with which they were connected. The leading feature in the French revolutionary character,
(said the minister) is a spirit of military enterprize, exerted not
for the purpose of systematic ambition, but every where in its
progress spreading terror and desolation. We are called in
the present age to witness the political and moral phenomenon
of a mighty and civilized people[e] formed into an artificial
horde of banditti, throwing off all the restraints which have
influenced men in social life, displaying a savage valour directed by a sanguinary spirit, forming rapine and destruction into
a system, and perverting into their detestable purposes all the
talents and ingenuity which they derived from their advanced
stage of civilization, all the refinements of art, and the discoveries of science. We behold them uniting the utmost savageness and ferocity of design with consummate contrivance and·
skill in execution, and seemingly engaged in no less than a
conspiracy to exterminate from the face of the earth all honour,
humanity, justice, and religion. In this state can there
be any question but to resist, where resistance alone can be
effectual, till such time, as by the blessing of providence upon
our endeavours, we shall have secured the independence of
this country, and the general interests of Europe. All the
succeeding parties which had prevailed from the deposition of
the king, however adverse to each other, had agreed in hostility to this country: the alternative of war and peace did not
at present exist. Before we could relinquish the principles on
which the war commenced, proof was necessary, either that
the opinions which he had conceived of the views of France
were erroneous, that the war was become desperate and impracticable, or that, from some improvement in the system
and principles of the French, the justice and necessity which
prompted us to commence the war, no longer co-operated.

Lord
Morning-
ton's
view of the
subject.
Lord Mornington spoke on the same side, and displayed very
extensive information and considerable ability. According to
the representation of his lordship, the French views of aggrandizement were unlimited. Their desire of conquest sprang
from principles which were subversive of all regular government. The avowals and exhortations of their most admired
writers fully proved their schemes of boundless agression, and
their determined hostility to this country.[f] But a still surer
proof was their conduct, which was uniformly and consistently hostile to this and every other nation within the reach of its
influence. Our cause was originally just; the whole series of

e Mr. Pitt's speech, 21st January, 1794. Ibid.

f To support his argument, his lordship quoted many extracts from
French writings, especially from a pamphlet by Mr. Brissot, which had recently reached England, and which breathed hostility to Britain,

events confirmed its justice. But an important point to be considered was the probability of success: the recent efforts of the French arose from causes that could not long exist; these were the atrocious tyranny of the present government, which embraced men, money, liberty, property, and life, within its grasp. The dreadful fire was consuming the fuel by which it was nourished: their expenditure was enormous; their finances must be speedily exhausted,[g] and leave them no longer the means of so formidable hostilities: they would be compelled to succumb to the just and systematic exertions of the allies. But it was by our warlike efforts only that we could secure ourselves from the inroads of revolutionary France. In proportion as this system of tyranny consumed the property of France, it must endeavour to repair its disordered finances by foreign plunder. It must be the immediate interest of a government founded upon principles contrary to those of surrounding nations, to propagate the doctrines abroad by which it subsists at home, and to subvert every constitution which can form a disadvantageous contrast to its own abilities. Nothing could secure us against the future violence of the French, but an effectual reduction of their power. That was a purpose which we had the most reasonable prospects of ultimately accomplishing, and the strongest inducements to persevere. But even were the French rulers, instead of being eagerly resolved to persevere in a war indispensably necessary to their usurped domination, disposed to accede to terms of equitable accommodation, where was the assurance of their stability? What reliance could we repose on the performance of their engagements? What was the purpose of attempting to negotiate with a government utterly unable to fulfil its stipulations. Not only the characters, the dispositions, and the interests of those who exercised the powers of government of France, but the very nature of that system they had established, rendered a treaty of peace upon safe and honourable terms impracticable at present, and consequently required a vigorous and unremitting prosecution of the war. A very great majority in parliament, A great convinced that peace could not be preserved with the present majority rulers of France, and confident that their extraordinary efforts approves of would speedily exhaust their own source, approved the continu- the contin- ance of the war, and its most vigorous prosecution. uance of the war.

g This was an argument often repeated by Mr. Pitt at different periods of the war. It was partly founded on the reports and calculations of sir Francis d'Ivernois, who very accurately and justly explained the sources of finance known to former experience; but in his estimate, not sufficiently allowing for the enthusiastic spirit by which the French republicans were now actuated, did not consider its creative effects. Thence it was that all predictions of French bankruptcy, founded in the application of common rules to a case totally beyond their reach, were completely falsified.

CHAP.   : Mr. Fox and Mr. Sheridan persevered in maintaining the
LIII.   inexpediency of the war, the improbability of success, and the
~~~~   wisdom of peace. They denied that France had been hostile
1794.   to this country. The chief charge of the present rulers
The oppo- against their predecessors was, that they involved their country
nents of   in a war with Britain contrary to the interests and wishes of
the war   the people. But whencesoever the war had originated, the
impute to
the combi- exertions and events afforded no reasonable ground for expecta-
nation the tion that the objects, even if just, were attainable. The efforts
astonishing of the French arose from the enthusiasm of conceived liberty
efforts of and patriotism. So devoted (it was said) are the whole people
France.
Messrs.   of France to the cause which they have espoused, so determined
Fox and   are they to maintain the struggle in which they have engaged,
Sheridan   so paramount and domineering is the enthusiastic spirit of liber-
predict the ty in their bosoms, so insignificant, comparatively, are all other
dissolution considerations, and finally, so bitter and active is their animo-
of the con- sity against the conspiring powers which surround them, that
federacy
and the tri- individual property has ceased to be regarded even by the pos-
umph of   sessor, but as subsidiary to the public cause; and the govern-
the French. ment which had demanded these unprecedented sacrifices, yet
           retains its power and does not appear to have impaired its popu-
           larity.[h] France, by the pressure of the allies upon her fron-
           tier, had become a school of military wonder; and if other
           governments persisted in their design of thus goading her to
           almost preternatural exertions, we should see a military repub-
           lic firmly established in the heart of Europe.[i] Such was the
           energetic spirit of the French, that we might be sure, with the
           resources that spirit would call into action, we could never
Discussion succeed. In answering the ministerial objection, with whom
of the
question   could we treat, we might negotiate with the existing rulers,
with whom and depend for adherence to pacific engagements neither on
shall we   the justice or stability of the present set, but on their interest,
treat.   and the interests of their successors, whoever they might be,
           and of the whole French nation. Interest and not good faith,
           had been our security in our various treaties with the despotic
           princes of France. The confederacy, in which we endeavour-
           ed to make an impression upon France, composed of hetero-
           geneous materials pursuing different objects, Mr. Fox strongly
           and repeatedly predicted, must be soon dissolved. If the
           objects of the war had been just and wise, the plans were dis-
           jointed, inconsistent and consequently ineffectual. But minis-
           ters, said Mr. Fox, never defined the object: they vaguely
           told us we were fighting for *security* ; but wherein was that
           security to consist. In former wars our objects had been defi-
           nite, to prevent aggrandizement of France,[k] by the acces-
           sion of one of her princes to the throne of Spain;[l] to, protect
           our merchantmen from the search of Spaniards;[m] to defend

h See Mr. Sheridan's speech on the first day of the session, 1794. Parliamentary Debates.
i See marquis of Lansdown's speech, on his motion for peace.
k War 1689.   l War 1702.   m War 1739.

our colonies from the encroachments of France:[n] to resist the interference of foreign nations, in disputes between us and our colonies.[o] There the objects, whether right or wrong, were definite : but here they were barren generalities, mere abstractions : if, as ministers professed, we were not warring for the restoration of the Bourbon princes to the throne of France. From their conduct, however, he was convinced they did propose that restoration which he predicted no foreign force would ever produce. He had spoken, and would always continue to speak against a war which sought no object beneficial to Great Britain ; required exertions that drained her resources, and anticipated the products of future industry. He prophesied that the war with France, like the war with America, would terminate in disappointment. We were incurring an enormous expense, in return for which we had no prospect of advantage or compensation. Such conduct might be varnished by splendid eloquence, or justified by sophistical logic, yet when viewed by common sense and common prudence, it was infatuated blindness that was producing consequences which the present and future ages would have strong reasons to lament and deplore. The minister merely played on the passions which he had himself inflamed, without addressing the reason or consulting the interest of his countrymen. These arguments were repeated both on direct motions for peace,[p] and various other questions connected with the war, but produced no effect on the majorities in parliament.

Next to peace and war, questions arising from internal discontent, projects of innovation, and the prosecutions which some abettors of these had undergone, occupied the chief share of parliamentary deliberation. Messrs. Muir and Palmer, and the sentenced members of the Scottish convention, in consequence of the power left by the judgment with his majesty and council to appoint the place of deportation, had been ordered to be sent to Botany Bay. In the execution of their sentence they had been sent on board transports at Woolwich, along with other convicts destined for the same place. Many who admitted the justness of the judgment, deprecated the severity of the treatment ; but a stronger ground was taken in parliament : it was maintained that the sentence was not legal, and that the criminal jurisprudence of Scotland required a revision which should render it more definite and precise, and put it on the same footing with the penal law of England. Motions to these intents were brought forward by Mr. Adam, a counsellor of great eminence, deeply conversant both in Scottish and English law, with moral and political science, which could appreciate their separate and comparative merits.

CHAP.
LIII.

1794.

Mr. Fox prophesies that the war with France like the war with America would terminate in disappointment.

Various motions for peace are ineffectual.

Questions respecting the trials for sedition in Scotland.

n War 1756.   o War 1778.
p February 17th, by the Marquis of Lansdown : May 30th, by the duke of Bedford and Mr. Fox, in their respective houses.

CHAP.
LIII.

1794.

Mr. A-
dam's pro-
posed a-
mendment
of the Scot-
tish crimi-
nal law.

With this view, he proposed to bring forward two bills; the one of which should grant an appeal to the lords of parliament from the judgment of the courts of justiciary and circuit in Scotland, in matters of law: the other should assimilate the criminal law of England and Scotland, that crimes and misdemeanors affecting the state should be on the same footing in both countries; that a grand jury should be held in Scotland in the same cases as in England; and that the power of the lord-advocate should be the same as the power of the attorney-general. These objects Mr. Adam had in view before, and in the preceding session had announced his intention of proposing alterations which should assimilate the criminal law of the two countries. But the recent trials in Scotland, in his apprehension, had rendered the discussion of the subject more urgently necessary; and made it adviseable to change the intended form of the propositions so as to include a declaratory and retrospective as well as an enacting and prospective operation. His first proposition was introduced to the house of commons on the 4th of February. Its purpose was, to establish an appeal from the court of justiciary to the lords, and to have a clause inserted which should subject the sentences of 1793 to the projected revisal. Having stated historically and juridically the facts and tendencies respecting the law as it now stood, and its administration; he observed, that there was not only a strong analogy between the criminal codes of England and of Scotland in the great purposes of all penal laws, but a striking resemblance also in their respective course of proceedings. Their mode of trial by jury was the same; every thing was the same except one circumstance; a right in the house of lords to revise the sentences of the court of justiciary and the circuit courts. With regard to the inconvenience that might accrue by bringing cases of criminal law from Scotland to a tribunal that did not understand the system of Scottish criminal law, this was an objection that applied much less to penal than civil cases, subjected by the union to the appeal which he now proposed.q Criminal laws had, in all countries, a considerable likeness, because there was in all countries an abhorrence of crimes; whereas civil laws greatly differed under different circumstances, objects, and pursuits of the several societies. Mr. Adam moved for leave to bring in a bill to give an appeal to the lords in parliament from judgments and sentences of the court of justiciary and circuit courts in Scotland, in matters of law, and that this be referred to a committee of the whole house. The motion was opposed on the following ground: it was a total change in the law, as it had existed both since and before the union. No appeal had ever lain from the justiciary court either to the parliament of Scotland

q Speech of Mr. Adam, introductory to his motion. Parliamentary Debates, 4th February, 1794.

or the parliament of Great Britain; there was no reason for CHAP. the proposed innovation, as no evil had been felt under the LIII. established mode. The greater number of the inhabitants of Scotland were perfectly satisfied with the administration of 1794. law as it now stood. They were persuaded of its excellence, and sensible of the blessings which they enjoyed under its protection. It was impolitic and hazardous to change a system experienced to be beneficial for a system untried, and consequently of doubtful operation in that country, and not sought by the people for whose benefit it was intended.[r] After a great display of legal and political ability by the mover, his supporters,[s] and his opponents,[t] the motion was negatived by a majority of a hundred and twenty-six to thirty-one. Defeated Proposed on the question of appeal, Mr. Adam proposed an inquiry inquiry which he had intended to have made a part of the same bill. into the He moved for a copy of the record of the trials of Messrs. conduct of Muir and Palmer, on the 24th of February, and on the 10th of tish March proposed the revision of the sentence passed upon these judges: two gentlemen. He undertook to prove, first, that the crimes his speech charged against Messrs. Muir and Palmer were what the law on that of Scotland calls *leasing making*, or public libel; that, by the subject. law of Scotland, the punishment annexed to leasing making was fine, imprisonment, or banishment, but not transportation : that the acts proved against these gentlemen did not amount to leasing making, the crime charged in the indictment. If the mover made good these positions, the obvious inference was, that the Scottish judges had, in the late sentences, greatly exceeded their power; and if they did so, the illegality would be, in imposing such a punishment, extremely tyrannical. The mover supported his legal positions by very extensive knowledge, jurisdical and historical, reciprocally illustrating and enforcing each other; he endeavoured from statute, analogy, and precedent, explained by their civil and political reasons, to establish his doctrines; and attempted to prove that the acts, cases, and decisions which he quoted, were not detached or insulated, but all resulted from the same spirit and principles, operating most effectually at the best times, under the most admired authorities and purest administrations of justice. He also contended, that transportation to places beyond seas neither was nor could be a part of the Scottish law before the union, because there were no places beyond seas in the possession of Scotland; and no act had since the union, been passed, allowing Scottish courts to transport in cases of sedition. On these grounds he denied the right of the Scottish judges to in-

r These arguments are to be found principally in the speech of Mr. Anstruther. See Parliamentary Debates, February 4th, 1794.

s Chiefly Messrs. Adair and Fox.

t Messrs. Anstruther, Watson, and the lord-advocate. See Parliamentary Debates.

CHAP.
LIII.

1794.

flict such a punishment if the crime had been established; and farther asserted that the charge was not proved: Having thus endeavoured to show that criminal justice had been perverted, he forcibly and eloquently stated the evils, moral and political, which must arise from such perversion; and concluded with moving the production of the records.

Reply of the lord-advocate.

The lord-advocate, chief law officer of the crown in Scotland had officially acted as the leading public accuser against those persons; and now vindicated the judgments in question as legal and meritorious. He endeavoured to prove, that though banishment, by the English law, might not be the same with transportation, they were regarded as synonymous by the Scottish law: this (he said) was their acceptation uniformly in the opinion of criminal courts and lawyers; and he quoted cases to illustrate his doctrine. Such construction, he argued, was perfectly conformable to the practice of the Scottish justiciary courts, and the Scottish privy-council; and he particularly stated instances that had occurred in the reign of Charles II. to justify his exposition. After endeavouring to prove that such was the law, he vindicated its recent exercise. The persons in question had been extremely active in sedition, and deserved exemplary punishment. The chief speakers[u] on both sides took a very active share in this debate, which produced a display of legal and political ability that has been rarely exceeded in parliament: the motion was negatived by a great majority. Notwithstanding these repeated disappointments, the manly spirit of Mr. Adam in the course which he conceived to be right. On the 25th of March he introduced a third motion for regulating the justiciary courts of Scotland: the general object of his proposition was the assimilation of the Scottish to the English criminal law in its substance, sanctions, rules, and forms of administration. The discussion of this subject necessarily introduced a repetition of certain arguments which had been already used; but also intermingled new matter. The mover endeavoured to prove by accurate enumeration, the general incompetence of the Scottish criminal system to answer the purposes of substantial justice; he kept his present proposition distinct from the special subjects and inquiries which, at his motion, the house had lately been discussing; and considered the present as a general question, which derived its reasons and importance from the general system of Scottish penal law and its administration. Mr. Se-

The motion is negatived.

Third proposition of Mr. Adam.

Masterly speech of Mr. Adam on that subject.

---

u Messrs. Sheridan and Fox on the one hand, and Mr. Pitt on the other, exerted themselves in respectively supporting Messrs. Adam and Dundas. Mr. Dundas's exhibition on this subject was universally allowed to be able, and worthy of the high office which he filled. Mr. Adam's speech was, by all parties, deemed one of the first that had ever been delivered upon a subject of law within that house, and made a very great addition to a character fast rising in eminence.

cretary Dundas denied the necessity or policy of a change in a
system with which the people subject to it were thoroughly
contented; instituted a comparison between the Scottish and
English law, and endeavoured to prove, that in many cases
the Scottish penal code was much superior. Respecting sedition, when he saw the attacks that were daily made on the
very vitals of the constitution; when he observed this systematically done; when he found that works in their nature hostile
to the government of the country, and addressed to the lower
orders of society were spread with indefatigable industry, he
must avow his conviction that the punishment annexed to this
crime by the law of England was not sufficiently severe to
deter persons from this practice, and that the legislature must
adopt a different mode of procedure upon that subject.[x] The
lord-advocate, with more minute specification, defended the
law of Scotland and its administration. The attorney-general,
with his usual acuteness and moderation, defended the criminal
justice of Scotland, as adapted to the general purposes of
penal codes; the sentiments, character, pursuits, and habits
of the people; and as firmly fixed by the articles of the union
but he delivered no opinion on the competency of the English
penal code, as it then stood, to restrain sedition. The seemingly incidental observations of Mr. Dundas respecting the
inadequacy of the English laws, did not escape the penetration
of Mr. Fox. He appeared to consider it not merely as an
illustrative remark on the subject before the house, but as an
indirect intimation of an agitated change, and intended to sound
the opinion and feelings of the commons: he warned him to
beware how he meddled with the liberties of Englishmen;
and to consider well before he increased punishment. This
third motion of Mr. Adam experienced a similar fate with the
two former; and was negatived by a very great majority. Petitions from Messrs. Muir and Palmer were laid before the house,
praying the reconsideration of the sentences; but the commons
refused to interpose in a judgment which had been regularly
pronounced by a competent court. Those important subjects
which Mr. Adam submitted to the discussion of the house of
commons, were also introduced before the lords by the earl of
Lauderdale. His lordship's motion was negatived without a
division; and the lord chancellor proposed a resolution, declaring " there was no ground for interfering in the established
" courts of criminal justice as administered under the constitu-
" tion, and by which the rights, liberties, and properties, of all
" ranks of subjects were protected." Thus finished the parliamentary consideration of subjects which warmly interested the
public mind. Messrs. Muir, Palmer, and also the condemned
members of the Scottish convention, were sent to Botany Bay.
Many out of parliament, who usually coincided with adminis-

x See Parliamentary Debates, March 25th, 1794.

CHAP.
LIII.

1794.

tration, reckoned this punishment extremely severe. Though unable to follow Mr. Adam through the researches of legal disquisition, or the depths of legal science, yet, conceiving the convicts in question to be rather mislead by enthusiasm than prompted by malignant intentions, they thought that the punishment far exceeded the moral guilt. Others who deemed severe punishment necessary, argued, that whatever the intention might be, the tendency was so pernicious as to require the most rigorous chastisement which the law permitted, for the future prevention of so dangerous incendiaries; but this last reasoning proceeding on a suspicion that the law did permit such sentences could make no impression on those who denied the premises.

Progress of the innovating spirit among the lower ranks.

Proceedings of the democratical societies.

Meeting at Chalk Farm.

The punishment of these agitators in Scotland did not deter innovating projectors in England from advancing with their schemes. During the preceding year clubs had met, both in full assemblies and detached committees, to project plans and devise expedients for effecting the manifold and radical changes which the British constitution required to suit the ideas which these persons had formed of the perfection of political systems. Of the three societies which we have already recorded to have congratulated the French convention on the downfall of monarchy, the revolution club appears to have ceased its collective existence; most of its members being probably joined to the other fraternities. The other two the constitutional and corresponding societies, very sedulously made certain results of their deliberations known to the world by advertisements, subscribed with the names, and *sanctioned by the authority* of Mr. Daniel Adams,[y] under clerk, and Mr. Thomas Hardy, shoemaker respectively, secretaries to the constitutional and corresponding society. These were seconded by handbills and pamphlets summoning the people to associate for the attainment of radical reform. In the course of their preparations they had called several meetings; especially one at Chalk Farm, near Hampstead. There several intemperate speeches were made; and when festivity intermingled with politics, very inflamatory toasts were proposed, and the meeting was undoubtedly seditious. Some of its most active members, not

[y] This Mr. Daniel Adams I have seen before he betook himself to his legislative occupations. He then appeared to be a common place, harmless, vain man, desirous of what, in colloquial language, is called *dashing*. His chief subject of conversation was the high company which he kept, and his own importance in the said company. I have no doubt but that the man was actuated by the same love of distinction in his reforming projects, and that no inconsiderable motive to his undertaking the office of secretary was to read his own name at the bottom of the advertisements. Indeed, as I have already said, after considerable inquiry and reflection, I think no one passion produced more votaries of change than vanity. But whatever might be the spring that set such an engine in motion, the dangerous operation was the same when it was actually moved.

only at that time, but in their habitual conduct, manifested themselves inimical to the British constitution, as far as their enmity could operate; hostile to kingly government of all kinds, and desirous of establishing a jacobinical democracy. Among these, one of the most noted was John Thelwal, destined to the same kind of perpetual remembrance which has followed John Ball, Wat Tyler, Jack Cade, and Kett, the tanner, those celebrated votaries of radical reform in their days. This John Thelwal. besides his joint efforts with others of the corresponding societies, was singly and separately instrumental to the purposes of sedition by a kind of periodical declamations, which he styled *political lectures.* These lectures were chiefly comments on Tom Paine's works-and similar performances, with abuse of the present constitution and government, more direct and pointed to its specific measures than even the efforts of Paine himself. With the most scurrilous invectives against establishments, which he called usurpation, his harangues mingled vehement exhortations[z] to revolution, or as he phrased it, to resume the rights of nature.[a] Government observed the 'open proceedings of these societies and individuals, and suspected the secret machinations of the ringleaders: to 'discover the truth they adopted the policy which is necessary in apprehended plots;[b] and employed despicable instruments that are easily to be found in all great cities, as spies that were to attend the conventicles of sedition, and to become members of the societies, in order to betray the secrets with which they might be intrusted. In consequence of discoveries which were obtained through these and other channels. ministers ordered Hardy and Adams to be arrested, and their papers to be seized; and immediately after Thelwal, Loveit a hair dresser, Martin an attorney, and two or three others, to be apprehended. In a few days the arrestations. extended to men of higher rank and reputation: Mr. Joyce, a respectable clergyman, chaplain to lord Stanhope : Mr. Kydd, a barrister of talents and fast rising character; the eminent and celebrated Mr. Horne Tooke, were among the numbers of the confined. The papers being examined, it was found that the two societies had concerted a project for assembling, by their joint influence; a national convention. This design, in combination with the many other proceedings of the

CHAP. LIII.

1794.

Lectures of John Thelwal against the British constitution and kingly government.

Leaders arrested, and their papers seized.

Plan of a national convention discovered by ministers.

z See Thelwal's Tribune, passim.   a See Rights of Nature, in opposition to the usurpation of establishment, by the same, passim.   b The anti ministerial writings of the times severely inveighed against government for employing wretches so very destitute of honour, and thence inferred to be so unworthy of belief. But the best and wisest statesmen, in investigating secret and associated villany, must often make use of worthless instruments. As well might. Cicero be blamed for employing the prostitute Fulvia in eliciting information respecting a conspiracy which he deemed dangerous to Rome, as ministers for employing such fellows as Goslin, Lynham, Taylor, and Groves, to elicit information concerning a conspiracy which they conceived dangerous to Britain.

CHAP.
LIII.

1794.

Commit-
tees of
houses ap-
pointed to
examine
the papers.
Report of
the com-
mittees.
Mr. Pitt
states his
view of the
substance.

societies, was construed by ministers to be a conspiracy against
the constitution; and consequently (they inferred), a conspiracy against the king, amounting to high treason. His majesty
sent messages to both houses, announcing the discoveries which
had been made, and referring to their consideration the voluminous papers that had been seized. The ministers proposed
a secret committee for the inspection of these documents. Mr.
Fox reprobated the projected secrecy as unconstitutional and
unnecessary, tending to promote that system of misery and delusion with which he had often charged the measures of administration. Whatever (he said) the criminality is, drag it
openly to light: besides, by a resolution of the house, the seizure of papers has been declared to be illegal, unless treason be
charged in the warrant, which authorizes such seizure. Ministers replied, that treason was charged in the warrant; that the
seizure, therefore, was not illegal; that not only prudent policy
directed, but the most imperious necessity dictated, secrecy in
their inquisitorial proceedings, as the very existence of parliament and the constitution was at stake. On the 12th of March,
at the instance of ministers, secret committees were nominated; and on the 16th, the first report being read to the commons, Mr. Pitt stated at great length his view of its contents,
He traced the history and proceedings of the societies for the
last two years: they had adopted, he said, the monstrous doctrines of the Rights of Man, which seduced the weak and ignorant to overturn government, law, property, security, and whatever was valuable; which had destroyed whatever was valuable in France, and endangered the safety, if not the existence,
of every nation in Europe. The object of all these societies
was the practical inculcation of such doctrines. A correspondence prior to the enormities of France had subsisted between
these societies and the French jacobin clubs. When the jacobin faction, which usurped the government, had commenced
hostilities against Great Britain, these societies as far as they
could, had pursued the same conduct, expressed the same attachment to their cause, adopted their appellations, and formed
the design of disseminating the same principles. Their operations were chiefly directed to manufacturing towns. They considered the convention at Edinburgh as the representatives of
the people, asserted the innocence of those members who fell
under the sentence of the law, and declared they could only
look for reform in such a convention. But the chief attention
of the house was required in considering a society, though
composed of the meanest and most despicable of the people,
who acted upon the worst jacobin principles, and had within it
the means of the most unbounded extension and rapid increase.
This society, comprehending thirty divisions in London, was
connected by a systematic correspondence with other societies
scattered through the manufacturing towns. It had arrived at
such a pitch of audacity as to declare its competence to watch

over the progress of legislation; to investigate its principles; CHAP.
LIII.
to prescribe limits for its actions, beyond which if it presumed to
advance, an end was to be put to the existence of parliament
itself. Recently this corresponding society had laid before the 1794.
constitutional society a plan for assembling a convention for all
England. The evident object of the proposed meeting, in Mr.
Pitt's opinion, was to exercise legislative and judicial capacities, to overturn the established system of government, and
wrest from the parliament the power which the constitution has
lodged in their hands. This plan was to be speedily carried into
execution, and a centrical spot[c] was chosen to facilitate the
meeting of their delegates. An assembly had been held on the
14th of April, and resolutions were passed which arraigned
every branch of the government; threatened the sovereign, insulted the house of peers, and accused the commons of insufficiency. Declarations were uttered, that if certain measures
were pursued, whether with or without the consent of parliament, they should be rescinded; and that the constitution was
utterly destroyed[d] The proofs of these allegations were their
own records; and it farther appeared from the report, that arms
had been actually procured and distributed by the societies;
and that, so far from breaking up this jacobin army, they had
shown themselves immoveably bent on their pursuit, and displayed preparations of defiance and resistance to government.
From all these facts Mr. Pitt inferred, there was a very dangerous conspiracy, which it became them, by seasonable interference, to prevent from being carried into execution.[e] In times
of apprehended rebellion it had been usual to enact a temporary
suspension of the habeas corpus law: that act had been suspended when the constitution and liberty of the country were
most guarded and respected; and such a suspension was more
particularly called for at this crisis, when attempts were made
to disseminate principles dangerous to that constitution for the
preservation of which the law had been made: Mr. Pitt, Mr. Pitt
therefore, proposed a bill, "empowering his majesty to secure proposes a
"and detain all persons suspected of designs against his crown bill for de-
taining sus-
"and government." Mr. Fox expressed his astonishment that pected per-
the committee should solemnly call the attention of the house to sons with-
facts so long notorious: the persons in question had for two out allow-
years openly and publicly avowed the acts now asserted to ing them
amount to a treasonable plot. If this was a conspiracy, it was the benefit
the most garrulous conspiracy that was ever recorded in history. of the ha-
beas cor-
Plots for overturning government had been published for two pus.
years in the daily newspapers; the real transactions reported Mr. Fox's
by the committee were chiefly repetitions of stale advertise- view of the
ments. What was the real amount, taken apart from the com- alleged
ments of Mr. Pitt's eloquence? Societies had been constituted conspi-
racy.

c Sheffield.
d Report of the secret committee of the house of commons concerning
the seditious societies. e Parliamentary Debates, May 16th, 1794.

CHAP. for the purposes of parliamentary reform; these had corre-
LIII. sponded, together; and they had corresponded with France
       when at peace with this country, To effect the purposes of
1794. parliamentary reform, a convention had been held in Edin-
       burgh: all these facts were notorious and stale; a convention
       was proposed for the purposes of reform in England; and this
       was *the only new information.* The project was in itself con-
       temptible and ridiculous, and could not really alarm the minis-
       ter, or any man in his senses. The remainder was not statement
       of facts, but inferences either of the committee or minister;
       containing an imputation of $intention$ to overturn government,
       without the slightest evidence that such intentions existed. No
       grounds were adduced that could possibly justify such a mo-
       mentous intrenchment on the liberties of the subject as this bill
       proposed. The minister, Mr. Fox believed, was not really
       alarmed,[f] but it was necessary for his views to keep up or create
       some new cause of panic, to gain a continuation of power over
       the people.[g] Why had not the law officers of the crown pro-
       secuted the authors of the writings or acts reported to the
       house, if they were so very mischievous? The bill underwent
       a very interesting discussion in both houses: its other supporters
       agreeing with Mr. Pitt, contended that the facts brought to
       light evinced the existence of a most dangerous conspiracy,
       requiring the proposed suspension in order farther to discover
       its extent, and to prevent its wider diffusion. The other oppo-
       sers agreed with Mr. Fox that no conspiracy or project of rebel-
The bill is lion existed, and that the bill was an unnecessary and destruc-
passed into tive infringement of British liberty; but the design of Mr. Pitt
a law.   prevailed, and the proposition of ministers was passed into a
         law. By persons who admitted criminality in the facts charged,
Ministers, different opinions were entertained concerning the degree of
including guilt which, if proved, they would constitute. The lord-chan-
the chan- cellor Loughborough, and several other eminent lawyers, con-
cellor, ceived that the allegations, if established, would amount to a
deem the
crimes   conspiracy against the king and government, and must be con-
charged to sidered as intending or compassing the king's death. No less
be high eminent lawyers, and at their head lord Thurlow, declared,
treason. that though proved, they would not amount to high treason;
Lord Thur
low asserts, that the interpretation by which they should be denominated
that by the high treason, was totally inconsistent with the letter of our
law of Eng- statutes, which precisely and accurately defined that crime;
land they and with the spirit of our laws, which rejected circuitous con-
are not struction. These thought that the allegations amounted to se-
treason. dition, and that the persons who should be proved actively
         guilty would well deserve the punishment annexed to sedition
The accu- by the laws of England. Government having adopted the
sed are chancellor's opinion, and resolved to prosecute the persons ar-
sent to the
Tower.   f Parliamentary Debates, 16th May, 1794.
         g This opinion was still more poignantly asserted by Mr. Sheridan.

rested for high treason, sent them to the Tower, there to be con- **CHAP.**
fined until evidence should be prepared for their trials.   **LIII.**

These were the principal discussions and measures concern-
ing subjects of internal tranquillity, whether retrospective or   **1794.**
prospective, that engaged parliament during the present ses-
sion. The other objects which chiefly occupied its deliberations Supplies
were warlike preparations both for defence and attack : the investigation of belligerent measures and events, and schemes of
finance.

An expedition having been projected to re-animate and assist
the insurgents of La Vendee, a body of Hessian troops was hired
as part of the force destined for that service : they reached the
coast of the Isle of Wight, and to prevent sickness, were disembarked until preparations should be ready. No objection was
made to the employment or destination of those troops ; nor Debate on
was the propriety or necessity of landing them called in question; the intro-
but it was maintained in parliament, that whenever the intro- Hessian
duction of foreign troops became necessary, ministers ought troops.
either to obtain the previous consent of parliament, or resort to
a bill of indemnity. Without discussing the general question
of prerogative, so as to form any precedent for future times, it
was determined that the specific exigency justified the measure
in the present case.

Among the military supplies proposed for the service of the Bill for the
current year, was a corps of emigrant volunteers. Mr. Pitt in- employ-
troduced a bill for that purpose, to enable the emigrant sub- ment of
jects of France to enlist in his majesty's service on the conti- emigrants.
nent of Europe, and to receive native officers. Such a corps
must be (it was said by its supporters) of wonderful efficacy,
especially if sent to assist the royalists of La Vendee. The
great body of the French was inimical to the terrible system,
and wanted nothing but the prospect of steady and effectual
aid to animate and invigorate them against the convention.
The present usurpation of France was incompatible with the
existence of other governments ; and till we could overthrow
their system of politics, we must not hope for peace or security.[h] In this endeavor he thought it right to unite with us
persons who had the same reasons with ourselves, and who called upon the British nation to give them arms. As the present
proposition, combined with the reasoning by which it was supported, appeared to approach nearer to interference in the internal affairs of France than ministers had before professed to
intend, it was very warmly promoted by Mr. Burke, who seemed
at last to conceive hopes that Britain would resolve,, and explicitly avow its resolution of carrying on war *for the restoration
of monarchy.* Mr. Dundas, indeed, has not stated the restitution of kingly government as synonymous with the overthrow

h See Mr. Dundas's speech on the bill for employing emigrants, when
before the committee.

CHAP. of the existing usurpation.   Mr. Burke, however, conceived
LIII. that the terrible system did not spring from the individual
        character of Robespierre, but from the revolution which over-
1794. turned the established orders, enabled and stimulated Robes-
        pierre's ambition to operate.   The emigrant corps, he hoped,
        assisting the La Vendeans, if powerfully and comprehensively
        supported by this country, would pave the way for a counter
        revolution.   Messrs. Fox and Sheridan, with some others, op-
        posed the bill: they alleged that it tended to render the war
        more ferocious, which must always be the consequence of
        arming citizen against citizen; raised a force that was totally
        inefficacious, and that would certainly be overpowered; em-
        ployed the votaries of the old government against the new go-
        vernment; and thus, contrary to the professions of ministers,
        really interfered in the internal affairs of France.   They far-
        ther represented the measure as inconsistent with humanity
        towards the emigrants themselves.   The French government
        had declared that no quarter should be given to Frenchmen
        caught in arms against the republic.   In its immediate opera-
        tion it must encourage the most cruel retaliation and ferocious
        vengeance; in its ultimate result, from the immense force of
        the present government, it would expose the emigrants to the
        most dreadful butchery.   On these grounds they opposed the
        bill; but their objections were overruled; it passed through
        both houses with very great majorities, and was enacted into a
        law.

Apprehen-   In the course of the session a message from the king an-
sions of an nounced the avowed intentions of the enemy to invade this
invasion.   kingdom.   A great augmentation of the militia, and an addition
             of volunteer fencible corps were accordingly voted: a letter
Voluntary   from the secretary of state to the lord-lieutenants of coun-
contribu-   ties, solicited voluntary subscriptions to levy troops.   The
tions for   solicitation was represented, by members of opposition, as an
raising   attempt to raise money without consent of parliament.   It
troops.   was contended by ministers, that voluntary contributions of
             the subject for the purpose of assisting levies, when they re-
             ceived the sanction of parliament were perfectly legal, and
             consonant to precedent and practice; and quoted the contribu-
             tions and levies during the rebellion in 1745; in the beginning
             of the seven years war; and in the American war, after the cap-
             ture of Burgoyne.   The supplies for the present year were
             very great and expensive: eighty-five thousand seamen, and
             a hundred and seventy-five thousand landsmen were voted,
             Besides the usual ways and means, there was a loan of eleven
Supplies   millions: new taxes on British and foreign spirits, bricks and
and taxes.   tiles slate crown and plate glass, met with little opposition:
             duties on paper and on attorneys were represented as oppres-
             sive, but on the whole it was allowed, that the imposts of Mr.
             Pitt, affecting the rich or middling classes, displayed financial
             ability and discrimination.   Various subsidies were voted to

fŏreign princes, and justified on the ground of contributing to
the great purposes of the war. But the most important of
these was the subsidy to the king of Prussia. On the 20th
of April his majesty sent to the house of commons a copy of
a treaty concluded by him with the states-general and the king
of Prussia, for the purpose of more effectually carrying on the
war. By the stipulations with Frederick William, Britain
had agreed to pay him 50,000l. a month ; 100,000l. a month
for forage ; in all,, for the remaining nine months of the present
year, thirteen hundred and fifty thousand pounds : the whole
year would amount to 1,800,000l., out of which the states-general were to pay 400,000l. Embarked (said Mr. Pitt) as
we were in war so just and necessary, it was material for us to
possess the aid of so powerful a force. The king of Prussia
was certainly a principal in the war, but unable to carry it on
without pecuniary assistance ; and his force, for which we
were engaged to pay, was to be employed for our advantage,
and the conquests to be made in the name of the maritime
states. The astonishing exertions of France rendered efforts
on our part additionally necessary ; and the object of the
war being so important, it would be the most preposterous folly to
slacken our exertions in order to spare expense.[i] Opposition
reprobated this policy as the height of profusion, and contended, first, that from the efforts of the king of Prussia, no benefit could accrue to this country which would compensate the
cost ; secondly, that we had no security that when the money
was contributed he would perform the engagements which he
incurred. The king of Prussia had originally begun the war :
this very beginning of his, whether through the French aggression or his own, had ultimately involved us in the contest.
Now, the king of Prussia having engaged other powers in the
quarrel, desired to withdraw himself, and must be bribed
to persevere in a war, which, but for himself, would have
never been begun.[k] His conduct contained such a mixture of
perfidy, fraud, and meanness, as was unparalleled in all
modern political history. No man of the least prudence
could repose any confidence in one by whom he had been
deceived, yet were the people of this country to pay to such
a person one million three hundred and fifty thousand pounds
the return for which was to depend upon his own honour : let
us not trust a prince whose good faith we had so much reason
to doubt. But if the king of Prussia was to be considered
merely as a hirer of troops, why were the soldiers which we
paid to be commanded by himself ? The direction of mercenaries
should belong to the power which purchased their service.
These arguments produced little effect : a great majority of
the house conceiving the proposed subsidy to the king of Prussia to be conducive to the purposes of the war, the advan-

i Parliamentary Debates, 29th April, 1794. k Ibid.

CHAP. tage and honour of this country, agreed to the motion which
LIII. was proposed by ministers.

1794.   While the British government adopted such measures as it
Bill to pre- thought most likely to strengthen our means of carrying on
vent sums the war, it also endeavoured to impair the resources of the
vested in enemy. As the public funds of Britain afforded the most un-
the British questionable security to the proprietors of money : there very
funds by large sums belonging to French subjects were vested. Agree-
French ably to their general principles of converting private property
subjects, to the use of the revolutionary government, the French rulers
from being had turned their attention to this subject. They had formed
seized by a resolution, directing the use of every possible expedient to
the French ascertain the property of French subjects in foreign funds, in
rulers. order that it might be delivered up to the state and become
public property; and that when the transfer was made, it
should be paid for in assignats estimated at par. Mr. Pitt discerned the object of this scheme, and proposed means to prevent its operation. The purpose, he saw, was to supply the
resources for carrying on the war by plundering individuals of
their property deposited in foreign countries, as they had
before grasped the property in their own country. A general
principle of our laws (he observed) was, that the payment of
any debt owing to an alien enemy may be suspended during
the war; and the king, if he thought fit, might attach it as belonging to an alien enemy : to continue, however, the benefits of
mercantile intercourse which were for the advantage of individuals, without trenching on public safety, the milder practice of
modern times long suffered the rigour of this law to relax. In
the present case Mr. Pitt proposed to secure the individuals by
withholding their property from the grasp of the revolutionary rulers; and thus, whilst private advantage was promoted,
resources sought by the enemy would be arrested. For this
purpose he proposed a bill to prevent the application to the
use of the present government of France, of all monies and
effects in the hands of his majesty's subjects, the property of
individuals of that country; and for preserving such money
and effects to the use of its owners. The bill with very little
opposition, passing into a law, answered the double purpose of
securing their property to individuals, and detaining from the
enemy means of carrying on the war.

Repeated motions made in both houses for the restoration of
peace, necessarily reiterated the arguments which were before
adduced; and indeed, the purposes of the propositions on that
subject appear to have been chiefly to procure from ministers
some declaration, or at least admission, of the specific objects
for which the war was continued ;[1] at least to induce them
expressly to disavow every intention of co-operation with the
continental powers to dictate her internal government to

[1] See Resolutions moved by the duke of Bedford and Mr. Fox, May 30th.

'France: they farther aimed at persuading the houses to disap- CHAP.
prove the conduct of the allies; especially of Prussia. Besides LIII.
these indirect attempts, a direct effort was made to expose as
impolitic the principle, system, and series of our foreign trea- 1794.
ties. Mr. Whitbread, on the 6th of March, proposed an address to his majesty, expressing the concern of the commons
that the king had entered into engagements totally incompatible with the avowed purposes of the present war; that he
had made a common cause with powers, whose objects, though
undefined, really appeared to be the restitution of monarchy;
and earnestly praying his majesty as far as was consistent
with the national faith, to extricate himself from such engagements as might impede the conclusion of a separate peace.
Next to the subsidiary treaty with the king of Prussia, a treaty Treaty
with the king of Sardinia, by which we engaged to continue with the
the war till Savoy was restored, incurred the strongest and king of
most explicit censure. Britain had stipulated a subsidy of Sardinia.
two hundred thousand pounds a year, to assist the king of
Sardinia in his efforts to defend his own dominions. Mr. Whitbread and others maintained, that the advantage which Britain could derive from such exertions was by no means adequate to the expense to be incurred; and that *the integrity of
the king of Sardinia's* dominions was not in the smallest degree, NECESSARY TO THE SECURITY OF BRITAIN; for which, according to ministers, we were engaged in the contest. Ministers endeavoured to prove that the whole system and series of
treaties subsidiary as well as others, were means necessary
to promote the grand ends of the war. The address was
negatived by the usual very great majority; and a similar
motion on the same subject experienced in the house of lords the
same fate.

Having in vain endeavoured to procure the termination of Proposi-
the war, and the dissolution of alliances deemed by govern- tion of an
ment and the majority in parliament, essentially conducive to to the con-
its purposes, opposition proposed to inquire how far, in the duct and
late campaign, its objects had been attained, and what the success of
probability of success was from perseverance in the contest. the last
Major Maitland, after a detailed review of the measures and campaign.
events of the last campaign, and an estimate of the result,
contended that the attainments of the French had been greater than their losses. They had been forced to evacuate Belgium, but they had suppressed the revolt of La Vendee, a
much more important event, since all their dangers arose from
internal disturbance. The strength of the allies had been
declining ever since the siege of Valenciennes. The empress
of Russia made protestations, but took no active share in hostilities; and the king of Prussia was manifestly meditating a
secession. The military plans lately adopted by the allies
deserved severe animadversion. While their armies were
united, their efforts had been crowned with success: the

separation of the forces he imputed to the influence of the
British · cabinet, as Britain alone was to be benefitted ·by
the capture of Dunkirk. If the attempt upon that fortress
by a detached force was expedient, the sole hope of success
must arise from promptitude of execution, and the complete-
ness of preparations; but neither of these attended the attack
upon Dunkirk: four weeks elapsed from the taking of Valenciennes before the siege of Dunkirk was undertaken. Neither artillery nor gun-boats were ready in proper time for
covering the operation. To the master-general of the ordnance, and to ministry, the failure of that enterprise must be
attributed. The evacuation of Toulon was still more severely
reprobated : why were not other troops sent to preserve the
conquest of Toulon? or why, when it was found untenable,
was not an evacuation at once determined upon, and the fleet
brought away to save the unhappy inhabitants from the fury
of those whom they had mortally offended ? On these grounds
major Maitland " moved a committee to inquire into the
" causes which led to the failure of the army under the duke of
" York at Dunkirk; and to inquire into the causes which led
" to the evacuation of Toulon under general Dundas and lord
" Hood." It was replied, that Dunkirk would have been to
Britain a very important acquisition; that it had every probable appearance of practicability ; that the attempt was therefore wise: that its failure arose from the enormous efforts of
the French, which could not have been foreseen or expected.
From the same cause proceeded the evacuation of Toulon:
those who censured us for leaving that place ought to recollect,
that we had there given such an effectual blow to the French
navy, that ages would elapse before they would be able to
recover their losses as a maritime power. On a general review of the events of the campaign, great glory was due to
the British councils and arms. These arguments appearing'
to the majority valid, the proposed motion was negatived.
About the same time a proposition was offered to the house
of commons respecting sinecure places and pensions. Since
a war was deemed necessary that called for all our resources,

**Proposi-
tion of a
tax on ·
places and
pensions.
Arguments
of Mr.
Burke
against the
proposi-
tion.**
it was prudent and expedient to retrench every unnecessary
expense: for this reason Mr. Harrison proposed a bill to
apply certain parts of salaries and pensions to the use of the
public during the continuance of the war; and also to appropriate part of the emoluments of efficient places, so that they
should not amount to more than a specific sum. This motion was
severely reprobated by Mr. Burke, as similar to the proceed-·
ings which had occasioned the ruin of France. It was the
peculiar province of the crown to measure and distribute the
portion of rewards according to the merits of its servants;
and he was astonished the house should be called upon to
interfere in a matter not within the scope of their ordinary
functions. Mr. Sheridan attacked this doctrine as totally un-

constitutional: did the crown possess the sole right of judging
what rewards were to be bestowed upon the public servants?
If it did, he would ask who was obliged to pay those rewards?
The money belonged to the public: the commons were the
servants of the people; and as the people contributed, they
had a right to expect and demand that the contributions
should be applied for their good. Entering into a detail upon
this general principle he gave a particular account of the
emoluments enjoyed by certain individuals, which he appeared
to think far surpassing their services; and that it was but fair
they should contribute part of the surplus towards the public
exigencies caused by a war which they warmly supported.
The opposite party replied, that the pension list and sinecure
places, during the administration of Mr. Pitt, had been very
greatly reduced, besides that it would be extremely unjust to
subject one body of men to an exclusive tax: On these grounds
Mr. Harrison's motion was rejected.

Mr. Dundas, as president of the board of control, presented
his annual statement of the finances of India; the result of
which was, that notwithstanding the late war with Tippoo,
and the stagnation of commerce at home until measures were
adopted for the support of mercantile credit, the affairs of the
company were in a prosperous situation, and he augured great
and rapid increase of their prosperity.

The slave trade was this session again resumed by Mr. Wilberforce; whose efforts, however, for the present were limited
to one branch of that traffic. He proposed to abolish that
part of the trade which supplied foreign territories with
slaves. The supporters of the slave trade rested their cause,
on the ground of its being necessary to the well being of our
West Indian possessions, which could not otherwise be supplied with labourers: They who were sincere in this objection
to the abolition must warmly defend the present motion: for,
instead of abridging that supply it tended to increase it, and
to prevent us from raising the colonies of foreigners into a competition with our own. A bill for the purpose being introduced
by Mr. Wilberforce, passed the commons, but was rejected by
the peers.

These were the chief subjects which occupied the attention **The ses-**
of the house during this very important session, which was **sion closes,**
closed by a speech from the throne on the 11th of July.

Before the narrative proceeds to the campaign of 1794, it is **Internal**
necessary to take a short view of the internal affairs of France, **proceed-**
which had a powerful influence on military transactions. We **ings of**
left the jacobin faction triumphant by the downfall of the Gi- **France.**
rondines; Robespierre paramount by his command over the **faction and**
populace; the system of terror completely established, and **Robes-**
producing the most direful effects within the country, but the **pierre par-**
most gigantic efforts against the enemies of its revolutionary **amount.**
system. The government of France was now become a government of blood, to be sustained by the terrors of the guillo-

CHAP.
LIII.

1794.

tine. This fell engine was employed to remove the obnoxious, to crush the suspected, and to destroy the unsuccessful. Misfortune, though totally blameless, was consummated on the scaffold:—thence Custine, a general of great ability and enterprise, was recalled from the northern army after the surrender of Valenciennes, and instantly committed to the prison of the Abbey. He was accused before the revolutionary tribunal of having maintained a traitorous correspondence with the Prussians while he commanded on the Rhine; and of having neglected various opportunities of throwing re-enforcements into Valenciennes. No evidence was adduced to prove the allegations; but proof was not necessary to sanguinary despotism : he speedily suffered death.

Situation
of the
queen.

The execution of Custine was soon followed by the trial of the unfortunate queen. This awful instance of the instability of human grandeur, after the murder of her ill fated husband, had been separated from her family in the Temple. On the first of August 1793, she was suddenly, and in the most cruel and insulting manner, removed to the Conciergerie, a prison destined for the reception of the vilest malefactors. In the midst of a nation recently so distinguished for loyalty, every effort of invention was employed in the most wanton and barbarous insults to the consort of their lately adored sovereign. In a metropolis, within a few years the centre of refinement, and devoted attention to the sex, the most brutal and savage ingenuity was exerted in oppression, insolence, and tyranny, to a poor, helpless, and forlorn woman. The cell in which she was immured was only eight feet square; her bed was a hard mattress of straw, and her food of the meanest kind; while she was never suffered to enjoy the privilege of being alone, two soldiers being appointed to watch her night and

Iniquitous
trial & con-
demnation.

day, without the intermission of a moment.[1] Confined in this loathsome dungeon, in such circumstances of aggravated brutality, on the 15th of October, she was brought before the revolutionary tribunal. The charges adduced against her were, that she had contributed to the derangement of the national finances, by remitting, from time to time, considerable sums to her brother the emperor Joseph: since the revolution continued to hold a criminal correspondence with foreign powers: attempted a counter revolution, particularly by applying to the officers at Versailles in October 1789; and at the same time, through the agency of certain monopolists, had created an artificial famine. According to her accusers she was the principal agent and promotor of the flight of the royal family in June 1791: induced the king to refuse his sanction to the decrees concerning the emigrants and refractory priests: in conjunction with a scandalous faction (the Gironde,) persuaded the king and the assembly to declare war against Austria, contrary to

1 See Otridge's Annual Register, 1793, p. 276.

every principle of sound policy and the public welfare: war being commenced, she had conveyed intelligence to the enemy, and was the cause of the massacre of the 10th of August. To these allegations, some of which were totally indifferent, whether true or false, and the rest supported by no proof, one was added for a consummation to the rest, as physically incredible, as morally infamous: it was affirmed by these brutes, in conception as well as in conduct, that she had an incestuous commerce with her own son, a child of eight years old.[m] The queen considered accusation by blood-thirsty despots as synonymous with condemnation: though she disregarded such accusers, yet out of justice to herself, her origin, her family, and her fame, she exerted her abilities in rebutting charges so horrid and flagitious. With the dignity of an elevated mind, attacked by the scorn and iniquity of the unworthy, she answered serenely and calmly to all their asseverations. Retaining, in this dreadful situation, that full possession of faculties which magnanimity secures to unmerited suffering, she, though totally ignorant of the allegations that were to be made, demonstrated their futility, and confuted the assertions of her enemies. Respecting the charge of incest, she appealed to those who were themselves mothers for the possibility of the crime. Though her defence completely overturned the evidence for the prosecution, it was, as she knew it would be, totally unavailing: she was pronounced guilty of all the charges, and doomed to die the following day.

The queen heard with resignation a sentence which announced her speedy release from a situation of such accumulated misery. She had one consolation to which the diabolical malignity of her murderers could not reach: she was a CHRISTIAN: she believed in a future state; and therein she looked for happiness which no revolutionary tribunal could disturb, no atheistical assassins could destroy. Before she was reconducted to her dungeon, it was four in the morning; and twelve the ensuing day was the hour fixed for her decapitation. She was not allowed a clergyman of her own choice, but provided with a constitutional priest. At half past eleven the queen was brought out of prison, and, like the lowest malefactor, was conducted in a common cart to the place of execution. Her hair was entirely cut off from the back of her head, which was covered with a small white cap; she wore a white undress; her hands were tied behind her; and she sat with her back to the horses. They who had seen her in the zenith of magnificence and splendour, could not but contrast her former with her present condition: those who had admired her exquisite beauty, could not but observe the premature depredations of sorrow on a face so fair: but if the changes impaired the gloss of her juvenile charms, they, together with their causes, to

---

[m] Otridge's Annual Register, 1793, p. 276.

CHAP.   feeling spectators (and all Frenchmen were not brutes) render-
LIII.   ed her faded countenance more interesting and impressive. She
~~~~   camly conversed ,with her priest, exhibiting neither ostentatious
1794.   indifference nor overwhelming anguish, but resigned submis-
        sion. Casting her eyes to the Thuilleries, one scene of her
        former greatness, which called up so many tender associations
        and melancholy ideas, she indicated a sorrowful emotion; but
        repelling this last intrusion of worldly recollection, she turned
Execution. to the instrument of death. At half past twelve the guillotine
        severed her head from her body; which the executioner exhi-
        bited, all streaming with blood, from the four corners of the
        scaffold, to an inveterate and insatiable multitude. The body
        of the murdered queen was immediately conveyed to a grave
        filled with quick lime, in the church-yard called De la Made-
        laine, where the remains of Louis XVI. had been interred
        with the same privation of pious regard to decent ceremo-
        nial.

Brissot and   The murder of the queen was soon followed by the death of
the other   the accused deputies. The trial of these persons was deferred
Gironde   from time to time, till the complete overthrow of their adherents
prisoners   should give security to their prosecutors. They were charged
put to   with having conspired against the unity and indivisibility of the
death.   republic, by exciting a rebellion in the departments of the
        south, and in Calvados. One article of the charges respect-
        ing foreign politics was, they were accused of having caused
        war to be declared, first against Austria, and afterwards
        against England and Holland. Thus arraigned, at the in-
        stance of the ruling party, they were all doomed to death:
        many others experienced a similar destiny, either undeservedly
Orleans   or illegally. The detestable and contemptible Orleans suffered
shares the   the same fate which, at his instigation, had overwhelmed so
same fate.   many others. A decree had been passed under the present
        rulers for removing the Bourbon family to Marseilles; and
        Orleans, who had latterly assumed the silly and fantastical name
        of Philip Egalite, was included in its operation. From Mar-
        seilles he was brought to Paris, on a charge of having aspired
        at the sovereignty from the commencement of the revolution.
        As this was an accusation which could scarcely admit of any
        evidence but conjectural, it was not substantiated so far as to
        justify the sentence of death to which he was doomed. Orleans
        experienced in his own person the tyrannic cruelty of the revo-
        lutionary system which he had been so ardent to promote; and
        however deserving he might be of capital punishment, he, ac-
        cording to the most probable accounts, suffered *illegally*. Pro-
        fligate and despicable as the character of this man had been,
        his sentence excited neither horror nor commiseration in any
        party; the last period of his life, however, appeared to indi-
        cate sentiments less disgraceful than those which had manifest-
        ed themselves in the invariable tenour of his former conduct.
        On the 6th of November he was conveyed to the place of his

execution, amidst the insults and reproaches of the populace; and met death, with a magnanimity less befitting the associate and tool of Robespierre and Marat than the descendant of Henry. Two days after the ignominious càtastrophe of Orleans, the lovely and accomplished madame Roland was brought to the scaffold. To the distinguished talents, varied and extensive knowledge of this celebrated lady, her domestic virtues were not inferior. Her husband, hated by Robespierre on 'account of his attachment to the Gironde party, was included in the proscription that followed the decree of the 3d of May: he accordingly quitted Paris, but his wife was apprehended and committed to prison. She was at length brought to trial, and the empty charge of a conspiracy was followed by a sentence of death. At the place of execution she maintained that firm undaunted spirit which had hitherto supported her; and bowing down before the statue of liberty, she exclaimed, "O liberty, "how many crimes are committed in thy name."

To take away property, liberty, and life, to inflict anguish and torment; to produce to human beings physical evil, did not satiate the inventive malignity of this extraordinary tyranny. Robespierre and his band, more comprehensive and more thoroughly diabolical, ardently, studiously, and systematically sought the increase of moral depravation. Projects for disseminating misery could not, they well knew, be so completely successful as by establishing the domination of sin. Sin could never attain so extensive an empire as by the total subjugation of religion; therefore to annihilate piety. with all its external forms and assistances, was one great object of Robespierre's devices. To effect this purpose, one means was to destroy the reverence for all the institutions which are deduced from the scriptures, and tend so powerfully to cherish sentiments of religion. Of these, none had been found more effectual than the exclusive devotion of one day in the week to the social worship of God; and the appointment of certain stated periods' for specific commemmorations. The calander, in all christian countries, taking its first origin from the birth of our Saviour, and enumerating the years by an event the most momentous to the christain world, had regulated the divisions of the year by epochs in the history of our Saviour's mission upon earth, or some other seasons connected with scripture narratives; and had intermingled religious associations with the several progressions of the seasons. Of these, the observance of the sabbath recurring most frequently is the most extensively beneficial. The government of Robespierre projected the abolition of these institutions, and actually effected a new calendar which destroyed all reference to christian history and precepts, commenced the æra from the downfall of monarchy, annihilated all terms' connected with christian history. 'and establishments, abolished the sabbath; and instead of the seventh day, enjoined by the commandment of God to be kept holy, they appointed

CHAP.
LIII.

1794.

Dreadful fate of France under Robespierre.

CHAP. the tenth as a spirit of mere civil respite, to the total exclusion
LIII. of all religious exercise. Having thus renounced christianity,
their new calendar partly adopted the phraseology and ar-
1794. rangement of pagans, denominated every space of four years
an Olympiad, in imitation of the Greeks, and the extraordinary
day of every fourth year an intercalary, in imitation of the Romans.[o] This innovation therefore, under the government of
Robespierre and his agents, tended strongly to promote that
impiety which the tribunitian government was so eager to
establish. Robespierre and his junto had often declared their
disbelief of the christian religion, and even denied the existence
of a supreme being; but they had not yet produced a formal
and public renunciation of the God and Saviour of the world.

The revo- An act so horrible remained for the legislature of a most en-
lutionary lightened nation, near the close of the eighteenth century. On
bishops ab- the 7th of November, in the frenzy of impiety, the republican
jure the   bishop of Paris, and his grand vicars, entered the hall of the
name of   convention along with the constituted authorities, abjured the
Christ,   name of Christ, renounced the office of christian priests, their
appointments as christian pastors, and their characters as christain men. Now they would own no temple but the sanctuary
of the law, no divinity but liberty, no object of worship but
their country, no gospel but the constitution. This abjuration
was received by the convention with the most rapturous applause. A number of allegorical deities, liberty, equality, indivisibility, and many others, were consecrated as objects of
worship. To promote this system of paganism, agents were
despatched to all the departments to complete the change. In
many parts the abjuration of religion, through the efforts of the
clergy, was very warmly received, while its various commenta-
tors added to the impiety, according to the measure of their
invention. One of the most zealous votaries of impiety was
the republican bishop of Moulins. Trampling on the cross
and the mitre, he assumed the pike and cap of liberty, and
preached the doctrine big with horror to reflecting men, but
and a fu- full of encouragement to diabolical natures, " that death is an
ture state. " eternal sleep." A common prostitute was placed on the altar
of the cathedral church of Paris, to receive adoration, as a
substitute for Jesus Christ. The convention combined intolerance with atheism and blasphemy, and passed a decree order-
The   ing the churches to be shut. Many of the priests who still
churches   attempted to officiate at their altars according to the rites of
are shut. christianity, were thrown into dungeons. Renunciation of
religion, as its abettors foresaw, promoted the most enormous
crimes. The populace, who in consequence of these proceed-

o They divided the year into twelve months consisting each of thirty
days, and distinguished by names expressive of their usual produce, temperature or appearance; while to complete the year, five supplementary
days are added, and denominated sans culotides.

ings reckoned themselves authorized to plunder every place of worship, public and private, divided with the convention large heaps of shrines, figures, and vessels, hitherto used in the offices of religion, while commissioners from the convention aided the sacrilegious pillage. The revolutionary frenzy had not totally overwhelmed every principle and sentiment of natural and revealed religion. The decree for shutting up the churches was received with so general horror and detestation, that the government found it necessary immediately to reverse it, and again to admit religious worship. Robespierre, though most active in enmity to religion, yet eagerly desirous to preserve and increase his popularity, promoted the restoration of divine service. By the influence which he established among the populace, be was able to acquire an ascendency over his associates. Of these, one of the ablest was Danton : this revolutionist, much superior to Robespierre in the talents and accomplishments which would have commanded attention in the Roman or British senate, did not equal him in the arts which conciliate an ignorant rabble. Conscious of his own powers, he intended Robespierre for a tool : and was active in overturning the Brissotines, in order to elevate himself; but at length fell like many of his revolutionary predecessors, by the instruments of his exaltation. So contrary to the interest of an able man it is to aggrandize a rabble that would level all distinctions. The Parisian populace loved and revered Robespierre, because in manners, appearance, and passions, he was one of themselves. His ruling affection was envy,[p] a desire of reducing all others to the level of his own meanness. This sentiment, together with fear, the natural passion of a despot without high talents, and greatness of mind, chiefly prompted all the enormities of this monster. He both hated and feared[q] the aristocracy of genius, as a superiority over himself, and the means of effecting his downfall. But his tyranny, dreadful as it was to France, by its very terrors produced most gigantic efforts against its enemies.

CHAP. LIII.

1794.

Fall of Danton.

The Parisian populace adore Robespierre. His real talents and character.

p See Adolphus's Memoirs of Robespierre.
q Domitian was the most timid of men ; the fearlessness of Julius Cæsar, on the contrary, hastened his assassination.

CHAP. LIV.

Jealousy among the allies —The emperor tries to raise his subjects in mass —is opposed by the king of Prussia.—Plan of the campaign —Respective force of the belligerent powers —The emperor joins the allied armies.— Energy of the revolutionary leaders in France.—Rebellion is quelled in La Vendee.—The confederates take the field.—Siege of Landreci.— Conflicts between the allies and the republicans.—Battle of the 24th of April between the duke of York and the republicans.—Our prince and countrymen are victorious.—Landreci is taken.— Testimony of the convention to the heroism of the English.—Pichegru—his new plan of warfare— well suited to the state of his army —System of incessant attack.— Co-operating line of French armies from the German Rhine to the sea — The French wisely avoid a close engagement with the British.—Separation of the confederates.—Jourdain advances with an army in mass — The prince of Cobourg attempts to oppose him without the assistance of the duke of York—receives a signal defeat at Fleurus, which decides the fate of the campaign.—Pichegru in West Flanders attacks and defeats Clairfait.—Dangerous situation of the duke of York—who retires to Antwerp.—Earl Moira is ordered to Flanders with his army.—The prince of Wales offers to act under him as a volunteer—it is not deemed expedient to risk the person of the heir apparent.—His lordship lands at Ostend—finds the place surrounded by enemies—determines to force his way to the duke of York—masterly execution and success of his design.— Advances of the French.—The Austrians entirely evacuate the Netherlands.—Intrepid stand of the British at Breda.—The duke of York and the prince of Orange are obliged to fall back—they retreat behind the Meuse.—Victories of the republicans on the Rhine.—The German troops cross the Rhine.—Address of the emperor to the German princes is totally unavailing —Faithlessness of the king of Prussia.—Opinions on the operations and events of this campaign.—Suspicions unfavourable to the prince of Cobourg—are not supported by proof—Cobourg a man of very moderate abilities.—Victories of the republicans over the gallant Clairfait.—The republicans reduce the whole left bank of the Rhine.—The British gain some advantages —Winter campaign in Holland —Sickness and mortality of the British troops—intrepid efforts of the exhausted remains.—Immense superiority of numbers obliges our reduced army to evacuate Holland—which yields to the French arms —Campaign of 1794 peculiarly disastrous to the British army.—Strictures of military critics on the plan of operations.—Strictures of political critics on the executive councils of Britain. Efforts of France beyond all evidence of experience or probable conjecture—the event therefore does not necessarily afford grounds of either military or political censure.—Signal successes of Britain when she fought alone—her fleets paramount in the Mediterranean— reduce Corsica, and protect Spain and Italy—in the West Indies she subdues Martinico, Guadaloupe, St. Lucie, and part of St. Domingo.— Operations of earl Howe and the channel fleet—skilful manœuvre to bring the enemy to battle—battle of the first of June—numbers, force, and courageous efforts of the enemy—unavailing against the British fleet—decisive, glorious, and momentous victory.

THERE was a great and evident want of concert among
the German powers engaged in the combination against France.
The duke of Brunswick was disgusted with the conduct of general Wurmser in abandoning the lines of Weissembourg without risking a battle, whence his serene highness had been
compelled to raise the siege of Landau. He had written a
letter to the king of Prussia, complaining of the want of concert, and extending his animadversions to the two campaigns.
On the other hand the emperor though he was far from blaming
the duke of Brunswick individually, was by no means satisfied
with the co-operation of the Prussian king. The truth appears Jealousy
to be that the jealousy which for half a century had subsisted among the
between the houses of Brandenburg and Austria, and which at allies.
the commencement of the war seemed absorbed in enmity to
the French revolutionists, was still alive, and strongly opera-
ting.q The king of Prussia considered the continental efforts
of the last campaign as aggrandizing Austria, without producing any benefit to him which could indemnify his own exertions, or balance the accession to his ancient and nearest rival.
He did not regard the operations on the frontiers of France as
necessary to the safety of the empire and security of his own
dominions, and therefore conceived himself not fighting his own
battles. If it was wise at all to combine against France, the
expediency of such a confederacy must have arisen from some
common object, which it imported the several members of the
alliance to pursue ; and if it was to be pursued, vigorous measures with concert of operations only could be efficient. If the
king of Prussia apprehended imminent danger from the progress of French principles, or of French power, in sound policy he ought to have made the repression of these his supreme
object; and to have restrained for the present his jealousy of
the house of Austria. If he did not apprehend danger from
France, prudence required he should withdraw from the confederacy ; honour and sincerity demanded that he should not
pretend to be an ostensive member of the alliance, if he was,
resolved to be inactive in its service, and indifferent about its
success. On the other hand, the same unity of object was the The empe-
real interest of the emperor, if it was his interest at all to be ror tries to
member of a combination against France. The separate ap- raise his
propriation of fortresses could not indemnify him for his bel- subjects in
ligerent exertions, must disgust his continental ally, and ulti- mass;
mately contravene the advancement of their common object.
In the beginning of this year the emperor, extremely anxious
to oppose fresh numbers of Germans to the republican host,
actively endeavoured to induce the Germanic states to arm in
mass. This mode the king of Prussia declared he would never is opposed
sanction, and would withdraw his troops if it were attempted. by the king
of Prussia.

q Segur, vol. iii. chap. xiii. .

CHAP.
LIV.

1794.

Plan of the campaign.

Respective forces of the belligerent powers.

The emperor joins the allied armies.

He however professed himself still an active member of the confederacy, and ready to support every prudent and practicable project for forwarding its ends. The emperor found it necessary to acquiesce in Frederick William's objections to a levy in mass, and to appear satisfied with his professions of zeal in the cause. The subsidiary treaty with England either empowered him to make vigorous efforts, or induced him to promise such, and accordingly he was still deemed one of the chief members of the confederacy, and upon the conviction of his co-operation the projects and plans of the campaign were formed. The confederates proposed this year to press upon the frontiers of France with numerous forces on various sides, and also to co-operate with the insurgents on the coast of Brittany. In the month of February the duke of York, and with him colonel Mack, came over from the continent to London to hold a conference with the British ministers on the operations of the campaign. The emperor undertook to furnish two hundred thousand men, the king of Prussia sixty-four, including thirty-two thousand in British pay, Britain forty thousand, the rest of the allies, the Dutch, German princes, and the Emigrants fifty-two thousand, so that the whole combined force to operate on the frontiers of France should amount to three hundred and fifty-six thousand men, besides the troops intended to be employed by Britain on the coast. The French army it appears at this time amounted to seven hundred and eighty thousand men, of whom four hundred and eighty thousand composed the armies on the frontiers, and the rest were employed either in watching the late scenes of insurrection, or on the frontiers of Spain and the Alps.

On the fifth of March the duke of York arrived on the continent, to take the command of the British army; on the seventeenth he proceeded with general Clairfait to Valenciennes, where a council of war was held with the prince of Saxe-Cobourg, after which the generals returned to their respective head-quarters. It was determined that the emperor himself should take the field, and should be invested with the supreme command.

On the ninth of April his imperial majesty arrived at Brussels, and was inaugurated duke of Brabant. This ceremony, performed with great pomp and splendour, it was presumed would strike the imaginations and hearts of the people, and stimulate them to the most vigorous efforts, in his and their own cause. The states in a body presented his imperial majesty with the keys of the Louvain; on the gate there was the following inscription : " *Cæsar adest, trement Galli;*" this sentence was by the courtiers construed to mean the French republicans tremble at the approach of the emperor Francis. Great numbers of children, decorated with white staves, drew the state coach solemnly along; at the principal church *Te Deum* was chaunted; verses were presented to the emperor, congratulating his inauguration, and celebrating the achievements CHAP. which he was to perform. His imperial majesty proceeding to LIV. Valenciennes, was joyfully received by the allied army; and on the 16th of April he reviewed the combined forces, previously to 1794. the commencement of military operations.

Meanwhile the French government had made the most pow- Energy of erful and efficient dispositions for opening the campaign. Hor- the revolu-rible as the decemviral system was, it possessed one quality so tionary momentous in war, that without it all other qualities supported leaders in by the most abundant resources are of little efficacy; it was dis- France. tinguished for extraordinary ENERGY. Every latent power was called into action, its immense resources were not only employ-ed, but converged into a focus. The immediate object was to repel foreign invasions and interference wheresoever they threatened, and wheresoever they were seconded; to concen-trate all the intellectual and physical force of France to this point; to crumble all opposition to this design and to the exist-ing rulers who were carrying it into execution. Some embers of rebellion rekindling early in spring, troops were sent with the usual rapidity to the scene of reviving insurrection. These Rebellion speedily subjugated the royalists, and punished them in the is quelled most summary and cruel manner. Rebellion was crushed by in La the dispersion of the Vendeans; faction was extinguished; and Vendee. hostile operations against foreign powers engrossed the sole attention. General Jourdain was removed from the command of the northern army, and succeeded by general Pichegru, whose uncommon military talents proved him deserving of this confidence. As Jourdain was permitted to retire without dis-grace, and indeed, in the express words of the decree, with honour to himself, and with the gratitude of his country, his retirement was but short, and he was afterwards appointed to command the army of the Rhine.

On the seventeenth of April the confederates advanced in The confe-eight columns to invest Landreci, a well fortified town in derates Hainault, on the right bank of the river Sambre. The first take the column, composed of Austrian and Dutch troops under prince Siege of ·Christian of Hesse Darmstadt, advanced upon the village of Landreci. Catillon, which was forced after some resistance. The second under lieutenant-general Alvintzy, forced the French intrench-ments at Mazinguer, Oisy, and Nouviou, and took possession of the whole forest of Nouviou. The third column, led on by the emperor in person and the prince of Cobourg, after carry-ing the villages of Ribouville and Wassigny, detached for-wards the advanced guards, which took possession of the heights called Grand and Petit Blocus. The fourth and fifth columns were intrusted to the duke of York; the first of these was under his own immediate direction: and the latter was commanded by sir William Erskine. The objects of these co-lumns were the redoubts and village of Vaux, and the strong intrenchments of the French in the wood called Bois de Bou-

CHAP.
LIV.

1794.
Conflicts
between
the allies
and the re-
·publicans.

Battle of
the 24th of
April be-
tween the
duke of
York and
the repub-
licans;

our prince
and coun-
trymen are
victorious.

Landreci is
taken.

chain. The sixth, seventh, and eighth columns, under the hereditary prince of Orange, were not engaged, being only a corps of observation on the side of Cambray.[r] The duke of York endeavoured, notwithstanding the strong position of the French army, to turn their right, and for that purpose ordered the whole column to move forwards under the cover of the high ground, leaving only sufficient cavalry to occupy their attention. The fire of the republicans was at first severe, but finding the British troops eager to press them to a close engagement, which they foresaw would terminate in their discomfiture, they thought it expedient to retreat. These successes of the British troops enabled the confederates to commence the siege. · The French assembled in considerable force at the camp of Cæsar, near Cambray, which as we have seen, they had occupied the former year. The duke of York, well knowing the efficacy of the British force, on the 23d of April sent general Otto to attack the enemy's position. Otto, finding the French strong, and firmly posted, delayed the assault till the arrival of a re-enforcement, when, charging them with impetuosity, he soon broke their line, and after killing twelve hundred drove the rest into Cambray, with the loss of their artillery.[s] Pichegru, not disheartened by these repeated disadvantages, still directed his own movements against the most formidable part of his enemies. On the 24th of April he attacked the duke of York on all sides. The consummate general of the republicans found in the British prince and his army a commander and soldiers not to be overcome even by his ability and efforts. Frederick vigorously receiving the assailants in front by grape-shot and musketry, judiciously despatched several regiments of cavalry round the right, and of infantry round the left wing of his enemy, while he himself opposed the powerful and numerous host in the front of the battle; the two detachments charging the enemy's flanks, broke their lines, and produced a most destructive carnage in both wings: such a combination of valour and skill completely defeated the French. This attempt of Pichegru was only part of a general plan of attack, extending from Treves to the sea, although he chose for himself the post of most difficulty and danger. On the right, the columns of the French attacking the enemy's army were repulsed with loss, though not nearly so great as the loss which they incurred in their conflict with the duke of York. On the left, they gained a trifling advantage by the reduction of Menin and Courtray. Other engagements took place during the siege, without any decisive event. Where the British fought, the French were uniformly repulsed; but in their other conflicts they were more successful. Their efforts, however, to relieve Landreci, were not effectual, as that

r See New Annual Register for 1794, p. 328.

s See Macfarlane's History, vol. iv. p. 469.

fortress was captured after an investment of ten days. The CHAP.
French rulers acknowledged in the convention, that though not LIV.
the most numerous, the most formidable opponents to Gallic valour were the English.[t]   . 1794.

Pichegru, a man of strong and comprehensive genius, re- Testimony
garded, precedented modes of warfare no farther than they of the con-
could serve his purpose, and formed a plan of attack at once the hero-
new and admirably adapted to the character of the French, ism of the
especially to the soldiers under his command. His system of English.
tactics consisted in pursuing the enemy without intermission; Pichegru.
courting opportunities of engagements; and keeping his whole His new
force together, without dividing it for the purpose of carrying warfare.
on sieges; to reduce only such as were necessary in order to
secure proper positions, without seeming to be at all concerned
about the reduction of such strong places as he had left behind.
This system was suitable to the state of military experience
among the greater part of the French soldiers, as well as to the
character of the people. The troops were mostly new levied,
and although nationally courageous, active, and impetuous,
and then inspirited by enthusiasm, yet they were not sufficiently
trained in stationary warfare to undertake any siege of difficulty. Besides, as an annalist[u] of the present campaign observes,
" The French soldier is too ardent and impatient to go through
" with a chain of operations that require perseverance. In
" the field he darts forth as an eagle, and fights like a lion. But
" a long and arduous siege repels and often even discourages.
" In order to have a military body of men perfect and invinci-
" ble, it would be necesary to carry on sieges with Swiss troops,
" and to have French armies of observation. But while a
" general has only Frenchmen under his command, he ought
" not to let them grow restive, by remaining long in one place,
" but keep them always in breath, and always within view of
" the enemy." This system of incessant attack was extended System of
in its operation to the several armies of the republicans, so as incessant
to render them really parts of one great host, closely connected attack.
together as one army over a wide expanse of country. From Co opera-
the German Rhine to the sea, there was one co-operating line ting line of
of armies. Though the victory of the duke of York, and the mies from
capture of Landreci retarded the progress of this grand the Ger-
scheme of advance and assault they did not prevent its final man Rhine
execution and success. The exertions and attainments of the to the sea,
British arms eventually promoted the accomplishment of the
French projects. After the battle of the 24th of April, they The
cautiously abstained from close engagement with the British French
wisely

t See Barrrere's speech in the convention, after the late victory of the avoid a
duke of York   close en-
u Histoire Chronoligique des operations de l'Armee du Nord, et de celle gagement
du Sambre et Meuse, par le citoyen David, temoin des plupart de leurs ex- with the
ploits.   British.

CHAP. forces, and bent their principal efforts, both on the right and
LIV. left, against the Austrians.

1794.

Separation
of the con-
federates.

Jourdan
advances
with an
army in
mass.

Battle of
Fleurus.

June 26.

Pichegru
in West
Flanders
attacks and
defeats
Clairfait.

To this plan of partial attack the movements of the allied
army were peculiarly auspicious. Soon after the siege of
Landreci it was judged expedient to divide the confederates
into three parts; the chief army under the immediate command of the prince of Cobourg, and having the emperor himself at his head, was posted near the Sambre; the duke of
York with the British forces, was stationed at Tournay; and
general Clairfait, with a third army, occupied West Flanders.
Pichegru directed his own principal efforts to the left against
Clairfait, and straitening the quarters of the duke of York;
and in attacking British posts and detachments, without
hazarding a decisive battle. Several very bloody conflicts,
however, took place in this kind of warfare, but without materially impairing his highness's force, though fresh numbers
were daily joining the French army. Jourdain, with the
army of the Rhine in the beginning of the campaign, had met
with severe checks, but had been ultimately successful against
general Beaulieu, whom he compelled to evacuate the duchy
of Luxemburg, and to fall back to Namur. Encouraged by
their career of success, the French now prepared to invest
Charleroi on the Sambre. The prince of Cobourg with the
main army advanced to its relief; but though the undertaking
was extremely important, trusted to his own troops, without calling for the aid of the duke of York from Tournay. On the
21st of June he reached Ath, and on the 24th he effected a
junction with the prince of Orange and general Beaulieu, at
Nivelles. The main body of the French army, under general
Jourdan was posted at this time at Templeuve, Gosselies, and
Fleurus, for the purpose of covering the siege of Charleroi.
A battle ensued: both armies fought with the most intrepid
courage, but the impetuous valour of the French succeeded.
The allied army wss defeated in every quarter, and forced with
immense loss to retreat to Halle, thirty miles from the field of
battle :[x] this victory decided the fate of the campaign. Charleroi, and soon after Brussels fell into the hands of the victorious
enemy. In West Flanders, Pichegru was equally successful
against Clairfait. Receiving large re-enforcements from Lisle,
he undertook the siege of Ypres, the key of Flanders. The
importance of this place induced general Clairfait to hazard
the whole corps under his command for its relief. On the 13th
of June he attacked the republicans; and drove them from their
first position; but fortune soon changed. The ability, courage,
and skill of Clairfait were in vain opposed to the immense host
of impetuous republicans. After a series of defeats he was
compelled to abandon Ypres, to retire to Ghent, while Pichegru

x New Annual Register, 1794, page 333.

overran West Flanders. The geographical reader. by tracing the progress of the French army, and the retreat of the Austrians, and observing the position of the duke of York, will see that he was in a very dangerous situation, surrounded on all sides by the conquering multitudes of the French troops. Ever since the enemy, by the defeat of Cobourg, were so much advanced on his left, the duke's position had been very perilous; but since the progress of Pichegru upon his right, his post was no longer tenable; he accordingly retired with great expedition to Antwerp. The emperor despairing of success, after in vain endeavouring to raise the people of the Netherlands in mass, returned to Vienna.

CHAP. LIV.

1794

Dangerous situation of the duke of York, who retires to Antwerp.

Part of the original plan of the campaign had been, as we have already seen, to co-operate with the insurgents of La Vendee. Britain had undertaken, with that view, to send an expedition to France, and proposed to intrust the command to the valour, ability, and conduct of earl Moira,[y] who as lord Rawdon had attained so high military distinction in America. But the suppression of the insurgents, already recorded, prevented this design from being carried into execution. His lordship's army was therefore ordered to Flanders. One illustrious personage, seeking a wider field for the exercise of his vigorous genius and active mind, and wishing to learn the military art from so able a master, desired to serve as a volunteer; this was George, prince of Wales. Fitted by natural abilities and acquirements for either the cabinet or the field, the heir apparent from the delicacy of his situation, had cautiously abstained from political business. His present proposition did not, he conceived, interfere with the line of conduct which filial duty had chalked to itself. But his royal parents not deeming it expedient to risk the person of the heir apparent, the execution of his intention was not permitted. In the latter end of June earl Moira, with ten thousand men, landed at Ostend, just as the Austrians had been obliged to evacuate West Flanders. The French, in the mean time, were advancing upon Ghent in great force, and but little expectation was entertained of general Clairfait's being able to make any effectual resistance in that quarter. In the situation in which the earl of Moira found the affairs of the allies, an alternative occurred of either defending Ostend, or proceeding to join the duke of York. To succour the confederates, and support the British army, appeared an object of more urgent importance than the precarious possession of a single town; whatever movement was to be made required despatch, lest the advance of the French armies might completely cut off the communication. A council of war was therefore called by the earl of Moira, and it was determined immediately to evacuate Ostend. This difficult and

Earl Moira is ordered with his army to Flanders. The prince of Wales offers to act under him as a volunteer.

It is not deemed expedient to risk the person of the heir apparent.

His lordship lands at Ostend; and finds the place surrounded by enemies; determines to force his way to the duke of York.

y His lordship had succeeded to that title in the former year by the death of his father.

laborious task was committed to colonel Vyse. . On the morning of the 1st of July he began to embark the troops on board
the shipping, which lay at single anchor in the harbour, and
the baggage and stores were in the vessels before night. The
French entered the town as the last detachment embarked.
While colonel Vyse was engaged in conducting the evacuation
of Ostend, lord Moira with his main army repaired to Malle,
about four miles from Bruges, on the great causeway to Ghent.

**Masterly
execution
and suc-
ce s of the
design.** The enemy pressing very fast, nothing was left but the most
rapid despatch. For that purpose they marched without tents
and baggage. The French general was extremely eager to attack this corps; but so skilfully had their masterly leader arranged them on their march, that passing through a country
overrun by myriads of enemies elated with victory, and eager
for combat, encountering numberless defiles, through flats intersected with canals. and lately inundated, he did not afford
them a single opportunity of attack. After undergoing incredible hardships, on the 8th of July he joined the duke of York.
Having conducted this important accession of strength in safety
to the prince, lord Moira returned to Britain. The French
generals were now advancing in all directions through the
Netherlands, and the allies were apprehensive that Holland
would again become the scene of invasion. The duke of York
remained at Antwerp, to afford the Dutch time to strengthen
Advances their fortifications, and prepare for a vigorous defence. The
of the · prince of Orange, in the beginning of the month, had taken
French. post at Waterloo; and here he was at first successful in repel-
The duke ling an advanced guard of the French. He was soon, however,
of York compelled to abandon this post, by the advance of the republi-
and prince can armies to Brussels. He attempted afterwards to make a
of Orange
are obliged stand along the canal of Louvain; but the French bringing up
to fall ' continual re-enforcements, he was obliged, with considerable
back. loss, to retreat on the 16th across the Dyle, and established,
for a short time, his head-quarters at Nyle. The stadtholder
solicited the Dutch, by repeated proclamations, to. levy one
man in ten throughout the United Provinces. But a great portion of the people were disaffected, and the rest were torpid.
The French generals advanced in front of the Dyle towards
Louvain. At the Iron Mountain, the brave though lately unfortunate Clairfait again attempted an ineffectual resistance,
but was completely defeated by general Kleber, with the loss,
in killed, wounded, and prisoners, of six thousand men; while
the generals Lefevre and Dubois seized on the position of the
abbey of Florival. It was at first the intention of the commanders of the combined armies to make a stand at Namur,
and to form a line of defence from that city to Antwerp; but
these successes of the republicans, and their rapid movements,
totally disconcerted this plan. Namur was abandoned by
general Beaulieu on the night of 16th, leaving behind him
only two hundred men, who surrendered both the city and

citadel on the first summons: a large quantity of artillery was found at Namur. On the 20th, the keys of the city were presented at the bar of the national convention.[z] In West Flanders the important pass of the Lier was forced about the same time: the French on the 23d sent a trumpeter to inform the inhabitants of Antwerp that they intended to visit them on the succeeding morning, which they did at eleven o'clock, and took quiet possession of that city. The allies had previously set fire to the immense magazines of forage which were there collected. Jourdain and his troops entered Liege, which immediately submitted to the victorious republicans. The fortresses of Lisle and Sluys were speedily captured;[a] the four towns taken from the French were successfully retaken. The Austrians entirely evacuated the Netherlands, which were now overspread by the republican armies. The British retreated from Antwerp, and in number about twenty-five thousand men proceeded to Breda, which it was determined to defend, and a Dutch garrison was stationed there for that purpose. The right column of the English marched through Breda on the 4th of August, while the left went round the town. They then took a position which had been previously marked out for them, about four miles distant. Having halted several days at Breda, which the prince of Orange was putting into a state of defence, they retreated in the end of August to Bois-le-duc, where a Dutch garrison of seven thousand men was posted. In the beginning of September general Pichegru approached with an army of at least eighty thousand men; and the advanced guard of the republicans attacked and stormed the posts on the Dommel, and the village of Boxtel, which though they made a most gallant resistance, found it impossible to withstand the numbers of the enemy. The duke, therefore, with so inferior a force, perceiving his situation totally untenable, on the 16th of September, recrossed the Meuse, and took a position which had been previously reconnoitred about three miles from Grave. So vigorous had been the resistance of the valiant British, that with twenty-five thousand men they withstood the republicans, who were more than eighty thousand, from the beginning of July to the middle of September; in which time they made very inconsiderable advances, where they had the duke of York and his band to combat.[b] On the Rhine similar success attended the energetic efforts of the republicans. The king of Prussia having long manifested the coldest indifference to the confederacy, had early in this year announced to the German princes his determination to withdraw from the alliance. But Britain, judging of his good faith by her own, had conceived that he would bring into the field the forces for which he had stipulated, and for which he had been paid; in short, that a monarch would

The Austrians entirely evacuate the Netherlands.

Intrepid stand of the British on the frontiers of Holland, but they are compelled to give way to immense superiority of numbers.

They retreat behind the Meuse.

Faithlessness of the king of Prussia.

---

z New Annual Register, 1794, page 400.   a Ibid. 401.
b See Macfarlane, vol. iv. page 489.

CHAP. not descended to an artifice so totally unbecoming a gentleman,
LIV. or an honest man, *as to procure the money from other people by
false pretences.* But our government and legislature had pro-
1794. ceeded on the supposition that Frederick William possessed
virtues with which they found by experience he was not endued.
The force which he furnished was very inferior to that which
he promised, and their efforts were not such as might have been
expected from a Prussian army, and were of little avail against
the sincere, zealous, and ardent enthusiasm of the republican
Victories troops. On the 12th of July, general Michaud attacked the
of the re- Prussians near Edickhoffen; and to favour his operations in
publicans that quarter, advanced at the same time upon the Austrians
on the before Spires. The contest was long and bloody, and both
Rhine. parties claimed the victory. On the following day the French
renewed the attack on the Prussians with redoubled vigour.
The battle lasted from early in the morning till nine at night.
They attacked seven times, and at length carried by assault,
amidst a terrible fire, the important posts fortified and occupied
by the Prussians on Platoberg, the highest mountain in the
whole territory of Deux -Ponts.[c]   The republicans captured
great numbers of prisoners, and nine guns, besides ammunition, waggons, and horses. Continuing their series of attacks,
the republicans successively defeated the German troops, and
Address of compelled them to seek safety by crossing the Rhine.[d]   The
the em- emperor, alarmed by such a multiplicity of successes, endea-
peror voured to stimulate the German princes to join him in efficacious
to the Ger-measures to defend the empire against the irruption of the re-
man publicans; and for that purpose he addressed a memorial to the
princes, circles. His own resources, he stated, were utterly inadequate
to the contest: the progress of the French was so rapid, that he
must be inevitably obliged to withdraw his troops, and station
them for the defence of his own frontiers, unless the empire
is totally should think proper to oppose the progress of the French with
unavailing a sufficient force: these exhortations did not produce the desired effect; and no vigorous efforts were made by the empire
to second its chief. The suspicion of treachery often springs
from discomfiture; and ideas of this sort were very prevalent
during this ill-fated campaign. Many of the Austrian officers
Opinions of incurred the imputation: it was said that a considerable number
the opera of these were infected with republican principles; and that
tions and not a few were corrupted with French gold. As, however, it
events of would exceed the bounds of history to repeat the various sur-
this cam- mises of suspicion, concerning which proof was not adduced
paign. to ascertain the truth of the rumours, the narrative shall not
follow their details. One result however, is, the conduct of
the Austrians in many instances was so extremely inconsistent
with the military ability which the officers of that nation have
generally possessed in a great degree, that it implied either

c New Annual Register, 1794, p. 401.
d Otridge's Annual Register, 1794.

treachery or incapacity. The prince of Cobourg has been CHAP.
severely censured for the operations which terminated in the LIV.
signal defeat at Fleurus, and the loss of the Netherlands. It
was said, that knowing the efficacy of the British troops, he 1794.
should not have left them at Tournay when he marched to encounter Jourdain : that the addition of such a force would have
insured victory : that the plan of separation in which the position of the British troops originated, was very inimical to the
objects of the campaign, and very unfit to oppose an enemy
whose grand scheme was an extensive and closely connected
line of co-operation : that the allies had stationed themselves
at three angles of a triangle, while the republicans, by a seg-
ment of a circle, at once encompassed the whole, and broke Suspicions
the communication of the parts. These allegations, if true, unfavoura-
might be all accounted for without any charge of disaffection ble to the
against Cobourg, and upon a supposition that will be very prince of
generally admitted, that Jourdain and Pichegru, especially the Cobourg,
latter, far surpassed Cobourg in inventive powers which formed
new combinations adapted to the case. Cobourg, indeed, ap- are not
pears to have been a man of mere tactical experience, without supported
genius, and therefore not fit to cope with skilful men of very by proof.
great genius. This prince, after the evacuation of the Netherlands, was dismissed from his command, not without a rumour
of imputed treachery ; the truth of which I have no grounds
to record as an historical fact; and I myself disbelieve, as his
character was fair and honourable ; as there is no evidence to Cobourg a
support such a charge, and as the disasters of the army under man of
his command appeared to have arisen from the superior ability very mode-
of the French generals, commanding a much more numerous rate abili-
force, inspired by the most ardent enthusiasm which, whence- ties.
soever it arises, has always inspired men to efforts far beyond
diplomatic calculation formed on the experience of common
wars. The emperor certainly did not receive in the Netherlands, the assistance from his Belgian subjects. the hopes of
which probably had a considerable influence in inducing him to
visit these dominions. His exhortation to them to rise in mass
was indeed very unlikely to be regarded, as they did not conceive that, like the French, they were fighting their own cause.
Their object was naturally their own security, and not the aggrandizement of the house of Austria : they did not choose to
rise in mass to fight for a master, though the French had risen
in mass to fight for themselves.

After evacuating the Netherlands, general Clairfait, leaving Able ef-
general Latour to cover Maestreicht, posted himself at Juliers. forts of
Jourdain in the beginning of September prepared to march Clairfait.
against Latour; but it was the middle of the month before
he was ready for the assault. On the 18th the French in four Victories
columns attacked the whole line, from the Aywaille to Emeux. of the re-
All the passages were forced with the bayonet, and the camps publicans.
taken at full charge. The Austrians left two thousand men

dead on the field of battle, and several of their battallions were reduced to one hundred and fifty men. Seven hundred prisoners, twenty-six pieces of large cannon, three pair of colours, one hundred horses, and forty ammunition waggons, were taken, as well as the general's own carriage, his secretary, and papers. The remnant of Latour's army was completely routed and dispersed : general Clairfait having endeavoured without effect to assist Latour, with great skill and ability fortified himself at Juliers; and thither the republicans directed their efforts. On the 29th the French advanced from Aix-la-Chapelle, crossed the Roer, and attacked all the Austrian general's extensive posts, from Ruremonde to Juliers and Dureu. The conflict lasted the whole of the 29th and 30th of September, and was renewed on the 1st and 2d of October. The battle was extremely fierce on both sides; but Clairfait having lost ten thousand men, found it necessary to retreat as rapidly as possible. Juliers was abandoned to the French, and Clairfait retreated across the Rhine : the republicans conquered Cologne, Worms, Bonn, and in short reduced the whole left bank of the river. Pichegru, meanwhile was pressing on towards Holland. He informed the national convention, that with two hundred thousand men he would subjugate the United Provinces : and though the whole force which he required was not immediately sent, yet so numerous an addition was despatched to his army, that he deemed himself able to proceed with his operations. In the beginning of October he invested Bois-le-duc, which in a few days surrendered. On the 20th of October, a sharp conflict took place between the republicans and the English, in which, though the event was not decisive, the loss was considerable. The duke of York now crossing the Waal, fell back to Nimeguen, and thither the French multitudes soon followed. The British army was posted to the left of Nimeguen, and the enemy in front of the town, where batteries were erected for the purpose of cannonade and bombardment. On the 4th of November a sortie was made in the night. The troops employed in the sally were about three thousand British, Hanoverians, and Dutch ; and their object was to destroy the batteries which were newly constructed to annoy the city. It appears that the French were by some means informed of this design, and were prepared to obstruct its execution. The conflict was extremely obstinate, but our troops were victorious, though with considerable loss. The British general, however, from the immense superiority of the enemy, found it necessary to evacuate Nimeguen. Philippine on the Scheldt also surrendered : the French army on the right was fast advancing, and after the victories over the Austrians laid siege to Maestreicht. This city stood a regular investment in the beginning of October. During this month the republicans carried on their approaches, and whilst their parallels were forming

The republicans reduce the whole left bank of the Rhine.

The British gain some advantages but are greatly outnumbered.

constructed their batteries. · They repeatedly summonded the town to surrender; this denunciation having on the 30th been made in vain, the besiegers began to pour a most dreadful shower of shot and shells from all their works, with which they had surrounded the place. This fire, lasting during the whole of the night, demolished many public buildings and private houses, wounded and killed great numbers of the inhabitants. During three days this destructive assault continued: the governor at length, moved by the entreaties of the magistrates and people, entered into a negotiation with general Kleber, and the city capitulated on the 4th of November. After the capture of Nimeguen and Maestreicht, the operations were inactive during the rest of the month. But the troops, though not engaged in battles, were exposed to the severest hardships. The winter began with extreme severity: the soldiers were in want of clothing and other necessaries for encountering a winter campaign, which had not been foreseen in time to make adequate provision. In a country so much colder and damper than Britain, 'that season far exceeded its usual rigour. The consequènce was sickness and mortality among the soldiers, augmented by the want of remedies and medical assistance sufficient for such an unexpected prevalence of distemper. It is probable, from the inaction of the French at this time, that they laboured under similar evils. Fresh and unmerous re-enforcements however, arriving, enabled them in December to proceed with their operations. On the 7th of this month they made a fruitless attempt to cross the Waal in four rafts, from Nimeguen; two of the rafts were sunk by the English forces, who were stationed on the opposite side, near the village of Lant; one floated to the side occupied by the Dutch; and only one of the four regained that which was in the possession of the republicans. On the 11th the attempt was renewed, and with better success: they crossed the river above Nimeguen and near the canal, in boats and on rafts to the number of about five thousand men. Another detachment, however, attempting the passage was repulsed with considerable loss. About the middle of December the frost became extremely intense and in a few days the Maese and the Waal were frozen over. On the 27th the army crossed the river; the duke of York had, together with the prince of Orange, endeavoured to rouse the Dutch to such energetic resistance as had formerly saved their country from French invaders; but the circumstances of the times, and the dispositions of the people, were totally changed. Great numbers of the Dutch were now unwilling to oppose the French, and most of the rest conceived opposition hopeless. The exhortations of the princes were, therefore, altogether unavailing; and the duke of York considered all efforts as useless to save a people not desirous of saving themselves. Seeing military exertions unlikely to be farther useful in that country, he returned to England. The

Winter campaign in Holland.

Sickness and mortality of the British troops.

Intrepid efforts of their exhausted remains.

Attempts of the duke of York and prince of Orange to rouse the Dutch.

remaining forces were now intrusted to the command of general Walmoden; and an attempt was made to force the enemy
to repass the Waal. For this purpose ten battallions of British infantry, with six squadrons of light cavalry, commanded
by major-general Dundas, assisted by four squadrons and
four battallions of Hessians, amounting in all to about six thousand five hundred infantry, and a thousand horse, advanced in
three columns. At day break on the 30th of December, attacking a great body of French at the village of Thuil, they carried it with the bayonet, and drove the republicans across
the river. This success, however, was only temporary; the
English army was from the dreadful effects of the climate
and season rapidly decreasing. Private liberality was added
to public expenditure in sending plentiful supplies of flannel
waistcoats, and other fences against the cold; but the inclemency of the frosts was superior to every expedient : the
chief part of the army was overcome with sickness. According to the reports of officers who were engaged in this dreadful
service, the professional attention bestowed upon the sick was
by no means adequate to the effectual discharge of that
momentous duty.[e] In the month of January the French again
crossed the Waal with seventy thousand men. This formidable
host attacked the remains of the British army, and compelled
them, though still making the most gallant resistance, to retire.
Without tents, and unable to procure cantonments, the distressed heroes were obliged to pass the night, in this severe season,
in the open tobacco sheds, or under the canopy of an incle-
ment sky. The Dutch now urged the stadtholder to conclude
a peace with the French, and finding him unwilling, their provinces and towns successively offered terms to the republicans,
which were accepted. Zealand, and soon after Holland, entered into a capitulation. The stadtholder with much difficulty
escaped from the Hague with his family, sought and found
refuge in England: by the beginning of February the provinces had concluded a treaty with the French. As the republicans now possessed all the country between the British army
and the coast of Holland, it was impossible to retreat in that
direction; they, therefore, were obliged to take a much more
circuitous route towards the north coast of Germany. They
repeatedly occupied strong positions, not with the vain intention of making a stand against three times their number, but
to secure their retreat. Therein they had also to encounter

Immense superiority of numbers forces the English to evacuate Holland, which yields to the French arms.

e The details on this subject, not once or twice mentioned, but very frequently repeated through the periodical works of the time, daily, weekly,
monthly, and yearly, and never contradicted, charge the medical department with extreme negligence. But candour must admit, that the prevalence of distemper was much greater than was to be foreseen or expected
when the medical appointments were made, and that therefore a less
minute attention could be bestowed on every individual patient, than the
case required.

many other difficulties. The partial thaws which occasionally took place only served to aggravate the misery of the troops, from the floods which succeeded these alterations in the temperature, and either impeded their progress, or obliged the soldiers to wade through torrents of mud and water, which sometimes reached even to their knapsacks. In this dreadful situation they were obliged to continue their march, or to be overwhelmed by the enemy. After a route perhaps unequalled in the annals of military hardship, the exhausted remains of our army arrived at Bremen; and having halted for some weeks they embarked for England.

Such was the melancholy termination of the British expedition to the continent: so little did the expenses, preparations, and military equipments of two years answer the purposes for which they were undertaken. Britain had gone to war to prevent an attack upon the rights of Dutch navigation: instead of one river, the whole seven provinces were now commanded by the republicans. She had gone to war to prevent French aggrandizement: one campaign had given France an accession of territory fertile, productive, and opulent, far surpassing all the conquests of her most ambitious and successful monarchs.

Campaign
of 1794,
disastrous
to the
British
army.

In Italy and Spain the republicans were successful as far as they employed their efforts: their exertions, however, in Piedmont, were not important. On the confines of Spain they made rapid advances: the Spanish government attempted to raise the subjects in mass: but this was an expedient that could succeed only in countries where the people, either being or conceiving themselves free, were inspirited by the ardour of liberty.

From such an issue to the efforts of the confederation, persons that did not exactly consider the specific case might very naturally draw unjust inferences. Such might conclude, that because the combination in question had been unsuccessful, that no future union for suppressing dangerous ambition could be successful, and therefore that the attempt would be vain. Were a concert to be proposed for reducing the exorbitant power of France, the events of 1794 might be quoted as warnings that the scheme would be impracticable; and assuredly the same means and conduct in similar circumstances would be unavailing. If the continental powers, pretending to join, were really to pursue different and even contrary objects; and if the French were inspired by the same spirit which, during their republican enthusiasm, animated and invigorated their exertions, the issue would certainly be discomfiture to the nominal coalition of really discordant parts. But if they were to unite in head, heart, and hand, to pursue an object which many might think more important for their ultimate safety than paltry indemnities; and if it were to happen that they had not to contend against enthusiasm, but torpid indifference, it would by no means follow that the events of 1794 would be repeated. Even respecting Holland singly, it would be extremely hasty to deduce a general conclusion from the untoward issue of this disastrous campaign. The reduction of Holland did not arise merely from the arms of Pichegru, but in a great degree from the Dutch themselves. The majority of them were democratical, and received the French not only without opposition, but with gratitude and joy, as their deliverers and brothers. They might have withstood Pichegru, when assisted by the gallant English, as without any assistance they withstood Turenne and Conde; and with much less aid they discomfited Alva and Parma. The Dutch have clearly manifested, that, if they exert themselves, no foreign power can keep their country in subjection, or even dependence. Should it ever happen that they choose to assert their independence, there is little doubt that they will be successful; whenever they have the will they have the power to be free.

Signal success of Britain where she fought alone.

Signal as had been the disasters of the British armies on the continent, where she acted alone, unincumbered with allies, and on her appropriate theatre, her success was momentous, and her glory transcendent. In the choice of naval commanders, our minister, through the war, has uniformly considered instrumentality; fitness for discharging the duties, and accomplishing the purposes of the appointment. The various commands, supreme and subordinate, were conferred on professional ability and character. Three powerful armaments were prepared for the campaign of 1794: one under lord Hood, commanded the Mediterranean, reduced the island of Corsica, and protected the coasts of Spain and Italy; a second, under sir John Jervis, with a military force headed by sir Charles Grey, reduced Martinico, Guadaloupe, St. Lucie, and some parts of St. Domingo. But the most illustrious monument of British naval glory was raised by earl Howe. During the preceeding part of the war, France, conscious of her maritime inferiority to Great Britain, had hitherto confined her exertions to cruisers and small squadrons for harrassing our trade. In the month of May the French were induced to depart from this system of naval warfare. Anxious for the safety of a convoy daily expected from America, conveying an immense supply of corn and flour, of naval stores and colonial productions, the Brest fleet, amounting to twenty-seven ships of the line, ventured to sea under the command of rear admiral Villaret. Lord Howe expecting the same convoy, went to sea with twenty ships of the line. On the 28th of May he descried the enemy to windward. Admiral Palsey in the evening gave signal to the vanmost ships to attack the enemy's rear. Lord Hugh Seymour Conway attacked the Revolutionarie of 120 guns, and being soon supported by captain Parker of the Audacious, so damaged the enemy's ship that she struck; but escaping during the night,

Her fleets paramount in the Mediterranean

Acquisitions in the West Indies.

Operations of earl Howe and the channel fleet.

she was towed into Rochfort. The next morning the fleets resumed the conflict, but the intermission of a thick fog prevented
its continuance. The fog lasted that and the greater part of the
two following days. The sun occasionally breaking through the
mist, showed to each other the direction of the fleets; and lord
Howe employed this time in most masterly manœuvres to obtain Skilful ma-
the weather-gage, that he might compel them to fight when the nœuvre to
atmosphere should clear, and at length he succeeded. On the bring the
1st of June, the fog being dispersed, our admiral, fróm his for- enemy to
mer excellent dispositions, found an opportunity of bringing the Battle of
French to battle. Between seven and eight in the morning, our the 1st of
fleet advanced in a close and compact line: the enemy, finding June.
an engagement unavoidable, received our onset with their accus- Numbers,
tomed valour. A close and desperate engagement ensued, pre- force, and
senting the French as combatants worthy of occupying the naval ous efforts
heroism of England. The Montague of 130 guns, the French of the ene-
admiral's ship having adventured to encounter the Queen Char- my; una-
lotte of 100, was, in less than an hour, compelled to fly: the other vailing a-
ships of the same division seeing all efforts ineffectual against gainst the
British prowess, endeavoured to follow the flying admiral; ten, fleet.
however, were so crippled that they could not keep pace with the Decisive,
rest; but many of the British ships were so damaged that some of glorious,
these disabled ships of the enemy effected their escape. Six re- and mo-
mained in the possession of the British admiral, and were brought mentous
safe into Portsmouth, viz. La Juste of 80 guns, La Sans Pereille victory.
of 80 guns, L'America 74 L'Achille 74, L'Impetueux 74, and
Northumberland 74: these, with Le Vengeur, which was sunk,
made the whole loss of the French amount to seven ships of the
line. The victorious ships arrived safe in harbour with their
prizes: the crews, officers, and admiral were received with those
grateful thanks and high applauses which Britain never fails to
bestow on her conquering heroes. Earl Howe was by all ranks
and parties extolled for his tactical skill, steady perseverance, and
determined courage; first, in forcing the enemy, after every evasion, to a close action; and then in obtaining so signal an advantage over a fleet superior in its number of ships and of men, as
well as in size and weight of metal.[f] The year 1794, surpassing in
disaster by land the unfortunate 1777[g] or 1781,[h] by sea equalled
the glories of 1759.

f See Macfarlane's History, vol. iv. p. 461.
g Capture of Burgoyne's army.   h Cornwallis's army.

CHAP. LV.

CHAP.
LV.

1794.
Internal
affairs of
France.

WHEN the victories of the French in the Netherlands removed their apprehensions from foreign enemies, their attention was turned to internal tyranny. After the jacobins had triumphed over the Girondists, they were themselves divided into two parties. A division in opposition to Robespierre was headed by Hebert, and called the faction of the Cordeliers; these men carried jacobinism to an extremity that even Robespierre himself did not approve, especially when he had made such strides to single despotism. In the frantic wildness of their

civil and political doctrines, they somewhat resembled the *fifth* CHAP.
monarchy men of this country. They proposed, without any   LV.
exception, equalization of property, and a community in every
kind of goods or desirable objects: but in a point of religious .1794.
doctrines they were totally different, or rather their frenzy took
a quite contrary direction. The English anarchists were possessed with the madness of fanaticism, the French with the
madness of atheism. Their inculcations of universal equality
by no means suited Robespierre, they were arrested at his instance, accused, and put to death. Anacharsis Clootz, one of
the number, preached, to his fellow sufferers atheism on the scaffold, and died blaspheming his God. The associates of Robespierre next followed: fear and envy doomed Danton to the
scaffold. The tenure of Robespierre's despotism was the Tenure of
alarms of the people: and as these decreased, his power de- the despot-
cayed. Rapidly susceptible in all their impressions, the French ism of Ro-
people no sooner began to consider the atrocities which he had bespierre,
been perpetrating, than they became enraged against the ty- the fear of
rant; his enemies stimulated the prevailing sentiment, and sug- foreign
gested that he desired to establish himself as dictator. Fear, enemies.
the most strongly operative of his two ruling passions, now
goaded the tyrant to fresh proscriptions: he had still the armed
force of Paris under his command, but he found that it was im-
bibing the sentiments of his adversaries. Encountering danger, his timidity palsied his usual sagacity. Billaud Varennus A power-
publicly accused him in the convention:[i] Barrere, his artful and ful party
versatile associate, perceived that his dominion was drawing to formed
an end, and supported the accusation. Robespierre finding so him.
powerful a party to be formed for his destruction, endeavoured
to interest the violent anarchists in his favour, and imputed the
charges against him to the machinations of loyalists and English: but his efforts being destitute of firmness and courage,
were totally inefficient. When he repaired to the convention,
Tallien rose, and in a vehement speech, painted in the most
vivid colours all the atrocities under which France had groaned
and of which he regarded Robespierre as the principle author.
He recapitulated the manifold details of his bloody tyranny,
all the crimes he had authorized, the atrocious laws of which
he had been the author, and the victims which he had sacrificed, earnestly endeavoured to make the convention blush at so
disgraceful a slavery, and turning towards the bust of Brutus,
invoked his genius, and drawing forth a dagger from his girdle,
he swore that he would plunge it into the heart of Robespierre,
if the representatives of the people had not the courage to order his arrestation, and to break their chains.[k] The tyrant
tryed to reply, but he was not suffered to be heard; the convention doomed him and his chief associates to imprisonment

i Segur, 111. 116.   Otridge's Annual Register, and New Annual Register, 1794.   k Segur, vol. iii. p. 117.

Attempts were made to excite an insurrection in his behalf; but his own cowardice prevented success.[1] Finding that all was lost, Robespierre shot himself with a pistol : but the justice of heaven would not suffer the scaffold to be deprived of so merited a victim ; his wound rendered his punishment more lingering and tormenting. During the twenty-four hours which preceded his execution, he beheld the universal joy inspired by his downfall, and the horror which his person excited; he heard the reproaches of his colleagues, whom he had abased, and over whom he had tyrannized ; the cries of joy of the victims whom he still wished to strike ; and the imprecations of the whole people, whom he had for such a length of time deceived and oppressed. An object of public execration, no kind remembrance to strengthen his courage, no friend by his tears to soften his torments, he was compelled to appear before that revolutionary tribunal, by which his fury had condemned his own accomplices. He was led to the scaffold, with his brother, Couthon, Saint Just, and Lebas, his colleagues, Henriot his general, and the members of the rebellious *communes*.[m] An immense crowd followed him, reproached him with his crimes and his baseness, loaded him with outrages, and announced to him, by their acclamations, the judgment of posterity, which would place him in the list of the most odious and contemptible tyrants. The executioner, tearing off with violence the bandage which covered his wound, drew from him a hideous shriek, exposed him for some time to the eager looks of vengeance and hatred, and at last despatched him by a death as infamous as his life.

Robespierre attained his power neither by extraordinary abilities nor intrepid courage. All government and subordination being destroyed, the mere brutal force of the mob was paramount; and he rose by the adaptation of his manners to the lawless rabble, and the coincidence of his disposition with the predominant savageness of infuriated passion. Terror for a time maintained the supremacy of this monster. Fearing and envying all excellence, he employed his dominion in the destruction not only of eminent and able men, but the very qualities which lead to distinction. The sway of such a wretch, though only temporary, is a warning lesson to abilities and genius enamoured of revolution, that by succeeding in its projects it is eventually a ladder for exalting the most execrable and contemptible of mankind. Robespierre having thus experienced THE MERITED DOOM OF TYRANNY, the convention pursued measures which tended to alleviate the mischiefs that had accrued from the reign of atrocity, and to prevent the recurrence of the system of terrorism.

The banished and imprisoned remains of the Gironde party were recalled or released, the most flagrant and infamous of Ro-

l Segur, vol. iii. p. 118.   m Ibid. p. 120.

bespierre's decrees were rescinded, inviolability was restored CHAP.
to the members of the convention; and, to crown the salutary LV;
changes, the jacobin club, that perennial source of anarchy and
every flagrant enormity was abolished. From this moment terror 1794.
by degrees ceased to rule over France, and the drawings of Dawnings
social order began to re-appear: religion again lifted up her hal- of return-
lowed voice, and a distant prospect of better days seemed to open ing order.
to France.

The internal events which chiefly attracted the public attention Britain.—
in 1794, were the trials for treason, both in Edinburgh and Lon- Trials for
don. In the Scottish metropolis, a person named Robert Watt, treason.
being a member of some of the corresponding societies, had of- burgh.
fered himself to government as a spy and an informer, but not Watt and
obtaining from the officers of the crown the sum which he ex- Downie.
pected and required, he seriously projected to seize by force the
castle of Edinburgh, the banks, and the excise office; also the
persons of the lord provost, and of the judges civil and criminal.
This project he communicated in a paper to one Downie, a me-
chanic, and several other members of the societies. Downie appeared to accede, but the others rejected the proposal, and one
of them being himself a spy, gave information to government:
Watt and Downie were apprehended and tried.

By the union, the treason laws of England extend to Scot- Watt's con-
land. Watt's conduct amounted to a conspiracy to levy war spiracy not
against the king, which though not treason by the statute of Ed- Edward
ward III. had been usually reckoned treason by judges interpre- III.'s sta.
ting that statute, as we have already observed.[n]. The president tute.
of the court of session was head of a special commission appoint- Treason by
ed to try these persons, and in his charge, adopted the judicial the judicial
construction,[o] instead of the legislative definition, he described tion of that
the crime to be treason, the jury admitted his explanation, and statute.
as the evidence of the fact was unquestionable, brought their
verdict guilty. The defence set up for the prisoner acknowledged most profligate baseness, but pretended that he had
proposed the plan to procure accomplices, that he might inform
against them, and betray their counsels. His most plausible.
defence would have been the irrelevancy of the charge, and
his counsel might have alleged, that the decisions of judges mi-,
litating against the express definition of a statute, did not constitute the law of the land; and as the treason law then stood, a
conspiracy to levy war was not one of its clauses: on this ground,
however, Watt did not insist. Downie was also condemned, but
recommended to mercy, and being found to be misled by igno- is condem-
rance rather than prompted by malignity, received a pardon; but ned, and
Watt was executed. suffers
death.

n See the account of lord Loughborough's charge to the grand jury after
the riots of 1780, vol. iii. p. 232.
o See lord president Campbell's charge to the jury of Edinburgh in
August, 1794.

CHAP.
LV.

1794.

Alleged
p ot to as-
sassinate
the king.

The allega-
tions sup-
ported by
no proof.

Trial of
Thomas
Hardy,
John Horne
Tooke, and
John Thel-
wal, for
high trea-
son.

About this time the public were greatly alarmed by the report of a plot to assassinate the king. The persons accused of
this nefarious intent were Le Maitre, a watch-maker's apprentice; Higgins, a chymist's apprentice; and Smith, who kept a
book-stall: the accuser was Upton, also a watch-maker's apprentice. According to this person's account, an instrument was to
have been formed like a walking stick, in the stick there was to
be a brass tube, through which one of the conspirators was to
blow a poisoned dart at his majesty, at a time and place to be
afterwards determined. Such mischievous machinations had
really been discovered, and so many more were believed, that
the nation in general was in a state of alarm, and great numbers
swallowed this improbable and absurd story. The men were
committed to prison; but ministers, after investigating the evidence, found it so contradictory and incredible, that the alleged
conspirators were set at liberty.

But the accused persons who chiefly occupied the thoughts
of all parties, and drew the public attention from the successes
of the French, were Messrs. Hardy, Tooke, Thelwal, and their
fellow prisoners in the Tower. During the greater part of summer and autumn they had been kept in close confinement. In
September a special commission was appointed, and in October
opened by the lord chief justice Eyre, who, in a charge to the
grand jury, appeared to consider the alleged facts, as, if proved, amounting to high treason.[p] The grand jury forming the
same opinion, found a bill of indictment against Thomas Hardy,
John Horne Tooke, J. A. Bonney, Steward Kydd, Jeremiah
Joyce, Thomas Wardell, Thomas Holcroft, John Ritcher, Matthew More, John Thelwal, R. Hodson, and John Baxter. John
Martin, attorney, was afterwards indicted in a separate bill.
On the 28th of October the trial of Thomas Hardy began: the
charge consisted of nine overt acts, the substance of which was,
that the accused had conspired to compass the king's death, by
a conspiracy to hold a convention which should overturn government; and thus had conspired to levy war against the king,
and to excite rebellion against his government, and that they
had procured arms for that purpose. The legal amount of the
charge therefore, was, a conspiracy against the constitution
and peace of the kingdom. A conspiracy to levy war, as we
have repeatedly observed, is not treason by the statute of Edward III. though it had been construed as treason by many interpreters of that statute. The evidence against Mr. Hardy
was partly written, partly oral. Many of the papers charged
as treasonable, had been communicated to the public in advertisements, and none of them were peculiar to him, but common to the whole corresponding society, in the name of which
he acted as secretary; and none of them by any reasonable construction could amount to treason. The oral evidence con-

p See judge Eyre's charge to the grand jury of Middlesex, in October,
1794.

sisted of two classes of men; the first, respectable persons of
unquestionable and unquestioned veracity; the second, of hired
spies, of course deserving no credit on their own account,
but to be believed or not according to the congruity of
their testimony with other circumstances. The evidence of
the first class proved little but what was more strongly expressed in the written documents; the evidence of the second set,
though very prompt[q] in general assertion, yet, when by inter-
rogation chained down to specific facts, whatever they advanced,
maintained nothing stronger than what had appeared from the
manuscripts and printed papers. The project of holding a convention indeed was proved, but there was no evidence that the
purpose was treasonable; and the general result was, that the
corresponding society, and Mr. Hardy as its secretary, had been
active in conduct of a seditious tendency, a proposition very
well known before, but totally irrelative to a charge of high
treason. The trial lasted seven days, a period unprecedented
in the history of capital prosecutions. The attorney-general, Abilities of
with a minuteness of detail, not only laudable but necessary in the lawyers
his professional situation, spoke for nine hours, and displayed on both
sides.
that candour of construction and liberality of sentiment which
he has uniformly manifested in the successive stations that he
has been called to fill.[r] The prisoner's defence was intrusted
to two counsellors, both of distinguished ability: The one was
Mr. Gibbs, eminent for extent and precision of legal knowledge,
for clear and logical pleading; who acquired very high reputation by his efforts. The other was the honourable Thomas Extraordi-
Erskine, who, though little more than forty years of age, and nary elo-
bred up to the profession of arms, for sixteen years he had been quence f
the shining ornament of the English bar, and exalted the judi- skine.
cial eloquence of his country to an equality with the best exertions of either Greece or Rome; and if in the Pitts, Fox, Burke,
and Sheridan, these realms presented rivals to Demosthenes and
Cicero in deliberative eloquence; they raised a rival to the best
pleading of Cicero, in the judicial efforts of Mr. Erskine. With
professional knowledge and science, this celebrated orator embodied a wide range of history and literature, and a thorough
conversancy with human life, moral and political philosophy:
such attainments, invigorated by genius, and adorned with persuasive grace, spoke through the heads to the hearts of his hearers; in the most impressive eloquence. His exhibition on this
trial, not inferior to Tully's defence of Milo, constituted a brilliant
epoch in the oratory of the British bar.

The jury having maturely weighed the law, allegations, and The ac-
proofs, returned a verdict, NOT GUILTY. The acquittal of Hardy cused are
gave very general satisfaction: impartial friends of the king respective-
and constitution were aware, that the best security of those ly acquitted.

q See evidence of Groves, Lingham, Gosling, and Taylor, in Gurney's account of the State Trials, 1794.   r See State Trials.

was the upright administration of law even towards their enemies; and were pleased that a person was acquitted, whose
proven acts had not contravened the statutes, which only established the crime of treason. Many who thought highly of
the ministers, yet did not wish liberty, property and life to be so
much in their power, as at their instance to subject freeborn Britons
to capital punishment upon such vague and circuitous construction. The verdict in favour of Hardy was considered as a very
favourable omen to the others who should be tried. After the
intermission of several days, Mr. Horne Tooke was brought to
the bar. The evidence for the crown, written and oral, consisted of nearly the same materials that had been already presented on the trial of Hardy. It appeared, however, that the
present defendant had been much more guarded and moderate
than most of the other votaries of reform, and had censured
them as exceeding wise and reasonable bounds. He indeed
appears never to have approved of annual parliaments or universal suffrage; and was friendly to the constitution of king,
lords, and commons; though he wished a change in the latter
branch, which he conceived would render it less liable to corruption. No treasonable act having been proved against the
accused, the verdict of course was, NOT GUILTY. Mr. Tooke
adduced, as exculpatory evidence, the duke of Richmond, Mr.
Pitt, and others, who had been advocates of parliamentary
reform. The questions put to these witnesses did not tend to
produce any defence of Mr. Tooke's conduct, their substance
related to the share taken by the witnesses themselves in
parliamentary reform at a totally different period; they are
therefore to be considered not as exculpations of the defendant
but as charges of inconsistency against the witnesses themselves,
in their political conduct. As the innocence or guilt of Mr.
Tooke did not depend on the facts which his majesty's ministers
might, as ministers, either acknowledge or deny, their testimonies
could answer no purpose relative to the charge, and were therefore unnecessary at his trial: other purposes, however, their adhi-
bition might answer, by reminding the public, that they who were
now inimical to one species of reform had once been favourable
to another, they impressed that numerous class which, in estimating conduct often disregards circumstances, with an opinion that
the ministers were apostates. The call upon Mr. Pitt and the
duke of Richmond to be witnesses at the trial of Mr. Tooke,
was evidently not a measure of judicial exculpation, where none
was required, but a political censure which so many were desirous of heaping upon ministers. The pleadings by Messrs.
Gibbs and Erskine, were worthy of their preceding efforts;
but Mr. Tooke himself was a very powerful counsel in his own
favour.

After this acquittal, which took place on the 22d of November, the attorney-general declined any farther prosecution of
the remaining members of the constitutional society; and on

Monday the 1st of December, a jury being impannelled *pro for-* ma, Messrs. Bonney, Joyce, Kydd, and Holcroft, were acquitted and discharged. Next came the trial of Thelwal: it appeared from the evidence that, in his conduct, and still more in his expressions, this person had been much more violent than the two others, but nothing which was proved against him amounting to treason, he was accordingly acquitted.

Whatever may have been the intentions of any of these individuals, as their acts by no means constituted legal guilt, their acquittal bearing so high testimony to the purity of trial by jury, manifested the excellence of our judicature, in constitution, and practice. No doctrine can be more inconsistent with the security of a free country than constructive treason, and none has the discriminating justice of the English law more severely reprobated. Constructive treason indeed is an engine of tyranny, under whatever forms it has been established. When the anti-monarchical party predominated in England, the first victim of its uncontroled injustice suffered for constructive and accumulative treason.[a] Earl Strafford, however morally culpable, or politically hurtful his conduct might be, was not legally guilty by any existing law, and was a sacrifice to party rage. Under Charles II. Russel and Sydney, by constructive treason, fell victims to monarchical tyranny. Instances have, in much more benignant reigns, occurred of men suffering from wrested interpretations, when obnoxious to the ruling party; but under the equitable and enlightened principles and sentiments of the present age, whoever might be the accusers, the accused were assured of strict and legal justice.

This summer there was great disturbance in the capital on account of villanies and cruelties asserted to have been committed in houses employed for enlisting recruits. It was affirmed, that various persons had been kidnapped to these abodes and confined until they consented to become soldiers. Some discoveries of this kind having been made, and many more having been reported, the populace became extremely outrageous, and destroyed various houses alleged to be the scenes of these atrocities. After being violent and riotous for about six days, the ferment of the people at last subsided.

This summer a treaty was concluded between Great Britain and America, tending powerfully to promote the political amity and commercial benefit of both countries. Several changes took place in administration, making room for the whigs. who had seceded from Mr. Fox at the commencement of the war: lord Fitzwilliam was made viceroy of Ireland, the duke of Portland third secretary of state, Mr. Windham secretary at war, and earl Spencer first lord of the admiralty.

Parliament met on the 30th of December 1794: his majesty's speech urged the necessity of perseverance in the war, not-

CHAP. LV.

1794.

Observations on their acquittal.

Riots in the metropolis about persons called crimps.

Treaty between Britain and America.

Meeting of parliament.

[a] See trial of lord Strafford; Humes's History vol. iii 2. and State Trials.

CHAP. withstanding our disappointments; and augured the ultimate
LV. success of the allies, from the progressive and rapid decay of
French resources, and the instability of every part of that un-
1794 natural system. The Dutch had, he observed, from a sense of
Mr Pitt present difficulties, made overtures for peace with the pre-
augurs the vailing party in France: but no established government could
downfall of
the present derive security from such a negotiation. The most effectual
system of. means had therefore been employed for the farther augmenta-
France, tion of the forces; on whose valour, as well as on the public
from the spirit of the people, his majesty professed he had the utmost
exhaustion
of her fi- reliance. In addition to the arguments frequently repeated for
nances. the continuance of the war, the minister laid great stress on
the exhaustion of the French finances. By a very copious detail of their pecuniary proceedings, illustrated and embellished
by his usual eloquence, he endeavoured to prove that France
was in the gulf of Bankruptcy, and that the ruin of the revolutionary system was inevitable, if we pressed them with vigour :
peace would be totally impolitic, even if attainable; and with
Opposition the present rulers it could not be permanent. In recommend-
contends ing peace, besides dwelling on the most unfortunate events of
that the
enthusias- the last campaign, opposition contended, that the French were
tic energy beginning to return to social order ; and that the hopes of sub-
of the duing them by the exhaustion of their finances were chimerical.
French What were the proofs of such a failure? Was it their extra-
would dis- ordinary energy of efforts and abundant supply of clothing
cover new
resources ; and provisions? The causes which brought a regularly go-
and alle- verned state to the last period of its military exertions, would,
ges France by no means, produce the same effect on a revolutionary go-
to be re- vernment, which possessed all the existing means and resources
turning to of the country. To reduce them to the last extremity, there
social or-
der. must be no land, no productions, no labourers, no soldiers, in
short, no faculties of any kind in the whole extent of the territory. France had been driven to unprecedented exertions by
an enthusiasm, the efforts of which the pressure of the confederacy had invigorated ; there being such a spring to their
enterprise, all calculations of resources formed on usual
principles, must be altogether erroneous. Whatever hopes of
success there might have been· at the beginning of the war,
they were now entirely vanished ; and the confederacy was
dissolved. Besides, let us consider the success of our arms:
all our preparations, financial and military, had been totally
useless. Why should we carry on a war in which all our efforts were to be wasted? The French were now very materially changed: the terrible system had entirely ceased;[t] jacobinism, so hostile to this country, was destroyed, and moderation was at least the assumption of a virtue, which showed the
real opinion of the people of France. This French republic-

t This argument was chiefly employed by Mr. Wilberforce ; who, though
he had voted for the war, was this session the advocate of peace.

ans were now probably not disinclined to peace; let us therefore propose a negotiation. Whether successful or not, it would
be extremely beneficial to this country: should our proffers be
rejected, the consequence would be, that as we should then
have right on our side, every person would unite in co-operating with government with the greatest vigour and firmness, in
what then would be a just and necessary war. It was replied,
that the disasters of the conflict arose from our allies : wherever
we had fought alone, we had been signally successful. The
balance of territorial acquisitions and pecuniary resources was
greatly in our favour; and France had lost more in permanent value and present means, than the losses of all the
allies united together. The alteration which had taken place
was only the change of a name, and not of a substance. The
present government was no more moderate than the government under Brissot, which had provoked this country to war.
Peace with such a system could not be secure ; we must, on
the contrary, increase our precautions. Hostilities would again
be commenced by France, when the military force of her enemies was reduced by a pretended peace. No treaty could be
stable that should be made with a government so totally unfettered by every principle of religion and justice. In spite of
partial disappointment, there was a moral certainty that we
should ultimately prevail in the contest. These arguments
were repeated in the discussion of sundry motions[u] for the attainment of peace; and the majority of parliament being determined to persist in the war, the pacific propositions were successively negatived. Lord Grenville moved, in lieu of a conciliatory motion by the duke of Bedford, that a vigorous prosecution
of the war was the most effectual means for producing a solid
and permanent peace.

In the course of these debates, the practicability of negotia- Discussion
tion with the present rulers, was very ably discussed on both respecting
sides. Ministers contended, that the French republicans en- the practi-
tertained an irreconcileable hatred to this country and its in- negotia-
habitants ; and that the principal motive of their willingness to tion.
make peace with the other members of the confederacy was,
that they might convert their whole rage against Britain. The
very principles of the French republic were such, that to acknowledge its legitimacy, which must be done in case of a

u By the earl of Stanhope, on the 6th of January, for no interference in
the internal affairs of France. By Mr. Grey, on the 26th of February, that
the present government ought not to be considered as precluding a negotiation for peace. By the duke of Bedford, on the 27th of February, to the
same purpose. By Mr. Wilberforce, on the 27th of May, that in the present circumstances of France, the British government ought not to object
to proposals for a general pacification ; and that it was the interest of the
nation to put an end to the war as soon as just and honourable terms could
be obtained. See parliamentary reports for 1795.

CHAP.   treaty, was to confess all other governments to be founded upon
LV.   injustice. A peace, built on such grounds, would be not only
        disgraceful, but fatal to our own constitution, by undermining its
1795.   principles, and empowering its many domestic enemies to repre-
        sent it as iniquitous and oppressive.

Whoever carefully reviews the ministerial speeches of this
session, will observe a very striking and important difference
between their general scope and that of the preceding years of
war. Their objections to peace now much more frequently
consisted of arguments taken from the internal constitution of
France. Though they did not directly and avowedly state the
restoration of monarchy as a condition of peace, yet professing
to make war for the sake of security, they very plainly intimated, that they knew of no other *means* of security, but the restoration of monarchy.[x] That they did not require the restoration of monarchy as an indispensable condition, but as the
means of another condition, was a nice and subtle logical distinction, though in point of practical effect, there was little real
difference; as peace upon that supposition could not be admitted unless the proposed *means* existed. This doctrine it may
be observed, approached much nearer to the AVOWED doctrines
of Mr. Burke than any which ministers had before expressed.
After the events of the last campaign, ministers could not really
suppose the probability of such a restoration by external pressure to be increased. They could not imagine that Britain and
Austria, after the loss of Belgium and Holland, were nearer
the establishment of the house of Bourbon, through their sole
efforts, than when, in conjunction with Prussia and the greater
part of Europe, they had been advanced on the frontiers of France.
Such expectations, if they at all existed, must have been built
on other grounds than the relative state of France and the confederates ; and this change is to be accounted for from different
causes.

Sentiments   The political objects and views of Mr. Burke, concerning
and rea-   the purpose of the war, as has been already shown, were ma-
sons of the terially different from those which ministers professed at its
whigs who   commencement to seek. His opinions had been adopted in a
separated   considerable degree by those members of the old whig aristo-
from Mr.   cracy who separated from Mr. Fox. They conceived the
Fox.   monarchical and aristocratical part of the constitution to be
endangered from the dissemination of democratical principles.
Mr. Fox's conduct they thought of a tendency too favourable
to the preponderance of democracy. Whatever might be their
diversities of opinion in other respects, Mr. Pitt and his party
agreed with them in supporting the privileged orders. Through
French principles, combined with a corresponding government,

---

x See speeches of Mr. Pitt, lord Grenville, and Mr. Windham, at the beginning of the session, and repeatedly afterwards when the subject was
agitated. See parliamentary debates for 1795.

they deemed the property, dignity, and privileges of the high- CHAP.
er ranks endangered; their ardent wish was. to re-establish LV.
monarchy in France, as the means of preserving the monarchy
and aristocracy of England. The introduction of so many of 1795.
their members into the British cabinet evidently influenced the
sentiments, or at least the counsels, of their colleagues, and
the support of the royal cause in France, probably in compliance with their wishes, became one of the chief objects of
military schemes; and hopes were sanguine as wishes were
ardent. These were warmly cherished by the representations
of the emigrants, who, either in their conception or reports, or
both extravagantly magnified the number and force of the
loyalists. Ministers, especially Mr. Windham and others who
had recently come into office, appear to have believed the
greater part of what the emigrants stated, and to have projected plans of powerful and effectual co-operation which
would, they fancied, promote the re-establishment of royalty
in France. These accessions to the cabinet, with the political
and military measures which they contributed to produce, had
probably their share in effecting this difference in the ministerial
reasonings of that session.

Perceiving ministers and a very great majority of parliament Motions
totally averse to every overture for accommodation with France, for an in-
opposition proposed to inquire into the state in which the nation quiry into
was placed by the war. The management of this momentous the man- agement
subject was undertaken by Mr. Fox; and on the 24th of March of the war,
he moved that a committee of the whole house should be ap- and state
pointed to consider the state of the kingdom. After our dis- of the na-
comfiture at Saratoga, in the American war, he had made a tion.
similar motion,y and it had been received, though our situation
was far from being equal in peril to the present. The most
evident necessity now dictated an inquiry: the war had lasted
only two years, and in that short period, the enemy had made
a progress unknown to former æras; they had overcome all resistance, and acquired such an extent of territory as placed
them in the most alarming state of superiority to the confederacy which had been formed for reducing their ancient power.
The losses of Britain had been immense, both in killed and
prisoners.[z] Our pecuniary expenditure had amounted to seventy millions, and the permanent taxes which it had occasioned, to three millions. What return was made to the nation,
for this enormous profusion of blood and treasure? Our subsidies to our allies had been equally useless as our own exertions. What did England gain by subsidizing Sardinia? Were
the British constitution, independence, and power; the liberty,
property, and lives of British subjects, more secure from the
guarantee of the king of Sardinia? What had been the effect

y See vol. i. p. 558.
z This position he attempted to prove by a detailed enumeration.

HISTORY OF THE

of our subsidy to the king of Prussia? that our money had been paid, and that he had not performed the stipulated service. If the war continued, other subsidies would be wanted, which would be equally unavailing. Affairs in Ireland also demanded investigation;[a] the extreme irritation of the great mass of the people ought to warn ministers not to render themselves responsible for the very possible event of its dismemberment from the British empire, by the refusal of an inquiry into the discontents of its inhabitants. In England, dissatisfaction was prevalent: an idea pervaded the mass of the people, that the commons could not fairly be reputed the representatives of the nation,[b] from their undeviating compliance with every measure proposed by ministry, notwithstanding the ill success with which they had conducted the war. What were the grounds for so extraordinary a confidence in men whose schemes were continually miscarrying? Even suppose the war had been just (which he was not now canvassing,) did the succession of plans and series of events afford reasonable grounds for reposing unlimited confidence in the present counsellors of his majesty, as wise, energetic, and effective war ministers? If they really deserved trust, they would not resist inquiry; men that dreaded a scrutiny into their conduct, afforded the clearest presumption that it would not bear examination. No man conscious of the able and upright discharge of his duty, will flinch from an investigation of his actions. Mr. Pitt objected to inquiry on the plan proposed by Mr. Fox, as too extensive to be compatible with the other business of parliament. Parts of his objects were inexpedient and unreasonable: Mr. Fox had exaggerated our losses, and detracted from our advantages, and on the whole had exhibited an unfair statement of our situation; and the inquiry at present would be productive of many mischiefs, and no benefit. It was replied, both by Messrs. Sheridan and Fox, that Mr. Pitt, instead of meeting it, had shifted the question; that if Mr. Fox had misrepresented the situation of the country, the means of confuting his statements were not the assertions of the party concerned, but a fair investigation of conduct. These arguments, though it must be owned not entirely without weight, did not impress the majority of the commons. Credit was given to ministers on their claims of confidence, and Mr. Fox's motion was negatived: a similar proposition by earl Guilford in the house of peers, was also rejected. Specific motions were afterwards made in both houses for an inquiry respecting Irish affairs, but with as little success.

The preparations for the ensuing campaign, early in the session came under the consideration of parliament. One im-

a Mr. Fox particularly alluded to the recall of earl Fitzwilliam, which is included in a subsequent part of the narrative.

b See parliamentary debates, March 27th, 1795.

portant branch of these was to strengthen our allies. The em- CHAP.
peror had signified his earnest inclination to make the most LV.
vigorous efforts against the common enemy, but intimated the
necessity of pecuniary assistance, in a loan of four millions, on 1795.
the credit of the revenues, which arose from his hereditary dominions. Through such an accommodation he proposed to
bring two hundred thousand men into the field. His Britannic
majesty expressed his wish that the emperor should not only
receive the desired supply, but also, that by means of a similar
loan to a greater extent, he might be enabled to employ a still
more considerable force. A message to that effect was, on Loan to
the 4th of February, delivered to the house of commons, and the emin a few days after to the house of peers. Mr. Pitt made a peror.
motion for the loan required: in discussing this proposition, the
anti-ministerial party naturally, took a view of the Prussian
subsidy, and its misapplication. The ministers, without justifying the conduct of the king of Prussia, contended that the
present loan would be powerfully conducive to the purposes of
the war; that there would be undoubted security from Austria
for the performance of the contract, and that the risk was not
so great as the probable advantage. Mr. Pitt therefore proposed that Britain should guarantee the loan: a similar proposition was made in the house of peers, and a law was passed
pledging the national faith for the security of the sums borrowed by the emperor. A convention, agreeable to the intimation
of the king, was concluded between his majesty and the emperor
of Germany, for enabling him to bring a still greater force against
the enemy. The whole amount raised for Austria under the
guarantee of parliament amounted to four million six hundred
thousand pounds.

The force required by Britain for the service of 1795, amount- Supplies.
ed to one hundred thousand seamen, one hundred and twenty
thousand regulars for the guard and garrisons of the kingdom,
sixty-six thousand militia, and forty thousand men employed
partly in Ireland and partly in the West Indies and the plantations, exclusive of fencibles and volunteers, foreign troops in
British pay, and embodied French emigrants. The sums required to maintain this force, with the extraordinaries and ordnance, for the Sardinian subsidy, and all the public services of
the year, amounted to twenty-seven millions, five hundred and
forty thousand pounds, requiring a loan of eighteen millions.
The taxes were upon wine, foreign and British spirits, tea, coffee, Taxes.
insurances, foreign grocery and fruits, timber, increase of post-
office duty by abridging the privilege of franking, and on hair
powder. The loan having been raised by private contract and
not by open competition, was severely censured; the terms were
alleged to be, at least, five per cent more favourable to the contractors than was necessary.

In furnishing the requisite force for the current year greatly
surpassing the demands of former, exigencies, it was necessary

Plan of Mr.
Pitt for
manning
the navy.

to consider the most speedy and effectual means for levying soldiers and sailors. Mr. Pitt proposed a new plan for manning the navy, and instead of attempting to throw the burthen on any particular class of society, to call upon the public, by requiring the contributions of all districts; he proposed as much as possible to supersede the necessity of pressing sailors, which besides its hardships, was accidental and partial in its operation towards the owners of ships; he therefore moved, that a supply should be required from the mercantile marine in general. The proprietors of merchantmen were the most deeply interested in maintaining the naval superiority, by which their valuable property was protected. Let them contribute one man out of every seven, with smaller proportion from the coasting trade; and also a certain number from those who were employed in inland navigation; and that besides one man should be furnished by each parish. After a few modifications the proposition was passed into a law, and officers were immediately despatched to superintend the several kinds of levy. Mr. Wyndham, as secretary at war, reviewed the means of internal defence, and proposed to render the militia more efficient, to augment its number, improve its discipline, and assimilate it as much as possible to the army. To effect this object it was necessary to employ expert subalterns, and to encourage such to offer their services, he proposed an additional allowance to be made to their pay in time of peace, and a bill for that purpose was introduced. Messrs. Fox and Sheridan opposed it as tending to increase the influence and patronage of ministers, and to place the whole military strength of the kingdom under their immediate direction; a step which was evidently preparatory to the complete establishment of arbitrary power; but their objections were overruled. With a view farther to promote the discipline of the militia it was judged requisite to introduce artillery into that body. The bill authorized the pressing into the regular corps, those militia men who should become expert in the management of artillery. It also permitted those privates who were inclined to enter into the navy, or in the artillery, to quit the militia service. These and other clauses tending to encourage militiamen to become soldiers, encountered strong objections; but the bill was passed by a great majority. This year had been remarkable for scarcity and dearth; the price of provisions was so high that the pay of soldiers was insufficient, and great complaints prevailed. Government, without communicating with parliament, had bestowed an extraordinary allowance to make up for the high price of bread. Though the measure was not only humane but necessary in itself, yet the mode of carrying it into execution was disapproved, as tending to establish a precedent for maintaining soldiers without the consent of parliament. The attempt was represented as the more inexcusable, as parliament was sitting, competent

Plan of Mr
Windham
for the improvement
of the militia.

and disposed to provide supplies according to the circumstan- CHAP. ces of the case; and a resolution was proposed, declaring it LV. illegal to augment the pay of the army without the consent of parliament. Ministers vindicated the measure as merely tem- 1795. porary and the result of necessity; that no increase was intended, but a mere occasional supply. After a warm discussion, in which many constitutional topics were introduced, the motion was negatived.[c]

Motions were made by the opposition in both houses to re- Discussion peal the suspension of the habeas-corpus act. The discussion of the late of that subject introduced a review of the prosecutions and acquittals. trials for high treason: the acquittals had been incidentally mentioned in various debates about the beginning of the session; but on the 5th of January, Mr. Sheridan made a direct motion on the following grounds: the preamble to the suspension stated, that a dangerous and treasonable conspiracy existed in this country: but a verdict in court had shown this conspiracy to be a mere fabrication. The parties had undergone the strictest trial, and no pains had been spared for their crimination. What were the proofs of the supposed conspiracy? An arsenal furnished with one pike and nine rusty muskets, and an exchequer containing nine pounds and one bad shilling. These were the ways and means with which the conspirators proposed to overturn the government of Great Britain. No treason had in fact been brought to light, the alleged ground of the suspension did not exist, therefore the suspension, which in fact suspended the whole British constitution, was an unnecessary infringement of the rights of Britons. Mr. Windham maintained, that the favourable verdict in the late trials arose from the ignorance and incapacity of the juries to discern the true state of the case. The real objects of the societies was to overturn the constitution, and the principles imported from France would produce the worst effects, unless they were opposed with the strictest vigilance. The determination of a jury was no proof of the non-existence of a conspiracy. There was, indeed, the strongest ground for believing that a desperate conspiracy had existed, and still existed. From their whole conduct was it not probable that the designs of the societies were the destruction of the monarch and the constitution? The guilty were often acquitted in courts of justice; not because they were considered as innocent, but merely because there was no strictly legal evidence produced to confirm the truth. A doubt of their guilt was sufficient in the breast of the jury, but by no means to clear the character of the accused. The verdict in their favour could not, therefore, operate as a motive for repealing the act, even were we to admit that their indictment for high treason had not been supported by legal proofs: if the judicious and un-

c See Parliamentary Reports of 1795.

CHAP.
LV.

1795.

biassed public looked upon them as guilty of an attempt for which the law had not provided a due punishment, it was the duty of parliament to make such provisions. The motion for repeal was rejected; and before the term of the act expired, it was renewed.

Statement of the affairs of the East India company.

Mr. Dundas brought forward his annual statement of the affairs of the East India company, in the month of June. The result of the details was, that the company's affairs were improved upwards of one million four hundred and twelve thousand pounds. Notwithstanding the discouragements and obstructions arising from the war, and while the European markets were shut against them, their sales were more extensive than ever. The surplus revenue would not be so large in future, on account of our appropriation of a part to the just claims of the army. There was now a great and necessary military establishment; but the company had no higher rank in their service than colonel; this deprived eminent military characters of that rank in which they often repose as the best part of their reward.: there was also, at present, but a slow progression of inferior stations. He proposed a certain proportion of general and field officers at the different settlements. He farther moved, that whereas before officers returning from India received no allowance from the company, those who had served twenty years in the army should retain full pay for life. If sickness required the return of an officer, he thought he ought to be allowed upon the opinion of a medical man, to leave India without loss of rank or pay.

Marriage of the prince of Wales with the princess Caroline of Brunswick.

During this parliamentary session an event of great national importance took place, in the marriage of the heir apparent to the throne of these kingdoms. His highness espoused his royal father's niece, princess Caroline, daughter of the duke of Brunswick, and his duchess Augusta of England. Lord Malmsbury was employed to conduct the royal bride from her father's court. Arriving at Hamburgh, her highness was conveyed in a squadron commanded by commodore Payne. On the 7th of April she landed at Greenwich hospital, and in one of his majesty's coaches attended by a suite of carriages, and escorted by a party of the prince's own regiment, she proceeded to town amidst troops of dragoons who were stationed on the road in honour of the princess. Hundreds of horsemen and carriages, with immense crowds of spectators, testified their joy at the arrival of the young and beautiful stranger. The people cheered the princess with loud expressions of love and loyalty, and she very graciously bowed and smiled at them as she passed along. Having arrived at St. James's, the people with the ardent eagerness of spontaneous loyalty, which flows from the generous and manly breasts of freeborn Britons, continued their congratulations. Her highness standing with the prince at the window, addressed them concisely, but impressively, in the English language: " Believe

" me, I feel very happy and delighted to see the GOOD 'and CHAP.
" BRAVE English people—the best nation upon earth."[d] The LV.
prince afterwards accosted his conntrymen with the grace by
which he is so eminently distinguished : both were received 1795.
with the most rapturous applause. On the eighth of April the
marriage of his royal highness George prince of Wales and
the princess Caroline of Brunswick was solemnized in the cha-
pel royal, by the archbishop of Canterbury. The nuptials were
celebrated with a magnificence suitable to the rank of the illustrious parties. The income of the heir apparent was greatly inferior
to the revenue of predecessors in that exalted situation, since his
illustrious family was called to the throne. It had never
amounted to more than 60,000l. in the present reduced value of
money ; whereas the establishment of his grandfather and great-
grandfather was 100,000l. when the value of money was so
much higher. Hence the benignant liberality of his highness
found it impossible to confine his expenditure within his annual
receipts.

On the 27th of April, a message from his majesty to the
commons announcing the marriage of the prince, expressed
the king's conviction that a provision would be made for the suitable establishment of the prince and princess. It also stated, Provison
that his highness was under pecuniary incumbrances, and for the es-
recommended to parliament his gradual extrication, by apply- tablish-
ing to that purpose part of the income which should have ment of
been settled on the prince, and appropriating to that object nesses.
the revenues of the duchy of Cornwall. When the message
was taken into consideration, it appeared that the debts of his
highness exceeded six hundred thousand pounds. The civil list
by no means could bear even the gradual liquidations of so heavy
a debt. It was not in the present state of public affairs proposed
to call upon the nation for such a sum, whence was it then to
be liquidated but by savings from the prince's income. It was
fair, reasonable, consistent with the dignity and policy of the
country, that his highness should be placed on an equal footing with former princes of Wales. One hundred thousand
pounds, eighty years ago, constituted the whole revenue of
his great-grandfather George II. then prince of Wales ; and
the income of his grandfather, thirty years after, amounted to
the like sum, exclusive of the duchy of Cornwall. A hundred and twenty-five thousand pounds at present, was not
more than a hundred thousand sixty years ago. It was pro- Arrange-
posed that a hundred and twenty-five thousand, together with ment for
thirteen thousand arising from the duchy of Cornwall should the pay-
be settled on the prince, of which seventy-eight thousand ment of the
pounds should be appropriated to the liquidation of his incum- prince's
brances, and that an arrangement should be made to prevent debts.
the contraction of farther debts. This proposition encoun-

d See Otridge's Annual Register for 1795, p. 15.

CHAP. tered several objections, and various substitutes were proposed :
LV.   why might not the prince's life interest in the duchy of Corn-
      wall be sold? It would fetch three hundred thousand pounds,
1795. successive ministers had appropriated the revenue of the
      duchy of Cornwall to the civil list: a contribution, therefore,
      from the civil list ought to have been made at present. It
      would be a gift from the civil list, but the payment of the ba-
      lance of an account. After repeated and various discus-
      sions the plan proposed by Mr. Pitt was adopted, and com-
      missioners were appointed to superintend the discharge of his
      incumbrances. Provisions were also made to prevent the far-
      ther contraction of debts; and a law was passed to prevent
      future princes of Wales from being involved in similar difficul-
      ties. A jointure of fifty thousand pounds per annum was settled
      upon the princess of Wales, if she should survive his royal high-
      ness.

Applica-   This session the West India merchants, especially of Grena-
tion from da and St. Vincent's laboured under great pecuniary embar-
the West rassments. In consequence of insurrections and other cala-
India mer- mities, they were much injured in their property, and suffered
chants.   great inconveniencies in their commerce. From these gentle-
      men a petition was brought to parliament, praying for such
      relief as might be judged most expedient. Mr Pitt reminded
      the house of the very great benefits which had accrued to
      the mercantile world two years before, from the means devi-
      sed for supporting commercial credit, and proposed a similar
      plan to answer the exigencies of these merchants, by issuing
      bills of exchequer for their accommodation. Mr. Fox strong-
      ly reprobated this interference of the public in private con-
      cerns; it tended to create an influence over the great com-
      mercial body, that would place it in the most abject depend-
      ence on ministers. Hence they would become the invariable
      supporters of all governments, good or bad, in expectation
      of assistance from them in every pecuniary difficulty. Of the
      many innovations lately introduced, this was one of the most
      dangerous and alarming: it would reduce a class of people,
      hitherto remarkable for their independent spirit, to a situation
      of subserviency, that would necessarily destroy all their for-
      mer importance, and subject them entirely to the direction and
      management of future administrations. These considerations
      not weighing with the majority of parliament, the proposed
      relief was granted. An attempt was made in the house of
      commons this session to attach blame to the conduct of sir
      Charles Grey and sir John Jervis; but the subject being dis-
      cussed, it was found that there was no reason for censure,
      and that every part of their proceedings had been highly me-
      ritorious. The thanks of the house, voted in the preceding ses-
Motion of sion, were confirmed.
Mr. Wil-
berforce   Mr. Wilberforce this year recalled the attention of the house
for   to a subject which appeared at present to be dormant; this was

the slave trade, so zealously reprobated by one party, as equally criminal and disgraceful; and no less warmly justified by
the other, as absolutely necessary in the actual situation of the
commercial and colonial affairs of Great Britain. He reminded
them, that a formal resolution had passed in the session of 1792, the aboli-
that after the expiration of the month of January 1796, it should tion of the
no longer be lawful to import African negroes into the British slave trade,
colonies and plantations. Besides repeating former arguments,
he mentioned the manifest disposition of the newly imported
negroes to rise against the white people, and of the consequent
necessity of maintaining a numerous military force to keep them
in awe and subjection. He proposed a final abolition of the
slave trade; but after a very warm debate, the motion was ne- is nega-
gatived. tived.

This session the trial of Mr. Hastings, after having lasted Termina-
seven years, terminated in his honourable acquittal. Out of tion of
twenty nine peers who pronounced judgment on the occasion, Hastings's
twenty-three declared him innocent. The East India company, trial by an
conscious of the immense advantages which they had derived acquittal.
from the exertions of this extraordinary man, discharged the
whole expense of the trial, and also presented him with a moderate pecuniary gift, to prevent from indigence so illustrious a
servant, who had always attended so much more effectually to
the interests of his employers than to his own. Though every
authentic and impartial historian must bestow high praise on
the political ability which saved India, yet he must allow, that
there were certain portions of his conduct manifestly inconsistent with the rules of justice which prevail in Britain. Whoever
considers the Rohilla war, the administration of the revenues,
the presents, the expulsion of Cheyt Sing, and the seizure of
the treasures of the begums, with the documents, testimonies,
and circumstances that appeared to the committee, and afterwards even on the trial, may find sufficient grounds for a man,
feeling and reasoning as an English man, to impute culpability
—great culpability, to Mr. Hastings. His subsequent justification of conduct, apparently blameable, does not render the in-
quirer into these appearances, and very prominent appearances,
of wrong, the object of censure. Men must judge from probability, until it be proved false: apparent culpability is a proper
subject of investigation, although, on inquiry, either proof
should be wanting, or even innocence or merit should be established. Those who consider the imputation of unworthy motives to the accusers of Mr. Hastings, confirmed by his acquittal, reason very inconclusively. Where is the evidence for such
allegations? The discussion of the conduct of the governor-
general came before a committee, in the unforeseen progress
of inquiry: Mr. Burke, a member of the committee, agreed
with all the other members in deeming certain proceedings stated before them, either in oral or written evidence, if true, extremely reprehensible. Examining the affairs of India still

CHAP.
LV.

1795.

farther, and not discovering the exculpatory matter which was afterwards established before the lords, he and many others of both the political parties which then prevailed, thought there were sufficient grounds to justify parliamentary impeachment. We can no more justly blame Burke, Fox, and Sheridan, for moving an impeachment on the chief subjects, and other gentlemen on less important charges, nor the house of commons for agreeing to the motions, although the peers afterwards acquitted the defendant, than we should blame an attorney-general for commencing a prosecution upon the probable grounds of oral and written evidence: or a grand jury for finding a bill, although the person arraigned should, on his trial, have a verdict in his favour of *not guilty*. The merits of Mr. Hastings are intrinsically great, and do not require any extraneous exaggeration: and those who wish to enhance his character by censuring his accusers, manifest an incorrect and inadequate idea of the subject of their deserved applause.

Such were the principal events during this session, which terminated on the 27th of June. His majesty's speech contained one passage totally different from the general tenor of ministerial reasonings, which had uniformly exhibited the existing government of France as incompatible with any ideas of secure peace. Mr. Pitt, indeed, had, in discussing one of the motions for peace, declared his majesty's willingness to terminate the war, on just and honourable grounds, with any government in France, under whatever form, which should appear capable of maintaining the accustomed relations of peace and amity with other countries; but he had constantly represented the government which then subsisted, as incapable of maintaining such relations. His majesty expressed hopes, that peace would eventually arise from the internal state which had now commenced. "It is impossible to contemplate the internal "situation of the enemy with whom we are contending, with- "out indulging a hope, that the present circumstances of "France may, in their effects, hasten the return of such a state "of order and regular government, as may be capable of main- "taining the accustomed relations of amity and peace with "other powers." Though this declaration afforded only a distant prospect of peace, yet intimating its attainableness without the restoration of monarchy, it gave great satisfaction to all those who did not think a counter revolution in France indispensably necessary to British security. By the party which reprobated every project of peace with the French republicans, it was strongly disrelished.[e]

Mr. Pitt declares his majesty's willingness to make peace, if attainable with security, without regard to the form of French government.

e To this declaration Mr. Burke alludes in the beginning of his Regicide Peace: he construed it in the following manner: "Citizens Regicides! "wheneve' you find yourselves in the humour, you may have a peace with us. That is a point you may always command as secure. We are constantly in

1795.
Irish
affairs.
Lord Fitz-
william
viceroy,

Irish affairs at this season were extremely interesting and important. When earl Fitzwilliam accepted the viceroyalty, as he afterwards declared, he had been authorized to complete the catholic emancipation;[f] and as soon as he entered upon his office he had prepared to put this popular measure into execution. The chief members of the Irish ministry at this time were the Beresford party, always inimical to the encouragement of catholics, but ardent supporters of most of the measures recommended by the English ministers. Lord Fitzwilliam dismissed from their offices' some of these persons, and chose in their place others favourable to the grand system which he had in view. The steps for accelerating the catholic emancipation passed without animadversion from the English ministry; but the dismissal of Mr. Beresford and his adherents gave great offence to the cabinet of London. Lord Fitzwilliam refusing to change his arrangements, he was recalled, and lord Camden, son to the illustrious judge, was appointed his successor. Lord Fitzwilliam arrived in Britain, made his appearance in parliament, challenged ministers to prove, that his measures deserved the blame which their conduct intimated, and demanded an inquiry. Ministers contended, that no blame was attached to lord Fitzwilliam, and therefore no inquiry was necessary for his vindication; and that there were reasons of state which rendered the discussion altogether improper: the motions in the respective houses for an inquiry were negatived.

misunderstanding between him and ministers, as to the extent and bounds of his powers. He is recalled, and succeeded by lord Camden.

In the ardent enthusiasm of misunderstood liberty, the French had proceeded, as we have seen, with rapid impetuosity, to break down, one after another, all the embankments of order and regular government, which reason and policy had constructed, or time had collected for restraining the torrent of impetuous passion. Many of the first national assembly had proposed a wise mixture of democracy, aristocracy, and monarchy; but the visionary theories of fanciful metaphysicians, conceiving in mankind a perfection which mankind do not possess, inculcated new schemes of legislation, totally unfit for human beings; and excluded religion, the great moderator of violent, and corrector of vicious passions. With these natural restraints upon the individual, they removed the artificial distinctions of rank and subordination, which conduced to the welfare of society; they destroyed the aristocracy, which best attempers and controls monarchical dictation, and popular fury. Allowing their king too feeble a power, the constitutionalists of 1789 rendered the multitude paramount, gave them unlimited sway, after they had loosened the principles that might have checked the most inordinate and outrageous abuses of their power; and thus they sowed the seeds of all future excesses.

Internal affairs of France.

attendance, and nothing you can do shall hinder us from the renewal of our supplications.

f See lord Fitzwilliam's letter to lord Carlisle.

CHAP.   The republicans of 1792, pursuing the same levelling principle
LV.   to a still greater extent, trusted that they could govern without
⁓   a monarch, as the constitutionalists of 1789 had governed with-
1795.   out separate orders and states. By the all-ruling mob, a junto
of scholars and ingenious men, with learning, eloquence, subtlety, and theoretical refinement, proposed to govern without a
king; but the engine which they moved they could not command. The constitutionalists unmuzzled, and the republicans
goaded, the wild beast that, though at first soothed by their
caresses, was soon turned upon themselves, with the unbridled
license of passion; impiety and cruelty increased; and democracy was swallowed up by anarchy. In five years, the French
had experienced all the changes from arbitrary monarchy,
through emancipation, liberty, licentiousness, anarchy, and

The go-   despotic terror. The æra of Robespierre, the season of atheism,
vernment   anarchy, and terror, was the lowest abyss of the French revolu-
of Robes-   tion. There is, as the first[g] of modern historians observes, and
pierre the one[h] of the first[i] repeats, an ultimate point of exaltation and
lowest   depression, which, when human affairs reach, they return in a
abyss of   contrary progress. From the destruction of Robespierre, the
revolution- proceedings of the French began to show some distinct ten-
ary anar-   deney to social order. The sway of the odious tyrant, terrible as
chy. Com-   it was while it lasted, was not without its salutary effects. It
mencing   very clearly demonstrated the terrible consequences of a poli-
return of   tical society without subordination, government, and religion.
social or- But the progress of the return from anarchy to social order,
der.   was slow, and often interrupted by formidable conspiracies.
The Mountain long predominated, and opposed, with all its
might, changes which tended to strengthen the Girondine party,
whose vengeance it dreaded. The Girondists, constitutionalists,
and other enemies to jacobin anarchy, gradually coincided in
one great object, the formation of a regular constitution, which
should contain a diversity of states, with reciprocal check and

Constitu-   control. The chief provisions of this new system were two
tion of   councils, both chosen by the electoral assemblies. The first,
1795 : two consisting of five hundred members, was styled the legislative
councils,   council; its object was to propose laws : the second, consisting
and an ex- of two hundred and fifty members, all above forty years of
ecutive di- age, was termed the council of elders; its object was to confirm
rectory of laws. One-third of the members were to be rechosen every
five.   year. The executive government was vested in a DIRECTORY
of five members. The directory was to be partially renewed,
by the election of a new member every year; none of the members who thus went out could be re-elected till after a lapse of
five years. The directory was to be elected by the two councils, in the following manner: the council of five hundred was
to make, by secret scrutiny, a list of ten persons; from which

g Hume, vol. ii. at the conclusion of Richard III.

h Robertson, Introduction to Charles V.   i Segur, vol. iii.

the senate, by secret scrutiny, was to select one; the judicial CHAP.
power was to reside in the judges of the department, chosen LV.
by the electoral assemblies; with a tribunal of appeal, chosen
by the same for the whole nation. The directors might invite 1795.
the legislative body to take a subject into consideration, but
could not propose any topic of discussion, unless concerning
peace and war. The directory was not invested with the power
of assembling or 'proroguing the legislative bodies. This con- French
stitution showed, that the French politicians had now formed politicians
some idea of the utility of a control of estates. It was, how- now con-
ever, extremely defective in its executive function, which was control of
not endued with sufficient power to prevent the encroachment estates is
of the legislative bodies. The bestowal of the executive power necessary.
upon five persons, necessarily produced distractions and contest.
It was impossible, in the nature of man, that five supreme
rulers should long act with harmony. In its executorial efficiency, this system bore some resemblance to the constitution
of 1789; in its two councils, it manifested a tendency to surpass
the democracy royal.

This year, the son of the late king, styled by the royalists Death of
Louis XVII. died in the temple; and the king's brother now the late
representative of the house of Bourbon, assumed the title of king's son.
Louis XVIII.

CHAP. LVI.

Effects of the French successes upon other powers.—The grand duke of
Tuscany and the king of Sweden acknowledge the French republic.—
Character and views of the king of Prussia.—After receiving a subsidy
from England, he abandons the alliance—and concludes a peace with
France.—Spain compelled to receive peace from France —German princes —Extensive dominion of the French republic —Renewal of the war
in La Vendee.—The French emigrants in England fancy and represent
royalism to prevail in France—plan of co-operation with the royalists
submitted to ministers—scheme adopted by them—expedition to Quiber-
ón—disastrous issue of.—Requisition from Holland.—The French armies
reduce the fortress of Luxemburg, and complete the conquest of Belgium.—Campaign upon the Rhine—indecisive —Armistice of three
months —Naval operations.—Engagement of admiral Cornwallis with a
much superior French force—by a stratagem he impels the enemy to fly.
—Lord Bridport defeats the French fleet off L'Orient, and captures their
large ships —Attempt of the French to recover their losses in the West
Indies.—War in Jamaica with the Maroon negroes.—Admiral Hotham
defeats the French off Corsica.—Admiral Elphinstone reduces the Cape
of Good Hope.—Internal affairs of France.—Ambitious views of the leaders of the convention.—Efforts of Napoleon Bonaparte, a young Corsican officer, excite general admiration.—The moderates at length prevail.

CHAP.
LVI.

1795.
Effects of
the French
successes
upon other
powers.

THE successes of the French struck all Europe with astonishment; and it was evident, that the confederacy must be
inefficient, without greater union of design, concert of counsels,
and vigour of conduct. Some of the princes had avowed, that
their object was the restoration of monarchy; but separate and
private views had interfered with the successful prosecution of
this purpose. It is probable that every sovereign would have
preferred, in so very powerful a nation, ancient establishment
to revolution. The effects and relations of the one were ascertained; of the other, could not be defined or comprehended.
The French monarchy, when vigilantly watched, had been
found compatible with the security of other countries: the
principle of the new system was universal change. Hitherto
no potentate had acknowledge the French republic, which
they either hoped or supposed must yield to so numerous and
strong an alliance; but the extraordinary progress of the Gallic
armies altered their opinions and policy; reasoning from operations and events, instead of combining them with their causes,
several princes conceived, that since the efforts of the confederates, planned and directed as they were, had been unsuccessful, no exertions could avail. Convinced of the stability
of the revolutionary scheme, sovereigns now began to deprecate
the anger and court the friendship of such a mighty people.
To the great surprise of politicians, the emperor's brother, the

grand duke of Tuscany, first acknowledged the French republic,
concluded peace, sent the count de Carletti as minister to Paris;
and, by a formal treaty, breaking his engagement with the coalition, promised in future to observe the strictest neutrality. One
crowned head soon followed the example of this prince: the re-The grand
gent of Sweden, in the name of his nephew, sent the baron de duke of
Staal to Paris; and that ambassador appeared in the convention, Tuscany
and assured the French nation of the friendship which the court and the
of Stockholm entertained for the republic. king of
Sweden ac-
The king of Prussia, for two years, had been a very cold knowledge
and inefficient ally: his jealousy of Austria had absorbed his the French
apprehensions from France; and the participation of Polish republic.
spoils engaged him much more powerfully than the restoration and views
of monarchy. Prematurely despairing to be able to reinstate of the king
the heir of the Bourbons on the throne of France, he became of Prussia.
disgusted with the war, and was not displeased that the hereditary rival of his family was weakened; and did not reflect,
that the power which overwhelmed the Netherlands, and
humbled Austria, was extending her means of eventually reducing Prussia. But examiners of conduct, who derive the
measures and actions of princes uniformly from public policy,
are apt to form very erroneous conclusions. Private passions
and personal habits influence the counsels of kings. Frederick
William was distinguished for his love of pleasure, and though
constitutionally brave, and occasionally active, a leading feature in his character was that indolence which is so usual
a companion or follower of sensual indulgence.[k] Like his
uncle he was rapacious. but from very different views: the
great Frederick sought and acquired territories and other possessions, for the aggrandizement and melioration of Prussia;
his nephew appears to have desired the property of others,
much more for the purposes of individual gratification. The
extravagance that rarely fails to attend luxurious sensuality,
had drained the coffers which the policy and economy of his
predecessor had so very fully replenished. The plunder of
Poland, and the sums which he received from England for
making a promise that he did not intend to perform, removed
his pecuniary difficulties, and created a new fund for pleasurable enjoyment: he could now revel in his seraglio without any
apprehension of fiscal embarrassments. These circumstances
and considerations, in the opinion of persons thoroughly acquainted with the disposition and private life of Frederick William, afforded an additional weight to the political reasons by
which he was determined to separate himself from the alliance.
"The king of Prussia (says Segur),[l] contented with his new
acquisitions in Poland, and disgusted with the war, forgot, in

k This account is strongly supported by Segur; a man of penetration,
who appears to have thoroughly comprehended the character of Frederick
William. See vol. iii. chap. xiii.
l Vol. iii. p. 206.

CHAP.
LVI.

1795.
After receiving a subsidy from England, he abandons the alliance, and concludes a peace with France.

Spain compelled to receive peace from France.

German princes.

"the arms of his mistresses, his former objects, his recent de-
"feats, the danger of the empire, the dispute of kings, and the
"interests of his sister, the princess of O$_r$ang$_e$."

During the year 1794, a negotiation was opened between
France and Prussia; and, in April, 1795, peace was concluded.
The articles of this treaty were entirely favourable to France;
such, indeed, was the temper, as well as the situation of the
French at this time, that no other would have been admitted.
The Prussian territories on the left bank of the Rhine were
ceded to France, and those only on the right restored to Prussia. The regulations for the internal settlement of the countries which were thus ceded, were referred, for final discussion,
to the period of a general peace between France and Germany.
It was agreed, that a cessation of hostilities should take place
and continue in the north of Germany, which henceforth should
be considered as neutral ground; and that those princes
whose dominions lay on the right side of the Rhine, should
be entitled to make proposals to France, and to be favourably treated; in behalf of whom; the king of Prussia
should interpose his good offices.[m] Having thus accomplished
by policy, peace with Prussia, the next object of France was
to compel Spain to withdraw from the confederacy. The war
of the republicans with that country had been uniformly successful. Their armies had surmounted the defiles of the Pyrenées, hovered over northern Spain, and threatened to penetrate into the heart of the country, and advance to Madrid.
The king of Spain saw no expedient to save himself from ruin,
but the conclusion of peace. All resources had been exhausted; the nobility, the gentry, the clergy, the monastic orders,
had all contributed; the orders of knighthood, which have large
possessions in Spain, had lately made liberal donations to government, besides a tax, laid on their revenues, of eight per
cent.[n] No class had been remiss in pecuniary assistance to
the state; but want of personal spirit, or discontent at the measures pursued by the ministry, seemed to pervade the mass of
the nation. In such a situation, the court of Madrid formed a
resolution to withdraw from the confederacy. Peace was
accordingly concluded, agreeably to the dictation of France.
The conditions were, that France should restore to Spain all
her conquests in that kingdom, and that Spain should cede to
France all its part of the island of Hispaniola in the West Indies; together with all the artillery and military stores deposited in that colony. France also concluded peace with the
greater number of the German princes. Holland was now
formed into a democratic republic, on the model of France;
and the power and wealth of these provinces was henceforward
entirely at the disposal of the French republic. "Never (as

m See Otridge's Annual Register, p. 62. n Ibid. p. 60.

" the able author[o] of the Annual Register[p] observes) since the
" days of Charlemagne, had the empire 'of France extended
" over so many regions and people." A list of recent conquests
'was printed, and affixed to a tablet which was hung in the hall
of the convention, and copies of it were sent to the armies, to-
'gether with an enumeration of the victories by which these acquisitions were obtained. They consisted of the ten provinces
of the Austrian Netherlands; the seven united provinces; the
bishoprics of Liege, Worms, and Spires; the electorate of
Treves, Cologne, and Mentz; the duchy of Deux Ponts; the
palatinate; the duchies of Juliers and Cleves. These accessions were all rich, fertile, and populous countries; abounding
with men as zealous in their cause, as the French themselves.
On the south side of France, their conquests were, the duchy
of Savoy, with the principalities of Nice and Monaco in Italy.
The population of all these countries was estimated at thirteen
millions; which, added to the twenty-four millions contained
in France, constituted a mass of thirty-seven millions, inhabit-
ing the centre of Europe, and capable, by that position alone,
if united under one government, to defy the enmity of all their
neighbours; to exercise an influence amounting almost to universal sovereignty.[q] So completely did the pressure of the
confederacy drive the French nation to military enthusiasm;
and such astonishing effects did that sentiment, operating upon
the genius and energy of this extraordinary people, produce
against an enemy who acted without a common principle or concerted union.

A disposition to insurrection still prevailed in La Vendee;
and at length broke out in new revolt. The objects of the
French during the campaign were, entirely to crush intestine
rebellion; and, in contending with their two remaining enemies,

CHAP.
LVI.

1795.

Extensive
dominion
of the
French re-
public.

Renewal
of the war
in La Ven-
dee.

---

o Generally believed to be Dr. William Thompson.   See life of that gentleman in Phillips's Public characters, for 1803.   p. Otridge's.
   q The means by which they arrived at such an extent of power, the
French exhibited in the following statement. In the space of seventeen
months, they had won twenty-seven battles, and been victorious in one hundred and twenty actions of less note. They had taken one hundred and
sixteen strong cities and fortified places; but what redounded chiefly to
the reputation of the French, these successes had been obtained over the
best disciplined armies of Europe, elated with their past triumphs over
warlike enemies; and commanded by generals of consumate experience,
and the most dazzling reputation. Their own armies, in the commencement of the contest, consisted of officers and soldiers, few of whom had
seen service, and their commanders were very far from eminent in their
profession. With these disadvantages, they resolutely ventured to face the
tremendous combination formed against them; and in less than twelve
months, from acting on the defensive, they assaulted their enemies in every
direction, and struck them every where with so much terror, that several
of them were meditating a retreat from the field of action, and total secession from the confederacy, by uniting with which they had sustained so
many losses. See Otridge's Annual Register, for 1795, p. 51.

Britain and Austria, to act on the defensive against the naval efforts of England, and on the offensive against the military force of the emperor. Persevering in the policy which common sense dictates to the objects of a hostile and powerful confederacy, they uniformly sought to detach its members separately and successively from the combination; and where negotiation would not avail, they employed force. Aware that against Austria their efforts would be much more effectual than against England, they directed their principal exertions towards their continental enemy. Luxemburg only remained in the possession of the Germans, on the left bank of the Rhine. The republicans proposed to reduce that fortress; afterwards, passing the Rhine, to make Germany the scene of war, and to press forward in Italy. Two armies were destined for the operations on the Rhine, respectively commanded by Pichegru and Jourdain. A considerable force was also sent against the insurgents, now consisting of the Vendeans and Chouans, and commanded by Charette. Large supplies of money sent from Britain, contributed to increase the number; and an expedition was undertaken from Britain, to co-operate with the French loyalists. Though this armament consisted chiefly of emigrants, the plan of operations was by no means conformable to their wishes and views. Certain emigrants represented to our ministers, that La Vendee and its neighborhood were far from being the sole scenes of French loyalty: that in Guienne, Languedoc, Provence, Lyonnois, and Alsace, there were numerous bodies attached to monarchy. They proposed a grand scheme of connected co-operation,[r] by an expedition in six divisions, in the maritime parts to consist chiefly of the English, and in the inland of Austrian, invaders. The votaries of Mr. Burke's sentiments and ideas eagerly seconded this proposition; but that part of the ministry which, to use the political language of latter times, was rather anti-gallican than anti-jacobin, which was more intent on the annoyance of French power, than the dictation of French government, was averse to so expensive and weighty an undertaking. Less ardent for the restoration of monarchy, they did not apprehend, that the numbers and force of its friends was nearly so great as conceived in the sanguine hopes of the emigrants and Burkites. These observed, that if any attempt was made, it must be with a view to be effectual; that a small equipment would be of no useful purpose; a scanty force could not expect to prevail against the numerous hordes of republicans; and it would be better not to send any expedition, than to send a handful, which, instead of really aiding the loyalists, would only stimulate them to certain destruction. The majority of the cabinet, however, appear to have

The
French
emigrants
in England
fancy and
represent
royalism
to prevail
in France.
Plan of co-
operation
with the
royalists
submitted
to minis-
ters;

r The proposed plan of operations, and the correspondence with which it was accompanied, was kindly communicated to me by an emigrant nobleman of high distinction, who bore a considerable part in the expedition.

intended merely a diversion, to weaken the efforts of the republi-   CHAP.
cans in other quarters : to the re-establishment of monarchy, the   LVI.
preparations were so totally inadequate, that it is morally certain
they could not be designed for that purpose.   1795.

In the beginning of June, the expedition sailed to the southern Expedi-
coast of Britanny; and as the Vendeans possessed no seaport tion to
to afford their friends a landing, the squadron proceeded to the Quiberon.
bay of Quiberon. Here a body of about three thousand men
landed on the 27th, and dispersed a small number of republicans. They besieged and took a fort garrisoned by six hundred men, and prepared to march farther into the country. A
considerable number joined the expedition, and a great quantity of arms had been sent; thence it was fondly expected, that
an army would be formed in a short time, capable of facing the
republican troops in the neighbourhood. Having increased to
about twelve thousand men, they advanced up the country, and
after gaining several skirmishes, attacking a large body of republican troops, they were obliged to retreat. Meanwhile,
Hoche having collected a numerous army, proceeded against
the emigrant forces; a bloody battle ensued, and was followed Disastrous
by a decisive victory on the side of the republicans; scarcely issue of.
three thousand escaped to their ships. The chiefs of the Chouans
for several months carried on a desultory war, were at length
overpowered by the republican armies, and punished as rebels
against the government which they had so lately acknowledged. The unfortunate emigrants captured on this disastrous
expedition were also treated as rebels, and suffered on the
scaffold.. Such was the melancholy termination of an expedition, from which no direct success could reasonably be expected.
In employing, however, the force of the enemy, this undertaking
was not without a considerable influence on the events of the
campaign.

Those statesmen who supposed that by the continuance of The ex-
the war the French would exhaust their resources, were in the pectation
event proved to be erroneous reasoners. War carried on with ing the
the energy which they exerted, and successful beyond all re- French
cords of history, was to them an instrument of acquisition : in finances
the spoils* of conquered countries they found their ways and proves
means : Holland and Belgium supplied the treasury of France. ground-
The Austrian Netherlands were formally incorporated with the The revo-
French republic; and to render this accession complete, they lutionists
besieged Luxemburg. With this operation they opened the find new
campaign; the garrison, though strong, yet being completely resources
                                                        in the con-

s This conversion of the property of the conquered to the use of the con- quered
querors has often been ascribed to jacobinism ; but the slightest attention countries.
to history proves, that both the principle and practice are not new, but as Requisi-
old as the records of war and plunder. One ingredient in their system dif- tion from
fered from Grecian and Roman plunder, a spirit of proselytism. But that Holland.
spirit was not peculiar to the French plunderers; the Spaniards in Mexico
and Peru were almost as eager to convert as to rob, the unoffending Indians.

invested, and finding that no succours ͵could approach, on the seventeenth of June capitulated. The French had only one place more to reduce, in order to compass that object which was to crown their military operations. This was, to make a conquest of the strong and important city of Mentz; by the acquisition of which they would regain the ancient boundary between Germany and Gaul, the river Rhine. But the situation of Mentz was extremely strong, and they found it necessary to convert the siege into a blockade. During the early part of the campaign, the French armies had been much less active than was expected from the successes of the former year. Their inaction, however, really arose from those very successes. Their victories, splendid and momentous as they were, had been earned by great profusion of lives; and though their armies were continually supplied with recruits, it required time to insure those to discipline. Though they might replace the numbers they were continually losing, they could not supply their places with an equal proportion of good soldiers. The French officers and commanders were fully aware of this deficiency, and, for this reason, were become less adventurous and enterprising. Besides, a considerable part of the republican force was employed against the revolters. The operations upon the Rhine were therefore, on the whole, indecisive and unimportant, compared with the events of the former year. It

was not till the month of August, that Jourdain crossed the Rhine; he captured Dusseldorf, and compelled the Austrians to retreat. Pichegru with his army followed a few days after, and having reduced Manheim, occupied a position on the right bank, which intercepted the Austrian armies on the north and south of the Main, respectively commanded by generals Clairfait and Wurmser. A division of his army having attacked the Austrians with the usual impetuosity, put them to the route. But the spirit of plunder was so predominant among the French, that as soon as they had defeated this part of Wurmser's army, they dispersed on all sides in quest of pillage. The Austrian cavalry, informed of their disorder, returning, completely surprised and defeated the plunderers, and compelled them to make a precipitate retreat. Clairfait meanwhile advanced upon Jourdain's army, which had invested Mentz from the right bank of the Rhine, attacked and defeated its rear, and took a large quantity of cannon destined for the siege; and after successive victories, his adversary compelled the Austrian to recross the Rhine. Pichegru also found the same retrograde movement necessary: the two Austrian armies, now enabled to form a junction, crossed the Rhine, obliged the republicans to raise the siege of Mentz, and reconquered the Palatinate and most of the countries between the Rhine and the Moselle. Alarmed at their progress, Jourdain collected all the troops, that were stationed in the proximity of the Rhine, and by forced marches reached, in a short time, the scene of action.

United with Pichegru, he had the good fortune to put a stop to ~CHAP.~
the rapid career of the Austrians. The successes of the Ger-   LVI.
mans encouraged them to project the siege of Luxemburg, but
the vigorous resistance of the republicans prevented them from   1795.
advancing so far. After various sharp conflicts, they were
obliged to recross the Rhine. Meanwhile, on the right bank
of the Rhine they were employed in besieging Manheim, which
a strong garrison of French so vigorously defended, that it
held out till the end of November, when it yielded to the Austrians. The campaign concluded by common consent of the Armistice
hostile generals, who agreed to a suspension of arms for three of three,
months, which was ratified by the respective powers; and the months.
armies of both parties withdrew into winter quarters. The
same languor marked the operations in Italy; the French
maintained their former acquisitions, but made no farther progress. The continental campaign of 1795 was, indeed, on
the whole inefficient. The French however had subdued the
revolters, and acquired Luxemburg. The French, at sea,
confined themselves to defensive efforts against our navy, and
depredations on our trade.

The naval operations of Britain were necessarily much less Naval ope-
important than in the former year, against an enemy that rations.
would not face them with any considerable force. They
were not, however, altogether deficient in brilliancy. Admi- Engage-
ral Cornwallis had, this summer, been stationed on the west ment of ad-
coast of France, to intercept the enemy's trade, and to corres- miral Corn-
pond with La Vendee: on the 16th of June, having only five wallis with
ships of the line, he met off Belleisle thirteen French ships of a much su-
the line. Against a force so greatly superior he kept a run- French
ning fight for the whole of the next day, without suffering the force.
enemy to gain the smallest advantage. At length his repeating By a strata-
frigate, to deceive the French, threw out a signal that a large gem he im-
British squadron was in sight. This ingenious stratagem im- pels the
pelled the republicans to betake themselves to a precipitate enemy to
flight. The Gallic squadron, six days after, fell in with lord fly.
Bridport, who defeated them, and took three of their largest port de-
ships, off port L'Orient. feats the

In the West Indies, the French formed a project of recover- French off
ing the islands which had been ceded to the English after for- L'Orient
mer wars. To promote this purpose, they sent emissaries to and cap-
St. Lucie, St. Vincent's, Grenada, and Dominica, who had con- largest
siderable success: St. Lucie was reduced through the efforts of ships.
the insurgents; and the three others with difficulty preserved. Attempt of
The French also reduced St. Eustatius, retook the island of the French
Guadaloupe, and the fort of Tiberon in St. Domingo. In Ja- to recover
maica, a war arose between the British and the Maroon In- in the West
dians, a very hostile and dangerous tribe, scattered in the Indies.
woods, and noted for robbery and murder. The militia and War in
soldiers turning out, completely subdued these savages; and Jamaica
to trace the fugitives employed blood-hounds: the island was Maroon
negroes.

CHAP.
LVI.

1795

Admiral
Hotham
defeats the
French off
Corsica.

Admiral
Elphin-
stone redu-
ces the
Cape of
Good
Hope

Internal af-
fairs of
France.

Ambitious
views of
the leaders
of the con
vention.

cleared of these marauders; the remainder of whom was transported to Upper Canada.

In the Mediterranean, admiral Hotham defeated the French
off Corsica; and on the coast of Africa, admiral Elphinstone
captured the Cape of Good Hope and a Dutch fleet. From
the time that Holland became a dependency of France, an order was issued for seizing all the Dutch ships in British ports;
and also letters of marque and reprisal were granted against the
Batavian republic. Such are the chief events of the third year
of the war in which Great Britain was engaged against the
French republic.

The internal proceedings of the French republicans were at
this time more active and energetic than the operations of their
armies. Having formed the new constitution on the overthrow
of the terrible system, the national convention was occupied in
preparing for its practical commencement, and in endeavouring
to destroy anarchy, did not lose sight of ambition. Before they
surrendered their authority into the hands of the nation, they
made provision for its renewal. They passed a decree, which
enjoined the electoral bodies to choose two-thirds of the deputies of the nation that were to be returned on this occasion, out
of the members of the present convention; and ordained, that
in default of an election of those two-thirds in the manner prescribed, the convention should supply the vacancies themselves.
The constitution, and these decrees, were formally transmitted
to the primary assemblies. These acts were by many considered as violations of the undoubted privileges of the people, and
attempts to perpetuate their own power against the sense of
their constituents. The Parisians declared, that henceforth the
convention had forfeited all title to any farther obedience. The
primary assemblies in the city having met by their own appointment, in defiance of the convention, insisted that they had chosen their electors, and that these being the direct representatives of the people, possessed a right to consult together as soon
as they judged it necessary. The convention, in order to ter-
rify the refractory, employed a military force to disperse this
assembly of Parisians. The Parisians forebore at that time
opposing the soldiers of the convention, but continued to in-
veigh against their designs. Both parties became inflamed
with the greatest rage. After warm and violent contests of
reasoning, they prepared to have recourse to force. On the
4th of October, the Parisian troops proceeded against the soldiers of their antagonists: a conflict taking place, was fought

Efforts of
Napoleon
Bonaparte,
a young
Corsican
officer, ex-
cite gener-
al admira-
tion.

with the greatest courage and ardour, when the skill and enterprise of a young Corsican gave a decisive victory to the conventional troops. The officer in question was Napoleon Bonaparte, who on this the first opportunity of exerting his talents
in military command, attracted the high admiration both of
those for whom, and against whom it was employed. The
numbers that fell did not exceed a thousand; and a great mul-

titude was preparing from different quarters to join the troops of the Parisians, but were overawed by the success of the opposite party. The metropolis was subjected to the power of the convention, which made a very severe use of the victory, punished, without mercy the Parisian insurgents; and in the apprehension of many of the more moderate republicans were about to revive the system of terror. The jacobins began to regain an ascendency in an assembly whose chief objects, like those of Robespierre, appeared to be uncontrolled dominion. They procured a commission to be appointed, consisting of five persons, who were empowered to consult together what measures were proper to be adopted in order to save the country. Such an arbitrary assumption of power alarmed all France: men were apprehensive that the days of Robespierre were about to be revived: but the circumstances were changed: the dread of foreign enemies being removed, the moderate republicans and constitutionalists were too numerous and powerful to submit to this new project of despotism. During the month of October, these contests were carried on with great warmth, and affairs appeared drawing to some important crisis; but they terminated favourably to the prospect of returning order. In the convention itself, the ablest men were among the moderates; and, though in a temporary minority, soon found means The mode rates at length prevail. to prevail over a considerable number of the others, and at length to overbalance the violent and jacobinical junto. It was proposed, in the name of the nation, that the commission of five should instantly be suppressed, and that the constitution decreed by the acceptance of the people should take place, and the convention be dissolved on the day appointed; and the moderate party being now predominent, these propositions were carried. The violent faction, aware of the odiousness of their conduct, and the decay of their power, endeavoured, by promoting or seconding popular acts, to regain the public favour. On the 26th of Dissolution of the convention, and character. October, this celebrated convention dissolved itself, after having sitten upwards of three years: and, in governing France, produced effects more momentous to Europe than any which had taken place for several centuries. Their character, operations, and efficiency, were astonishing, and surpassed all the experience and records of history. Their chief collective characteristic was promptitude of intellectual and active powers, which discovered and called into effectual operation all the faculties and resources of the country: and made every species of inanimate and rational beings engines for compassing their ends. Exempt themselves from all moral and religious restraints, they destroyed or suppressed these principles in others, in order to insure their instrumentality; in all qualities and means, they regarded merely efficacy; and in seeking their objects, they simply employed sagacity, invention, courage, resolution, and expedition. Genius, vigour of mind, indefatigable and rapid exertion, moving directly on to their end, and totally regardless of conscience, and of all the laws

of God and man, making no account of human happiness or misery, may certainly do numberless acts in a private station, which,
must surprise all who, with equal power, have not thrown off the
fetters of piety and virtue. Enormous however as their crimes
might be, they were mixed with most extraordinary efforts, brilliant actions, and astonishing success against the enemies of their
country. Never had a government greater obstacles to surmount ;
internal dissensions that rose to rebellion, extensive, powerful,
and formidable ; a confederacy of nations, two of which sent forth
armies, that in numbers, courage, discipline, and military skill,
were equal to the Roman legions ; and assisted by other states no
less brave and hardy ; with a kingdom which commanded the
fountains of silver and of gold ; had been once the rival of France
herself, and, of continental powers, was still the second in naval
greatness : but, beyond all, an insular empire, which united the
genius of Greece, with the persevering valour and constancy of
Rome ; the opulence of Carthage and Persia ; military prowess
superior to any heroes of modern Europe,[t] and a maritime force
which far surpassed any related in the annals of mankind. Such
a combination of resources and warriors never before had one
state to oppose. Yet did the French convention, with the executive governments which it successively created, not only resist
their immense efforts, by crushing internal revolt, and driving the
enemy from their frontiers, but acquired accessions of territory
more extensive than any which have been procured by conquest
in modern Europe ; whose fertility, industry, skill, riches, and the
means of force, far surpassed any conquest achieved by the Romans during half a century of their most warlike history. If in
compassing objects of such magnitude, they were guilty of many
enormities ; they possessed most uniformly, and signally exerted,
one quality, without which the highest intellectual and moral excellencies avail little, in the conductors of momentous and dangerous wars, or any other arduous situations in active life :—this
was ENERGY,[u] constant in object, rapid in exertion, and decisive
in effect.

   t If this should be thought an unfounded assertion, it must be by those
who do not recollect the pitched battles between the British and any opponents, from Cressy to Alexandria : they never were beaten by equal, or nearly equal, troops, and very rarely by much superior numbers.
   u This quality no observer of their conduct more explicitly and fully
allows, than one author, who will never be accused of partiality in favour of
the French revolutionists. See Burke on Regicide Peace ; and his other
writings concerning the French revolution, subsequent to the commencement of the war.

CHAP. LVII.

Britain.—Many who had approved of the war, tired of its continuance—are disappointed in its results—they conceive the advantages gained do not balance the loss incurred.—Scarcity and dearness of provisions.—Discontents.—Active endeavours of the innovating societies.—Multiplication of lecturers—who represent war as ministerial jobs for plundering the people —Frequency of seditious meetings —Meetings of the corresponding society at Chalk farm and Copenhagen house.—Abuse of government.—Behaviour of the mob to the king in his way to and from parliament—a bullet is shot into the king's coach. Indignation of the public—Proclamation.—Proceedings of parliament.—Lord Grenville introduces a bill for the safety of his majesty's person—principle and details —arguments against it—for it.—Mr. Pitt's bill for preventing seditious meetings—objects and provisions of—arguments against it.—Mr. Fox reprobates the bills—exhibits the rights of the people to state their grievances—declares the bills intended to prevent the exercise of that right —and to shield ministers—he alleges, they subvert constitutional freedom —Active efforts of him and his coadjutors both in and out of parliament.—Petitions.—Arguments for Mr. Pitt's bill—required by the circumstances of the times—somewhat modified, both pass into laws.—Impartial view of the new acts.—Restrictions on the freedom of the press.—Mr. Pitt apprehended to undervalue literary effort —Majority of the literary class inimical to his administration —Writers represent the series of his measures as more conducive to the power of his crown than the rights of his people —State of ministerial popularity.—Ministers intimate his majesty's disposition to open a negotiation for peace—remarks of Mr. Fox on this declaration.—The conduct of the war is severely censured.—Supplies—immense loan.—The taxes financially judicious, laid on the luxuries or conveniencies, and not the necessaries of life.—Able speech of earl Moira on revenue.—Proposed remonstrance of opposition.—Dissolution of parliament.

CHAP. LVII.

1795.

Britain.—Many who had approved of the war, tire of its continuance: are disappointed in its results; they conceive the advantages gained do not balance the loss incurred.

THE war had been begun with the approbation, and even applause, of a very great majority of the British nation; and, during the first campaign, these sentiments continued to prevail: but the distresses of our army in Holland, and the apparent hopelessness of the contest at the expiration of the second, began to damp their eagerness. When a third campaign was concluded, many of the former promoters of war conceived, that the exertions of three years had not brought Britain any nearer the purpose of hostilities, than they were at its commencement, and now became tired of its continuance. Its expenses retrenching the comforts of life, came home to their feelings: like the bulk of mankind, judging from the event, they began to think that the war must have been wrong in the outset, which in its progress had so totally disappointed their expectation; at any rate, that it must be unwise in the continuance, when, in their apprehensions, it produced no benefit to balance the very heavy loss. In addition to the pressure of

1795.
Scarcity
and dear-
ness of
provisions.
Discon-
tents.

the war, a scarcity prevailed throughout the kingdom, and was woefully felt by the poorer sort, several of whom perished for want. The means for procuring sustenance were narrowed from various causes: but the discontented attributed this evil to the war; and the sufferers, through defect of employment, were ready enough to believe those who represented all the calamities that affected the nation, as proceeding chiefly, if not solely, from the hostilities. Multitudes, not only of the lower, but even the middling classes, very ardently desired peace, and began to cherish displeasure against ministers for not endea-

Active en-
deavours
of the in-
novating
societies.

vouring to procure that blessing to the country. The members of the innovating societies were now extremely bold and ac-tive: the acquittals, at the trials for high treason, had swelled their exultation, and inspired their courage. They regarded the ministers as a junto, who had desired and plotted against them unjust death, without the power of perpetrating their de-signs. The most zealous democrats eagerly stimulated disaf-

Multipli-
cation of
lecturers,

fection to government. Declamatory lecturers multiplied in the metropolis; the demagogues did not confine themselves to the topics which had been so often agitated in democratic societies, addressed to their own peculiar cast; but watched the tone of dissatisfaction beginning to be heard among persons who were well affected to the constitution of their country: and pointed their invectives and sarcasms, not merely against what they called the aristocratic principles and objects of the war, but what came much more home to the hearts of the people, its ef-

who re-
present
wars as
ministerial
jobs for
plundering
the people.

fects on their purses and means of livelihood. Lecturers[u] both stationary and itinerant, represented wars, and beyond them all, this war, as contrived by courts and ministers, to afford them pretexts for plundering the people, that they and their adherents might wallow in luxury; while the multitude, by whose hard earnings their profusion was supported, were stint-ed in the necessaries of life. These inflammatory arts opera-ting on minds already sore with the pressure of the war and scarcity, brought many loyal and constitutional, though not considerate and discriminating men, into the vortex of discon-tent. A multiplicity of publications, periodical and occasion-

Frequency
of sedi-
tious meet-
ings.

al, strongly forwarded the same purposes; but the most point-ed and effectually conducive to aversion against the present government, were the lectural and political conventicles which abounded in 1795, beyond all former periods; the private ca-bals of innovating associators and the numerous public meetings

Meetings
of the cor-
responding
society at
Chalk farm
and Co-
penhagen
house.

to which these gave rise. The corresponding society again meet at Chalk farm and other places, repeatedly in the course of the summer and autumn. A meeting, held at Copenhagen

u The author had the curiosity to go to hear some of the once noted John Thelwal's effusions, and also to read a certain production of his, styled, The Tribune; he recollects, that the declamation mentioned in the text, constituted the substance of both.

house near Islington, of these conventions, was the most re- .CHAP.
markable. The numbers that attended, either through zeal in LVII.
the cause, or through curiosity, were computed at about fifty
thousand. Some very daring addresses were made to the mul- 1795.
titude; the conduct of ministers was arraigned in the most un- Abuse of
qualified language; and a remonstrance to the king, on the govern-
necessity of peace, and a reform in parliament, was universally ment.
adopted. The chief abettors of the proceedings against government, were apprehended to be emissaries from France,[x] who,
though natives of Great Britain or Ireland, had thrown off all
attachment to their country, and were become its most violent
and rancorous enemies. The difficulty of detecting individuals
connected with our foes, enabled them to assume the appearance
of patriotism, and to delude with facility the majority of their
hearers into a persuasion, that they spoke and acted from principle, and had no other intention than to expose abuses, and to
induce the people to assert their rights.[y] The increasing frequency of those meetings, and the growing audaciousness of their
directors, called for preventive measures.

The internal state of the kingdom, as well as its foreign rela- Behaviour
tions, determined his majesty to call his parliament together of the mob
at an earlier period than usual. It accordingly assembled on to the king,
the 29th of October; a memorable day on account of the to and from
events which it witnessed, and the consequences which ensu- parlia-
ed. A report had been spread, that an immense multitude ment.
of discontented people had agreed to take this opportunity of manifesting their sentiments to the king in person. This
of course excited the curiosity of the public, and the park
was crowded in a manner unprecedented since his majesty's
accession to the throne. In his way to the house of lords
through the park, his coach was surrounded on every side,
by persons of all descriptions, demanding peace,[z] and the
dismission of Mr. Pitt. Some voices were even heard, ex-
claiming, "No king;" and stones were thrown at the state
coach as it drew near to the horse guards. In passing through
palace yard, one of the windows was broken, it was said, by a bul- A bullet is
let discharged from an air gun. These outrages were repeated shot into
on the king's return from parliament, and he narrowly escaped the king's
the fury of the populace in his way back from St. James's palace coach.
to Buckingham house.

Every loyal and patriotic Briton felt with indignation the Indigna-
unmerited insult offered to his sovereign; and saw the neces- tion of the
sity of restraining the rebellious spirit which such attempts public.

x Annual Register, 1796, chap i.   y Ibid.
z First in a melancholy, but soon after a menacing tone. As his majesty's equipage turned towards the horse guards, the populace were become very insolent. His majesty displayed his usual magnanimity, and
conversed with the lords without appearing to notice the disposition to riot.
So far I was an eye witness; but apprehending a tumult, I then left the park.

CHAP.
LVII.

1795.
Proclama-
tion.

indicated. A proclamation was published offering a large pecuniary reward for the discovery of the perpetrators; and also stating, that previously to the opening of parliament, a meeting had been held in the vicinity of the metropolis, where inflammatory speeches were made, and divers means used to sow discontent and excite seditious proceedings; requiring all magistrates and other well affected subjects to exert themselves in preventing and suppressing all unlawful meetings, and the dissemination of seditious writings.

Proceed-
ings of par-
liament.

A conference was held between the two houses as soon as his majesty had withdrawn, and witnesses were examined in relation to the outrages that had been committed. Their testimony was communicated to the commons, and both houses unanimously concurred in the addresses which were proposed. It was by no means deemed sufficient to investigate past guilt, and testify abhorrence of its treasonable enormity; it was necessary to prevent the recurrence of such dangerous wickedness.

Lord Gren-
ville intro-
duces a bill
for the safe-
ty of his
majesty's
person.
Principles
and de-
tails.

To secure his majesty against future effects of so disloyal and unconstitutional a spirit, lord Grenville proposed a bill, entitled, "An act for the safety and preservation of his majesty's "person and government against treasonable and seditious "practices and attempts." This law consisted of two parts; the first made a very momentous change, and extension of the crime of treason: it declared the commission, by deed, or by words spoken, written, or printed, or in any other open manner, or any act *tending* to the imprisonment, deposition, or death, of the king, or his heirs and successors, a conspiracy to levy war, in order to overawe the parliament, and to effect a change of counsels, or to instigate any foreigner or stranger by force to invade any of the king's dominions, to be high-treason, during the king's natural life, and till the end of the next session of parliament, after the demise of the crown. The second part extended the crime, and aggravated the punishment, of sedition: to excite dislike, and hatred to the person of the king, or to the persons of his heirs and successors, or to the government and constitution of this realm as by law established, by deed, by advised speech, or by words written or printed, was, for the first offence, rendered liable to the penalties incurred by the commission of a high misdemeanor, and, for the second, to the usual punishments prescribed by law, or to transportation for not more than seven years, at the discretion of the court. "The provisions (lord Grenville said) were conform-
"able to the principles admitted in the acts of Elizabeth, and
"Charles II. and were as similar as circumstances would per-
"mit. Difficulties having arisen in the construction of the laws
"relating to treason, already in force, the intent of this bill was
"to explain and fix the meaning of those laws. It would
"not prohibit any act allowed to be legal, but only provide
"a more suitable punishment according to the degree of cri-

" minality, than that which was ordained by the laws now in CHAP.
" force; as in various cases, notwithstanding criminality was LVII.
" evidently proved, an opposite law had not been enacted."
This bill was strongly opposed, though but by a very small 1795.
number in the house of peers. Its most active impugners arguments
·were the duke of Bedford and the earl of Lauderdale. These against it:
lords expressed the utmost horror of the daring outrage which
had been committed against his majesty; but alleged that the
bill did not tend to procure more safety to the person of the
sovereign than the laws that already existed; there was· no
sufficient proof that the outrages committed were connected
with the meetings to which they were attributed: the present
law was evidently an innovation in the constitution, and ·an
abridgment of the liberty of the subject: it opened a dangerous
latitude for constructive treason, one of the most pernicious
instruments of tyrannical government. One of the strongest
bulwarks of our freedom was the treason law of Edward III.
by which, accurate definition of crime fenced the liberties and
lives of ·English subjects against the capricious displeasure, or
arbitrary designs of a king or his ministers. This law had
guarded former monarchs through barbarous ages and periods of
turbulence and violence, and it was certainly sufficient to protect
the king's life and safety in the present age of civilization and
very general loyalty. But the proposed measure was neither
calculated nor intended for the security of the king; it was
designed to deter the people from exercising their constitutional
right of stating grievances, lest thereby they might incur, from
the vengeance of ministers, prosecutions for high treason, for
acts, the *tendency* of which, by this new law, they might pretend
to be treasonable. Ministers were aware that the eyes of the
people were open to the folly and madness of their infatuated
and ruinous war; and that their measures had excited general
disapprobation and discontent: they unhinged the laws of the
land, threw down the strongest props of our freedom, to fright-
en a distressed ·people from declaring their sufferings and
requesting relief. The same motives dictated the second part
of the bill, by which the most innocent acts were declared to
be sedition, and the punishment was aggravated far beyond
its proportion to the crime, and was totally inconsistent with
the constitutional spirit of the English penal laws: our criminal code was to change its clearness, precision, accurate and
enlightened justice, to accommodate either the wickedness, the
imbecility, or infatuation of ministers. These were the arguments of the opponents of this law.

Ministers on the contrary used the following arguments: for it.
laws must be adapted to changing circumstances; the ingenuity of human wickedness often devises modes of mischief, which
lawgivers could not foresee in all their varieties; and hence,
in human actions, instances of moral guilt and political injury,
not provided against by law, occur in the history of depravity,

CHAP.   as flagitious in motive, heinous in circumstances, and hurtful
I.VII.   in effect, as any which are described in the penal code.   Ed-
         ward III.'s law had not been the only fence round the persons
1795.   and rights of our kings ; various statutes had been added as
         new occasions or circumstances of danger occurred : acts had
         been passed in the time of Charles II. as guards against the
         machinations of the republican party, because from them dan-
         ger was apprehended : at subsequent periods, treason had
         been extended to conspiracies in favour of the pretender ; be-
         cause, from such, danger was then apprehended.   It was
         certainly true, that hitherto a conspiracy to overawe parlia-
         ment, by whatever overt act carried on, had not been made
         treason, and the law in that respect was new.   In point of fact,
         a conspiracy to overawe parliament had never till very recent-
         ly occurred : the remedy and preventive had not been devis-
         ed until the disease had appeared ; but a conspiracy to control
         legislature was as inimical to the public welfare as the treasons
         already defined.   The general principle was preserved, and
         the treason laws were extended to a new case which endan-
         gered the public safety.[a]   The act imposed no restraint which
         loyalty and patriotism did not impose : its capital penalties
         were to be dreaded only by those who were conspiring to con-
         trol the legislature, or to dethrone the king ; and by ceasing
         to conspire, they avoided the penalties ; and its subordinate
         enactments were dreadful only to the disseminators of sedition.
         Legal proceedings upon this law, as upon all others, were
         subject to an impartial investigation of a British jury.   On
         these grounds, very forcibly urged by ministerial peers, espe-
         cially lords Grenville and Loughborough, the bill after under-
         going some modifications from the discriminating wisdom of
         Thurlow, passed the house of peers, was carried to the com-
         mons, and underwent a similar discussion.

Mr. Pitt's   Meanwhile, a collateral bill was introduced by Mr. Pitt into
bill for pre- the house of commons, to root up a principal cause of the
venting se- crimes described in lord Grenville's law, by preventing sedi-
ditious   tious meetings.   These assemblies, as we have said, had mul-
meetings :   tiplied very rapidly under various forms and denominations ;
         but most regularly and constantly, for hearing inflammatory
         invectives against the government and constitution, under the
object and name of political lectures.   To prevent such mischievous con-
provisions venticles, Mr. Pitt's bill proposed that all assemblies exceeding
of,   fifty in number, and not already recognised by law, if convened
         for addressing the king or parliament, with the view, or on the
         pretext of considering grievances, or procuring an alteration
         in church or state, should be declared unlawful, and liable to
         dispersion by a magistrate, after reading a specific proclama-
         tion ; unless the assembly were collected by a public adver-
         tisement, signed by seven resident householders, and a true

         a See Parliamentary Debates of Nov. and Dec. 1795.

copy of it subscribed by them, were left with the publisher, who,
under a penalty of fifty pounds, must deliver it to any justice of
the peace by whom it should be demanded. It farther provided,
that disobedience for more than one hour to the magistrate's order to disperse, should subject any individual, of a number above
twelve, to the punishment of death; and even an assembly held
by regular advertisement, in the same manner and with the same
risk to the disobedient, might be dispersed if any measure subversive of the constitution, or tending to incite the people to hatred, or dislike, or contempt to the royal family, or of the parliament, were proposed. To prevent certain political lecturers from
gaining a livelihood by preaching sedition, a house opened for
any political discussion, without a license, was to incur a penalty
of a hundred pounds.

Mr. Fox was the first that rose to impugn this bill. There arguments
was, he alleged, no evidence but the assertions of ministers, against it:
that the outrages, which he reprobated as much as any man,
arose from the meetings described in the bill. But if the closest Mr. Fox
chain of connexion could have been traced between certain reprobates
meetings and the attack upon our sovereign, the abuse did the bill,
not justify the proscription of the rights of the people. Public discussion on national subjects, was not only legal, but the
very life of the English constitution: and without these no
liberty could subsist. The people had an unalienable right to exhibits
deliberate on their grievances, and to demand redress from the the rights
legislature; but by this bill were forbidden to exercise those of the peo-
rights without the attendance of a magistrate, and previous notice ple to state
to him of their intention. A PERSON APPOINTED BY GOVERNMENT their grie-
vances,
was empowered to arrest any one present, whose words he
might think proper to call sedition, and even to dissolve the
meeting at his own pleasure. Behold the state of a free declares
Englishman: before he can discuss any topic which involves the bill in-
his liberty, or his rights, he is to send to a magistrate, who tended to
is to attend the discussion; that magistrate cannot prevent prevent the
the meeting, but he can prevent their speaking, because he can exercise of
allege that what is said has a tendency to disturb the peace that right,
of the kingdom. Can a meeting, under such restrictions, be and to
shield mi-
called a meeting of free people? Is it possible to make the nisters:
people of this country believe that the plan is any thing but a
total annihilation of their liberty? If the people's complaints
were groundless, the less they were noticed the sooner they
could cease, as false surmises would very soon be discovered
and lose their effect: but if well-founded, the efforts made
to repress them must terminate either in a base-minded submission of the people, or in a resistance fatal to their rulers as
well as to themselves. Revolutions were not owing to popular meetings, but to the tyranny which was exerted to enslave
men. The French revolution arose from ministerial oppressions, and the arbitrary proceedings of a despotic government,

CHAP.
LVII.

1795.
he alleges
they sub-
vert consti-
tutional
freedom.
Active ef-
forts of him
and his co-
adjutors,
both in and
out of par-
liament.
Petitions.

that held the people in continual dread, and silenced their very
fears by the terror of the punishments suspended over those who
dared to utter their sentiments. "Say then at once (exclaimed
" the orator), that a free constitution is no longer suitable to Bri-
" tain : conduct yourselves openly as the senators of Denmark
" did : lay down your freedom, and acknowledge and accept de-
" spotism : but do not mock the understandings and feelings of
" mankind, by telling the world that you are free. These strictures, seconded by all the brilliancy, ingenuity, and acuteness of
Sheridan, the constitutional and legal knowledge, and impressive
eloquence of Erskine, being added to the efforts of opposition in
the house of peers against the other bill, stirred up a great ferment in the country. Numerous petitions flocked in from every
quarter, deprecating the bills as an annihilation of the liberties of
the people. In promoting petitions, the lead was taken by the
whig club, consisting of men in point of talents rank, property,
and character, equal to any association of the same number in the
kingdom. On the other hand, addresses were presented in
favour of the bills, which, though not near so numerous, came
from persons *aggregately* superior in rank and property to the
petitioners.

Arguments
for Mr.
Pitt's bill:

required
by the cir-
cumstan-
ces of the
times.

The arguments of the addressers and of the parliamentary
supporters of Mr. Pitt's bill, were the wicked designs of those
who directed the meetings which were proposed to be suppressed, and their destructive tendency if suffered to continue.
The pretence of these meetings was to petition the legislature
for rights withheld from the people; but the real motive was,
to promulgate opinions that were inimical to government, and
calculated to bring it into contempt. If the executive power
were not invested with sufficient authority to control these
meetings, they would finally endanger the existence of the
state. It was the indubitable right of the people to pass their
judgment upon ministers and their measures, and freely to express their sentiments on all political subjects, as also to petition the different branches of the legislature; but these rights
ought to be kept within their intended limits, and it was the
duty of parliament to prevent them from becoming instrumental
to the subversion of the established government. The rights
of the people doubtless ought to be respected, but it was
equally indispensable to obviate their abuse. A precise and
acknowledged power was wanted in the magistrate to disperse
such meetings as threatened disorder. The bill proposed to
restrain no meetings, but those which were evidently calculated to incite ignorant and unwary men against the constitution.

somewhat
modified
both pass
into laws.

It permitted innocent and lawful assemblies, and only prohibited conventions hostile to the existing polity. These arguments
convincing the majority in both houses, the bill was passed

into a law: lord Grenville's bill also passed about the same CHAP.
time.[b]   LVII.

These acts tended greatly to shake the popularity of Mr.
Pitt through the kingdom. However efficient they might be   1795.
for remedying the specific evils that prevailed, yet even many Impartial
friends of government thought they did much more than the views of
necessity of the case justified. Persons unconnected with party the new
admitted the expediency of extending the treason laws to con- acts.
spiracies for levying war against the sovereign and constitution;
but disapproved of the vague and general description of this
new species of treason including in its overt acts whatever had
a *tendency* to rebellion against the king, government, or legislature. This clause they considered as a deviation from the
spirit of English laws: it opened, they said, a door for the arbitrary and oppressive constructions which characterize absolute and tyrannical systems; and was therefore contrary to the
principles and objects of the British constitution. . The restrictions upon the press, imposed by the same act, by many well Restric-
affected to government were deemed to admit also too much tions on
latitude of construction; to subject literary effort to the control dom of the
of ministers, and to enchain the freedom of the press. It was press.
allowed by every candid and impartial man, that the harangues
and lectures of demagogues, in periodical and occasional conventicles, were extremely dangerous, and required to be prevented; but, on the other hand, it was asserted, that the laws
in existence were sufficient for punishing whatever sedition
could be proved to have been uttered; that the whole community ought not to be debarred from assembling, because incendiaries had, in certain assemblies, violated the laws. The right
of discussing public measures belongs to every free-born Briton;
its exercise promotes his sense of personal importance; the
best nourisher of liberty and independence. Other Britons
were not to be debarred from enjoying such privileges, because
a foolish, virulent, or malignant lecturer, abused his exercise of
the same right. The restriction tended to enervate the spirit
of freedom, and thus to effect a great, general and permanent
evil, in order to remedy a partial and temporary evil. The
most solid and effectual answer to these very forcible objections
was, that the obnoxious laws were only intended to be temporary.

The abilities of Mr. Pitt often manifested themselves in turning public opinion into the current which best suited his political views; but one engine he appears not to have estimated with
his usual perspicacity: Mr. Pitt laid too little stress upon litera- Mr. Pitt
ry efficacy: while the press is free, literary power will produce hended to
great effects on public opinion. The minister was not deemed underva-
favourable to writers, as a class: perceiving that they had fre- lue litera-
quently done much mischief in France, he appeared to have ry effort.

b For the details of the debates, see Parliamentary Reports.

CHAP.
LVII.

1795.

Majority of
the literary
class inimi-
cal to his
adminis-
tration.

Writers re-
present the
series of his
measures
as more
conducive
to the
powe of
the crown
than the
rights of
the people.

State of
ministerial
popularity.

drawn an inference too hasty, that they ought to be discouraged
in England. The laws in question, and other acts, tended to
restrain the market for literary commodities, consequently to do
an aggregate hurt to the profession. This effect literary men
felt, and many of them strongly and efficiently expressed their
feelings : habits of combination, analysis, comparison, and deduction of general principles, enabled them to view and estimate the character of the legislative measures of Mr. Pitt. In
these they professed to discover, that the greater part of our
new laws had a reference, either to public revenue, or to the
security of the monarchical part of the constitution; and that
few, of any extensive operation, are of the class that may be
denominated popular.[c]
     The violence of some partisans in their promotion of the
bills, far transcended the limits which were observed by the
minister himself, and added to the dislike with which many
regarded those laws. While the minister justified the restriction as a necessary expedient, in a temporary case, without in-
trenching upon the whig principles on which the British constitution rests, high tories who supported him in defending the
church and monarchy, promulgated their own peculiar doctrines; and manifesting a desire of degrading the just authority
of a free people, revived exploded doctrines of passive obedience to the existing power. Ingenious men, adverse to ministers, did not fail to impute to the supreme leader these sentiments of too vehement and ardent subalterns; and an opinion
now pervaded the lower classes, and infected many of the middling, and some of the higher, that Mr. Pitt was anxious not
only to fortify, but extend the power of the crown, to weaken
and contract the power of the people. Such an apprehension
once entertained, affected the construction of his subsequent
conduct; and from this time, his popularity diminished, though,
perhaps, his power increased. The financial ability of Mr. Pitt,
during the whole of his administration, secured to him the support of the great capitalists, and the monied interest. In part
of his ministry, the landed interest had been considerably divided, but through the alarms entertained from the French revolution, the greater number had joined his standard. At the beginning of the war, high rank and great property, with comparatively few exceptions, ranged themselves on the side of the
minister. By much the greater proportion of the middling and
lower ranks, having moderate or small property, joined the
cause, which they, as well as the superior orders, conceived to
protect their property, and other benefits which they held ; but
now many of the middling classes, and most of the lower rank,
took the opposite side, while high rank and great opulence continued to favour ministers. In parliament, nearly the usual majorities supported the continuance of war, on the original ne-

c See Annual Register for 1796, p. 46.

cessity still remaining, and the expected exhaustion of the enemy's finances. Its opponents repeated their allegations of its original impolicy and folly; denied the probability of a decay of resources, arising from the ardent spirit of freedom; from the events of the last campaign, enforced their former assertions that the contest was hopeless; and adduced new reasons for peace, in the returning disposition to order in the French republicans, which was manifested since the overthrow of Robespierre and of the system of terrorism; they reminded ministers of the hopes held out at the conclusion of the former session in his majesty's speech, and insisted that the meliorated state therein mentioned was now arrived.

Though ministers repeated their usual arguments for the vigorous prosecution of the war while it lasted, they had not dwelt as in the former years, on the impractability, from the internal state of France, of its termination. His majesty's speech at the beginning of the session, delivered while the contest between the terrorists and the moderates in the national convention, was at the most violent height, contained the following declaration: " The distraction and anarchy which have so " long prevailed in that country, have led to a crisis, of which " it is as yet impossible to foresee the issue, but which must, in " all human probability, produce consequences highly impor- " tant to the interests of Europe. Should this crisis terminate " in any order of things compatible with the tranquillity of " other countries, and affording a reasonable expectation of se- " curity and permanence in any treaty which might be conclu- " ded, the appearance of a disposition to negotiate for a gene- " ral peace, on just and suitable terms, will not fail to be met, on " my part, with an earnest desire to give it the fullest and speedi- " est effect."[d] The moderates having at length prevailed, his majesty began to entertain hopes of the practicability of a peace with the government that now subsisted in France. According-ly, on the 8th of December, he sent a message to the houses, stating, that the crisis depending at the commencement of the session had led to such an order of things in France, as would induce his majesty, conformably to the sentiments which he had already declared, to meet any disposition for negotiation on the part of the enemy; and expressing his earnest desire to give it the fullest and speediest effect, and to conclude a general peace as soon as it could be accomplished justly and honoura-bly for Britain and her allies. After this declaration, the argu-ments for and against peace ceased to turn on the *competence* of the existing French government to conclude a treaty. Mr. Fox contended that, there never existed an obstacle to negotia-tion in any of the successive governments of France, it was like every former discussion of peace and war with either French or other enemies, a mere question of justice and expe-

Ministers intimate his majesty's disposition to open a negotiation for peace.

Remarks of Mr Fox on this declaration.

d See State Papers for 1795, p. 131.

1796.

diency, belonging to the Spanish nations in their relations to each other, without any connexion with the internal government of either.[e] He rejoiced, however, that ministers professed to return to a disposition, from which they ought never to have departed, and to which he had so often exhorted them in vain. Motions were afterwards made in the houses of parliament, for addresses to the king, requesting him to communicate to the executive government in France, his readiness to embrace an opportunity of coinciding with them in mutual endeavours for the re-establishment of peace.[f] These propositions were resisted by ministers: the conduct of a negotiation belonged solely to the executive government; if ministers were deemed unworthy of such a trust, their opponents ought to petition for their removal; but while they continued in office, they alone could be the proper agents in such a transaction; they ought, on this principle, to act unitedly, not only among themselves, but with the allies of this country, to whom no cause should be given to suspect us of duplicity, or of a separate policy. If they remained entire, so powerful a confederacy could not, in the nature of things fail, by perseverance and unanimity, to obtain an advantageous peace; but this desirable object depended on the moderation of the enemy. All had been done which honour and interest admitted, to bring France to this issue; but neither honour nor interest would be sacrificed. On these grounds the several motions[g] were negatived. The conduct of the war underwent severe animadversions: it was asserted by opposition, that the miscarriages of the campaign had manifested a total want of concert in our plans; that our military measures were a mere succession of detached experiments, directed to no uniform and consistent object; that they showed a total want of the wisdom and energy, the combination of which was necessary to a war minister. The expedition to Quiberon was reprobated with peculiar severity; ministers were also strongly reprehended for their inadvertence, in not furnishing the troops sent to the West Indies with a sufficient quantity of medical stores, and for maintaining at present, without necessity, no less than a thousand staff officers. The number to which the fencible cavalry amounted, were attributed to the ministerial plan of keeping the people in subjection and dread; the regular cavalry, was equal to every just and proper purpose, without loading the public with so much additional expense. In the preceding summer a great addition had been made to the barracks before erected, and many regiments had been raised, and placed under the command of gentlemen, or noblemen, who had never been in the army. Opposition re-

The conduct of the war is severely censured.

e See Parliamentary Reports, Dec. 8, 1795.
f Motion of Mr. Grey, 15th Feb. 1796.
g By Mr. Fox and lord Guilford, on the 10th of May, in their respective houses.

probated these measures, as tending to increase the influence of the crown by lucrative jobs and appointments; the more dangerous, because not a few of these commanders were members of parliament; the barrack system, by separating soldiers from the people, tended to destroy that coincidence of sentiment, without which soldiers would be the mere tools of the executive power, instead of being defenders of the community.[z] Ministers defended the expedition of Quiberon, as the result of the best information and reasoning that could be derived from officers of experienced skill, and thoroughly acquainted with the country. In the West Indies, an ample supply of medicinal stores had been sent, but had fallen into the hands of the enemy; they were, however, repairing with all possible expedition. The staff officers were numerous, but not more than were required by the manifold exigencies of the service. The system of barracks was neither new, nor unconstitutional while the war lasted, it was necessary to hold men in readiness, and the present was the most convenient mode for that purpose; they also prevented the inconvenience, trouble, and expense accruing to subjects from quartering soldiers. Men of opulence and distinction had been preferred to commands, in their respective counties, as more able to procure levies than others; besides, in a war of which so important an object was the defence of rank and property, it was consistent and prudent to employ persons who had so much at stake.

The national expenditure was also a subject of discussion. Besides the annual income of the country, two loans were this year required; the first, including a vote of credit, consisted of twenty millions and a half; and the second of seven millions and a half. So enormous a sum added to the preceding debts incurred since the war, made the additional amount of the national incumbrances near eighty millions in three years. The censurers of the war viewing this immense burthen, asked its supporters what benefit would accrue to the country to balance the loss? To what end were we carrying on a contest of such unparalleled cost? the minister had asserted, we were warring for security and indemnity? how was a repetition of disaster to strengthen security? Failing in our enterprises, whence were we to derive a compensation? Ministers contended that the war had been undertaken for the most important objects, that the greatest and most vigorous preparations were necessary, not only for defending Britain if the war should continue, but for inclining the enemy to peace. Our commercial situation, notwithstanding the war, was more prosperous than at any an-

CHAP.
LVII.

1796.

Supplies.

Immense Loan.

---

[z] These arguments were urged in repeated motions; especially a proposition by Mr Grey, on the state of the nation, on the 10th of March; by Mr. Sheridan, for inquiring into the mortality in the West Indies, on the 21st of April; and by Mr. Grey, for an impeachment of his majesty's ministers on the 24th of April. See Parliamentary Reports.

CHAP.
LVII.

1796.

tecedent period. The average of exports, during the three last years of peace, the most flourishing ever known in this country, was twenty-two millions five hundred and eighty-five thousand pounds; and the same average for the last three years of war was twenty-four millions four hundred and fifty-three thousand. The expenditure of war was doubtless immense; but the exertions, to which it was applied were of no less magnitude. Never was the energy of this country so astonishingly displayed, nor its resources so wonderfully proved; our fleets and our armies were in a far superior condition, both as to numbers and equipment, to those which were maintained in the American war. Besides, the decreased value of money made a very great real difference in sums nominally the same; and compared with the importance of the object, and the magnitude of our efforts, the amount was not excessive.

The taxes financially judicious; laid on the luxuries and conveniences, and not on the necessaries of life.
Able speech of earl Moira on revenue.

Every impartial observer, reviewing the taxes both of the present and the former years of the war, admitted, that if politically necessary, they were financially judicious. The principal subjects were wines, spirits, tea, coffee, silk, fruit, tobacco, hair powder, and various other articles of luxury, without any encroachment upon the necessaries of life. Opposition, however, contested the financial expediency of the imposts. In the house of peers, the earl of Moira exhibited a very able discussion upon the revenue, the taxes, the imports and exports, and the other financial circumstances of the nation, at the close of the American war, and at the present period. The inferences from the arguments and statements produced by the respective parties were extremely opposite. The one represented the situation of this country as replete with the most arduous difficulties, and almost verging to ruin; and the other described it as full of opulence and resources of every denomination; and able, with proper management, to encounter and surmount every obstacle, and to flourish with more lustre than ever.

Proposed remonstrance.

Opposition, not understanding that ministers were taking any steps for the attainment of peace, charged them with insincerity; and in both houses proposed a very strong address in the nature of a remonstrance, professing to exhibit the leading features, principles, and character of ministerial conduct from the beginning of the war; and attempting to prove that they had transgressed every rule of prudence and policy; and praying his majesty to adopt maxims more suitable to the public exigencies. On a review (this remonstrance set forth) of so many instances of gross and flagrant misconduct, proceeding from the same pernicious principles, and directed with incorrigible obstinacy to the same mischievous ends, we deem ourselves bound in duty to your majesty, and to our constituents, to declare that we see no rational hope of redeeming the affairs of the kingdom, but by the adoption of a system radically and fundamentally different from that which has produced our present calamities; unless your majesty's ministers shall, from a

real conviction of past errors, appear inclined to regulate their CHAP.
conduct upon such a system, we can neither give any credit to LVII.
the sincerity of their professions of a wish for peace, nor repose
any confidence in them for conducting a negotiation to a pros- 1796.
perous issue: the proposed address was combatted on the usual is nega-
grounds, and negatived by a very great majority.   tived.

Mr. Wilberforce, this year, made a new motion for the abolition of the slave trade, which, though supported by Messrs. Pitt
and Fox, was rejected. On the 19th of May parliament was Dissolution
prorogued, and a few days after it was dissolved.   of parlia-
                                                             ment.

CHAP. LVIII.

Views of the belligerent powers.—French decree for the irrevocable annexation of Belgium to the republic.—Hopes of Britain and of Austria —
The governments of the contending countries are little disposed to peace
—the people on both sides desire to terminate the evils of war—the
respective governments profess a pacific disposition—indirect overtures
of Britain to France—the answer of the French for the present prevents
negotiation.—Belligerent policy of the French government.— French objects of the campaign—La Vendee, Germany, and Italy.—The reduction
of La Vendee.—Tendency of revolution to call forth abilities —Numbers
of able commanders who sprang up among the French.—This year displays an extraordinary general —Bonaparte appointed to command the
French army in Italy.—Numerous and well disciplined army of the emperor—assisted by the Italian princes.—Inferior force of the French.—
Bonaparte commands the minds of his soldiers—he attacks and defeats
the Austrians—repeated victories.—Bonaparte separates the Austrian
and Piedmontese armies.—By a victory at Mondovi he compels the king
of Sardinia to yield at discretion—who receives peace from his dictation.
—Bonaparte surmounts the natural ramparts of Italy—wise measures to
keep up the spirits of his troops.—Battle at the Bridge of Lodi—signal
exploit and victory of Bonaparte—he imitates the Romans in their rapacity as well as valour—but mingles conciliatory policy, especially towards
the populace.—Conspiracies at the instance of the nobles and clergy—are
disconcerted—and punished. —Bonaparte gains to his interest the men of
genius and literature—and endeavours to bring every kind of talent into
efficient action—result of his political efforts—he resumes military operations—marches from Italy towards Germany.—Wurmser takes the field
with a fresh army of Austrians—Is repulsed by the French.—Bonaparte
invests Mantua—Wurmser approaches to its relief.—Bonaparte is surrounded at Lonado—he extricates himself by a stratagem, and induces a
much superior army to surrender —Successive victories of Bonaparte—
decisive victory at Arcola—capture of Mantua.—Commotions at Rome—
conduct of the papal government—the pope attempts to make war against
Bonaparte—the French general makes conciliatory overtures—reply of
the pope.—Bonaparte invades the Roman territories, and compels the
pontiff to sue for a peace —Amount of the French acquisitions in Italy
in this campaigne—Political administration of Bonaparte.—Germany invaded by Jourdain and Moreau.—The archduke Charles—successive battles of, with Jourdain—Danger of the empire—is warded off by the
valour of the archduke—who compels Jourdain to evacuate Germany.—
Progress and situation of Moreau—masterly and successful retreat in the
face of the German host —Britain continues signally successful where
she fights alone—retakes St Lucie—quells insurrections in the other
islands—captures seven Dutch ships of the line in Saldana bay—reduces
Ceylon and other Dutch settlements in the east—judges it expedient to
relinquish Corsica.—Ineffectual attempts of the French upon Ireland —
Internal events —Birth of a princess, heir to the prince of Wales.—General election—the least contested of any in the eighteenth century.—
British government proposes to send an ambassador to Paris to negotiate
a peace.—France agrees to receive a British ambassador.

DURING the last campaign the efforts of the French ré-
publicans had been much less successful than from the victories
and acquirements of the former year, together with the diminution of the confederacy, they had probable grounds for expecting: they were anxious to recover their superiority of military powers, and with this view the directory made vigorous
preparations to place the numerous armies of the republic on
the most formidable footing. It was proposed to the legislature,
and solemnly decreed to annex their acquisitions in the Low
Countries, and on the left side of the Rhine, irrevocably to the
dominions of the republic. In the relative circumstances· of
the belligerent powers, a resolution of this nature precluded all
ideas of peace. The retention of those fertile and spacious
provinces could not be submitted to, without an evident alteration of the political system of Europe, of which France would
possess a control that would perpetually disturb the peace, if
not endanger the safety of all her neighbours. The inhabitants
of Belgium, so long habituated to the sway of the Austrian
princes, which, though occasionally oppressive, had been generally mild, still retained a willingness to return to their obedience, provided they could be secured in the enjoyment of their
ancient customs and liberties. Sensible of this disposition, and
exaggerating the success of the last campaign, the Austrian
cabinet preserved the hope of recovering those fertile provinces.
The British ministers were no less bent on the restoration of the
Austrian Netherlands to their former owner. The accession
of such immense and valuable territories to France in so close
a proximity, seriously alarmed all men who reflected on the
power, energy, and enterprise of the French ; and their violent
resentment against this country. The government of Britain
and her ally on the one hand, and of the French on the other,
were, from this contention of adverse purposes, little inclined
to peace ; but the people, in all the conflicting countries were
anxiously desirous to be relieved from a war, the pressing evils
of which they immediately felt ; and the eventual advantages
of which, if any, they either did not comprehend, or did not
think sufficient to counterbalance the present burthens and losses.
The belligerent governments, therefore, to gratify the people,
found it expedient to assume the appearance of a pacific disposition ; in which, from the subsequent acknowledgements[a] of our
ministers, it is certain, and from the conduct of the French di-
reetors it is very probable, that they were respectively inimical
to peace. The French, meanwhile, were employing their usual
ingenuity and address, in endeavouring to detach various members from the hostile confederacy, and Basle, a considerable city
in Switzerland, was on account of its neutral state and central

Marginal notes:
1796.
Views of the belligerent powers.
French decree for the irrevocable annexation of Belgium to the republic.
Hopes of Britain and of Austria.
The governments of the contending countries are little disposed to peace.
The people on both sides to terminate the evils of war.
The respective governments profess a pacific disposition.

a See Mr. Pitt's speech on the first consul's proposals for peace, in Jan. 1800.

CHAP.
LVIII.

〰〰〰

1796.

Indirect
overtures
of Britain
to France.

The an-
swer of
the French
for the
present
prevents
negotia.
.ion.

Bellige.
rent policy
of the
French go.
vernment.

French ob.
jects of
campaign ;
La Ven-
dee, Ger-
many, and
Italy.

position, the scene of their negotiations. There the celebrated M. Barthelemi had concluded the treaty with Prussia, and was still engaged in diplomatic agency. Mr. Wickham, the British ambassador to the Swiss cantons, was instructed to apply to this gentleman, to sound the disposition of the French government, and to learn whether the directory were desirous to negotiate with Britain and her allies, on moderate and honourable conditions, and would agree to the meeting of a congress for this purpose, and specify the terms on which it would treat, or point out any other method of procedure. The answer received from M.. Barthelemi, in the name of the directory, was, that it felt the sincerest desire to terminate the war on such conditions as France could reasonably accept, and which were specified in the answer ; but one of these positively insisted on the retention of the Austrian dominions in the Low Countries, and assigned as a reason, their formal annexation to the republic by a constitutional decree that could not be revoked. This reply expressing a decided resolution not to part with their acquisitions, displayed in the opinion of the British ministers, a disposition so arrogant, that the negotiation was suspended, and both parties proceeded to open the campaign.

The French directory had now to contend with two potent enemies ; the one. of which surpassed most nations, but was inferior to France in land forces ; the other far exceeded all nations, and even France herself, in maritime strength. With a policy much more profound than that which dictated the belligerent measures of the Bourbon princes, the revolutionary rulers employed their exertions in the scenes of probable victory, instead of probable defeat : their armies, still superior to their valiant and disciplined opponents, occupied their principal attention, and their fleets, subjects of only secondary consideration, did not divert, as in former wars, to hopeless efforts a grand portion of their resources.

The directory had three objects in contemplation : an invasion of Germany, another of Italy, and the complete reduction of domestic insurgents. The subjugation of La Vendee was indispensably necessary, before they could carry into execution their grand projects against the Austrian dominions. The connexion of the insurgents with the most formidable and dangerous rivals of France—the English, made it evident, that while the royal party subsisted unsubdued, it would probably, as it had done in the preceding year, throw such embarrassments in the military operations intended against foreign enemies, as would clog and impede the plans that were proposed. The discomfiture of the expedition from En land, and the severe punishment of its abettors, had frightened the Vendeans. The leaders of the insurrection, however, found means to excite the people to a new revolt, attended with all the disorders usual in civil war. Charette and Stoflet published a manifesto charging the republicans with breach of faith, and the most outrageous cruelty. In consequence of the revolutionary enormities, they declared themselves determined to take up arms again, and never to lay them down till the heir of the crown was restored, and the catholic religion re-established.[b] They held out every motive that had formerly been prevalent; attachment to their religion, love of their king, and hatred to the present innovations. Many were induced accordingly to enlist again under their banners: but the greater part remained quiet in their habitations, and the flower of the insurgents was not, as before, composed of the Vendeans, but of the mixed and numerous mass of the inhabitants of the several provinces of Britanny, Poitou, Maine, Anjou, and others, which are situated on the banks of the Loire.[c] Hostilities raged with great fury during the winter; the republican government sent general Hoche early in the season against the insurgents: Charette was completely defeated, and his followers dispersed. The directory, wishing to adhere to the moderate measures which from the beginning of their power they professed to adopt, enjoined their commanders and troops to employ conciliation as much as possible; and to abstain from all unnecessary severity. An amnesty of the past was accordingly published to all who should return to their duty; every district which surrendered its arms, and punctually conformed to the conditions prescribed, was immediately placed under the protection of the laws. Conciliatory policy, the wisest that can be adopted in intestine insurrections, for terminating revolt already broken by successful force, proved ultimately effectual, and the rebellion was crushed. The government was now at liberty to direct the whole force of its efforts against Germany and Italy.

The reduction of La Vendee.

As the directors by personal efforts had reached the pinnacle of executive power, by success only could they hope to retain eminence. The insurance of success depended on the choice of instruments in the various departments of public service. In revolutionary governments which have levelled pre existing establishments, promotion according to qualification, exclusively, is much more practicable than in old and regular constitutions, which contain fixed gradations of rank and of orders. In the very best systems of polity that have been long settled, splendid ancestry, high rank, extensive property, or political connexions, attach to certain families or individuals such an authority, that few ministers can avoid employing them in services for which their talents and characters by no means render them the fittest that could be chosen. A British minister, even if he should be desirous, would find it difficult to fill either military or political departments with the most efficacious men that could be found, without respect to rank, situation, and influence: even Mr. Se-

Tendency of revolution to call forth abilities.

b Otridge's Annual Register, 1796.
c See Otridge's Annual Register, for 1796, p. 82.

CHAP. cretary Pitt, who carried the principle of employing men accord-
LVIII. ing to their respective abilities farther than any other English
～～～ minister, in *politics* was obliged to admit the co-operation of cer-
1796. tain men of rank and influence, whom his penetrating judgment
would assuredly never have selected, on account of their personal qualities, as his associates in great designs. Forming his naval
and military appointments without control, and choosing that
class of executive servants on the simple principle of instrumentality, he obtained such brilliant successes both by sea and land.
The French government, totally unfettered from prescription
and authority,[d] possessed without control the power that might
Numbers be instrumental to success. Thence sprang so many able gene-
of able rals, whose genius, without neglecting the lessons of experience,
command- disdained mere precedent, and invented new combinations of de-
ers who fence and attack, new modes of advance and retreat, to suit the
sprang up
among the circumstances of their situation.
French.   The campaign 1796 exhibited a young leader, who, in prowess,
This year energy, and exploits, equalled any commander that the late war
displays an had discovered and exercised : this was Napoleon Bonaparte, a
extraordi-
nary gene- native of Corsica, born about 1769. The youth possessed talents
ral. and qualities which peculiary fitted him for attaining distinctions
Bonaparte. in the ferment of revolution, and the dangers of war. To a head
sagacious and inventive, instantaneous in comprehension, and
rapid in efforts, he joined a heart that was ardent, resolute, intrepid, and courageous; with an aspiring ambition, and an impetuous temper. One prominent feature of his character was
determined perseverance in his purposes, and he would scruple
no sacrifice to compass his ends. His object being to exalt himself, he joined the parties that were successively paramount ;
was a monarchist, constitutionalist, and terrorist. To Robespierre he adhered as long as fortune adhered ; and with no less
eagerness devoted himself to that monster's successors, and became a prime favourite with Lepaux : he was at equal pains to
Appointed win the attachment of the troops. The directors discerned the
to com- vigorous and fertile genius of Bonaparte, knew his military ar-
mand the
French ar- dour and $_e$n$_e$r$_g_y$, and his popularity among the soldiers. Such
my in Italy. qualifications they conceived to overbalance his youth and limited experience ; and they conferred on him the command of the
army of Italy.

d Although it be a fact, that in revolutions abilities generally rise to a
greater elevation than in established governments, yet it does not follow
that it is a beneficial fact, as the able heads which are thus raised, commonly attain and preserve their power by the most mischievous qualities of
the heart : such possessors of supremacy, far beyond their original rank and
station, have usually proved unprincipled adventurers, who regarded neither justice, patriotism, nor the good of mankind, in comparison with their
own ambition. For instance, Cæsar, Cromwell, &c.

The emperor was joined by the king of Sardinia, the king CHAP.
of Naples and the pope; and during the three preceding LVIII.
years, the French had in vain attempted to pierce through
Piedmont into the interior parts of Italy. The immense bar- 1796.
riers of mountains which divide that country from Savoy
seemed to oppose an insurmountable obstacle to their progress.
The republicans were indeed in possession of the coast from
Nice to Genoa; but the passes in Lombardy were guarded
with such care that no apprehension was entertained by the
court of Turin with respect to the future.[e] The emperor's Numerous
forces amounted to eighty thousand well disciplined men, and well
commanded by excellent generals and able officers, and pro- disciplined
vided with every species of warlike necessaries. The king of army of the
Sardinia's army was sixty thousand strong, exclusive of militia: emperor,
the pope and the king of Naples were occupied in embody- the Italian
ing as many troops as their circumstances would permit, and princes.
the latter had despatched two or three thousand horse to serve
in the imperial army. Such obstacles opposed by nature,
joined to so great a hostile army, only served to rouse the
genius and spirit of Bonaparte. · The whole force which the Inferior
French could afford to this general, before La Vendee was force of the
reduced, did not exceed fifty thousand, not so well supplied French.
as the much more numerous host of his veteran adversaries;
with this army he took the field in the month of April. According to the common calculation of probabilities, in a war
stimulated by the usual principles of enmity among sovereigns,
the project of forcing the passes of the Italian mountains against
such numerous and powerful foes, would have been extravagant and romantic. A tactician of mere experience,[f] without penetration and invention, reasoning very fairly from *his*
knowledge and views, would have concluded, that such an
attempt must terminate in disappointment and disaster: but
Bonaparte, penetrating into the French mind and springs of Bonaparte
action, saw that the republicans were animated by an enthu- commands
siasm which would overbear all the regular but phlegmatic the minds
valour of the Germans. The Austrian army was commanded diers.
by general Beaulieu, an officer of great military experience,
though in the Netherlands, as we have seen, he had been
overpowered by the republicans. The imperialists being inspirited with the successes of their countrymen in the preceding year, and his troops being so numerous, he did not hesitate
to act on the offensive: and, in the beginning of April, he
advanced towards the French lines. On the 9th he attacked
an outpost with success; and, on the 11th, he attempted the

e See Belsham's History, vol. v. p. 419.

f A very common objection against the military efforts of Bonaparte was,
that they deviated from the established practice; and with those *judges*
who in MEANS regard *usage* more than ADAPTATION TO ENDS, the objection
must have weight.

CHAP.
LVIII.

1796.
He attacks
and defeats
the Aus-
trians.
other intrenchments.ᵍ Bonaparte, by a rapid movement, turning the enemy's flank and rear, assailed them with impetuous
vigour, at a place called Montenotta, and gained a complete
victory, having killed fifteen hundred men, and taken two
thousand prisoners. Like Cæsar, Bonaparte was not only energetic, but rapid in energy: eager to improve his victory, he
pursued the Austrians, who had retreated to a strong situation on an eminence called Millasimo; but general Angereau
having forced the avenues to their position, the imperialists
retired to the ruins of an old castle, and having fortified themselves, they recovered from the disorder into which they had
been thrown by their late defeat. Conceiving his forces,
after this respite, still superior to the republicans, Beaulieu
again, on the 16th of April, attacked the French army. The
troops on both sides were animated with extraordinary courage,
the Austrians regarding with indignation their route at Montenotta, which they imputed to a stratagem, and not to the
prowess of the enemy, were eager to efface the remembrance

of the disaster. The French elated with their victory, which
had so auspiciously commenced the campaign, and operated
so powerfully on their susceptible and impetuous minds, glow-
ed with an ardent desire of overwhelming the superior numbers of their enemies. The Austrian charge was extremely
vigorous, but was withstood with an intrepidity and strength that
could not be moved. While the imperialists were bending
the whole force of their attack on the front of the enemy's
centre, Bonaparte, with the most dexterous celerity, moved
his wings round the right and left of the Germans, and in a
short time assailed them in both flanks and rear. Thus unexpectedly surrounded, the imperialists sustained a dreadful defeat,
two thousand were slain in the field, and eight thousand
made prisoners. Among the killed were some officers of high
distinction; and of the taken, one was a general, and near
thirty colonels, besides inferior officers. Between twenty and
thirty cannon fell into the hands of the French with fifteen
standards, and an immense quantity of stores and field equipage. Beaulieu, not disheartened by these disasters, collected
as many as possible of his scattered soldiers, and the following
day attacked the French, who did not expect an assault from
troops they had just vanquished, and were indulging themselves
in that repose which comes so grateful after the successful
completion of arduous labour. The onset at first disconcerted
the republicans, thus relaxed in their vigilance; but they soon
rallied. Bonaparte, agreeably to his plan already twice successful, formed a large body in front of the enemy, to occupy
their attention, while another division going round should
charge them in flank. The celerity of the French movements

ᵍ See Campaigns of Bonaparte for the military details both of this and
succeeding actions; and also the Austrian accounts, as inserted in our
gazettes of 1796.

soon obliged the enemy to act on the defensive. Having long made a resolute stand, the Austrians were compelled to give ground, and leave the field to the French, with the loss of near two thousand men, of whom about fifteen hundred were made prisoners. On the side of the French, great numbers also fell, and among these Caussa, one of their best officers. In the course of these battles, Bonaparte effected a separation between the Austrian and Piedmontese armies, and now directed his efforts against the troops of the king of Sardinia. On the 22d of April, he came up with the Italians at Mondovi, and attacked them though strongly intrenched: the Piedmontese made a very vigorous resistance, but totally unavailing against the republican impetuosity and force. The royal army was completely routed, and the fate of the king's dominions decided by the defeat.[h] His Sardinian majesty saw that the only means of escape from utter ruin was to accept peace from the dictation of the victorious general. He was compelled to cede Savoy and Nice: to withdraw from the coalition; to apologize for his conduct towards the French republic; and, retaining the name of king, to become a mere dependent on France. Thus Bonaparte, in the first month of his command, effected what his predecessors had for three years, without any misconduct, attempted in vain. He had stormed the ramparts of Italy, and, like Hannibal,[i] had its delightful vales, and fertile fields lying within his grasp. Their astonishing successes could not fail to inspire the French armies with the highest degree of exulting joy; nor did their commander forget to improve the sentiments of self applause and confidence manifested by them, into that disposition of mind which would lead them on to those farther exploits that he had in contemplation. He issued an address, concisely and forcibly recapitulating the achievements which they had already performed, and the objects which lay within the reach of their valorous efforts.[k] They were come (he said) into Italy to deliver the inhabitants from the government of strangers, and the tyranny of domestic rulers. Bonaparte being now freed from his Sardinian enemy, advanced against the Austrians. The German general and his troops, bravely as they fought, being repeatedly defeated, retired near Milan, the capital of Lombardy, and made a stand at a very strong post at Lodi,[l] determined to venture a battle, which was necessary to save Milan and the whole Austrian interest in Italy. Between Bonaparte and the imperialists was the river Adda, over which there was a long bridge, that Beaulieu had intended to break down, but was prevented by the quick approach of the French general. It was protected, however, by so numerous an artillery, that

Bonaparte separates the Austrian and Piedmontese armies.

April 22d, by a victory at Mondovi, he compels the king of Sardinia to yield at discretion, who receives peace from his dictation.

Bonaparte surmounts the natural ramparts of Italy.

Wise measures to keep up the spirit of his troops.

Battle at the bridge of Lodi.

---

h Campaigns of Bonaparte.   i See Livy, book xxi.
k Annual Register, 1796, p. 91.   l Ibid. p. 94, and Campaigns of Bonaparte.

CHAP. the Austrians did not imagine the French would be able to
LVIII. force a passage Bonaparte saw the tremendous danger, but
instantaneous in reasoning, he perceived the exact predicament
· 1796. in which he stood. The astonishing successes which sprang
from his direction of valorous enthusiasm, had been carried
to their present pitch by the opinion that his troops entertained
of themselves and their general; and failure in an attempt
however arduous, by lessening their conception of their resistless force, would damp their glowing animation, and diminish
the energy of their future efforts. In such circumstances the
most adventurous boldness was solid wisdom. Guided by
these reflections and sentiments, he determined to try every
effort, and to encounter every personal danger, in order to
carry a point on which such momentous interest appeared to
Signal ex- depend. Forming together the selectest bodies of his army, in
ploit and the midst of a most tremendous fire, he led them in person to the
victory of attack of the bridge. His presence, and that of all the chief
Bonaparte. officers in the French army, animated the soldiers to such a degree that they rushed forward with an impetuosity which nothing
was able to withstand. They crossed the bridge and assailed the
whole line of the Austrian artillery, which was instantly broken.
They fell with equal fury on the troops that advanced to the
charge, threw them into disorder, and put them to flight on
every side; and the victory was complete. Bonaparte having
thus defeated the principal army of the imperialists, after taking
Pavia, proceeded to Milan, and, with its capital, subdued the
greater part of Lombardy before the end of May. The Austrian army retreated towards the frontiers, and the imperialists being no
longer able to protect Italy, the pope and the king of Naples
sued for an armistice, which was granted to the king of Naples
on condition of his observing a neutrality, but the pope was required to pay a large sum of money, and also to deliver a great
number of pictures, busts, and statues. The victorious French
The required from the Italian princes, as a condition of peace, the
French delivery of the various monuments of art. Imitating the Romans
imitate the in rapacity as well as valour, they sent the pictures, statues, and
Romans in sculptures, to the national repositories. This spoliation of monu-
their rapa- ments, which bearing signal testimony to the taste and genius of
city as well the Italians, were regarded with national pride and veneration,
as valour. and which had escaped the irruptions of all former plunderers,
excited the most poignant regret and indignation among the
conquered, and was universally condemned and execrated by all
civilized nations.[m]

m In this part of his narrative, the author of Otridge's Annual Register
makes the following observations : "To deprive the poor Italians of objects
so long endeared to them by habit and possession, seemed an act of tyranny exercised upon the vanquished in the wantonness of power. Those objects had been respected by all parties, in the vicissitude of those events

Wherever Bonaparte carried his victorious arms, as soon as he had effected conquest, and exacted the contributions to which, as a conqueror, he deemed his efforts entitled, he endeavoured to mingle conciliation,[n] especially in his treatment of the lower classes. The commons, who were by no means indisposed towards the French republicanism, which promised protection against aristocratical domination and tyranny, he treated with the greatest mildness, professing that he had entered Italy to vindicate their rights, and to promote their happiness. But the irreligious and democratical spirit of the French revolution, excited his army to express and manifest the most contemptuous irreverence towards the priests, whom they represented as impostors; and detestation against the nobles, whom they painted as oppressors. These two orders were no less incensed against the French, whom they regarded with equal abhorrence and dread, as the destroyers of religion, and the levellers of the privileged orders. As they still retained a considerable influence, they endeavoured to employ it in inciting the commonalty against the republicans. A conspiracy was formed for a general insurrection, and commotions were prevalent throughout Lombardy: Pavia was intended to be the principal scene of the plot: but the active vigilance of Bonaparte discovered the designs before they were ripe for execution, and his force soon crushed their machinations: he ordered the chief conspirators, to be shot, and the others to find two hundred hostages for their peaceable behaviour in future. Thither, for the same reason, he also sent the nobles and priests of the insurgent districts, and denounced the same punishment against all who should afterwards be found instigating insurrection. He next issued a proclamation, declaring, that those who did not lay down their arms within twenty-four hours, and take an oath of obedience to the French republic, should be treated as rebels, and their houses committed to the flames. Having employed these effectual means to crush insurrection, Bonaparte was enabled to return to conciliatory efforts. He with great activity and success endeavoured to attach Italian partisans to the French cause. Besides the commonalty, who rejoiced at the idea of the freedom proffered by the French, Bonaparte gained great numbers of another class. The literary men of Italy were, as in France, with very few exceptions, inimical to the existing orders, and eager for changes under

CHAP.
LVIII.

1796.
Bonaparte mingles conciliatory policy, especially towards the populace.

Conspiracies at the instance of the nobles and clergy,

are disconcerted,

and punished.

Bonaparte gains to his interest the men of genius and literature,

that had so frequently subjected the places that contained them to different masters: the French were the first who had conceived the idea of seizing them as a matter of mere property. Herein they were accused of consulting their vanity rather than their taste for the fine arts. The Romans in their triumphant periods, had plundered the Greeks of all the master pieces they could find in their country. This appeared to the French a precedent fit for their imitation, and a sanction for robbing the Italians of what they esteem the most valuable part of their property, and the most honourable proof they still retained of their former superiority in those departments of genius.   n See Annual Register, 1796, p. 97. ·

CHAP. which they hoped to attain higher power and importance than
LVIII. they possessed under the clergy and nobles. Bonaparte read-
        ily saw that they might be rendered very useful instruments in
1796.   directing public opinion as long as insinuation and persuasion
        should be necessary or expedient ; and that votaries of physical
        studies might be employed in promoting the productiveness of
and endea- the new conquests. So far did Bonaparte apply conciliation,
vours to
bring eve- as to court those who would readily join against the possessors
ry kind of of property; and so far did he patronize literature and philo-
talent into sophy, as to make them labouring tools for his accommodation,
efficient emolument, and aggrandizement. His soldiers pretending to
action.   HONOUR, he merely *used ;* they were a different kind of tools,
        which he never failed to employ, when conciliation, literary
        patronage, or any other persuasives, would not suit his pur-
        pose.
He re-   Mantua only, of the Austrian dominions. remained in the
sumes mi-
litary oper- possession of the emperor. Bonaparte, not having a sufficient
ations :   train of artillery to reduce that strong fortress immediately by
marches   storm, resolved to pursue the Austrian army. The broken for-
from Italy ces of the Germans had, in their retreat, taken refuge in the
towards   Venetian territory ; and thither they were closely pursued by
Germany.   the French. Bonaparte published an address to the govern-
        ment of Venice, assuring them, that, in following the enemies
        of France into the Venetian territories, he would observe the
        strictest discipline, and treat the inhabitants with all the amity
        and consideration that were due to the ancient friendship sub-
        sisting between the two nations.   Meanwhile, the Austrians
        took possession of Peschiera, by the connivance[o] of the Vene-
        tians, to whom that town belonged. Here Beaulieu hoped to
        be able to make a stand, till succours should arrive from Ger-
        many. Bonaparte, desirous to drive him from Italy, or to com-
        pel him to surrender, advanced to that town, intending to cut
        off his retreat to the Tyrol by the eastern side of the lake of
        Garda. On the 30th of May, several divisions of the French
        approached the bridge of Borghetto, by which Bonaparte pro-
        posed to effect a passage over the Mincio, and surround Beau-
        lieu's army. The Austrians employed the utmost efforts to de-
        fend the bridge; but the French crossed it after a warm action;
        —and the German general, perceiving their intent, withdrew
        in haste from his position at Peschiera, and retired with the ut-
        most expedition to the river Adige, which, having passed, he
        broke down all the bridges to prevent the French from contin-
        uing the pursuit, and by these means he secured his retreat to
        Tyrol. The Venetians had given refuge to the brother of the
        late king of France, who was called by the royalists Louis
        XVIII. : but, anxious to prevent or avert the displeasure of the
        French republic, they directed Louis to quit the Venetian ter-
        ritories. Bonaparte, on the 3d of June, took possession of the

        o See Annual Register for 1796, p. 98.

city of Verona, the late residence of the French prince, and
continued his progress. The emperor finding the victorious
republicans advancing from Italy to Germany, gave the command of his troops to marshal Wurmser, who having collected
a powerful force, marched to encounter Bonaparte. The Aus- Wurmser
trian troops contained the flower of the emperor's army, which takes the
far exceeded the conception of the enemy, and inspired both field with
a fresh ar-
the emperor and his ally with hopes of retrieving the fortune of my of Aus-
the campaign. Bonaparte had found it necessary to divide his trians:
troops,. in order to secure the conquered territory, and the
situation of the French at this period was extremely critical:
they had subdued an extensive range of country, to preserve
which they had been obliged to detach considerable numbers
from their main body. The remains of Beaulieu's army and
the re-enforcements which arrived with marshal Wurmser,
composed a much more formidable strength than that which
Bonaparte commanded; but the confidence which he placed in
the valour of his soldiers, and that which they reposed in his
superior genius and skill, were more than adequate to numbers and even disciplined valour. The Austrians had secured
the passes into the Tyrol, by works which extended from the
lake of Garda to the river Adige. Here Wurmser posted himself in the end of June; But the French generals Massena and
Joubert, at the head of a select body, broke into his lines, by
turning his right and left: they seized his baggage and stand- is repul-
ing camp, and forced him to retreat with the utmost precipita- sed by the
tion. Bonaparte, meanwhile, had crushed a new insurrection French
in Lago, an ecclesiastical town; and, from the many fortresses
which he captured, having collected a formidable train of artillery he determined to invest Mantua. About the middle of Bonaparte
July, he commenced a regular siege, and pressed on his opera- invests
tions with incessant vigour; he summoned the town to sur- Mantua.
render, but without effect. Having erected batteries for firing
red-hot balls, he cannonaded the city, and reduced several parts
of it to ashes. Meanwhile Wurmser, having received very
great re-inforcementss, resolved to repair his recent defeat by Wurmser
raising the siege of Mantua. Having attacked the divisions of approach-
the French that were placed near lake Garda, he dislodged es to its
relief.
them from their positions; and, with a very numerous and
formidable host, advanced between them and Bonaparte's army. He marched towards Mantua, while another division of
Austrians also approached. Bonaparte, aware that the force
which he now had with him was unequal to a conflict with the
combined armies of Austria, resolved to encounter them separately. This purpose, however, he could not execute without
abandoning the siege of Mantua, which he most reluctantly
raised on the 30th of July. Several engagements were fought
between the Austrians and the French, in which the republicans were generally superior, though without a decisive event.

CHAP.
LVIII.

1796.

Bonaparte is sur-. rounded at Lonado; he extri- cates him-. self by a stratagem, and indu- ces much superior army to sunrender

Successive victories of Bona- parte.

Bonaparte, in examining one of his advanced posts, found him- self surrounded at Lonado by four thousand Austrians, while he had only twelve hundred. With ready presence of mind, he impressed the German commander with a belief that his whole army was at hand, under which notion that leader sur- rendered himself with his detachment. Escaped from this danger, the French general determined to bring the contest to a final issue ; but to cover his intentions, he feigned to be desi- rous of avoiding an engagement. Wurmser, imputing his con- duct to consciousness of inferior force, hastened to bring on a battle. On the 5th of August, while deceived by appearances, he was advancing the French army by one of its rapid move- ments, was formed into two divisions, the one of which receiv- ed the enemy in front, whilst the other, having doubled the right wing during the night, attacked them in the rear. Wurmser, hemmed in by this dexterous stratagem, made, with his vete- ran host, a most gallant and obstinate resistance ; but the impe- tuous valour of the republicans bore down all before them, and obtained a still greater victory than even at the battle of Lodi. The losses of the Austrians amounted to seventy pieces of can- non, all the carriages belonging to their army, more than twelve thousand prisoners, and six thousand slain. The Austrian go- vernment, still unbroken by continued disaster, raised numer- ous levies, and Wurmser once more made head against Bona- parte in the field. A succession of conflicts ensued, in which the French, without gaining any signal victory, were greatly superior. At length, in the month of November, a battle was fought at Arcola, in which, after a vicissitude of attacks and re- pulses, during the fifteenth and sixteenth, and a very obstinate and doubtful contest, the French finally gained a signal victo- ry,[p] and the Austrians did not again encounter the French in the field, during the present campaign. This event was complete- ly decisive : the troops, that were beaten, were chiefly vete- rans; those who came with Wurmser, were deemed the flower of the Austrian army, that had so obstinately contended with the best troops of France upon the Rhine. Wurmser himself was reputed an officer second to no one in the imperial service, or indeed in Europe, for valour, skill, and experience, and was deemed the last hope of Austria for the recovery of Italy. The Austrians, their allies, and all the friends of the cause in which they were engaged, had conceived the most sanguine expecta- tions from the military talents of Wurmser, and the force by which they were supported. Both he and his soldiers did all that courage, discipline, and skill could perform, but against the impetuous enthusiasm of the republican forces, and the overpowering genius of Bonaparte, their efforts were unavail- ing. Throughout the whole course of this arduous trial, the powers and exertions of this leader astonished both friends and

Decisive victory at Arcola ;

p See Campaigns of Bonaparte.

foes. Surrounded by difficulties of every sort, he acted with a CHAP. clearness of penetration that foresaw and obviated them all : he LVIII. removed impediments as fast as they arose, and took his mea- sures with so much prudence and sagacity, that he could not 1796. be charged with having committed one false step. His body and his mind appeared reciprocally calculated for the support of each other : both were incessantly employed, the one in plan- ning, and the other in personally forwarding every design that was conceived.[q]

Of Austrian Italy, Mantua still remained unsubdued; thither the republican force was now bent, and the imperialists once more collected a formidable army for its preservation. Various conflicts ensued, in which Austrian firmness and intrepidity made a most vigorous stand against the impetuous valour and enthusiastic animation of the republicans. At length they again at Rivoli. encountered each other in a pitched battle, at Rivoli; the impe- rialists in valour and conduct equalled any of their former most heroic efforts, and once appeared to be on the eve of victory; when Bonaparte, with the usual rapidity of his genius and ener- gy, made an instantaneous movement, which surrounded a great body of Austrians, entirely defeated them, and facilitated the dis- comfiture of their principal strength : by this disaster all hopes of defending Mantua were vanished; and the garrison was obliged Capture of to capitulate. Mantua.

While the contest appeared doubtful between the imperial Commo- and republican generals, the Italian clergy, hoping the Aus- tions at trians might prove successful, again renewed their machina- Rome. tions to incite the people to insurrection; but the victories of the French soon suppressed these attempts throughout the north of Italy. In Rome the anti-gallican party was much more vio- lent and open in its proceedings than in other Italian districts. The pope, having heard that the siege of Mantua was raised, without waiting either to examine the reasons, or observe the consequences of this movement, sent a legate to retake posses- sion of Ferrara, in direct opposition to the convention con- cluded with Bonaparte, and to the wishes of the people, who were noted for dislike to the Roman government. Priests and monks that swarm in the seat of ancient heroism, deviated from their habitual indolence, and were incessantly active in stimu- lating their votaries to outrage against the French republicans who happened to be in the papal dominions. Intelligence soon arriving of the victories of the French general, repressed these instigators of discord; but Bonaparte was too much occupied in pursuing the Austrians for the present to attend to the coercion of these puny opponents.

As the season was too far advanced for continuing warfare among the mountains of the Tyrol, Bonaparte now directed his attention to the internal settlement of Italy, and to the punish-

See Otridge's Annual Register for 1796, p. 108.

CHAP. ment of revolt. The power of the French-republic, over all
LVIII. Italy, now deserted by the Austrians, was so extensive and ir-
‿‿‿ resistible, as to render opposition, however just, totally inexpe-
1796. dient; and not only useless, but ruinous. The secular princes
of Italy had faithfully adhered to the treaties which they had
concluded with the French republic, and were paying the sti-
Conduct of pulated contributions. The court of Rome alone was guilty of
the papal the most unwise violation of its engagements. In order more
govern- effectually to inflame the minds of the people against the re-
ment. publicans,[r] the pope and his priests, his only counsellors, had
recourse to the stale artifices and despicable tricks known by
the name of *pious frauds.* They pretended the intervention of
heaven, and positively asserted the performance of miracles,
in many of the churches, in vindication of the catholic faith
and the papal supremacy, outraged and menaced by the conduct
of the French. The streets were filled with processions of
saints and images, who were to arrest the progress of the French
general. He who was fit to have combatted a Scipio or a
Cæsar, was to be overcome by friars; he whom the Austrian
eagle could not withstand, was to yield to a Romish owl. This
ridiculous mummery, however, had its effect; though eventually very pernicious to its contrivers. In the papal metropolis
there is, as among all Italians, a considerable portion of sagacity; and among the higher ranks of the laity, no small
share of literature; yet, those who could most easily detect
and expose these impostures, would not find it safe to interfere
in baulking their clerical promoters. On such occasions, therefore, gentlemen and liberal scholars, including some of the clergy themselves, carefully avoided attempts to counteract decep-
The pope tion that was practised on credulity. At present the zeal of all
attempts to classes and conditions was kindled; the populace was impelled
excite war to the utmost fury against all who did not readily believe the
against Bo- asserted miracles, or presumed to trust more to reason and their
naparte. senses than to the infallibility of the church; manifested the most
ardent eagerness to go to war against the republicans and infidels of France; and, like the mahometan bigots, they trusted
to supernatural assistance in combating the enemy; a very
great majority joined in preparations for war. The French envoy at Rome was active in endeavouring to convince the administration, that by perseverance in hostility they would expose
themselves and their country to very great evils, which they
might avoid merely by adhering to the terms of pacification: but
his admonitions and remonstrances were altogether unavailing.
The Bonaparte desirous of conciliating the affections of the Italians,
French ge- ardently wished for a pacification with the head of the Romish
neral church, a respectful treatment of whom, he was conscious,
makes con-
ciliatory would be highly gratifying to all the Roman catholic states and
overtures. people. Resolved, therefore, to forbear coercive measures, he

wrote a letter to cardinal Mattœi, prime minister to his holiness, requesting him to prevail on the pope to recommend pacific negotiations, in order to prevent the march of the French armies into his territories, and to represent to him the inutility of arming his subjects against men who had overcome so many formidable enemies. To this letter no answer was made until after the battle of Arcola had finally crushed all hopes that the Austrians could save Italy from the French. The pope instructed his minister in his reply,[i] to state to the general the anxiety of his holiness to remedy the disorders which had so long distracted France, and to restore amity between France and the Roman see: the French, elated with the success of their arms, had made requisitions incompatible with the dictates of his conscience, and subversive of all christian and moral principles; grieved at such intolerable demands, he had implored the assistance of heaven to direct him how to act in so difficult a situation: doubtless he was inspired on this occasion by that holy spirit which had animated the primitive martyrs in the cause for which they suffered: having laboured in vain to bring the directory to a more equitable way of thinking, he thought it necessary to resist them by open force: the death that awaited men in battle was the commencement of eternal life and happiness to the righteous, and everlasting misery to the wicked: though infidels and pretended philosophers ridicule the idea of assistance from heaven, yet, if providence were pleased to interpose, the French would contend in vain against the power of the Almighty: if the French were desirous of peace, the Roman see desired it still more, if attainable on conscientious and equitable terms. Such a letter, addressed to a victorious general at the head of a resistless army, that little regarded spiritual admonitions, was not likely to interrupt the republican career, or change their resolution. The pope, meanwhile, persisted in preparing for war, and endeavoured to interest those powers, to whose predecessors in former times, the will of a pontiff served for a law. But now, both circumstances and sentiments were totally changed: even the court of Spain, heretofore the chief prop of papal domination, sent an answer, recommending to the pope the demission of all temporal power, and the confinement of future proceedings to the exercise of the heavenly virtues.[k]

i Otridge's Annual Register, 1797.

k The Spanish minister, denominated the prince of peace, replied to the pope's nuncio soliciting the interference of Spain, to the following effect: " That the conduct of the court of Rome respecting the French, was temporizing and insincere; and that those who were intrusted with the administration of its political concerns, had, by their imprudence and erroneous management, brought them into so critical a situation, that it seemed adviseable for the preservation of the personal safety of the pope, that he should resign his temporal possessions, in order to secure the rights of the

CHAP. LVIII.

1796.

Bonaparte invades the Roman territories,

and compels the pontiff to sue for peace.

Amount of the French acquisitions in Italy in this campaign.

Bonaparte, finding no prospect of overawing his holiness to submission, resolved to recommence actual hostilities. Publishing a manifesto, he charged the pontiff with a breach of the convention; and turned against the papal effeminate Romans, genius, courage, and conduct, which the disciplined heroism of republican Rome, under her most consummate generals, would have found arduous difficulty in resisting. Bonaparte was too artful, wantonly to shock the religious prejudices of a country which he wished to govern: having entered the Roman territories, he issued a proclamation, assuring the inhabitants that he would protect religion as well as property, and maintain the public peace: he warned them to abstain from all acts of enmity, which would certainly draw down upon them vengeance and all the horrors of war: every town and village that sounded the tocsin on the approach of the French, was threatened with instant destruction: and it was denounced that every district where a Frenchman was assassinated, should be declared hostile, and subjected to heavy contributions. The papal army having ventured to encounter the republicans, was completely defeated. Bonaparte compelled the pontiff to sue for peace,[1] to cede part of his territories, and to pay a sum that would amount to thirty millions of French livres, on account of the last rupture, besides fulfilling the conditions of the armistice in the preceding summer.

Thus, in one campaign, Bonaparte overcame four successive armies of the bravest and best disciplined troops, much more numerous than his own, commanded by skilful and able generals: extended the territories of the French republic from the gulf of Genoa to the Adriatic Sea, from the Alps to the Tiber, and her commanding influence over all Italy, where his versatile dexterity seemed to secure what his military abilities had acquired. Those who estimate conquerors merely by their warlike achievements, without considering either *the justness of the cause, or the wisdom of the pursuit,* must regard Bonaparte with high honour. He undoubtedly displayed all that combination of intellectual and active powers which rendered Alaric, Genseric, and Attila, with their respective Goths, Vandals, and Huns, irresistibly successful in subjugation and plunder. But in one instrument of iniquitous acquisition, the Corsican surpassed the northern invaders: they simply employed force, whereas he used artifice and deceit, as well as violence and rapine. But exceeding Attila, or any of his co-operators, in craft and versatility, he resembled them in sentiment. With all the in-

church, and to prove his disinterestedness, and the fervour of his piety, by an example that would prove so edifying to all the christian world."—See Otridge's Annual Register, for 1797, p. 12.

1 This peace was not concluded till February 1797; but being part of a series of military and political conduct belonging to 1796, to preserve the unity of action unbroken, I have included in the narrative of the present year.

trepidity, resolution, and courage of a valiant combatant, he was totally deficient in elevation of mind, and bore no resemblance to the grandeur of a Roman, much less the Macedonian conqueror. Besides, Bonaparte found auxiliaries to which the lofty soul of an Alexander would have disdained to resort: he successfully employed money,[m] as well as arms, in promoting his victories. In this his most difficult campaign, Bonaparte proved himself an able, energetic, and dexterous adventurer; but in no instance manifested either the magnanimous hero, or the wise statesman.

In Germany also the French generals displayed distinguished ability, and made very forcible exertions, though with less permanent success. Jourdain entered the empire by the Upper Rhine, while Moreau marched through Suabia. Charles of Austria, brother to the emperor, a young prince of heroic courage and great military enterprise, at this time headed the Austrian army. At the village of Ettingen, the gallant prince encountered the republican general on the 8th of July, and, after a very bloody battle, was obliged to give way to the impetuous valour of the French. Moreau was now master of Suabia, was penetrating into Bavaria; Jourdain had entered Franconia, and from the confines of Bohemia to the mountains of Tyrol the advancing chain of the republican armies extended, menacing the invasion of Austria itself, and the capture of the Austrian capital. The duke of Wirtemberg, and the other princes of the empire who had still remained in alliance with their imperial head, were now obliged to sue for peace, and to receive it from the victorious republicans on such terms as they chose to grant. The emperor, thus deserted by his auxiliaries, was in dreadful consternation; but for the present the efforts of his gallant brother relieved him from his fears. On entering the empire, the French forces had found the commonality in general favourable to principles and projects which they conceived would reduce their domineering tyrants; but the rapacity of their exactions,[n] though in some degree necessary for the supply of the troops, yet oppressive and injurious to the forced

CHAP.
LVIII.

1796.

Germany invaded by Jourdain and Moreau.
The archduke Charles.
Successive battles with Jourdain.
Danger of the empire.

m I am assured by gentlemen who resided at Vienna during a great part of the war, that it was generally thought there that many of the Austrian officers were bribed.

n Their levies of money and other requisitions, excited universal alarm. The duke of Wirtemberg had been assessed four millions: the circle of Suabia, twelve millions, besides to furnish eight thousand horses, five thousand oxen, one hundred and fifty thousand quintals of corn, one hundred thousand sacks of oats, a proportionable quantity of hay, and one hundred thousand pair of shoes: eight millions were demanded from the circle of Franconia, with a very large supply of horses: great sums were also required from the cities of Franckfort, Wurtzburg, Bamberg, and Nuremberg, together with an immense quantity of other articles, for the subsistence and clothing of the French troops.—See Otridge's Annual Register for 1796, p. 136.

CHAP.
LVIII.

1796.
is warded
off by the
valour of
the arch-
duke,
who com-
pels Jour-
dain to
evacuate
Germany.
Progress
and situa-
tion of
Moreau.
Masterly
and suc-
cessful
retreat in
the face of
the Ger-
man host.

contributors, changed their attachment into hatred. After his adverse conflict with Moreau, the archduke Charles had lost no time in recruiting, collecting, and rallying his forces. Jourdain's army was now advanced near Ratisbon : prince Charles, leaving a strong body to watch the motions of Moreau, repaired with his main army against Jourdain ; being daily reinforced, he after several bloody, but partial conflicts, on the 28th of August, engaged Jourdain in a pitched battle, and compelled him to retreat with considerable loss. The Austrians continued to molest him as he fell back towards the Rhine : Jourdain faced, and sometimes repulsed his pursuers, and at last arriving at the Rhine, repassed the river.

Moreau, deprived of the co-operation of Jourdain, was now exposed to the whole force of the German armies, and found it necessary to retreat. A superior host assailed his rear, and a large detachment harassed his front, while the peasants rose in every direction and intercepted his convoys : but Moreau repulsed his pursuers, defeated all the bodies that opposed his march ; with masterly skill and rapid execution, changing his front according to the direction of the enemy, he by offensive operations secured his defence. Latour, a very able and enterprising general, commanded the pursuers, and notwithstanding reiterated defeats, still continued to harass the French rear. Moreau now advanced to the middle of Suabia, but still at a great distance from the Rhine, he perceived that he must again resist a general action, and unless he again defeated the Austrians who were nearest, they speedily would be joined by such numerous re-enforcements, that all resistance would be vain. On the 2d of October, a select body attacked the right wing of the Austrian army posted between Biberach and the Danube: after routing this division, they advanced upon the centre, which was at the same time vigorously assailed by the centre of Moreau's army. The contest lasted six hours, and was extremely bloody on both sides : at length the Austrians gave way, and were so completely defeated, that they retired with the utmost expedition to a great distance from the field of battle. Their loss amounted to near five thousand men killed and taken, twenty pieces of cannon, several standards and a quantity of ammunition.[o] Still, however, there was a strong army between Moreau and the Rhine. He proceeded with caution and firmness through every impediment, and driving the Austrians before him, crossed the Danube. On the 9th, his army entered a defile called the Valley of Hell, from the frightful appearance of the rocks and mountains that hang over it on each side, and in many places are hardly the space of thirty feet asunder. At the outlet of the valley, a powerful body of Austrians were stationed ; behind was Latour, who having again collected a considerable army, pressed the French rear ; and every inlet

o See Otridge's Annual Register for 1796, p. 140.

on each side was lined with troops ready to assail the flanks of CHAP.
the republicans as they passed. To guard against this multi- LVIII.
plicity of dangers, Moreau disposed of his right and left in such
a manner, that the rear of them protected his entrance into that 1796.
valley, by facing the forces under Latour; and the van, by advancing upon Navaudorf and Petrasch on their respective wings,
obliged them to divide their strength and attention. Having
made these dispositions, the French marched in a compact order
along the valley. The enemy on the rear were repulse; and, on
the right and left, did not venture an attack of troops so prepared
for terrible resistance; the Austrians stationed in front, durst not
attempt their molestation. Moreau passed the defile, marched
on to Friburg, and brought his army in safety to the Rhine, by as
masterly a retreat as any recorded in the annals of history.[p]

During this campaign, the attention of the French was so much Britain sig-
directed to land efforts, that Britain encountered little opposition nally suc-
in her maritime exertions, and those military enterprises which cessful
depended chiefly on naval co-operation. A considerable arma- fights
ment had been fitted out under general Abercrombie, to prose- alone.
cute our successes in the West Indies. In April, leaving Bar- West In-
badoes, he sailed to the valuable settlement of Demarara, belong- dies.
ing to the Dutch, which speedily surrendered to the British arms. General
In the month of May, he recovered the island of St. Lucie, and, Abercrom-
soon after quelled the insurrections which had been excited by St. Lucie,
the noted Victor Hughes. The British still maintained their and quells
conquests in the very valuable island of St Domingo : the French insurrec-
had entirely abandoned that settlement; the people of colour, tion in the
and the negroes possessed the interior country, whilst the other islands.
English occupied various parts of the coast. But here they had
to encounter an enemy much more dreadful than the French Progress in
forces, in a pestilence so fatally known by the name of the yellow St. Do-
fever; which, having raged with most destructive violence in all mingo.
tropical latitudes of the west, and extended to the northern climate of Philadelphia and even New-York, had been still more
generally mortal in St. Domingo.

In Saldanna bay, a Dutch fleet of seven sail of the line, which Capture of
had sailed in hopes of retaking the Cape, was captured by ad- Dutch
miral Elphinstone. The Dutch settlements in the east were ships and
reduced by our fleets; among the rest the island of Ceylon, one settle-
of the most important possessions in European India. In the ments.
Mediterranean, the Corsicans showing themselves inclined to
return to their connection with the French republicans, Britain
judged it expedient to relinquish a settlement, the expense and
trouble of protecting which so totally overbalanced the advantages
of the possession. At the close of the year, the French, encouraged by reports of disaffection in Ireland, and supposing

p The impartial historian cannot even except Xenophon's retreat with the
ten thousand, since, though the space was much more extensive, the opponents were only desultory marauders, and not regular troops; the opposition was only occasional, not constant and systematic.

our navy would be less vigilant in the winter season, made an attempt with thirteen ships of the line, and a large body of troops, to make a descent at Bantry Bay; but the stormy season dispersing the armament, the commander in chief, who had arrived at his place of destination, returned to Brest with the loss of a ship of the line, and two frigates. Thus ended a campaign in which Britain, acting on her own element, was uniformly successful; and without any very brilliant or difficult enterprise, made most important acquisitions. Her ally, stimulated by the British spirit, and assisted by British money, made extraordinary efforts, acquired partial advantage and signal honour; but, on the whole, incurred severe, extensive, and multiplied disasters and losses; her enemies, inefficient by sea, by land displayed military ability, attained splendid success. and warlike glory, which have been rarely equalled, and never surpassed, in the annals of history.

Birth of a princess, heir to the prince of Wales. General election.

Among the domestic events of this year, was the birth of a princess, at present heir to the prince of Wales, and who appears likely to give to England, in the next age, a female reign. During this summer there was a general election, but with much less contention than on any former occasion throughout the eighteenth century.

British government proposes to send an ambassador to Paris to negotiate a peace.

British ministers had during the recess, applied to the Danish ambassador at London, to transmit, through the Danish envoy at Paris, a declaration, stating, his Britannic majesty's desire to conclude a peace, "on just and honourable conditions, and de- "manding the necessary passports for a person of confidence, " whom his majesty would send to Paris, with a commission to " discuss with the government there all the measures the most " proper to produce so desirable an end." The Danish minister having conveyed to the directory this manifestation of the British intentions, it was replied by the French government, " that the

France agrees to receive an ambassador from Britain and lord Malmsbury is sent.

" executive government would not receive or answer, from the " enemies of the republic, any overture transmitted through an " intermediate channel; but that, if England would send persons " furnished with full powers and official papers, they might, upon " the frontier, demand the passports necessary for proceeding to " Paris." The court of London having applied for passports, nominated Lord Malmsbury as ambassador to Paris, who accordingly set out the beginning of October.

CHAP. LIX.

Meeting of the new parliament—the king-announces pacific intentions.—
Difference of opinion on this subject between ministers and the votaries
of Burke.—Burke's publication against a peace with regicides.—Earl
Fitzwilliam reprobates negotiation, unless monarchy be restored.—
Ministers declare security attainable without the restoration of monarchy ·-Opposition declare they do not believe the ministers really to
desire peace.—Apprehensions of an invasion.—Powerful and extensive
preparations for defence.—Law for establishing a militia in Scotland.—
Army, navy, and pecuniary supplies.—Imposts begin to be severely felt
by the lower and middling classes.—Negotiation of Lord Malmsbury at
Paris—basis proposed by Britain, reciprocal restitution ·France will not
relinquish Belgium.—Abruptly requires the *ultimatum* of the ambassador -which he is not empowered immediately to deliver he is ordered
to quit France —British manifesto, charging France with the rupture.—
Splendid eloquence of Mr. Pitt on this subject —Mr. Erskine's view of
the causes and consequences of the war.—Reasoning of Mr. Fox —Motions for the removal of ministers—are negatived by a great majorities —
Gloomy aspect of affairs at the commencement of 1797—enormous increase of national debt—advances and state of the bank - correspondence
between the bank and ministers—alarms for public credit—fears of an
invasion—unusual demand for specie—rapid decrease of cash in the bank
—public agitation—application to government—order of council to suspend payments in cash—the subject is discussed in parliament—opposition declare the bank to be in a state of insolvency from the infatuation
of ministers—ministers allege, and the bank proves, its property far to
exceed its engagements—bill to enable the bank to pay in notes instead
of cash—Complaints of the sailors—artifices of disaffected agitators—
alarming mutiny at Portsmouth is quieted by lord Howe —An augmentation of pay is granted by parliament —More outrageous and dangerous
mutiny at the Nore—Parker—the insurgents block up the Thames—
alarm in London ·the sailors at length return to obedience.—Parker tried
and executed.—Law rendering the instigation of mutiny capital felony —
State of Ireland —Lord Moira's proposed address to his majesty on the
subject—negatived.—Motion for parliamentary reform, and inquiries into
the state of the nation—negatived.—Marriage of the prince of Wirtemberg to the princess royal of England—portion bestowed on her highness.
Parliament rises.

THE new parliament met on the 6th of October; and
his majesty informed the houses that he had omitted no endeavours for setting on foot negotiations to restore peace to Europe,
and to secure for the future the general tranquillity. But nothing (he observed) could contribute so effectually to this end,
as to manifest that we possessed both the determination and
resources to oppose, with increased activity and energy, the
farther efforts with which we might have to contend.[q] On the

CHAP.
LIX.

1796.
Meeting of
the new
parlia-
ment: the
king an-
nounces
pacific in-
tentions.

q King's Speech, State Papers, October 6th, 1796.

CHAP. general propriety of a negotiation, there was a division of
LIX. opinion between those who had promoted the war and support-
~~~~~ ed its continuance. We have already stated that Mr. Burke,
1796. in inculcating hostility against revolutionary France, chose dif-
Difference ferent grounds from ministers. In the progress of the war he
of opinion had adhered to his original opinion, that the restoration of
on this sub-
ject be-
monarchy and the ancient orders, under certain modifications,
tween mi- ought to be the sole and avowed purpose of the war; and that
nisters and no peace could be secure until that object was effected. Under
the vota- that impression, he wrote his " Thoughts on a Regicide
ries of
Burke.
"Peace." intended to prove, that the system of France was
Burke's impious, enormously wicked, and destructive to all who were
puulica- within its sphere: we must either conquer the revolution, or
tion against be destroyed ourselves: peace would enable it to operate ra-
a peace pidly to our ruin: let us, therefore, avoid peace. Earl Fitz-
with regi-
cides.
william, the intimate friend of Mr. Burke, in a considerable
Earl Fitz degree adopted these opinions, and reprobated negotiation.
william re- To restore order (he said;) to defend the civilized states of
probates Europe against the danger that threatened them; to protect
negotia- persons and property from a fatal devastation, and suppress
tion.unless
monarchy
the tendency of innovating and pernicious doctrines; were the
be restor- ostensible objects of the war, and upon these principles they
ed. had supported its continuance. If it were wise to negotiate
now, the same wisdom ought to have been manifested four
years ago; for the causes of war, which then existed, still
operated with equal force, and proved the necessity of perse-
Ministers, verance in hostility to the French system. Ministers declared
declare se- they had never stated, that the existence of a republic in
curity at-
tainable
France was an insurmountable bar to peace: they had expres-
without sed what they still believed, that the best issue to the contest
the restor would be, the re-establishment of monarchy in France; yet
ation of they had never pledged themselves, much less the parliament,
monarchy, to an opinion so extravagant, as that without the attainment of
this object there was no hope or possibility of peace. They
were always resolved to seek peace with France, whenever it
was attainable with SECURITY. The French government now
appeared to have some tendency to moderation; our own country was very much improved in point of tranquillity, which
might be chiefly imputed to the wise laws against sedition and
treason that had been enacted in the last session. Those who
had always reprobated the war, expressed their hearty appro-
Opposition bation of the declared intention to negotiate. Judging how-
declare
they do not
ever (they said) from the conduct, and not from the profession
believe the of ministers they did not give them full credit for sincerity.[r]
ministers Mr. Pitt strongly represented, that the surest way of obtain-,
really to ing favourable conditions of peace, was to be prepared for war;
desire
peace.
and exhibited a very flattering account of the flourishing con-

r See speeches of Messrs, Fox and Sheridan, Parliamentary Debates,
October 1796.

dition of the country, and the extent of her resources, which were CHAP.
increased beyond all former calculations or hopes. LIX.

A clause in his majesty's speech had declared the king's apprehension that the enemy were preparing an invasion upon this 1796.
island. Mr. Pitt very early in the session recommended adop- Apprehen-
tion of measures for repelling the designed, as well as future sions of an
attempts. For this purpose he formed a plan for levying fif- invasion.
teen thousand men from the different parishes for the sea service, and another for recruiting the regular regiments. In the
projected levies for the land service, he considered two objects;
first, the means of calling together a land force sufficient of itself
to repel an invasion, even independently of our naval armaments; and, secondly, to adopt such measures in the levies as
should not materially interfere with the agriculture, commerce,
and general industry of this kingdom. The primary object was Powerful
to raise, and gradually train, such a force as might in a short and exten-
time be fit for service. For this purpose he proposed a supple- parations
mentary levy of militia, to be grafted on the old establishment, of for de-
the number of sixty thousand men; not to be immediately cal- fence.
led out, but to be enrolled, officered, and completely trained, so
as to be fit for service at a moment of danger. He also proposed to provide a considerable force of irregular cavalry, to be levied in the following manner; every person who kept ten horses,
should be obliged to provide one horse, and one horseman, to
to serve in a corps of militia; and those who kept more than ten,
should provide in the same proportion; and that those that kept
fewer than ten, were to form themselves into classes, in which it
should be decided by ballot who, at the common expense, should
provide the horse and the horseman; these troops were to be
furnished with uniform and accoutrements, arranged into corps,
and put under proper officers. The whole number of cavalry
proposed to be raised by this mode was twenty thousand: the
other supplementary troops amounted to seventy-five thousand
men. Among the means proposed for internal defence, a bill Law for
was introduced by Mr. Dundas, for raising and embodying a establish-
militia in Scotland, and an act for that purpose was passed with- ing a mili-
out opposition. The whole land forces of the country, intended land.
for the year 1797, were to consist of one hundred and ninety-five Army, na-
thousand, six hundred and ninety-four; and the navy was to vy, and
amount to a hundred and twenty thousand men. The pecuniary pecuniary
supplies of the year were thirty one millions borrowed, besides supplies.
the annual income.

Mr. Pitt still continued to display great financial skill in ex- Imposts
empting the very lower class from the severest pressure of the begin to be
new taxes, though the principal part bore very heavily on the severely
comforts and accommodations of the middling ranks; the fresh felt by the
imposts were upon tea, coffee, spirits, sugars, and various other lower and
articles of daily and general consumption; upon assessed middling
taxes, postage, stage coaches, and canal navigation; and in the classes.

CHAP.
LIX.

1796.

Negotia-
tion of
lord
Malmsbu-
bury at
Paris.

Basis pro-
posed by
Britain re-
ciprocal
restitu-
tion.

minister's plans of finance, it began to be complained that the very high and opulent did not contribute so much more than the lower classes, as the proportion of their property would have admitted.

While preparations were making for carrying on the war, lord Malmsbury was at Paris conveying from his court professions of a desire to negotiate a peace. The French government, elated with the brilliant successes of the campaign, were far from relinquishing their determination to retain in their possession the whole of the left bank of the Rhine; this resolution they had intimated to Britain, and to it they were resolved to adhere. Lord Malmsbury arrived at Paris on the 22d of October. His first reception by the French government manifested a distrust of the sincerity of his employers: the negotiation was however opened by a proposition from lord Malmsbury for reciprocal restitution. Great Britain had made very valuable acquisitions, and had incurred no losses herself; seeking from war, not the possessions of her adversary, but the general security, she was willing to restore her own conquests, in lieu of the acquisitions which France had won from her allies, as a basis for a treaty: therefore Britain proposed a general principle of reciprocal restitution. The directory replied, that receiving the British Ambassador as the agent of Britain only, and not understanding him to have a commission to act for the allies of Britain, they could not now enter into the concerns of those powers: the mode which he proposed of an intermixture of other discussions with a treaty, they represented to be circuitous and dilatory; but to show their sincere and ardent desire of peace, if he procured the credentials from the other belligerant states, they would take into consideration such specific proposals as he might then make. To these observations they added an opinion, that the British court was insincere in its overture; that its purposes were to prevent other powers from negotiating a separate peace; and to facilitate the attainment of the supplies from the people of England, through a persuasion that the French refused an accommodation. To this assignation of motives which, whether true or fanciful, was irrelevant to the discussion, the British minister, with becoming dignity, forbore to reply: confining himself to the answer, he stated, that he had not been commissioned to enter upon a separate treaty; that Great Britain proposed to make in this transaction a common cause with her allies. The directory rejoined, that in a question of reciprocal restitution, the chief object of consideration was the relative condition of the respective parties. Of the original confederates, somewhere become the friends of France, and others observed a strict neutrality. The remaining allies of Britain were now weakened by their losses, and the desertion of their associates. France, it was insinuated, would not in a negotiation of terms forget the circumstances in which she was placed. Besides the assertions and replications con-

tained in official notes, conferences were carried on between lord
Malmsbury and De la Croix, the French minister.[s] In these
they respectively unfolded in more detailed statements the objects and resolutions of their employers.

CHAP.
LIX.

1796.

The Netherlands constituted one of the principal topics of
discourse. The British ambassador stated the restitution of
Belgium as an indispensable article from which his Britannic
majesty would not recede. From the outset indeed of the discussions, we find in his own letter, that he told the French
minister that he must entertain no hopes that his majesty would
ever consent to see the Netherlands a part of the French dominions. From the same official documents it appears, that
the French minister proposed several schemes of equivalent
for Belgium, but that lord Malmsbury considered himself as
bound by his instructions to admit no proposition by which
Belgium should continue annexed to France. On the other
hand, the French minister declared, that the republic was resolved not to relinquish Belgium. In the course of their conferences, lord Malmsbury delivered his opinions freely on certain
effects of the revolutionary system, which, extending to the
West Indies, influenced the conduct of some of the British
islands, and produced confusion and disorder; at length the
directory agreed to the general principle of compensation, but
required a specific description of the reciprocal restitutions
proposed by Britain. The British ambassador stated the terms
in contemplation to be, the restitution by France of her conquests from the emperor, the inclusion of Russia and Portugal
in the treaty, and the restoration of the stadholderian government in Holland. To these outlines, containing propositions
so very contrary to the declared views of the French government, De la Croix answered by requiring the whole of his final
demands, or, according to diplomatic language, his *ultimatum*,
to be delivered in twenty-four hours. To this peremptory requisition lord Malmsbury replied, that it precluded at once all
farther negotiation; that if they disapproved of his propositions, or refused to take them into consideration, they ought to
bring forward their own, that he might lay them before his sovereign. But he received no other answer than, that they
could listen to no terms inconsistent with the constitution, and
the engagements that were formed by the republic. They
farther signified to him, that since he was obliged to consult
the British ministry previously to all replies and communications, it evidently appeared that his powers were inadequate to
the conduct of a treaty; and if the British ministry were inclined to pacific measures and determined to treat on their present plan, farther communications might be as well forwarded
by an epistolary correspondence: his residence, therefore, in
Paris being totally unnecessary they ordered him to depart in

France
will not re-
linquish
Belgium;

abruptly
requires
the ultima-
tum of the
ambassa-
dor, which
he is not
immedi-
ately em-
powered to
deliver.

He is or-
dered to
quit
France.

s See State Papers, December 20th, 1796.

CHAP.   forty-eight hours.   This injunction was notified to him on
LIX.   the 20th of December; and thus terminated the first nego-
        tiation for peace between Great Britain and the French re-
, 1796. public.

British   The British ministers professed to consider the abrupt con-
manifesto,   clusion of these overtures as arising totally from France, and
charging   published a manifesto,[t] on the 27th of December, setting forth
France   the pacific dispositions of the British government, and the ma-
with the   lignant hostility of France. "The repeated endeavours of the
rupture.   " French government (this document states) to defeat this mis-
        " sion in its outset, and to break off the intercourse thus open-
        " ed, even before the first steps towards negotiation could be
        " taken ; the indecent and injurious language, employed with a
        " view to irritate ; the captious and frivolous objections raised
        " for the purpose of obstructing the progress of the discussion ;
        " all these have sufficiently appeared from the official papers
        " which passed on both sides, and which are known to all
        " Europe: the failure of the present negotiation arises exclu-
        " sively from the obstinate adherence of France to a claim
        " which never can be admitted ; a claim that the construction
        " which that government affects to put on the internal constitu-
        " tion of its own country, shall be received by all other nations
        " as paramount to every known principle of public law in
        " Europe, as superior to the obligations of treaties, to the ties
        " of common interest, to the most pressing and urgent consi-
        " derations of general security." On these allegations minis-
        ters justified the continuance of the war as indispensably neces-
        sary : they endeavoured to prove that the rupture of the nego-
        tiation was to be attributed to a systematical aversion to peace
Dec. 30th. in the governing party in the French republic. The manifesto
        being laid before the houses of parliament, ministers assumed
        this declaration as a text, expatiated upon it in eloquent and
        impressive comments and suitable exhortations, and animated
        the indignant resentment of the parliament and country against
Splendid   the government of France. Mr. Pitt addressed the house in
eloquence   that style of splendid amplification which his oratory so hap-
of Mr.   pily assumes when his object is to strike the fancy, or rouse
Pitt on this
subject.   the passions. The question (he said) is not how much you will
        give for peace; but, how much disgrace you will suffer at the
        outset, how much degradation you will submit to as a prelimina-
        ry? In these circumstances, then, are we to persevere in the
        war, with a spirit and energy worthy of the British name, and
        of the British character? or are we, by sending couriers to
        Paris, to prostrate ourselves at the feet of a stubborn and su-
        percilious government, to yield to what they require, and to
        submit to whatever they may impose? I hope there is not a
        hand in his majesty's councils which would sign the proposal ;
        that there is not a heart in this house which would sanction the

        t See State Papers, December 27th, 1796.

measure; and, that there is not an individual in the British CHAP.
dominions who would act as the courier. In answering the LIX.
speech of Mr. Pitt, Mr. Erskine took a general view of the
causes and consequences of the war with France,[u] and endea- 1796.
voured to prove that the ostensible was not the real grounds of Mr Er-
the rupture; but that we were actually to be at war for Belgium. skine's
Mr. Fox argued, that the whole amount of the minister's causes and
splendid oration that night, was to admit that we had been four conse-
years engaged in a war unprecedented in expense and force, quences of
and had done nothing: after all the efforts so honourable to the war.
Britons; after an addition of no less than two hundred millions Reasoning
to the national debt, and of nine millions to the permanent taxes of Mr. Fox.
of the country; after an enormous effusion of human blood,
and an incalculable addition to human wretchedness; so far
were we from having gained any object for which we had set
out in the war, that the minister had this night come forward,
in a long and elaborate speech, to show that the only effect of
all our efforts had been, that the enemy had, from success, become more unreasonable in their pretensions, and that all hopes
of peace were removed to a greater distance than ever. To
persevere in an undertaking productive of such prodigious expense and loss, without the least probability of advantage, or
even indemnification, was altogether inconsistent, not only with
wisdom but with common prudence and common sense. In
private life, a person who should persevere in a ruinous undertaking, which wasted large property, and incurred overwhelming debts, without receiving any returns, would be, by all men
in their senses, deemed an infatuated projector. The nature
and character of such public conduct was the same; the only
difference was, that the madness of the former involved a few
individuals: the madness of the latter, a great, populous, and
powerful nation, in its destructive effects. Persisting in a hostile spirit against the French republic, fondly wishing to restore
their beloved arbitrary monarchy, ministers, in the face of the
clearest and most decisive experience, still cherished their delusive hopes, embraced the most futile and often exploded theories,
and still conceived that France, exhausted by her efforts, would
yield to our dictates. With these ideas and views, they had
resolved to prosecute this war, surpassing in its miseries our
pernicious project of subjugating and enslaving America. So
obstinate in madness, they had pretended to negotiate, merely
to induce the people to acquiesce in the expenses which they so
severely felt. The negotiation, as it appeared from its circum-

u His reasonings and sentiments upon this subject were afterwards expanded in his celebrated and popular publication so very universally read,
and called for in so many editions. On the acuteness, ingenuity, and eloquence of this production, as well as its candid and liberal spirit, all impartial critics bestowed high praise, whether they agreed or disagreed in
his statements, reasonings, and inferences, concerning the causes and consequences of the war.

CHAP. stances and propositions, was never intended to be conciliatory.
LIX. The British minister had categorically declared, that he could
not recede from demanding the cession of Belgium; the
1796. French government as peremptorily declared, they would not
recede from their refusal. The French, whether wisely or not,
had merely availed themselves of the advantages which they
had acquired in war. In denying to our demands the restitution of Belgium, they knew they could, by their power, support
that denial; whereas we insisted on a concession which we had
no means to enforce. As a question of expedience, it was extremely absurd to continue, on account of Belgium, so dreadful
a war, when we were morally certain, that all our exertions to
regain it would be unavailing. Our offers of compensation
were totally inadequate to this valuable acquisition of the
French; therefore we could not reasonably hope that they
would have been accepted. We already saw, in the unexampled depreciation of the national funds on lord Malmsbury's return, the dreadful shock which public credit received; and we
might reasonably expect, that, as the pressure of the new incumbrances came to be felt, the shock would be much greater:
dejection and despondency were spread through the country;
1797. the nation was never in so deplorable and dreadful a situation.
Motions for On these and similar grounds, Mr. Fox in the house of com-
the remo- mons, and lord Oxford in the house of peers, proposed addresses
val of min-
isters, to the king, representing the conduct of ministry, in the whole
of the war, as ruinous; in this negotiation, as a compound of
folly and deceit; and describing the country as hastening to
destruction, through their infatuated counsels. These addresses,
are nega- however, were negatived, and opposite addresses, approving
tived by highly of the general system of ministers, of the principles and
great ma- conduct of the negotiation, and throwing the whole blame of the
jorities. rupture upon the French, were carried by most numerous majorities.

The sentiment, of parliament, however, concerning ministers
and the public affairs, were now very far from being general.
Instead of deeming the country prosperous, great numbers went
into the opposite extreme, and thought it, from the grievous
burthens of the war, about to sink to ruin.

Gloomy In the earlier part of 1797, the aspect of affairs was gloomy
aspect of and dismal. We were involved in a war, distressing beyond all
affairs at historical record, without seeing any likelihood of an end;
the com-
mence- national credit seemed to totter from its base; rebellion was
ment of ready to burst out in the sister island; and, while foreign in-
1797. vasion threatened, those who had so long been the champions
of Britain upon her own element, refused to obey orders issued
for her defence, and turned their mutinous arms against their
country.
Enormous
increase of The rapid and enormous increase of the national debt, had,
the na- for two years, created an alarm among many proprietors in the
tional debt. public funds; and, under this impression, sums to a great

amount were sold out of the stocks, and vested in other securities. After the failure of the negotiation, the sellers became
much more numerous, and the prices fell proportionably. With
fears of the downfall of national credit, were joined fears for
the grand national repository, the bank. Visionary as, when
examined, those apprehensions proved; there was a concurrence of circumstances which, without affecting the ultimate
responsibility of the most opulent body recorded in commercial
history, menaced their immediate solvency according to the
literal tenor of their engagements. In the course of the war,
the bank had advanced immense and extraordinary sums to
government, far beyond its usual accommodation to the treasury. A considerable part of these advances consisted of re-
mittances to foreign powers, and especially to the emperor of
Germany; and being necessarily in coin, instead of promissory
notes, greatly diminished the gold and silver of the kingdom.
So early as 1795, the directors had strongly expressed to Mr. Advances
Pitt their expectations " that he would arrange his finances for and state
" the year in such a manner as not to depend on any farther bank.
" assistance from the bank." They repeated their remonstrances at different periods in the same year; and, on the 8th
of October, they concluded a written representation, by stating Corres-
" the absolute necessity which they conceived to exist, for di- pondence
" minishing the sum of their present advances to government, between
" the last having been granted with great reluctance on their the bank
" part, on his pressing solicitations." In 1796, however, the and minis-
urgency of Mr. Pitt representing the pressing demands of the ter.
public service, induced them to continue large accommodations
to government. In the beginning of 1797, the minister requested farther advances; and also stated, that one million five hundred thousand pounds beyond the accommodation of the English treasury, would be wanted as a loan for Ireland. On the Alarms for
9th of February 1797, the directors ordered the governor to in- public
form Mr. Pitt, " that, under the present state of the bank's ac- credit.
" commodation to government here, to agree with his request of
" making a farther advance of 1,500,000l. as a loan to Ireland,
" would threaten ruin to the bank, and most probably bring Fear of an
" the directors to shut up the doors."x But besides the remit- invasion.
tance of specie, and the advance to government, another
cause powerfully co-operated: the dread of invasion induced
the farmers, and others resident in parts distant from the metropolis, to withdraw their money from the hands of those bankers with whom it was deposited. The run, therefore commenced upon the country banks, and the demand for specie Unusual
soon reached the metropolis. From Monday the 20th of Fe- demand
bruary, a great run began upon the bank. which increased the Rapid de-
21st, and still more rapidly on the Wednesday and Thursday. crease of
                                                                cash in the
x See correspondence between Mr. Pitt, and the bank, Annual Register, bank.
1797.

CHAP.
LIX.

1797.
The public
agitation.
Applica-
tion to go-
vernment.
Order of
council to
suspend
payments
in cash.
The sub-
ject is dis-
cussed in
parlia-
ment.
Opposition
declare the
bank to be
in a state
of insolven-
cy, from
the infatu-
ation of
ministers.

Ministers
allege, and
the bank
proves its
property
far to ex-
ceed its
engage-
ments.

The bank was extremely alarmed. On the 24th, the drafts and demands of cash for bank notes were so numerous and large, that a deputation of the directors hastened to the chancellor of the exchequer, to state the amount of cash in hands and notes demandable by bearer ; and also the drafts of the preceding and present day ; and to ask him how far he thought the bank might venture to go on paying coin, and when he would think it necessary to interfere, before the cash was so reduced as might be detrimental to the immediate service. Government thought itself compelled to interpose ; and, on, the 26th of February, an order of the privy-council was issued, prohibiting the directors of the bank from "issuing any cash in "payment till the sense of parliament should be taken." This subject being announced to the respective houses, the opponents and supporters of ministers formed totally different opinions of the amount of the actual case ; the former construed the discontinuance of cash payments which the national repository was pledged to perform, into an inability to discharge its pecuniary engagements: under that impression, they declared the bank of England to be in a state of insolvency and bankruptcy: this opinion was founded in the usual definitions and practice of merchants, according to which, any individual or company that did not pay his or their own notes or acceptances, was certainly insolvent as long as the disability lasted. and bankrupt or not according to its permanency. The notes of the bank had been commonly considered merely as the representatives of gold and silver ; and their convertibility into coin had been regarded by the people as the criterion of their value ; and thence an obstruction to the readiness of their exchange for gold or silver was esteemed a depreciation. Ministers considered the present as a case to be viewed on great and general principles, without being confined to the daily usage of ordinary stations : the present was not a question of definition, but of expediency and provision. The bank of England had been stated by its directors to possess, in its corporate property, effects infinitely beyond all the demands to which it was subject ; but, from unfounded alarms, was not suffered to retain the usual quantity of gold and silver : they believed this statement to be true ; and denied that if it was found so, the bank could be justly denominated insolvent and bankrupt. Money, whether in coin, metal, or any other material, was merely a medium of exchange, and an agreed representative of commodity : where there was abundance of effects, they would soon bring gold and silver, as well as other merchandise to market.[y] The first step to be taken was to ascertain the assets of the bank : for that purpose, a second committee was proposed, and appointed in both houses in the beginning of March. The result of the reports was, " that on the 25th of February, the last day of pay-

y See Smith's Wealth of Nations, vol. i. passim.

" ing gold and silver, there was a surplus of effects belonging CHAP.
" to the bank, beyond the total debts, amounting to the sum of LIX.
" 3,826,890l. exclusive of a permanent debt of 11,666,800l. due
" from government ; that the bank of England had lately ex- 1797.
" perienced an universal drain of cash ; that this drain was ow-
" ing to drafts from the country, which arose from local alarms
" of invasion ; that demands had been of late progressively in-
" creasing, but particularly in the last week ; and that there
" was every reason to apprehend, that these demands, and the
" consequent progressive reduction of cash, would continue,
" and even increase, insomuch that if it were to proceed in the
" same proportion, the bank of England would be deprived of
" the means of supplying the cash which might be necessary for
" pressing exigencies of public service." Grounded on these Bill to en-
reports, Mr. Pitt proposed a bill, enabling the bank of England able the
to issue notes in payment of demands upon them. instead of bank to
pay in
cash, agreeably to the late order of council to that effect : and notes, in-
after various discussions, and several modifications, the bill was stead of
passed into a law. This measure saved the credit of the bank, cash.
and of the public funds, which had been injured by the alarm ;
recalled to circulation the concealed hoards of the valuable
metals, and made money of the various denominations much
more plentiful than before. The predictions of the ablest men
in opposition, that bank notes would soon be sold at a great
discount, proved totally unfounded ; and the interference of
the privy-council in the affairs of the bank, on the alarming
disappearance of the precious metals, has from experience been
demonstrated not only prudent, but indispensably necessary.

Scarcely had the public alarm from the bank subsided, when Complaints
other imminent dangers occasioned dread and consternation. of the
The soldiers and sailors of Britain had long complained of the sailors.
smallness of their pay, as totally inadequate to their comfortable
subsistence and accommodation, in the present diminished value of money : with these grievances, still unredressed, other
causes co-operated to produce and desseminate discontents
throughout the army and navy. The democratic doctrines Artifices
of universal equality had been circulated by inflammatory agi- of disaffec-
tators, but more especially in the navy ; great numbers of po- ted agita-
tors.
litical innovators entered themselves aboard the fleet ; they
knew the principal grievances in the estimation of sailors, to be
severe punishment when aboard, and the want of means of
pleasure when ashore : they, therefore, directed their animadversions to the harsh behaviour of several of the officers, and to
the striking disproportion observed in the distribution of prize
money.[z] This inequality they represented not only as unjust,
but as a proof of the contempt in which sailors were held by
their officers ; and yet it was evident, that, to the bravery of
the seamen was principally owing the success in most engage-

z See Annual Register, 1797.

CHAP.
LIX.

1797.

Alarming
mutiny at
Ports-
mouth.

ments. The promoters of these doctrines conducted their inculcations and measures with such secrecy and sagacity, as
showed very considerable ability and skill : the means employed were dexterously and comprehensively fitted to the end proposed,—the incitement of a general mutiny through the fleet.[a]
With so much address were their schemes conducted, that the
existence of discontent was not suspected by the officers until
mutiny was publicly announced. Several anonymous petitions
in the month of March, were sent from the channel fleet to lord
Howe, begging his interference to procure such an increase of
pay as would enable them in those dear times to support their
families. Earl Howe, then at London, wrote to the commanding officer at Portsmouth, lord Bridport, to inquire whether
there was any dissatisfaction. His lordship, after examining his
officers, reported that there was none ; and that it was merely
an attempt of certain individuals to persuade government that
the sailors disapproved of its conduct. The admiralty being
informed by lord Howe of the petitions and inquiries, drew the
same conclusion. But at this time it was settled by all the sailors of the channel fleet, that no ship should heave an anchor till
a redress of grievances was obtained. On the 13th of April,
lord Bridport ordered the signal for weighing anchor : which,
instead of obeying, the sailors in the Queen Charlotte, lord
Howe's own ship, set up three cheers, as the signal for commencing mutiny ; and every other ship followed the example.
The officers exerted themselves to the utmost to recall the sailors to obedience ; but their attempts were unavailing. The sailors
were now supreme masters of the fleet; every crew appointed
two delegates to form a convention, which should carry on its
deliberations in lord Howe's own cabin. On the 17th, an oath
was administered to every man in the fleet, to support the cause
in which they had engaged : ropes were then reefed to the yard
arm in every ship, as the signal of punishment that would be inflicted on those that betrayed the cause; and several officers were
sent ashore who were particularly obnoxious to their respective
crews. Meanwhile, though the admiral could not lead his fleet
to sea, both he and the officers were treated with the greatest
respect and attention, and the whole routine of naval duties were
regularly performed. On the 18th, two petitions, one to the
admiralty, and the other to the house of commons, were drawn
up, and signed by the delegates. The petition to the commons
stated, in very respectful language and correct composition, the
inadequacy of their pay (unchanged since the reign of Charles II.)
to their subsistence in the present state of prices ; and their inferiority in various articles to the soldiers. Their petition to the
admiralty stated the low rate of their pay, and the insufficiency
of their allowance of provisions ; demanding an increase of both,
together with the liberty of going ashore while in harbour ; and
the continuance of pay to wounded seamen, till they should be
cured and discharged.

a Annual Register, 1797.

These proceedings so greatly alarmed government, that the CHAP. LIX.
lords of the admiralty went down to Portsmouth to inspect the
transactions of the fleet themselves: finding the firm determination of the sailors to persist in their demands, and aware of   1797.
the dreadful consequences that must ensue if the defenders of
our country continued refractory, they authorized lord Bridport
to inform the ship's company, that they would recommend to
the king to propose to parliament an augmentation of their pay,
and a redress of their other complaints. The delegates answer- April 21st.
ed, that it was the determination of the crew, to agree to nothing that should not be sanctioned by parliament, and guaranteed by the king's proclamation. This declaration being made
in a conference with several commanders, admiral Gardner was
so irritated, that he seized one of the delegates by the collar,
and swore he would have them all hanged, with every fifth man
throughout the fleet.   This conduct so much enraged the
sailors, that the brave officer with difficulty escaped alive; the
ships loaded their guns, and put themselves in a state of defence.   The next day, however, they wrote a letter to the
lords of the admiralty, stating the motives of their conduct on
the preceding day; and another to lord Bridport, expressing
for him personally the highest respect and attachment.   On
the 23d, his lordship pathetically addressing his crew, informed
them that he had brought with him a redress of all their grievances, and the king's pardon for what had passed.   These offers being communicated to the other crews, after some deliberation, were accepted, and every sailor returned to his duty.
For a fortnight the fleet remained tranquil, expecting from par- On the
liament a confirmation of their demands, but finding no steps ${}^{17\text{th of}}$
hitherto taken for that purpose, they renewed their former me- May.
naces. Alarmed at this intelligence, government sent to quell Is quieted
the tumult, lord Howe, an officer universally beloved through- by lord
out the British fleet. This illustrious commander having pledged Howe.
his word to the seamen that government would faithfully keep its
promises, they declared their unlimited confidence in lord Howe's
assurance, and returned to their duty.   A mutinous disposition
which had also appeared at Plymouth, subsided upon hearing of
these transactions at Portsmouth.

· Parliament now proceeded to consider the case of the sea- An aug-
men: Mr. Pitt proposed an augmentation which was unani- mentation
mously agreed to as necessary both in justice and policy; but ${}^{\text{of pay is}}_{\text{granted by}}$
Mr. Fox very strongly censured the procrastination of minis- parliament
try, to which he imputed the renewal of the disturbances.   It
was hoped that these compliances of government, sanctioned
by legislature, would have prevented any fresh tumults; but More out-
a mutiny broke out at the Nore, on the 22d of May, much rageous
more outrageous and dangerous than the proceedings of the ${}^{\text{and dan-}}_{\text{gerous mu-}}$
Portsmouth or Plymouth fleets.   The sailors at the Nore tiny at the
blamed those of Portsmouth, for having omitted to insist on a Nore.

CHAP. more equal distribution of prize money. The crews took pos-
LIX.   session of their respective ships, chose delegates, stated their
       demands, including not only a much larger distribution of prize
1797. money,[h] but many privileges and exemptions from duty, which
       were totally inconsistent with the subordination of the navy, and
       objects of the service. At the head of this mutiny was a person
Parker. named Richard Parker, a man of good abilities, not unedu-
       cated, a bold and resolute character. The lords of the admi-
       ralty, directed admiral Buckner, the commanding officer at
       the Nore, to inform the seamen, that their demands were totally
       inconsistent with the good order and regulations necessary to
       be observed in the navy, and could not for that reason be com-
       plied with; but, that on returning to their duty, they would
       receive the king's pardon for their breach of obedience. To
       this offer Parker replied by a declaration, that the seamen had
       unanimously determined to keep possession of the fleet, until
       the lords of the admiralty should repair to the Nore and re-
       dress the grievances which they had stated. Meanwhile,
       on the 6th of June, the mutinous fleet was joined by four
       ships of the line, from the squadron which, under admiral
       Duncan, was watching the motions of the Dutch in the North
       sea. The lords of the admiralty hastened to Sherness, and
       held a board at which Parker and the other delegates attend-
       ed: but their behaviour was so audacious, that the commis-
       sioners returned to town without the least success. Embolden-
       ed by the strength of men and shipping in their hands, and
       resolved to persevere in their demands till they should extort
       compliance, the mutineers proceeded to secure a sufficiency of
       provisions for that purpose, by seizing two vessels laden with
The insur- stores, and sent notice ashore that they intended to block up
gents   the Thames, and cut off all communication between London
block up
the   and the sea, in order to force government to a speedy ac-
Thames. cession to their terms; they began the execution of their me-
       nace by mooring four of their vessels across the mouth of the
       river, and stopping several ships that were coming from the
Alarm in metropolis.   While these transactions excited great alarm in
London. the nation, they were violently reprobated by the seamen
       belonging to the two divisions of the fleet lying at Portsmouth
       and Plymouth; each of them addressed an admonition to their
       fellow seamen at the Nore, warmly condemning their proceed-
       ings as a scandal to the name of British sailors, and exhorting
       them to be content with the indulgence already granted by
       government, and to return to their duty without insisting on
       more concessions than had been demanded by the rest of the
       navy. These warnings proved ineffectual : the delegates
       commissioned lord Northesk, whom they had kept confined in
       the Montague which he commanded, to repair to the king in
       the name of the fleet, and to acquaint him with the conditions

h See Annual, Register 1797.

on which they were willing to deliver up the ships. The CHAP.
petition which he was charged to lay before the king, was LIX.
highly respectful and loyal to his majesty, but very bitter against
his ministers; and they required an entire compliance with 1797.
every one of their demands, threatening, on the refusal of any,
to put immediately to sea. Lord Northesk undertook to convey their petition; but told them, that, from the unreasonable-
ness of its contents, he could not flatter them with the hope
of success. No answer being returned to the message, and
information being brought to the fleet that the nation at large
highly disapproved of their proceedings, great divisions took
place among the delegates, and several of the ships deserted
the others; not, however, without much contest and bloodshed.
The mutineers, despairing now of accomplishing their designs, The sailors
struck their flag of mutiny: every ship was left at its own at length
command, and they all gradually returned to obedience. Par- return to
ker was seized and imprisoned, and after a solemn trial that Parker is
lasted three days, on board the Neptune, he was sentenced tried and
to death. He suffered with great coolness and intrepidity, executed.
acknowledging the justice of his sentence. With him the
other chief ringleaders, after a full proof of their guilt, were
condemned and executed; but mercy either immediately, or at
a more distant period, was extended to the rest. This mutiny,
so much more dangerous than the disturbances in the other
fleets, attracted the very serious attention of parliament, to which
it was communicated by a message from his majesty: measures
were adopted for preventing communication between the well
affected and the present mutineers, and also precautions were
employed to hinder and punish future attempts to seduce soldiers
or sailors from their duty and allegiance, or to excite mutiny
and sedition. With this view, Mr. Pitt proposed a bill purport- Law ren-
ing, that persons who should endeavour to seduce either sol- dering the
diers or sailors from their duty, or instigate them to mutinous instigation
practices, or commit any act of mutiny, or form any mutinous of mutiny
assemblies, should on conviction, be deemed guilty of felony, felony.
and suffer death.[c] The duration of the act was limited to one
month after the commencement of the next session; and the
law at the present crisis, was so evidently necessary that it passed by an unanimous vote. Having suppressed this insurrection
of the sailors, government turned its attention to the army,
which complained of the smallness of pay. An increase had
been granted about two years before, and now a farther augmentation was established by which every soldier was to receive a
shilling per day.

Great discontents prevailed at this time in Ireland, which State of
ministers imputed to the dissemination of jacobinical principles; Ireland.
and opposition to the system of government which had been
adopted since the recall of earl Fitzwilliam. Ministers re-

c See Acts of Parliament, 1797.

presented the country as having been almost in a state of rebellion: insurrection had been prevented by the firmness of government, and could be hindered in future only by a continuance of the vigorous measures which were now employed. The opponents of ministers denied that the Irish people were disposed to rebellion; and declared there existed great discontents, arising from the arbitrary, coercive, and unconstitutional system of the Irish government, tending to drive the people of Ireland to rebellion.[d]   Earl Moira moved an address, praying his majesty's interference to allay the discontents in Ireland.   The motion was resisted, first as an interposition of the British legislature in Irish affairs, contrary to the independence of the Irish legislature; secondly, as mischievous, since it tended to render the Irish disaffected towards their own parliament and government, whose conduct was the most conducive to their welfare that could possibly be adopted. Motions of a similar nature were made in the house of commons, and rejected upon similar grounds.   In supporting their respective propositions, lord Moira and Mr. Fox reprobated the present system of administering Ireland, described the various classes and sects of men whom the system of terror tended to alienate, but especially the catholics in the south, and presbyterians in the north.   The arguments however did not influence government, which continued to approve of a system that was styled by its supporters provident and wholesome firmness: by its opponents, violent and impolitic tyranny: but the full illustration of the grounds of these contrary opinions, will be found in the narrative of the Irish rebellion in the following year.

The ministers, since the rupture of lord Malmsbury's negotiation, had greatly declined in popularity, and numerous petitions were presented to the king for their dismission.   Induced by the calamitous events of the war, and encouraged by the sentiments which were now becoming prevalent, their opponents proposed, in both houses of parliament, addresses[e] to his majesty to remove from his councils his present servants. The grounds both of attack and defence were the same that had been so often discussed in many propositions, and various forms, and included the commencement and continuance of war; its conduct and events; the rupture of the negotiation; the management of finance; the enormous addition of debt and taxes; and the distresses of the nation; with the replies

LordMoira proposes an address on the subject to his majesty. His motion is negatived.

Motions for the removal of ministers,

d See Parliamentary Debates, 1797.

e The respective motions were made by the earl of Suffolk in the house of peers, March 27th; and by Mr. alderman Combe in the house of commons, May 19th.   The former limited his proposition to the dismissal of the first lord of the treasury; the latter included all the cabinet ministers. See Parliamentary Reports for 1797.

often repeated. The motions were respectively rejected by both houses.

Mr. Grey, this season, renewed his propositions of parliamentary reform: and his scheme was more definite and explicit than at preceding periods: that the number of county members should be increased from ninety-two to a hundred and thirteen, eligible not only by freeholders, but by copyholders and leaseholders; and that the other four hundred members should be chosen by all householders. The arguments for and against the proposition, were, with some new details and illustrations, the same that had been so repeatedly employed. Near the close of the session, a motion was made in the house of peers for an inquiry into the state of the nation; but opposed by ministers, as intended to produce a change of measures, which change they affirmed would be ruinous to the country.

In the course of this session, Charlotte Matilda, the princess royal, a young lady of great beauty and accomplishments, and highly distinguished for ability, knowledge, and literary taste, was married to Frederick William hereditary prince of Wirtemberg. On the 18th of May, the ceremony was performed by the archbishop of Canterbury, assisted by the archbishop of York, in presence of the royal family. Our sovereign gave the hand of his amiable and beloved daughter to her destined husband. The domestic sensibility of that affectionate and happy family, was very striking and impressive on an occasion that was to separate them from so dear a member: fraternal, sisterly, and, above all, parental feelings, when combined with the character and relations of the illustrious personages, rendered the scene at once solemn and pathetic. Her highness received a portion of eighty thousand pounds. Parliament rose the 20th of July, after having sitten between nine and ten months.

CHAP. LIX.

1797.

Motion for parliamentary reform are negatived.

Marriage of the princess royal.

Parliament rises.

CHAP. LX.

Campaign of 1797 —Operations in Italy—settlement of Italy—displays the political abilities of Bonaparte— Address and versatility of Bonaparte—attempts to revolutionize the minds of the people.— He marches against the Austrians.—The archduke Charles is appointed general of the Austrians.— Formidable armies of the arch uke and Bonaparte.—After successive victories, Bonaparte advances towards Vienna— Bonaparte offers peace to Austria—a negotiation is opened —Bonaparte changes the government of Venice—and of Genoa.—Treaty of Campo Formio—iniquitous disposal of the territories of, Venice.— Britain only remains to combat the ambition of France—France proposes to overmatch our navy, exhaust our finances, and excite rebellion—mighty preparations in the ports of Spain, France, and Holland—and plan of the naval campaign.— Distribution and disposition of the British navy—admiral Jervis encounters a Spanish fleet of superior force off St. Vincent's—able and dexterous scheme for dividing the enemy's force—bold and masterly execution—decisive and important victory—totally disconcerts the plans of the enemy —Powerful armament equipped by the Dutch—proposes to join the French at Brest—opposed by admiral Duncan—battle off Camperdown—Duncan, fearless of a lee shore, breaks the enemy's line—the British fleet gains a most brilliant victory—admirals Jervis and Duncan are called to adorn the peerage —This year, repeating the lesson of former wars, shows France and her allies the futility of contending with the navy of England.—Internal state of France—the royalists revive—alleged conspiracy—arrestation and banishment of the suspected persons without any proof —New negotiation for peace—Lord Malmsbury sent to Lisle—propositions on the part of Britain—preliminary requisitions of France—farther demands—propose entire restitution without any equivalent.— Lord Malmsbury declares so unreasonable a proposition totally inadmissible—French temporize and pretend a disposition to modification—dilatory pretexts of, until their internal changes were fixed—resume their proposition of restitution without any equivalent—Britain refuses such dishonourable conditions—lord Malmsbury ordered to depart.—The rupture of this negotiation unquestionably owing to France —Causes of the hostile disposition of France.- Discontents in Scotland—misapprehension of the militia bill—riots— alarming tumults in Perthshire—illustrating the operation of democratic principles—leaders fortunately ignorant, though daring—riots quelled.

CHAP.
LX.

1797.
Campaign
of 1797.

ENCOURAGED by the signal successes of the former year, the French republic made most powerful dispositions for commencing the campaign against Austria. The progress which she had effected by her land operations, she apprehended also enabled her to devote a considerable portion of her efforts against the maritime power of England. Having the direction of the navies of both Spain and Holland, her plan was to employ the united force of these countries with her own, in an attempt to deprive Britain of the dominion of the ocean, whilst her military energies continued to be exerted in extend-

ing the acquisitions of the former campaign. Italy had been CHAP.
the great scene of her military success, though not the sole field LX.
of her military glory. In that quarter the republic determined
most strenuously to push her advantages, without invading 1797.
Germany on the side of the Rhine. Bonaparte, having driven Operations
the Austrians from Italy, and quelled insurrection at Rome, be- in Italy.
fore he resumed his pursuit of the enemy, devoted his attention
to civil arrangements. He proposed to give the northern Italian Settlement
states such strength as would eventually enable them, in depend- of Italy,
ence upon France, to sustain themselves against the attacks of displays
Austria on the one side, or of Rome on the other. In the for- the politi-
mer year, a republican confederation had been framed under ties of Bo-
his auspices, composed of the four cities of Reggio,[f] Modena, naparte.
Bologna, and Ferrara, on the southern confines of the Po. This
scheme he now extended, and formed two republics on the model of the French constitution; the Transpadane, consisting of
the states on the north, and the Cispadane, of the states on the
south, of the Po. The population of the countries on the north
and south of the Po, that composed the two republics, was
computed at upwards of four millions. This was amply adequate to their defence against their neighbours, without requiring the assistance of France, which would only be needed to
protect them from the hostile designs of Austria; and thus they
would soon be able to co-operate in resistance. The influence
of France in Italy would henceforth be established on the surest foundation, the necessity of adhering faithfully to it by
those states that depend on it for their preservation. In order Address
to conciliate the minds of the people to republican institutions, and versa-
Bonaparte carefully attended to those rules and manners which tility of
republicans adopt and value. He cautiously avoided all osten- Bonaparte.
tation, and, in his personal demeanour, readily put himself on
a footing of perfect equality with all persons of decent situations in society: hence he acquired a number of friends, not
only among the French, but among the Italians, who had hitherto experienced little of that condescension, especially from
the Germans, who seldom studied to make their authority ac-
ceptable among the natives.[g] One great purpose of his expe- He at-
dition was to revolutionize the minds of the Italians: the better tempts to
to fit them for those changes in their various governments that ize the
would assimilate them to the system of France. This end he minds of
completely attained, and established his influence very exten- the people.
sively in Italy. The solicitude he manifested, in effecting and
consolidating the federal union between the republics, of which
he had encouraged the foundation, more than any other circumstance, raised his fame and credit among the Italian politicians,

f The geographical reader will recollect that there is another Reggio,
much more noted, in the southern extremity of Italy (the ancient Rhegium.)
The Reggio, mentioned in the text, is a few leagues from Modena, nearer
the Po.

g See Otridge's Annual Register for 1797, p. 21.

CHAP.
LX.

1797.
He march-
es against
the Aus-
trians.

The arch-
duke
Charles is
appointed
general of
the Aus-
trians.

Formid-
able armies
of the
archduke
and Bona-
parte.

After suc-
cessive vic-
tories, Bo-
naparte ad-
vances to-
wards Vi-
enna.

who had long wished for the revival of such systems in their country, recollecting how much it had formerly flourished under their influence. Having completed his civil arrangements, Bonaparte now resumed military operations : he proposed to pursue the enemy in the Tyrol: to drive them before him to Vienna, and either to dictate peace, or capture the metropolis and overwhelm the power of Austria. Meanwhile the Austrians were making preparations, not for longer disputing the empire of Italy, but for defending their country. Animated by that generous and indignant patriotism which strains every nerve to resist foreign invaders, they made most formidable efforts to vindicate their independence, which they now conceived to be at stake. Generals of ability, skill, and reputation, the Austrians possessed; but as the first purpose was not to conduct armies, but to inspirit and invigorate the people, and to recruit the exhausted force, the primary consideration was, from their many capable generals, to select one in whom the nation reposed the greatest confidence. The conduct and successes of the archduke Charles, in compelling the republican armies to evacuate Germany, raised the public voice in his favour. All their other great commanders had been defeated; he alone was victorious ; to render his appointment supremely popular, this single circumstance was sufficient. He was nominated commander in chief against Bonaparte, and all possible vigour and expedition were employed in equipping an army adequate to the service. The patriotism, honour, and loyalty of the brave Germans, stimulated them to flock to the standard of the gallant young prince.[h] If this were to be their last effort in defending their country, they were resolved it should be an effort worthy of the Austrian glory. In the end of February, prince Charles took the field. Valiant and meritorious as this young commander was, yet unequally was he matched when placed opposite to Bonaparte. He brought enterprise and heroism to combat enterprise and military talents, supported by a victorious army, elated with success, and confident of future victory. The soldiers of the archduke were chiefly new raised, whereas Bonaparte commanded veterans. New troops, however valiant, engaged against a disciplined army, inspirited by enthusiasm, and so long accustomed to uninterrupted triumph, were and must be inferior. The archduke Charles was unequal to his opponent because their respective forces were not equally habituated to war; commanding recruits against victorious veterans, the magnanimous youth found himself overmatched, like Hanibal in similar circumstances. After various conflicts, one battle was fought near Tarvis,[i] in which the Austrians were completely and decisively defeated : a line of French armies, severally headed by Massena, Bernadotte, and Joubert, with the principal force under the immediate command of Bonaparte.

h Annual Register 1797, chap. ii.   i Annual Register 1797, p. 26.

himself, extending from the Tyrolese mountains to Carniola, ra- CHAP.
pidly proceeded towards Vienna. The Austrians, repeatedly LX.
vanquished, renewed the contest; the republicans still advancing, reduced the strong fortress of Carniola and Carinthia; and 1797.
having entered Stiria, were within a hundred miles of the Austrian capital. Charles again made a stand at Hundmark, upon
the river Murh, but was again defeated: this last army by repeated losses being entirely broken, no means appeared to remain of defending Vienna, but by terminating the war. With
some renowned heroes war appears to have been an end; with Bonaparte
Bonaparte, war seemed only a means; and when triumphant, he offers peace to
uniformly professed to offer peace. After the last victory, he to Austria.
wrote a letter to the archduke Charles, expressing his desire of
accommodating a contest, which was ruinous to the vanquished,
and wasteful to the conquerors. " Brave soldiers made war, but
" desired peace: the war had now lasted six years; men enough
" had been slaughtered, and evils enough committed against suf-
" fering humanity." The archduke declared himself equally desirous of peace, and sent Bonaparte's letter to Vienna: a suspension of arms was appointed. One part of the consumate policy of Bonaparte, consisted in offering liberal terms to a vanquished enemy. With a view to secure permanent peace with A negotia-
the emperor; he proposed such conditions as might have even tion is
satisfied alternate victory: and a negotiation was opened at Cam- opened.
po Formio.

Whilst this treaty was pending, Bonaparte directed his views Bonaparte
to the situation and conduct of Venice;[k] which republic had changes
long viewed with dissatisfaction the victorious progress of the the govern-
French in Italy. The house of Austria, though at all times ment of Venice,
formidable, had never been an object of terror to Venice, not
even when it united Spain and Germany in the same family.
The turbulent and restless disposition of the French, and their
propensity to democratical innovation, alarmed the Venetian
aristocracy, which feared that the changes might extend to the
subversion of their authority: they took no open share in the
contest, but they favoured the imperialists, and rendered them
as much service as they could without avowing hostilities
against their adversaries. Bonaparte was far advanced into
Austria, and reports were spread that the French army had
been drawn into a defile, and were about to capitulate: the
Venetians believing this rumour, in an evil hour sent a large
army of their desultory troops to attack the posts which Bonaparte had left in Italy. In executing these orders, the Venetians massacred the French wherever they were to be found.
Being informed of the outrages, Bonaparte ordered a great body
of troops to march into the Venetian territories. The republicans easily defeated such opponents; and, on the 16th of May,
took possession of the city of Venice. Bonaparte established a

k Annual Register, 1797, chap. iii,

CHAP.   new government on the French model, instead of the aristo-
LX.   cracy which had lasted for so many centuries, and acquired
        such eminence among European nations: he also compelled
1797.   them to pay a contribution amounting to upwards of three mil-
        lions sterling.

and of   In Genoa also the nobles were friendly to the Austrian cause,
Genoa. but the people were attached to the French, and desirous of a
        popular government: Bonaparte, soon after the revolution of
        Venice, established a democratical government in Genoa; but
        as the nobles had never been active in hostility, and did not op-
        pose the change, they escaped exactions. Meanwhile, the ne-
        gotiation at Campo Formio was proceeding, the preliminaries
        were signed in the month of July, and the definitive treaty on the
        17th of October.[1]

Treaty of   By the peace of Campo Formio, the emperor ceded in full
Campo   sovereignty to the French republic, the whole of the Austrian
Formio. Netherlands; and consented to their remaining in possession of
        the Venetian islands of Corfu and Zante, Cephalonia, and all
        their other isles in the Adriatic, together with their settlements
        in Albania, situated in the southeast of the gulf of Lodrino:
        he acknowledged the republic, newly constituted under the name
        Cisalpine, to be an independent state; he ceded to it the sove-
        reignty of the countries that had belonged to Austrian Lom-
Iniquitous bardy, and consented to its possessing the cities and territories
disposal of of Bergamo, Brescia, and others, late the dependencies of Ve-
the terri- nice; together with the duchies of Mantua and Modena; the
tories of principalities of Massa and Carrara; and the cities and territo-
Venice. ries of Bologna, Farrara, and Romagna, lately belonged to the
        pope. The cessions of the French republic to the emperor
        were Istria, Dalamatia, with all the Venetian Islands in the Adri-
        atic, lying to the northwest of the gulf of Lodrino, the city of
        Venice, with a large portion of the dominions of that republic,
        chiefly those lying between the Tyrol, the lake of Guarda, and
        the Adriatic. Besides these public articles, there was a secret
        convention, by which it appears the dismemberment of the Ve-
        netian territories was determined, and the emperor was to com-
        pensate his losses in the Netherlands by the iniquitous seizure of
        dominions before independent. Here, indeed the emperor chose
Britain for his model his neighbours of Russia and Prussia.
only re-   One enemy now only remained to oppose the victorious ca-
mains to reer of the French republic, but that was the most formidable
combat the
ambition of that they did or could encounter. Having now at their com-
France. mand the navy of Spain as well as that of Holland, the French
France   government proposed to combat Britain upon her own element:
proposes naval warfare, however, was only a part of their intended hos-
to over-
match our tilities. Their objects in their contest with England were prin-
navy, ex- cipally three; to overmatch our navy, exhaust our finances, and
haust our excite rebellion. In the earlier part of 1797, the circumstances
finances,
and excite   [1] See State Papers, Oct. 17th, 1797.
rebellion.

of England appeared favourable to the realization of these CHAP.
hopes: the bank was, as we have seen, represented by very LX.
eminent senators as insolvent; the sailors were mutinous, and
great discontents prevailed, especially in Ireland. Immense 1797.
preparations were made in the ports of Spain and Holland.
The French plan of the naval campaign was, that the greater Mighty
part of the Spanish navy should be formed into one armada, prepara-
sail early in the spring to Brest, join the French ships, meet a the ports
powerful Dutch fleet, and bear down upon England with more of Spain,
than seventy sail of the line. As it was the policy of France France,
to effect a junction of the three naval armaments, so it was the and Hol-
policy of England to keep them separate. Admiral Duncan land, and
was appointed to watch the motions of the Dutch in the Texel, plan of th'
and sir John Jervis to intercept the Spaniards on their own paign.
coast; the Spanish fleet consisted of six ships of a hundred and Distribu-
twelve guns, one of a hundred and thirty-two, reckoned the tion and
largest vessel in Europe; two of eighty-four, and eighteen of disposition
seventy-four guns: the squadron destined to oppose this arma- of the Bri-
da, amounted to fifteen ships of the line, and some frigates. On Admiral
the 14th of February, cruising off cape St. Vincent, Jervis de- Jervis en-
scried the hostile fleet; so inferior in force, the British admiral counters a
saw that his policy was to divide the enemy: rapid in execu- Spanish
ting as well as wise and bold in planning, he formed his line fleet of su-
with wonderful despatch, passed through the Spanish fleet, se- force off St.
parated one-third of it from the main body, and by a vigorous Vincent's.
cannonade compelled it to remain to leeward, and prevented Able
its junction with the centre till the evening. After having thus scheme for
broken through the enemy's line, and, by this daring and for- dividing
tunate measure, diminished his force from twenty-seven ships my's force:
to eighteen, he perceived that the Spanish admiral, in order to
recover his superiority, was endeavouring to rejoin the ships
separated from him, by wearing round the rear of the British
lines; but commodore Nelson, who was in the rearmost ship,
directly wore, and by standing towards him prevented his design. He had now to encounter the Spanish admiral of one Bold and
hundred and thirty-two guns, aided by two others, each of masterly
them three-deckers: he was happily relieved from this dangerous execution:
position by the coming up of two ships to his assistance, which
detained the Spanish admiral and his seconds, till he was attacked by four other British ships; when, finding that he could
not execute his design, he made the signal for the remainder of
his fleet to form together for their defence. The British admiral, before they could get into their stations, directed the rearmost of them, some of which were entangled with others, to
be attacked, and four were captured. In the mean time, that
part of the Spanish fleet which had been separated from its
main body had nearly rejoined it, with four other ships, two of
which were not in the engagement: this was a strength more
than equal to that which remained of the British squadron, fit,
after so severe a contest, for a fresh action. The Spaniards,

CHAP. however, would not adventure to face the British force in close
LX. battle, and retreated. The victorious squadron of Britain carried off the four captured vessels, two of them bearing one
1797. hundred and twelve guns, one eighty-four, and the other seven-
decisive ty-four. The slain and wounded on board of these, before
and im- they struck, amounted to six hundred; and on board of the
portant British squadron to half that number: the killed and wounded
victory. on board the other Spanish ships were also computed to
amount[m] to about six hundred. The vanquished fleet withdrew
to Cadiz, whither it was immediately followed by the victors,
who blocked it up in so close a manner, that not one of the
numerous ships of force belonging to Spain in that capacious
harbour-durst venture out beyond the reach of the many powerful batteries that were erected for its defence. There the British
squadron commanded the seas, and took many prizes. Various
attempts were made to bombard Cadiz, under the immediate direction of commodore Nelson, and in one of them great execu-
Totally tion was done. Thus the victory of Jervis entirely disconcerted
disconcert the plan of the three allied powers.
the plans of
the enemy. The Dutch made mighty preparations, with a view, it was
Powerful supposed, of joining the Brest fleet, and invading Ireland: but
armament the vigilance of admiral Duncan rendered it impracticable for
equipped them to venture out of port without risking an engagement.
by the A violent storm having arisen about the autumnal equinox,
Dutch: obliged Duncan to return to Yarmouth to repair his ships: the
propose to Batavian government ordered admiral De Winter to sail with
join the all possible expedition, hoping they might proceed so far on
French at their way to Brest that it would be impracticable for Duncan
Brest: to prevent their junction with the French fleet: but they soon
found it would be impossible to elude the vigilance of our ad-
is opposed miral. Apprized by the signals of his advanced cruisers that
by admiral the Dutch fleet had left the Texel, Duncan, on the 10th of Oc-
Duncan. tober, sailed from Yarmouth roads: reaching the coast of Holland late in the evening, he stationed his squadron so as to pre-
Battle off vent the enemy from regaining the Texel. On the 11th of Oc-
Camper- tober, early in the morning, he descried the Dutch fleet formed
down. in a line of battle, about nine miles to leeward between Egmont
Duncan, and Camperdown. To prevent them from approaching nearer
fearless of a the shore, Duncan resolved to break their line: this movement
lee shore, he speedily executed, and, about twelve o'clock, a close action
breaks the began,[n] wherein admiral Duncan's division attacked the van of
enemy's the Dutch, and admiral Onslow the rear. The ship mounted
line. by Duncan lay near three hours along side of the Dutch admiral De Winter, and the conflict between these two brave
commanders was remarkably obstinate and destructive. The
latter did not strike his flag till all his masts were overboard,
half of his crew was slain or wounded, and it was utterly im-

m See London Gazette extraordinary, for March 3d, 1797.
n See London Gazette extraordinary, Oct. 16th, 1797.

possible to make any more resistance. The Dutch vice-admi- CHAP.
ral yielded to admiral Onslow, after he had been reduced to   LX.
the same condition; and all the Dutch ships that struck had
defended themselves with equal bravery, being almost every   1797.
one totally disabled. About four in the afternoon the battle The Bri-
terminated in a decisive victory to British valour and British tish fleet
skill. Our fleet, by this time, was within five miles of the shore, gains a
and in no more than five fathoms water; so that the admiral's most bril-
chief care now was to prevent his victorious fleet from being liant vic-
entangled in the shallows. This necessary precaution, and the tory.
approach of night, compelled him to discontinue the pursuit,
which saved a remnant of the enemy's fleet: no fewer, however, were captured than eight ships of the line, two of fifty-six
guns, and two frigates. The loss of men, on both sides, in
this bloody and well fought battle, was very great: in the British
squadron it amounted to seven hundred; but in the Dutch, to
twice that number; and they were the choicest of their seamen.
Naval critics impute this victory to the united boldness and
judgment which carried the British fleet between the enemy and
the shore. It is indeed an instance of a position which the
series of facts in this history illustrates, that, TO BRITAIN EN-
GAGED IN WAR, THE MOST ADVENTUROUS COURAGE IS THE WISEST
POLICY. This grand victory entirely overturned the naval projects of France. The two illustrious admirals, who in their re- Admirals
spective stations broke the maritime power by which France had Jervis and
expected to invade and annoy England, besides the praise and Duncan are
gratitude of the nation, received the honour of the peerage, with called to
the titles taken from the scenes of their respective victories: adorn the
Jervis was created earl St. Vincent, and Duncan viscount Dun- peerage.
can of Camperdown. These were the chief naval transactions repeating
of a year, that so strongly repeated the lesson of former wars, the lesson
that France or her auxiliaries waste their efforts in seeking to of former
humble the navy of England.   wars,
  During this year, great internal dissension manifested itself France and
in France; the royalists were becoming so powerful, as to rouse her allies
the jealousy and apprehension of the republicans. At a new the futility
election of the national councils, a considerable proportion of of contend-
members friendly to royalty, was returned; among these were ing with
Pichegru with his friends and adherents. Bonaparte on the the navy of
other hand, though at a distance from Paris, was the strenuous England.
supporter of directorial government. Angereau, one of his Internal
generals, a brave and enterprising officer, and beloved by the state of
soldiers, undertook to support the directorial leaders in their France.
attempts to crush the royalists. Having concerted measures The royal-
for striking a decisive blow, Barras, Reubel, and Lareveillere, ists revive.
three of the directors, intrusted Angereau to repair to the na- Alleged
tional council, and arrest sixty of the deputies whom they conspi-
charged with conspiracy for re-establishing royalty. Among racy.
the accomplices they included Carnot and Barthelemi, the two
remaining directors. Angereau executed his commission on

CHAP.
LX.

1797.
Arresta-
tion and
banish-
ment of the
suspected
persons,
without a
proof.

the 4th of September, with the most summary and decisive expedition: the specified deputies were arrested, and also Barthelemi; Carnot made his escape. The directory published
addresses to the French people, declaring that this arrestment
was necessary to the salvation of the republic. As a great majority of the people was attached to a republican form of constitution, they were easily persuaded that the conduct of the
directors was right and expedient. The directors having ascertained their superiority and present stability, professed themselves disposed to lenient punishment, and that they would not
suffer any blood to be spilt; but that the chief conspirators should
be transported. In opposition to these professions of mercy, it
was answered, that the directory grossly transgressed the first
principles of justice; that the alleged conspirators were never
tried; and that instead of a free constitution, the government was
an arbitrary oligarchy, rendering the property, liberty, and life of
every Frenchman dependent on the directors, and the army which
was at their devotion.

New nego-
tiation for
peace.

Meanwhile, attempts were made by the British government
to renew the negotiation for peace: an official note, dated the
1st of June, was sent to the French minister for foreign affairs,
intimating a willingness to enter into a negotiation for the re-
establishment of peace, and for the regulation of preliminaries, to be definitively arranged at a future congress. The answer of the directory expressed an equal disposition to pacific
measures; but signified, at the same time, a desire that negotiations should at once be set on foot for a definitive treaty. The
directory was anxiously intent upon giving the law to England,
as it had done to other countries, and was desirous, for that
purpose, to remove all obstructions that must have arisen
from a junction of the common interests of its allies together
with its own. In transmitting the passports for the expected
minister, they specified that he was to be furnished with full
power, to negotiate a definitive and separate treaty. As the
republican party and the army were paramount in France, the
government depending upon their support for its own stability
and power, it was necessary in conducting the negotiation to
regard the opinion and sentiments of both. The republicans
were solicitous that no concessions should be made favourable
to the interests of royalty or its partisans, either in France, or
even its proximity. The soldiers and officers were no less
anxious, that the vast acquisitions made by their valour should
be retained; and, that after so many victories, the fruits of their
exploits should not be relinquished. Neither disposed nor able
to thwart these inclinations, and guided by similar sentiments,
the directory sent their minister to meet lord Malmsbury, at

Lord
Malms-
bury is sent
to Lisle.

Lisle. The British ambassador proposed the plan of pacification which his constituents had formed. This scheme demanded from Spain a cession of the island of Trinidad; and from

the Batavia republic a cession of the Cape of Good Hope, Cochin in the East Indies, and its possessions in Ceylon. On these conditions, an entire restitution would be made, on the part of Great Britain, of all that it had taken from France and its allies, in the course of the war. It required that the prince of Orange s property should be restored to him, or an equivalent in money be allowed; and that France should engage to procure for him at the general peace, a compensation for the loss of his offices and dignities in the united provinces. The queen of Portugal should also be included in this treaty, without being subjected to demands of any kind. On the part of France, the minister required as preliminaries to any treaty, first, a full and unequivocal recognition of the French republic; secondly, that the king of Great Britain should henceforward desist from assuming the title of king of France; monarchy having been totally abolished by the French, they could no longer permit any claim, though nearly nominal and inconsequential, to remain in the possession of any prince; and therefore expected and required that it should be relinquished by the British monarchs in future thirdly, that the ships taken by the English at Toulon should be restored, or an equivalent for them, and those that had been destroyed. The French republic was acknowledged in the addresses of the British ambassador to its plenipotentiary.[p] The renunciation of the title of king of France, lord Malmsbury deemed a claim hardly worthy of serious reasoning. The demand of the restitution of the captured ships, was a matter of real importance; he, therefore, by the instructions of his court, forbore giving any decisive answer, until the French should state their propositions, or, in diplomatic language, their *contre project*. The French note stated another preliminary, more important and comprehensive than any of the former; that England should engage to make an entire restitution of all the possessions it had taken, not only from France, but from Spain and the Batavian republic: they required the ambassador to accede to this proposal, and if already not sufficiently authorised, to despatch a messenger to the British court, in order to procure the necessary powers. The argument on which they founded this peremptory requisition was, that the treaties between France and its Spanish and Batavian allies respectively guaranteed to each other the territories they possessed previously to the war. Lord Malmsbury declared such an imperious and unqualified demand must speedily break the negotiation, as it proposed cession on the one side, without any compensation on the other: if this were the resolution of the directory, the negotiation was at an end; and it only remained for Great Britain to persevere in maintaining, with an energy and spirit proportioned to the exigency, a war that could not be

CHAP. LX.

1797.
Proposition on the part of Britain.

Preliminary requisition of France.

Farther demands.

The French propose restitution, without any equivalent.

Lord Malmsbury declares so unreasonable a proposition totally inadmissible,

p See successive State Papers between lord Malmsbury and the French ministers, at Lisle, in July, August, and September 1797.

The
French
temporize,
and pre-
tend a dis-
position
to modifi-
cation.

Dilatory
pretexts
of, until
their inter-
nal chan-
ges are
fixed.

Resume
their pro-
position of
restitution
without
any equi-
valent.

Britain re-
fusing
such dis-
honourable
conditions,
lord
Malmsbu-
ry is or-
dered to
depart.

The rup-
ture of this
negotia-
tion is un-
questiona-
bly owing
to France.

Causes of
the hostile
disposition
in France.

ended but by yielding to such disgraceful terms. The French ministers hinted, that some modification might be devised, and professed to apply to the directory for fresh instructions. The whole month of August passed without any decisive answer from France: the republican negotiators, in frequent conference with lord Malmsbury, intimated that the directory was endeavouring to dispose its allies to terms more consonant to the views of England. Lord Malmsbury was fully aware that these pretences were totally unfounded, and that both Spain and Holland were driven to hostilities by the power of France, and were desirous of peace: nevertheless, he yet continued to wait a positive answer. For a fortnight more the procrastination continued: meanwhile the republican party completely accomplished their purpose of subjugating their adversaries; and immediately after the revolution of the 4th of September, new ambassadors were appointed to negotiate with lord Malmsbury. These ministers, after some prefatory professions of the desire of the French government for peace, peremptorily repeated the impracticability of a negotiation, except on the principle of complete restitution on the part of Britain, without any compensation.[q] Finding Britain in the plenitude of power and resources, would not accede to such dishonorable conditions, the French government ordered lord Malmsbury to depart from Lisle. Whether the rupture of the first negotiation is imputable to Britain or France, is a subject which admits of such very strong arguments on both sides,[r] that the impartial historian, satisfied with stating the facts, will not rashly give judgment; it was indeed a question of prudence, balancing probabilities, was, or was not the retention of Belgium by France so important as to counterpoise the miseries of war? If it was, were our means of compelling its restitution such as to render success likely? In the second negotiation, we were not merely called to acquiesce in possessions acquired by the French, and which it would be evidently difficult to extort from them by force; but to relinquish, without a compensation, our acquisitions, which they could not extort from us by force. Here the historian may safely give judgment, that the hostile conclusion of the second negotiation arose from the French republic. We have uniformly seen that peace is the permanent interest of the two first nations of the world; and that every war has left both the conquered and the conqueror in a worse situation than they would have been if no conquest had arisen: national rivalry unfortunately produced animosity and enmity, and overwhelmed all views of mutual and reciprocal interest. This hostility had been strongly inflamed by the events of the present war. Irre-

q See in State Papers, 1797, the notes and conferences between the respective ambassadors, from the 15th of September to the 1st of October, 1797.

r See Erskine on the causes and consequences of war, and answer by John Giffard, esq. also, answer by John Bowles, esq.

sistibly triumphant over all other enemies, France had experi- CHAP.
enced the most powerful and effectual opposition from Eng- LX.
land: not only resentment, nor even ambition, but pride stimulated her to show herself superior in combat to England as 1797.
well as to the rest of the world. Republican energy inspiring
and invigorating immense military force, afforded, she conceived, the means of humbling, or even subjugating, her most
formidable and potent rival. Their recent victory over interior
adversaries enabled the government to employ its spirit, resources, and instruments, without interruption, against the only
enemy which the total dissolution of the coalition had now left.
These inclinations were cherished by their most brilliant and
captivating orators: England was represented as another Carthage, long paramount in opulence, and in power resting upon
that opulence; but which France, as another Rome, would
overwhelm by superiority of military strength. These sentiments and ideas impressed in both the government and the nation, contributed powerfully to the dismassal of lord Malmsbury,
and to the persistance in war with England.

The spirit of discontent which had existed both in England Discon-
and in Scotland, with a fluctuation of increase and decrease ten's in
ever since the first diffusion of the revolutionary doctrines, this Scotland.
year was in Scotland brought into alarming action, by a misconception of the militia act: misrepresented by jacobin dema- Misappre-
gogues, many of the ignorant peasants appear to have consider- hension of
ed it as a press act, compelling the persons drawn to become the militia
soldiers. Various partial tumults arose in the manufacturing Riots.
towns as well as agricultural villages and districts in the low
countries of Scotland, and were not suppressed without the intervention of military force. These, however, possessing neither
unity of design nor system, were without much difficulty quelled through the vigilance of the magistrates aided by military
activity. In more sequestered districts, where soldiers were
rarely stationed, tumult, and indeed insurrection, rose to such a
height as to overpower the civil magistrates, and, for a time, to
suspend all regular government. In the highlands of Perth- Alarming
shire, on the banks of the Tay and its tributary rivers, and in tumults in
the adjacent glens and fastnesses of the Grampians, the com- Perth-
mon people were remarkable for industry, sobriety, and other shire.
virtues[s] that render this useful station respectable: pious and
attentive to the essential duties of religion, without the purtan-
ical fanaticism of some of the adjacent districts. They were
characteristically respectful to the higher ranks; in some cases
even to the submissiveness of feudal ideas, and beyond the necessary subordination of regular liberty. As, however, they
advanced in civilization and knowledge, agricultural skill, successfully exerted, in various instances produced independence

[s] See Statistical Accounts of the parishes of Blair, Moulin, Logieraite,
Little Dunkeld, Weem, Dull, and Fortingal.

CHAP. of situation ; independence of sentiment began to follow ; and,
LX.   about the commencement of the French revolution, they had
      reached a very proper medium between servility and arrogance,
1797. and were what British peasants may always be wished to con-
      tinue. Intelligent and inquisitive, they were anxiously desi-
      rous to know the state of public affairs : newspapers found their
      way into those recesses, and they became extremely interested
      in the transactions of the continent.[t] When the contest seem-
      ed to be between the mass of the people and their former lords,
      their minds, being alive to such discussions, were the more easi-
      ly impressed by the works of Thomas Paine, which were stu-
      diously spread among them, as well as the rest of our country-
      men. At first they did not clearly apprehend what benefits
      " The Rights of Man" held forth ; but understood its scope in
      general to be the redress of all grievances under which they
      might fancy themselves to labour.[u] Those highlanders were,
      in most respects, contented with their lot, and, for several years,
      were not driven to dissatisfaction, though they gradually relax-
      ed in deference to their lay superiors, and also to their clergy,
      whom they had hitherto regarded with peculiar veneration.
      The country not affording provision for all its natives, many of
      these migrate to more productive districts, whence some of
      them returning to visit the habitations of their fathers, bring
      back with them the ideas of their new residence. Hence prin-
      ciples and doctrines of Glasgow and of Paisley found their way
Causes and to Athol. Somewhat before this time, two noted agitators,
instiga- named Menzies and Cameron, having returned to the High-
tors.   lands from the chief scenes of Scotch conventionalists, pitched
      their abode in populous part of the districts in question ; there
      they actively disseminated the revolutionary ideas, and made
      very great progress among their countrymen ; and, by the be-
      ginning of 1797, had succeeded in inclining the people to dis-
      like the constituted authorities, and to wish for a revolution :
      but though these fellows were laying the train, matters did not
      appear fit for lighting the match. Such was the state of things
      when the report of the militia act reached the country, together
      with very exaggerated accounts of the resistance of the people
      in the south. About the 1st of September, the populace were
      all in a ferment, and then only did the gentlemen receive any
      intimation of the spirit that was predominant. In two days the
      country was a scene of tumult, and even insurrection : the mob
      visited the house of every magistrate, clergyman,[x] or other gen-

---

t See Statistical Account of Little Dunkeld by Mr. John Robertson, clergyman of the parish, written in 1792.
    u They first conceived that Tom Paine was to put an end to *excisemen*,
whose office, enhancing the price of the favourite beverage, whiskey, is
peculiarly unpopular
    x Their treatment of one clergyman of the most estimable character, ad-
vanced in years, brought on an illness that terminated in his death, long before the previous vigour of his constitution taught his friends to expect
his decease.

tleman of respectability, and proffered them oaths and engagements to join in opposing the militia act; but such still was the
influence of habitual ideas, that they drew up those compulsory
stipulations *on the stamps required by the law for legalizing*
agreements : in their violation of all law, they rendered homage
to the conventional and social securities which law establishes.
The mob threatened recusants with the destruction of their
houses; and, to show themselves prepared for conflagration,
carried with them fire and combustibles; and the watch-word,
which they roared with infuriate yell as they approached the
seats of gentlemen, was "straw and burning coals!" Most of
the gentlemen, to preserve their property, yielded to the mandates of the mob, and professed to incur obligations that could
not be binding, and there being no military force, did not attempt a resistance, which, if the insurgents were resolute, must
have certainly proved destructive; a few argued with some
reason, that persons so new to riot and outrage could not immediately proceed to atrocity; they therefore refused to make
a promise which they did not intend to perform; and some gentlemen made very vigorous dispositions for defence. The event
demonstrated that, in the precise circumstances of the case, repugnance was the most effectual; resolute refusal was followed by no outrage, whereas concession to lawless demands produced some violence, and much insult. As the insurgents pro- Revolu-
ceeded, they assumed a considerable degree of organization; tionary
the respective rioters, in their operations, changed districts, so objects.
as to be less easily recognised, should order return, and judicial
inquiry be instituted. The first exercise of the legislative functions with which they had invested themselves, they proposed
to be the annihilation of three classes of men, clergymen, lairds
(landholders), and excisemen, and thus to commence revolution by the abolition of religion and revenue, and the confiscation of property.[y] Fortunately for the peace of the country,
their leaders, though active and daring, were not able; and prematurely exulting in success, through their own security, were
the more easily surprised and arrested in a career which was
hurrying on to rebellion.

The chief person in that part of Scotland, from rank, fortune,
and his official situation as lord-lieutenant of the county, was
the duke of Athol: his house was in considerable danger, but
was preserved by a mixture of prudence and resolution, the
most efficacious that could be employed in encountering a mob
that was furious in violence, without being desperate in atrocity.
The rioters had advanced to a park wall that separates the
public road from a lawn before Athol house, and urged their
demands in a tone of imperious dictation. The duke explained

[y] The reader, by recurring to this vol p. 263, will see a striking resemblance between the objects of the French peasants in 1789, and these highlanders in 1797.

to them their misconception of the act, calmly expostulated with them on their conduct, and advised them to return to the occupations of the season. Many of his hearers were disposed to listen to this salutary advice, but others, more outrageous, would persevere; and some of them threatened to break into the grounds, and set the house on fire. Lord Henry Murray, brother to the duke, agreeably to the prompt execution of Military procedure, proposed an immediate attack upon the insurgents, with the servants, adherents, and guests of the family, and a small party of light horse that was at hand; but his grace was averse to a measure which must have produced the effusion of blood, and might drive the populace to desperation. Finding them about to enter the grounds, he gave directions to load and point cannon that were placed in the lawn for festive occasions, with all the arms of his house to be in readiness; with much danger to himself, he walked to the paling, and told the rioters that, if one of them entered his grounds, he would order a general fire. Finding them intimidated by his resolution, he, after some time, resumed a milder strain, and appealed to feelings which, though suspended, he knew were not yet extinguished; and at length they departed, though not without leaving an apprehension that they might be brought back by Menzies and Cameron, who were believed to intend coming to the same place the following day, with a very large body, from an equally populous district as Athol; and the next was expected to be a very critical day; but the prompt measures which were contrived or adopted by his grace, disconcerted the insurgents. The ringleaders, apprehending no interruption from government, passed the night at their respective habitations with as confident security as if they had returned to enjoy repose after the fatigue of lawful business. · The direct roads between their mansions and the station of any military force, were all either possessed or observed by their friends and votaries. The duke, aware of this circumstance, sent the light horse, not above twelve in number, by a circuitous route across the mountains; which, not being suspected, he naturally conceived would not be watched. The party, with professional expedition, arrived, before day break, at the place of their destination, seized the fellows, and escorted them in a chaise along the road to Edinburgh. The intelligence spread instantaneously through the country, where the people were before hastening to the places of rendezvous. And here I cannot avoid mentioning a circumstance which shows how naturally men, totally unacquainted with military occupations, adopt the schemes of soldiers in circumstances that appear to them to require force, either for defence or aggression. The object of the populace was to rescue the ringleaders: expresses were despatched to have the defiles seized, so that smaller bodies might detain the convoy until the great mass of the people should arrive. The different passes were beset with a skill worthy of regular soldiers; and though the insurgents could not obstruct, they considerably retarded the dragoons, who were unwilling to proceed to extremities as long as they could be avoided. The mob, with considerable judgment, spent no more time at smaller defiles in opposing the escort, than to enable great numbers to press forward to that on which they fixed as the chief position of resistance. This was a bridge over the Bran, a rapid river that falls into the Tay, that may be considered as one of the entrances to the ghauts of the Grampians. There the insurgents, besetting the bridge, seized the horses of the carriage. The mob were many thousands in number: the commander used every peaceable effort in his power to persuade the populace to let the party pass without opposition; but finding all unavailing, he ordered his men to form for a charge. The rioters seeing the swords drawn and ready for action, and being hitherto the votaries of speculative error rather than of practical guilt, as much awed by the crisis that must begin bloodshed and rebellion as intimidated by the danger, suffered the carriage to pass on, and to proceed to the seat of justice. The ringleaders being seized, the misguided peasants returned by degrees to their usual occupations. This insurrection caused a dreadful alarm, not only in the scene of its operation, but throughout Perthshire and the neighbouring counties. Though being quelled in a short time, it was less memorable in event than at one time it threatened, yet it appears to me sufficiently important to deserve historical record: it illustrates the close connexion between levelling doctrines and revolutionary attempts. It farther proves that, in tumults which arise from mischievous error rather than criminal intention, implicit concession is far from being the most effectual policy; submission to even absurd claims of the ignorant, instead of giving satisfaction, encourages still more unreasonable demands. To meet such insurgents, the most successful means were, a prudent moderation that did not uselessly exasperate passion already violent, and a resolute firmness that would not yield to insolent and lawless demand. In individual cases the concessions might be necessary, but it was firmness that proved effectual to the public tranquillity. Menzies and Cameron were carried over to Edinburgh, to be tried by the justiciary court; but, by some unaccountable neglect, they were suffered to fly from prison, and thus escaped the punishment which, as there was abundance of evidence, they must have unquestionably incurred.[z]

z I have derived the materials for this part of the narrative from various gentlemen who resided in Athol at the time; and, among others, from my own father, the clergyman to whom I have alluded in the preceding note.

CHAP. LXI.

State of public opinions and sentiments at the meeting of parliament.—Effects of British victories, and the haughty conduct of France.—Discontent is much less prevalent than in former years—the nation regards the continuance of war as unavoidable, and bravely resolve to meet the exigency —the king publicly states the progress and rupture of the negotiation— the nation in general is disposed to support government.—Meeting of parliament—encouraged by the public sentiment, the minister adopts a new scheme of finance—he proposes to alleviate the funding system by raising a great part of the supplies within the year—and projects a multiplication of assessed taxes, which he presumes to be a criterion of income—details—arguments against and for—voluntary contributions proposed by Mr. Addington—the finance scheme is passed into a law—liberal contributions of all ranks and conditions—redemption of the land tax— object to absorb a large quantity of funded stock—plan of national defence introduced by Mr. Dundas—voluntary associations—the whole nation becomes armed against foreign and domestic enemies—revival of the alien bill—apprehensions of an invasion.—Motion of the duke of Bedford for the removal of ministers—is negatived—prorogation of parliament. Rebellion in Ireland—treatment of Ireland from the latter years of the American war—the penal statutes against catholics repealed—the catholics desire a participation of political privileges, which is refused—effects of the French revolution—united Irishmen—Wolfe Tone—professed objects, reform in parliament and catholic emancipation—real object— counter association of Orange men—catholic defenders— French mission to Ireland—proposed plan of insurrection to facilitate a French invasion—apprehension of Jackson, and discoveries through him —hopes of the catholics from the appointment of lord Fitzwilliam—consequences of his recall—farther progress of the united Irishmen—they send ambassadors to France—vigilance of the British government—martial law is proclaimed—mission of Macnevin to France—his proposed scheme of military operations—the whig party propose conciliatory measures—which are rejected as inapplicable to the case—proclamations and proffers of pardon—are totally disregarded—the united Irishmen concert measures for a general insurrection—disappointed by Duncan's defeat of the Dutch fleet—want of concert between the Irish conspirators and the French republic—arrestation of the delegates—hurries on rebellion before their designs were ripe—rebellion—insurgents near Dublin—are subdued—alarming insurrection in Wexford—successes of—at length are defeated—rebellion is suppressed in the south—insurrection in the north. —advances, but is subdued—lord Camden desires to be recalled—marquis Cornwallis is appointed his successor—wise policy of—the French attempt to revive rebellion—are vanquished—squadron defeated by sir John Borlase Warren—Irish rebellion extinguished.

CHAP.   IN England discontent was much less prevalent than in
LXI.   former years. The signal victories of our naval commanders
〰〰 gratified the national sense of honour and glory, and promised
1797. security against foreign invasion; the re-appearance of gold
State of and silver proved the responsibility and extensive property of
public opi- the bank, and dispelled apprehensions concerning national credit.
nions and

The desertion of our allies, while it stimulated the energies of the country, pleased its patriotism, as our efforts were to be entirely for ourselves. The abrupt termination of the embassy at Lisle, that obviously arose from the determined hostility of France, roused indignant resentment against an enemy which durst presume to dictate to Britain. The nation in general deemed the continuance of the war now a measure of necessary self defence, and was disposed to make the greatest exertions. With most patriots the question no longer was, were we prudent in going to war, or might we not before this time have made a peace; but we are now in a situation of great difficulty and danger, how can we best extricate ourselves? To common sense the answer was obvious: as the enemy will not make peace upon admissible terms, we must continue to fight. Before the meeting of parliamet, his majesty published a declaration, stating the progress, difficulties, and result of the negotiation; and showing that its rupture was owing to the unreasonable demands of France; calling on Britons to exert themselves adequately to the difficulty of the contest, and the importance and value of the objects at stake: he trusted that the resources of his kingdoms, and the spirit of his people, would vindicate the independence of their country, and "resist with "just indignation the assumed superiority of an enemy against "whom they fought with the courage, the success, and glory "of their ancestors: and who aimed at nothing less than to "destroy at once whatever has contributed to the prosperity "and greatness of the British empire; all the channels of its "industry, and all the sources of its power; its security from "abroad, its tranquillity at home; and above all, that consti- "tution on which alone depends the undisturbed enjoyment of "its religion, laws, and liberties."[a] Still his majesty was disposed to conclude peace upon the same equitable terms which he had now proposed. This address, appealing to the best feelings, most powerful sentiments, and dearest interests of Britons, had a very general effect, which his majesty's speech at the opening of parliament, tended strongly to increase. Ministers showed very clearly, that the continuanee of the war, by the rupture of the negotiation at Lisle, was owing to the enemy, not to Britain; thence they justly inferred the necessity of extraordinary efforts. Parliament, in an address to the throne, said, WE KNOW THAT GREAT EXERTIONS ARE NECESSARY: WE ARE PREPARED TO MAKE THEM: and the public in general coincided in this opinion and resolution. Aware not only of the state and circumstances of the nation, but of the sentiments and determination which recent events had diffused through the country, ministers from the joint result formed their schemes of finance, of internal vigilance and defence, and external armaments. The antecedent efforts of Britain had produced immense expendi-

CHAP. LXI.

1797.

Effects of British victories, and the haughty conduct of France.

Discontent is much less prevalent than in former years.

The nation regards the continuance of war unavoidable, and bravely resolves to meet the exigency. The king publicly states the progress and rupture of the negotiation.

The nation in general is disposed to support government.

Meeting of parliament.

Encouraged by the public sentiments, the minister adopts a new scheme of finance.

a State Papers, October 25th, 1797.

ture, and an enormous increase of debt, which, added to the burthen of taxes, contributed to the depression of the funds, rendered loans if not more difficult as to the attainment of principal, yet more disadvantageous as to the rate of interest; this was one ground on which the enemy rested their expectations. To render these hopes vain, to prevent the necessity of such an additional loan as would farther depress the funds, and to confirm public credit, was one of the primary objects which called for the attention of the legislature. The funded debt was already so great, that to add to it all the supplies that were necessary for the year, would have been extremely inconvenient, and would have postponed an evil, that must increase by con-

He propo-
ses to alle-
viate the
funding
system, by
raising a
great part
of the sup-
plies within
the year,
and pro-
jects a
multiplica-
tion of as-
sessed
taxes,
which he
presumes
to be a cri-
terion of
income.
Details.

tinuance, instead of meeting it immediately and boldly. The minister, therefore, proposed to raise a capital within the year, in order to prevent that increase of permanent debt from which the enemy expected the downfall of our credit. It was wise (he said) to sacrifice a part, even though a considerable part, for the preservation of the whole. With this view he proposed to treble the assessed taxes; the greatest contribution, he calculated, would not exceed a tenth part of the income of the highest class of those by whom it was to be paid: to prevent evasion, not future but past assessments were to be made the basis of the new contribution; because the most impartial evidence that could be obtained of the ability of each individual to contribute to the exigencies of the state, was the amount of his expenditure before he had any temptation to lower it that he might elude the impost. The minister divided the assessed taxes, already paid, into different classes; those who were charged for male servants, carriages and horses, luxuries of life, were to pay for both these articles of luxury, and for their houses, windows, clocks, watches, the necessaries and conveniences of life, a sum varying according to their former amount from treble to quintuple. Those who paid for houses, windows, clocks, and watches, were charged an additional duty from one-fourth to five times the former amount, in proportion to its magnitude, from whence the ability of the contributor was inferred. Thus, he whose assessed taxes before amounted to one pound, was to pay for this new plan, only one pound five; but he that before contributed fifty, by this new scheme, was to pay two hundred and fifty. But as large houses and numerous windows were, in many employments, instruments of profession or trade, a very considerable abatement was allowed in such circumstances; and the utmost contribution was not more than double the amount of the former assessments. There was besides, allowed to persons whose income did not exceed two hundred pounds, a gradation of reduction; the highest new assessments were to be one-tenth of that income descending to sixty pounds, which was to contribute only a hundred and twentieth part; and incomes below that sum were to contribute nothing towards the additional impost. Thus whatever the establishment was, even if it included male servants, horses, and CHAP. carriages, a person whose income did not exceed two hundred LXI. pounds, was not liable to pay more than twenty pounds of additional assessment. 1797.

During the former session, Mr. Fox had absented himself Arguments from parliament, together with several other gentlemen of op- against position, declaring their attendance totally unavailing: on the and for. discussion of the assessed taxes, however, both he and Mr. Sheridan made their appearance. The arguments of these illustrious senators,[b] as well as other opponents to government, embraced grounds not immediately relative to the subject which was before parliament. Before they investigated the proposed scheme of finance, they contended that ministers throughout the war had demonstrated such incapacity and infatuation, that parliament ought to pledge itself to no measures for supporting government, until they received an assurance that ministers would be dismissed; they ought not to vote such an enormous sums to be levied from their constituents, without security that the present weak and wasteful stewards were no longer to be intrusted with the management. Their reasoning they followed with strictures on the financial merits of this new scheme of pecuniary provision: it was, they said, a requisition the same in principle with the exactions of Robespierre; and from its retrospective operation, much more iniquitous; it was a change of system imposing an immense burthen without promoting any advantage. The funded system was not exhausted: the difficulty attending great loans was, the difficulty of providing the interest; but how could ministers insist upon this, when they were ready to impose so large a sum on the country in one year? The measure would be as oppressive in its operation as it was unjust in its principle. Ministers answered, that the funded system was not abandoned, as only a comparatively small part of the supplies this year was to be raised by the new mode; that assessed taxes resulting from probable expenditure, were a fair criterion of income; and that the various modifications would prevent the apprehended inconveniences of the operation. An Voluntary additional clause was proposed by Mr. Addington, allowing contributions pro- voluntary contributions, and adopted; and the finance scheme, posed by after being farther combatted in the house of peers, with this Mr. Ad- annexation, on the the 12th of January, 1798, was passed into a dington. law. Voluntary contributions commenced from the most opu- The fi- lent classes and individuals: the first personage in the nation nance manifested his love to his subjects and his country by a sacrifice scheme is amounting to one third of his personal income. The highest in a law. rank co-operated with the most abounding in wealth: the no- Liberal bility, the gentry, and farmers contributed very liberally, ac- contribu- cording to their respective stations and circumstances: the civil tions of professions joined in the patriotic effort: the navy and army all ranks and condi- tions.

b See Parliamentary Debates, Dec. 1797.

CHAP.
LXI.

1798.

Redemp-
tion of the
land tax.

Object to
absorb a
large
quantity of
funded
stock.

vied with each other in that species of exertion for a king and
country, which their professional services and personal dangers
had so strenuously and successfully defended, secured, and vindicated. Corporate bodies united with individuals ; tradesmen
and mechanics followed the example of bankers, merchants,
companies, and corporations ; journeymen and menial servants
made such exertions as manifested their attachment to the
king and constitution, under whom the fruits of industry are as
sacred to the menial as to the greatest merchant ; his rights and
property to the labourer as to the lord. Nor were the contributions confined to men : the fair sex' joined their donations for
the service of a country in which their situation is pre-eminently
respectable ; a pre-eminence arising from the superiority of
their virtues and accomplishments, joined to the superior discrimination of those who appreciate the British female character.[c] The highest personage set the example, an example that
was liberally followed by her sex : even children sacrificed a
great part of their means of gratification and amusement, to
prove their zealous love for a country and constitution which
they were themselves one day to support ; and as they were to
receive it from their fathers, to transmit it unimpaired to their
posterity.[d] The amount of this contribution, calculated at
about a million five hundred thousand pounds, was of less consequence as a fund of supply, than as a manifestation of the
public resolution. Besides these supplies, there was a loan of
seventeen millions. and Mr. Pitt now proposed a financial measure for the redemption, or rather the commutation, of the land
tax : its object was, to absorb a large quantity of stock, and in
the process to transfer a great portion of the national debt into
a landed security. The quantity of stock thus transferred was
in its amount to equal, at least, the quantity of land tax, which,
by this means, should be extinguished, and become applicable
to the public service. The amount of the land tax is two millions sterling ; the ministers proposed to set it up at twenty years
purchase, when the three per cent. were at fifty with a proportionable rise of purchasage according to their increasing price.
Forty millions sterling, the present amount of the land tax, at
twenty years purchase, would amount to eighty millions three
per cent. stock at fifty, affording an interest of 2,400,000l. and
leaving a clear gain to the revenue of 400,000l. a year. To
simplify to the operation, the purchase was to be made in stock,
and not in money : the proprietor was to have the opportunity
of pre-emption, as the land tax was not to be offered to sale to

c For a detailed account of the subscriptions, see the periodical journals
of the times, copied from the lists which were officially published at the
royal exchange, and in other parts.

d The contributions were considerable, both from public schools and
private academies ; of which last I remember various instances very honourable to the pupils and preceptors.

third persons until the expiration of a certain period, to be given to the proprietor of the land to make his arrangements for the purchase; afterwards it was redeemable by the proprietor, on replacing to the original purchaser the same quantity of three per cent. stock which he paid as the price of his purchase.[e] Even if a gentleman of landed property were not able to raise the sum necessary for the purchase of his tax, without selling a part of his land for that purpose, he would still find the operation extremely advantageous. Were he to sell in order to purchase his land tax, for his land he would receive twenty-eight years purchase at the average value; he would only have to pay twenty for his land tax, so that he would be a clear gainer of eight years purchase. This scheme encountered strong objections, the most important was, that, " by consenting to vote " the land tax perpetual, instead of bestowing it annually, par- " liament would give up one of the great checks which it had " in the privilege of voting or withholding the public money." It was farther said to be intended to benefit the monied interest at the expense of the landed, but these objections were overruled, and a bill conformable to Mr. Pitt's scheme was passed into a law.

With financial resources, parliament considered and devised other means of defence. A plan for the security and protection of the realm was drawn by Mr. Dundas, and introduced into parliament in the form of a bill. Its object was to encourage loyal and patriotic associations for the defence of the country; to enable the lords-lieutenants of counties to embody those who might be willing to come forward for the protection of their laws, religion, and property. The bill was passed into a law, and produced very speedy and extensive effects; loyal associations to arm in their country's defence, which had before been confined to particular places, now became universal. The whole kingdom, and every one of its parts, exhibited those constitutional guardians, resolute to defend their king and country against foreign and domestic enemies. To make their resolution effectual, the volunteers learned the use of arms, and paid an equally implicit obedience to the officers of their recommendation as if they had been under military law. While the members of the volunteer corps were zealous to increase their skill, utility, and numbers, zeal did not transport them beyond the bounds of prudence: the use of the military exercise depended upon the character and dispositions of the persons that made it a study; therefore a strict inquiry was instituted into the behaviour and political sentiments of those who proposed to be members. In London and the adjacent districts, two housekeepers of known integrity, respectability, and constitutional loyalty, testified the qualifica-

CHAP.
LXI.

1798.

Plan of national defence introduced by Mr. Dundas.

Voluntary associations.

The whole nation becomes armed against foreign and domestic enemies.

[e] For a minute and detailed explanation of this subject, see Wright's Weekly Examiner, for the 19th of March, and the 7th of May, 1798.

tions of the candidates: throughout the kingdom, that, or some
other mode of a similar kind, was adopted for ascertaining
eligibility. The persons chosen after this investigation were
men, who in their variety of stations, had the welfare and
honour of themselves, their families and friends, involved in
the welfare and honour of their country: whose private and
public affections and interests led to the same conduct; from
whom their aged parents, beloved wives, and infant children,
called for the same exertions as their king and country. Another measure of preventive policy, for the defence of the
kingdom, adopted in the course of this session of parliament,

was the revival of the alien bill. It was introduced in the
house of commons on the 29th of March, and having undergone some amendments, passed on the 27th of April. The
clauses added to the alien bill, were for obliging the letters of
lodging to give regular accounts to government of the foreigners who resided in their houses: and for enabling his majesty
to detain foreigners; and to prevent aliens from landing in
Great Britain, until the master of the vessel had authority to

let them come on shore. On the 20th of April, a message was
brought to the house of commons from his majesty, stating
the advices he had received of great preparations for invading
his dominions; and that in this design the enemy was encouraged by the correspondence and communications of the traitorous and disaffected persons and societies of these kingdoms.
In such circumstances legislature deemed it expedient to renew
a bill for detaining suspected persons. Mr. Wilberforce this
session renewed his motion, for the abolition of the slave trade,
but his proposition was rejected; several regulations however
were made for alleviating the sufferings of the Africans in their

Motion of
the duke of
Bedford
for the re-
moval of
ministers
is negati-
ved.

passage, and a law was enacted for the purpose. In the course
of the session, the duke of Bedford made a motion for an address to the king, to remove ministers: the debate on this subject necessarily consisted of arguments often repeated; and his
proposition was rejected.

Ireland was a subject of frequent inquiry and animadversion; but ministers represented the circumstances as too critical for public discussion; and, on the 29th of June, parliament

Proroga-
tion of par-
liament.
Rebellion
in Ireland.
Treatment
of Ireland
from the
latter years
of the Ame
rican war.
The penal
statutes
against the
catholics
repealed.

was prorogued. Before the prorogation, the storm which long
had been gathering in Ireland at length burst out, and the
sister island became a scene of rebellious uproar. Having
seen the fatal effects of coercion that was attempted towards
h colonies, the British minister, from the latter years of the
American war, adopted towards Ireland a much more liberal
and enlightened system of policy. The penal statutes against
the Roman catholics were repealed; they held their land on
the like terms with the protestants; they enjoyed, in short,
every right and franchise in common with the former, saving
only the offices of state, and the privilege of sitting in parliament. The Irish catholics deemed themselves injured by the

restrictions which continued, instead of being favoured by the CHAP. relief bestowed ; and desired a participation in the privileges LXI. that were still withheld. The protestants, considering the catholics as still unaltered, conceived that the admission of a 1798. sect so superior to their own in number, to an equality of pri- The catho- vileges, would be eventually a surrender of their own acquisi- lics desire tions and possessions : outnumbering them and overpowering a participa- them in parliament, the catholics might claim and recover the litical pri- possessions of their ancestors, of which they very naturally vileges, deemed the protestants usurpers. The lower classes of catho- which is lics, grossly ignorant and superstitious, and governed by their refused. priests, were inflamed with the greatest rancour against the protestants, whom they abhorred as heretics, as well as detest- ed as interlopers. These were their relative sentiments at the Effects of time the French revolution began to agitate all the neighbour- the French ing countries. Whatever sentiments might be entertained of revolution. the concomitant excesses, the revolution itself was imputed to the obstinate perseverance of the old government in its abuses. When the extraordinary events happened, on the 10th of Au- gust 1792, which overturned the French monarchy, the hopes of the reforming parties, both in England and Ireland, were equally elated : they now thought their wishes would infallibly be accomplished, and that the dread of the people would ope- rate so powerfully upon their rulers, that these would hardly venture any longer to reject their demands, with such terrify- ing consequences before their eyes, of the king of France's opposition to popular demands. To promote the changes United which they desired, certain persons formed a society to which Irishmen. they gave the name of United Irishmen.[f] This institution, Wolfe projected and organized by Wolfe Tone, proposed to connect Tone. the whole Irish nation together, with the professed purpose of Professed a general melioration of their condition, by a reform of par- objects, re- liament, and an equalization of catholic with protestant privileges, form in without any exceptions civil or political. The plan of union parlia- was formed on unity of object, connexion of instruments, and ment, and a co-operation of means, that combined secrecy of proceeding catholic emancipa- with efficacy of counsel and conduct. No meeting was to tion. consist of more than twelve persons ; five of these meetings were represented by five members in a committee, vested with the management of all their affairs : from each of these com- mittees, which were styled " baronial," a deputy attended in a superior committee, that presided over all those of the barony or district.[g] One or two deputies from each of these superior commit- tees, composed one of the whole county, and two or three from every county committee composed a provincial committee. The provincial committees chose in their turn five persons to superin- tend the whole business of the union: they were elected by ballot,

f See reports of the committees of the Irish parliament, 1797 and 1798.
g See reports of the committees.

CHAP.
LXI.

1798.

Real Ob-
ject and
progress
of.

and only known to the secretaries of the provincial committees, who were officially the scrutineers. Thus, though their power was great, their agency was invisible, and they were obeyed without being seen or known. Whether the designs of these associates were originally to effect a complete separation of Ireland from Britain, has not been ascertained as a fact; but there is no doubt that, in the progress of their concert, they had formed such a project;[h] and that parliamentary change, and catholic emancipation, were only pretexts with the heads and principal agents of this confederacy, in order to unite the greater numbers in the execution of their designs. The protestants, persuaded that whatever their purpose might be, the ferment which they were agitating must be inimical to the existing establishments, under the protection of which they held their privileges and property, formed counter associations, and assumed the name of *Orangemen*, in honour of king William the vindicator of protestant security, and the establisher of protestant property and power in Ireland. The Orangemen proposed to disarm the catholics. Bodies of these associated to resist the attempts, and assumed the name of *defenders*. Between the Orangemen and defenders various feuds took place, accompanied with great disorder, ferocity, and depredations, with some bloodshed on both sides. The united Irishmen did not immediately amalgamate with the defenders, who were rather violently outrageous than systematically designing In them, however, they saw ready and willing instruments, when their own deep laid schemes should be mature for open and avowed execution. Neither the prevalent broils nor the several machinations, were unknown to the French rulers; they despatched one Jackson, a native of Ireland, and a protestant clergyman, but now an emissary of France, as a spy, to Britain and to Ireland, in order to sound the dispositions of the people. Jackson, in Ireland, formed a connexion with Wolfe Tone, Hamilton Rowan, and some of their associates, and proposed a plan of insurrection, in order to facilitate a French invasion. In England, Jackson had trusted his treasonable schemes to an intimate friend, one Cockayne, an attorney. This person communicated the projects to Mr. Pitt; and undertook to accompany his friend to Ireland, in order farther to discover his intentions and plots to government, from which he was to receive the sum of three hundred pounds, if, through his means, the capital conviction of his friend should ensue.[i] Cockayne being thus engaged to accompany his friend to Ireland, and pretending to partici-

Counter as-
socia ion
of Orange-
men.

Catholic
defenders.

French
mission to
Ireland.

Proposed
plan of in-
surrection
to facilitate
a French
invasion.

h See reports of the committees of the Irish parliament, especially the committee of 1798.

i From what has been already said about Messrs. Goslin, Taylor, &c the witnesses in the state trials of 1794, the readers, I trust, have perceived the absolute necessity often imposed in conspiracies, on the most upright minis-

pate in the plot, was introduced to Rowan and other conspira- CHAP.
tors. A plan was formed for concerting a French invasion of LXI.
Ireland : Jackson wrote several letters to correspondents
abroad, explaining the state of Ireland and the outlines of 1798.
the project. The letters being sent to the post-office, Cockayne, who had perused them all, gave information to govern- Appre-
ment : the letters were seized; Jackson was tried; Cockayne hension of
was the sole oral evidence; but the papers coinciding with Jackson,
his testimony, rendered the case so clear, that the jury with- coveries
out hesitation found the defendant guilty. Jackson was con- through
demned to die; but by suicide anticipated execution. By this him.
discovery the correspondence with France was suspended:
Tone and Rowan made their escape. Lord Fitzwilliam was
now arrived in Ireland, commissioned, as he conceived, to terminate all disputes in that country, by making the concessions which the Roman Catholics demanded. Such also was Hopes of
the general persuasion of the Irish themselves : but as it was the catho-
frustrated, and lord Fitzwilliam recalled, the discontents lics from
became deeper and more extensive than ever. From this the appointment
time the united Irishmen proceeded with more despatch and of lord
decision in their arrangements; a military organization took Fitzwil-
place in the several provinces; arms were procured, pikes liam.
fabricated, and every preparation was made to enter upon Conse-
the execution of their schemes. The chiefs, and men of supe- quences of
his recall.
rior abilities and weight that had now joined the association, Farther
intended nothing less than a thorough revolution, and an progress of
abolition of all church establishments; while the common peo- the united
ple sought principally to be discharged from the payment of Irishmen.
tithes and ecclesiastical dues to the protestant clergy; in order
to obtain which it was easy to persuade them that a total
change of government was necessary. The activity of the
leaders was indefatigable, and most extensively successful:
those of their numbers who had absconded on the discoveries
made by or through Cockayne, were now in France, and had

---

ters, to employ spies and informers. Cases may even occur, as Cicero has well
shown in his offices, in which a person is bound by conscience and duty to
become an informer; but not *for hire* How far Mr Cockayne's motives
would come under Cicero's moral exceptions may be best learned from his
own evidence, as recorded in the State Trials. Mr. Cockayne and Jackson had been very intimate friends : in the course of their intimacy, money transactions had taken place, rendering by Mr Cockaney's account,
Jackson his debtor three hundred pounds When Cockayne communicated
his discoveries to the minister, it was intimated that, as the matter must
become the subject of legal investigation, it would be necessary for him to
substantiate the allegations : Mr. Cockayne was averse to give evidence
against his friend, *because*, if the friend should be capitally convicted, he
would lose the sum that was owing ; but government agreeing to liquidate
this account, his scruples were removed ; he went to Dublin to become a
witness for the crown. See Cockayne's evidence on Jackson's trial, Irish
State Trials.

CHAP.   settled a correspondence between their Irish associates and the
LXI.   French government. ; A proposal was made; by which the
        French were to assist the Irish with a considerable body of
1798.   forces, to enable them to throw off their connexion with Eng-
        land, and form themselves into a republic.[k]   The offer was
They send accepted; and lord Edward Fitzgerald, and Mr. Arthur
ambassa- O'Connor were appointed to settle the terms of a treaty.
dors to For this purpose they went to France, met general Hoche. in
France. the summer of 1796, and arranged the business of the project-
        ed invasion, which was destined to be executed the follow-
        ing November.   In the latter end of autumn, intelligence[l] arriv-
        ed from France that the expedition was deferred to the follow-
        ing spring, when England should be invaded at the same time.
        Hence it happened that, when the French armament arrived
        on the coast of Ireland, towards the close of the year, the
        Irish that were to second them, being wholly unapprized of
        their coming, were in no state of preparation, and the deter-
        mined spirit of loyalty displayed by the friends of government,
        awed its adversaries: thence the French had not landed, but
Vigilance had returned to their own coast.   The government was indeed
of the Bri- very vigilant, and had long before this time procured an act
tish go- to be passed authorizing the magistrates to proclaim martial
vernment law, in case of imminent danger. A proclamation accordingly
Martial was made, and put in force at the arrival of the French.   The
law is pro- disappointment of this expedition did not discourage the con-
claimed spirators from prosecuting their plans.   The chiefs of the
Mission of Irish association sent doctor Macnevin, an able man, of great
Macnevin importance in the combination, as minister to France.   He into France. formed the French government that if they would invade Ire-
        land, the numbers ready for insurrection were immense, that a
        hundred and fifty thousand would rise in Ulster alone.[m]   He
His pro- also laid before them a plan of attack, demanded a supply of
posed   arms and money and particularly recommended that the
scheme of French plenipotentiaries, then treating at Lisle with lord Malms-
military
operations. bury, should be instructed to make the dismemberment of
        Ireland, from England a condition of the peace; he solemn-
        ly engaged, that all the advances made for the service of
        Ireland, and all the expenses already incurred, should be

        k See reports of the committees of both houses of the Irish parliament
     in 1798, from which a considerable portion of the text is digested and
     formed.
        l Whence this information came has never transpired: some have
     thought it a deception; fabricated by some secret partisan of the English:
     by others it has been attributed to the French themselves, with a view of
     lulling friends and foes into general tranquility, thereby to effect their de-
     signs without opposition or interference.
        m To this expected insurrection may probably be referred the fol-
     lowing verse—
            " In the north I see friends, too long was I blind oh !" ·
     in the celebrated song of Erin go brah ; in which pathetic music and se-
     ductive eloquence so powerfully propel ignorance to outrage and revolt.

reimbursed as soon as affairs were settled, and its independence secured. France agreed to their other requests, but the
government declared its inability at present to supply them
with money. Meanwhile this conspiracy proceeded with such
secrecy, that, though the penetration of the Irish government
discovered there were strong grounds for suspicion, yet no precise information was procured: they did not till the month of
April 1797, obtain certain intelligence of the transactions that
were carried on in many parts of the kingdom. Government
learned that, on the 14th, a number of seditious people were
to meet at a house at Belfast: on this information, it was entered by a party of the military, and two of the association committees were found actually sitting: their papers were seized,
and sufficient documents appeared to bring at once to light
the nature and extent of the plot in agitation. This important
discovery led to others in various places, and the danger and
magnitude of the conspiracy was clearly ascertained. Government immediately employed precautions of every kind; enforced
the act against illegal conventions; searched for arms, and seized
great quantities. In operations requiring military force and
summary execution, where there is a collision of attack and
resistance, bloodshed is unavoidable; but the malcontents set
the example of atrocious violence, by plundering houses and
murdering the innocent inhabitants. The soldiers were not
slow in retaliation, nor always discriminating in punishment.
Both parties of Irishmen were inflamed by reciprocal suffering,
and the acts of both bore the stamp of infuriated passion, and
unrestrained licentiousness. The conspirators, first in recent
transgression, were the more atrocious in barbarous acts;
but their advocates imputed their conduct to the indignant
resentment of men that had suffered long under systematic
oppression, and in endeavouring by the most violent exertions
to break their chains on the heads of their oppressors, little
cared though these oppressors should be crushed in the struggle; and Ireland was now a scene of disorder, robbery, and
massacre. In this situation of things, the whig party, consist- The whig
ing chiefly of men of similar sentiments both in general and party pro-
temporary politics with those of Messrs. Fox, Sheridan, pose conci-
Erskine, and their coadjutors in England, in May, proposed liatory
the conciliatory measure of parliamentary reform. In conten- measures,
tions between government and numerous bodies of the governed, conciliation is generally the soundest policy, if adopted
before the passions be violently inflamed, and the projects
matured. Conciliatory measures when adopted, appeased
America, and if the system had been uniform, there is a moral
certainty, that the war and all its dreadful consequences might
have been prevented: spontaneous sacrifice on the part of
the French monarchy, if offered at the first appearance of a
spirit of liberty, might have preserved the greater part of what
by too long tenacity it was compelled to relinquish: but, con-

CHAP. LXI.

1798.

which are rejected as inapplicable to the case.

ciliation to be effectual, must be offered in the early stage of discontent, before resentment contracts inveteracy, and concerted resistance requires force. After rigid rejection of suppliant petitions, concession offered to men in $a_r m_s$, appears either the retraction of precipitancy, or submission of fear; and, instead of restoring confidence and attachment, encourages revolt by representing it likely to succeed. Lenient measures were then too late; government and legislature acted wisely in rejecting them at so advanced a period of the conspiracy: thwarted in this attempt, the whigs withdrew from parliament.

Ireland was at this time in a deplorable state: the occupations in civil life were deserted, and the people were intent every where on preparations for war: those who were peacefully disposed could promise themselves no security; they were plundered by the malcontents, who collected in numerous armed bodies, and committed every species of outrage and devastation.

Proclamations and proffers of pardon are totally disregarded.

Proclamations were issued, threatening severe punishments on the offenders; but they were as little regarded as the offers of pardon to those who forsook the rebellious associations. The conspirators projected a general insurrection, to take place in the summer of this year, and to be seconded by France.

The united Irishmen concert measures for a general insurrection.

In July they received information that two armaments, one from Holland and the other from Brest, were ready to sail for Ireland whenever they could elude the British fleets; they therefore postponed the intended rise, and waited with impatience for the arrival of the promised auxiliaries; but the defeat of the Dutch fleet in October was a fatal blow to their hopes.[o] France they knew had for maritime effort trusted chiefly to Spain and Holland, and their expectations from both had been blasted by Jervis and Duncan.

Disappointed by Duncan's defeat of the Dutch fleet.

But another fortunate circumstance for the British interests in Ireland was, that the object of the malcontents and of the French republic were totally different. The Irish conspirators sought the formation of their country into a republic, independent of Britain and also of France. The French proposed to subdue Ireland, and to form it into a government like the Batavian republic, dependent on themselves. The Irish, considering their own object, desired the directory to send ten thousand men, which would be a very efficient body of auxiliaries, without being dangerous to the principals. The French, to promote their purpose, proposed to send fifty thousand men, which they did not doubt would be able to model the whole island according to their views and pleasure. Finding the Irish, however, averse to their plan of invasion, they turned their attention to objects which they deemed more advantageous and more practicable. They now therefore received the propositions of the conspirators with great coolness; and the Irish despairing of any effectual

Want of concert between the conspirators and the French republic.

o See Reports of the Secret Committees of the Irish parliament, 1798.

assistance from the French republic, prepared for insurrection, without waiting for co-operation from the continent. In spring 1798, they employed themselves in dispositions for war: and meanwhile, in every part of the country, were guilty of the most savage atrocities. The benevolent spirit of lord Moira, still hoping that conciliation might be effectual, proposed pacificatory measures, but government assured his lordship that any proffers of the kind would be unavailing, and lord Moira's conciliatory motion was rejected. Such was the secrecy of the chief conspirators, that though the plot was discovered, yet the names of the plotters were not found out. At last one Reynolds, who had become an united Irishman, reflecting on their atrocious designs, was struck with remorse, and communicated their intentions to a friend, who prevailed on him fully to disclose the business and agents to government. On this discovery, fourteen of the chief delegates were seized in the house of Mr. Oliver Bond.[p] Lord Edward Fitzgerald escaped, but being afterwards discovered, he resisted the officers sent to apprehend him, in the scuffle was mortally wounded, and died a few days after. The remaining conspirators, now grown desperate, proposed a general insurrection, to be executed in the night of the 24th of May: but captain Armstrong, a militia officer, who had insinuated himself into their confidence, and pretended to be an accomplice, apprized government of their designs. The two Sheares of Dublin, Neilson of Belfast, and several other chiefs, were arrested on the 23d of May, and the metropolis was put into a state of perfect security against any attempt. The conspirators thus deprived of their leaders, though scantily provided with arms and necessaries, determined notwithstanding to execute their project of general insurrection. They began rebellion, on the 24th of May, by attacking Naas, a town fifteen miles from Dublin; but they were repulsed by a body of Irish militia, under lord Gosford. A band of insurgents at the same time took possession of the heights near Kilcullen, but they were dislodged by general Dundas, and between one and two hundred were killed and taken. To detail the various engagements which took place in this warfare, would exceed the space which the plan of the history allows; I shall therefore confine myself to the chief agents, operations, and results. The insurgents fighting with undisciplined courage, were frequently victorious over smaller numbers; but inflamed by their furious priests, where they prevailed, they exercised a savage barbarity unknown in the annals of civilized society.[q] The regular soldiers of the loyalists were not numerous, but the Irish militia fought with distinguished fidelity, valour, and effect, against the rebels. The English militia being at their own instance permitted by

CHAP.
I.XI.

1798.

Arrestation of the delegates,

hurries on rebellion before their designs were ripe.

Rebellion.

The insurgents near Dublin are defeated.

p See Annual Register, 1798.
q See Narrative of the sufferings of Jackson, published in 1798.

CHAP. LXI.

1798.

Alarming insurrection in Wexford;

successes of;

at length they are defeated.

Rebellion is suppressed in the south. Insurrection in the north advances, but is subdued.

Lord Camden desires to be recalled; marquis Cornwallis is appointed his successor; wise policy of.

The French attempt to revive rebellion, are vanquished. Squadron defeated by Sir John Borlase Warren.

Irish rebellion extinguished.

an act of parliament to assist their loyal fellow subjects, several regiments crossed the channel, and were most powerfully instrumental in supporting the cause of government. To pass over desultory skirmishes, the first great scheme of rebel operation was in the counties of Carlow and Wexford : a large body of them having been repulsed at the former place, being reenforced, proceeded to Wexford, amounting to fifteen thousand : part of the garrison marched out to give them battle, but they were surrounded and entirely defeated.[r] In a few days after the insurgents took the town of Wexford, and a great number of prisoners. In their farther progress being repulsed, and infuriated by revenge and priestly instigation, they murdered their prisoners in cold blood. General Lake, on the 21st of June, gained a complete victory, the consequence of which was, that this tumultuary insurrection was entirely crushed.[s] In the north of Ireland a rebellion also broke out, but the insurgents were completely overcome at Ballynahinch, and the whole rebellion was quelled before the end of June. After that time, various scattered parties, taking refuge in the fastnesses and mountains, infested the adjacent country, but were rather marauding banditti that disturbed the police than insurgents that rebelled against the government. The most formidable of these parties was commanded by the daring and noted adventurer, Holt, who at length surrendered himself to government. The discovery and seizure of the principal conspirators prevented this rebellion being carried on with any efficient concert, in the south, it consisted of detached multitudes driven by their priests to desperate valour and savage cruelty ; in the north, chiefly inhabited by protestant dissenters, it was by no means so general in extent, nor so merciless in operation. The rebellion of Ireland, appearing both to the viceroy and to his majesty to require a lord-lieutenant who could act in a military as well as civil capacity, lord Camden therefore requested to be recalled, and the king appointed marquis Cornwallis his successor. The rebellion being finished, the new viceroy adopted a plan of mingled firmness and conciliation, which executed with discriminating judgment, tended to quiet Ireland, and prepare matters for a permanent plan to prevent the recurrence of such pernicious evils, and to promote the industry and prosperity of the country. The French with a small body attempted to revive rebellion in Ireland, and surprising our troops by their unexpected appearance, gained a temporary advantage ; but were soon overpowered and captured by lord Cornwallis. A French squadron of one ship of the line (the Hoche) and eight frigates, with troops and ammunition on board, destined for Ireland, was, on the 1st of October, taken or dispersed by a

r Otridge's Annual Register, 1798. p. 163.
s See letters of general Lake, dated June 22d, and inserted in the London Gazette extraordinary of June 26,

British squadron under sir John Borlase Warren:[t] the whole CHAP.
French equipment, with the exception of two frigates, fell ulti-   LXI.
mately into the hands of the English. Among the prisoners
taken in the Hoche was Wolfe Tone, who being tried and con-   1798.
demned, hastened out of life by a voluntary death.

t See letter from commodore Warren, in the London Gazette extraordinary, Oct. 21st, 1798.

CHAP. LXII.

1798.

THE inattention of the French to the affairs of Ireland,
by no means arose from supineness: they were occupied with
very grand and soaring projects. Their power was at this time
enormous: Holland, Spain, and Italy, were appendages of the
French empire; Austria was prostrate at its feet; the mountains
and fastnesses of Switzerland had not escaped the invading ambition of this potent neighbour; unprovoked by aggression, the
republicans had entered, pillaged, and revolutionized those
brave cantons. Ireland they saw was inaccessible to their
schemes of subjugation: England, always terrible was in the
year 1798, become a nation of soldiers. From Caithness to
Kent and Cornwall, the united nations were in arms: internal
conspiracies were quashed, and all hearts and hands were joined in defiance of the French. The leaders of opposition,[u] who
had so often predicted the evils that would arise from persistance
in the war, were among the readiest to meet the enemy, if he
invaded Britain. Bonaparte was aware that Britain contained

French
threats of
an invasion
rouse the
spirit and
stimulate
the efforts
of Britain.
Animated
and ener-
getic pa-
triotism.

[u] No man showed himself more loyally and patriotically resolute to
combat in the field an invasion, than that illustrious nobleman, who in the
vigour of a life devoted so warmly, wisely, and effectually, to the benefit
of his country, has within these few days[*] been prematurely cut off in the
middle of a benevolent and beneficial career, which entitled him to a much
more estimable reputation, than any statesman or general could acquire by
planning or carrying on aggressive war. See his proposed address to the
king, March 1798, and the speech by which it was supported.
[*] Written in March 1802, soon after the death of the duke of Bedford.

more formidable opponents than he had ever encountered; the defiles and precipices of the Alps and Appenines, guarded by myriads of Austrians fighting for their *masters*, could be surmounted; but the plains of Sussex and of Kent, containing hands and hearts of free-born Englishmen, fighting for THEMSELVES, would, he well knew, be impassable. Convinced of the hopelessness of any direct attempt upon England, the French government and the general, formed a very grand scheme of conquest, which would ultimately extend to the richest possessions of Great Britain. The project was to subdue Malta, invade and reduce Egypt, and establish the French power in that country, with the double purpose of possessing the riches of the Nile, and extending their sway to the wealth of the Ganges: the empires of Turkey and Hindostan they proposed to render either parts or dependencies of the French republic. The projects for an invasion of England were apparently continued for a considerable time after the design was laid aside, that their real purposes might be the better concealed and accomplished. While certain bodies of troops, and stores, were drawn towards the coasts of Normandy and Britanny, others were collected at Toulon; this port was the rendezvous of the expedition which sailed under the orders of Bonaparte, on the 20th of May, 1798. It consisted of thirteen ships of the line, of which one carried a hundred and twenty guns, three eighty, and nine seventy-four, seven frigates of forty guns, besides smaller vessels, making altogether forty-four sail. The transports amounted to nearly two hundred, carrying about twenty thousand men, regular troops, with a proportionable number of horses, and artillery, and immense quantities of provisions and military stores. Bonaparte in all his-expeditions and designs included the advancement of knowledge, the subjection of matter to mind, and the subserviency of mind to his own views; with his *physical artillery* so tremendous to opponents, he carried an INTELLECTUAL AND MORAL ARTILLERY, tending still more effectually to break down all opposition. In his fleet there were scientific men and artists of every kind: astronomers, mathematicians, chemists, mineralogists, botanists, physicians, and many other classes of ingenious and learned men; certainly a much more rational assortment of attendants, than buffoons, parasites, priests, and prostitutes, the usual retinue of French monarchs when heading their army.[y] A variety of conjectures were formed with regard to the destination of this formidable armament: the largest that had ever been equipped in France, for any distant expedition. Malta and Egypt were generally pointed out as its principal objects; which they proved accordingly. The riches of the former were deemed a sufficient temptation for France to seize them, in its present need of resources, exclusive of the abundant supply of skilful mariners to be drawn from that island, were the French to retain it: the

CHAP. LXII.

1798.
The nation starts up in arms to defend their king, constitution and country. Against a people so disposed and so powerful, Bonaparte sees all attempts must be vain. France turns her ambition to less hopeless projects. Grand scheme of distant conquest. Expedition under Bonaparte, sails from Toulon.

Learned and philosophical attendants of the expedition.

[y] See Campaigns of Louis XV. in Flanders.

CHAP.
LXII.

1798.

latter appeared an acquisition of the highest importance to the commercial interests of France, which would enable it to intercept and ruin the trade of England in India, one of the principal resources of our opulence and naval grandeur. On the 9th of June, the fleet arriving at Malta, Bonaparte attacked that country, upon no better principle than Cyrus, Alexander or Cæsar attacked Babylon, Persia, and Gaul; and annexed it to the possessions of France.[z] Departing on the 20th of June, on the 1st of July he reached the bay of Alexandria.

Lands in Egypt.

The project of seizing and colonizing Egypt had been suggested by the count Vergennes, to the French government, during the monarchy. At present its seizure was extremely desirable to the French, because, besides its commercial benefits both actual and prospective, it opened a probable opportunity of revolutionizing Greece, long and ardently desirous of breaking the fetters of Turkish despotism. The French commander sent to the Greek states the strongest assurances of powerful aid, if they would vindicate their liberties. His ability, however, to perform his promises, depended upon an element, the command of which Providence had bestowed on another; a truth of which France had many warnings, but now was to receive a most fatally signal lesson.

Lord St. Vincent commanded this year, as before, the fleet destined to watch the coast of the ocean, and was cruizing off Cadiz when intelligence arrived of the departure and operations of the Gallic armament. While he himself continued to block the Spanish fleet, he detached a squadron in quest of the French expedition, and conferred the command on rear-admiral sir Horatio Nelson. This armament consisted of thirteen ships of the line and one of fifty guns.[a] The captains were all men of unquestionable zeal and professional talents, assisted by officers who highly merited their respective statious; and these were supported by crews who had been long practised in the habits of all that appertains to naval war; and the greater number of the ships had been engaged in distinguished actions.

Admiral Nelson sails in pursuit of the French fleet.

The British admiral first sailed towards Naples, and on the coast of Sicily learned that the enemy's fleet had visited Malta. Thither he hastened: but on his arrival was informed, they had departed from thence a few days before, and steered to the eastward. Conceiving that the French expedition was destined for Egypt, he proceeded directly thither: but arriving off

z See details of the capture and voyage, in Denon's Travels, chap. i and ii.
a The ships were, the Vanguard, 74, rear-admiral sir Horatio Nelson, captain Berry; Orion, 74, sir J. Saumarez; Culloden, 74, Troubridge; Alexander, 74, Ball; Zealous, 74, S. Hood; Goliah, 74, captain Foley; Bellerophon, 74, captain Darby; Minotaur, 74, captain Louis; Defence, 74, captain Peyton; Audacious, 74, captain Gould; Majestic, 74, captain Westcott; Swiftsure, 74, captain Hallowel; Theseus, 74, captain Miller; Leander, 50, Thompson.

Alexandria, he heard that they had not appeared on that coast. CHAP.
Eager to meet the enemy, and confident that they were in the LXII.
Mediterranean, he proceeded in a course which he had not
hitherto essayed; the British squadron was led northward to   1798.
Rhodes. There hearing no tidings of the enemy, Nelson again He tra-
returned to the westward; sailing along the coast of Morea, verses the
he learned from a Turkish governor that the French fleet had Mediter-
proceeded to Egypt, though they had not reached that country ranean.
so soon as their pursuers. Sailing as quickly as possible, the
British squadron again arrived on the coast of Egypt. The He descries
Alexander and Leander, being before the rest, descried the them in
Pharos of Alexandria, and, immediately after, the fleet perceiv- Aboukir
ed the armament of the enemy lying at anchor in a line east- bay.
ward from the point of Aboukir.[b] The two ships which had
first perceived Alexandria, by this time had advanced nearer
the coast on the right hand, so that the others, which were farther out to sea, were before them in rounding the cape. The
Culloden being obliged to tow a vessel laden with wine, was somewhat behind the rest.

The genius of Nelson united that comprehensive foresight Disposi-
which completely provides for every probable occurrence, with tions for
the ready invention and prompt decision which meet unfore- attack.
seen circumstances. Conceiving it likely that the enemy would
be moored near the coast for easy and expeditious communication with their land forces, and knowing that the dexterity and
boldness of English seamen could venture nearer land than the
French would judge prudent, on this foundation he concerted
his plan; and resolved that if it could be found at all practicable, part of his fleet running between them and the shore should
attack them on the one side, while the rest should bear down
upon the other, and thus inclose the foe between two fires.
Having formed this general design, and reposing the highest
confidence in the ability and courage of his officers and sailors,
he directed that in its execution the captains should exercise
their judgment in the time and place, and that every ship should
begin battle where she could act most powerfully. On this oc- Emulous
casion, there were such displays of emulation by every ship to ardour of
gain an advanced post in the attack, as must have tended to in- the British
spire each other with an invincible confidence. So alert were heroes.
the whole, that no ship could get ahead of another that was in Rapidity of
the smallest degree advanced forward.[c] The admiral gave or- movement.
ders for attacking the enemy's van and centre, and soon after
hoisted a signal for close engagement. As the British fleet was Strong po-
closing upon the enemy, a cannonade was begun by the French sition of
ships, supported by batteries from the castle of Bequires on the enemy,
Aboukir promontory. The enemy's fleet lay in a line with and collateral ad-
vantages.

b Denon says, that one of the French ships descried our fleet.

c Besides gazettes and other documents, I have received many particulars
from gentlemen who were present.

their heads towards the west. Having on their left, or larboard, the coast abounding with shoals, they had no apprehension that the British ships would make any attempt on that side, where, besides shallow water, they would be so much annoyed by the batteries on shore: their defence was directed to the starboard, where only they expected an attack: but one adventurous movement of the British totally disconcerted the Gallic plan of combat. Captain Foley, in the Goliah, leading the British van, darted in ahead of the enemy's vanmost ship, Le Guerrier, doubled her larboard side, and having poured a destructive fire into the Frenchmen, moved on to the second, whom he charged with tremendous fury. Next followed the Zealous, captain Hood, who attacked the enemy's vanmost ship, also on her side next the shore. Thirdly proceeded the Orion, sir James Saumarez, and took her station on the inside of the enemy's third ship. The Theseus, captain Miller, following the same example, encountered the enemy's fourth. Fifth came the Audacious, captain Gould, who moved round to the enemy's fifth. Sixth advanced the Vanguard, carrying the heroic Nelson, with his gallant Berry, and took his station opposite to the enemy's starboard, where, expecting the British efforts, they were prepared. The enemy's first and second, which had longest encountered our ships, being considerably damaged before Nelson came up, the admiral assailed that which was still fresh; the seventh, eighth, and ninth ships stationed themselves opposite to the fourth, fifth, and sixth ships of the enemy. Thus by the masterly seamanship and conduct, with the dauntless valour of the British commanders, nine of our ships were so disposed as to bear their force upon six of the enemy. The seventh of the French was L'Orient, a ship of immense size, being a hundred and twenty guns: this stupendous adversary was undertaken by the Bellerophon, captain Darby; while the Majestic, captain Westcott, attacked an antagonist farther astern. The British ships, thus arranged, played upon the enemy with the most tremendous effects. The heroic admiral himself was wounded in the head: but his soul animating his valiant countrymen the ardour of their efforts was undiminished. Meanwhile the Leander and Alexander, captains Thompson and Ball, though by having been foremost on the side of Alexandria, they were behind the others in passing Aboukir, yet reached the enemy in time to partake of the most dreadful dangers of the conflict. The enemy fought with a valour and impetuous heroism which no efforts of courage and skill could have withstood but the extraordinary courage and skill which they had to encounter; they resolutely persevered in their exertions after the close of the evening till the approach of midnight. The conflict was now carried on in the darkness of the night in the southern latitudes, and the only light to guide their operations were the flashes of cannon. About twelve o'clock, the enemy's enormous ship the L'Orient, was blown up with a terrible explosion, and a blaze that displayed at one glance the promontory of Aboukir, the capacious bay, and the magnificence of the Nile. The French now found all their endeavours hopeless; they however continued a languid fire, with increasing intermissions, and at length entirely desisted from opposition so unavailing. Morning opened a view, exhibiting at once the intrepid valour and obstinate resolution of the vanquished, the stupendous efforts and decisive victory of the conquerors. Of the French fleet two ships only and two frigates escaped fire or destruction; so complete was the victory of British heroism and ability. The French transports in the harbour, and garrison in Alexandria, waited, in suspense, for their personal doom, as well as the fate of the French navy. Even as far as Rosetta, distant about thirty miles from Aboukir, the battle, by the aid of glasses, was seen by French officers, from its minarets and towers.[d] An interesting part of the prospect afforded by the dawning morn was, the adjacent shores all lined with natives, regarding with astonishment both in the conquered and conquerors, the terrible heroes of the north. As a sublime effort of naval genius, the history of ENGLAND HERSELF affords no instance more brilliant than the battle of the Nile. The head that projected the plan of attack, the hearts and hands that carried it into execution, deserve not merely the cold narrative of the historian, but the ardent description of the epic poet. Were Homer to rise from the dead, he would find a subject worthy of his muse in the British sailors and the British officers, headed by the British Nelson.

While the renown of this action reached every quarter of the globe, its political effects were instantaneous and surprising over all Europe. The enemies of France every where recovered from the despondency by which they were oppressed previously to this glorious event; and an evident re-animation took place in all their councils, which were now occupied with the means of improving so signal a success. Reaching England, the news of this extraordinary victory filled the nation with joy and generous pride.

Government, anticipating its political effects, were animated with the hopes of reviving and extending the combination against France. There were various circumstances favourable to this expectation: the Austrians regarded the treaty of Campo Formio as merely an armed truce, during which they were to make dispositions for renewing the combat.[e] The emperor himself, a harmless prince, and intent upon frivolous amusement, little comprehended the political interests of his dominions; but extremely plastic, was guided by his counsellors, and

Marginal notes:
CHAP. LXII.

1798.

in vain combat the naval heroism of England.

Decisive and splendid victory of Nelson.

Estimate of this achievement.

Political effects.

Extensive and momentous consequences of the battle of Aboukir.

d See Denon's Travels, vol i.
e Annual Register 1798, chap ix.; and 1799, ch. viii.

CHAP.
LXII.

1798.

stimulates
all Europe
to resist
the power
of France.

Russia.

Character
of Paul.

Internal
regula-
tions and
external
policy.

State of
the Ame-
rican re-
public as
affected by

acted wisely or unwisely according to the directions he received. His ministers having now time to recover from the consternation under which they had concluded a peace that left to
France such valuable possessions, and finding a great portion
of the French force, with its formidable leader, by the late victory separated from the country, began to perceive the practicability of recovering some of their lost advantages. A congress had been opened at Rastadt between the various princes
of the Germanic empire and the French republic, for the adjustment of their respective pretensions; but the settlements went
on very slowly, and many differences were either found or made.
Catharine, empress of Russia, at first had only been in name a
member of the confederacy; but after the secession of Prussia,
had judged it expedient to become serious, and was preparing
a great force, when suddenly arrested by the hand of death.
Her successor and son, Paul, though weak, was extremely imperious, and having the most despotic notions of kingly right,
considered the Bourbon family as unjustly and iniquitously ejected from a rightful possession, which they derived from heaven;
and not individuals, excluded from the executive office held by
their ancestors, when the majority of the people conceived such
an exclusion conducive to the public welfare: he therefore determined to attempt their restoration, which, after Nelson's
victory, he thought practicable. Throughout his empire, but
especially in the metropolis, he was chiefly anxious to preserve
the gradation of ranks, and to resist novelty. The minuteness
of his arrangements for this purpose extended to orders for
wearing cocked hats instead of round, coats without capes,
waistcoats with flaps, stocks instead of stiffened handkerchiefs,
breeches and shoes with buckles instead of strings; prohibited
half boots; and manifested a petty mind pursuing a great object, which was in its careless ease and appendages to reprobate republicanism, and to cherish monarchy in its stiff and
formal ceremonials. His proclamations about shoe buckles and
neck handkerchiefs as clearly demonstrated the intentions of
such a man, as an edict for preventing an influx of revolutionists.
Paul very directly and explicitly avowed his abhorrence of the
French republic, and indicated such dispositions to overthrow
the present revolutionary system, and re-establish monarchy.
The Turks also were incensed at the French invasion of Egypt,
and manifested a determination to use their utmost efforts to
drive them from that country, and to combine with their enemies. The British ministers were not slow in discovering these
views, and endeavoured to form a confederacy more powerful
than the preceding alliance: nor were their views confined to
Europe, but extended to the American republic.

France, considering herself as the nurse of American liberty,
from the confederacy of 1778, had cultivated a close connexion
with the new commonwealth. From the commencement of the
French revolution, the Gallic republicans had eagerly desired

to spread their own peculiar doctrines beyond the Atlantic: they had procured many votaries, but were not able to succeed with the more respectable and powerful classes in the United States: maintaining solid and beneficial liberty, property, and religion, these presented three potent bulwarks against the French revolution. The necessary precautions of Britain for preventing importation of stores into France, had given umbrage to the Americans; but on fully considering the necessity of the case, and the fairness and equality with which the British government had acted, they had been perfectly reconciled; and, in 1794, had concluded a treaty of amity and commerce. In 1796, the haughtiness of the directory on the one hand, and the prudence of America on the other, coincided with the policy of Britain in drawing the ties of confederation closer between this country and the United States. The French republicans, considering the United States as indebted to France for their independence, bore with impatience and indignation that so great a benefit should be overlooked, and that, in this struggle for liberty, with so many powers combined against them from every quarter, in Europe, they should be forsaken by that people, in whose cause they had acted with so much zeal and success. But they were particularly displeased with the treaty of 1794, which they deemed inconsistent with the engagements between France and America. The French government breathed nothing but revenge; and its agents were extremely active in exertions to revolutionize America. Two parties now existed in the states, which, from their objects, may be deemed the constitutional, or supporters of the established government; and the revolutionary, or abettors of innovations on the model of the French changes. Of the former were the greater number of men of property, character, and importance in the state, of the latter were demagogues and their votaries, and the same kind of men that were agitators of discontent in Great Britain, and that are agitators of discontent in all countries where circumstances afford an opportunity. The object of the constitutional party was peace and neutrality, not to be interrupted by the contests of Europe. These would, in the course of a few years, raise the United States to a condition of prosperity and power, that must render them formidable to all the world, and secure to them tranquillity at home, and respect from abroad. The French having intercepted a letter from the United States to the ambassador at London, expressing these sentiments, considered this avowal of neutrality as inimical to the republic of France, and hoped to effect such a change in America as would render them dependent on France; and, by their agents, ardently endeavoured to spread principles of jacobinical revolution. Meanwhile, they made very imperious remonstrances to the government of the United States; and at length passed a decree directing her privateers to capture the vessels of neutral nations. In consequence of this decree, numerous captures of American vessels were made by the cruisers of the French republic, and of some of those of Spain, during the year 1797. A farther decree, on the subject of maritime affairs, was issued in January 1798, " That all ships, having for their cargoes, in " whole or in part, any English merchandise, should be held " lawful prizes, whoever might be the proprietor of that mer- " chandise; which should be held contraband from the single " circumstance of its coming from England, or any of its foreign " settlements ." It. was also enacted, that the harbours of France should be shut against all ships, except in cases of dis- tress, that had so much as touched at any English port; and, that neutral sailors, found on board English vessels, should be put to death. The execution of this last degree was prevented by a declaration on the part of Britain, threatening retaliation. But these hostile proceedings extremely incensed the Ameri- cans, and disposed them to enmity with the country that they considered as the universal disturber of other states. Couvin- ced, however, of the policy of persevering in neutrality, the American government still attempted conciliatory measures; and instructed their envoy to endeavour to re-establish harmony between the French and the American republics : but the di- rectory haughtily refused an audience. Imputing to intimida- tion the American desire of preserving peace, the directory re- solved to make the most of their supposed fears; and intima- ted, that if a treaty was to be renewed between France and America, the states must contribute, in return for this friend- ship, a very large sum of money; and farther intimated, that' it would be impossible for America to resist the power of France. The American government was well aware, that boasts of a power to be exerted by France on the ocean, where Britain was her opponent, were not to be dreaded as the means of conquest; still however, should a rupture take place, their trade they knew would be very materially injured : they there- fore made such a reply as showed that they still desired peace, though they would not be bullied to concession ; and they de- clared themselves solicitous to avoid a contest with the French republic. One object only was dearer to them than the friend- ship of France, their national independence : America, they observed, had taken a neutral station : to lend a sum of money to a belligerent power, abounding in every thing requisite for war, but money, would be to relinquish their neutrality, and take part in the contest. To lend that money, under the lash and coercion of France, would be to relinquish the government of themselves, and to submit to a foreign government imposed by force. They would make one manly struggle before they surrendered their national independence. America· was not like the petty nations of Europe that had become subject to the Gallic yoke : they were competent to their own defence against all hostile attacks; they could maintain their own rights. The

French still continued to demand a loan,[f] to capture American
ships, and to employ the most imperious and insulting language,
which a free, brave, and independent people, regarded with equal
indignation and contempt, and prepared to repel force by force.
Liberty was granted by congress to individuals to fit out privateers to make reprisals: measures were adopted for forming
and establishing a powerful navy, to protect and defend the American flag. The army was strengthened, and the command was
bestowed on general Washington: the destruction of the French
fleet at Aboukir spread joy over the constitutional Americans, and
stimulated their preparations against a power which they had
good reason to deem the disturber of all established society; and
thus the exertions of America were expected by the European
enemies of republican France, to co-operate with their efforts.

Amidst the signal successes of Britain in preventing invasion,
suppressing rebellion, and crushing the naval force of the enemy,
she experienced one disappointment: an expedition was undertaken against Ostend, with a view of seizing the ships and stores
there deposited by the enemy. The armament consisted of a
naval force, commanded by captain Home Popham, and a body
of troops, commanded by general Coote. Their first effort was
successful, but great numbers of republican forces having been
rapidly assembled at Ostend, overpowered the British troops, and
compelled them to surrender; but captain Popham brought off
his department of the expedition. This miscarriage was but little
regarded in a year of such extraordinary efforts, brilliant and momentous achievements, as the renowned 1798 was to Great,
Britain.

f See the correspondence and conferences between the French minister
and the American envoys, with the proceedings of the American government thereon, as detailed in State Papers, 1798 The publication of this
correspondence (as the Annual Register observes) between Talleyrand and
the American ministers of peace, made a lively and deep impression on all
the nations of Europe. Not all their actual depredations in Germany, the
Netherlands, Holland, Switzerland, and Italy; no, not their plunder of the
Papal territories, afforded to the minds of men so convincing a proof, that
the French republic was governed no more by a thirst of universal dominion, than by a rage for plunder, as even an attempt to subject the Americans to tribute.

CHAP. LXIII.

CHAP.
LXIII.
⁓
1798.
Britain.
Effects of
the late
glorious
campaign.

AS the disposition of the nation had been much more
favourable to the ministers, in the close of 1797 than at the
end of 1796, so at the termination of 1798, they were more
generally popular than at any period since the first year of the
war. The assessed taxes, having undergone so many modifications, were not much felt but by the higher classes, who with
few exceptions were favorable to government. Among the
middling ranks, and also including some of the lower orders,
the royal associations superinduced a military character on the
civil ideas and sentiments of their members, and had a powerful tendency to render them well affected to government and
administration, with whom they naturally deemed themselves

Discontent
is silenced.

co-operators in defending their country from foreign invasion,
and internal disturbance.   Discontent was silenced; the subjugation of rebellion in Ireland strengthened the power of the
British government : the splendid battle of the Nile, so gratifying to the generous pride of British patriotism, encircling the
whole nation with the rays of glory, reflected part of its lustre
on those ministers who had furnished the force and selected the
commanders. The contemplation of magnificent victory acquired by national prowess, engrossing the thoughts of the multitude, suspended all retrospective inquiry into the wisdom of

Ministers
recover a
high de-
gree of po-
pularity.
Meeting of
parlia-
ment.

the contest, the energy and skill of preceding plans, the consequent events, and the general result of benefit to Great Britain.
As our arms had been so eminently successful, the counsels of
the ministers recovered a very considerable share of popularity
and applause. Such was the state of things and the disposition
of the people, when parliament met November 20th, 1798.
His majesty's speech having bestowed the just tribute of ap-

plause on the glorious achievements of the campaign, mentioned his hopes that our efforts and successes would inspirit other
powers to such exertions as might lead to the general deliverance of Europe. He entertained great expectations from the
example of Russia and the Ottoman Porte, which, joined to
the disposition manifested almost universally in the different
countries struggling under the yoke of France, must be a powerful encouragement to other states, to adopt that vigorous line
of conduct, which experience had proved to be alone consistent
with security and honour. The supreme objects of parliamentary provision were propositions of finance and force for internal Grand ob-
defence, and for invigorating the confederacy which was now ject, to
forming ; and propositions of permanent union between Great provide for
Britain and Ireland. The army demanded for the year 1799, was defence,
somewhat greater and more expensive than for the former. For strengthen
the navy, a hundred and twenty thousand were required, instead the confed-
of a hundred and ten thousand. The assessed taxes, from the eracy, and
number of modifications, had failed in productiveness : in lieu union with
of it, the minister therefore proposed a direct tax upon income, Ireland.
requiring one-tenth on all incomes exceeding two hundred Supplies.
pounds. To this proposition various objections were made : it Income
was said to be a requisition similar in principle to the reproba- tax :
ted exactions of the French rulers ; and an application of the
revolutionary maxim, that all property belongs to the state. It
compelled a disclosure of property, in many respects extremely
inconvenient to mercantile men. To these general objections
to the principle, were added more special arguments against
the provisions ; that two hundred pounds was much too low a
rate to admit a subtraction of one-tenth ; that the gradation objections
ought to continue to at least five hundred, to be balanced by in- and argu-
creased contributions from larger incomes. It was farther said, and
that the source of income ought to be considered ; that persons against.
deriving a revenue from professional industry and skill, or trade,
ought not to pay the same proportion as landed and monied
capatalists ; because part of their income might be equitably
allowed to be reserved for accumulating a capital. It was said
that Mr. Pitt, in resisting modifications to those effects, rather
employed that trimming dexterity which courted the favour of
landed and monied capitalists, than the liberal and wise policy
which sought the least burthensome mode of necessary impost.
Having undergone these objections, Mr. Pitt's new scheme of
finance was by a very great majority passed into a law. From
the income tax he expected about ten millions, and the rest of
the supplies were to be raised by a loan amounting to about fifteen millions. The taxes in addition to income were new imposts upon sugar and coffee, on bills of exchange and stamps.
The British government, deeming the co-operation of the Russian emperor against the French republic as of the first importance, had so successfully made application to his present dispositions, that an alliance was concluded between the two powers.

CHAP. A provisional treaty was concluded between Great-Britain and
LXIII. Russia, December 18th, 1798,[g] the general object of which
was to concert such measures as might contribute, in the most
1798. efficacious manner, to oppose the successes of the French arms,
and the extension of the principles of anarchy, and to bring
about a solid peace, together with the re-establishment of the
balance of Europe. His Britannic majesty engaged to furnish
the pecuniary succours : 225,000*l.* sterling for the first and most
urgent expenses ; of which, 75,000*l.* was to be paid as soon as
the troops should have passed the Russian frontier ; and that
the other two moieties of a like sum each. It was also stipulated, that his Britannic majesty should pay for a campaign of
eight months, a subsidy of 112,500*l.* per month, two-thirds of
the sum to be immediately paid, the other third at the conclusion of a peace.[h] The emperor, on his part, was to bring to
the field forty-five thousand men, in cavalry and infantry, with
the necessary artillery. The contracting parties engaged not
to make either peace or armistice, without including each other
in the treaty. A message from his majesty stated this convention to parliament, and the requisite subsidy was proposed by
ministers. The proposition did not pass without objection :
the opponents of ministers asked what benefit was to accrue to
England from the services of Russia, to balance a present of
two hundred and twenty-five thousand pounds, and an annuity
of thirteen hundred and fifty thousand. Might not Paul apply
the money to his own purposes, like another prince who had so
completely duped the ministers. Mr. Pitt, in a very eloquent
speech, enlarged on the merits of the prince who now swayed
the Russian sceptre : he expatiated on Paul's magnanimity, zeal
for religion, justice, property, and social order. From this assemblage of virtues, which the brilliant genius of the minister
painted with his usual force of delineation and splendour of
colour, he inferred fidelity and consistency in the emperor. His
striking eulogy made a most powerful impression upon the
house, and on the faith of Paul's pious, honourable, and conscientious character, the house, without any other security,
voted the sums which were required. Three millions more were
granted to his majesty for making good such other engagements
as he might contract. The opponents of the administration, apprehending that such projects of new alliance might continue
hostilities, proposed an address to his majesty, deprecating any
negotiation that might be inimical to the peace. We were
likely to be again engaged in a crusading confederacy against

Subsidy to
the empe-
ror of Rus-
sia.

Argu-
ments for
and
against.

Splendid
speech of
Mr. Pitt,
in praise of
the empe-
ror Paul.

Powerful
impres-
sions of on
the house.

The subsi-
dy is
granted.

Motion for
peace.
Opposition
reprobate a
new con-
federacy.

g See State Papers.
h Russian subsidy—first expense   -   -   225,000
   Monthly 75,000l for eight months   -   -   600,000*l.*
   A balance of 37,500l. for said eight months payable after
   the peace   -   -   -   -   -   -   300,000
                                         1,125,000*l.*

France, which; we might be assured,.would prove inefficient.
If ministers, as they professed, did not fight for the restoration
of the Bourbon family, what did they mean to effect? They
professed to fight for SECURITY; how were the Russian or
Austrian efforts to produce the security of England? The
safety of this country depended on her own power, and especially her maritime exertions. The victory at Aboukir afforded,
if properly improved, a most favourable opportunity for concluding a peace: now was the time to offer terms of accommodation to France, when she was so deeply impressed with the
impossibility of encountering the navy of England. These
arguments having no weight with the majorities in parliament,
the proposed address was negatived. That ministers did not
propose the restoration of the house of Bourbon, we are assured
by their reiterated professions and declarations. Since the re-
establishment of monarchy was not their purpose, the historian,
judging from their conduct, must find it difficult to discover
what other object they could, by reviving a confederacy, propose to pursue. Here, however, the declarations of British
ministers are uniformly consistent—we were fighting for SECU-
RITY. If we subsidized Prussia, the benefit which was to compensate the price paid, was to be *security*. If we subsidized
Austria and Russia, we were to be gainers by the additional
security which their purchased efforts were to produce. Security is a kind of metaphysical generality, the import and application of which might admit very different and contrary system of efforts. If we proposed to go on in war until we
attained what metaphysical politicians might call security, wisdom would of course examine the probable trouble and cost of
the means, with the probable practicability and value of the ends;
wisdom would ascertain, before she engaged deeply in supporting Russia and Austria by the resources of England, how far
the advances of these powers, in a remote part of Europe, were
to make England more secure than we could be, with less trouble
and cost, through our own army and navy. Government and
legislature, appeared however to think that immense advantages
might be derived from a new confederacy, and the great object
of Britain in her foreign politics at present was to inspirit and invigorate a coalition of continental powers, to act offensively against
France in 1799.

While these schemes of external operation were forming, the
ministers were actively employed in proposing measures for the
better management of the sister kingdom. Ireland had, for
many centuries, formed one dominion with England, and, allowing to this country a superiority in the nomination of her king,
she claimed and enjoyed, in every other respect, an equality of
rights with Englishmen. As the privileges subjects in both
kingdoms were the same, the king's prerogatives were also the
same. What the English parliaments were doing in England,
the Irish parliaments imitated in Ireland; but as different in-

CHAP.
LXIII.

1798,

The mo-
tion is ne-
gatived.

Great ob-
ject of the
British go-
vernment
to excite
and invigo-
rate a coa-
lition
against
France.

Measures
for the bet-
ter admi-
nistration
in Ireland.

CHAP. terests and different views predominated in the parliament of
LXIII. each kingdom, different commercial regulations followed of
course, and the opposite shores of the Irish channel became,
1798. by degrees, mutually inimical. A wall of separation was raised
between the two kingdoms, to the prejudice of both, and commercial concerns, which in the beginning, we were directed by a
law of uniformity, came thus to be directed by a law of diversity. For want of a more regular and more defined system of
connexion between the two islands, since the abolition of the
feudal tenures, the undefined supremacy of the English parliament over Ireland was regarded as the sole remaining anchor
that held Great Britain and Ireland together; as the only principle that made them one in political power and dominion.
This system however was abolished under the Rockingham administration, in 1782; the motion for the abolition of the old
constitution was followed by another proposition, declaring the
absolute necessity of forming a new polity, which might connect the interests and privileges of the two kingdoms. But
though the wisdom, and even necessity, of this connexion were
admitted, yet no measures were adopted for carrying it into
effect. The three great objects to be accomplished for the
formation of a constitutional connexion between the two nations were, an equality of interests, an equality of privileges,
and an unity of power.[i] The two first of these purposes were
already in a great measure provided for, and very little remained indeed that could be urged by any peaceable and well disposed Irishmen, as a subject of complaint against the British
government; but the unity of power or unity of defence between Great Britain and Ireland remained unsettled. To the
want of a close political connexion between Great Britain and
Ireland, both eminent statesmen and political writers imputed
the growth of disaffection to such an alarming height. The
following is the substance of their arguments :—If there had
been a union between Britain and Ireland, we should not have
been exposed to the evils of rebellion, co-operating with foreign
enemies. Many as were the political and commercial advantages which must accrue to both countries from union, so as to
render such a measure generally expedient, the recent transactions rendered close connexion more imperiously necessary at
the present time; when the safety of the sister kingdom was
assailed both by domestic treason and foreign force, what preserved the country but the aid of Britons? The only effectual
remedy was to identify the interests of the two countries, to secure the same advantages in prosperity and in war, a free communication of the bravery, the resources, and the power of the
empire for its common defence! The internal situation of Ireland strongly demonstrated the necessity of a union. While
Ireland continued disjoined, any attempt to provide a salu-

Reason-
ings of
statesmen
and politi-
cal writers,
favourable
to union
between
Britain and
Ireland.

i Annual Register for 1799, chap. xii.

tary cure for her intestine divisions, or to allay the animosities
which arise out of her religious difference,[k] would be impracticable. By considering the sects into which the population
is divided, the remains of hostility between the English settlers and the native inhabitants, together with the unfortunate
want of civilization more conspicuous there than in most
parts of Europe, and the prevalence of jacobin principles[l]
among the very lowest classes of the people, we might comprehend the disastrous state of Ireland. For these evils no remedy could be devised but an imperial legislation aloof from the
prejudices, uninflamed by the passions, and uninfluenced by the
jealousies, to which a local legislature must be liable.[m] " The
" leading distinction in Ireland (said the unionists) is that of
" protestant and catholic : the protestant feels that the claims
"of the catholic for power and privilege (for this now is all)
"'threatens his ascendancy'; and the catholic considers his ex-
" clusion as a grievance. Ireland in this respect forms an ex-
" ception to every country in Europe, and runs counter to all
" received principles concerning religious establishments.[n] The
" religion of the government and that of the multitude, are
" different, and the mass of property is in the hands of a smal-
" ler number. In the present state of things, full concession
" cannot be made to the catholics without endangering the ex-
" isting constitution; but under a united constitution, privileges
" may be extended to the catholics with much more safety.
" Ireland at present wants industry and capital : capital may be
" imparted, and industry stimulated by close connexion with
" England. It is like a co-partnery proposed by a great capitalist
" with a small, upon equal terms, and which consequently must
" be extremely beneficial to the poorer party:" for these reasons, union between Great Britain and Ireland was ardently
desired, not by government only, but by many enlightened
patriots totally unconnected with administration. On the other
hand, many who were not in the general tenor of their conduct
adverse to administration, were inimical to a union between
the two countries: some of these were evidently actuated by
the most generous motives ; they dreaded union, as the destroyer
of Irish independence ; they conceived that the projected connexion would be, not a relation of equality between two states
agreeing to unite for common benefit, but a relation of superiority and dependence; that Ireland so joined to England,
would be merely a province; that England would be the great
receptacle of wealth, into which would be drawn all the products of Irish fertility, ingenuity, industry, and skill; that the
transfer of the legislature to the British metropolis, would bring

Arguments
of states-
men and
writers ad-
verse to
union, from
patriotic
considera-
tions.

k This argument is powerfully enforced in Mr. Pitt's introductory
speech, which was published.
l Arthur Young, passim.
m Mr. Pitt's speech on the 31st Jan. 1799.   n Ibid.

the nobility and gentry from Ireland to Britain; that the provincial towns of Ireland, and the metropolis itself, would be
deserted; that capital, at present so much wanted to commerce
and manufactures, would become still more defective, because
so great a portion of its constituents would be absorbed into
another country; that industry, long so languid, and recently
in some parts beginning to be excited, would, when such incentives were withdrawn, become more languid than ever; that
Ireland would again revert to the idleness and barbarity from
which, left recently to herself, she was emerging. While a
dependent on Britain, she had been in the most miserable and
distressed state; from the time that these fetters had been
relaxed, she had begun to flourish: this recent and contrasted
experience strongly forbade recurrence to real vassalage, under
the pretext of an equal union. Ireland, as an independent
kingdom, though not supremely powerful, would be more respectable and prosperous than as a tributary appendage of a
great and extensive empire:[o] besides, Britain, with all her commercial opulence and political power, was encumbered with an
enormous debt; must the growing enterprise and wealth of
Ireland be subjected to burthens not incurred by herself, nor
on her account; must Irish agriculture, manufactures, and commerce, be taxed to liquidate the accumulated profusion of the
British government in all its belligerent projects for more than
a century? As to a co-partnery, it was not like a very rich man
admitting a poor man upon his firm; it was a man of very extensive concerns, including immense engagements and respon-
sibilities, proposing to take into his company an active, enterprising, and industrious trader, of growing prosperity, who
might at once bear a share in his burthens, and promote his
trade. Ireland was likely to prosper much more by separate
adventure, than by a joint stock company so circumstanced.
These were the sentiments and reasonings of Irish patriots,
who, whether their conceptions or inferences were right or
wrong, were actuated by regard for the honour and prosperity
of their country. The citizens of Dublin were very hostile to
a design, which they apprehended might desolate their beautiful and flourishing metropolis; they indeed appeared to have
imbibed the same fears respecting their city, that during the
discussion of the British union, combining with a creative
fancy, dictated the celebrated prophecy of lord Belhaven, so
beautiful and eloquent as a poetic vision, and so totally falsified
by experience.[p] Irish imagination, not less vivid and fertile
than Scottish, conceived that by union, grass would grow on
the main streets of Dublin. There were others, who, without
being inimical to the British ministers, were averse to the union

o These arguments were employed by earl Moira and Mr. Sheridan in
parliament; and by many writers, especially Dr. Duigenan.

p See Somerville's History of Queen Anne.

from much less liberal and patriotic motives; who did not so
much consider the honour and general good of Ireland, as the
exclusive advantages which their own parties and classes had
long enjoyed. Many of the protestants conceived that a union
was intended to be a prelude to catholic emancipation, which
it would certainly facilitate. A junto of these, usually known
by the name of the Beresford party, had long governed Ireland,
and stimulated the most coercive measures in the various
stages of progressive discontent: this combination was very
inimical to union, which they apprehended might extend the
supreme power and influence to other parties and denominations. Ireland indeed was ruled by an oligarchy, which very
naturally reprobated a measure likely to produce a more extended and popular system of authority. Of the Irish lawyers, many were inimical to a change of legislature, which,
transferring the supreme judicial court to the metropolis of
Britain, would, they apprehend, carry a great part of their
parliamentary business to English counsellors. Whilst from
different motives, totally unconnected with opposition to government, great numbers of various classes and denominations
deprecated a union between the two countries, the malcontents
not only detested every additional scheme of connexion, but
desired a total separation. The united Irishmen, who though Views of
repressed were still extremely numerous, desired a democrati- the disaf-
cal republic entirely independent of England; they concurred fected;
with the unionists in considering the proposed connexion as
intended and fitted to counteract their project of complete
disunion, and not only encouraged aversion to the scheme
among their own associates, but very actively inflamed the
other causes of dislike. To these different opponents of a of anti min-
closer connexion between the two islands, may be added the isterialists.
usual party in both countries, which had been uniformly anti-
ministerial; these professing to regard with jealousy and suspicion every important design of administration, reprobated
the project of union as a scheme of ministerial patronage in
the various branches of the constitution. While union was
known to be in contemplation, and before its several impugners
had arranged and disposed their respective arguments, one preliminary position was advanced in which they all appeared to
have concurred though very different from the doctrines which
some of them had maintained and practically exemplified in
their late discussions with the votaries of disaffection; this
was, that the Irish parliament was not competent to conclude
a treaty of union; that so important a resolution could not be
santioned but by the general consent of the people.

Such was the state of sentiments and affairs, when on the
22d of January, the king sent a message to both houses of
parliament, stating the unremitting industry with which our
enemies preserved in their avowed design of effecting the
separation of Ireland from this kingdom; he recommended to

CHAP.
LXIII.

1799.

Mr. Pitt's
reasoning
on the ad-
vantages of
a union.

the lords and commons to consider the most effectual means of finally defeating that design, by disposing the parliaments of both kingdoms, to provide in the manner which they should judge the most expedient, for settling such a complete and final adjustment, as might best tend to improve and perpetuate a connexion essential for their common security, and consolidate the strength, power, and resources of the British empire. Mr. Pitt, in supporting the propriety of a union, exhibited a view of the settlement of 1782,[p] which he contended was not designed to be final, and had really been found by experience totally inadequate to its purpose. Since that time nothing had been attempted to provide for that defective settlement, but the partial and inadequate measure of the Irish propositions, which were defeated by the persons who framed the resolution, out who formed no substitute in their room. Was there no probable case in which the legislatures of both kingdoms might differ? Had not one case actually arisen within the short space of sixteen years, the measure of the regency: the difference of object was evident, the Irish parliament had decided upon one principle, and the British parliament upon another. If in the present contest the opposition should have as much influence in Ireland, a vote for peace might be passed by the Irish parliament, and the efforts of Great Britain might be paralized by the sister kingdom.[q] Ireland in such a state might neutralize its ports, prevent levies of recruits for the army and navy, and might endanger the very existence of the empire. Parliament undoubtedly wished to render the connexion between Great Britain and Ireland perpetual, but they would not promote a purpose so beneficial to both countries, if they neglected to bring forward some proposition which might secure the safety and advance the prosperity of Ireland, and remedy the miserable imperfections of the arrangement which was formed in 1782. It had been asserted by persons inimical to a union, that the Irish parliament was not competent to establish a measure which effected such a change in the constitution and relations of the country. He conceived that the parliament of Ireland, as of Britain, was fully competent to every purpose of legislation, and to enact laws for joining the two kingdoms as well as for any other purpose: a union was necessary to the interest of both countries, to improve their respective powers of productive industry, and to defend each other against internal commotion and foreign invasion: very great impediments now existed to the prosperity of Ireland, which would be entirely removed by a union with Great Britain.[r] The union with Scotland had been as much opposed, and by nearly the same arguments, prejudices and misconceptions, creating simi-

p Parliamentary Debates, on the 31st of January 1799.
q Ibid
r Mr. Pitt's speech, Jan. 31st, 1799.

lar alarms, and provoking, similar outrages, to those which had CHAP.
lately taken place in Dublin; yet the advantages which the LXIII.
northern part of the united kingdom had derived from the
union were abundantly apparent from the prosperity of the 1799.
capital, manufacturing towns, and of the country in general.
After this introductory speech, he submitted to the house
various propositions, the objects of which were to establish the
advantages which might be derived from the union; to explain
the principles by which such a connexion might be more beneficial; to present the outlines of a plan which he framed for
the purpose; and to declare the willingness of the British parliament to concur with the parliament of Ireland in effecting a
union between the two kingdoms. He proposed that the king His plan of
doms of Great Britain and Ireland, on a day to be appointed, union be-
should be joined into one kingdom by the name of the United tween Bri-
Kingdom of Great Britain and Ireland.[a] That the succession tain and
of the crown of the united kingdom should be limited and Ireland.
fixed agreeably to the present settlement of the crowns of the
separate kingdoms, according to the existing laws, and conformably to the terms of the union between England and Scotland. That the kingdoms so united should have one parliament, to be denominated the parliament of the united kingdom
of Great Britain and Ireland; that such a number of lords
spiritual and temporal, and such a number of commons, as
should hereafter be fixed by the contracting parties, should be
appointed to sit in the united parliament, and that on the part
of Ireland they should be summoned, chosen, and returned as
the Irish parliament should fix before the destined union. The
churches of England and Ireland, the doctrine, worship, discipline, and government thereof, should continue the same in
both countries as was established by the existing laws. His
majesty's subjects in Ireland should be entitled to the same
privileges, and should be on the same footing, in respect of
trade and navigation, in all ports and places belonging to Great
Britain, and in all cases with respect to which treaties might
be made by his majesty, his heirs or successors, with any
foreign power, as his majesty's subjects in Great Britain. The
import and export duties of Great Britain and Ireland should
be reciprocally equalized. The expenses of the united kingdom should be defrayed by Great Britain in proportions to be
established by their respective parliaments previously to the
union: that for the like purpose it would be fit to propose,
that all laws in force at the time of the union, and that all the
courts of civil or ecclesiastical jurisdiction within the respective
kingdoms, should remain as now by law established within the
same, subject only to such alterations or regulations, from time
to time, as circumstances might appear to the parliament of the
united kingdom to require. These are the outlines of Mr.

a Parliamentary Reports, Jan. 31st, 1799.

CHAP.
LXIII.

1799.
Union proposed to
the Irish
parliament:

discussed
and very
vehement-
ly opposed.

Opposition
to this
scheme in
the British
parlia-
ment.
-Argu-
ments of·
Mr. Sherl-
dan and
lord Moira.

Pitt's scheme of union between Great Britain and Ireland, which he wished to be submitted to the Irish parliament, that if agreeable to that body it might be carried into effect.

While Mr. Pitt submitted these propositions to the English house of commons, the subject had been introduced into the Irish parliament, and a discussion had taken place, which having given the tone to British opposition, it is proper to mention, before the narrative proceeds to the arguments adduced here against the minister's project. In the upper house of the Irish parliament, an address friendly to the union, was carried by a decisive majority ; in the lower it passed by a majority of one, and a motion consequent on it was afterwards lost. The opponents of the measure, in the Irish house of commons, did not enter into a full consideration of the advantages or disadvantages that might be likely to accrue from the scheme, nor prove that there was reason to induce the legislature to reject the proposition, but contented themselves with denying the competency of lawgivers to conclude such an agreement. To prove the incompetency of parliament, they did not reason from experience of fact and tendency, but from abstract principles, and the admission of theories that in no case had been reduced to practice : they rested their system on Mr. Locke's social compact, an hypothesis which, however well it might be intended by its wise and benevolent author, is one of the principal sources of modern democracy. On these speculative grounds, they maintained the incompetency of the legislature to make such a contract without consulting their constituents : they also pressed the various arguments from expediency, patriotism, and national honour which have been stated. The leading opponents in the British parliament were, in their respective houses, Mr. Sheridan and Lord Moira; and the ground on which they principally rested, in the first discussion, was the declared disapprobation of the Irish house of commons. As the commons of Ireland were avowedly averse to the project of union, it ought to be no farther agitated by England, until a more favourable disposition should appear in the other party. It was absurd to persist in pressing a union with a party unwilling to join, unless intimidation or force were intended. It was at present evident that there could be no voluntary union between Britain and Ireland, therefore it would be much more prudent to suspend the subject until the parties should have time coolly to reflect on its probable advantages and disadvantages. Afterwards, if the parties became willing to take it into consideration let it undergo a fair and impartial discussion: no measures could improve and perpetuate the amity and connexion between Great Britain and Ireland, unless their basis were the free and manifest consent and approbation of their respective parliaments. They who should endeavour, by corruption or intimidation, to obtain the appearance of consent, would deserve to be branded as enemies to the king and consti-

s Irish Parliamentary Debates on the union, January 1799.

tution. Having disavowed every intention of intimidation, Mr. Pitt strongly contended that the subject should be discussed at present. Let Ireland (he said) completely know what is proposed, then let her judge. By the judgment of her parliament we must ultimately abide; but we wish to state every general principle, and every particular circumstance, on which we ground our proposals; and doubt not that, when coolly and dispassionately weighed, their ultimate decision will be different from their determination of the preliminary questions. With this view he proposed a committee for examining the articles, and the house agreed to his motion. In a more advanced stage of the business, Mr. Dundas very ably showed the beneficial effects of the union between Scotland and England. He here took a view of the evils apprehended by the Scotch anti-unionists, and demonstrated not only the complete failure of their predictions, but the immense advantages that have accrued to Scotland from its incorporation with England.[t] Of these predictions lord Belhaven's were the most remarkable, as they exhibited in one view the apprehensions and arguments of the opposers of the union: " I think I see," said his lordship, " the royal state of boroughs "walking their desolate streets." So far, Mr. Dundas said, are these prophecies from being verified, that most of the boroughs are ten times increased in population, industry, and wealth. To prove this, it is only necessary to mention the names of Edinburgh, Glasgow, Aberdeen, Perth, Montrose, Dundee, and, in short, every other town of any name or consequence in that part of the united kingdom. These were strong facts, tending to controvert the reasoning of persons who asserted that a union would lessen the population, manufactures, and commerce of Dublin and other Irish cities and boroughs. The Scottish anti-unionists had prophesied that a preference would be given to Englishmen over Scots in every employment; the event, as Mr. Dundas observed, proved, totally different: natives of North Britain are almost exclusively employed in offices belonging to their own country, and a much greater number are established in England, than if no union had taken place; we need only look into every profession throughout England from the Scotch gardener, baker, and hair dresser, up to the Scotch merchant, physician, lawyer, general, and admiral, to prove that, since the union, merit has been equally rewarded throughout the whole island, whether its possessor was rocked in his cradle on the south or on the north side of the Tweed. The Scottish union tended to break asunder the bonds of feudal vassalage that had prevailed to so mischievous an excess in that country, and had allowed separate tyrants to exercise arbitrary power. The abolition of heritable jurisdictions resulting from the union, had promoted agriculture[u] to a very

CHAP. LXIII.

1799.

Mr. Dundas argues from the commercial effect of union with Scotland; his remarks on the celebrated prophecy of lord Belhaven in the Scottish parliament.

t Parliamentary Debates, February 1st, 1799.

u In point of agriculture, Scotland, as is obvious to every one the least great and rapidly increasing degree of improvement; like causes produced like effects; beneficial consequences of a similar kind would result to Ireland from union. Agriculture, manufactures, and commerce, mutually and reciprocally advanced each other; and whereas in the country of Scotland, there before existed only lord and dependent; the improvements from the union conjointly formed that middling class which in England had ever been found the most efficacious supporters of our laws, liberty, and constitution, from the oppression of feudal aristocracy in former times, and the licentious of democracy in latter. One of the chief causes of the evils under which Ireland laboured, was the want of this intermediate class: a parliament, with local interests and prejudices, was not likely to devise, at least steadily to employ, means for the establishment of so important an order: by an imperial legislature only could so desirable a change be effected. The subject was also discussed in the house of peers, and great eloquence was displayed on both sides; and both houses of British parliament concurred in approving Mr. Pitt's propositions of union, and, in an address to the king requesting his majesty to communicate to Ireland their views and resolutions. The king accordingly instructed the viceroy to lay the proffers and proceedings of the British before the Irish parliament.

acquainted with the country, has undergone most extraordinary melioration from the time that the union completely operated, on pursuits of a much more gradual improvement than commerce: this change has, no doubt, arisen in a considerable degree from the increase of capital that flowed into the country, from the time that the poor trader was admitted into partnership with the rich. It has not, however, been solely owing to commercial advantages, but in a great measure to political regulations resulting from the union. Whoever has spoken or written on this subject, considers the destruction of feudal vassalage as an event that would have never happened had Scotland possessed a separate parliament; because most of the members of that parliament, by vanity, pride, and ambition, would have been engaged to oppose a measure which reduced them from being petty princes on their own estates, to an equal submission to the laws with their vassals, and even poorest tenants. The vassals had before bestowed a servile attendance on their chieftain, at whose call they had been obliged to repair to his castle, and neglect their own private affairs. In that dependent state, they had estimated themselves, and each other, according to their place in the favour of their liege lord; and their chief occupation had been to court his good graces, by being lounging retainers about his mansion. Emancipated from their thraldom, they attended to the cultivation of their lands. The generous pride of personal independence succeeded the contemptible vanity which had been gratified by second hand importance. To independence the surest road was industry; the subject for the employment of their industry was their hitherto neglected land: to their inferiors they communicated a portion of that independence which they themselves possessed, and began to enjoy; they let their farms upon long leases, and dispensed with the most humiliating services. The tenants were, by the security of their tenures stimulated to unusual industry.

So important a subject occupied a great portion of literary CHAP.
ability[x] on both sides, and the press teemed with works on the LXIII.
justness and expediency of a union, with the means of carrying it most effectually into execution.

1799.

The farther parliamentary proceedings of the present session Farther
chiefly regarded external defence and internal tranquillity. provisions
There was now very little ground for fearing an invasion, and for inter-
the measures adopted respecting Ireland tended to prevent the nal de-
recurrence of rebellion : still, however, it was necessary to be fence and
vigilant. The supplementary militia, therefore, without being security.
increased, were continued on the same footing as in the former
years. The discontent and sedition which had so strongly pre- Renewed
vailed, were now in a great measure dissipated; still, however, suspicion
so much of malignity was by ministers and their supporters pre- of the ha-
sumed to remain, as to render the suspension of the habeas cor- beas corpus still necessary to be continued. A bill for continuing to pus act.
his majesty the power of detaining suspected persons was introduced into parliament, and passed into a law.

Mr. Wilberforce renewed his annual motion for the abolition
of the slave trade, but his efforts were again unavailing : parlia- Parliament
ment was prorogued on the 12th of July.   is proro-
                                                                 gued.

x Of these, one of the most eminent was a treatise published by dean
Tucker, many years before, strongly recommending union with Ireland.
It is to be hoped that his predictions respecting that connexion will be as
fully verified as the prophecies which he uttered concerning America. See
vol. i. of this history, p. 419.

CHAP. LXIV.

CHAP.
LXIV.

1799.
Congress
at Rastadt.

AT the treaty of Campo Formio it had been agreed, that a congress should be held at Rastadt, composed solely of the plenipotentiaries of the Germanic empire and of the French republic, for the purpose of concluding a negotiation between those powers; and this congress had met in December 1797. To follow the meeting through the various details which occupied their attention, would be foreign to the purpose of the present history and the accounts shall be confined to such proceedings as produced the rupture with France, and the renewal of the confederacy with Britain.

Project of
indemni-
ties.

By the treaty of Campo Formio it was agreed, that the Rhine should form the boundary between the French and German empires, and that a system of indemnities should make up to the princes of the Germanic empire for the losses which they should incur by this extension of the French empire; the proposed project was to be the secularization of the ecclesiastical estates; but in applying this general principle, there was a great interference of interests. Prussia and Austria proposed first the secularization of the chief ecclesiastical possessions;

Principle
that the
weaker,

·in other words, that because the great powers had sustained
losses by the conquests of the French, the smaller should indemnify them for these losses. The ecclesiastical electors
thought it vain to controvert the general principle of making
the weak pay for the losses of the strong: but were for shifting
the losses from themselves to a lower order: the electorial
archbishops proposed to be indemnified for their sacrifices to
the high powers, from the possessions of the prince bishops.
The prince bishops required the suppression of abbeys, monasteries, and the inferior prelacies. *Simple as the principle*
of secularization was, yet the adjustment of such an intermixture of pretensions was not without difficulty. France indeed
was not to be charged with enhancing the difficulty by any
intricacy of her own claims, these were very explicit and definite: she, in the first place, was to occupy all the left bank
for her share, and was afterwards to assist the Germans on
the other, in settling their respective boundaries. The reason
which she adduced for appropriating such an extent of territory was, not the love of dominion, *but the convenience of demar-*
cation. The Rhine was a natural boundary which the republic did not demand for the purpose of aggrandizement, but for
fixing a secure and determined frontier. Meanwhile the directory aud its agents entered into the Germanic discussions of
secularizations, and eagerly endeavored to sow discord between the various states and members of the empire: they
farther proposed to take under their own special protection
the very opulent cities of Franckfort, Bremen and Hamburg,
which they alleged to be coveted by German potentates; and
that therefore it behoved the French republic to interpose its
powerful meditation in their behalf. For these and other
purposes, it was necessary that France should possess a weighty
influence beyond the Rhine. The king of Prussia continued
to favour France, and she thoroughly accomplished the appropriation of the left bank. France farther proposed the free
navigation of the river to the opposite bank as well as her
own, the re-establishment of commercial bridges, and a division of the islands on the Rhine, by which France was to possess those which best suited the convenience of her own
boundary. France, possessing the left bank, was to strength-
en and fortify it as she pleased, while she required the demolition of fortifications on the other hank, because they might
interfere with the secure navigation of the French upon the
river.ʸ The fortress of Ehrenbreitstein, situated upon the right
bank of the Rhine, commands the entrance into Germany on
the side of Westphalia, the Upper Rhine, and Hesse; this
strong post the French desired to be destroyed. The evident
object of this demand was to secure an entrance into Germa-

CHAP.
LXIV.

1799.
should pay
for the
losses of
the
stronger,
through
the power
of the
strongest.
New requi-
sitions of
the
French.

ʸ See note of the French ministers to the deputation of the empire, May ·
31st, 1798.

CHAP. ny, whenever the republicans judged the opportunity favourable
LXIV. for the purposes, both general and special, which they had so very
clearly manifested. Elated with success, and conceiving them-
1799. selves irresistible by any continental effort, the French added to
their boundless ambition an overweening and dictatorial insolence which none of its objects could tolerate but from dread of
the French power. The Austrians were now recovering from
their disasters; incensed by the arrogance of France, which had
manifested itself even in the heart of the Austrian capital,[z] and
are resist- inspirited by the proffers of military aid from Russia, and of pe-
ed. cuniary supply from Britain, they prepared for force, by which
only the exorbitant demands of France could be resisted. The
directory easily discovered[a] sentiments and designs so naturally
resulting from their own series of ambition and haughtiness;
learning that the Russians were on their march to the south, they
no longer doubted that they were destined to co-operate with
the imperial army in Italy: having three great armies ready for
motion, they threatened to cross the Rhine, unless the Russians
should retreat from the confines of Germany; and finding that
Austria would not yield to their demands, they ordered their
War. ambassadors to leave Rastadt, and immediately prepared to commence a war.

The French, as we have seen, had totally changed the plan
of war: their system consisted wholly in pursuing the enemy
without intermission; courting opportunities of engagements;
and keeping their whole force together, without dividing it for
the purpose of carrying on sieges: the armies of France,
instead of investing particular forts and towns, attacked whole
countries. Fortresses which heretofore arrested, occupied
and consumed armies, were passed with unconcern, insulated
French as it were by the enormous mass. To this extension of the
plan of the theatre of war they were invited by their numbers, the superi-
campaign. ority of their artillery, and the provision that was made by
their moveable columns for the celerity of their motion. The
plan of the directory was the same that had been pursued
in 1796 and 1797; the invasion of the hereditary states of the
house of Austria, and the junction of the French armies under
the walls of Vienna. Of three hundred and twenty thousand
men who at this time composed the French army, forty-five
thousand, under the orders of general Massena, occupied Switzerland and the left bank of the Rhine, almost from its
source to the western extremity of the lake of Constance, and
from that point the two banks of the river as far as the Basle.
Between that town and Dusseldorf were stationed about sixty-

z Especially in the conduct of Bernadotte the ambassador, who hoisted
the three coloured flag of revolutionary democracy in sight of the Imperial
palace. See Periodical Journals of the year 1798.
a See State Papers, Note of the French ministers to the deputation of the
empire, January 2d, and January 31st, 1799.

five thousand men, commanded by general Jourdain, and form- CHAP.
ing what was called the 'army of Mentz. It was intended LXIV.
that the army of Jourdain should cross the Rhine, traverse the
defiles of the Black Forest, extend itself into Suabia, turn the   1799.
lake of Constance, and the southern part of the Tyrol, and
that the army of Switzerland should drive the Austrians from
the country of the Grisons, attack the Tyrol in front, and seize
the vallies of Leck and of the Inn ; while the army of Italy
should penetrate into Germany, either through the Tyrol or Plan of the
Friuli.   confede-
   The situation and the views of the Austrians were as follow : rates.
more than sixty thousand were concentrated under the archduke on the Leck. Twenty thousand were collected in the
Palatinate, in the environs of Auberg, or at Wurtzburg, under
the orders of General Sztarray : a like number was headed by general Hotze, in the Voralberg and the country of the
Grisons. Near twenty-five thousand, commanded by general
Bellegarde, were on the frontiers of the Grisons and the Tyrol,
part of which was on the Adige ; and the rest in Friuli and
Carinthia, was reckoned to be more than sixty thousand. Thus
the emperor had to oppose to the French one hundred and
eighty-five thousand fighting men, ninety thousand of whom
were in a situation for acting against Jourdain and Massena,
But the Austrians being determined not to commence hostilities,
acted at first on the defensive. Jourdain, through Suabia, and
Massena, through Switzerland, advanced towards Tyrol ; be- The
tween them during a part of the march, was the Rhine and French ar-
the lake of Constance ; and on the eastern side of that great mies in-
body of water they intended to form a junction. Jourdain, vade Ger-
with this intent, marched eastward with the left bank of the many and
Rhine on his right, and his left extending northward to the the Gri-
                                                                  sons, under
duchy of Wirtemberg. Their armies being so far advanced, Jourdain
the directory threw off the mask, and declared war against and Mas-
the emperor. Jourdain, occupying the space between the lake sena.
and the Danube, advanced to meet the archduke coming from
the Leck. Not restraining his troops from plundering the
country, he, as in 1796, incensed the inhabitants, whose resentment communicated to the soldiers. Already indignant against
the French for what they deemed a breach of the treaty, and
an unprovoked invasion of their country, they were ardently
desirous of chastising their insulting foe ; the archduke skilfully availed himself of this spirit, and being somewhat superior
in force, offered Jourdain battle. The French general had
been endeavouring to execute the plan of conjunction with Massena ; but the defiles, rivers, mountains, and other obstacles
which the latter was obliged to encounter, had hitherto obstructed the scheme. A successful battle, Jourdain conceived,
would effectually accomplish that object, and decide the fate
of the campaign ; and, confident of victory, he resolved to
hazard a conflict. On the 21st, a partial engagement took

CHAP.
LXIV.

1799.
Battle be-
tween the
archduke
Charles
and Jour-
dain.

the French
are defeat-
ed, and
for ed to
evacuate
Germany.

Advances
of Massena
in the Gri-
sons.
By the de-
feat of
Jourdain
he is oblig-
ed to re-
treat.

place, in which great numbers. were killed on both sides ; but
the Austrians were superior. On the 27th of' April, Jourdain
hazarded a pitched battle : he advanced in three columns to
attack the archduke ; the battle was fought with wonderful
obstinacy, and the French had almost proved victorious, when
the archduke, dismounting himself, led his infantry to the
charge, and, by his presence and example, inspirited his soldiers to prodigious efforts : still, however, the French were
unbroked : when the archduke, sending some battallions of
grenadiers, charged them in flank, and throwing the enemy
into confusion, completed the victory. The next day the
republican general endeavoured to renew the combat ; but,
finding his army so much reduced[b] as to be incapable of
making head against the enemy, he retreated, and recrossed
the Rhine ; and thus ended 'the French expedition to Germany in 1799. . Jourdain was dismissed from the command
of the army, and Massena was appointed generalissimo of the
whole French force from the Alpine frontiers of Italy to Mentz.
The army immediately under himself in the beginning of the
campaign, made considerable advances in the Grisons ; but
after the retreat of Jourdain, the force sent from the Austrian
army on the Danube to assist Bellegarde and Hotze on the
Upper Rhine, rendered the imperialists so powerful, that
Massena found it necessary to return to the left bank.[c] But
the subsequent operations in Switzerland were so much affected
by the transactions in Italy, that it is necessary to turn the narrative to Cisalpine operations.

The republican forces in Italy, at the commencement of
1799, consisted of nearly eighty thousand French soldiers,
and more than fifty thousand Poles, Swiss, Piedmontese, Geno-
ese, Romans, or Neapolitans ; they were formed into two
armies, one of which was called the army of Italy, and the
other of Naples : the army of Italy, consisting of ninety thousand, occupied the Modenese, the state of Genoa, Piedmont,
Milanese, the Valteline, and the countries of Brescia, Bergamo, and Mantua. This dispersion of force, which a general
hatred of the French rendered necessary, reduced the number
of men who could be employed' in active operations to about
fifty thousand.[d] They were in cantonments on the banks of
the lake of Garda, of the Mincio, and of the Po ; from the
frontier of the Tyrol to the mouth of the Po. The army of
Naples, consisting of about forty thousand, occupied the capital, and the conquered part of his Sicilian majesty's dominions ;
as also Rome, and the different provinces of the church.
The object proposed through the army of Italy was, general
co-operation with the army of Switzerland in attacking the
Austrian dominions, from the Adriatic, through Stiria and

b Annual Register, 1799, chap. xiii.
c Annual Register, 1799, chap. xiv.   d Ibid. chap. xv.

Carinthia, in the direction to Vienna. Thus, if Jourdain had
been successful, the grand line of approach, in three divisions,
towards Vienna, would have extended from the gulf of Venice
to the confines of Belgium. The emperor's ministers having
taken a view of the various causes of discomfiture in the
former part of the war, found treachery to have prevailed
among Austrian officers; and dismissing all those whom there
were grounds to suspect, substituted others in their place.
The French had also derived great benefit from their train of
artillery: the Austrian counsellors in this campaign took care The Aus-
that the imperial forces should equal their adversaries in ord- trians in-
nance. Scherer, the French commander took the field in March : vade Italy.
on the 26th of that month, encountering the Austrians command- Successes.
ed by general Kray, he was repulsed and compelled to fly
towards Mantua. Successively defeated, the republicans were
driven from the left bank of the Adige. The Italians now They reco.
joining the Austrian army, assisted in annoying the retreating ver the
French, and all the territories that had been extorted from northeast
the Venetians were evacuated; when marshal Suwarrow, with of Italy.
twenty-five thousand men, joining the Austrians, took the chief
command.

· Leaving Kray to invest the fortresses of Peschiera and Man- Arrival of
tua, the Russian commander pursued the enemy that had re- marshal
tired to the Milanese: overtaking their army at Adda, on the Suwarrow
27th of April, he entirely defeated them, and compelled them Russian ar-
to evacuate the Milanese. Peschiera was, meanwhile, cap- my.
tured by Kray; and, except Mantua, the whole northeast of Military
Italy was recovered from the republicans. Meanwhile Moreau operations
was placed at the head of the French; who, seeing the force and victo-
of the enemy, determined on a plan of defence, by occupy- Skilful
ing successive posts and defiles, which should prevent the con- movement
federates from any material advantage, and retard their pro- of Moreau.
gress until effectual re-enforcements might arrive. He therefore occupied a position which secured a communication between France and Switzerland on the one hand, and Macdonald
on the other.

· General Macdonald had been prevented from extending his Affairs of
conquests in Naples, by the gradual diminution of his army. Naples;
By the threats of descent from the Turks, the Russians, and the French
the English, who hovered over the coasts of the upper and evacuate
lower seas, he had been obliged to content himself with secur- of Italy,
ing the submission of the capital, putting the coast in a state and con-
of defence, and completing the reduction of the two provin- centrate
ces of Abruzzo and Capitana, and of the two principalities. their force
Such was the situation of Macdonald, when he received from north.
the directory an order to evacuate the kingdom of Naples,
and join Moreau. According to his instructions, he deposited
all power in the hands of the patriots; leaving for their support, republican corps that had been raised in the country, and
the garrisons of St. Elmo, of Capua, and Gaeta. Having

traversed the Roman estates, he arrived at Florence on the 24th of May; and having there joined several detachments of republican troops, he found himself at the head of twenty-five thousand men. With this force, Macdonald proposed to join Moreau, who was at a hundred and fifty miles distance; and to overcome the multiplied obstacles which were presented both by the nature of the country and the enemy. To effect a union with his colleague, he had two roads, on different sides of the Appenines: the one goes along the Riviera di Po-nente, and is known under the name of the Corniche; but it could not admit of the passage of artillery or even of bag-gage. The second road was that between the Appenines and the Po, across the duchies of Modena, Parma, and Placentia. This last route, though the more circuitous, he chose for his march; but secured the road by the Corniche, in order to retain that communication with Moreau. Suwar-row saw that if Macdonald should join Moreau, he would have a much more formidable force to encounter than any which he had before combated in the present campaign, and applied for re-enforcements. Accordingly, eleven thousand Russians, and fourteen thousand Austrians commanded by general Bellegarde, arrived to his assistance in the beginning of June. The month of June was occupied by Macdonald and Moreau in attempting to effect a junction; and extraordi-nary efforts of generalship were exerted by the three com-manders, both in forming schemes, and in reciprocally discon-certing antagonists. Suwarrow proposed to combine defen-sive with offensive operations, to occupy a strong line of posts on the west, in order to check the advances of Moreau, and on the east to bend his principal efforts against Macdonald. Both Moreau and Macdonald, on the other hand, wished severally to avoid a general engagement, that their strength might not be impaired when they should be united. Macdonald, after several conflicts with detachments of imperialists, was, on the 16th of June, advanced as far as the river Trebia;[e] and Suwarrow had now reached the same place. On the 17th, a couse of battles commenced, which, lasting three days, called forth from both the Russian and French generals, efforts not unworthy of the Carthagenian hero[f] who first gave celebrity to the scene of action. Macdonald being at length defeated, was for several weeks retarded from accomplishing his purpose, and his force was considerably reduced. Hastening back to meet Moreau, Suwarrow compelled that general to retreat. Macdonald meanwhile had retraced his own course back to Tus-cany: foiled in the first route which he had for so good reason chosen, there now remained for him only the left hand tract

e See Annual Register, 1799, chap. xvi.
f See account of the battle of Trebia, between Hannibal and the Roman consul Sempronius, Livy, book xxi. near the end.

by the Corniche, impassable as we have seen to baggage and artillery. He had no other means of saving his artillery and baggage, including the spoils of Italy, than by sending them by sea, and this was a very dangerous expedient, as the English men of war hovered over the coast. Impelled however by necessity, he sent his various stores to Leghorn to be embarked. Meanwhile, Suwarrow, having compelled Moreau to retreat, endeavoured to improve his victory over Macdonald by reconquering Tuscany. To this attempt the dispositions of the inhabitants were extremely favourable; and they were farther inspirited by the English envoy, Mr. Windham, to profit by the disasters of the French, re-assert their independence, and re-establish their sovereign. About 25,000 took arms with this intention, and were soon joined by very considerable re-enforcements. Diminished as his force was, Macdonald might easily have matched a feeble and desultory multitude; yet such an attempt was not at present his object. Freed from every incumbrance, he now took the route of the Corniche, and made his way towards Moreau, whom, near the end of July, he joined in the neighbourhood of Genoa, with the remainder of his army, now reduced to about thirteen thousand men: the whole army of the French in Italy amounted to about fifty thousand. During this period, Mantua and Alexandria had been captured by the imperialists; and while affairs were so prosperous in the north, they were no less flourishing in the south of Italy. After the evacuation of Naples by Macdonald, cardinal Ruffo, at the head of the royalist army, consisting of more than twenty thousand men, and some hundreds of Russians, defeated the republican levies of men which were opposed to him, and marched against the capital; which, on the 20th of June, surrendered by capitulation. A few days after an army of allies came into port, animated by the activity and directed by the talents of admiral Nelson, and his gallant and able second, captain Trowbridge. A body of English, Russian, and Portuguese troops, having obtained possession of the castles of Ovo and Nuovo, on the 26th; under the command of captain Trowbridge, invested the castle of St. Elmo, on the 29th. The garrison, unable to resist such a force and such commanders, capitulated: the other towns successively surrendered; and the king of the two Sicilies was restored to his throne and dominions by the British hero, whose splendid achievements had excited and invigorated, in various parts of the globe, the most courageous efforts for vindicating the independence of nations against the boundless ambition of revolutionary conquest. From Naples lord Nelson turned his attention to the papal territories, and sent captain Trowbridge with a small armament towards Rome. The inhabitants joyfully flocked to the standard of their deliverers:

the republicans finding resistance hopeless, surrendered by capitulation and evacuated the Roman dominions before the end of July. Tuscany was by this time completely recovered. Piedmont was chiefly in the possession of the confederates; and the French, who in the end of March had been masters of all Italy, now occupied only a small corner in the north-west. In the beginning of August, Joubert was appointed to command in the place of Moreau, who was sent to head the army on the Rhine. The confederates were now employed in the siege of Tortona, the last fortress which remained to the republicans in Piedmont; and twenty thousand men were on their march from Alexandria and Mantua to join Suwarrow. Joubert, desirous of making one attempt to relieve Tortona, resolved to attack the Russian general before the re-enforcement should arrive. The French amounted to about forty thousand men: the combined force was more considerable; and, besides the superiority of the latter in point of numbers, they were choice troops, better disciplined, and flushed with recent victories. The republicans, on the 15th of August, prepared to offer battle: and with that view, were formed in an encampment placed upon the hills which are situated behind the town of Novi; and, though not very high, yet are extremely steep. Notwithstanding the strength of this position, Suwarrow, the next morning at five o'clock, advanced to engage the enemy. The republicans received the attack of the imperial troops with their usual firmness and intrepidity, and drove back their centre and right wing three several times. The French appeared to be immoveable in their position, and sustained with equal valour repeated charges: at noon they confidently expected the victory; but sixteen battallions of Austrians arriving on the right flank of the enemy, made such an impression, that it was thrown into confusion; and general Joubert, endeavouring to rally his men, was himself mortally wounded. Deprived of their commander, and out-numbered by their opponents, the republicans were at length completely overpowered. Suwarrow obtained a most signal victory, which finally decided the fate of the campaign. Tortona was captured; Piedmont was entirely recovered; and of the acquisitions of Bonaparte in Italy, there now remained to the French only the small territory of Genoa. Suwarrow having so effectually accomplished the purposes of his command in Italy, prepared to carry his victorious arms against the republicans in Switzerland.

While the French by the combined armies were driven from their Cisalpine conquests, Massena was engaged in the most strenuous efforts on the Rhine. The successes in Italy invigorated the allies in their operations among the Alps, and compelled Massena to act upon the defensive. He was driven from the Grisons, and the Austrians, crossing the Rhine, established themselves on the left bank. Advancing in the

CHAP.
LXIV.

1799.
Successe
of the Au
trians.

career of victory, the Germans drove the French from the
strong and important position at St. Gothard, established themselves in Switzerland, and opened with the army of Italy, a line
of communication, which, on the other side extended through
Suabia to the banks of the Maine; so that from Mentz to Italy,
there was a chain of forces advancing against the French republic, of which the army of the Alps constituted the central
link.' During the month of June the imperialists proceeded
rapidly into Switzerland; and after the most obstinate conflicts,
made themselves masters of Zurich. But considerable detach-'
ments of the Austrians having been drafted to Italy, and a very
great body of Russians being still expected, the archduke,
without farther pursuing his conquests. contented himself. with
preserving his acquisitions, until the allies should arrive. The
present force of Massena being too much reduced for immediately resuming offensive movements, he employed himself in
preparations. This state of inaction continued, with no important interruption on either side, from the end of June till near
the end of August. The exertions and successes of the confederates meanwhile produced accessions to the alliance. The
duke of Wirtemberg and duke of Bavaria, the greatest secondary princes of southern Germany, joined the house of Austria
in its efforts against the republicans. The soul of the combination was England, which afforded money to assist the Austrians, prompt the Russians, and stimulate the German princes.
The great allied powers continued their attempts to induce the
king of Prussia to take a share in a combination which they represented as necessary to their own safety. This prince, however, still more jealous of Austria than of France, would not
join in exertions by which he conceived, that if successful,
Austria would be ultimately aggrandized: and, if unsuccessful,
the disasters would fall upon himself. Against revolutionary
doctrines and designs, he thought that the best antidote was to
preserve for his people the comforts of peace, which prevented
the necessity of oppressive imposts, promoted industry and
prosperity, and thereby precluded the most powerful causes of
discontent: he therefore persisted in avoiding all interference
in the contest. The secondary and other princes of northern
Germany were retained in their neutrality by the influence and
power of the king of Prussia. The elector of Bavaria and
the duke of Wirtemberg, respectively engaged to furnish ten
thousand and six thousand men, for which they were to be subsidized by England.

From this time, it is believed, that a difference subsisted between the courts of Viennna and Petersburg concerning farther
operations. The Austrians, considering their acquisitions as
ends, wished to preserve what they had obtained.[b] The Russians regarding their conquest merely as *means* of re-establish-'

b Annual Register, 1799. chap. xv.

ing the house of Bourbon, desired to pursue the successful career. Britain, without avowing the same object as Russia, agreed
in her policy, and was anxious to press as extensively and effectually as possible upon France. This diversity of views and
schemes between the two imperial courts soon manifested itself
in the belligerent operations.

The French government, in order to preserve Switzerland,
proposed to create a diversion on the western borders of Germany, and the execution of this project was the object of the
army which Moreau was called from Italy to command. In
consequence of this project, a powerful host of republicans,
passing the Rhine, invaded Germany near the end of August,
and entering Suabia, levied various contributions. About this
time, general Korsakow arrived at Switzerland, with a great
body of Russians; and Suwarrow, after his signal victories in
Italy, was advancing to the same quarter. The Russian general had expected that the archduke Charles was in Switzerland,
to co-operate with his efforts; but that prince, when the republicans entered the empire, marched towards the Lower
Rhine, in order to repress the incursion of the French; and
the defence of Switzerland was now chiefly left to the Russians.
The force of the allies being so much weakened by the departure of the archduke, Korsakow, and Hotze (left commander
of the Austrians in Switzerland), contracted their plan of offensive operations. It was now projected merely to recover the
possessions of the small cantons, and compel Massena to retire
to the Aar. Korsakow had several obstinate conflicts with
the republicans, with various success; but in the course of the
battles, the French had acted with so much skill in the management of their positions, that the Russians, when they were
apparently victorious by their intripid and impetuous valour,
were really surrounded from the masterly skill of their antogo-
nists. At Zurich, Korsakow was encompassed on all sides;
and Massena, knowing the terrible prowess of the Russian soldiers, endeavoured to profit by the advantage which he had gained, without driving them to desperation. He had it in his power
to intercept their retreat, but not with a force sufficient to overcome them, if driven to extremity; ' he therefore left, by the
road to Winterthur, one outlet unobstructed. Meanwhile he
offered to Korsakow a capitulation, by which he might quietly
retreat to the Rhine; but this proposal was totally disregarded.
Korsakow began his retreat by the outlet left for him; and
Massena, with much pleasure, permitted his departure without
attempting any obstruction. The Russian, however, having
merely begun his march in the undisputed course, suddenly
took a different direction, and attacked a great body of the republicans who were advantageously posted on heights that commanded the road. The French, though they had not expected
an attack, yet soon prepared themselves for skilful resistance.
They suffered the Russians to approach, and then opened a

tremendous fire of musketry and artillery. The Russians fought with astonishing courage, but without concert and design, and were therefore totally unequal to the valour, skill, and ability of their adversaries. Overwhelmed along the whole of their column by the grape shot of the French, whose flying artillery operated on this occasion with terrible effect, they rushed repeatedly with fixed bayonets on the enemy: and forced them, for some moments, to give way. But, as the prodigies of valour performed by the Russian infantry, neither were, nor indeed could be, turned to any account by the superior officers, in their present circumstances, they served only to render the defeat more complete, as well as sanguinary. General Korsakow, with the remains of his army, forced forward and passed the Rhine. Such was the situation of affairs when marshal Suwarrow arrived in Switzerland, in the month of September. The Russian general having successfully executed his march into Switzerland, expected a very powerful co-operation, which would enable him to be equally successful as he had been in Italy. Not apprized of the circumstances which had compelled the retreat of Korsakow, he fully relied on the aid of that general, as well as of the Austrians; and in that confidence advanced into the country which was now possessed by the enemy. But, on penetrating into Switzerland, he found that his countrymen were departed, and that he had very little co-operation to expect from the Austrians. He was now obliged to act on the defensive, and to retreat towards the Rhine. Korsakow, rallying his troops, recrossed the river to support his countrymen; and various bloody engagements took place between the Russians and republicans. Suwarrow, though compelled to retire, never suffered a defeat; and at last, in October, seeing no assistance from the Austrians, passed the Rhine.

Prince Charles having deemed it necessary, instead of co-operating with the Russian generals, to march into Suabia, there had to encounter the French army. After various and indecisive operations, he was informed of the misfortunes in Switzerland, and departed towards Suwarrow. Between the army which he left, and the republicans, repeated conflicts took place, without any important event; and the French repassed the Rhine: and thus the Rhine from its source to the ocean, again became the boundary of the republic.

The departure of the archduke for Suabia was, by military critics, deemed unnecessary, as a detachment might have sufficed. This movement, however, was not imputed to an error of the commander, but to political jealousy of the cabinet. The event of the campaign in Italy was favourable to the allies; but in Switzerland they lost in the end the advantages of the beginning; and besides the causes and circumstances of the discomfiture, tended to break the combination through which only they could succeed against France. Paul, about this time, published a manifesto, declaring his intention to restore the ancient

CHAP.
LXIV.

1799.
defeats
Korsakow
the Russian
general.

Suwarrow
marches
into Swit-
zerland,

not proper
ly support
ed by the
Austrians,
he retires
towards
Germany.

CHAP. government of France, and to replace all the conquests of the
LXIV. republic on the footing which they were on before the war. · If
the German princes would co-operate with him, he would exert
1799. his whole strength by sea and land; but if they withheld their
assistance, he would withdraw his forces.[i]

The British While the allies were thus engaged in endeavouring to make
fleets block an impression upon France, Britain undertook an expedition
up the to detach the Batavian republic from its connexion with the
ports of French; and to extricate her ancient ally from that domination
France,
Spain, and which she naturally supposed a great portion of the inhabitants
Holland. to bear only from necessity. The efforts of our illustrious commanders, in the two preceding years, had so reduced the maritime strength of France and her dependencies, that though both
Spain and she had a great number of ships, they had no efficient
naval force; and their harbours, during 1799, were under a state
of blockade.

Expedition Thus free from the apprehensions of maritime interruption
of the duke or invasion, government determined to send a powerful armaof York to ment to Holland. The chief command was conferred on the ·
Holland. duke of York: the land force was to consist of about thirty
thousand men, including a body of Russian auxiliaries. On the
13th of August, sir Ralph Abercrombie set sail from Deal with
the first part of the army, and a fleet commanded by rear-admiral Mitchel, joining lord Duncan in the north seas, on the 21st
they came in sight of the Dutch coast; but from weather extremely boisterous, notwithstanding the season of the year,
Troops could not attempt to land till the 27th. Admiral Mitchel, with
land at the very great skill and ability, covered the landing of the troops,
Helder. which sir Ralph superintended with equal intrepidity and vigour. Inspired by mutual confidence, sameness of wish, and
a thorough reliance on the courage, professional knowledge,
and wisdom of their respective leaders, both the army and the
Battle and navy acted with the most perfect unanimity.[k] The enemy postvictory. ed at the Helder, had made a vigorous opposition to our troops;
but were entirely defeated; and some days afterwards, the
Dutch fleet Dutch fleet in the Texel surrendered to admiral Mitchel. From
surren- this time to the 13th of September, the rest of the British forces,
ders. together with the Russians, arrived; and his royal highness having that day joined the army, found himself at the head of
British thirty thousand men.[l] The prince resolved on a general atroops ad- tack; and on the 19th, advanced with his army, extending in
vance to four columns from the right to the left, towards the eneAlkmaer. my, who were posted at Alkmaer. The column to the exBattle of
September tremity of the right, consisted chiefly of the Russians, in twelve
19th.

i See State Papers, Paul's declaration, September 15th, O. S. 1799.
k In the strong professional language of admiral Mitchel, *"they pulled
heartily together."*
l See the duke of York's letters to Mr. Dundas, London Gazette, September 19th.

battallions, assisted by the seventh light dragoons, and general CHAP.
Manners's brigades, and was commanded by the Russian lieu- LXIV.
tenant-general De Hermann, and extended to the sand hills on
the coast near the famous Camperdown; on which heights a 1799.
column of the enemy was very advantageously posted. The
second division, commanded by lieutenant-general Dundas, consisted of two squadrons of the eleventh light dragoons, two brigades of foot guards, and major-general his highness prince
William's brigade. Its object was to force the enemy's position at Walmen-huysen and Schoreldam, and to co-operate with
the column under lieutenant-general De Hermann. The third
column, commanded by lieutenant-general sir James Pulteney,
consisted of two squadrons of the eleventh light dragoons, major-general Don's brigade, and major-general Coote's brigade.
This column was intended to take possession of Ouds Carspel
at the head of the Lange dyke, a great road leading to Alkmaer.[m] The fourth and left column, under the command of
lieutenant-general sir Ralph Abercrombie, consisted of two
squadrons of the eighteenth light dragoons, major-general the
earl of Chatham's brigade, major-general Moore's brigade,
major-general the earl of Cavan's brigade, first battallion of
British grenadiers of the line, first battallion of the light infantry of the line, and the twenty-third and fifty-fifth regiments, under colonel Macdonald, and was destined to turn the
enemy's right on the Zuyder Zee. To the attainment of these
manifold and important objects, the most formidable obstacles
presented themselves. To the right, on which side the Russians
were to advance, the country was almost covered with woods,
especially near the village of Bergen, where the principal force
of the enemy was placed. The Russians, advancing with an
intrepidity that overlooked the powerful resistance they were
to meet, were, by their impetuous courage, transported beyond
the bounds of that order which would have insured safety and
success; and, after a most valliant contest, obliged to retire with
considerable loss. Both the second and third columns had also
great difficulties to encounter in the deep ditches and canals by
which the scene of their operations was intersected. The second, under general Dundas, after renewing the battle with
promising success, was at length obliged to retire. Lieutenant-
general sir James Pulteney, with the third, effected his object
in carrying by storm the post of Ouds Carspel at the head of
the Lange dyke; but the disappointment of the right preventing our army from profiting by this advantage, it became expedient to withdraw the third column. The same circumstances
led to the necessity of recalling the corps under lieutenant-general sir Ralph Abercrombie, who had proceeded without interruption to Hoorn, of which city he had taken possession, to-

m See the Duke of York's letter to Mr. Dundas, London Gazette extraordinary, September 24th, 1799.

CHAP.
LXIV.

1799.
Battle of
Bergen,
October
2d.

gether with its garrison. The whole of the army, returned to
its former position. Autumn 1799 was remarkably rainy, and
even tempestuous; such weather in a country naturally so wet,
and also intersected by canals and ditches, for some time suspended the operations of the British army. On the 2d of October the storm having abated, the British army commenced an
attack on the whole of the enemy's line. A severe and obstinate action ensued, which lasted from six in the morning until
the same hour at night. The right wing of the British army
was commanded by sir Ralph Abercrombie, the centre division
by general Dundas, and the left by major-general Burrard : all of
whom eminently distinguished themselves on this day by their cool
courage and excellent conduct.[n] The first impression was made
on the adverse line by the right wing of our army : the next
by the centre; and lastly, the left wing also overcame all resistance. The enemy being entirely defeated, retired in the
night from the positions which they had occupied on the Lange
dyke, the Koe dyke at Bergen, and on the extensive range of
sand hills between this last and Egmont-op-Zee. On the night
after the battle, the British troops lay on their arms ; and on the
3d of October moved forwards, and occupied the positions of
Egmont-op-Hoof, Egmont-op-Zee, the Lange dyke, Alkmaer,
and Bergen.

The enemy's force was computed to be about twenty-five
thousand men, of which, by far the greater part were French.
The duke of York, in the account he gave of the action
of the second of October, bestowed warm and liberal praise
on the whole army under his command. " Under the Divine
" Providence," says his royal highness, " this signal victory ob-
" tained over the enemy, is to be ascribed to the animated and
" persevering exertions which have been at all times the cha-
" racteristics of the British soldier, and which, on no occasion,
" were ever more eminently displayed : or has it often fallen to the
" lot of any general to have such just cause of acknowledge-
" ment for distinguished support. I cannot in sufficient terms
" express the obligations I owe to general sir Ralph Abercrom-
" bie and lieutenant-general Dundas, for the able manner in
" which the conducted their respective columns; whose suc-
" cess is in no small degree to be attributed to their personal
" exertions and example: the former had two horses shot un-
" der him." Very distinguished praise is also bestowed by his
highness on colonel Macdonald, lord Paget, major-general Coote,
general sir James Pulteney, and many other officers. The loss
sustained by the enemy exceeded four thousand men killed,
about three hundred prisoners, seven pieces of cannon, and a
great many tumbrils. But the victory obtained by the British
army was dearly purchased by the loss of about fifteen hun-

n See letter of the duke of York to Mr. Dundas, London Gazette extraordinary, October 24th, 1799.

dred men killed and wounded.[o]   The exhausted state of the
troops, from the vast difficulties and fatigues they had to
encounter, prevented the British commander from taking that advantage of the enemy's retreat, which, in any other country, and
under any other circumstances, would have been the couse-
quence of the operations of the 2d of October.

   The French general having taken post at the narrow isthmus between Beverick and the Zuyder Zee, the duke of York
determined, if possible, to force him from thence, before he
should have an opportunity of strengthening by works the
short and very defenceless line which he occupied; and to
oblige him still further to retire, before he could be joined by
the re-enforcements which he was informed were upon their
march.   Preparatively, therefore, to a general and forward
movement, he ordered the advanced posts which the army had
taken on the 3d, in front of Alkmaer and the other places already mentioned, to be pushed forward; which was done accordingly on the 4th.   At first, little opposition was shown,
and the British succeeded in taking possession of the villages
of Schermerhoorn, Archer Sloot, Limnen, Baccum, and of a
position on the sand hills near Wyck-op-Zee.   The column,
consisting of the Russian troops, under the command of major
general D'Essen, attempted to gain a height in front of their
intended advanced post at Baccum which was material to the
security of that point; but was vigorously opposed by a strong
body of the enemy, which obliged sir Ralph Abercrombie to
move up for the support of that column with the reserve of
his corps.   The enemy, on their part, advanced their whole
force : the action became general along the line from Limnen
to the sea, and was maintained on both sides until night, when
the Batavian and French army retired, leaving the British masters of the field of battle.   This conflict was as severe as any
of those that had been fought since the arrival of our troops
in Holland; and, in proportion to the numbers engaged, attended with as great a loss.   Of the British 600 were killed or
wounded; of the Russians, not less than 1200.   The loss of
the enemy was also very great, in the killed, wounded, and
prisoners which fell into our hands to the number of 500.   The
post to which the British army directed its march was Haer-
lem ; but intelligence was received from the prisoners taken in
this action, that the enemy, who had been just re-enforced by
6000 infantry, had strengthened the position of Beverwick, and
thrown up very strong works in its rear; and farther, that they
had stationed a large force at Parmirind, in an almost inaccessible position, covered by an inundated country ; the debouches
from which were strongly fortified, and in the hands of the enemy ; and farther still, that as our army advanced, this corps

Battle of
Limnen.

   o Among the wounded was the brave and accomplished marquis of Hunt-
ley ; who for many months suffered very severely, but at length recovered.

CHAP.
LXIV.

1799.

was placed in our rear. Informed of all these circumstances; the British commander naturally paused. The obstacles here enumerated might have been overcome by the persevering courage of the troops under his command, had not the state of the weather, the ruined condition of the roads, and the total want of the necessary supplies, arising from the above causes, presented additional difficulties which demanded the most serious consideration. From the people, instead of co-operation, he experienced hostility; indeed, if they had been disposed, of which they manifested no appearance, fear of the French republicans would have impelled them to distress the British troops. The duke of York, therefore having naturally weighed the situation in which the army under his command was thus placed, thought it adviseable, with the concurrence of general Abercrombie and the lieutenant-generals of the army, to withdraw the troops from this advanced position, and fall back to Shagenbrug. There the enemy harrassed our line of defence by daily, though partial attacks; the most serious of which was made by general Daendels in person. That general, on the 10th of October, assaulted the right wing of the British forces, upon an advanced post near Winckle, under the command of prince William of Gloucester; and with six thousand men and six pieces of cannon, endeavoured to force this post by every exertion. To resist this formidable attack, the prince had only twelve hundred men, and two pieces of cannon; yet he obliged the Dutch general to retreat, with the loss of two hundred men killed, and one French general. But general Daendels being almost immediately re-inforced by four thousand Dutch troops, the prince of Gloucester was under the necessity of falling back to Cohorn. The loss of the English in this action did not exceed three killed and about twelve wounded. The prince, during the action, had his horse shot under him; but he received no injury himself, though exposed to the greatest personal danger, under a heavy fire, being frequently in the front of the line, animating the exertions of his troops by his example.

The British troops fall back.

Indecisive success in the Zuyder Zee.

The efforts of our marine, under the conduct of admiral Mitchel, in the Zuyder Zee, and on the other parts of the coast, were continued, amidst these transactions on land, with unabated activity. Many gunboats, and several light ships of war, were taken from the enemy; and an attack that, on the 11th of October, they made on the town of Lemmer, which had come into our possession, as above related, was gallantly repulsed by the British sailors and marines, under the command of captain Boorder of the Wolverene bombship.

Difficult situation of the army.

On considering the various obstacles to his expedition, the duke of York despatched his secretary, colonel Brownrig, to London, in order to give a circumstantial account of the state of affairs in Holland, and to receive his majesty's farther instructions. The colonel soon returned to the army, with or-

ders for the immediate evacuation of Holland. Transports CHAP.
were sent for this purpose, and works were thrown up on the LXIV.
commanding heights of Keckdown, to cover the embarkation
of our troops. On the 17th of October, a suspension of arms   1799.
in Holland was agreed on between the captain-general of the Suspension
English and Russian army, on the one part, and the generals of arms.
Brune and Daendels on the other. It was stipulated by the
parties, that all prisoners should be given up on both sides,
those on parole, as well as others. It was further stipulated,
as the price of permission to the British troops to re-embark on
board their transports without molestation, that eight thousand
of the seamen, whether Batavian republicans or French, who
were prisoners in England, should be given up to the French
government. The combined English and Russian army was
to evacuate Holland before the end of November. No time British
was lost in the embarkation of the British and Russian troops; troops
and, together with these, a great number of Dutch royalists, withdraw
to the amount of near two thousand, came to England. The land.
Russians were quartered in Jersey and Guernsey.

The efforts of the British nation in the contests with the
Batavian republic, were, as usually in the history of Britain,
more successful at sea than on land; and not only in the northern sea, but beyond the Atlantic. The rich colony of Suri- Capture of
nam, in which there is so striking an assemblage of luxuriancy Surinam.
of soil, accumulation of riches, and luxury of manners, was
added to our colonial possessions.p This Dutch settlement
voluntarily surrendered August 20th, to lord Hugh Seymour,
commander in chief of his majesty's land and sea forces in the
Leeward and Windward Caribbee Islands, who conducted
against it a small squadron of ships, with troops collected from
Greneda and St. Lucie. The principal articles of the capitulation were nearly the same that, in an earlier period of the
war, had been granted to French islands. The inhabitants
were to enjoy full security to their persons, and the free exercise of their religion, with the immediate and entire possession
of their private property, whether on shore or afloat. All
ships of war, artillery, provisions, and stores in the public
magazines and warehouses, as well as the effects of every description, belonging to the public, were to be given up to his
Britannic majesty, in the state they then were; regular lists
being taken by officers appointed for this purpose by each of
the contracting parties. In case the colony of Surinam should
remain in the possession of his Britannic majesty, at the conclusion of a general peace, it should enjoy every right and
every commercial privilege enjoyed by the British colonies in
the West Indies. The troops then in Surinam, as well as the
officers belonging to the different corps serving under its present government, should have it in their option to enter into his

p See London Gazette, October 15th, 1799.

CHAP. Britannic majesty's service, on the same footing, with respect
LXIV. to appointments and pay, as the rest of his army, provided that
they took the oath of fidelity and allegiance to his majesty,
1799. which they would be required to take.

Short   The situation of affairs on the continent, and the part which
meeting of the British government had undertaken to act in the confedera-
parliament tion against the French republic, caused a short meeting of
in Septem- parliament, at so early a season as the month of September.
ber.
The object of this extraordinary convocation was to pass a law
for extending the voluntary service of the militia, while the
regular forces were employed on the expedition; and also to
vote some pecuniary supplies on account of the unforeseen
expenses. The projected bill respecting the militia, permitted
three-fifths of that body to enlist into such corps of regulars
as his majesty should appoint; each volunteer to receive ten
guineas, to serve in Europe only, and to continue attached to
the corps in which he first entered. If companies (not less than
eighty privates) should volunteer together, they might continue
to form the same corps, and either to be joined into separate
battallions; or if their number did not admit of such an arrangement, they were to be attached to regular regiments.
Every officer belonging to such a company of militia should
have temporary rank in the regulars equal to that which he had
before held; if the corps was reduced, he should enjoy either
half-pay, or permanent military rank, and full pay like any
military officer. The bill, being accompanied with numerous
regulations concerning the mode of its execution, underwent
considerable opposition, as tending to diminish by donative the
constitutional and patriotic force of the militia, and to increase
the standing army dependent on the crown. The object of
Mr. Pitt had uniformly been (his opponents said) to extend the
influence and authority of the monarchical branch of the constitution beyond its due and salutary bounds. His system of
policy, in order to effect this general end, had been to propose
some special or temporary evil to be removed, or good to be attained, from the restriction of popular privileges, and the en-
largement of kingly force. The pretext for suspending the
habeas corpus was the existence of a conspiracy; as if a conspiracy, if it had really existed, might not have been discovered
and crushed by the constitutional laws of the land. The pretext for extending the laws of treason, and controling popular
assemblies, was the existence of seditious meetings and rebellious designs. The pretended causes had totally ceased, but
the laws, so conducive to the real purpose of ministers still continued. The ostensible reason for alluring the militia to become soldiers was, to give effect to our military operations
abroad; the real intention was, at once to increase the standing army and ministerial patronage. These objections, though
strongly urged, were, by a great majority of the house, deemed
futile; and the bill was passed into a law. The supplies

granted at present amounted to between six and seven millions, CHAP.
including two milion five hundred thousand to be raised by ex- LXIV.
chequer bills. Bills were also passèd for granting relief to
West India merchants, and for supporting commercial credit. 1799.
These were the chief acts of this short session, which lasted Supplies.
only from the twenty-fourth of September, till the twelfth of Parliament
October is proro-
gued.

CHAP. LXV.

Ultimate purpose of the French expedition to Egypt—their views concerning India.—Tippoo Sultan recovers a considerable part of his former
strength—forms a new confederacy for driving the English from India—
his schemes are discovered, and he is admonished by the British government to relinquish his projects—disregards the admonition—British
armies from the two coasts take the field—Tippoo retires into Seringapatam—British army storm that city—death of Tippoo, and reduction of
Mysore—humane and wise policy of the British governor.—Proceedings
in Egypt—situation of Bonaparte after the battle of Aboukir—difficulties
with which he had to contend—exercise his extraordinary genius—military progress—battle of the pyramids—he addresses the passions and prejudices of the Egyptians—he promises the French will protect them from
the Mamalukes—he professes a respect for the Mahomedan faith—plan of
Bonaparte to amalgamate the prejudices of the Mahomedans with the
pretensions of the French—his undertaking more difficult than the undertaking of Mahomet.—Civil and political administration—his innovations
are disregarded by many of the Egyptians—discontents—are quelled—
Bonaparte proposes to march into Syria—object of this design—march
and progress of the French army—Bonaparte defeats the Syrians—captures Joppa—advances towards Acre—state and importance of that fortress—situation—the French army invests the city—sir Sidney Smith,
with a British squadron, arrives at Acre—captures a French flotilla—he
perceives the importance of here repressing the progress of the French—
his masterly view of the situation of affairs—his first purpose to inspirit
the Turks—he diffuses moral energy into their physical strength—the
French effect breaches in the wall—assaults on the town—inspirited and
headed by the English, the Turks repel the attack—grand assault by the
French—Smith employs his sailors as soldiers—efficacious efforts and
example of this heroic band—the French are entirely vanquished—retreat from Acre—Bonaparte returns to Egypt—the Turks send an army
to Aboukir, but are defeated—measures of Bonaparte for the improvement of Egypt.

CHAP.
LXV.

1799.
Ultimate
purpose of
the French
expedition
to Egypt;
concerning
India.

THE contest between the French republic and Britain
and her allies was not confined to Europe and the contermi-
nous ocean, but extended in a diagonal line to India and its
environs. The grand object of the expedition from Toulon
was to give a fatal blow to the commercial and maritime greatness of England. Among the various measures pursued, or
suggested for this end, none seemed to the French more effectual for the execution of their designs, than the formation
of alliances with the native powers of India. Greatly as Tippoo Sultan had been reduced in the war with lord Cornwallis,
he had not been entirely subdued. His ambition, though so
severely repressed, was not totally crushed; and he still cherished hopes of ultimately succeeding in its gratification. The
humiliating conditions to which he had been obliged to submit,
inflamed his pride to resentment and revenge, and co-operated

with his love of power to stimulate hostility against England. He watchfully observed every circumstance in the politics of Asia, or of Europe, which might be improved into the means of humbling the British power in India. Like the Carthagenians, after the signal overthrow that closed their second war with the Romans, though compelled to deliver hostages, to pay a tribute, to confine themselves within much narrower limits than they possessed at the beginning of the war, instead of succumbing under misfortune, he employed peace in recovering his strength and improving his resources. It is customary for the princes of Hindostan, according to their faculties and views, to entertain different portions of European troops, for the purpose of training, animating, and conducting their own people in wars with their neighbours; in much the same manner that the different princes and states of Italy, enervated after a lapse of time since the irruption of their ancestors from the north, by a delicious climate and exuberant soil, were wont to retain leaders of bands,[q] with their followers, from the hardy regions beyond the Alpine mountains. Tippoo, very soon after the pacification of 1792, began to increase his European military establishment. All European adventurers, especially the French, found ready admittance into his service, and as much encouragement as can be given under a despotic form of government. The common enmity of the sultan and the French to the British nation, formed a kind of tacit alliance between those two powers, and a predisposition to define and ratify it by express stipulation, whenever an opportunity should be presented in the vicisitudes of Asia and of Europe. The preponderating power of Great Britain at sea, and her dominion in the east, by the cession of Mysorean-territory at once more extended and compacted than ever, suppressed the hostile emotions and intentions that burned within the bosom of Tippoo Sultan, though naturally daring and impetuous, until the unparalleled successes of the tremendous Bonaparte in Italy, and on the southern frontiers of the Austrian dominions, encouraged him to take some steps towards a formal confederation with the French against the English. The expanded genius of Bonaparte, seeking physical and moral instruments wherever they could be found, immediately, in the power and hatred of Tippoo, perceived an engine and springs which might be directed with effect against the commercial and maritime greatness of a nation, in enmity so formidable to the French republic; nor was he slow in setting it in motion. Having corresponded with the French general, Tippoo renewed his hopes and expectations of being able, at last, to effect the object which he and his father had so often attempted in vain. Aware of the disposition of his neighbours in the peninsula, and despairing of procuring the alliance of the Nizam and the

Tippoo Sultan recovers a considerable part of his former strength.

Forms a new confederacy for driving the English from India.

q Condottieri.

Mahrattas, he had carried his plans of alliance to more distant powers, and projected an invasion from the northern kingdoms of Candahar and Cabul, extensive and populous countries situated between the river Indus and the southern extremities of the Caspian sea, and between the eastern confines of Persia, and great Bucharia or the country of the Usbeck Tartars; including, besides, Lahore, and the celebrated province of Cachemire, and governed by Zemaun Shab, a prince of great abilities.[r] In the mean time, Tippoo, while augmenting his whole army, laboured to increase the army of the Nizam of the Decan, though the ally of the English. A scheme was concerted between the sultan and certain French officers, for gradually raising the European force in the army of that prince above his control, and for bringing over to the side of the Mysoreans, this force, together with as many of the native troops as might be induced, according to the manner of the Asiatics, to join the party prevailing at the moment. The natural indolence of eastern sovereigns, acting in every thing by delegation, and the mode of subsisting the army by allotments of land, and not by the disbursement of money from a treasury under their own inspection, conspired to facilitate conspiracy; and above 10,000 Europeans, French and others, were incoporated, and began to take the lead in the army of the Nizam, when this circumstance was discovered to lord Hobart, governor of Madras, by colonal Halcot, an officer commanding the military force in one of the company's establishments, in the north western parts of the presidency of Madras. In the mean time, two events happened, which contributed to disconcert the schemes of the confederacy between Tippoo and the French arms, against the British power in India. The dismission of the French faction from the Nizam's army, was happily accomplished at Hydrabad, and a new subsidiary treaty ratified with that prince: and a decisive and glorious victory had been obtained by the English over a French fleet on the coast of Egypt.

His schemes are discovered, and he is admonished by the British government to relinquish his project: disregards the admonition

The governor-general had discovered the machinations of Tippoo, and notified to the sultan that he was acquainted with his intercourse with the French nation. He mentioned the success of the British fleet against the French in Egypt, the revival of our defensive alliance with the Nizam, and the destruction of the French influence in the Decan; he farther intimated the military preparations of the British on both coasts, and he admonished him of the danger which would accrue from proceeding in his hostile schemes. Tippoo professed to negotiate, but was really persevering in warlike preparations. The governor-general made repeated efforts to preserve peace, but finding his endeavours unavailing, determined to commence the

[r] Annual Register, 1799, chap. civ.

war as effectually as possible.[s] Lord Mornington ordered two   CHAP.
armies from the coasts of Malabar and Coromandel, command-   LXV.
ed respectively by generals Stewart and Harris, to meet in Mysore. The Nizam's army took the field, and made the proper   1799.
dispositions for forming a junction with that of Madras: this
army consisted of six thousand native forces, nearly an equal
number of the company's troops, subsidized by his highness,
and a great body of cavalry; it then joined that of Madras under major-general Harris, about twenty-four thousand strong,
which entered the Mysore country on the fifth of May, with
orders to proceed immediately to Seringapatam. ' In the mean British ar-
time, the Malabar army equipped and put in motion with equal mies from
promptitude and judgment under general Stewart, on the 1st the two
of February, marched from Cannanore, and ascended the coasts take
Ghauts on the 25th; his army was divided into four different the field.
corps, and these moved successively into such a situation as
might enable him to form the earliest possible junction with the
principal army: with the same view he occupied a post at
Seedaseer, near to which there is a high hill that commands a
view of the Mysore, almost to the environs of Seringapatam;[t]
hence our troops beheld the enemy's encampment, and perceived that they were in motion; but their movements were so
well concealed (March 5th) by the woodiness of the country,
and the haziness of the atmosphere, that it was impossible to
ascertain their object; nor was it discovered, until they had
penetrated a considerable way into the jungles, and commenced an attack upon our lines, which happened between the
hours of nine and ten on the 7th. The enemy pierced through
the jungles with such secrecy and expedition, that they attacked our front and rear almost at the same instant. This despatch prevented more than three of the Bombay corps being
engaged; as the fourth, which was posted two miles and a half
in the rear, was unable to form a junction, from the enemy having posted themselves between them and Seedaseer: the communication was completely obstructed by a column which, according to the reports of prisoners, consisted of upwards of
five thousand men, under the command of Baber Jung. The
brigade was on every side completely surrounded, and had to
contend against a vast disparity of numbers. General Stewart,
informed of the danger of this corps, marched to their assistance
with the flank companies of his majesty's 75th regiment, and
the whole of the 77th.[u] Attacking the enemy, he, after an obstinate resistance, gained a victory, which enabled him to effect a junction with the main army. Tippoo now took refuge Tippoo re-
in his metropolis, which the British troops advanced to besiege. tires into
Their batteries being erected, the artillery began to play, and Seringapatam.

s Despatches of lord Mornington to the company.
t Annual Register, 1799 :
u Annual Register, 1799, chap. iv.

CHAP. had, on the evening of the 3d of May, so much destroyed the
LXV. walls against which they were directed, that the arrangement
        was made for assaulting the place next day, when the breach
1799. was reported practicable. The troops which were intended
        to be employed, were stationed in the trenches early on the
        morning of the 4th, that no extraordinary movement might
        lead the enemy to expect the assault, which general Harris de-
        termined should be made in the heat of the day, as the time
British ar- best calculated to ensure success, for their troops would then
my storm be least prepared for making opposition. At one o'clock, the
that city. troops moved from the trenches, crossed the rocky bed of the
        Cavary,[x] under an extreme heavy fire, passed the glacis and
        ditch, and ascended the breaches in the *fausse braye* and ram-
        part of the fort; surmounted in the most gallant manner every
Death of obstacle in their way, and were completely successful. Tip-
Tippoo, poo defended himself to the last with a courage and ability
and reduc- worthy of his former fame: he made a stand at post after post,
tion of My- till at last driven to his palace, he fell among crowds of his brave
sore. defenders. His body was found under a heap of slain, and in-
        terred with all the honours due to his rank in the mausoleum of
        his father. Thus fell that bold, enterprising, and able barbarian,
        and with him the house of Hyder, which, though low in its origin,
        was ennobled by its exploits, splendid in its progress, and great
        even in its fall: it is eminently distinguished from all the families
        or dynasties that have ever appeared in such quick succession in
        Hindostan, by a more extensive cultivation and application of
        European arts and arms, than had been known before in the
        dominions of any native power of Asia. On the reduction of
        Seringapatam, and the excision of Tippoo, lord Mornington re-
        solved to make such arrangements as might establish the British
Humane influence and authority in the subdued country. Commissioners,
and wise appointed on the part of the company, and also in behalf of
policy of the Nizam, on the 24th of June, promulgated a scheme of par-
the British tition and settlement: the capital, with its fortress, and the island
govern- in which it is situated, with some extensive districts, including
ment. Mangalore and a very considerable extent of sea coast, were
        allotted to the English: a large portion was assigned to the
        Nizam; and a separate territory was subjected to the sway of
        the Mihissour, Maha Rajah Kishennai Wuddiar, a descendant
        of the ancient rajahs of Mysore, whose throne had been seized
        by Hyder Ally. The sons of Tippoo were taken into the pro-
        tection of the English.
Proceed- The ability of Bonaparte, powerful as it was, could not effect
ings in every object through means remote from his own energy; yet
Egypt. where he was placed himself, he displayed an astonishing com-
Situation bination of talents. We left this extraordinary personage land-
of Bona-
parte after ed in Egypt, and, by the terrible discomfiture of his fleet, ap-
the battle
of Aboukir. [x] See letter of general Harris in the London Gazette extraordinary, Sept.
        14, 1799.

parently cut off from all intercourse with his country. It was
not with mamalukes and Arabs. alone that the French general
had to contend, but with the climate, endemical distempers, and
the usual perfidy of barbarians, united with the malignity of a
proud and illiberal superstition. But these circumstances served only to exercise the elasticity of genius and heroism tried by
difficulty and danger. Bonaparte examined into the resources,
parties, sects, opinions sentiments, and dispositions of the people in the country wherein he arrived. The chief military
force ·in Egypt consisted of the mamalukes: besides these,
there were in Egypt a great number of Arabs, Jews, Greeks,
and Copts, (who were christians, and the descendants of the ancient Egyptains.) His own force now consisted of about forty
thousand soldiers, with a considerable number of transports,
and some of the sailors. His first object was to manifest his
force to procure a firm footing in the country; and afterwards,
to extend his power as much as possible by his moral artillery.[y]
He took Alexandria by storm,[z] and soon after received the submission of Rosetta and Damietta. To conciliate the good will
of the people, he published a declaration purpörting, that the
French were the friends and allies of the grand signior; that
they were come to chastise the beys, and would pay every respect to the Türkish laws and religion; provide and convey regularly the due tribute to the Sublime Porte. Having secured
his acquisitions on the coast, he marched towards Cairo, defended by Murad bey, a distinguished chief of the mamalukes,
who were in great force, to the number, it has been said, of
twenty thousand, but wholly composed of cavalry. The mamalukes made several brave but ineffectual charges on the
French, who had only infantry. At Cairo, Murd bey assembled all his forces, and advanced into that vast plain where
stand the pyramids. He was at the head of a numerous army,
commanded under him by three inferior beys, all men of determined bravery, but used, like their soldiers, to fight only on
horseback: they were all mounted on the finest horses, provided with the most splendid arms, and, along with these, rich
purses of gold; it being the custom of the mamalukes to carry
. along with them what they deem most valuable. Being excellent horsemen, well acquainted with the defiles and contour
of the country, and of intrepid courage and resolution, though
barbarians, they were no contemptible enemies. They attacked the French with much courage and impetuosity, endeavouring to surround them or at least to make an impression upon
their flanks and rear; but were every where repulsed with
such slaughter that they were compelled to fly on all sides,
leaving two thousand killed or wounded on the field: an in-

CHAP.
LXV.

1798.
Difficulties
with
which he
had to con-
tend, ex-
ercises his
extraordi-
nary abili-
ties.

Military ·
progress.

Battle of
the pyra-
mids.

y Annual Register, 1798, chap. x. and 1799, chap. v.
z To the vanquisher' of the Austrian host, this was an inconsiderable
achievement. See sir Robert Wilson, p. 17.

CHAP.
LXV.

1799.

trenchment, which they 'threw up to protect their camp, was carried, together with fifty pieces of cannon that defended it, and all their baggage: many of the beys were killed or wounded. Cairo, evacuated in the night, was taken possession of by the French the next morning.[a] Thus established, Bonaparte prepared his conciliatory projects; he first considered the most generally prevalent affections of the people with whom he had now to deal. The predominant passions of the inhabitants of Egypt were religious bigotry and superstition, and a jealousy and indignation against any degree of familiarity with their women. Bonaparte, therefore, deemed it necessary to instruct and caution his army on these two important and delicate subjects: he explained to them the principal articles of the Mahomedan creed; exhorted them to show the same respect to its ceremonials as to those of the popish faith : and inculcated universal toleration, according to the example of the Roman legions. He farther enjoined abstinence from pillage, as enriching only a few, but dishonouring the whole army. Having thus cautioned his soldiers, he addressed himself to the prejudices and sufferings of the Egyptian people; they had long languished under the tyranny of the beys; Frenchmen would vindicate their natural rights, protect their property, and promote their religion. All men (he said) are equal in the eyes of God; UNDERSTANDING, INGENUITY, and SCIENCE, alone make a difference between them; and what WISDOM, what talents, what virtues distinguish the mamalukes, that they should have exclusively, all that renders life sweet and pleasant ? Is there a beautiful woman? she belongs to the mamalukes. Is there a handsome slave, a fine horse, a fine house? they belong to the mamalukes. All the Egyptians are entitled to the possession of all places: the wisest, most enlightened and most virtuous, will govern, and the people will be happy. You had once great cities, large canals, much trade ; who has destroyed them but the avarice, injustice, and tyranny of the mamalukes. Thus persuading, what may be called the Egyptian democracy, that, through France, they would be emancipated from aristocratical tyranny, and the ancient splendour and glory of Egypt restored ; he stimulated love of independence, patriotism, and pride, to co-perate with his efforts. The astonishing versatility of this extraordinary man applied itself to their religious prejudices, not only to protection, but by pretending to coincidence of opinion : he insinuated that he was actually and expressly commissioned by the prophet to resist, repel, and overthrow the tyranny of the beys, to reform certain errors and abuses, and to promote justice, mercy, and piety, the great ends of the Mahomedan religion. He also adopted the figurative and proverbial language of eastern countries. By these means he extended his influence, not only through Egypt, but through Arabia,

He addresses the passions and prejudices of the Egyptians.

He promises the French will protect them from the Mamalukes.

He professes a respect for the Mahometan faith.

Plan of Bonaparte to amalgamate the prejudices of the Mahomedans with the pretensions of the French.

a See Otridge's Annual Register for 1798, p. 150.

Syria, and more northern parts of Asiatic Turkey. The task **CHAP.** undertaken by Bonaparte, to amalgamate the prejudices of the **LXV.** Mahomedans with the pretensions of the French, was difficult almost beyond example, and even more arduous than the pro-   1799. ject of Mahomet: the plan pursued by Mahomet was great, His under- but simple; the spirit of it was terror; the instruments, or taking means of execution, were great and simple also—God, war, cult than and fate. It was a more complicated and a nicer undertaking the under- to mingle terror with reasoning, the rights of man with the pri- taking of vileges or rather prerogatives of mussulmen, and the submission Mahomet. of the followers, to strangers, at best only dubious friends to the prophet. To accomplish that design, Bonaparte made pre- sents to Turks, Copts, Greeks, and Arabs. He patronized strict justice between man and man; he gave free passage and protection to the pilgrims going to and from Mecca; and encou- raged all kinds of commerce. He found a number of predial slaves, whom he encouraged to industry, by giving them lands to be cultivated on their own account. He gave equal right of Civil and inheritance to all the children of the same parents. He improv- political ed the condition of women, by giving them a certain portion of adminis- the goods of their husbands at their discease, and the right of tration. disposing of such property. He encouraged marriage between his soldiers and the natives, and endeavoured to restrain poly- gamy. He established schools for the instruction of the young French, Copts, and Arabs, in French, Arabic, geography, and mathematics. He was a friend to shows, festivals, games, and other diversions; in all which he wished the French and the natives to mingle together; and he submitted as a problem to the institute by what musical instruments and airs the minds of these last might be the more readily and effectually impressed, through the power of music: by his orders, issued about the middle of September, a general assembly was to be held on or before the 12th of October, of all the notables throughout the fourteen provinces into which Egypt is divided. Deputations from each of these provinces were to form a general council, or divan for the government of the nation, at the capital Grand Cairo. These innovations however were at length discovered His inno- to be contrary to the koran, and caused several insurrections; vations are but they were speedily quelled; and the French were masters disrelished of all Lower, and a great part of Upper Egypt.[b] The Turks by many had now entered into an alliance offensive and defensive with of the Russia, and were the declared enemies of France. Informed Egyptians. of the hostile intention of the Ottomans, Bonaparte concluded that a combined operation would take place against the French, in an expedition from Syria, and an attack by sea. Ghezzar Discon- Oglou, the bashaw of St. John d'Acre, had given a kind recep- tents. tion to Ibrahim bey, with about a thousand mamalukes, after he had been driven out of Egypt into Syria; he himself had

b See Denon, vol. ii.

CHAP.
LXV.

1799.

Bonaparte proposes to march into Syria. Object of his design.

March and progress of the French army.

Bonaparte defeats the Syrians at El Arisch.

assembled a very considerable force. The bashaw of Damascus was also in motion; and multitudes of Arabs appeared ready to join the enemies of the French, if likely, to prevail. The collection of an army in Egypt, or on its confines, Bonaparte apprehended, would revive the courage of the inhabitants, and overturn an authority not yet confirmed by the lapse of time, the abatement of prejudice, or the change of habit: he therefore determined to anticipate the expected attack, and made dispositions for marching into Syria; but, before he began hostilities, he professed to seek satisfaction first by conciliatory methods. He despatched an envoy with a letter to Ghezzar, assuring him that the French nation was desirous to live at peace, and preserve friendship with the grand signior; but he insisted that Ghezzar should dismiss Ibrahim with his mamalukes. Ghezzar, who, in his military preparations, had acted by the orders of the Porte, made no answer to this letter from Bonaparte, but sent back the officer who carried it, and put the French at Acre into irons.[e] Bonaparte therefore proceeded in his preparations, including various political precautions. The force of the army destined for this expedition amounted to above twelve thousand men.[d] The obstacles to be encountered in the passage of the desert did not admit of heavy artillery being transported by land; the ordnance that had been employed in the siege of Alexandria was put on board three frigates, which were to cruise off Jaffa, and to maintain a communication with the army. Camels and mules were provided with extraordinary expedition at Cairo, for carrying the light artillery, ammunition, and provisions, of which, the most bulky, as well as the most necessary article, was water. The army was parted into four divisions, under generals Kleber, Regnier, Bon, and Lannes; the cavalry was commanded by general Murat, the artillery by general Domnartin, and the engineers by general Chafferell. A junction was formed, February 4th, 1799, between the division of Kleber and the advanced guard of Regnier, under the command of general Grange, at Cathick; from whence they proceeded to Larissa, otherwise called El Arisch, a village pleasantly situated on the river Peneus, and the seat of a Greek archbishop, as well as of mosques for the votaries of the Mahomedan religion. Bonaparte ordered one of the towers of the castle to be cannonaded, and the breach being opened, he summoned the place to surrender: the garrison was composed of Arnauts and Maugrabins, all rude barbarians, without leaders, and uninformed in any of the principles of war that are acknowledged by civilized nations: their answer was, that they were willing to come out with their arms and bag-

c See Annual Register for 1799, p. 21.

d Division of Kleber 2,349, division of Bon 2,449, division of Lannes 2,924, division of Regnier 2,160: cavalry 800, engineers 340, artillery 1,385, guides for the infantry and cavalry 400, dromedaries 88. See Berthier's Narrative.

gage, as it was their wish to go to Acre. Bonaparte professed
himself anxious to spare the effusion of blood; he therefore delayed the assault;[e] and, on the 21st of February, the garrison
surrendered on condition of being permitted to retire to Baydat
near the desert. On the 24th of February the army arrived at
Kan Jounesse, the first village of Palestine beyond the desert:
they now reached the cultivated plain of Gaza; and next day
they marched against the city. The Asiatics, under Abdallah
bashaw, first made a show of resistance, but soon evacuated
the town. At Gaza the republicans found a considerable supply of provisions and military stores. On the 21st of March,
the main army of the French began to move towards Jaffa (the
ancient Joppa,) a seaport in Palestine, between which and Damietta, along the coast, the whole is desert and wild. This city
is surrounded by a wall, without a ditch, and defended by
strong towers provided with cannon. Trenches were opened, Capture of
batteries were erected, and a practicable breach was made in Jaffa.
the wall: notwithstanding two desperate sorties, and every exertion on the part of the garrison, about 4000 strong, the principal
tower was taken, and the greater part of the brave defenders
put to death; with a view, no doubt, of striking terror into
other parts of Palestine, and wherever Bonaparte might direct
his march. About three hundred Egyptians, who escaped
from the assault, were sent back into Egypt, and restored to
their families. The French found in the towers of Jaffa, ten
pieces of cannon, and about twenty siege pieces, either iron or
brass. Having taken possession of Jaffa, he ordered that the
inhabitants should be spared: in the harbour he found fifteen
small trading vessels. Having formed a divan, consisting of
the most distinguished Turks in the place, Bonaparte took the
necessary measures for restoring it to a state of defence, and
also established an hospital. Jaffa was to the army a place of
the highest importance, as it became the *entrepôt* of every thing
that was sent to them from Alexandria and Damietta. From
Jaffa, Bonaparte again wrote to Ghezzar a letter, dated the 9th
of March: therein he avowed his friendly intentions towards
the Turks and Syrians; but announced his determination to
march against Acre, unless the bashaw should become disposed
for peace. To this menace Ghezzar returned the following
verbal answer: "I have not written to you, because I am re-
"solved to hold no communication with you: you may march
"against Acre when you please: I shall be prepared for you,
"and will bury myself in the ruins of the place, rather than let Advances
"it fall into your hands." On receiving this answer, Bonaparte towards
proceeded towards Acre. Acre.

The city of Acre, called St. Jean d'Acre, because it was State and
the residence of the knights of Jerusalem, which they defended tance of
that for-
tress.

against the Saracens, is situated near the southern extremity of
the Phœnician coasts, on the confines of Palestine. After being
wrested from the christians by the Turks and Arabs, it had
been recovered by the crusaders; and afterwards captured by
Saladin; it was taken a second time by the romantic valour of Richard I. and given to the knights of St. John, who
held it about one hundred years with great bravery: but a dispute concerning the possession of it among the christians.
themselves, gave an opportunity to Sultan Melech Seraf, with
an army of one hundred and fifty thousand men, to reduce it
again under the Ottoman yoke; and it has since continued dependent on the Turks.[f]

Situation.   Acre is encompassed on the north and east by a spacious and
fertile plain; on the west by the Mediterranean, and on the
south by a large bay, which extends from the city to mount
Carmel. So frequently the object of contention, it was by its
successive possessors more strongly fortified than cities have
generally been under those desultory and barbarous warriors.
On the 18th of March, late in the evening, the French army
arrived at the mouth of the little river of Acre, which is at the
distance of about 1500 fathoms from the fortress: the river
runs through a very marshy ground. Bonaparte did not think
it adviseable to attempt so perilous a passage during the night,
and the more so as the enemy had pushed forward riflemen in
infantry and cavalry, to the opposite side of the river. The
night was employed in constructing a bridge; on the 18th,
at break of day, the whole army passed over.[g] Bonaparte
that day ascended an eminence that commands a view of St.
Jean d'Acre, at the distance of about a mile: he ordered his
troops to attack the Syrians, drawn up in gardens that envi-
roned the town, and compelled them to retire within the fortress: the republican army was encamped upon an insulated
eminence that runs near to, and parallel with the sea, and
which extends as far as Cape Blanc, about a league and a half
to the northward, commanding to the east a plain about a
league and three quarters in length, terminated by the mountains that lie between Acre and Jordan. The French had
seized magazines at Caiffa and adjacent villages which were
much wanted for the sustenance of the army. Having employed the 19th in reconnoitring the fortress, Bonaparte resolved to attack the front of the salient angle, at the eastward of
the town: no intelligence had yet arrived of the siege artillery
that was sent by sea. On the 20th, the trenches were opened

[f] In the fifteenth century, the Danes, descendants from the christian
crusaders, wrested Acre from the Turks: and in one age Faccardanio, an
able and eminent chief, becoming connected with the Tuscan princes of
Medici, introduced various improvements in the arts and literature; but,
after his death, Acre again fell into the hands of the Turks; and was overwhelmed like their other dominions, by Turkish barbarism.

[g] See Berthier's Narrative.

at about 150 fathoms from the fortress; and advantage was CHAP.
taken of the garden, and ditches of the old town, and of an LXV.
aqueduct that unites ·with the glacis of the town: posts were
stationed to blockade the place, so as to keep·the Syrians with- 1799,
in their walls, and to repulse them with advantage and effect, in
case they should attempt a sortie. In defending the fortress,
Ghezzar was to be supported by an army which was to march
from Damascus; and the combined operation of these forces
from Syria, was to be favoured by a·diversion, towards the mouth
of. the Nile, by Mourad bey, who, though compelled to retreat
before the French, was yet in considerable strength, and would
be joined by bodies of Arabs.

To direct and assist the execution of this plan, sir Sidney Sir Sidney
Smith hastened to Acre. This. distinguished officer had left Smith with
Portsmouth the preceding autumn, and was now commander of a British
the British naval force in the Archipelago, consisting of the Tigre squadron
of 80 guns, the Theseus of 74 guns, and the Alliance of 20 guns. Acre.
Informed of the first movements of Bonaparte, he endeavoured
to detain him by bombarding Alexandria, but found that without
troops he could do the enemy no effectual injury in that city.
Finding that Bonaparte had marched to Syria, he hastened to
Acre, to concert with the Turkish governor the plan of defence: he arrived two days before the French army. On the Captures a
16th, an achievement of the commodore greatly facilitated the French
progress of defensive preparations; he chased and captured off flotilla.
the cape.of Carmel,, the whole French flotilla, under the command of Eydoun, chief of division, laden with heavy cannon,
ammunition, platforms, and other articles necessary for Bonaparte's army to undertake the siege. This artillery, consisting
of forty-four pieces, was immediately mounted on the ramparts
of Acre, against the line and batteries of the enemy, as well as
on the gun vessels.

Sir Sidney Smith, a man of genius as well as military and He per-
naval skill, clearly and fully comprehended the exact situation ceives the
in which he was placed, and the characters on which he was tance of
to act. The adherence of the Asiatics, either to one side or here re-
the other, would, he saw, depend on events: if Bonaparte after pressing
such signal successes in Egypt, were to continue in his course the proof advancing conquest, the Asiatics, deeming him invincible, gress of the
would desist from farther opposition, and many of them would French.
even join the French invaders, in the hopes of plunder. If,
on the other hand, he were repelled, the Asiatics would unite
with their enraged mahomedan brethren in harassing and annoying the subduer of mussulmen. The physical force of the His mas-
Syrians, and their auxiliaries from Egypt and Arabia, was very terly view
considerable; but their intellectual and moral energies were by of the situ-
no means equal to the French. Both France and Britain knew affairs.
well, from the experience of India, that mahomedan valour, directed, methodized, and fortified by christian genius and skill,
formed very efficacious troops. Smith was fully convinced that

CHAP.
LXV.
1799.
His first
purpose to
inspirit th
Turks.

the soldiers of western Asia were naturally as brave as those of eastern; and considered how their courage and prowess could be most speedily animated and directed to effectual action. The time did not admit of that regular and systematic discipline which assimilates sepoys to British soldiers; it was necessary not only to stimulate exertion, but to prompt such speedy effort as would immediately influence Asiatic opinion: the first and grand object of Smith's comprehensive mind, was to infuse into the strength and courage of the Turkish soldiers, the energies of a British soul; by a kind of mental alchemy to transmute gross metal into the purest and most valuable. This was the great principle of sir Sidney Smith's policy: he sought to give unity of wish and pursuit to very great diversity of sentiment, prejudice, and views; to make the mamalukes of Egypt, the Turks of Syria, the bedouins of Arabia, and the christians of Palestine, unite as instruments in the hands of En-

He diffuses
moral
energy into
their phy-
sical
strength.

glishmen, for opposing the French. In moral artillery, so successfully as we have seen prepared and employed by the French commander, the British officer also shewed himself supremely conversant. He found that different as the various tribes were from one another, and immensely different as they all were from Englishmen, there were some principles which they had in common. They all regarded religion, their property, and their independence. Sir Sidney Smith very ably and eloquently called on believers to unite against infidels, on all who valued their own effects, their own country, families, and the government which was most consonant with their habits and sentiments, to combine against systematic plunderers, invaders, and revolutionizers. These representations being strongly urged in all the cities and provinces of the neighbourhood, made a very powerful impression, and great bodies of natives were excited to approach to Acre. But Bonaparte so posted his troops as to render the arrival of succours by land very difficult. The English commander therefore, while by his political negotiations, stirring up armies of Asiatics against the French, was obliged to form his military plans from the garrison that was already at Acre: the co-operation of the Asiatics without would depend upon the effects of the efforts within.

Bonaparte pressed the siege with his usual vigour and skill. The figure of Acre is rectangular, having the sea on the west and south sides. Though Bonaparte had approached from the south by mount Carmel, which is washed by the bay, he had carried on the siege on the north and east sides, both to intercept the Syrian army from the country, and to be as much as possible out of the reach of the British ships. On the 3d of April, having effected a breach in the wall on the northeast part of the town, he attempted to take it by assault, but was vigorously repulsed with very great loss. The British commander made dispositions for a sortie, to be executed under the orders of colonel Douglas, and the direction of colonel Philipeaux.

The
French
effect
breaches in
the wall.
Assaults on
the town.

On the 7th of April it was proposed that the British marines CHAP. and seamen should force their way into a mine which the LXV. French were forming towards a tower that protected the north-east angle of the wall; while the Turks should attack the ene-   1799. my's trenches on the right and left. The British seamen succeeded in destroying all that part of the enemy's preparations; and great numbers of the French were slain. But a much Inspirited more important advantage was attained than even the destruc- andheaded tion of the work: the example of the British forces inspired by the Enthe Turks to the most determined and resolute efforts: they glish, the were filled with admiration of their valiant defenders, and Turks rewished to vie with them in prowess and skill. Bonaparte, pel the meanwhile, was successfully engaged in repelling the approaches attack. of the Syrian army, and his generals, Kleber and Murat gained repeated victories in Syria; while he himself continued before Acre. During the month of April, various sorties were made, in which the garison was generally successful. In the beginning of May, a fleet of transports appeared in the road of Acre, bringing a strong re-enforcement of troops, commanded Grand asby Hassan bey. Bonaparte determined on a vigorous assault sault by before those troops should be disembarked. The constant fire the of the besiegers was suddenly increased ten fold, and they had French. raised epaulements which shielded them from the fire of the British ships. Several batteries, managed by sailors, were planted on shore, which, added to the Turkish musquetry, did great execution. Still, however, the enemy gained ground, and made a lodgment in the second story of the northeast tower. The upper part being entirely battered down, and the ruins in the ditch forming the ascent by which they mounted: day-light showed the French standard on the outer angle of the town. The fire of the besieged was much slackened in comparison to that of the besiegers, and the British flanking fire was become of less effect, the enemy having covered themselves in this lodgment, and the approach to it by two traverses across the ditch. Hassan bey's troops were in the boats, though as yet but half way to shore. This was a most critical point of the contest, and an effort was necessary to preserve the place for a short time till their arrival. Here the genius of Smith emsir Sidney Smith, in the midst of danger and alarm, retaining ploys his the completest self possession and a thorough command of all sailors as his faculties, devised one of those happy movements which soldiers. have frequently decided the fate of battles, and even of nations: he landed his crew at the mole, and, arming them with pikes, led them to the breach, where the Turks, having made a very brave resistance, were fast becoming feeble and hopeless, and many of them, in despair, were leaving the conflict; when the sight of such a re-enforcement re-animated their valour and inspirited the most astonishing efforts. The grateful acclamations of the Asiatics, men, women, and children, went feelingly home

1799.

Efficacious
efforts and
example of
this heroic
band.

to the hearts of our generous tars,[h] and invigorated their glad-
dened co-adjutors. With the heroic sailors, the fugitive Asiatics
returned to the breach; which was defended by a few brave
Turks, whose most destructive missile weapons were heavy
stones; these, striking the assailants on the head, overthrew
the foremost down the slope, and impeded the progress of the
rest. A succession, however, ascended to the assault, the
heaps of ruins between the two parties serving as a breastwork
for both. The muzzles of their muskets touched one another,
and the spear heads of the standards were locked together.
Ghezzar, hearing that the English were on the breach, quitted
his station, where, according to the ancient Turkish custom, he
was sitting to reward such as should bring him the heads of
the enemy, and distributing musket catridges with his own
hand. The energetic old man, coming behind, forcibly pulled
them down, saying, if any harm happened to his English
friends, all was lost.[i] This amicable contest, as to who should
defend the breach, occasioned a rush of Turks to the spot, and
thus time was gained for the arrival of the first body of Hassan's troops. It was necessary to combat the bashaw's repugnance to the admission of any troops but his Albanians into the
garden of his seraglio, become a very important post, as occupying the terre-plein of the rampart. There were not above
two hundred of the original thousand Albanians left alive.
The eloquence of sir Sidney overruled the bashaw's objections:
a regiment, called the Chifflic, was introduced, consisting of a
thousand men, armed with bayonets, and disciplined after the
European method, under sultan Selim's own eye; and placed,
by his orders under sir Sidney's immediate command. The
garrison, animated by the appearance of such a re-enforcement, was now all on foot, and there being consequently enough
to defend the breach, sir Sidney proposed to the bashaw to get
rid of the objects of his jealousy, by opening his gates to let
them make a sally, and then to take the assailants in flank.
Ghezzar readily complied: the gates were opened, the Turks
rushed out; but were repulsed with loss. The French now
renewed the attack, and in a massive column advanced to the
breach. Ghezzar proposed not to defend the opening this time:
but to suffer a certain number of them to enter, and close with
them before they were joined by the rest. The French column
thus mounted the breach unmolested, and descended from the
rampart into the bashaw's garden, where, in a very few minutes, the bravest and most advanced among them lay headless
corpses; the sabre, with the addition of a dagger in the
other hand, proving more than a match for the bayonet.[k]   Re-

h See letters of sir Sidney, London Gazette, September 10th, 1799.
i Ibid.
k See sir Sidney Smith's letter of May 9th, in the Gazette of September
10th, 1799.

taining the spirit which the energetic heroism of the British
seamen had inspired, the Turks charged the republicans with
so impetuous and persevering vigour, as finally to accomplish
sir Sidney's design, by a complete repulse of the enemy. During this conflict, multitudes of spectators covered the surround- The
ing hills, ready, as usual with those unprincipled hordes, to join French are
the conqueror; and, through the efforts of Smith, taught that entirely
the French invader was not irresistible, were the more disposed vanquish-
to join the opposite party. Continuing his purpose of availing ed.
himself of the turns of opinion with great skill and genius, the
British commander sent circular letters to the native tribes, recalling them to a sense of their duty and interest, and engaging
them to cut off supplies from the French camp. The repulse
of the eighth of May, so glorious in effort, proved more speedily
decisive in event than even its illustrious author himself expected.[1] From this time, Bonaparte appears to have been convinced
of the impolicy of farther perseverance against Acre, and the
impracticability of farther advances into the Turkish empire.
As he himself had wared partly by moral artillery, he perceived he had met with an antagonist who applied himself to
the same species of engine: he saw, that without the co-operation of Asiatic opinion and assistance, it would be impossible
for him, with his reduced army, to proceed; and he saw that
British heroism and genius, followed by success, had given an
effectual turn to the natives. Nor was enmity to him, he well
knew, confined to Turkish Asia, disaffection had been studiously
promoted by the beys in Egypt, which the reports of his disappointment would encourage to manifest itself. His own presence only could effectually repress attempts so extremely probable. Persistance in his present undertaking was wasteful
and ruinous. Farther advance, from the impulse communicated by sir Sidney Smith, was totally impracticable. To retreat Retreat
alone remained: and on this movement Bonaparte resolved. from Acre.
May 20th, he began his departure towards Egypt. His batter- Bonaparte
ing train of artillery, consisting of twenty-three pieces fell into returns to
the hands of the English; the lighter artillery, which had been Egypt.
brought through the desert, was sent back by sea: but captured
by sir Sidney Smith. The British officers, whom sir Sidney
mentioned as, after Philipeaux and Douglas, the most eminently
distinguished, were, major Oldfield, killed in one of the first
sorties; captain Wilmot, and captain Miller, of the navy, of
whom the former lost his life; lieutenants Wright, Brodie, and
Canes; and Summers, the midshipman; and indeed all our
force, naval and marine, are included in the high praises of
their brave and meritorious commander. Thus terminated the

---

1 In the close of his letter of May 9th, sir Sidney was still doubtful of the
immediate issue of the contest; though he was convinced it had so much
weakened the republican army, that it would ultimately prevent the progress of their invasion. See last paragraph of his letter.

CHAP.
LXV.

1799.
The Turks
send an
army to
Aboukir,
but are de.
feated.

Measures
of Bona-
parte for
the im-
provement
of Egypt.

siege of Acre, after having lasted sixty-four days. The garrison consisting originally of undisciplined troops, and possessing
scarcely any artillery, must have soon fallen before the republican host, if the brave bands of England, with a Douglas and
a Smith, had not intervened. But it was not merely the physical force, not exceeding fifteen hundred men, that could combat the Gallic multitudes of victorious veterans, so commanded; it was the energy which their example infused into the
Asiatic defenders, that foiled the enemy. By this successful
defence of Acre, it is morally certain that the able and heroic
Smith saved the rich provinces and cities of Asiatic, and even
European Turkey, from becoming a prey to. the French republic; swelling the possessions of our enemy, already so
enormous, with the addition of territory and its spoils, that
would have afforded the means of farther aggrandizement and
spoiliation, dangerous to every other country. As sir Sidney
Smith first showed that even BONAPARTE was not invincible by
ENGLISHMEN, he first effectually repressed Gallic schemes
of boundless ambition, which invaded, revolutionized, and despoiled unoffending nations. Such must impartial history transmit to posterity, sir Sidney Smith, the defender of Acre, and the
repeller of Bonaparte.

Bonaparte, in the end of June, after being much harrassed by
the Asiatics in his retreat, arrived at Cairo. The successes of
the Turks, in defensive operations, encouraged them to attempt
a plan of offence for the recovery of Egypt; and a considerable Turkish army landed at Aboukir. Bonaparte being at
Cairo, informed of the arrival of this armament, after making
proper dispositions for the defence and peace of Upper Egypt
and Cairo, and for preserving a communication with both,
marched to Alexandria; thence he proceeded to Aboukir,
where the Turks were posted. On the 25th of July a battle
was fought, in which, as the French veterans had only to contend with undisciplined Ottomans, they gained a signal victory.
The Turks immediately left Egypt, and Bonaparte returned to
civil arrangements. Having repelled this invasion, and also
crushing several attempts of the mamalukes, he, during the
rest of his stay, devoted his attention to the internal state of
the country, natural, civil, and political; and to devising improvements. He was ardently desirous to promote the interests
of literature and science, and to bring every kind of intellectual ability into efficient action. With this view the learned
men, whom he took with him to Egypt, were employed in determining latitudes; examining the state, and taking the sur-
veys of canals and lakes; in repairing canals ;[m] in examining
and describing plants and animals, in mineralogical researches;
and, what is nearly connected with these, chymical experiments;
in making observations, geological, nosological, and meteorolo-

<hr>

m See Denon, passim.

gical; in drawing plans of towns, edifices, and various monuments of, antiquity; in improving agriculture; in erecting a
chymical labaratory, founderies, windmills, and other useful
works. Bonaparte formed a library, and an institution for promoting art, science, and philosophy. He also paid particular
attention to navigation and commerce. He took a very detailed survey of the towns, and adjacent coasts, and ordered the
construction of certain works for the defence of this important
post. For the encouragement of commerce he lowered the
duties paid to the bashaws and mamalukes; and for carriage
of goods, established regular caravans from Suez to Cairo and
Belbies. He discovered the remains of the canal of Suez, and
taking a geometrical survey of its course, ascertained the existence of one of the greatest and most useful works in the world.
Indeed few generals, recorded in ancient or modern times, surpassed Bonaparte, in uniting with the progress of arms the researches of investigation, the deduction of science with their
practical applications to the purposes of life. Such were the
pursuits of this conqueror, when the affairs of France recalled
him from the banks of the Nile to the banks of the Seine.

CHAP. LXVI.

Internal affairs of France—the directory becomes unpopular—the revival
of the system of terror threatened—Bonaparte unexpectedly arrives
from Egypt—character and views of the able Sieyes—popularity of Bonaparte—he is adored by the army—plan of a new constitution—Bonaparte is invested with the command of the army—the legislative bodies
translated to St. Cloud—Bonaparte's address to the army—he enters the
council of elders—and is favourably received—opposed in the council of
five hundred—but is seconded by grenadiers with bayonets—the partisans of Bonaparte pray for his assistance, to enable them to deliberate
peaceably—the grenadier guards remove the refractory members—dissolution of the legislature—new constitution—Bonaparte is chosen chief
consul—offers peace to his Britannic majesty.—Britain—gloomy prospect
—people again wish for a peace—meeting of parliament—proposals of the
consul to our king—answer rejecting his proposals—submitted to parliament—arguments of ministers, insincerity and instability of Bonaparte—
of opposition, that Bonaparte is disposed and competent to make peace
—the rejection of the overtures is approved by great majorities.—German subsidies—motion for an inquiry into the expedition to Holland—
rejected by a great majority—progress of the intended union with Ireland—proposed articles—arguments for and against—the plan of union,
and time of commencement are finally fixed by both parliaments—dearness of provisions—corn and bread bill—bill of lord Auckland concerning the marriage of divorced persons—the duke of Clarence's view of
the subject—arguments for and against—is rejected—warmly engages
the public attention—attempt at the theatre to assassinate our sovereign
—is found to arise from lunacy—anxious alarm of the public—amendment of the insanity bill—parliament rises.

CHAP.
LXVI.

1799.
Internal
affairs of
France.

THE war in Italy under Bonaparte, had not only fed and
supported itself, but afforded a surplusage of finance to the
treasury of Paris. Scarcely had that renowned chief embarked
on board the French squadron at Toulon, when a remissness
was visible in the military affairs of France. Neither was the
genius of the directory, Barras alone excepted, suited to war;
nor did the system on which they aimed at the establishment of
their own power and fortune, admit of that pure, faithful, and
prompt distribution of the resources of the nation, which was
necessary to a vigorous exertion in so many scenes on such an
extended theatre. A majority of them, Reubel, Lepaux, and
Merlin, bred lawyers, were jealous of military renown and
influence; and wished not for any greater number of troops
than might be necessary barely to secure the frontier, and, above
all, their own despotism in the internal affairs of the republic.
The possession of authority, and the new avenues for governing by corruption, diminished in their eyes the necessity of supporting themselves by supporting the army. The French
were divided into two great parties, the lovers of order, and the
jacobins. The former were the most numerous, as well as

respectable; the latter the most united, daring, and active. The
directory endeavoured to acquire popularity, by forbearing the
imposition of fresh taxes: supplies of men, and all necessaries
were wanting to the armies; nor were the sums which were
raised honestly applied to public services; and the directory
became odious and despicable. The discomfiture and defeats The direc-
that every where attended the French armies, in the earlier tory be-
part of 1799, united with a general contempt and detestation comes un-
of the executive government, awakened the courage with the popular.
hopes of the jacobins, and threatened the moderate and peaceable part of the nation with a revival of the system of terror.
The directors through fear resigned, and a new directory was The reviv-
substituted in their place; the nation was in the greatest confu- al of the
sion; and thought with regret on the absence of the renowned system of
general who had given them victory and glory. Bonaparte threaten-
was warned how much his political weight was wanted, and ed.
conceived what important effects his presence might produce
at Paris; he therefore resolved to leave Egypt. At his departure, he wrote a letter to the army, expressing the necessity
of his immediate return to France, and declaring his regret to
part from the brave men to whom he was so tenderly attached.
Kleber he appointed commander in chief, during his absence,
and Dessaix general of Upper Egypt. He set sail from Aboukir
with two frigates and two sloops. On the 24th of August,
without fearing interception, he encountered the Mediterranean; and in the end of September arrived at Corsica. Sailing
from thence in the beginning of October, when he approached
the coast of France, he was nearly overtaken by some English
cruisers, but dexterously escaped the danger, by striking into a
small seaport in Provence. As he passed from the south to
Paris, he was received with triumphal honours. The courier Bonaparte
who had been despatched before him, to announce his arrival unexpect-
to the directory, and to prepare relays of horses for his journey, edly ar-
called out for them every where in his name; and from every rives from
town and village the people rushed out to meet him, and accom- Egypt.
panied him beyond their respective communities: so immense
was the crowd, even in the roads, that the carriages found it
difficult to go forward. At Lyons, but most of all at Paris, he
was the object of enthusiastic admiration. These sentiments
facilitated, and indeed probably produced the revolution of
1799.

One of the new directors was the abbé Sieyes, a man of great Character
metaphysical ability, combined with political address, who, and views
though unamiable in his manners, had acquired very great of the abbé
sway with the moderate party of republicans. The abbé Sieyes.
Sieyes had early foreseen, or apprehended, the discordant and
fluctuating nature of the various forms of government that had
been adopted since the overthrow of the monarchy. He had
attempted, in vain, the introduction of a constitution, which,
though still retaining the name, and in some degree the form of

a republic, should be consolidated and swayed by one chief magistrate and a constitutional jury, or conservative senate; and, in the various changes that took place from time to time, he was a friend to. an increase of power in the hands of the executive government. The abbé Sieyes had gained an ascendency in the public councils, but had to contend with the democratical party; and to overthrow the principles and plans of this faction by an opposite system, in which his own project of a single chief and a constitutional jury should be adopted, was the leading principle in his conduct, and the great object of his incessant contrivance. In the returning disposition to the government of a single person, the sentiments of Sieyes, supported by his distinguished abilities, produced him very great influence among the moderate and much more numerous party; and at the return of Bonaparte, he was deemed the most profound political character in the civil department of the French republic; and indeed none could surpass him in the power of compassing his ends by intellectual dexterity and skill. His great object was to command the minds of men, and rather by convincing their understandings, or at least impressing on them his doctrines and views. than by interesting their passions. He spoke more to the opinions, than the feelings of men; was more desirous of obtaining proselytes than partisans. To employ an analogy which has been before used in the history, the artillery of Sieyes was rather logical than moral; the predominancy of his intellectual deductions, he seems to have sought more than external splendour and power. It was at first doubted whether the metaphysical depth of Sieyes, or the sublime conception, invention, and design, the penetrating genius, firm and undaunted spirit, conciliating policy, and military renown of Bonaparte, would acquire the ascendency: but a subtile and profound metaphysician, applying exclusively to reason, if he come into competition with one whose intellectual meditation is combined with a versatile and soaring imagination, with energy of affection and of active powers, applying not only to the reason but to the fancy and passions, will soon find himself totally surpassed in the power of commanding men. The profound philosophers might have greatly influenced transcendent genius engaged in energetic actions, but the acting statesman or heroes would always, if really men of superior ability, preside and govern. In no human society could a Locke, if he had turned statesman, have outstripped a secretary Pitt or a Marlborough; a Hume or a Montesquieu, a Frederick; an Aristotle, an Alexander. Among the susceptible, ardent, and impetuous French, so fond of glory, and not only of great, but of striking and brilliant actions and characters, there could be little doubt to whom the preference would be given, if a contest had actually taken place between Sieyes and Bonaparte; but, in fact there is no evidence that such a competition ever was in agitation. Indeed, their respective

characters and circumstances rendered concert expedient and CHAP.
practicable. Bonaparte uniformly professed himself the votary LXVI.
of that moderate and regulated government, which suited the
metaphysical delineation of Sieyes; and Bonaparte, from his 1799.
talents, his popularity, and estimation among Frenchmen, was Popularity
the most efficient person that could be found for carrying such of Bona-
a system of legislation into execution, and for undertaking the parte.
supreme active functions of such a government. Bonaparte
soon manifested that he was inimical to jacobinical licentiousness, and joined the moderate party. He also showed himself
very conscious that the fate of France was in his power. The He is ador-
army was at his devotion, through all its ranks and gradations; ed by the
among the people he was the object of idolizing admiration. army.
Sieyes and Bonaparte admitted into their councils Rœderer;
these associates, assured that the multitude, both civil and military, would follow Bonaparte, concerted a new plan of govern Plan of a
ment: the ostensible and avowed object of this junto was to new con-
deliver the republic from the evils of jacobinism, which had stitution.
produced such enormous mischiefs, and dreadful miseries.
The associates communicated their scheme to several members
of the legislative assemblies, whom they reckoned confidents
and friends. The prevalence of jacobinism and anarchy,
they, with reason, imputed to too great preponderance of democracy in the legislature and government, notwithstanding
the various correctives they had undergone since the dissolution of the national convention. The control of the council of
elders was too feeble for restraining the violence and licentiousness of a popular assembly; the executive authority distributed among five, was totally inefficient and inadequate to its
purposes. The principles of the projected change were, an
increase of control upon the popular part of the legislature,
and an increase of executive power, that for this purpose, there
should be one supreme executive magistrate. The plan for
effecting this alteration, was a representative assembly: the
members of the senate were to have a much more durable
power than the former council of elders: to lessen farther the
popular character of the legislative bodies, the chief part of
their business was to be transacted by committees of twenty-
five each, who were to arrange objects of police, legislation,
and finance, in conjunction with the executive power : thus,
the real deliberative body, instead of being excessively democratical, was now proposed to be oligarchical. The executive
power was to be vested in three consuls, one of whom was to
be the supreme magistrate. This executory was to possess the
administrative functions in every department, and to appoint
all the officers civil and military, for internal tranquillity, defence against foreign enemies, every kind of intercourse with
foreign powers; in short, for every purpose of executorial conduct. More closely to unite the deliberative oligarchy with
the executorial monarchy, influence was to be added to power;

the members of the legislative bodies were not only allowed but invited to accept and exercise the manifold offices of honour, trust, and emolument, dependent on the chief consul. The abettors of this project enlarged the circle of their communications, and gained over a considerable number of the council of elders, who either really deemed such a change necessary for the suppression of jacobinical anarchy, or individually hoped for a much larger share of emolument and power, now that the management of the nation was to be contracted into so narrow a circle. Though many were trusted, yet with such discrimination and caution was the confidence imparted, that the secret was kept inviolate, until the moment of intended manifestation. Having concerted their plan, the associates with firmness, energy, and consummate ability, carried it into execution. By an article of the constitution of 1795, it was established, that the council of elders might change, whenever they should think proper, the residence of the legislative bodies; that, in this case, they should appoint a new place and time for the meeting of the two councils; and that, whatever the elders should decree with regard to this point, should be held irrevocable. Paris, where the jacobins were still so numerous, was not the scene for effecting the change with that ease and tranquillity which the projectors deemed most effectual to the promotion of their scheme. A majority of the council of elders were now gained over to their views. A committee of inspectors had been appointed to investigate the conspiracies alleged to be carried on by jacobins. This commission being in the interests of the associates, represented jacobin conspiracies as about to burst forth upon Paris. Early in the morning of the 9th of November, they sent letters of convocation to all the members of the council of elders, except noted jacobins. The members thus convoked, not in the real secret, were told that a terrible conspiracy of jacobins was preparing, and that the most effectual measures ought to be adopted for averting the danger. Carnot expatiated on the impending mischiefs, and the necessity of speedy and effective measures for deliverance. Regnier adopted the same tenor of reasoning, as to the alarming plots of jacobins, but was more particular and specific in recommending the means of delivery. They ought to transport the legislative body to a place near Paris, where they might deliberate safely on the measures necessary for the salvation of the country. Bonaparte was ready to undertake the execution of any decree with which he might be charged: he, therefore, proposed that the councils should be transferred to St. Cloud; and the motion was carried by a great majority. It was farther moved and resolved, that this translation should take place on the following day; that Bonaparte should be charged with the execution of the decree, and to take the necessary measures for the security of the national representation; that, for this end, he should be invested with

the general command of every kind of armed force at Paris; CHAP.
that he should be called into the council to take the requisite LXVI.
oaths; and finally, that a message, containing the resolution of
the council, should be sent to the directory, and to the council of 1799.
five hundred.

An address was voted to the French people, stating, the right Transla-
possessed by the council of elders, to remove the legislative tion of the
body to St. Cloud, and also the motives which had induced body to St.
them to use the privilege in the present circumstances.[n] The Cloud.
general avowed object of the council, was to repress the spirit
of insubordination, faction, and commotion. The Parisians
moved by this address, desirous of peace, and confident in
Bonaparte, waited calmly for the developement of the catastrophe. Bonaparte by the decree of the council invested with
irresistible military force, appeared in the hall of the assembly, accompanied by several generals; he informed the council that he would execute the decree in his own name, and that
of his companions in arms; "assisted (he said) by my brave
" companions, I will put a stop to the prevailing disturbances:
" *we* want a republic *founded on civil liberty*, or a national
" representation; we shall have it—I swear we shall." The
message of the elders being read at the bar of the council
of five hundred, the deputies not intrusted with the secret
were struck with astonishment, observed silence, and suspended all deliberation. Various proclamations were published on
the occasion, by the supporters of Bonaparte's schemes: one Bona-
of these was by himself addressed to the army, he therein parte's ad-
informed the soldiers of the command which had been con- dress to
ferred on him; inviting them to second him with their accustom- the army.
ed courage and firmness, promising them liberty, victory, and
peace, and to restore the republic to the rank which two years
ago it had held in Europe, and which incapacity and treason
had brought to the verge of destruction: he announced to the
national guard at Paris, that a new order of things was on the
point of being settled; that the council of elders was going to
save the state, and that *whoever should oppose their designs,
should perish by the bayonets of the soldiers.* Still the supporters of the intended revolution endeavoured to represent their
project as the result of rectitude and patriotism; and for this
purpose they employed various engines of conciliation, especially the press.[o]

n See Annual Register for 1800, p. 14.
o On the celebrated 9th of November, a pamphlet was distributed at the
door of the two councils, entitled, " A Dialogue between a Member of the
Council of Elders, and a Member of the Council of Five Hundred." This
production was in the usual style of dialogues, written by a party author,
between a champion of his own side, and of the opposite; in which the former has the argument all his own way; or if his shadowy antagonist urges
any objections, they are feeble, and easily overcome. The advocate of the
elders endeavours to remove the scruples and to allay the fears of the other,

Bonaparte sent a considerable force to the council house of
the elders; he himself, with a great number of staff officers
repaired to the Thvilleries, the approaches to which were shut
up from the public; a strong detachment of cavalry was stationed near the hall of the council of five hundred: these different bodies were re-enforced in the morning by additional
troops, and particularly by cavalry and artillery: the directory were invited to resign, but did not all immediately comply;
the refractory were put under a guard; the decree was sealed
for translating the legislative bodies; the directorial guard joined with Bonaparte: the general with an immense military force
repaired to St. Cloud where the assemblies were to meet,
under the superintending protection of the general and army.
The directors now all resigned their offices; motions were
made for inquiring into the reasons of the translation, but these
He enters were immediately overruled. Bonaparte now entered the
the council council of elders, and in a speech informed them, that he was
of elders, come with his brave companions in arms devoted to their service, and to the good of their country; he was *not* a (rom-
well or a Cæsar, coming with bands of supporters to establish
a military government; but *a friend to freedom* and his country, joined with his valiant fellow patriots, who had so often
been crowned with signal victory, to save them from intestine
destruction: conspiracies were going forward; cherished by
these, rebellion was again rearing its head; the nation was in
the most emminent danger; the most vigorous and decisive
measures were necessary. The present constitution (he said)
has been a pretext for all manner of tyranny; for the preservation of the republic it must be completely changed: the constitution, too often violated, is utterly inadequate to the salvation of the people: it is indispensably necessary to have
recourse to means fitted to carry into execution the sacred
principles of the sovereignty of the people, civil liberty and
freedom of speech as of thought, and in a word the realization
of ideas hitherto only chimerical. Some members of the coun-

by observing, that the translation of the councils was a constitutional measure, that in the present circumstances, it was necessary to the freedom
of deliberation and debate; that as to ensuring the execution of this measure by an armed force, this also must be considered as a thing constitutional, or clearly within the powers of the council of elders, who, if they
could change the residence of the legislature, must also be supposed to
possess the means of changing it in peace and safety Protection would be
afforded to liberty and property, the constitution would be restored, the
reign of terror and jacobinism would be entirely overthrown This *reasoning* convinces the advocate of the five hundred, but he expresses his apprehensions from the interference of Bonaparte These the other advocate re-
moves by expatiating on Bonaparte's character, and quoting Bonaparte's
professions and conduct. *His very acceptance of the commission* which he
was called upon to execute, was an unequivocal proof of his moderation and
patriotism.

cil manifested a spirit of opposition to the general; but in
the council of five hundred, he had to encounter much more
serious obstacles than that. which he had experienced in the
elders; and there was a very general cry of "support the
" constitution, no dictators, we are not afraid of bayonets."
This last declaration was soon put to the test; while the assembly was engaged in debate, the door opened, Bonaparte
entered, accompanied by a party of grenadiers, while vast multitudes of soldiers beset the entrance. The assembly was in
an uproar; many called out, " dare armed men enter the legis-
" lative assembly of a free people ! down with the dictator !"
Many darting from their seats, seized the general by the collar, and pushed him towards the door; one person aimed a
dagger at his breast, which was parried by a grenadier. General Le Febre now rushed in with a much larger body of soldiers than had at first rescued Bonaparte. The president of
the assembly was Lucien Bonaparte, the general's brother:
the meeting being in a most violent ferment, the chairman was
in imminent danger. Bonaparte himself meanwhile harangued
his soldiers, who declared they would stand by him to the
last extremity. A party entering the assembly hall, rescued
Lucien from the enraged deputies, whom the general described
as factious assassins, opposing patriotic efforts for the salvation
of the republic. The president exhorted the general to deliver
the representatives of the people from conspirators of their own
number, that they might deliberate peaceably concerning the
destiny of the republic. To secure the peaceful exercise of
their legislative functions to patriotic members, application
was made to the grenadier guards. The soldiers were ordered to re-enter the hall; and without firing upon the refractory
members, simply to charge bayonet: they entered accordingly with drums beating, and marched up the hall. Before he
gave the signal for charge, the commanding officer of this
brigade took the speaker's chair, and first called out, citizens
representatives, this place is no longer safe; I invite you to
withdraw. Plain as this hint was, it did not prove sufficient;
and his next address was still plainer. Representatives, withdraw, it is the general's orders: Many of the members continuing reluctant, the officer's next address was still shorter,
and directed his men to present bayonets; the drums beat to
the charge, the house was immediately cleared, or to use a
word more historically appropriate, was *purged* p The council
of elders now declared that the factious assassins of the other
house did not deserve the name of representatives ; and therefore that they, the council of elders, were the whole of the
national representation. They however invited those in the
other council, who had not opposed their measures, to resume

CHAP.
LXVI.

1799.
and is fa-
vourably
received.
He is op-
posed in
the council
of five hun-
dred; but
is seconded
by grena-
diers with
bayonets.

The parti-
sans of Bo-
naparte
pray for his
assistance
to enable
them to
deliberate
peaceably.

The grena-
diers re-
move the
refractory
members,

Dissolu-
tion of the
legislature

p See colonel Pride's process in the house of commons, under the direction of Oliver Cromwell.

their meeting. Having accordingly met, they joined in reprobating the factious malignity of their late jacobinical brethren;
in bestowing the highest praises on the intentions, councils, and
efforts of Bonaparte; and in testifying the warmest gratitude
to the officers and soldiers who, by repressing outrageous violence, had proved themselves such efficacious friends of moderation and freedom. They farther declared their resolution
to co-operate in the measures of the general and council of
elders for saving the country. In this harmonious disposition
of the legislative bodies, was presented the project, of which
the outlines are already exhibited: and after some detail of
discussions and illustrations, very unanimously adopted. Those
members of the lower council, who had so violently opposed
the projectors of the new revolution, were entirely excluded

New con-
stitution.

from a seat. The supreme objects of the new constitution
were to be the re-establishment of tranquillity, virtue, prosperity, and happiness at home; and to restore peace with foreign
nations. The consuls chosen for executive administration,

Bonaparte
is chosen
chief con-
sul.

were Ducos and Sieyes, two of the late directors; the chief
consul, and supreme executive magistrate, now elected, was
Bonaparte. The first measures of this extraordinary man,
now at the head of the French nation, were directed to conciliation, both domestic and foreign. He had uniformly, when
less exalted in station, professed himself determined to bestow
peace upon Europe: he regarded the British nation with the
warmest admiration of its character, enhanced by the astonishing
exertions by which she combated the gigantic efforts of the French
republic. He saw it was the interest of the two chief nations of

Offers
peace to
his Britan-
nic majes-
ty. Britain.

the world not to exhaust themselves in unavailing war. The
first act of foreign policy in his consular supremacy was to bring
the two chief nations of the world to peace.

In Britain, the energy of 1798 had continued through a
considerable part of 1799; the battle of the Nile re-animating
Europe, had encouraged the imperial powers to hostilities.
These hostilities had been attended in the first part of the
campaign with signal success. The discomfiture of Jourdain
in Germany, and the expulsion of the French from Italy, was
imputed to the spirit and contributions of Britain, as the ultimate cause and means of the operations. The retreat of Bonaparte from the siege of a fortress, which Englishmen undertook to defend, being his first failure in any military attempt,
added to the national exultation. He that had conquered all
with whom he contended, from Britons only found he was
not invincible. It was not doubted but Britain and her allies
would now succeed in repressing the ambition of France,
driving her back within her ancient limits, and permanently
securing her neighbours from future encroachments. Those
who considered the restoration of the Bourbon family as necessary to re-establish in France, and maintain in other countries, religion, justice, property, and social order, trusted that,

under Providence, the Russians, wisely seconded and supported, CHAP.
would recall civilization and humanity to France, and prove LXVI.
the saviours of Europe from the barbarizing doctrines and conduct of the republicans. Not those only who considered the 1799.
revival of French monarchy as indispensably necessary to the
safety of Britain, but the greatest number of the more moderate
supporters of the war, expected the campaign of 1799 would
be decisively successful. The formidable armament prepared
against Holland added to the general hopes. It was confidently expected that such a force, co-operating with the multitudes reported and supposed to be inimical to French supremacy, would recover the united Netherlands, and even co-
operate with the archduke in regaining Belgium. The failure
of this expedition was a gloomy disappointment. By far the Gloomy
greater majority, estimating plans and execution from the prospect.
event, without allowing for unforeseen obstacles, supposed that
an army of forty thousand men, supported by such a fleet, might
have been much more effectual ; or that the difficulties might
have been foreseen, and that, therefore, the expedition ought
not to have been undertaken. They saw that British valour
and skill had been exerted in the successive operations, but that
the result had been disaster and injurious concussion. They
hastily and rashly concluded, that either the destination of so
very powerful, gallant, and well officered an army, was unwise,
or its conduct unskillful, merely because it had not been completely successful. Such precipitance of judgment spread
great dissatisfaction throughout the country : and severe censure was bestowed, before an investigation of facts could ascertain its merits. Accounts also arriving in the close of the year,
of the failure of the Russians in Switzerland, and their retreat into Germany, despondency again began to prevail, the
people revived their wishes for peace, because they again People
conceived that no purpose could be answered by continuing the again wish
war.   for peace.

Parliament met on the 2d of February 1800. The first con-   1800.
sul of France had at this time indicated to his Britanic majes- Meeting of
ty a desire of peace. In his letter declaring such a disposi- parlia-
tion, he appealed to our king in the following terms : " How Proposals
" can the two most enlightened nations of Europe, powerful of the con-
" and strong beyond what their safety and independence re- sul to our
" quire, sacrifice to ideas of vain greatness, the benefits of king.
" commerce, internal prosperity, and the happiness of families?
" How is it that they do not feel that peace is of the first
" necessity, as well as the first glory ? These sentiments can-
" not be foreign to the heart of your majesty, who reigns over
" a free nation, and with the sole view of rendering it happpy.
" France and England, by the abuse of their strength, may
" still for a long time, for the misfortune of all nations, retard
" the period of their being exhausted ; but I will venture to
" say, the fate of all civilized nations is attached to the termi-

CHAP.
LXVI.

1800
Answer re-
jecting his
proposals;

submitted
to parlia-
ment.

Argu-
ments of
ministers

"nation of a war which involves the whole world." To this letter, conciliatory in spirit, concise and forcible in argument, an answer was returned, much more copious in detail, but by no means conciliatory : its perport was, that the French government afforded no grounds for trust : the most effectual way to convince Great Britain that France was disposed to resume its former relations, would be the re-establishment of that line of princes, which for so many centuries maintained the French nation in prosperity at home, and in consideration and respect abroad. The king, however, did not prescribe to France the disposition of her executive authority ; as soon as he saw that peace could be made with security, he should most readily concert with his allies the means of pacification ; but as, in the present state of France, he could not hope for the stability of any treaty, he with other powers must persist in a just and defensive war. The chief consul of France, made another attempt at negotiation : Talleyrand, the foreign ministers, in a letter to the foreign ministers of England, vindicated the conduct of France from the censures contained in lord Grenville's note, and proposed that a suspension of arms should be immediately concluded ; and plenipotentiaries sent to Dunkirk, or any other convenient place of meeting ; the reply to the second proposal like the first consisted of often repeated charges of French aggression, and declared that no peace could be made unless such as was likely to be secure and permanent. The propositions to be French government being laid before parliament, the rejection of the overtures was by ministers defended upon two grounds : the first was, that France still retained those sentiments and views which characterized the dawn, and continued to march with the progress of her revolution : the second, that no safe, honourable, and permanent peace could be made with France in her present situation.[q] From a long detail of his conduct they endeavoured to prove that no confidence could be reposed in the sincerity of Bonaparte ; and though he himself were inclined to preserve good faith, that there was no security for his stability. The censurers of the rejection argued, that abuse of the personal character of the man whom the contending nation had chosen for its head, was neither conciliatory nor beneficial : it was far from tending to procure peace, and certainly did not promote the purpose of war : our glorious successes in wars with France, had come from fighting, not from railing ; ministers (Mr. Fox said) in their rage against the adversaries of the old French monarchy, had formed a very indiscriminate idea, that they were all unanimously profligate and unprincipled : such accumulation of abuse had been often bestowed upon the Americans, still we had found it necessary to treat with them at last. Of Bona-

insincerity
and insta-
bility of
Bonaparte.
Of opposi
tion, that
Bonaparte
is disposed
and com-
petent to
make
peace.

q See Parliamentary Debates.

parte's character they had formed a very inadequate estimate:
however, even supposing the chief magistrate of France to
be as faithless and iniquitous as ministers represented, he could
see no inference they could draw from the admission, justificatory of their rejection: were we to enter into no agreement
with persons or states whose conduct was demonstrably unjust?
Had we not made peace with the Bourbon princes, the tyrants
of their own country, and plunderers of their neighbours? Did
we reject overtures with Louis XIV. and proclaim as our
reason, that he had in the midst of peace, seized the provinces of enfeebled Spain, and carried butchery and havoc into
the peaceful Palatinate?[r] Did we forbear alliance with the
plunderers of Poland? What was our security for either peace
with one, or alliance with the other? Certainly their interest;
not their faith nor their virtue. We had the same security
with Bonaparte: he, like all other statesmen, no doubt, wished
to make a peace advantageous to himself and the nation over
which he presided. With regard to stability, whether Bonaparte remained chief consul or not, peace and not war was
the interest of France. If ministers really wished to continue
the war eternally, unless the Bourbon princes were restored,
let them reflect on its practicability; the external force of the
confederacy had tried it in vain, and from internal efforts it was
not to be hoped. The whole property of France, real or personal, in the hands of its present possessors, depended on the
existence of the present, or some similar government: it was
impossible to restore the princes of the house of Bourbon, without restitution to those who had been exiled in its defence,
which in effect raised up the whole property in the nation to
support the republic, whatever they might feel concerning its
effects: the attempt was as hopeless as the intention was unjust; inconsistent with the objects of the British constitution,
and the rights of an independent nation. This country, from
an accumulation of causes, principally originating in the war,
was in very great distress: ministers had for seven years persevered in their ruinous system; taught by woful experience,
they ought to have at last admitted proposals for peace.
These arguments might perhaps appear to many hearers or The rejec-
readers not to be without weight, but they made little impres- tion of the
sion on the majorities in parliament; and addresses were voted, overtures
highly approving of the answer returned by government to of by great
Bonaparte. majorities.

Perseverance in the war being still determined, prepara- German
tions for the ensuing campaign came under their consideration. subsidies.
Messages to the respective houses from the king, stated that
his majesty was at present employed in concerting such engagements with the emperor of Germany, the elector of Bavaria,

r Parliamentary Debates, Feb. 3d, 1800.

CHAP. LXVI.

1800.

and other powers of the empire, as might strengthen the ef-forts of his imperial majesty, and materially conduce to the ad-vantage of the common cause, in the course of the ensuing campaign.[s] Certain advances would be necessary if the trea-ties were concluded, and he recommended to his parliament to make provision for such eventual engagements. The argu-ments against the proposed subsidy, were the inefficacy of all our former subsidies in the present war, and the distressed state of the country, from the enormous load of taxes, and the unprecedented price of the necessaries of life. It was also in-ferred, that ministers were well assured of the secession of the Russians from the confederacy. The parliamentary majority overruled all objections, and the required subsidies were voted. The military and naval force appointed for the service of the year 1800, was nearly the same as in the former year. The income tax was continued; and including a vote of credit,

Motion for an inquiry into the ex-pedition to Holland,

there was a loan of twenty-one millions. Amidst the arrange-ments for the future campaign, opposition proposed an inquiry into the past.[t] An army of forty thousand men had been em-ployed in Holland: had fought most valiantly; but no good pur-pose, they averred, had been effected; very great losses had been incurred, and very humiliating conditions had been accept-ed. Did the miscarriage arise from weakness of plan, or tardy preparations? from defective execution: or from resistless bad fortune? To ascertain the cause, they proposed an inquiry. If the disasters were entirely owing to fortune, an inquiry would acquit both the planners and executors; without an inquiry, the one or the other, or both, might be unjustly accused. Ministers endeavoured to prove that the proposers of the expedition had not failed; as besides the ships that surrendered to our fleet, our army had caused a very powerful diversion, and had no doubt contributed to the signal successes of our allies. As the expedition could not be properly said to have failed, an inquiry was totally unnecessary. The opponents replied, that the capi-tulation to an inferior force required to be investigated, both for the honour and interest of the country; but the motion was re-

rejected by a great ma-jority.

jected by a great majority.

Progress of the in-tended union with Ireland. Proposed articles.

The union between Great Britain and Ireland underwent an ample discussion in both houses of the Irish parliament; eight articles were proposed by the secretary of state as the founda-tion of this measure. The first imported, that the two king-doms should be united on the 1st of January 1801: the second, that the succession to the crown should continue limited and settled, in the same manner as it now stands limited and settled according to the union between England and Scotland; the third, that the same united kingdom should be united in one and the same parliament; the fourth, that four lords spiritual

s Parliamentary Debates, Feb. 13th, 1800.

t Parliamentary Debates, Feb. 10th.

of Ireland, by rotation of sessions, and twenty-eight lords temporal of Ireland, elected for life by the peers of Ireland, should
be the number to sit and vote, on the part of Ireland, in the
house of lords in the parliament of the united kingdoms; the
fifth, that the churches of England and Ireland should be united into one protestant episcopal church, to be called " The
" united Church of England and Ireland;" the sixth article
proposed a fair participation of commercial privileges; the seventh left to each kingdom the separate discharge of its public
debt, and arranged the proportions of national expense; fifteen
parts to be defrayed by Britain and two by Ireland; the eighth
ordained, that the laws and courts of both kingdoms, civil and
ecclesiastical, should remain as they were now established,
subject however to such alterations as the united legislatures might hereafter deem expedient: all laws, at present
in force in either kingdom, which should be contrary to any
of the provisions that might be ordained by any act for carrying the above articles into effect, from and after the union,
should be repealed. Irish ministers supported the union as in
its principle and objects mutually beneficial to the contracting
parties; in its articles, thoroughly consonant to these principles,
conducive to the commercial and political improvement of both,
and peculiarly advantageous to Ireland. The legislative
weight of the respective countries was, they said, apportioned
to the compound result of the population and contribution, and
a majority of the people was favourable to the union. The
measure was opposed, as tending to render Ireland a dependence upon England. The legislative portion allowed by
these propositions to Ireland was inadequate. The two nations Argu-
were now identified by this junction of legislature: the trans- ments for
fer of legislature from Ireland to England would drain the and a-
country, without affording any adequate reflux to Ireland. gainst.
No authentic documents had established the arguments of the
unionists, that legislation by was this treaty apportioned to population and contribution. It was merely an assertion without
a proof, and therefore ought not to be the foundation of a political arrangement. Before so great a change was permitted,
an appeal should be made to the people: if the Irish in general
did not oppose the new scheme, their inaction was owing, not
to conviction of its utility, but to fear of the immense military
force employed by government in Ireland. These reasons
were urged both in debates and protests; the project of union The plan
however was adopted by a great majority in both houses. The of union
concurrence of the Irish parliament with their plan of union be- and time of
ing communicated to the British, the respective resolutions mence-
were reciprocally ratified, and a bill founded on them was in- ment are
troduced. On the 2d of July, it received the royal assent; and finally fix-
it was provided that the union between Great Britain and Ire- ed by both
land should commence on the 1st of January 1801, being the parliaments.

CHAP.
LXVI.

1800.
Dearness
of provi-
sions.

Corn and
bread bill.

Bill of lord
Auckland
concerning
the mar-
riage of
divorced
persons

first day of the nineteenth century. The suspension of the ha-beas corpus was, after a considerable discussion, continued.

Provisions being during this session uncommonly high, attracted the attention of parliament. Mr. Pitt, on the soundest principles of political economy, sanctioned by the authority of the ablest writers,[u] had abstained from all interference in the corn market. The speculations of individuals he conceived were more likely to produce an adequate supply of foreign wheat at the present crisis, than any other measure that could be adopted. The legislature confined its attention to the contrivance of substitutes, and diminution of consumption. Committees appointed by both houses reported, that, although a considerable importation of wheat from foreign countries had already taken place, and more might be expected, yet they felt they should not discharge their duty, unless they strongly recommended to all individuals, to use every means in their power to reduce the consumption of wheaten flour in their families, and encourage in the districts in which they lived, by their example, influence, and authority, every possible economy in this article. They farther recommended, that all charity and parochial relief should be given, as far as was practicable, in any other article except bread, and flour; and that the part of it which was necessary for the sustenance of the poor, should be distributed in soups, rice, potatoes, or other substitutes. They were of opinion that, if this regulation were generally adopted, it would not only, in a very great degree, contribute to economize at that time the consumption of flour, but that it might have the effect of gradually introducing into use a more wholesome and nutritious species of food than that to which the poor were at present accustomed. From the evidence of bakers it appeared, that the consumption of bread baked for some hours was much less considerable than if eaten new. At the instance of the committee, a bill was brought in, prohibiting bakers from exposing any bread for sale which had not been baked twenty-four hours; and immediately passed into a law. In considering the scarcity, opposition, investigating its causes, derived them chiefly from the war; and various incidental debates took place on the subject. Mr. Pitt from a detailed view of the price of provisions during the whole contest, argued that if the scarceness had arisen from the war, the increase would have been progressive; whereas the prices in 1796, 1797, and 1798, had been as low as in peace, and the rise had not taken place till 1799; and was obviously imputable to the wet, late, and unproductive harvest.

With the necessaries of life, public morals occupied the attention of the legislature. The crime of adultery being extremely prevalent, was by many supposed to exceed in frequency the dissolution of former times. It was conceived by various poli-

u See Wealth of Nations, on the corn laws.

tical moralists, that the permission granted to the offending parties, after a divorce, to intermarry, was one powerful cause of
the seduction of married women.   To remove this incentive, lord
Auckland proposed a bill, making it unlawful for any person, on
account of whose adultery a bill of divorce should be applied for
in that house, to intermarry with the woman from whom the complaining party might be divorced.   This restriction, his lordship
observed had always prevailed, and still did prevail in Scotland,
where the parties, after being divorced, were never permitted to
marry.   The diversity of the case here, in his opinion, in a great
measure accounted for the prevalence of the crime.   This bill
was strongly contested in the house ; both the supporters and opponents admitted and lamented the frequency of a crime, cutting asunder the most important ties of social life ; both showed
themselves friends of religion and morality, pursuing the same
object, through different means   Lord Auckland reasoned, that
the certain preclusion from subsequent marriage would in many
cases operate as a preventative of the crime ; the force of their
reasoning obviously depended upon the admission of a general
fact, that the hopes, or at least the probability, of a future permanent relation, facilitated the temporary success of a seducer. The
opponents of the bill, the most active of whom was the duke of
Clarence, took a different view of the tendency of circumstances
and situation, in determining female affections and conduct: the
prohibition would not act as a discouragement of the vice ; the
obstacle might inflame the passion, and furnish new materials to
the dexterity of an accomplished seducer.   Inefficacious to the
prevention of the crime, it would produce the most pernicious
consequences to the weaker of the parties concerned in the commission.   Heinous and hurtful as this vice was, still it was possible that the seduced person might not be entirely profligate and
abandoned.   To the preservation of virtue, next in moral wisdom
was recovery from vice, before it became habitual and inveterate :
the present bill, if passed into a law, would drive the females to
desperation and unrestrained licentiousness.   Lord Carlisle also
very strenuously opposed the bill in question : the law lords, and
the bishops in general supported lord Aukland's proposition ;
but it was rejected by a considerable majority.   This bill attracted the public attention much more than any measure which was
introduced into parliament, in the course of the whole session.
It was supported by the highest political, legal, and ecclesiastical
authority: was evidently devised from the best intentions, and
framed with great ability: it may however, be doubted whether
the prospect of the restriction, would in many instances prevent
the crime ; and it was morally certain that after it was committed,
the restriction itself must powerfully tend to drive a female to infamous profligacy.

An incident that happened near the close of this session warmly
interested the feelings, not only of both houses of parliament, but the
of the whole nation.   On the 15th of May, his majesty went to

CHAP. LXVI.

1800

to assassinate our sovereign:

is found to arise from lunacy.

Anxious alarm of the bublic.

Amendment to the insanity bill.

Parliament rises.

the theatre royal Drury lane : as he was entering the box; a man in the pit near the orchestra, on the right hand side, suddenly stood up and discharged a pistol at the royal person. The king had advanced about four steps from the door : on the report of the pistol, his majesty stopped, and stood firmly. The house was immediately in an uproar, and the cry of " seize him !" resounded from every part of the theatre : the king, not the least disconcerted, came nearly to the front of the box. The man who had fired it was immediately dragged into the orchestra, and carried behind the scenes : his name was found to be Hadfield. Being examined by a magistrate, he exhibited symptoms of insanity; though some of his answers were rational. The veneration and love that the nation bore to his majesty's person, was by this accident awakened into an enthusiastic joy at his escape; even the spirit of faction was lost in a general stream of loyalty and exultation. Addresses of congratulation on the king's escape were presented by both houses of parliament, the universities, the corporation of London, and, in a word, by all the other corporations as well as the counties. Hadfield was tried in the court of king's bench for high treason; and it was proved that he had been for some years insane, chiefly in consequence of wounds received in his head, when he acted as a serjeant in the army, in 1794, in Holland : he was therefore acquitted, but not discharged. In consequence of Hadfield's act, and repeated instances of insanity, being directed against a personage whose safety was so dear and important to the state, two additional clauses, by way of amendments, were added to the insanity bill. The first was to hinder individuals confined for alleged lunacy, from being bailed, in any circumstances, without the concurrence of of one of the magistrates who committed him; except by the judges, or at the quarter sessions of the peace. The second clause proceeded on a principle similar to the first, namely, security. The second clause provided more especially for the personal safety of the sovereign, repeatedly endangered by insane persons. These provisions were the last important acts of this session of parliament, which was prorogued on the 29th of July.

CHAP. LXVII.

France—conciliatory efforts of Bonaparte—he invites the emigrants to return—insurrection not entirely crushed—he reduces the royalists—army of reserve—state of the confederates and of France—plan of the campaign - state of affairs in Italy—the Austrians invest Genoa—assisted by the British fleet--gallant defence of the republicans—Massena is permitted to evacuate Genoa.—Bonaparte prepares to restore the French affairs in Italy—Moreau invades Germany—his able manœuvres to divert the enemy, while he assisted the army of Italy.—Bonaparte takes the field to retrieve the affairs of the French in Italy—rapid and astonishing march over the Alps—progress in Italy—battle of Marengo—danger of the consular army—means of extrication—signal victory—decides the fate of Italy—armistice between the chief consul and the Austrians commander—Italy surrenders to Bonaparte—measures of Bonaparte for settling the country—having effected his purpose, Bonaparte returns to Paris.—Moreau advances into Bavaria—armistice and overtures for peace. —The emperor receives a new subsidy from England—proposes to include Britain in the negotiation—Bonaparte refuses—prolongation of the armistice—expiration, and renewal of hostilities—operations—partial successes of the Austrians—battle of Hohenlinden—the French gain a decisive victory—the emperor sues for peace—review of this extraordinary campaign—war is terminated between France and Austria.—Operations of the British forces—expedition on the coast of France—attempt on Ferrol—on Cadiz—reduction of Malta—Egypt—convention for the evacuation of it by the French—guaranteed by sir Sidney Smith—ministers, not knowing this guarantee, refuse to ratify the convention—Kleber, the French general, renews hostilities—new negotiation is broken off.—West Indies—capture of Curacoa.—East Indies—wise administration of the governor-general.

THE principal and most memorable events of 1800, arose from Bonaparte. The glory of the French arms, had in the absence of the conqueror of Italy, begun to decline: he now appeared, on his return, to be the only arbiter who could change the course of affairs, and the destinies of France; and the name of king or emperor alone was wanting to Bonaparte. With a senate appointed by himself, and recruited from year to year by his sole influence; he possessed the nomination of all officers, civil, political, military, and naval; the command and distribution of the whole military and naval force of the empire; the power of foreign negotiation on peace, war, and commerce; a complete, though indirect, control over the treasury; the sole privilege of proposing laws, and withdrawing them in any stage of deliberation or discussion. Being established as executive magistrate of France, he perceived the staggering state of the interior parts of the republic, and learned the consequence of the defeats which the French had suffered in Italy. Encouraged by the late failures of the republicans, the royalists

Concilia-
tory efforts
of Bona-
parte.

CHAP. in Britanny and Normandy had again taken arms; and their
LXVII. numbers in November amounted to sixty thousand. Bonaparte
1800. saw that effectual as a force might be against the internal enemies of the republic, conciliation was much more beneficial.
His general plan was to conciliate as many enemies of the republic as possible : he and all the members of the new government expressed a desire of peace, not only with the royalist armies of France, but even emigrants; and published a procla-
He invites mation, inviting exiles to return. Great numbers of loyalists,
the emi-
grants to on the faith of government, daily came back to France; among
return. these the *constitutionalists*, or favourers of mixed monarchy and
democracy, were permitted to come back : the greater number
of those that fled in the time of Robespierre, or at the convul-
sion in September 1797, were invited to their country : even
estates were restored so far as the restitution did not violate the
Insurrec- new tenures of landed property. Notwithstanding the anxious
tion entire- endeavours of Bonaparte, the Chouans still persisted in revolt,
ly crushed. and cultivated a correspondence with the British fleet. In the
beginning of the year, the chief consul detached a considerable
part of the insurgents from the hostile confederacy against the
French republic : where pacific measures did not succeed, he
He reduces very effectually employed force and severity, and early in
the royal-
ists. spring entirely crushed the insurrection.
Having established intestine tranquillity, and endeavoured in
vain to negotiate a peace with foreign opponents, Bonaparte
prepared for prosecuting the war. He published a proclamation in February, complaining of the obstinate resolution of the
English to continue hostilities, and inviting the French to furnish
the subsidies and men that were necessary for acquiring peace
Army of by force of arms. It was also at the same time deemed expedi-
reserve. ent by the consuls, that an army of reserve should be raised, to
consist of sixty thousand men, composed of conscripts, and to
be assembled at Dijon, where the first consul himself was to
take the command of it in person. The Austrians had now recovered all Italy, except the small republic of Genoa, and their
army was distributed in winter quarters through Piedmont and
State of Lombardy. The Austrians, seconded by the English, prepared
the con-
federates, for military operations with great alacrity and vigour: even
and of the abettors of peace, and among these the archduke Charles
France. knew, that the most effectual instruments of a fair and favourable accommodation, were an immense body of troops ready for
action. The armies were recruited, and a very strong and numerous force was prepared. The imperial forces of Switzerland and Italy occupied a semicircular line of communication,
extending from the frontiers of Suabia to the coasts of the Mediterranean. The republican armies occupied the positions
facing their enemy in an irregular line from Genoa to the valley of the Rhine; but the army of Genoa being blockaded by
an English fleet under lord Keith, they were extremely strait-
ened for provisions, and were in number very much inferior

to the enemy: from the Var to Genoa, there were scarcely CHAP.
twenty-five thousand, almost all infantry. A re-enforcement of LXVII.
fifteen thousand men from Switzerland and France were on
their march to join the army of Italy; others were likewise 1800.
promised; but those which had arrived, were few in number;
and so great was the void in the ranks of the French army,
produced by an epidemic fever, and by desertion, that Massena,
in the month of April, had not more than thirty-five thousand.
men in the whole extent of the country of Nice, and of the
state of Genoa: the distresses of the troops, during the rigours
of winter, were very severe, and many of the soldiers were
either dispirited or discontented. Notwithstanding those un- Plan of the
promising appearances, Bonaparte proposed a bold, vigorous, campaign.
and comprehensive plan of offensive operations: to invade
Germany, drive the enemy from Switzerland, and recover
Italy, by a co-operating line of armies. Moreau commanded
the army of the Upper Rhine, which, by the indefatigable activity of the chief consul, amounted to 100,000 men, extending from Switzerland to Mentz; on the left wing was secured
by Prussian neutrality, on the rear was protected by its communication with France and Belgium, and on the right was
covered by the Helvetic Alps: with this formidable host he
directed his course towards Vienna. Ill health, together with
court intrigues, obliged the archduke Charles to resign the chief
command of the army of the Rhine, and he was succeeded by
general Kray, an officer well fitted for so high and important a
trust. Bonaparte in his efforts on the side of Germany, had a
double purpose, and intended not only to make an impression
on that quarter, but to draw off the attention of the enemy
from his plans for the recovery of Italy: which, by those who
in considering military situations had not included extraordinary genius, was supposed desperate. The chief consul appointed Massena, who had so eminently distinguished himself in
Switzerland, to maintain the French positions there, until he
should put his own grand designs in execution. Melas, early State of af-
in spring, made dispositions for investing Genoa, which was fairs in
already so closely blockaded from maritime intercourse by lord Italy.
Keith. Massena endeavoured to obstruct their approach, and
effected all that skill, valour, and discipline could perform
against skill, valour, discipline, and superior numbers. He repulsed them in various conflicts: but was more frequently overpowered, and at length compelled to retreat; and on the 30th The Aus-
of April, the Austrians appeared before the city. On land the trians in-
French were pressed by the German army; from the sea, the vest Ge-
city was bombarded by the English fleet; within the walls, fa- noa, assist-
mine, and its never failing attendant pestilence, joined with British
conflagration in making the people loudly clamorous for a sur- fleet.
render, and with difficulty they were restrained from actual in- Gallant de-
surrection. Amidst these complicated evils, the republicans fence of
during the whole month of May, not only resisted, but often the republicans.

CHAP. defeated the Austrians, until they were at length exhausted
LXVII. by their own victories, Massena, aware that relief was approaching, wished to maintain it much longer, but found it im-
1800. practicable; he accordingly opened a negotiation with the
Massena is British admiral and the Austrian general, and obtained very
permitted favourable and honourable terms. He was permitted to eva-
to evacuate cuate Genoa with his troops, and procured provisions and a safe
Genoa. conduct. In his conference, the sagacious Frenchman penetrated into the acuteness and intelligence of the English commander,
and bestowed a just tribute of praise on the superiority of the
British character, and the efficacy of the British force. By the
fall of Genoa, many politicians considered the fate of Italy as
entirely decided, and the hopes of France as totally destroyed;
Bonaparte but the imperialists had still another general to encounter, whom
prepares to they were destined never to combat without defeat and discom-
relieve the fiture. In stationing his army of reserve in the plains of Bur-
French af- gundy, the chief consul intended to afford assistance either in
fairs in
Italy. Italy or Germany, as occasion might require; but he was chiefly
anxious to direct his efforts to Italy, where they were most wanted. With Moreau he had concerted the plan of the campaign,
according to which their operations, though distant, might be
managed in concert, on a great scale, and with as much precision as the evolutions of the two wings of the same army. The
object of Moreau's expedition was, by a series of feints, not less
than attacks, to occupy the attention of general Kray, to strike
terror into the heart of Germany, to alarm the Austrians for the
safety of the capital, and, at the same time, to maintain a communication with the French army in Italy, and send seasonable
re-enforcements.

Moreau in To execute his part of the plan, Moreau, on the 25th of
vades Ger- April, crossed the Rhine in four divisions, and formed a Junc-
many. tion of the whole army in Suabia, with the lake of Constance
on his right: by various feints and other manœuvres he turned
the right wing of the enemy's army; and in a series of engagements very bravely fought on both sides, he was so successful
in the result, as to command Franconia and Suabia on the left,
lay both under contributions, and intercept supplies, and destroy magazines. In front he occupied the attention of the
whole Austrian army, while on the right he was able to send
His able detachments to the south. He kept Kray so completely em-
manœu- ployed in counteracting his pretended designs, that he did not
vres to di- dive into his real intentions; and for near two months, Moreau
vert the sought nothing further than to amuse general Kray; by marches
enemy, and counter-marches, by threatened sieges, and feigned irrup-
while he tions, to alarm the Austrians for the safety of the hereditary
assists the states, and prevent them from paying any attention to the affairs
army of
Italy. of Italy.
Bonaparte . While professional experience and tactical skill were thus,
takes the in Germany, overborne by the paramount power of genius; in
field to re- Italy its efficacy was still more forcibly, brillantly, and suc-

cessfully exercised. Informed of the critical situation of Massena, the chief consul resolved to march into Italy with the utmost expedition, and to surmount every difficulty in the passage of the Alps, in order to attack the rear of the Austrian army. On the 15th of May, his army reached St. Bernard, where the transportation of the artillery was extremely difficult: but by soldiers inspired with enthusiastic admiration for their renowned general, the difficulty was speedily overcome; every piece of cannon was dismounted, and placed in troughs hollowed out of trees cut down for the purpose. These were drawn by five or six hundred men, according to the size and weight of the piece; the wheels fixed to poles, were borne on men's shoulders; tumbrils were emptied, and placed on sledges, together with the axeltrees. This difficult march he executed with such rapidity, that notwithstanding an immense train of artillery, he had made his way through all the defiles in spite of the opposing enemy, by the 26th of May. The Austrians were obliged to evacuate Milan and Pavia. The French vanguard having crossed the Po, encountered an advanced corps of imperialists, and defeated them with considerable loss at Montebello; not however decisively. The main body of the Austrian forces now arrived from Genoa, and fixed its headquarters at Alessandria. Bonaparte came forward into a plain between Alessandria and Tortona, and both sides prepared for a general engagement. The French commander with the van of the army, on the 15th of June, had advanced as far as the village of Marengo. Early the following morning, he saw the Austrian line extending opposite to him, about six miles in length. Dessaix, with the rear division of the French, was not yet arrived. About noon the battle began: Bonaparte, though with so inferior a force, withstood the weight of the Austrian column with equal intrepidity and ability. The immense host however of the imperialists was making a very powerful impression. The left wing of the French began to give way, the centre and right to follow the example, and disorder was evident through the whole line. The Austrians perceiving the advantage, pressed forward, with an impetuosity which was inspirited by confident expectations of certain victory, to strike a finishing blow. The garison of Tortona, seeing the confusion of the enemy, sallied out, and nearly surrounded the consular troops. Every movement appeared to forebode the total overthrow of Bonaparte. Undismayed by the impending danger, the general was foremost among the ranks. rallied his troops, and led them again to battle : his grand purpose was to prevent a route, until Dessaix, who was now near, should arrive. To render the overpowering numbers of the enemy less efficient, he seized a defile flanked by the village, there made a firm stand, bayonet to bayonet, though the Austrian infantry were seconded by a battery of thirty pieces of cannon, that played with tremendous effect. This unyielding resistance

CHAP. LXVII.

1800.
trieve the affairs of the French in Italy.
Rapid and astonishing march over the Alps.

Progress in Italy.

Battle of Marengo.

Danger of the consular army.

Means of extrication.

CHAP. produced the consequence which the general had hoped; the
LXVII. rear division now arrived; the French combatants revived by
~~~~~ this re-enforcement, and assisted by a fresh corps, charged the
1800. enemy with enthusiastic ardour: but still the event was extremely doubtful, when a movement of the Austrian general
gave a fatal turn. Melas found he could not force the defile;
but elated with success, and not informed that the re-enforcement was arrived, he extended his line in order to surround the
enemy. Bonaparte, perceiving this change of position, instantaneously saw how it might be improved: hastily he abandoned the defile; and, formed into a strong column, the consular troops pressed on the Austrians where their front was
weakened by extension. Of the French, besides the strength
of their disposition, a great portion was quite fresh; the Austrians, besides their weakened arrangement, were fatigued and
Signal vic exhausted, by the proceding efforts of the day. The French
tory, broke the line of the imperialists, bore down all before them,
put the enemy completely to the route, and obtained a victory
decides which decided the fate of Italy. All the united efforts of
the fate of Suwarrow and his Russians, of the Austrian generals and their
Italy. gallant troops, which had rendered the Italian campaign of
1799 so signally successful to the confederates, were now un-
done by the overwhelming genius of Bonaparte. The fruits of
all the British subsidies which set those operose bodies in motion, were blasted at Marengo.

Armistice The Austrian general finding it impossible any longer to de
between fend Italy, applied for an armistice until a message should be
the chief sent to Vienna. Bonaparte granted his request, on agreeing to
consul and a conditional convention, the validity of which was to depend
the Aus- upon the ratification of the emperor, and the consul sent an
trian com- envoy offering peace. The terms proposed by the conqueror
manders. were, in the relative state of the belligerent powers, wisely moderate. The Austrian army should retire within the line established by the treaty of Campo Formio; the Austrians should
occupy the northeast corner of Italy, bounded by the Po on the
south, and the Mincio on the west: Tuscany was to be a neutral state. Whatever answer should be returned from Vienna
to these propositions, it was agreed that the armistice should
Italy sur- not be broken without ten days previous notice. Meanwhile
renders to the fortresses, cities, and country, in the north and northwest of
Bonaparte. Italy, all surrendered to his arms.

Measures Having reconquered Italy, Bonaparte next considered its
of Bona- political settlement. He now resolved that Lombardy and
parte for Liguria should form, instead of two, one very powerful repub-
settling lic; and declared that the resolution in a speech at Milan. He es-
that coun- tablished a provincial administration, an a *consult* for prepar-
try. ing for the republic a constitution and legislature: he gave
orders for respecting religion, and the property of all citizens
without distinction. Citizens, who had fled from their country, were invited to return; with the exception of such as had

taken arms against the Cisalpine republic, after the treaty of
Campo Formio. The chief consul having effected those
momentous changes in the state of affairs in Italy, returned to
Paris.

Meanwhile Moreau, in co-operation with Bonaparte, resumed
an offensive campaign. Having already manifested his genius
in the dexterous and consumate prudence which suited his
situation, Moreau now showed enterprize as active. energetic,
and decisive, as his caution had been wise. The republicans
were now arrived at Blenheim, so fatal to their monarch when
contending with a British hero. The cross the Danube, the
French general had neither bridges nor boats, as both had been
destroyed by the Austrians; who possessing the opposite bank,
rendered it apparently impossible. To remove this obstacle,
Moreau bethought himself of an expedient, manifesting that
combination of courage and genius, which has so eminently
distinguished the republican warriors of France in this arduous
contest. Eighty soldiers undertook to swim across the river;
and when armed with muskets and knapsacks, sent in two small
boats for their use, to secure the bank. This enterprise they
effected: they took possession of the villages of Grensheim
and Blenheim, seized several pieces of cannon, these they
manned with artillery men, who had passed upon ladders,
placed on the wrecks of the bridge. The republicans thus occupying the left bank, maintained their positions with extraordinary courage, while a great number of miners and bridge
builders, though exposed to the enemy, completed the repairs,
and enabled the army to cross the river. The republicans
having succeeded in their attempt, the Austrian Army fell back
from Ulm, and retired towards Bavaria. Moreau took possession of Munich, and laid the Bavarian territories under heavy
contributions: the elector was compelled to pay to the French
a great part of the subsidy of five hundred thousand pounds
which he had received from Britain: the republicans also laid
the duchy of Wirtemberg under a severe contribution. The
right wing commanded by Lecourbe, drove the Austrians entirely from the Grisons, and entered the Tyrol; while on the
left, a new army of French and Batavians were preparing to
enter Germany, to penetrate into Franconia and Bohemia.
Animated by the exhortation and example of Britain, and supplied by her treasures, the emperor had hitherto refused the
terms offered by the republicans; but, as their armies now
menaced the very heart of his domains, he judged it expedient to sue for an armistice, which Moreau, with the approbation of Bonaparte, granted on the 14th of July. On the 28th
of the same month, St. Julien, envoy from Francis, in the name
of his imperial majesty, signed at Paris the preliminaries of
peace, on the basis of the treaty of Campo Formio; on the
part of the French, they were signed by the ministers of foreign
affairs, the ex-bishop Talleyrand. Meanwhile, the emperor

Having ef-
fected
his purpo-
ses, Bona-
parte re-
turns to
Paris.
Germany.
Moreau
resumes
offensive
operations.

Moreau ad-
vances into
Bavaria.

Armistice,
and over-
tures for
peace.

CHAP.
LXVII.

1800.
The empe-
ror re-
ceives a
new subsi-
dy from
England.
Proposes
to include
Britain in
the nego-
tiation
Bonaparte
refuses.

received a subsidy of two millions sterling from England, and had concluded a new treaty, by which the contracting parties stipulated for the one not to make peace without comprehending the other: the emperor adhering to this engagement, endea-voured to include Britain in the negociation. But it was the uniform policy of Bonaparte, to detach the members of the confederacy, and to listen to no terms but of separate peace. The emperor refused to ratify the preliminaries, alleging that St. Julien had exceeded his powers. The armistice was to ex-pire on the 7th of September; the French government directed its generals to begin hostilities that day. The emperor im-puting the rupture to the French, put himself at the head of the army, and endeavoured to rouse the force of Germany in defence of the empire; but the king of Prussia, in neutrality hostile, kept the whole north of Germany in the same inaction with himself, and intimidated its weaker princes from sending assistance to the head of the empire, and contributing to the repression of such formidable invaders. His imperial majesty proposed the prolongation of the armistice: the chief consul declared, that he would not waste the rest of autumn in idle conferences, or expose himself to endless diplomatic discus-sions: the securities which he demanded were Philipsburg, Ulm, and Ingolstadt, with their dependent forts. This condi-tion, though it laid the hereditary dominions of Austria in a great measure at the mercy of the enemy, being agreed to at Hohenlinden, a suspension of arms was concluded for forty-five days commencing from the 21st of September. This interval was occupied by both parties in formidable preparations. Moreau's army was seconded on the left by Angereau, prepar-ed with the French and Batavians to invade Germany, from the Maine; and on the left the army of the Helvetic Rhine, commanded by Macdonald, advanced as far as the entry of the Tyrol, and was ready to proceed on the first signal. The armistice expiring, the army of the left crossing the Rhine, defeated the Austrians in a series of engagements, penetrated through Franconia to the confines of Bohemia, and ascertained its communication with the army of the centre in Bavaria. Macdonald, defying the severities of an Alpine winter, pushed forward from the Grisons to the Valteline, drove the Austrians before him wherever he came, and supported by the army of Italy, was ready to advance to Austria, menaced by a still more formidable danger from the west. Moreau, with the grand and centrical army, resumed offensive operations on the 29th of November. The Austrians commanded by the archduke John, fourth brother of the emperor. making a very powerful resistance, repulsed the French army, and in their turn attack-ing their posts, obtained considerable advantages. Encouraged by these successes, the young prince ventured a general assault on the lines of the enemy at Hohenlinden, on the 3d of De-

Prolonga-
tion of the
armistice.

Expira-
tion, and
renewal of
hostilities
Opera
tions, par-
tial success
of the Aus-
rians.

They as-
sault the
French
lines.

cember. The archduke had no sooner begun his march, than CHAP.
there fell a heavy shower of snow and sleet, by which he was LXVII.
so much retarded, that only the central column had arrived at
the place of destination, at a time when all the divisions ought 1800.
to have been ready for action. A division of the French, con- Battle of
ducted by Richepanse, pierced between the left wing of the Hohenlin-
Austrians, and the centre, reached the great road behind the den.
centre, and assaulted the left flank and rear of that column, at
a moment when it had formed in front, and commenced an attack.[x] The Austrians with their usual courage maintained the The
conflict for several hours, but were at length broken by the French
impetuosity of the French, thrown into irretrievable confusion, gain a de-
and entirely defeated with the loss of fifteen thousand men cisive vic-
killed or taken prisoners. The battle of Hohenlinden decided tory.
the contest: the emperor found it impossible to stand against
the rapidly advancing line of armies, every where victorious.
The British court, sensible of the alarming situation in which
the emperor were placed, released him from his engagements:
he renewed his negotiations with the French, which have since The empe-
terminated in the peace of Luneville: and thus ended a cam- ror sues for
paign between Austria and France, in which German valour, peace
discipline, tactical skill, and military experience, having to con- Review of
tend with French valour, discipline, experience, and skill, in- this extra-
vigorated and guided by genius, demonstrated the inefficacy of campaign.
mere customary expertness and precedented usage, when, in
new combinations and arduous circumstances, they had to contend with rapid, fertile, and energetic invention. The grand design of Bonaparte comprehended every vulnerable point of the
enemy; uniform in object, and consistent in plan, he, with rapid
versatility, varied operations as circumstances changed; choosing his generals and officers according to their fitness; he
brought or sent with the mass of French courage and force
transcendent ability to guide it to its ends; and thereby completely effected his purposes: he recovered what had been War is ter-
lost, and compelled his enemy to sue for peace, which had minated
been constantly and avowedly the object of his stupendous ef- between
forts in war.   France
                                                             and Aus-
While the chief consul thus crushed every hope that Bri- tria.
tain had derived from continuing the war on the continent, this Operation
country undertook several expeditions, either entirely mari- of the Bri-
time, or in which her naval power could co-operate with her tish forces.
efforts by land. A squadron, under the command of sir Ed- Expedi-
ward Pellew, attacked the southwest of the peninsula of Qui- tions on
beron, on the coasts of Bretagne, silenced the forts, and clear- the coast
ed the shore of the enemy; a party of soldiers then landed and of France.
destroyed the forts.[y] An attack was afterwards made on various posts, and six brigs, sloops, and gun vessels, were taken,

x See Annual Register for 1800, p 208.
y Annual Register, 1800, p. 212.

a corvette burned, and a fort dismantled. This success was soon followed by an interception of supplies destined for the use of the French fleet at Brest On the 8th of July, an attempt was made to take or destroy four frigates in the road of Dunkirk: captain Campbell,[z] of the Dart, took the La Desiree, but the other ships, in number three, escaped, though not without considerable damage. An exploit performed by lieutenant Jeremiah Coghlan, about this time, excited high admiration, and is . a signal instance of the personal prowess, energetic courage, and unyielding intrepidity which combine in British heroism. This young gentleman was commandant of the Viper Cutter, under the orders . of sir Edward Pellew, and watching port Louis, near L'Orient in Britanny:' he conceived a design of cutting out some of the gunboats that were at the entrance of the harbour: with the permission of Pellew, he made the attempt in a ten oared cutter: with a midshipman and eighteen sailors, the gallant youth determined on boarding a gun. brig, mounting three twenty-four pounders, and four six pounders, having her full complement of men, and within pistol shot of three batteries. On the night of the 29th of July, he and his valiant comrades undertook the enterprise: they boarded the brig, and though her crew consisted of eighty-seven, charged the enemy, who made a gallant resistance, and repeatedly repulsed their assailants; but the British handful returned to the charge, and with the loss of one killed and eight wounded, including the commandant himself, our twenty countrymen overpowered their eighty-seven enemies, and made a prize of the brig.[a] Sir Charles Hamilton[b] appearing with a small squadron near Goree, on the coast of Africa, the governor surrendered, and a British garrison took immediate possession of the forts, and of Joul, a dependent factory. In August, a fleet under the command of sir John Borlase Warren, with a military force under the orders of sir James Murray. Pulteney, set sail on a secret expedition. One object of this was, the conquest of Belleisle; but the strong works that had been provided for the defence of that island, discouraged the attempt. The armament therefore proceeded to the coast of Spain; and on the 25th of August, arrived before the harbour of Ferrol. Our troops effected a landing, but finding, on examining the ground, that an attempt to storm the place would be impracticable, they re-embarked. Sir Ralph Abercrombie, with an army of about twenty thousand men, and a fleet of twenty ships of the line, commanded by lord Keith, appeared off Cadiz. An epidemic disease now raged in this city with pestilential violence. The governor of Cadiz sent a letter to

z See London Gazette, July 12th, 1800.

a See letters of sir Edward Pellew and lord St. Vincent, in the London Gazette of August 9th, 1800.

b London Gazette, July 8th, 1800.

the English admiral, stating to him the situation of the inhabi- CHAP. tants, and the universal odium which must attend an attack on LXVII. a city so afflicted by the visitation of heaven. The British com- mander replied that as the ships in the harbour were to be em- 1800. ployed in increasing the naval force of the French republic, they could avert an attack only by surrendering the vessels. To this requisition the governor would not agree, and declared a resolution of defending the place to the last extremity. The works were very strong ; the strength, however, of the place was much less formidable than the dreadful distemper, which indeed was a species of plague. The armament proceeded to the Mediterranean, where as it afterwards appeared, it was principally destin- ed to act. A detachment reduced the island of Malta: there, Reduction and in Minorca, lately captured from Spain, the troops were of Malta. chiefly stationed, until dispositions were made to carry into effect the ultimate purpose of the expedition.

When Bonaparte left Egypt, in the close of 1799, he had Egypt. conferred the chief command of the army on general Kleber. Before his departure he had made overtures for a pacification with the Ottomans ; and a convention for the evacuation of Egypt Convention was settled between the French republic and the Turks, January for the eva- 24th, 1800, and agreed to by sir Sidney Smith.[c] The British cuation of, ministers heard of the convention before they were informed that by the it was guaranteed by sir Sidney Smith ; and apprehensive that if guaran- the French army returned, such a force might powerfully affect teed by sir the war in Italy and Germany, they ordered lord Keith not to Sidney ratify any convention formed for that purpose. Kleber having Smith. demanded from lord Keith a safe conduct for the return of his army to France, the British admiral, agreeably to his instructions, declared he would not suffer him to pass unmolested. Mean- while the grand vizer, with a Turkish army, having taken pos- session of many posts which the French had evacuated, demand- ed the immediate surrender of Cairo. General Kleber, urging Kleber the that the English were hostile to the convention, refused to de- French prive his endangered army of so important a station, and an- general re- nounced his intention of renewing the war. On the 18th of news hosti- March, he attacked a body of Turks, and routed them : he then lities. engaged the grand army, and obtained a complete victory. The British court, understanding that the convention had been sanc- tioned by sir Sidney Smith, though not pleased with an act in which they considered him as having exceeded his instructions, to preserve the character of British faith, ordered the treaty to be ratified. Kleber consented to renew the negotiation ; but be- New nego. fore matters were brought to a conclusion, he was himself as- tiation is sassinated by a Turkish aga, and succeeded in the command broken off. by general Menou. From this time the negotiation appears to have been discontinued, and Menou to have resolved to defend Egypt to the last. Such was the state of affairs in that quarter

c See state Papers, January 24th, 1800.

CHAP. of the world at the end of 1800. In the West Indies, the im-
LXVII. portant island of Curacoa, belonging to the Dutch, was reduced by Britain. In the East Indies, the remains of the war
with Mysore were completely crushed, and earl Mornington,
now created marquis Wellesley, was wisely and successfully
employed in promoting the civil, commercial, literary, and political improvement of a country, which he had so effectually
freed from the great military disturber of its peace and happiness.

1800.
West In-
dies, cap-
ture of
Curacoa.
East In-
dies, wise
adminis-
tration of
the go-
vernor
general.

CHAP. LXVIII.

Britain—high price of provisions—riots in September—disturbance in London -vigour and activity of the volunteer associations -- the tumults are quelled without bloodshed. Negotiations for peace with France—French propositions deemed, inadmissible by Britain.—Last meeting of the British parliament—inquiries concerning the price of corn—the scarcity is, by opposition, imputed to the war, which ministers deny—propositions for the interference of the legislature in the price of corn—rejected with, great disapprobation—regulations for diminishing consumption, and encouraging importation—discussion of the late negotiation—supplies. -State of affairs at the meeting of the united parliament—disputes with the northern powers—public law of Europe, relative to belligerent and neutral nations.—Conduct of the northern powers-- Denmark—and Sweden—discussion with Denmark.—Russia rise and progress of Paul's enmity to Britain—interest of all nations to cultivate peace with Britain -efforts of Bonaparte to promote the hostile intentions of Paul towards England—lawless acts of Paul—embargo on British shipping.—Northern confederacy -the subject is discussed in the united parliament—unexpected change of ministry.—Short review of the late eventful administration—Mr. Pitt's situation, the most arduous of any recorded in the history of cabinets—new administration—alarming illness of the king—anxious concern of the people—recovery -In-quiries concerning the last campaign—supplies—loans—taxes—additional imposts upon paper -effects of—liberal and wise bill of lord Moira, for the relief of insolvent debtors--farther regulations for encouraging the importation of wheat—session rises.

IN Britain, the year 1800 was chiefly distinguished by the exorbitant price of the necessaries of life. This dreadful evil had progressively increased during the summer; but was borne with meritorious patience, in the hopes and belief, that the growing crop, alleged to be generally promising, would remove the calamity. When harvest commenced, the prices fell with considerable rapidity, upwards of one-fourth. But in September, while the belief still continued general that the crop was abundant, bread again rose; and reports were spread that the evils proceeded chiefly from monopolizers combining to enrich themselves by the public distress; and facilitating the efficacy and extent of their combinations by paper currency. Ever prone to judge and to act from present impulse, without investigation of cause, or reflection on consequence, the multitude easily swallowed these opinions; and many persons thought, by intimidation and force, to reduce the price of bread. In manufacturing towns riots began, especially at Birmingham; thence they reached London. In the night preceding Monday the 15th of September, inflammatory bills were posted on the monument, urging the people to rescue themselves from famine by their own exertions, and to take ven-

CHAP.
LXVIII.

1800.

géance on monopolists and forestallers. In the morning a mob appearing in Mark-lane, insulted the corn dealers, and clamorously demanded the reduction of the price of bread. Mr. Combe, the lord-mayor, justly and forcibly represented to the populace that turbulence and violence could only aggravate the evil of which they complained. Being obliged by their obstinacy, to read the riot act, he at length succeeded in dispersing them without military aid. The riot was afterwards renewed; and though the mob was violent, the chief magistrate, now supported by the volunteers, still hoping to quell them without bloodshed, did not order the associations to fire. For several days there were tumults in different parts of the city; but the ready attendance and firmness of the volunteers intimidated the populace, and without actual use of arms repressed the commotions.

Vigour and activity of the volunteer associations. The tumults are quelled without bloodshed.

Negotiations for peace with France.

While negotiations had been carrying on between Austria and France, the British government intimated a desire of being included in a treaty for peace. The chief consul, informed of this intimation, authorized Mr. Otto, a gentleman who was then employed in England as agent for the exchange of prisoners, to demand an explanation of the British proposals, and to request that a truce should immediately be concluded between the French and British forces by sea and land. The British government declared its readiness to send a plenipotentiary to congress; but observed that a naval armistice had never been established between France and England during a negotiation, nor until the preliminaries had been actually signed; that such a step, giving rise to disputes, might obstruct rather than promote a pacification. M. Otto answered, that the proposal of the chief consul was made in consequence of the offer of Britain to negotiate jointly with the emperor. In that view an English armistice would be an equivalent to the French, for the obvious disadvantages from prolonging the truce with Austria. The armistice proposed to England, as a joint negotiator with Austria was, that the ships of Great Britain and France should enjoy a freedom of navigation as before the war: that Belleisle, Malta, and Alexandria, should be in a similar predicament with Ulm, Philipsburg, and Ingolstadt; and that accordingly, all French and neutral vessels should be permitted to supply each garrison with provisions and stores; and that the squadrons which formed the blockade of Flushing, Brest, Cadiz, and Toulon, should return into their own harbours, or at least retire from the respective coasts. Lord Grenville, as secretary of foreign affairs, after objecting to the principle of the armistice, as affording an advantage to France, in the discontinuance of the blockade, without any equivalent to England, proposed a counter project more equal in principle. This plan prohibited all means of defence from being conveyed into the island of Malta, or any of the parts of Egypt, but allowed the necessaries of life to be introduced

from time to time; it provided for the discontinuance of the
blockade at Brest,[d] Toulon, and other French ports, but tended
to prevent all naval or military stores from being conveyed
thither by sea; and the ships of war, in those ports, from being
removed to any other station. The French government, not
satisfied with these propositions, offered this alternative: if Great
Britain would agree to a separate negotiation, her scheme would
be adopted; but, if she should insist on a general negotiation,
the French project must be accepted. Lord Grenville insisted French
on the the terms that had been already offered by Great Britain. proposi-
After a fruitless discussion, M. Otto intimated that the joint ne- tions deem-
gotiation was at an end; but added, that the first consul was dis- ed inadmis-
posed to receive any overtures, for a separate treaty with Great Britain.
Britain: to which proposal the British government, true to their
ally, gave a decided negative.

The last British parliament met on the 10th of November Last meet-
1800, in order to despatch the most urgent business previous to ing of the
the meeting of the united legislature. The subjects which British par-
chiefly occupied their attention were, the overtures to a peace Inquiries
with the French republic; the high price of provisions; and concerning
the immediate supplies for the national service. The oppo- the price of
nents of ministry endeavoured, as in the former year, to charge corn
the scarity on the account of the war; but ministers still con- The scarci-
tinued to resist this allegation. In considering dearth, the first position
point was to ascertain whether its cause was an insufficiency in imputed to
the crop. Committees of the houses were appointed to investi- the war,
gate facts; and reported that the result of their inquiry was, which mi-
that the crop was defective about one-fourth. To supply this nisters'
deficiency, the greater number in both houses proposed the en- deny.
couragement of importation both of corn and rice, the prevention of export, the use of substitutes in the mixture of quality,
and diminution, both by precept and example, of the quantities consumed. Propositions were offered for positive interfe- Proposi-
rence, in order to compel the sale of wheat, both in corn and tions for
flour, at prices not to exceed a certain sum, which, according the inter-
to the calculation of the proposers, should allow an equitable the legisla-
benefit to the venders and raisers of these commodities. It was ture in the
argued, that there were certain prices which sufficiently remu- price of
nerated the farmer in point of labour, profit, and rent, which corn,
might be ascertained in defective as well as abundant crops:
and that the present circumstances required a deviation from
the usual principles of policy. But it was answered, that com- rejected
pulsory means, employed by the legislature, respecting that with great
species of property, were totally inconsistent with the security bation.
of every kind of property; regard to which so peculiarly distinguished the British laws and constitution. Upon what principle could you compel the farmer or corn merchant to bring

d The substance of this part of the narrative is taken from the State
papers on the negotiation, from September 4th to October 9th.

Regula-
tions for
diminish-
ing con-
sumption,
and encou-
raging im-
portation.

that article to market upon less advantageous conditions than other commodities? by diminishing the security of the corn dealer's property, you impel him to withdraw, and deter others from employing so much capital in that commodity as would be otherwise applied, and lay the foundation for future scarcities. These views being adopted by great majorities in parliament, without interfering in the price, they proposed to remedy the evil by diminishing consumption, and encouraging supply. Acts were passed for enjoining, for a specified time, the use of mixed and inferior kinds of bread, and for encouraging importation by granting very extraordinary bounties. Recommendations were added to all families and individuals, to be as economical as possible in the use of bread. Distillation of spirits was also suspended, that luxury might not employ grain, so much wanted for necessaries. These were the general objects of the enactments or exhortations of legislature, for meeting the scarcity.

Discussion
of the late
negotia-
tion.

Discussing the negotiation, a great majority in parliament approved highly of the resolution of government, not to conclude a separate peace. The opponents of administration predicted that Britain would ultimately be compelled to accede to a separate plan of pacification. The supplies required were voted, the British parliament was prorogued in the end of December, and the united parliament of Great Britain and Ireland met for the first time, January 22d, 1801.

Supplies.

1801.
State of
affairs at
the meet-
ing of the
united par-
liament.

Besides the war in which Britain was actually engaged, she was now likely to be exposed to hostilities from a confederacy of the northern powers. The right of a belligerent state to prevent neutral ships from conveying to the opposite party ammunition or stores that may enable him more effectually to carry on the war, is involved in the laws of self preservation and self defence. The general principle has been admitted in modern Europe by maritime states, and various treaties have been formed, defining the articles thus to be prohibited. To exercise this right, it was obviously necessary that the nations at war should have a discretionary power of searching ships suspected to be carrying contraband commodities to the enemy. This power had been uniformly admitted, till the American war; when a wish to humble Britain, and the desire of finding for their merchandize a freer vent than was allowed by the existing maritime code of public law, produced the naval confederacy styled the *armed neutrality*, consisting of Holland and the northern powers. During a great part of the present war, Russia, the principal member of that alliance, being inimical to France, had avoided every kind of commerce that could interfere with the efforts of England. Sweden and Denmark had often engaged in contraband traffic, and ships had been seized by the vigilance of the British cruisers, employed to prevent unlawful imports into the harbours of the enemy. Remonstrances and replies had been reciprocally and repeatedly made, and had terminated on the one hand without rupture, and on the other

Disputes
with the
northern
powers.
Public law
of Europe
relative to
belligerent
and neutral
nations.

Conduct of
the north-
ern powers,
Denmark
and Swe-
den.

without preventing the continuance either of the northern con-
traband traffic, or of the British search of ships which traded.
In this situation affairs were, when a dispute between a Danish
frigate, conveying a fleet of merchantmen, introduced into dis- 1801·
cussion a new general principle of the maritime law of nations.[e] Discus-
The Dane had admitted to Britain, as a billigerent power, a sion with
right of searching vessels not sailing under convoy, but had as- Denmark.
serted that the company of a ship of war protected trading
vessels from being liable to examination. The British envoy
at Copenhagen stated to the minister of Denmark, the act that
had taken place, and the principle alleged in its justification.[f]
The Dane admitted his knowledge of the facts, and maintained
the principle to be agreeable to public law. The English
minister showed, first, that in point of history and actual convention, no such principle had ever been recognized; secondly, that its admission would amount to a virtual renunciation of
the right of search; because the smallest ship of war by ac-
companying the largest fleet of merchantmen, might secure the
import of any quantity of contraband stores into the harbours
of the enemy. The Danish minister continued to support the
principle, but without either documents or apposite arguments.
He alleged that the belligerent party had, in the honour of the
neutral party, sufficient security that ships of war should not
be employed to guard the conveyance of contraband articles.
To rest upon the honour of another state the maintenance of
any right which she could enforce by her own power, little
suited the policy or greatness of Britain. Our ambassador
firmly, but temperately, stated and repeated the determination
of Britain to search neutral ships steering towards the enemy's
country, by whatever convoy they might be attended. Similar
discussions and intimations took place at London between the
Danish ambassador and lord Grenville. Britain, averse to
hostilities, if they could possibly be avoided, released the Freya,
a frigate belonging to Denmark which had been taken in pro-
teeting contraband stores, but maintained her right to the support of the principle. Sweeden also took a part in the dispute,
and maintained the principles of public law asserted by Denmark.[g] Demark and Sweden, however, could not have ventured
to persist in maintaining a naval claim which Britain chose to Russia.
dispute. But another state now not only joined, but headed the
contest. The emperor Paul, in 1799 so eagerly a co-operator
with Austria and Britain, was now become violently hostile to
both. Conscious that, in Italy, the brilliant events of that cam- Rise and
paign had been principally owing to the Russian host, he saw progress of
 Paul's en-
 mity to
e See State papers, April 10th, 1800. Britain.
 f See correspondence between the British and Danish ministers, from
April 10th to December 31st, 1800, both inclusive. State Papers.
 g See State Papers 1800, memorials between Sweden and other courts
of Europe, from September 17th, to the end of the year.

CHAP.
LXVIII.

1801.

that the court of Vienna regarded the efforts of the Russians with jealousy, and forbore granting them the praise which they deserved. This disposition which had before partially appeared, the court of Petersburgh readily perceived in the Austrian gazette account of the battle of Novi. The exposure of his armies in Switzerland in the latter end of the campaign, by the departure of the Austrians, he imputed to the same malignant and unwise jealousy, and conceived that the court of Vienna wished the Russians to encounter the chief danger, while the Austrians should reap the glory as well as the benefit. Under these impressions, he had withdrawn his troops from the scene of war. Not without reason offended with the illiberal and hurtful policy of Austria, so very inimical to the great objects of the combination, he had included the other ally in his suspicion and displeasure. The carnage of the Russians in Holland arising from their own precipitate valour, he imputed to intentional exposure by their British allies: with these causes of disgust, real respecting Austria, and imaginary towards England, many other circumstances were combined to impell a monarch, that had neither sagacity nor patience for separating truth from falsehood, to withdraw from the confederacy. Since his secession, he rapidly became hostile to his former allies: his enmity to England fast growing in his weak and violent mind, was roused into immediate action by the capture of Malta, without being ceded to him as grand master: he was now seized with a desire of giving law to the first naval power in the world by sea, as the former year he had proposed to dictate to the first military power by land. Bonaparte comprehending the character and learning, the present dispositions of Paul immediately conceived a design of rendering the mighty power of this weak and capricious monarch an instrument for promoting the schemes of France against England: his genius formed and directed the northern confederacy, that all maritime Europe might join in enmity to the mistress of the ocean. Paul, the puppet of passion and caprice, no sooner declared his resolution to renew and extend the armed neutrality, than, contrary to ever principle of justice and the law of nations, he laid an embargo upon all the shipping and property of British subjects, though he professed not to be at war with this country. Against such an act of flagrant and lawless injustice, mere diplomatic remonstrance, British ministers knew, could be of little avail: they, therefore, prepared a maritime force, which should teach the weak and capricious tyrant that neither the subjects nor the rights of Britain were to be violated with impunity. While the armament was preparing, however, attempts were made between Britain and the two smaller powers of the north, to adjust their differences amicably; but as they continued to insist upon their claims, and Britain would not renounce her valuable right which she well knew she had force to maintain, it appeared that force alone must decide the contest. An embargo

Efforts of
Bonaparte
to promote the
hostile intentions of
Paul towards
England.

Embargo
on British
shipping.
Lawless
acts of
Paul.

was laid on the ships of northern powers. Nothing is more
evident than that the commercial exertions of Great Britain,
promoting the industry and arts of the various countries, with
which she traffics, and exchanging surplus for supply, benefits
respectively and jointly every country within the wide range of Interest of
her trade : it is therefore the interest of all those countries, all nations
that her commerce should continue and increase, by which vate peace
their emolument and gratification continue and increase in the with Bri-
same proportion : her capital, ability, and skill, stimulate their tain.
most lucratively productive labours, and enables them to purchase imported accommodation and luxuries : as the commerce
of England is so much connected with her navy, it is advantageous to all other industrious nations, that her maritime greatness should flourish : enmity to the naval power of England in
any country that has valuable commodities to export, and wishes
with these to purchase necessary or pleasurable imports, is
contrary to every principle of sound policy, and must arise
from envy, jealousy, or some illiberal or unwise motive, and
not from well digested projects either of accumulation or ambition : yet, not Paul only, the dupe of every whim and caprice,
but other monarchs of much more respectable understanding,
were persuaded, or impelled from jealousy, to seek hostility,
which both indirectly and directly must impair their commercial resources, and diminish their naval power. Denmark The sub-
and Sweden manifested a determination to co-operate with ject dis-
Paul. cussed in
The discussion with the northern powers was one of the parliament.
principal subjects which occupied the attention of the first session of the united parliament. The question which thence Northern
arose, called forth on both sides very ingenious and able inves- confedera-
tigations of the maritime public laws, which both parties en- cy.
deavoured to ascertain from natural jurisprudence, and consideration of the end of all laws, the mutual and reciprocal protection and benefit of the parties concerned from general and
acknowledged usage, and definitive and specific contract. A
great majority of both houses concurred in thinking, that the
pretended claims of the states in question violated the law of
nations ; that it was, therefore, just in England to resist their
attempts ; and considered the assistance which this illegal traffic
might convey to the enemy as so important as to render it expedient to employ force for its prevention.

In the month of February, a very unexpected alteration took
place in the British cabinet by the resignation of Mr. Pitt and
his principal[h] coadjutors. For this unforseen change, various
causes were alleged ; a prevalent and popular opinion was,
that in the present situation of the country, peace was deemed
necessary, and that ministers who had manifested such hostility
against the rulers of France, could not consistently be ostensi-

h Except the duke of Portland.

ble counsellors of peace: this, however, was an hypothesis that displayed neither a discriminating nor comprehensive view of the objects and policy of Mr. Pitt. From the commencement of the war, the minister uniformly professed to seek security, and to desire peace whenever it should be attainable with security: he had repeatedly tried negotiation with the French republic, ministers even had made overtures to the chief consul. When Bonaparte, in the beginning of 1800, proffered negotiation, the chief ground of rejection was the instability of the new government. In autumn, 1800, after the events of the summer had ascertained the firmness of the consular establishment, our cabinet offered to treat, and the negotiation was broken off merely by a difference about terms. Before the close of the year the power of the French rulers, from signal success, acquired additional strength. Britain being left by her continental ally, and likely to be engaged in new hostilities, there were more forcible reasons to incline Mr. Pitt to peace, than at any of the periods when he made overtures for conciliation: recollecting and considering these circumstances, I can see no sufficient reason to justify the theory that Mr. Pitt resigned his office from unwillingness to be the adviser of peace; and his subsequent conduct contradicts, instead of confirming the supposition. Of the other ministers, arguing from their former measures and policy, I can find none that could be fairly inferred to be hostile to conciliation with France, except Mr. Windham, the friend and votary of Mr. Burke. The grounds alleged by ministers themselves for their retreat from their posts, have a much greater share of intrinsic probability, and are supported by various evidences direct and circumstantial.

In the discussion of union with Ireland, Mr. Pitt and his supporters repeatedly mentioned the satisfaction of the catholics, as more practicable under an extended and united legislation, than a confined and separate; and he either by express stipulations had pledged himself, or by general assurances had impressed many others with a persuasion, that when the union should be effected, he would be the advocate of the catholic claims. I have indeed unquestionable information, that many before adverse, were induced to support the union by a conviction, that Mr. Pitt would speedily follow it by a proposition satisfactory to the catholics; that strenuous unionists considered Mr. Pitt as bound to introduce and support such a measure; and little doubt was entertained that a project which should be proposed by such a minister, would be finally adopted. But another difficulty arose which proved to be unsurmountable;' the virtues by which our monarch is distinguished, are not mere effusions of pleasing temper, or even amiable dispositions; his is a benevolence confirmed by moral principle, and conscience, at once expanded and directed by religion: in his relations and conduct to man, he regarded his duty to God; and in contemplating the engagements which he had incurred, he considered the Being to whom he had called as a witness ; by his coronation oath, he bound himself to maintain the protestant religion, established by law ; the proposed changes he regarded as inconsistent with that oath, and would agree to no project of policy which was not sanctioned by his conscience. Mr. Pitt, it appears, was so far engaged to support the claims of the catholics, that when unable to execute such an important measure, he deemed it expedient to resign ; and this is the most probable and best authenticated account of the motives and causes which terminated one of the most eventful administrations that English history can record.

I trust that the narrative, regarding neither panegyrists nor detractors, but viewing conduct, has not altogether failed in presenting to the reader a just picture of the late ministry ; a short parting view shall now therefore suffice. From the time of Cecil, except sir Robert Walpole, none was so long prime minister of England as Mr. Pitt, and without excepting any statesman, none had to encounter such arduous and trying situations. To direct the counsels of a great nation in difficult circumstances, requires chiefly patriotic intention, wise deliberation, and energetic execution ; all fortified by a magnanimity, which will be deterred by no paltry, or ignoble motives, from beneficial pursuits, plans, and conduct. That William Pitt possesses transcendent talents, none of his most virulent opponents, who have any talents themselves, will venture to deny ; but it is on the exercise of his powers, and the co-operation of his moral qualities, that the ministerial character of the statesman rests. To an understanding which unites extraordinary sagacity, force, and compass, to comprehend the situation of affairs in all their bearings and circumstances, to see what objects ought to be pursued, he unites that combination of invention and discernment which readily discover and estimate opposite means, with an unyielding firmness, that will act according to his own judgment and choice : his mind is in a high degree endowed with self-possession ; he is neither to be impelled to speak or to act in any other way than he thinks suitable to the occasion : and perhaps there never was a minister, who, in all the contentions of debate, and the irritation of invective, so completely retained the command of his own powers and passions : neither the poignancy of a Sheridan, nor the strength of a Fox, could move him from the spot on which he resolved to stand. The integrity of William Pitt the second, as of William Pitt the first, was unimpeached. After seventeen years, he retired from office, with an annuity scarcely five thousand pounds ; an infinitely less provision than his talents might have secured by the exercise of his original profession : but to such a mind, money must be a very secondary object : a passion much more appropriate than avarice to superior minds is ambition. Mr. Pitt, at a very early age, sought power, and acquired it by the fame of his personal qualities ; how he

employed it may be best seen from results. When he became
minister, he found the country in a very exhausted state, he
readily perceived that the extension of commerce, improvement of finance, and promotion of public credit, were objects
of the most urgent and immediate concern: justly concluding that peace was much more favourable to trade and revenue than war, he set out as the votary of a pacific policy.
During many years of his administration, commerce, finance,
and credit were extremely flourishing: his scheme for paying
off the national debt, was very effectual during the continuance of peace, and diminished the burthens of the war.[i] His
principles of foreign policy were those which his ablest predecessors had adopted; that the interposition of Britain in the
affairs of the continent is expedient, so far as it tends to
preserve the balance of power, for the security of Britain, and
the independence of Europe: the application of this principle
to Holland, was by all approved; in the case of the imperial
confederacy, the vigour and energy of Pitt repressed, and in
a great measure dissolved, a combination that was extremely
dangerous to neighbouring states. No part of his policy was
more discriminately wise than his conduct in the first years of
the French revolution; he carefully avoided not only interposition, but even the expression of an opinion concerning the
new system and doctrines, while they did not disturb this
country. Even when they became prevalent here, while he
adopted the most effectual precautions for preventing their
pernicious operation in Britain, he carefully forebore any allusion to their consequences in France; he and his coadjutors
observed the strictest neutrality between the internal parties
of France, and the contending powers of France and of Germany.
In the war, on a fair view of the evidence[k] on both sides, there
now remains little doubt that the French were the aggressors;
but on the broad question of expediency, the possibility and
prudence of avoiding a war, there still exists a great diversity
of opinion which must influence the estimate of the administration from that time. On the supposition that war was unavoidable, its conduct becomes the test for appreciating Mr.
Pitt's talents, as a war minister; and here we must again refer
to the results; where Britain acted in confederacy with other
powers, she and they failed in most of the objects which they
sought; going to war to defend Holland, and to prevent the
aggrandizement of France, we suffered Holland to become a
province, and France to acquire a power unprecedented in the
annals of modern Europe; but where Britain fought alone, and
where the councils of her ministers, as well as the efforts of her
champions could fully operate, she was uniformly victorious:

i See accounts presented to the house of commons, of the public funded
debt, and the reduction thereof, No. 6. p. 8.
k See this volume, chap. 1.

if, therefore, war was necessary, as far as Mr. Pitt's talents could operate, it was successful: his plans animating the spirit, for invigorating the energy, and promoting the resources of the country, were unquestionably efficient. During his belligerent administration, Britain was instigated to efforts which she had never before exhibited. After a contest which reduced the other contending nations to be dependents on France, Britain alone preserved her power and importance. One of the most alarming evils with which Mr. Pitt had to contend, was intestine disaffection, arising from the contagion of revolutionary principles: the means which were employed to repress such agitators, were in Britain completely successful, and sedition was restrained before it ripened into treason. In vigorously pursuing an object right within certain bounds, it is extremely difficult not to overstep the limits. The extravagant projects of the corresponding societies required vigilance and counteraction, but it appeared that both ministers and parliament misapprehended the case in supposing such machinations to be treason by the English law: to prohibit the daily utterance of inflammatory lectures, was certainly necessary in the state of the popular mind: but the laws for imposing the restrictions probably outwent the professed purpose. The watchfulness of government respecting Ireland, brought to a premature explosion the rebellion, that might have proved tremendous had it been allowed time to be fully charged: not satisfied with efficacious remedy to existing evil, Mr. Pitt extended his policy to preventives, and endeavoured by union to indify the sentiments as well as the interest of the Irish and British. The union between Britain and Ireland, one of the most momentous measures of Mr. Pitt, even as to present effects, will probably, in future ages, be much more distinguished, when the consequences of British and Irish connexion are experimentally ascertained, as are now the consequences of English and Scottish.

Persons who deny the necessity or prudence of the war, may probably little value the abilities which it has called forth, and if they give credit to Mr. Pitt for genius and energy, may deny him wisdom, and assert, that for the last eight years his great powers were employed in remedying evils which he might have before prevented: this, however, is a mere matter of opinion, that resolves itself into the original expediency of the war, combined with the opportunities of afterwards making peace. It is less the province of the historian to obtrude upon his readers his own judgment, than to furnish to them facts on which to ground theirs: without therefore presuming to solve so very contested a question, I cannot help declaring my thorough conviction, founded on an impartial and accurate view of his whole conduct, that Mr. Pitt, in advising the commencement of the war, and at various stages of its continuance, acted conscientiously, and according to the best of his judgment; and sought the benefit of his king and country, whose

affairs he so long administered. Whether unbiassed posterity
shall regard the war of 1793 as a necessary or unnecessary
measure, peace in 1796 and in 1800 as attainable or not attainable, they must account Mr. Pitt, in the whole series of his
administration, a statesman of great ability and strength of
mind, who rendered momentous services to his country; and
must allow that never was the force of the British character
tried by such dangers, or graced by more splendid achievements, than under the administration of William Pitt.

This celebrated statesman was supported by able and efficient colleagues; of these the first for practical talents, readiness of useful plan, removal of obstacles, and expeditious despatch of important business, was Henry Dundas, supreme in
devising and executing the most effectual schemes of national
defence, and for the improvement of British India. For assiduity, research, information, firmness, and perseverance, lord
Grenville was highly esteemed. Acuteness, ingenuity, and
literary ability, with erudition and taste, constitute the principal features in the intellectual character of William Windham;
while his prominent moral virtues are honour, justice, sincerity, and benevolence, though not without a tinge of enthusiasm;
and probably this loyal and patriotic senator, like his proto-
type, Burke, was fitter for acquiring eminence by speculative
genius, learning, and eloquence, than the arts of a practical
statesman. A most respectable member of the late administration, was the earl Spencer, formerly known as a munificent patron and ardent votary of literature and the arts; but
by his recent conduct destined to be transmitted to posterity,
not only as proprietor of a most valuable collection of erudition, but as the minister who supplied the means for those heroic naval efforts, of which adequate recital will in future ages
be the brightest ornament that can adorn a British library;
and when some descendant of the present Spencer, in a hereditary reservoir of learning, shall dwell on the splendid exploits
which Britain performed in the last years of the eighteenth
century, with proud pleasure he may say, my ancestor presided
in preparing the fleets with which a Jervis, a Duncan, and a Nelson conquered.[1]

Mr. Pitt was succeeded by Mr. Addington, who for many
years had held the office of speaker of the house of commons,
to the very great satisfaction of the house; lord Grenville,
by lord Hawkesbury, eldest son to the earl of Liverpool;
and the other members by gentlemen or noblemen who had
belonged to the party of the late administration, except
the earl St. Vincent, who was appointed first lord of the
admiralty.

[1] The fleet which obtained the splendid victory of Howe, was prepared
under the auspices of lord Chatham.

In the end of February, the nation was extremely alarmed by a fit of illness which seized the king, and tended if possible to manifest more strongly than ever the patriotic and affectionate loyalty of all ranks of his faithful subjects; to demonstrate the tender and anxious love of his queen; the affectionate and dutiful attachment of the royal children; and to place in a most striking light, the filial piety, judgment, prudence, and delicacy of his eldest son and heir apparent. Less decided in nature, and much shorter in duration, than his former malady, the illness of the king did not severely afflict his majesty more than a fortnight; though followed by a languor, and lassitude which gradually giving way to returning vigour, in a few weeks more totally disappeared, and enabled the monarch to resume his executorial and legislative functions. Inquiries were proposed into the expedition to Ferrol and Cadiz, and also concerning the convention of El-Arish, which if observed by England, it was said, might have prevented the necessity of sending troops to Egypt: but all these motions were negatived by the usual very great majorities. The supplies additional to those which were voted before the meeting of the united parliament, included a loan of twenty-five millions, four hundred thousand pounds; the taxes were numerous in detail, embracing various conveniences, and indeed by habit necessaries of life; especially tea and sugar : one of the most severely felt by numerous classes, was the tax upon paper of ten per cent. additional duty. This article was before so extremely dear, from the war enhancing the price of materials, that the impost operating as a prohibition, very much diminished the productiveness of the tax.

In the first session of the united parliament, a peer of both realms, the humane and generous Moira, at length succeeded in procuring an act for relieving all such insolvent debtors as without fraud had incurred debts not exceeding 1500l. and demonstrated their willings to do every justice in their power to their creditors, by a complete surrender of their effects. The general principle was to relieve the debtor from a confinement which could not promote the payment of the creditor, and to surrender to the creditor the debtor's funds; from which only, and not from abridgement of his liberty, the creditor could receive any portion of his demand. Such being the scope of the bill, the clauses and provisions were framed with equal benevolence and discrimination, to relieve misery, without granting impunity to guilt. In the course of the session various new regulations were made for farther encouraging the importation of wheat, American flour, and rice, to lessen the growing pressure of scarcity. On the 1st of July, the session of parliament terminated.

CHAP. LXVIII.

1801.

Alarming illness of the king.

Anxious concern of the public.

Inquiries concerning the last campaign.

Supplies.

Loan.

Taxes.

Additional impost on paper;

effects on.

Liberal and wise bill for the relief of insolvent debtors.

Farther regulations for encouraging the importation of wheat.

The session rises.

·CHAP. LXIX.

CHAP.
LXIX.

1801.
The king
of Prussia
promotes
the confe-
deracy.
Short
sighted po-
licy of an
attempt to
intimidate
Britain.
Project of
Britain re-
specting
the nor-
thern
powers.

THE king of Prussia earnestly promoted the northern
confederacy, in hopes, as it afterwards appeared, of deterring
the British government from proceding with the expedition,
and impelling them to liberate the Swedish and Danish ships;
and with this view sent an army to Hanover ; and the king of
Denmark also sent a body of troops to Hamburgh, where there
was British mercantile property to a great amount.   Short
sighted was the policy which supposed that Britain was to be
intimidated by any confederation, from vindicating her rights.
Finding the hostile disposition of the northern powers, his
majesty resolved on measures at once decisive and pacificatory, somewhat resembling the proposition of Mr. Secretary
Pitt,[m] forty years before, for enforcing diplomatic ultimatum
from the mouths of cannon ; our king determined in the present
dispute to employ a policy consonant to the combined justice

m See vol. 1. p. 167.

and power of the British nation. This scheme was to send negotiators for peace to Copenhagen, and to second their nego- tiations by a strong fleet, which should beset the sound. The armament destined for this service consisted of eighteen ships of the line, four frigates, and a great number of bomb and gun- boats; it amounted in all to fifty-two sail, and had on board several regiments of marines, and of riflemen. The command *Expedi-* of this equipment was bestowed on sir Hyde Parker: second *tion to the* was the hero of the Nile, who went to seek fresh glory in the *Baltic, un-* Baltic. On the 12th of March, the fleet sailed from Yarmouth *Hyde Par-* Roads and proceeded towards the Cattegate. The northern con- *ker and* federates made dispositions for their reception, with a vigour and *lord Nel-* precaution worthy of wiser policy than that which dictated their *son.* hostility against the mistress of the ocean. Aware that no naval *Disposi-* force was fit to contend with the British, where they had plenty *tions and* of sea-room, they endeavoured to obstruct our progress, by seiz- *northern* ing the straits, and guarding them on both sides with tremendous *confede-* batteries. The Danish navy consisted of twenty-six ships of the *rates.* line, with a considerable number of frigates, bomb-ketches and gun-boats. The Swedes possessed eighteen ships of the line, with a proportionable number of smaller vessels. The Russians had forty-seven sail of the line in the north, neither so well equip- ped, manned, or officered, as the Danish and Swedish ships. The first force which the British had to meet, was the navy of Denmark.

The wind being contrary during part of their voyage, the *Our arma-* British armament did not reach the Cattegate, till the 25th; *ment ar-* and proceeding to the Sound, on the 27th, sir Hyde Parker *rives in the* wrote to the governor of Cronberg castle, which commands *Cattegate;* the entrance into the straits, desiring to be informed whether he had received orders to fire on the British fleet as it passed into the Sound; and intimating that he would deem the firing of a gun a declaration of war on the part of Denmark. The Danish governor replying, that he was instructed to oppose such an entrance,[n] on the 30th they entered the Sound. The *passes the* admiral, together with the vice-admiral lord Nelson, and rear- *Sound.* admiral Graves, reconnoitred the formidable line of ships, radeaux, pontoons, galleys, fireships, and gun-boats, stationed in the road of Copenhagen; they were flanked and supported by batteries on the two islands called the Crowns, the largest of which batteries was mounted with from fifty to seventy pieces of cannon. They were again commanded by two ships of 70 guns, and a large frigate, in the inner road of Copen- hagen; and two 64 gun ships, without masts, were moored on the flat, on the starboard side of the entrance into the arse- nal. The day after, the wind being southerly, the admiral *Parker re-* *solves to* *attack the* n See in London gazette extraordinary of April 15th, copies of four Let- *Danes.* ters, No. 1, 2, 3, 4, that passed between sir Hyde Parker and Stricker, com- mander of Cronberg castle; and transmitted by sir Hyde to the admiralty.

CHAP.
LXIX.

1801.
Nelson offers his services to conduct the attack.

Battle of Copenhagen,

and victory of Nelson.

The victorious admiral proposes an armistice.

The prince of Denmark agrees on amicable negotiation.

again examined their position; and came to the resolution of attacking the Danes, from the southward. Lord Nelson having offered his service for conducting the attack, after having examined and buoyed the outer channel of the middle ground, proceeded with twelve ships of the line, all the frigates, bombs, fireships, and all the small vessels; and on the same evening of the 1st of April, anchored off Draco Point, to make his disposition for the attack, and wait for the wind to the southward.[o] In the morning of the 2d of April, lord Nelson made the signal for the squadron to weigh, and to engage the Danish fleet, consisting of six sail of the line, eleven floating batteries from twenty-six 24 pounders to eighteen 18 pounders, and one bombship, besides schooner gun vessels. These were supported by the Crown islands, mounting eighty-eight cannon, and four sail of the line moored in the harbour's mouth, and the batteries on the island of Amack. The bomb ship and schooner gun vessels made their escape; the other seventeen sail, being the whole of the Danish line to the southward of the Crown islands, after a battle of four hours, were sunk, burnt, or taken. The result of the success was, that the remaining ships of the enemy, and the batteries of Copenhagen, were in the power of Nelson. The narrow passage which was the scene of their efforts, prevented admiral Parker's division from taking a share in the conflict.[p] The damage suffered by Nelson's division was very considerable, and three of our ships, the Bellona, Russel, and Agamemnon, were aground, and exposed to the batteries of Crown islands. With his squadron generally victorious, and these ships in imminent danger, the ready genius of Nelson immediately formed a project which should at once give effect to the victory, and extricate the ships from their perilous situation. As soon as the cessation of Danish resistance enabled him to descend to his cabin, he wrote a letter to the prince royal, representing the expediency of allowing a flag of truce to pass; and stating, that if this were denied, he should be under the necessity of destroying the floating batteries, now in his power, while it would be impossible to save those brave men by whom they were defended.[q] The note was addressed to " the brothers of Englishmen, the Danes." The application of Nelson produced an interview with the prince, the immediate consequence of which was an armistice, which termi-

o See gazette extraordinary, April 15th, 1801.

p See London gazette extraordinary for April 15th, the letter of admiral Parker to the admiralty, dated on the 6th of that month off Copenhagen roads.

q I have been informed of a circumstance, attending the letter, which admirably displays the self possession and coolness of our magnanimous hero. When the letter was finished, the secretary, from the urgency of the case, was going to put a wafer in it, to save the time that would have been occupied by sealing-wax. " No (said Nelson) it must be properly and correctly sealed; lest, by the appearance of hurry, we indicate our anxiety, and thereby defeat our purpose.

nated in an amicable convention. The Swedish fleet was
detained by contrary winds from joining the Danes; and the
successes of the British at Copenhagen, strongly impelled them
to unite in conciliation: and an event, the intelligence of which
now reached both Denmark and Sweden, determined them to Sweden.
renounce the northern confederacy.

On the night of the 22d of March, Paul, emperor of Russia, Russia—
was found dead in his bed. His son and successor, Alexander, Death of
no sooner ascended the throne, than he demonstrated his de-Paul.
termination to abandon the late projects of his father, and tread
in the steps of his renowned grandmother. One of the first Conduct of
acts of this prince was redress for violated justice; by remov-Alexan-
ing the embargo on British shipping and property, releasing der; his
British sailors, and sending them to the several ports from which on with
they had been taken. He immediately despatched an envoy Britain.
to Britain, expressing his desire to have every difference ami-
ably terminated; and a negotiation was opened for that purpose, in which Sweden and Denmark were now very willing
to be included. Both these powers had received fresh warnings of the impolicy of a contest with Britain: the capture of
the valuable islands of Santa Cruz and St. Thomas, with other
settlements of smaller note, belonging to Sweden and Denmark,
showed that hostilities with Britain were no less destructive
to their commerce than to their marine. The negotiation ter-Amicable
minated in an amicable convention between Britain and Russia,[r] adjust-
concluded on the 17th of June 1801; to which Denmark[s] ac-ment be-
ceded on the 23d of October 1801; and Sweden[t] on the 30th tween Bri-
of March 1802. By the settlement between Britain and the tain and
northern powers, all the contested points were so clearly ascer-ern pow-
tained, as to preclude any likelihood of future contest: the ers.
right of search was accurately defined, and the enumeration
of contraband articles was more definite and specific[u] than at
any former period. Such were the effects of seconding negotiation by formidable force. After the month of April, there
were no actual hostilities; and the British fleet, having effected
its purpose, returned to England.

Disappointed in his expectations of being seconded by a proceed-
northern confederacy, the chief consul was engaged in conclud-ings of Bo-
ing the treaty of Lunéville, and arranging the internal affairs naparte.
of Germany with the emperor and king of Prussia; he also
settled Italy; prepared to invade Portugal: and attempted to
amuse England with feints of invasion, to prevent the British
from sending re-enforcements to Egypt. After the treaty of Germany,
Luneville was completed, a diet was held at Ratisbon, wherein the emperor received full powers, in concert with the courts
of Berlin and Petersburg, to adjust the secularizations. In Italy.

r See State Papers, June 17th, 1801.   s October 20th, 1801.
t State Papers, March 30th, 1802.
u See the respective conventions above quoted.

CHAP.
LXIX.

1801.

Italy, peace was concluded between the king of Naples and the French republic. · The ecclesiastical territories were restored to the pope. If the emperor had agreed to the first proposals made by the chief consul at Marengo, Tuscany would have been permitted to remain governed by a prince of the house of Austria: but being invaded and conquered by the French troops, it became subject to the disposal of the republic: Bonaparte, erecting it into a kingdom, conferred the government on the youngest branch of the house of Bourbon, under the denomination of the king of Etruria; a title which has probably been dormant ever since the time of Porsenna, who entered into a confederacy for the restoration of monarchy in republican Rome.

Naval campaign.

Britain, finding Portugal menaced with invasion on account of her fidelity, generously released her from engagements, adherence to which must involve her in ruin. She at the same time granted her a subsidy to defend herself until peace could safely and honourably concluded. Unable to cope with such powerful enemies as Spain, assisted and headed by France, she prudently entered into a negotiation. Various British squadrons, both in the Atlantic and Mediterranean, watched the motions of the French and Spaniards; but taught by the events of former years, the enemy's fleet prudently avoided encountering us in open seas. It was the object therefore of our commanders, to attempt the destruction of their force in harbour or near the shore. A very signal exploit of this sort was performed by sir James Saumarez: finding some French ships at anchor near Algeziras, he attacked them; but the wind rising very strong from the sea, and the water being very shallow in that part of the bay, the Hannibal ran aground, and was taken. The British commander in these circumstances found it necessary for the present to desist. A few days after he attacked the Spanish ships, sent from Cadiz to convoy the prize from Algeziras: he took a seventy-four gun ship, and set fire to two first rates, which were consumed, and near two thousand four hundred men perished. The French continued to menace an invasion; and were reported to have assembled great numbers of gun-boats on their north coast. Lord Nelson undertook an expedition to Dunkirk and Boulogne where the greatest number were understood to be collected. In this undertaking, though he incurred considerable loss, yet he was on the whole successful.

Enterprise of sir James Saumarez.

Threats of an invasion.

Destruction of the gun-boats.

The splendid successes of the British arms during this war, had hitherto arisen principally from her navy. Her soldiers indeed had fought with as much valour and skill, as at the most brilliant periods of her military history; and in the campaigns of 1793, 1794, and 1799, efforts of heroism had been exhibited, which fully equalled the glorious æras of Blenheim, Ramillies, and Quebec; but the event was very different. In the recent war, our champions were encumbered, not assisted by allies;

where we acted alone, we were victorious: in concert we were
not vanquished, but were compelled to relinquish our objects.
The history now comes to exploits and achievements of the
British Army, which have never been surpassed in the annals of
war.

The death of Kleber, and the succession of Menou to
the command, prevented the evacuation of Egypt.   The
French general resolved to violate the treaty, which had been
concluded by his predecessor, and actually kept possession of
the country, which it had been stipulated to abandon.   Justifiable reasons for transgression of compact are not to be found;
but the motives for a deviation from good faith, were easily discovered.   Egypt was well known to be a favourite object with
Bonaparte, and that he attached much more importance to it,
than the directorial government.   Kleber had concluded the convention of El-Arish before intelligence had arrived that Bonaparte was supreme magistrate, with uncontrolled power; and
was no sooner informed of the elevation of the general, than
he began to make dispositions for retaining possession of Egypt.
The misunderstanding with the British government respecting
the capitulation allowed him a pretext for re-possessing strong
holds.   The British ministers, agreeably to the good faith of
the nation, ratified the treaty as soon as they were assured
that it had been actually concluded.   The negotiation had
been renewed, as we have seen, but the asssssination of Kleber intervened before any decisive measure was effected.
Besides the views of Bonaparte, the wishes of Menau himself
were eager for retaining Egypt: he had declared himself a
mussulman, married an Egyptian lady, was desirous of erecting Egypt into a colony, and extremely hostile to all who proposed to return to France.   Some asserted, that he even intended to render Egypt an independent principality, of which
he himself might be the head.   This opinion is not very
probable; because without the protection of France, he could
have no reasonable hopes of being able to maintain his ground;
and there are no proofs that he ever had such an object in
contemplation.   But whatever might be his purpose in keeping
possession of Egypt, it was an end of the first importance to the
British government, to drive the French enemy from a settlement which was in itself advantageous and productive;
and might pave the way for enabling them to annoy British
India.   To achieve such a momentous purpose, was the ultimate object of the expedition, in which sir Ralph Abercrombie commanded the army, and lord Keith the fleet. After our
armament had witdrawn from Cadiz, in October 1800, they
entered the Mediterranean, and during some time anchored in
the bay of Tetuan. On the 3d of November, part of the fleet
sailed from Minorca, and the remainder, with sir Ralph Abercrombie to Malta, where it arrived on the 30th, and was joined by lord Keith, with the other divisions, on the 14th of De-

The
French
still keep
possession.

Britain re-
solves to
dispossess
them.

Expedition.
of sir
Ralph
Abercrom-
bie and
lord Keith,
for that
purpose,

CHAP.
LXIX.
⌣⌣⌣
,1801.

Arrive at
Marmo.
rice.

cember.   At Malta the troops disembark, while the ships were cleaning: the abundance of fresh provisions, the comforts of the beautiful city of la Valette, and the luxuriancy of the scenery soon re-animated the troops, and rendered them completely fit for service.   On the 20th and 21st, the first and second division sailed from Malta, and instead of proceeding directly to Egypt, bent their course to Asia Minor, and anchored in Marmorice bay, between the continent and the island of Rhodes.   The object of this diagonal movement was to be assured of the military co-operation of the Turks, and also their assistance in furnishing horses, gun boats, and other necessary articles:[x] here also they procured supplies of fresh provisions.   During the month of January, and a considerable part of February, the expedition continued in this station and every endeavour was employed to learn the nature and local circumstances of the country, the force and disposition of the enemy.   On the first subject, the only officer that could give them any information was sir Sidney Smith; the coasts that commander had seen, surveyed with his usual accuracy, and comprehended with his usual ability; but to the interior parts of the country his knowledge did not extend.   Captain Boyle, who had been wrecked off Damietta, and, contrary to the usages of war, was made a prisoner, had omitted no opportunity of learning the number, condition, and situation of the French army; but it appears the intelligence actually received by the British commanders, from such confined sources was extremely imperfect, and the power of the enemy was much greater than they had any reason to apprehend. The French force which now possessed Egypt, it was afterwards found, amounted to thirty thousand, besides natives, who were reckoned about fifteen thousand more.   The Gallic troops were habituated to the country, elated with success, inured to danger, aware of the importance of Egypt to their government, determined to defend the possession of it, and encouraged in this determination, no less by the assurance of speedily receiving effectual succours, than by the promise of reward, and the love of glory.   The English army that was to dispossess this formidable force, amounted to fifteen thousand, of whom from sickness only twelve thousand were effective; and thus twelve thousand troops, totally unacquainted with the country, and unused to the climate, were to attack what thirty thousand of the best troops of the continent of Europe, thoroughly conversant in all the local advantages, and familiarized to the climate, were to defend.   Such was the relative state of the parties: let us now follow them to their conduct in that state.

Proceed to
Egypt.

On the 23d of February, the fleet weighed anchor; the number of vessels of every kind amounted to about a hundred

x Sir Robert Wilson, p. 3.

and seventy-five sail; and, says the historian of the expedition,
" a nobler sight could not be beheld. The greatness of the
" armament, the gaiety of the brave men on board, exciting
" reflections on the awful destiny of the expedition, not only as
" relating to those immediately acting in it, but as affecting the
" dearest interests of Great Britain, afforded a scene for con-
" templation, in the highest degree gratifying and impressive."[y]
The armament steered a southern course : on the 1st of March
the leading frigate discovered land, which proved to be the
coast near Arabs Tower ; and on the next morning the whole
fleet moored in Aboukir bay, and the men of war occupied the very ground on which had been fought the battle of
Nelson.

The coast from Aboukir bay round to the Nile presented an   Attempt to
appearance at once picturesque, striking, and formidable. The   land at
sea full of shoals rendered disembarkation extremely difficult,   Aboukir.
and even dangerous, though it should not be interrupted by an
enemy. The shore and the adjacent country were 'covered
with sand hills ; among these the French were disposed in very
great numbers and force, with batteries in front; towards the
Nile to the left extremity of the British ; and on our right
along the promontory of Aboukir. The batteries and sand
hills afforded to the artillery and musketry such positions as
could dreadfully annoy our troops in their attempt to land, and
be secure themselves : while they fired on our soldiers, our ships
could not return the fire, because thereby they must bear upon
their friends more than upon their foes. Tremendous as were
these obstacles to landing, they served only to rouse the energy
of British heroism : but for some days the extreme roughness
of the surf prevented an attempt to disembark. On the 8th of
March, the weather being less boisterous, it was resolved on that
day to effect a landing. Early in the morning, the first division of the army, consisting of the reserve under the orders of
major-general Moore ; the brigade of guards under major-
general Ludlow ; and part of the 1st brigade, composed of the
royals, 1st battallion of the 54th, and two hundred of the 2d
battallion ; the whole amounting to about five thousand five
hundred men, under the command of major-general Coote, assembled in the boats ; the remainder of the 1st and 2d Brigade
being put into ships close to the shore, that a support might be
quickly given after the first landing was effected.[z] At nine
o'clock the signal was made for the boats to advance, and the
troops proceeded towards the shore. The French posted   Battle and
among the sand hills, and forming the concave arch of a circle,   victory.
looked with wonder at the preparation ; and, as they afterwards confessed, did not believe such an adventurous attempt

y Sir Robert Wilson, p. 7.
z General Abercrombie's Letter, dated March 16th, 1801, in the London
zette of May 9th; sir Robert Wilson, page 12.

CHAP. could be made : but when they saw the boats moving with ex-
LXIX. traordinary rapidity, they were convinced that the British were
in earnest, and they immediately poured from the heights, and
1801. Aboukir castle, all the shot and grape-shot that their musketry
and artillery could issue : the effect was tremendous ; in a situation in which they could not return the fire, and seeing their
comrades fall about them, under these fell messengers of multiplied death, instead of being dismayed, our heroic soldiers were
the more indignantly eager to reach the shore, where, bringing
arm to arm of Briton against Frenchman, they knew they
would soon avenge their fellow countrymen. The boats arrived at the destined point: springing on land, in the face of
cannon, our champions formed on the beach, and advanced in
a line, which, in the deep sands, piles of sand hills, and in the
face of the enemy, was as well observed as if they had been
exercising on a parade.[a] Marching coolly and steadily up to
the foes, they were enabled to use the surest instrument of victory to British courage, supported by British muscular strength
—the bayonet. And now the artillery from our ships could
operate against the batteries of Aboukir, without exposing our
soldiers to danger. The French made a stand worthy of their
national heroism : but when British sailors can use their cannon, and British soldiers their bayonets, the most valiant
Frenchmen are destined to yield. In the conflict between such
combatants, the battle was obstinate and bloody : but our
heroes prevailed. The French found they had more formidable foes to encounter than even those whom they had met at
Lodi and Arcola ; and that a British handful at Acre had merely given a specimen of what they might expect from a British
army.

The country in which this astonishing landing was effected,
is an oblong peninsula; having on the east a branch of the
Nile ; on the north the ocean ; on the south the canal of Alexandria, called by the French lake Maadie ; and on the west, situated on the isthmus, the city of Alexandria. The peninsula
was from two to three miles in width, from the sea to the canal:
from the vanguard of the army, now facing the west, to Alexandria, the space was about sixteen miles, but full of ruins, and
other posts of very strong defence. On the right was the sea,
with the British fleet at anchor in the bay ; behind was the
Nile ; on the left the canal ; and in front sand hills, terminated by the metropolis, flanked by its sublimely towering Pharos.

On the 9th of March the army advanced to the westward,
leaving two regiments to blockade Aboukir, which refused to

a Lieutenant-colonel James Stewart, of the 42d regiment, told me he
had never seen the ranks more exactly dressed, or a better and more harmonious line on a review day, than was here formed and maintained in the
face of so many obstacles and dangers. That gentleman himself, with
colonel Dickson, the first lieutenant-colonel, were wounded in this engagement.

surrender. The 10th and 11th were employed in reconnoitring
the enemy, bringing stores from the ships, and forming hospitals and depots. On the 12th some partial skirmishes took
place, but with no material consequences. The French army
was posted on a ridge of heights, about four miles from Alexandria; the British resolved to attack them in this position:
and on the 13th commenced the assault, by the left of our Battle of
army, hoping to turn the right flank of their antagonists. The the 13th of
enemy made a very vigorous resistance, and by their cavalry March.
and artillery cut off a great number of our men, and prevented
us from attacking them in flank; but the British, forming in two
lines, made such a charge in the front, as compelled them to
retire to the heights, before Alexandria. Ardent to pursue their
victory, the gallant British pushed on to force the strong position
of the enemy; but the French artillery played with such tremendous effect, that it was found prudent to desist; and the loss of
our troops in this arduous enterprise was very considerable. The
detachment that was employed in the siege of Aboukir proceeded in its operations, and on the 17th day that fortress surrendered. The army was meanwhile employed in getting their
heavy cannon on shore, and procuring supplies of water and
provisions. Menou was now arrived from Cairo, and the whole
force of the French was concentrated at Alexandria. By his
memorable defence of Acre, sir Sidney Smith had obtained very
great influence among the Arabs, who communicated to him
every information which they deemed important. On the even- Menou pro-
ing of the 20th, an Arab chief sent a letter to this commander, jects a
acquainting him that general Menou was arrived, and intended night at-
the next morning to attack the British camp. Sir Sidney be- tack.
lieved the intelligence:[b] the commanders did not think it probable that such an attempt would be made: but the information
proved authentic.

The British army, at this time was encamped across the
peninsula, about four miles from Alexandria; the right consisted of various regiments, in front of which, on the extremity,
was the 28th; in a redoubt the 42d to the left, a little more
advanced,[c] with Stewart's foreign regiment on the left in front;
immediately behind, the 28th, the 23d, and 58th, and about
five other regiments farther back. Such was the plan of our
right division: between which and the left there intervened a
considerable space. Between the right of the British and the
beach there was a narrow tract of ground; in day-light covered
by the British frigates and gunboats that were nearest the shore,
but at night, without such a collateral defence. Menou proposed to turn the right flank of our right division on the one
hand, and attack the left flank of the same division on the
other, so as to surround that part of the army, and cut it off

b Sir Robert Wilson, p. 29.

c See Sir Robert Wilson's plan of the Battle of the 21st.

CHAP. LXIX.

1801.
Battle of the 21st.

British 42d regiment.
Bonaparte's Invincibles.

Surprised and encompassed.

Heroism of the whole army.

from the support of the left: to facilitate the intended assault on the right, the French made a feint on the other division. At half past three in the morning, some musketry was heard on the extremity of the left; and when anxious attention was turned to that quarter, loud shouts were heard on the right: a roar of musketry succeeded, and the action became general. The enemy had turned our right flank, and the 28th, from its position, bore the first brunt of the battle, and maintained their ground against unequal numbers with the intrepid heroism of British soldiers. The 58th and 23d, which were behind the 28th, with equal intrepidity, marched to its assistance, but the numbers of the French were extremely great. Colonel Alexander Stewart marched the 42d to support their fellow soldiers, and became engaged with a corps, styled by the French, IN-VINCIBLES (and till that morning they had deserved the name); THE HIGHLANDERS COMPLETELY VANQUISHED THE INVINCIBLES, and took their standard; but while pursuing their victory, a body of cavalry coming round, charged them in the rear, while a fresh column marched up to them in front. In this double danger, Stewart[d] made every disposition that the exigency could admit; and the highlanders at the same time fought in front, flank, and rear. The company of major Robert Bisset was first engaged with the French cavalry; and, after a most intrepid resistance, their commander being first wounded with a pistol, and afterwards mortally with a sabre, a great part of the company was cut to pieces; and, combatting quadruple their number, the whole corps performed the most splendid efforts of prowess worthy of their heroic character so long earned and uniformly maintained; but they were oppressed by numbers, and in very imminent dangers: yet, though broken, the gallant band was not defeated: individually its heroes resisted, and the conduct of each man exalted the renown of the regiment.[e]—But why, in recounting the extraordinary feats of British heroism, should we dwell on the achievements of one part: fighting for their king and country, every column, Lowland, English, and Irish, had the hearts and hands of Royal Highlanders. Nor were the efforts of the army, at this critical juncture, confined to the native subjects of his majesty: foreign troops displayed equal valour, and gave an important turn to the contest. The 42d and 28th were almost overpowered, when general Stewart with the foreign brigade, consisting of

d Alexander Stewart, first major of the regiment, and then commander : Dickson, and James Stewart, the two lieutenant-colonels, having been wounded on the 8th. Alexander Stewart, though but little turned of forty, has been twenty eight years an officer in that regiment: he is the eldest son of a very respectable gentleman, Robert Stewart, esq. of Clochfollidgh, in the county of Perth. James, his younger brother, was on this expedition, captain of lord Keith's ship.

e Sir Robert Wilson, p. 32.

three regiments, advanced to their assistance, and poured in
such a heavy and well directed fire, that nothing could withstand it: the enemy fled in confusion. Though the battle was
hottest in the front division of the right wing, yet the attack of
the enemy extended to the rear, and part of the left was en- Enemy re-
gaged: but the valour of our troops was every where propor- pulsed
tionate to the dangers by which it was assailed. Next to the slaughter.
regiments that have been already mentioned, the 40th, 44th,
30th, and Queen's, appear to have been chiefly exposed in the
battle. Soon after daybreak, the French were repulsed on every
side. A fresh column attempted to turn the right flank of the
guards, who were in the right extremity of the left wing, but the
steady and vigorous fire of those troops soon compelled the enemy to fly, and the repulse was complete.

During the charge of cavalry, the veteran hero, sir Ralph
Abercrombie, received his mortal wound. On the first alarm
he had hastened to the scene of combat; and having despatched his aides-du-camp with orders to the different brigades, he
was alone when some French dragoons attacked him, threw
him from his horse, and attempted to cut him down with a
sword; the gallant old man sprang up to defend himself, and
wrested the sword from his antagonist, who was immediately
bayonetted by a soldier of the 42d: but our general himself
had received wounds, which at the time he little regarded, and
he kept the field, giving his orders with his usual coolness and
intrepidity. When the flight of the enemy rendered exertion no
longer necessary, his spirit yielded to nature, he became faint,
and was placed in a hammock. Hailed on every side by the Death of
blessings of his soldiers, he was carried to a boat, and conveyed sir Ralph
on board lord Keith's ship; and after languishing for several Abercrom-
days, died on the 28th.   bie.

Sir Ralph Abercrombie was one of the most distinguished
generals in the British service. His commands were important, and uniformly successful; the means which he employed
were indeed the most efficacious for ensuring victory. To his
officers and soldiers he united every practicable and useful indulgence, with the strictest discipline and the most rigid exaction of professional duty. He was beloved and revered by the
army, and they went on with the assurance of victory when he
was at their head. In private life, he was as amiable and estimable as in public meritorious and admirable. To his family,[f]
friends, and connexions, of every rank and degree, he was endeared by the habitual practice of all the relative and social

[f] Sir Ralph Abercrombie was the representative of the very ancient and
respectable family of Tullibodie, in the county of Clackmannon; he married
miss Menzies, of the family of Castle Menzies, and cousin-german to sir
Robert Menzies, head of that name and house As a testimony of his majesty's regard, his widow has been created a baroness, the honours to descend to their son and heir.

CHAP. duties, the agreeableness of his manners, the warmth and ten-
LXIX. derness of his affections, the honour and integrity of his con-
⌇⌇⌇ duct: but to use the words of an illustrious judge;[g] " it is some
1801. " consolation to those who tenderly loved him, that, as his life
"was honourable, so was his death glorious: his memory will
" be recorded in the annals of his country, will be sacred to
" every British soldier, and embalmed in the recollection of a
" grateful posterity." Of officers of rank, major-general Moore
was wounded in the head, but not dangerously; brigadier-
general Oakes was dangerously wounded; colonel Paget, of
the heroic 28th, was wounded at the first onset, but less severely
than general Moore, The field officers killed were, lieutenant-
colonel David Ogilvy,[h] of the 44th; lieutenant-colonel Peter
Dutens,[i] of one of the foreign regiments; and major Robert
Bisset.[k] The other officers killed and wounded were not numerous, but in their respective ranks also merited and earned high
commendation.

Invincible   As every circumstance belonging to this momentous and glo-
standard. rious day must be interesting to readers, it may not be deemed
improper to say a few words on a subject which has greatly
engaged the public attention: the capture, loss, and re-capture,
of the invincible standard. Of the various statements that have
been presented concerning this trophy, the following, admitted
by sir Robert Wilson, is in itself the most probable, reconciles
different testimonies, and shows that evidence which has been
represented as contrary, is merely a variety of parts which
easily harmonizes into one whole. Major Stirling, of the 42d,
took the standard,[l] just as they had marched to the relief of the
28th, delivered it to serjeant Sinclair, and directed him to retire
to the rear. By the surrounding cavalry, Sinclair was wounded,
and lost the standard;[m] here ends the evidence of the capture

g See general Hutchinson's letter to Mr. Dundas, dated the 5th of April,
1801, and inserted in the gazette extraordinary of the 15th of May.

h An officer of very high character, whom I knew from a boy; he was
my class fellow at St. Andrew's college, with captain Charles Campbell,
who twenty-two years before (as I mentioned in the account of the campaign 1779,) fell in an earlier stage of the same honourable course. Colonel Ogilvy was the son of the late sir John Ogilvy, head of a very ancient
and honourable family in the county of Angus, and brother to the present
sir Walter.

i Dutens was in high estimation for enterprise, and adventurous boldness
and generosity, and was a distinguished favourite with the officers and soldiers.

k Of my friend and relation, major Bisset, his brother officers and soldiers
of the 42d, best attest the merits by their esteem and regret.

l See narrative (by authority) of the movements of the 42d, on the 21st
of March, and signed A. Stewart, major and lieutenant-colonel of the 42d R.
H. regiment; and James Stirling, major and lieutenant-colonel of the 42d
R. H. regiment.

m Sinclair himself, in his declaration before the Highland Society, testified, that from his wound he fell into a swoon; and before he recovered,
the standard was gone.

and loss. Anthony Lutz, a private of the Minorca regiment, brought the standard to the head quarters; and in addition to the fact of his having it in his possession, adduced two witnesses to prove that he had taken it from the French: and such is the testimony of the recapture. The result of the whole evidence is, that major Stirling took the standard, and delivered it to Sinclair; who being wounded, and in a state of insensibility, lost the same; and that it was re-taken by sir Anthony Lutz. Taking no part in the dispute, the historian has only to express his wish, that future narrators of British wars may ever have to celebrate such valour as was exhibited by the 42d and foreign regiments, the captors and re-captors of a standard that was termed invincible till it was borne against the troops of Britain.

CHAP.
LXIX.
1801.

On the death of general Abercrombie, Hutchinson succeeded to the supreme command, under circumstances the most trying and difficult. The victories of the 8th, 13th, and 21st, must naturally impress many with an idea, that French Egypt was subdued, and that nothing remained but to take possession of the conquest: such is the opinion all those would form, who regard fighting as the only arduous service of a soldier. The British had impaired the force of the enemy, but still they were much more numerous than the invading army; and our troops had to contend against foes, which military heroism often encounter in vain: they had to penetrate an unknown country; to traverse trackless deserts; to wade through burning sands, exposed to the rays of the scorching sun, fast approaching to vertical heat; they had to meet with difficulties unessayed in the history of British warfare,—difficulties so numerous and complicated, as to exceed any that had been experienced among the mountains of Hindostan, or the woods of St. Domingo: to undergo such hardships required not only British prowess, but magnanimity, and the moral energy of professional duty. To animate and invigorate these principles, was the first and grand object of the new general. To attack Alexandria was at present impracticable; since it was so strongly fortified that the exertions must reduce his army; and even success in that enterprise tend ultimately to defeat the object of the expedition. Hutchinson, therefore, resolved to penetrate into the country, reduced Lower Egypt, and make his way to Cairo; thence that Alexandria would be insulated, and if not taken by storm compelled to capitulate. Completely to debar the French army from communication with the interior country, he cut the canal of Alexandria, to let the sea into the lake Mareotis, and thus render the capital an island. Having effected this change, Hutchinson proceeded in this plan of reducing Lower Egypt; and while lord Keith commanded the coast to intercept communications between France and her troops, sir Sidney Smith headed a squadron of gunboats that sailed up the Nile to co-operate with the army.

General Hutchinson succeeds to the command.

Great difficulties that still remained in the enterprize.

Plan of operations.

In exhibiting pursuits requiring patience, constancy, and for titude, more frequently than active prowess, there is less room for minute description of operation than general exhibition of object, conduct, progress, and result. In proposing to reduce Egypt, on both sides of the Nile up to Cairo, one purpose of Hutchinson was; to facilitate the way for a junction of troops from India, that were expected soon to reach Suez, so that not only advances were necessary for the general objects of the expedition, but such advances as would secure the route of the expected re-enforcements : it was requisite, therefore, to obtain a footing in the esst as well as the west of Egypt, and with this view our general proceeded. By the 19th of April, forts Julien and Rosetta, on the left bank of the river, were captured ; and being now joined by a considerable number of Turks, they proceeded up the banks to Rhamanich, which was at once a magazine of provisions to the enemy, and commanded the entrance into the Delta : here the French made a stand, but were vanquished, and retreated towards Cairo ; and the British troops took possession of the town. This was a very important stage of our progress, since we thereby cut off the communication between Menou in Alexandria, and Belliard the French general in Upper Egypt ; commanded the Delta, and had the means of intercepting the convoys of provisions for the enemy. On the 11th of May, the army continued its match up the river, in a fine country. Accustomed to Mahomedan and French depredators, the people regarded the new comers at first with dread, but afterwards with wonder when they found that not a single soldier of the British committed the slightest pillage ;[n] and at last with gratitude hailed them as their deliverers from a plundering banditti. The only gratuitous contribution which our champions required was water, this beverage with gladened eagerness the natives brought, and readily supplied with every provision in their power, heroes, who in the midst of war and scanty stores, strictly observed the principles of justice, and showed that British troops are soldiers, not robbers. On the 15th of May, intelligence was received that Belliard was in full march from Cairo towards the British army : Hutchinson resolved to anticipate the expected attack. On the 16th, the Turks commenced the onset, the French took post in a wood of date trees which they maintained for three hours, but at length were compelled to retreat.[o] These successes encouraged great numbers of Arabs to join the British army, and while they were making such progress on the left bank of the Nile, they also made advances in the Delta, and

n See sir Robert Wilson, p. 99. · Every officer with whom I have conversed, agrees in this account so singularly honourable to the British soldiers.
o See in London gazette extraordinary, letter of major Halloway, dated the 20th of May.

took a very valuable convoy on the canal of Menouf,[p] which
joins the Rosetta to the Damietta branch of the river. Being
secure on both sides, our army advanced up the bank, but were
obliged to traverse deserts that came down to the very edge of
the Nile; and at the summer solstice, under a vertical sun, our
soldiers were digging their way through the burning sands of
Africa; but their constancy and resolution, in encountering the
soil and climate, were equal to their heroic courage, in forcing
the sabres and cannon of hostile men. At length they crossed
the wilderness, the pyramids of Egypt presented themselves to
their astonished view, and the difficulties of nature which they
had just surmounted, were absorbed in their wonder at the stupendous monuments of art which they beheld. At Gizeh the
camp was placed, and dispositions were made for investing
Cairo from both sides of the Nile; but the French garrison,
conscious of their inability to withstand the efforts of the British,
offered to capitulate. A convention[q] was accordingly conclud- Surrender
ed on the 27th of June, by which it was agreed that the French of Cairo.
were to be conveyed to their ports in the Mediterranean, with
their arms, artillery, baggage, and effects, within fifty days
from the date of the ratification; men of letters and naturalists
were permitted to retain their papers and collections; an ex-
oneration was granted to such of the people as had adhered to
the cause of France; and it was stipulated, that Menou might
avail himself of these conditions, for the surrender of Alexandria, provided his acceptance of them were notified to the
general commanding before that city, within ten days of the
date of the communication being made. And thus the efforts
of our commander and army, surmounting very arduous obstacles, effected a momentous part of their purpose; and it depended upon Menou, whether the whole was not compassed by
the convention of Cairo. A few days after this treaty, the army from India arrived on the banks of the Nile, and it was extremely mortifying to our brave troops from the east, that after
tasting so deeply of the toils and hardships of war, fortune did
not permit them to participate on this occasion in its glories.

Menou was far from approving of the article in the capitulation of Cairo, by which he might have been included in the convention. He had long expected a re-enforcement which was
under the convoy of admiral Gantheaume, and that commander
had spared no diligence to reach Alexandria : but the vigilance
and ability[r] of lord Keith rendered his approach impracticable :

p See Ibid letter of general Hutchinson to lord Hobart, dated June 1st.
q State Papers, June 27th, 1802.
r Naval heroism and ability appears to be hereditary in the family of
Elphinstone. Captain Charles Elphinstone Flemyng, son to lord Elphinstone, the elder brother of lord Keith, though several years under thirty,
distinguished himself throughout the war; but especially in 1797, in the
West Indies, where commanding a frigate, he cut out several Spanish ships
from a harbour, under the cover of batteries, and in the face of frigates.

after having advanced within thirty leagues of the coast, being descried by the English fleet, he departed with all possible expedition; so that Menou had only the garrison with which in April he had been enclosed in Alexandria.

Meanwhile the British forces were at Cairo, and had time to survey the famed capital of Saracenic Egypt, which was found to be totally different from what it had been reported by travellers, and very unlike the magnificence which has so often delighted the reader of the Arabian Nights Entertainments.[s] The manners and customs of the people, however, were found to be much more similar, and it is not difficult to account for either the diversity or resemblance. The vicissitudes of war, and political revolutions, may dissipate or transform cities; but the Mahomedan character and manners are stationary and uniform : topographical and statistical reports of Egypt, however, come not within the plan of the history.

Informed that Menou would not accede to the capitulation, Hutchinson prepared to proceed against Alexandria. The French were sent, under the escort of general Moore, to Rosetta; and as quickly as possible embarked for Europe. In the beginning of August, Hutchinson being now on the coast, made dispositions for besieging Alexandria. On the 15th he invested that city, on the eastern and western front; while lord Keith[t] co-operated from the north with his fleet, and on the south with the gun-boats that were assembled in lake Mareotis : Alexandria was thus completely surrounded. On the 21st the British fleet forced its way into the great harbour. On the 22d, general Coote, who commanded the western detachment, protected by the gun-boats in the Mareotis on the right, and by light vessels belonging to the fleet on the left, moved forward near the walls of the town. On the east, so recently the scene of British heroism, Hutchinson with the main army pressed.[u] By the 26th, Menou, finding resistance totally hopeless, offered to capitulate : and received the same terms which had been granted to Bel-

Capture of Alexandria, and expulsion of the French from Egypt.

r Captain Charles Elphinstone, son to William, India director, second brother of lord Keith, several years younger than his cousin, has also acquired high reputation; and captain Charles Adam, (son to a sister of lord Keith and to Mr Adam, whom this history has repeatedly mentioned,) only twenty-three years of age, in the Sybil frigate, at the close of the war, captured the French Chipone, of much superior force, and terminated hostilities by an achievement as brilliant as any performed by a single ship during the arduous contest.

s Sir Robert Wilson informs us, that Mr. Hammer procured in Cairo a complete edition of the Arabian Nights Entertainments, in Arabic manuscript, containing many more stories than have as yet been published, and which he means to translate; see p. 154.

t See letter of lord Keith, dated the 27th of August, and inserted in the London gazette of the 17th of November; and sir Robert Wilson, from p. 187 to 206.

u Sir Robert Wilson, p. 187.

liard at Cairo. Such was the issue of Bonaparte's expedition
to Egypt: there, as in all their undertakings during the last
war, the French prospered until they encountered the forces of
Britain: there Bonaparte learned, that in vain he might project schemes of maritime and commercial conquest, when opposed by the naval and military heroes of Britain. All the
mighty preparations and boasted achievements of four years in
pursuit of the favourite object of the chief consul, perished without leaving a wreck behind. The whole, and every part of
this expedition, displayed the British character in its manifold excellencies. Adventurous courage guided by wisdom,
united with patience and magnanimous constancy, and were all
inspired by patriotism and loyalty, and enhanced by justice.
Such were the qualities that rendered Britain triumphant in the
signally glorious campaign of Egypt, in such Britain may always confide, and such let her enemies dread. If *ambitious
pride* should overlook more remote events, when she seeks war
with Britain, let her REMEMBER EGYPT.

CONCLUSION.

The new ministers of England, following the example of
their predecessors, uniformly declared themselves desirous of
peace, whenever it should be attainable with security, and a negotiation was opened with M. Otto. The chief difficulty arose
from Egypt, which Bonaparte was resolved if possible to retain; and the British government was determined to dispossess
the French of a settlement which would prove so injurious to
the interests of England. That difficulty, however, lessened,
as intelligence was received of the progress of our arms. Both
parties wisely observed the strictest secrecy concerning the
overtures, the advances, and the obstacles: the hopes of the
people of Britain and France had been extremely sanguine in
summer, but in autumn they began to fear that the reciprocal
discussions were not likely to terminate in pacification. Various circumstances convinced the public that the crisis was fast
approaching, and it was generally suspected that a few days
would announce the continuance of war. With such antici-
pations September closed; and never were hopes of immediate peace more distant throughout London, than during the
greater part of the 1st of October. Such were the opinions
that prevailed, when the next day opened with intelligence
that peace was concluded between Great Britain and the French
republic. The tidings spread through the country a joy that
was natural and just, on the supposition that the peace would
be secure and permanent; and that supposition was founded in
an idea that the chief consul of France would regard the real
interest and welfare of the people, and would not provoke dismission from his office, by rendering it the instrument of na-

CHAP. tional misery.   The reasoning was fair ; the hopes of durable
LXIX. tranquillity were founded on probable grounds, and the rejoic-
       ings were general.[x]   They were not however universal, as from
1801. the situation and character of the chief consul, a small number
       augured inveterate hostility to Britain.

    The objects which the former ministers had professed to seek
by war, and in the succesive negotiations, were, the security
of Britain, restitution to her allies, and the independence of
Europe.   From the events of the war; and the separate treaties which had been concluded by her first confederates. it was
impracticable for Britain to provide for their independence any
farther than they chose to co-operate themselves.   Restitution
to allies was become a much narrower proposition than before,
because allies were so few : it now comprehended only demands for the evacuation of Egypt;[y] and for the restoration of
places which were taken from the queen of Portugal.   The
conquests of France had been immense, but ceded by their
former possessors, could not with any hopes of success be reclaimed from her by Britain ; and all the restitution which
we sought to our allies was obtained.   Respecting Britain herself, ministers did not think it necessary to insist on retaining
all the acquisitions of our volour : we did not fight to subdue
the possessions of others, but to secure ourselves.   We agreed
to restore all our acquisitions, except the island of Trinidad,
and the Dutch possessions in the island of Ceylon.   The Cape
of Good Hope was to be opened to both parties : and the island
of Malta was to be evacuated by Britain, but to be placed on
such a footing as to render it totally independent of France.[z]
As a mere question of terms and equivalents, it may be doubted
whether we might not have commanded greater extent of territory, if acquisition had been our object ; but acquisition was
an object which the present, like the former ministry, uniformly
disclaimed ; and the retention of a plantation more or less was
held to be a very inadequate ground for incurring the expense
and loss of another campaign.   The preliminaries, signed at
London, on the first of October, were ratified by the chief consul on the 7th ; and so terminated the memorable war between
Great Britain and the French republic.

    The treaty of Amiens opened new subjects of discussion,
which for the reasons mentioned in the preface, appear to me

---

    [x] I must acknowledge that I was one who rejoiced at the peace. I
thought it would be lasting, because it was the interest of France, and the
chief consul himself, that it should be permanent; and Bonapar.e had
repeatedly declared his regret that the two first nations in the world should
waste their resources and power in enmity.

    [y] The news of the capture of Alexandria, as our readers will recollect,
had not reached Britain ; though by many.it was supposed to have reached
the chief consul ; and that he readily consented to evacuate a country from
which he knew his troops had been driven by force.

    [z] See State Papers, October 1, 1801.

to belong more properly to a subsequent period, which shall embrace the history and progress of that pacification ; the state and sentiments of the two countries, and of other nations during the peace; the rise and progress of the rupture, with the events which may ensue until hostilities be brought to a permanent conclusion. The most important object which Britain ascertained at the termination of the late war, was her own security : for this valuable blessing, under providence, she was indebted to her own extraordinary efforts during the whole of the contest, but especially since the rupture of the first negotiation at Paris. She had proved, even beyond her own exertions in former times, that she was superior to the whole naval world combined against her in war. Every attempt to disturb her rights, to invade her dominions, either directly or indirectly to impair the sources of her commercial prosperity and political greatness, have recoiled on the authors : never had her commerce been so flourishing, or her power so resistless, as during the most arduous war which her history has to record. Threatened, and actual rebellion only demonstrated paramount loyalty and patriotism : attempts on her finances,[a] displayed beyond former conception, the extent of her resources; leaving their bounds far beyond calculation; resources exhaustless, because flowing from minds which afford perennial supply : menaced invasion served only to show the number and force of her voluntary defenders. Every means that fertile genius could devise, or gigantic power execute, was essayed against our country : if she could have been subdued by any human effort, in the late arduous contest she must have fallen : the stupendous exertions that were employed against Britain, but employed in vain, demonstrate her invincible. HERE RESTS OUR SECURITY, IN THE MANIFESTATION OF RESOURCES NOT TO BE EXHAUSTED, A SPIRIT NOT TO BE BROKEN, AND A FORCE NOT TO BE SUBDUED : OUR SECURITY IN INVULNERABLE WHILE WE CONTINUE WHAT WE HAVE BEEN, AND ARE TRUE TO OURSELVES.

a From the account presented to the house of commons, it appears that the national income amounts to the wonderful sum of sixty-three millions two hundred and forty five thousand five hundred and fifty-nine pounds four shillings and eight pence, exceeding the expenditure by six hundred and seventy thousand and eighty pounds six and eight-pence, besides the annual million. From the same vouchers it appears, that so rapid has been the operation of Mr. Pitt's plan for the reduction of the national debt, that in sixteen years and a half, sixty seven millions two hundred and fifty-five thousand nine hundred and fifteen pounds have been paid off.—See No. 6; Accounts respecting the Public Funded Debt, p. 8, column second.

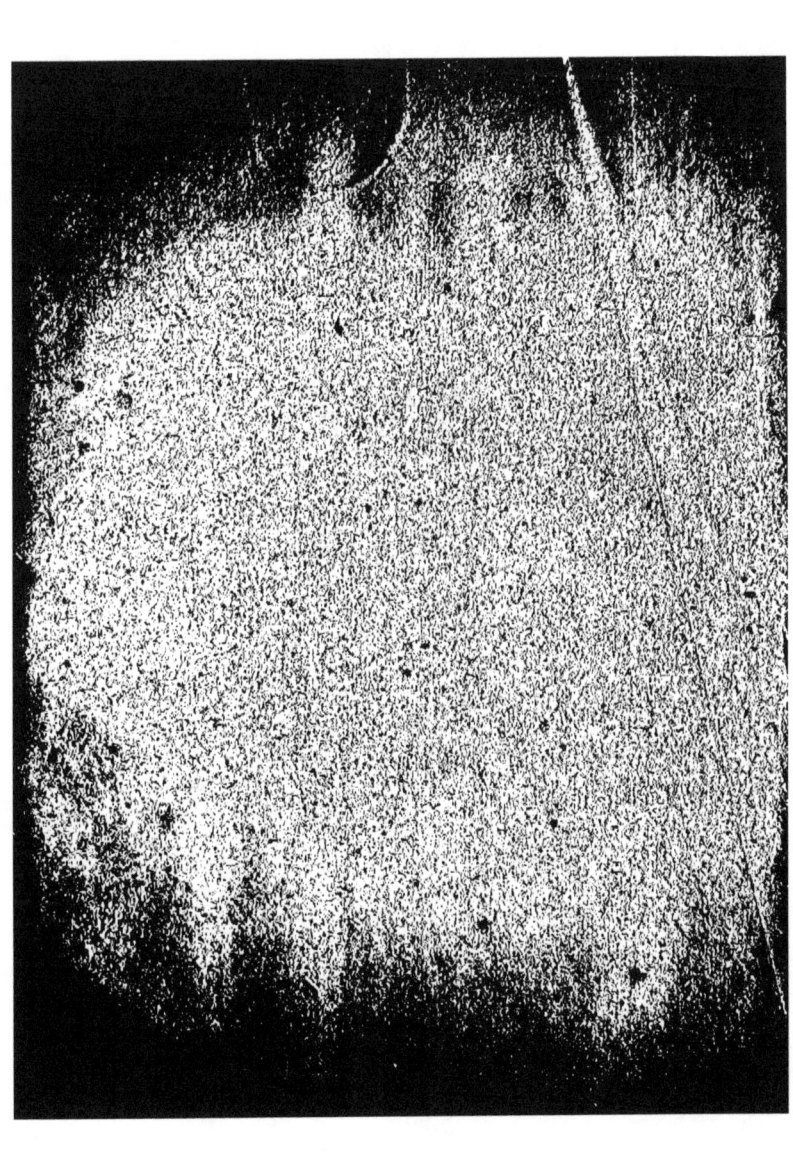

CPSIA information can be obtained
at www.ICGtesting.com
Printed in the USA
BVHW081445061118
532319BV00008B/183/P